WE ARE THEIR HEAVEN

This Large Print Book carries the
Seal of Approval of N.A.V.H.

WE ARE THEIR HEAVEN

ALLISON DUBOIS

THORNDIKE PRESS

An imprint of Thomson Gale, a part of The Thomson Corporation

THOMSON
✷
™
GALE

Detroit • New York • San Francisco • New Haven, Conn. • Waterville, Maine • London • Munich

LIBRARY OF CONGRESS CATALOGING-IN-PUBLICATION DATA

DuBois, Allison.
    We are their heaven : why the dead never leave us / by Allison DuBois.
        p. cm.
    ISBN 0-7862-8999-6 (hardcover : alk. paper)
        1. DuBois, Allison. 2. Mediums — United States — Biography. 3. Large
type books. I. Title.
    BF1283.D82A3 2006
    133.9'1—dc22   2006021799

ISBN 13: 978-0-7862-8999-8

Published in 2006 by arrangement with Simon & Schuster, Inc.

Printed in the United States of America on permanent paper
10 9 8 7 6 5 4 3 2 1

This book is dedicated to Joe, my fantastic husband, and my incredible little girls. They have made my life sweet and meaningful. Words can never express my gratitude for their love.

To those who live and those who live again. Especially, little Lindsey Whelchel who died young but touched many.

I also dedicate *We Are Their Heaven* to some of the best mediums/friends to have ever lived. You have helped pave the way for those who will follow behind us and who will learn from us and hopefully exceed us.

I would like to thank Laurie Campbell, who will never be surpassed as a medium or friend; George Dalzell, who has more energy and heart of most anyone I know; and Sally Owen, not only a great medium but a woman whose character can never be questioned — it's outstanding. We have all since left the lab, having contributed many years of our lives to science, and now we move forward helping clients and law enforcement to bring the change that we were born to bring.

CONTENTS

FOREWORD 9
INTRODUCTION 19

Chapter 1: Here Again 23
Chapter 2: Out of Sight, Not Gone . . 90
Chapter 3: *Medium* 146
Chapter 4: Living with Gifts 171
Chapter 5: Somebody's Baby 188
Chapter 6: Angels of the Hospice . . 220
Chapter 7: The Hard Questions . . . 240
Chapter 8: A Little Wiser 270

ACKNOWLEDGMENTS 281

FOREWORD
JOE DUBOIS

How Do I Know?

Even before Allison completed her first book, her mind was already working on this one. She already knew the title would be *We Are Their Heaven* and had a clear idea of what it would be about. She told me that people often ask her about heaven. I began thinking, What a great idea, I love heaven! I also enjoyed writing a chapter in her first book and hoped to be able to do it again, but who am I to write about heaven? I am not a heaven expert. I have not been there, but I hope to go (no time soon). I have only read one book on the topic, which is helpful but hardly exhaustive research.

I am an expert at some things. I do know my wife, Allison. She *is* an expert on what happens after we die. That may seem like a bold statement, but it is one I am confident in making. I have known this wonderful woman for thirteen years. I know her daily life. I have seen her at her strongest, when her guard is up and she is ready to take on the world. I have seen her win a war of words with radio interviewers who are more interested in their own agenda than in getting to know Allison or learning about life after death. I have seen her in her most vulnerable state, when her guard is down and she is loving her family as a mother and a wife. At these times, her heart is open to us and she lets me in. It is an amazing privilege to go there with her. If I need to be clearer, I love my wife and I am very proud of her.

I also know a thing or two about aerospace engineering, aka "rocket science." Much debate can be held over a cold beer as to who is permitted to don the moniker "rocket scientist," and I am actually a little embarrassed when people call me this. I am embarrassed because I would reserve the title for heroes of mine like Robert Goddard or Wernher von Braun, who were both geniuses in the development of modern rocketry. Allison quickly reminds me that I have spent my career in aerospace on projects including experimental satellites, jet engine valves, and yes, as a matter of fact, rocket engine valve performance analysis and control system design.

At this point you are asking yourself, "If this is a book about heaven, why is he writing about himself?" I am writing about myself because I want to establish that I am a critical thinker. When I am confronted with an anomalous situation, I do not immediately jump to any conclusion. I try to thoughtfully and rationally come to terms with the very interesting things that happen around my house. I now tell you what I have learned about Allison and what she does as a medium so that you may hear her message and take it to heart.

Allison's mediumship ability is a natural talent, a gift, some would say. She did not go to school to develop her abilities. However, she has spent a life honing her skills by practicing and not accepting mediocrity. Her talent is not different from what many people experience on a daily basis. Hers is just clearer and more obvious.

Since she has had this ability her entire life, she has known that a person's consciousness, whatever that may be, survives the death of the body. This has profoundly shaped who Allison is. Whereas most of us have to rely on belief and faith to comprehend heaven, Allison has to deal with it in a more visual sense.

Allison grew up knowing that when people

die, they remain closely connected with the people left behind. They are close, yet they might as well be a million miles away because they can rarely be seen or heard by their living loved one. She was taught as a child to believe in an ethereal heaven that was described in an abstract way and involved many rules for proper entry, yet she plainly saw people who had died all around her. Being put in a situation where she saw one thing and was taught something slightly different would prove to be very frustrating. Thankfully, Allison worked through it and developed a very strong sense of self and the ability to be strong in her convictions. Allison sees the world in black and white with no gray. Allison does not live by rules, she lives by what she feels is right and is guided by her heart.

Allison and I have had the "why me" conversation several times. This is the conversation where she questions why she has her gift. The most recent time was this past summer. It was a family Sunday. We went swimming with our children, then followed up with a delicious barbecue. In typical American fashion, I grilled the hamburgers and Allison made a nice macaroni salad. I have a great secret hamburger recipe that Allison loves. I suggest that every dad should have one, even if it is just adding a little teriyaki sauce to the beef. Mine is more complicated and does not involve teriyaki, but it lets my kids know that I love them because I take extra time to make the meal just the way they like it. Fallon often helps me make the burgers. One time she snuck a pinch of sugar into the sauce. I did not tell anyone, and everyone loved the burgers that night. Now she is in charge of her own special secret ingredient. Please don't tell her that I shared her secret ingredient.

After this wonderful day, our children decided to go inside to play, and Allison and I remained on the patio to enjoy a glass of wine. This is when the "why me" conversation started. This question was asked not in a woeful way but more as part of a search for purpose. In Allison's life, she searches for the purpose of events. I, on the other hand, am more content to believe that some things just are the way they are without greater purpose. Time and time again, Allison will point out how a series of seemingly random and unconnected events, when taken as a whole, show a bigger plan.

I reminded Allison of what makes her so special besides the fact that she is a medium. She is also very intelligent, beautiful, strong-willed, honest, charitable, wise, and young at heart, and she has integrity. To put it simply, Allison is the best person I know. Allison is a handshake kind of person. If she makes a promise, she will keep it. She likes to play it off that she somehow has cowboy blood in her. She was raised in Phoenix and the older Phoenicians were straight shooters, but I believe Allison would have been this way regardless of where she was born. Allison is who she is because she is who she is!

To explain this seemingly ridiculous sentence, I must share a brief story about Allison when she was visiting Hawaii as a teenager. Through a series of choices made by the then sixteen-year-old Allison, she found herself on a surfboard far from the beach being circled by a large shark. At that point, she told God that if he kept her safe, she would do whatever he asked and that she would "help people." God sent a current to carry her safely to shore. He kept his side of the deal, now she is keeping hers. The first "she is who she is" means that she is doing what God has asked of her; the second part, "because she is who she is," means that she knows no other way than to have integrity in her word. Allison is the only person I know who argues with God. This does not mean that she is irreverent. It means that God is always in Allison's life. She talks (prays) to God and listens to God. She has never told me that God speaks to her directly, but she describes his indirect acknowledgment and guidance. Since she is honest, she will let God know if she is unhappy about what is being asked of her. It was a little unnerving at first, but I have gotten used to it. This is a lesson that I am learning from Allison: be honest with yourself and live knowing that you are bare in front of God.

I know that my dad shares in my life today, even though he passed away over thirteen years ago. Allison has talked to my dad for me on many occasions. What I really mean is that Allison will listen to my dad and tell me what he says. She's my interpreter. I know that he can hear me, and now I recognize that the little feeling I get sometimes that he is around is right. Now that I have acknowledged that he is around, I don't need to have Allison tell me quite so much.

My dad does not always talk in subtle ways. He has had the opportunity to mysteriously set off fire alarms. Without a doubt the most amazing sign that he was near was that Fallon was born on the fifth anniversary of his death in the same hospital where he died. The hospital was not the closest one to our house, but Allison thought the nurses were nicer there. At the time, I thought my dad had died April 28, but it turned out that he had died April 29. My mom informed me that he had died after midnight in the middle of the night. I didn't learn this until we had Fallon, and it made her birth even more special.

I also know when my father-in-law is around. He was quite a man and I love him very much. He has an incredible way of playing just the right song on the radio, right when you need it. He also has the knack of making Allison happy. I just wish I could hear him better when I am picking out anniversary presents. I am sure if I could hear him right now, he would be saying, "Don't listen to me, listen to your wife. She will tell you what makes her happy."

I have learned by being married to Allison that we are here on this earth to live and love one another. I have learned why it is so important to be yourself, to be honest, and to have integrity. I have learned that my father, grandparents, and ancestors are here with me because they love me. They could be off doing other things, but they choose to visit me instead. As Allison says, "We are their heaven." The journey of writing this chapter has helped me to realize that I do know what heaven is. Allison is my heaven.

INTRODUCTION

While writing this book, I decided that giving my perspective is good, but giving my perspective and the perspective of the person whom I read will be more beneficial to my readers. I think it's important for people who are grieving to have others to relate to, people who walk their same path. In this book, the people whom I've read speak in their own words about how they moved forward and what our meeting did for them. I share details about the process of each reading. I also illustrate why being a medium has such a great impact on my life, as well as the lives of my family.

I met a lot of new people through the media tour for my first book, during radio and television interviews and question-and-answer sessions before book signings. I noticed there are common threads of questions. Many people ask what heaven is like. There is an obvious concern around what

19

happens to our deceased loved ones. People wonder about the connection of the dead to the living. I often get questions from people who are concerned that their mourning a loved one is preventing the loved one from fully passing over to the other side.

This book addresses some of the various ways in which people die, for example by suicide or accident, and the different ways in which they show us that they remain. A question that I hear often is, Why do the deceased want to remain after death? Well, of course because they love us, but there are other reasons as well. Our deceased relatives want to connect with the living because our lives are based on emotion and continuing to learn and grow, as are their own. They willingly stay with us to share in our emotion and to help teach us what we need to learn. Often they want to make sure that we don't repeat their mistakes, the things they ended up regretting and would do differently if they had the chance. It also brings them a great deal of joy to share in our lives, especially when we're talking about them or to them. It's important to stay open to the messages that are sent from those who go before us, those who are still a part of us. Part of my book's purpose is to open the living up to the spirits who continue to share in their loved ones' lives. Loving people who have died doesn't hold them here, as some think. It gives them life. They stay around us because we are what they consider utopia, their "heaven."

There is a heaven, a flawless place where we exist after we die. There are white skies and blue water that the eyes of the living cannot see. There are children running through perfect blades of brilliant emerald grass with sunshine bouncing off every strand of their hair. There are old men fishing on the same banks that they fished from when they were boys, with the puppy that died when they were small. Couples who were married for fifty years now look like they did when they were first married, as they stroll hand in hand down a path by a tree. It's all that and more.

Yet even with all that, it's not entirely heaven to those who've died because, usually, not all their loved ones are there. Try to understand: it's the flaws of the living, our attempts to figure out who we are, how to connect with others, and how to spend our time on earth that interests those who've passed. They want to see how our character stands up when we're challenged. They want to see their namesakes move through life. They want to see children born and anniversaries celebrated, help the sick get better, lend strength to us in times of weakness. Parents who die still want to be there for their kids on the days they're needed most. Children who die want to see their parents, siblings, and friends laugh again and, most important, "feel" their presence and continuing love. So, yes, they have a beautiful sanctuary where everything is as it should be, but never forget that *we* are their heaven.

CHAPTER 1
HERE AGAIN

The loss of a child has to be the hardest loss to endure. I have three daughters who mean the world to me, and I know that every parent's biggest fear is to outlive his or her child. There is not a day that goes by that I don't thank God for my kids, and I know for parents whose children have died, they thank God for every day that they had with their child. I hope my readers will find some comfort and inspiration in the stories shared in this chapter. The connection between parent and child can never be broken, not even by death. Our children are a part of us not just physically but spiritually as well. Parents are the caretakers, the protectors of a helpless little life that grows under our love and guidance. I believe that is why there is a certain amount of guilt that follows the loss of a child, more so than with other losses. Love is indivisible, so there can never really be a good-bye, only "Till we meet again."

I asked a woman whom I read to detail the loss of her daughter and her experience with me. I also have included how I was impacted by the reading personally.

A Mother's Love

Oddly enough, the first time I "met" Allison DuBois was in the spring of 2005. However, my very first contact with her was the sound of a soft-spoken, sweet voice with a western drawl coming to me over two thousand miles of phone lines connecting me in New York to Allison in Arizona. What I was not prepared for that day was that we would have a party line connection!

Looking back, I see that the events leading up to this meeting were like the perfect choreography of a professional dance ensemble. My daughter Candace died at the age of fifteen, in September of 2002, in an automobile accident while riding with her brother in his car. The accident left our son in a coma for several days. We began to experience signs of our daughter's presence from the day of her funeral, first through close friends, and then personally. It was clear to me she was around, and that gave me the strength to get up every day. But my husband could not grasp the concept of a world beyond this physical one. His pain and his doubt were unshakable and even made me question my own convictions.

Meanwhile, lightbulbs went out in our home, only to turn back on as we stood there with a replacement bulb in our hands. Electronic sounds emanated from our bedroom thermostat. It seemed the electrician, at my husband's request, was suddenly spending way too much time at our house.

By now, we had finished reading books on grief and had both concluded that they offered little help. We moved into religious books for an explanation of why such a wonderfully bright, vivacious, and talented young child could be taken from this world. Where was the justice? Weren't we taught that God was all-loving? When you lose a child, it is hard to understand why the child had to go. Questioning God seems to make sense.

And then one day, while waiting for a conference with our son Jon's rehabilitation team, we stopped at a nearby bookstore for a cup of coffee. And there on a display, just a few feet from our table, was a book that included accounts of mediums being studied in a university laboratory. Of course we bought it, along with a few other books. We wanted to explore spirituality and look outside the box.

A few days later, I experienced the most unbelievable sign from the other side . . . except this time it wasn't from my daughter. I was on my way to pick up Jon from a physical therapy session when I suddenly had to stop driving, as I became over-whelmed with the gnawing need to know the age of a little girl who had lost her life days after being crushed by a gym door in a nearby elementary school in 1991. I didn't know why, I just felt compelled to find out. Once composed, I got back on the road and continued on to pick up my son. Upon our arrival home, we were greeted by my hus-band, Tom, who had just located a meeting of The Compassionate Friends (a grief sup-port group for anyone who's had a loss), and we needed to eat our dinner quickly in order to arrive on time. (Newcomers were asked to arrive early to chat with "buddies" before the meeting got started.) On the way there, I shared with Tom the strange experi-ence of the day.

The meeting ritual at this chapter of The Compassionate Friends was to go around the room so that each person would have the opportunity to speak about who they were and whom they had lost. The woman seated behind me took her turn; as she introduced herself to the group, I recognized her as the mother of the little girl who had "visited" me earlier in my car. I had had this awesome interaction with this other mother's deceased child. It was as if I was being prepped to see my own daughter. I dug my nails into my husband's arm as I took in the enormity of the moment.

When we broke for coffee, I went to talk with her and I told her of the "coincidence" earlier in the day. "How nice," she replied. "Today is my daughter's birthday. She would have been twenty-one years old."

Well, Tom and I have been married for more than thirty years. He had never known me to lie or even bend the truth, but had I not shared the story with him on the way to The Compassionate Friends meeting, he never could have truly appreciated the experience of a spirit child's finding a way to let her mom know that she was there with her on this very special birthday.

By this time, my husband had finished reading the book on mediumship testing and had decided to contact the university mentioned in the book. Our goal was to have a personal reading with each one of the mediums who had taken part in the experiments in the book. If he could find a scientific explanation for the little girl's "visit," then we might also have a method by which to reach our daughter.

In February 2003, we received a response from a scientist at the university. In March 2003, we had a phone conversation with our first research medium, Laurie Campbell. Later, in August, we flew to Arizona to meet with Laurie and to participate in an experiment. It was all so wonderfully healing for me, but Tom, so grounded in the physical world, wanted still more proof!

Eventually I received a call from the laboratory at the university saying we were invited to participate in a large experiment that was about to begin. They didn't have to ask me twice. I was even ready to hop on a plane, until the coordinator explained it was all to take place over the phone!

A few weeks later, on a predetermined day, I sat home as instructed, awaiting the call from the scientist. Just the thought of connecting to my daughter again lifted me higher than I had felt since before her passing.

When the phone finally rang, the scientist explained that I could not say a word; as soon as she got the medium on the other line, we were to hang up! *Hang up?* Yes, this was one of many parts to the experiment. I would be called back again in half an hour.

I held on as the scientist dialed another number to conference the call. The soft-spoken, sweet voice with a western drawl at the other end said, "Hello."

The scientist said, "Hi, Allison, are you ready? When we hang up, you are to begin part 1A," and then everyone hung up. Part 1A was where the medium gave her information on the deceased to the scientist. I sat there for a moment waiting for something special to happen to me — a special feeling, a sign, something to tell me that this other world was busy with the science of the afterlife, or at least that my daughter was nearby waiting her turn to speak.

By the time the phone rang again half an hour later, I was filled with anticipation. Allison was now introduced to me. I was introduced as the "sitter" to Allison and reminded that I was to remain silent. The discarnate (deceased) was introduced as the "daughter of the sitter."

I took nineteen pages of notes as Allison brought through facts about Candace as if my daughter were standing right in front of her! And perhaps she was. Allison mentioned a cat on the other side with Candace. She described some of her passing, my dad and how he passed, the sports that Candace enjoyed, her shyness before warming up to new people, how she always sat in the kitchen watching me cook chocolate pudding on the stove, how she loved to go to the movies. Allison relayed the message "I can take care of you now like you took care of me."

The messages came fast and furious. But one message in particular helped me with a feeling common among those who are grieving — guilt.

"*The King and I*," Allison said. "She says, 'Mom was watching.' "

I wanted to speak, but I bit my tongue.

As a mother of three, I literally lived in my car, driving from Little League to karate to birthday parties to school events. As the kids got involved in more and more activities, Tom and I had to start picking and choosing the events we could attend, and more often than not we would have to split up. Tom always opted to attend our daughter's events. The two of them always had a very special bond. But it was the presentation of *The King and I* at the elementary school that I and not my husband had attended. With her death, it haunted me that I had missed so many of her games and performances, and here was Allison showing me that Candace was pointing out the play that she had been so excited to be in and I had been so proud to attend.

We could have hung up then, and I would have been grateful, although I really wanted this reading to go on forever. The connections, no matter how frequent or significant, are never enough when you have lost a child.

Allison continued, as Candace talked about leaving behind her brother, "I miss him, and I'm still teasing him." She reported that she no longer had to eat the green vegetables I insisted be consumed with each dinner, and that she knew about the new puppy our cousin had just gotten.

The information continued to flow. Half of me wanted it to stop, so I could let Allison know just how significant these tidbits of information were; the other half wanted to sit and listen to Candace for eternity.

We had been on the phone for almost two hours now, completing parts 1b, 2b, and 2c of the experiment with a fifteen-minute break in between. Each part was different. In the first there was no living sitter present. Then a living sitter was on the phone to listen but not respond while a researcher asked the medium a series of questions. The process was in depth and very structured because it was a scientific experiment. We finally came to part 3, described in the lab instructions as "You and the medium will engage in a traditional reading in which you are no longer silent and an open dialogue can occur."

Yippee! I can talk. I was not interested in a "traditional reading." What I needed from this fabulous woman was to share with her some of the things that she was bringing through that told me in no uncertain terms that Candace had joined us on this party line. I was now formally introduced to Allison DuBois.

What I didn't expect at this point was that Candace had not hung up the phone. And so, as I attempted to chat with Allison about *The King and I*, Candace was busy calling her brother "butthead." And as I mentioned the new toddler who had moved in next door with the unusual name of Cole (whom Allison had mentioned previously in the reading by name!), Candace also told us in all certainty that Cole knows she's there!

And I now could hear Allison weeping at the other end. "She loves you. She says you're a 'great mom,' and she felt very close to you. And she said, Dad, he hurts himself physically by keeping this all inside."

And then, just to make certain we all knew it was she, Candace threw us some of her teasing humor. Allison described my mother-in-law, focusing on the very thing that Candace had always teased Grandma about: she showed Allison a little woman with platinum hair and her eyebrows drawn on. My positive response to Allison, elicited one word from Candace. " 'Grammy!' " Allison told me. "She sends her love by name."

And then there was the picture that Allison had described early on in the experiment: "A picture of her with a best friend or sister . . . a female, just the two of them with their arms around each other, smiling towards the camera." Before I hung up, I wanted Allison to know that she had described the photo I looked at every day on my desk in my office. No sooner had the words left my mouth, when Allison said, "Happy Valentine's Day. She says to tell you, 'Happy Valentine's Day.' "

For a moment I was confused; February was months away! Then I recalled that it had been Valentine's Day when the lab had finally responded to the many e-mails and letters that my husband had written. It was 4:30 p.m. when we said our thanks and our good-byes. I was now in a new place emotionally. It wasn't just because of Allison's ability to connect with dead people. It was because Allison had visited with Candace. She saw her. She spoke with her, and my little girl spoke back, telling her things only she and I knew, and then sending messages of love, guarantees that she was well, happy, and where she needed to be, promises to be there watching us, confirmation that she had been spending time with us, even sitting and having dinner with us. I couldn't wait to go over my notes with Tom.

The next morning, I awoke feeling different. Yes, I checked. The hole in my heart was still there, but it wasn't bleeding anymore. I dressed and went down to my office. There was the picture. Candace with her sister — her best friend, her confidante — dressed up, arms around each other and smiling into the camera, just as Allison (or was it Candace?) had described.

I lovingly removed the photo from its display, turning on my scanner so I could e-mail it to the laboratory to back up the data of the experiment. This is the science, I thought. This is what my husband needed, and this is what the lab must have to back up the data. I flipped the photo over.

And written on the back was "Valentine's Day Dance."

Looking back now, it seems that marked the moment when my life journey profoundly changed. Soon after that, Tom had his first "visit" from Candace (feeling her presence and seeing her in a dream), and her sister experienced a "visit" on the same day. However, we all learned very quickly that we could not share this excitement with just anybody. Instead, we needed first to be certain that we were talking to "believers."

It wasn't long before we realized that we were not alone in either the experiences we were having or our fear of sharing them. Talking to others about seeing the deceased in dreams or feeling their presence around you, even seeing them before your eyes, is hard. You don't want to talk to nonbelievers and deal with their personal hang-ups about the afterlife and have their reaction somehow take away from your special experience.

Throughout my life, I have not been afraid of affecting change. It was clear to me that the Western way of thinking denied the existence of a powerful force — a force that many people report experiencing firsthand, a force that can provide wonderful healing to the bereaved — and that this mind-set clearly needs to change.

Bringing Candace Through

In 2003 I was set up for a mediumship test through a university. I was contacted via telephone by a scientist with a series of questions pertaining to a formal test. I was asked not only to answer questions but to provide the information that I received from the deceased. There were two different readings to be administered for two different people who had never met and had each experienced a loss.

For the first test, I kept seeing a young girl who showed herself playing volleyball. She also kept talking about "*The King and I*" and the "play," as she put it. I told the scientist that she'd either been in this play or somehow it was her favorite. The "sitter," who wasn't allowed to speak in the first phase of the test, was asked to hit a button on the phone to confirm that she felt all the information given was indeed that of the deceased she wished to contact. She did. After the initial phase, the sitter along with the scientist were permitted to comment as I continued to provide information. The deceased spoke of a Chinese restaurant as being important to her. Among many other pieces of information, she revealed that her head hurt at the time of her passing. She said volleyball was important to her. These are typical examples of the kind of information that can come through in a reading.

After a few months (the lab was a little slow giving the results), the test was scored by the parents of the deceased and I was able to see the accuracy of my information in the reading. The scoring is important because the sitter scores each piece of information individually. There are a lot of pieces, each scored between a one and a six, one meaning nothing like the deceased, six meaning uniquely specific to the deceased. Then the hundreds of pieces of information are averaged and placed on a scale between one and six to reveal the level of specificity that the medium achieved during the test. It turned out that the deceased was an amazing, beautiful teenage girl who had passed away in a car accident. She had played on her school volleyball team. She had also been in a school production of *The King and I.* Her head hurt from her injuries in the fatal car accident that had occurred after she'd had dinner with her parents at a Chinese restaurant. These were all important details shared by Candace. I won't include all of the details of the reading because there are too many, but you get the gist of what took place that day.

I cannot tell you how much I enjoyed bringing her through and how lucky I felt to be able to experience the love this mother and daughter have for each other. It was an emotional reading, especially because I have daughters and could empathize with the parents of the deceased. People sometimes tell me how they couldn't do what I do; they place a lot of emphasis on the sorrow involved. It is important to me that people understand my view. I believe that I am one of the luckiest people in the world. Even though my job is emotional, I have learned through reading many people how to put aside my own feelings to make room for others to share. When things get really tough, most mediums have found other people, often other mediums, to listen to us as we unload those feelings. I am privileged to be in a position to ease people's pain and reach their loved ones who've passed on. Mediums don't want to be martyrs; we see a lot of good things in our readings. We feel the love between the client and the deceased. We are voyeurs to the special memories held by the deceased. Mothers who pass show pictures like a home movie running in my head. They show their children blowing out candles on birthday cakes. Children who pass let their living parents know how special they felt to have been born to them. Dads show their children small and dancing with them, sometimes standing on their shoes while Dad waltzes with them in his own clumsy way. We see the love, we see the pain, but most important, we see that the dead are not gone.

You will remember that earlier I said there were tests with two different sitters. With the second sitter, I stopped fifteen minutes into the test and told the scientist that I could not complete it because the deceased was someone I recognized from a reading two years before. That was amazing in itself, that I could identify a deceased person from a prior reading. I was given a score of six by the sitter in the first reading, where I connected with Candace, but when the same data was put before the dad from the second reading, who'd lost his son, I received a one, which is great! It means that nothing from the first reading meant anything to the second sitter, even though it meant everything to the first. This showed that specifics that came through could not fit people across the board, as a skeptical mind might argue.

Candace's mom found me, and I am happy that I was able to bring her daughter through to her. Sometimes, though, it is the person from the other side who makes the initial connection, finding me and then guiding their living relative to me as well.

Son

My nineteen-year-old son Brian and his girlfriend traveled more than a thousand miles by car to spend Christmas 2003 with me, his stepdad, and his little sister, then five years old. It was not only a holiday to treasure but one I will surely never forget.

After Christmas was over, my son left Arizona, heading back for New Year's Eve in New Orleans. I didn't hear from my son on New Year's Eve and I sensed that something was terribly wrong, but my son was grown and I didn't want to be an overbearing mom. The next time I heard from Louisiana was four days later, January 4, 2004. It was a detective from Baton Rouge calling me. He told me that my son was dead. In an instant, I was certain my life was over!

After Brian's death, I had three weeks before I had to return to work. Three weeks to wrap my mind and heart around my son's death to try and make sense out of the loss. The loss was so fresh that I was emotionally raw. I was crying incessantly in the car, wherever I drove. There was no end in sight to this unbearable pain and sadness that consumed my heart.

Three weeks into my son's death, my sister-in-law saw Allison's Web site on a local news program and told my husband about it. She suggested that I e-mail Allison. My husband had to do it, as I was not open to anything or anyone because my pain was just so overwhelming. I think it's normal to shut down and put up your guard when you lose someone you love.

On February 7, approximately a month after his death, I received a phone call confirming a date and time to have a reading with Allison. It was scheduled for approximately six weeks after Brian's death. My husband and I left our house early, to find Allison's home and to be there on the dot. Allison greeted my husband and me, stating that our son had been with her for three days. She told us that she had copious notes providing the information communicated to her by Brian that she wanted to confirm with me. I would like to mention that there is no other way and no magic that could produce the knowledge that Allison had about my son. I've always heard that when someone dies, that person is still with you, in your heart. Until I lost my son, I had no real understanding of that idea. In the last five years, I have lost both my parents, an infant child, and my teenage son, and when I say that I did not want to live any longer, I truly mean it. When I tell you that Allison saved my life, again, I mean it.

Allison began describing the coloring, size,

and personality characteristics of a dog that she saw standing beside my son. I immediately recognized the dog through the description and fondly reflected on a furry family member that had died before my son. I thought it was pretty funny that right off the bat my son appeared to Allison with one of our four pet schnauzers, named Glitche. I thought it humorous because this was the least favorite of his dogs. I know he knew that it would be important for me to know that Glitche was all right because Glitche meant so much to me. Glitche is now his faithful companion on the other side.

My son said that he wanted me to locate two boxes that would verify much of the reading that I didn't understand at the time. For example, Allison said, "Your son spends a lot of time with Alexander."

I said, "You mean Alexandra."

Allison responded, "No, Alexander."

I wasn't sure about the boxes or Alexander. Two days after the reading, I received a call from an old landlord. We had lived in her building three years before my son's death. She stated that she had found two boxes labeled "keepsakes" along with the name "Brian." She wanted to know if I knew who that was. I guess since it had been so long, she didn't remember my son's name. Her call was a godsend. As the shock of the call settled in, I pondered what could be in the boxes.

Anyone who's lost anyone knows how valuable getting that call was to me. To be able to have something that belonged to my son and to know that he orchestrated that gift from the other side to let me know he is still here with me was invaluable. Not just anything, but childhood mementos — it doesn't get any better than that.

I immediately retrieved the boxes. Upon opening the first, I found a folder with a project that Brian had completed in school, titled "Old Families of Louisiana." The biography of "Alexander Stirling from the 1700's" was the first thing that I laid my eyes on. He was a family ancestor whom my son had wanted to know more about.

Allison also described seeing a large body of water with paddlewheel boats. "This is where your son likes to be. He spends time there."

Allison said that she's never been to Louisiana or the Mississippi River. She described every detail of the area to a tee. Keep in mind that she knew nothing of our Louisiana background and I have no accent.

Allison went on to explain how my son had died, that he had been administered something that he had had a bad reaction to. She described how quickly it happened and how he left this world in no pain.

She described his spirit, his personality; she used words and expressions that he would use.

Allison gave me names of songs that Brian would play for me, and after his passing he did play them consistently for months. Whether I was in the car or an elevator, I heard the songs that she named. She explained how spirits have almost an electric energy and that they can manipulate other objects with electric energy like computers, radios, and such to give signs that they're still around.

She described my son's relationship with his little sister, before he died and after.

She talked about an older man whom he plays checkers with. When I spoke with my son's biological dad in Louisiana, I was informed that his great-grandfather played checkers all the time.

Allison also said, "He says he still calls you on your phone."

I immediately grabbed my purse and pulled out my cell phone. I had to show her the text message that Brian had sent me *after* his passing. The message said that he loved me. Allison had confirmed that he had indeed called me when he left the text message on my cell phone. This occurred three days after he had died. The message was not traceable. In October, nine months after his death, he text-messaged me again when my dad died. I believe he was letting me know that he was around my dad. The calls would pop my son's name up on the screen.

Allison continued, "Your son says he misses barbecued ribs."

She explained that those who have passed often come through with their favorite food dishes. Kind of like a calling card and also because favorite foods bring good feelings in life.

This is his favorite food in the whole world. When we have ribs for dinner, Brian always gives us a sign that he's with us. Whether it's lights flickering or a small animal running up to us in our yard and looking eye to eye with us.

Allison confirmed that my daughter's little toy airplane with no batteries would light up and turn around on top of our television. This was a regular occurrence. Allison validated what we had suspected, that my son was the culprit. Apparently, by affecting objects, spirits communicate that they're around the objects' owners. The toy is my daughter's, so my son is just letting us know he's watching over her.

Allison gave me many other messages and family members' names that I validated for her. There are too many to mention, but the signs that are there — daily, weekly, all the time — are what mean the most to me. That's the gift that Allison gave to me. She put me on the same page energetically as Brian so that I can appreciate the signs instead of dismissing them. Allison's recognition of signs that I already suspected were from Brian, without her having heard them from me, confirmed to me that my son is contacting me. The truth is, in my heart I already knew this. I know that my son is around me always. Now I can enjoy the signs and talk to my son knowing that he hears me.

Not only did Brian contact Allison, he communicated through her. My son's reaching out to me saved my life. Was I skeptical? Of course. Did I want it to be true? Again, of course. However, I had no idea the amount of detailed information that would be passed from my son to Allison. I found myself amazed at the absolute proof that my son still existed. That proof would surface over and over again, reassuring me that my son would never leave his mom. He's not gone.

If by telling my story and sharing my relationship with Allison, I can help one person who has lost a child to cope a little better, then Brian would be happy. I truly feel that what happens in life is all a part of a bigger plan, bigger than any of us can comprehend. I am Catholic. I always believed in heaven and hell. I don't have all the answers about religion or spirits, but I am telling you that I don't think I could have moved forward without Allison DuBois's giving me a little nudge in the right direction. She helped me to understand that my child is still with me, watching over his sister, giving us signs all the time that he's around. Does it still hurt? Of course. Do you still miss your child? Yes! You always will; your children are a part of you. I still cry and sometimes get so sad that I literally cry myself to sleep. You always look back and wonder what you could've or should've done differently. Would it have changed this tragic event? Did you do something wrong in life? But my son told Allison to tell me something very important. His words were "Mom, you couldn't have prevented my passing. It was out of your hands." He also said that he knows I love him and that I'm a good mom. So when I go to bed at night, I can lay my head o⌐

that for comfort.

Allison has a gift. It is a gift from God. It's been a year and a half since Brian's death. I now spend much of my time telling stories about him, laughing about him, remembering him in the most wonderful ways. I know that I couldn't have changed the fact that he was slated to leave this world when he did and that gives me some peace. I have emerged in a positive way since my readings with Allison. If I can touch one reader and help that person, then my pain becomes more bearable because my son's tragic death wasn't in vain.

Once you believe that your child's spirit is truly with you, you will be more open to signs. The signs are there, but you have to believe in their existence. I'm a fortunate woman to have had an incredible son for nineteen years, and I'm blessed to have a seven-year-old daughter. I know how lucky I am to have them. Still, in the first reading that I had, my son stated that he knew that I wanted to be with him and that I was thinking that I didn't want to live any longer, but that he would give me signs all the time and help me to move forward. He would give me his strength so that I could make it through the day. He reminded me that I need to be here for his sister. He said when it's my time, when I'm *reeeaaallly* old, that he'd be there to welcome me into heaven. So I'll keep making the barbecued ribs and talking to my daughter about Brian. He is a part of me that I will never let go.

A Persistent Young Man

I will always remember the persistent young man who inhabited my house for three days. If I went in my backyard, he was there. Walked in the kitchen, he was there. He would pop in and out of my house and yard throughout the day, demanding my attention, standing before me waiting for me to drop everything for him, making me feel an urgency within to act as a secretary and take notes for him. By the time his mom and stepdad arrived for their reading, I was relieved to relay his messages so that I could have some alone time again. Just kidding! He was only in my house because he knew that his parents would be there soon. I don't usually summon the dead. They most often use me as a go-between, knowing that their loved ones are making their way toward me. I believe my clients have been brought to me by the deceased through strange "co-incidences." Sometimes the dead whisper in the ear of the living, saying, "Her, go to her."

It was interesting how Brian's mom even got an appointment with me. I was booked for almost a year at that time. Somehow my booker, who was learning how to use her computer, had slid the grieving mother into a cancellation spot. She was on the waiting list, but not near the top, oops! Not only that, but I have a policy that three months need to pass after a death before I do the reading so that there's time for things to unfold in the client's life and to give the client some time to find their footing again after the loss. It had only been a few weeks for her, which I found out during the reading. Brian did pretty good orchestrating that one!

Brian, who knew how much his mom needed to hear from him, pulled a lot of strings, which just shows the lengths he'll go to for his mom.

What I remember the most about the reading is the moment when I told her, "He still reaches you on your phone."

She seemed a little shocked. Then she reached into her purse and pulled out her cell phone. She ran through her saved messages, and there was a text message sent from Brian *after* his death. His name was on the screen with the message, "I love you mom."

I was also struck by the boy's mention of the boxes that would confirm the information that I gave the mother. It's always hard to look at a client and say, "It'll make sense to you at some point." This is an important part of the process of a reading, because being told something that has yet to happen reinforces that the spirit was there.

I never question spirits in these circumstances because I've seen them work their magic before. I look at my clients and reassure them as I say, "Really, they'll come through for you."

I also remember feeling my client's pain and also feeling Brian's attempt to ease it for her. Looking at my client, I saw the same face that I see every time that I read a person who's lost a child. I'm glad I not only got to know my client but also had the pleasure of knowing her mischievous son. I'm also not advising everyone to run out and book with a medium. I'm just trying to give others a glimpse into a place they themselves may not be able to see. And I want to reassure those who mourn lost children that their children are always a part of them, even after death. For those of you who know that your children are still with you after death, talk to them. They can hear you. If you decide to book a medium, do

51

your homework. I find word of mouth from a family member or trusted friend to be the best indicator of a medium's ability.

I often see parents who carry a heavy burden. It's the burden of "What if? What if I had known? What if I could have changed things?" I'm talking about parents of children who have some specific self-destructive behavior that leads to their death. This was the case with Christine.

This wonderful woman lost her precious teenage daughter to addiction. Let me state that addiction was only a part of this girl. She was also tenacious, intelligent, beautiful, and sensitive.

Christine's daughter Dallas had a chemical imbalance. Because of Dallas's age, it's easy to see why Christine thought that Dallas was just experiencing "growing pains." Most parents can relate to this, as they are often told by their friends, "Oh, she'll grow out of it." Unfortunately, some kids are not given the chance to. Dallas, like many kids, had experimented with drugs. As far as Christine knew, Dallas had only tried smoking marijuana. But Dallas's drug use had turned into something much bigger. It had evolved into an addiction to crystal meth. By the time Christine found out about the severity of her daughter's problem, it was too late. I explained to Christine that many people will benefit from her story, recognizing similarities between her story and their own. It's important for people to grasp that many people with chemical imbalances turn to drugs or alcohol to "find balance." From my experience bringing through the deceased who had chemical imbalances, I have noticed that the more severe the imbalance, the more they reached for drug or drink.

There is a vital purpose to Christine's story — to prevent any preventable deaths and to teach by example. I want you all to know that there is a ripple effect to every death, one that touches many and helps some that are in jeopardy to be pushed back to shore.

Christine

I never thought that Dallas wouldn't outlive me. She was definitely choosing the difficult path, but we were always hopeful that she would "grow up" and become the beautiful, fun daughter that we had before. We didn't know that she had been using crystal meth for more than six months before it took her away from us. This is how devastating and quick this drug can be. It can change and take a life without remorse or warning. If any parents think that their child is involved with drugs, I beg them to do *whatever* it takes to save their child. I know that I wish every day that I had done more or somehow could have saved my daughter.

My husband and I have two other children, Tori and Mason, and *they* are why we keep going. I thank God for them every day.

I used to pray to God every night for my children to be safe, happy, and healthy. After Dallas died, I was telling a friend of mine at work about my prayers and how God hadn't listened to me. She responded with "Have you ever thought that maybe Dallas is happy now?"

Those few words have stayed with me. I think they are true. Dallas wasn't happy here when she was alive. The next best thing to having Dallas with us is having Allison talk to her and relay to us her messages letting us know that she is in a much better place. I know now that she is much more content where she is.

There were some specific pieces of information that Allison gave me in my reading that really touched me. When I feel sad, I can look back on them to remind myself that my little girl is still with me.

One of the first things out of Allison's mouth was "Dallas is around a male who skateboards, a younger male whom she loves."

Her brother Mason, who is only eleven, skateboards just about every day of his life! It meant a lot for Dallas to acknowledge her brother.

Allison mentioned an "Ashley" connected to Dallas. She said that Dallas is around Ashley now. Ashley is her closest girl cousin, my brother's daughter. Again, it's comforting to know that she's still with us.

Allison also mentioned a "Jason" and that he may be someone whom I "blame." This is the name of the boy she was living with at the time of her death, a boy who I believe was giving her the drugs. He died one year after Dallas as a result of his own poor choices.

Allison stated, "Dallas likes to spend time around your dad, Christine."

Well, my dad lives in Arkansas and we had just spent a long weekend with him. I guess she was there with us!

Allison also said, "She is around a favorite uncle."

My brother died 360 days before her. They were like brother and sister, so there is no doubt in my mind that they are together having a grand ole time. I sat with Allison as she provided me with information that validated to me that my daughter is doing well and is still an "active" member of our family.

Allison also brought through my brother Eric, who had passed away. It was the first time that Allison and I had met, and *wow,* did he ever come through loud and clear. The very first thing she said was "Now don't take this the wrong way. He is laughing and saying he is a menace to society."

That is so Eric! After he died, I could hear him laughing like he was standing right next to me for at least two weeks. Allison also mentioned a Ron "connected" to Eric. Ron is our dad's name and also the name of one of Eric's close friends. I could feel Eric there in the room with us. He had a huge presence in life, as he still does in the afterlife!

Thank you, Allison, for reconnecting my family.

Dallas

In February of 2003 I was asked to do a reading at a news station that would be taped to air. The news station would pick the sitter, who would sit behind me during a controlled experiment. I was up for the challenge, so I accepted. Aside from any science that I participated in, it was always the sitter and the soothed soul that were the greatest incentive for me to participate.

When I arrived at the news station, I met a producer named Jim, who seemed friendly but guarded. He pulled up a chair for me, and I perched myself on it. I was a little nervous. To calm my nerves, I pulled out one of my favorite gifts of all time, my iPod. I put in my tiny earphones and tried to go to a more relaxed place in my head, tuning out the hustle and bustle of the cameramen, spectators, and others. If a medium is too distracted by surroundings, we tend to lose some of the information that we receive in readings. I had my big, white pad of paper to jot down the information that I receive before a reading about the sitter and the people they have asked to hear from. I was given the signal that my sitter was in place behind me ready to go. As I moved through the information piece by piece, I was so focused on receiving, I was unaware that my sitter behind me was in tears. When we were finished, I stood up and turned around to hug my sitter, who turned out to be a woman named Christine. She reminded me very much of my own friends, and I liked her immediately. I also liked her daughter Dallas, whom I had brought through. I had also brought through her brother who had recently passed. He was a kick in the pants.

Her daughter was sorry she had left so soon but was more concerned about her mom. I would not see Christine again for almost two years.

After the news segment aired, I was asked by the news producer if I would read his wife, Wendy, as a Valentine's Day gift from him. I obliged. His wife was a young woman with long brown hair and eyes that were big, friendly, green welcome mats. She was tall and thin, with an air of laughter wrapped around her. She sat down and I read her for an hour. Afterward, I walked her out. Little did I know that she would become one of my closest friends. She was the person who had suggested to her TV producer husband that he invite Christine to be the sitter. So, almost two years later, while I was working on this chapter, Wendy said, "Why don't you call Christine and share her story?"

"Oh, I don't want to bother her."

"Allison, it's no bother. She'd probably like to talk about Dallas."

This led to Christine's coming back to see me. I told her that I was thinking of a follow-up reading for her. Christine replied that she had received the information she needed from Dallas the first time we met and that I shouldn't go to any trouble. I said, "Well that's nice to hear, but Dallas showed up to talk to me last night and I have five pages of notes from her, if you want them."

So I went through the pages with Christine, and it was great to see that her daughter was in an even better place than before. Dallas was also still giving messages to reassure her mom and remind her that she remains around her family out of love, not because she's bound here for some sad reason. Christine's brother who passed is a real joker and caught my attention with his Cheshire cat grin. Her brother showed me himself riding around a lake on a Jet Ski, waving, smiling, and, as he put it, "living." Dallas said she was with Christine's wonderful granddad and that "he died far too soon." Only one of Christine's granddads had passed. He had died of a heart attack beside her crib when he was in his forties. So it was very nice for Christine to know that her daughter was with her granddad. Dallas kept talking about the VW bug and said she would have had one had she lived longer. Christine found this touching since she herself had had one when she was younger and she used to tell her kids about it and all of her adventures in it. This led to Christine's affection for "slug bug," which is a game that she played regularly with her kids. It seemed that Dallas was also saying that she really wanted to be like her mom, which is the biggest compliment that any parent can receive. It's the obscure little details that can carry the biggest impact in a reading. The details that would mean nothing to another person mean everything to the bereaved. I am quite sure I will be hearing from Dallas again, and I look forward to that day.

All in the Family

This story is unusual for many reasons. It deals with the death of a beloved son born into a family of mediums/psychics who span at least three generations and without a doubt many more. It's important for people to understand what it's like to "know" that something bad is going to happen and not be able to stop it. I think many people will be able to relate to this feeling because most parents are innately connected to their children on many levels. From the moment their child is born and, for some people, before that, there is an unbreakable bond. People who would say they've never pre-dicted anything in their life seem to sense when their children are in trouble. So, whether you're a medium/psychic or just highly connected to those you love, it's not hard to relate to Mark Ireland's loss of his son. We may also empathize with his ability to embrace his son's soul after his death and admire his ability to begin to turn his family's pain into healing for others. I also think that it's nice to see a dad's perspective. Mark has been gracious enough to share his with us.

Fathers and Sons

It occurred to me that my background is probably very different from that of most other people who experience a reading with Allison. You see, my father was a prominent psychic-medium, so I experienced the phenomenon of predictions coming to pass on a firsthand basis every day growing up. From the 1950s until his passing in 1992, Dad counseled celebrities like Mae West and Amanda Blake, in addition to high-ranking government officials, who had total trust in his guidance. My father appeared on television programs, gave lectures, and demonstrated his abilities worldwide. He was also a deeply spiritual minister who worked with religious leaders from all faiths, using his gifts to spread the message, "There is no death and there are no dead." Despite my dad's outstanding abilities and achievements, very few people today know the name Richard Ireland. Looking back, I guess Dad was ahead of his time, a sort of trailblazer, if you will.

Living with someone who has these gifts is a double-edged sword. When your father knows *everything* that's going on, you really can't get away with much. On the other hand, seeing my dad's gifts displayed on a daily basis, I came to fully appreciate that psychic phenomena and spirit communication are real. It was comforting to know that there's something more than just this brief physical existence.

Moving into adulthood, I suppressed any personal psychic leanings and focused on a mainstream lifestyle. While I experienced intuitive feelings on many occasions, it was rare for me to trust them. So while I loved my father, I deliberately chose a different and more stable path than a life centered on the metaphysical. I was practical, driven, and focused on business and family, pushing aside part of my lineage to concentrate on my own life. Working hard over the years, I enjoyed success, which allowed me to build a beautiful home for my family — a loving wife and two wonderful sons, one in high school and the other in college. In January 2004, however, my calculated, comfortable life was rocked to its foundation.

My younger son, Brandon, had just turned eighteen and was entering the final semester of his senior year in high school. Good-natured and easy to please, Brandon was invariably considerate of others. He was tall and lanky, with long, curly brown hair and eyes reflecting a loving and caring nature. His strong jaw line, dimpled chin, and the ridge on his forehead were a fresh minting of my features.

Brandon had become quite proficient on the bass guitar after six years of lessons. He showed a strong aptitude for mathematics, which correlated to his exceptional musical skills. His mathematical ability also led him to an interest in physics, which he intended to study in college. Brandon's college plans were well outlined and bolstered by good SAT scores. In concert with his friends, he was excited and ready to embark on future goals.

Despite my pragmatic nature, I was disturbed by vivid premonitions that came as a feeling of certainty, a gut feeling of impending disaster, on the morning of January 10, 2004. Brandon shared his intention to embark on a very difficult hike with friends to the summit of the McDowell Mountains near our home in Scottsdale, Arizona. He enjoyed hiking as a regular hobby and had hiked three times earlier that week.

Because of my strong feelings, I asked Brandon to stay home.

In response, my son looked me and said, "We're going, Dad," as if to convey the message "Stop worrying."

I got the sense that my son thought I was just being a worried dad.

So, in spite of my warnings, Brandon began his trek toward the McDowell Mountains with four of his good friends. On that particular day, ominously strong winds pushed pollutants from the Greater Phoenix valley toward the mountains where Brandon was hiking. The impure air made the vigorous climb all the more stressful. Brandon suffered a severe asthma attack, which resulted in reduced levels of oxygen in his bloodstream. I was later told that Brandon had rested in an effort to regain his strength and ability to breathe. Brandon also used his prescription inhaler, hoping to improve his deteriorating respiration. Unfortunately, these actions were ineffective, and Brandon's condition grew progressively worse.

Evidently, Brandon attempted to climb back down to the base of the mountain with two of his friends (the other two had gone ahead at a faster pace), which further depleted the oxygen supply he needed to sustain his heart and brain. He became light-headed and had to rest repeatedly. The gradual decline in blood oxygen levels eventually caused Brandon's heart to fail. Because of the unique symptoms, which included a rapid heartbeat and numbness of limbs, neither Brandon nor his good friend Stuart recognized his condition as an asthma attack. While Brandon used his inhaler to see if it might help, both boys thought something else was wrong because the symptoms were unlike anything my son had ever experienced. I later learned that Brandon was joking the entire time and never seemed panicked. Apparently, he failed to recognize the severity of the situation, which turned out to be a blessing in disguise. Just before collapsing, Brandon told Stuart that "Everything was shining."

This statement evokes images of what heaven might have looked like to my son.

Needless to say, I repeatedly kicked myself for failing to heed my intuitive warning. Although I initially thought I might have been able to alter the outcome, I now believe that the outcome was a matter of destiny. Perhaps the warning was intended to prepare me emotionally for the inevitable.

The fact is that I could have demanded that Brandon stay home on Saturday only to have him hike on Sunday with the same conclusion. In fact, I've come to recognize that there is no value in playing the blame game.

I love my son Brandon more than words can describe, and I've had great difficulty imagining life without him. After his passing, I would often break down and cry and still do on occasion. Nothing can prepare a parent for the loss of a child.

After losing Brandon, I recalled teachings that my dad shared many years ago, teachings focused on God's love and the continuity of life. My father wrote books and even documented his own psychic work, leaving behind a legacy of valued training materials. I found renewed interest in these writings and began poring over them.

I also recalled that spirit communication was available to me. Immediately I called my uncle Robert, a medium psychic and retired minister. I asked my uncle, "Please share anything you may receive or feel that pertains to Brandon. Any information that you receive on him at all."

At about 2 p.m., on Monday, January 12, 2004, I was standing in the Desert Hills mortuary in Scottsdale, Arizona, when my cell phone rang. Realizing that the call was from my uncle, I felt a mixed sense of hope and anxiety. I then listened with great anticipation as my uncle proceeded to tell me, "I tried hard to make a connection last night but got nothing. This morning, however, your dad came to me during meditation. He told me that Brandon's heart failed due to a lack of oxygen and, while he experienced shortness of breath, Brandon suffered no pain. When he first left his body, Brandon was confused, but your dad came to meet him and helped him adjust. [Sometimes when a person dies, it takes him or her a while to realize what happened.] Brandon also had a message for you and Susie. He wants you to know that you were the best parents he ever could have had."

This might seem like a general statement to most, but coupled with the specific details that my uncle had already given pertaining to Brandon and my personal relationship with my uncle, I had no reason to doubt him. As a matter of fact, coming from him, the information meant even more, and it was something that I needed to hear. While we were still reeling from the loss of Brandon, my uncle's words provided immeasurable comfort for my family.

When I spoke to my uncle, there had been

nothing confirmed by the authorities about the cause of Brandon's death. The authorities would not share any information with us regarding the suspected cause, nor were they even willing to speculate. It was about a week after speaking to my uncle that I received validation of my uncle's description of Brandon's cause of death. When I spoke to the physician who performed the autopsy, she explained that Brandon's death was attributed to a severe asthma attack. In an effort to process more oxygen, his lungs had become oversized to the point of nearly touching in the middle. Evidently, this condition occurs only in cases of drowning and severe asthma. Brandon's inability to process oxygen eventually led to cardiac arrest, thus the official cause of death matched the description given by my uncle. Not knowing our son's cause of death for a week was terrible; my uncle's assurance that it was a natural death was comforting at a time when nobody else could give us the answer to the question, "Why did our son die?"

At this time, I also felt inspired to begin daily meditation in hopes of enhancing my perceptive abilities and connecting with Brandon. I didn't expect to develop skills anywhere near my dad's level but did aspire to become more "connected." As a result of these efforts, my sensitivity became heightened to some degree.

Just a few days after Brandon's passing, I sat meditating quietly. During this time I saw an image of Brandon's face, which seemed to be surrounded by warmth and joy. I can only describe this feeling as a simultaneous melding of different sensory input. After the vision of Brandon's face I saw a symbol, which was a cross with an oval loop at the top. I was not familiar with this particular image, so I searched for information on the Internet. As a result of my research, I learned that the cross was an ankh, an ancient Egyptian symbol that predates the cross of the crucifixion. The lower cross portion of the symbol represents physical life, while the oval loop portion at the top symbolizes eternal life. Ultimately, I believe that the message was a symbolic way of confirming that Brandon is indeed alive and well.

My older son, Steven, also began meditating after Brandon died. About a week into the process — two weeks after his brother's passing — Steven experienced a vivid dream that I believe was an astral experience. Astrals, commonly referred to as "out-of-body experiences," are very different from everyday dreams. They are astonishingly lucid experiences. During astrals, our senses are exceedingly sharp and surroundings seem exceptionally real. While in this state, our physical body remains asleep while our soul or "spiritual body" (described by the apostle Paul, in the New Testament) travels in other realms, dimensions, or "planes."

While asleep, Steven heard music emanating from our living room. Walking toward that room, he saw Brandon playing the bass guitar, a previously common scene in our home. Steven immediately ran to his brother and gave him a hug, noting that the embrace was so real, he actually *felt* the fabric of Brandon's shirt. Steven then asked Brandon, "What's it like?" and Brandon replied, "At first it was so weird, but now it feels incredible." Brandon then said to Steven, "Why don't you come visit me more often?"

After the encounter with his brother, while still physically asleep, Steven experienced hovering above his own body and observing the time on a clock in his room. As he awoke, Steven opened his eyes and looked at the clock, finding that the time was exactly the same as what he had just seen in his "dream" without the aid of his physical senses. It seemed that the validation with the clock allowed Steven to recognize that what he had experienced with his brother was very real.

My wife also experienced a profound connection. While sitting alone at the foot of our bed, Susie suddenly felt Brandon's presence very strongly. She was then able to see Brandon, as a shadow figure, discernible through her peripheral vision for about thirty seconds. She was absolutely certain that this was Brandon: she could *feel* it. One day later, Susie received a phone call from a musician friend, James Linton, who was shaken and needed to talk. Before even hearing of Susie's experiences, James described a similar set of circumstances, where he felt the presence of someone else while recording music in his studio. James also saw a shadow figure through his peripheral vision in the exact same manner as Susie had.

In February 2004 I was contacted by one of my dad's friends, who called to share his condolences and provide a helpful suggestion. This gentleman, Jerry Conser, asked me how I was doing and then said, "Mark, I know of a quality medium in Phoenix who can help you get in touch with your son." Intrigued by Jerry's words, I listened with a sense of heightened anticipation as he continued, "Her name is Allison DuBois." I was stunned by Jerry's comments because I'd just seen a news clip about Allison one day earlier.

As a result of Jerry's call, I contacted Allison's assistant to arrange a reading. It was a few months before I could see her, because she was booked through the balance of the year, but the experience was well worth the wait. Allison provided highly compelling evidence that my father and son were both still quite alive, as evidenced in the following reading excerpts:

Brandon's presence was immediately apparent in Allison's first words, "I see a son connected to you. I'm not sure if he passed or if I'm seeing a son who is yet to be born." Given that Allison was unaware that I had a son on the other side, I was greatly encouraged by this start and hoping for even more.

Allison continued, "Your dad is referencing a Susan as being connected to you. He notes that he is around Susan. Do you understand?" Greatly impressed, I responded, "Why yes, that's my wife!"

Allison then delivered one of the most compelling validations of the day, speaking to a matter that was a complete secret, "I see him signing a book and handing it over to you. I believe this was his book and he is handing it over to you. Do you understand this?" Delighted beyond words, I burst out, "Totally!"

Just a week earlier, I'd been contacted by one of my father's friends, who handed me an unpublished manuscript that my father authored back in 1973. Before receiving this call, I was completely unaware that the book, entitled *ESP Development Course*, even existed. Apparently, just before his passing, my dad asked this friend to hold the book for safekeeping. Now for some inexplicable reason, *twelve years later,* this person suddenly felt compelled to share the book with me. I started thinking this was just too coincidental to be a coincidence.

Allison assumed a new path, which garnered my immediate attention: "Your dad mentions 'having the boy.' Your son is with your dad, and he says 'that's how it should be.'" This statement made me flash back to my uncle's description of how my dad greeted Brandon at the time of his passing. The validation was even more significant because I knew that Allison was unaware that I'd lost a son. (Before the reading, I had verified that Jerry Conser had not spoken to her.)

Now sharing information from my son, Allison said, "Twenty-five years is being shown as important for you and your wife.

Have you hit your twenty-fifth anniversary?" Pleasantly surprised, I responded, "Yes, we had our twenty-fifth anniversary, on June thirtieth." Allison then said, "Happy anniversary. These are the things that matter to them after they pass — the happy times." I was thrilled by this wonderful validation, which referenced a milestone event that had occurred less than two months earlier.

I then began a determined pursuit of top mediums throughout America and Europe in a personal search for answers to some very deep questions. In the course of my readings with all the mediums, I was amazed at the specific, accurate information that was provided. Even more compelling was the consistency of the messages that began to overlay and form a sort of mosaic.

I also found it therapeutic to talk about Brandon with other people and to allow myself to cry whenever the feeling came. My wife, son, and I like to be around other people who knew and loved Brandon and are not afraid to talk about him, sharing special memories. You may find that some people are afraid to discuss topics pertaining to loved ones who have passed. What these folks don't understand is that we want to talk about our mothers, fathers, sons, and daughters who have crossed over because it helps us feel connected to them and it keeps them fresh in our minds. If you encounter people who shy away from mentioning those who have passed, give them permission to talk openly by letting them know that you want to share stories about your loved ones. Ultimately, there is no "one size fits all" approach to the healing process, but I hope my story will help others who are struggling through loss.

Connecting with Brandon

I remember the day that I met Mark. He was a good-looking man whose hair had just begun to pepper in a very distinguished way. He was a little anxious and very focused. I invited him to have a seat in my office, and I explained to him that if he sees me scribbling on a pad of paper, it's my protocol when I read. Writing down the information helps me to focus and "process out" the energy that I'm bringing through, which is the deceased. He seemed very pleasant. He reminded me a little bit of the engineers that my husband worked with, so I knew he was very intelligent and a little aloof.

I began his reading by getting a "son" connection to him. I asked him if he had a son who had died. I couldn't tell if his son had died or if this was a son yet to be. He said yes, his son had passed away. I remember feeling drowning, heaviness in the lungs. I felt an urgency around the son. The problem for me was that Mark had another son who's living, so I wanted to be thorough. I said, "If your deceased son didn't have asthma or pass with a feeling of water in the lungs, then keep an eye on your living son." Mark then said that his son who had passed had asthma and the M.E. indeed had said that it would have felt as though there were water in his lungs even though he died in the desert. I also remember very well that Mark's dad made an appearance, saying that he's with his grandson as he should be. I was very happy when Mark's deceased dad mentioned the name "Susan" and said he is fond of her and is connected to her. Mark said this is his wife's name and was happy to hear his dad acknowledge her. I was very moved by Mark's love for his son. He is without question a wonderful dad. I have no doubt that Mark's son and dad will be there for Mark when his time comes for a reunion. I've since met Susan and Mark's son Steven. They are a uniquely centered family, not only spiritually healthy but a lot of fun to be around. I won't forget that reading because I brought through my first professional psychic-medium. He was very easy to understand and to relay messages from. Interestingly, skeptics are like pulling mud through a colander. I think the more open-minded and spiritual people must be doing something right, because they certainly are more pleasant in death.

When I asked Mark to contribute his story to this chapter, I asked him to include advice for people walking his same path. (I asked the same from all of the parents in this chapter; their responses are immeasurably helpful.) Mark not only "gets it," his account is eloquent and heartfelt: "Those you've lost are not gone, and you will never be alone."

Lost Children

While writing this chapter, I tried to be thorough and cover different parents and their own experiences, as well as mine. I also know that some children who die pass at the hands of others. This is a different kind of pain, often because the parents have a face that represents the person who took their child's life. Sometimes parents don't have that, and they spend a lot of time sizing people up, wondering if they're looking at the face of the person who unjustly took their child's life.

In 2005 I was faced with one of the most

rewarding yet heavy experiences that I have ever faced. I was asked to be a guest speaker at a grief support group. I never hesitated to accept their invitation, and I was honored to be asked. I was also well aware that this task would not be easy and would be a challenge to recover from. When the night came for me to speak at the meeting, I knew that I would meet many wonderful people, both the living and those who had passed.

Joe and I pulled into the parking lot behind the building where the group meeting was being held. I found it hard to collect myself to face the overwhelming nature of the roomful of traumatic deaths that awaited me. Previously I had "read" for people who had lost their children to murder, but this was on a much larger scale with a clear focus on murder. I didn't want to walk in looking shaken. I was there to comfort the parents. I reminded myself that any empathy that I felt for them didn't even come close to what they had been through. So I took a deep breath and walked through the door.

I asked myself, If I lost a child in this way, what are the words that could bring some relief?

My goal in coming to the meeting was to send the people there home in a better place energetically than when they first walked through the door.

I stood in a room that had many broken hearts inside. I could feel and see the kids who had had their lives cut short. We were seated in a large circle, and behind the parents and siblings of the murder victims stood the figures of the deceased. Some had their hand on their dad's shoulder; some were just smiling at those who came for them. They were all there, ready to come through and have their words be heard by their parents. There were children who had been adults at the time of their death; nevertheless they were somebody's child. There were boys and girls of all ages, and they knew that I could see them. I suspect they are there every week to support their parents. They were children of all skin colors and heights, children who'd died of gunshots wounds, died in hand-to-hand combat after being attacked, died in many terrible ways at the hands of others.

I was given a little white stuffed bear with angel wings that was made specifically for this support group. I clung to this little bear for comfort and to keep my focus. I searched the faces of the people present, hoping I could somehow relieve a small part of their pain. In this room full of people who'd lost a child in the most painful way, I thought, This is why I do what I do!

I asked those who had died to please come through "loud and clear" because I would only have a couple of minutes for each living person. I have to tell the dead exactly what I need from them so they can work with me. I started off by sharing that sometimes siblings like to come through to their brothers and sisters through music that they play on the radio, or they tell me that in death they passed their record collection to their sibling. This is one way to let the living know they are still with them. Often "their song" will play in the most obscure place; other times it will play everywhere you go. I shared with the group that people who liked to talk on the phone in life tend to be behind the phone calls where we find silence on the other end when we pick up. This is the deceased's way of telling us that they can still reach us. Many present acknowledged having experiences where they "knew" it was their child saying, "I'm still here."

I spent part of the evening trying to explain to parents why someone would shoot and kill their child. I had to answer the question "Why would God let a child die?" One boy who died was killed by his own parent. "Why?" is an enormous question. From what I can tell, it's because without loss we don't appreciate what we have. Premature death causes a tidal wave of emotions that inspire others to hold their children more, some to start support groups to help others like them, others to fight for tougher laws that will in turn prevent the deaths of many others. There is always a backlash from pain that creates a stronger consciousness.

We are human and are feeling beings who sometimes get caught up in ourselves and we forget why we are here to begin with. We are here to make it better for someone else, to learn what matters in life, to see and experience love. With love comes loss, but that loss is temporary and the love stays forever. Sometimes this is little comfort for the grieving, but it is something to think about. Grief brings people together in search of happiness again. Grief builds our awareness, and relationships change.

After an emotional evening with this group, I felt both wiped out and renewed. I left the meeting having gotten to know a group of wonderful people, both the living and the deceased. I looked deep into the eyes of people who are forced to be resilient without any choice in the matter. I studied their faces, which I will always remember, and I willingly felt their pain. I wasn't going to be one of those who distance themselves from these people. I would be one who embraces them, even if it meant sharing their pain. Sometimes you have to feel someone's pain in order to help take some of it away. The members hugged me good-bye and walked out the door with smiles on their faces. I didn't solve all of their problems, but I did help cast light on the faces of their children so they could be seen on that special night.

At that meeting I was asked, as I often am, about "dreams" where the people we love appear. I explained that a dream is like being able to fly or drive a race car through the sky. When someone who died appears in our dreams, it's a visit. It's that person's way of telling us that he or she is still with us and a part of our life. People I've talked to who've had this experience know the feeling and how unmistakable a dream visit is. You can feel the difference in your heart because your heart feels lighter. Those who have died just want us to acknowledge that we know that they're still here. If you feel tension or irritation from the spirit, it's for that reason. Once they're acknowledged, they relax, and you won't get such a feeling of urgency.

Also, please remember that when you lose people you love, they still continue to share in your day. They will still sit in their favorite chair. They'll still talk to you. Their personality will largely determine what signs they choose to send you. Do you want to share sorrow and pain with them daily? I think they would like to share in your good times. Of course, you're going to have bad days from time to time, but if you make an effort to share a good day with those who've passed, they get to take part in your joy. Nothing makes them happier. Talk to those who have passed and laugh with them again. Pore over their pictures, and you'll find that one will stand out. That's how they communicate to you what they look like now. Love those you love enough to live for them.

Your loved ones don't want you to suffer for the rest of your life, paying homage to them through your tears. They sit there with you while you cry, and the harder you cry, the louder you get. But if you are drowning them out with sobs, then how can they be heard? Allow peace to enter your heart, take a deep breath, and ask them to let you know they're with you. They will find a way. They want to continue to share in your life and in the memories you're making. Live life "large" for yourself. That allows them to continue living.

As many of you know, my dad passed away in 2002. Sometimes, to feel closer to him, I eat a big cheeseburger or go to the movies. Why? Because burgers and movies are two things we used to enjoy together when I was little. The more connections you make to those who've passed, the stronger you'll feel their presence. By extending your energy to them and embracing their presence in your life, you will find some of the pain you carry slip away, to be replaced by the love your loved ones still have for you.

Visits are a fantastic gift from the person who passed. When a child dies, the loved ones experience grief in many different ways. Usually mothers feel torn to pieces from within and, bound by grief, can't move forward. They have a lump in their throat that appeared the day they lost their child and it has never left them. They often can't speak without crying. They remember holding their baby in their arms and making a favorite sandwich when the child was small. (Children usually keep those favorites no matter how old they get, because their mom made it for them and that made them feel loved.)

People mourning the loss of a loved one

feel guilt for having a good day, which turns into a no-win situation. It is important, healthy, and necessary to relearn how to live after any great loss. Parents who've lost children must move forward for the rest of their family. It is easy for the siblings and other family members of the deceased to see only the focus on the child who died; the living may feel unseen and unheard. Those who've passed on don't want their death to take the focus off the living. Parents need to own that their child wants Mom and Dad to be happy and wants to share their good days with them but will also share their bad days, if that's all there is. Mothers gave life to their child and are challenged to allow themselves to move forward and know that their child is indeed still with them. Easier said than done: this is by no means an easy task. But it's important for anyone mourning a loss to make an effort to move through the pain for their own well-being. Moms, or anybody who has lost someone they love, have to find a new way of loving that person, since hugs and kisses are no longer an option. Talk to those who've passed, eat their favorite food, or find a picture that draws you in and helps you to share their love. Remember, they can hear you and touch you still, so it's a matter of your learning how to reach them again. You're playing catch-up with them. They've been trying to reach you since the day they died. It's also essential for parents who've lost children to reach out to other parents who understand their grief. Very few things will be more comforting than connecting with someone who's walked in your same shoes. There are others who understand what it's like to pick up the pieces of a broken heart. So please, reach out for those connections of understanding.

From my readings I've noticed that dads tend to retreat from others emotionally and hold their pain inside. I know this because the child who died often tells me this so that I can relay it to my client. It seems that dads feel like they're supposed to be able to fix anything, so they grapple with the fact that they couldn't "fix" or save their child. I think many people agree that males are taught to hold their feelings inside from a young age. But the loss of a loved one can bring overwhelming feelings. Your passed loved one can feel your pain and wants you to release it. It's not healthy to hold on to this sorrow. Sometimes all you need to release it is an understanding person to talk to who will listen and not judge you.

Dads hurt every bit as much as moms,

but sometimes they aren't provided the same support system. So if you know a man who has lost a child, make an extra effort to reach out to him. Provide a shoulder for him to cry on or an ear to listen to anything that a grieving father has to say.

I've seen people distance themselves when someone dies because they don't know what to say or do for the grieving. They don't know how to make it right. Even though supporting someone who's hurting is not an easy thing to do, it's the right thing to do. To step away from people when they need you most is like kicking them when they're down. So be aware of how your actions, good or bad, can affect others. The grieving person will never forget your kindness and will never need it more than after such a great loss.

There are simple ways you can reach out and remind the grieving that you care. Bring dinner over for their family, help to clean their house, send a card to cheer them up, or phone them once a week to see how they are holding up. Any effort will mean the world to them. Try to be sensitive to their needs. Instead of asking them if they are doing well, which is unlikely, ask them if they are feeling "decent" today. That is probably the best they can hope for, for quite some time. They don't need to hear "Be strong." If you can't fall apart after losing a loved one, then when can you fall apart? Falling apart is what must happen so that you can put yourself back together again in a new form.

People who suffer a great loss will never completely be who they were before the loved one died — just as the deceased aren't exactly what they were before their death. But you know what? Just as you have to learn how to love those who've passed in a new way, they too have to learn how to reach you again. Remember, your loved ones are better than okay, and they remain here to watch you become whole again. They stay to love you and show you how fantastic they are now. They marvel at who you will become through growth and change. Make every day count, creating magic moments and stories to share with those who've passed away.

When my dad died, I was emotionally and physically maimed. I didn't want to sleep because every day that passed was a day that took me further away from the last day of his life, and it hurt. What I came to realize was that every day that carries me forward took me one day closer to the moment that my dad and I would reunite energetically.

He will walk me through the thin veil that separates the living and those who live again.

Chapter 2
OUT OF SIGHT, NOT GONE

The desire for intimate connection with another person is universal. Yet the connection that is created between two people is entirely unique. When people fall in love and decide to build a life together, get married, buy a house, and have kids, they eventually develop a shorthand with each other. They can communicate with fewer words, predict each other's needs, sometimes even read each other's thoughts. This can help us during the busy times of life, when we're bogged down with who's going to wash the laundry or who's going to put away the dishes.

In readings, I find the living often end up missing the things about their spouse that they used to complain about the most. They miss their spouse's cold feet being stuck on them for warming at bedtime. Often a man misses his wife's ability to soothe him by her words and shut down his defenses with her silly "I love you" smile. These are some of the things that seem to be universal. Then there are things in readings that are completely unique, such as the deceased coming through and showing me ten boys and three girls and relaying to me that the couple have thirteen children. A husband might come through and tell me that his wife makes the best chocolate chip, blueberry pancakes in the world! Well, I think that's pretty unique in itself, but universal in that many people come through and name their favorite food and tell me they felt loved when it was made for them.

In life, we know our partner's routine, for instance that a wife is cranky in the morning without her coffee and you better not say a word until she's had it, or that when a husband has a cold, he turns into a two-year-old and needs babying. Or you might know never to give your spouse the checkbook because he or she will double up payments to pay off the balance faster, thinking he or she is doing a good thing, but end up emptying your bank account. We kiss, pout, say we're sorry, and laugh at how fast the years go by. These examples are just a drop in the bucket compared to the ocean of memories and familiarities that we experience with those we love every day. I try to remember the lessons I've learned through those who've died and those who live and miss them. When Joe rides my nerves, I take a very deep breath and I thank God for the times I've had with him and for my extraordinary daughters. I sometimes stare at Joe and the kids, memorizing every detail of their faces, and my heart swells with gratitude. Sometimes it feels like it will break, because I love them so much. It's hard for me to imagine the walls of any heart's being strong enough to contain the love that my family give me every day and the love that I have an abundance of for them. It's awfully crowded in there, and that's why God gave us hearts that were made to expand.

When a great love dies, it's devastating. There is no replacing the love of your life and your best friend. It's hard enough to fall in love and to trust someone with your deepest feelings. To hold that person in a place inside your heart that is sacred is to render yourself vulnerable. We allow ourselves to risk getting hurt because we can't imagine an end to the love that we feel. In reality, there is no end to this love. Even when we physically lose that person, the one we love has become a part of us and we are a part of him or her. The loss of a spouse or someone we love romantically is exceptionally painful. The song "The Way We Were" sung by Barbra Streisand is, I feel, a powerful telling of what losing a love can be and often is. I find this song very moving, haunting in a way. The lyrics speak of "scattered pictures" and all the happy memories from before life changed. Although the song seems to be more about losing a loved one through a breakup or divorce, you can see how the words can be applied to the death of a loved one. I know from personal experience, both from losing my dad and from seeing through the eyes of the deceased, that for pictures to be scattered around the person who is grieving is a very real occurrence that happens every day.

I've brought through many people who were and are the love of a lifetime to someone. I assure you that moving on doesn't have to mean letting go. Those who have passed still sit with you at the kitchen table, and they often sit with and touch the living loved one at bedtime, whether it's through dreams or continuing to lie on their side of the bed. Because this was their routine in life, they often continue it even after death. They do this out of love and for the comfort they feel they still bring the living. Also, the living provide comfort for those who have passed when we mention their name, talk to them directly, stare at their picture, and include them in our lives. The deceased don't exactly cry, but I have felt their heart ache for the living person they're trying to reach. It pains them to see you cry, so they will try harder to reach out to you through others, signs, or dreams until you acknowledge their presence in words or just by thinking about them — the "I know you're there" being screamed in your head and your heart.

I believe that the deceased comfort the living in many ways. Often they appear to loved ones in dreams to say they're all right. They let us "feel" their presence. They're simply reminding us that we're not alone, that they haven't left. They send us songs to communicate to us; I've talked to people who are very aware when it's a dedication being sent to them from the other side. The deceased give us all sorts of signs that they remain. People smell the perfume their mom used to wear or the cigar their grand-dad used to smoke. Some see orbs of light, unmistakably not of this world, appear in photographs. The deceased make toys run without batteries to say they're around the kids. They communicate through children, who lack the hang-ups that grown people have. My youngest daughter says, "Grandpa's not gone, Mom. I see him in my room. He talks to me." You get what I'm saying. They are often trying so hard to communicate that they'll try different ways to reach out to you until they are heard. Be careful not to harden your mind and heart, dismissing every sign they send you. Signs will be clear. If you keep an open mind and an open heart, you may be able to verify the presence of your loved one.

When your love story seems to end with a death, please remember that love stories never really end. That's what makes them so special. There are countless ways that we connect and communicate with our loved ones both in life and in death. Remember this: "till death do us part" doesn't apply in the afterlife. People are rejoined and whole again, and they always are where they want to be the most.

As a footnote, significant others who pass do want their loved one to be happy, and if that entails remarriage, then they're fine with that. You're not minimizing the love you have for the person who died by loving someone else for different reasons. The deceased don't sit around and watch your physical contact with other people. They are here on an emotional level to support you when you need it and advise you when you'll listen, because they know what pitfalls await you. Those who have passed have a wide view.

People often wonder which one of the men/women they loved in life will be with them after they have all passed away. This is a valid concern but one that requires no real thought or guilt. I say this because when you die, your energy seems to be emotionally based. You will be where your heart truly wants to reside. If that means around more than one person, then so be it. It's usually not, but I have had a few instances of this. I had one guy come through with three wives who had all passed before him. He seemed happy, can't imagine why. Just kidding. If a spouse dies young, then even though the living partner may remarry and live for years with another spouse, he or she often chooses to be with that first spouse. Remember, this sorting out is based on emotional energy, not thought. There tends to be unfinished business between the first couple. They often will look exactly as they did around the time of the young spouse's death. Even if a husband lived to be ninety-five, he will revert to twenty-one, if that was his age when they were parted by death. Trust me, the level of joy that I see on these spirits' faces is pure magic. This doesn't mean that a second wife from later in life is left out in the cold when she passes. The husband may choose to be with her. It depends on where he *feels* he needs to be.

Once there is no one left in the living world whom they love, there is very little incentive for the deceased to reach the living. If there was a house, saloon, church, or other place that a deceased person spent a lot of time, he or she will sometimes remain there for comfort. For the deceased, it's not the current day; it's whatever year they were happiest in connection with the structure. This presence is sometimes referred to as a "haunting." The deceased are there usually not to hurt others but because they like being where you also happen to want to be. When there is absolutely no interest for spirits here in our world, they return to their own heaven and "live" with their loved ones who have also died.

I do, however, believe that sometimes spirits will appear back here when they are needed for intervention to save the life of a living person or to help shape a person into who he or she was meant to be by attempting to guide that person down the right path. Usually this will be a person who reminds them of themselves and whom they want to keep from walking down the wrong path — often the path that the deceased themselves had traveled.

Music to My Ears

I learned of Allison DuBois in March of 2004. Reading news articles on the Internet, I came across one that mentioned the "Michael Jordan" of mediums. Allison had been involved in experiments at an Arizona university. The article said that she communicates with dead people. I had lost my dear husband, Bill, on 9/11/2001 at the World Trade Center. He was on the 100th floor of the North Tower, the first building to be attacked. I did not hear from Bill, and the exact circumstances of his death would be lost to me forever. Dying there was horrible, but I knew some deaths were worse than others. Some people were burned alive. Many jumped to their deaths to escape the flames and extreme heat. Of course, my imagination spun some very gruesome scenes. But when I read about Allison and the attempts of scientists to back her up, I figured this was my only chance to quench my need to know what happened to Bill.

My reading was in late August of 2004. I was very nervous. I did not want to convey any hints, to supply any information. I wanted it all to come from Bill. Allison explained that she would give me all the information that she received because she didn't want to edit anything important out. During the course of the reading, Allison asked if I wanted any specific questions answered. I said I wanted to know the circumstances of my husband's death.

She immediately said that he was in a building that was on fire. He was with other people and that he was very afraid to die and that he loved his life very much. She said that he was looking at a picture of our family before he died. Bill was just at the World Trade Center for a two-day meeting and didn't have an office there. The picture was the one that he always carried in his wallet. She said the ceiling caved in and that he "was gone" instantly. Then she said, "How is it that you don't know how your husband died?"

When I revealed his location, Allison was taken aback. Since Bill was inside the building, she couldn't see the outside. She had no idea that he was in the WTC. Information concerning other circumstances were talked about, such as information about our children, friends, and family that came through. He also talked about deceased people related to us whom he spends time around now.

When the reading was almost over, Allison said, "By the way, Bill says that when it's your turn to pass, 'We're going dancing . . . *and it's a date!*' " Before Bill's death, our local community arts center would occasionally offer ballroom dancing lessons. He was not much of a dancer, but he encouraged me to sign us up. I missed the deadline, and when the fall 2001 schedule came out, he reminded me to sign us up. I promised him I would. A week later 9/11 happened. Since his death, I would speak to him all the time. I would end our conversations by saying, "And when I cross over, we're going dancing!"

What Allison shared with me that day chased away a paralysis caused by grief that had gripped my heart. I did approach her with an open mind and heart. My belief in a life after this was already a part of me, all through blind faith. Allison's reading gave me affirmation and a link with my better half that I desperately needed.

Second anniversary of 9/11:

I decided to stay home alone that day and face my sadness privately. I don't like to carry grief around 24/7 because it is such an energy drain, but I do pull it out at appropriate times, and the 9/11 date always qualifies. After watching various ceremonies on television, I decided to do some laundry. I went through some pants' pockets and found some change and laid it on the kitchen counter. I later came back to put the coins away. As I glanced down, I noticed an old wheat penny. I was thrilled because every time my husband saw one, he would joyfully point it out, saying that he would save it with other old coins that he treasured. Finding the coin and remembering made me smile. I was happy with that little sign on 9/11. But I was even happier after I picked up the coin. As I turned it over and saw the imprint of Bill's birth year, I knew that the coin was a gift. I knew that he was all around me at that moment. He was joyous, and playful, and whole. The sadness was my own, definitely not his. I liked his feelings better and spent the rest of my day with his mind-set instead of the one I had woken up with.

After my second reading with Allison on September 16, 2005:

Bill proved to Allison his skills in the kitchen by showing her his favorite food — scrambled eggs. He always enjoyed making them for the family when he was alive, especially for his beloved boxer dogs, Mike and Zelda. It was so important that Allison talked about Bill's fondness for scrambled eggs because it's specific to his personality, further letting me know he's with me. It's nice to know that cholesterol problems don't cross over with us!

Bill talked about being with relatives who had died in recent years. Allison spoke of them by name. Everyone is together. There isn't any loneliness or longing. There seems to be a sense of universal love that is private and special for each individual, yet it belongs to everyone.

Allison says that our loved ones know of our time that is yet to come, good or bad, but they understand that while we are here, we must move through, even stumble through, our humanness. And their new way of understanding is out of our realm of thinking. We will be reunited one way or another, and with the knowledge that we will someday be in their wonderful place, we should be inspired to live better lives and to make wiser choices. Allison said that Bill wanted to acknowledge the plaque that was erected in his honor. In fact, Bill's former employer had put a plaque up for Bill in the office in his honor. Allison said that Bill spoke of wanting me to take a trip and be happy. She shared details about our life together as well as things that have happened since.

I am so very happy that Allison contacted me during the fourth anniversary of 9/11. The things that she shared with me from the other side not only lessened my burden of sorrow and grief but also gave me great hope for my future, here and beyond. Every negative particle will simply fall away in an instant. Relish the spirit of those who have gone before us. There truly is no end.

Reading 9/11

When I contacted Betty about my book, I only had her name and phone number from my assistant's old records. Having read three hundred people the year that I read her, I didn't remember that she was a 9/11 widow. I e-mailed her a few days before the fourth anniversary of 9/11. I have every confidence that Bill arranged for his wife to be read around the time of his passing. I had only sent e-mails out to five random former clients out of three hundred to see if they wanted to share their story in my book, and the only chapter that I hadn't written was "loss of spouse." She was the only one out of the five who had lost a spouse, so I'm quite sure Bill's behind this. Good job, Bill!

Betty e-mailed me back that after she

returned from her trip to a 9/11 tribute, she would contact me to share the details of her reading with me. After she returned and called me, I felt compelled to reread her. The timing was right, and Bill had some things to say.

Betty called me on the day that we had agreed on for a phone reading. I told her that her husband said he sends her birds so that she knows he's around.

She shared with me that just the other day she had had a little bird fly up around her head, and she said, "I know that's you, Bill."

Sometimes birds can symbolize freedom to the deceased, a way to let the living know that they're soaring in the sky and not in the ground or in an urn. Birds are a sign of life and an expanded consciousness. Birds usually look down on us and observe us, and that's not so different from angels/spirits.

So it was nice for her to have acknowledgment from her husband that indeed this was an attempt to get her attention. They're also sort of a calling card from him, which means birds will be his way to share his presence with his wife so she doesn't dismiss him.

He shared names of family members whom he is around on the other side, names that Betty easily verified — except for one. I thought it was interesting that I kept getting the name "James." Betty said, "You kept getting that name last year, and I couldn't figure that one out."

I had a lightbulb moment. "Betty, it's a last name. Do you know someone close to your husband with the last name James?"

It then clicked in her head. She realized that Bill was talking about a friend, a Dr. James, who had also passed away. Whew! Sometimes it's harder than other times, but that was great that Bill finally got me to realize that it was a last name. Every person Bill named and said he was with was now accounted for and was someone close to his heart.

Bill also kept talking about a plaque that was for him that he loved. He wanted his wife to know how much it meant to him. It had been erected for him at his office and had his image etched onto the front.

Many pieces of information were conveyed to Betty that day from Bill, but I thought the most important was that he was thinking of her in his final moments at the World Trade Center and he still is carrying her with him. He will continue to guide and love his family as well as give them occasional urges to make his famous scrambled eggs just the way he likes them.

I would like to thank Betty for courageously sharing her story with others. Many people who lost loved ones on 9/11 will no doubt relate to her as well as empathize with her. To all of those who've loved and lost, please remember that you're blessed having loved so greatly and that love will never die.

Hurricane Katrina

In August 2005 the worst natural disaster to hit America in modern times tore through the South. Hurricane Katrina blew through Louisiana and Mississippi and left utter devastation in its wake. My friend Wendy called me distraught because her husband Jim, the news producer, had decided to head for the ruins left by Katrina. Wendy was worried about his safety, which is understandable. All I could do was reassure her. Jim thankfully returned safely a few days later.

The following week his news station held a telethon to raise money for the disaster relief fund. I called Wendy and said, "Let's go sort clothes or take food down to the coliseum in Phoenix for the evacuees. Let's do something to help!"

Wendy said, "Allison, why don't you come tonight and answer phones at the news station for the telethon?"

So that's exactly what I did. It was a great night with many ups and downs. There were pizza parlors that called in donating $4,000, there were people who offered to house an evacuee, and there were children who called in to donate the contents of their piggy banks! As I always say, much can be learned from children.

Anyway, I sat next to a nice guy named Dave, who was my age. We started chatting between phone calls. He asked me what I do for a living, so I told him, "I'm a medium."

His response was "No way!"

Then he started telling me about his friend Jason, whose wife had just died tragically. He then got on his cell phone and called Jason to tell him who was sitting next to him. All I could hear was "No way!" You can tell why those two are friends! I gave the excited friend my e-mail address, and he contacted me the next day.

Jason had lost his wife four months before our introduction. He had two daughters to take care of. My empathy was enormous, and I knew his wife orchestrated our meeting. She was taking care of him from the other side. So I told him I would bring his wife through, and I set up a reading for the following week. Jason shared that he had looked up my Web site a couple of months earlier but saw that I had a long waiting list. He had been disappointed when he wasn't able to book an appointment with me. Apparently his wife took care of this for him by cutting through the red tape and going right to the source!

Jason mentioned that he had a friend, Karla, who had had a reading with me. Her husband had died in a car accident along with their youngest daughter and oldest daughter's best friend. He had met Karla in a support group she had founded called Safe Harbor. I immediately remembered her reading from a little over a year before. I thought, I'm going to call her because the coincidences keep adding up.

I explained to Jason what some of the information his wife might come through with would be like. I know that when I give examples to someone who is grieving, it helps the person to know what I'm actually seeing in my head. Joe, who never tires of my giving people an example, has observed that the example resonates on their faces as they begin to experience their own unique connections and realize that my example is their reality. One example that I gave Jason was "Your wife might say, I'm going to be at the little girl's birthday party."

I visualized birthday balloons held in the hand of Jason's wife, but Jason said nothing about my birthday example, so I thought I'd save it for his reading the following week. I was baffled, I must admit. The examples I give are usually very important to the deceased, so I'm used to their clicking with the living. I hung up with Jason and I called Karla to say hi.

She was quite taken aback to hear from me. As we talked, I asked her about her support group. She said it focuses on deaths involving car accidents. I asked if I could add the group's information to my Web site as a resource for others who had lost loved ones in this way, and she agreed. Karla then shared something else. Today was her daughter's birthday. She knew it was no coincidence that I called that day. We talked about how much she misses her family and that she was taking balloons to the cemetery for her daughter today. For me, this greatly reinforced the fact that we are purposely placed into people's lives when they need us the most. No doubt Karla's daughter and husband had a hand in leading me to her during this chain of "coincidences." I told Jason the next day that it was Karla's daughter's birthday. I knew that Jason's wife, Nicole, had been trying to let Karla know that she was taking care of her little girl. I knew this because when people who've passed on show me something like birthday balloons in their hand, I know they're showing a physical connection between themselves and whoever the object belongs to. A feeling of certainty that I am reading the visual correctly can also reinforce the visual that I receive. After learning of Karla's daughter's birthday, I was kicking myself for not having taken the information further, but I did share with Karla that I had mentioned the little girl's birthday to Jason. Karla knew her husband and daughter were letting her know that they saw the balloons she'd brought for her daughter and that they were with her. People who pass on find themselves connected through the relationships that the living have.

Jason and Karla have included their stories, hoping to touch others who have lost their lovers and spouses.

Mrs. Jason Sherman

My name is Jason Sherman. My life and the lives of my family and close friends were forever changed on May 15, 2005, at 2:15 a.m., on a sad stretch of the 101 freeway in Phoenix, Arizona. My wife, Nicole, and I had just spent the evening with some childhood friends of hers whom she had recently reconnected with. We had a blast! Eating, drinking, dancing, and catching up on old times.

Her friends asked if we wanted to stay at their place since the drive home was so far and it was so late. We decided that we should go home. There is nothing like sleeping in your own bed after a night out. Besides, later that morning we were going to see a medium who was in town because my wife was interested in the topic of life after death.

On our way home, we saw what looked to be a horrific accident in the opposite lane of traffic. The vehicles were at a standstill. We couldn't see if anyone had been hurt. I have an EMT license and had been trying to join various fire departments in the valley for the last five years, so Nicole immediately said, "Oh my God, we should pull over and help!"

I did just that, quickly pulling over to the side of the road that we were closest to, on the opposite side of the freeway from the accident. It looked as though the two vehicles involved in the accident had smashed into the center dividing cables of the median and had thrown debris all along the freeway, even across to the other side. I jumped out and I dialed 911 as I raced across the freeway on foot. I told them to send police and fire because it looked really bad. Just then I saw the two people in one car run away, one right past me! I asked if he was okay, and he said yeah and kept running. As I got to the median, I noticed that on their side of the freeway, there were a bunch of street racers who had pulled over. As soon as they heard the sirens, they yelled, "Cops! Let's go!" They all sped off.

Nicole had crossed with me to the other side of the street to look inside the cars to check for casualties. Meanwhile we could hear the police sirens getting closer. I told her that she should go back to the car and stay there, since it was apparent that nobody was hurt. I told her I'd finish exploring the scene and be right there. So she nodded and returned to our car. I still remember seeing her cross back over the freeway to our car and move our car more parallel to the accident.

I started to advise another person who had stopped to give assistance, letting him know nobody was hurt. We began moving debris out of the vast roadway. One car's front bumper and trim were in the lanes closest to the center on our side! Cars were still flying by us and running over debris! I thought to myself, "Man, they're going too fast. Why don't they slow down!" Just then a highway patrol vehicle pulled up on the side the cars were on. The officer got out and started assessing the scene. I had turned my back to the freeway so that I could talk to him to let him know what I had witnessed.

The next thing I knew, I heard this heavy sound of a large object hitting something solid and then the sickening sound of it hitting the ground. This was followed by the screech of a car hitting the brakes. I turned and I saw something maybe ten or so feet away from me in the lane right next to the median, which was where I was standing. I remember thinking that what I was looking at didn't look real. I actually thought that someone playing a joke had dropped a mannequin out of a vehicle. It looked very unnatural.

I heard someone say it was a body, and I turned to see people with a horrified look on their faces while they backed away. I was in the road. I turned back to look closer, thinking to myself, "No way, it's fake." That's when I noticed the clothes. They were identical to what Nicole was wearing. I felt this wave of panic and shock and sickness wash over me.

"Oh my God . . . Oh my God!"

I started to step back so that I could see into our car, which was across the freeway. I asked an officer who was out in the middle of the road to check my car. I told him that my wife was supposed to be in the car. He shined his flashlight into my vehicle . . . nothing. She was not there. By this time I had backed away from where the unnatural-looking body lay. The body dressed in Nicole's clothes.

I realized what I had been looking at all along was Nicole. She must have tried to cross back over the freeway to be with me. When I had turned to talk with the officer, she was simultaneously being hit by a car. I felt a kind of sick feeling that is beyond comparison to any other in the world, so massive I couldn't think. My head was swimming. My first thought was about our girls and how they would never see her again. How was I going to tell them? They had had no clue, as they kissed her earlier in the night at the babysitter's, that this would be their last kiss, their last time to see their mommy alive. I had no idea that as I watched her dance that night, that as she turned to me and said, "I love you," that would be the last time I would hear those words from her. No idea that as we slowly danced and held each other, an hour later she would be gone from my life.

I am forever grateful for that last dance and those last words of "I love you."

My Reading with Allison

Before I met Allison, I was in a pretty dark place. I was doing my best to get through each day. It was hard enough getting myself up to go in to work in the morning. I used to wake up to Nicole every morning and the thoughts of what the day would bring — things we had to do or were looking forward to. Now I was waking up and she was no longer next to me. My new tragic reality was the first thing I thought of upon awakening, and the last fleeting thought as I drifted off to sleep at night was of her. I was just surviving. I felt lost.

But now I had a new list of responsibilities that were solely mine. Our ten-year-old daughter, Hailey, and our seven-year-old daughter, Mckenna, were at the top of this list. I had many things to learn. I have had a shaved head for the last seven or so years. There's not a lot of thought that goes into what I'm going to do with my hair in the mornings. It is safe to say that I haven't had a lot of practice fixing the girls' hair! Ponytails, scrunchies, hair clips — forget it! I feel really bad for them. I'm trying, but they get frustrated and say, "Never mind, Dad." Does anyone know of a class to teach dads how to fix their daughters' hair? I would gladly sign up.

Losing Nicole has really made me take a hard look at my life and the things that are really important. Many times we take for granted that our partners will always be there — be there when the girls get home from school, or to go clothes shopping with them, or to fix their hair before going out anywhere. Nicole always made sure the girls looked cute. Cute hair, cute clothes. Now I'm left in charge of that — the guy who would holler out from the closet, "Honey, what should I wear when we go out tonight?"

I admit that I beat myself up because I can't do the things that she was able to do as well as she could. It's hard to accept that I might not be able to do everything and be everywhere. I feel like it's my responsibility to try to make up for their mom's not being there. I feel as if I am letting Nicole down if I can't handle everything at once — the girls, work, my feelings and emotions, cleaning the house, doing the yard. The list goes on and on. I am doing the best I can. I have to keep telling myself this.

I believe that Nicole saw me struggling and pulled some strings to lead me to Allison. After I met Allison, I began to feel less alone. Not as lost. I'm not magically better, and I'm aware that the girls and I have a long road ahead of us. It's a start, though. Allison talked about so many things that she could not have known about except through Nicole. After the funeral, we wrote messages to Nicole on pieces of paper and attached them to balloons and let them go. Allison said, "Nicole got the balloons you sent her." My jaw just dropped. There were so many things that just blew me away.

There were some things that didn't make sense at first but did later. One in particular was a message Nicole had for her best friend, Larissa. She mentioned Larissa and showed the color purple around her — *all* around her! She also kept showing Larissa driving past a Burger King, over and over again. Nicole kept showing Allison the Burger King sign through the window of a car driving by. I know, I thought the same thing: what the heck are you talking about! About a week later, I was able to share with Larissa the things Allison brought through from Nicole. When I told her about the color purple around her, she told me how the house she just bought was entirely purple on the inside! Obviously Larissa and her husband had some painting to do before moving in. When I mentioned driving past the Burger King over and over, she said, "What day was it that you went to Allison?"

I told her that it was last Tuesday, and she got quiet. She said that same day she went to a department store near where we live. She went over and over; she must have gone five or six times. Well, guess what's right in front of the department store. You guessed it — Burger King!

Larissa cried. She has struggled with losing Nicole like all of us have. But she has kept it pretty private. She is a firefighter, and as she does so many times in her work, she pushed aside her own fears and emotions to be there for other people. She and her husband, Jeff, were there for me and my girls from the start, and they just dove into helping me out where they could with the funeral and food and everything. Larissa is also very religious and looks to the Bible as a source of strength and guidance in her life. My reading with Allison blew her away. I think she is afraid that if she believes in it too much, it will take away or cloud her beliefs in God and heaven. But she is still so sad and lonely, as we all are early in our loss of a loved one.

What has helped me is learning that Nicole is always around us. That she is only gone in the physical sense and that she influences the girls and my life every day. This has helped to ease my sadness and loneliness. No, I can't hug her or kiss her anymore, or feel her body next to mine. But I can "feel" her presence around me if I pay close attention. I talk to her every day, telling her how much I love her and asking her to help me out when things get overwhelming with the girls. I know that when my heart lightens some more, and the anger and the guilt and the sadness lessen, she will come into my dreams again. I long for this day and I know that we will be together again someday, when it's my time.

Medium Affected

When I met Jason for the first time, I had already written four pages of information from his wife and I was eager to share it with him. I opened the door to a friendly young man with a heavy heart. I could feel his pain. I invited him in to sit down and we began the reading.

First, I told him how amazed I was at the lengths his wife went to orchestrate a reading for the husband she still very much loves. She didn't cause a hurricane to get my attention. She did use it as an opportunity to reach me through a chain of events that were meant to happen to bring me to Jason. Spirits are very creative in setting up circumstances to get our attention. I asked his wife, "Come through loud and clear, and if there's something you want to say to your husband, now would be a good time."

Before Jason arrived, Nicole had kept showing me "her" ring around Jason's neck on a chain. I had written it down on a pad of paper. I now had my tablet of paper on my lap. As I looked at Jason, I said, "Jason, is that Nicole's ring around your neck?"

He responded yes.

"Jason, I'm going to turn my pad of paper towards you so that you know I wrote this before you got here."

I had answered the door myself with it in my hand, and Jason knew I hadn't written anything since we'd shaken hands. He looked confused and squinted at the paper: "Jason wears wedding ring on chain because then it's close to his heart."

Jason was clearly moved, and this is important. It's why I write information before a reading. There is a heavier impact when information is received before a reading. Then no one can argue that I "saw" the necklace and inferred my information. Which is great; it removes doubt.

"Jason, Nicole keeps talking about the lock of her hair that was saved. She also keeps talking about Disneyland and your taking your girls there after her passing. So this trip is important to her, and if you didn't just take them, then you plan to. She also talks about a little boy connected to her little sister whom she's around now. She also says she 'whispers' in your ear."

Jason was busting to tell me what the information meant. I asked him to wait until I finished giving him what I had, although I understood why it was difficult to refrain.

"She's also talking about ambulance lights that were a tribute to her?" I was a little confused by that one, but it would all make sense later. "She says she got the balloons that were released to her. She says to thank the ladies that brought all of the food after her passing. She was happy that you were taken care of by the "ladies," because she would have made dinner for you in life and appreciates it that they cared so much. Don't forget to thank them for her. She keeps showing me her necklace with the heart pendant as being important to her. She says she was well liked, and she says there were a lot of females she was around who were crying for her when she passed. She acknowledges a tattoo that was created in memory of her. She says she loved Mexican food and that she's with Jack on the other side."

This is some of the information that I gave Jason that emphasized to me who Nicole is and what she's about.

Jason then came back with responses to my information. "I do hear Nicole whisper in my ear. I do have a lock of her hair that means a lot to me. I did take our girls to Disneyland after Nicole passed. She has a little sister with a small son named Cole. There was a fire engine at her funeral that turned the lights on in tribute to Nicole. We did release balloons to her. Mexican food is her absolute favorite, and my deceased grandfather's name is Jack."

Well, I did think the fire engine was an ambulance, but that's still pretty close. I was moved that Nicole kept showing herself around her nephew, whose name is Cole. Cole/Nicole — the names side by side are pretty telling. He will always be a part of her, just as he is in name.

After the reading was over, as Jason was leaving, I hoped that what I told him would help him move a tiny bit forward and help him start to heal. He'll never fully move through the loss, but he will see her again and be reunited. I was very moved by meeting Jason. I saw the similarities between me and my Joe and Jason and his Nicole. They'd been married eleven years and had two daughters. Joe and I had been married eleven years and had three daughters.

Jason said to me, "I don't understand. Nicole and I were supposed to grow old together. There were so many things we had planned on doing together."

I looked at Jason, and it resonated with me that at any moment life can throw you a curveball. I knew that from all the readings I had done and from losing my father. I was looking at a man who had married the same time I did, had children the same age that my kids are, and yet I was afforded the luxury of being able to look at my husband from across the dinner table every night. I also took in that spouses, myself included, argue over silly things, things that later we realize are unimportant. I explained to Jason that it's just life — arguing, making up and moving on. No guilt needs to exist. It's the struggles that make us strong and later cause us to either return to or reflect upon those we love.

Jason had already walked out of my house

with Joe. I was still inside. Nicole whispered in my ear to go "Tell him I love him."

It seems general to some, but so what; it matters and she meant it. You bet I told him.

Nicole Sherman was planning her birthday party before she died and had picked out the band and everything. Jason and her family decided to hold the event anyway. It was the first birthday party that I ever attended for someone I brought through in a reading. As Nicole mentioned in the reading, Mexican food was her favorite, so her family catered her party from her favorite restaurant, El Charro. I also found it interesting that balloons with a note seem to be something both Karla and Jason have done for their loved ones. Both readings mentioned balloons.

In Jason's reading, Nicole had talked about wanting her two little girls to have heart necklaces. Jason explained that he had two made that had a small bit of Nicole's ashes inside the heart. He'd give them to his daughters when they are much older. Although Nicole understood why Jason was waiting, she still wanted her girls to have something right now to hold onto from her. So before the birthday party, my two younger girls and I set out in search of the perfect heart pendants for the Sherman girls. A mall on Saturday is something I only do when I absolutely have to, argghh! But brave it we did. We had been to four different jewelry stores when my second daughter, Fallon, upon entering another store, announced that this is where we would find the right necklace. She was right. We found the two perfect necklaces for the girls, and we took them to be engraved. I asked Nicole what she wanted to have inscribed on the back, and she said simply, "Mom."

Going to the party, gifts in hand, I hoped I wasn't overstepping my bounds. My girls met Nicole's. I handed one of the necklaces to Hailey, the older daughter, and she seemed happy with it. I gave Jason the necklace for the younger to be given later. My girls ran off to play as I stood and admired the cake with Nicole's young and flawless angel face on it staring back at me. I told Nicole that I was sorry that I couldn't do more for her, as I emotionally noted that I was one of many who would have liked to pull her back to our side of the veil. As my girls ran around me, I felt guilty and thankful all at the same time for being able to hug my little girls.

Sometimes after a reading with the loss of a spouse or child, I hug my family and then retreat to separate myself from them because I need to grieve privately for the deaths that hit too close to home. Sometimes I just watch my kids sleep to remember that moment forever. I "feel" for my clients that those sleeping, playing, laughing moments are the most important in life, so I remember to take in as many as humanly possible. When people die, they don't show me how much money or how many things they had. They show me the people who made them live well. It's the memories they banked that made them truly rich. I was deeply touched by Jason and Nicole's life together, and I hope their reading lets others know that there is no division of love.

After writing Jason's section for my book, I reflected on Karla and her family. I wanted to convey Karla's story in just the right way. Karla not only has experienced the loss of a spouse, which is the topic of this chapter but also lost her child at the same time. I think her story is the right one to conclude two very important and emotionally charged chapters; I hope it will add healing as well. This chapter includes three love stories that many people can relate to and admire. Karla's story is different from the other two in that she can't miss her husband without missing her daughter too, and vice versa. Karla has written a tribute for her husband that includes their love story. It's important to Karla that you feel like you know her family. She hopes her story will help others who have lost or will lose someone they love.

Karla

The day that I received that phone call from Allison was another hard day. It was my daughter Lindsey's birthday. She would have been fourteen years old. I woke up that morning, got my older daughter off to school, and headed for the gym, thinking that was going to make me feel better. I came home, took a shower, and got dressed for the day. I remember standing in the middle of my kitchen, feeling like I wanted to go back to bed. I stood there in the kitchen crying, talking to my daughter, telling her it is another sad day. I was feeling extremely depressed. I told her I needed something to bring a smile to my face that day. Then out of the blue, I received a phone call from Allison DuBois, asking me if I would like to do a tribute to my husband and daughter. Before I could tell her it was Lindsey's birthday, Allison already knew.

Two years ago, I lost part of myself when we were driving home from a family vacation. We were approximately one hour away from home when we had a tire blow out.

Our SUV rolled several times. My daughter Lindsey, age eleven, my husband, age thirty-six, and my older daughter's best friend, Tawnee Hogan, age fifteen, died at the scene of the accident. My life would never be the same. Although I can no longer see them, I am grateful for having them be a part of who I am.

To give you a little background on my husband and me, allow me to go back to where it all began for us.

I have known my husband forever, and when I say forever, I mean it. You see, our mothers were good friends at the time they were pregnant with us in Wichita, Kansas. We were born six weeks apart. I loved to tease him about being older than me. When I was five years old, my parents moved to California, and his parents moved to Colorado. When I was twelve, his father came to live with us while he found a job and a home to move his family to. I remember my mom calling me to come downstairs and meet the Whelchel boys — Brent, my future husband, and Todd. My husband told me that the moment he laid eyes upon me, he left there telling his brother Todd that I was the girl he was going to marry!

Several years passed, and although my husband tried several times to get me to be his girlfriend, it didn't happen. He was best friends with my brother, also named Brent. So, as Brent and Brent became close friends, he was like another brother in the house to me.

For our graduation, our mothers planned a party for the two of us. We talked until the early morning hours, and I realized that I was in love with Brent.

We dated for two years and were married at the young age of twenty and twenty-one. On our wedding day, Brent strolled in twenty minutes before the wedding. Time enough to raise a beer with his brothers and put on a tux. He told me surfing was great that day; the waves were too good to leave.

He was the kind of man who loved being the center of attention. Brent loved to make people laugh; he never minded others' calling him a smart-ass. (I think he enjoyed it.) He made a joke of everything; sometimes it was hard to get him to be serious. He never lost the child inside him.

His motto was "Work hard, and play hard." Brent never held back when it came to work. He looked for ways to learn and improve along the way.

Brent loved music. He played acoustic guitar and electric guitar. In the last three years of his life, he taught himself to sing, just as he had taught himself to play the guitar and drums. Brent always had a crowd cheering as he belted out songs from Stone Temple Pilots at a local sushi bar where he enjoyed karaoke. He could hear any song and immediately know the right chords to play. His love for rock and roll and playing in a band started when he was fourteen and continued until the day he died.

Brent loved to watch the Discovery channel. He especially loved anything that had to do with airplanes. So, at the age of thirty-five, he decided to take lessons to learn how to fly. He never seemed afraid of anything.

One of his brothers died almost ten years to the day before Brent died. He knew life was short, and he always told me, "Never look back. Yesterday is gone. Make the best of today, and keep your head looking forward."

It seemed as though the last few years of his life, Brent did everything he wanted to do. He took up cooking. He loved creating his own recipes and arranging his dishes on plates to make them look like they came from a gourmet restaurant. He loved serving the girls and me.

Brent was loyal to his work, family, and friends. He loved being a father, although he was a softie when it came to his girls.

His light lives on in his daughter Bridget, and his music will continue to play in the hearts of all who knew him.

Brent, I will love you always and forever.

Your special Kay.

How I Met Allison DuBois and the Details from My Reading

During the summer of 2004 I had been working with a therapist weekly to help me through the pain that I was still feeling. My therapist had a good idea of what I believed in spiritually. So during our session, she asked me what I thought about mediums. I told her I was very open, and did she know of anyone? She told me she had seen this lady on television and had looked up her Web site. Her name was Allison DuBois. She told me that she was going to have a reading with her soon. I remember going home that day and visiting Allison's Web site. She was booked for several months, so I decided that it was not meant to be.

Toward the end of the summer I walked into my therapist's office. She looked happy and peaceful. When I told her I recognized a change in her, she smiled and told me she had had her reading with Allison. She had lost a son. Not knowing what I would say, she said she asked if she could play the first part of the tape for me. She believed my husband had come through first, to try to reach me. I believe when you lose someone suddenly, especially in a car accident, you immediately have survivor's guilt, as I did. My therapist and I were working on my survivor's guilt. The first part of the tape, Allison starts off by saying that she is seeing a young man with two very young females, one on each side of him. "He wants you to know it is not your fault. He also wants you to know that he misses sitting out by the pool and sharing a good bottle of wine with you."

None of this made sense to my therapist, but everything made perfect sense to me. Brent was with Tawnee and Lindsey, who were in the accident with him, he knew I had survivor's guilt, and he wanted me to know that it was not my fault and that he cherished our evenings in Arizona sitting out by the pool with a good bottle of wine. Allison then got through to my therapist's son, who controlled the rest of the reading. That is typical of my husband, to go after exactly what he wants.

That evening I was sitting at my computer. Out of nowhere I heard this voice that came over me, *"E-mail Allison now!"*

I went to her Web site and did just that.

The next day her assistant e-mailed me saying that she had had a cancellation, and then she clicked on my e-mail. Would I like a reading in two weeks? Absolutely!

The middle of September 2004, I went to Allison's for a reading with my daughter. I made certain that I didn't give her assistant any information.

Allison immediately came through with my husband. He was standing with two very young girls, one on each side of him. Allison's eyes filled with tears. She looked at my daughter and me and asked, "Is this your father?"

Bridget answered, "Yes."

Allison explained that within the last week she had read someone who had died in 9/11. She told me that she thought the woman's husband who had passed was very strong as he came through, and my husband was coming through very clearly as well. This other woman turned out to be Betty, who's also in this chapter, what a coincidence. Allison told me and my daughter that she could feel a lot of love among our family.

Allison continued, "This was a car accident. There was something wrong with the tire, and the vehicle rolled."

In fact, our back left tire blew, and our

SUV rolled.

Brent came through his usual way. Allison laughed because she heard Brent singing "Happy Birthday" to himself in a comical manner. This meant a lot to me because Brent's birthday is September 24, and Lindsey's is September 8.

Allison said, "Brent wants you to know that he likes the way he looks now. He looks better than ever." Allison also said that Brent wanted Bridget to know that the song she keeps playing over and over again in her room is the song that he sends to her, "Dance with My Father" by Luther Vandross. He wanted her to know that "although she struggles with not being able to connect with him, he sits at the end of her bed every night as she sleeps."

I had experienced several wonderful dreams of my husband, Lindsey, and Tawnee. Bridget struggled with not having dreams or signs of their being with her.

At the scene of the accident in Tonapah, Arizona, a desolate town on the outskirts of Phoenix, I was severely injured. With a severed wrist, broken bones, and contusions everywhere, I somehow managed to get myself out of my seat belt. Our vehicle was upside down. As I crawled out, Brent was seated right next to me. I kept shouting for him to wake up and help us. Allison said, "Brent wants you to remember him the way he was before the accident, not at the scene of the accident." (I struggled with this in therapy.)

I managed to get Bridget out of her seat belt — she was conscious — and to get my younger daughter's friend, who was also conscious, away from the SUV. Immediately, we had help at the scene. There were two RNs who showed up to help right away. When we finally were air evacuated to the hospital, I was rushed into surgery. I had two surgeries back to back, one on my left wrist and one on my right foot. The doctor called my sisters and their husbands and said that I had a 50 percent chance of living. I had lost a lot of blood. At the scene of the accident, after the first roll, I remember there being a tunnel of light. My daughter Lindsey and my husband were waiting for me. The next thing I remember is their pushing me back, and the next thing I heard was my older daughter Bridget's scream for help.

Allison told me, "Brent knew that you wanted to come with them, but it was not your time. He said he knew that you would understand that he had to go be with Lindsey." After working in a hospice for seven years, every once in a while I would want to talk with Brent about what we would do if something happened to one of us. Brent always told me he did not want to talk about it, because he was "going to go first." He said he could not handle life without me.

Brent told Allison that he was sorry for not leaving me financially secure. A few months before, we had someone come out and talk to us about life insurance. With Brent's pilot lessons, our rate was very high. I had decided that we should hold off for a few more months, when our SUV would be paid off. Brent told Allison for me to never worry, he would always take care of me financially. (Funny, I have never once had to worry about money. It has always been there when I needed it.)

After the accident, I decided to do research on vehicles. I bought a Volvo. Allison told Bridget that when she starts to drive, "Your dad wants you to get a tank, an old Volvo."

Of course, this is exactly what I told Bridget she was going to get when she started driving. I have a tendency to be overprotective these days with my daughter Bridget. Allison told us not to worry, "Brent is really watching her now!"

Allison laughed because Brent wanted

Bridget to know her dad was "always watching her" and she should keep that in mind.

Over the years Brent had developed a strong relationship with his dad. He wanted us to know that he was worried about his dad, something about his heart. Not like a heart attack; he knew his dad had a broken heart.

Brent knew our anniversary was coming up soon, and he wanted me to go celebrate. He would be there with me. I had already made reservations to the Sanctuary (a project that Brent had personally worked on). He told Allison he wanted me to take a picture of him and set it at the table. He said that roses would be coming to me.

After my reading with Allison, I went home. My sister had a dozen roses waiting for me on the table. So I asked her, "Why did you get me roses?"

She replied, "I don't know. I was at the store with some flowers in my hand for you, and something made me walk back and return the flowers that I had and pick up the roses for you."

So I shared with my sister what Allison had said earlier. We both knew it was Brent.

That same week I went out to eat at the restaurant that my husband had helped build and there were roses at the table waiting for me. I don't know who sent them or where they came from, but I suspect Brent had something to do with my flowers. None of the other tables had any flowers. Bridget and I did take his pictures with us so that we would feel like he was dining with us.

Allison told Bridget and me that Brent wanted us to take a trip to Hawaii together.

Over that summer Bridget and I had talked about if we could take a trip, where would it be? Bridget told me, "I want to go to Hawaii."

I told her I didn't know if she remembered that her dad and I went to Hawaii for two weeks on our first wedding anniversary. I was seven months pregnant with her.

Allison asked if there was anyone else we wanted her to try to get through. I told her yes, my daughter. Allison immediately got Lindsey through. She told me she thought she was seven or eight. Lindsey "was very happy and playing with animals." (Lindsey loved animals.)

She said there was an older lady with her, who wore glasses. (My grandmother, I believe.)

Allison said, "She loved the balloons that she got on her birthday, and she is so touched that all her friends got together." Her last two birthdays, all her friends got together celebrating what they have made "Lindsey's Day." They bring a big cake and balloons. Together we release the balloons in front of her school, where a memorial wall and two benches sit in honor of her and her dad.

Allison said, "Lindsey was scared at first when she crossed over, but then her daddy took her hand."

Allison tells me that Lindsey says, "She lies with you at night in your bed with her dog, Sara. She doesn't like it that you cry so much. She knows that you have the TV on, but she knows that you are not watching it." Every night, Lindsey's dog sleeps with me. I stare at the TV, unaware of what is on. I used to cry, thanking God that I had made it through another day, and wishing God would take me that night.

Lindsey wants Bridget to know "that she knows they fought like sisters do, but she loves her and there is no need for her to feel guilty." Bridget had argued with her sister two days before the accident and was having a hard time forgiving herself.

The older lady is there with her, and she is wondering if it is okay if Lindsey goes and plays now for a while.

Bridget asked Allison if she could get her best friend to come through.

Tawnee came through. She told Bridget, "She likes being there with Bridget's dad. She is worried about her mom, and for us to please watch over her." Tawnee's family has had a very difficult time.

She told Bridget that when the dogs bark for no reason, this is her talking to us. She makes them bark. The dogs still bark for no reason. Now we just tell Tawnee, "We hear you, Tawnee."

Tawnee "loves the tattoo her mom got of her. She loves the butterfly with her name on it."

Allison asked if we had any questions.

I asked why I keep having dreams of Lindsey in which she is seven or eight, and why when Allison got her to come through, that was her age. (Lindsey was eleven when she died.)

Allison paused and answered, "Lindsey says that as she got older, things started to become more confusing to her, so when she died, she returned to the age that she was the happiest." Lindsey liked being small and babied. Somewhere between seven and eight. I have had several dreams of Lindsey in the past two years; she is always younger than she was when she died.

I enjoyed my reading and look back on it knowing my family really is still together.

For all of you who end up dealing with your own loss, the best advice that I can give you is try to connect with others who have had a similar ordeal. Although you feel all alone, there is someone out there who has more than likely gone through a very similar loss.

The Medium's Perspective

I remember meeting Karla and her daughter. Karla is a remarkable woman with a need to talk to her husband and little girl. That's what I do, so she has found the right person. I gave her reading everything I had and just hoped it was enough to ease some of the pain. I remember feeling the pain of the family, but more than that I felt the love they have for each other. As I experienced the car accident and recited the details to Karla, I reminded myself of how fragile life is.

I was astounded that Karla and Betty both had readings that were pivotal in September, and I got in touch with both of them again for my book in September. Karla's husband and daughter had September birthdays, which came out in the reading, and Betty lost her husband on September 11, 2001. So it made sense that to add their stories to this book in September would be very much a tribute to those they love. I was also struck by the coincidences that had to occur to bring Jason to me, me back to Karla and Betty. The mention of Betty, a total stranger to Karla, a year before my writing this book during Karla's reading tells me that Bill, Brent, and Lindsey already knew they were going to be a part of this book that would bring their loved ones together. The fact that I would reconnect with Karla more than a year after her reading — and through Jason Sherman and a hurricane, no less — is amazing in itself.

I think it's important to know a person's story to better understand ourselves. It's not that if you don't get a traffic ticket in your whole life, you go to a better place than everyone else. It's not that anyone who has suffered a loss could have prevented the passing if they had prayed harder or made a deal with God to stop it. I tried that one myself. It didn't work; my dad still passed. Karla "gets" what her life with Brent was, and she didn't take it for granted. She emotionally drank it in and now lovingly recounts her life with him. I remember when I "read" Karla as she was trying to process her enormous loss. She wasn't mourning the love of her life singularly — that's unimaginable by itself — she also was grieving losing her baby, Lindsey, and her daughter's best friend.

I reflect on how I see people pick themselves up after such great loss time and time again, and I'm in awe. I see them fueled by the love they still have for the loved ones who exited too early. People who live well ultimately die well too. By this I mean, they leave people who know how strong the love exchanged is, and they know that it remains. When you take the time to show others that they matter to you and live life large, you become a person whom others learn from. Others then look at their own life and remember to make it count.

This is not to say that you have to live a flawless life. My dad, for example, would have taken back some of the decisions he made. When I sat with him before he died, he apologized for not attending my wedding because of a falling-out he had with my family. Because he said this to me in life, as much as I'd love to have that day back to spend with him, I have no more pain in my heart about my wedding day. He removed that simply by saying he was sorry and that he'd do it differently now. His apology came at my aunt Olivia's funeral. Following the apology, my dad said, "You never know when the next funeral will be your own."

And it was — his own.

See how easy it is to live and die well. My dad fixed something that bothered me in life that would have gnawed at me even more after his death. He lived well because he put his ego aside and asked for forgiveness. Usually all it takes is an "I'm sorry" when you love somebody.

Brent loves Karla and she knows that, and she knows he's still with her. Brent spent his life wisely. You can see by what Karla wrote in tribute to Brent that he did it right. Learn your lessons in life, love while you're here, swallow your pride. Love yourself enough to allow others entry to love you too. Five minutes after finishing Karla's section, I walked outside and a huge butterfly circled my head. My eight-year-old said, "Mommy! Look at the butterfly. It landed on your head."

Joe confirmed the size of it, and I sat back reflecting on the call that I had just received from Karla half an hour before my brush with the beautiful butterfly. Karla had spoken of the bird and the huge butterfly that had fluttered very close to her as she chronicled her contribution to the book. She knew they were sent to her from her family. Personally, I think the butterfly was her daughter. The bird, I think, was her beloved. That's just my impression. Karla would know best.

CHAPTER 3
MEDIUM

I included this chapter for all of the fans of *Medium*. I am often asked, "Did that really happen?"

Meaning, did what happens in the episodes happen in my real life? The answer is it depends on which episode you're talking about.

First, I want to thank all the *Medium* fans for giving us such a warm reception. I've heard from thousands of you who can relate to my character Allison, Joe, and their girls. I appreciate and can relate to your feeling that you are finally seeing that you belong. I also hear from many of you who have lost someone you love, and you express how nice it is just to know those who have passed remain with you.

I've included some of the many episodes that I'm asked about from the first season of *Medium.* I hope this scratches an itch for all of the inquisitive ones out there.

I can understand the curiosity around shows based on real people and the desire to know how much of the show parallels the life of the real person. I think both the show and my books are resources that many people can relate to, since we've all felt to some extent misunderstood for, even burdened by, who we are. The show has the benefit of outstanding writers who successfully capture the world as seen through my family's eyes. And even though our family seems unique, we actually face a lot of the same problems that any family does.

Most of the episodes do have at least one story line that is true to my life. Sometimes this is the family relationship story, rather than the investigation. Such as Joe tries to surprise me with a trip for my birthday, and I reach under the bed and pull out a suitcase already packed. Joe can never surprise me with a gift because I already know what it is, and usually how much it cost. There are thirteen years of these instances that the show could draw from and that I could share with you, so I'll share a recent one. In September 2005 we were going to the Emmys. Joe bought me a beautiful ring to surprise me. I looked at him and rattled off the cost of the ring to the exact penny, which made Joe's jaw drop. He jokingly said, "Get out of my head, Allison!"

It is possible for me to be surprised as long as he doesn't say to me, "You'll never guess what I got you."

That only starts my mind wandering, which results in an object's popping into my head. Many people who can predict future events hear motives and thoughts from others, which results in a picture of the object in question popping into our heads. So I told Joe a long time ago, "If you don't bring it up, I can usually ignore images of your surprises popping into my psyche."

He's had to learn how to be married to someone he can't hide gifts from in a closet or under a bed. Unlike most husbands, he has to worry about hiding them from me in his head. When I touched the ring and knew exactly how much it cost, even I was amused with myself. I thought his surprise was pretty great and he did a good job keeping it from me, except that I spent a couple of weeks feeling deception around him. To me, deception feels like when you know you are telling a lie or you're leaving something out and you feel like everyone's staring at you because they don't believe you. For me, that feeling is followed by my face getting warm. When I'm being deceived, I experience the same feelings as if I myself were doing the deceiving. It's the senses in my body giving me the forecast. I was happy when he gave me the ring, because the deception feeling went away. Whew! Lucky for him, I was preoccupied writing this book, so I didn't let these feelings make me hell-bent on getting to the bottom of his secret.

This past Christmas Joe again made the mistake of saying, "You'll never guess what I got you." He said that he figured that if he waited until the last minute to decide on and buy my present, there wouldn't be a picture in his head for me to see. So when he asked the question I couldn't stop myself. I smiled, ran toward him, and jumped into his arms.

"You got me a frozen margarita machine! I can't wait to have my friends over."

I looked up and I saw Joe's face fall. I felt bad and said, "I'm sorry, Joe."

He looked down at me and smiled. "I'm glad you like your present. I know that you like to entertain. Besides, you were surprised when you saw the picture in my head."

That's true. After all, I am surprised one way or another, so I do get the same initial rush of excitement that everybody gets. Joe is relentless in his efforts to surprise me, and I'm always looking forward to what he'll think of next. Maybe next time I'll have a better poker face and look surprised.

When you watch *Medium*, sit back and enjoy a great television program knowing that I'm watching it with you.

Like Glenn Caron, the creator of the show, says both in play and truth, "Allison, the wheels of justice turn slowly, and you can't work cases fast enough to fill all the episodes."

Not all the cases on the show are cases I've worked, but it's not the cases themselves that are important to the story line of the show but the way they affect my character and the family. One of the most important facets of *Medium* is how it shows a family learning to deal with what comes their way and how they become closer and stronger for it.

Just the Facts

In the opening episode of *Medium* I am an intern at the district attorney's office. That is in fact true; I interned in my graduating semester at Arizona State University, where I met the man I respectfully refer to as "Chief," who's wonderfully portrayed by Miguel Sandoval. Glenn has met the real DA, and they seemed to both think a lot of each other. I think a lot of them both too.

One of my jobs as an intern was to sort the crime scene photos, and while doing so, I noticed that I could see flashes of what happened before the victim in the photo was killed. I could also see details around the killer, such as a name, cars, accomplices, motive, and other details. It was unnerving, and I wasn't sure what to make of what I was seeing. I mean, I had seen things that had happened in my life in the form of flashes of pictures in my head, but I guess because I had never been exposed to actual crime scene photos, this flash of images all seemed new to me. I toyed with the idea that maybe I was an overworked mother of three girls who needed a break. This seemed plausible but still didn't fully explain what was happening to me. I wasn't even sure that I wanted to explore the possibility that I was seeing flashes of the actual violent crime. The first episode of *Medium* is a very real depiction of what happened in my real life.

I am actually married to an aerospace engineer (rocket scientist) named Joe. We challenge each other intellectually, and we can be very playful with each other. The relationship on the screen is very "us." It's strange to have a portrayal of our relationship out there to be critiqued. I wouldn't change the way Joe and I are together; it works for us. People who know us constantly comment on how much the relationship in the show is similar to our real-life relationship. We also have three fantastic little girls who share my gift, a gift that I believe is genetic.

While I was interning, I told Joe what was happening to me. We thought it might help to test the theory to see if I was just "seeing things" or if it was something far bigger than that. So I chose three random murder/ missing cases and created "write-ups," which is my term for writing down any information that comes to me that is connected to the victim. There was a large part of me that wanted to prove that I wasn't doing what I thought I was doing. We faxed these write-ups to law enforcement across the country, expecting to hear nothing. To my surprise, I was contacted by the Tarrant County Sheriff's Office in conjunction with the Texas Rangers. After a couple of phone conversations with them, I decided to go out there to see if I could help in any way. I still wasn't quite sure how this all worked. I wasn't sure how to read all the signs or if I was even supposed to be a part of this case at all. I nervously and hesitantly headed to Dallas. The law enforcement officials picked me up at the airport, not at a private airstrip as in the show. I wish!

They did take me to areas that the victim had "potentially" been taken to test me. I then said to the officer, "He did not bring the child here."

A few minutes later the officer acknowledged knowing that already, because scent dogs had been brought through those areas before my visit. At the time I was a little miffed by this treatment, but it was naïve of me to think that I wouldn't be tested by the police. Still, we didn't have much time before the sun would go down, and I wanted to cover as much territory as I could. Their tests were wasting my time. Then again, it was my first case, so I was unsure exactly what it was that I was expected to do or what I should expect from law enforcement. It was frustrating, frightening, and exhilarating all at the same time. In the five and a half years since my first write-up, and thousands of people's personal tests later, I've come to understand it's human nature to challenge others. I now try not to take it personally.

I did tell the sheriff that the perpetrator had shared his information with the guy in the next cell, which was also acknowledged by the police to have occurred but could not be used in court. Unfortunately, my information alone can't fix injustices. We have to work within the confines of the law. We also have to have the support of a higher power, which can have a bigger plan that we can't always see the full scope of. We don't always know how someone's life is supposed to be changed by a serious set of events.

The real sheriff from the story line of the first episode did indeed have a heart problem that I talked to him about when he said, "Tell me something about me."

The female officer in the car burst out laughing when I shared that I picked up on a physical defect with his heart that would need surgery and serious treatment. Apparently the sheriff had had heart surgery just shortly before my visit. Unfortunately, he had another heart attack after I left. You may recognize some of these details from the first episode.

There indeed was a Hurricane Alison that came through before it was arranged to have scent dogs taken out. I did throw a temper tantrum when I got home, not being able to understand what good my abilities are if I couldn't produce the Texan child's remains. I also struggled with hearing Joe's thoughts and feeling that he didn't fully believe me and didn't know what to think of me. I would look into his eyes, and his eyes looked uncertain of me, which was painful for me, since I had never seen this look before. I could hear his thoughts, questioning what to say to me, how to choose his words carefully so as to not offend me. Our real-life experience over this incident was very much like that in the first episode of *Medium*, where our characters have words over whether or not Joe believes Allison and he doubts her claims of what she "sees."

In August of 2001 I flew to Dallas to be met by officers from the sheriff's department of the county where the missing child lived when she was abducted. I was also met at the airport by a couple of cars full of Texas Rangers. We shared a lovely lunch together at a local Chinese restaurant. I have never felt as safe as I did having ten to twelve Rangers, sheriffs, and police officers with me at 7-Eleven while I purchased a Big Gulp. It was very intimidating at times, absorbing that I was in the company of such authority as I struggled with understanding my visions as well as wondering how the hell I had gotten myself into this situation.

One brave officer actually was kind enough and secure enough to go on the record for me in 2002 when channel 12 news in Phoenix ran a story on me and some of the cases that I've profiled locally in Maricopa County. The sergeant issued a public statement for channel 12, saying that he worked with me on this particular missing child's case and that I provided information on the case that "impressed" him. I provided information that had never been released publicly, such as accomplices and multiple vehicles used in the crime. Since it's a matter of public record, meaning his name was run on the evening news, I feel comfortable publicly thanking Sergeant Bobby Atteberry. Bobby was the person who first told me about the Amber Alert, which I hadn't heard of until that day. I don't think he realizes how many Arizona children he helped by sharing his emotional recollection of the death of Amber Hagerman (abducted and murdered in Texas), the child who inspired the Amber Alert. I spoke of initiating this system for Arizona in my book *Don't Kiss Them Good-Bye*. I was able to initiate the program and serve on the task force to design it. Thank you, Bobby. Meeting you was a pivotal moment in my life that I will never forget.

One of the many Rangers who picked me up at the airport that day and who was willing to take a chance on my information was

Ranger Ted Poling. He was a genuinely nice man who clearly took the abducted girl's case personally. She affected every officer I came in contact with that day so intensely that I'm sure at the end of the day they all took her home with them in their heart. I know I did. I think officers who use valid psychic profilers should be applauded for putting the victim first and ignoring naysayers who, in truth, can't bring them any closer to resolving their case.

I think anyone with good sense can understand why I tend to avoid broadcasting the names of law enforcement officials whom I work with, since clearly I have to make sure these fine people aren't harassed by skeptics with too much time on their hands.

The way I look at it is, I'll keep working cases, reading people, and helping when I can, while others argue about whether or not it's possible.

Medium, Extra-Small

In another episode of *Medium*, my middle daughter, Fallon, regularly talks to "an imaginary friend" who turns out to be a child who died. This was true. She did experience this. In reality, her "imaginary" friend was a little girl who had passed away. Fallon was four when this happened and now, four years later, she still occasionally brings her up. My daughter used to make us set a place at the table for her unusual friend, and being who we are, we did! On *Medium* she met the deceased child on the playground; our little girl acquired her "imaginary" friend in her preschool classroom.

She also had trouble making other friends because she was too busy playing with her "imaginary" friend, so Joe and I set out to make an effort to expand her social calendar. You may remember that our characters on the show do the same. It wasn't easy for us, because our daughter definitely lives in her own world, and of my three daughters, she is the quirky one, but I really love and appreciate that about her. She has since found friends who are little mediums themselves or are simply unique kids too.

This is one of my favorite episodes. I like it because it shows nonmediums what the children who are mediums go through trying to understand why everyone doesn't see what they see. It was also like scratching an itch for me, because when I was a child, I didn't have anyone to guide me through the growing pains of being a young medium. This episode of *Medium* will continue to open many eyes and hopefully resonate with the young.

All of my daughters' personalities portrayed in the show are accurate. My oldest daughter, Aurora, whose character is named Ariel on the show, is very much an eldest child. She's a go-getter. She's well liked. She's used to winning. She doesn't know her limitations yet because she's so busy giving it her all in whatever sport she's in. Aurora's made a sport out of picking on her little sister Fallon, which we're trying to break her of, as on the show. She's also inherited her father's math ability — very much as on the show, except it turns out on the show that her math aptitude comes from her pulling the answers out of my husband's head. In reality, she really is advanced in math. Her father has bragging rights there.

My middle daughter, Fallon, is an exceptional little singer, a very vocal little girl and very wise for such a little kid. When Fallon was four years old, Joe and I had the girls outside looking at the stars. Fallon looked at the moon and said, "Look, it's a new moon!" Joe looked at me and said, "Allison, you can see just a sliver, it is a new moon." She never ceases to amaze us. She's also very generous. When she was in the second grade, her school was collecting money to clothe and feed an orphan. Fallon came home at high speed, went straight to her "hidden" tooth fairy money, collected it up, and asked us if it was okay for her to give it to the school for the orphan. You can tell what your child is made of from a pretty young age. I must admit, she makes me proud and grateful to be her mom. Joe and I gave her a little extra money to take in and she was elated. Fallon mixes her food together and makes animal figurines out of her mashed potatoes. She is stubborn yet sensitive and one of the most comedic kids I've ever seen. What makes it more funny is that she's not trying to be funny, she just is.

Sophia is my baby. Everybody just adores her because she's tiny and bubbly, and she reminds me a lot of my dad. She's a natural little dancer who loves to play dress-up. Her bedroom looks like a fairy tale. Her ceiling is painted to look like the sky. While tucking her in one night, I said, "Look, honey, it looks like heaven." She whispered to me, "Mommy, I think I can see the angels." She melts me on a regular basis, and although the character inspired by her on the show is still very young, she gives you a glimpse at what a doll my little one is. They're both pretty far up there on the cute meter.

As my daughters begin to experience their

gift, I walk them through their various senses and I explain how to "read" what they see and hear as little mediums. It really is special to me to be able to be their guide through life and to share in their excitement when they one-up their mom through a great prediction.

My husband, Joe, is a brilliant aerospace engineer who has recently retired for obvious reasons. He's tall, handsome, and sarcastic. On the show *Medium*, Jake Weber does a fantastic job portraying my Joe. It is true that Joe dotes on his little girls. He is usually the only person who can talk sense to me, and he defuses my cranky moods with his sarcasm and humor just as on the show. I think he may have raised the bar a little for husbands around the world, not bad. Unlike in the show, I don't wake up screaming all that often, and in reality my Joe's a much heavier sleeper than his character on the show. He's also working on developing that wonderful "six-pack" that Jake Weber sports on the show in his abdominal area. The real Joe isn't quite there yet, but no worries, he makes up for it in his infectious laugh and his immeasurable patience.

Oh Brother!

The episode of *Medium* called "Lucky" shows my brother Michael and his struggle with trying to both understand and ignore his ability to see and hear those who've died. He was in the army and went to war, where he used his instinct to return home to us in one piece. That is all true to my real brother Michael. In real life, he's older than me by five years. He's not my younger brother, as in the show. Also, my brother is much more intelligent than his character and wouldn't put up with bullying from anybody! He is, however, proud and, in the end, does the right thing, as the character demonstrates. He also is not a fan of X-rated movies as in the episode of *Medium*, but he does like the ladies.

My real brother Michael grapples with his abilities. He sees images, but hearing those passed is something he still works on. He can hear them talking but can't always make out the words being said. I can imagine how frustrating that must be. He also knows when things are going to happen before the fact. He has a great sense of danger, as well as a great instinct concerning people and their motives, which helped to bring him back to us from a war that killed some of the men who were ranked above him in his group. He's very brave and can be very modest. This episode was difficult for me to watch. It's hard to see right before my eyes the pain and confusion that exists in mediums, including my brother, whom I love dearly. Sometimes we talk about what we see and hear from the other side, and I think we help each other. We can joke medium to medium. This ability is not an easy thing to talk to just anyone about. Also, having it doesn't obligate you to make a career out of it. Sometimes just trying to understand it is enough.

As in the episode "Lucky," I did work a case where I was asked to sit in front of a house that was severely burned and write my impressions down for the DA's office. I told them that I saw that a woman was murdered. I told them what room she was murdered in and who committed the crime. It was very difficult to sit in my car writing down what I saw and what the victim was telling me. Now, in the episode "Lucky," the victim was a child. In real life, the victim was a grown woman and the perpetrator was a different family member. These are the sort of details that are changed for the show's story lines in order to protect the surviving loved ones of the deceased. It's never easy to fathom that a person could take the life of another without remorse, but unfortunately it happens all the time. That episode from *Medium*'s first season is hard to watch for me but still remains one of my favorites. Oh, and in the episode my brother's friend kills their commander. I'm sure that you can guess that didn't happen in my real life, but that's a good thing.

Like Mother, Like Daughter

There was an episode of *Medium* where my eldest daughter, "Ariel," worked a murder case with me that involved a young girl. This happened in reality, although I hadn't shared that with the writers of *Medium*, so that episode semi-paralleling my life was just an eerie coincidence. In reality, I wrote the first name of the missing girl on a piece of paper and gave it to my daughter, telling her to just write down whatever she saw or felt. I really wasn't expecting anything from her, but I wanted to see if she could profile.

I was stunned when she handed the paper back to me with a profile of the perpetrator similar to mine. She looked at me and said, "Mom, it felt like I was guessing."

This is a term little mediums use because details pop into their head and it can seem too easy to receive information. I explained this to her and told her how well she did. I had never shared anything about any missing cases with her. In fact, I had just spent the weekend with Laurie Campbell and Janet Mayer, who are also profilers. I wrote the same name on a piece of paper for each of them. We spent less than an hour on our write-ups. We then took turns reading what we had received. Many pieces of information overlapped, and some added different information, great clues. We then shared our information with the detective who had requested it. The interesting thing with my oldest daughter is that she drew diagrams of the street that the perpetrator lived on that coincided with our own drawings. Not every profiler draws diagrams. I do, and apparently so does she. She also got the correct description of the suspect's vehicle, misspelling the make of the vehicle, which just reminded me how young she really is.

Aurora didn't see any grim details because she doesn't have a reference in her head for some of the things that older mediums/profilers see, thank God. I couldn't allow her to profile otherwise, because I couldn't subject her to that. I know that one day that will change and she will have references in her head to compare her feelings and impressions to. Nonetheless, I was proud of her and impressed with her abilities. I saved her first write-up for her scrapbook. That's one of many ways that my family is different from some others. Not good, not bad, just different.

My daughter still talks to the murdered girl and passes messages to me. She feels friendship connections with those who've passed, just as I do. Once you've emotionally connected to a person who's passed on, you feel like you know them and still think about them from time to time. Sometimes they'll return to you when something's up with the living person you read when you brought the deceased through. You feel especially close to the deceased who died traumatically because they're sharing information about their death, and that's pretty personal stuff.

In the episode of *Medium* in which my character works with her daughter to get a wider assortment of information, the missing girl was still alive. In reality, unfortunately, our missing girl is deceased. Of course this means that we did not charge up to the house and save the living girl. In real life, I have devoted many hours to trying to move this case forward, and I believe I've helped to do that. Recently we've pinpointed an incarcerated suspect who needs to be cracked, a work in progress. I just want to bring the girl home to be buried and make sure the guys responsible can't hurt anyone else.

"Mother-in-Law"

This episode was particularly important to my husband, Joe, since it dealt with his mother and the loss of his father.

I enjoyed that this episode illustrated what many women already know, which is what a mother-in-law can be like. In this episode, my mother-in-law, played by Kathy Baker (whom I loved in *Picket Fences*), was widowed. My real-life mother-in-law is widowed as well. I think Glenn Caron beautifully showed the regret that my father-in-law had when he died and he saw the mistakes that he'd made, including not being there enough emotionally for his wife. My real-life mother-in-law married Joe's dad when she was nineteen. He passed away from cancer when she was around fifty-eight years old. My father-in-law, as I described him to Glenn, was a tough bird. He was very intellectual (an MIT grad). He was also not terribly emotionally available to his family, but he loved his family very much. He indeed enjoyed smoking cigars, as illustrated in this episode.

My real father-in-law does spend a great

deal of time around Joe's mom since his death, and I formed a relationship with him at his insistence. I met him after he died, not before. He was never shy about telling me how I could do things better. But I'm sure that when I had to pass my math class to graduate from college and I asked him to "help" me, he was the one who showed me the answers so that I could graduate. I only squeaked by in college math; I am not mathematically inclined. He also came through and gave me information for Joe's mom, including an apology with information that was something only he'd known. That rattled her because it involved her keeping a secret and he spoiled it for her. Jim has a wicked sense of humor; I like that about him.

Joe's mom did enjoy coming over and sharing with me her wisdom concerning homemaking, and I'm quite sure that she's had moments when she thought I wasn't doing a chore, like making dinner, efficiently enough or with the right ingredients. I don't think she's unlike other mothers-in-law that way; they mean well. We all love her. It was very significant for Joe to be able to watch this episode of *Medium* and feel some comfort, seeing a scenario unfold on the screen that I had described to him years before when I brought his dad through.

Not an Exact Science

I can't break down every episode of *Medium* because it would take forever. Please keep in mind that *Medium* is inspired by my life but not a biography of my life. There will be some episodes that are just great writing and nothing more. One episode that comes to mind is the one about a professor named Dr. Caldwell, who thinks that his brother died only to find out many years later that he's still alive. This is a fictitious character, not based on a real person. Yes, it's true that I was studied by real scientists in a university lab, but Dr. Caldwell is just a character created by Glenn Caron and his fantastic staff of writers. The real scientists whom I have worked with are not like Dr. Caldwell in any way, and they will not be characters on the show.

I have worked many cases where the missing person was thought to be deceased and was in reality alive. I live for these cases, because they show that there are happy endings out there in the world. So the real similarity, I guess, is that I've worked other cases with the same happy outcome, but that's it. I've never been studied by a scientist who specializes in sleep disorders, but I can understand why Allison (the character on *Medium*) would be a candidate for that kind of study. I'm glad that so many people enjoyed this episode, and I'm sure Glenn will keep you all guessing which characters are real and which are his creations.

To all of the fans of *Medium*, thank you for watching and thank you for sharing my life.

Chapter 4
LIVING WITH GIFTS

All people with intuitive gifts must learn how to comprehend signs. The best way for me to illustrate how a medium/predictor learns is by using myself as an example. For all of you with your own stories of predicting people's death, picking up on vibes that others put out, and other intuitive gifts, this chapter will reassure you that you're not alone. I get many letters from people who find solace in knowing that, although they thought they were isolated in their gift, they are in truth a part of a far bigger family. My dad always said, "Make no apologies for who you are." For those of you who feel overly responsible for everything around you and even burdened by your awareness and your abilities, I have a suggestion. Try writing "Make no apologies for who you are!" on your mirror or somewhere that you will see it when you wake up in the morning. This will serve as a reminder to deflect any shame that you have owing to others' closed minds.

Any saying/mantra that inspires you is worth recognizing regularly and taking in so frequently that it becomes a part of who you are. For the longest time I had "Go to your destiny!" written in lipstick on my bedroom mirror. I heard it for the first time on *Oprah* when two Olympic runners who came from a troubled neighborhood explained how they beat the odds and emerged as successful people from a place where most people didn't emerge at all. They inspired me to live by those words. Instead of hesitantly climbing out of bed, wondering what obstacles I would face, I sprang out of bed ready to "Go to my destiny," whatever that might be.

There is nothing to be ashamed of in just being who you are. As a matter of fact, you should feel blessed to be given the ability to connect with others in such a profound way. Instead of saying, "It's a curse to know when someone is going to pass ahead of time," try, "How fortunate am I to be given the opportunity to say good-bye to someone I love and sometimes even to allow myself to be used as an instrument to help save someone's life."

For those people who share your gifts in

other ways, like being the nurse with unbeatable bedside manner most of us pray for when our loved ones are in need, know that your gifts are just as great. You might be the grocer the elderly look forward to seeing every week because you brighten their day. There are so many gifts that a person can have. What they all have in common is that only sharing your gift with others makes it meaningful. Mediums/predictors can share our gifts in ways that aren't overstepping our bounds. We can listen to those who need to talk and mix in a little of our intuition with good advice for a person who needs a friend. There's a time and a place for everything, and as with any gift, sharing it is only helpful when it's welcome.

Living well is partially about perspective, and then action. If you have a moment of inspiration about how you might improve the quality of another person's life and don't act on it, then you've really done nothing with that inspiring idea. So know you're being guided, and take that next step. Not only will you be helping another, but by helping that person, you will find the true definition of who you are, one that was written long ago but is being looked at for the first time.

Can You Feel It?

I urge you to pay attention to what is around you. I think many of you experience a heightened sense on a daily basis. It's nothing that will be outwardly validated: you won't be born with a special birthmark; no Red Sea will part for you. It's a human ability that you can learn to rely on and trust completely. You must be validated from within, not by others. I find that as human beings, we often doubt ourselves and punish ourselves for things that are beyond our control. This chapter illustrates the importance of trusting your instincts and encourages those who sense presences not to deny their existence.

For those of you who "feel" as though someone is standing behind you, or "feel" as though someone is standing at the foot of your bed, or even sitting on it, for that matter, I hope this chapter will speak to you. You aren't imagining a presence. In fact, you are a sensitive being with the ability to "feel" on a grand scale. I will try to guide you through understanding your special sense.

Some people reading this chapter who may be able to sense illness need to learn more about what they feel. In my first book, *Don't Kiss Them Good-Bye*, I talked about being six years old when I had my first spiritual encounter: my great-granddad appeared at the foot of my bed after his funeral. I described feeling "on edge." Part of what I meant by that has to do with sensing illness. My great-granddad had passed from intestinal cancer, which is not such a nice way to pass. I felt sick to my stomach and had an almost static-electrical sensation on the surface of my skin. Once I became an adult medium, I learned to recognize that feeling as something that would occur only when I was in the presence of someone with cancer. When I bring a person through who is dead, the deceased makes me feel something physical connected to the cause of death, almost like a calling card to identify who it is for the living. This doesn't mean that the dead are still in pain; they're not. It's just a way for them to communicate who they are to us.

I also realized that I would have the same feeling when I was in the presence of a living person with a specific disease, such as cancer. Some people don't know why they sense something that they can't explain or define, like illness or deception around a person. Many people in the health professions may have a special knack for this sense, partially from being exposed to illnesses over and over, and they learn to trust different feelings for various sicknesses. We are all individuals, so we may sense things in different ways. What feels like a heart attack to me may feel like something else to another intuitive person. I'll share what it feels like for me. Perhaps it's the same for many others. If your feeling is different from mine, it doesn't mean you're wrong, it just means that the same information is coming to you in a different way. When I sense a heart attack in someone who is living, it feels different from the heart attack of someone who has already died. In the presence of someone who died of a heart attack, I feel like I've had a small punch to the chest. It takes my breath away a little bit. That's how the dead communicate the cause of their passing to me.

If you experience these feelings and they're too much for you, acknowledge to the person passed that you understand the cause of his or her passing and ask the deceased person to ease up on that message. The deceased are fine with that and just need to be reminded sometimes that they are coming through loud and clear. They need to know that they can use less energy because they are being "felt" by the living. You can imagine how frustrating it is for them to not be heard after their death. They learn to turn up their energy as loud as they can as they walk through a room full of people with ear plugs/blinders until they find someone who doesn't have ear plugs/blinders. Imagine their relief. Once acknowledged, they will turn down their volume if you ask them to. If you have a loved one who passed away who does this to you, tell the person you're glad he or she is here and you'd love to have his or her love and guidance in your life. This will remove the feeling of frustration or aggravation that you might be feeling from the person. All the deceased want is to be acknowledged and accepted.

When I feel heart trauma around the living, it comes in different levels of seriousness. The least serious is when someone will need heart medication. I see this and hear "treatable." Sometimes I'll feel a heartburn sensation and will visualize it as being in the chest, but I sense that the damage isn't yet severe and can be treated through diet and minor medication. In other words, it's not taking the person's life anytime soon but could become more severe, so I recommend seeking medical attention. Sometimes it's the beginning stages of a blockage in an artery or plaque forming, something that's just beginning. Also, I tell people to be persistent and make sure they find a doctor they feel comfortable with. Never second-guess your own sense, most especially when it has to do with your health or the health of someone you love.

On occasion, when it's a more severe heart problem, I literally see surgery in the future or the living person standing in a hospital gown, but I also sense a "fixability" around their heart, as if he or she is not going to die right now from it but still has time. Intervention is possible at this point because the damage is not so severe.

The most severe level of heart disease I experienced with my own father. I would hug him good-bye, and when he pressed against me, his chest felt heavy to me, as if his heart wasn't beating — which in that moment made letting go of him nearly impossible. His energy felt like it was nearly gone, which meant to me that the life he still contained was very little and would soon run out. Sadly it did. There is also a sense that I get when anyone's days are short. It feels like the person's story has come to an end and there's no more left to "read." It's like reading a good book and knowing you're close to the last page and feeling disappointed there's no more to enjoy. You close the cover of your book and feel puzzled, wondering what other exciting things might happen if the book could just last a little bit longer.

After you do what I do for a while, you learn to gauge how long a person has to live by the level of energy that you feel the person still carries. There are pros and cons to this ability. On the one hand, you know when you need to say and do all the things that will matter to you and the person who will pass away. On the other hand, you're saying good-bye every time you see or talk to that person, and you don't have the luxury of thinking that everything is just fine. I spoke of this in my first book, *Don't Kiss Them Good-Bye*, when I shared the prediction of my own father's death and my inability to stop it from happening. Two years of sending him to heart specialists just wasn't enough. Oddly, they all said that his heart was fine, but it wasn't. When somebody's time is up, it's up, and, for whatever reason, only some predictions can be affected by intervention. I've told many clients of pitfalls that I see before them, such as a car accident, or I suggest that they get their chest X-rayed. It seems that I can touch most events in a positive way, but there are also some that cannot be stopped.

I try to remember to have faith that things happen the way they're supposed to, but I'm only human. The way I look at it is the grass is always greener on the other side of the fence, and you just have to enjoy your own landscape.

On the television show *Medium*, the character Allison DuBois sees bad things before they happen, and sometimes she intervenes in time and sometimes she doesn't. She often finds out that her vision was part of a bigger picture, that the victim was not to be saved. My life is no different.

The only people who read signs are the ones intuitive enough to acknowledge them as signs and to accept them as a form of communication from the unseen to us. Signs, sent by relatives or friends who've passed, come in many forms. They are sent to us because those who have passed are trying to guide us through life. I asked for a sign when I was deciding whether to be a medium professionally or to go through law school. I didn't get the answer at the time that I had hoped for, but we can all see that I am where I'm supposed to be. After I asked for a sign — and this is where you have to be careful what you ask for — I received numerous signs. While driving I took a wrong turn and ended up behind a car with a license plate that said "Oracle." Another said "Medium." Then I passed a sign that said "Oracle" and ended up on a street called Campbell, which is the last name of another medium who was studied in the laboratory with me and whom I've now come to know very well. That's how it started. Then so many signs were thrown my way that I never actually caught my breath again, and now I'm here where I belong. It was frustrating though. I sent out all my law school applications after triple-checking each one. I sent them several months in advance. Two days before the deadline I received every application back in the mail. Each one had a note that said, "You're missing something," then each went on to identify an item that was checked off on my checklist but that I was being told wasn't in there. It was something different for each application. I had to again stare at the words "You're missing something" and laugh or cry. I looked at Joe and said, "I don't think I'm supposed to go to law school."

He said, "I was wondering how long it would take you to figure that out."

Don't get me wrong, I'm proud to be a medium, but when you have your mind set on what you want, it's hard to see another picture.

I've heard stories from other people who were changing jobs and weren't sure which direction to go and asked for a sign. They received a call the same day from an associate starting a new business venture, wondering if they were interested. When my cat Sinbad was sick, I asked for a sign to know whether I should put him to sleep. I had a dream that night where my friend Domini thumbed through my scrapbooks, then she waved at me to follow her, and she walked me through a door. As I walked through, I found myself standing in my vet's office. Domini smiled at me, letting me know it would be all right. My mom took Sinbad to the vet the next day. I couldn't go because I knew he wouldn't be coming home with me, and it broke my heart. The vet looked at Sinbad and said that he had terminal cancer and that it was painful. So we did the humane thing and let him go. Not easy, but Domini's sign let me know that it was the right thing to do and that she'd take care of him. Signs come in many forms for many different reasons. They serve as both comfort and guidance when heeded. If you're lucky enough to be given a sign, pay attention. Sometimes the consequences of ignoring them are minor, but often we think back and we could kick ourselves for ignoring a sign sent to guide us.

May 8, 2005, was not only a beautiful Sunday afternoon but Mother's Day. Joe, my mom, myself, and our three girls were off to the mall for a shoe-shopping spree because my mom and I agreed nothing would be more fun. My plan was to pick up my grandma after our shopping trip and have her join us for dinner. While we were driving, I informed my mom that I wanted to get Grandma Jenee later for dinner.

My mom began joking and said, "Do we have to?" She had just taken Grandma to lunch earlier and was teasing, as most daughters will.

I turned to my mom to say, "Mom, this is Grandma's last Mother's Day, so be nice."

In between the words *Mother's* and *Day*, a huge pigeon hit my windshield. My face and the bird were separated only by a piece of glass. We were all completely floored. In my whole life I've never hit an animal in my car, ever. The bird came out of the sky and flew right into our windshield. It wasn't just the bird, it was the bird coupled with the words that were coming out of my mouth at the time. I was speaking of my grandmother's imminent death! I had just talked to my brother Michael about it the night before.

He had said, "Something's different with Grandma. Al, Grandma *feeeels* different. I know she's gonna go this year, but I can't put my finger on the feeling."

I said, "Michael, the feeling is that she's already gone."

"Yes!" he said. "That's it! That's what it feels like."

"Michael, whenever you get that feeling in the future, you'll know the person's days are numbered. That's how mediums learn to read things."

I snapped back to the ride to Grandma's house, thinking of what I'd miss the most about her. There are so many things. The fact that she loves hummingbirds and has had a feeder for them my whole life. Her great laugh and the way she lights up when Joe and I take the kids over to her house to visit.

This was indeed a special Mother's Day. I made an emotional note to savor the day. As I gazed at my grandma from across the dinner table, I remembered her taking me to the park to feed the ducks and how she'd braid my hair too tight when I was little. So tight I thought my eyes would reach my ears. Okay, that was a slight exaggeration, but you know what I mean. I handed Grandma her Mother's Day gift. She loves cash, so she squealed with delight as she reached for her purse. She pulled out a picture of a lavender dress, hat, and purse, along with an order form. She explained how badly she wanted this outfit but that it required she save money in order to buy it. I knew what this dress was; it was what she was going to be buried in. I knew it, my mom knew it, and even Joe knew it.

"Grandma, can I see that?"

She handed me the form, where she had already filled in all her information ready to send to buy this outfit that she adored. I flipped open my cell phone and dialed the number.

My grandma said, "Allison, what are you doing?"

I noticed my grandma had added the amount wrong, and I wanted to make sure that she had this outfit to enjoy when it mattered the most, *before* her final day of rest.

As we sat waiting for dinner, I ordered my grandma that outfit, and she couldn't have smiled any bigger. Everyone at our table was so moved to see Grandma so happy. Sometimes it's the little things in life that mean everything. I'm sharing this with you because I want you to see my life and walk through it with me. Maybe one day you will relate to my experiences. Maybe you already do.

In the spring of 2004 I made a prediction. I said that I would lose my grandmas within twelve months of each other. My grandmas are very different women, nothing alike. My grandma Lesa (stepgrandma, but I loved her) was Italian, fiery, and enormously loving. Grandma Maria (my dad's mom) was Hispanic, adored my dad, and loved to cook. The grandma I'm the closest to, my grandma Jenee (my mom's mom), is European, tall, friendly, loves to play the piano, and is a medium.

In October 2004 my grandma Lesa passed away to join my grandfather Joseph, whom I adore. In December 2004 my grandma Maria died to join her son, my dad, where I know she's the happiest. My grandma Jenee is not doing so well, and I'm trying to spend time with her and let her know how much she means to me. Although I am fortunate enough to still have my grandma Jenee with me, I know I won't have her forever. My grandma knows she is getting up there and jokes that she's so bad that hell doesn't even want her. This cracks me up, and I know it's not true. I tell her she's "still needed," that's all.

I always tell her she can't go anywhere, because "then I'll be the bad one in the family," and we laugh. I was shaken by the bird's hitting the windshield, as was everyone in the car. I read it as a sign, and I understand that an end is most likely coming. For now, I'm just keeping my fingers crossed that last Mother's Day, when the bird incident happened, won't be the last one that I get to spend with my grandmother.

CHAPTER 5
SOMEBODY'S BABY

This chapter is dedicated to all the children who miss their mom or dad. Whether you were eight weeks old or eighty years old when your parent died, we are all little kids inside when it comes to our mom and dad. Some parents I bring through in readings express regret for not spending more time with their kids. They share that they'd do things differently now and that they try to take care of you from the other side, make it up to you, if it's in their power. The problem with dying and leaving behind wounded people is that, once you've passed, often the wounded no longer want your help. That's why I tell people if you live well, you die well. In other words, when you paint the portrait of your life, be sure it's a picture you can look at forever, because you will. This doesn't mean we can't forgive people after their death. It's just nicer to have those moments while you can still hold them.

Maybe your dad was father of the year because he was always your rock during your emotional storms and your pillow when you needed a place to cry. Or he could have been one of those men who had to learn later on how to be a good dad. Maybe he wasn't good at "I love you." Or maybe he missed all those nights when you were small, failing to tuck you in. The same goes for moms. Maybe you were blessed enough to have a mom who could rival Carol Brady for the ultimate mom award. Maybe you weren't raised by your mom and didn't get to bond with her in life. Either way, I hope this chapter reminds you all that you are loved and adored by those who gave you life. Even those who had to see with their own eyes where they went wrong and how they can help you now.

As a medium, I am glad to lend my assistance to others, helping them to move through their pain after losing someone they love. After my dad died, I found myself needing solace from the other side and had to learn to accept the kindness of others. I was accustomed, being a medium, to my ability to make contact with the other side at my will. This is how I had planned on moving myself forward when my dad died, because it was the best way I knew to heal myself. Now I would be taught an unfamiliar lesson, how to accept the help I needed from someone who had no agenda other than to act as a mirror of myself, showing me what I do for others, putting me in the seat of the client.

Should I Take a Message?

When my dad passed away in September 2002, I found myself unable to see him or hear him for quite some time, which frustrated me greatly. I received a call a little less than a year after my dad died from a fellow research medium named Laurie Campbell. She apologized for not having called sooner, but she had just learned that my dad had died several months ago. She also shared that her own dad had passed recently. We spoke of the frustration of being mediums and being able to see the dead but not being able to see our own dads. This didn't sit well with us, not because of ego, but because we live in the trenches of life and death in our profession. Our work is a part of who we are, and so are our fathers, yet neither of us seemed to be able to communicate with our own father. As Laurie and I spoke on the phone, it occurred to us that we could see and hear each other's father. Could we read each other? Give closure to another medium?

Laurie confidently stated, "Allison, your dad says he prefers blondes."

She laughed hysterically and so did I.

I responded, "Laurie, you could have told me anything about my dad, and you said what was paramount to who my father was and is. My dad *loooved* blondes and always said so." She continued to talk about his being dressed in a tuxedo and how regal he looked. She continued to fill my head with details about my dad that were very personal. I was immersed in a comfort that I recognized as something that I was used to providing for others, and I then understood why my clients were so full of gratitude after a reading.

I told Laurie, "I see your dad too, and he's cracking nuts and eating them. He's also referring to your daughter Amanda as 'Peanut.'" This turned out to be a nickname he had called his granddaughter. Laurie's dad likes to share things with me such as what's in Laurie's kitchen pantry, or what object is sitting in front of Laurie while we talk on the phone. I told her that her dad kept talking about the man in the navy and the name Ronald connected to him. She confirmed for me that her uncle (her mom's brother) was in the navy and his name is

Ron. I kept seeing a 1957 Chevy in my head that was connected to her family. She confirmed that it belonged to her parents and she still has pictures of it. Her dad kept talking about Santa Cruz as a place where a family member had lived, which I conveyed to Laurie. She said that her grandma used to live there and they drove there in the '57 Chevy when Laurie was two or three years old to visit. Her dad then showed me a Felix the Cat clock with the eyes shifting from side to side. Laurie said that her grandma from Santa Cruz had one in her house. I kept seeing salmon and eggs, and her dad said they used to make them a lot, which Laurie confirmed. Laurie's dad spoke fondly about the ham and scalloped potato casserole that they used to make. This was special to Laurie, having him acknowledge something that she used to make for him. He kept talking about a black skillet that Laurie's mom always cooked with when she'd make him fried eggs.

I kept seeing a patchwork cat that her dad kept showing me, and he said they had one. Laurie confirmed the patchwork cat that her mom had made in her house growing up. Her dad also talked about being around "Bill" on the other side, and Laurie shared that he was her dad's father. Her dad kept saying the name "Scooter" and talked about being around Scooter, and it turned out that was the name of Laurie's sister's cat that had died. I was shown horses and cowboy boots as connected to Laurie's dad. Laurie's sister ended up getting a new horse around that time that matched the description of the horse that her dad had shown me. Her dad also said that he had to go "in order to keep Laurie's kids here." I shared this with Laurie. Although it didn't make sense at the time, being a medium, she knew it would mean something someday. A couple of years after Laurie's dad's death, Laurie found out that her son needed a heart transplant. Laurie was naturally frantic and she said, "Allison, is he going to get a heart?" I told her he would.

Some months after that, her son was offered a heart that I had a bad feeling about. Laurie shared this feeling. Laurie called and asked, "Allison? Should I take the heart? If I pass on it, he may die before he's offered another one." It's an emotional and difficult question to answer for a client who's frantic. It was tearing me apart to hear my answer for my friend. "Laurie, reject the heart. It's a weak heart, and it will make him ill."

She did, she turned it down, and it was one of the most difficult choices that she's ever had to make. It was also one of the most difficult things that I've ever had to say. The next day Laurie learned that there was a question about the donor's using drugs, which would have compromised the heart. As relieved as we were, we still knew that Laurie's son needed a heart for transplant.

Some weeks after that, Laurie was getting worried because another donor heart hadn't come up for her son. It was May at the time, and Laurie asked me if I could tell about what time a donor heart would come for him. I was nervous about being off on my prediction; this after all was life or death for a friend's son. "The Fourth of July, Laurie, he'll get it on the Fourth of July." The Fourth of July weekend came, and we celebrated my youngest daughter's fifth birthday. There were little girls everywhere and red, white, and blue cake smeared across their pretty little faces. My phone rang. It was Laurie: "Allison, they have a heart that's a match. They're performing the transplant on the fourth, just like you said."

I gave her my love and prayers, and we hung up. Her son had the transplant and everything went smoothly. Her dad did keep him here and watched over him during the heart transplant and after. Laurie's dad and my dad shared too many details, names, places, and other information to name them all, but you get the gist of what I'm saying.

Laurie was moved by her dad's words and knew he was beside her, as I knew my dad was beside me from Laurie's information.

As time passed, we continued to read each other and laugh with our dads, something we thought we'd never do again. That was definitely a bonding experience, and since then we've had many conference phone calls for the four of us.

Another occasion that I had to put my pride aside and accept the supporting words of another was provided to me not by another medium but by a client.

I had a colleague call in a favor one Sunday afternoon when I was asked to give a reading for a friend of his. I normally don't work on Sunday, but I made an exception for him. My client showed up, a very vibrant woman with an air of wisdom about her. I invited her in and we sat down. I looked at her and said, "I get the issue is your dad." I then went into special details about her dad, who had passed away. At the end of her reading, I shared with her that my dad too had passed and I understood her pain. It's strange when you lose someone you love; sometimes the only comfort you really find is in those who have walked your same path. For me it was another daughter who'd lost the first man she'd ever loved too, her dad. You'd think that would be the end of the story, but not so. Later that day, after my client left, I received an e-mail from her. She wrote, "I know this is going to sound crazy, but after I left the reading, while I was driving home, I could hear what I believe was your dad, Allison. He was singing a song called "Last Dance" by, I think, Donna Summer. Does that make sense to you? I know I don't know you or your dad, but I thought I'd tell you anyway."

I sat back in my office chair and stared at the words on my computer screen as though I were consuming the words with my eyes. Does that make sense to me? I thought. Well, let me tell you how much that means to me. After Dad died, every time I walked into a building, that song would come on. I knew it was my dad saying we had our "last dance." When I had to change the title on his car and remove his name and add mine, it was a particularly difficult day. I stopped at a little tavern to process my pain, and like clockwork, "Last Dance" was the first song that came on when I sat down. Of course, I bawled like a baby, but still I knew the song was sent with love. Sometimes the things that remind us of those we love cause us pain, because the connection from the other side reminds us that our loved one isn't here on earth with us. But later those are the moments we will crave. I don't remember the exact moment, but after two years of hearing that song and choking back tears, I found that one day the pain became a smile. For an instant I caught myself smiling and I felt a little guilty, but I know my dad would rather I smile when I think of him than cry. I have given that time a great deal of thought, and I think that once I cracked my first smile and I fully owned that my dad was with me by not mourning him but embracing him, his energy, and love, the curtain between us fell. Now I say, "Hey, Dad, it's our song!" and I know he hears me.

My dad was a professional ballroom dancer for fifty years. We had our last dance together in September 1999 at my cousin Juan's sixtieth birthday party. My family certainly knows how to throw a memorable party. I was seated with my husband, Joe, and my dad at a round table that afforded me the luxury to be able to take in everyone at the table at once. It was a calm night, and light hearts engulfed the moments that would connect like dots, ending in the last dance that I shared with my dad. My dad stood before me. "Come on, Allison, let's dance! Dance with your old dad."

"Oh Dad! I'm not good at the West Coast swing."

"Sure you are, you're my daughter."

"Oh yeah, what was I thinking?"

We laughed and we danced, my dad with an enormous smile on his face that left anyone helpless but to notice him. His infectious smile had a domino effect throughout the celebration, reminding all that my dad was never anything less than the life of the party. My dad danced with me from the time that I was an infant until, like any good party, his life came to an end. Anyone who has loved another will understand how important a song can be and the power that a song has to resurrect memories and share good times as though they were happening in real time.

And remember that, even though you may not be a "medium," that doesn't mean there won't ever be a day that you will have a medium-like experience. Some people have fleeting medium-like experiences, some people only once in a lifetime. I see it like any ability; some people have more of a certain talent than others. When you're ten years old, you can have the baseball game of a lifetime, a game that is still legendary in your family or your town, to be recounted for generations to relive. You won the big game against the town rival, and you were a hero for it. You grow up and never have that experience again, but you know it's possible, and you recognize the feeling. Another ten-year-old child goes on to play pro ball and eventually enters the Hall of Fame. A town hero and a Hall of Famer can both experience their moment of greatness and revel in it.

It is these moments that bring us fulfillment in life. Sometimes a moment of greatness comes in the form of a homemade birthday card that your little one made for you. This is no regular card but a one-of-a-kind card that displays your child's love for you, which can be seen on her little cherry-drink-stained smile as she hands you the card that she meticulously crafted with pride. People walk different paths and often wonder why they can't do something that you can and vice versa. It's because, sometimes, a taste of an experience is all that you needed to know that you're a part of something bigger than you are and to be reminded how much you've loved being a part of it.

If you're given a message from the other side, don't be afraid to share it. My client shared my father with me by confirming his sign to me through the title of the song. Even though she wasn't a professional medium, her words meant everything to me because I knew she had delivered a message from him. You never know how much the most seemingly obscure detail will mean to the recipient. Be sensitive to the message and circumstances. If it's a downer of a message that won't help anybody, then write the message down and throw it away. Energetically tossing it out rids you of the negativity. It's kind of like making a big statement that you aren't going to internalize the information. Most of us are aware that bad news can manifest physically within us if we carry too much baggage. This is a good exercise for anyone who needs to get distance from a bad situation. Usually, big problems come with a first name, and writing the name down and throwing it away lets you affirm your decision to move on. Works for me!

If it's upbeat information, then share it. Be sure the recipient is open to life after death. If you don't know the person well enough to know this about him or her, then a warm smile is more appropriate than a message from those passed. Either way, appreciate the gift of the message and the knowledge that we're not alone.

I had another experience after my dad died that brought me a lot of comfort and acted as a shining example of how mediums can also be blocked by pain and have to receive messages from their clients or another source. Occasionally the sign will benefit more than either a client or the medium; it may help all involved.

I was meeting with a wonderful woman in November of 2004 for a reading. She was a client, and hers had been the last private reading that I would be able to do that year because of the time demands of the holidays, family, *Medium*'s debut, press, and so on. Joe had thought about rearranging the date of the reading, but I told him, "I'm supposed to read her. It's important, so messing with the schedule could be bad."

When she arrived, we sat down and exchanged pleasantries. Her mom came through and shared many personal details with me that I passed along to her. So as we sat and laughed at her mom's effervescent sense of humor, my client said to me, "Allison, that's all great and it means a lot, really, but could she tell you the nickname she had for me?"

I said, "I can ask, but I can only give you what she gives me."

So I asked her mom for the nickname, and I concentrated and listened with everything I had, and I heard nothing. The silence was deafening; the moments were long and empty. In actuality, it was only a minute, but it felt like forever. I apologized to her because I could see how disappointed she was.

Just then I heard my dad, whom I had only recently started to hear two years after his passing. He said, "Allison, tell her about the nickname I have for you."

So I looked at her, and I said, "For some reason my dad wants me to share my nickname with you that he called me for thirty years until his death. It's a little embarrassing though."

She smiled politely and said, "What is it?"

"Jellybean. He called me Jellybean because I was so physically tiny when I was little. Even when I grew bigger, he still called me Jellybean."

I saw her face fall, and I wondered if I had said something to offend her.

"Oh my God! Allison, that's the nickname my mom called me!"

Well, you could have knocked both of us over with a feather. Jellybean is not a common nickname. We were both stunned. We stared at each other for a few minutes with smiles on our faces and tears in our eyes. This happened at the end of her reading, and it put her over the top. I will never, as long as I live, forget that night. Neither one of us ever thought we'd be called that name again, and clearly our parents worked in concert to touch us both and remind us how loved we are by them and they by us. My client walked away with the satisfaction of knowing that she had visited with her mom that night and that her mom had had a lot to say. My client also had a lot to share with her living family, letting them know that she had been reassured firsthand that her mom would always be close by.

In September 2005, while finishing this book, I was summoned out of town by the fifty-seventh annual Emmy Awards. Patricia Arquette was nominated for Best Actress in a Drama for the show *Medium*. This was a moment in my life I will never forget, not just because of the honor involved, but because my dad paid me a visit.

I'm always telling people to watch the chairs at their family gatherings, because during the holidays our deceased relatives and friends want to be there too. They love to be there for special occasions. They will show up around whoever made them the happiest in life. Sometimes they show up to a house where they were the most content, and especially they'll appear if they get both of these things in one place. Most of the time, their visits have more to do with the people than the structure, though. I find it amusing to watch a common spirit interaction with the living. There will be a chair that nobody will sit in; the living will even walk around the chair and stare as though there's something in front of them that can't be seen but is felt. People will even prefer standing before sitting in the only chair in the room that's empty, and they don't really know why that is. Well, it's because the seat is already taken by a well-intending spirit who wants in on the occasion, so save them a seat!

This very occurrence happened to me at the Emmys. So, I'm at the Emmys, and Joe and I take our seats, drinking in the moment. Me and the mister are sitting at the Emmys for a show that was inspired by my life story, and the woman who plays me (Patricia Arquette) is up for an Emmy for Best Actress. Yeah, that was hard to wrap my mind around. So, the place is full of people all dressed up, and I have a knot in my stomach that keeps reminding me how nervous I am. I wanted Patricia to win, she deserved to win, and she plays me, so I felt a vested interest.

Joe was sitting to my right at the end of the row. The seat next to me was empty; even the seat fillers who are on standby wouldn't sit there. This was a three-hour event, and my publicist's boss sat there for twenty minutes halfway through the night, and then it was vacant again. I looked at Joe and said, "Isn't it funny that nobody will sit there. Every chair is filled but that one."

Even the publicist who sat there briefly seemed uncomfortable, leaned over to me, and said, "I'm gonna go to the lobby. I'll see you later."

The moment of truth came before they were going to announce the winner of Best Actress in a Drama. The knot in my stomach grew, and I said, "Dad, I know you've been beside me tonight, and this is in no way a challenge. If Patricia wins, I will know that you, Patricia's dad, and Granddad had something to do with tonight, and I'll never question that you were here beside me."

The next words that I heard were "The winner is Patricia Arquette for *Medium*!"

I cried and looked down at my father's ring, which looked so out of place on my hand, and I rubbed it.

"Thanks, Dad, not for the win, but for being here with me on this special night. It means so much to me to have you here."

I kissed Joe and took all of the hugs headed my way, and we were off to the parties. When I walked into the Paramount/*Entertainment Tonight* party, I saw Patricia standing at a table that was clearly composed of people connected to *Medium*. I walked over, and she whirled around, handed me the Emmy, gave me a great hug, and said, "Thank you."

I was out of pithy responses, so I replied, "You're welcome."

A moment in time, that's what that was. She looked beautiful, and she was having the time of her life on a night that celebrated her talent. We posed for pictures and had a glass of champagne to toast the occasion, and as my glass and Joe's touched, the song "Last Dance" came on. Joe shot me a knowing look, and I was forced to lip-sync the rest of the song. Okay, not forced, but how could I resist? As of September 22, 2005, three years since Dad died, that song has gone from being a heartbreaker for me to a moment of celebration on a night that is a once-in-a-lifetime experience. Although I will always miss the way it was when my dad was living, I still have the comfort of knowing that when it's important to me, whether it be good times or bad times, he'll be there. It was icing on the cake that Patricia is a blonde and my dad had a clear affinity for blondes. Don't think that little detail escaped me.

There are many ways that our loved ones, especially parents, take care of us still, even after their demise. I've seen it for my clients, and I've seen it for myself. In September 2004, I got a really bad feeling that I was going to have a car accident. So I slowed down, took alternate routes, and guess what, I still got into a car accident.

Sometimes we're warned, but that doesn't mean we get to avoid it. The warning just helps to prepare us for a shaky situation.

So anyway, I was hit by a pickup truck, and I was really mad. I loved my car. So I called Joe to come get me from the scene of the accident. Of course, he wanted to take me to the hospital, but I'm thickheaded like everyone else in my family.

So I said, "Joe, I have a concussion, but I'm fine. Just wake me up from time to time for a day or two."

Joe was pretty annoyed with me but is well aware he can't change my mind.

I went out to my back porch and sat down

to collect myself, which was not easy. I looked up at the sky and said, "Wow, I was hit in the head pretty hard. Maybe I won't be able to see or hear the dead anymore."

As I nervously laughed, I heard my father clearly say, "You can hear me."

I almost fell off my chair. I knew my dad was with me when I was in my accident because I could feel him, but that was the first time in two years that I was able to really hear him. When I left the scene of the accident, the first song that came on the radio was "Circle of Life" by Elton John, and I knew Dad was letting me know he was with me, which reinforced what I had already felt. My dad used to play "name that tune" with me. I was quite good, as he expected from me. So my dad communicates with me a lot through music when I'm experiencing something traumatic.

Dad's music would become especially important to me on August 30, 2005. I had spent a couple of days with Craig from *TV Guide* and Jennifer, my publicist from Paramount. Craig was writing a story on a day in the life of the real Allison DuBois. My life is never boring, so the first day they accompanied me to a radio interview with Tim and Willy from KNIX radio. These are two of my favorite radio personalities, and they happen to be in Phoenix. Later that night Craig, Jennifer, Joe, and I had dinner with a couple of the district attorneys whom I work with. We went to one of my favorite restaurants, Durant's in Phoenix; they have the best steaks and strawberry shortcake ever!

When I woke up the next day, I told Joe I was feeling "off" and irritated. Later that day I went to a farewell lunch with Craig and Jennifer. My cell phone rang and it was Joe: *"The girls are okay. Allison, I was in an accident. You need to come to the scene."*

Craig ran out the door with me, and we jumped into my car. The radio came on when I started the engine. The song that was on was "Circle of Life."

I knew my dad was letting me know that he was with Joe and the girls and that everything would be okay. It didn't fall short on me that the same song had played one year ago, almost to the day, after my accident. I arrived at the scene. My two younger girls ran to me and held on tight. My eyes met Joe's. I saw his arm that had lost many layers of skin. I've brought through many spouses who have died in car accidents. Now my clients' feeling of loss all came rushing back to me. I counted myself immediately lucky and thanked God that my family was all right. The old lady who had hit my husband's car was being wheeled by on a paramedic's gurney. She apparently didn't see Joe and took a left into his car. While she was being wheeled by, my middle daughter looked at Craig and said, "It's okay, she doesn't have long to live anyway."

Obviously Craig and Jennifer were shocked. My youngest daughter then looked at Craig and said, "She has a TV in her head. She sees these things."

My other daughter angrily scolded her baby sister for telling anyone about that. Jennifer looked at my concerned daughter and said, "It's okay, your mom has a TV in her head too."

This is one of the ways little predictors and mediums express themselves and is good to note for parents who think that their kids might be gifted. I talked to my daughter later: "Honey, you can't say things like that about people you see dying. It's a big deal, and you need to be sensitive."

At the accident, my daughter said she was sorry, and with a crimson face, I apologized to Craig and Jennifer, who were incredibly supportive and understanding.

Joe looked at me and said, "You not only told me in the last three weeks that you saw me getting into a car accident, which made me be more cautious, but you told me a year ago when I bought the car that you saw me getting into an accident and to be careful."

I knew he was going to be in an accident, which clearly I couldn't stop. I saw the driver's side front fender being hit. It's very hard to "see" something that will hurt someone you love, but by being with Joe, I knew my dad was saying, "You couldn't save me, but I could save him." Without a doubt, with a wink of his eye. Thanks, Dad!

This is one of the ways they show us they love us from the other side, by intervening when they're permitted to. By the way, I wasn't the only one to see the accident before it happened. My eight-year-old daughter saw the accident in her head that day at lunch, right before it happened, and told her dad to "drive carefully."

As a footnote, just so you know, I did have a concussion and I am just fine. Joe's fine too. I told him to leave the crash dummy testing to me and never to scare me like that again. We laughed and hugged. Know this, that those we love and lost continue to protect us and when necessary give us a good swift kick in the posterior. Sometimes that's just what we need.

The loss of a parent is always tragic, but

even more so when the children didn't have the opportunity to get to know their mom or dad or to make memories that they can find comfort in after their parent has passed. For these children, mediums can sometimes provide the first and most special details of a relationship that a parent has built from the other side.

Eileen

The day was January 29, 1970; my father lay dead on the floor, a single gunshot wound to his head. I was a baby resting in my cradle, only a few feet away from a father I'd never know. At just under four months old, I wasn't a very good witness.

"Suicide," the cops declared. The same cops who for years would arrest my father for any petty crime that took place in our town. The same police force his brother served. No investigation, no fuss. Never mind that the gun he was holding in one hand didn't match the side of his head with the entrance wound. All agreed, suicide.

Our family knew another story. It seems that at some point he had made an enemy of an acquaintance who was part of organized crime. One night, badly beaten and left for dead outside, my dad, his friends, and our family were threatened. He was told that if he showed his face in a certain part of town again, he would not live to see his next birthday.

It seems my father did not heed the warning. His birthday was January 30 but he would not live to blow out birthday candles this year. He had been so proud to be a father, and he was really trying to turn his life around. He was doing public service speaking engagements to children in local schools, on the radio, and on TV.

Anyone who knew Chris said he would not have taken his own life. To this day his policeman brother says he never believed his death to be suicide. Friends have teased that his vanity was so great, he certainly wouldn't have ever shot himself in the head.

Fast-forward to October 2, 2004. I met Allison for the first time. Having lived with this pain in my heart throughout my life, I longed to find some peace. I'd hoped she would confirm what I've always believed to be true. During my reading my father "came through," and he apologized to me for my having to live with the shame involved with his death. He wanted me to know that someone else "had a hand" in his death. He said he knew it was coming and wanted to stop it, but he couldn't. He wanted to say he was sorry for not being there for my mother, and he acknowledged that she has not been there for me. He thanked my husband for loving me and being there for me to share my life "the way he would have been." He wanted to thank me for naming my children after him. No one, he said, had ever done anything so special for him in his life.

"Did you?" Allison asked after the reading.

Indeed. All five of our daughters' middle names are after my dad.

My fifth child was born twenty-nine years after he died on January 29, the anniversary of my dad's death, when I was twenty-nine years old. She was born spontaneously (in the bathtub) within the same half hour listed on his death certificate.

At my reading with Allison, my father then wished me a happy birthday. The lights in the room flickered. We all looked up, and Allison asked, "Is it your birthday?" As I answered in the affirmative, the lights flickered again. We all laughed.

The person responsible for taking my father's life will never be held accountable. But to receive validation from Allison has helped fill a void with some peace. I've always known the truth in my heart, but to hear it from Allison, after having only just met her that day, was overwhelming. The fact that she could tell me details unique between my father and me was incredibly special. She has given me such an amazing gift. She's provided me with a playback of the last moments of my dad's life, ending the not-knowing that had eaten at me for years. She also spoke all the words that I have waited my whole life to hear. I'll always be grateful to her for that.

My Take on Eileen's Reading

I ask my client to not give me information before a reading on the person who passed away, their relationship to my client, or the cause of passing. A medium should be able to give the client the information. Clients can feel free to confirm and ask questions after the initial information has already been provided, but it's necessary for the medium to give information first. It makes a reading more compelling.

Eileen had seen me on a news program in Phoenix, where I was tested on the air when I was asked to read a person that the news station had selected. After watching me, she decided that she wanted to book a reading. Her reading was scheduled for October 2, 2003, which coincidentally is my wedding anniversary. Before a client comes, I always write a few pages of information that is given to me by the deceased connected to my client. When I met Eileen and her husband, Paul, I had the information that I had previously written down on her dad and his passing on a pad of paper resting in my lap. Eileen walked into my office — a statuesque, dark-haired woman, not only a classic beauty on the outside, but every bit as pretty within. Paul, her husband, reminded me of my Joe. He's supportive of Eileen, and it is easy to see the deep love he has for his wife. I told Eileen that I was picking up on a father figure who had passed away. He was very insistent that I tell her that he did not take his own life and that he'd never have willingly left her.

He also kept showing a money transaction as being involved in his murder. He knew the killer and let him into his house willingly, not expecting that it would be the last person he would see before he died. Chris showed me this event in slow motion because not a lot of time passed and he wanted me to feel the enormity of those few last moments of his life. When Chris showed me the scene, it was slightly out of focus, so I had to look hard to understand why. Sometimes when a person has had a drink of alcohol at the time of death, it can impair what I see too. This is only the case when they show me the scene through their eyes.

Chris talked me through the details surrounding his death, which I shared with Eileen. Some of the details I'm leaving out because they're personal to Eileen and not appropriate to share. Of all the details that Chris shared, I find the most important information to be the way he died. He did not commit suicide; he was murdered by a hired hit man. He said that he loves his little girl and would never have left her for any reason. That he was at Eileen's wedding in spirit and thought she looked beautiful. That he's honored to have five granddaughters named after him. He spends a lot of time around the girls, all of his lovely granddaughters, but most important and especially his little girl.

When spirits show me a meaningful moment that they are a part of, sometimes it's through their eyes. Sometimes it's just an overview of the room where a pivotal action took place. When greed is involved, and a money transaction is a part of why they died, they often show me a black bag full of money so that I understand the motive for their murder. Spirits find many ways to communicate, but their main goal with a medium is to get us to understand what they're saying and to help us to deliver their message to those they love.

Losing a parent is like losing a part of yourself. Every day after is a journey forward that teaches us perseverance. Our love for those we lost provides us incentive to strengthen our memory so as to not forget all the little details of their faces, their laughs, anything that brings them back to us, if only for a moment. Children find different ways to heal or at least to move forward. We who have lost parents will find them again in the faces of our children or in a dream where they make a special appearance. For the daughters and sons who still have their parents in the living world, enjoy every Mother's Day, Father's Day, every moment when they remind you of when you were small, because right now you are creating the very moments that you will replay in your mind over and over later.

I still miss my dad. I think that never really goes away. Sometimes I watch *Father of the Bride* with Steve Martin and bawl like a baby, but you know what? I couldn't possibly cry like that if my dad hadn't done something right in life. I know I'm not the only daughter who cries when she watches movies like that, thinking of the dad she lost. I know how hard it is, especially for the kids who lost their parents young, and my heart goes out to them. I think I speak for everyone on that note. My dad used to call me "Jellybean." As I grew older, I hated it, but now I love that he saw me as little and sweet. It's funny how your perspective changes, isn't it?

Chapter 6
ANGELS OF THE HOSPICE

While writing this book, I have ventured where most people can't bear to go, into a hospice, where I watched a friend let go. My friend's name was Shari.

Shari wasn't my biological parent, although she was like a mom to me for all of my life. I met Shari when I was an infant. My closest childhood friend, Susie, is her daughter. Shari was my mom's best friend, and boy, did they have fun together. I can't remember a time in the beginning of my life when she wasn't there. Shari and my mom took Susie and me to Knott's Berry Farm when I was ten, and we had so much fun that our heads hurt from laughing so much. We drove from Arizona to California in a big, pale yellow station wagon with my boom box thumping. I'm sure that my mom drove as fast as that wagon would take us so that she could get away from the same two songs that I played all the way there. I believe one of the songs was "Girls Just Want to Have Fun" by Cyndi Lauper, and wasn't it the truth? We were making a memory so special that when I grew up, it would be a part of the soul that makes up this book.

Yeah, it seemed like it was Shari and my mom against the world. Sitting by our swimming pool, laughing together, is how I remember Shari and my mom. We never quite knew what they had in those big, bright plastic tumblers that they drank out of when Susie and I were small. Susie and I laugh about it now, because we can wager a guess on what beverage would make our moms increasingly giggly as they drank another round. Susie and I were splashing around in the water with a beautiful big sun watching over us. The promise of Happy Meals from our moms guaranteed a big "Yeah!" from our little mouths.

Yep, our moms were the coolest. Shari was larger than life with her red hair and her hippie bandana wrapped around her head, tied at the nape of her neck. My mom, the stunning blonde, turned heads with her floppy, big-brimmed hat and her Hollywood good looks. They were young and setting the world on fire together.

Now I had to realize that, as much as I'd

like to turn back the clock to give Shari a day of being healthy again, it was not in my power. Many others out there understand what I'm saying because they too have their memories and their own clock that they'd like to turn back.

I had just found out that Shari was going to die. She had pancreatic, lung, and liver cancer. There was no hope for survival. I ventured into the hospice where she had been moved after a stay in the hospital. Visiting a hospice is like no other experience. Hospices are full of people who are sick and terrified and who know that they'll never go home again.

I stared down at the woman who tried to feed me carrots when I was two. She always laughed, telling the story of the stubborn two-year-old who tried to explain to her that I was "leeergic to carrots." I wasn't and she knew it; I just didn't want to eat them. So she made me something else to pacify me. I'm sure it involved a high sugar content, because Shari was always baking pastries of some sort. Shari was not only a vibrant, loving, funny woman, she was a nurse who cared for the sick and dying herself. She worked until the day she entered the hospital, never to walk out again.

I learned something sitting beside Shari. I

learned that the dying force us to feel things that we would never voluntarily feel. They make us face our own mortality and force us to ask why. They force us to put ourselves in their shoes, and then force us to tell them all the things that we love about them, words that we shouldn't have waited so long to say. Some people never say the words at all, which is a shame. They fight to hold on to life out of the habit of living. They need to hear you say that it's okay to let go. Otherwise they just keep on fighting. A voice they trust, telling them to let go, telling them you love them and always will love them, is an enormous comfort to those who are dying.

I watched my mom hold her dying friend's hand firmly, yet with loving care. I watched my mom carefully apply Shari's favorite color of bright pink lipstick to Shari's lips. She called Shari "princess" and gave her a manicure. She was learning how to love Shari in a way that made it comfortable for Shari to let go and allowed my mom to let go of the way things had been in the past.

I sat beside Shari's bed and replayed every memory that I had stored of my mom and Shari getting into mischief together in the 1970s and 1980s, when they were learning how to be single moms together. We lived in the same cul de sac, and when one would be down and out, the other one was there, either with money to make ends meet or a shoulder to cry on. I stared at Shari, the woman who had decided long ago that the best medicine for a skinned knee was for her to bake you a chocolate cake. She wasn't so wrong.

I sat next to Shari and I read her funny jokes and anecdotes by nurses, and Mom and I laughed. I stared at a poster board on the wall that said, "My name is Shari. I like rock music, funny movies, and pizza. I have two daughters and five granddaughters." I read it out loud to Shari, announcing who she is and letting her know that she's not just a person who happens to be dying. She's our friend, and she matters to many. We were there simply to love her and for no other reason. When people are dying, it's crucial that they have people with them who can reminisce with them and hold their hand. Shari was a natural comedian, so my telling nurse jokes was my way of connecting with that part of her. My mom has always been very aware of appearance and personal care. She showed Shari love by pampering Shari. My mom expanded the energy that Shari didn't have as a deep way of showing love.

The last moments of a person's life are as pivotal for the living as for the dying. Death allows us to perform those last acts of love for the person who's passing on. Shari kept saying "hot," she was burning up, and we couldn't do much to comfort her. Her organs were shutting down, and her body was not cooling itself well. We fed her ice chips and applied cool cloths to her forehead. It was all that we could do. I prayed that if Shari was not to be saved, God would please take her home so that she didn't have to suffer anymore. It physically pained me to hug her because I could feel her cancer, yet I didn't know how to let go. I asked my dad to help Shari over. I gazed at Shari one last time, knowing that I would never see her alive again. At the same time — and I'm sure many people can relate to this — as I looked at Shari, I knew that "my" Shari was already gone. The woman who was always laughing and pulling practical jokes on us, the woman who made us raspberry tarts for Christmas, the woman I grew up around had no more happy memories to create for herself or the ones who love her.

Just before we left, a friend of Shari's, who is also a nurse, walked in to see her. He shared that he hadn't seen Shari in a while before she was wheeled into the hospice.

He gazed down at his dying friend with love, compassion, and, of course, heartbreak. It was profound to view the relationship between two people who, as nurses, had always cared for strangers as though they were family. Shari was now the patient, and it was something to see her friend, in the ultimate act of friendship, take care of the nurse whom he just happened to also love.

Even besides the hardship of facing the death of a friend, I find a hospice a particularly difficult place to be. I was bumping into those who had died as I walked down the hall. I felt numb, except for the prickly feeling on the surface of my skin that I always get when I'm around death or spirits. In this case, it was both. I felt like my senses were overloading. The dead would steal my breath every couple of minutes when they would try to move through me or talk to me. I glanced out of the window at the sunshine and the Christmas decorations that lined the houses in the area. All of a sudden, I felt like I was standing in a nucleus of death and beyond the walls resided the living. Part of me longed to rejoin the living, but right now I was needed by the dying. I wanted to walk into each room and hold the dying who had no visitors and let them know they're not invisible and remind them that they're still here. To tell all of them that they matter and, even when it seems they're alone, they're not.

I think a lot of people who are dying have the line blurred between "here" and "there." They lose track of where life ends and eternal life begins. Most hospice nurses will tell you that the dying start talking about being little kids or telling detailed stories about their parents, who have been deceased for decades. The dying do this because they're sensing their youth again; they're feeling those who are waiting for them and are there to receive them. I've spoken with hundreds of people who've been in the room of the dying and witnessed the dying talking about being small or younger, or the dying saying they saw the deceased in their room in the last days of their life. I've also brought people through who talk about seeing the people who'd previously died right before they themselves passed and now say that they're together. The spirits give me names and physical descriptions of the visitors they had when they were alive.

I was deeply impressed with the hospice that Shari stayed in. It was warm, personal, and soothing. It was in a large house called the Gardener Home in Phoenix, donated to the hospice by the family that had lived there. It was being run by Hospice of the Valley. Such a good idea. I had never thought of what a gift donating a house to the dying would be. As I was thinking about this great gift, my mom said to me, "Should we have a chaplain come see Shari?"

I thought it a grand idea, one of the few comforts that we could provide for Shari. Although Shari didn't belong to a specific religion, she definitely believed in God. My mom and I told Shari we had to go but that we loved her. Shari whispered, "I love you too."

As we walked out of her room, a handsome older man with piercing blue eyes walked out of another patient's room and approached us.

"Can I help you? I'm a chaplain. Would you like for me to pray with your friend?"

This was no coincidence. He looked like an angel, he sounded like an angel, and that day he was our angel.

We joined hands with each other and Shari as he prayed for her and with her and, for the first time, I saw a look of peace cross Shari's face. That day there were many angels in that hospice. The nurses who are in the death trenches every day are angels; those dying, preparing to get "their wings," are angels; those who have already died and await their loved ones, those who died in the same hospice who stay to help others cross, the people who value the last wishes and moments of those who held them when they were children or sit beside those who were the children they held, they're all angels. Sometimes just someone whom you allowed to hold your hand is an angel.

As I said good-bye to a friend I love, it pained me because all I really wanted to do was pull Shari back, to give her my strength, and take some of her pain away. I know that this is unreasonable, but who wants to be reasonable when it comes to losing a friend? If love were enough, I suppose nobody would ever die. To the people who sit in hospices and say good-bye to the way things were, know that you're not alone. To those who work there, know that we appreciate you. To those who will die there, know that angels are tending to you and that you will not be forgotten.

The morning after I visited the hospice, I was emotionally wrung out, so I called my friend Kelly. I told her I wanted to call the hospice but was told by an inner voice, "Don't call right now."

As I sat on the phone talking to Kelly about Shari, just then I saw Shari in front of me. She always had an overstated sense of humor that I loved. Shari appeared before me in her peach-colored fairy godmother Halloween costume that she wore a couple of years back. Wings and wand included! The picture of her in this costume was hung on the wall of her hospice room. As I admired her healthy appearance and her always great humor, I had to crack a smile.

She said, "I'm gone."

"Kelly, Shari just showed herself to me and she said she's gone."

"Oh, Allison, I'm sorry." (It's nice having friends who don't question you because they already know your capabilities.)

Fifteen minutes later my other line rang. "Kelly, it's Hospice of the Valley. Hold on."

It was the news that I needed to hear from someone else. "Allison, Shari just passed away a little bit ago."

Me and my big mouth responded softly with "I know."

The family friend who was relaying this bad news to me was okay with what I had said, but I have to be careful, it's not always easy to explain to others exactly where I'm coming from. I clicked back to my other line and shared the news with Kelly. It's not easy to get the words out with a lump in your throat. Just then a song came on by Bread (for those of you old enough to know who they are). It's called "Everything I Own." As I drank in the words, I knew it was from Shari. People who die like to reach the living through songs on the radio. Spirits seem to have an electric energy that can manipulate electronic items. What are radios? Boxes full of words about emotion, so it makes sense that spirits try to speak to us through the songs. They send their love that way, and many people know when a song has been sent to them by a loved one who passed away. They are and should be sure of it.

Shari had passed away. The only comfort for me is that I know when people die, they're strong, vibrant, happy, and beautiful. I see them in their new form after they pass; it's an immediate transformation. I know this because I saw Shari minutes after she passed and she looked radiant. Amazing, I saw Shari moments after she passed away, what a gift! She was glorious and smiling again. Till we meet again, Shari! I love you.

A few days after Shari died, I attended her funeral along with other friends and family. I took my seat waiting for the sermon. When I looked up, the same man with the piercing blue eyes who had prayed with us in the hospice was standing at the podium. He spoke lovingly and with conviction about Shari's life, a woman he had sat with in the last days of her life in the Hospice of the Valley, the woman whose hand he held and whose forehead he had placed his hand on as Shari struggled with dying. When he finished, I asked Shari's daughter, Susie, how they had arranged for him to give her mother's sermon. Susie was unaware of the connection between the blue-eyed man and her mother. She said that a friend of her mother's was across town at the hospital and met this really nice man who turned out to be a minister. He asked the man to speak at his friend's funeral, and the man accepted.

"Wow!" was all I could muster to say.

The minister was at a hospital at least forty minutes away from the hospice where he had met Shari when he was asked to speak at her funeral. He didn't realize that he was speaking at a funeral for a dying woman he had met across town days earlier. He spoke of his surprise when he laid eyes on Shari's picture placed on the table beside the podium at her funeral and realized that this was the same woman whom he had prayed for. Phoenix has millions of people in it. I know that it was no coincidence that this "angel" of a man, who gave Shari peace at the end of her life, also gave her peace in death. I cannot convey the look of shock on my face and my mother's when we laid eyes on him at Shari's funeral, but maybe you can imagine the calm he provided us in our hearts when we knew he was sent to us. We are sent whom and what we need when we need them the most.

The word P-A-I-N can never sum up what it feels like to lose someone. There is no word in any language that can fully describe the loss of one's self when someone dies. After writing this chapter, I realized something. Every moment that you take a step forward by making it through another day, no matter how good or bad you feel, you can't run fast enough or far enough to escape loss. This is because you can never leave behind the love inside your heart. It moves with you. It moves with you because the person who died stands beside you.

It's ironic. I see people who are living who walk through life feeling dead inside, just passing time until they die. Then there are those who have died who want to stay with the living and have never felt more alive. There are people who had a chemical imbalance in life who, now dead, want to join the living because they see how beautiful life can be. There are also souls who just had such a great life that they still want to share it with their loved ones. And there are people who died too soon who choose to remain with the living who are the same age so they can live through their experiences. There are people who fought to live an extra day, or to see one last sunset, and they fight for these things out of a love of life. Life is meant to inspire us to take a chance, to reach down into the very core of who we are and bring that to the surface to share.

I guess the trick is to "think outside the body" while you are living. How have you touched people and made their life better? Do you remember to send a birthday or Christmas card to relatives who have become distant and who might be alone? Do you plan a special night for you and your spouse to let your love know you appreciate him or her? I know widows/widowers who would give anything to have another day with the love of their life. Do you take the time to compliment people in passing to brighten their day? I do! I love making people smile, because it seems so much of my life involves people crying because they miss the ones they love. I love asking my grandma Jenee about her parents and when she was little. It makes her so happy to talk about them. I love bringing grandma her favorite foods and calling her for no other reason than to brighten her day. Grandma still has a lot to teach us in her older years, and she still needs company and acknowledgment, she's human! So I won't waste any time that I still have with my grandma, no regrets!

In my life, I know my oldest daughter will always remember me springing her from school to go shopping. It's not the shopping that mattered, it was that her mom was creating a moment with her. We ate junk food and laughed. I revel in my children. I ride roller coasters with them, hold them when they feel the world is against them. I will always fight for their happiness. I teach them to touch others. We take them to the mall every Christmas, and we buy a whole tree of Salvation Army Christmas Angels for kids without Christmas. My girls pick out everything personally. They will grow up to take the time to care about others, as Shari did in her life.

Caretakers

After going through the pain of losing Shari, I remembered fondly the hospice nurses. Nurses and people who work in hospices experience loss on a daily basis. They're often with the dying when no family or friends are there. I wanted to share with you a wonderful woman named Joani Roberts. She is a caretaker, and she serves as a surrogate family member for the dying and the family of the dying. I came to know her because my friend Brian's grandfather was ill in 2005. She took care of him during this time, and she was able to make his final moments of life better. She also brought Brian a great deal of comfort in knowing that his granddad was not just being taken care of but was being cared for like family.

Joani has many memories of sharing someone's final moments. I've asked her to relate one of them to you to show that almost anyone who chooses a career that deals with death will be faced with life after death.

Suzette

Suzette was an eighty-year-old, white female who came into hospice service with colon cancer. She had been married to Phil for fifty-five years. One night, sixteen hours before her passing, I was sitting quietly at her bedside, in the dark, when she asked me to please turn the TV off. I gently took her hand and told her that the TV wasn't on. She spoke of a movie screen playing above her bed. She asked, "You don't see it? You don't see the nuns? I'm sitting there in my uniform, it's me."

I said, "No, but tell me about it."

She said, "It's my life, and it's loud. Will you turn it off?"

I said, "I sure will."

I sat quietly for a few moments, and inquired, "Is that better?"

She said, "Yes."

I thought she had drifted peacefully to sleep. Fifteen minutes later, in the darkness, she asked, "Have you met my father?"

I said, "No, I've never had the pleasure." (Out of respect, I went along with her.)

She said, pointing to the empty chair beside me, "Well, let me introduce you."

As sure as I sit here today, I know he was right there with her during her final hours, to welcome her to the other side. Hours later, Suzette passed peacefully, and I am comfortable in my belief that her father was with her.

It is not uncommon in my profession to work with a hospice client whose spouse has recently died. There is often a familiar "presence" in the house after the first partner dies that is lasting evidence of their union. Tangible treasures include family photos, ashes, clothing never discarded, and projects that will not reach completion. But the strangest phenomena I experience include flickering lights, unusual reflections in mirrors, feeling a spiritlike presence, comforting aromas, objects often moved out of place, and pictures askew. Although most people would find these events unsettling, I often feel comforted, knowing that loved ones are "checking in" and awaiting a reunion with their beloved. I am learning lessons with every patient, every client I sit with, knowing as sure as I shake their hand in our first meeting that I am there to help them to die comfortably. We don't have all the answers in life, but there are some patterns of dying that cannot be ignored. I think we can all agree that although some things cannot be fully explained, that doesn't mean that there's no explanation; it's just beyond us.

Joani's Memory of Suzette

I am comforted every time I hear a story like Joani's because it teaches me that life goes by fast, but death happens like lightning. Life in comparison is long, and death is quick, so focus on life, make it good. Because even though death can be sad and painful, it's sadder and more painful to think that people squandered their life worried about what others think of them more than what they think of themselves. Live well, be there for your friends and family, be proud to be who you are, and remember that just because something feels hard to do for another, that doesn't mean you shouldn't do it. It was hard for me to sit with Shari, it hurt to hold her, and it was even harder to say good-bye, but I was there out of love and she knew it. Love is about sacrifice, and I promise that the sacrifices that you make for another will not only be worth every tear that you shed, they will one day be made *for* you instead of *by* you.

CHAPTER 7
THE HARD QUESTIONS

I am often asked what happens to people who commit suicide. I want to dispel some myths that surround suicide, the most damaging being that people who commit suicide go to "hell." I also want to touch on religion and touch on the interpretation of the Bible. I get so many letters from people who think their son or daughter has gone to a bad place for committing suicide. So I will give you not only my perspective but the perspective of a priest who is also a medium.

People often ask me about reincarnation, so I want to say, for the record, that I don't know the answers around reincarnation. What I do know is that people on the other side remain available for me to communicate with as long as there is someone alive with whom they have an emotional connection. I do believe that reincarnation is entirely possible. People seem to be eerily drawn to a specific place and time in history, as if they'd been there before. But on this, I am not an expert. I personally have tried to focus on the here and now in life and not reach back to possible past lives. I believe in making the present a priority, and I try to live well and be happy. There are many wonderful authors who have researched reincarnation, and I encourage people to search for the answers they need in life. If reincarnation is important to you, then by all means, find your truth.

Because of my work and because of the show, people also seek me out to better understand the passing of someone who has been murdered.

Murder

I want to shed some light on what happens to people who pass at the hands of others. People who die at the hands of a killer carry a distinct energy, different from that of people who die in natural ways or in suicide or accidents.

It's important for families to understand that people who are murdered do not roam the earth unsettled. The deceased join family and friends who've already passed — the same family and friends who were not permitted by a bigger plan to intervene on behalf of the victim. There are circumstances where the death of one person would serve to change many lives through inspiring change for the better and serves as a powerful, positive rippling effect that moves more people than could be moved by the living. On the flip side, there are also occasions when a person's life plan included their being saved, when it was not in their "grand plan" to leave just yet. Although it seems greatly unfair sometimes, the living don't always see all the ways that a tragedy can invoke inspiration into a life. For instance, the child who was my first missing person's case was a stranger to me. Through looking for her, I learned about the child abduction alert system, Amber Alert, which was, at the time, very new. I came home from that case and set my sight on making Arizona a part of this valuable and necessary alert system. Once our system was up and running, it immediately saved many children's lives in Arizona. Without the child from my first case, who had died tragically, it may have taken Arizona much longer to create a statewide alert. Eventually, it would have happened, but which of the first saved would have fallen without the alert? In this way, the little victim saved other children from meeting a similar death. I will again remind you that we don't always see the many reasons to have faith in a "bigger plan." Sometimes we only see glimpses of the greater purpose, but those glimpses are only one small part of the plan. Those glimpses are most visible when held up against dark times for contrast. So when people wonder why bad things happen, I always believe that with good comes bad, but what we make of the bad is up to us.

The biggest tragedy is when people fail to change a life for the better. It's never too late to decide to share your special gifts. These are the gifts that can only be found deep within the recesses of who you are. Sometimes a tragedy serves to call out these gifts lodged deep within us.

The deceased feel the pain of the living people whom they love, and they try to support them with their presence. Victims also serve as a reminder to the person who took their life. Not only is the deceased victim a reminder, but the living family members who lost a part of their future through the death of a loved one serve as reminders. I'm always moved when I see a family member of a victim on television talking to the parole board, telling them why the person who murdered his or her loved one should never come out of prison. My stance on murder is that if you willingly take an innocent life, you forfeit yours. I think the victim's family, who have to reach into their own pockets to pay to travel to stand before a parole board, are more important than the perpetrator. Hopefully, one day, there will be reform that will ease the lives of the victims and their families rather than the lives of the people who created the pain in the first place. We innately fight for those we love. The families of victims fight not only for the deceased but to remind everyone that the one they lost should matter to all. They're right for thinking so.

Families of victims will still be serving their sentence long after the perpetrator's ends. I want to help the families that deal with that kind of pain. I find a particular visual exercise helpful in processing the pain around loss. One such exercise is to lie on your bed and visualize a person you feel connected to who has passed away. Visualize the person standing at the foot of your bed holding a basket. Look at the detail of the basket and follow upward slowly with your eyes to the person's face. He or she is smiling and is backed by a white light. The person is capable of removing your pain and your worries. You're going to reach forward and place your problems in the basket. You can add as many as you want because the deceased has the ability to take all you have and gladly will do so. I once personally visualized my dad holding the basket. He was beaming light through his grin, and every hair was in place. I took my biggest problem at the time, which was a man whom I trusted but who turned out to not be so nice. I said, "Are you sure, Dad?"

He laughed and nodded his head. "Yes."

So I visualized the man himself being placed into the big basket feet first, until all you could see was the balding top of his head and his eyes peering angrily over the top of the basket. I've got to tell you, this is a great exercise. That helped me so much and allowed me to have a good laugh with my dad. My dad winked at me, turned, and carried away my troubles. Whenever I need him to take away my spiritual junk for me, I repeat the exercise. Anything that causes your heart to be heavy is worth placing in the basket. This exercise is also fantastic in strengthening the bond between yourself and those who've passed. They remain to help the ones they love, and even more so, they love to be needed still. So no worries about burdening the ones we love. They only feel burdened by their unfulfilled desire to be needed. So give them what they need, connection to us.

Another great exercise for people with a heavy heart is to visualize your heart filled with a magnificent white light. I've heard from healers that green is the heart chakra, which is great too. I like white, it works for me, like it's blowing away the painful rocks and cobwebs that can fill a heart. Like opening a window to a room that sometimes can feel cold and dark. I let in white because it reminds me of the spectacular white background that surrounds our loved ones when they appear from the other side. I always say, do what works for you! Green, white, whatever radiance you decide to introduce to your heart will be an improvement. Visualize the light until it not only fills every wall of your heart, but also spills over in all directions like a star. You can do this with your stomach if it's in knots or any part of your body that ails you.

You can also ask your deceased loved one to please add back to your heart what you feel was taken from you when he or she died. Close your eyes, take a deep breath, and allow the deceased to reinvest part of themselves back into your heart. It's a very uplifting exercise that also can be physically felt. Be sure to fully open your heart and mind to receive them back into your heart.

Don't confuse desperation with openness. It's important to take a really big breath in through your nose and exhale through your mouth so that you can hear the air passing through. A quiet room is a big help for this exercise. This breathing puts you on the same energetic "page" as your deceased loved ones. They want to help. Let them remove your guilt/pain and replace it with their love.

As a footnote, victims who died are aware of everything that awaits the person who took their life. But that aside, spirits are more concerned with their loved ones than with the perpetrator. Families of victims often wonder what the deceased can see. They can see everything that awaits us, and when our lives are affected by the murderer, as they always are in a homicide, then the deceased care about the perpetrator only because the crime affects their own family and those they love. Victims care that a killer not be allowed to victimize another person, and they care about their own family. Other than that, the killer is unimportant to the deceased now.

On the flip side of death, people who have passed, even when they have been mur- dered, are aware of every emotion that the family feels, and they look for even the smallest joys over things like new puppies and celebrations. They want us to remember them and still love them, but they want us to move beyond our pain and experience joy again. Remember, they are there for each and every moment of happiness that you find or create. They love hearing us tell stories about them and watching us put up pictures of them at their zenith around the house — the portrait taken the day they were married; the WWII picture that they held onto with pride, the soldier looking handsome in his uniform; pictures of a mother who used to resemble a young Elizabeth Taylor, as she held her baby so close to her face with adoration; pictures of a father dancing with his daughter on her wedding day, the same little girl who wrapped her tiny infant hand around her daddy's finger years ago and stole his heart, which he'd never get back. Those pictures are the galleries of their life, the pictures that captured images of their existence, the ones that told the story of all they ever dreamt of having or being.

Those we love put thoughts into our heads, trying to prod us to join them in a walk down memory lane, or they talk us into making their favorite snack, which they loved but we never saw the value of until they died. Now it seems familiar and wonderful, even lovable! Isn't that just the way life works? Grandpa's deviled ham sandwiches with pickle relish on wheat bread that smelled so strong we held our noses every time he'd eat it has now become something that we crave ourselves. Whether for emotional comfort, or changing taste buds, we crave it. There are so many things to savor in life; it's sometimes hard to choose. Many families of murder victims feel guilty about being joyful, and they are sometimes too devastated to continue the experience of their loved one's life. I want to assure you that it is okay to move toward happiness. It's what preserves and protects the word *love*. And, yes, sometimes Grandpa's sandwich can remind us how much we love him.

Those who pass on insist on being remembered as they were when things were happy and untainted. They don't like their death to define their life. They are well loved and highly protected and often connecting with others who passed in a similar way. They also help support the living families of other victims who are now their friends. I find this predominantly the case with murders. It seems to be because most natural deaths don't usually cause people to reach out to strangers for support. Once the victim's family has reached out to another victim's family, the victims on the other side are brought together because two families who were previously strangers have now emotionally adopted each other. They have a common goal to help others. Also, the families tend to mention their new friends' loved one who was victimized almost in concert with their loved one, forming a deep bond.

I witnessed this bonding when I was a guest speaker for a grief counseling group that dealt with the topic of murder. Just talking to the members and seeing how they are there for each other was inspiring. On top of that, to see that they willingly experience the pain contained in the other members, as well as their own pain, made me sit back and fully feel this connection. At a time in a person's life when you would think the wounds are so severe that recovery would be impossible, I watched those people put their own grief aside to comfort another. I can honestly say, I have witnessed the best that a person is capable of being. When they had nothing left inside, they still reached into the depths of their soul and found strength for another in need. Not all of us can say that about ourselves, but as long as we are willing to try, we take a step closer to becoming someone's lifeline. Which is really a gift that you will one day get back.

Addressing a killer's bad acts is important. I find it necessary to let people know that as bad as the killer's act was, it can no longer affect the person who died, who is now completely surrounded by immeasurable love and strength. He or she can never be touched again by anything bad, ever. This is important to express to the families of murder victims because their pain is so much deeper than in other types of losses. To lose a loved one at the hands of a person who had such hate and disregard for life resurrects images that are disturbing to the living, and far more scarring than other deaths. And for those of you who have been lucky enough never to be touched by murder, reach out to those who don't have the luxury of saying that. Even if all you can do is listen to them when they feel life has brought them to their knees, your kindness will help them to stand again. More important, this is for those who have been touched by murder: I hope you can look through my eyes, to know that the ones taken from you were surrounded with the arms of unbreakable love as soon as they crossed.

My heart and prayers go out to all the

families of murder victims. Remember that every day forward is a day closer to your reunion with the ones who await you.

Suicide

Suicide is a way that few can understand. For the record, when a person commits suicide, he or she does not "go to hell." I know that religion has shared a different opinion on suicide; I am just sharing with you what I've seen myself. People who commit suicide are often good people who have a good heart. They also happen to be people who have a biological, chemical imbalance. We are not held responsible by the higher power for what we cannot help.

I often bring through people who have committed suicide, and they do express regret. They also express undying love and concern for their family and friends. They show me their childhood and what made them happy. They tell me how excited they are about their loved ones' lives since their passing. The babies born, the vibrant birthday parties, well-deserved graduations, blissful holidays, and visits they've made to their loved ones from the other side all are important to them. There are endless instances, but you get the idea. The living and dead are forever connected through our emotions and a continual attachment to one another that sees no reason to let go but every reason to hold on. Also, the deceased often acknowledge the people in the family who have passed away after them, and they convey the presence of the "newer" members that they now stand with to bring comfort to the living family members and friends, so that you know they're reunited with those who've more recently passed away. This is a communication that most deceased find important to mention to the living, letting them know that they are acting as a sort of host to those who have died more recently. It makes sense, since the deceased mostly remain to comfort the living, so of course they will ease minds and hearts by making their presence with the newly departed known to their living family. They often come through asking for forgiveness from the living and apologize for any pain they've caused. They often explain that if in life they had had the clarity they now have, they wouldn't have been suicidal. They seem to express their own grief over the loss of their life. At the same time they seem very happy to be healthy and to feel better than they ever could have imagined.

When I hear certain Christmas songs, my

heart swells with love and pride in reflection of not only elegant words but the captivating sentiment being expressed. I'm not physically touching anything, but I'm moved by the words. When we die, all of the personality traits and preferences that we had in life move with us, but the feelings that seem to have the most strength in remaining present with the living are the experiences and emotions that caused us to feel good. It almost feels as though those moments prompted our soul to expand and deepen. So when our body no longer remains, the energy and depth we have inside breaks free and becomes even more awe-inspiring than before. Our limitations are removed and our real power, which was inside all along, can connect to anything, as well as gain for us a great sense of understanding. It seems as though the little traits stay with us. For instance, I'm a redhead, and all my life people have pointed out that redheads are feisty. Well, this may be true, but above that, I find being a redhead is part of who I am. So when I die, I expect that I will probably appear with red hair even if I die with gray, because it's a signature of who I am. We're all made up of these traits that affect how we feel inside or how we react in life. Some people have a great sense of humor. Often I bring them through telling jokes, because it's a part of who they are. Physical limitations die; our true selves live as we never could before and expand in our new form.

For the people left behind who lost a loved one to suicide, know this: you were loved by the person who died. Don't think that you're not loved and that maybe if the person loved you more, he or she wouldn't have committed suicide. It's not true. Those who died were not thinking straight, and they hurt as they observe the devastation they left behind. They often share with me in readings that they crave to hear that you know they love you and that they were overtaken by their inner imbalance. They don't think rationally about the person who has to find their body or the people who plan their funeral and cry for them. They only know they feel like they can't live in their body because it hurts, and they just want their inner suffering to stop. Anyone touched by a suicide will understand what I mean. For those who haven't had the experience, I can only say that some people feel such anguish inside that it feels like they're giving it everything they have just to stay another day. The solution of ending the bad feelings within them seems obvious to them.

They see no other way. It's almost as if you had your emergency brake on in your car. You're driving with it fully pulled. Not only does driving feel difficult, but other things inside the car are breaking down because of that difficulty. Eventually, the car will break down.

Sometimes people who commit suicide are unstoppable, and survivors shouldn't beat themselves up thinking that somehow they could have prevented the passing. Many depressed or imbalanced people hide how they feel from those around them until it's too late. This is not to excuse the pain they cause, only to explain how they were feeling when they took their life. Often they feel undeserving of the love people have for them and see the living as better off without them. We know suicidal people are deserving of our love, but often they irrationally don't believe us. We all like to think that everyone else thinks and feels the way we do, but that's not the case. We're all different combinations of energy and often see things very differently from the people we stand next to. I think we've often listened to a person explain why he or she is justified in making a choice that others don't agree with, but as you look into the person's eyes, he or she truly doesn't see it the way you do. People are who they are; they may defy who we are, but we still can't change them, no matter how much we might want to.

People who survive those who commit suicide are often left with abandonment issues. If that is your situation, please hear this: you are without question worth living for.

You lost someone who couldn't continue. When you feel low and it hurts, remind yourself that you are worth living for. You lost someone who you love who was unreachable when living, but without a doubt, that person is still with you, now balanced and able to understand you completely.

Since they've shed the physical ailment that was driving them, suicides have also lost feelings that they don't have control of themselves. Once the body is gone, they discover a clearer way of thinking and an even clearer ability to connect with others.

You carry an inner strength they didn't feel they had. From what I've seen and learned through readings from people who've committed suicide, their stories have some similarities. Their imbalance started out as mild depression early in youth. As they got older, it became harder to suppress and hide from others. Often they looked for a way to suppress their up-and-down tides of depression and resentment through alcohol or drugs. Some outgrew the level of medication they were prescribed to control their irrational highs and lows but didn't realize that the medication itself had become part of the problem. Some chemically imbalanced people just weren't heard by those whom they talked to about their problematic feelings. Not because the people didn't care, but because it can sometimes be hard to tell if someone is experiencing a chemical imbalance or feeling overwrought from having a really bad day.

Although they found it necessary to leave this life, they want you to continue your life and to be happy, because they love you. They'll walk through your life with you, grateful just to be a part of you. Remember, you're the part of them that gave them the glimmers of happiness in life. You'll see that eventually. Live your life without regret and "feel" their presence. They are now balanced, and they are your biggest cheerleader.

I want to stress that prevention of suicide is possible for some. Many depressed people are treatable by a physician or therapist who can help them achieve some clarity. The yellow pages have listings of suicide hotlines for most cities. There are many resources waiting to help.

I also want to remind people who are judgmental of families who have lost a loved one to suicide or who condemn the deceased to remember that people who commit suicide are human and deserve compassion and understanding. They shouldn't be seen as weak or shameful; rather, they were born with a combination of physical and emotional baggage that brought about their demise. We do have free will, but the other variables must also be considered. When I bring through a person who has recently passed from suicide, their energy to me feels like confusion or scattered energy. Their energy stabilizes over the first year after their passing. It's an energy adjustment that takes place within their soul, lending to a balance of their energy that they didn't have in life. They still have family around them, like any other person passed does. They have memories, love, and messages. They are not incomplete people. It was simply in their energy from birth to be challenged on many levels.

Some people may not understand this. Most people have experienced depression on one level or another and can relate to a feeling of grief and being misunderstood. People who are suicidal feel grief inside that consumes them; the pain feels to them as if someone died. Anyone who's loved and lost knows how deeply that hurts. The difference is it's everything within them that they feel die little by little, until they feel like a shell of a person. So to them they're already gone; suicide is a way of making it official.

If you see any signs that someone you love is depressed, reach out to him or her. Don't just say, "Hey, everything will be fine!" because the person is not hearing you. If there are chemical imbalances in the family, you might acknowledge this and share what you know with the person you're concerned about: "We come by this feeling naturally. It wouldn't hurt to go to the doctor and check this out together."

In some families, big noses are common; in others, green eyes. Some families have chemical imbalances; the condition is usually treatable. All we can do in life is reach out and try to meet people on familiar terms, and if it's not enough, at least you did *something*. All you can do is try. And remember, there is something greater than all of us that has a hand in death. You are not solely responsible for protecting a person from his or her genetics or own decisions. I see people carry a burden that somehow they should have been able to "fix" the person who committed suicide. Unfortunately, love and tears are not always enough to keep a person here. You did your best, and the person loves you for it, remember that.

Compassion for the families who have lost their loved one to suicide is key. I've talked to families who've been cast out of churches, shunned by their friends, and treated with contempt. How do you punish people who had no control over what the victims did to themselves? They'd give anything to have them back, and the person who committed suicide has paid the ultimate price. So when you're presented with an opportunity to be there for someone who's walked this path, be a good person and lend a shoulder.

I had an interesting experience after I wrote this section. I had dinner with a Catholic priest — who's a *medium*. A chance to ask all the questions I've ever had about being a medium who also believes in God. As I sat with him I thought, The idea that a priest could also be a medium goes against everything I've had to fight.

I asked him, "How do you balance your collar with being a medium? How do you balance what you teach with what you know inside to be true?"

He explained to me that there is interpretation in reading the Bible and he finds that his beliefs line up most of the time with what is written in the Bible.

I looked at him and I said, "People who commit suicide don't go to hell." (Did I just say that out loud? Me and my big mouth.)

I sat back and waited for him to show anger toward me. He leaned forward and said, "I know, I see them too. I counsel both the living and the dead."

My head was spinning as I tried to wrap my mind around this one. "So does that mean you're not going to call me the Antichrist?" I laughed.

"Not unless I'd apply that same term to myself," he said.

He and I spent a few moments studying each other, and both of us had a bit of a smirk.

I stared at the chain around his neck that existed only to hold a precious cross. His eyes were cool and contemplative. He almost seemed relieved to have another person like him to talk to. I had so many questions to ask him. This was an opportunity that most mediums never have, to speak to a priest who understands what it is to be a medium. He shared a story from his childhood that included parochial school and a nun who seemed to understand his path. He had questioned her about animals that die and his belief that they were in heaven.

She responded, and I paraphrase, "If we love animals, then God loves them too, so why wouldn't they go to heaven?" The father explained to me that this form of belief is called "theology from below," meaning common sense of the faithful people. I found this all terribly interesting and enlightening. I think that was a good answer from the sister, an honest, gentle response for a child.

We talked about many things that night, and he had questions for me, as I did for him. He wanted to know why sometimes the deceased appear in our head and sometimes they appear in front of us. I responded, "It has nothing to do with the medium. It seems to have everything to do with the deceased. It depends on how much energy the spirit has to come through with. This is usually determined by the life the person lived. If people knew how to connect to others emotionally in life, that carries over in their spirit and allows them to still reach the living easily as they did when alive. If people were isolated or didn't care for others in life, then that too carries over, and they will have a difficult time communicating still. It takes spirits far less energy to appear in our head than before our eyes. People who really had fun, dramatic, loving energy come through with more ease than someone who was confused, had troubled connecting with others emotionally, and didn't communicate well. It doesn't mean that one was bad, it's just an energy issue, and a question of whether they have the ability to express their energy well enough to reach the living.

"Father, you say that you know suicides cross over too. You don't believe that God would punish people with chemical imbalances as though they were in control of their actions, do you?" I'm aware that although this was in the form of a question, it was more of a statement.

He said, "No, I know they go to a good place to be with their family and friends. I see them. Sometimes they seek me out. God knows chemically imbalanced people are people trying to deal with their own pain and they sometimes act in haste."

He went on to tell me that the church no longer takes the stance that those who commit suicide go to hell. The church allows that people who commit suicide are people not in control of themselves, so God wouldn't punish them. I don't know if this information is widely known. People still seem to think that those who commit suicide aren't heaven-bound. It's good to know that they are looked at by the church with understanding.

We talked about the church's feeling about mediums. I asked him, "Weren't we created in God's image?"

"Yes, Allison, we all were."

"Didn't Jesus appear to people after his death?"

"Yes, Allison, and King David appeared to a woman who summoned him after his death. It's in the Bible. This also testifies to the fact that life after death is possible. Not only to exist after your body dies, but for the living to communicate with those who've passed away. Allison, I'm sold on the fact that we're eternal.

"And Allison, the Church acknowledges that mystics truly exist, but the Church worries about evil spirits being able to be brought through by mediums. That's a concern."

"Father, I've never brought through anyone who's hurt anyone after death, have you?"

"No."

"Father, I witness evil more in the living

265

than in those who are on the other side. For instance, when I'm at a murder trial, sitting within feet of evil, I often see the defendant sit there with a smile on his or her face while people testify how they witnessed the defendant carry out a killing. I'm more worried and shaken by them than I am by any spirit."

As our conversation continued, the father and I agreed that all babies are born in the image of God, but as we get older, we can find darkness within ourselves that we either embrace or try to change for the better.

I also wanted to ask him about the term "false prophets." "Father, does the church mean people who *pretend* to predict or *pretend* to commune with the dead?"

"Yes, people who don't actually have these abilities and are pretending to be a mystic not to help people but to harm them."

I'm glad I cleared that up, because it means that the church doesn't view mediums or mystics as bad. It means people who aren't what they claim to be are "false."

I can't begin to tell you how much I enjoyed meeting and breaking bread with such a rare man of the cloth. Then I wondered, Is he really so rare? I bet there are many people of God who can communicate with those who've passed on. I decided that yes, he is rare, because he's willing to understand and own both his priesthood and his mediumship abilities.

As I took in the enormity of this validation, I thought, I will never forget tonight, and it's true that anybody can be cut from the medium cloth. Anybody at all — a mother, a beggar, a child, a priest, *anyone.*

Because it's human and natural to connect with people we love, even after their physical body dies, their spirit remains and is stronger and clearer than ever. I realize I am just trying to learn all I can about life and living. It is comforting to me to know that throughout the Bible there are mentions of spirits appearing before the living and communicating. It's also comforting to know that there were many mediums who came before me, and there will definitely be many who come after me. I already know of three little girls in particular who will follow in my footsteps!

As I left the restaurant, saying good-bye to the father, I turned to my friend who had joined us and told her how blown away I was. In fact, it was she who had introduced us. I thanked her for an experience that I will continue to learn from the rest of my life.

■ ■ ■ ■

Recently I was watching Larry King. He had a rabbi on who had negative energy, a man of the cloth, no less. Anyway, he was on the show arguing against three mediums who were also guests on the show, talking about life and death. Callers had glowing things to say about the mediums, who'd read them, and how they'd had a life-changing, uplifting experience through their readings. The skeptics smirked and ridiculed the callers. One even tried to "cold read" a caller (ask certain ambiguous questions that supposedly let anyone appear to read a person) but failed miserably at it, as the caller pointed out. One of the mediums then read the caller and demonstrated immediate results, and the caller was happy with his reading. So I sat back and observed this angry exchange of energy, and I thought, As far as religion goes, how is it so different when a medium asks to be believed, in that we can see something that may not be visible to all others? When you hold our reality next to that of a man of religion who's asking people to believe in a God that can't be seen? It's not so different. Both claims center around one's belief and personal spiritual experiences. Both are leaps of faith.

I believe in God, I believe I'm being taught many lessons in my life, and I'm paying attention to learn all that I can while I'm here. I'm not minimizing anyone's religion. I'm just drawing an obvious comparison of the two faiths. Often the faiths overlap, as they should, because both focus on something bigger than the living.

Being a compassionate person and embracing people when it's not the easiest thing to do or the most convenient time to do it are tests of character. If this chapter opens one mind and heart, then it has succeeded in changing a life for the better. What we learn in life and teach others is all a part of the domino effect. Differences are good, and keep in mind: as long as nobody's being hurt, to each his own.

And remember, as the father said, "We are eternal."

CHAPTER 8
A LITTLE WISER

While preparing to write my final chapter of this book, I searched my soul for the words that could convey to my readers what I've learned in the year that's followed the debut of *Medium* and my first book, *Don't Kiss Them Good-Bye.*

I shook many hands in 2005, read many letters about loss, and placed myself in too many others' shoes to count. I was almost "blinded by the light" this year, excuse the humor, but I cling to it. Before becoming so public, I had successfully read many people, dismissed many skeptics, and asked the question so many of us ask every day, "Why me?"

Recently my friend Rich asked, "Allison, what do you want to do with your life?"

I hadn't been asked that in a long time, so I pondered the question. I responded, "Rich, I guess I want to help put away some more bad guys."

Rich looked at me with a look of friendship and sadness stirred together. "No, Allison, what do you want to do with your life that makes you happy?"

Wow! I don't think anyone had ever asked me that before. I have spent so much time being consumed by deep topics like murder and death that I didn't know that I was permitted another option. I thought, Well, my girls and Joe make me happy. If I have a lifetime with them, and my kids are healthy and passionate about life, then that sounds like a utopia to me.

I'm sharing this because, until Rich asked me that simple yet poignant question, I hadn't been outside the box that holds who I am inside it — the box of expectations and appearances, responsibility, and becoming set in one's ways. So I'm asking the same question of all my readers, "What are you going to do with your life that makes you happy?"

To answer this question, you must peek in every corner of your soul, look under every solid element of who you are. All it really takes is to do what most people do every day — analyze their past deeds that led them to where they are today. Except instead of beating yourself up for walking the road that led to who you became, look at who you *can* be. Some of you will say you have become who you set out to be, others will have to think long and hard about who that was that you dreamed of being.

When I was small, I wanted to grow up to help put bad guys away and make the world safer for kids. Check, I've done that, not on the scale I wanted to, but I am only one person. One, I've come to realize, is a great number. Even when you acknowledge that as one person you can't end world hunger by yourself or doctor everyone in the world, you still must know that you mattered to someone. Mattering to one person in life still changes the world through a domino effect. I love making others happy, and now I'm going to spend the next year finding out not only how to not apologize for who I am, but how to not let the problems of the world get me down. I'm going to concentrate on shaking more hands and hugging my kids.

On January 3, 2005, *Medium* first aired, and I lost my anonymity and opened myself up to a world of interesting, enlightened people, as well as some people who are constructed of anger and criticism. Patricia Arquette gave me some sound advice, "Don't read what the critics write. It can consume you."

Although, I must admit, I do love looking back at some of the TV critics' write-ups before the debut of *Medium*. Most were encouraging and wonderful, but I remember a couple that were along the lines of, and I paraphrase, "You don't have to be psychic to know this show will not last a season." I laugh when I read that one. These are the same critics who scoffed when I said that Patricia would be nominated for an Emmy Award, so what do they really know? They're people like anyone else, and I've come to realize that. You have to have a sense of humor in life and not become hardened by others. Humor will prolong your life and save you from becoming a callous individual.

When you feel empty inside or consumed by anger and think that you have all the answers to the world's problems, you become hardened. Although I feel very strongly about what I believe, I'm not trying to convert anyone. I share my experiences and hope they strike a chord with the people who feel that this example might be right for them. For those who haven't had my experiences, I try to be understanding. For those who condemn what I do, I try to be tolerant, knowing that I feel sorry for them in many ways. Everyone's born with a certain complex energy that will evolve as they get older, as long as they allow it to. There are those who've been on a soapbox so long they don't even hear whom they're talking at anymore. I say this because I've talked to many people who've had a moving reading that truly touched them, given either by myself or another medium, and they go home to have their spouse, friend, whoever ruin this special experience for them with snide remarks. It's necessary for me to point out to people that you can't let someone else's beliefs overshadow or carry more importance than your own. If someone you care about feels alleviated of a burden thanks to a reading, why would you or anyone want to negate that feeling? What could possibly motivate the spouse or friend who then steps in and deliberately hurts the person they're supposed to love?

When a person does this to you, you really need to look at whether this person is thinking about you or simply reacting from his or her own fear and anxiety. If you're lucky enough to have a great reading, don't let anyone steal your thunder.

When you contemplate what makes you happy in life and what will make your life feel well lived, remember this: thinking about something is only the first step. You must take action. Don't wait for someone to come along and hope the person brings a big bag of happiness. Go get your own.

Last year I was given the opportunity to observe people from around the world. I noticed a common thread connecting all of them. I traveled to Australia and New Zealand for a book tour. It was beautiful, and the people were friendly as well as comfortable with themselves, which was nice to see. I visited Sydney, Melbourne, Auckland, and Christchurch, and each city was special in its own way. Sydney was breathtaking with its Opera House and, let's not forget, Pancakes on the Rocks, which has yummy food. It's definitely a city that must be visited at least once. I will be returning, and I will make sure that this time I get to visit the magical carnival on the pier that at night lights up and looks straight out of a child's dream, junk food and all. Melbourne was memorable, where I met the Sisters in Crime when I was a speaker at their memorable meeting of female crime authors, forensic scientists, and such. Auckland was my first stop. It has a small-town charm, and the people were very kind. Christchurch had great Belgian suds and was picturesque to boot.

When you travel, you will always notice

some local differences, such as the food or the style of clothing. The most valuable part of my trip, though, was that I learned firsthand that people who have lost someone are the same no matter where they live. They feel pain, they need support from others, and each individual will deal with the pain the best he or she can, one way or another. I was met with some very enlightened faces who know their loved ones remain. They need no convincing because in their heart they already know that those who've died live again, just in a different form. They reside in a place of peace and faith. On the flip side, I had a skeptic stand up at a book signing, and I thought that my fans were going to lynch him, but I took care of that on my own with my words and soaked up their kind applause. Again, you have to learn to roll.

While I was writing this book, my husband, Joe, reminded me of a time when we were in our hotel room in New Zealand watching TV. We saw a commercial advertising a blanket. A man being interviewed about the blanket said, "Well, I was skeptical at first . . ."

Joe and I cracked up, because if there are people in the world who are skeptical of a blanket's performance, then truly anything in the world is capable of drawing skeptics. You have to take other people's opinions of what you do with a grain of salt. So the next time you're down on yourself about someone's criticism of *you,* remember that whether it be a man whose fiancée's family is skeptical of his ability to be a good husband, or a sixteen-year-old girl who has people doubting her ability to graduate from high school, *everyone* is open to skepticism in life. Apparently, even inanimate objects aren't safe from criticism! Once you understand that, everyone in the world can work on letting it go and being happy, if for no other reason than because you deserve to be happy.

Don't be a person with a smile on your face and a sob on the inside. Be happy from the inside out. Consider that not every little exchange of energy in life, good or bad, is all up to you. We're all part of a bigger picture, and part of that picture is learning to release the burdens that we collected along the way in life. There will always be people who share my beliefs and others who will criticize both who I am and what I do. Guess what? It's okay. It's all a part of life. People question you so that you question yourself and deeply search your soul to find the answers within you that all add up to and equal you. And I'm not only talking about people who are skeptical about other people. I'm talking about people who are skeptical about religion, science, humanity, whatever. I realize they're necessary, because both action and reaction can show force, and force moves things, or else nothing would change.

So as I travel and meet people, I see why I have to keep being who I am. I have to because I too bring change in the world, as does every person who breathes. When you ignore who you are in order to please others or make them more comfortable, you deny your true energy and keep it from the world, replacing it with the stale ideas of people who are afraid to act and react and to participate in their own dynamic life force. I think that getting to the bottom of who we are can take a lifetime. That is truly the most challenging and rewarding puzzle of all. Skeptics aside, what really matters here is learning to stand tall in life and, when life calls for it, to kneel.

You better believe I pray. I recommend it. Sometimes it's what you need to carry you through an impossible time. Life is a series of choices. The more hands you shake in life, the more people you connect with, the more you learn about others and yourself.

Everyone has something to teach and everyone has something to learn.

I've had an amazing year, never to be forgotten. I'm going to start my list of things to do next year, including taking my girls to SeaWorld for a family vacation. Also, I'm going to take my hubby, Joe, to Maui for some R and R and, although I think I'm already a pretty good friend, I'm going to work on spending more time with my friends. So, what would you add to your own list to make sure you live well, to make sure that life doesn't pass you by? Because it's never too late to make it count.

After a busy yet spectacular year, I've watched my family's life change. Joe has taken up golf and loves it and is jokingly called "Mr. Medium" by his friends. He's retired early to support the girls and me. He wants to be there for us when we need him.

My oldest daughter is every bit like her character on the show. She's the sixth-grade class representative, an honors math student, and the youngest girl on the Junior High Cheer Line, yikes!

My middle daughter, whom I lovingly call my "centered" daughter (Get it? I know, bad joke), is in the third grade. She's also very much the same as the character on

279

Medium. She's my quirky one, and she can be heard in her school choir singing louder than all the other kids. You gotta love her. She marches to the beat of her own drummer.

My youngest daughter, my baby, who was born on the Fourth of July, is in the first grade now. She's taking ice-skating lessons, which she loves, Brownies too! And she still has me wrapped around her little finger. So although their mom has a show based on her life, writes books, and traipses through the desert in hiking boots looking for the missing, my girls still think I'm just another overbearing mom who they know loves them more than anything.

To all of you who've sent me letters asking about my family and sending me cards thanking me for writing my books, I hope I've answered your questions. Thank you for taking the time to write me, to read my books, and to watch *Medium.* Although it has been an incredible year, I hope to spend each year making other people's lives a little easier and becoming a little bit wiser.

ACKNOWLEDGMENTS

I want to acknowledge my editor, Nancy Hancock; my publicist, Ellen Silberman; and the rest of the team at Simon & Schuster for standing behind my books and inviting me into their family. Glenn Caron for his passion in writing. Patricia Arquette for capturing me and sharing my story. And Paramount and NBC for continuing a show that enlightens many. A special thank you to Drew Gomez and John Pagoto at Dilemma.

Last, but certainly not least, I want to thank the people who are mentioned and whose stories are shared in this book. Please know we are all connected and those who've moved on are never gone from you.

ABOUT THE AUTHOR

Allison DuBois's unique story, the inspiration of the hit NBC TV show *Medium,* started during her final semester at an Arizona university, while she was an intern at the district attorney's office. Soon after, researchers at the university documented her ability through a series of tests in which she scored exceptionally high on accuracy and specificity. This validation bolstered Allison's confidence in her decision to become a professional medium and profiler instead of a prosecuting attorney.

In her short career, Allison has conducted over two thousand personal readings. In those readings, she helps to ease the pain people feel from losing a loved one. She had spent four years participating in various tests for the university.

Allison donates her time to missing and murdered persons and criminal cases for agencies across the country. She is contacted by law enforcement agencies and families to help find missing and murdered people. Allison also assists in jury selection for district attorneys' offices. Each of these activities is a means for her to give back to the world for being so blessed.

Allison maintains close ties to the show *Medium* as a consultant.

Allison has been featured on *The Today Show*, *The Big Idea with Donny Deutsch*, and *Last Call with Carson Daly*, and in countless magazines and newspapers.

The employees of Thorndike Press hope you have enjoyed this Large Print book. All our Thorndike and Wheeler Large Print titles are designed for easy reading, and all our books are made to last. Other Thorndike Press Large Print books are available at your library, through selected bookstores, or directly from us.

For information about titles, please call:

(800) 223-1244

or visit our Web site at:

www.gale.com/thorndike
www.gale.com/wheeler

To share your comments, please write:

Publisher
Thorndike Press
295 Kennedy Memorial Drive
Waterville, ME 04901

Street by Street

LONDON

S0-ACZ-454

7th edition April 2010
© AA Media Limited 2010

Original edition printed May 2001

Enabled by Ordnance Survey This product includes map data licensed from Ordnance Survey® with the permission of the Controller of Her Majesty's Stationery Office.
© Crown copyright 2010.
All rights reserved.
Licence number: 100021153.

The copyright in all PAF is owned by Royal Mail Group plc.

RoadPilot® Information on fixed speed camera locations provided by RoadPilot © 2010 RoadPilot® Driving Technology.

Published by AA Publishing (a trading name of AA Media Limited, whose registered office is Fanum House, Basing View, Basingstoke RG21 4EA. Registered number 06112600).

Produced by the Mapping Services Department of The Automobile Association. (A03956)

A CIP Catalogue record for this book is available from the British Library.

Printed by Oriental Press in Dubai.

The contents of this atlas are believed to be correct at the time of the latest revision. However, the publishers cannot be held responsible or liable for any loss or damage occasioned to any person acting or refraining from action as a result of any use or reliance on any material in this atlas, nor for any errors, omissions or changes in such material. This does not affect your statutory rights. The publishers would welcome information to correct any errors or omissions and to keep this atlas up to date. Please write to Mapping Services, The Automobile Association, Fanum House, Basing View, Basingstoke, Hampshire, RG21 4EA.
E-mail: *streetbystreet@theaa.com*

Ref: MN037u

Key to map pages	ii–iii
Key to map symbols	iv–1
Enlarged map pages	2–49
Main map pages	50–163
Index – towns & villages	164–165
Index – streets	168–296
Index – featured places	296–340
Acknowledgements	340

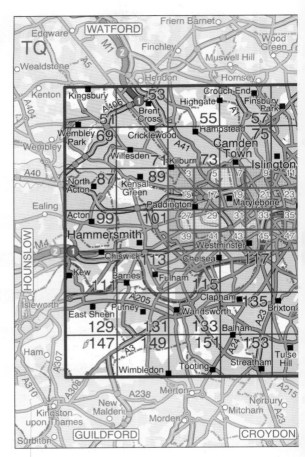

Enlarged scale pages **1:10,000**   6.3 inches to 1 mile

| 0 | | miles | 1/4 |
| 0 | | 1/4 | kilometres | | 1/2 |

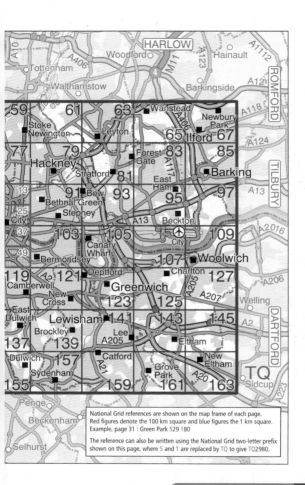

National Grid references are shown on the map frame of each page.
Red figures denote the 100 km square and blue figures the 1 km square.
Example, page 31 : Green Park 529 180

The reference can also be written using the National Grid two-letter prefix
shown on this page, where 5 and 1 are replaced by TQ to give TQ2980.

3.2 inches to 1 mile   **Scale of main map pages 1:20,000**

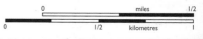

Junction 9	Motorway & junction
Services	Motorway service area
	Primary road single/dual carriageway
Services	Primary road service area
	A road single/dual carriageway
	B road single/dual carriageway
	Other road single/dual
	Minor/private road, access may be restricted
← ←	One-way street
	Pedestrian area
=========	Track or footpath
	Road under construction
	Road tunnel
30 **V**	Speed camera site (fixed location) with speed limit in mph or variable
40 **V**	Section of road with two or more fixed camera sites; speed limit in mph or variable
50→ ←50	Average speed (SPECS™) camera system with speed limit in mph
P **P+**	Parking, Park & Ride
	Bus/coach station
	Railway & main railway station
	Railway & minor railway station

⊖	Underground station
⊖	Docklands Light Railway (DLR) station
⊖	London Overground station
⊖	Light railway & station
+++++++	Preserved private railway
_LC_	Level crossing
•—•—•	Tramway
---------	Ferry route
··········	Airport runway
▬ ▬·▬·▬	County, administrative boundary
	Congestion Charging Zone *
	Charge-free routes through the Charging Zone
	Low Emission Zone (LEZ) (visit **theaa.com** for further information)
93 **7**	Page continuation 1:20,000 Page continuation to enlarged scale 1:10,000
	River/canal, lake, pier
	Aqueduct, lock, weir
	Woodland
	Park
	Cemetery
	Built-up area

* The AA Central London Congestion Charging map is also available

Industrial/business building	Abbey, cathedral or priory
Leisure building	Castle
Retail building	Historic house or building
Other building	Wakehurst Place (NT) National Trust property
City wall	Museum or art gallery
A&E Hospital with 24-hour A&E department	Roman antiquity
PO Post Office	Ancient site, battlefield or monument
Public library	Industrial interest
i Tourist Information Centre	Garden
Petrol station, 24 hour Major suppliers only	Garden Garden Centre Association Member
† Church/chapel	Garden Wyevale Garden Centre
Public toilets	Arboretum
Toilet with disabled facilities	Farm or animal centre
PH Public house AA recommended	Zoological or wildlife collection
Restaurant AA inspected	Bird collection
Madeira Hotel Hotel AA inspected	Nature reserve
Theatre or performing arts centre	Aquarium
Cinema	Visitor or heritage centre
Golf course	Country park
▲ Camping AA inspected	Cave
Caravan site AA inspected	Windmill
Camping & caravan site AA inspected	Distillery, brewery or vineyard
Theme park	

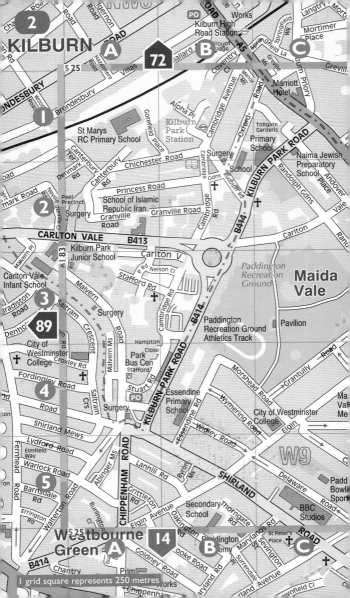

2 KILBURN

St Marys RC Primary School

School of Islamic Republic Iran

Kilburn Park Junior School

Carlton Vale Infant School

City of Westminster College

Essendine Primary School

Paddington Recreation Ground Athletics Track

Paddington Recreation Ground

Maida Vale

Pavilion

City of Westminster College

BBC Studios

Secondary School

Westbourne Green

Naima Jewish Preparatory School

Marriott Hotel

Kilburn Park Station

Kilburn High Road Station

Padd Bowl Sport

St Peter's Place

1 grid square represents 250 metres

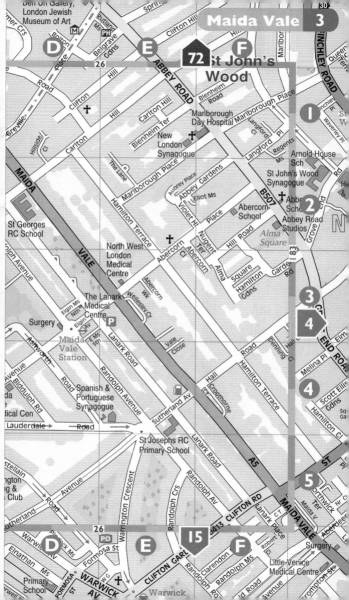

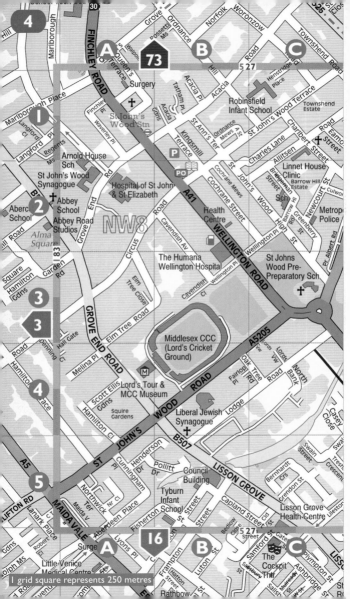

4

30

FINCHLEY ROAD

A Queen's Terrace Grove Possetti Ms Ordnance **B** Norfolk Woronzow Townshend Road 325 Clos

Wapping **73** Acacia Pl Acacia St Ann's Ter 5 27 Hensbridge Place Townshend Estate

Surgery Tatham Pl Acacia Gdns Robinsfield Infant School St John's Wood Terrace Road Eamon

Finchley Pl Waverley Pl St John's Wood Stn St Ann's Ter Ordnance Mews St Charles Lane Charlbert Street Eamont Street

Kingsmill Terrace John's Allitsen Linnet House Clinic

P Cochrane Mews St Wood Street Barrow Hill Estate Newcourt Culwor

Arnold House Sch **PO** St Greenberry Metropo

St John's Wood Synagogue Hospital of St John & St Elizabeth A41 Barrow Hill Sch St Police

Abbey School Grove End Rd Health Centre High Pl Albert Rd

Aberc **2** Abbey Road Studios **NW8** Cavendish Av Wellington Pl St St Johns Wood Pre-Preparatory Sch

School Alma Square Circus Road **WELLINGTON ROAD** Wellington Pl

Square Hamilton Gdns 83 Garden Rd The Humana Wellington Hospital Wellington

3 **3** Elm Tree Close Cavendish Cl

Road Hall Gate Fleming Grove End Road Elm Tree Road

Hamilton Place **4** Melina Pl Middlesex CCC (Lord's Cricket Ground) A5205 Lords Vw Lords Oak Tree Road Fairog Pl North Bank

M Scott Ellis Gdns Lord's Tour & MCC Museum WOOD Casey Close

A5 Squire Gardens Hamilton Cl Lodge Liberal Jewish Synagogue ROAD Swain

ST JOHN'S Henderson Dr B507 **LISSON GROVE** Bernhardt Crs Swa

CLIFTON RD **5** Cunningham Pollitt Dr Council Building Grendon St Tresh Crescen

Northwick Ter Tyburn Infant School Capland Street Lisson Grove Health Centre

MAIDA VALE Aberdeen Place Fisherton Street Bellow 5 27 Samford St St Gate

Lanark Place Maida V. Nr Cl Street Street street liss

Robert St Surge **16** **A** Lyons Pl **B** Luton St Salisbury Samford St **C** Plympton St LISS

Little Venice Medical Centre Frampton Hatton The Cockpit Ashbridge

Gdns Lanark Rathbow Luton St St St Thi

1 grid square represents 250 metres

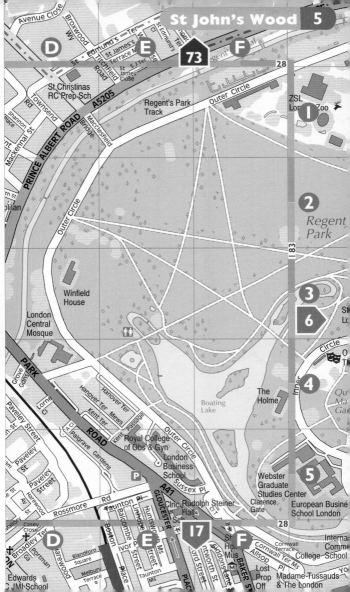

D **E** **F**

Avenue Close
Bronwood Wy
St Edmund's Ter
St James's Terrace Ms
Litchfield Road
St S J Ter
St James's Close

73

Regent's Cal

28

St Christinas RC Prep Sch

Townsend Rd
Shannon Pl
Mackennal St

PRINCE ALBERT ROAD A5205

Macclesfield Bridge

Regent's Park Track

Outer Circle

ZSL London Zoo

1

North St
Metropolitan
politan

Outer Circle

2

Regent Park

I 83

3

6

Si
Lo

Winfield House

London Central Mosque

Circle

PARK

Grove Gdns
Lorne Cl
Paveley Street
Paveley St
Paveley Street

Hanover Ter Mews
Hanover Ter
Kent Ter
Kent Passage

ROAD

Inner

4

The Holme

Qu
Ma
Gar

Boating Lake

Royal College of Obs & Gyn

London Business School

Outer Circle

Palgrave Gardens

Sussex Pl

Rossmore Rd

A41 GLOUCESTER

Taunton Pl
Balcombe St
Linhope St
Huntsworth Ms
Ivor Street
Boston Pl

Clnc Rudolph Steiner Hall

Webster Graduate Studies Center

Clarence Gate

5

European Busine School London

Interna
Comm
College School

D **E** **F**

Casey Close
Broadley Ter
Portman
Harewood
Mallory St
AV St
Harewood St

Edwards C JMI School

Blandford Square
Melbury Terrace
Taunton Ms

17

PLAC

ford Street
ntworth St
Siddons Lane

St
Ho
Mus

Cornwall Terrace
Cornwall Ter Ms
Allsop Pl

BAKER ST

Lost Prop Off

Madame Tussauds & The London

28

M

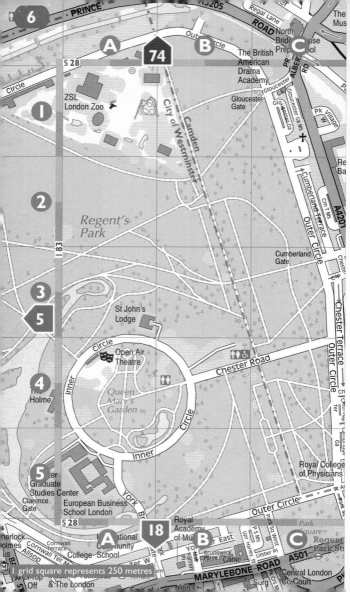

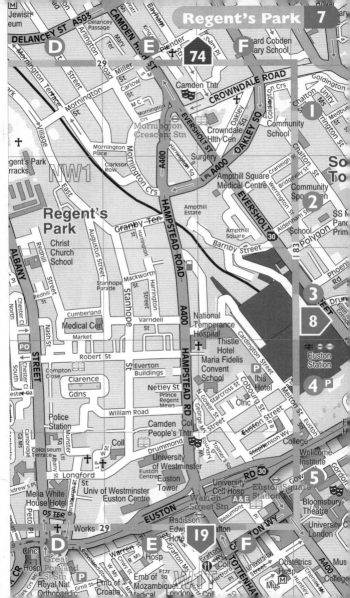

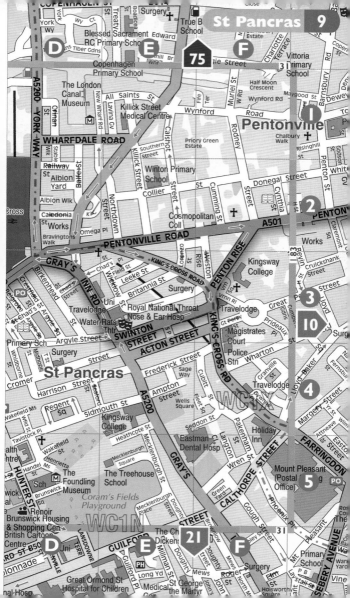

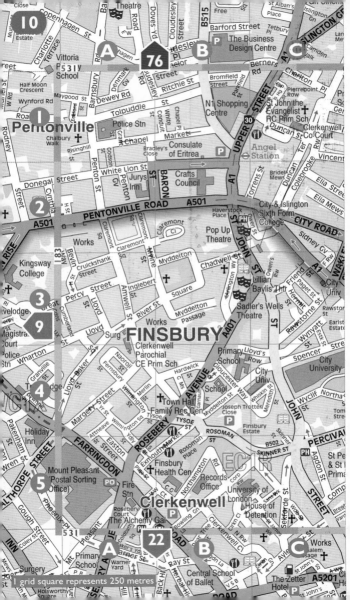

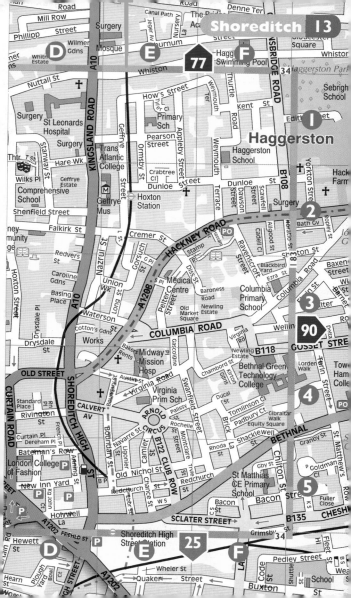

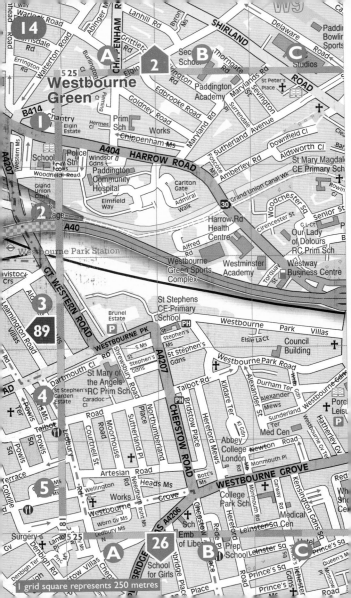

D **E** **F**

26

PO

Sutherland Avenue

Warwick Av

Pindock Ms

Warrington Crescent

Randolph Crs

B413

CLIFTON RD

MAIDA VALE

Elnathan Ms

Einathan Ms

Primary School

Formosa St

WG

WARWICK AV

FORMOSA ST

Bristol Mews

Bristol Gdns

Clifton Villas

Warwick Avenue Station

CLIFTON GARDENS

Clarendon Gdns

Randolph Road

Randolph Ms

Blomfield Road

Avenue

Surgery

Little Venice Medical C

Crompton St

I

PH

Delamere Terrace

Blomfield Road

Chichester Ter

Lapworth Ct

Warwick Pl

Warwick Vis

Little Venice

Maida Park Pl Villas

Howley Place

Paddington Green Primar School

St Mary's

St Mary's Ter

2

Primary School

Chichester Rd

Canal Cafe Theatre

D St

Warwick Ter Rd

Warwick Crs

John Aird Ct

Porteus Rd

St Mary's Hogan

St Mar

Warwick Estate

Fire Station

Gilpin Close

WESTWAY

Sheldon Sq

BISHOP'S BRIDGE ROAD

3

16

Royal Oak Station

Celbridge Ms

Westbourne Terrace

P

Paddington Sta

4

Gloucester Ter

Orsett Ms

Orsett Terrace

BRIDGE

ROAD

A4205

EASTBOURNE TERRACE

Pad

PORCHESTER

Porchester Sq

Porchester Ter

Gloucester Gdns

Westbourne Ms

Cleveland Ter

Eastbourne Ms

Eastbourne Terrace

Porchester Square Mews

P

BISHOP'S

A4206

Cleveland Ter

CLEVELAND TER

Westbourne Terrace

Chilworth Street

Gloucester Terrace

Chilworth Mews

Uni

PICKERING

RD

Queensway

Ms

Emb of Dominican Rep

Halifield Estate

Halifield Clinic

Gloucester Ms West

Cleveland Gdns

Westbourne

Upbrook Ms

Gloucester Terrace

5

CRAVEN ROAD

B410

Com Mews

Westbn Ter

Whiteleys opping Centre

QUEENSWAY

PO

Halifield Infant School

Inverness Ms

Leinster Ter

Porchester Gdns

Cleveland Sq

Queen's Gardens

Devonshire Ms

Craven Ter

Brook Ms

Westbourne Crs

Westbourne Crescent Mews

UCI

Leinster Gdns

Queen's Gardens

27

Craven Hi Gdns

Craven HL

Lancaster

Emb of

Queen's Ms

Salem Rd

26

Porchester Gdns

Queensborough

Bayswater

C HI Gdns

CRAVEN HL GDNS

M London Rd

D **E** **F**

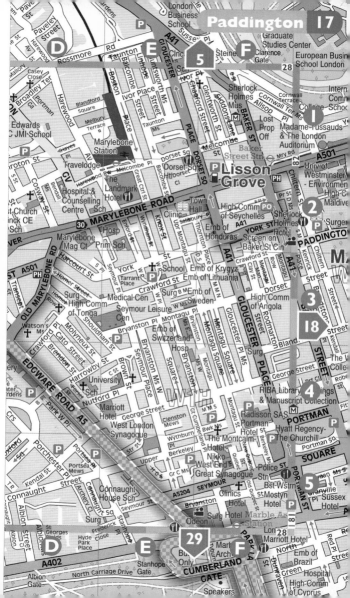

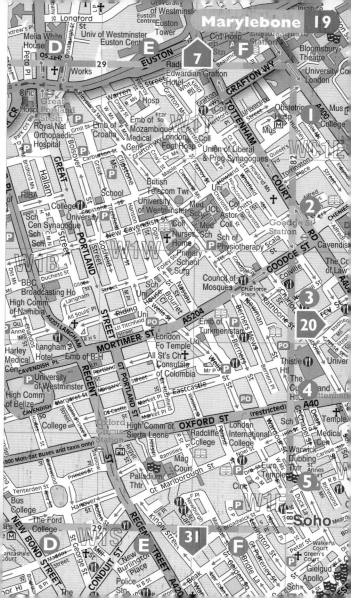

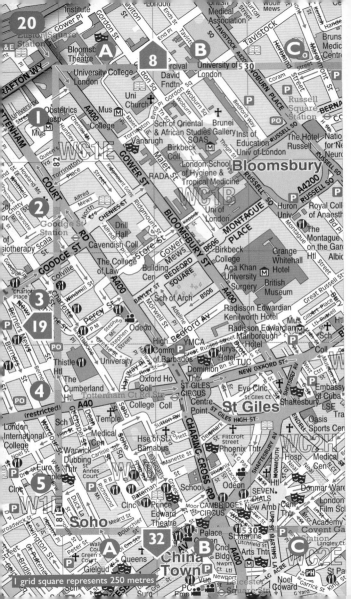

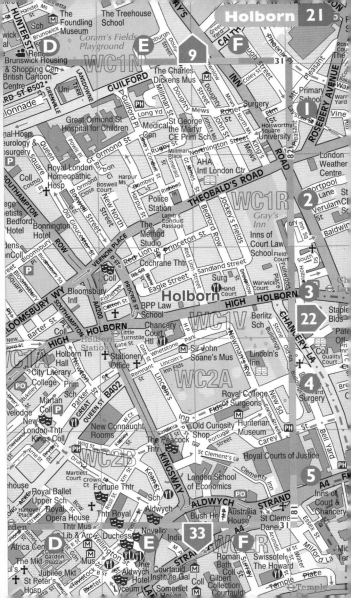

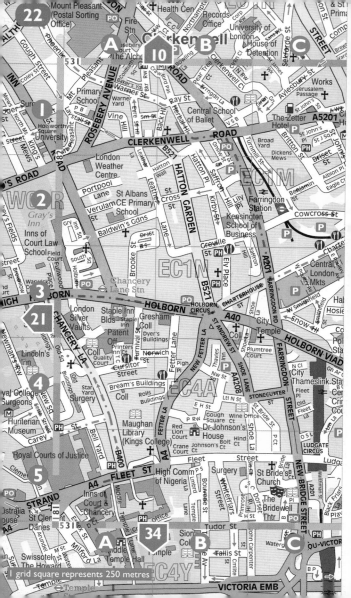

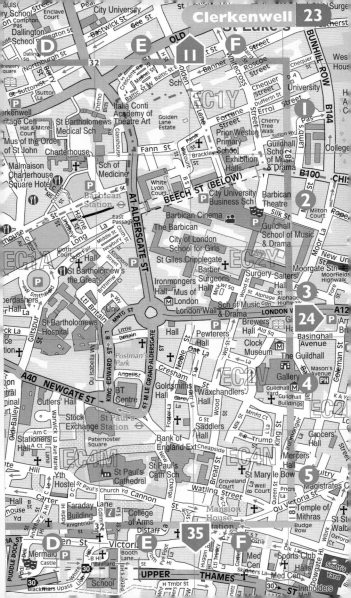

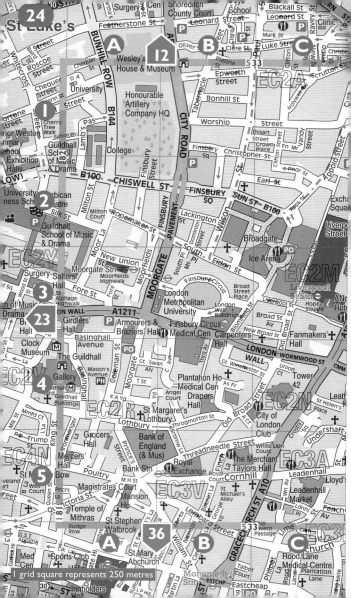

24 St Luke's

Surgery Cen
Featherstone St

Shoreditch
County Court
Leonard Street

Blackall St
Leonard St

School

A
Wesley's
House & Museum
12

B
Clere St
Platina St

C
Mark St
St Luke St
Clifton St
Clinic

Roscoe Street

Chequer Street

University

Epworth Street
EC2A
Scrutton St

Honourable
Artillery
Company HQ

Bonhill St

Worship Street

Dysart Street
Crown Place

Guildhall School
of Music
& Drama

B100

CHISWELL ST

Finsbury Street

FINSBURY
SQ

Christopher St
Clifton Street

Earl St

Exchange
Square

University
ness Sch

2
P

Barbican
Theatre
Milton Court

Guildhall
School of Music
& Drama

Ropemaker St

FINSBURY
PAVEMENT

Lackington St

South St
Eldon St

SUN ST-B100

Wilson

Broadgate

Ice Arena

PO

EC2M
Liverpool
Street

Liverpool
Street

EC2V

Surgery
Salters'
Hall

3
St Alphage
Highwalk

Moorgate Stn
Moorfields
Highwalk
Fore St

New Union

Moorgate

London
Metropolitan
University

Finsbury Circus

Broad
Street
Place

Broad St
Av

Liverpool St

Hope
Square

And
Hotel

of Music
Drama

23
ON WALL

A1211

Girdlers'
Hall

Armourers &
Braziers' Hall

London
Wall
Buildings

Finsbury Circus
Medical Cen

Broad St
Av

New Broad St

Carpenters
Hall

Broad St

LONDON

Fanmakers'
Hall

EC2N

Clock
Museum

Basinghall
Avenue

PO

Gt Swan
Aly

Gt Winchester St

Union
Ct

WORMWOOD ST

Tower
42

The Guildhall

Mason's
Avenue
PH

Coleman St

Moorgate

Plantation Ho
Medical Cen

Old Broad Street

St Helen's
Place

4
Gallery
Guildhall
Buildings

EC2R

St Margaret's
Lothbury

Angel Court
Drapers'
Hall

City of
London
Club

EC2N

EC4N

Mercers'
Hall
Bow

Grocers'
Hall
Prince's Street

Lothbury

Throgmorton St

Threadneedle Street

White Lion
Court

Crosby

Undershaft

5
Well
Court

Magistrates'
Court

Bank
of
England
(& Mus)

Bank Stn

Royal
Exchange

Cornhill

The Merchant
Taylors' Hall

Leadenhall

EC3A

Lloyd's

Poultry

Victoria
Temple
of
Mithras

Mansion
Ho

St Stephen
Walbrook

M H St

Lombard Street

Royal
Court

EC3V

St
Michael's
Alley

Leadenhall
Market

Fenc

A

St Mary
Abchurch

36

B

GRACECHURCH ST A10

Lime St

Rood Lane
Medical Centre

C
hurch

Med
Cen

Sports Club

William St

Monument
Sm

ESTCHP
Eastcheap

Talbot
Court

Plantation
Lane

I grid square represents 250 metres

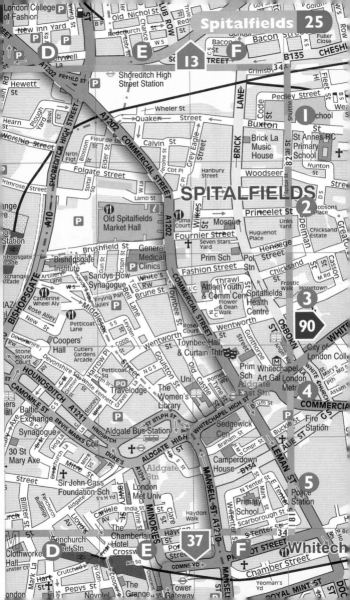

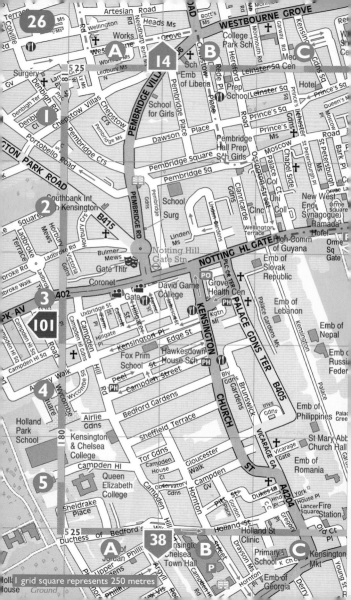

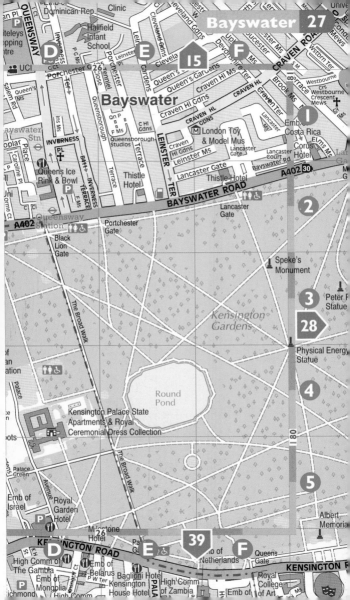

Queensway
Whiteleys
Shopping
Centre

UCI

Queen's Rd

Salem Rd

Bayswater
Stn

Poplar
Place

Caroline Pl

Orme Ct

Uni

Inverness Pl

Queensway

D

Porchester Gdns

Porchester Ter

PG Ms

Inverness

Hallfield
Infant
School

Dominican Rep.

Clinic

Leinster Gdns

Cleveland Gdns

Cleveland Sq

Porchester Gdns

E

Leinster
Gardens

Queensborough
Studios

Queensborough Terrace

QnP

C HI Gdns

FM's

Clevela

Queen's Gardens

Bayswater

Craven HI Gdns

CRAVEN
GDNS

Craven
HI Gdns

Leinster Ms

Craven HI Ms

LEINSTER TER

Leinster Ms

Lancaster Gate

Queen's Gardens

15

Devonshire Ter

Upbrook Ms

Gloucester Ter

CRAVEN HL

CRAVEN HL

F

Lancaster
Gate

M London Toy
& Model Mus

Craven Ter

CravenTer

Lancaster Ms

CRAVEN ROAD

Brook Ms

Westbourne Cr

Westbourne
Crescent
Mews

Westbourne Ter

Embo
Costa Rica

Corus
Hotel

La

I

Inverness
Terrace

INVERNESS

PL

Queens Ice
Rink & Bowl

INVERNESS TERRACE

Thistle
Hotel

Elms

Thistle Hotel

BAYSWATER ROAD

A402 **30**

Lancaster
Court

Bayswater Rd

Lancaster
Gate

M
G

A402

Queensway
Station

Porchester
Gate

Black
Lion
Gate

2

The Broad Walk

Speke's
Monument

*Kensington
Gardens*

3

Peter P
Statue

28

Physical Energy
Statue

4

Round
Pond

I 80

Kensington Palace State
Apartments & Royal
Ceremonial Dress Collection

The Broad Walk

5

Palace
Green

Emb of
Israel

Palace
Avenue

Royal
Garden
Hotel

Milestone
Hotel

Pal
G

E

Emb of
Netherlands

39

Albert
Memoria

Queens
Gate

F

KENSINGTON ROAD

D

KENSINGTON R

High Comm of
The Gambia

Emb of
Mongolia

Emb of
Belarus

P W Ter

Baglioni Hotel

Kensington
House Hotel

High Comm
of Zambia

KENSINGTON PALA

Royal
College
of Art

Emb of

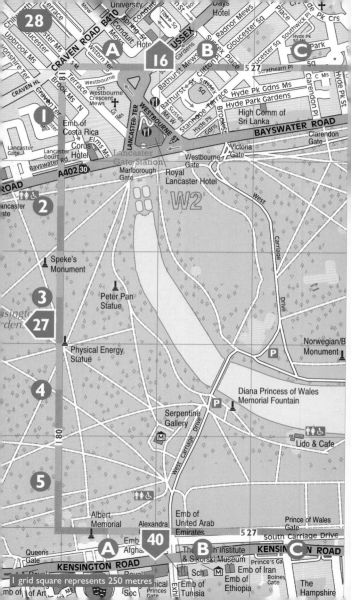

28

A **B** **C**

University
Conduit
Mew
B410 Conduit St
Spring St
Tibde St
Days Hotel
Radnor Mews
Gloucester Sq
Southwick Pl
Hyde Pk
Scho

CRAVEN ROAD
Westbn Ter
16
USSEX
Gardens
Bathurst Mews
St
Clifton Pl
Sussex Pl
Gloucester Sq
527
Strathearn Pl
Hyde Pk St
Sq
C

CRAVEN HL
Craven Ter
Chil
Gloucester Ms
onshire Ter
M
Westbourne
Terrace
Westbourne
Crescent
Mews
Clifton Pl
Bathurst St
Sussex
Sq
Stanhope Terrace
Hyde Pk
Gdns
Hyde Pk Gdns Ms
Hyde Park Gardens
Clarendon Pl
c Ms
Clarendon Pl

Upbrook Ms

1
Emb of
Costa Rica
Corus
Hotel
Elms Ms
WESTBOURNE ST
LANCASTER TER
Brook St
High Comm of
Sri Lanka
BAYSWATER ROAD
Clarendon
Gate

Lancaster
Gate
Lancaster
Court
Hotel
Bayswater Rd
A402 **30**
Marlborough
Gate
Lancaster
Gate Station
Westbourne
Gate
Victoria
Gate
Royal
Lancaster Hotel

ROAD

Lancaster
Gate
2

West
Carriage

W2

Speke's
Monument
3
Peter Pan
Statue

nsington
rden
27

Physical Energy
Statue
4
Drive

Norwegian/B
Monument

180

P
Diana Princess of Wales
Memorial Fountain

Serpentine
Gallery
P
West Carriage Drive
M
Lido & Cafe

5

Albert
Memorial
Alexandra
40
The
Emb of
United Arab
Emirates
Prince of Wales
Gate
527
South Carriage Drive

A
Emb of
Afgha
B
h Institute
& Sikorski Museum
KENSING
Prince's Ga
N ROAD
C

Queens
Gate
KENSINGTON ROAD
Sch
M
Emb of
Tunisia
Emb of Iran
Bolney
Gate
The
Hampshire

mb of f Art
hical
Princes
Gate
Soc
Emb of
Ethiopia
Exhi
Royal

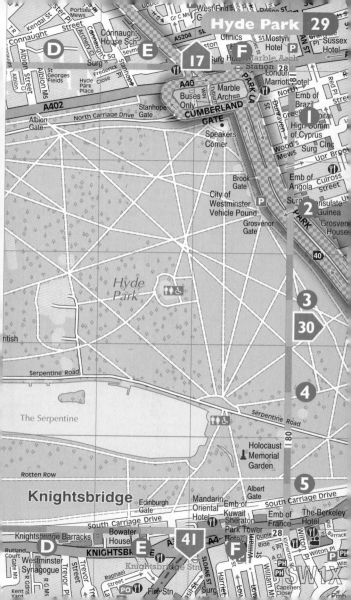

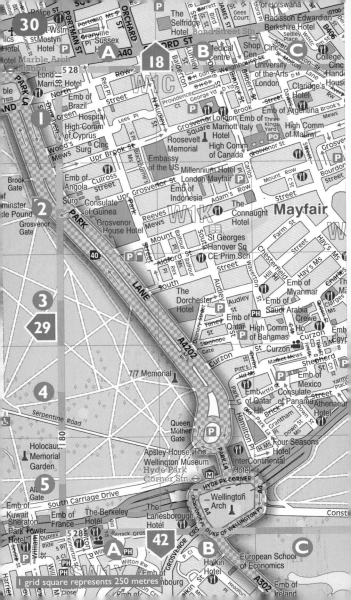
I grid square represents 250 metres

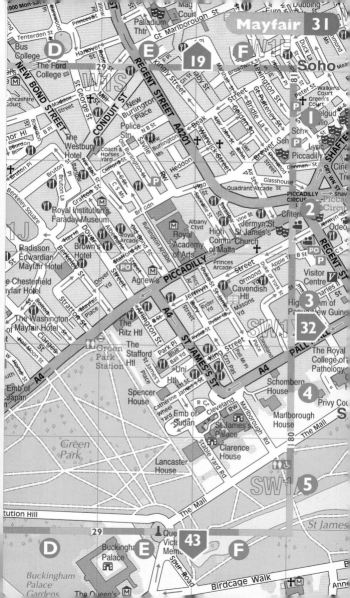

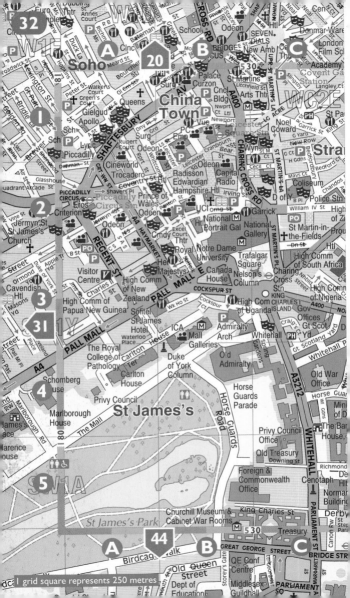

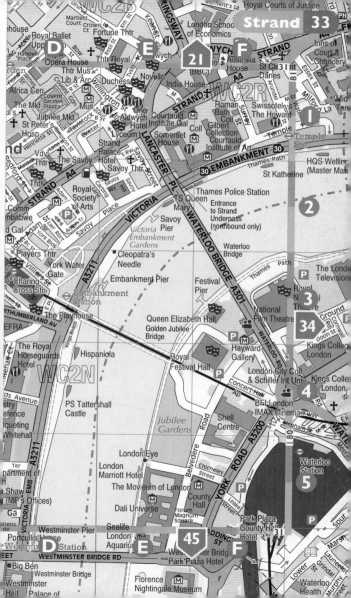

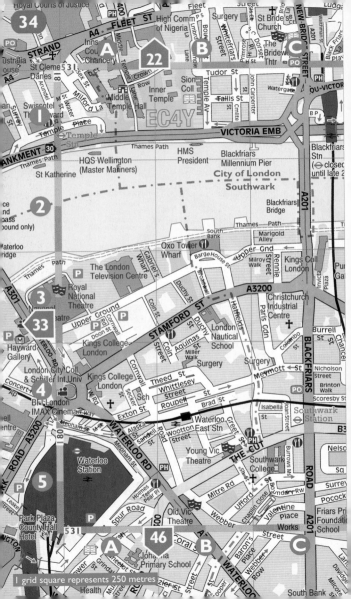

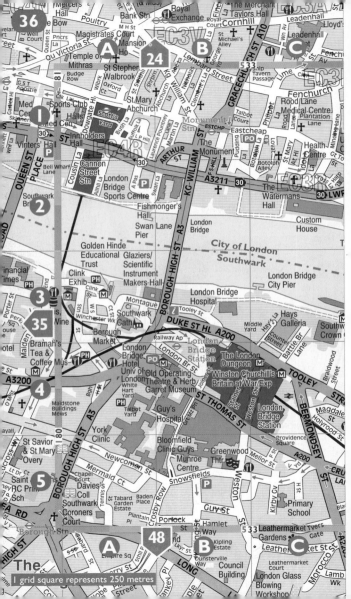

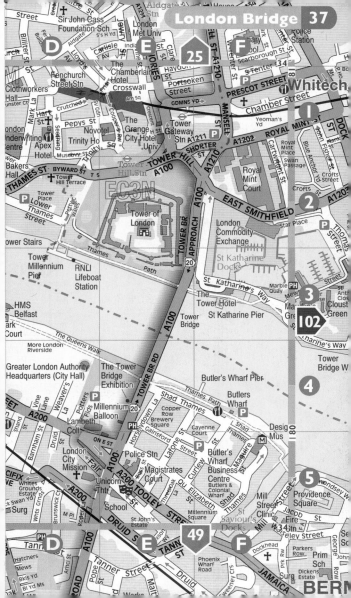

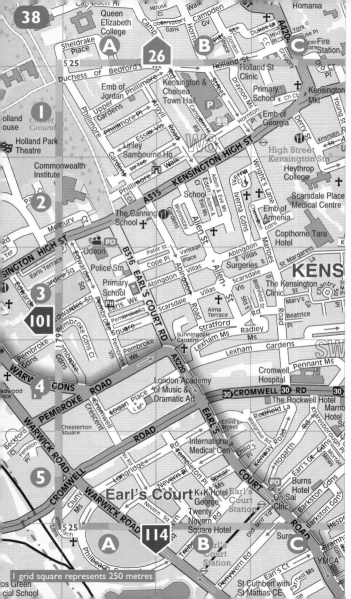

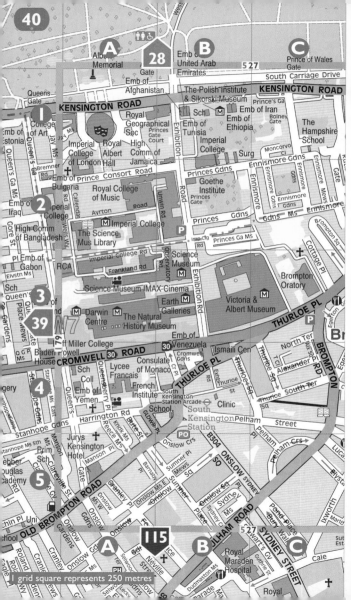

40

A · B · C

28

Albert Memorial
Gate
Emb of United Arab Emirates
5 27
Prince of Wales Gate

South Carriage Drive

KENSINGTON ROAD

Queens Gate

I **KENSINGTON ROAD**

The Polish Institute & Sikorski Museum
Prince's Ga
Emb of Iran
Bolney Gate

College of Art
Emb of Estonia

Royal Geographical Soc
Princes Gate Court
High Comm of Jamaica

Sch
Emb of Tunisia
Emb of Ethiopia
Imperial College
Surg

Moncorvo Cl
The Hampshire School

Jay Ms
Queen's Ga Ms
Bremner Rd

Imperial College of London
Royal Albert Hall

Ennismore Gdns

Ennismore Mews

Gate

Prince Consort Road

Emb of Bulgaria
Royal College of Music
Goethe Institute
Princes Gate

Ennismore Gdns
Ennismore Gdns Ms

2
Imperial College
Emb of Iraq

Callendar Rd
Ayrton Road
Unwin Rd

Princes Gdns

Princes Gdns Ms

Brompton

High Comm of Bangladesh
Emb of Gabon
Elvstn Ms

Wells Wy

M Imperial College
The Science Mus Library

P
inn Clg Rd
princes Ga Ms

Pl
RCA

Imperial College Rd
Observatory
Frankland Rd

Science Museum

M

Cottage Pl

Sch
Queen's
Place Mews
Gardens

3

39
W7

Science Museum IMAX Cinema
M Darwin Centre
The Natural History Museum
Earth Galleries
M
Exhibition Rd

Victoria & Albert Museum
M

Brompton Oratory

THURLOE PL

P
Egerton

Br

f Miller College
Baden Powell House

Rd 179
Emb of Venezuela
30
Ismaili Cen

North Ter
Thurloe
Sq
Thurloe Sq

THURLOE PL

BROMPTON RD

CROMWELL 30 **ROAD**
Cromwell Gdns
Cr Pl

Alexander Sq
South Ter

Eg

4
Sch
Coll
Lycee Francais
Queensberry Pl
Queensberry Pl
Consulate of Monaco
CP
Exhth
Thurloe
St
Thurloe Sq

South Ter

gery
Emb of Yemen
French Institute
School
Harrington Rd
Knick Ms
Reece Ms
Bute St
South Kensington Station Arcade
South Kensington Station
Clinic
Pelham Street

Luca

Stanhope Gdns
Stanhope
Gdns East
De Vere Gdns
Gloucester
PO
Onslow Crs
Pelham Crs

Elvstn

gery
Stanhope Ms sth
Prim Sch
Jurys Kensington Hotel
Manson Pl
Sumner Pl
Sumner Pl Mews
Onslow Sq
SQ
ONSLOW
SYDNEY

5
ebber
uglas ademy
Clareville Gr
Clareville St
Gloucester Rd
Onslow Gardens
Onslow Ms W
Onslow Ms E
Barnaby Pl
Onslow Pl
Onslow Sq
Onslow Sq
Sydney Ms
Sydney Pl

Pond Place
Petyward

Pelham Cr

xworth

OLD BROMPTON ROAD
Cranley Gardens
Onslow Gardens
Onslow Gardens
Sydney St

FULHAM ROAD
5 27
SYDNEY STREET

hln Pl Uni
chool
Roland Gdns
Cranley
Selwood Ter
Neville St
Ice
Neville Tce
PH
Royal Marsden Hospital

Swan's Cv
Guthrie St
Cale
Sut Est

A · **I 15** · B · C

Royal

Matt's Cv

`I grid square represents 250 metres`

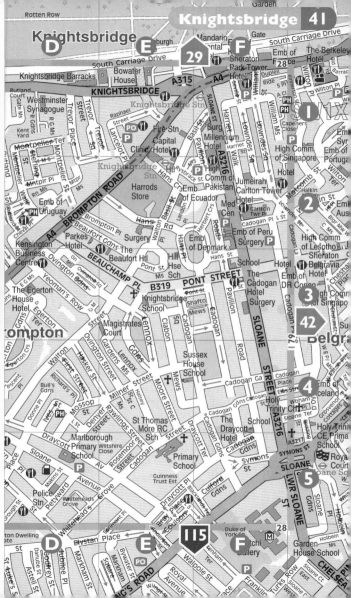

42

Garden

Hyde Park
Corner Stn

Wellington Museum

HYDE PK CORNER

Wellington
Arch

C

Consti

Gate

South Carriage Drive

A

30

ough

B

Emb of
Kuwait

Sheraton
Park Tower
Hotel

Emb of
France

The-B
Hotel

Grosvenor
Ms

DUKE OF WELLINGTON PL

GROSVENOR PL

European School
of Economics

Duplex
Ride

Barrack

Wilton Pl

PH

PH

PH

SW1X

Wilton Pl

Emb of
Luxembourg

GROSVENOR CRS

The
Halkin
Hotel

Headfort

Wilton Crs

Chapel St

Emb of
Ireland

A302

GROSVENOR PLACE

I

Capeners
Close

Emb of
Syria

High Comm
of Malaysia

Emb of
Turkey

Chester Cl Chester

Harriet
Walk

High Comm
of Singapore

Emb of
Portugal

BELGRAVE SQ

Halkin

Wilton

Halkin St

High Comm
of Trinidad &
Tobago

Groom
Place

Chester Street

Chester
St

Dorset

Lowndes Sq

Emb of
Côte d'Ivoire

Wilton
St

Chester
Street
Mews

Lowndes Sq

Jumeirah
Carlton Tower
Hotel

Hotel

Halkin
Arcade

W Halkin St

High Comm
of Brunei

Emb of
Austria

Emb of
Norway

Belgrave Ms
South

St Peter's
Church

London
Tourist
Board

HOBART PL

2

Cadogan Pl

Surgery

High Comm
of Lesotho

Sheraton
Belgravia

Emb of
Finland

Emb of
Germany

Emb of
Spain

BELGRAVE PL

Eaton Place

Eccleston
Mews

Eaton Rw

Belgrave

Mews N

EATON SQUARE

Grosvenor
Gdns Mews
North

Emb of Peru

Hotel

Chesham
Place

Emb of
Hungary

Emb of
Bolivia

St Peters St

Eaton Square
CE Prim Sch

School

The
Cadogan
Hotel

Emb of
DR Congo

Emb of
Belgium

Lyall
Mews

Eaton Ms N

Ebury Ms N

Prep
School

PO

Eccleston

3

High Comm
of Singapore

Cadogan Place

Lyall

Eaton

SQUARE

Eaton MS S

Surgery

Eccleston
Place

4 I

Surgery

Belgravia

A3217

EATON SQUARE

ECCLESTON ST

Eaton MS N

Eaton
Square
Sch

Boscobel

Chester

Chester Sq

Ebury Mews E

Surg

Ebury Mews

The
Colonn
Shoppi
Centre

4

Emb of
Iceland

Wpham

Surgery

Eaton Ter

Eaton
West

Elizabeth
St

Gerald
Rd

Ebury

Surgery
Victoria
Coach Sta
(arrivals)

A3216

Holy
Trinity CH'H

Grosvenor
Cottages

Eaton

Minera Ms

Burton Ms

Street

Eccleston Place

Victoria
Coach Station

BUCK

Holy Trinity
CE Primary
School

Eaton
Cl

Caroline
Terrace

Chester Terrace

A3214

Symons
St

Royal
Court

Bourne

Francis Holland
School

Graham

Ebury

Cundy

Semley Place

Police
Station

5

SLOANE
SQ

Sloane Sq
Stn

Whitaker

Ebury
Sq

Elizab

Saatchi
Gallery

LWR SLOANE
ST

Garden
House School

A

PIMLICO R

116

PIMLICO RD

Council
Building

Blim Ter

B

St Barnabas
CE Prim Sch

Surgery

A3214

Barnabas
St

ROAD

C

Abbo
Mano

Bridge

Abb
Man
Est

I grid square represents 250 metres

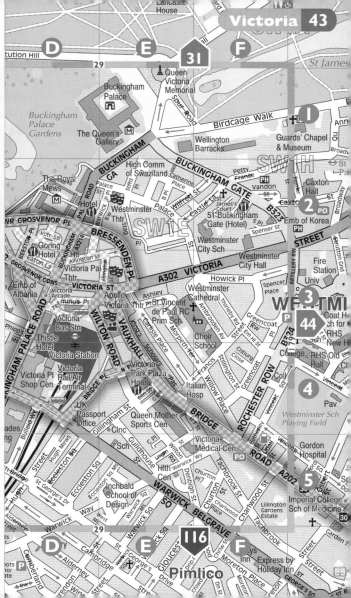

44 SW1A

Richmond De

Foreign & Commonwealth Office

Bowling St

Cenotaph

Norman Building

Derby

A St James's P

32 urchill um & binet War Rooms

B King Charles St

C PARLIAMENT ST

Treasury

Canon Ra

Birdcage Walk

GREAT GEORGE STREET

I dcage W

Anne's Ga

Old Queen Street

Storey's Gate

QE Conf Centre

PARLIAMENT SQ

BRIDGE STR

Guards' Chapel & Museum

Dept of Education

Middlesex Guildhall

St Margaret's

Westminster Abbey

Old Palace Yard

Broadway

Tothill St

Central Hall

Little Cloisters

ABINGDON STREET

SW1H

St James's Park Stn

Deans Yard

Jewel Tower

Petty France

Caxton Hall

Dacre St

Department of Trade & Industry

Choir School

Westminster Church School

College

Vic Ga

GATE Vandon St PH

New Scotland Yard

Abbey Orch

Little Dean's yard

A3212

Caxton St

Gt College St

Cowley

Emb of Korea PO

St Ann's St

Barton

Tuffon

Lord

St John's Concert Hall

Spenser st PH

Old Pye St

Peter

Surg

St

Dn stanley St

ck Pl

Westminster City Hall

Fire Station

Matthew St

Great

Chadwick St

Lord Chancellors Department

Home Office

Tufton Street

Smith Sq

Dn Stanley St

Transport House

Spencer St

Univ

3 P

WESTMINSTER

43 P

Grey Coat Hospital Sch for Girls

Medway St

Magistrates Court

Romney Street

Bradley

B323

Coburg Close

Greencoat

RHS New Hall

Surg

A St

HORSEFERRY ROAD

MARSHAM STREET

Royal Coll of Veterinary Surgeons

Thames House

RHS Old Hall

Col Clinic

Coroners Court

Dept for Transport

Page Street

Dean Ryle

Thorney St

4

College

Vincent

SW1P

P

Millbank Tower

ROCHESTER ROW

Westminster Sch Playing Field

High

Fynes St

Vincent St

Marsham St

John Islip St

Clore Gallery

A202

Gordon Hospital

Regency St

Millbank Estate

Montaigne Cl

Erasmus St

Herrick St

Tate Britain

30

PO

5

Imperial College Sch of Medicine

30

Douglas St

The Greycoat Hosp

Fairley House Sch

Millbank Primary School

Cureton St

JOHN ISLIP STREET B326

ATTERBURY ST

M

Lillington Gardens Estate

Charlwood

30

Gaterden St

A Days Inn Express by Holiday Inn

117

VAUXHALL BR ROAD

GATE

B JOHN ISLIP ST

Ponsonby Pl

C Chelsea Coll of Art & Design

MILLBANK

Pimlico

Westminster

M

RD BESSBOROUGH

I grid square represents 250 metres

Waterloo

Ter
partment of
Shaw
(MP's Offi
Ga

London
Marriott Hotel
The Moviem of London
Dali U

County

33

Park Plaza
County Hall
Hotel

P

D

E

F

hens
de
Portcullis House
Westminster Station

Westminster Pier

Sealife
London
Aquarium

Westminster Bridge
Park Plaza Hotel

WESTMINSTER BR

A23

Waterloo
Health
Centre

I

BAY

EET

WESTMINSTER BRIDGE RD

Big Ben
Westminster
Hall

Westminster Bridge

Westminster
Palace of
Westminster
Houses of
Parliament

PO

Florence
Nightingale Museum

M

A&E

ADDINGTON
ST

Upper Marsh

WESTMINSTER BR R

Marsh

Grindal

Murphy

St

St Thomas'
Hospital

Royal Street

Lane

Carlisle

Newnham

Carmuir St

Virgil St

Rd

McAuley Cl

2

ME

St
Str

oria Tower
rdens

City of Westminster
Lambeth

United Medical
& Dental
Schools

Hercules

Cosser Street

Morton
Place

Days
Hotel

A3036

Thames Path

LAMBETH PALACE ROAD

Archbishop's
Park

Sidford
Place

LAMBETH

3

Thames Path

Lambeth
Palace

M

46

Sun

Museum of
Garden History

A3203

Part
Walk

Sail Street

Lambeth

Walnut Tree Wa

Beedha

Mews

Hornbeam

Walnut
Tree Walk
Primary Sch

4

Lambeth Bridge

A3203

Juxon st

Street

Fitzal

Saunders

Street

Distin

St

Novotel

Old Paradise St

Norfolk Row

Ingram

Saperton
Walk

Lollard

bank
ennium

Lambeth Bridge

Fire
Brigade
HQ

Lambeth High Street

Whitgift Street

Works

Riverbank
Park Plaza
Hotel

P

Salamanca
Street

Black

Dragon Road

Gibson
Road

Lollard Street

Marylee

Beaufoy
Walk

Way

Ethe
Esta

Lollard

5

SE11

ALBERT EMBANKMENT

Newport Street

Lilac Pl

Prince

St

Lillian Baylis
School

Road

St Thoma
Day Hospital

Childrens

Hotsur

Orsett St

D

E

117

F

Tinworth
Street

Graphite
square

Randall Road

Citadel

Randall RW

Walk

Vauxhall

Nathan

Tyers

Wickham

Morgan St

PO

Glass

St

Works

I grid square represents 250 metres

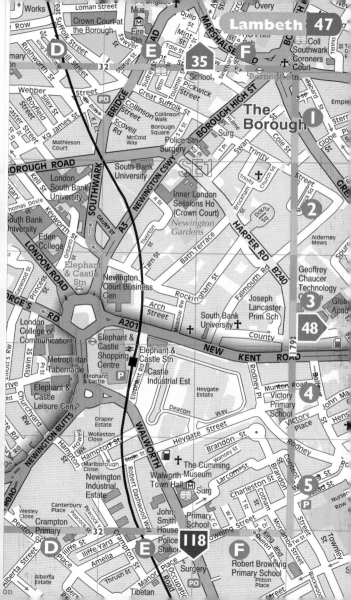

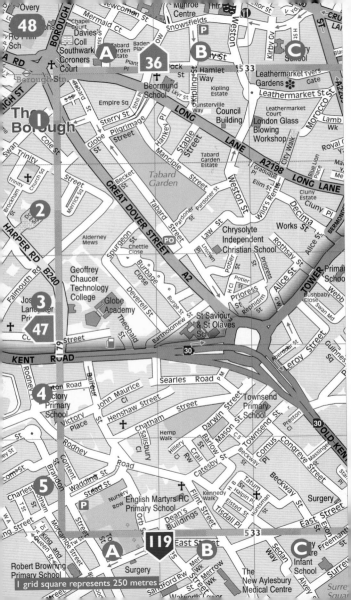

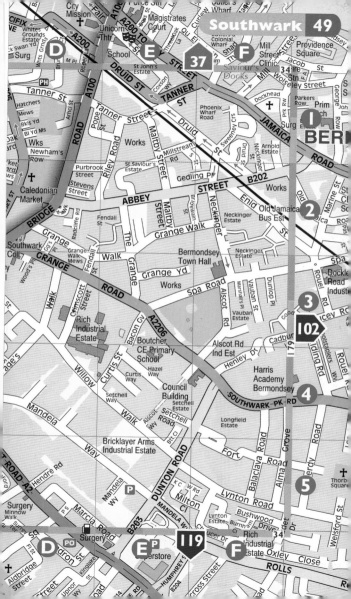

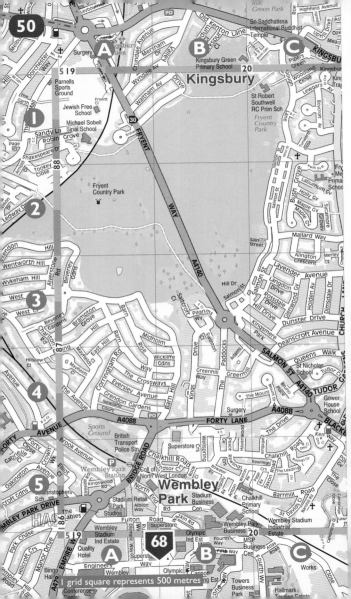

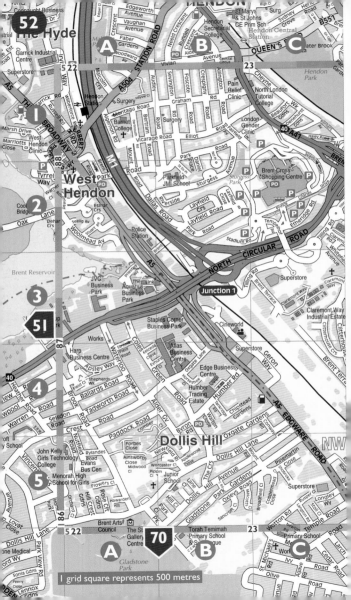

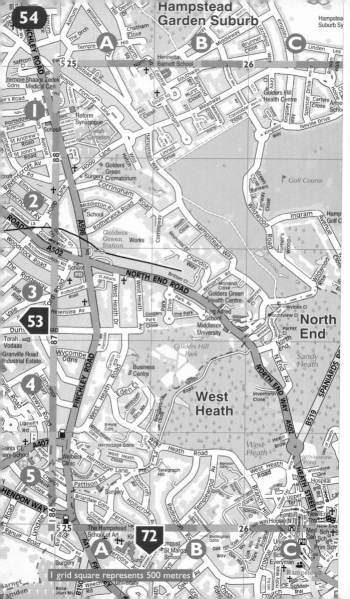

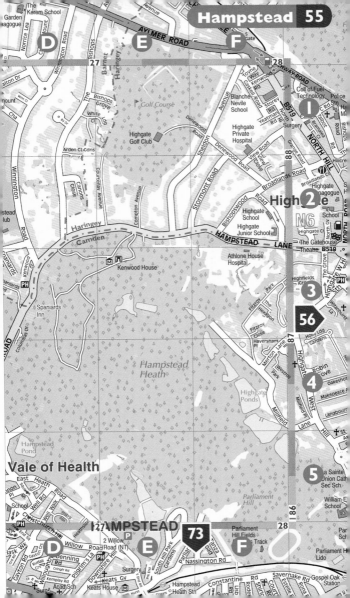

The Kerem School

Garden Synagogue

AVENUE

AYLMER ROAD

D   **E**   **F**

27   Barnet   Haringey   28

HIGHWAY ROAD

Coll of Fuel Technology   Police Stn

I

Norrice Lea

Wilmington Road

Bishops Avenue

The Bishops Grove

White Ldg

Arden Ct Gdns

Canons Close

Courtenay Avenue

Compton Avenue

Golf Course

Highgate Golf Club

Denewood Road

Shelton Road

Denewood Road

Towne Oxenden Kenwood Rd   Blanche Nevile School   storey   Yeatman

View Close   Surgery

Highgate Private Hospital

Broadlands Road

B519

NORTH HILL

Clinton Rd   C Rd

Clifton

Hillcre

7

Broadlands Rd

2 High e

Synagogue

School

N6

Winnington Road

Haringey

Camden

Kenwood

Spaniards Rd

PH

Columbus Dr

Spaniards Inn

Kenwood House

Bishopswood Road

Stormont Road

HAMPSTEAD LANE

Highgate School

Highgate Junior School

High

Highgate Cl

North Hill

NORTH HILL

School

Highgate Rd   The Gatehouse Theatre

B519

The Grove

Athlone House Hospital

Highfields Gro   **3**

Fitzroy Park   The Hexagon

Fitzroy Close   Haversham Pl

56   87

Merton Lane   Westhill   Park

Highgate

How Lodge Gardens

Robin Grove

Oakeshot

4

Makepeace Av

West

Millfield Lane

Langbourn

Hampstead Heath

Highgate Ponds

Millfield Ln

Hill

St

Av

Vale of Health

Hampstead Pond

East Heath Road   Well Rd

PH

Christchurch

5   a Sainte Union Cath Sec Sch

William E School

Parliament Hill

Pa

Parliament H Lido

I 86

D   Willow Road   **P**   **E**   **73**   Parza   **F**   Parliament Hill Fields   Track   27   28   Gospel Oak Station

Savernake Road

Carlton Rd   Denning Rd   Pilgrim's Rd

Rudall   Cithgft Rd

Kemplay Rd   Downshire

2 Willow Road (NT)   PH   Surgery   South Hill Park Gardens   Parlat   Nassington Rd

Keats Gv

Keats House   Hampstead Heath Stn   Constantine

Gospel Oak

Mask Rd   Acad Sch   Hunt   Constantine   Rd   Rode   Str   Court   Estelle   Savernake Rd

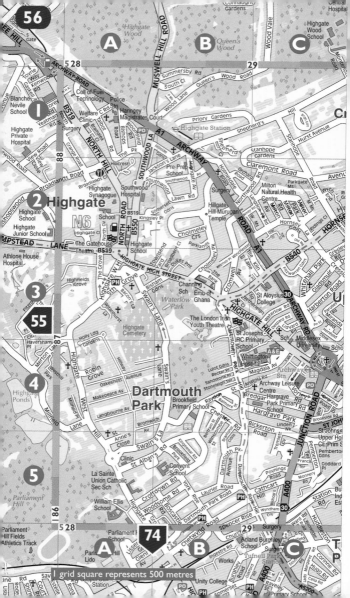

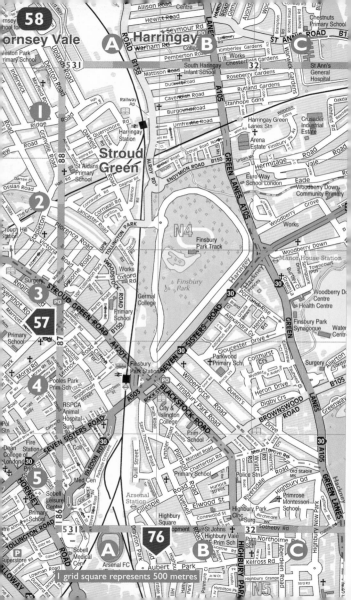

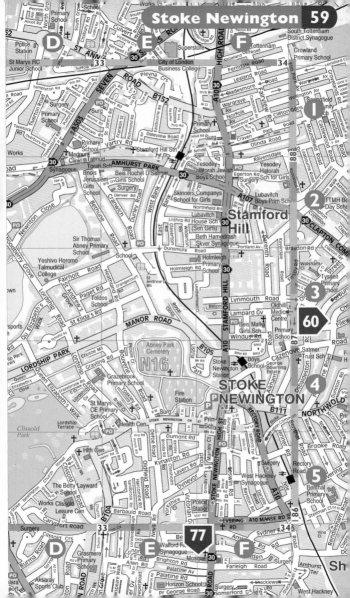

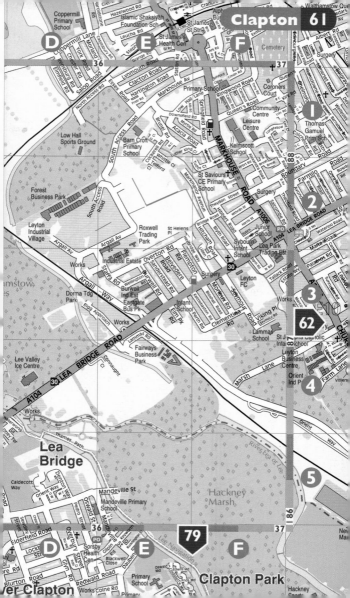

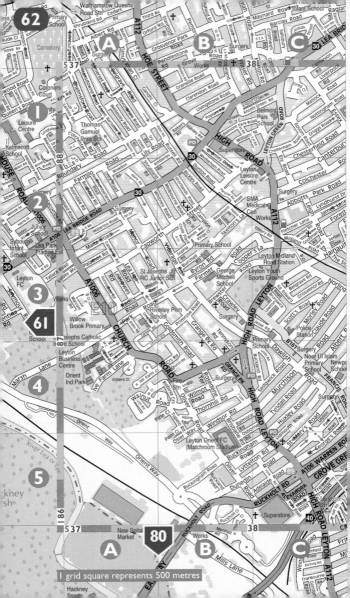

I grid square represents 500 metres

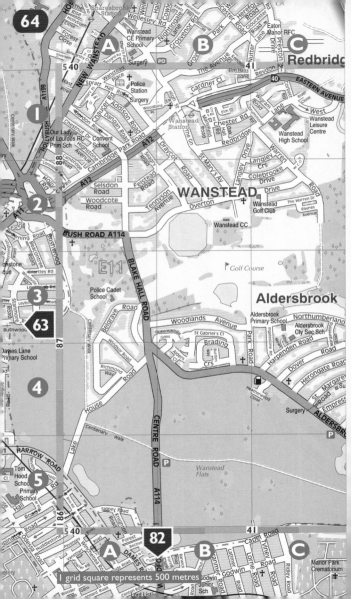

64

A **B** **C**

Sharesbrook Station
Wellesley Rd
Cowie
Wanstead CE Primary School
Grosvenor Rd
Northumberland Rd
Eaton Manor RFC
Preston Drive

Redbridge

Hollybush Rise
Hollybush Close
Forest Close

NEW WANSTEAD

HOLLY

5 40

A1199

A1199

Surgery
PO

The Avenue

41

Elm Hall Gdns
Reydon

40

EASTERN AVENUE

spratt Hall

Police Station
Surgery

Addison Road
Dangan Road
Convent School

Gardner Cl

Chester Rd

River Close

West Wanstead Leisure Centre

Woodbine

Wigram Road

I

Centenary Walk

HOLLYBUSH

HOLLY Rd

Our Lady of Lourdes RC Prim Sch

Chestnut Dr
Cambridge Avenue

Hainstone Rd

Cambridgevale Rd

Lorraine Rd

A12

Wanstead Station

Redbridge
Oak
Elm Cl

Wanstead High School

Gordon Rd

Cambridge
A12

Selsdon Road

Woodcote Road

Draycot Road
Feilstead Road

Tennyson Avenue

St Mary's Av

Langley Drive
Colebrooke Drive

Warren Rd

WANSTEAD

Overton

Wanstead Golf Club

The Warren Dr
Raynes Avenue

2

A11

Browning Road
Beacontree Ave

Bushwood

BUSH ROAD A114

E11

Wanstead CC

3

63

Stanmore Rd
Lister
Bushwood

Leyton Rd

Police Cadet School

Belgrave Road

Waldorf Road

BLAKE HALL ROAD

Woodlands Avenue

Queenswood Gdns

St Gabriel's Cl

Brading Crs

Aldersbrook Primary School

Park Road

Northumberland

Aldersbrook Cty Sec Sch

Ingatestone Rd
Dover Rd

Harpenden Road

Herongate Rd

Aldersbrook

Golf Course

Davies Lane
Primary School

4

87

Lake House

Centenary Walk

Richmond Way

Aldersbrook Rd
Burnett Way

Heatherwood Close

St Margaret
Su
Empress

Surgery

ALDERSBR

P

HARROW ROAD

Tom Hood School

Primary School

Hall

CENTRE ROAD A114

P

Wanstead Flats

P

5

86

Sidney Road

Forest

5 40

82

A

DAVIES Rd

Winchelsea Road

Godwin Junior Sch

B

Banner Road
Latimer Rd
Lorne Rd

41

Cadet Road

Tylney Rd

C

Manor Park Crematorium

Ridley Road

I grid square represents 500 metres

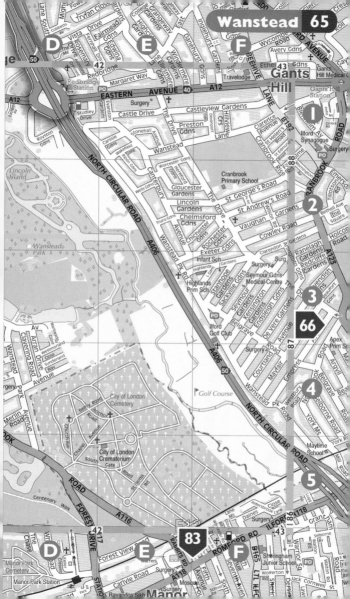

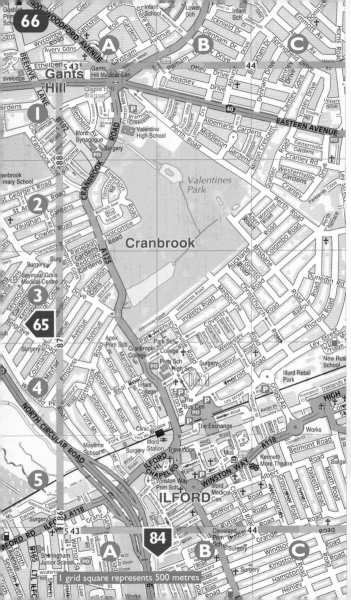

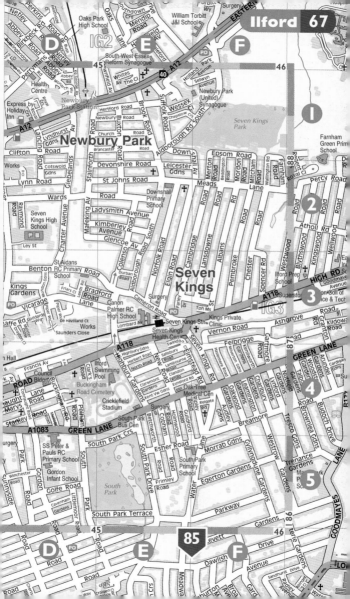

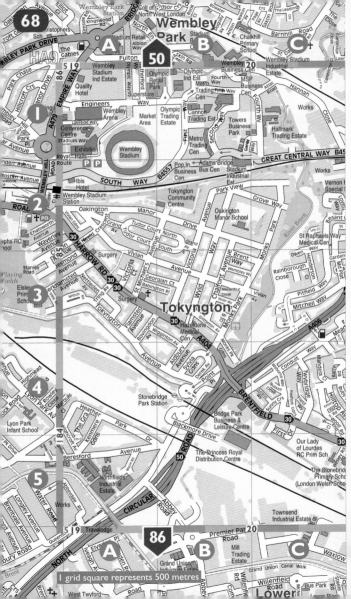

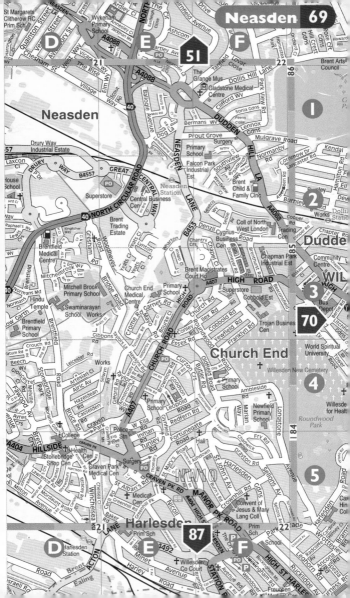

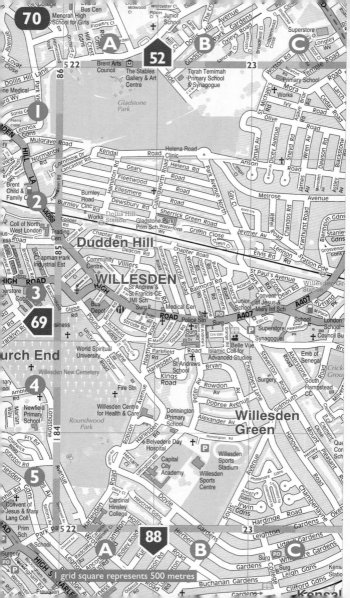

I grid square represents 500 metres

I grid square represents 500 metres

1 grid square represents 500 metres

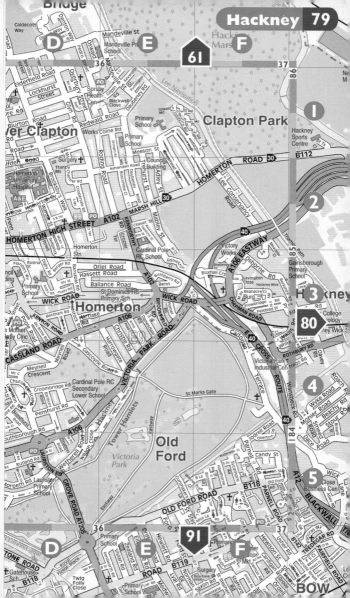

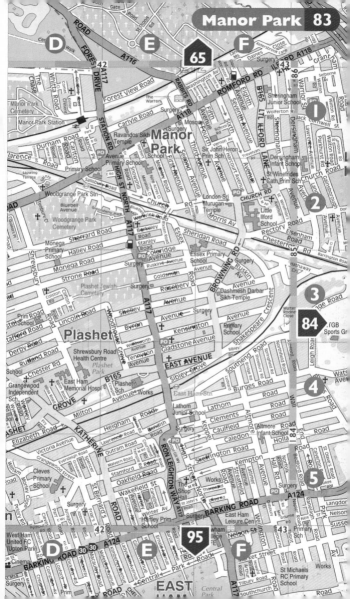

D E F

65

Manor Park

Plashet

95

D E F

EAST

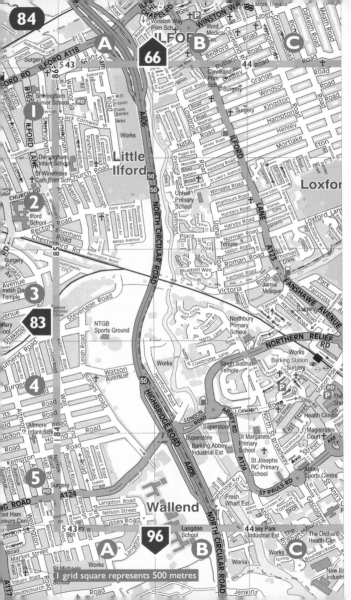

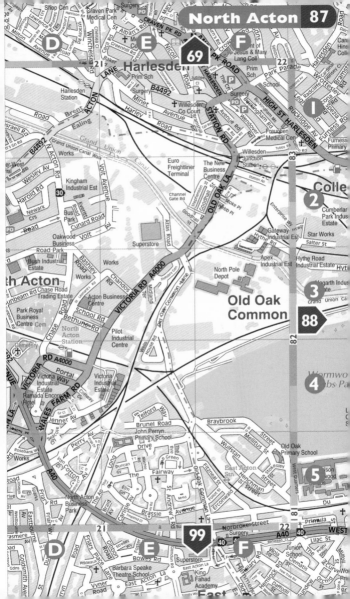

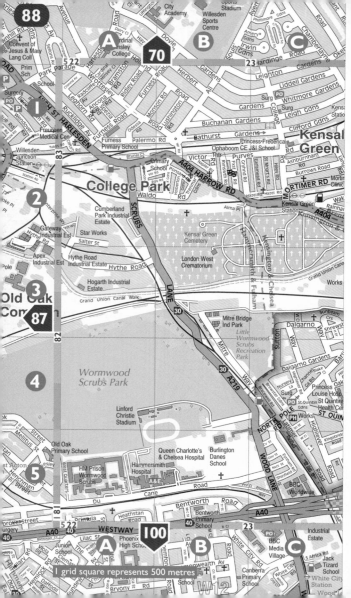

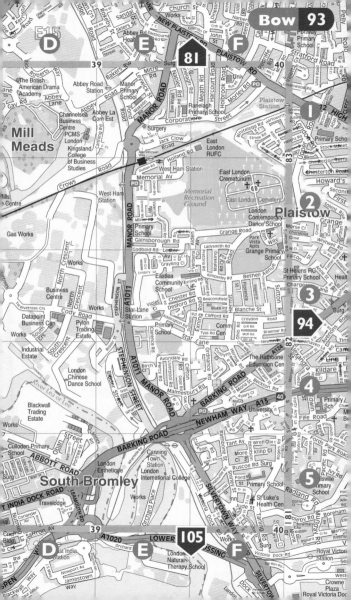

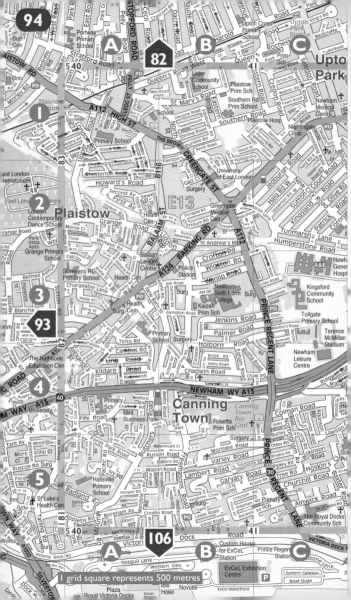

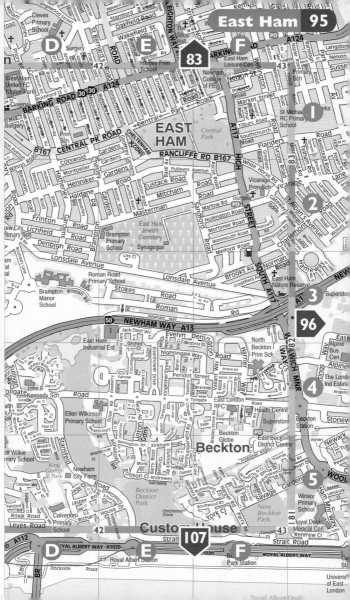

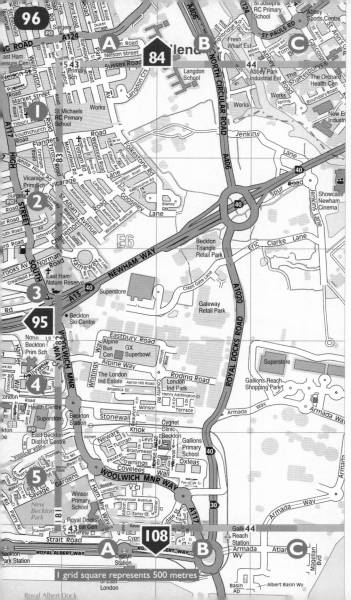

I grid square represents 500 metres

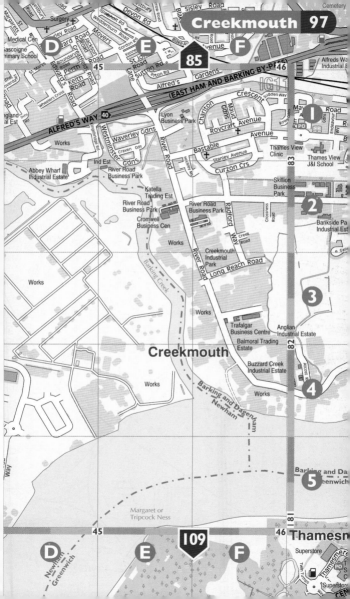

Cemetery

Surgery
Medical Cen
Gascoigne
Primary School
St Mary's

Sisley Road
Devon Rd
Spashott Rd
Wedderburn Road
Jackson
Sutton Road
St Jac
Ripon Rd

D 45 **E** Cordon Rd **F**

Alfred's Way
Industrial E

85

Alfred's
Gardens
EAST HAM AND BARKING BY-PASS
IG11 46

Charlton
Crescent
Sudden way
Lyon Business Park
Maud Gdns
Roycraft Avenue
Mayo Road
PO

I

ALFRED'S WAY 40
Westminster
Waverley Gdns
Craven Gdns
River Road
Bastable
Avenue
Thames View Clinic
Thames View J&I School

Works
Ind Est
River Road
Business Park
Stanley Avenue
Curzon Crs

Abbey Wharf
Industrial Estate
Katella
Trading Est
River Road
Business Park
Cromwell
Business Cen
River Road
Business Park
Radford
Way
Creek Road
Crossness Road
Skillion
Business
Park

2

Bankside Pa
Industrial Est

Works
Works
Creekmouth
Industrial
Park
Long Reach Road

3

Works
River Road
Barking Creek

Works
Trafalgar
Business Centre
Balmoral Trading
Estate
Anglian
Industrial Estate

Creekmouth
Buzzard Creek
Industrial Estate
Works
Alcott R

4

Works
Barking and Dagenham
Newham

Barking and Da
Greenwich

5

Margaret or
Tripcock Ness

D 45 **E** **109** **F** 46 **Thamesn**

Superstore

Newham
Greenwich

Superstore
PO
Superstore

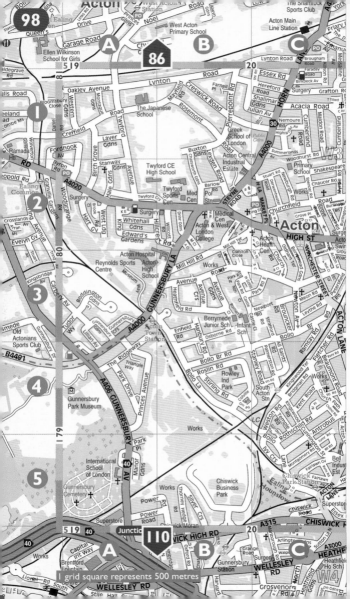

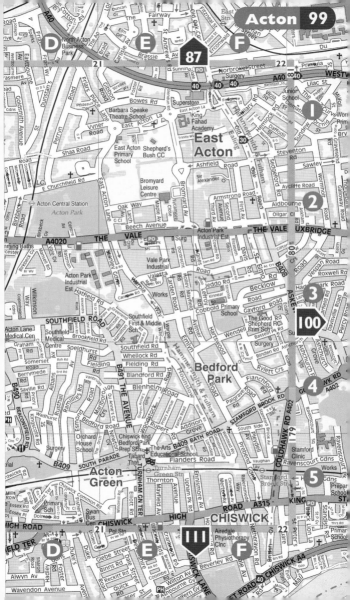

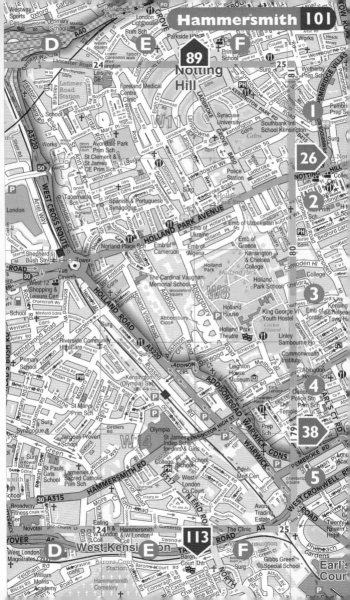

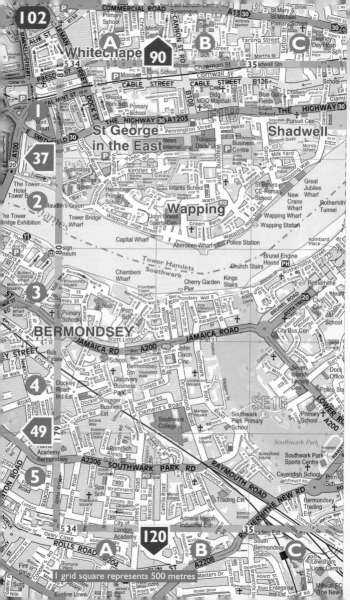

grid square represents 500 metres

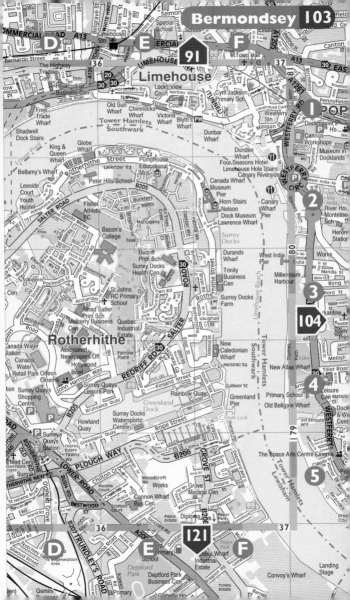

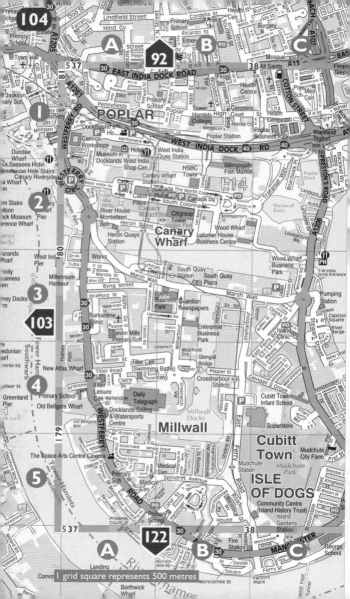

grid square represents 500 metres

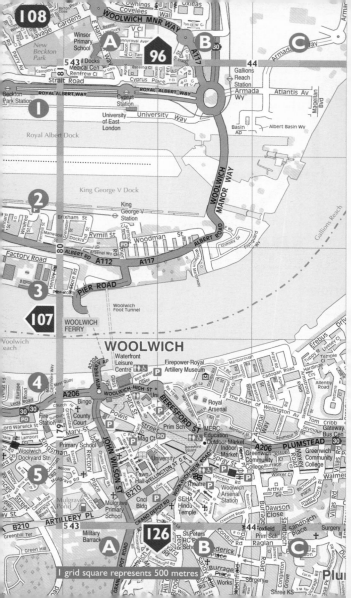

I grid square represents 500 metres

D   E   **97**   F

45   46

Margaret or
Tripcock Ness

Newham
Greenwich

Tripcock Point
Development Site

Thamesm

Superstore

Thamesmere

I

Superstore

CEN

A2041

Woolwi
Polyte

2

SI

Waterside
Drive

Barnham

Newmarsh Rd
haven

Newmarsh Rd

Reference Murray

Miles Dr

Warrior Bailey Cl

Hill View Drive

Discovery
Prim Sch

Hill Vw La

Marathon

Sunset
Road

Birchmere
Bus

3

A2041

Martin Rd

Denise Rd

Merbury

Top Cl

Levett Cl

New Acres Rd

Battery Rd

Battery Rd

Kentlea Rd

Battery Rd

Maretmore Vw

Birchmere Rd

Silver

Pitfield Cr

Courtauds

Lakes Av

WESTERN WAY

Harness Rd

Nathan Way

Wholnt Dr

Warspoint Dr

Ridge
Close

Nuthatch
Gardens

Nuthatch
Gdns

Harrier Mews

Avocet Ms

WESTERN WAY A2016

Goldtrip

Griffin Manor Way

Tugboat Rd

Magistrates Court

Woolwich
Crown Court

HM Prison
Belmarsh

Boughton

Nathan Way

Hadden Road

Works

North Rd

Nathan Way

Kellner Road

Works

West Thamesmead
Business Park

White

Avenue

Hart

Works

Broadreach
College

4

Manor Way

St Thomas a' Becke
RC Primary Sch

Mottisfont
Ro

ombwe

Camel Ct

Whinchat
Road

Heronsgate
Primary
School

Harrier Mews

Camel Ct

Whinchat
Road

Crescent

Pier Way

Surg

Garside

PETTMAN

A206

CRESCENT

Road

Works

ROAD

Plumstead
Station

Terrace

thorne
Gv

Reidhaven

Barth
Ms

Marmadon

Road

Braconda

Birkdale Road

Church

5

ithdale

Road

PLUMSTEAD

White Hart Road

Garland

Aber

Brookdene

Benares

Road

Road

Manton

Woodhurst

Amrose St

Myra St

HIGH STREET

Primary
School

Police

Ceres

Myrtledene Rd

Bendmore

London
Robert St

St Patricks
RC Primary
School

Conway
Primary
School

Conway
Medical C

Council
Building

A206

D   E   **127**   F

45   46

Waterside
Prim Sch

prim Sch

Elmer

Earl

Conway Rd

Colwell Rd

Orissa Rd

Miriam Rd

Mt Pleasant

Leisure
Cen

Granite St

Primary
School

Surgery

Gatling

Rockmount

Leonhorn Rd

Lei Zang

Congo Rd

Majendie

Ancona Rd

Brewery Road

Philimore
Close

Wetland Rd

Saunders
Road

stead

Plumstea

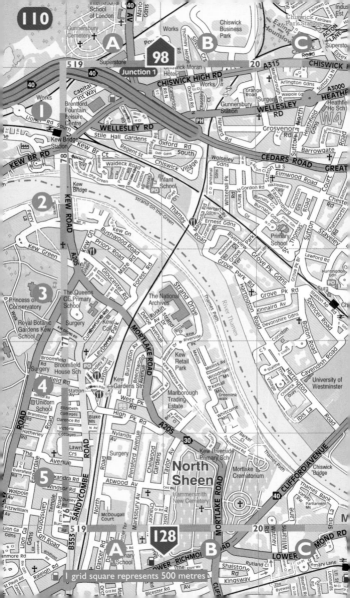

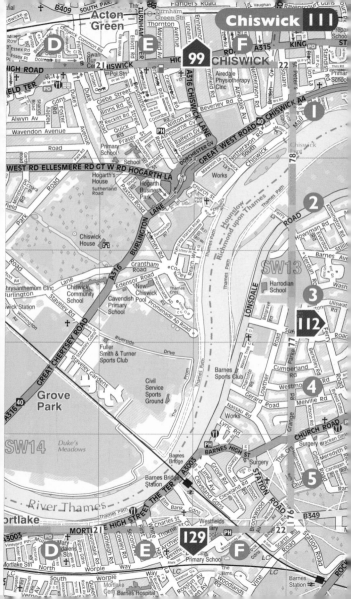

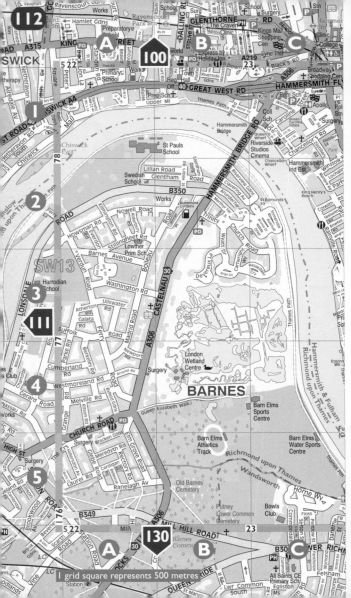

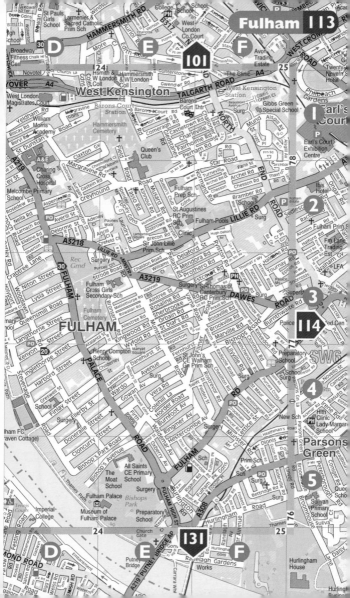

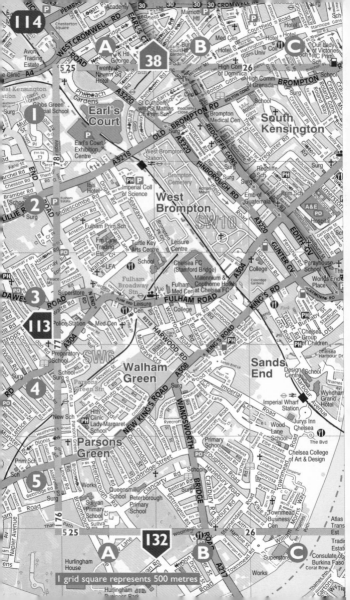

A 42 B C

VAUXHALL BRIDGE ROAD

WARWICK WAY 29 BELGRAVE RD

Pimlico

1

CHELSEA

SW1W

2

EMBANKMENT

River Thames

GROSVENOR ROAD

Chelsea Bridge

Grosvenor Bridge

Battersea Power Station (disused)

Tideway Industrial Est

NINE E

SW

Cringle

Sleaford Industrial Estate

3

BAT 115 SEA

Southside Industrial

St Georges CE Prim Sch

BATTERSEA PARK ROAD

4

BATTERSEA PARK ROAD

Abbey Business Centre

Michael Manley Industrial Est

CLAPHAM

5

Queenstown Road Battersea Station

ROAD

30

A 134 B WANDSWORTH NORTH C

I grid square represents 500 metres

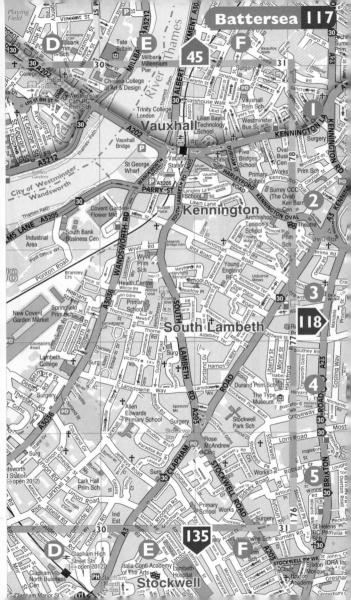

1 grid square represents 500 metres

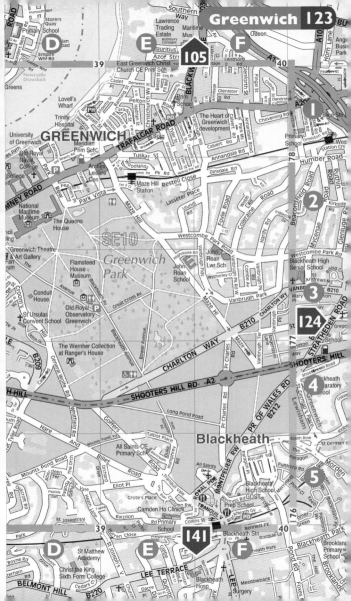

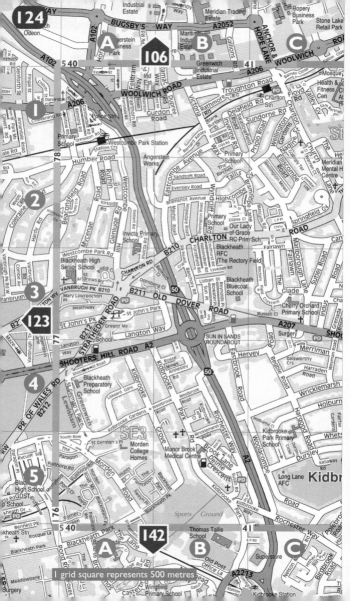

124

Industrial Estate

BUGSBY'S WAY

Willoughby

Meridian Trading Estate

A2052

Ropery Business Park

Stone Lake Retail Park

Odeon

A Angerstein Business Park

Maritime Industrial Estate

B

ANCHOR & HOPE LANE

C

106

Greenwich Industrial Estate

WOOLWICH

A206

ROAD

Mosque

Health & Fitness Cen

WOOLWICH ROAD

Troughton Road

Charlton Stn

PO

Floyd Rd

Barney Close

1 Chevening Rd

A206

Police Stn

Rathmore Rd

Charlton

Delafield Rd

Wellington Gardens

Nadir

Church

Meridian Mental Health Centre

Primary School

Westcombe Park Station

Station Crs

Ormiston Rd

Gurdon Road

Victoria Way

Sundorne Rd

Swallowfield

Inverine Rd

Ransome Rd

Fossdene Rd

Philip Rd

Elliscombe Road

Humber Road

Angerstein Works

Eastcombe Avenue

Sandtoft Road

Eversley Road

The Birches

Primary School

Tallis

Springfield Gv

2 Coraline Rd

Hardy Rd

Combe Av

Beaconsfield Road

Ruthin Road

Westcombe Road

Mycenae Road

Glenluce Road

Bramshot Avenue

Maryhill Rd

Hopedale Road

Highcombe

Copse Cl

Primary School

Our Lady of Grace RC Prim Sch

Fairlawn

Marlborough Lane

Fairlawn

Suffield Road

Kirkside

Invicta Primary School

CHARLTON

ROAD

Vanbrugh Pk Rd W

St Andrews

Blackheath High Senior School

CHARLTON RD

B210

Dornberg Cl

Blackheath RFC (The Rectory Field)

St Reynolds Cl

Blackheath Bluecoat School

The Glade

Cherry Orchard Primary School

3 Vanbrugh

TON WAY

Mary Lawrenson

PO

B210

Lizban St

Bowater Pl

Sun Pl

Russell Cl

Surgery

Heathway

St John's Pk

St John's Park

Gregor Ms

OLD

DOVER

ROAD

A207

SHOO

B2

123

Langton

STRATHEDEN ROAD

Langton Way

SUN IN SANDS ROUNDABOUT

Hervey

Merriman

Galsworthy Crs

Harraden Road

Wricklemarsh

77

SHOOTERS HILL ROAD A2

Rosse Mews

Annesley

Bebbe Road

Holburn

4 PR OF WALES RD

B212

Shooters

Blackheath Preparatory School

Greenwich Place

Lewisham

Kidbrooke

Liskeard Gdns

Westbrook Road

Westbrook Park

Rochester Way

Woolcombe

Kidbrooke Park Primary School

Harwood Road

Dursley

Whets

Kidbrooke

Long Lane AFC

Kidb

South Row

St German's

Morden College Homes

Manor Brook Medical Centre

Brook Lane

Penn

A2

Rochester

Road

5 Black High School

GDST

p School

PO

Rycliff Cl

Futhrop Rd

The Paragon

Corner

The Glebe

Hunts

Swan Rd

Pond Rd

Brook Lane Crescent

PO

Kidbrooke Way

Kellaway Rd

Superstore

Bennett Pk

Rocque La

540

Blackheath Park

The Lane

Pond Rd

A

142

Thomas Tallis School

Old Post Office La

B

41

Nelson Road

C

Blackheath Park

Meadowbank

Wingfield Primary School

A2213

Kidbrooke Station

1 grid square represents 500 metres

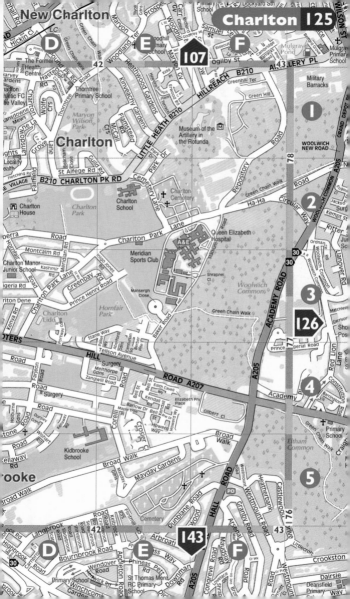

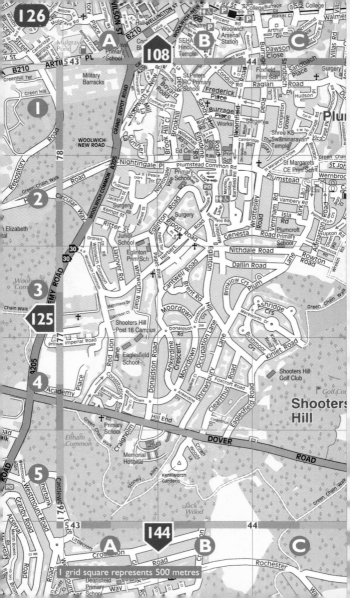

I grid square represents 500 metres

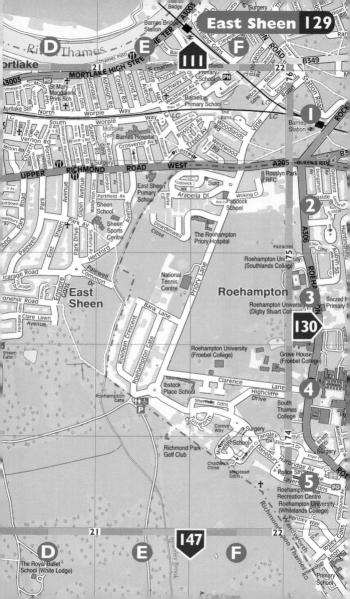

Barnes Bridge Station

D River Thames **E** **F**

Mortlake

MORTLAKE HIGH STREET

St Mary Magdalens Prim Sch

Mortlake Stn

Barnes Primary School

Barnes Hospital

Barnes Station **I**

UPPER RICHMOND ROAD WEST A205 QUEEN'S RIDE

Rosslyn Park RFC

East Sheen Primary School

Sheen School

Paddock School

2

Sheen Sports Centre

The Roehampton Priory Hospital

Roehampton University (Southlands College)

Fairacres

East Sheen

Palewell Common

National Tennis Centre

Priory Lane

Roehampton

Roehampton University (Digby Stuart College)

Sacred Heart Primary

3

I30

Roehampton University (Froebel College)

Grove House (Froebel College)

Clarence Lane

Highcliffe Drive

South Thames College

4

Bank Lane

Roedean Crescent

Ibstock Place School

Roehampton Gate

Sherfield Gdns

Cleeve Way

Surgery

Richmond Park Golf Club

Chadwick Close

Minstead Gdns

Police Stn

5

Roehampton Recreation Centre

Roehampton University (Whitelands College)

Richmond Thames

Wandsworth

21

I47

D The Royal Ballet School (White Lodge)

Beverley Brook

E **F**

22

Primary School

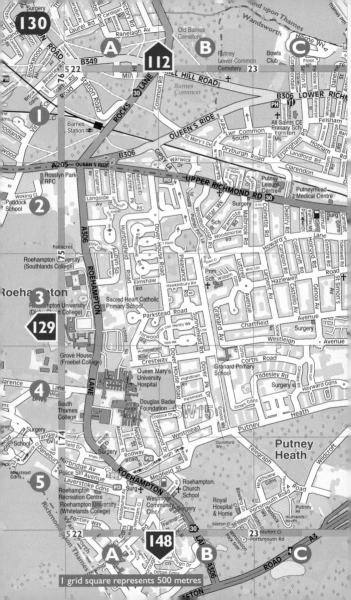

I grid square represents 500 metres

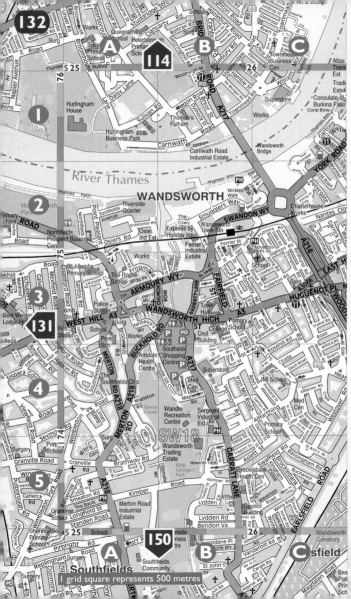

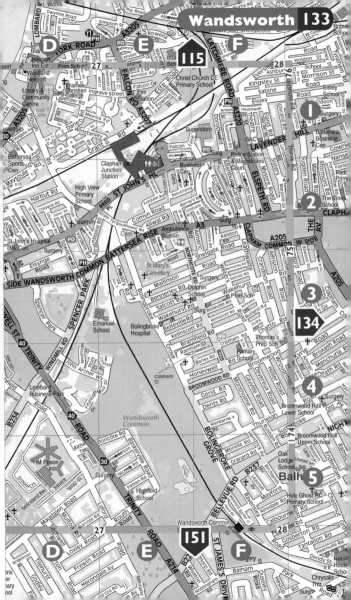

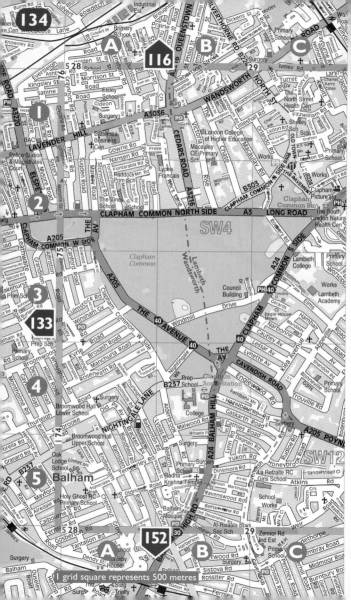

Stockwell

Clapham Park

117

153

136

2

3

4

5

SW2

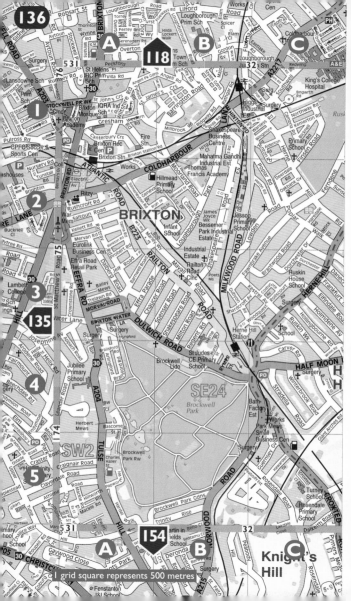

I grid square represents 500 metres

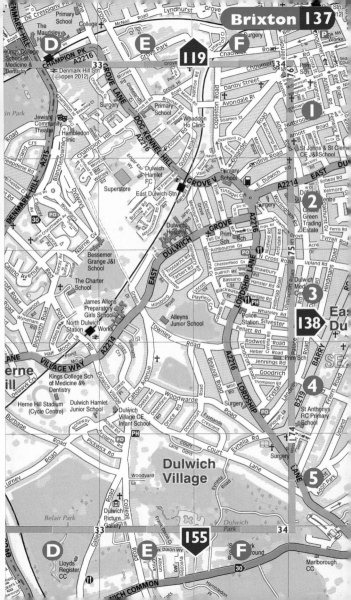

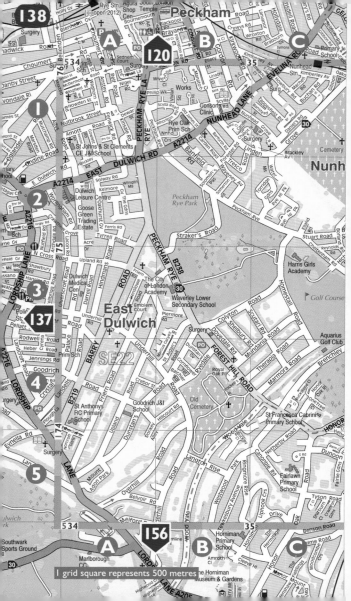

1 grid square represents 500 metres

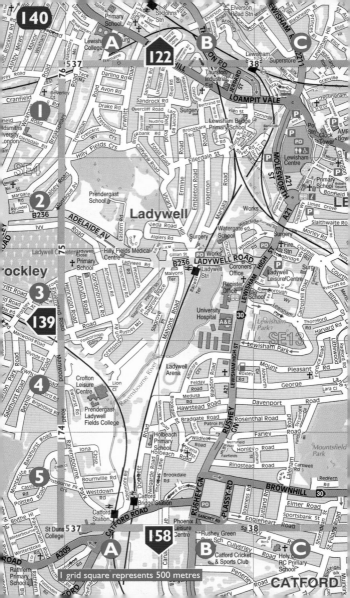

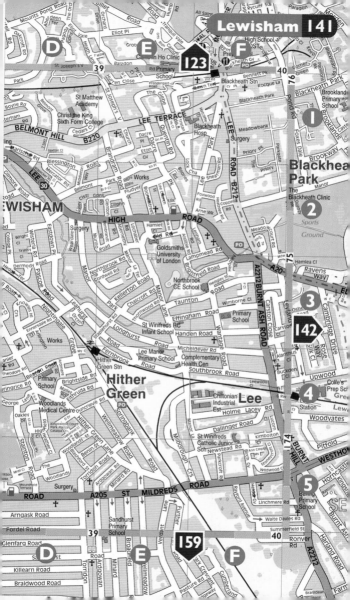

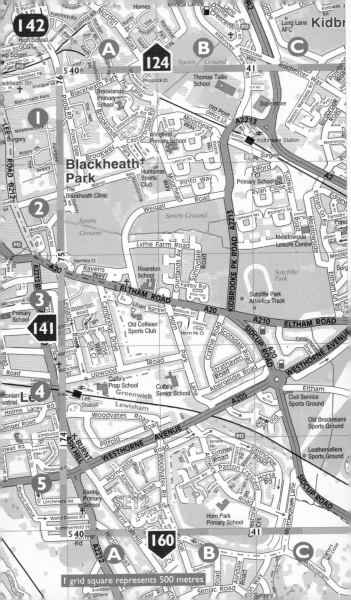

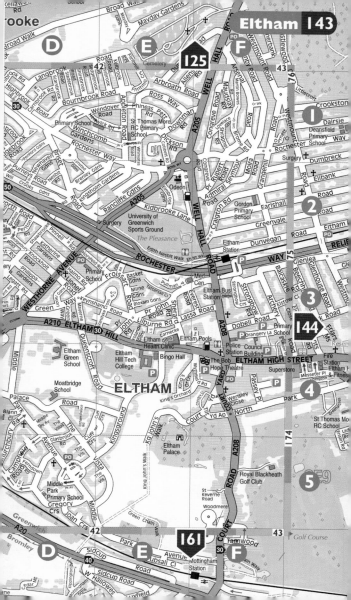

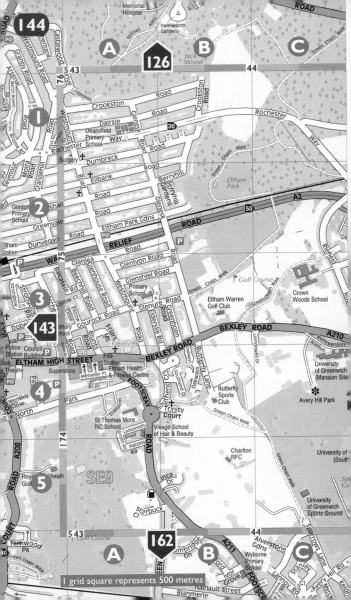

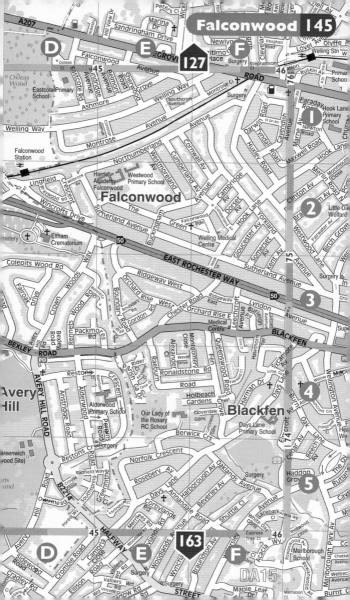

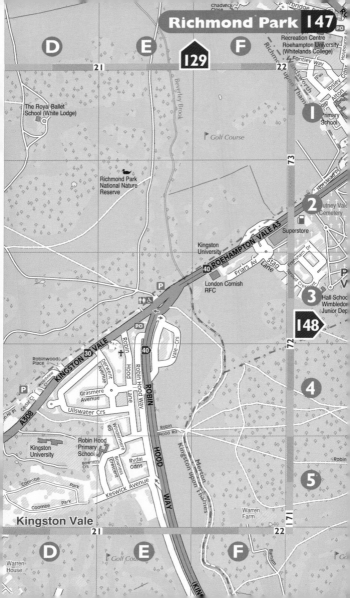

I grid square represents 500 metres

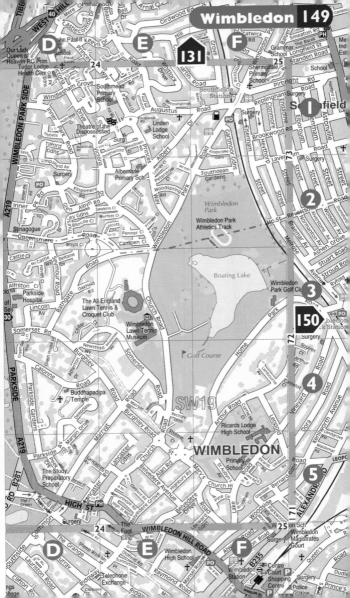

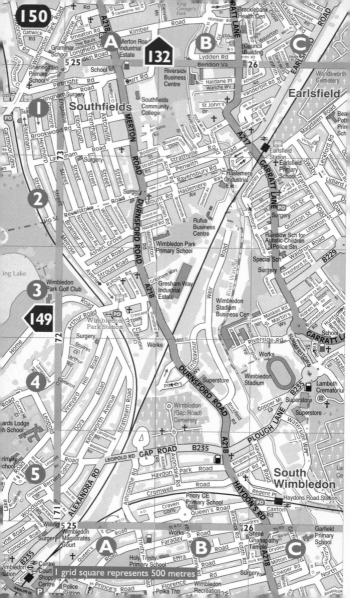

I grid square represents 500 metres

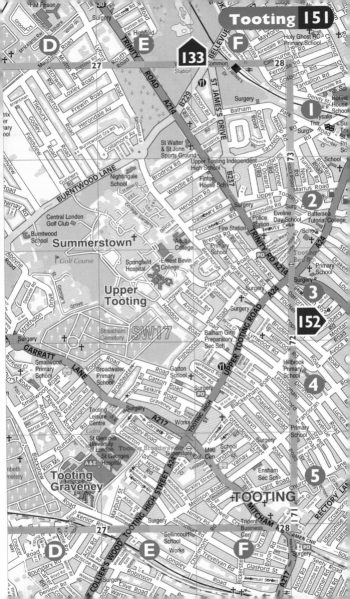

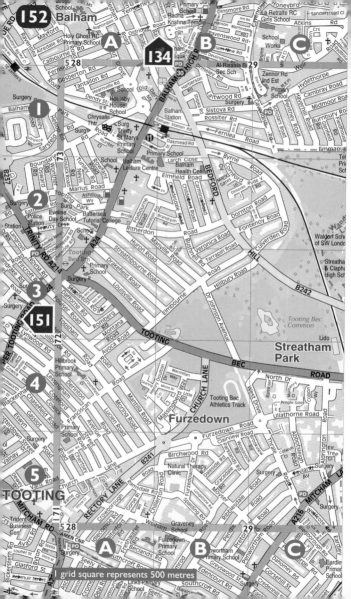

152 Balham

School

Holy Ghost RC
Primary School

A

134

B

La Retraite RC
Girls School

Sandersted Cl

Atkins   Rd

C

School
Works

Primary
School

Radha
Krishna Temple

Dinsmore Rd

Ravenswood Rd

Al-Risaala Bi 29
Sec Sch

Zennor Rd
Ind Est

Hydethorpe

Mayford

Airedale Rd

Calbourne

Ravenscroft

Fernside

5 28

Gosberton Rd

Tantallon Rd

Hearnville Rd

Hornsby
House
School

Denby St

Ormeley Rd

Harperson

Fitwood Rd

Sistova Rd

Rossiter Rd

Fernlea   Road

Cambray Rd

Midmoor Rd

Burnbury Rd

Balham Station

Oakmead Rd

Byrne   Road

Emmanue

Surgery

Balham

Bexley Rd

Hertop Rd

Sarsfeld Rd

I

Chrysalis
Thtr

Surg

Road

St Marys
Primary
School

Trinity

Larch Close
Balham
Health Cen

2

Boundaries
Oswald

Womthe

Tooting
Surg
Park

Eveline
Day School
Trinity

Battersea
Tutorial College

Marius Road

Ashdon

WY

Nevis

Bedford
+

Cornford

Ritherdon   Road

Dornton   Road

Fonteney Road

Waldorf Scho
of SW Londo

Police
Station

Crescent

School

Brandreth

Chillerton Road

Cavendish Road

Ryde

Dimocks Rd

Streatha
& Claphi
High Sch

Trinity Rd A214

Langford

Ravenscroft

3

Stapleton Rd

Darfenne Rd

Huron   Road

Manville   Road

Bushnell Road

Veronica Road

Terrapin Road

Hillbury Road

HILL

Culverden Road

B242

Streatha
Stati

Surgery

Dakefield Road

Louisville Road

Embourne

Dr Johnson Avenue

Tooting Bec
Common

Lido

151

Toulser Road

Topsham

Romberg

Montana

Avoca   Road

TOOTING   **BEC**   **ROAD**

Streatham
Park

Trident
Business
Cen

Hillbrook
Primary
School

Tessington

Cofford

Derinton

Mantilla Road

Morcha Road

Lucien Road

MacMillan
Way

Doulton

de Lisle

North Dr

West Drive

Rambler
CI

Ullathorne Road

Alborstagh

Elr
Tree
Cl

4

Chatefield

Cowick

Enwin Street

Gassiot

Franciscan   Avenue

CHURCH   LANE

Tooting Bec
Athletics Track

Pringle Gdns

Colton

Furzedown

Aldrington

Surgery

5

TOOTING

Vant   Road

Church   Lane

RECTORY   LANE

Ramsdale Rd

Chillerton Rd

Furzedown Road

Clairview Road

Birchwood Rd

B241

Natural Therapy
Clinic

Dalmore Rd

Bracknell Rd

Thrale   Road

Colvin

Eyland Rd

Surgery

PO

MITCHAM   LA

Surgery

Mitcham Rd

5 28

Av

Loubet St

Glasford St

Idlecombe

Franxdd

Becrands Rd

Cowze   Rd

Wellam

Graveney
School

Furzedown
Primary
School

Perdle

29

Streatland

Perntham   Road

Credenhill

Dahomey
Rd

Westcote

A216

Corsehill

Ender
Prima
Scho

A

B

C

I grid square represents 500 metres

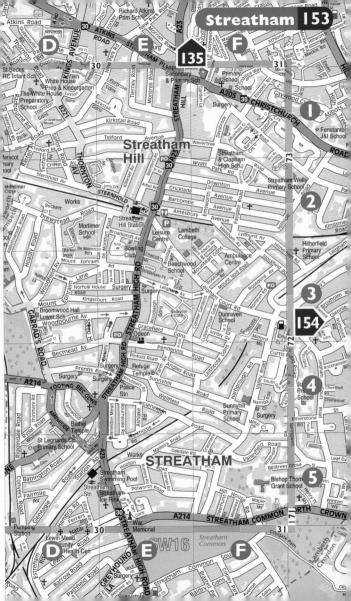

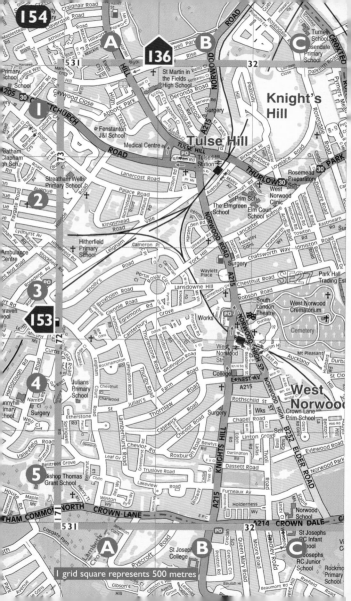

I grid square represents 500 metres

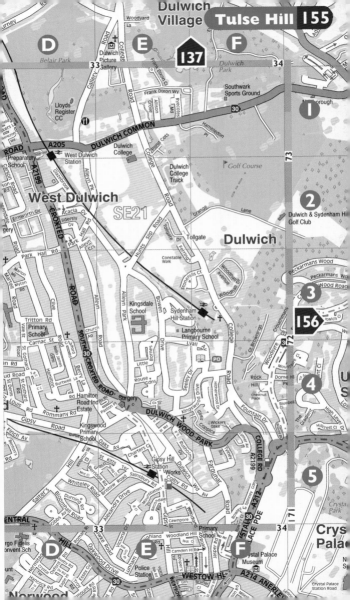

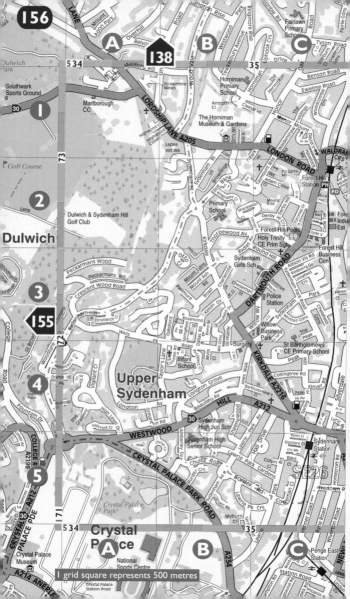

I grid square represents 500 metres

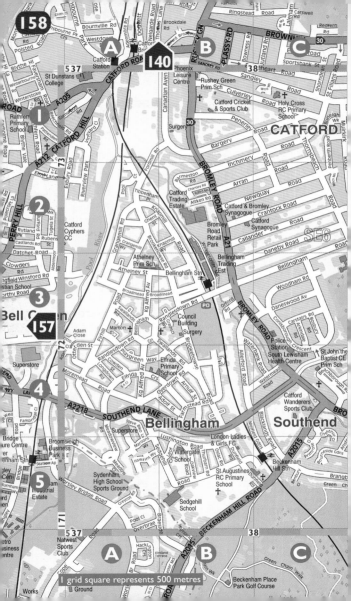

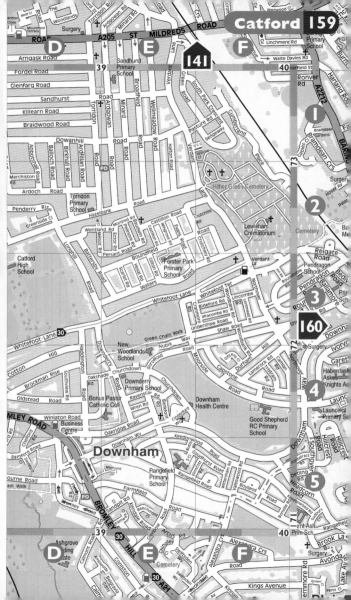

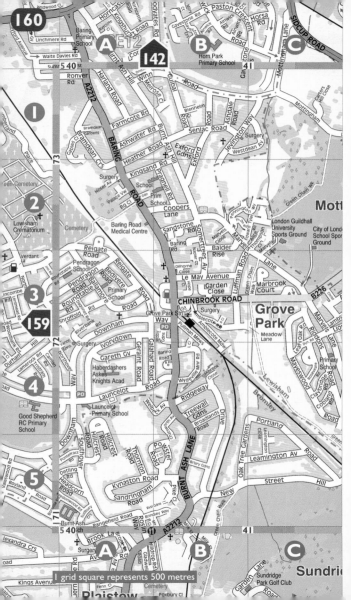

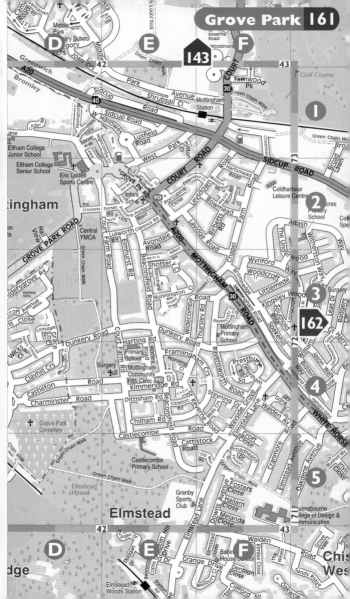

D E 143 F

A20 Greenwich
Bromley

Golf Course

I

SIDCUP ROAD

43

Keverne
Road
Woodmere

Farnwood
Pk

Green chain Walk

Bro

Green Chain Walk

Mottingham
Station

Sidcup Road

Shrubsall Cl.

Park Avenue

W Hallowes

Luxfield
Road

West Park

Coldharbour
Leisure Centre

Acres
Primary
School

Col
Spo

Altash

The Underwood

Witherston Way

Eltham College
Junior School

Eltham College
Senior School

Eric Liddell
Sports Centre

ingham

Hall
View

Central
YMCA

The Crossway

Infant
Scho

Dorset Rd
Portland
Road

Porcupine
Close

Hartsmead
Road

Powntley Cl
Leysdown Wy
Bownead
Birbetts
Chapel Farm
Bromhedge

Wynford
Way

Woodcroft

3 Surgery

Littlemede

Kingsley Wood
Southold
Slakenhill

Leas Di

Badgers

GROVE PARK ROAD

COURT FARM ROAD

GROVE PK RD

COURT ROAD

Avondale
Road

Elmhurst Rd

Court Farm Road

Beaconsfield Road

Tulworth Rd
Clarence Rd
Albert
shotter
Nunnington

Lavidge Road

162

MOTTINGHAM ROAD

Haven Cl
Raven

Mottingham
Primary
School

Gt
William
Bidder
Jason Walk

Aldersgrove Av

Grace
Close

Wicks Cl

Clavhill Crs

Castleton
Road

Charminster Road

StaField
Gdns

Lonsdale
Close

Dunkery Road

Harting
Road

Court Farm
Road

Mottingham
Community
Hlth Clinic

Framlingham Crs

Horning

Kimmeridge Rd

Dittisham Rd
Ickleton
Rd

Widecombe

Dunkery Road

Thursley Rd

Ravensworth
Road

Steyning Gv

Prestbury
Chenham
Sq

Jay Gdns

Walden Av
4

WHITE HORSE

Walden Av

Green Chain Walk

Grove Park
Cemetery

Castlecombe
Road

Chilham Rd

Keverne Road
St Croft
Close

Cattistock
Road

Broadheath
Dr
Old Wy

Crannore Avenue

Oakdene Avenue

5

Rushall Wy
Inv
Close

Castlecombe
Primary School

Elmstead
Wood

Elmstead

Green Chain Walk

Granby
Sports
Club

Fosters
Close

Hallam
Close

Melanda
Close

Elmstead Lane

Downs Avenue

Walden Road

Ravensbourne
College of Design &
Communication

Chis
Wes

Grove Road

D E 143 F 42

Langton Dr
John Hill
Wood Dr
Benetts Copse

Grange Drive

Babin
House School

Emlee Close

Denbigh
Close

Clifford
Rd

Melbury Rd

Sandy Ridge

Oxtwo

Invi

dge

Elmstead
Woods Station

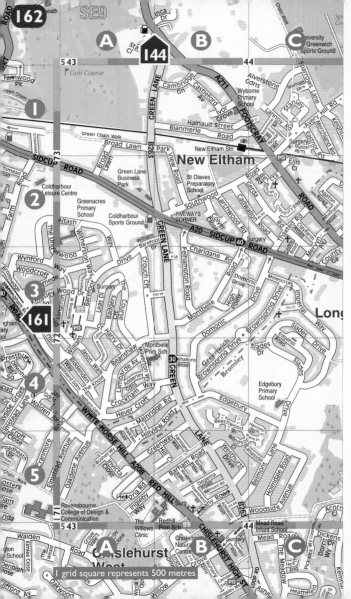

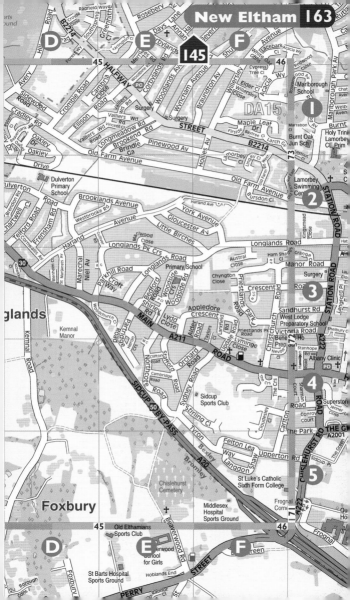

Acton	98	C2
Acton Green	99	D5
Aldersbrook	64	C3
Avery Hill	144	C4
Balham	133	F5
Barking	85	D4
Barnes	112	B4
Barnsbury	75	F4
Battersea	115	F3
Bayswater	27	E1
Beckton	95	F5
Bedford Park	99	F4
Belgravia	42	A4
Bell Green	157	F5
Bellingham	158	A4
Bethnal Green	90	B2
Blackfen	145	F4
Blackheath	123	F5
Blackheath Park	142	A2
Blackwall	105	D1
Bloomsbury	20	B2
The Borough	47	F1
Bow	92	A1
Bow Common	92	A4
Brixton	136	A2
Brockley	139	F3
Bromley	92	B2
Brompton	40	C3
Brondesbury	71	E5
Brondesbury Park	71	D5
Brook Green	100	C4
Camberwell	119	F4
Camden Town	74	A4
Canary Wharf	104	A2
Canning Town	94	B4
Canonbury	76	C3
Catford	158	C1
Charlton	125	D1
Chelsea	116	A1
Child's Hill	53	E4
China Town	32	B1
Chiswick	99	F5
Church End	69	F4
City of London	35	D1
Clapham	116	B5
Clapham Park	135	D4
Clapton Park	79	F1
Clerkenwell	10	A5
College Park	88	A2
Cranbrook	66	A2
Creekmouth	97	E4
Cricklewood	71	D1
Crouch End	56	C1
Cubitt Town	104	C5
Custom House	107	F1
Dalston	77	F4
Dartmouth Park	56	A4
De Beauvoir Town	77	E5
Deptford	121	F2
Dollis Hill	52	B5
Downham	159	D5
Dudden Hill	70	A2
Dulwich	155	F2
Dulwich Village	137	E5
Earl's Court	38	C1
Earlsfield	161	G5
East Acton	99	F1
East Dulwich	138	A3
East Ham	95	E1
East Sheen	129	D3
Elmstead	161	E5
Eltham	143	E4
Fair Cross	85	F2
Falconwood	145	E2
Finsbury	10	A3
Finsbury Park	57	E4
Forest Gate	82	A2
Forest Hill	157	D1
Foxbury	163	D5
Fulham	113	D3
Furzedown	152	B4
Gants Hill	65	F1
Globe Town	91	D2
Golders Green	55	E1
Gospel Oak	74	A2
Greenwich	123	D1
Grove Park	111	D4
Grove Park	160	C3
Hackney	78	C3
Hackney Wick	80	A3
Haggerston	13	F1
Hammersmith	100	B5
Hampstead	73	D1
Harlesden	87	E1
Herne Hill	136	C4
Highbury	76	B2
Highgate	55	F2
Hither Green	141	E4
Holborn	21	E3
Homerton	79	D3
Honor Oak	139	D4
Honor Oak Park	139	E4
Hoxton	12	C2
Ilford	66	B5
Isle of Dogs	104	C5
Islington	76	A5
Kennington	117	E2
Kensal Green	88	C1
Kensal Rise	89	D1
Kensal Town	89	E3
Kensington	38	C3
Kentish Town	74	C3
Kidbrooke	124	C5
Kilburn	71	E5
Kingsbury	50	B1
Kingsland	77	E4
Kingston Vale	157	D4
Knightsbridge	29	D5
Knight's Hill	154	C1
Ladywell	140	A2
Lambeth	46	A2
Lea Bridge	61	D5
Lee	141	F4
Lewisham	140	C2
Leyton	63	D5
Leytonstone	63	F3
Limehouse	105	E1
Lisson Grove	17	F2
Little Ilford	84	A2
Longlands	162	C3
Lower Clapton	78	C1
Lower Holloway	75	F2
Lower Place	86	C1
Lower Sydenham	157	D4
Loxford	84	C2
Maida Vale	2	C3
Maitland Park	73	F3
Manor Park	83	E1
Marylebone	18	A3
Mayfair	30	C2
Mile End	91	E3
Mill Meads	93	D1
Millwall	104	B4
Mortlake	110	C5
Mottingham	160	C2
Neasden	69	D1
Newbury Park	67	D1
New Charlton	107	D5
New Cross	121	E5
New Cross Gate	121	E4
New Eltham	162	B2
Newington	46	B3
North Acton	86	C3
North End	54	C3
North Kensington	89	D4
North Sheen	110	B5
North Woolwich	107	E5
Notting Hill	101	E1
Nunhead	138	C2
Old Ford	79	E5
Old Oak Common	87	F3
Paddington	16	A3
Park Royal	86	A2
Parsons Green	114	A5
Peckham	120	B5
Pentonville	9	F1
Pimlico	116	C1
Plaistow	93	F2
Plashet	83	D3
Plumstead	126	C1
Plumstead Common	127	F2
Poplar	104	A1
Primrose Hill	73	F5
Putney	131	D3
Putney Heath	130	C5
Putney Vale	148	A3
Queen's Park	89	E1
Regent's Park	7	D2
Roehampton	129	F3
Rotherhithe	103	D4
St Giles	20	B4
St James's	32	A4
St Johns	122	A5
St Luke's	11	F5

St Pancras	9 D4		Tokyngton	68 B3
Sands End	114 C4		Tooting	151 F5
Seven Kings	67 E3		Tooting Graveney	151 D5
Shacklewell	78 A1		Tufnell Park	74 C1
Shadwell	102 C1		Tulse Hill	154 B1
Shepherd's Bush	100 B2		Upper Clapton	60 A3
Shooters Hill	126 C4		Upper Holloway	56 C3
Shoreditch	12 B4		Upper Sydenham	156 A4
Silvertown	106 C3		Upper Tooting	151 E3
Soho	20 A5		Upton	82 B4
Somers Town	8 A2		Upton Park	82 C5
South Bromley	93 D5		Vale of Health	55 D5
Southend	158 C4		Vauxhall	117 E1
Southfields	150 A1		Walham Green	114 A4
South Hackney	78 C5		Wallend	84 A5
South Hampstead	72 B4		Walworth	118 C2
South Kensington	39 E5		Wandsworth	132 A2
South Kensington	114 C1		Wanstead	64 B2
South Lambeth	117 E3		Wapping	102 B2
South Wimbledon	150 C5		Welsh Harp	51 D3
Spitalfields	25 E2		Wembley Park	50 A5
Stamford Hill	59 F2		West Acton	86 A5
Stepney	90 C4		West Brompton	114 B2
St George in the East	102 A1		West Dulwich	155 D2
Stockwell	135 E1		West Hampstead	72 A2
Stoke Newington	59 F4		West Heath	54 B4
Strand	32 C1		West Hendon	52 A2
Stratford	80 C4		West Hill	131 E5
Stratford Marsh	80 B5		West Kensington	113 D1
Stratford New Town	80 C3		West Kilburn	89 E2
Streatham	153 E5		Westminster	43 F3
Streatham Hill	153 E1		West Norwood	154 C4
Streatham Park	152 C4		Whitechapel	37 F1
Stroud Green	58 A1		Willesden	70 A5
Summerstown	151 D2		Willesden Green	70 B4
Swiss Cottage	73 D5		Wimbledon	149 E5
Sydenham	157 D5		Woolwich	108 A4
Temple Mills	80 B2			

USING THE STREET INDEX

Street names are listed alphabetically. Each street name is followed by its postal town or area locality, the Postcode District, the page number, and the reference to the square in which the name is found.

Standard index entries are shown as follows:

1 Av *WOOL/PLUM* SE18......................**108** B4

Street names and selected addresses not shown on the map due to scale restrictions are shown in the index with an asterisk:

Abbeville Ms *CLAP* SW4 * **135** D3

Entries in red indicate streets located within the London Congestion Zone. Refer to the map pages for the location of the Zone boundary.

GENERAL ABBREVIATIONS

ACC	ACCESS		CO	COUNTY
ALY	ALLEY		COLL	COLLEGE
AP	APPROACH		COM	COMMON
AR	ARCADE		COMM	COMMISSION
ASS	ASSOCIATION		CON	CONVENT
AV	AVENUE		COT	COTTAGE
BCH	BEACH		COTS	COTTAGES
BLDS	BUILDINGS		CP	CAPE
BND	BEND		CPS	COPSE
BNK	BANK		CR	CREEK
BR	BRIDGE		CREM	CREMATORIUM
BRK	BROOK		CRS	CRESCENT
BTM	BOTTOM		CSWY	CAUSEWAY
BUS	BUSINESS		CT	COURT
BVD	BOULEVARD		CTRL	CENTRAL
BY	BYPASS		CTS	COURTS
CATH	CATHEDRAL		CTYD	COURTYARD
CEM	CEMETERY		CUTT	CUTTINGS
CEN	CENTRE		CV	COVE
CFT	CROFT		CVN	CANYON
CH	CHURCH		DEPT	DEPARTMENT
CHA	CHASE		DL	DALE
CHYD	CHURCHYARD		DM	DAM
CIR	CIRCLE		DR	DRIVE
CIRC	CIRCUS		DRO	DROVE
CL	CLOSE		DRY	DRIVEWAY
CLFS	CLIFFS		DWGS	DWELLINGS
CMP	CAMP		E	EAST
CNR	CORNER		EMB	EMBANKMENT

EMBY	EMBASSY
ESP	ESPLANADE
EST	ESTATE
EX	EXCHANGE
EXPY	EXPRESSWAY
EXT	EXTENSION
F/O	FLYOVER
FC	FOOTBALL CLUB
FK	FORK
FLD	FIELD
FLDS	FIELDS
FLS	FALLS
FM	FARM
FT	FORT
FTS	FLATS
FWY	FREEWAY
FY	FERRY
GA	GATE
GAL	GALLERY
GDN	GARDEN
GDNS	GARDENS
GLD	GLADE
GLN	GLEN
GN	GREEN
GND	GROUND
GRA	GRANGE
GRG	GARAGE
GT	GREAT
GTWY	GATEWAY
GV	GROVE
HGR	HIGHER
HL	HILL
HLS	HILLS
HO	HOUSE
HOL	HOLLOW
HOSP	HOSPITAL
HRB	HARBOUR
HTH	HEATH
HTS	HEIGHTS
HVN	HAVEN
HWY	HIGHWAY
IMP	IMPERIAL
IN	INLET
IND EST	INDUSTRIAL ESTATE
INF	INFIRMARY
INFO	INFORMATION
INT	INTERCHANGE
IS	ISLAND
JCT	JUNCTION
JTY	JETTY
KG	KING
KNL	KNOLL
L	LAKE
LA	LANE
LDG	LODGE
LGT	LIGHT
LK	LOCK
LKS	LAKES
LNDG	LANDING
LTL	LITTLE
LWR	LOWER
MAG	MAGISTRATE
MAN	MANSIONS
MD	MEAD
MDW	MEADOWS
MEM	MEMORIAL
MI	MILL
MKT	MARKET
MKTS	MARKETS
ML	MALL
MNR	MANOR
MS	MEWS
MSN	MISSION
MT	MOUNT
MTN	MOUNTAIN
MTS	MOUNTAINS
MUS	MUSEUM
MWY	MOTORWAY
N	NORTH
NE	NORTH EAST
NW	NORTH WEST
O/P	OVERPASS
OFF	OFFICE
ORCH	ORCHARD
OV	OVAL
PAL	PALACE
PAS	PASSAGE
PAV	PAVILION
PDE	PARADE
PH	PUBLIC HOUSE
PK	PARK
PKWY	PARKWAY
PL	PLACE
PLN	PLAIN
PLNS	PLAINS
PLZ	PLAZA
POL	POLICE STATION
PR	PRINCE
PREC	PRECINCT
PREP	PREPARATORY
PRIM	PRIMARY
PROM	PROMENADE
PRS	PRINCESS
PRT	PORT
PT	POINT
PTH	PATH
PZ	PIAZZA
QD	QUADRANT
QU	QUEEN
QY	QUAY
R	RIVER
RBT	ROUNDABOUT
RD	ROAD
RDG	RIDGE
REP	REPUBLIC
RES	RESERVOIR
RFC	RUGBY FOOTBALL CLUB
RI	RISE
RP	RAMP
RW	ROW
S	SOUTH
SCH	SCHOOL
SE	SOUTH EAST
SER	SERVICE AREA
SH	SHORE
SHOP	SHOPPING
SKWY	SKYWAY
SMT	SUMMIT
SOC	SOCIETY
SP	SPUR
SPR	SPRING
SQ	SQUARE
ST	STREET
STN	STATION
STR	STREAM
STRD	STRAND
SW	SOUTH WEST
TDG	TRADING
TER	TERRACE
THWY	THROUGHWAY
TNL	TUNNEL
TOLL	TOLLWAY
TPK	TURNPIKE
TR	TRACK
TRL	TRAIL
TWR	TOWER
U/P	UNDERPASS
UNI	UNIVERSITY
UPR	UPPER
V	VALE
VA	VALLEY
VIAD	VIADUCT
VIL	VILLA
VIS	VISTA
VLG	VILLAGE
VLS	VILLAS
VW	VIEW
W	WEST
WD	WOOD
WHF	WHARF
WK	WALK
WKS	WALKS
WLS	WELLS
WY	WAY
YD	YARD
YHA	YOUTH HOSTEL

POSTCODE TOWNS AND AREA ABBREVIATIONS

ABYW	Abbey Wood
ACT	Acton
ALP/SUD	Alperton/Sudbury
ARCH	Archway
BAL	Balham
BANK	Bank
BARB	Barbican
BARK	Barking

Abbreviation	Full name
BARN	Barnes
BAY/PAD	Bayswater/Paddington
BECK	Beckenham
BERM/RHTH	Bermondsey/Rotherhithe
BETH	Bethnal Green
BFN/LL	Blackfen/Longlands
BGVA	Belgravia
BKHTH/KID	Blackheath/Kidbrooke
BLKFR	Blackfriars
BMLY	Bromley
BMSBY	Bloomsbury
BOW	Bow
BROCKY	Brockley
BRXN/ST	Brixton north/Stockwell
BRXS/STRHM	Brixton south/Streatham Hill
BTFD	Brentford
BTSEA	Battersea
CAMTN	Camden Town
CAN/RD	Canning Town/Royal Docks
CANST	Cannon Street station
CAT	Catford
CAVSQ/HST	Cavendish Square/Harley Street
CDALE/KGS	Colindale/Kingsbury
CEND/HSY/T	Crouch End/Hornsey/Turnpike Lane
CHARL	Charlton
CHCR	Charing Cross
CHEL	Chelsea
CHST	Chislehurst
CHSWK	Chiswick
CITYW	City of London west
CLAP	Clapham
CLKNW	Clerkenwell
CLPT	Clapton
CMBW	Camberwell
CONDST	Conduit Street
COVGDN	Covent Garden
CRICK	Cricklewood
DEPT	Deptford
DUL	Dulwich
EA	Ealing
ECT	Earl's Court
EDUL	East Dulwich
EFNCH	East Finchley
EHAM	East Ham
ELTH/MOT	Eltham/Mottingham
EMB	Embankment
FARR	Farringdon
FENCHST	Fenchurch Street
FITZ	Fitzrovia
FLST/FETLN	Fleet Street/Fetter Lane
FSBYE	Finsbury east
FSBYPK	Finsbury Park
FSBYW	Finsbury west
FSTGT	Forest Gate
FSTH	Forest Hill
FUL/PGN	Fulham/Parsons Green
GDMY/SEVK	Goodmayes/Seven Kings
GINN	Gray's Inn
GLDGN	Golders Green
GNTH/NBYPK	Gants Hill/Newbury Park
GNWCH	Greenwich
GTPST	Great Portland Street
GWRST	Gower Street
HACK	Hackney
HAMP	Hampstead
HBRY	Highbury
HCIRC	Holborn Circus
HDN	Hendon
HDTCH	Houndsditch
HGT	Highgate
HHOL	High Holborn
HMSMTH	Hammersmith
HNHL	Herne Hill
HOL/ALD	Holborn/Aldwych
HOLWY	Holloway
HOM	Homerton
IL	Ilford
IS	Islington
KENS	Kensington
KIL/WHAMP	Kilburn/West Hampstead
KTBR	Knightsbridge
KTN/HRWW/WS	Kenton/Harrow Weald/Wealdstone
KTTN	Kentish Town
KUTN/CMB	Kingston upon Thames north/Coombe
LBTH	Lambeth
LEE/GVPK	Lee/Grove Park
LEW	Lewisham
LEY	Leyton
LINN	Lincoln's Inn
LOTH	Lothbury
LSQ/SEVD	Leicester Square/Seven Dials
LVPST	Liverpool Street
MANHO	Mansion House
MBLAR	Marble Arch
MHST	Marylebone High Street
MNPK	Manor Park
MON	Monument
MORT/ESHN	Mortlake/East Sheen
MUSWH	Muswell Hill
MV/WKIL	Maida Vale/West Kilburn
MYFR/PICC	Mayfair/Piccadilly
MYFR/PKLN	Mayfair/Park Lane
NKENS	North Kensington
NOXST/BSQ	New Oxford Street/Bloomsbury Square
NRWD	Norwood
NTGHL	Notting Hill
NWCR	New Cross
OBST	Old Broad Street
OXSTW	Oxford Street west
PECK	Peckham
PGE/AN	Penge/Anerley
PIM	Pimlico
PLSTW	Plaistow
POP/IOD	Poplar/Isle of Dogs
PUT/ROE	Putney/Roehampton
RCH/KEW	Richmond/Kew
RCHPK/HAM	Richmond Park/Ham
REDBR	Redbridge
REGST	Regent Street
RSQ	Russell Square
SCUP	Sidcup
SDTCH	Shoreditch
SEVS/STOTM	Seven Sisters/South Tottenham
SHB	Shepherd's Bush
SKENS	South Kensington
SOHO/CST	Soho/Carnaby Street
SOHO/SHAV	Soho/Shaftesbury Avenue
SRTFD	Stratford
STBT	St Bart's
STHWK	Southwark
STJS	St James's
STJSPK	St James's Park
STJWD	St John's Wood
STLK	St Luke's
STNW/STAM	Stoke Newington/Stamford Hill
STP	St Paul's
STPAN	St Pancras
STRHM/NOR	Streatham/Norbury
SYD	Sydenham
THMD	Thamesmead
TOOT	Tooting
TOTM	Tottenham
TPL/STR	Temple/Strand
TWRH	Tower Hill
VX/NE	Vauxhall/Nine Elms
WALTH	Walthamstow
WALW	Walworth
WAN	Wanstead
WAND/EARL	Wandsworth/Earlsfield
WAP	Wapping
WBLY	Wembley
WBPTN	West Brompton
WCHPL	Whitechapel
WELL	Welling
WEST	Westminster
WESTW	Westminster west
WHALL	Whitehall
WIM/MER	Wimbledon/Merton
WKENS	West Kensington
WLSDN	Willesden
WNWD	West Norwood
WOOL/PLUM	Woolwich/Plumstead

1

1 Av WOOL/PLUM SE18.... 108 B4

A

Aaron Hill Rd EHAM E6.... 96 A4
Abberley Ms BTSEA SW11.... 134 B1
Abbess Cl BRXS/STRHM SW2.... 158 B1
Abbeville Ms CLAP SW4 *.... 135 D3
Abbeville Rd CLAP SW4.... 134 C4
Abbey Dr TOOT SW17.... 152 A5
Abbeyfield Est BERM/RHTH SE16.... 102 C5
Abbeyfield Rd BERM/RHTH SE16.... 102 C5
Abbeyfields Cl WLSDN NW10.... 86 A2
Abbey Gdns HMSMTH W6.... 113 E2
  STHWK SE1.... 102 A3
  STJWD NW8.... 3 E2
Abbey La SRTFD E15.... 92 C1
Abbey Orchard St WEST SW1P.... 48 B2
Abbey Rd BARK IG11.... 84 B4
  GNTH/NBYPK IG2.... 67 D1
  SRTFD E15.... 81 E5
  STJWD NW8.... 72 C5
  WLSDN NW10.... 68 B5
Abbey St PLSTW E13.... 94 A3
  STHWK SE1.... 49 E2
Abbotsbury Cl PECK SE15.... 138 C1
Abbotsbury Rd WKENS W14.... 101 E3
Abbotshade Rd BERM/RHTH SE16 *.... 103 D1
Abbotshall Rd CAT SE6.... 159 D1
Abbotsleigh Rd STRHM/NOR SW16.... 152 C4
Abbots Pk BRXS/STRHM SW2.... 154 A1
Abbot's Pl KIL/WHAMP NW6.... 72 B5
Abbots Rd EHAM E6.... 83 D5
Abbots Ter CEND/HSY/T N8.... 57 E1
Abbotstone Rd PUT/ROE SW15.... 130 C1
Abbotswell Rd BROCKY SE4.... 139 F3
Abbotswood Rd EDUL SE22.... 137 E2
  STRHM/NOR SW16.... 153 D3
Abbott Rd POP/IOD E14.... 92 C4
Abbotts Cl IS N1 *.... 76 C4
Abbotts Park Rd LEY E10.... 62 C2
Abchurch La MANHO EC4N.... 36 B1
Abdale Rd SHB W12.... 100 B3
Aberavon Rd BOW E3.... 91 E2
Abercorn Cl STJWD NW8.... 3 E2
Abercorn Pl STJWD NW8.... 3 E3
Abercorn Rd STJWD NW8.... 3 E3
Abercorn Wy STHWK SE1 *.... 120 A1
Abercrombie St BTSEA SW11.... 115 E5
Aberdare Gdns KIL/WHAMP NW6.... 72 B4
Aberdeen La HBRY N5.... 76 B2
Aberdeen Pk HBRY N5.... 76 B2
Aberdeen Pl BAY/PAD W2.... 16 A1
Aberdeen Rd HBRY N5.... 76 C1
  WLSDN NW10.... 69 F2
Aberdeen Ter BKHTH/KID SE3.... 123 D5
Aberdour Rd STHWK SE1.... 48 C5
Aberfeldy St POP/IOD E14.... 92 C5
Aberford Gdns WOOL/PLUM SE18.... 125 E4
Abergeldie Rd LEE/GVPK SE12.... 142 B4
Abernethy Rd LEW SE13.... 141 E2
Abersham Rd HACK E8.... 77 F2
Abery St WOOL/PLUM SE18.... 109 E5
Abingdon Cl STHWK SE1 *.... 119 F1
Abingdon Rd KENS W8.... 38 B3
  WEST SW1P.... 44 C1
Abingdon Vls KENS W8.... 38 A3
Abinger Gv DEPT SE8.... 121 F2
Abinger Ms MV/WKIL W9.... 2 A5
Abinger Rd CHSWK W4.... 99 F4
Ablett St BERM/RHTH SE16.... 120 C1
Abney Park Cemetery
  STNW/STAM N16 *.... 59 F4
Aboyne Rd TOOT SW17.... 150 C3
  WLSDN NW10.... 51 E5
Abyssinia Cl BTSEA SW11.... 133 E2
Abyssinia Rd BTSEA SW11 *.... 133 E2
Acacia Cl DEPT SE8.... 103 E5
Acacia Gdns STJWD NW8.... 4 B1
Acacia Gv DUL SE21.... 155 D2

Acacia Pl STJWD NW8.... 4 B1
Acacia Rd ACT W3.... 98 C1
  STJWD NW8.... 4 B1
  WALTH E17.... 61 E1
  WAN E11.... 63 E4
Academy Pl WOOL/PLUM SE18.... 125 F4
Academy Rd WOOL/PLUM SE18.... 125 F3
Acanthus Dr STHWK SE1 *.... 120 A1
Acanthus Rd BTSEA SW11.... 134 A1
Accommodation Rd GLDGN NW11.... 53 F2
Acfold Rd FUL/PGN SW6.... 114 B4
Achilles Cl STHWK SE1 *.... 120 A1
Achilles Rd KIL/WHAMP NW6.... 72 A2
Achilles St NWCR SE14.... 121 E3
Acklam Rd NKENS W10.... 89 F4
Ackmar Rd FUL/PGN SW6.... 114 A4
Ackroyd Dr BOW E3.... 91 F4
Ackroyd Rd FSTH SE23.... 139 D5
Acland Cl WOOL/PLUM SE18.... 127 D3
Acland Crs CMBW SE5.... 137 D4
Acland Rd CRICK NW2.... 70 B3
Acol Rd KIL/WHAMP NW6.... 72 B4
Acorn Cl CHST BR7.... 162 C5
Acorn Gdns ACT W3.... 87 D4
Acorn Pde PECK SE15 *.... 120 B3
Acorn Wy FSTH SE23.... 157 D3
Acre Dr EDUL SE22.... 138 A2
Acre La BRXS/STRHM SW2.... 135 F2
Acris St WAND/EARL SW18.... 132 C3
Acton Hill Ms ACT W3 *.... 98 B2
  WLSDN NW10.... 86 C2
Acton La CHSWK W4.... 98 C4
Acton Ms HACK E8.... 77 F5
Acton St FSBYW WC1X.... 9 F1
Acuba Rd WAND/EARL SW18.... 150 B2
Ada Gdns POP/IOD E14.... 93 D5
  SRTFD E15.... 81 E5
Adair Rd NKENS W10.... 89 E3
Adam Cl CAT SE6.... 157 F4
  FSTH SE23.... 156 C2
Adam & Eve Ms KENS W8.... 38 B2
Adams Cl WBLY HA9.... 50 B4
Adams Ct OXST EC2N.... 24 B4
Adams Ms TOOT SW17.... 151 F2
Adamson Rd CAN/RD E16.... 94 A3
  HAMP NW3.... 73 D4
Adams Pl HOLWY N7.... 75 F2
Adamsrill Rd SYD SE26.... 157 D4
Adam's Rw MYFR/PKLN W1K.... 30 A1
Adam St CHCR WC2N.... 33 D2
Adam Wk FUL/PGN SW6 *.... 112 C3
Ada Pl BETH E2.... 78 A5
Adare Wk STRHM/NOR SW16.... 153 E2
Ada Rd CMBW SE5.... 119 E3
Ada St HACK E8.... 78 B5
Adderley Gdns ELTH/MOT SE9.... 162 B4
Adderley Gv BTSEA SW11.... 134 A3
Adderley St POP/IOD E14.... 92 C5
Addington Gv SYD SE26.... 157 E4
Addington Rd BOW E3.... 92 A2
  CAN/RD E16.... 93 E3
  FSBYPK N4.... 58 A2
Addington Sq CMBW SE5.... 118 C3
Addington St STHWK SE1.... 45 F1
Addison Av NTGHL W11.... 101 E2
Addison Bridge Pl WKENS W14.... 101 E5
Addison Crs WKENS W14.... 101 E4
Addison Dr LEE/GVPK SE12.... 142 B3
Addison Gdns WKENS W14.... 101 D4
Addison Gv CHSWK W4.... 99 E4
Addison Pl NTGHL W11.... 101 D2
Addison Rd WAN E11.... 64 A1
  WKENS W14.... 101 E3
Addison Ter CHSWK W4 *.... 98 C5
Addle Hl BLKFR EC4V.... 35 D1
Addle St CITYW EC2V *.... 23 F4
Adelaide Av BROCKY SE4.... 140 A2
Adelaide Gv SHB W12.... 100 A2
Adelaide Rd CHST BR7.... 162 B5
  HAMP NW3.... 73 F4
  IL IG1.... 66 B4
  LEY E10.... 62 C5
  PUT/ROE SW15.... 132 A3
  STJWD NW8.... 73 D4
Adelaide St CHCR WC2N *.... 32 C2
Adela St NKENS W10.... 89 E3
Adelina Gv WCHPL E1.... 90 C4
Adelina Ms BAL SW12.... 153 D1
Adeline Pl RSQ WC1B.... 20 B3
Adeliza Cl BARK IG11.... 84 C4
Adelphi Ter CHCR WC2N.... 33 D2

Adeney Cl HMSMTH W6 .... 113 D2
Aden Gv STNW/STAM N16 .... 77 D1
Adenmore Rd CAT SE6 .... 140 A5
Aden Rd IL IG1 .... 66 B2
Adie Rd WCHPL E1 * 100 C4
Adine Rd PLSTW E13 .... 94 A3
Adler St WCHPL E1 .... 90 A4
Adley St CLPT E5 .... 79 E2
Admaston Rd WOOL/PLUM SE18 .... 126 C3
Admiral Ms NKENS W10 .... 89 D3
Admiral Pl BERM/RHTH SE16 .... 103 E3
Admiral Seymour Rd ELTH/MOT SE9 . 143 F2
Admiral's Ga CNWCH SE10 .... 122 B4
Admiral Sq WBPTN SW10 * 114 C4
Admiral St DEPT SE8 .... 122 A4
Admiral's Wk HAMP NW3 .... 54 C5
Admirals Wy POP/IOD E14 .... 104 A3
Admiralty Cl DEPT SE8 * 122 A4
Adolf St CAT SE6 .... 158 A4
Adolphus Rd FSBYPK N4 .... 58 B4
Adolphus St DEPT SE8 .... 121 F3
Adpar St BAY/PAD W2 .... 16 A2
Adrian Ms WBPTN SW10 .... 114 B2
Advance Rd WNWD SE27 .... 154 C4
Adys Lawn CRICK NW2 * 70 B3
Adys Rd PECK SE15 .... 137 F1
Affleck St IS N1 * 9 F2
Afghan Rd BTSEA SW11 .... 115 E5
Aftab Ter WCHPL E1 * 90 B3
Agamemnon Rd KIL/WHAMP NW6 ... 71 F2
Agar Gv CAMTN NW1 .... 75 D4
Agar St CHCR WC2N 32 C2
Agate Cl CAN/RD E16 .... 95 D5
Agate Rd HMSMTH W6 .... 100 C4
Agatha Cl WAP E1W * 102 B2
Agaton Rd ELTH/MOT SE9 .... 162 C2
Agave Rd CRICK NW2 .... 70 C1
Agdon St FSBYE EC1V 10 C5
Agincourt Rd HAMP NW3 .... 73 F1
Agnes Av IL IG1 .... 84 A1
Agnes Cl EHAM E6 .... 108 A1
Agnes Riley Gdns CLAP SW4 * 134 C5
Agnes Rd ACT W3 .... 99 F5
Agnes St POP/IOD E14 .... 91 F5
Agnew Rd FSTH SE23 .... 139 E5
Ailsa Rd POP/IOD E14 .... 92 C4
Ainger Rd HAMP NW3 .... 73 F4
Ainsdale Dr STHWK SE1 .... 120 A1
Ainsley St BETH E2 .... 90 B2
Ainsty St BERM/RHTH SE16 * 102 C3
Ainsworth Cl CMBW SE5 .... 119 E5
  CRICK NW2 .... 52 A5
Ainsworth Rd HOM E9 .... 78 C4
Ainsworth Wy STJWD NW8 .... 72 C5
Aintree Av EHAM E6 .... 83 E5
Aintree St FUL/PGN SW6 .... 113 E5
Airdrie Cl IS N1 * 75 F4
Airedale Av CHSWK W4 .... 111 F1
Airedale Av South CHSWK W4 * 111 F1
Airedale Rd BAL SW12 .... 133 F5
Airlie Gdns IL IG1 .... 66 B3
  KENS W8 .... 26 A4
Air St REGST W1B 31 F2
Aisgill Av WKENS W14 .... 113 F1
Aislibie Rd LEE/GVPK SE12 .... 141 E2
Aiten Pl HMSMTH W6 .... 100 A5
Aitken Cl HACK E8 .... 78 A5
Aitken Rd CAT SE6 .... 158 B2
Aitman Dr BTFD TW8 * 110 A1
Ajax Rd KIL/WHAMP NW6 .... 71 F1
Akehurst St PUT/ROE SW15 .... 130 A4
Akenside Rd HAMP NW3 .... 73 D2
Akerman Rd BRXN/ST SW9 .... 118 B4
Alabama St WOOL/PLUM SE18 .... 127 D3
Alan Hocken Wy SRTFD E15 .... 93 E1
Alan Rd WIM/MER SW19 .... 149 E5
Alanthus Cl LEE/GVPK SE12 .... 141 F4
Alaska St STHWK SE1 .... 34 A4
Albacore Crs LEW SE13 .... 140 B4
Alba Gdns GLDGN NW11 .... 53 E1
Albany Cl MORT/ESHN SW14 .... 128 B2
Albany Ctyd MYFR/PICC W1J 31 E2
Albany Ms CMBW SE5 .... 118 C2
  IS N1 * 76 A4
Albany Rd CHST BR7 .... 162 B5
  CMBW SE5 .... 119 E2
  FSBYPK N4 .... 57 F1
  LEY E10 .... 62 A2
  MNPK E12 .... 83 D1
  WALTH E17 .... 61 E1
  WALW SE17 .... 119 D2

  WIM/MER SW19 .... 150 B5
Albany St CAMTN NW1 .... 7 D3
Alba Pl NTGHL W11 .... 89 F5
Albatross St WOOL/PLUM SE18 .... 127 E3
Albatross St WOOL/PLUM SE18 .... 127 E3
Albemarle Ap GNTH/NBYPK IG2 .... 66 B1
Albemarle Gdns GNTH/NBYPK IG2 .... 66 B1
Albemarle St CONDST W1S 31 E2
Albemarle Wy FSBYE EC1V 22 C1
Alberta Est WALW SE17 .... 118 B1
Alberta St WALW SE17 .... 118 B1
Albert Av VX/NE SW8 .... 117 F3
Albert Basin Wy EHAM E6 .... 108 C1
Albert Br BTSEA SW11 .... 115 E3
Albert Bridge Rd BTSEA SW11 .... 115 E3
Albert Bridge Rd BTSEA SW11 .... 115 E3
Albert Carr Gdns STRHM/NOR SW16 . 153 E5
Albert Cl HOM E9 .... 78 B5
Albert Cots WCHPL E1 * 90 A4
Albert Dr WIM/MER SW19 .... 149 E2
Albert Emb STHWK SE1 .... 117 E1
Albert Gdns WCHPL E1 .... 91 D5
Albert Ga KTBR SW1X 29 F5
Albert Ms BROCKY SE4 * 139 F2
  FSBYPK N4 * 57 F3
  KENS W8 .... 39 E2
  POP/IOD E14 * 103 E1
Albert Pl KENS W8 * 39 D1
Albert Rd CAN/RD E16 .... 107 E2
  ELTH/MOT SE9 .... 161 E3
  FSBYPK N4 * 57 F3
  IL IG1 .... 66 C5
  KIL/WHAMP NW6 .... 89 F1
  LEY E10 .... 62 C4
  SEVS/STOTM N15 .... 59 E1
Albert Sq SRTFD E15 .... 81 E2
  VX/NE SW8 .... 117 F3
Albert Terrace Ms CAMTN NW1 * 74 A5
Albert Ter CAMTN NW1 .... 74 A5
  WLSDN NW10 * 69 D5
Albert Wy PECK SE15 .... 120 B3
Albion Av VX/NE SW8 .... 117 D5
Albion Cl BAY/PAD W2 .... 29 D1
Albion Dr HACK E8 .... 77 F4
Albion Est BERM/RHTH SE16 * 102 C3
Albion Ga BAY/PAD W2 .... 29 D1
Albion Gv STNW/STAM N16 .... 77 E1
Albion Ms BAY/PAD W2 .... 17 D5
  HMSMTH W6 .... 100 B5
  IS N1 * 76 A3
Albion Pl FARR EC1M 22 C2
  HMSMTH W6 .... 100 B5
Albion Riverside BTSEA SW11 .... 115 E3
Albion Rd STNW/STAM N16 .... 77 D2
Albion Sq HACK E8 .... 77 F4
Albion St BAY/PAD W2 .... 17 D5
  BERM/RHTH SE16 .... 102 C3
Albion Ter HACK E8 .... 77 F4
Albion Villas Rd SYD SE26 .... 156 C3
Albion Wk IS N1 .... 9 D2
Albion Wy LEW SE13 .... 140 C2
  STBT EC1A 23 E3
  WBLY HA9 .... 50 A5
Albion Yd IS N1 .... 9 D2
Albrighton Rd EDUL SE22 .... 137 E1
Albury Ms MNPK E12 .... 64 C3
Albury St DEPT SE8 .... 122 A4
Albyn Rd DEPT SE8 .... 122 A4
Alcester Crs CLPT E5 .... 60 B4
Alconbury Rd CLPT E5 .... 60 A4
Aldborough Rd South
  GDMY/SEVK IG3 .... 67 E3
Aldbourne Rd SHB W12 .... 99 F3
Aldbridge St WALW SE17 .... 119 E1
Aldburgh Ms MHST W1U 18 B4
Aldbury Av WBLY HA9 .... 68 B4
Aldebert Ter VX/NE SW8 .... 117 F3
Aldeburgh St GNWCH SE10 .... 124 A1
Alden Av SRTFD E15 .... 93 F2
Aldenham St CAMTN NW1 .... 7 F2
Aldensley Rd HMSMTH W6 .... 100 B4
Alderbrook Rd BAL SW12 .... 134 B4
Alderbury Rd BARN SW13 .... 112 A2
Alder Cl PECK SE15 .... 119 F2
Alder Gv CRICK NW2 .... 52 A4
Alderholt Wy PECK SE15 * 119 E3
Aldermanbury CITYW EC2V * 23 F4
Aldermanbury Sq CITYW EC2V 23 F3
Aldermoor Rd CAT SE6 .... 157 F3
Alderney Ms STHWK SE1 .... 48 A3
Alderney Rd WCHPL E1 .... 91 D3

Alderney St *PIM* SW1V 42 C5
Alder Rd *MORT/ESHN* SW14 .... 129 H1
  SCUP DA14 .... 163 E3
Aldersbrook La *MNPK* E12 .... 65 F5
Aldersbrook Rd *MNPK* E12 .... 64 B4
Alders Cl *WAN* E11 .... 64 B4
Aldersey Gdns *BARK* IG11 .... 85 D5
Aldersford Cl *BROCKY* SE4 .... 139 D2
Aldersgate St *CITYW* EC2Y 23 E4
  STBT EC1A 23 E4
Aldersgrove Av *ELTH/MOT* SE9 .... 160 C3
Aldershot Rd *KIL/WHAMP* NW6 .... 71 F5
Aldershot Ter *WOOL/PLUM* SE18 * 126 A5
Alders St *NKENS* W10 .... 89 E3
The Alders *STRHM/NOR* SW16 * 152 C4
Alderton Cl *WLSDN* NW10 .... 51 D5
Alderton Rd *HNHL* SE24 .... 136 C1
Alderville Rd *FUL/PGN* SW6 .... 113 F5
Alderwood Rd *ELTH/MOT* SE9 .... 145 D4
Aldford St *MYFR/PKLN* W1K 30 A3
Aldgate *FENCHST* EC3M 25 D5
Aldgate Barrs *WCHPL* E1 * 25 F4
Aldgate High St *TWRH* EC3N 25 D5
Aldine St *SHB* W12 .... 100 C3
Aldington Rd *CHARL* SE7 .... 107 D3
Aldis Ms *TOOT* SW17 .... 151 E5
Aldis St *TOOT* SW17 .... 151 E5
Aldred Rd *KIL/WHAMP* NW6 .... 72 A2
Aldren Rd *TOOT* SW17 .... 150 C3
Aldrich Ter *WAND/EARL* SW18 .... 150 C2
Aldridge Road Vls *NTGHL* W11 .... 89 F4
Aldrington Rd *STRHM/NOR* SW16 .... 152 C5
Aldsworth Cl *MV/WKIL* W9 .... 14 C1
Aldwick Cl *ELTH/MOT* SE9 .... 163 D5
Aldworth Gv *LEW* SE13 .... 140 C4
Aldworth Rd *SRTFD* E15 .... 81 E4
Aldwych *HOL/ALD* WC2B 21 E5
Alestan Beck Rd *CAN/RD* E16 .... 95 D5
Alexander Av *WLSDN* NW10 .... 70 B4
Alexander Cl *BFN/LL* DA15 .... 145 E3
Alexander Evans Ms *FSTH* SE23 .... 157 D2
Alexander Ms *BAY/PAD* W2 .... 14 A3
Alexander Pl *SKENS* SW7 .... 40 C4
Alexander Sq *CHEL* SW3 .... 40 C4
Alexander St *BAY/PAD* W2 .... 14 B4
Alexandra *DEPT* SE8 .... 121 F2
Alexandra Av *BTSEA* SW11 * 116 A4
Alexandra Cots *NWCR* SE14 .... 121 F4
Alexandra Dr *NRWD* SE19 .... 155 F5
Alexandra Ga *SKENS* SW7 .... 28 A5
Alexandra Gv *FSBYPK* N4 .... 58 B3
Alexandra Pl *STJWD* NW8 .... 72 C5
Alexandra Rd *CHSWK* W4 .... 99 D3
  EHAM E6 .... 96 A2
  LEY E10 .... 62 C5
  MORT/ESHN SW14 .... 129 D1
  STJWD NW8 .... 72 C4
  WALTH E17 .... 61 F1
  WIM/MER SW19 .... 150 A5
Alexandra St *CAN/RD* E16 .... 94 A4
  NWCR SE14 .... 121 F3
Alexis St *BERM/RHTH* SE16 .... 102 A5
Alfearn Rd *CLPT* E5 .... 78 C1
Alford Pl *IS* N1 .... 11 F2
Alfreda St *BTSEA* SW11 .... 116 B4
Alfred Cl *CHSWK* W4 .... 99 D5
Alfred Ms *GWRST* WC1E 20 A2
Alfred Pl *GWRST* WC1E 20 A2
Alfred Rd *ACT* W3 .... 98 C2
  BAY/PAD W2 .... 14 B2
  SRTFD E15 .... 81 F2
Alfred's Gdns *BARK* IG11 .... 97 E1
Alfred St *BOW* E3 .... 91 F2
Alfred's Way (East Ham & Barking
  By-Pass) *BARK* IG11 * 97 D1
Alfreton Cl *WIM/MER* SW19 .... 149 D3
Alfriston Rd *BTSEA* SW11 .... 133 F1
Algarve Rd *WAND/EARL* SW18 .... 150 B1
Algernon Rd *HDN* NW4 .... 52 A1
  KIL/WHAMP NW6 .... 72 A5
  LEW SE13 .... 140 A2
Algiers Rd *LEW* SE13 .... 140 A2
Alice La *BOW* E3 .... 79 F5
Alice St *STHWK* SE1 .... 48 C3
Alice Thompson Cl *LEE/GVPK* SE12 .... 160 C2
Alice Walker Cl *HNHL* SE24 * 136 B2
Alie St *WCHPL* E1 .... 25 F5
Alington Crs *CDALE/KGS* NW9 .... 50 C3
Alison Cl *EHAM* E6 .... 96 A5
Aliwal Ms *BTSEA* SW11 * 133 E2
Aliwal Rd *BTSEA* SW11 .... 133 E2

Alkerden Rd *CHSWK* W4 .... 111 E1
Alkham Rd *STNW/STAM* N16 .... 59 F4
Allan Barclay Cl *SEVS/STOTM* N15 .... 59 F1
Allan Wy *ACT* W3 .... 86 C4
Allardyce St *CLAP* SW4 .... 135 F2
Allcroft Rd *KTTN* NW5 .... 74 A3
Allenby Rd *FSTH* SE23 .... 157 E3
  WOOL/PLUM SE18 .... 108 C4
Allendale Cl *CMBW* SE5 .... 119 D5
  SYD SE26 .... 157 D5
Allen Edwards Dr *VX/NE* SW8 .... 117 E4
Allen Rd *BOW* E3 .... 91 F1
  STNW/STAM N16 .... 77 E1
Allensbury Pl *CAMTN* NW1 .... 75 D4
Allen St *KENS* W8 .... 38 B2
Allenswood Rd *ELTH/MOT* SE9 .... 143 E1
Allerford Rd *CAT* SE6 .... 158 B4
Allerton Rd *STNW/STAM* N16 .... 58 C4
Allerton St *IS* N1 .... 12 B2
Allestree Rd *FUL/PGN* SW6 .... 113 E3
Alleyn Crs *DUL* SE21 .... 155 D2
Alleyn Pk *DUL* SE21 .... 155 D2
Alleyn Rd *DUL* SE21 .... 155 D3
Allfarthing La *WAND/EARL* SW18 .... 132 C4
Allgood St *BETH* E2 .... 13 F2
Allhallows La *CANST* EC4R 36 A2
Allhallows Rd *EHAM* E6 .... 95 E5
Alliance Rd *ACT* W3 .... 86 B3
  PLSTW E13 .... 94 C3
Allied Wy *ACT* W3 * 99 E3
Allington Cl *WIM/MER* SW19 .... 149 D5
Allington Rd *NKENS* W10 .... 89 E2
  BGVA SW1W 43 D3
  WESTW SW1E 43 D3
Allison Cl *GNWCH* SE10 .... 122 C4
Allison Gv *DUL* SE21 .... 155 E1
Allison Rd *ACT* W3 .... 86 C5
Allitsen Rd *STJWD* NW8 .... 4 C2
Alloa Rd *DEPT* SE8 .... 121 D1
Alloway Rd *BOW* E3 .... 91 E2
Allport Ms *WCHPL* E1 * 90 C4
All Saints Dr *BKHTH/KID* SE3 .... 123 F5
All Saints Pas *WAND/EARL* SW18 * 132 A3
All Saints' Rd *ACT* W3 .... 98 C4
  NTGHL W11 .... 89 F4
All Saints St *IS* N1 .... 8 E1
Allsop Pl *CAMTN* NW1 .... 17 F1
All Souls' Av *WLSDN* NW10 .... 88 B1
All Souls' Pl *REGST* W1B 19 D3
Allwood Cl *SYD* SE26 .... 157 D4
Almack Rd *CLPT* E5 .... 78 C1
Alma Gv *STHWK* SE1 .... 49 F5
Alma Pl *WLSDN* NW10 .... 88 B2
Alma Rd *WAND/EARL* SW18 .... 132 C3
Alma Sq *STJWD* NW8 .... 3 F1
Alma St *KTTN* NW5 .... 74 B3
  SRTFD E15 .... 81 D3
Alma Ter *BOW* E3 .... 79 F5
  KENS W8 .... 38 B3
  WAND/EARL SW18 .... 133 D5
Almeida St *IS* N1 .... 76 B5
Almeric Rd *BTSEA* SW11 .... 133 F2
Almington St *FSBYPK* N4 * 57 E3
Almond Cl *PECK* SE15 .... 120 A5
Almond Rd *BERM/RHTH* SE16 .... 102 B5
Almorah Rd *IS* N1 .... 77 D4
Alnwick Rd *CAN/RD* E16 .... 94 C5
  LEE/GVPK SE12 .... 142 B5
Alnwick Ter *LEE/GVPK* SE12 .... 142 B5
Alperton St *NKENS* W10 .... 89 E3
Alpha Cl *CAMTN* NW1 .... 5 D1
Alpha Gv *POP/IOD* E14 .... 104 A3
Alpha Pl *CHEL* SW3 .... 115 E2
  KIL/WHAMP NW6 .... 2 B1
Alpha Rd *NWCR* SE14 .... 121 F4
Alpha St *PECK* SE15 .... 120 A5
Alpine Gv *HOM* E9 .... 78 C4
Alpine Rd *BERM/RHTH* SE16 .... 102 C5
  LEY E10 .... 62 B4
Alpine Wy *EHAM* E6 .... 96 A4
Alric Av *WLSDN* NW10 .... 69 D4
Alroy Rd *FSBYPK* N4 .... 58 A2
Alsace Rd *WALW* SE17 .... 119 E1
Alscot Rd *STHWK* SE1 .... 49 F3
Alscot Wy *STHWK* SE1 .... 49 E4
Alston Rd *TOOT* SW17 .... 151 D4
Altash Wy *ELTH/MOT* SE9 .... 161 F2
Altenburg Gdns *BTSEA* SW11 .... 133 F2
Althea St *FUL/PGN* SW6 .... 114 B5
Althorp Rd *TOOT* SW17 .... 151 F1
Altmore Av *EHAM* E6 .... 83 F4

Alton Rd PUT/ROE SW15....148 A1
Alton St POP/IOD E14....92 B4
Alvanley Gdns KIL/WHAMP NW6....72 B2
Alverstone Av WAND/EARL SW18....150 A2
Alverstone Gdns ELTH/MOT SE9....162 B1
Alverstone Rd CRICK NW2....70 C4
  MNPK E12....84 A1
Alverton St DEPT SE8....121 F1
Alvey St WALW SE17....119 E1
Alvington Crs HACK E8....77 F2
Alwold Crs LEE/GVPK SE12....142 C4
Alwyn Av CHSWK W4....111 D1
Alwyne La IS N1 *....76 B4
Alwyne Pl IS N1....76 C3
Alwyne Rd IS N1....76 C4
Alwyne Sq IS N1....76 B3
Alwyne Vls IS N1....76 B4
Alwyn Gdns ACT W3....86 B5
Alyn Bank CEND/HSY/T N8 *....57 D1
Alyth Gdns GLDGN NW11....53 F1
Amar Ct WOOL/PLUM SE18....109 F5
Amardeep Ct WOOL/PLUM SE18....127 F1
Amazon St WCHPL E1....90 B5
Ambassador Gdns EHAM E6....95 F4
Ambassador Sq POP/IOD E14....104 B5
Ambergate St WALW SE17....118 B1
Amber Gv CRICK NW2....53 D3
Amberley Gv SYD SE26....156 B4
Amberley Rd LEY E10....62 A2
  MV/WKIL W9....14 B2
Amber St SRTFD E15 *....81 D3
Amblecote Cl LEE/GVPK SE12....160 B3
Amblecote Meadow LEE/GVPK SE12....160 B3
Amblecote Mdw LEE/GVPK SE12 *....160 B3
Amblecote Rd LEE/GVPK SE12....160 B3
Ambler Rd FSBYPK N4....58 B5
Ambleside Av STRHM/NOR SW16....153 D4
Ambleside Cl HOM E9....78 C2
  LEY E10....62 B2
Ambleside Rd WLSDN NW10....69 F4
Ambrosden Av WEST SW1P....43 F3
Ambrose Av GLDGN NW11....53 F1
Ambrose St BERM/RHTH SE16....102 B5
Amelia Cl ACT W3....98 B2
Amelia St WALW SE17....118 B1
Amen Cnr STP EC4M....23 D5
Amen Ct STP EC4M....23 D5
America Sq TWRH EC3N....37 E1
America St STHWK SE1....35 E4
Amerland Rd PUT/ROE SW15....131 F4
Amersham Gv NWCR SE14....121 F4
Amersham Rd NWCR SE14....121 F5
Amersham V NWCR SE14....121 F5
Amery Gdns WLSDN NW10....70 B5
Amesbury Av BRXS/STRHM SW2....153 E2
Ames Cots POP/IOD E14 *....91 E4
Amethyst St SRTFD E15....81 D1
Amhurst Pde STNW/STAM N16 *....59 E2
Amhurst Pk STNW/STAM N16....59 E2
Amhurst Rd STNW/STAM N16....77 F1
Amhurst Ter STNW/STAM N16....78 A1
Amiel St WCHPL E1....90 C3
Amies St BTSEA SW11....133 F1
Amina Wy BERM/RHTH SE16....102 A4
Amity Rd SRTFD E15....81 F4
Ammanford Gn CDALE/KGS NW9 *....51 E1
Amner Rd BTSEA SW11....134 A4
Amor Rd HMSMTH W6....100 A4
Amott Rd PECK SE15....138 A1
Ampthill Est CAMTN NW1....7 E2
Ampthill Sq CAMTN NW1....7 F2
Ampton St FSBYW WC1X....9 E4
Amroth Cl FSTH SE23....156 B1
Amroth Gn CDALE/KGS NW9 *....51 E1
Amsterdam Rd POP/IOD E14....104 C4
Amwell St CLKNW EC1R....10 A3
Amyruth Rd BROCKY SE4....140 A3
Amy Warne Cl EHAM E6....95 E4
Anatola Rd ARCH N19....56 B4
Ancaster St WOOL/PLUM SE18....127 E3
Anchorage Cl WIM/MER SW19....150 A5
Anchor & Hope La CHARL SE7....106 B4
Anchor Ms MNPK....65 D4
Anchor St BERM/RHTH SE16....102 B5
Anchor Ter WCHPL E1 *....90 C3
Anchor Yd FSBYE EC1V *....11 F5
Ancill Cl HMSMTH W6....113 D2
Ancona Rd WLSDN NW10....88 A1
  WOOL/PLUM SE18....127 D1
Andalus Rd BRXN/ST SW9....135 E1
Anderson Cl ACT W3....87 D5
Anderson Rd HOM E9....79 D3

Anderson Sq IS N1 *....76 B5
Anderson St CHEL SW3....115 F1
Andover Av CAN/RD E16....95 D5
Andover Pl KIL/WHAMP NW6....2 C2
Andover Rd HOLWY N7....57 F4
Andover Ter HMSMTH W6 *....100 B5
Andre St HACK E8....78 A2
Andrew Borde St LSQ/SEVD WC2H *....20 A1
Andrewes Gdns EHAM E6....95 E5
Andrew Pl VX/NE SW8....117 D4
Andrew Rd BETH E2....92 A2
Andrew St POP/IOD E14....92 C5
Andrews Wk WALW SE17....118 B2
Anfield Cl BAL SW12....134 C5
Angela Carter Cl BRXN/ST SW9....136 A1
Angel Aly WCHPL E1....25 F5
Angel Ct LOTH EC2R....24 B4
Angelica Dr EHAM E6....96 A4
Angel La SRTFD E15....81 D3
Angell Park Gdns BRXN/ST SW9....136 A1
Angell Rd BRXN/ST SW9....136 A2
Angell Town Est BRXN/ST SW9 *....118 A5
Angel Ms PUT/ROE SW15....130 A5
  WCHPL E1....102 B1
Angel Pas CANST EC4R....36 A2
Angel Sq FSBYE EC1V *....10 C2
Angel St STBT EC1A....23 E4
Angel Wk HMSMTH W6....100 C5
Angerstein La BKHTH/KID SE3....123 F5
Anglers La KTTN NW5....74 B3
Anglesea Ms WOOL/PLUM SE18....108 B5
Anglesea Rd WOOL/PLUM SE18....108 B5
Angles Rd STRHM/NOR SW16....153 E4
Anglo Rd BOW E3....91 F1
Angus Rd PLSTW E13....94 C2
Angus St NWCR SE14....121 E3
Anhalt Rd BTSEA SW11....115 E3
Ankerdine Crs WOOL/PLUM SE18....126 B4
Anley Rd HMSMTH W6....101 D5
Annabel Cl POP/IOD E14....92 B5
Anna Cl HACK E8....77 F5
Annandale Rd BFN/LL DA15....145 E5
  CHSWK W4....99 E5
  GNWCH SE10....123 F1
Anna Neagle Cl FSTGT E7....82 A1
Anne Compton Ms LEE/GVPK SE12....141 F5
Annesley Cl WLSDN NW10....51 E5
Annesley Rd BKHTH/KID SE3....124 B3
Annesmere Gdns BKHTH/KID SE3....143 D1
Anne St PLSTW E13....94 A3
Annette Rd HOLWY N7....57 F1
Annexe Market WCHPL E1 *....25 E2
Annie Besant Cl BOW E3 *....79 F5
Anning St WCHPL E1....13 D5
Annis Rd HOM E9....79 E3
Ann La WBPTN SW10....115 D3
Ann Moss Wy BERM/RHTH SE16....102 C4
Ann's Cl KTBR SW1X....41 F1
Ann St WOOL/PLUM SE18....109 D5
Ansdell Rd PECK SE15....120 C5
Ansdell St KENS W8....39 D2
Ansdell Ter KENS W8....39 D2
Ansell Rd TOOT SW17....151 F3
Anselm Rd FUL/PGN SW6....114 A2
Ansford Rd BMLY BR1....158 C5
Ansleigh Pl NTGHL W11....101 D1
Anson Rd ARCH N19....74 C1
  CRICK NW2....70 B2
Anstey Rd PECK SE15....138 A1
Anstice Cl CHSWK W4....111 E3
Anstridge Rd ELTH/MOT SE9....145 D4
Antelope Rd WOOL/PLUM SE18....107 F4
Anthony's Cl WAP E1W....102 B2
Anthony St WCHPL E1....90 B5
Antill Rd BOW E3....91 E2
Antill Ter WCHPL E1....91 D5
Anton Pl WBLY HA9....50 B5
Anton St HACK E8....78 A2
Antrim Rd HAMP NW3....73 F3
Antrobus Rd CHSWK W4....98 C5
Apollo Pl WAN E11....115 (check)
  WBPTN SW10 *....115 D5
Apollo Wy THMD SE28....109 D4
Apothecary St BLKFR EC4V *....22 C5
Appach Rd BRXS/STRHM SW2....136 A3
Apple Blossom Ct VX/NE SW8 *....117 D3
Appleby Rd CAN/RD E16....94 A5
  HACK E8....78 A4
Appleby St BETH E2....13 E1
Appledore Cl TOOT SW17....151 F2
Appledore Crs SCUP DA14....163 E3

Appleford Rd *NKENS* W10	89	E3
Applegarth Rd *WKENS* W14 *	101	D4
Apple Rd *WAN* E11	63	E5
Appleton Rd *ELTH/MOT* SE9	143	E1
Apple Tree Yd *STJS* SW1Y	31	F3
Applewood Cl *CRICK* NW2	52	B5
Applewood Dr *PLSTW* E13	94	B3
Appold St *SDTCH* EC2A	24	C2
Apprentice Wy *CLPT* E5	78	B1
Approach Rd *BETH* E2	90	C1
The Approach *ACT* W3	87	D5
April Gln *FSTH* SE23	157	D3
April St *HACK* E8	77	F1
Apsley Wy *CRICK* NW2	52	A4
MYFR/PICC W1J *	30	C4
Aquila St *STJWD* NW8	4	B1
Aquinas St *STHWK* SE1	34	B4
Arabella Dr *PUT/ROE* SW15	129	E2
Arabin Rd *BROCKY* SE4	139	E2
Arbery Rd *BOW* E3	91	E2
Arborfield Cl *BRXS/STRHM* SW2	153	F1
Arbour Sq *WCHPL* E1	91	D5
Arbour Cl *BAY/PAD* W2	17	D5
Arbutus St *HACK* E8	77	F5
Arcade Chambers *ELTH/MOT* SE9 *	144	A4
The Arcade *ELTH/MOT* SE9 *	144	A4
LVPST EC2M *	24	C3
Arcadian Pl *WAND/EARL* SW18	131	E5
Arcadia St *POP/IOD* E14	92	A5
Archangel St *BERM/RHTH* SE16	103	D5
Archbishop's Pl *BRXS/STRHM* SW2	135	F4
Archdale Rd *EDUL* SE22	137	F3
Archel Rd *WKENS* W14	113	F2
Archer Sq *NWCR* SE14	121	E2
Archer St *SOHO/SHAV* W1D	32	A1
Archery Cl *BAY/PAD* W2	17	D5
Archery Rd *ELTH/MOT* SE9	143	F5
The Arches *SOHO/SHAV* W1D	33	D1
Archibald Rd *HOLWY* N7	75	D1
Archibold St *BOW* E3	92	A2
Arch St *STHWK* SE1	47	E3
Archway Cl *ARCH* N19 *	56	B4
NKENS W10	89	D4
WIM/MER SW19	150	B4
Archway Rd *HGT* N6	56	B1
Archway St *BARN* SW13	129	E1
Arcola St *HACK* E8	77	F2
Arctic St *KTTN* NW5	74	B2
Ardbeg Rd *HNHL* SE24	137	D4
Arden Court Gdns *EFNCH* N2	55	D1
Arden Crs *POP/IOD* E14	104	A5
Arden Est *IS* N1	12	C2
Ardfillan Rd *CAT* SE6	159	D1
Ardgowan Rd *CAT* SE6	141	D5
Ardilaun Rd *HBRY* N5	76	C1
Ardleigh Rd *IS* N1	77	D3
Ardley Cl *CAT* SE6	157	E5
WLSDN NW10	51	E5
Ardlui Rd *WNWD* SE27	154	C2
Ardmere Rd *LEW* SE13	141	D4
Ardoch Rd *CAT* SE6	159	D2
Ardshiel Cl *PUT/ROE* SW15	131	D1
Ardwell Rd *BRXS/STRHM* SW2	153	E2
Ardwick Rd *CRICK* NW2	72	A1
Arena Est *FSBYPK* N4 *	58	B1
Argall Av *LEY* E10	61	D2
Argall Wy *LEY* E10	61	D3
Argenta Wy *WLSDN* NW10	68	B4
Argon Ms *FUL/PGN* SW6	114	A3
Argyle Pl *HMSMTH* W6	100	A3
Argyle Rd *CAN/RD* E16	94	B5
IL IG1	66	A4
SRTFD E15	81	E5
WCHPL E1	91	D3
Argyle Sq *STPAN* WC1H	9	D3
Argyle St *CAMTN* NW1	8	C3
STPAN WC1H	9	D4
Argyle Wk *STPAN* WC1H *	8	C4
Argyle Wy *BERM/RHTH* SE16	120	A1
Argyll Cl *BRXN/ST* SW9	135	F1
Argyll St *KENS* W8	38	A1
WOOL/PLUM SE18	108	C4
Argyll St *SOHO/SHAV* W1D	19	E5
Arbchie St *STHWK* SE1	49	D1
Arica Rd *BROCKY* SE4	139	E2
Ariel Rd *KIL/WHAMP* NW6	72	A3
Ariel Wy *SHB* W12	100	C2
Aristotle Rd *CLAP* SW4	135	D1
Arkindale Rd *CAT* SE6	158	C3
Arklow Rd *NWCR* SE14	121	F2
Arkwright Rd *HAMP* NW3	72	C2

Arlesford Rd *BRXN/ST* SW9	135	E1
Arlingford Rd *BRXS/STRHM* SW2	136	A4
Arlington Av *IS* N1	76	C5
Arlington Cl *BFN/LL* DA15	145	E5
LEW SE13	141	D3
Arlington Gdns *CHSWK* W4	110	C1
IL IG1	65	F2
Arlington Pde *BRXS/STRHM* SW2 *	135	F3
Arlington Rd *CAMTN* NW1	74	B5
Arlington Sq *IS* N1	76	C5
Arlington St *MYFR/PICC* W1J	31	E3
Arlington Wy *CLKNW* EC1R	10	B3
Armadale Rd *FUL/PGN* SW6	114	A3
Armada St *DEPT* SE8	122	A2
Armada Wy *EHAM* E6	96	B4
EHAM E6	96	C4
Armagh Rd *BOW* E3	79	F5
Arminger Rd *SHB* W12	100	B2
Armitage Rd *GLDGN* NW11	53	E5
GNWCH SE10	105	F5
Armour Cl *HOLWY* N7	75	F3
Armoury Rd *DEPT* SE8	122	B5
Armoury Wy *WAND/EARL* SW18	132	A3
Armstrong Cl *EHAM* E6	95	F3
Armstrong Rd *ACT* W3	99	F2
WLSDN NW10	69	E4
WOOL/PLUM SE18	108	C4
Arnal Crs *WAND/EARL* SW18	131	E5
Arne St *LSQ/SEVD* WC2H	21	D5
Arne Wk *LEW* SE13	141	F2
Arneway St *WEST* SW1P	44	B3
Arnewood Cl *PUT/ROE* SW15	148	A1
Arngask Rd *CAT* SE6	141	D5
Arnheim Pl *POP/IOD* E14	104	A4
Arnold Circ *BETH* E2	13	E4
Arnold Est *STHWK* SE1	49	F4
Arnold Rd *BOW* E3	92	A2
Arnott Cl *CHSWK* W4	99	D5
Arnould Av *CMBW* SE5	137	D2
Arnside Rd *WALW* SE17	118	C2
Arnulf St *CAT* SE6	158	B4
Arodene Rd *BRXS/STRHM* SW2	135	F4
Aragon Rd *EHAM* E6	83	D5
WAND/EARL SW18	150	A1
Arran Dr *MNPK* E12	65	D3
Arran Rd *CAT* SE6	158	B2
Arran Wk *IS* N1	76	C4
Arrow Rd *BOW* E3	92	B2
Arsenal Rd *ELTH/MOT* SE9	125	F5
Arsenal Wy *CAN/RD* E16	108	A3
WOOL/PLUM SE18	108	C5
Artemis Pl *WAND/EARL* SW18	131	F5
Artesian Cl *WLSDN* NW10	69	D4
Artesian Rd *BAY/PAD* W2	14	A5
Arthingworth St *SRTFD* E15	81	E5
Arthurdon Rd *BROCKY* SE4	140	A3
Arthur Gv *WOOL/PLUM* SE18	108	C5
Arthur Rd *EHAM* E6	95	F1
HOLWY N7	75	F1
WIM/MER SW19	150	A5
Arthur St *CANST* EC4R	36	B2
Artichoke Hl *WAP* E1W	102	B1
Artichoke Pl *CMBW* SE5 *	119	D4
Artillery Cl *GNTH/NBYPK* IG2	66	C1
Artillery La *LVPST* EC2M	25	D3
SHB W12	88	A5
Artillery Pas *WCHPL* E1 *	25	D3
Artillery Pl *WOOL/PLUM* SE18	125	F1
Artillery Rw *WEST* SW1P	44	A3
Artizan St *WCHPL* E1	25	D4
Artwell Cl *LEY* E10	62	B1
Arundel Cl *BTSEA* SW11	133	E5
SRTFD E15	81	E1
Arundel Gdns *NTGHL* W11	101	F1
Arundel Gv *IS* N1	77	E2
Arundel Pl *HOLWY* N7	76	A3
Arundel Sq *HOLWY* N7	76	A3
Arundel St *TPL/STR* WC2R	33	F1
Arundel Ter *BARN* SW13	112	B2
Arungford Ms *BRXS/STRHM* SW2	136	A3
Arvon Rd *HBRY* N5	76	A2
Asbaston Ter *IL* IG1	84	C2
Ascalon St *VX/NE* SW8	116	C3
Ascham St *KTTN* NW5	74	C2
Ascot Pde *CLAP* SW4 *	135	E2
Ascot Rd *EHAM* E6	95	F2
Ashanti Ms *HACK* E8 *	78	B3
Ashbourne Gv *CHSWK* W4	111	E1
EDUL SE22	137	F3
Ashbridge Rd *WAN* E11	63	E2
Ashbridge St *STJWD* NW8	16	C1

Ashbrook Rd *ARCH* N19	57	D4
Ashburn Gdns *SKENS* SW7	39	E4
Ashburnham Gv *GNWCH* SE10	122	B3
Ashburnham Pl *GNWCH* SE10	122	B3
Ashburnham Retreat		
GNWCH SE10	122	B3
Ashburnham Rd *WBPTN* SW10 *	114	C3
WLSDN NW10	88	C2
Ashburn Pl *SKENS* SW7	39	E4
Ashburton Av *GDMY/SEVK* IG3	85	F1
Ashburton Rd *CAN/RD* E16	94	A5
Ashbury Rd *BTSEA* SW11	133	F1
Ashby Gv *IS* N1	76	C4
Ashby Ms *BROCKY* SE4	139	F1
Ashby Rd *BROCKY* SE4	121	F5
Ashby St *FSBYE* EC1V	11	D1
Ashchurch Gv *SHB* W12	100	A3
Ashchurch Park Vis *SHB* W12	100	A4
Ashchurch Ter *SHB* W12	99	F4
Ashcombe Pk *CRICK* NW2	51	E5
Ashcombe Rd *WIM/MER* SW19	150	A5
Ashcombe St *FUL/PGN* SW6 *	114	B5
Ashcroft Rd *BOW* E3	91	E2
Ashdale Rd *LEE/GVPK* SE12	160	B1
Ashdown Crs *KTTN* NW5 *	74	A2
Ashdown Rd *WLSDN* NW10	69	G3
Ashdown Wy *TOOT* SW17	152	A2
Ashen *EHAM* E6	96	A5
Ashenden Rd *CLPT* E5	79	E2
Ashen Gv *WIM/MER* SW19	150	A3
Asher Wy *WAP* E1W	102	A2
Ashfield Rd *ACT* W3	99	F2
FSBYPK N4	58	C1
Ashfield St *WCHPL* E1	90	B4
Ashfield Yd *WCHPL* E1 *	90	C4
Ashford Cl *WALTH* E17	61	F1
Ashford Rd *CRICK* NW2	71	D1
EHAM E6	83	F3
Ashford St *IS* N1	12	C3
Ash Gv *CRICK* NW2	71	D1
HACK E8	78	B5
Ashgrove Rd *GDMY/SEVK* IG3	67	F3
Ashington Rd *FUL/PGN* SW6 *	113	F5
Ashlake Rd *STRHM/NOR* SW16	153	E4
Ashland Pl *MHST* W1U	18	A2
Ashlar Pl *WOOL/PLUM* SE18	108	B5
Ashleigh Rd *MORT/ESHN* SW14	129	E1
Ashley Crs *BTSEA* SW11	134	A1
Ashley Pl *WESTW* SW1E	43	E5
Ashley Rd *ARCH* N19	57	E3
FSTGT E7	82	C4
Ashlin Rd *SRTFD* E15	81	D1
Ashlone Rd *PUT/ROE* SW15	113	D5
Ashmead Ms *DEPT* SE8	122	A5
Ashmead Rd *DEPT* SE8	122	A5
Ashmere Gv *BRXS/STRHM* SW2	135	E2
Ash Ms *KTTN* NW5 *	74	B2
Ashmill St *STJWD* NW8	16	C2
Ashmole St *VX/NE* SW8	117	F2
Ashmore Cl *PECK* SE15	119	F3
Ashmore Gv *WELL* DA16	145	D1
Ashmore Rd *MV/WKIL* W9	89	F2
Ashmount Rd *ARCH* N19	56	C2
Ashness Rd *BTSEA* SW11	133	F3
Ashridge Crs *WOOL/PLUM* SE18	126	C3
Ash Rd *SRTFD* E15	81	E2
Ashtead Rd *STNW/STAM* N16	60	A2
Ashton Rd *SRTFD* E15	81	D2
Ashton St *POP/IOD* E14	104	C1
Ashurst Dr *GNTH/NBYPK* IG2	66	B1
Ashurst Gdns *BRXS/STRHM* SW2 *	154	A1
Ashvale Rd *TOOT* SW17	151	F5
Ashville Rd *WAN* E11	63	D4
Ashwater Rd *LEE/GVPK* SE12	160	C1
Ashwell Cl *EHAM* E6	95	F5
Ashwin St *HACK* E8	77	F3
Ashworth Cl *CMBW* SE5	119	D5
Ashworth Rd *MV/WKIL* W9	3	D3
Aske St *IS* N1	12	C3
Askew Crs *SHB* W12	99	F3
Askew Rd *SHB* W12	99	F3
Askham Rd *SHB* W12	100	A2
Askill Dr *PUT/ROE* SW15	131	E3
Asland Rd *SRTFD* E15	81	D5
Aslett St *WAND/EARL* SW18	132	B5
Asmara Rd *CRICK* NW2	71	D2
Aspen Cl *HACK* E8 *	78	A3
Aspenlea Rd *HMSMTH* W6	113	D2
Aspen Wy *POP/IOD* E14	104	C1
Aspern Gv *HAMP* NW3	73	E2
Aspinall Rd *BROCKY* SE4	139	D1
NWCR SE14	139	D1

Aspinden Rd *BERM/RHTH* SE16	102	B5
Aspley Rd *WAND/EARL* SW18	132	B3
Assam St *WCHPL* E1	90	A5
Assata Ms *IS* N1	76	B3
Assembly Pas *WCHPL* E1	90	C4
Astbury Rd *PECK* SE15	120	C4
Astell St *CHEL* SW3	115	E1
Asteys Rw *IS* N1	76	B4
Astle St *BTSEA* SW11	116	A5
Astley Av *CRICK* NW2	70	C2
Aston Gv *POP/IOD* E14	91	E5
Aston Ter *BAL* SW12 *	134	B4
Astonville St *WAND/EARL* SW18	150	A1
Astoria Pde *STRHM/NOR* SW16 *	153	E3
Astoria Wk *BRXN/ST* SW9	136	A1
Astrop Ms *HMSMTH* W6	100	C4
Astrop Ter *HMSMTH* W6	100	C4
Atwood Ms *WESTW* SW1E	39	D4
Asylum Rd *PECK* SE15	120	B3
Atalanta St *FUL/PGN* SW6	113	D4
Atheldene Rd *WAND/EARL* SW18	150	B1
Athelney St *CAT* SE6	158	A3
Athelstane Gv *BOW* E3	91	F1
Athelstane Ms *FSBYPK* N4	58	A3
Athelstan Gdns		
KIL/WHAMP NW6 *	71	E4
Athenlay Rd *PECK* SE15	139	D3
Athens Gdns *MV/WKIL* W9 *	14	A1
Atherden Rd *CLPT* E5	78	C1
Atherfold Rd *BRXN/ST* SW9	135	E1
Atherstone Ms *SKENS* SW7	39	F4
Atherton Dr *WIM/MER* SW19	149	D4
Atherton Ms *FSTGT* E7	81	F3
Atherton Rd *BARN* SW13	112	A3
FSTGT E7	81	F2
Atherton St *BTSEA* SW11	115	E5
Athlone Cl *CLPT* E5	78	B2
Athlone Rd *BRXS/STRHM* SW2	135	F5
Athlone St *KTTN* NW5	74	A3
Athol Sq *POP/IOD* E14	92	C5
Atkinson Rd *CAN/RD* E16	94	C4
Atkins Rd *BAL* SW12	134	C5
LEY E10	62	B1
Atlantic Rd *BRXN/ST* SW9	136	A2
Atlantis Av *EHAM* E6	108	C1
Atlas Gdns *CHARL* SE7	106	C5
Atlas Ms *HACK* E8	77	F3
Atlas Rd *PLSTW* E13	94	A1
WBLY HA9	50	B3
WLSDN NW10	87	E2
Atley Rd *BOW* E3	80	A5
Atney Rd *PUT/ROE* SW15	131	E2
Atterbury Rd *FSBYPK* N4	58	A1
Atterbury St *WEST* SW1P	44	A5
Attewood Av *WLSDN* NW10	51	E5
Attneave St *FSBYW* WC1X	10	A5
Atwell Rd *PECK* SE15 *	120	A5
Atwood Av *RCH/KEW* TW9	110	A5
Atwood Rd *HMSMTH* W6	100	B5
Aubert Pk *HBRY* N5	58	C5
Aubert Rd *HBRY* N5	76	B1
Aubrey Pl *STJWD* NW8	3	E2
Aubrey Rd *NTGHL* W11	101	F2
Aubrey Wk *KENS* W8	101	F2
Auburn Cl *NWCR* SE14	121	E3
Aubyn Hl *WNWD* SE27	154	C4
Aubyn Sq *PUT/ROE* SW15	130	A2
Auckland Hl *WNWD* SE27	154	C2
Auckland Rd *BTSEA* SW11	133	E2
IL IG1	66	B3
LEY E10	62	B5
Auckland St *LBTH* SE11	117	F1
Auden Pl *CAMTN* NW1	74	A5
Audley Cl *BTSEA* SW11	134	A1
Audley Dr *CAN/RD* E16	106	B2
Audley Gdns *GDMY/SEVK* IG3	67	F4
Audley Rd *HDN* NW4	52	A1
Audley Sq *MYFR/PKLN* W1K *	30	B3
Audley St *MYFR/PKLN* W1K	30	B3
Audrey Rd *IL* IG1	66	B5
Audrey St *BETH* E2	90	A1
Augurs La *PLSTW* E13	94	B2
Augustine Rd *HMSMTH* W6	101	D4
Augustus Cl *SHB* W12	100	B3
Augustus Rd *WIM/MER* SW19	149	D1
Augustus St *CAMTN* NW1	7	D2
Aulton Pl *LBTH* SE11	118	A1
Auriga Ms *IS* N1	77	D2
Auriol Rd *WKENS* W14	101	E5
Austen Cl *FSTH* SE23	139	E5
Austin Friars *OBST* EC2N	24	B4
Austin Friars Sq *OBST* EC2N *	24	B4

Austin Rd *BTSEA* SW11 .... 116 A4
Austin St *BETH* E2 .... 13 E4
Austral Cl *BFN/LL* DA15 .... 163 F5
Australia Rd *SHB* W12 .... 100 B1
Austral St *LBTH* SE11 .... 46 C4
Autumn St *BOW* E3 .... 80 A5
Avalon Rd *FUL/PGN* SW6 .... 114 B4
Avebury Rd *WAN* E11 .... 63 D3
Avebury St *IS* N1 .... 77 D5
Aveline St *LBTH* SE11 .... 117 F1
Ave Marie La *STP* EC4M 25 D5
Avenell Rd *HBRY* N5 .... 58 B5
Avening Rd *WAND/EARL* SW18 .. 132 A5
Avening Ter *WAND/EARL* SW18 ... 132 A4
Avenons Rd *PLSTW* E13 .... 94 A4
Avenue Crs *ACT* W3 .... 98 B3
Avenue Gdns *ACT* W3 .... 98 B3
  MORT/ESHN SW14 .... 129 E1
Avenue Park Rd *WNWD* SE27 ...... 154 B3
Avenue Rd *ACT* W3 .... 98 B3
  CEND/HSY/T N8 .... 57 D1
  FSTGT E7 .... 82 B1
  HGT N6 .... 56 C2
  STJWD NW8 .... 73 D4
  WLSDN NW10 .... 87 F1
The Avenue *CHSWK* W4 .... 98 B5
  CLAP SW4 .... 134 A3
  GNWCH SE10 .... 123 D3
  KIL/WHAMP NW6 .... 71 E4
  WAN E11 .... 64 B1
Averill St *HMSMTH* W6 .... 113 D2
Avery Farm Rw *BGVA* SW1W * ... 42 C5
Avery Hill Rd *ELTH/MOT* SE9 ..... 162 C1
Avery Rw *MYFR/PKLN* W1K 30 C1
Aviary Cl *CAN/RD* E16 .... 93 F4
Avignon Rd *BROCKY* SE4 .... 139 D1
Avington Wy *PECK* SE15 * 119 F3
Avis Sq *WCHPL* E1 .... 91 D5
Avoca Rd *TOOT* SW17 .... 152 A4
Avocet Cl *STHWK* SE1 .... 120 A1
Avocet Ms *THMD* SE28 .... 109 D4
Avondale Av *CRICK* NW2 .... 51 E5
Avondale Park Gdns
  NTGHL W11 .... 101 E1
Avondale Park Rd
  NTGHL W11 .... 101 E1
Avondale Pavement *STHWK* SE1 * .. 120 A1
Avondale Ri *PECK* SE15 .... 137 F1
Avondale Rd *CAN/RD* E16 .... 93 E4
  ELTH/MOT SE9 .... 161 E2
  MORT/ESHN SW14 .... 129 D1
  WALTH E17 .... 62 A2
  WIM/MER SW19 .... 150 B5
Avondale Sq *STHWK* SE1 .... 120 A1
Avonley Rd *NWCR* SE14 .... 120 C3
Avonmore Gdns *WKENS* W14 * ... 101 F5
Avonmore Pl *WKENS* W14 .... 101 F5
Avonmore Rd *WKENS* W14 .... 101 F5
Avonmouth St *STHWK* SE1 .... 47 E2
Avon Rd *BROCKY* SE4 .... 140 A1
Awliscombe Rd *WELL* DA16 .... 127 F5
Axe St *BARK* IG11 .... 84 C5
Axis St *GNWCH* SE10 .... 123 E2
Axminster Rd *HOLWY* N7 .... 57 E5
Axon Pl *IL* IG1 .... 66 C4
Aybrook St *MHST* W1U 18 A3
Aycliffe Rd *SHB* W12 .... 99 F2
Aylesbury Cl *FSTGT* E7 .... 81 F3
Aylesbury Rd *WALW* SE17 .... 119 D1
Aylesbury St *CLKNW* EC1R 22 C1
  WLSDN NW10 .... 51 D5
Aylesford St *PIM* SW1V 117 D1
Aylestone Av *KIL/WHAMP* NW6 ... 71 D4
Aylmer Rd *SHB* W12 .... 99 E3
  WAN E11 .... 63 F2
Aylton Est *BERM/RHTH* SE16 * ... 102 C3
Aylward Rd *FSTH* SE23 .... 157 D2
Aylward St *WCHPL* E1 .... 91 D5
Aymhoe Rd *WKENS* W14 .... 101 D5
Ayres Rd *PLSTW* E13 .... 94 A2
Ayres Crs *WLSDN* NW10 .... 69 D4
Ayres St *STHWK* SE1 .... 35 F5
Aysgarth Rd *DUL* SE21 .... 137 D4
Aytoun Pl *BRXN/ST* SW9 .... 117 F5
Aytoun Rd *BRXN/ST* SW9 .... 117 F5
Azalea Cl *IL* IG1 .... 84 B2
Azania Ms *KTTN* NW5 .... 74 B2
Azenby Rd *PECK* SE15 .... 119 F5
Azof St *GNWCH* SE10 .... 105 E5

B

Baalbec Rd *HBRY* N5 .... 76 B2
Babington Ri *WBLY* HA9 .... 68 A3
Babington Rd *STRHM/NOR* SW16 .. 153 D5
Babmaes St *STJS* SW1Y 32 A3
Bache's St *IS* N1 .... 12 B4
Back Church La *WCHPL* E1 .... 102 A1
Back Hl *CLKNW* EC1R 22 B1
Back La *HAMP* NW3 .... 72 C1
Back Rd *WAN* E11 .... 63 D1
Bacon Gv *STHWK* SE1 .... 49 E4
Bacon's La *HGT* N6 .... 56 A3
Bacon St *BETH* E2 .... 13 F5
Bacton St *BETH* E2 .... 90 C2
Baden Pl *STHWK* SE1 .... 36 A5
Baden Rd *IL* IG1 .... 84 B2
Badgers Cft *ELTH/MOT* SE9 ...... 162 A4
Badminton Ms *CAN/RD* E16 .... 106 A2
Badminton Rd *BAL* SW12 .... 134 A4
Badsworth Rd *CMBW* SE5 .... 118 C3
Bagley House
  WOOL/PLUM SE18 * 125 E3
Bagley's La *FUL/PGN* SW6 .... 114 B4
Bagshot Ct *WOOL/PLUM* SE18 * .. 126 A4
Bagshot St *WALW* SE17 .... 119 E1
Baildon St *DEPT* SE8 .... 121 F3
Bailey Cl *THMD* SE28 .... 109 E2
Bailey Cots *POP/IOD* E14 * 91 E4
Bailey House *WOOL/PLUM* SE18 * .. 125 E3
Bailey Ms *BRXS/STRHM* SW2 .... 136 A3
  CHSWK W4 .... 110 B2
Bainbridge St *NOXST/BSQ* WC1A .. 20 B4
Baird Cl *CDALE/KGS* NW9 .... 50 C1
  LEY E10 .... 62 A3
Baird Gdns *NRWD* SE19 .... 155 E4
Baird St *STLK* EC1Y 11 F5
Baizdon Rd *BKHTH/KID* SE3 ...... 123 E5
Baker Rd *WLSDN* NW10 .... 69 E5
  WOOL/PLUM SE18 .... 125 E3
Bakers Av *WALTH* E17 .... 62 B1
Bakers Fld *HOLWY* N7 .... 75 D1
Bakers Ms *MHST* W1U 18 A4
Baker's Rents *BETH* E2 .... 13 E3
Bakers Rw *SRTFD* E15 .... 93 E1
Baker's Rw *CLKNW* EC1R 22 A1
Baker St *CAMTN* NW1 .... 17 F1
  MHST W1U 18 A3
Baker's Yd *CLKNW* EC1R * 22 A1
Bakery Cl *BRXN/ST* SW9 * 117 F3
Balaam St *PLSTW* E13 .... 94 A2
Balaclava Rd *STHWK* SE1 .... 49 F5
Bala Gn *CDALE/KGS* NW9 * 51 E1
Balantyne Cl *ELTH/MOT* SE9 ..... 161 E4
Balcaskie Rd *ELTH/MOT* SE9 .... 143 F5
Balchier Rd *EDUL* SE22 .... 138 B4
Balcombe St *CAMTN* NW1 .... 5 E3
Balcorne St *HOM* E9 .... 78 C4
Balder Ri *LEE/GVPK* SE12 .... 160 B2
Balderton St *OXSTW* W1C 18 B5
Baldock St *BOW* E3 .... 92 B1
Baldwin Crs *CMBW* SE5 .... 118 C4
Baldwin Rd *BTSEA* SW11 .... 134 A4
Baldwin's Gdns *FSBYW* WC1X 22 A2
Baldwin St *FSBYE* EC1V 12 A4
Baldwin Ter *IS* N1 .... 11 E1
Baldwyn Gdns *ACT* W3 .... 98 C1
Bale Rd *WCHPL* E1 .... 91 E4
Balfern Gv *CHSWK* W4 .... 111 E1
Balfern St *BTSEA* SW11 .... 115 E5
Balfe St *IS* N1 .... 9 D2
Balfour Ms *MYFR/PKLN* W1K 30 B3
Balfour Pl *MYFR/PKLN* W1K 30 B2
  PUT/ROE SW15 .... 130 B2
Balfour Rd *ACT* W3 .... 86 C4
  HBRY N5 .... 76 C1
  IL IG1 .... 66 B4
Balfour St *STHWK* SE1 .... 48 A4
Balgowan St *WOOL/PLUM* SE18 .. 109 F5
Balham Gv *BAL* SW12 .... 134 A5
Balham High Rd *BAL* SW12 .... 152 B1
Balham Hi *BAL* SW12 .... 134 B5
Balham New Rd *BAL* SW12 .... 134 B5
Balham Park Rd *BAL* SW12 .... 151 F1
Balham Station Rd *BAL* SW12 .... 152 A1
Balkan Wk *WAP* E1W * 102 B1
Balladier Wk *POP/IOD* E14 .... 92 B4
Ballamore Rd *BMLY* BR1 .... 160 A3
Ballance Rd *HOM* E9 .... 79 D3

Ballantine St *WAND/EARL* SW18 .... 132 C2
Ballards Rd *CRICK* NW2 .... 52 A4
Ballast Quay *GNWCH* SE10 .... 123 D2
Ballater Rd *BRXS/STRHM* SW2 .... 135 E2
Ballina St *FSTH* SE23 .... 139 D5
Ballingdon Rd *BTSEA* SW11 .... 134 A4
Balliol Rd *NKENS* W10 .... 88 C5
Ballogie Av *WLSDN* NW10 .... 69 E1
Ballow Cl *CMBW* SE5 * 119 D3
Ball's Pond Pl *IS* N1 * 77 D5
Balls Pond Rd *IS* N1 .... 77 D5
Balmer Rd *BOW* E3 .... 91 F1
Balmes Rd *IS* N1 .... 77 D5
Balmoral Cl *PUT/ROE* SW15 * 131 D4
Balmoral Gv *HOLWY* N7 .... 75 F3
Balmoral Ms *SHB* W12 .... 99 F4
Balmoral Rd *CRICK* NW2 .... 70 B3
  FSTGT E7 .... 82 C1
  LEY E10 .... 62 B4
Balmore St *ARCH* N19 .... 56 B4
Balmuir Gdns *PUT/ROE* SW15 .... 130 C2
Balnacraig Av *WLSDN* NW10 .... 69 E1
Balniel Ga *PIM* SW1V 117 D1
Baltic Pl *IS* N1 * 77 E5
Baltic St East *STLK* EC1Y 23 E1
Baltic St West *FARR* EC1M 23 E1
Baltimore Pl *WELL* DA16 .... 127 F5
Balvaird Pl *PIM* SW1V 117 D1
Balvernie Gv *WAND/EARL* SW18 .... 131 F5
Bamber Rd *PECK* SE15 .... 119 F4
Bamborough Gdns *SHB* W12 .... 100 C3
Bamford Rd *BMLY* BR1 .... 159 D5
Bampton Rd *FSTH* SE23 .... 157 D5
Banbury Ct *COVGDN* WC2E * 32 C1
Banbury Rd *HOM* E9 .... 79 D4
Banbury St *BTSEA* SW11 .... 115 E5
Banchory Rd *BKHTH/KID* SE3 .... 124 B3
Bancroft Rd *WCHPL* E1 .... 90 C3
Banfield Rd *PECK* SE15 .... 138 B1
Bangalore St *PUT/ROE* SW15 .... 130 C1
Banim St *HMSMTH* W6 .... 100 B4
Banister Rd *NKENS* W10 .... 89 D2
Bank End *STHWK* SE1 .... 35 F5
Bankfoot Rd *BMLY* BR1 .... 159 E4
Bankhurst Rd *CAT* SE6 .... 139 F5
Bank La *PUT/ROE* SW15 .... 129 E3
Bankside *STHWK* SE1 .... 35 E2
Bankside Av *LEW* SE13 .... 140 C1
Bankside Rd *IL* IG1 .... 84 C2
Banks Wy *MNPK* E12 .... 84 A1
The Bank *HGT* N6 .... 56 B3
Bankton Rd *BRXN/ST* SW9 .... 136 A2
Bankwell Rd *LEW* SE13 .... 141 E2
Banner St *STLK* EC1Y 23 F1
Banning St *GNWCH* SE10 .... 123 E1
Bannister Cl *BRXS/STRHM* SW2 .... 154 A1
Bannockburn Rd *WOOL/PLUM* SE18 ..... 109 E5
Banstead Ct *SHB* W12 * 99 F1
Banstead St *PECK* SE15 .... 138 C1
Bantry St *CMBW* SE5 .... 119 D3
Banyard Rd *BERM/RHTH* SE16 .... 102 B4
Baptist Gdns *KTTN* NW5 .... 74 A3
Bardolph Rd *HOLWY* N7 .... 75 E1
Bard Rd *NKENS* W10 .... 101 D1
Bardsey Pl *WCHPL* E1 .... 90 C4
Bardsey Wk *IS* N1 * 76 C3
Bardsley La *GNWCH* SE10 .... 122 C2
Barfett St *NKENS* W10 .... 89 F3
Barfield Rd *WAN* E11 * 63 F3
Barford St *IS* N1 .... 76 A5
Barforth Rd *PECK* SE15 .... 138 D1
Bargate Cl *WOOL/PLUM* SE18 .... 127 F1
Barge House Rd *CAN/RD* E16 .... 108 B3
Barge House St *STHWK* SE1 .... 34 B3
Barge La *BOW* E3 .... 79 F5
Bargery Rd *CAT* SE6 .... 158 B1

Bargrove Crs *CAT* SE6 .... 157 F2
Barham Cl *CHST* BR7 .... 162 B5
Barham Rd *CHST* BR7 .... 162 B5
Baring Cl *LEE/GVPK* SE12 .... 160 A2
Baring Rd *LEE/GVPK* SE12 .... 160 B4
Baring St *IS* N1 .... 77 D5
Barker Cl *RCH/KEW* TW9 .... 110 B5
Barker St *WBPTN* SW10 .... 114 C2
Barker Wk *STRHM/NOR* SW16 .... 153 D5
Barking Rd *EHAM* E6 .... 95 D1
  POP/IOD E14 .... 92 B1
Bark Pl *BAY/PAD* W2 .... 26 C1
Barkston Gdns *ECT* SW5 .... 38 C5
Barkworth Rd *BERM/RHTH* SE16 .... 120 B1
Barlborough St *NWCR* SE14 .... 121 D3
Barlby Gdns *NKENS* W10 .... 88 B3
Barlby Rd *NKENS* W10 .... 88 C4
Barleycorn Wy *POP/IOD* E14 .... 103 F1
Barley Mow Pas *CHSWK* W4 .... 111 D1
Barlow Dr *BKHTH/KID* SE3 .... 125 E4
Barlow Pl *MYFR/PICC* W1J 31 D2
Barlow Rd *ACT* W3 .... 98 B2
  KIL/WHAMP NW6 .... 71 F3
Barlow St *WALW* SE17 .... 48 B4
Barmeston Rd *CAT* SE6 .... 158 B2
Barmouth Rd *WAND/EARL* SW18 .... 132 C4
Barnabas Rd *HOM* E9 .... 79 D3
Barnaby Pl *SKENS* SW7 .... 40 A5
Barnard Ms *BTSEA* SW11 .... 133 E2
Barnard Rd *BTSEA* SW11 .... 133 E2
Barnardo Gdns *WCHPL* E1 * 91 D5
Barnardo St *WCHPL* E1 .... 91 D5
Barnby St *CAMTN* NW1 .... 7 F2
  SRTFD E15 .... 81 E5
Barn Cl *KTTN* NW5 * 75 D2
Barnes Av *BARN* SW13 .... 112 A3
Barnes Br *CHSWK* W4 .... 111 E5
Barnes Cl *MNPK* E12 .... 83 D1
Barnes High St *BARN* SW13 .... 111 F5
Barnes Rd *IL* IG1 .... 84 C2
Barnes St *POP/IOD* E14 .... 91 E5
Barnes Ter *DEPT* SE8 .... 121 F1
Barnet Gv *BETH* E2 .... 90 A2
Barnett St *WCHPL* E1 .... 90 B5
Barney Cl *CHARL* SE7 .... 124 C1
Barn Fld *HAMP* NW3 * 73 F2
Barnfield Cl *FSBYPK* N4 .... 57 E2
  TOOT SW17 .... 150 C5
Barnfield Gdns *WOOL/PLUM* SE18 * 126 B2
Barnfield Pl *POP/IOD* E14 .... 104 A5
Barnfield Rd *WOOL/PLUM* SE18 .... 126 B2
Barnham Dr *THMD* SE28 .... 109 F2
Barnham St *STHWK* SE1 .... 37 D5
Barn Hl *WBLY* HA9 .... 50 B4
Barnhill Rd *WBLY* HA9 .... 50 C5
Barningham Wy *CDALE/KGS* NW9 .... 50 C1
Barn Ri *WBLY* HA9 .... 50 A3
Barnsbury Est *IS* N1 .... 75 F5
Barnsbury Gv *HOLWY* N7 .... 75 F4
Barnsbury Pk *IS* N1 .... 76 A5
Barnsbury Rd *IS* N1 .... 76 A5
Barnsbury Sq *IS* N1 .... 76 A4
Barnsbury St *IS* N1 .... 76 A4
Barnsbury Ter *IS* N1 .... 75 F4
Barnsdale Av *POP/IOD* E14 .... 104 B5
Barnsdale Rd *MV/WKIL* W9 .... 89 D3
Barnsley St *WCHPL* E1 .... 90 B3
Barnstaple La *LEW* SE13 .... 140 C2
Barnston Wk *IS* N1 * 76 C5
Barn St *STNW/STAM* N16 .... 59 E4
Barn Wy *WBLY* HA9 .... 50 A3
Barnwell Rd *BRXS/STRHM* SW2 .... 136 A3
Barnwood Cl *MV/WKIL* W9 .... 14 C1
Baroness Rd *BETH* E2 .... 13 F3
Barons Cl *IS* N1 * 10 A1
Baron's Court Rd *WKENS* W14 .... 113 E1
Barons Keep *WKENS* W14 * 113 E1
Baronsmead Rd *BARN* SW13 .... 112 A4
Baron's Pl *STHWK* SE1 .... 46 B1
Baron St *IS* N1 .... 10 B2
Barque Ms *DEPT* SE8 .... 122 A2
Barrett's Green Rd *WLSDN* NW10 .... 86 C1
Barrett's Gv *STNW/STAM* N16 .... 77 E2
Barrett St *MHST* W1U 18 B5
Barrhill Rd *BRXS/STRHM* SW2 .... 153 E4
Barriedale *NWCR* SE14 .... 121 E4
Barrier Point Rd *CAN/RD* E16 .... 106 C2
Barringer Sq *TOOT* SW17 .... 152 A4
Barrington Cl *KTTN* NW5 .... 74 A2
Barrington Rd *BRXN/ST* SW9 .... 136 B1

MNPK E12	84 A3
Barrington Vls *WOOL/PLUM* SE18	126 A4
Barrowgate Rd *CHSWK* W4	110 C1
Barrow Hill Est *STJWD* NW8	4 C2
Barrow Hill Rd *STJWD* NW8	4 C2
Barrs Rd *WLSDN* NW10	69 D4
Barry Av *SEVS/STOTM* N15	59 F1
Barry Pde *EDUL* SE22 *	138 A2
Barry Rd *EDUL* SE22	138 A4
EHAM E6	95 E5
WLSDN NW10	68 C4
Barset Rd *PECK* SE15	138 C1
Barston Rd *WNWD* SE27	154 C1
Barstow Crs *BRXS/STRHM* SW2	153 F1
Barter St *NOXST/BSQ* WC1A	21 D3
Barth Ms *WOOL/PLUM* SE18	109 E5
Bartholomew Cl *STBT* EC1A	23 E3
WAND/EARL SW18	132 C2
Bartholomew La *OBST* EC2N	24 B4
Bartholomew Rd *KTTN* NW5	74 C3
Bartholomew Sq *FSBYE* EC1V	11 F5
Bartholomew St *STHWK* SE1	48 A3
Bartholomew Vls *KTTN* NW5	74 C3
Bartle Av *EHAM* E6	95 E1
Bartle Rd *NTGHL* W11	89 D5
Bartlett Cl *POP/IOD* E14	92 A5
Bartlett Ct *FLST/FETLN* EC4A *	22 B4
Barton Cl *EHAM* E6	95 F5
HOM E9	78 C2
Barton Rd *WKENS* W14	113 E1
Barton St *WEST* SW1P	44 A1
Bartram Rd *BROCKY* SE4	139 E3
Bartrip St *HOM* E9	79 E3
Barwick Rd *FSTGT* E7	82 A1
Bascome St *BRXS/STRHM* SW2	136 A4
Baseing Cl *EHAM* E6	108 A1
Basevi Wy *DEPT* SE8	122 A2
Bashley Rd *WLSDN* NW10	87 D3
Basil Av *EHAM* E6	95 E2
Basil Gdns *WNWD* SE27	154 C5
Basil St *CHEL* SW3	41 E1
Basin Ap *EHAM* E6	108 B1
POP/IOD E14	91 E5
Basing Ct *PECK* SE15	119 F4
Basingdon Wy *CMBW* SE5	137 D2
Basinghall Av *CITYW* EC2V	24 A3
Basinghall St *CITYW* EC2V	24 A4
Basing Hl *GLDGN* NW11	53 F3
Basing Pl *BETH* E2	13 D3
Basing St *NTGHL* W11	89 D5
Basire St *IS* N1	76 C5
Baskerville Gdns *WLSDN* NW10	69 E1
Baskerville Rd *WAND/EARL* SW18	133 E5
Basket Gdns *ELTH/MOT* SE9	143 E3
Baslow Wk *CLPT* E5	79 D1
Basnett Rd *BTSEA* SW11 *	134 A1
Bassano St *EDUL* SE22	137 F3
Bassant Rd *WOOL/PLUM* SE18	127 F2
Bassein Park Rd *SHB* W12	99 F3
Bassett Rd *NKENS* W10	89 D5
Bassett St *KTTN* NW5	74 A3
Bassingham Rd *WAND/EARL* SW18	132 C5
Basswood Rd *PECK* SE15	138 B1
Bastable Av *BARK* IG11	97 F1
Bastwick St *FSBYE* EC1V	11 D5
Basuto Rd *FUL/PGN* SW6	114 A4
Batavia Ms *NWCR* SE14	121 E3
Batavia Rd *NWCR* SE14	121 E3
Batchelor St *IS* N1	10 A1
Bateman Rd *BARK* IG11	84 C5
Bateman's Blds *SOHO/SHAV* W1D	20 A5
Batemans Cnr *CHSWK* W4 *	111 D1
Bateman's Rw *SDTCH* EC2A	13 D1
Bateman St *SOHO/SHAV* W1D	20 A5
Bate St *POP/IOD* E14	103 F1
Bath Cl *PECK* SE15	120 B3
Bathgate Rd *WIM/MER* SW19	149 D3
Bath Gv *BETH* E2	90 A1
Bath Pl *SDTCH* EC2A *	12 C4
Bath Rd *CHSWK* W4	99 E5
FSTGT E7	83 D3
Baths Ap *FUL/PGN* SW6 *	113 F3
Bath St *FSBYE* EC1V	11 F4
Bath Ter *STHWK* SE1	47 E3
Bathurst Gdns *WLSDN* NW10	88 B1
Bathurst Ms *BAY/PAD* W2	28 B1
Bathurst Rd *IL* IG1	66 B3
Bathurst St *BAY/PAD* W2	28 B1
Bathway *WOOL/PLUM* SE18	108 A5
Batley Pl *STNW/STAM* N16	59 F5
Batley Rd *STNW/STAM* N16	59 F5
Batman Cl *SHB* W12	100 B2
Batoum Gdns *HMSMTH* W6	100 C4
Batson St *SHB* W12	100 A3
Batten Cl *EHAM* E6	95 F5
Batten Cots *POP/IOD* E14 *	91 E4
Batten St *BTSEA* SW11	133 E1
Battersby Rd *CAT* SE6	159 D2
Battersea Br *WBPTN* SW10	115 D3
Battersea Bridge Rd *BTSEA* SW11	115 D3
Battersea Church Rd *BTSEA* SW11	115 D4
Battersea High St *BTSEA* SW11	115 D5
Battersea Park Rd *BTSEA* SW11	116 A4
Battersea Ri *BTSEA* SW11	133 E3
Battersea Sq *BTSEA* SW11 *	115 E3
Battery Rd *THMD* SE28	109 E3
Battishill St *IS* N1	76 B4
Battle Bridge La *STHWK* SE1	36 C4
Battledean Rd *HBRY* N5	76 B2
Batty St *WCHPL* E1	90 A5
Baudwin Rd *CAT* SE6	159 E2
The Baulk *WAND/EARL* SW18	132 A5
Bavaria Rd *ARCH* N19	57 E4
Bavent Rd *CMBW* SE5	118 C5
Bawdale Rd *EDUL* SE22	137 F3
Bawtree Rd *NWCR* SE14	121 E3
Baxendale St *BETH* E2	90 A2
Baxter Rd *CAN/RD* E16	94 C5
IL IG1	84 B2
IS N1	77 D3
Bayfield Rd *ELTH/MOT* SE9	143 D2
Bayford Ms *HACK* E8 *	78 B4
Bayford Rd *WLSDN* NW10	89 D2
Bayford St *HACK* E8	78 B4
Bayham Pl *CAMTN* NW1	74 C5
Bayham Rd *CHSWK* W4	99 D4
Bayham St *CAMTN* NW1	74 C5
Bayley St *FITZ* W1T	20 A3
Baylis Rd *STHWK* SE1	46 A2
Bayne Cl *EHAM* E6	95 F5
Baynes Ms *HAMP* NW3	73 D3
Baynes St *CAMTN* NW1	74 C4
Bayonne Rd *HMSMTH* W6	113 E2
Bays Cl *SYD* SE26	156 C5
Bayston Rd *STNW/STAM* N16	59 F5
Bayswater Rd *BAY/PAD* W2	27 E2
Baythorne St *BOW* E3	91 F4
Baytree Cl *BFN/LL* DA15	163 F1
Baytree Rd *BRXS/STRHM* SW2	135 F2
Bazely St *POP/IOD* E14	104 C1
Beacham Cl *CHARL* SE7	125 D2
Beachborough Rd *BMLY* BR1	158 C4
Beachcroft Rd *WAN* E11	63 E5
Beachy Rd *BOW* E3	80 A4
Beacon Cl *NWCR* SE14	139 D1
Beacon Hl *HOLWY* N7	75 E2
Beacon Rd *LEW* SE13	141 D3
Beaconsfield Cl *BKHTH/KID* SE3	124 A2
CHSWK W4	110 C1
Beaconsfield Rd *BKHTH/KID* SE3	124 A2
CAN/RD E16	93 F3
CHSWK W4	99 D4
ELTH/MOT SE9	161 E3
LEY E10	62 C5
WALTH E17	61 F1
WALW SE17	119 D2
WLSDN NW10	69 F5
Beaconsfield Terrace Rd *WKENS* W14	101 E4
Beaconsfield Wk *FUL/PGN* SW6	113 F4
Beacontree Rd *WAN* E11	63 F2
Beadman Pl *WNWD* SE27 *	154 B4
Beadman St *WNWD* SE27	154 B4
Beadnell Rd *FSTH* SE23	157 D1
Beadon Rd *HMSMTH* W6	100 C5
Beak St *REGST* W1B	31 E1
Beale Pl *BOW* E3	91 F1
Beale Rd *BOW* E3	79 F5
Beal Rd *IL* IG1	66 A4
Beames Rd *WLSDN* NW10	69 D5
Beamish Rd *ED* N9	18 C2
Beanacre Cl *HOM* E9	79 F5
Beanshaw *ELTH/MOT* SE9	162 A4
Beardsfield *PLSTW* E13	82 A5
Beardsley Wy *ACT* W3	99 D3
Bear Gdns *STHWK* SE1	35 E4
Bear La *STHWK* SE1	35 D3
Bearstead Ri *BROCKY* SE4	139 F3
Bear St *LSQ/SEVD* WC2H	32 B1
Beatrice Cl *PLSTW* E13	94 A3
Beatrice Pl *KENS* W8	38 C3
Beatrice Rd *FSBYPK* N4	58 A2
STHWK SE1	102 A5
Beatty Rd *STNW/STAM* N16	77 E1

Beatty St *CAMTN* NW1 *	7	E1
Beauchamp Cl *CHSWK* W4	98	C4
Beauchamp Pl *CHEL* SW3	41	D3
Beauchamp Rd *BTSEA* SW11	133	E2
FSTGT E7	82	B4
Beauchamp St *HCIRC* EC1N	22	A3
Beauchamp Ter *BARN* SW13	130	B1
Beauclerc Rd *HMSMTH* W6	100	B4
Beaufort *EHAM* E6	96	A4
Beaufort Cl *PUT/ROE* SW15	148	C1
Beaufort Gdns *CHEL* SW3	41	D2
HDN NW4	52	A1
IL IG1	66	A3
Beaufort St *CHEL* SW3	115	D2
Beaufoy Wk *LBTH* SE11	45	F5
Beaulieu Av *CAN/RD* E16	106	B2
SYD SE26	156	B4
Beaulieu Cl *CMBW* SE5	137	D1
Beaulieu Pl *CHSWK* W4	98	C4
Beaumaris Gn *CDALE/KGS* NW9 *	51	E1
Beaumont Av *WKENS* W14	113	F1
Beaumont Crs *WKENS* W14	113	F1
Beaumont Gdns *HAMP* NW3	54	A4
Beaumont Gv *WCHPL* E1	91	D3
Beaumont Ms *MHST* W1U *	18	B2
Beaumont Pl *FITZ* W1T	7	F5
Beaumont Ri *ARCH* N19	57	D3
Beaumont Rd *CHSWK* W4	98	C4
LEY E10	62	B2
PLSTW E13	94	B2
WIM/MER SW19	131	E5
Beaumont Sq *WCHPL* E1	91	D4
Beaumont St *CAVSQ/HST* W1G	18	B1
Beaumont Ter *LEW* SE13 *	141	E5
Beaver Wk *HAMP* NW3	73	F4
Beaverbank Rd *ELTH/MOT* SE9	137	F4
Beaverwood Rd *CHST* BR7	163	D1
Beavor La *HMSMTH* W6	100	A5
Bebbington Rd *WOOL/PLUM* SE18 *	109	E5
Beccles Dr *BARK* IG11	79	E5
Beccles St *POP/IOD* E14	91	F5
Beck Cl *GNWCH* SE10	122	B4
LEW SE13	122	B4
Becket Av *EHAM* E6	96	A2
Becket St *STHWK* SE1 *	48	A2
Beckett Cl *STRHM/NOR* SW16	153	D2
WLSDN NW10	69	D3
Beckford Dr *WKENS* W14	101	F5
Beckford Pl *WALW* SE17 *	118	C1
Becklow Rd *SHB* W12	99	F3
Beck Rd *HACK* E8	78	B5
Beckton Rd *CAN/RD* E16	93	F4
Beckway St *WALW* SE17 *	48	B5
Beckwith Rd *HNHL* SE24	137	D5
Becmead Av *STRHM/NOR* SW16	153	D4
Becondale Rd *NRWD* SE19	155	F5
Bective Rd *FSTGT* E7	82	A1
PUT/ROE SW15	131	E2
Bedale St *STHWK* SE1 *	36	A4
Beddington Rd *GDMY/SEVK* IG3	67	F2
Bedford Av *RSQ* WC1B	20	B3
Bedfordbury *CHCR* WC2N	32	C1
Bedford Cl *CHSWK* W4	111	E2
Bedford Cnr *CHSWK* W4 *	99	E5
Bedford Ct *CHCR* WC2N	32	C2
Bedford Gdns *KENS* W8	26	A4
Bedford Hl *BAL* SW12	152	B2
Bedford Ms *CAT* SE6	158	B2
Bedford Pl *RSQ* WC1B	20	C2
Bedford Rd *BFN/LL* DA15	163	E3
CEND/HSY/T N8	57	F1
CHSWK W4	99	D4
CLAP SW4	135	E2
EHAM E6	84	A5
IL IG1	66	B5
Bedford Rw *GINN* WC1R	21	F2
Bedford Sq *RSQ* WC1B	20	B3
Bedford St *COVGDN* WC2E	32	C1
Bedford Wy *STPAN* WC1H	20	B1
Bedgebury Gdns *WIM/MER* SW19	149	E3
Bedgebury Rd *ELTH/MOT* SE9	143	D2
Bedivere Rd *BMLY* BR1	160	A3
Bedlam Ms *LBTH* SE11	45	F4
Bedlow Cl *STJWD* NW8	16	B1
Bedser Cl *LBTH* SE11 *	117	F2
Beeby Rd *CAN/RD* E16	94	B4
Beech Av *ACT* W3	99	E2
Beech Cl *DEPT* SE8	121	F2
PUT/ROE SW15	130	A5
Beech Ct *ELTH/MOT* SE9 *	143	E4
Beechcroft Av *GLDGN* NW11	53	F2

Beechcroft Cl *STRHM/NOR* SW16	153	F5
Beechcroft Rd *MORT/ESHN* SW14 *	128	C1
TOOT SW17	151	E3
Beechdale Rd *BRXS/STRHM* SW2	135	F4
Beechen Pl *FSTH* SE23	156	C2
Beeches Rd *TOOT* SW17	151	E2
Beechfield Rd *CAT* SE6	157	F1
FSBYPK N4	58	C1
Beechhill Rd *ELTH/MOT* SE9	144	A3
Beechmont Cl *BMLY* BR1	159	E5
Beechmore Rd *BTSEA* SW11	115	F4
Beechmount Av *RCH/KEW* TW9	110	B4
Beechwood Av *RCH/KEW* TW9	110	A3
Beechwood Gv *ACT* W3	99	E1
Beechwood Ri *CHST* BR7	162	B4
Beechwood Rd *HACK* E8	77	F3
Beechworth Cl *HAMP* NW3	54	B4
Beecroft La *BROCKY* SE4	139	E3
Beecroft Ms *BROCKY* SE4	139	E3
Beecroft Rd *BROCKY* SE4	139	E3
Beehive Cl *HACK* E8	77	F4
Beehive La *IL* IG1	65	F1
Beehive Pl *BRXN/ST* SW9	136	A1
Beeston Cl *HACK* E8	78	A2
Beeston Rd *BGVA* SW1W	43	D3
Beethorpe St *NKENS* W10	89	E2
Begbie Rd *BKHTH/KID* SE3	124	C4
Begonia Cl *EHAM* E6	95	E4
Beira St *BAL* SW12	134	B5
Bekesbourne St *POP/IOD* E14 *	91	E5
Belfast Rd *STNW/STAM* N16	59	F4
Belford Gv *WOOL/PLUM* SE18	108	A5
Belfort Rd *PECK* SE15	120	C5
Belfry Cl *BERM/RHTH* SE16 *	120	B1
Belfry Rd *MNPK* E12	65	D4
Belgrade Rd *STNW/STAM* N16	77	E1
Belgrave Ct *ACT* W3	98	C3
Belgrave Gdns *STJWD* NW8	71	F5
Belgrave Ms South *KTBR* SW1X	42	B2
Belgrave Ms West *KTBR* SW1X	42	A2
Belgrave Pl *KTBR* SW1X	42	B3
Belgrave Rd *BARN* SW13	111	F3
IL IG1	65	F3
LEY E10	62	B3
PIM SW1V	43	E5
PLSTW E13	94	C3
WALTH E17	62	A1
WAN E11	64	A3
Belgrave Sq *KTBR* SW1X	42	A2
Belgrave St *WCHPL* E1	91	D4
Belgrove St *CAMTN* NW1	8	C3
Belinda Rd *BRXN/ST* SW9	136	B1
Belitha Vs *IS* N1	76	A4
Bellamaine Cl *THMD* SE28	109	F5
Bellamy Cl *POP/IOD* E14	104	A3
WKENS W14	113	F1
Bellamy St *BAL* SW12	134	B5
Bellarmine Cl *THMD* SE28	109	F5
Bellasis Av *BRXS/STRHM* SW2	153	E1
Bell Dr *WAND/EARL* SW18	131	E5
Bellefields Rd *BRXN/ST* SW9	135	F1
Bellegrove Cl *WELL* DA16	127	F5
Bellegrove Rd *WELL* DA16	127	E5
Bellenden Rd *PECK* SE15	119	F5
Belleville Rd *BTSEA* SW11	133	E3
Bellevue Pl *WCHPL* E1 *	90	C3
Bellevue Rd *BARN* SW13	112	A5
TOOT SW17	151	D2
Belew St *TOOT* SW17	150	C3
Belfield Rd *BKHTH/KID* SE3	124	B3
Bell Gdns *LEY* E10	62	A3
Bellgate Ms *KTTN* NW5	74	B1
Bell Gn *SYD* SE26	157	E4
Bell Green La *SYD* SE26	157	F5
Bellina Ms *KTTN* NW5	74	B1
Bellingham Gn *CAT* SE6	158	A3
Bellingham Rd *CAT* SE6	158	C3
Bell La *CAN/RD* E16	105	F2
WCHPL E1	24	C3
Bell Meadow *NRWD* SE19	155	E4
Bello Cl *HNHL* SE24	154	B1
Bellot St *GNWCH* SE10	123	E1
Bell St *BAY/PAD* W2	16	C2
WOOL/PLUM SE18	125	E4
Belltrees Gv *STRHM/NOR* SW16	153	F5
Bell Water Ga *WOOL/PLUM* SE18	108	A4
Bell Wharf La *CANST* EC4R	35	F2
Bellwood Rd *PECK* SE15	139	D2
Bell Yd *LINN* WC2A	22	A5

Bell Yard Ms *STHWK* SE1	49	D1
Belmont Av *WELL* DA16	127	E5
Belmont Cl *CLAP* SW4	134	C1
Belmont Gv *CHSWK* W4	99	D5
LEW SE13	141	D1
Belmont Hl *LEW* SE13	141	D1
Belmont La *CHST* BR7	162	C4
Belmont Pde *CHST* BR7 *	162	B5
Belmont Pk *LEW* SE13	141	D2
Belmont Park Cl *LEW* SE13	141	E2
Belmont Park Rd *LEY* E10	62	B1
Belmont Rd *CHST* BR7	162	B5
CLAP SW4	134	C1
IL IG1	66	C5
Belmont St *CAMTN* NW1	74	A4
Belmont Ter *CHSWK* W4	99	D5
Belmore La *HOLWY* N7	75	D2
Belmore St *VX/NE* SW8	117	D4
Beloe Cl *PUT/ROE* SW15	130	A2
Belsham St *HOM* E9	78	C3
Belsize Av *HAMP* NW3	73	E2
Belsize Court Gdns *HAMP* NW3.	73	D2
Belsize Crs *HAMP* NW3	73	D2
Belsize Gv *HAMP* NW3	73	E3
Belsize La *HAMP* NW3	73	D3
Belsize Ms *HAMP* NW3 *	73	D3
Belsize Pk *HAMP* NW3	73	D3
Belsize Park Gdns *HAMP* NW3.	73	D3
Belsize Park Ms *HAMP* NW3	73	D3
Belsize Pl *HAMP* NW3	73	D3
Belsize Rd *KIL/WHAMP* NW6	72	B5
Belsize Sq *HAMP* NW3	73	D3
Belsize Ter *HAMP* NW3	73	D3
Belson Rd *WOOL/PLUM* SE18	107	F5
Beltane Dr *WIM/MER* SW19	149	D3
Belthorn Crs *BAL* SW12	134	C5
Belton Rd *WAN* E11	81	E1
WLSDN NW10	70	A3
Belton Wy *BOW* E3	92	A4
Beltran Rd *FUL/PGN* SW6	114	B5
Belvedere Av *WIM/MER* SW19	149	E5
Belvedere Blds *STHWK* SE1	47	D1
Belvedere Dr *WIM/MER* SW19	149	E5
Belvedere Gv *WIM/MER* SW19	149	E5
Belvedere Ms *PECK* SE15	138	C1
Belvedere Pl *BRXS/STRHM* SW2	135	F2
Belvedere Rd *LEY* E10	61	D3
STHWK SE1	33	E5
Belvedere Sq *WIM/MER* SW19	149	E5
The Belvedere *WBPTN* SW10 *	114	C4
Bembridge Cl *KIL/WHAMP* NW6	71	E4
Bemerton St *IS* N1	75	F5
Bemish Rd *PUT/ROE* SW15	131	D1
Benares Rd *WOOL/PLUM* SE18	109	F5
Benbow Rd *HMSMTH* W6	100	B4
Benbow St *DEPT* SE8	122	A2
Benbury Rd *BMLY* BR1	158	C5
Bendall Ms *CAMTN* NW1	17	D2
Bendemeer Rd *PUT/ROE* SW15	131	D1
Bendish Rd *EHAM* E6	83	E4
Bendon Va *WAND/EARL* SW18	132	B5
Benedict Rd *BRXN/ST* SW9	135	F1
Bengal Rd *IL* IG1	84	B1
Bengeworth Rd *CMBW* SE5	136	C2
Benhill Rd *CMBW* SE5	119	D3
Benhurst La *STRHM/NOR* SW16	154	A5
Benin St *LEW* SE13	141	D5
Benjamin Cl *HACK* E8	78	A5
Benjamin Ms *BAL* SW12	134	C5
Benjamin St *FARR* EC1M	22	C2
Ben Jonson Rd *WCHPL* E1	91	E4
Benledi St *POP/IOD* E14	93	D5
Bennelong Cl *SHB* W12	100	B1
Bennerley Rd *BTSEA* SW11	133	E3
Bennet's Hl *BLKFR* EC4V	35	D1
Bennett Cl *LEW* SE13	122	B4
Bennett Pk *BKHTH/KID* SE3	141	F1
Bennett Rd *BRXN/ST* SW9	118	A5
PLSTW E13	94	C3
Bennett St *CHSWK* W4	111	E2
WHALL SW1A	31	E3
Benn St *HOM* E9	79	E3
Bensbury Cl *PUT/ROE* SW15	130	B5
Ben Smith Wy *BERM/RHTH* SE16	102	A4
Benson Rd *PLSTW* E13	94	C1
Benson Quay *WAP* E1W	102	C1
Benson Rd *FSTH* SE23	156	C1
Benthal Rd *STNW/STAM* N16	59	F4
Bentham Rd *HOM* E9	79	D3
Ben Tillet Cl *CAN/RD* E16 *	107	F2
Bentinck Ms *MHST* W1U	18	B4

Bentinck St *MHST* W1U	18	B4
Bentley Cl *WIM/MER* SW19	150	A3
Bentley Dr *CRICK* NW2	53	F5
GNTH/NBYPK IG2	66	C1
Benton Rd *IL* IG1	67	D3
Benton's La *WNWD* SE27	154	C4
Benton's Ri *WNWD* SE27	155	D5
Bentworth Rd *SHB* W12	88	B5
Benwell Rd *HOLWY* N7	76	A1
Berwick Cl *BERM/RHTH* SE16	102	B5
Benworth St *BOW* E3	91	F2
Benyon Rd *IS* N1	77	D5
Benyon Whf *IS* N1	77	D5
Berber Pde *WOOL/PLUM* SE18	125	E4
Berber Rd *BTSEA* SW11	133	F3
Bercta Rd *ELTH/MOT* SE9	162	C2
Berenger Wk *WBPTN* SW10 *	115	D3
Berens Rd *WLSDN* NW10	89	D3
Beresford Av *ALP/SUD* HA0	68	A5
Beresford Rd *HBRY* N5	77	D2
Beresford Sq *WOOL/PLUM* SE18	108	B5
Beresford St *WOOL/PLUM* SE18	108	B4
Beresford Ter *HBRY* N5	76	C2
Berestede Rd *HMSMTH* W6	111	F1
Bere St *WAP* E1W	103	D1
Berger Rd *HOM* E9	79	D3
Bergham Ms *WKENS* W14	101	D4
Bergholt Crs *STNW/STAM* N16	59	E2
Bergholt Ms *CAMTN* NW1	74	C4
Bering Sq *POP/IOD* E14	122	A1
Bering Wk *CAN/RD* E16	95	D5
Berisford Ms *WAND/EARL* SW18	132	C4
Berkeley Gdns *KENS* W8	26	B4
Berkeley Ms *MBLAR* W1H	17	F4
Berkeley Rd *BARN* SW13	112	A4
MNPK E12	83	E2
SEVS/STOTM N15	59	D1
Berkeley Sq *MYFR/PICC* W1J	31	D2
Berkeley St *MYFR/PICC* W1J	31	D2
Berkley Rd *CAMTN* NW1	73	F4
Berkshire Rd *HOM* E9	79	F3
Bermans Wy *WLSDN* NW10	69	E1
Bermondsey St *STHWK* SE1	36	C4
Bermondsey Wall East		
BERM/RHTH SE16	102	A3
Bermondsey Wall West *BERM/RHTH* SE1	102	A3
Bernal Green *BETH* E2		
Bernard Ashley Dr *CHARL* SE7	124	B1
Bernard Cassidy St *CAN/RD* E16	93	F4
Bernard Gdns *WIM/MER* SW19	149	E5
Bernard St *BMSBY* WC1N	20	C1
Bernay's Gv *BRXN/ST* SW9	135	F2
Berners Ms *FITZ* W1T	19	E3
Berners Pl *FITZ* W1T	19	F4
Berners Rd *IS* N1	76	A5
Berners St *FITZ* W1T	19	F3
Berner Ter *WCHPL* E1 *	90	A5
Bernhardt Crs *STJWD* NW8	4	C5
Berridge Ms *KIL/WHAMP* NW6	72	A2
Berridge Rd *NRWD* SE19	155	D5
Berriman Rd *HOLWY* N7	57	F5
Berry Cots *POP/IOD* E14 *	91	E5
Berryfield Rd *WALW* SE17	118	B1
Berryhill *ELTH/MOT* SE9	144	B2
Berryhill Gdns *ELTH/MOT* SE9	144	B2
Berry La *DUL* SE21	155	D4
Berryman's La *SYD* SE26	157	D4
Berrymead Gdns *ACT* W3	98	C2
Berrymede Rd *CHSWK* W4	99	D4
Berry Pl *FSBYE* EC1V	11	D4
Berry St *FSBYE* EC1V	23	D1
Bertal Rd *TOOT* SW17	151	D4
Berthon St *DEPT* SE8	122	A3
Bertie Rd *WLSDN* NW10	70	A3
Bertram Rd *HDN* NW4	52	A1
Bertram St *KTTN* NW5	56	B5
Bertrand St *LEW* SE13	140	B1
Berwick Crs *BFN/LL* DA15	145	E4
Berwick Rd *CAN/RD* E16	94	B5
Berwick St *SOHO/CST* W1F	19	F5
Berwyn Rd *HNHL* SE24	154	B1
RCHPK/HAM TW10	128	B2
Beryl Av *EHAM* E6	95	E4
Beryl Rd *HMSMTH* W6	113	D1
Besant Cl *CRICK* NW2 *	53	E5
Besant Pl *EDUL* SE22	137	F1
Besant Rd *CRICK* NW2	54	A1
Besant Wy *WLSDN* NW10	68	C2
Bessant Dr *RCH/KEW* TW9	110	B3
Bessborough Pl *PIM* SW1V	117	D1
Bessborough Rd *PUT/ROE* SW15	148	A1
Bessborough St *PIM* SW1V	117	D1

Bessemer Rd *CMBW* SE5	118	C5
Bessie Lansbury CI *EHAM* E6	96	A5
Besson St *NWCR* SE14	120	C4
Bessy St *BETH* E2 *	90	C2
Bestwood St *DEPT* SE8	103	D5
Beswick Ms *KIL/WHAMP* NW6	72	B2
Betchworth Rd *GDMY/SEVK* IG3	67	G2
Bethell Av *CAN/RD* E16	93	F3
IL IG1	66	A2
Bethnal Green Rd *BETH* E2	13	F5
Bethune Rd *STNW/STAM* N16	59	D2
WLSDN NW10	87	D3
Bethwin Rd *CMBW* SE5	118	B3
Betterton St *LSQ/SEVD* WC2H	20	C5
Bettons Pk *SRTFD* E15	81	E5
Bettridge Rd *FUL/PGN* SW6	113	F5
Betts Ms *WALTH* E17	61	F1
Betts Rd *CAN/RD* E16	94	B5
Betts St *WAP* E1W	102	B1
Bevan St *IS* N1	76	C5
Bev Callender CI *VX/NE* SW8	134	B1
Bevenden St *IS* N1	12	B3
Beveridge Rd *WLSDN* NW10	69	E4
Beverley Av *BFN/LL* DA15	145	F5
Beverley CI *BARN* SW13	112	A5
BTSEA SW11	133	D2
Beverley Ct *BROCKY* SE4	139	F1
Beverley Gdns *BARN* SW13	129	F1
GLDGN NW11	53	E2
WBLY HA9	50	A3
Beverley Rd *BARN* SW13	129	F1
CHSWK W4	111	F1
EHAM E6	95	D2
Beversbrook Rd *ARCH* N19	57	D5
Beverstone Rd *BRXS/STRHM* SW2	135	F3
Beverston Ms *MBLAR* W1H *	17	E3
Bevin CI *BERM/RHTH* SE16	103	E2
Bevington Rd *NKENS* W10 *	89	E4
Bevington St *BERM/RHTH* SE16	102	A3
Bevin Sq *TOOT* SW17	151	F3
Bevin Wy *FSBYW* WC1X	10	A2
Bevis Marks *HDTCH* EC3A	25	D4
Bewdley St *IS* N1	76	A4
Bewick Ms *PECK* SE15	120	B3
Bewick St *VX/NE* SW8	116	B5
Bewley St *WCHPL* E1	102	B1
Bewlys Rd *WNWD* SE27	154	B5
Bexhill Rd *BROCKY* SE4	139	F4
MORT/ESHN SW14	128	C1
Bexley Rd *ELTH/MOT* SE9	144	A3
Bianca Rd *PECK* SE15	119	F2
Bibury CI *PECK* SE15	119	E2
Bicester Rd *RCH/KEW* TW9	128	A1
Bickenhall St *MHST* W1U	17	F2
Bickerton Rd *ARCH* N19	56	B4
Bickles Yd *STHWK* SE1	49	D1
Bickley Rd *LEY* E10	62	B2
Bickley St *TOOT* SW17	151	E5
Bicknell Rd *CMBW* SE5	136	C1
Bicborough St *STPAN* WC1H	8	C4
Biddenden Wy *ELTH/MOT* SE9	162	A4
Bidder St *CAN/RD* E16	93	E4
Biddestone Rd *HOLWY* N7	75	F1
Bidduiph Rd *MV/WKIL* W9	3	D4
Bideford Rd *BMLY* BR1	159	F5
Bidwell St *PECK* SE15 *	120	B4
Biggerstaff Rd *SRTFD* E15	80	C5
Biggerstaff St *FSBYPK* N4	58	A4
Bigg's Rw *PUT/ROE* SW15	131	D1
Big Hl *CLPT* E5	60	B3
Bigland St *WCHPL* E1	90	C5
Bignell Rd *WOOL/PLUM* SE18	126	B1
Bignold Rd *FSTGT* E7	82	A1
Bigwood Rd *GLDGN* NW11	54	B1
Bill Hamling CI *ELTH/MOT* SE9	161	F2
Billingford CI *BROCKY* SE4	139	D2
Billing PI *WBPTN* SW10 *	114	B3
Billing Rd *WBPTN* SW10 *	114	B3
Billing St *WBPTN* SW10 *	114	B3
Billington Rd *NWCR* SE14	121	D3
Billiter St *FENCHST* EC3M *	25	D5
Billiter St *FENCHST* EC3M	25	D5
Bilson St *POP/IOD* E14	104	C5
Bina Gdns *ECT* SW5	39	E5
Binden Rd *SHB* W12	99	F4
Binfield Rd *CLAP* SW4	117	E4
Bingfield St *IS* N1	75	E5
Bingham Ct *IS* N1 *	76	B4
Bingham St *MHST* W1U	18	A2
Bingham St *IS* N1	77	D3
Bingley Rd *CAN/RD* E16	94	C5
Binney St *MYFR/PKLN* W1K	30	B1
Binns Rd *CHSWK* W4	111	E1
Birbetts Rd *ELTH/MOT* SE9	161	F2
Birch CI *CAN/RD* E16	93	E4
Birchdale Rd *FSTGT* E7	82	C2
Birchen CI *CDALE/KGS* NW9	51	D4
Birchen Gv *CDALE/KGS* NW9	51	D4
The Birches *CHARL* SE7	124	B2
CMBW SE5 *	137	G1
Birchfield St *POP/IOD* E14	104	A1
Birch Gv *ACT* W3	98	A1
LEE/GVPK SE12	141	F5
WAN E11	63	E5
Birchington Rd *CEND/HSY/T* N8	57	D1
KIL/WHAMP NW6	72	A5
Birchin La *BANK* EC3V	24	C5
Birchlands Av *BAL* SW12	133	F5
Birchmere Av *BKHTH/KID* SE3	123	F5
Birchmore Wk *HBRY* N5	58	C5
Birchwood Dr *HAMP* NW3	54	B5
Birchwood Rd *TOOT* SW17	152	B5
Birdbrook Rd *BKHTH/KID* SE3	142	B1
Birdcage Wk *WESTW* SW1E	43	F1
Birdhurst Rd *WAND/EARL* SW18	132	C2
Bird In Bush Rd *PECK* SE15	120	A3
Bird-In-Hand Ms *FSTH* SE23	156	C2
Bird-In-Hand Pas *FSTH* SE23	156	C2
Birdsfield La *BOW* E3	79	F5
Bird St *MHST* W1U	18	B5
Birdwood Av *LEW* SE13	141	D4
Birkbeck Av *ACT* W3	98	C1
Birkbeck Gv *ACT* W3	99	D1
Birkbeck Hl *DUL* SE21	154	B2
Birkbeck Ms *ACT* W3 *	98	C1
HACK E8	77	F2
Birkbeck PI *DUL* SE21	154	B1
Birkbeck Rd *ACT* W3	99	D1
HACK E8	77	F2
WIM/MER SW19	150	B5
Birkbeck St *BETH* E2	90	B2
Birkdale CI *BERM/RHTH* SE16 *	120	B1
Birkenhead St *CAMTN* NW1	9	D3
Birkhall Rd *CAT* SE6	159	D1
Birkwood CI *BAL* SW12	135	D5
Birley St *BTSEA* SW11	116	A5
Birnam Rd *FSBYPK* N4	57	F4
Birse Crs *WLSDN* NW10	69	E1
Biscay Rd *HMSMTH* W6	113	D1
Biscoe Wy *LEW* SE13	141	D2
Bisham Gdns *HGT* N6	56	A3
Bishop King's Rd *WKENS* W14	101	E5
Bishops Av *PLSTW* E13	82	B5
Bishop's Av *FUL/PGN* SW6	113	D5
The Bishops Av *EFNCH* N2	55	D1
Bishop's Bridge Rd *BAY/PAD* W2	15	D4
Bishops CI *CHSWK* W4	110	C1
ELTH/MOT SE9	162	C2
Bishop's Ct *STP* EC4M	22	C4
Bishopsgate *LVPST* EC2M	25	D3
Bishopsgate Ar *LVPST* EC2M	24	C3
Bishops Gv *EFNCH* N2	55	D1
Bishops Md *CMBW* SE5 *	118	C5
Bishop's Park Rd *FUL/PGN* SW6	113	D5
Bishops Rd *FUL/PGN* SW6	113	F4
HGT N6	56	A1
Bishop's Ter *LBTH* SE11	46	B4
Bishopsthorpe Rd *SYD* SE26	157	D3
Bishop St *IS* N1	76	C5
Bishop's Wy *BETH* E2	90	C1
Bishopswood Rd *HGT* N6	55	F2
Bisson Rd *SRTFD* E15	92	C1
Bittern St *STHWK* SE1	35	E5
Blackall St *SDTCH* EC2A	12	C5
Blackbird HI *WBLY* HA9	50	C4
Blackbird Yd *BETH* E2	13	F3
Blackburne's Ms *MYFR/PKLN* W1K	30	A1
Blackburn Rd *KIL/WHAMP* NW6	72	B3
Blackdown Ter *WOOL/PLUM* SE18 *	125	F4
Blackenham Rd *TOOT* SW17	151	F4
Blackett St *PUT/ROE* SW15	131	D1
Blackfen Rd *BFN/LL* DA15	145	F3
Blackfriars Br *STHWK* SE1	34	C2
Black Friars La *BLKFR* EC4V	22	C5
Blackfriars Pas *BLKFR* EC4V	34	C1
Blackfriars Rd *STHWK* SE1	34	C1
Blackfriars U/P *BLKFR* EC4V	35	D1
Blackheath Av *GNWCH* SE10	123	D3
Blackheath Gv *BKHTH/KID* SE3	123	F5
Blackheath Hl *GNWCH* SE10	122	C4
Blackheath Pk *BKHTH/KID* SE3	124	A5
BKHTH/KID SE3	141	F1
Blackheath Ri *LEW* SE13	122	C5

Blackheath Rd *GNWCH* SE10 .... 122 B4
Blackheath V *BKHTH/KID* SE3 .... 123 E5
Black Horse Ct *STHWK* SE1 * 48 B3
Blackhorse Rd *DEPT* SE8 .... 121 E2
Blacklands Rd *CAT* SE6 .... 158 C4
Blacklands Ter *CHEL* SW3 .... 41 E5
Black Lion Ga *BAY/PAD* W2 .... 27 D2
Black Lion La *HMSMTH* W6 .... 100 A5
Blackmans Yd *WCHPL* E1 * 13 F5
Blackmore Dr *NW10* 68 B4
Blackpool Rd *PECK* SE15 .... 120 B5
Black Prince Rd *LBTH* SE11 .... 48 B5
Blackshaw Rd *TOOT* SW17 .... 151 D5
Black's Rd *HMSMTH* W6 .... 112 C1
Blackstock Rd *FSBYPK* N4 .... 58 B4
Blackstone Est *HACK* E8 .... 78 A4
Blackstone Rd *CRICK* NW2 .... 70 C2
Black Swan Yd *STHWK* SE1 .... 36 C5
Blackthorn Av *IL* IG1 .... 85 D2
Blackthorn St *BOW* E3 .... 92 A3
Blacktree Ms *BRXN/ST* SW9 * 136 A1
Blackwall *GNWCH* SE10 .... 105 D2
Blackwall Tunnel *POP/IOD* E14 .... 105 C3
Blackwall Tunnel App *POP/IOD* E14 .... 104 C1
Blackwall Tunnel Northern Ap
  BOW E3 .... 80 A5
Blackwall Wy *POP/IOD* E14 .... 104 C1
Blackwater St *EDUL* SE22 .... 137 F3
Blackwell Cl *CLPT* E5 .... 79 E1
Blackwood St *WALW* SE17 .... 119 D1
Blade Ms *PUT/ROE* SW15 .... 131 F2
Blagdon Rd *CAT* SE6 .... 140 B4
Blagrove Rd *NKENS* W10 .... 89 E4
Blair Av *CDALE/KGS* NW9 .... 51 E2
Blair St *BFN/LL* DA15 .... 145 E3
  IS N1 .... 76 C3
Blairderry Rd *BRXS/STRHM* SW2 .... 153 E2
Blair St *POP/IOD* E14 .... 92 C3
Blake Av *BARK* IG11 .... 85 E5
Blake Cl *NKENS* W10 .... 88 C4
  WELL DA16 .... 127 E4
Blake Gdns *FUL/PGN* SW6 .... 114 A4
Blake Hall Rd *WAN* E11 .... 64 A3
Blake Ms *RCH/KEW* TW9 .... 110 A4
Blakemore Gdns *BARN* SW13 .... 112 B2
Blakemore Rd *STRHM/NOR* SW16 .... 153 E3
Blakeney Cl *CAMTN* NW1 .... 8 A1
  HACK E8 .... 78 A2
Blaker Ct *CHARL* SE7 * 124 C3
Blaker Rd *SRTFD* E15 .... 93 F3
Blakes Cl *WLSDN* NW10 .... 80 C5
Blakes Rd *PECK* SE15 .... 119 E3
Blake's Rd *PECK* SE15 .... 119 E3
Blanchard Cl *ELTH/MOT* SE9 .... 161 E3
Blanchard Wy *HACK* E8 * 78 A3
Blanch Cl *PECK* SE15 .... 120 C3
Blanchedowne *CMBW* SE5 .... 137 D2
Blanche St *CAN/RD* E16 .... 93 F3
Blandfield Rd *BAL* SW12 .... 134 A4
Blandford Rd *CHSWK* W4 .... 99 E4
Blandford Sq *CAMTN* NW1 .... 17 D1
Blandford St *MHST* W1U 17 F4
Blann Cl *ELTH/MOT* SE9 .... 143 D2
Blaney Crs *EHAM* E6 .... 96 B2
Blanmerle Rd *ELTH/MOT* SE9 .... 162 B1
Blann Cl *ELTH/MOT* SE9 .... 143 D4
Blantyre St *WBPTN* SW10 .... 115 D3
Blantyre Wk *WBPTN* SW10 * 115 D3
Blashford St *LEW* SE13 .... 141 D5
Bleak Hill La *WOOL/PLUM* SE18 .... 127 F2
Blechynden Gdns *NKENS* W10 .... 101 D1
Blechynden St *NKENS* W10 * 101 D1
Bleeding Heart Yd *HCIRC* EC1N * 22 B3
Blendon Ter *WOOL/PLUM* SE18 .... 126 C1
Blendworth Wy *PECK* SE15 .... 119 E3
Blenheim Av *GNTH/NBYPK* IG2 .... 66 A1
Blenheim Cl *LEE/GVPK* SE12 .... 160 B1
Blenheim Ct *ARCH* N19 .... 57 E2
  BFN/LL DA15 .... 163 D3
Blenheim Crs *NTGHL* W11 .... 89 E5
  WELL DA16 .... 127 F4
Blenheim Gdns *BRXS/STRHM* SW2 .... 135 F4
  CRICK NW2 .... 70 C2
Blenheim Gv *PECK* SE15 .... 119 F5
Blenheim Pas *STJWD* NW8 * 3 E1
Blenheim Rd *CHSWK* W4 .... 99 E4
  EHAM E6 .... 95 D2
  STJWD NW8 .... 3 F1
  WAN E11 .... 81 E1
Blenheim St *CONDST* W1S 18 C5
Blenheim Ter *STJWD* NW8 .... 3 E1

Blenkarne Rd *BTSEA* SW11 .... 133 F4
Blessington Rd *LEW* SE13 .... 141 D2
Bletchley St *IS* N1 .... 11 F1
Bletsoe Wk *IS* N1 .... 11 F1
Blincoe Cl *WIM/MER* SW19 .... 149 D2
Blissett St *GNWCH* SE10 .... 122 C4
Bliss Ms *NKENS* W10 .... 89 E2
Blithfield St *KENS* W8 .... 38 C5
Bloemfontein Av *SHB* W12 .... 100 B1
Bloemfontein Rd *SHB* W12 .... 100 B1
Blomfield Rd *MV/WKIL* W9 .... 15 D2
Blomfield St *LVPST* EC2M 24 B3
Blomfield Vls *BAY/PAD* W2 .... 15 D3
Blondel St *BTSEA* SW11 .... 116 A5
Blondin St *BOW* E3 .... 92 A1
Bloomfield Crs *GNTH/NBYPK* IG2 .... 66 B1
Bloomfield Pl *MYFR/PKLN* W1K 31 D1
Bloomfield Rd *HGT* N6 .... 56 A1
  WOOL/PLUM SE18 .... 126 B1
Bloomfield Ter *BGVA* SW1W 116 A1
Bloom Gv *WNWD* SE27 .... 154 B3
Bloomhall Rd *NRWD* SE19 .... 155 D5
Bloom Park Rd *FUL/PGN* SW6 .... 113 F3
Bloomsbury Pl *NOXST/BSQ* WC1A 21 D3
Bloomsbury Sq *NOXST/BSQ* WC1A 21 D3
Bloomsbury St *GWRST* WC1E 20 B2
Bloomsbury Wy *NOXST/BSQ* WC1A 20 C3
Blore Cl *VX/NE* SW8 .... 117 D4
Blossom St *WCHPL* E1 .... 25 D1
Blount St *POP/IOD* E14 .... 91 E5
Bloxam Gdns *ELTH/MOT* SE9 .... 143 E5
Bloxhall Rd *LEY* E10 .... 61 D3
Blucher Rd *CMBW* SE5 .... 118 C3
Blue Anchor La *BERM/RHTH* SE16 .... 102 A5
Blue Anchor Yd *WCHPL* E1. .... 102 A1
Blue Ball Yd *WHALL* SW1A 31 E4
Bluebell Av *MNPK* E12 .... 83 D2
Bluebell Cl *HOM* E9 .... 78 C5
  SYD SE26 .... 155 F4
Bluebell Wy *IL* IG1 .... 84 B3
Bluebird Wy *THMD* SE28 .... 109 D3
Blue Lion Pl *STHWK* SE1 .... 48 C2
Blundell Cl *HACK* E8 .... 78 A1
Blundell St *HOLWY* N7 .... 75 E4
Blurton Rd *CLPT* E5 .... 79 D1
Blythe Cl *CAT* SE6 .... 139 F5
Blythe Hl *CAT* SE6 .... 139 F5
Blythe Hill La *CAT* SE6 .... 139 F5
Blythe Hill Pl *FSTH* SE23 * 139 F5
Blythe Ms *WKENS* W14 * 101 D4
Blythe Rd *WKENS* W14 .... 101 D4
Blythe St *BETH* E2 * 90 B2
Blytheswood Pl *STRHM/NOR* SW16 .... 153 F4
Blythe V *CAT* SE6 .... 157 F1
Blyth Rd *WALTH* E17 .... 61 F2
Blythwood Rd *FSBYPK* N4 .... 57 E2
Boadicea St *IS* N1 * 75 F5
Boardwalk Pl *POP/IOD* E14 .... 104 C2
Boathouse Wk *PECK* SE15 .... 119 F3
Boat Lifter Wy *BERM/RHTH* SE16 .... 103 E5
Boat Quay *CAN/RD* E16 .... 106 C1
Bob Anker Cl *PLSTW* E13 .... 94 A2
Bobbin Cl *CLAP* SW4 .... 134 C1
Bob Marley Wy *HNHL* SE24 .... 136 A2
Bocking St *HACK* E8 .... 78 B5
Boddicott Cl *WIM/MER* SW19 .... 149 E2
Boddington Gdns *ACT* W3 .... 98 A3
Bodmin St *WAND/EARL* SW18 .... 150 A1
Bodney Rd *CLPT* E5 .... 78 B2
Bofors House *CHARL* SE7 * 125 E3
Bohemia Pl *HACK* E8 .... 78 C3
Bohn Rd *WCHPL* E1 .... 91 E4
Boileau Rd *BARN* SW13 .... 112 A3
Bolden St *DEPT* SE8 .... 122 B5
Boldero Pl *STJWD* NW8 * 16 C1
Boleyn Rd *EHAM* E6 .... 95 D1
  FSTGT E7 .... 82 A4
  STNW/STAM N16 .... 77 E2
Bolina Rd *BERM/RHTH* SE16 .... 120 C1
Bolingbroke Gv *BTSEA* SW11 .... 133 E3
Bolingbroke Rd *WKENS* W14 .... 101 D4
Bolingbroke Wk *BTSEA* SW11 * 115 D5
Bollo Bridge Rd *ACT* W3 .... 98 B4
Bollo La *ACT* W3 .... 98 B4
  CHSWK W4 .... 98 C5
Bolney Ga *SKENS* SW7 .... 40 C1
Bolney St *VX/NE* SW8 .... 117 F3
Bolsover St *GTPST* W1W 19 D1
Bolt Ct *FLST/FETLN* EC4A 22 B5
Bolton Crs *LBTH* SE11 .... 118 A2

Bolton Gdns *ECT* SW5........................ 114 B1
  WLSDN NW10............................. 89 D1
Bolton Gardens Ms *WBPTN* SW10.... 114 B1
Bolton Pl *IS* N1 *.................................. 76 B4
Bolton Rd *CHSWK* W4.......................... 110 C3
  SRTFD E15.................................... 81 F3
  STJWD NW8................................... 72 B5
  WLSDN NW10............................... 69 E5
Boltons Pl *ECT* SW5............................ 114 C1
The Boltons *WBPTN* SW10 *............... 114 C1
Bolton St *MYFR/PICC* W1J................. 31 D3
Bombay St *BERM/RHTH* SE16............ 102 B5
Bomore Rd *NTGHL* W11........................ 101 D1
Bonar Rd *PECK* SE15........................... 120 A3
Bonchurch Rd *NKENS* W10.................. 89 E4
Bond St *SRTFD* E15.............................. 81 E2
Bondway *VX/NE* SW8............................ 117 E2
Boneta Rd *WOOL/PLUM* SE18............ 107 F4
Bonfield Rd *LEW* SE13......................... 140 C2
Bonham Rd *BRXS/STRHM* SW2........... 135 F3
Bonheur Rd *CHSWK* W4....................... 99 D3
Bonhill St *SDTCH* EC2A....................... 24 B1
Bonita Ms *PECK* SE15.......................... 139 D1
Bonner Rd *BETH* E2.............................. 90 C1
Bonner St *BETH* E2 *............................. 90 C1
Bonneville Gdns *CLAP* SW4................. 134 C4
Bonnington Sq *VX/NE* SW8.................. 117 F2
Bonny St *CAMTN* NW1........................... 74 C4
Bonsor St *CMBW* SE5........................... 119 E3
Bonville Rd *BMLY* BR1.......................... 159 F5
Boones Rd *LEW* SE13........................... 141 E2
Boone St *LEW* SE13.............................. 141 E2
Boord St *GNWCH* SE10........................ 105 E4
Boothby Rd *ARCH* N19.......................... 57 D4
Booth Cl *HOM* E9.................................. 78 B5
Booth La *BLKFR* EC4V........................... 12 A4
Boot St *FSBYE* EC1V.............................. 12 C4
Border Crs *SYD* SE26........................... 156 B5
Border Rd *SYD* SE26............................ 156 B5
Bordon Wk *PUT/ROE* SW15................. 130 A5
Boreas Wk *IS* N1................................... 11 D2
Boreham Av *CAN/RD* E16.................... 94 A5
Boreham St *WAN* E11........................... 62 C3
Borgard House *CHARL* SE7 *............... 125 E3
Borgard Rd *WOOL/PLUM* SE18........... 107 F5
Borland Rd *PECK* SE15........................ 138 C2
Borneo St *PUT/ROE* SW15.................. 130 C1
Borough High St *STHWK* SE1............. 47 F1
Borough Rd *STHWK* SE1...................... 46 C2
Borough Sq *STHWK* SE1 *.................... 47 E1
Borrett Cl *WALW* SE17......................... 118 C1
Borrodaile Rd *WAND/EARL* SW18...... 132 B4
Borthwick Ms *WAN* E11 *..................... 81 E1
Borthwick Rd *CDALE/KGS* NW9.......... 51 F1
  SRTFD E15.................................... 81 E1
Borthwick St *DEPT* SE8........................ 122 A1
Bosbury Rd *CAT* SE6............................ 158 C3
Boscastle Rd *KTTN* NW5..................... 56 B5
Boscobel Pl *BGVA* SW1W.................... 42 A4
Boscobel Rd *BAY/PAD* W2................... 78 E2
Boscombe Av *LEY* E10.......................... 63 D2
Boscombe Cl *CLPT* E5.......................... 79 E2
Boscombe Rd *SHB* W12........................ 100 A3
Boss St *STHWK* SE1.............................. 37 E5
Boston Gdns *CHSWK* W4..................... 111 E3
Boston Pl *CAMTN* NW1......................... 17 E1
Boston Rd *EHAM* E6.............................. 95 E2
  WALTH E17.................................. 62 A1
Boswell Rd *BMSBY* WC1N.................... 21 D1
Boswell St *BMSBY* WC1N..................... 21 D1
Bosworth Rd *NKENS* W10.................... 89 E3
Botha Rd *PLSTW* E13........................... 94 B4
Bothwell Cl *CAN/RD* E16...................... 94 A4
Bothwell St *HMSMTH* W6..................... 113 D1
Botolph Aly *MON* EC3R......................... 36 C2
Botolph La *MON* EC3R.......................... 36 C2
Bott's Ms *BAY/PAD* W2......................... 14 B5
Boughton Rd *THMD* SE28..................... 109 E4
Boulcott St *WCHPL* E1.......................... 91 D5
The Boulevard *FUL/PGN* SW6.............. 114 C5
Boultwood Rd *EHAM* E6....................... 95 F5
Boundaries Rd *BAL* SW12.................... 151 F2
Boundary Av *WALTH* E17...................... 61 F2
Boundary Cl *GDMY/SEVK* IG3............. 85 E1
Boundary La *CMBW* SE5....................... 118 C2
  PLSTW E13.................................. 95 D2
Boundary Ms *STJWD* NW8................... 72 C5
Boundary Pass *WCHPL* E1.................. 13 E5
Boundary Rd *BARK* IG11...................... 96 C1
  BFN/LL DA15................................ 145 E3
  PLSTW E13.................................. 94 C1
  STJWD NW8.................................. 72 C5

Boundary Rw *STHWK* SE1................... 34 C5
Boundary St *BETH* E2........................... 13 E4
Boundfield Rd *CAT* SE6....................... 159 E5
Bourchier St *SOHO/SHAV* W1D.......... 32 A1
Bourdon Pl *MYFR/PKLN* W1K............. 31 D1
Bourdon St *MYFR/PKLN* W1K.............. 30 C2
Bourke Cl *CLAP* SW4............................ 135 E4
  WLSDN NW10............................. 69 E3
Bourlet Cl *GTPST* W1W........................ 19 E3
Bournbrook Rd *BKHTH/KID* SE3......... 143 D1
Bourne Est *HCIRC* EC1N *.................... 22 A2
Bourne Rd *BAY/PAD* W2...................... 14 C2
Bournevale Rd *STRHM/NOR* SW16..... 153 E4
Bournville Rd *CAT* SE6......................... 140 A5
Bousfield Rd *NWCR* SE14..................... 121 D5
Boutcher Rd *BTSEA* SW11................... 133 E2
Boutique Hall *LEW* SE13 *.................... 140 C2
Bouverie Ms *STNW/STAM* N16............ 59 E4
Bouverie Pl *BAY/PAD* W2.................... 16 B4
Bouverie Rd *STNW/STAM* N16............ 59 E4
Bouverie St *EMB* EC4Y......................... 22 B5
Boveney Rd *FSTH* SE23........................ 139 D5
Bovill Rd *FSTH* SE23............................ 139 D5
Bovingdon Av *WBLY* HA9..................... 68 A3
Bovingdon Rd *FUL/PGN* SW6.............. 114 B4
Bovington Dr *ARCH* N19...................... 56 C4
Bowater Cl *BRXS/STRHM* SW2............ 135 E4
Bowater Pl *BKHTH/KID* SE3................. 124 B3
Bowater Rd *WBLY* HA9......................... 50 B5
  WOOL/PLUM SE18....................... 107 D2
Bow Bridge Est *BOW* E3...................... 92 B2
Bow Churchyard *STP* EC4M *.............. 23 F5
Bow Common La *BOW* E3..................... 91 F3
Bowden St *LBTH* SE11.......................... 118 A1
Bowditch *DEPT* SE8.............................. 121 F1
Bowdon Rd *WALTH* E17........................ 62 A2
Bowen Dr *DUL* SE21............................. 155 E3
Bowen Rd *POP/IOD* E14....................... 92 B5
Bower Av *GNWCH* SE10....................... 123 E4
Bowerdean St *FUL/PGN* SW6.............. 114 B4
Bowerman Av *NWCR* SE14.................. 121 E2
Bower St *WCHPL* E1............................. 91 D5
Bowes Rd *ACT* W3............................... 99 E1
Bowfell Rd *HMSMTH* W6...................... 112 C2
Bowhill Cl *BRXN/ST* SW9..................... 118 A3
Bowie Cl *CLAP* SW4............................. 135 D5
Bowland Rd *CLAP* SW4........................ 135 D2
Bowland Yd *KTBR* SW1X *.................... 41 F1
Bow La *STP* EC4M................................ 23 F5
Bowl Ct *WCHPL* E1............................... 25 D1
Bowley La *NRWD* SE19........................ 156 A4
Bowley St *POP/IOD* E14...................... 103 F1
Bowling Green Cl *PUT/ROE* SW15..... 130 B5
Bowling Green La *CLKNW* EC1R *....... 22 B1
Bowling Green Pl *STHWK* SE1 *......... 36 A5
Bowling Green Rw
  WOOL/PLUM SE18 *...................... 107 F5
Bowling Green St *LBTH* SE11............. 118 A2
Bowling Green Wk *IS* N1...................... 12 C3
Bow Locks *BOW* E3 *............................ 92 C3
Bowman Av *CAN/RD* E16...................... 94 A5
Bowman Ms *WAND/EARL* SW18......... 149 F1
Bowmans Lea *FSTH* SE23.................... 138 C5
Bowmans Ms *WCHPL* E1...................... 102 A1
Bowman's Ms *HOLWY* N7..................... 57 E5
Bowman's Pl *HOLWY* N7 *.................... 57 E5
Bowmead *ELTH/MOT* SE9.................... 161 F2
Bowmore Ms *CAMTN* NW1................... 75 D4
Bowness Cl *HACK* E8 *.......................... 77 F5
Bowness Crs *PUT/ROE* SW15............. 147 D5
Bowness Rd *CAT* SE6........................... 140 B5
Bowood Rd *CLAP* SW4.......................... 134 A2
Bowrons Av *WBLY* HA9........................ 68 A2
Bow Rd *BOW* E3.................................... 92 A2
Bow St *COVGDN* WC2E......................... 21 D1
  SRTFD E15.................................. 81 E2
Bowyer Cl *EHAM* E6............................. 95 F4
Bowyer Pl *CMBW* SE5.......................... 118 C3
Bowyer St *CMBW* SE5.......................... 118 C3
Boxall Rd *DUL* SE21.............................. 137 E4
Boxley St *CAN/RD* E16......................... 106 B2
Boxworth Gv *IS* N1............................... 75 F5
Boyard Rd *WOOL/PLUM* SE18............ 126 B1
Boyce Wy *PLSTW* E13.......................... 94 A3
Boycroft Av *CDALE/KGS* NW9............. 50 C5
Boydell Ct *STJWD* NW8........................ 73 D4

Boyd St *WCHPL* E1	90	A5
Boyfield St *STHWK* SE1	47	D1
Boyland Rd *BMLY* BR1	159	F5
Boyne Rd *LEW* SE13	141	D1
Boyne Terrace Ms *NTGHL* W11	101	F2
Boyson Rd *WALW* SE17	118	C2
Boyton Cl *WCHPL* E1	91	D5
Brabazon St *POP/IOD* E14	92	B5
Brabourne Cl *NRWD* SE19	155	E5
Brabourn Gv *PECK* SE15	120	C5
Bracewell Rd *NKENS* W10	88	C4
Bracey Av *FSBYPK* N4 *	57	E4
Bracken Av *BAL* SW12	134	A4
Brackenbury Gdns *HMSMTH* W6	100	B4
Brackenbury Rd *HMSMTH* W6	100	B4
Bracken Cl *EHAM* E6	95	F4
Bracken Gdns *BARN* SW13	112	A5
Brackley Av *PECK* SE15	138	C1
Brackley Rd *CHSWK* W4	99	F5
Brackley St *BARB* EC2Y	23	F2
Brackley Ter *CHSWK* W4	111	E1
Bracklyn St *IS* N1	12	A1
Bracknell Gdns *HAMP* NW3	72	B2
Bracknell Wy *HAMP* NW3	72	B2
Bradbourne St *FUL/PGN* SW6	114	A5
Bradbury St *STNW/STAM* N16	77	E2
Braddyll St *GNWCH* SE10	123	E1
Bradenham Cl *WALW* SE17	119	D2
Braden St *MV/WKIL* W9 *	14	C1
Bradfield Rd *CAN/RD* E16	106	A5
Bradford Cl *SYD* SE26	156	B4
Bradford Rd *ACT* W3	99	E3
IL IG1	67	D3
Bradgate Rd *CAT* SE6	140	B4
Brading Crs *WAN* E11	64	B4
Brading Rd *BRXS/STRHM* SW2	135	F5
Brading Ter *SHB* W12	100	A4
Bradiston Rd *MV/WKIL* W9	89	F2
Bradley Cl *HOLWY* N7	75	E4
Bradley Stone Rd *EHAM* E6	95	F5
Bradmead *VX/NE* SW8	116	B4
Bradmore Park Rd *HMSMTH* W6	100	B4
Bradshaw Cots *POP/IOD* E14 *	91	E5
Bradstock Rd *HOM* E9	79	D3
Brad St *STHWK* SE1	34	B4
Bradymead *EHAM* E6	96	A5
Brady St *WCHPL* E1	90	B5
Braemar Av *WIM/MER* SW19	150	A2
WLSDN NW10	51	D5
Braemar Gdns *BFN/LL* DA15	163	D3
Braemar Rd *PLSTW* E13	93	F3
Braeside *BECK* BR3	158	A5
Braes St *IS* N1	76	B4
Braganza St *WALW* SE17	118	B1
Braham St *WCHPL* E1	25	F5
Braid Av *ACT* W3	87	E5
Braidwood Rd *CAT* SE6	159	D1
Braidwood St *STHWK* SE1	36	C4
Brailsford Rd *BRXS/STRHM* SW2	136	A4
Braintree St *BETH* E2 *	90	C2
Bramalea Cl *HGT* N6	56	A1
Bramall Cl *SRTFD* E15	81	F2
Bramber Rd *WKENS* W14	113	F2
Bramblebury Rd *WOOL/PLUM* SE18	127	D1
Bramble Gdns *SHB* W12	88	A5
The Brambles *WIM/MER* SW19 *	149	F5
Bramcote Gv *BERM/RHTH* SE16	120	C1
Bramcote Rd *PUT/ROE* SW15	130	B2
Bramdean Crs *LEE/GVPK* SE12	160	A1
Bramdean Gdns *LEE/GVPK* SE12	160	A1
Bramerton St *CHEL* SW3	115	E2
Bramfield Rd *BTSEA* SW11	133	E4
Bramford Rd *WAND/EARL* SW18	132	C2
Bramham Gdns *ECT* SW5	114	B1
Bramhope La *CHARL* SE7	124	B2
Bramlands Cl *BTSEA* SW11	133	E1
Bramley Crs *CNTH/NBYPK* IG2	66	A1
VX/NE SW8	117	D3
Bramley Rd *NKENS* W10	101	D1
Brampton Cl *CLPT* E5	60	B4
Brampton Gv *WBLY* HA9	50	A3
Brampton Rd *EHAM* E6	95	D3
Bramshaw Rd *HOM* E9	79	D3
Bramshill Gdns *KTTN* NW5	56	B5
Bramshill Rd *WLSDN* NW10	87	E1
Bramshot Av *CHARL* SE7	124	B2
Bramston Rd *WLSDN* NW10	88	A1
Bramwell Ms *IS* N1	75	F5
Brancaster Rd *CNTH/NBYPK* IG2	67	D1
STRHM/NOR SW16	153	E3
Branch Hl *HAMP* NW3	54	C5
Branch Pl *IS* N1	77	D5
Branch Rd *POP/IOD* E14	91	E5
Branch St *CMBW* SE5	119	E3
Brand Cl *FSBYPK* N4	58	B3
Brandlehow Rd *PUT/ROE* SW15	131	F2
Brandon Ms *BARB* EC2Y *	24	A2
Brandon Rd *HOLWY* N7	75	E4
Brandon St *WALW* SE17	47	F4
Brandram Ms *LEW* SE13 *	141	E2
Brandram Rd *LEW* SE13	141	E1
Brandreth Rd *EHAM* E6	95	F5
TOOT SW17	152	B2
Brand St *GNWCH* SE10	122	C3
Brangbourne Rd *BMLY* BR1	158	C5
Brangton Rd *LBTH* SE11	117	F1
Branksea St *FUL/PGN* SW6	113	D4
Branksome Rd *BRXS/STRHM* SW2	135	E3
Branscombe St *LEW* SE13	140	B1
Bransdale Cl *KIL/WHAMP* NW6	72	A5
Brantwood Rd *HNHL* SE24	136	C3
Brasenose Dr *BARN* SW13	112	C2
Brassey Rd *KIL/WHAMP* NW6	71	F3
Brassey Sq *BTSEA* SW11	134	A1
Brassie Av *ACT* W3	87	E5
Brasted Cl *SYD* SE26	156	C4
Brathway Rd *WAND/EARL* SW18	132	A5
Bratley St *WCHPL* E1	90	A3
Braundton Av *BFN/LL* DA15	163	F1
Bravington Pl *MV/WKIL* W9	89	F3
Bravington Rd *MV/WKIL* W9	89	F2
Bravingtons Wk *IS* N1	9	D3
Braxfield Rd *BROCKY* SE4	139	E2
Brayard's Rd *PECK* SE15	120	B5
Braybrook St *SHB* W12	87	F4
Brayburne Av *VX/NE* SW8	116	C5
Bray Crs *BERM/RHTH* SE16	103	D3
Braydon Rd *STNW/STAM* N16	59	F3
Bray Dr *CAN/RD* E16	105	F1
Brayfield Ter *IS* N1	76	A4
Brayford Sq *WCHPL* E1 *	90	C5
Bray Pl *CHEL* SW3	115	F1
Braywood Rd *ELTH/MOT* SE9	145	D2
Bread St *STP* EC4M	23	F5
Breakspears Ms *BROCKY* SE4	122	A5
Breakspears Rd *BROCKY* SE4	139	F1
Bream Gdns *EHAM* E6	96	A2
Breamore Cl *PUT/ROE* SW15	148	A1
Breamore Rd *GDMY/SEVK* IG3	67	F4
Bream's Blds *LINN* WC2A	22	A4
Bream St *BOW* E3	80	A4
Breasley Cl *PUT/ROE* SW15	130	B2
Brechin Pl *SKENS* SW7	114	C1
Brecknock Rd *ARCH* N19	74	C1
Brecknock Road Est *ARCH* N19 *	75	D2
Brecon Gn *CDALE/KGS* NW9 *	51	E1
Brecon Ms *KTTN* NW5	75	D3
Brecon Rd *HMSMTH* W6	113	E2
Brede Cl *EHAM* E6	96	B2
Bredgar Rd *ARCH* N19	56	B4
Breer St *FUL/PGN* SW6	132	B1
Breezer's Hl *WAP* E1W *	102	A1
Bremans Rw *WAND/EARL* SW18	150	C2
Bremner Rd *SKENS* SW7	39	F2
Brenda Rd *TOOT* SW17	151	F2
Brendon Av *WLSDN* NW10	69	E1
Brendon Rd *ELTH/MOT* SE9	163	D2
Brendon St *MBLAR* W1H	17	D4
Brenley Gdns *ELTH/MOT* SE9	143	D2
Brent Cross F/O *HDN* NW4	52	C2
Brentfield *WLSDN* NW10	68	B4
Brentfield Cl *WLSDN* NW10	69	D3
Brentfield Gdns *CRICK* NW2 *	53	D2
Brentfield Rd *WLSDN* NW10	69	D3
Brenthouse Rd *HACK* E8	78	B4
Brenthurst Rd *WLSDN* NW10	70	A3
Brenton St *POP/IOD* E14	91	E5
Brent Park Rd *CDALE/KGS* NW9	52	A3
Brent Rd *CAN/RD* E16	94	A5
WOOL/PLUM SE18	126	B3
Brent Ter *CRICK* NW2	52	C4
Brent View Rd *CDALE/KGS* NW9	52	A3
Brent Wy *WBLY* HA9	68	B3
Brentwood Cl *ELTH/MOT* SE9	162	C1
Bressenden Pl *WESTW* SW1E	43	D2
Brett Cl *STNW/STAM* N16	59	E4
Brett Crs *WLSDN* NW10	69	D5
Brett St *WALW* SE17	119	D1
Brett Pas *HACK* E8	78	B2
Brett Rd *HACK* E8	78	B2
Brett Vls *ACT* W3 *	87	D4

Brewer St *REGST* W1B........................ 31 F1
Brewery Rd *HOLWY* N7........................ 75 E4
  WOOL/PLUM SE18................. 127 D1
Brewery Sq *FSBYE* EC1V...................... 23 D1
  STHWK SE1
Brewhouse La *WAP* E1W...................... 102 B2
Brewhouse Rd *WOOL/PLUM* SE18........ 107 F5
Brewhouse St *PUT/ROE* SW15.............. 131 E2
Brewhouse Wk *BERM/RHTH* SE16......... 103 E2
Brewhouse Yd *FSBYE* EC1V.................. 10 C5
Brewster Gdns *NKENS* W10................... 88 C4
Brewster Rd *LEY* E10........................... 62 B3
Briant St *NWCR* SE14......................... 121 D4
Briardale Gdns *HAMP* NW3.................. 54 A5
Briar Rd *CRICK* NW2............................ 70 C1
Briar Wk *NKENS* W10............................ 89 E3
  PUT/ROE SW15
Briarwood Cl *CDALE/KGS* NW9 *........... 50 C1
Briarwood Rd *CLAP* SW4...................... 135 D3
Briary Cl *HAMP* NW3 *.......................... 73 E4
Briary Gdns *BMLY* BR1........................ 160 B5
Brickbarn Cl *WBPTN* SW10 *............... 114 C3
Brick Ct *EMB* EC4Y............................. 22 A5
Brick Farm Cl *RCH/KEW* TW9.............. 110 B4
Brickfield Cots *WOOL/PLUM* SE18....... 127 F2
Brickfield Rd *BOW* E3......................... 92 B3
  WIM/MER SW19................. 150 B4
Brick La *WCHPL* E1............................ 25 F1
Brick St *MYFR/PKLN* W1K................... 31 E3
Brickwood Ct *SYD* SE26...................... 156 B5
Bridale Cl *PECK* SE15......................... 119 F2
Bride Ct *EMB* EC4Y............................. 22 C5
Bride La *EMB* EC4Y............................. 22 C5
Bridel Ms *FSBYE* EC1V........................ 10 C2
Bride St *HOLWY* N7............................. 75 F3
Bridewain St *STHWK* SE1.................... 49 E2
Bridewell Pl *BLKFR* EC4V..................... 22 C5
  WAP E1W.......................... 102 B2
Bridford Ms *GTPST* W1W..................... 19 D2
Bridge Av *HMSMTH* W6....................... 112 C1
Bridge Cl *NKENS* W10 *....................... 89 D5
Bridge House Quay *POP/IOD* E14......... 104 C2
Bridgeland Rd *CAN/RD* E16................. 106 A1
Bridge La *BTSEA* SW11........................ 115 E4
Bridgeman Rd *IS* N1............................ 75 F4
Bridgeman St *STJWD* NW8.................... 4 C2
Bridge Mew *NWCR* SE14 *................. 121 D2
Bridge Pde *STRHM/NOR* SW16 *......... 153 E6
Bridge Pk *WAND/EARL* SW18............. 132 A3
Bridge Pl *PIM* SW1V............................ 43 D4
Bridgepoint Pl *HGT* N6......................... 56 B3
Bridgeport Pl *WAP* E1W *.................... 102 A2
Bridge Rd *EHAM* E6............................ 83 F4
  LEY E10............................ 61 E4
  SRTFD E15........................ 81 D5
  WALTH E17........................ 61 F2
  WBLY HA9......................... 50 A3
  WLSDN NW10..................... 69 E3
Bridges Ct *BTSEA* SW11.................... 133 D1
Bridge St *CHSWK* W4.......................... 99 D5
  WHALL SW1A..................... 44 C1
Bridge Ter *LEW* SE13 *..................... 141 D2
  SRTFD E15........................ 81 D4
Bridgetown Cl *NRWD* SE19................ 155 E5
Bridgeview *HMSMTH* W6.................. 112 C1
Bridge Vis *MHMR* SW19 *................. 150 A5
Bridgewater Sq *BARB* EC2Y *.............. 23 E2
Bridgewater St *BARB* EC2Y................. 23 E2
Bridgeway *BARK* IG11.......................... 85 F4
Bridgeway St *CAMTN* NW1.................... 5 F4
Bridgford St *WAND/EARL* SW18.......... 150 C3
Bridgman Rd *CHSWK* W4...................... 98 C4
Bridle La *SOHO/CST* W1F..................... 31 F1
Bridport Pl *IS* N1................................ 77 D5
Bridstow Pl *BAY/PAD* W2..................... 14 B4
Brief St *BRXN/ST* SW9...................... 118 B4
Brierley Rd *BAL* SW12........................ 152 C1
  WAN E11.......................... 81 D1
Brierly Gdns *BETH* E2 *....................... 90 C1
Brigade St *BKHTH/KID* SE3................ 123 F5
Briggeford Cl *CLPT* E5......................... 60 A4
Brightfield Rd *LEE/GVPK* SE12.......... 141 E3
Brightling Rd *BROCKY* SE4................. 140 B4
Brightlingsea Pl *POP/IOD* E14........... 103 F1
Brightman Rd *WAND/EARL* SW18........ 151 D1
Brighton Rd *EHAM* E6.......................... 96 A2
  STNW N16.......................... 77 E1
Brighton Ter *BRXN/ST* SW9................ 135 F2
Brightside Rd *LEW* SE13................... 141 E4
Bright St *POP/IOD* E14........................ 92 B5
Brightwell Crs *TOOT* SW17................. 151 F5
Brig Ms *DEPT* SE8.............................. 122 A2

Brill Pl *CAMTN* NW1.............................. 8 B1
Brindle Ga *BFN/LL* DA15.................... 163 E1
Brindley St *BROCKY* SE4.................... 121 F4
Brindley Wy *BMLY* BR1....................... 160 B5
Brinklow Crs *WOOL/PLUM* SE18......... 126 B3
Brinkworth Wy *HOM* E9........................ 79 F3
Brinsley St *WCHPL* E1 *...................... 90 C5
Brinton Wk *STHWK* SE1........................ 34 C4
Brion Pl *POP/IOD* E14.......................... 92 C4
Brisbane Rd *IL* IG1............................... 66 C2
  LEY E10............................ 62 B4
Brisbane St *CMBW* SE5...................... 119 D4
Briscoe Cl *WAN* E11............................ 63 F4
Briset Rd *ELTH/MOT* SE9................... 143 D1
Briset St *FARR* EC1M.......................... 22 C2
Briset Wy *HOLWY* N7........................... 57 F4
Bristol Gdns *MV/WKIL* W9................... 15 D1
Bristol Ms *MV/WKIL* W9...................... 15 D1
Bristol Rd *FSTGT* E7........................... 82 C3
Briston Gv *CEND/HSY/T* N8................. 57 E1
Bristowe Cl *BRXS/STRHM* SW2.......... 136 A4
Bristow Rd *NRWD* SE19..................... 155 E5
Britannia Cl *CLAP* SW4...................... 135 D2
Britannia Ga *CAN/RD* E16................. 106 A2
Britannia Rd *FUL/PGN* SW6............... 114 B3
  IL IG1.............................. 66 B5
  POP/IOD E14................... 104 A5
Britannia Rw *IS* N1.............................. 76 B5
Britannia St *FSBYW* WC1X................... 9 F3
Britannia Wk *IS* N1............................. 12 A2
Britannia Wy *FUL/PGN* SW6............... 114 B3
  WLSDN NW10..................... 86 B3
British Est *BOW* E3............................. 91 F2
British Gv *HMSMTH* W6..................... 111 F1
British Grove Pas *CHSWK* W4 *......... 111 F1
British St *BOW* E3............................... 91 F2
Brittage Rd *WLSDN* NW10.................. 69 E4
Britten Cl *GLDGN* NW11...................... 54 B3
Britten St *CHEL* SW3......................... 115 E1
Brittidge Rd *WLSDN* NW10 *............... 69 E4
Britton Cl *CAT* SE6............................ 141 D5
Britton St *FARR* EC1M........................ 22 C1
Brixham Gdns *GDMY/SEVK* IG3........... 85 E2
Brixham St *CAN/RD* E16.................... 107 F2
Brixton HI *BRXS/STRHM* SW2............ 135 F4
Brixton Hill Pl *BRXS/STRHM* SW2...... 135 E5
Brixton Ov *BRXS/STRHM* SW2............ 136 A2
Brixton Rd *BRXN/ST* SW9................... 136 A2
  LBTH SE11....................... 118 A2
Brixton Station Rd *BRXN/ST* SW9...... 136 A1
Brixton Water La *BRXS/STRHM* SW2... 135 F3
Broadbent Cl *HGT* N6.......................... 56 B3
Broadbent St *MYFR/PKLN* W1K *.......... 30 C1
Broad Bridge Cl *BKHTH/KID* SE3....... 124 A3
  STNW/STAM N16 *.............. 60 A3
Broad Ct *COVGDN* WC2E *.................... 21 D5
Broadfield Cl *CRICK* NW2.................... 52 C5
Broadfield La *CAMTN* NW1................... 75 E4
Broadfield Rd *CAT* SE6...................... 159 E1
Broadfields Wy *WLSDN* NW10.............. 69 F2
Broadgates Rd *WAND/EARL* SW18..... 151 D1
Broadheath Dr *CHST* BR7.................. 161 F5
Broadhinton Rd *CLAP* SW4................. 134 B1
Broadhurst Av *GDMY/SEVK* IG3........... 85 F1
Broadhurst Cl *KIL/WHAMP* NW6 *......... 72 C3
Broadhurst Gdns *KIL/WHAMP* NW6...... 72 B3
Broadlands Av *STRHM/NOR* SW16..... 153 E2
Broadlands Cl *HGT* N6.......................... 56 A2
  STRHM/NOR SW16.............. 153 E2
Broadlands Rd *BMLY* BR1................... 160 B4
  HGT N6............................ 55 F2
Broad Lawn *ELTH/MOT* SE9................ 162 A1
Broadley St *STJWD* NW8...................... 16 C2
Broadley Ter *CAMTN* NW1.................... 17 D1
Broadmead *CAT* SE6.......................... 158 A3
Broadstone Pl *MHST* W1U.................... 18 A3
Broad Street Av *LVPST* EC2M.............. 24 B3
Broad Street Pl *LVPST* EC2M................ 24 B3
Broadview *CDALE/KGS* NW9................. 50 A1
Broad Wk *BKHTH/KID* SE3................ 124 C5
Broadwalk La *GLDGN* NW11................. 53 F2
The Broad Wk *BAY/PAD* W2................. 27 D3
Broadwall *STHWK* SE1........................ 34 B3
Broadwater Rd *THMD* SE28................ 109 D4
  TOOT SW17..................... 151 E4
Broadway *BARK* IG11.......................... 84 C5
  SRTFD E15........................ 81 D4
  STJSK SW1H..................... 44 A1
Broadway Market *HACK* E8.................. 78 B5
Broadway Market Ms *HACK* E8............. 78 A5
Broadway Ms *STNW/STAM* N16............ 59 F2

The Broadway *ACT* W3 *.................... 98 A3
   CDALE/KGS NW9................... 51 F1
   CEND/HSY/T N8..................... 57 E1
   PLSTW E13........................... 94 A1
Broadwell Pde *KIL/WHAMP* NW6 *..... 72 C3
Broadwick St *SOHO/CST* W1F........... 31 F1
Broadwood Ter *WKENS* W14 *.......... 101 F5
Broad Yd *FARR* EC1M..................... 22 C1
Brocas Cl *HAMP* NW3.................... 73 E4
Brockdish Av *BARK* IG11.................. 85 F2
Brockenhurst Gdns *IL* IG1................ 84 C2
Brockham Cl *WIM/MER* SW19............ 149 F5
Brockham Dr *BRXS/STRHM* SW2......... 135 F5
   GNTH/NBYPK IG2..................... 66 C1
Brockham St *STHWK* SE1................. 47 F2
Brockill Crs *BROCKY* SE4................. 139 E2
Brocklebank Rd *CHARL* SE7............. 106 B5
   WAND/EARL SW18.................. 132 C5
Brocklehurst St *NWCR* SE14............. 121 D3
Brockley Cross *BROCKY* SE4.............. 139 E1
Brockley Gv *BROCKY* SE4................. 139 E3
Brockley Hall Rd *BROCKY* SE4........... 139 E3
Brockley Pk *FSTH* SE23.................. 139 E5
Brockley Ri *FSTH* SE23................... 139 E5
Brockley Rd *FSTH* SE23................... 139 E4
Brockley Vw *FSTH* SE23.................. 139 E5
Brockley Wy *FSTH* SE23................. 139 D3
Brockman Ri *BMLY* BR1................... 159 D4
Brock Pl *BOW* E3........................... 92 B3
Brock Rd *PLSTW* E13...................... 94 B4
Brock St *PECK* SE15 *..................... 138 C1
Brockway Cl *WAN* E11..................... 63 E4
Brockwell Park Gdns *HNHL* SE24...... 136 B5
Brockwell Park Rw
   BRXS/STRHM SW2................... 136 A5
Brodia Rd *STNW/STAM* N16............. 59 E5
Brodie St *STHWK* SE1.................... 119 F1
Brodlove La *WAP* E1W.................... 103 D1
Brodrick Rd *TOOT* SW17.................. 151 E2
Broken Whf *BLKFR* EC4V................. 35 E1
Brokesley St *BOW* E3..................... 91 F3
Broke Wk *HACK* E8 *....................... 78 A5
Bromar Rd *CMBW* SE5................... 137 E1
Bromehead St *WCHPL* E1................. 90 C5
Brome House *CHARL* SE7 *............... 125 E3
Bromell's Rd *CLAP* SW4.................. 134 C2
Brome Rd *ELTH/MOT* SE9............... 143 F1
Bromfelde Rd *CLAP* SW4................. 135 D1
Bromfield St *IS* N1........................ 10 B1
Bromhedge *ELTH/MOT* SE9............. 161 F3
Bromley Hall Rd *POP/IOD* E14......... 92 C4
Bromley High St *BOW* E3................. 92 B2
Bromley HI *BMLY* BR1..................... 159 D5
Bromley Rd *CAT* SE6...................... 158 B5
   LEY E10.............................. 62 B2
Bromley St *WCHPL* E1..................... 91 D4
Brompton Ar *CHEL* SW3 *................. 41 E1
Brompton Cots *WBPTN* SW10 *......... 114 C2
Brompton Park Crs *FUL/PGN* SW6..... 114 B2
Brompton Pl *CHEL* SW3.................. 41 D2
Brompton Rd *CHEL* SW3.................. 40 C2
Brompton Sq *CHEL* SW3.................. 40 C2
Brompton Ter *WOOL/PLUM* SE18 *.... 126 A4
Bromwich Av *HGT* N6...................... 56 A4
Bromyard Av *ACT* W3...................... 99 E2
Brondesbury Ms *KIL/WHAMP* NW6 *.... 72 A4
Brondesbury Pk *KIL/WHAMP* NW6..... 70 C4
Brondesbury Rd *KIL/WHAMP* NW6..... 89 F1
Brondesbury Vls *KIL/WHAMP* NW6..... 89 F1
Bronsart Rd *FUL/PGN* SW6.............. 113 E5
Bronte Cl *FSTGT* E7 *...................... 82 A1
Bronti Cl *WALW* SE17..................... 118 C1
Bronze St *DEPT* SE8....................... 122 A3
Brookbank Rd *LEW* SE13................. 140 A1
Brook Cl *ACT* W3.......................... 98 A2
   TOOT SW17.......................... 152 A2
Brookdale Rd *CAT* SE6................... 140 B5
Brookdene Rd *WOOL/PLUM* SE18 *.... 127 F1
Brook Dr *LBTH* SE11....................... 46 B3
Brookehowse Rd *CAT* SE6............... 158 A2
Brookend Rd *BFN/LL* DA15.............. 163 E1
Brooker Cl *POP/IOD* E14................. 91 F4
Brooke Rd *STNW/STAM* N16............ 60 A5
Brooke's Market *HCIRC* EC1N *......... 22 A2
   HCIRC EC1N *........................ 22 A3
Brookfield Pk *KTTN* NW5................. 56 B5
Brookfield Rd *CHSWK* W4................ 99 D3
   HOM E9............................... 79 F2
Brook Gdns *BARN* SW13................. 129 F1
Brook Ga *MYFR/PKLN* W1K.............. 29 E1
Brook Gn *HMSMTH* W6................... 100 C4

Brook Hill Cl *WOOL/PLUM* SE18....... 126 B1
Brookhill Rd *WOOL/PLUM* SE18....... 126 B1
Brooking Rd *FSTGT* E7.................... 82 A2
Brooklands Av *BFN/LL* DA15............ 163 D2
   WIM/MER SW19..................... 150 B2
Brooklands Ct *KIL/WHAMP* NW6....... 71 F4
Brooklands Pk *BKHTH/KID* SE3......... 142 A1
Brook La *BKHTH/KID* SE3................. 124 B5
Brook Ms North *BAY/PAD* W2 *......... 27 F1
Brookmill Rd *DEPT* SE8................... 122 A4
Brook Rd *CRICK* NW2..................... 52 A4
   GNTH/NBYPK IG2.................... 66 B1
Brooks Av *EHAM* E6....................... 95 F3
Brooksbank St *HOM* E9 *................. 79 D3
Brooksby Ms *IS* N1........................ 76 A4
Brooksby St *IS* N1......................... 76 A4
Brooksby's Wk *HOM* E9.................. 79 D2
Brookside Rd *ARCH* N19................. 56 C4
   GLDGN NW11........................ 53 E1
Brooks La *CHSWK* W4..................... 110 A2
Brook's Market *HCIRC* EC1N *........... 30 C1
Brooks Rd *CHSWK* W4.................... 110 A1
Brook St *BAY/PAD* W2.................... 28 B1
   MYFR/PKLN W1K.................... 30 B1
Brooksville Av *KIL/WHAMP* NW6....... 71 E5
Brookview Rd *STRHM/NOR* SW16..... 152 C5
Brookville Rd *FUL/PGN* SW6............ 113 F3
Brookway *BKHTH/KID* SE3............... 142 A1
Brookwood Av *BARN* SW13.............. 129 F1
Brookwood Rd *WAND/EARL* SW18..... 149 F1
Broome Wy *CMBW* SE5................... 119 D3
Broomfield *WALTH* E17................... 61 F1
Broomfield St *POP/IOD* E14............. 92 A4
Broomgrove Rd *BRXN/ST* SW9.......... 117 F5
Broomhill Rd *WAND/EARL* SW18....... 132 A5
Broomhouse La *FUL/PGN* SW6.......... 114 A5
Broomhouse Rd *FUL/PGN* SW6......... 114 A5
Broomsleigh St *KIL/WHAMP* NW6 *.... 72 A2
Broomwood Rd *BTSEA* SW11............ 133 E4
Broseley Gv *SYD* SE26................... 157 E5
Brougham Rd *ACT* W3.................... 86 C5
   HACK E8............................... 78 A5
Brougham St *BTSEA* SW11............... 115 F5
Brough Cl *VX/NE* SW8.................... 117 E3
Broughton Dr *BRXN/ST* SW9............ 136 A2
Broughton Gdns *HGT* N6................. 56 C1
Broughton Rd *FUL/PGN* SW6........... 114 B5
Broughton Road Ap *FUL/PGN* SW6 *.. 114 B5
Broughton St *VX/NE* SW8................ 116 A5
Brownfield St *POP/IOD* E14............. 92 B5
Brown Hart Gdns *MYFR/PKLN* W1K.... 30 B1
Browning Cl *MV/WKIL* W9................ 15 F1
   WELL DA16.......................... 127 E4
Browning St *WALW* SE17................. 118 C1
Browning Rd *MNPK* E12.................. 83 F3
   WAN E11............................. 63 F2
Brownlow Ms *CAVSQ/HST* W1G *....... 18 B3
Brownlow Ms *BMSBY* WC1N............. 9 F5
Brownlow Rd *FSTGT* E7.................. 82 A1
   HACK E8.............................. 77 F5
   WLSDN NW10........................ 69 E4
Brownlow St *HHOL* WC1V................ 21 F3
Brownspring Dr *ELTH/MOT* SE9....... 162 B5
Brown St *MBLAR* W1H..................... 17 E4
Brownswood Rd *FSBYPK* N4............ 58 B3
Broxash Rd *BTSEA* SW11................. 134 A4
Broxbourne House *BOW* E3............. 92 A5
Broxbourne Rd *FSTGT* E7................ 64 A5
Broxholm Rd *WNWD* SE27............... 154 A3
Broxted Rd *FSTH* SE23.................... 157 F2
Broxwood Wy *STJWD* NW8.............. 73 E5
Bruce Cl *NKENS* W10...................... 89 D4
Bruce Rd *BOW* E3.......................... 92 B2
   WLSDN NW10........................ 69 D4
Bruckner St *NKENS* W10................. 89 E2
Brudenell Rd *TOOT* SW17................ 151 F5
Bruford Ct *DEPT* SE8...................... 122 A2
Bruges Pl *CAMTN* NW1................... 74 C4
Brunel Cl *WLSDN* NW10................... 88 A2
Brunel Est *BAY/PAD* W2................... 14 A3
Brunel House *WOOL/PLUM* SE18 *.... 125 E3
Brunel Ms *NKENS* W10................... 89 D2
Brunel Rd *ACT* W3......................... 87 E4
   BERM/RHTH SE16................... 102 C3
   WALTH E17.......................... 61 E1
Brunel St *CAN/RD* E16................... 93 F5
Brune St *WCHPL* E1....................... 25 E5
Bruno Pl *CDALE/KGS* NW9............... 50 A3
Brunswick Ct *STHWK* SE1................ 49 D1

Brunswick Gdns *KENS* W8	26 B4
Brunswick Ms *MBLAR* W1H	17 F4
Brunswick Pk *CMBW* SE5	119 D4
Brunswick Pl *CAMTN* NW1	18 B1
IS N1	12 B4
Brunswick Quay *BERM/RHTH* SE16	103 D4
Brunswick Rd *LEY* E10	62 C5
Brunswick Sq *BMSBY* WC1N	9 D5
Brunswick Vls *CMBW* SE5	119 E4
Brunton Pl *POP/IOD* E14	91 E5
Brushfield St *WCHPL* E1	25 D1
Brushwood Cl *POP/IOD* E14	92 B4
Brussels Rd *BTSEA* SW11	133 D2
Bruton La *MYFR/PICC* W1J	31 D2
Bruton Pl *MYFR/PICC* W1J	31 D2
Bruton St *MYFR/PICC* W1J	31 D2
Bryan Av *WLSDN* NW10	70 B4
Bryan Rd *BERM/RHTH* SE16	103 F3
Bryanston Ms East *MBLAR* W1H	17 E3
Bryanston Ms West *MBLAR* W1H	17 E3
Bryanston Pl *MBLAR* W1H	17 E3
Bryanston Sq *MBLAR* W1H	17 E4
Bryanston St *MBLAR* W1H	17 E5
Bryant St *SRTFD* E15	81 D4
Bryantwood Rd *HOLWY* N7	76 A2
Bryden Cl *SYD* SE26	157 E5
Brydges Pl *CHCR* WC2N	32 C2
Brydges Rd *SRTFD* E15	81 D2
Brydon Wk *IS* N1	75 E5
Bryett Rd *HOLWY* N7	57 F4
Brymay Cl *BOW* E3	92 A1
Brynmaer Rd *BTSEA* SW11	115 F4
Bryony Rd *SHB* W12	100 A1
Buchanan Gdns *WLSDN* NW10	88 B1
Buchan Rd *PECK* SE15	138 C1
Bucharest Rd *WAND/EARL* SW18	132 C5
Buckden Cl *LEE/GVPK* SE12	141 F4
Buckfast St *BETH* E2	90 A2
Buckhold Rd *WAND/EARL* SW18	132 A4
Buckhurst St *WCHPL* E1	90 B3
Buckingham Av *WELL* DA16	145 E2
Buckingham Dr *CHST* BR7	162 B5
Buckingham Ga *WESTW* SW1E	43 E2
Buckingham La *FSTH* SE23	139 E5
Buckingham Ms *IS* N1	77 E3
WESTW SW1E *	43 E2
WLSDN NW10	87 F1
Buckingham Palace Rd *BGVA* SW1W	42 C4
Buckingham Pl *WESTW* SW1E	43 E2
Buckingham Rd *IL* IG1	67 D4
IS N1	77 E3
LEY E10	62 B5
SRTFD E15	81 F2
SRTFD E15	81 F1
Buckingham St *CHCR* WC2N	33 D2
Buckland Crs *HAMP* NW3	73 D4
Buckland Rd *LEY* E10	62 C4
Buckland St *IS* N1	12 B2
Bucklersbury *MANHO* EC4N *	24 A5
Buckle St *WCHPL* E1	25 F4
Buckley Cl *FSTH* SE23	138 B5
Buckley Rd *KIL/WHAMP* NW6	71 F4
Buckmaster Rd *BTSEA* SW11	133 D2
Bucknall St *NOXST/BSQ* WC1A	20 C4
Bucknell Cl *BRXS/STRHM* SW2	135 F2
Buckner Rd *BRXS/STRHM* SW2	135 F2
Buckstone Cl *FSTH* SE23	138 C4
Buck St *CAMTN* NW1	74 B5
Buckters Rents *BERM/RHTH* SE16	103 D2
Buckthorne Rd *BROCKY* SE4	139 E4
Buddings Cir *WBLY* HA9	50 C5
Budge Rw *MANHO* EC4N *	36 A1
Buer Rd *FUL/PGN* SW6	113 E5
Bugsby's Wy *GNWCH* SE10	105 F5
Bulinca St *WEST* SW1P *	44 C5
Bullace Rw *CMBW* SE5	119 D4
Bullards Pl *BETH* E2	91 D2
Bulleid Wy *BGVA* SW1W	43 D5
Bullen St *BTSEA* SW11	115 E5
Buller Cl *PECK* SE15	120 A3
Buller Rd *BARK* IG11	85 E4
WLSDN NW10	89 D2
Bullivant St *POP/IOD* E14	104 C1
Bull Rd *SRTFD* E15	93 F1
Bulls Aly *MORT/ESHN* SW14 *	129 D1
Bull's Gdns *CHEL* SW3	41 D4
Bull Yd *PECK* SE15	120 A4
Bulmer Ms *NTGHL* W11	26 A3
Bulstrode Pl *MHST* W1U	18 B3
Bulstrode St *MHST* W1U	18 B4
Bulwer Court Rd *WAN* E11	63 D3
Bulwer Rd *WAN* E11	63 D3

Bulwer St *SHB* W12	100 C2
Bunhill Rw *STLK* EC1Y	12 A5
Bunhouse Pl *BGVA* SW1W	116 A1
Bunkers Hl *GLDGN* NW11	54 C2
Bunning Wy *HOLWY* N7	75 E4
Bunsen St *BOW* E3	91 E1
Bunton St *WOOL/PLUM* SE18	108 A4
Buonaparte Ms *PIM* SW1V	17 D1
Burbage Cl *STHWK* SE1	48 A3
Burbage Rd *HNHL* SE24	137 D4
Burcham St *POP/IOD* E14	92 B5
Burchell Rd *LEY* E10	62 B3
PECK SE15	120 B4
Burcher Gale Gv *PECK* SE15	119 E5
Burcote Rd *WAND/EARL* SW18	151 D1
Burdenshott Av *RCHPK/HAM* TW10	128 C3
Burden Wy *WAN* E11	64 B4
Burder Cl *IS* N1	77 E3
Burder Rd *IS* N1	77 E3
Burdett Rd *BOW* E3	91 F3
POP/IOD E14	91 F5
Burfield Cl *TOOT* SW17	150 C4
Burford Rd *CAT* SE6	157 F2
EHAM E6	95 E2
SRTFD E15	81 D4
Burford Wk *FUL/PGN* SW6 *	114 B3
Burges Gv *BARN* SW13	112 B3
Burges Rd *EHAM* E6	84 A4
Burgess Av *CDALE/KGS* NW9	51 D1
Burgess Hl *CRICK* NW2	72 A1
Burgess Rd *SRTFD* E15	81 E1
Burgess St *POP/IOD* E14	92 A4
Burge St *STHWK* SE1	48 B3
Burghill Rd *SYD* SE26	157 D4
Burghley Hall Cl *WIM/MER* SW19 *	149 E1
Burghley Rd *KTTN* NW5	74 B1
WAN E11 *	63 E5
WIM/MER SW19	149 D4
Burgh St *IS* N1	11 D1
Burgon St *BLKFR* EC4V	23 D5
Burgos Gv *GNWCH* SE10	122 B4
Burgoyne Rd *BRXN/ST* SW9	135 F1
FSBYPK N4	58 B1
Burke Cl *PUT/ROE* SW15	129 E2
Burke St *CAN/RD* E16	93 F4
Burland Rd *BTSEA* SW11	133 F3
Burleigh Av *BFN/LL* DA15	145 F3
Burleigh Pl *PUT/ROE* SW15	131 D5
Burleigh St *COVGDN* WC2E	33 D1
Burleigh Wk *CAT* SE6	158 C1
Burley Rd *CAN/RD* E16	94 C5
Burlington Ar *CONDST* W1S	31 E2
Burlington Av *RCH/KEW* TW9	110 A4
Burlington Cl *EHAM* E6	95 E5
MV/WKIL W9	2 A5
Burlington Gdns *ACT* W3	98 C2
CHSWK W4	110 C1
CONDST W1S	31 E2
Burlington La *CHSWK* W4	110 C3
Burlington Ms *ACT* W3	98 C2
Burlington Pde *CRICK* NW2 *	71 D1
Burlington Pl *FUL/PGN* SW6	113 E5
Burlington Rd *CHSWK* W4 *	110 C1
FUL/PGN SW6	113 E5
Burma Rd *STNW/STAM* N16	77 D1
Burma Ter *NRWD* SE19 *	155 E5
Burmarsh Rd *TOOT* SW17	152 A1
Burnaby Crs *CHSWK* W4	110 B2
Burnaby Gdns *CHSWK* W4	110 B2
Burnaby St *WBPTN* SW10	114 C3
Burnbury Rd *BAL* SW12	152 C1
Burnell Wk *STHWK* SE1 *	119 F1
Burnels Av *EHAM* E6	96 A2
Burness Cl *HOLWY* N7	75 F3
Burne St *CAMTN* NW1	16 C2
Burnet Cl *HOM* E9	78 C2
Burney St *GNWCH* SE10	122 C3
Burnfoot Av *FUL/PGN* SW6	113 E4
Burnham Cl *STHWK* SE1	49 F5
Burnham St *BETH* E2	90 C2
Burnham Wy *SYD* SE26	157 F5
Burnley Rd *BRXN/ST* SW9	117 F5
WLSDN NW10	69 F2
Burnsall St *CHEL* SW3	41 D5
Burnside Cl *BERM/RHTH* SE16	103 D2
Burns Rd *BTSEA* SW11	115 F5
Burn's Rd *WLSDN* NW10	69 F5
Burnt Ash Hl *LEE/GVPK* SE12	141 F4
Burnt Ash La *BMLY* BR1	160 B5
Burnt Ash Rd *LEE/GVPK* SE12	141 F3
Burnthwaite Rd *FUL/PGN* SW6	113 F4

Burntwood Cl *WAND/EARL* SW18 * 151 D1
Burntwood Grange Rd
   WAND/EARL SW18 ...... 151 D1
Burntwood La *TOOT* SW17 ...... 151 D2
Burntwood Vw *NRWD* SE19 * 155 F5
Buross St *WCHPL* E1 ...... 90 B5
Burrage Gv *WOOL/PLUM* SE18 ...... 108 C5
Burrage Pl *WOOL/PLUM* SE18 ...... 126 B1
Burrage Rd *WOOL/PLUM* SE18 ...... 108 C5
   KIL/WHAMP NW6 ...... 72 A2
Burr Cl *WAP* E1W 102 A2
Burrells Wharf Sq *POP/IOD* E14 ...... 122 B1
Burrels Wlf *POP/IOD* E14 ...... 122 B1
Burroughs Cots *POP/IOD* E14 * 91 E4
Burrow Rd *EDUL* SE22 ...... 137 E2
Burrows Ms *STHWK* SE1 ...... 34 C5
Burrows Rd *WLSDN* NW10 ...... 88 C2
Burr Rd *WAND/EARL* SW18 ...... 150 A1
Bursar St *STHWK* SE1 * 36 C4
Bursdon Cl *BFN/LL* DA15 ...... 165 F2
Burslem St *WCHPL* E1 ...... 90 B5
Burstock Rd *PUT/ROE* SW15 ...... 131 E2
Burston Rd *PUT/ROE* SW15 ...... 131 D3
Burtley Cl *FSBYPK* N4 ...... 58 C3
Burton Bank *IS* N1 * 77 D4
Burton Gv *WALW* SE17 ...... 119 D1
Burton La *BRXN/ST* SW9 * 118 A5
Burton Ms *BCVA* SW1W 42 B5
Burton Pl *STPAN* WC1H 8 B1
Burton Rd *BRXN/ST* SW9 ...... 118 A5
   KIL/WHAMP NW6 ...... 71 F4
Burtons Ct *GTPST* E15 ...... 81 D4
Burton St *STPAN* WC1H 8 B5
Burt Rd *CAN/RD* E16 ...... 106 C2
Burtwell La *WNWD* SE27 ...... 155 D4
Burwash Rd *WOOL/PLUM* SE18 ...... 127 D1
Burwell Cl *WCHPL* E1 ...... 90 B5
Burwell Rd *LEY* E10 ...... 61 E3
Burwood Pl *BAY/PAD* W2 ...... 17 D4
Bury Cl *BERM/RHTH* SE16 ...... 103 D2
Bury Ct *HDTCH* EC3A 25 D4
Bury Pl *NOXST/BSQ* WC1A 20 C3
Bury St *HDTCH* EC3A 25 D5
   ST/S SW1Y 31 E3
Bury Wk *CHEL* SW3 ...... 40 C5
Busby Pl *KTTN* NW5 ...... 75 D3
Bushbaby Cl *STHWK* SE1 ...... 48 C3
Bushberry Rd *HOM* E9 ...... 79 E3
Bush Cots *WAND/EARL* SW18 ...... 132 A5
Bushell Cl *BRXS/STRHM* SW2 ...... 153 F2
Bushell Wy *CHST* BR7 ...... 162 A5
Bushey Hill Rd *CMBW* SE5 ...... 119 F4
Bushey Lees *BFN/LL* DA15 * 145 F4
Bushey Rd *PLSTW* E13 ...... 94 C1
   NRWD/STOTM N15 ...... 59 E1
Bush Gv *CDALE/KGS* NW9 ...... 50 C2
Bush House *WOOL/PLUM* SE18 * 125 E3
Bush La *CANST* EC4R 36 A1
Bushmoor Crs *WOOL/PLUM* SE18 ...... 126 B3
Bushnell Rd *TOOT* SW17 ...... 152 B2
Bush Rd *DEPT* SE8 ...... 103 D5
   HACK E8 ...... 78 B5
   WAN E11 ...... 63 F2
Bushwood *WAN* E11 ...... 63 F3
Bushwood Dr *STHWK* SE1 ...... 49 F5
Bushwood Rd *RCH/KEW* TW9 ...... 110 A2
Butcher Rw *WAP* E1W 91 D5
Butchers Rd *CAN/RD* E16 ...... 94 B5
Bute Gdns *HMSMTH* W6 ...... 101 D5
Bute St *SKENS* SW7 ...... 40 A4
Bute Wk *IS* N1 * 77 D3
Butler Rd *WLSDN* NW10 ...... 69 F4
Butlers & Colonial Whf *STHWK* SE1 ...... 37 F5
Butler St *BETH* E2 * 90 C2
Butterfield Cl *BERM/RHTH* SE16 * 102 A3
Butterfield House *CHARL* SE7 * 125 E2
Butterfield Ms *WOOL/PLUM* SE18 ...... 126 B2
Butterfield Sq *EHAM* E6 ...... 95 F5
Butterfly La *ELTH/MOT* SE9 ...... 144 B4
Butterfly Wk *CMBW* SE5 * 119 D4
Buttermere Cl *SRTFD* E15 ...... 81 D1
   STHWK SE1 ...... 49 E5
Buttermere Dr *PUT/ROE* SW15 ...... 131 E3
Buttermere Wk *HACK* E8 ...... 77 F3
Butterwick *HMSMTH* W6 ...... 100 C5
Butterworth Ter *WALW* SE17 * 118 C1
Buttesland St *IS* N1 ...... 12 B3
Buttmarsh Cl *WOOL/PLUM* SE18 ...... 126 B1
Buttsbury Rd *IL* IG1 ...... 84 C2
Butts Rd *BMLY* BR1 ...... 159 E5

Buxhall Crs *HOM* E9 ...... 79 F3
Buxted Rd *EDUL* SE22 ...... 137 D2
   HACK E8 ...... 77 F4
Buxton Gdns *ACT* W3 ...... 98 B1
Buxton Ms *CLAP* SW4 ...... 117 D5
Buxton Rd *ARCH* N19 ...... 57 D3
   CRICK NW2 ...... 70 B3
   EHAM E6 ...... 95 E2
   GNTH/NBYPK IG2 ...... 67 E1
   MORT/ESHN SW14 ...... 129 E1
   SRTFD E15 ...... 81 E2
Buxton St *WCHPL* E1 ...... 25 F1
Byam St *FUL/PGN* SW6 ...... 114 C5
Byelands Cl *BERM/RHTH* SE16 ...... 103 D2
The Bye *ACT* W3 ...... 87 E5
The Byeway *MORT/ESHN* SW14 ...... 128 C1
Byfeld Gdns *BARN* SW13 ...... 112 A4
Byfield Cl *BERM/RHTH* SE16 ...... 103 E5
Byford Cl *SRTFD* E15 ...... 81 E4
Bygrove St *POP/IOD* E14 ...... 92 B5
Byng Pl *GWRST* WC1E 20 B1
Byng St *POP/IOD* E14 ...... 104 A3
Byron Av *MNPK* E12 ...... 83 E3
Byron Cl *HACK* E8 ...... 78 A5
   SYD SE26 * 157 E4
Byron Ms *HAMP* NW3 ...... 73 D1
   MXN/WKIL W9 ...... 2 B5
Byron Rd *CRICK* NW2 ...... 52 B4
   LEY E10 ...... 62 B3
Byron St *POP/IOD* E14 ...... 92 C5
Bythorn St *BRXN/ST* SW9 ...... 135 F1
Byward St *MON* EC3R 37 D2
Bywater Pl *BERM/RHTH* SE16 ...... 103 E3
Bywater St *CHEL* SW3 ...... 115 F1
Bywell Pl *GTPST* W1W * 19 E3

C

Cabbell St *CAMTN* NW1 ...... 16 C3
Cable Pl *GNWCH* SE10 ...... 122 C4
Cable St *WCHPL* E1 ...... 102 A1
Cable Trade Pk *CHARL* SE7 * 124 A1
Cabot Sq *POP/IOD* E14 ...... 104 A2
Cabot Wy *EHAM* E6 ...... 83 D5
Cabul Rd *BTSEA* SW11 ...... 115 E5
Cactus Cl *CMBW* SE5 * 119 E5
Cadbury Wy *BERM/RHTH* SE16 ...... 49 F3
Caddington Rd *CRICK* NW2 ...... 53 E5
Cadell Cl *BETH* E2 ...... 13 E3
Cade Rd *GNWCH* SE10 ...... 123 D4
Cadet Dr *STHWK* SE1 ...... 119 F1
Cadet Pl *GNWCH* SE10 ...... 123 D5
Cadiz St *WALW* SE17 ...... 118 C1
Cadman Cl *BRXN/ST* SW9 ...... 118 B3
Cadmus Cl *CLAP* SW4 ...... 135 D2
Cadogan Cl *HOM* E9 * 79 F4
Cadogan Gdns *CHEL* SW3 ...... 41 F4
Cadogan Ga *KTBR* SW1X 41 F4
Cadogan La *KTBR* SW1X 42 A2
Cadogan Pl *KTBR* SW1X 41 F2
Cadogan Rd *WOOL/PLUM* SE18 ...... 108 C4
Cadogan Sq *KTBR* SW1X 41 E3
Cadogan St *CHEL* SW3 ...... 41 E5
Cadogan Ter *HOM* E9 ...... 79 F3
Cadoxton Av *SEVS/STOTM* N15 ...... 59 F1
Cadwallon Rd *ELTH/MOT* SE9 ...... 162 B2
Caedmon Rd *HOLWY* N7 ...... 75 F1
Cahill St *STLK* EC1Y * 23 F1
Cahir St *POP/IOD* E14 ...... 104 B5
Caird St *NKENS* W10 ...... 89 E2
Cairnfield Av *CRICK* NW2 ...... 51 E5
Cairns Rd *BTSEA* SW11 ...... 133 E3
Caister Ms *BAL* SW12 ...... 134 B5
Caistor Park Rd *SRTFD* E15 ...... 81 F1
Caistor Rd *BAL* SW12 ...... 134 B5
Caithness Gdns *BFN/LL* DA15 ...... 145 F4
Caithness Rd *WKENS* W14 ...... 101 D4
Calabria Rd *HBRY* N5 ...... 76 B3
Calais St *CMBW* SE5 ...... 118 B4
Calbourne Rd *BAL* SW12 ...... 133 F5
Caldecot Rd *CMBW* SE5 ...... 118 C5
Caldecott Wy *CLPT* E5 ...... 61 D5
Calderon Rd *WAN* E11 ...... 80 C1
Caldervale Rd *CLAP* SW4 ...... 135 D3
Calderwood St *WOOL/PLUM* SE18 ...... 108 A3
Caldew St *CMBW* SE5 ...... 119 D3

Caldicote Gn *CDALE/KGS* NW9 *...... 51 E1
Caldwell St *BRXN/ST* SW9.......... 117 F3
Caldy Wk *IS* N1 *.................. 76 C3
Caledonian Rd *IS* N1............... 75 F4
Caledonian Sq *CAMTN* NW1 *....... 75 D3
Caledonian Wharf Rd *POP/IOD* E14. 105 D5
Caledonia St *IS* N1................. 9 D2
Caledon Rd *EHAM* E6................ 83 F5
Cale St *CHEL* SW3.................. 115 E1
Caldore Rd *BRXS/STRHM* SW2 *.... 135 F4
Callaby Ter *IS* N1 *................ 77 D3
Callaghan Cl *LEW* SE13............. 141 E2
Callaghan Cots *WCHPL* E1 *........ 90 C4
Callander Rd *CAT* SE6.............. 158 B2
Callcott Rd *KIL/WHAMP* NW6........ 71 F4
Callcott St *KENS* W8............... 26 A3
Callendar Rd *SKENS* SW7........... 40 A2
Callingham Cl *POP/IOD* E14 *....... 91 F4
Callisons Pl *GNWCH* SE10........... 123 E1
Callis Rd *WALTH* E17............... 61 F1
Callow St *WBPTN* SW10.............. 114 C2
Calmington Rd *CMBW* SE5............ 119 E2
Calonne Rd *WIM/MER* SW19.......... 149 D4
Calshot St *IS* N1................... 9 E1
Calthorpe St *FSBYW* WC1X.......... 9 F5
Calton Av *DUL* SE21................ 137 E4
Calverley Gv *ARCH* N19............ 57 D3
Calvert Av *WCHPL* E1............... 13 D4
Calverton Rd *EHAM* E6............. 84 A5
Calvert Rd *GNWCH* SE10........... 123 F1
Calvert St *CAMTN* NW1............. 74 A5
Calvin St *WCHPL* E1................ 13 E3
Calydon Rd *CHARL* SE7............. 124 E1
Calypso Crs *PECK* SE15............ 119 E3
Calypso Wy *BERM/RHTH* SE16....... 103 F4
Camarthen Gn *CDALE/KGS* NW9 *.... 51 E1
Cambalt Rd *PUT/ROE* SW15.......... 131 E3
Camberley Av *WIM/MER* SW20 *..... 149 D4
Cambert Wy *BKHTH/KID* SE3........ 142 B2
Camberwell Church St *CMBW* SE5.. 119 D4
Camberwell Glebe *CMBW* SE5....... 119 D4
Camberwell Gn *CMBW* SE5........... 119 D4
Camberwell Gv *CMBW* SE5........... 119 D4
Camberwell New Rd *CMBW* SE5...... 118 C3
Camberwell Rd *CMBW* SE5........... 118 C2
Camberwell Station Rd *CMBW* SE5.. 118 C4
Camborne Ms *WAND/EARL* SW18 *.. 132 A5
Camborne Rd *WAND/EARL* SW18..... 132 A5
  WELL DA16.......................... 127 E5
Cambourne Ms *NTGHL* W11 *......... 89 E5
Cambria Cl *BFN/LL* DA15........... 163 D1
Cambria Cl *WNWD* SE27.............. 154 B3
Cambrian Rd *LEY* E10............... 62 A3
Cambria Rd *CMBW* SE5.............. 136 C1
Cambria St *FUL/PGN* SW6........... 114 B3
Cambridge Av *KIL/WHAMP* NW6...... 2 A1
  WELL DA16.......................... 145 F2
Cambridge Barracks Rd
  WOOL/PLUM SE18................... 107 F5
Cambridge Circ *SOHO/SHAV* W1D ... 20 B5
Cambridge Cl *WALTH* E17............ 61 F1
  WLSDN NW10........................ 50 C5
Cambridge Crs *BETH* E2............ 90 B1
Cambridge Dr *LEE/GVPK* SE12...... 142 A3
Cambridge Gdns *KIL/WHAMP* NW6... 2 A1
  NKENS W10......................... 89 D5
Cambridge Ga *CAMTN* NW1.......... 6 C4
Cambridge Gate Ms *CAMTN* NW1.... 7 D4
Cambridge Gn *ELTH/MOT* SE9....... 162 B1
Cambridge Gv *HMSMTH* W6.......... 100 B5
Cambridge Heath Rd *BETH* E2...... 90 B2
Cambridge Pk *WAN* E11.............. 64 A1
Cambridge Park Rd *WAN* E11....... 63 F2
Cambridge Pas *HOM* E9............. 78 C4
Cambridge Pl *KENS* W8.............. 39 D1
Cambridge Rd *BARK* IG11........... 84 C4
  BARN SW13......................... 111 F5
  BTSEA SW11........................ 115 F4
  CDMY/SEVK IG3..................... 67 E3
  KIL/WHAMP NW6..................... 2 A3
  RCH/KEW TW9....................... 110 A3
  SCUP DA14......................... 163 E4
  WAN E11........................... 64 A1
Cambridge Rd *CHSWK* W4............ 110 B1
Cambridge Rd North *CHSWK* W4..... 110 B1
Cambridge Rd South *CHSWK* W4.... 110 B1
Cambridge Rw *WOOL/PLUM* SE18..... 126 B1
Cambridge Sq *BAY/PAD* W2......... 16 C4
Cambridge St *PIM* SW1V............ 116 B1
Cambridge Ter *CAMTN* NW1......... 7 D4
Cambridge Terrace Ms *CAMTN* NW1 *. 7 D4
Cambus Rd *CAN/RD* E16............. 94 A4
Camdale Rd *WOOL/PLUM* SE18....... 127 F3

Camden Gdns *CAMTN* NW1 *......... 74 B4
Camden High St *CAMTN* NW1........ 74 B5
Camdenhurst St *POP/IOD* E14...... 91 E5
Camden Lock Pl *CAMTN* NW1 *...... 74 B4
Camden Ms *CAMTN* NW1.............. 74 D4
Camden Park Rd *CAMTN* NW1........ 75 D3
Camden Pas *IS* N1................. 10 C1
Camden Rd *CAMTN* NW1.............. 74 B5
  WALTH E17......................... 61 F1
  WAN E11........................... 64 B1
Camden Road Permanent Wy
  CAMTN NW1 *...................... 75 D5
Camden Rw *BKHTH/KID* SE3.......... 123 D5
Camden Sq *CAMTN* NW1.............. 75 D3
Camden St *CAMTN* NW1.............. 74 C5
Camden Ter *CAMTN* NW1 *........... 75 D3
Camden Wk *IS* N1.................. 76 B5
Camelford Wk *NTGHL* W11 *......... 89 E5
Camellia St *VX/NE* SW8............ 117 E3
  WIM/MER SW19...................... 149 E5
Camelot Cl *THMD* SE28............. 109 D3
Camel Rd *CAN/RD* E16............. 107 D2
Camera Pl *WBPTN* SW10............. 115 D2
Cameron Pl *STRHM/NOR* SW16....... 154 A3
Cameron Rd *CAT* SE6............... 157 F2
  CDMY/SEVK IG3..................... 67 E3
Cameron Ter *LEE/GVPK* SE12 *..... 160 B3
Camerton St *HACK* E8.............. 77 F5
Camilla Rd *BERM/RHTH* SE16....... 102 B5
Camlan Rd *BMLY* BR1............... 159 F4
Camlet St *BETH* E2................ 13 E5
Camley St *CAMTN* NW1.............. 75 D5
Camomile St *HDTCH* EC3A........... 25 D4
  OBST EC2N......................... 24 C4
Campana Rd *FUL/PGN* SW6........... 114 A4
Campbell Rd *STRHM/NOR* SW16...... 153 D5
  WOOL/PLUM SE18.................... 126 A4
Campbell Gordon Wy *CRICK* NW2.... 70 B1
Campbell Rd *BOW* E3............... 92 A2
  EHAM E6........................... 83 E5
  SRTFD E15......................... 81 E1
Campbell Wk *IS* N1 *.............. 75 D5
Campdale Rd *HOLWY* N7............. 57 D5
Campden Gv *KENS* W8............... 26 A5
Campden Hi *KENS* W8............... 26 A5
Campden Hill Gdns *KENS* W8....... 26 A4
Campden Hill Pl *NTGHL* W11 *...... 101 F2
Campden Hill Rd *KENS* W8......... 26 A5
Campden Hill Sq *KENS* W8......... 101 F2
Campden House Cl *KENS* W8........ 26 A5
Campden House Ter *KENS* W8 *..... 26 A4
Campden Sq *KENS* W8............... 26 A4
Campden Ter *CHSWK* W4 *........... 111 E1
Campen Cl *WIM/MER* SW19.......... 149 E2
Camperdown St *WCHPL* E1.......... 25 E5
Campfield Rd *ELTH/MOT* SE9....... 143 D5
Campion Cl *EHAM* E6.............. 107 F1
Campion Rd *PUT/ROE* SW15......... 130 C2
Campion Ter *CRICK* NW2........... 53 D5
Camplin St *NWCR* SE14............. 121 D3
Camp Rd *WIM/MER* SW19............ 148 B5
Campsbourne Rd *WIM/MER* SW19 *... 148 B5
Campshill Pl *LEW* SE13........... 140 C3
Campshill Rd *LEW* SE13........... 140 C3
Campus Rd *WALTH* E17............. 61 F1
Camp Vw *WIM/MER* SW19............ 148 B5
Cam Rd *SRTFD* E15................ 81 D5
Canada Crs *ACT* W3............... 86 C4
Canada Rd *ACT* W3................ 86 C4
Canada Sqaure *POP/IOD* E14....... 104 B2
Canada St *BERM/RHTH* SE16........ 103 D3
Canada Wy *SHB* W12............... 100 B1
Canadian Av *CAT* SE6............. 158 B1
Canal Ap *DEPT* SE8............... 121 E1
Canal Bvd *KTTN* NW5.............. 75 D3
Canal Cl *NKENS* W10.............. 89 D3
  WCHPL E1.......................... 91 E3
Canal Gv *PECK* SE15.............. 120 A2
Canal Pth *BETH* E2............... 77 E5
Canal St *CMBW* SE5............... 119 D2
Canal Wk *IS* N1.................. 77 D4
  WLSDN NW10 *...................... 68 C4
Canal Wy *NKENS* W10.............. 89 D3
Canberra Rd *CHARL* SE7........... 124 C2
  EHAM E6........................... 83 F5
Canbury Ms *SYD* SE26............. 156 A3
Cancell Rd *BRXN/ST* SW9.......... 118 A4
Candahar Rd *BTSEA* SW11.......... 115 E5
Candle Gv *PECK* SE15............. 138 B1
Candlelight Ct *SRTFD* E15........ 81 E1
Candler St *SEVS/STOTM* N15 *..... 59 D1
Candover St *GTPST* W1W *......... 19 E3

Candy St *BOW* E3	79	F5
Caney Ms *CRICK* NW2	53	D4
Canfield Gdns *KIL/WHAMP* NW6	72	B4
Canfield Pl *KIL/WHAMP* NW6	72	C3
Canford Rd *CLAP* SW4	134	A2
Canham Rd *CHSWK* W4	99	E3
Cann Hall Rd *WAN* E11	81	F1
Canning Cross *CMBW* SE5	119	E5
Canning Pas *KENS* W8 *	39	F2
Canning Pl *KENS* W8	39	E2
Canning Place Ms *KENS* W8 *	39	E2
Canning Rd *HBRY* N5	58	B5
SRTFD E15	93	E1
Cannon Dr *POP/IOD* E14	104	A1
Cannon HI *KIL/WHAMP* NW6	72	B2
Cannon La *HAMP* NW3	55	D5
Cannon Pl *CHARL* SE7	125	E1
HAMP NW3	54	C5
Cannon St *BLKFR* EC4V	23	E5
Cannon Street Rd *WCHPL* E1	90	B5
Canon Beck Rd *BERM/RHTH* SE16	102	C3
Canonbie Rd *FSTH* SE23	138	C5
Canonbury Crs *IS* N1	76	C4
Canonbury Gv *IS* N1	76	C4
Canonbury La *IS* N1	76	C5
Canonbury Pk North *IS* N1	76	C3
Canonbury Pk South *IS* N1	76	C3
Canonbury Rd *IS* N1	76	B4
Canonbury Sq *IS* N1	76	B4
Canonbury St *IS* N1	76	C4
Canonbury Vls *IS* N1	76	B4
Canonbury Yd East *IS* N1	76	B5
Canon Rw *WHALL* SW1A	44	C3
Canons Cl *EFNCH* N2	55	D2
Canon St *IS* N1	15	D1
Canrobert St *BETH* E2	90	D1
Cantelowes Rd *CAMTN* NW1 *	75	D1
Canterbury Av *IL* IG1	65	E2
Canterbury Cl *CMBW* SE5 *	118	C5
EHAM E6	95	F5
Canterbury Crs *BRXN/ST* SW9	136	A1
Canterbury Gv *WNWD* SE27	154	A3
Canterbury Pl *WALW* SE17	47	D5
Canterbury Rd *KIL/WHAMP* NW6	2	A2
LEY E10	62	C2
Canterbury Ter *KIL/WHAMP* NW6	2	A1
Cantley Gdns *GNTH/NBYPK* IG2	66	C1
Canton St *POP/IOD* E14	92	A5
Cantrell Rd *BOW* E3	91	F3
Cantwell Rd *WOOL/PLUM* SE18	126	B3
Canvey St *STHWK* SE1	35	E3
Cape Cl *BARK* IG11	84	B4
Capel Gdns *GDMY/SEVK* IG3	85	F1
Capel Rd *FSTGT* E7	82	B1
Capeners Cl *KTBR* SW1X *	41	F1
Capern Rd *WAND/EARL* SW18	150	C1
Cape Yd *WAP* E1W	102	A2
Capital Interchange Wy *BTFD* TW8	110	A1
Capland St *STJWD* NW8	4	B5
Caple Pde *WLSDN* NW10 *	87	F1
Caple Rd *WLSDN* NW10	87	F1
Capstan Rd *DEPT* SE8	105	F5
Capstan Sq *POP/IOD* E14	104	C3
Capstan Wy *BERM/RHTH* SE16	103	E2
Capstone Rd *BMLY* BR1	159	F4
Capulet Ms *CAN/RD* E16	106	A2
Capworth St *LEY* E10	62	A3
Caradoc Cl *BAY/PAD* W2	14	A4
Caradoc St *GNWCH* SE10	123	E1
Caradon Ct *WAN* E11	63	E3
Caravel Cl *POP/IOD* E14	104	A4
Caravel Ms *DEPT* SE8	122	A2
Caraway Cl *PLSTW* E13	94	B4
Carbis Rd *POP/IOD* E14	91	F5
Carburton St *GTPST* W1W	19	D2
Cardale St *POP/IOD* E14	104	C3
Carden Rd *PECK* SE15	138	B1
Cardiff Rd *WOOL/PLUM* SE18	127	E3
Cardigan Pl *LEW* SE13 *	123	D1
Cardigan Rd *BARN* SW13	112	A5
BOW E3	91	F2
Cardigan St *LBTH* SE11	118	A1
Cardigan Wk *IS* N1 *	76	C4
Cardinal Bourne St *STHWK* SE1 *	48	B3
Cardinal Hinsey Cl *WLSDN* NW10 *	88	A1
Cardinal Pl *PUT/ROE* SW15	131	D2
Cardinals Wy *ARCH* N19	57	D3
Cardine Ms *PECK* SE15	120	B3
Cardington St *CAMTN* NW1	7	F3
Cardozo Rd *HOLWY* N7	75	E2
Cardross St *HMSMTH* W6	100	B4
Cardwell Rd *HOLWY* N7	75	E1
Cardwell Ter *HOLWY* N7 *	75	E1
Carew Cl *HOLWY* N7	57	F4
Carew St *CMBW* SE5	118	C5
Carey Gdns *VX/NE* SW8	116	C4
Carey La *CITYW* EC2V	23	E4
Carey Pl *SMW* SW1V	44	A5
Carey St *LINN* WC2A	21	F5
Carey Wy *WBLY* HA9	68	C2
Carfax Pl *CLAP* SW4	135	D2
The Carfax *SYD* SE26	156	C3
Carfree Cl *IS* N1	76	A4
Cargill Rd *WAND/EARL* SW18	150	C1
Carholme Rd *FSTH* SE23	157	F1
Carisbrooke Gdns *PECK* SE15 *	119	F3
Carker's La *ARCH* N19	57	D2
KTTN NW5	74	B2
Carleton Gdns *ARCH* N19 *	74	C2
Carleton Rd *HOLWY* N7	75	D1
Carleton Vls *KTTN* NW5 *	74	C2
Carlile Cl *BOW* E3	91	F1
Carlingford Rd *HAMP* NW3	73	D1
Carlisle Av *ACT* W3	87	E5
TWRH EC3N	25	D5
Carlisle Gdns *IL* IG1	65	E1
Carlisle La *STHWK* SE1	45	F2
Carlisle Pl *WEST* SW1P	43	E3
Carlisle Rd *FSBYPK* N4	58	A3
KIL/WHAMP NW6	71	E5
LEY E10	62	A3
Carlisle St *SOHO/SHAV* W1D	20	A5
Carlisle Wk *HACK* E8	77	F3
Carlisle Wy *TOOT* SW17	152	A5
Carlos Pl *MYFR/PKLN* W1K	30	B2
Carlow St *CAMTN* NW1	7	E1
Carlton Cl *HAMP* NW3	54	A4
Carlton Dr *PUT/ROE* SW15	131	D3
Carlton Ga *MV/WKIL* W9	14	B2
Carlton Gv *SCUP* DA14	163	F4
Carlton Gv *PECK* SE15	120	B4
Carlton HI *STJWD* NW8	3	D1
Carlton House Ter *STJS* SW1Y	32	A4
Carlton Ms *KIL/WHAMP* NW6 *	72	A2
Carlton Rd *CHSWK* W4	99	D3
FSBYPK N4	58	A2
MNPK E12	83	D1
MORT/ESHN SW14	128	C1
SCUP DA14	163	F5
Carlton Sq *WCHPL* E1 *	91	D3
Carlton St *STJS* SW1Y	32	A2
Carlton Ter *SYD* SE26	156	C4
Carlton Tower Pl *KTBR* SW1X	41	F2
Carlton V *KIL/WHAMP* NW6	2	A3
Carlwell St *TOOT* SW17	151	E5
Carlyle Cl *EFNCH* N2	54	C1
WLSDN NW10	69	D5
Carlyle Ct *WBPTN* SW10 *	114	C4
Carlyle Pl *PUT/ROE* SW15	131	D2
Carlyle Rd *MNPK* E12	83	E1
Carlyle Sq *CHEL* SW3	39	F5
Carmalt Gdns *PUT/ROE* SW15	130	C2
Carmel Ct *KENS* W8	26	C5
Carmelite St *EMB* EC4Y	34	B1
Carmel Wy *RCH/KEW* TW9	110	A5
Carmen St *POP/IOD* E14	92	B5
Carmichael Cl *BTSEA* SW11 *	133	D1
Carmichael Ms *WAND/EARL* SW18	133	D5
Carminia Rd *TOOT* SW17	152	B2
Carnaby St *SOHO/CST* W1F	19	E5
Carnac St *WNWD* SE27	155	D4
Carnarvon Rd *LEY* E10	62	C1
SRTFD E15	81	F5
Carnbrook Rd *BKHTH/KID* SE3	143	D1
Carnecke Gdns *ELTH/MOT* SE9	143	E3
Carnegie Pl *WIM/MER* SW19	149	D3
Carnegie St *IS* N1	75	F5
Carnoustie Dr *IS* N1	75	F4
Carnwath Rd *FUL/PGN* SW6	132	A1
Carolina Cl *SRTFD* E15	81	E2
Caroline Cl *BAY/PAD* W2	27	D2
STRHM/NOR SW16	153	F3
Caroline Gdns *BETH* E2	13	D3
PECK SE15 *	120	B3
Caroline Pl *BAY/PAD* W2	27	D1
BTSEA SW11	116	A5
Caroline Place Ms *BAY/PAD* W2 *	27	D1
Caroline St *WCHPL* E1	91	D5
Caroline Ter *BGVA* SW1W	42	A5
Caroline Wk *HMSMTH* W6	113	E2
Carol St *CAMTN* NW1	74	C5
Carpenters Ms *HOLWY* N7 *	75	E2
Carpenter's Pl *CLAP* SW4	135	D2

Carpenters Rd *SRTFD* E15 .... 80 C4
Carpenter St *MYFR/PKLN* W1K 30 C2
Carrara Ms *HACK* E8 .... 78 A2
Carrara Wharf *FUL/PGN* SW6 .... 131 E1
Carre Ms *CMBW* SE5 .... 118 B4
Carriage Dr East *CHEL* SW3 .... 107 E5
Carriage Dr North *BTSEA* SW11 .... 116 A4
Carriage Dr South *BTSEA* SW11 .... 115 F4
Carriage Dr West *BTSEA* SW11 .... 115 F3
Carriage Ms *IL* IG1 .... 66 C3
Carrick Ms *DEPT* SE8 .... 122 A2
Carrington Gdns *FSTGT* E7 .... 82 A1
Carrington Rd *RCHPK/HAM* TW10 .... 48 A2
Carrington St *MYFR/PICC* W1J 30 C4
Carroll Cl *KTTN* NW5 .... 74 B1
Carroll Cl *SRTFD* E15 .... 81 D2
Carronade Pl *THMD* SE28 .... 108 C4
Carron Cl *POP/IOD* E14 .... 92 B5
Carroun Rd *VX/NE* SW8 .... 117 F3
Carr St *POP/IOD* E14 .... 91 E4
Carslake Rd *PUT/ROE* SW15 .... 130 C4
Carson Rd *CAN/RD* E16 .... 94 A4
DUL SE21 .... 154 C2
Carstairs Rd *SE5 .... 138 C3
Carston Cl *LEE/GVPK* SE12 .... 141 F3
Carswell Rd *CAT* SE6 .... 140 C5
Carter Cl *CDALE/KGS* NW9 .... 51 D1
Carteret St *STJSPK* SW1H 44 A1
Carteret Wy *DEPT* SE8 .... 103 E5
Carter La *BLKFR* EC4V 23 D5
Carter Pl *WALW* SE17 .... 118 C1
Carter Rd *PLSTW* E13 .... 82 B5
Carters Cl *KTTN* NW5 .... 75 D3
Carters Hill Cl *ELTH/MOT* SE9 .... 160 C1
Carter St *WALW* SE17 .... 118 C2
Carters Yd *WAND/EARL* SW18 * 132 A3
Carter's Yd *WAND/EARL* SW18 * 132 A3
Carthew Rd *HMSMTH* W6 .... 100 B4
Carthew Vis *HMSMTH* W6 .... 100 B4
Carthusian St *FARR* EC1M 23 E2
Carting La *TPL/STR* WC2R 33 D2
Cartwright Gdns *STPAN* WC1H 8 B4
Cartwright St *WCHPL* E1 .... 37 F1
Cartwright Wy *BARN* SW13 .... 112 B3
Carver Cl *CHSWK* W4 .... 98 C4
Carver Rd *HNHL* SE24 .... 136 C4
Cary Rd *WAN* E11 .... 81 E3
Carysfort Rd *STNW/STAM* N16 .... 59 D5
Casella Rd *NWCR* SE14 .... 121 D3
Casewick Rd *WNWD* SE27 .... 154 B5
Casey Cl *STJWD* NW8 .... 4 C3
Casimir Rd *CLPT* E5 .... 60 B5
Casino Av *HNHL* SE24 .... 136 C3
Caspian St *CMBW* SE5 .... 119 D3
Caspian Wk *CAN/RD* E16 .... 95 D4
Casselden Rd *WLSDN* NW10 .... 69 D4
Cassidy Rd *FUL/PGN* SW6 .... 114 A3
Cassilis Rd *POP/IOD* E14 .... 104 A3
Cassland Rd *HOM* E9 .... 79 D4
Casslee Rd *CAT* SE6 .... 139 F5
Casson St *WCHPL* E1 .... 25 F5
Castellain Rd *MV/WKIL* W9 .... 2 C5
Castellane Av *PUT/ROE* SW15 .... 130 C3
Castelnau *BARN* SW13 .... 112 B3
Casterbridge Rd *BKHTH/KID* SE3 .... 142 A1
Casterton St *HACK* E8 .... 78 B3
Castile Rd *WOOL/PLUM* SE18 .... 108 A5
Castlands Rd *CAT* SE6 .... 159 E2
Castle Baynard St *BLKFR* EC4V 157 F2
Castlebrook Cl *LBTH* SE11 .... 35 D1
Castle Cl *ACT* W3 .... 46 C1
WIM/MER SW19 .... 98 B3
Castlecombe Dr *WIM/MER* SW19 .... 131 D5
Castlecombe Rd *ELTH/MOT* SE9 .... 161 E5
Castle Ct *BANK* EC3V 24 B5
SYD SE26 .... 157 F3
Castle Dr *REDBR* IG4 .... 65 E1
Castleford Av *ELTH/MOT* SE9 .... 162 B1
Castlehaven Rd *CAMTN* NW1 .... 74 B4
Castelelnau La *WESTW* SW1E 43 E2
Castlemaine St *WCHPL* E1 * 90 B4
Castle Md *CMBW* SE5 * 118 C3
Castle Ms *CAMTN* NW1 .... 74 B3
TOOT SW17 .... 151 E4
Castle Pl *CAMTN* NW1 .... 74 B3
Castlereagh St *MBLAR* W1H 17 F4
Castle Rd *CAMTN* NW1 .... 74 B3
Castle Rw *CHSWK* W4 * 111 D1
Castle St *EHAM* E6 .... 94 C1
Castleton Rd *ELTH/MOT* SE9 .... 161 D4

Castletown Rd *WKENS* W14 .... 113 E1
Castleview Cl *FSBYPK* N4 .... 58 C3
Castleview Gdns *IL* IG1 .... 65 E1
Castle Vis *CRICK* NW2 * 70 A3
Castle Wy *WIM/MER* SW19 .... 149 E5
Castlewood Dr *ELTH/MOT* SE9 .... 125 F5
Castlewood Rd *STNW/STAM* N16 .... 60 A1
Castle Yd *HGT* N6 * 56 A2
STHWK SE1 * 35 D3
Castor La *POP/IOD* E14 .... 104 B1
Catalpa Ct *LEW* SE13 .... 141 D4
Caterham Rd *LEW* SE13 .... 140 C1
Catesby St *WALW* SE17 .... 48 B5
Catford Broadway *CAT* SE6 .... 140 B5
Catford Hl *CAT* SE6 .... 157 F1
Catford Island *CAT* SE6 .... 140 B5
Catford Rd *CAT* SE6 .... 158 A1
Cathall Rd *WAN* E11 .... 63 E5
Cathay St *BERM/RHTH* SE16 .... 102 B3
Cathcart Hl *ARCH* N19 .... 56 C5
Cathcart Rd *WBPTN* SW10 .... 114 B3
Cathcart St *KTTN* NW5 .... 74 B3
Cathedral St *STHWK* SE1 .... 36 A3
Catherall Rd *HBRY* N5 .... 58 C5
Catherine Griffiths Ct *CLKNW* EC1R 10 B5
Catherine Gv *GNWCH* SE10 .... 122 B4
Catherine Pl *WESTW* SW1E 43 E2
Catherine St *HOL/ALD* WC2B * 33 E1
Catherine Wheel Aly *LVPST* EC2M 25 D3
Catherine Wheel Yd *WHALL* SW1A 31 E4
Cathles Rd *BAL* SW12 .... 134 B4
Cathnor Rd *SHB* W12 .... 100 B3
Catling Cl *FSTH* SE23 .... 156 C3
Catlin St *BERM/RHTH* SE16 .... 120 A1
Cato Rd *CLAP* SW4 .... 135 D1
Cator St *PECK* SE15 .... 119 F2
Cato St *MBLAR* W1H 17 D4
Cattistock Rd *ELTH/MOT* SE9 .... 161 E5
Catton St *RSQ* WC1B 21 E5
Caudwell Ter *WAND/EARL* SW18 * 133 D4
Caulfield Rd *EHAM* E6 .... 83 F4
PECK SE15 .... 120 B5
The Causeway *WAND/EARL* SW18 .... 132 B2
WIM/MER SW19 .... 148 C5
Causton Cots *POP/IOD* E14 * 91 E4
Causton Rd *HGT* N6 .... 56 B2
Causton St *WEST* SW1P 44 B5
Cautley Av *CLAP* SW4 .... 134 C3
Cavalry Gdns *PUT/ROE* SW15 * 131 E3
Cavaye Pl *WBPTN* SW10 * 54 F1
Cavell St *WCHPL* E1 .... 90 B4
Cavendish Av *STJWD* NW8 .... 4 B2
WELL DA16 .... 145 F1
Cavendish Cl *KIL/WHAMP* NW6 .... 71 F3
STJWD NW8 .... 4 B3
Cavendish Dr *WAN* E11 .... 63 D3
Cavendish Gdns *BARK* IG11 .... 85 F2
CLAP SW4 .... 134 C4
IL IG1 .... 66 A3
Cavendish Ms North *GTPST* W1W 19 D2
Cavendish Ms South *GTPST* W1W 19 D3
Cavendish Pde *CLAP* SW4 * 134 C4
Cavendish Pl *CAVSQ/HST* W1G 19 D4
CRICK NW2 .... 71 D3
Cavendish Rd *BAL* SW12 .... 152 C1
CHSWK W4 .... 110 C4
CLAP SW4 .... 134 B4
FSBYPK N4 .... 58 B1
KIL/WHAMP NW6 .... 71 E4
Cavendish Sq *CAVSQ/HST* W1G 19 D4
Cavendish St *IS* N1 .... 12 A2
Cavendish Ter *BOW* E3 * 91 F2
Cavenham Gdns *IL* IG1 .... 67 D5
Cave Rd *PLSTW* E13 .... 94 B1
Caverleigh Flats *CHEL* SW3 * 115 F4
Caversham Rd *KTTN* NW5 * 74 C3
Caversham St *CHEL* SW3 .... 115 F2
Caverswall St *SHB* W12 .... 88 C5
Cawnpore St *NRWD* SE19 .... 155 E5
Caxton Gv *BOW* E3 .... 92 A2
Caxton Rd *SHB* W12 .... 101 D2
WIM/MER SW19 .... 150 C5
The Caxtons *BRXN/ST* SW9 * 118 B5
Caxton St *STJSPK* SW1H 43 F2
Caxton St North *CAN/RD* E16 .... 93 F5
Cayenne Ct *STHWK* SE1 * 37 E4
Cayton Pl *FSBYE* EC1V 12 A4
Cazenove Rd *STNW/STAM* N16 .... 59 F4
Cdiamond Ter *GNWCH* SE10 .... 122 C4
Cecil Av *BARK* IG11 .... 85 D5
Cecil Ct *CHCR* WC2N * 32 C1
LSQ/SEVD WC2H 32 B2

Cecile Pk *CEND/HSY/T* N8 .... 57 E1
Cecilia Rd *HACK* E8 .... 77 F2
Cecil Rd *ACT* W3 .... 86 C4
  IL IG1 .... 84 B1
  PLSTW E13 .... 82 A5
  WAN E11 .... 63 E4
  WLSDN NW10 .... 69 E5
Cedar CI *BOW* E3 * 79 F5
  DUL SE21 .... 155 D3
  IL IG1 .... 85 D2
  KUTN/CMB KT2 .... 147 D4
Cedar Ct *CHARL* SE7 * 124 C2
  ELTH/MOT SE9 * 143 F4
  WIM/MER SW19 .... 149 D3
Cedarhurst Dr *ELTH/MOT* SE9 .... 142 C5
Cedar Mt *ELTH/MOT* SE9 .... 161 D1
Cedar Rd *CRICK* NW2 .... 70 A3
Cedars CI *LEW* SE13 .... 141 D1
Cedars Cots *PUT/ROE* SW15 * 130 A4
Cedars Ms *CLAP* SW4 * 134 B2
Cedars Rd *BARN* SW13 .... 111 F5
  CHSWK W4 .... 110 C3
  CLAP SW4 .... 134 B3
  SRTFD E15 .... 81 E3
The Cedars *HOM* E9 * 79 D4
  SRTFD E15 * 81 F5
Cedar Tree Gv *WNWD* SE27 .... 154 B5
Cedar Wy *CAMTN* NW1 .... 75 D4
Cedric Rd *ELTH/MOT* SE9 .... 162 C5
Celandine CI *POP/IOD* E14 .... 92 A4
Celandine Dr *HACK* E8 .... 77 F4
Celandine Wy *SRTFD* E15 .... 93 E2
Celbridge Ms *BAY/PAD* W2 .... 15 D4
Celestial Gdns *LEW* SE13 .... 141 D2
Celia Rd *ARCH* N19 .... 74 C1
Celtic St *POP/IOD* E14 .... 92 B4
Cemetery La *CHARL* SE7 .... 125 E2
Cemetery Rd *FSTGT* E7 .... 81 F2
Cenacle CI *HAMP* NW3 .... 54 A5
Centaur St *STHWK* SE1 .... 45 F2
Centenary Ms *MNPK* E12 .... 65 D5
  .... 63 F1
Central Av *WAN* E11 .... 63 D4
Central Hall Blds *ARCH* N19 * 56 C4
Central HI *NRWD* SE19 .... 154 C5
Central Pde *ACT* W3 * 98 A3
  STRHM/NOR SW16 * 97 F5
Central Park Rd *EHAM* E6 .... 95 D1
Central Sq *GLDGN* NW11 .... 54 A1
Central Wy *WLSDN* NW10 .... 86 C2
Centre Av *ACT* W3 .... 99 D2
Centre Rd *FSTGT* E7 .... 64 A5
  WAN E11 .... 63 F1
Centre St *BETH* E2 .... 90 B1
Centric CI *CAMTN* NW1 * 74 B5
Centurion CI *HOLWY* N7 .... 75 F4
Centurion La *BOW* E3 .... 91 F1
Centurion Sq *CHARL* SE7 .... 125 E4
Century Ms *CLPT* E5 * 78 C1
Cephas Av *WCHPL* E1 .... 90 C3
Cephas St *WCHPL* E1 .... 90 C3
Ceres Rd *WOOL/PLUM* SE18 .... 109 F5
Cerise Rd *PECK* SE15 .... 120 A4
Cerney Ms *BAY/PAD* W2 .... 28 A1
Cervantes Ct *BAY/PAD* W2 .... 15 D5
Ceylon Rd *WKENS* W14 .... 101 D4
Chabot Dr *PECK* SE15 .... 138 B1
Chadbourn St *POP/IOD* E14 .... 92 B4
Chadwell St *CLKNW* EC1R 10 B3
Chadwick CI *PUT/ROE* SW15 .... 129 F5
Chadwick Rd *IL* IG1 .... 66 B5
  PECK SE15 .... 119 F5
  WAN E11 .... 63 E2
  WLSDN NW10 .... 69 F1
Chadwick St *WEST* SW1P 44 A5
Chadwin Rd *PLSTW* E13 .... 94 B4
Chagford St *CAMTN* NW1 .... 17 E1
Chailey St *CLPT* E5 .... 60 C5
Chalbury Wk *IS* N1 .... 9 F1
Chalcot Crs *CAMTN* NW1 .... 73 F5
Chalcot Gdns *HAMP* NW3 .... 73 F3
Chalcot Ms *STRHM/NOR* SW16 .... 153 E3
Chalcot Rd *CAMTN* NW1 .... 74 A5
Chalcot Sq *CAMTN* NW1 .... 74 A4
Chalcroft Rd *LEW* SE13 .... 141 E3
Chaldon Rd *FUL/PGN* SW6 .... 113 E3
Chale Rd *BRXS/STRHM* SW2 .... 135 E4
Chalfont Av *WBLY* HA9 .... 68 B3

Chalfont Ms *WAND/EARL* SW18 .... 149 F1
Chalford Rd *DUL* SE21 .... 155 D4
Chalgrove Rd *HACK* E8 .... 78 C3
  HOM E9 .... 78 C3
Chalk Farm Pde *HAMP* NW3 * 74 A4
Chalk Farm Rd *CAMTN* NW1 .... 74 A4
Chalk Hill Rd *HMSMTH* W6 .... 101 D5
Chalkhill Rd *WBLY* HA9 .... 50 A5
Chalklands *WBLY* HA9 .... 50 C5
Chalk Rd *PLSTW* E13 .... 94 B4
Challenge CI *WLSDN* NW10 .... 69 E5
Challin Wy *BRXS/STRHM* SW2 .... 153 F1
Challoner Crs *WKENS* W14 .... 113 F1
Challoner St *WKENS* W14 .... 113 F1
Chalmers Wk *WALW* SE17 * 118 B2
Chalsey Rd *BROCKY* SE4 .... 139 F2
Chalton St *CAMTN* NW1 .... 8 A1
  .... 5 F3
  THMD SE28 .... 66 C5
Chamberlain Cots *CMBW* SE5 * 119 D4
Chamberlain St *CAMTN* NW1 * 73 F4
Chamberlayne Rd *WLSDN* NW10 .... 70 C5
Chambers Garages *HMSMTH* W6 * 100 B5
Chambers La *WLSDN* NW10 .... 70 B4
Chambers Rd *HOLWY* N7 .... 75 E1
Chambers St *BERM/RHTH* SE16 .... 102 A3
Chamber St *WCHPL* E1 .... 37 F1
Chambon PI *HMSMTH* W6 .... 100 A5
Chambord St *BETH* E2 .... 13 F4
Champion Crs *SYD* SE26 .... 157 E4
Champion Gv *CMBW* SE5 .... 137 D1
Champion HI *CMBW* SE5 .... 137 D1
Champion Pk *CMBW* SE5 .... 137 D1
Champion Rd *SYD* SE26 .... 157 E4
Champness CI *WNWD* SE27 .... 155 D4
Champness Rd *BARK* IG11 .... 85 F4
Chancellor Gv *DUL* SE21 .... 154 C2
Chancellor's Rd *HMSMTH* W6 .... 112 C1
Chancellors St *HMSMTH* W6 .... 112 C1
Chancellors Whf *HMSMTH* W6 * 112 C1
Chancel St *STHWK* SE1 .... 34 C3
Chancery La *LINN* WC2A 21 F3
Chance St *BETH* E2 .... 13 E5
Chanctonbury CI *ELTH/MOT* SE9 .... 162 B3
Chandler Av *CAN/RD* E16 .... 94 A4
Chandlers CI *LEE/GVPK* SE12 .... 160 B2
Chandlers Ms *POP/IOD* E14 .... 104 A3
Chandler St *WAP* E1W 102 B2
Chandler Wy *PECK* SE15 .... 119 E2
Chandos PI *CHCR* WC2N 32 C2
Chandos Rd *CRICK* NW2 .... 70 C2
  SRTFD E15 .... 81 D2
  WLSDN NW10 .... 87 E3
Chandos Wy *GLDGN* NW11 .... 54 B3
Channel Gate Rd *NKENS* W10 .... 88 C4
  WLSDN NW10 .... 87 E2
Channel Islands Est *IS* N1 .... 76 C3
Channelsea Rd *SRTFD* E15 .... 81 D5
Chantrey Rd *BRXN/ST* SW9 .... 135 F1
Chantry CI *MV/WKIL* W9 * 89 F3
Chantry Crs *WLSDN* NW10 .... 69 E2
Chantry Sq *KENS* W8 .... 38 C2
Chantry St *IS* N1 .... 76 B5
Chant Sq *SRTFD* E15 .... 81 D4
Chant St *SRTFD* E15 .... 81 D4
Chapel Av *MNPK* E12 .... 65 D5
Chapel CI *WLSDN* NW10 .... 69 F2
Chapel Ct *STHWK* SE1 .... 36 A5
  WOOL/PLUM SE18 .... 127 F2
Chapel Farm Rd *ELTH/MOT* SE9 .... 161 F2
Chapel House St *POP/IOD* E14 .... 122 B1
Chapel Market *IS* N1 .... 10 A1
Chapel PI *CAVSO/HST* W1G 18 C4
  IS N1 .... 10 B1
Chapel Rd *IL* IG1 .... 66 A5
  WNWD SE27 .... 154 B4
Chapel Side *BAY/PAD* W2 .... 26 C1
Chapel St *BAY/PAD* W2 .... 16 C3
  KTBR SW1X 42 B2
Chaplin PI *STHWK* SE1 .... 42 B2
Chaplin Rd *CRICK* NW2 .... 70 A3
  SRTFD E15 .... 93 E1
Chapman Rd *HOM* E9 .... 79 F2
Chapman Sq *WIM/MER* SW19 .... 149 D3
Chapman St *WCHPL* E1 .... 102 B1
Chapter CI *CHSWK* W4 .... 98 C4
Chapter Rd *CRICK* NW2 .... 70 A2
  WALW SE17 .... 118 B1
Chapter St *WEST* SW1P 44 A5
Chara PI *CHSWK* W4 .... 111 D2

Chardin Rd *CHSWK* W4 * 99 E5
Chardmore Rd *STNW/STAM* N16 .... 60 A3
Chardwell Cl *EHAM* E6 .... 95 E5
Charecroft Wy *WKENS* W14 .... 101 D3
Charford Rd *CAN/RD* E16 .... 94 A4
Chargeable La *PLSTW* E13 .... 94 A3
Chargeable St *CAN/RD* E16 .... 93 F3
Chargrove Cl *BERM/RHTH* SE16 .... 103 D3
Charing Cross *CHCR* WC2N * 32 C3
Charing Cross Rd *LSQ/SEVD* WC2H 32 B1
Chariot Cl *BOW* E3 .... 80 A5
Charlbert St *STJWD* NW8 .... 4 C1
Charlbury Gdns *GDMY/SEVK* IG3 .... 67 F4
Charldane Rd *ELTH/MOT* SE9 .... 162 B3
Charlecote Gv *SYD* SE26 .... 156 B3
Charlemont Rd *EHAM* E6 .... 95 F2
Charles Cl *CLAP* SW4 * 134 C1
Charles Coveney Rd *CMBW* SE5 * 119 F4
Charlesfield *ELTH/MOT* SE9 .... 160 C3
Charles Flemwell Rd *CAN/RD* E16 * 106 A2
Charles Grinling Wk
    WOOL/PLUM SE18 .... 108 A5
Charles Haller St *BRXS/STRHM* SW2 ...... 136 A5
Charles II PI *CHEL* SW3 * 115 F1
Charles II St *STJS* SW1Y 32 A3
Charles La *STJWD* NW8 .... 4 C2
Charles PI *CAMTN* NW1 * 7 F4
Charles Rd *FSTGT* E7 .... 82 C4
Charles Sq *IS* N1 .... 12 B4
Charles Square Est *IS* N1 .... 129 E1
Charles St *BARN* SW13 .... 106 C2
    CAN/RD E16 .... 30 C3
    MYFR/PICC W1J 30 C3
Charleston St *WALW* SE17 .... 47 F5
Charles Whincup Rd *CAN/RD* E16 .... 106 B2
Charleville Circ *SYD* SE26 .... 156 A5
Charleville Rd *WKENS* W14 .... 113 E1
Charlotte Despard Av *BTSEA* SW11 .... 116 B4
Charlotte Ms *FITZ* W1T 19 F2
    NKENS W10 .... 89 D5
    WKENS W14 * 101 E5
Charlotte Pde *FSTH* SE23 * 157 E2
Charlotte PI *FITZ* W1T 19 F3
    PIM SW1V 43 E5
Charlotte Rd *BARN* SW13 .... 111 F4
    SDTCH EC2A 12 C4
Charlotte Rw *CLAP* SW4 .... 134 C1
Charlotte St *FITZ* W1T 19 F2
Charlotte Ter *IS* N1 * 75 E1
Charlow Cl *FUL/PGN* SW6 .... 114 C5
Charlton Church La *CHARL* SE7 .... 124 C1
Charlton Dene *CHARL* SE7 .... 124 C3
Charlton King's Rd *KTTN* NW5 .... 75 D2
Charlton La *CHARL* SE7 .... 125 D1
Charlton Park La *CHARL* SE7 .... 125 D3
Charlton Park Rd *CHARL* SE7 .... 125 D2
Charlton PI *IS* N1 .... 10 C1
Charlton Rd *BKHTH/KID* SE3 .... 124 A3
    CHARL SE7 .... 124 C2
    WLSDN NW10 .... 69 E5
Charlton Wy *BKHTH/KID* SE3 .... 123 F3
    GNWCH SE10 .... 123 E4
Charlwood PI *PIM* SW1V 43 F5
Charlwood Rd *PUT/ROE* SW15 .... 131 D1
Charlwood St *PIM* SW1V 43 F5
Charlwood Ter *PUT/ROE* SW15 .... 131 D2
Charminster Rd *ELTH/MOT* SE9 .... 161 D4
Charnock Rd *CLPT* E5 .... 60 B5
Charnwood Gdns *POP/IOD* E14 .... 104 A5
Charnwood Rd *SNWD* SE25 .... 60 A4
Charnwood St *CLPT* E5 .... 60 A4
Charrington St *CAMTN* NW1 .... 8 A1
Charsley Rd *CAT* SE6 .... 158 B2
Charter Av *GNTH/NBYPK* IG2 .... 67 D3
Charterhouse Bids *FARR* EC1M * 23 E1
Charterhouse Ms *FARR* EC1M 23 D2
Charterhouse Rd *HACK* E8 .... 78 A1
Charterhouse St *HCIRC* EC1N 22 B5
The Charterhouse *FARR* EC1M * 23 D1
Charteris Rd *FSBYPK* N4 .... 57 F3
    KIL/WHAMP NW6 .... 71 F5
Charters St *NRWD* SE19 .... 155 E5
Chartfield Av *PUT/ROE* SW15 .... 130 B3
Chartfield Sq *PUT/ROE* SW15 * 131 D3
Chartham Gv *WNWD* SE27 .... 154 A3
Chartley Av *CRICK* NW2 .... 51 E5
Chartley Pde *CRICK* NW2 * 51 E5
Chart St *IS* N1 .... 12 B3
Chartwell Cl *ELTH/MOT* SE9 .... 163 D2
Charwood *STRHM/NOR* SW16 .... 154 A4
Chasefield Rd *TOOT* SW17 .... 151 F4
Chaseley Ct *CHSWK* W4 * 110 B1

Chaseley St *POP/IOD* E14 * 91 E5
Chase Rd *ACT* W3 .... 87 D3
The Chase *CLAP* SW4 * 134 B1
    FSTGT E7 .... 83 E2
Chatfield Rd *BTSEA* SW11 .... 132 C1
Chatham PI *HOM* E9 .... 78 C3
Chatham Rd *BTSEA* SW11 .... 133 F4
Chatham St *WALW* SE17 .... 48 A4
    WOOL/PLUM SE18 .... 108 B4
Chatsworth Av *BMLY* BR1 .... 160 B5
Chatsworth Cl *CHSWK* W4 .... 110 C2
Chatsworth Est *CLPT* E5 * 79 D1
Chatsworth Gdns *ACT* W3 .... 98 B1
Chatsworth Rd *CHSWK* W4 .... 110 C2
    CLPT E5 .... 60 C5
    CRICK NW2 .... 71 D5
    SRTFD E15 .... 81 F2
Chatsworth Wy *WNWD* SE27 .... 154 B3
Chatterton Ms *FSBYPK* N4 * 58 B5
Chatterton Rd *FSBYPK* N4 .... 58 B5
Chatto Rd *BTSEA* SW11 .... 133 F3
Chaucer Av *RCH/KEW* TW9 .... 110 A5
Chaucer Dr *STHWK* SE1 .... 49 F5
Chaucer Rd *ACT* W3 .... 98 C2
    FSTGT E7 .... 82 A3
    HNHL SE24 .... 136 A3
    WAN E11 .... 64 A1
    WELL DA16 .... 127 F4
Chaundrye Cl *ELTH/MOT* SE9 .... 143 F4
Chaunler Rd *CAN/RD* E16 .... 94 B5
Cheam St *PECK* SE15 * 138 B1
Cheapside *CITYW* EC2V 23 F5
Cheesemans Ter *WKENS* W14 * 113 F1
Chelford Rd *BMLY* BR1 .... 159 D5
Chelmer Rd *HOM* E9 .... 79 D2
Chelmsford Cl *EHAM* E6 .... 95 F5
    HMSMTH W6 .... 113 D2
Chelmsford Gdns *IL* IG1 .... 65 E2
Chelmsford Rd *WALTH* E17 .... 62 A1
    WAN E11 .... 63 D5
Chelmsford Sq *WLSDN* NW10 .... 70 C5
Chelsea Br *VX/NE* SW8 .... 116 B2
Chelsea Bridge Ga *VX/NE* SW8 .... 116 A2
Chelsea Bridge Rd *BGVA* SW1W 116 A1
Chelsea Cl *WLSDN* NW10 .... 69 D5
Chelsea Crs *CRICK* NW2 * 71 F3
    WBPTN SW10 * 114 C4
Chelsea Emb *CHEL* SW3 .... 115 F2
Chelsea Gdns *BGVA* SW1W * 116 A1
Chelsea Harbour Dr *WBPTN* SW10 .... 114 C4
Chelsea Manor Gdns *CHEL* SW3 * 115 E2
Chelsea Manor St *CHEL* SW3 .... 115 E1
Chelsea Park Gdns *CHEL* SW3 * 115 D2
Chelsea Sq *CHEL* SW3 .... 115 D2
Chelsea Towers *CHEL* SW3 * 115 E2
Chelsea Village *FUL/PGN* SW6 * 114 B3
Chelsfield Gdns *SYD* SE26 .... 156 C3
Chelsham Rd *CLAP* SW4 .... 135 D1
Chelsworth Dr *WOOL/PLUM* SE18 .... 127 D2
Cheltenham Gdns *EHAM* E6 .... 95 E1
Cheltenham PI *ACT* W3 .... 98 C3
Cheltenham Rd *LEY* E10 .... 62 C1
    PECK SE15 .... 138 C2
Cheltenham Ter *CHEL* SW3 .... 115 F1
Chelverton Rd *PUT/ROE* SW15 .... 131 D2
Chelwood Gdns *RCH/KEW* TW9 .... 110 A5
Chenappa Cl *PLSTW* E13 .... 94 A2
Cheneys Rd *WAN* E11 .... 63 E5
Chenies Ms *GWRST* WC1E 20 A1
Chenies PI *CAMTN* NW1 .... 8 B1
Chenies St *GWRST* WC1E 20 A2
Cheniston Gdns *KENS* W8 .... 38 B2
Chepstow Cl *PUT/ROE* SW15 .... 131 E3
Chepstow Cnr *BAY/PAD* W2 * 14 B3
Chepstow Crs *GDMY/SEVK* IG3 .... 67 E1
    NTGHL W11 .... 26 A1
Chepstow PI *BAY/PAD* W2 .... 14 B5
Chepstow Rd *BAY/PAD* W2 .... 14 B4
Chepstow Vls *NTGHL* W11 .... 101 F1
Chequer St *STLK* EC1Y 23 F1
Cherbury St *IS* N1 .... 12 B2
Cheriton Dr *WOOL/PLUM* SE18 .... 127 D3
Cheriton Sq *TOOT* SW17 .... 152 A2
Cherry Cl *BRXS/STRHM* SW2 .... 136 A5
Cherry Garden St *BERM/RHTH* SE16 .... 102 B3
Cherry Orch *CHARL* SE7 .... 124 C2
Cherry Tree Cl *HOM* E9 * 78 C5
Cherry Tree Dr *STRHM/NOR* SW16 .... 153 E3
Cherry Tree Rd *SRTFD* E15 .... 81 E2
Cherry Tree Wk *STLK* EC1Y 23 F1

Cherrywood Cl *BOW* E3 .... 91 E2
Cherrywood Dr *PUT/ROE* SW15 . 131 D3
Chertsey Rd *IL* IG1 .... 85 D1
   WAN E11 .... 63 D4
Chertsey St *TOOT* SW17 .... 152 A5
Cheryls Cl *FUL/PGN* SW6 .... 114 B4
Cheseman St *SYD* SE26 .... 156 B3
Chesham Cl *KTBR* SW1X * 42 A3
Chesham Ms *KTBR* SW1X 42 A2
Chesham Pl *KTBR* SW1X 42 A2
Chesham St *KTBR* SW1X 42 A3
   WLSDN NW10 .... 51 D5
Cheshire St *BETH* E2 .... 90 A3
Chesholm Rd *STNW/STAM* N16 .. 59 E5
Cheshunt Rd *FSTGT* E7 .... 82 B3
Chesilton Rd *FUL/PGN* SW6 ...... 113 F4
Chesley Gdns *EHAM* E6 .... 95 D1
Chesney St *BTSEA* SW11 .... 116 A4
Chesson Rd *WKENS* W14 .... 113 F2
Chester Cl *BARN* SW13 * 130 B1
   KTBR SW1X 42 B1
Chester Cl North *CAMTN* NW1 ... 7 D3
Chester Cl South *CAMTN* NW1 ... 7 D4
Chester Crs *HACK* E8 .... 77 F2
Chesterfield Gdns *GNWCH* SE10 * 123 D3
   MYFR/PICC W1J * 30 C3
Chesterfield Gv *EDUL* SE22 ...... 137 F5
Chesterfield Hl *MYFR/PKLN* W1K 30 C3
   LEY E10 .... 62 C2
Chesterfield Rd *CHSWK* W4 .... 110 C2
Chesterfield St *MYFR/PICC* W1J . 30 C3
Chesterfield Wy *PECK* SE15 ...... 120 C3
Chesterford Gdns *HAMP* NW3 ... 72 B1
Chesterford Rd *MNPK* E12 .... 83 F2
Chester Ga *CAMTN* NW1 .... 6 C4
Chester Ms *KTBR* SW1X 42 C2
Chester Pl *CAMTN* NW1 .... 6 C3
Chester Rd *ARCH* N19 .... 56 B4
   BFN/LL DA15 * 145 E3
   CAMTN NW1 .... 6 B4
   CAN/RD E16 .... 93 E3
   FSTGT E7 .... 83 D4
   GDMY/SEVK IG3 .... 87 F3
   WAN E11 .... 64 B1
Chester Rw *BCVA* SW1W 42 A5
Chester Sq *BCVA* SW1W 42 B4
Chester Square Ms *BCVA* SW1W * 42 C3
Chester St *BETH* E2 .... 90 A3
   KTBR SW1X 42 B1
Chester Ter *CAMTN* NW1 .... 6 C3
Chesterton Cl *WAND/EARL* SW18 132 A3
Chesterton Rd *NKENS* W10 .... 89 D4
   PLSTW E13 .... 94 A2
Chesterton Sq *KENS* W8 .... 101 F5
Chesterton Ter *PLSTW* E13 .... 94 A2
Chester Wy *LBTH* SE11 .... 46 B5
Chestnut Av *FSTGT* E7 .... 82 B1
   MORT/ESHN SW14 .... 129 D1
Chestnut Cl *CAT* SE6 .... 158 C4
   NWCR SE14 .... 121 F4
   STNW/STAM N16 .... 59 D4
   STRHM/NOR SW16 .... 154 A4
Chestnut Dr *WAN* E11 .... 64 A1
Chestnut Gv *BAL* SW12 .... 134 A5
Chestnut Pl *SYD* SE26 .... 155 F4
Chestnut Ri *WOOL/PLUM* SE18 .. 127 E1
Chestnut Rd *WNWD* SE27 .... 154 B3
Chettle Cl *STHWK* SE1 .... 48 A2
Chetwode Rd *TOOT* SW17 .... 151 F2
Chetwynd Rd *KTTN* NW5 .... 74 B1
Chetwynd Vls *KTTN* NW5 * 74 B1
Cheval Pl *POP/IOD* E14 .... 41 D2
Cheval Pl *POP/IOD* E14 .... 104 A4
Chevening Rd *GNWCH* SE10 ...... 123 F1
   KIL/WHAMP NW6 .... 89 D1
Cheverton Rd *ARCH* N19 .... 57 D3
Chevet St *HOM* E9 .... 79 E2
Chevington *CRICK* NW2 * 71 F3
Cheviot Gdns *CRICK* NW2 .... 53 D4
Cheviot Rd *WNWD* SE27 .... 154 A5
Chevron Cl *CAN/RD* E16 .... 94 A5
Cheyne Gdns *CHEL* SW3 .... 115 E2
Cheyne Ms *CHEL* SW3 .... 115 E2
Cheyne Pl *CHEL* SW3 .... 115 E2
Cheyne Rw *CHEL* SW3 .... 115 E2
Cheyne Wk *CHEL* SW3 .... 115 E2
   HDN NW4 .... 52 C1
   WBPTN SW10 .... 115 D3
Chichele Rd *CRICK* NW2 .... 71 D2
Chicheley St *STHWK* SE1 .... 33 F5
Chichester Cl *BKHTH/KID* SE3 ... 124 C3

   EHAM E6 .... 95 E5
Chichester Gdns *IL* IG1 .... 65 D5
Chichester Rd *BAY/PAD* W2 ...... 15 D2
   KIL/WHAMP NW6 .... 2 A2
   WAN E11 .... 63 D5
Chichester St *PIM* SW1V 116 C1
Chichester Wy *POP/IOD* E14 ...... 105 D5
Chicksand St *WCHPL* E1 .... 25 F3
Chiddingstone St *FUL/PGN* SW6 114 A5
Chigwell Hl *WAP* E1W 102 B1
Childebert Rd *TOOT* SW17 .... 152 B2
Childeric Rd *NWCR* SE14 .... 121 E3
Childerley St *FUL/PGN* SW6 ...... 113 E4
Childers St *DEPT* SE8 .... 121 E2
Child La *GNWCH* SE10 .... 105 F4
Child's Ms *ECT* SW5 * 38 C5
Child's Pl *ECT* SW5 .... 38 C5
Child's St *ECT* SW5 .... 38 B4
Child's Wk *ECT* SW5 * 38 C5
Chilham Rd *ELTH/MOT* SE9 .... 161 E4
Chillerton Rd *TOOT* SW17 .... 152 A5
Chillingford St *BTSEA* SW11 ...... 132 C2
Chillingworth Rd *HOLWY* N7 ..... 75 F3
Chiltern Gdns *CRICK* NW2 .... 53 D5
Chiltern Pl *CLPT* E5 .... 60 B4
Chiltern Rd *BOW* E3 .... 92 A3
Chiltern St *MHST* W1U 17 F2
Chilthorne Cl *CAT* SE6 .... 139 F5
Chilton Gv *DEPT* SE8 .... 103 D5
Chilton Rd *RCH/KEW* TW9 .... 128 A1
Chilton St *BETH* E2 .... 13 F5
Chilver St *GNWCH* SE10 .... 123 F1
Chilworth Ms *BAY/PAD* W2 .... 15 F5
Chilworth St *BAY/PAD* W2 .... 15 F5
China Hall Ms *BERM/RHTH* SE16 102 C4
China Ms *BRXS/STRHM* SW2 ...... 135 F5
Chinbrook Crs *LEE/GVPK* SE12 .. 160 B3
Chinbrook Rd *LEE/GVPK* SE12 ... 160 B3
Chipka St *POP/IOD* E14 .... 104 C3
Chipley St *NWCR* SE14 .... 121 E2
Chippendale St *CLPT* E5 .... 61 D5
Chippenham Ms *MV/WKIL* W9 ... 14 A1
Chippenham Rd *MV/WKIL* W9 .... 2 A5
Chipstead Gdns *CRICK* NW2 ...... 52 B4
Chipstead St *FUL/PGN* SW6 ...... 114 A4
Chisenhale Rd *BOW* E3 .... 91 F1
Chisley Rd *SEVS/STOTM* N15 .... 59 E1
Chiswell Sq *BKHTH/KID* SE3 ...... 124 B5
Chiswell St *CMBW* SE5 .... 119 D3
   STLK EC1Y 24 A2
Chiswick Br *CHSWK* W4 .... 110 C5
Chiswick Common Rd *CHSWK* W4 99 D5
Chiswick High Rd *CHSWK* W4 .... 110 A1
Chiswick House Grounds
   CHSWK W4 * 111 D2
Chiswick La *CHSWK* W4 .... 111 E1
Chiswick La South *CHSWK* W4 ... 111 F2
Chiswick Ml *CHSWK* W4 .... 111 F2
Chiswick Pk *CHSWK* W4 * 98 C4
Chiswick Pier *CHSWK* W4 .... 111 F3
Chiswick Quay *CHSWK* W4 .... 110 C5
Chiswick Rd *CHSWK* W4 .... 98 C5
Chiswick Sq *CHSWK* W4 * 111 E2
Chiswick Staithe *CHSWK* W4 ..... 110 C4
Chiswick Village *CHSWK* W4 ..... 110 A2
Chiswick Whf *CHSWK* W4 .... 111 F2
Chitty St *FITZ* W1T 19 F2
Chivalry Rd *BTSEA* SW11 .... 133 E3
Chobham Gdns *WIM/MER* SW19 149 D2
Chobham Rd *SRTFD* E15 .... 81 E3
Cholmeley Cl *HGT* N6 * 56 B2
Cholmeley Pk *HGT* N6 .... 56 B3
Cholmley Gdns *KIL/WHAMP* NW6 72 A2
Cholmondeley Av *WLSDN* NW10 . 88 A1
Chopwell Cl *SRTFD* E15 * 80 D4
Choumert Gv *PECK* SE15 .... 120 A5
Choumert Ms *PECK* SE15 .... 120 A5
Choumert Rd *PECK* SE15 .... 137 F1
Chow Sq *HACK* E8 * 77 F2
   HACK E8 * 77 F2
Chrisp St *POP/IOD* E14 .... 92 B4
Christchurch Av *KIL/WHAMP* NW6 . 72 A5
Christchurch Hl *HAMP* NW3 .... 55 D5
Christchurch Rd *BFN/LL* DA15 ... 163 F4
   BRXS/STRHM SW2 .... 153 F1
Christ Church Rd *CEND/HSY/T* N8 57 E1
Christchurch Rd *IL* IG1 .... 66 A4
   MORT/ESHN SW14 .... 128 B3
Christchurch Sq *HOM* E9 * 78 C5
Christchurch St *CHEL* SW3 .... 115 F2
Christchurch Ter *CHEL* SW3 * 115 F2

Christchurch Wy GNWCH SE10 ..... 123 E1
Christian St WCHPL E1 ..... 90 A5
Christie Rd HOM E9 ..... 79 E5
Christina Sq FSBYPK N4 ..... 58 B3
Christina St SDTCH EC2A 12 C5
Christopher Cl BERM/RHTH SE16 ..... 103 D3
　BFN/LL DA15 ..... 145 F3
Christopher Pl CAMTN NW1 * 8 B3
Christophers Ms NTCHL W11 * 101 E2
Christopher St SDTCH EC2A 24 B1
Chryssell Rd BRXN/ST SW9 ..... 118 A3
Chubworthy St NWCR SE14 ..... 121 E2
Chudleigh Crs GDMY/SEVK IG3 ..... 85 E1
Chudleigh Rd BROCKY SE4 ..... 139 F3
　KIL/WHAMP NW6 ..... 70 C4
Chudleigh St WCHPL E1 ..... 91 D5
Chulsa Rd SYD SE26 ..... 156 B5
Chumleigh Gdns CMBW SE5 * 119 D5
Chumleigh St CMBW SE5 ..... 119 E2
Church Ap DUL SE21 ..... 155 D3
Church Av ACT W3 ..... 74 B3
　MNPK E12 ..... 65 D4
　MORT/ESHN SW14 ..... 129 D2
Churchbury Rd ELTH/MOT SE9 ..... 143 D5
Church Crs HOM E9 ..... 79 D4
Churchcroft Cl BAL SW12 * 134 A5
Churchdown BMLY BR1 * 159 E4
Churchfield Rd ACT W3 ..... 98 C2
Churchfields GNWCH SE10 ..... 122 C2
Church Garth ARCH N19 * 57 D4
Church Ga FUL/PGN SW6 ..... 131 E1
Church Gn BRXN/ST SW9 * 118 A5
Church Gv LEW SE13 ..... 140 B2
Church Hl WIM/MER SW19 ..... 149 F5
　WOOL/PLUM SE18 ..... 107 F4
Church Hyde WOOL/PLUM SE18 * 127 E2
Churchill Gdns ACT W3 * 86 A5
Churchill Gardens Rd PIM SW1V 116 B1
Churchill Pl POP/IOD E14 ..... 104 B1
Churchill Rd CAN/RD E16 ..... 94 C5
　CRICK NW2 ..... 70 A1
　KTTN NW5 ..... 74 B1
Churchill Wk HOM E9 ..... 78 C2
Church La CDALE/KGS NW9 ..... 50 C3
　TOOT SW17 ..... 151 F5
　WAN E11 ..... 63 E3
Churchley Rd SYD SE26 ..... 156 B4
Church Md CMBW SE5 * 118 C3
Churchmead Rd WLSDN NW10 ..... 70 A3
Church Pth MORT NW10 * 98 C4
Church Ri FSTH SE23 ..... 157 D1
Church La LEY E10 ..... 62 B4
Church Rd ACT W3 ..... 98 C3
　BARK IG11 ..... 84 C3
　BARN SW13 ..... 112 A5
　GNTH/NBYPK IG2 ..... 67 E1
　HGT N6 ..... 56 A3
　IS N1 ..... 76 C3
　LEY E10 ..... 62 A3
　MNPK E12 ..... 83 E2
　WIM/MER SW19 ..... 149 E4
　WLSDN NW10 ..... 69 E3
Church Rw FUL/PGN SW6 * 114 B3
　HAMP NW3 ..... 72 C1
　WAND/EARL SW18 ..... 132 B3
Church St BAY/PAD W2 ..... 16 B2
　CHSWK W4 ..... 111 E2
　SRTFD E15 ..... 81 E5
Church Street Est STJWD NW8 ..... 16 B1
Church St North SRTFD E15 ..... 81 E5
Church Ter BKHTH/KID SE3 ..... 141 E1
　FUL/PGN SW6 * 114 B5
Church V FSTH SE23 ..... 156 C2
Church Vw FSTH SE23 ..... 157 D2
Church Wk CDALE/KGS NW9 ..... 51 D4
　CRICK NW2 ..... 53 F5
　STNW/STAM N16 ..... 77 D1
Churchway CAMTN NW1 ..... 8 B3
Churchyard Rw LBTH SE11 ..... 47 D4
Churston Av PLSTW E13 ..... 82 B5
Churston Cl BRXS/STRHM SW2 * 154 B1
Churton Pl CHSWK W4 * 110 B2
　PIM SW1V 43 F5
Churton St PIM SW1V 43 F5
Chyngton Cl BFN/LL DA15 ..... 163 F5
Cibber Rd FSTH SE23 ..... 157 D2
Cicada Rd WAND/EARL SW18 ..... 132 C4
Cicely Rd PECK SE15 ..... 120 A4
Cinderford Wy BMLY BR1 ..... 159 E4
Cinnamon Cl PECK SE15 ..... 119 F5
Cinnamon St WAP E1W 102 B2

The Circle CRICK NW2 ..... 51 E5
Circular Wy WOOL/PLUM SE18 ..... 125 F2
Circus Ms MBLAR W1H * 17 E2
Circus Pl LVPST EC2M * 24 B3
Circus Rd STJWD NW8 ..... 4 A5
Circus St GNWCH SE10 ..... 122 C5
Cirencester St BAY/PAD W2 ..... 14 C2
Citadel Pl LBTH SE11 ..... 117 F1
Citizen Rd HOLWY N7 ..... 58 A5
Citron Ter PECK SE15 * 138 B1
City Barracks SHB W12 * 100 C2
City Garden Rw IS N1 ..... 11 D2
City Rd FSBYE EC1V 10 C2
　STLK EC1Y 24 B1
City Wk STHWK SE1 ..... 48 C2
Clabon Ms KTBR SW1X 41 E3
Clack St BERM/RHTH SE16 ..... 102 C5
Clacton Rd WALTH E17 ..... 61 E1
Claire Pl POP/IOD E14 ..... 104 A4
Clairview Rd STRHM/NOR SW16 ..... 152 B5
Clancarty Rd FUL/PGN SW6 ..... 114 A5
Clandon Cl ACT W3 ..... 98 B3
Clandon Rd GDMY/SEVK IG3 ..... 67 E4
Clandon St DEPT SE8 ..... 122 A5
Clanricarde Gdns BAY/PAD W2 ..... 26 B2
Clapham Common North Side
　CLAP SW4 ..... 134 A2
Clapham Common South Side
　CLAP SW4 ..... 134 B3
Clapham Common West Side
　CLAP SW4 ..... 134 A2
Clapham Court Ter CLAP SW4 * 135 E3
Clapham Crs CLAP SW4 ..... 135 D2
Clapham High St CLAP SW4 ..... 135 D2
Clapham Manor St CLAP SW4 ..... 134 C1
Clapham Park Est CLAP SW4 * 135 D5
Clapham Park Rd CLAP SW4 ..... 134 C2
Clapham Park Ter
　BRXS/STRHM SW2 * 135 E3
Clapham Rd BRXN/ST SW9 ..... 117 E5
Claps Gate La EHAM E6 ..... 96 B3
Clapton Common CLPT E5 ..... 78 A3
Clapton Pas CLPT E5 ..... 78 C2
Clapton Sq CLPT E5 ..... 78 B2
Clapton Ter CLPT E5 ..... 60 A2
Clapton Wy CLPT E5 ..... 78 A1
Clara Pl WOOL/PLUM SE18 ..... 108 C1
Clare Cnr ELTH/MOT SE9 ..... 144 B5
Claredale St BETH E2 ..... 90 A1
Clare Gdns BARK IG11 ..... 85 F3
　FSTGT E7 ..... 82 A1
　NTGHL W11 * 89 E5
Clare La IS N1 ..... 76 C4
Clare Lawn Av MORT/ESHN SW14 ..... 129 D3
Clare Ms FUL/PGN SW6 ..... 114 B3
Claremont Cl BRXS/STRHM SW2 ..... 153 F1
　CAN/RD E16 ..... 108 A3
　IS N1 ..... 10 B2
Claremont Gdns GDMY/SEVK IG3 ..... 67 E4
Claremont Gv CHSWK W4 ..... 111 E3
Claremont Rd CRICK NW2 ..... 52 C2
　FSTGT E7 ..... 82 B2
　GLDGN NW11 ..... 53 D5
　HGT N6 ..... 56 B2
　MV/WKIL W9 ..... 89 E1
　WAN E11 ..... 63 D5
Claremont Sq IS N1 ..... 10 A2
Claremont St GNWCH SE10 ..... 122 B2
Claremont Vls CMBW SE5 * 119 D3
Claremont Wy CRICK NW2 ..... 52 C3
Clarence Av CLAP SW4 ..... 135 D4
　IL IG1 ..... 65 F1
Clarence Crs CLAP SW4 ..... 135 D4
Clarence Gdns CAMTN NW1 ..... 7 D4
Clarence Ga CAMTN NW1 ..... 5 F5
Clarence La PUT/ROE SW15 ..... 129 F3
Clarence Ms BERM/RHTH SE16 ..... 103 D2
　CLPT E5 ..... 78 B3
　TOOT SW17 ..... 150 C3
Clarence Pas CAMTN NW1 * 8 C2
Clarence Pl CLPT E5 ..... 78 B3
Clarence Rd CAN/RD E16 ..... 93 E3
　CHSWK W4 ..... 110 A1
　CLPT E5 ..... 78 B1
　DEPT SE8 ..... 122 B2
　ELTH/MOT SE9 ..... 161 E2
　KIL/WHAMP NW6 ..... 71 F4
　MNPK E12 ..... 82 C1
Clarence Ter CAMTN NW1 * 117 E5
Clarence Wk CLAP SW4 ..... 135 E1
Clarence Wy CAMTN NW1 ..... 74 B4
Clarendon Cl BAY/PAD W2 * 28 C1

HOM E9	78	C4
Clarendon Cross NTGHL W11	101	E1
Clarendon Dr PUT/ROE SW15	130	C2
Clarendon Gdns IL IG1	65	F3
MV/WKIL W9	15	F1
Clarendon Ga BAY/PAD W2	28	C1
Clarendon Ms BAY/PAD W2	28	C1
Clarendon Pl BAY/PAD W2	28	C1
Clarendon Ri LEW SE13	140	C1
Clarendon Rd NTGHL W11	101	E1
WALTH E17	62	B1
Clarendon St PIM SW1V	116	B1
Clarendon Ter MV/WKIL W9	3	F5
Clarens St CAT SE6	157	F2
Clare Rd NWCR SE14	121	F5
WAN E11	63	D1
WLSDN NW10	81	G5
Clare St BETH E2	90	B1
Clareville Gv SKENS SW7	39	F5
Clareville St SKENS SW7	39	F5
Clarges Ms MYFR/PICC W1J	30	C3
Clarges St MYFR/PICC W1J	30	C3
Claribel Rd BRXN/ST SW9	118	B5
Clarissa St HACK E8	77	F5
Clarkers La KTTN NW5	74	B2
Clarkes Ms CAVSQ/HST W1G	18	B2
Clarkson Rd CAN/RD E16	93	F5
Clarkson Rw CAMTN NW1	7	E2
Clarkson St BETH E2 *	90	B2
Clark's Rd IL IG1	67	D4
Clark St WCHPL E1	90	C5
Claude Monet Ct EDUL SE22 *	138	A3
Claude Rd LEY E10	62	C3
PECK SE15	120	B5
PLSTW E13	82	B5
Claude St POP/IOD E14	104	A5
Claudia Pl WIM/MER SW19	149	A5
Claughton Rd PLSTW E13	94	C1
Claverdale Rd BRXS/STRHM SW2	135	F2
Clavering Av BARN SW13	112	F2
Clavering Rd MNPK E12	65	D3
Claverton St PIM SW1V	116	B1
Clave St WAP E1W	102	C2
Claxton Gv HMSMTH W6	113	F1
Claybank Gv LEW SE13	140	B1
Claybridge Rd LEE/GVPK SE12	160	C4
Claybrook Rd HMSMTH W6	113	D2
Claydon Ms WOOL/PLUM SE18	126	A1
Clayfarm Rd ELTH/MOT SE9	162	C2
Clayhill Crs ELTH/MOT SE9	161	D4
Claylands Pl VX/NE SW8	118	A3
Claylands Rd VX/NE SW8	117	F2
Claypole Rd SRTFD E15 *	92	C1
Clay St MHST W1U	17	F3
Clayton Av EHAM E6	95	F5
Clayton Crs IS N1	75	E5
Clayton Dr DEPT SE8	103	D4
Clayton Ms GNWCH SE10	123	D4
Clayton Rd PECK SE15	120	A4
Clayton St LBTH SE11	118	A2
Cleanthus Cl WOOL/PLUM SE18	126	B4
Cleanthus Rd WOOL/PLUM SE18	126	B4
Clearbrook Wy WCHPL E1	90	C5
Clearwater Ter NTGHL W11	100	C5
Clearwell Dr MV/WKIL W9	14	C1
Cleaver Sq LBTH SE11	118	A1
Cleaver St LBTH SE11	118	A1
Cleeve Hl FSTH SE23	156	B1
Cleeve Wy PUT/ROE SW15	129	F4
Clegg St PLSTW E13	82	A1
WAP E1W	102	B2
Clematis Cots SHB W12 *	100	A1
Clematis St SHB W12	99	F1
Clem Attlee Ct FUL/PGN SW6 *	113	F2
Clem Attlee Pde FUL/PGN SW6 *	113	F2
Clemence St POP/IOD E14	91	E5
Clement Av CLAP SW4	135	D2
Clement Cl CHSWK W4	99	D5
KIL/WHAMP NW6	70	C4
Clementina Rd LEY E10	61	F3
Clement Rd WIM/MER SW19	149	E5
Clements Av CAN/RD E16	106	A1
Clements Inn LINN WC2A	21	F5
Clements La IL IG1	66	B5
Clement's La MANHO EC4N	36	B1
Clements Rd BERM/RHTH SE16 *	102	A4
EHAM E6	83	F4
IL IG1	66	B5
Clement's Rd BERM/RHTH SE16	102	A4
Clendon Wy WOOL/PLUM SE18	109	D5
Clennam St STHWK SE1 *	35	F5
Clenston Ms MBLAR W1H	17	E4
Clephane Rd IS N1	76	C3
Clere Pl SDTCH EC2A	12	B5
Clere St SDTCH EC2A	12	B5
Clerkenwell Cl CLKNW EC1R	10	B5
Clerkenwell Gn CLKNW EC1R	22	B1
Clerkenwell Rd CLKNW EC1R	22	A1
Clermont Rd HOM E9	78	C5
Cleveland Av CHSWK W4	99	F5
Cleveland Gdns BARN SW13	111	F5
BAY/PAD W2	15	E5
CRICK NW2	53	D4
Cleveland Gv WCHPL E1	90	C3
Cleveland Ms FITZ W1T	19	E2
Cleveland Pl STJS SW1Y	31	F5
Cleveland Rd BARN SW13	111	F5
CHSWK W4	98	C4
IL IG1	66	B5
IS N1	77	D4
WELL DA16	127	F5
Cleveland Rw WHALL SW1A	31	F4
Cleveland Sq BAY/PAD W2	15	E5
Cleveland St CAMTN NW1	19	D1
Cleveland Ter BAY/PAD W2	15	E5
Cleveland Wy WCHPL E1	90	C3
Cleveleys Rd CLPT E5	60	B5
Clevely Cl CHARL SE7	107	D5
Cleverly Est SHB W12 *	100	A2
Cleve Rd KIL/WHAMP NW6	72	A4
Cleves Rd EHAM E6	83	D5
Clifden Ms CLPT E5	79	D1
Clifden Rd CLPT E5	78	C2
Clifford Av MORT/ESHN SW14	110	C5
RCH/KEW TW9	128	B1
Clifford Cl PLSTW E13 *	94	B2
Clifford Dr BRXN/ST SW9	136	B2
Clifford Gdns WLSDN NW10	88	C1
Clifford Rd CAN/RD E16	93	F3
CONDST W1S	31	E2
Clifford Wy WLSDN NW10	69	F1
Cliff Rd CAMTN NW1	75	D3
Cliff Ter DEPT SE8	122	A5
Cliffview Rd LEW SE13	140	A1
Cliff Vls CAMTN NW1	75	D3
Cliff Wk CAN/RD E16	93	F4
Clifton Av SHB W12	99	F3
Clifton Crs PECK SE15	120	B3
Clifton Gdns CHSWK W4	99	D5
GLDGN NW11	53	F1
MV/WKIL W9	15	E1
SEVS/STOTM N15	59	F1
Clifton Ga WBPTN SW10 *	114	C2
Clifton Gv HACK E8	78	A3
Clifton Hl STJWD NW8	3	D1
Clifton Pl BAY/PAD W2	16	A5
BERM/RHTH SE16	102	C3
WBPTN SW10 *	114	C2
Clifton Ri NWCR SE14	121	E3
Clifton Rd CAN/RD E16	93	E4
CEND/HSY/T N8	57	D1
FSTGT E7	83	D5
GNTH/NBYPK IG2	67	D1
MV/WKIL W9	3	F5
SCUP DA14	163	E4
WLSDN NW10	88	A1
Clifton St SDTCH EC2A	24	C1
Clifton Ter FSBYPK N4	58	A4
Clifton Vls MV/WKIL W9	15	D2
Clifton Wy PECK SE15	120	C3
Clink St STHWK SE1	36	A3
Clinton Rd BOW E3	91	E2
FSTGT E7	82	A1
Clinton Ter DEPT SE8 *	122	A2
Clipper Cl BERM/RHTH SE16	103	D3
Clipper Wy LEW SE13	140	C2
Clipstone Ms GTPST W1W	19	E2
Clipstone St GTPST W1W	19	D2
Clissold Crs STNW/STAM N16	77	D1
Clissold Rd STNW/STAM N16	59	D5
Clitheroe Rd BRXN/ST SW9	117	E5
Clitterhouse Crs CRICK NW2	52	C3
Clitterhouse Rd CRICK NW2	52	C3
Clive Ct WLSDN NW10	69	F4
Cliveden Pl BGVA SW1W	42	A4
Clive Rd DUL SE21	155	D3
Cloak La CANST EC4R	35	F1
Clockhouse Av BARK IG11	84	C5
Clockhouse Cl WIM/MER SW19	148	C3
Clockhouse Pl PUT/ROE SW15	131	E3
Clock Mews IS N1	76	C5
Clock Tower Pl HOLWY N7 *	75	E3
Cloister Rd ACT W3	86	C4

CRICK NW2		
Clonbrock Rd *STNW/STAM* N16	77	E1
Cloncurry St *FUL/PGN* SW6	113	D5
Clonmel Rd *FUL/PGN* SW6	113	F3
Clonmore St *WAND/EARL* SW18	149	F1
Clorane Gdns *HAMP* NW3	54	A5
The Close *GNTH/NBYPK* IG2	128	B1
RCH/KEW TW9		
WBLY HA9	50	C5
Cloth Ct *STBT* EC1A	23	D3
Cloth Fair *STBT* EC1A	23	D3
Clothier St *HDTCH* EC3A	25	E3
Cloth St *STBT* EC1A	23	E2
Clothworkers Rd *WOOL/PLUM* SE18	127	D5
Cloudesdale Rd *TOOT* SW17	152	B2
Cloudesley Cl *SCUP* DA14	163	F4
Cloudesley Pl *IS* N1	76	A5
Cloudesley Rd *IS* N1	76	A5
Cloudesley Sq *IS* N1	76	A5
Cloudesley St *IS* N1	76	A5
Clova Rd *FSTGT* E7	82	A2
Clove Crs *POP/IOD* E14	104	C1
Clovelly Rd *CHSWK* W4 *	99	D5
Clovelly Wy *WCHPL* E1	90	C5
Clover Cl *WAN* E11 *	63	D4
Cloverdale Gdns *BFN/LL* DA15	145	E3
Clover Ms *CHEL* SW3	115	F2
Clove St *PLSTW* E13	94	A3
Clowders Rd *CAT* SE6	157	F3
Cloysters Gn *WAP* E1W *	102	A2
Club Rw *BETH* E2	13	E5
Clunbury St *IS* N1	12	B2
Cluny Est *STHWK* SE1	48	C2
Cluny Ms *ECT* SW5	38	A5
Cluny Pl *STHWK* SE1	48	C2
Clutton St *POP/IOD* E14	92	B4
Clyde Ct *CAMTN* NW1	9	F5
Clyde Flats *FUL/PGN* SW6 *	113	F3
Clyde Pl *LEY* E10	62	B2
Clydesdale Gdns *RCHPK/HAM* TW10	128	B2
Clydesdale Rd *NTGHL* W11	89	F5
Clyde St *DEPT* SE8	121	F2
Clyde Ter *FSTH* SE23	156	C2
Clyde V *FSTH* SE23	156	C2
Clyston St *VX/NE* SW8	116	C5
Coach & Horses Yd *CONDST* W1S	31	D1
Coach House La *HBRY* N5 *	76	B1
WIM/MER SW19		
Coach House Ms *FSTH* SE23	138	C4
NWCR SE14 *	121	D4
Coach House Yd *WAND/EARL* SW18 *	132	B2
Coalecroft Rd *PUT/ROE* SW15	130	C2
Coates Av *WAND/EARL* SW18	133	E4
Coate St *BETH* E2	90	A1
Cobbett Rd *ELTH/MOT* SE9	143	E1
Cobbett St *VX/NE* SW8	117	F3
Cobble La *IS* N1	76	B4
Cobble Ms *HBRY* N5	58	C5
Cobbold Ms *SHB* W12 *	99	F3
Cobbold Rd *SHB* W12	99	F3
WAN E11	63	F5
WLSDN NW10	69	F3
Cobb St *WCHPL* E1	25	E4
Cobden Ms *SYD* SE26	156	B5
Cobden Rd *WAN* E11	63	E4
Cobham Cl *BTSEA* SW11	133	E4
Cobham Ms *CAMTN* NW1 *	75	D4
Cobham Rd *GDMY/SEVK* IG3	67	E4
Cobland Rd *LEE/GVPK* SE12	160	C4
Coborn Rd *BOW* E3	91	F2
Coborn St *BOW* E3	91	F2
Cobourg Rd *CMBW* SE5	119	F1
Cobourg St *CAMTN* NW1	7	F4
Coburg Cl *WEST* SW1P	43	F4
Coburg Crs *BRXS/STRHM* SW2	153	F1
Coburg Dwellings *WCHPL* E1 *	102	C1
Cochrane Ms *STJWD* NW8	4	B2
Cochrane St *STJWD* NW8	4	B2
Cockerell Rd *WALTH* E17	61	E2
Cock La *STBT* EC1A	22	C3
Cockspur Ct *STJS* SW1Y	32	B3
Cockspur St *STJS* SW1Y	32	B3
Code St *WCHPL* E1	25	F1
Codling Cl *WAP* E1W	102	A2
Codrington HI *FSTH* SE23	139	E5
Codrington Ms *NTGHL* W11	89	E5
Cody Rd *CAN/RD* E16	93	D3
Coffey St *DEPT* SE8	122	A3
Coin St *STHWK* SE1	34	A3
Coity Rd *KTTN* NW5	74	A3
Cokers La *DUL* SE21	154	C1
Coke St *WCHPL* E1	90	A5
Colas Ms *KIL/WHAMP* NW6	72	A5
Colbeck Ms *SKENS* SW7	39	D5
Colberg Pl *STNW/STAM* N16 *	59	F2
Colby Rd *NRWD* SE19	155	D5
Colchester Rd *WALTH* E17	62	A1
Coldbath Sq *CLKNW* EC1R	22	A1
Coldbath St *LEW* SE13	122	B4
Cold Blow La *NWCR* SE14	121	D3
Coldharbour *POP/IOD* E14	104	C2
Coldharbour Crest *ELTH/MOT* SE9 *	162	A5
Coldharbour La *BRXN/ST* SW9	136	A2
Coldharbour Pl *CMBW* SE5	118	C5
Coldstream Gdns *WAND/EARL* SW18	131	F4
Colebeck Ms *IS* N1	76	B3
Colebert Av *WCHPL* E1	90	C3
Colebrooke Dr *WAN* E11	64	B2
Colebrooke Rw *IS* N1	76	B5
Colebrooke Rw *IS* N1	10	C2
Coleby Pth *CMBW* SE5 *	119	D3
Coleford Rd *WAND/EARL* SW18	132	C3
Colegrave Rd *SRTFD* E15	81	D2
Colegrove Rd *PECK* SE15	119	F2
Coleherne Ms *WBPTN* SW10	114	B1
Coleherne Rd *ECT* SW5	114	B1
Colehill Gdns *FUL/PGN* SW6 *	113	E4
Colehill La *FUL/PGN* SW6	113	E4
Coleman Flds *IS* N1	76	C5
Coleman Rd *CMBW* SE5	119	E3
Colemans Heath *ELTH/MOT* SE9	162	A5
Coleman St *CITYW* EC2V	24	A4
Colenso Rd *CLPT* E5	78	C1
GNTH/NBYPK IG2	67	E3
Colepits Wood Rd *ELTH/MOT* SE9	145	D5
Coleraine Rd *BKHTH/KID* SE3	123	F2
Coleridge Av *MNPK* E12	83	E3
Coleridge Cl *VX/NE* SW8	116	B5
Coleridge Gdns *KIL/WHAMP* NW6	72	C4
WBPTN SW10	114	C3
Coleridge Rd *CEND/HSY/T* N8	57	D1
FSBYPK N4	58	A4
Coles Green Rd *CRICK* NW2	52	A3
Colestown St *BTSEA* SW11	115	E5
Cole St *STHWK* SE1	47	F1
Colet Gdns *WKENS* W14	113	D1
Coley St *FSBYW* WC1X	21	D1
Colfe & Hatcliffe Glebe *LEW* SE13 *	140	B3
Colfe Rd *FSTH* SE23	157	E1
Colinette Rd *PUT/ROE* SW15	130	C2
Coliston Rd *WAND/EARL* SW18	132	A5
Collamore Av *WAND/EARL* SW18	151	E1
Collard Pl *CAMTN* NW1	74	C4
College Ap *GNWCH* SE10	122	C2
College Crs *HAMP* NW3	72	C3
College Cross *IS* N1	76	A4
College East *WCHPL* E1 *	25	F3
College Gdns *TOOT* SW17	151	E2
College Gv *CAMTN* NW1	75	D5
College HI *CANST* EC4R *	23	F1
College La *KTTN* NW5	74	B1
College Ms *IS* N1	76	A4
WEST SW1P	44	C2
College Pde *KIL/WHAMP* NW6 *	71	E5
College Park Cl *LEW* SE13	140	C2
College Pl *CAMTN* NW1	74	C5
WBPTN SW10 *	114	C3
College Rd *DUL* SE21	137	E5
NRWD SE19	155	F5
WLSDN NW10	88	C1
College Rw *CANST* EC4R *	35	F1
College Vw *ELTH/MOT* SE9	161	F1
College Yd *KIL/WHAMP* NW6 *	71	E5
KTTN NW5 *	74	B1
Collent St *HOM* E9	78	C3
Collett Rd *BERM/RHTH* SE16	102	A4
Collier Cl *EHAM* E6	96	C5
Collier St *IS* N1	9	E2
Collingbourne Rd *SHB* W12	100	B2
Collingham Gdns *ECT* SW5	39	D5
Collingham Pl *ECT* SW5	38	C5
Collingham Rd *ECT* SW5	39	D4
Collington St *GNWCH* SE10	123	D1
Collingtree Rd *SYD* SE26	156	C4
Collingwood St *WCHPL* E1	90	B3
Collinson St *STHWK* SE1	47	E1
Collinson Wk *STHWK* SE1 *	47	E1
Collins Rd *HBRY* N5	76	C1
Collins Sq *BKHTH/KID* SE3 *	141	F1
Collins St *BKHTH/KID* SE3	123	E5
Collyer Pl *PECK* SE15 *	120	A4
Colman Rd *CAN/RD* E16	94	C4
Colmar Cl *WCHPL* E1	91	D3
Colmore Ms *PECK* SE15	120	B4

Colnbrook St STHWK SE1 ... 46 C3
Colne Rd CLPT E5 ... 79 D1
Colne St PLSTW E13 ... 94 A2
Cologne Rd BTSEA SW11 ... 133 D2
Colombo Rd IL IG1 ... 66 C3
Colombo St STHWK SE1 ... 34 C4
Colomb St GNWCH SE10 ... 123 E1
Colonial Dr CHSWK W4 ... 98 C5
The Colonnade DEPT SE8 * ... 103 F5
Colonnade BMSBY WC1N ... 20 C1
Colosseum Ter CAMTN NW1 ... 7 F3
Colson Wy STRHM/NOR SW16 ... 152 C4
Colston Rd FSTGT E7 ... 83 D3
  MORT/ESHN SW14 ... 128 C2
Colthurst Crs FSBYPK N4 ... 58 B4
Colts Yd WAN E11 * ... 63 F3
Columbus Dr HAMP NW3 ... 55 D4
Columbia Rd BETH E2 ... 13 E3
  PLSTW E13 * ... 93 F3
Columbine Av EHAM E6 ... 95 E4
Columbine Wy LEW SE13 ... 122 C5
Colveiw Ct ELTH/MOT SE9 ... 161 D1
Colvestone Crs HACK E8 ... 77 F2
Colville Est IS N1 ... 77 D5
Colville Gdns NTGHL W11 ... 89 F5
Colville Houses NTGHL W11 ... 89 F5
Colville Ms NTGHL W11 ... 89 F5
Colville Pl FITZ W1T ... 19 F3
Colville Rd ACT W3 ... 98 B4
  NTGHL W11 ... 89 F5
  WAN E11 ... 62 C5
Colville Sq NTGHL W11 * ... 89 F5
Colville Square Ms NTGHL W11 * ... 89 F5
Colville Ter NTGHL W11 ... 89 F5
Colvin Cl SYD SE26 ... 156 C5
Colvin Rd EHAM E6 ... 83 E4
Colwell Rd EDUL SE22 ... 137 F3
Colwick Cl HGT N6 ... 57 D2
Colwith Rd HMSMTH W6 ... 112 C2
Colworth Gv WALW SE17 ... 47 F5
Colworth Rd WAN E11 ... 63 F1
Colwyn Cl STRHM/NOR SW16 ... 152 C5
Colwyn Gn CDALE/KGS NW9 ... 51 E1
Colwyn Rd CRICK NW2 ... 52 B5
Colyer Cl ELTH/MOT SE9 ... 162 B2
Colyton La STRHM/NOR SW16 ... 154 A5
Colyton Rd EDUL SE22 ... 138 B3
Combe Av BKHTH/KID SE3 ... 123 F5
Combedale Rd GNWCH SE10 ... 124 A1
Combemartin Rd WAND/EARL SW18 ... 131 E5
Comber Cl CRICK NW2 ... 52 A4
Comber Gv CMBW SE5 ... 118 C3
Combermere Rd BRXN/ST SW9 ... 135 F1
Comberton Rd CLPT E5 ... 60 B4
Combeside WOOL/PLUM SE18 ... 127 F3
Comeragh Ms WKENS W14 ... 113 E1
Comeragh Rd WKENS W14 ... 113 E1
Comerford Rd BROCKY SE4 ... 139 E2
Comet Cl MNPK E12 ... 83 D1
Comet Pl DEPT SE8 ... 122 A3
Comet St DEPT SE8 ... 122 A3
Comfort St PECK SE15 ... 119 E3
Commercial Rd WCHPL E1 ... 90 A5
Commercial St WCHPL E1 ... 25 E1
Commercial Wy CMBW SE5 ... 119 F4
  WLSDN NW10 ... 86 B1
Commerell Pl GNWCH SE10 ... 123 F1
Commerell St GNWCH SE10 ... 123 F1
Commodore St WCHPL E1 ... 91 D4
Commondale PUT/ROE SW15 ... 112 C5
Common Rd BARN SW13 ... 130 A1
The Common SRTFD E15 ... 81 F3
Commonwealth Av SHB W12 ... 100 B1
Community Rd SRTFD E15 ... 81 D2
Como Rd FSTH SE23 ... 157 E2
Compayne Gdns KIL/WHAMP NW6 ... 72 B4
Compton Av EHAM E6 ... 95 D1
  HGT N6 ... 56 B3
  IS N1 ... 76 B3
Compton Crs CHSWK W4 ... 110 C3
Compton Pas FSBYE EC1V ... 10 C5
Compton Rd IS N1 ... 76 B3
  WLSDN NW10 ... 89 D2
Compton St FSBYE EC1V ... 10 C5
Compton Ter IS N1 * ... 76 B3
Comus Pl WALW SE17 ... 48 C5
Comyn Rd BTSEA SW11 ... 133 E2
Comyns Cl CAN/RD E16 ... 93 F4

Conant Ms WCHPL E1 ... 102 A1
Concanon Rd CLAP SW4 ... 135 F2
Concert Hall Ap STHWK SE1 ... 33 F4
Concord Rd ACT W3 ... 86 B3
Concorde Dr EHAM E6 ... 95 F4
Concorde Wy BERM/RHTH SE16 ... 103 D5
Concord Wy BERM/RHTH SE16 * ... 103 D5
Condell Rd VX/NE SW8 ... 116 C4
Conder St POP/IOD E14 ... 91 E5
Condover Crs WOOL/PLUM SE18 ... 126 B3
Condray Pl BTSEA SW11 ... 115 E3
Conduit Ct COVGDN WC2E * ... 32 C1
Conduit La BAY/PAD W2 ... 16 A5
Conduit Ms BAY/PAD W2 ... 16 A5
Conduit Pl BAY/PAD W2 ... 16 A5
Conduit Rd WOOL/PLUM SE18 ... 126 B1
Conduit St CONDST W1S ... 31 D1
Conduit Wy WLSDN NW10 ... 68 C4
Conewood St HBRY N5 ... 58 B5
Coney Wy VX/NE SW8 ... 117 F2
Congleton Gv WOOL/PLUM SE18 ... 126 C1
Congo Rd WOOL/PLUM SE18 ... 126 C1
Congreve Rd ELTH/MOT SE9 ... 143 F1
Congreve St WALW SE17 ... 48 C5
Conifer Gdns STRHM/NOR SW16 ... 153 F3
Coniger Rd FUL/PGN SW6 ... 114 A5
Coningham Ms SHB W12 ... 100 A3
Coningham Rd SHB W12 ... 100 B3
Coningsby Rd FSBYPK N4 ... 58 B2
Conington Rd LEW SE13 ... 122 B5
Conisborough Crs CAT SE6 ... 158 C3
Coniston Av BARK IG11 ... 85 E4
  WELL DA16 ... 148 A1
Coniston Cl BARN SW13 ... 111 E3
  CHSWK W4 ... 110 C4
Coniston Ct BAY/PAD W2 * ... 17 D5
Coniston Wy HOLWY N7 ... 75 E2
Coniston Wk HOM E9 ... 78 C2
Conlan St NKENS W10 ... 89 E3
Conley Rd WLSDN NW10 ... 69 E3
Conley St GNWCH SE10 ... 123 E1
Connaught Av MORT/ESHN SW14 ... 128 C1
Connaught Br CAN/RD E16 ... 107 D1
Connaught Cl BAY/PAD W2 * ... 16 C5
  LEY E10 ... 61 E4
Connaught La IL IG1 ... 66 C4
Connaught Ms FUL/PGN SW6 * ... 113 E2
  HAMP NW3 ... 73 E2
  WOOL/PLUM SE18 ... 126 A1
Connaught Rd CAN/RD E16 ... 107 D2
  FSBYPK N4 ... 58 A2
  IL IG1 ... 67 D4
  WAN E11 ... 63 D3
  WLSDN NW10 ... 87 E1
  WOOL/PLUM SE18 ... 126 A1
Connaught Sq BAY/PAD W2 ... 17 D5
Connaught St BAY/PAD W2 ... 17 D5
Connor Cl WAN E11 ... 63 E3
Connor St HOM E9 * ... 79 D5
Consort Rd PECK SE15 ... 120 B5
Cons St STHWK SE1 * ... 34 B3
Constable Av CAN/RD E16 ... 106 B2
Constable Cl GLDGN NW11 ... 54 B1
Constable Wk DUL SE21 ... 155 E3
Constance Rd CAN/RD E16 ... 107 E2
Constantine Rd HAMP NW3 ... 73 E2
Constitution Hl MYFR/PICC W1J ... 30 C5
Constitution Ri WOOL/PLUM SE18 ... 126 A4
Content St WALW SE17 ... 47 F5
Convent Gdns NTGHL W11 ... 89 F5
Conway Gv ACT W3 ... 87 D4
Conway Ms FITZ W1T ... 19 E2
Conway Rd CRICK NW2 ... 52 C4
  WOOL/PLUM SE18 ... 109 D5
Conway St FITZ W1T ... 19 E1
Conybeare HAMP NW3 ... 73 F2
Conyers Rd STRHM/NOR SW16 ... 153 D5
Conyer St BOW E3 * ... 91 E1
Cookes Cl WAN E11 ... 63 F4
Cooks Rd WALW SE17 ... 118 B2
Cook's Rd SRTFD E15 ... 92 B1
  WALW SE17 ... 118 B2
Coolfin Rd CAN/RD E16 ... 94 B5
Coolhurst Rd HGT N6 ... 57 D1
Cool Oak Br CDALE/KGS NW9 ... 51 F2
Cool Oak La CDALE/KGS NW9 ... 51 F2
Coomassie Rd MV/WKIL W9 ... 89 F3
Coombe Ldg CHARL SE7 ... 124 C2
Coombe Pk KUTN/CMB KT2 ... 146 C5
Coombe Ridings KUTN/CMB KT2 ... 146 C5
Coombe Rd CHSWK W4 ... 111 E3
  SYD SE26 ... 156 B4
  WLSDN NW10 ... 51 B5

Coombe Vls WAND/EARL SW18 * 132 A5
Coombe Wood Rd KUTN/CMB KT2 .... 146 C5
Coombs St IS N1 .... 11 D2
Coomer Ms FUL/PGN SW6 * 113 F2
Coomer Pl FUL/PGN SW6 .... 113 F2
Cooper Cl STHWK SE1 .... 46 B1
Cooper Rd HDN NW4 .... 53 D1
WLSDN NW10 .... 69 F2
Coopersale Rd HOM E9 .... 79 D2
Coopers Cl WCHPL E1 .... 90 C3
Coopers La CAMTN NW1 .... 8 B1
LEE/GVPK SE12 .... 160 B2
Cooper's La LEY E10 .... 62 B3
Coopers Rw TWRH EC3N 37 F1
Coopers Rd STHWK SE1 .... 119 F1
Cooper St CAN/RD E16 .... 93 F4
Coopers Yd IS N1 * 76 B4
Copeland Rd PECK SE15 .... 120 C3
Cope Pl KENS W8 .... 156 C5
Copenhagen Gdns CHEL SW3 .... 115 D1
CHSWK W4 .... 99 D3
Copenhagen Pl POP/IOD E14 .... 91 F2
Copenhagen St IS N1 .... 75 D3
Cope St BERM/RHTH SE16 .... 103 D5
Copford St IS N1 .... 76 C5
Copleston Rd PECK SE15 .... 137 F1
Copley Cl WALW SE17 .... 118 B2
Coppelia Rd LEE/KID SE3 .... 141 F2
Copperas St DEPT SE8 .... 122 B2
Copperfield Rd BOW E3 .... 91 E3
Copperfield St STHWK SE1 .... 35 D5
Coppermead Cl CRICK NW2 .... 52 C5
Copper Mill La TOOT SW17 .... 150 C4
Coppermill La WALTH E17 .... 60 C1
Copper Rw STHWK SE1 * 37 E4
Coppice Dr PUT/ROE SW15 .... 130 A4
Coppock Cl BTSEA SW11 .... 115 E5
Copse Cl CHARL SE7 .... 124 B2
Copsewood Cl BFN/LL DA15 .... 145 E4
Copthall Av LOTH EC2R 24 B4
Copthorne Av BAL SW12 .... 135 D5
Coptic St NOXST/BSQ WC1A 20 C4
Copton Cl BOW E3 .... 92 A4
Coral Rw BTSEA SW11 * 132 C5
Coral St STHWK SE1 .... 46 B1
Coram St STPAN WC1H 20 C1
Corbet Pl WCHPL E1 .... 25 E2
Corbett Rd WAN E11 .... 64 C1
Corbett's La BERM/RHTH SE16 ..... 102 C5
Corbicum WAN E11 .... 63 E2
Corbridge Crs BETH E2 .... 90 B1
Corbylands Rd BFN/LL DA15 .... 145 E5
Corbyn St FSBYPK N4 .... 57 E3
Corby Rd WLSDN NW10 .... 86 C1
Cordelia Cl HNHL SE24 .... 136 B2
Cordelia St POP/IOD E14 .... 92 B5
Cording St POP/IOD E14 .... 92 B1
Corelli Rd BKHTH/KID SE3 .... 125 E4
Corfield St BETH E2 .... 90 B3
Coriander Av POP/IOD E14 .... 93 D3
Corinne Rd ARCH N19 .... 74 C1
Cork Sq WAP E1W 102 A2
Cork St CONDST W1S 31 E2
Corlett St CAMTN NW1 .... 16 C2
Cormont Rd CMBW SE5 .... 118 B4
Cormorant Rd FSTGT E7 .... 81 F2
Cornelia St FSBYPK N4 .... 75 F3
Corner Fielde BRXS/STRHM SW2 * 153 F1
Corner Gn BKHTH/KID SE3 .... 124 A5
Corney Reach Wy CHSWK W4 .... 111 E3
Corney Rd CHSWK W4 .... 111 E2
Cornflower Ter EDUL SE22 .... 138 B4
Cornford Rd BAL SW12 .... 152 B2
Cornhill BANK EC3V 24 B5
Cornmill La LEW SE13 .... 140 B1
Cornmow Dr WLSDN NW10 .... 69 F2
Cornthwaite Rd CLPT E5 .... 60 C5
Cornwall Av BETH E2 .... 90 C2
WELL DA16 .... 145 E1
Cornwall Cl BARK IG11 .... 85 F3
Cornwall Crs NTGHL W11 .... 101 E1
Cornwall Gdns SKENS SW7 .... 39 D5
WLSDN NW10 .... 70 B3
Cornwall Gdns Wk SKENS SW7 ..... 39 D5
Cornwall Gv CHSWK W4 .... 111 E1
Cornwallis Av ELTH/MOT SE9 ...... 163 D2
WOOL/PLUM SE18 .... 108 A1
Cornwallis Rd ARCH N19 .... 57 E4
Cornwallis Sq ARCH N19 .... 57 E4
Cornwallis Wk ELTH/MOT SE9 ..... 143 F1
Cornwall Ms South SKENS SW7 ..... 39 E3
Cornwall Ms West SKENS SW7 * 39 E3
Cornwall Rd FSBYPK N4 .... 58 A2
STHWK SE1 .... 34 A3
Cornwall Sq LBTH SE11 * 118 A3
Cornwall St WCHPL E1 .... 102 B1
Cornwall Ter CAMTN NW1 .... 17 F1
Cornwall Terrace Ms CAMTN NW1 . 17 F1
Corn Wy WAN E11 .... 80 C5
Cornwood Dr WCHPL E1 .... 90 C5
Corona Rd LEE/GVPK SE12 .... 142 A5
Coronation Av STNW/STAM N16 * .. 94 C2
Coronation Rd PLSTW E13 .... 94 B3
WLSDN NW10 .... 86 B3
Coronation Vls WLSDN NW10 * 86 B3
Coronet St IS N1 .... 12 C4
Corporation Rw CLKNW EC1R 10 B5
Corporation St HOLWY N7 .... 75 E2
SRTFD E15 .... 93 E1
Corrance Rd BRXS/STRHM SW2 ... 135 E2
Corringham Rd GLDGN NW11 .... 54 A2
WBLY HA9 .... 50 A3
Corringway GLDGN NW11 .... 54 B2
Corris Gn CDALE/KGS NW9 * 37 D2
Corry Dr BRXN/ST SW9 .... 136 B2
Corscombe Cl KUTN/CMB KT2 ..... 146 C5
Corsham St IS N1 .... 12 B4
Corsica St HBRY N5 .... 76 B3
Cortayne Rd FUL/PGN SW6 * 113 F5
Cortis Rd PUT/ROE SW15 .... 130 B4
Cortis Ter PUT/ROE SW15 .... 130 B5
Corunna Rd VX/NE SW8 .... 116 C4
Corunna Ter VX/NE SW8 .... 116 C4
Coryton Rd MV/WKIL W9 .... 89 F3
Cosbycote Av HNHL SE24 .... 136 C3
Cosmo Pl BSQ W1B * 21 D2
Cosmur Cl SHB W12 .... 99 F4
Cossall Wk PECK SE15 .... 120 B4
Cossar Ms BRXS/STRHM SW2 * 136 A4
Cosser St STHWK SE1 .... 46 A2
Costa St PECK SE15 .... 120 A5
Cosway St CAMTN NW1 .... 17 D2
Cotall St POP/IOD E14 .... 92 A5
Coteford St TOOT SW17 .... 151 F4
Cotesbach Rd CLPT E5 .... 60 C5
Cotham St WALW SE17 .... 47 F5
Cotherstone Rd BRXS/STRHM SW2 153 F1
Cotleigh Rd KIL/WHAMP NW6 ...... 72 A4
Cotman Cl GLDGN NW11 .... 54 C1
Cotswold Gdns CRICK NW2 .... 53 D4
EHAM E6 .... 95 D2
GNTH/NBYPK IG2 .... 67 D2
Cotswold Ga CRICK NW2 .... 53 E3
Cotswold Ms BTSEA SW11 .... 115 D4
Cotswold St WNWD SE27 .... 154 B4
Cottage Gn CMBW SE5 .... 119 D3
Cottage Gv BRXN/ST SW9 .... 135 E1
Cottage Pl CHEL SW3 .... 40 C2
Cottage Rd HOLWY N7 .... 75 F2
Cottage St POP/IOD E14 .... 104 B1
Cottesbrook St NWCR SE14 .... 121 E3
Cottesloe Ms STHWK SE1 .... 46 B2
Cottesmore Gdns KENS W8 .... 39 D2
Cottingham Rd VX/NE SW8 .... 117 F3
Cottington St LBTH SE11 .... 118 A1
Cotton Av ACT W3 .... 87 D5
Cotton Cl WAN E11 .... 63 E4
Cotton Gardens Est LBTH SE11 .... 46 C5
Cotton Hl BMLY BR1 .... 159 E4
Cotton Rw BTSEA SW11 .... 133 D1
Cotton's Gdns BETH E2 .... 13 D3
Cotton St POP/IOD E14 .... 104 C1
Coulgate St BROCKY SE4 .... 139 E1
Coulson Cl CHEL SW9 .... 115 F1
Coulter Rd HMSMTH W6 .... 100 B4
Councillor St CMBW SE5 .... 118 C4
Counter St STHWK SE1 .... 36 C5
Countess Rd KTTN NW5 .... 74 C2
County Gv CMBW SE5 .... 118 C4
County Rd EHAM E6 .... 96 B4
PLSTW E13 .... 94 B1
County St STHWK SE1 .... 47 F3
Coupland Pl WOOL/PLUM SE18 .... 126 C1
Courland Gv VX/NE SW8 .... 117 D4
Courland St VX/NE SW8 .... 117 D4
The Course ELTH/MOT SE9 .... 162 A3
Courtauld Rd ARCH N19 .... 57 D3
Court Cl STJWD NW8 * 73 D4
Court Cl STJWD NW8 * 73 D4
Courtenay Av HGT N6 .... 55 E2
Courtenay Rd WAN E11 .... 63 F5
Courtenay Sq LBTH SE11 * 118 A1
Courtenay St LBTH SE11 .... 117 F1

Court Farm Rd ELTH/MOT SE9..............161 D2
Courtfield Gdns ECT SW5....................39 D5
Courtfield Ms ECT SW5.......................39 D5
Courtfield Rd SKENS SW7....................39 E4
Court Gdns HOLWY N7.........................76 A3
Courthill Rd LEW SE13.........................133 F2
Courthope Rd HAMP NW3......................73 F1
WIM/MER SW19.................................149 E5
Courthouse La STNW/STAM N16.............77 F1
Courtland Av IL IG1............................65 F4
Courtland Rd EHAM E6.......................83 E5
Courtlands RCHPK/HAM TW10.............128 A3
Courtlands Av LEE/GVPK SE12.............142 B3
RCH/KEW TW9...............................110 B5
Court La DUL SE21............................137 F5
Court Lane Gdns DUL SE21..................137 F5
Courtmead Cl HNHL SE24....................136 C4
Courtmeil St BAY/PAD W2....................14 A4
Courtney Rd HOLWY N7.......................76 A2
Courtrai Rd FSTH SE23.......................139 E4
Court Rd ELTH/MOT SE9......................161 F1
Courtside HGT N6..............................57 D1
SYD SE26 *.....................................156 C5
Court St WCHPL E1............................91 D1
Court Vw HGT N6 *............................56 B4
Court Wk ACT W3.............................86 C4
Court Yd ELTH/MOT SE9......................143 E4
The Courtyard IS N1..........................75 F4
Cousin La CANST EC4R.......................36 A1
Couthurst Rd BKHTH/KID SE3...............124 B3
Coutts Crs KTTN NW5 *.......................56 A5
Coval Gdns MORT/ESHN SW14...............128 B2
Coval La MORT/ESHN SW14...................128 B2
Coval Rd MORT/ESHN SW14..................128 C2
Covelees Wall EHAM E6......................96 A5
Covent Gdn COVGDN WC2E...................33 D1
Covent Garden Piazza
COVGDN WC2E..............................33 D1
Coventry Cl EHAM E6.........................95 F5
KIL/WHAMP NW6 *...........................2 B1
Coventry Cross Est BOW E3..................92 C3
Coventry Rd BETH E2 *.......................90 B2
IL IG1...66 B3
WCHPL E1.......................................90 B3
Coventry St SOHO/SHAV W1D...............32 A2
Coverdale Rd CRICK NW2....................71 E4
SHB W12...100 B2
The Coverdales BARK IG11...................97 D1
Coverley Cl WCHPL E1 *......................90 A4
Coverton Rd TOOT SW17.....................151 E4
Cowbridge La BARK IG11......................84 B4
Cowcross St FARR EC1M......................22 C2
Cowden St CAT SE6............................158 A4
Cowick Rd TOOT SW17........................151 E4
Cow Leaze EHAM E6..........................96 B4
Cowley Ct WAN E11 *..........................63 E5
Cowley La WAN E11 *..........................63 E5
Cowley Rd ACT W3.............................99 F2
BRXN/ST SW9...................................118 A4
IL IG1..65 F2
MORT/ESHN SW14............................129 E1
Cowley St WEST SW1P........................44 C3
Cowling Cl NTGHL W11........................101 E1
Cowper Av EHAM E6...........................83 E4
Cowper Rd ACT W3.............................99 D2
STNW/STAM N16..............................77 E1
Cowper St STLK EC1Y.........................12 B5
Cowper Ter NKENS W10 *.....................89 D4
Coxmount Rd CHARL SE7.....................125 D1
Coxson Wy STHWK SE1.......................49 E1
Coxwell Rd WOOL/PLUM SE18..............127 D1
Crabtree Cl BETH E2...........................13 E2
Crabtree La FUL/PGN SW6...................113 D3
Craddock St KTTN NW5 *......................74 A3
Cradley Rd ELTH/MOT SE9...................163 D1
Craigen Gdns IL IG1...........................97 F2
Craigerne Rd BKHTH/KID SE3...............124 B3
Craigholm WOOL/PLUM SE18................126 A5
Craignair Rd BRXS/STRHM SW2.............135 F5
Craig's Ct WHALL SW1A.......................32 C3
Craigton Rd ELTH/MOT SE9..................143 F2
Crail Rw WALW SE17...........................48 B5
Cramer St MHST W1U.........................18 B3
Crammond Cl HMSMTH W6..................113 E2
Cranberry La CAN/RD E16.....................93 E3
Cranborne Rd BARK IG11......................85 D5
Cranbourne Rd MNPK E12....................83 E2
SRTFD E15......................................80 C1
Cranbourn St LSQ/SEVD WC2H.............32 B1
Cranbrook Ri IL IG1.............................65 F1

Cranbrook Rd CHSWK W4....................111 E1
DEPT SE8.......................................122 A4
GNTH/NBYPK IG2..............................66 A1
Cranbrook St BETH E2.........................91 D1
Cranbury Rd FUL/PGN SW6..................114 B5
Crane Av ACT W3...............................98 C1
Crane Ct FLST/FETLN EC4A.................22 B5
MORT/ESHN SW14 *..........................128 C2
Crane Gv HOLWY N7..........................76 A3
Crane Md BERM/RHTH SE16................103 D5
Crane St PECK SE15...........................119 F4
Cranfield Rd BROCKY SE4....................139 F1
Cranford Cots WAP E1W *.....................103 D1
Cranford St WAP E1W.........................103 D1
Cranhurst Rd CRICK NW2.....................70 C2
Cranleigh Gdns BARK IG11...................85 D4
Cranleigh Ms BTSEA SW11...................115 E5
Cranleigh St CAMTN NW1.....................7 F2
Cranley Dr GNTH/NBYPK IG2................66 C2
Cranley Gdns SKENS SW7....................114 C1
Cranley Ms SKENS SW7.......................114 C1
Cranley Pl SKENS SW7........................40 A5
Cranmer Rd GNTH/NBYPK IG2..............66 C1
PLSTW E13......................................94 B4
Cranmer Rd BRXN/ST SW9..................118 A3
FSTGT E7..82 B1
Cranmer Ter TOOT SW17.....................151 D5
Cranmore Rd BMLY BR1......................159 E3
CHST BR7.......................................161 F5
Cranston Est IS N1.............................12 B1
Cranston Rd FSTH SE23......................157 E1
Cranswick Rd BERM/RHTH SE16...........120 B1
Crantock Rd CAT SE6..........................158 C2
Cranwell Cl BOW E3...........................92 B3
Cranwich Rd STNW/STAM N16..............59 E2
Cranwood St FSBYE EC1V...................12 B4
Cranworth Gdns BRXN/ST SW9.............118 A4
Craster Rd BRXS/STRHM SW2..............135 F5
Crathie Rd LEE/GVPK SE12..................142 B4
Craven Cl STNW/STAM N16 *................60 A2
Craven Gdns BARK IG11.......................97 E1
WIM/MER SW19.................................150 B5
Craven Hl BAY/PAD W2........................27 F1
Craven Hill Gdns BAY/PAD W2...............27 E1
Craven Hill Ms BAY/PAD W2.................27 F1
Craven Ms BTSEA SW11 *....................134 A1
Craven Pk WLSDN NW10......................69 D4
Craven Park Ms WLSDN NW10...............69 E4
Craven Park Rd SEVS/STOTM N15.........59 F1
WLSDN NW10..................................69 E5
Craven Pas CHCR WC2N.....................32 C3
Craven Rd BAY/PAD W2.......................27 F1
WLSDN NW10..................................69 D5
Craven St CHCR WC2N........................32 C3
Craven Ter BAY/PAD W2 *...................27 F1
Craven Wk CLPT E5.............................60 A2
Crawford Ms MBLAR W1H *..................17 E3
Crawford Pas CLKNW EC1R..................17 E2
Crawford Pl MBLAR W1H......................17 D4
Crawford Rd CMBW SE5.......................118 C5
Crawford St MBLAR W1H......................17 E3
MHST W1U......................................17 E3
WLSDN NW10..................................69 D4
Crawley Rd LEY E10............................62 B3
Crawthew Gv EDUL SE22....................137 F2
Craybury End ELTH/MOT SE9...............162 C2
Crayford Rd HOLWY N7........................75 E1
Crealock St WAND/EARL SW18..............132 B4
Crediton Hl KIL/WHAMP NW6................72 B2
Crediton Rd WLSDN NW10...................71 D5
Credon Rd BERM/RHTH SE16...............120 B1
PLSTW E13......................................94 C2
Creechurch La HDTCH EC3A.................25 D4
Creechurch Pl HDTCH EC3A.................25 D5
Creed La BLKFR EC4V..........................23 D5
Creek Rd BARK IG11...........................97 F2
DEPT SE8..122 C2
GNWCH SE10..................................122 C2
Creekside DEPT SE8...........................122 B3
Creeland Gv CAT SE6..........................157 F3
Crefeld Cl HMSMTH W6......................113 D2
Creffield Rd ACT W3............................98 A1
Creighton Av EHAM E6.........................95 D1
Creighton Cl SHB W12.........................100 B1
Creighton Rd KIL/WHAMP NW6.............89 D1
Cremer St BETH E2.............................13 E2
Cremorne Est WBPTN SW10 *...............115 D2
Cremorne Rd WBPTN SW10.................114 C3
Crescent TWRH EC3N..........................37 E1
Crescent GNWCH SE10.......................122 C2
Crescent Gdns WIM/MER SW19............150 A3

Crescent Gv CLAP SW4 .... 134 C2
Crescent La CLAP SW4 .... 135 D3
Crescent PI CHEL SW3 .... 40 C4
Crescent Rd BFN/LL DA15 .... 163 F3
   CEND/HSY/T N8 .... 57 D1
   LEY E10 .... 62 B4
   PLSTW E13 .... 82 A5
   WOOL/PLUM SE18 .... 126 B1
Crescent Rw STLK EC1Y 23 E1
Crescent St IS N1 * 75 F4
The Crescent ACT W3 .... 87 E5
   BARN SW13 .... 111 F5
   CRICK NW2 .... 52 B5
   GNTH/NBYPK IG2 .... 66 A1
   SCUP DA14 .... 163 F4
   WIM/MER SW19 .... 150 A3
Crescent Wy BROCKY SE4 .... 140 A1
Crescent Wood Rd SYD SE26 .... 156 A1
Cresford Rd FUL/PGN SW6 .... 114 B4
Crespigny Rd HDN NW4 .... 52 B1
Cresset Rd HOM E9 .... 78 C3
Cresset St CLAP SW4 .... 135 D1
Cressida Rd ARCH N19 .... 54 B5
Cressingham Rd LEW SE13 .... 140 C1
Cressington Cl STNW/STAM N16 .... 77 E2
Cresswell Pk BKHTH/KID SE3 .... 141 F1
Cresswell Pl WBPTN SW10 .... 114 C4
Cressy Ct HMSMTH W6 .... 100 B4
   WCHPL E1 .... 90 C4
Cressy Houses WCHPL E1 * 90 C4
Cressy Pl WCHPL E1 .... 90 C4
Cressy Rd HAMP NW3 .... 73 F1
Crestfield St CAMTN NW1 .... 9 D3
Crest Rd CRICK NW2 .... 52 A4
The Crest HOLWY N7 * 75 F1
Crestway PUT/ROE SW15 .... 130 A4
Creswick Rd ACT W3 .... 98 B1
Creukhorne Rd WLSDN NW10 * 69 E4
Crewdson Rd BRXN/ST SW9 .... 117 F3
Crewe Pl WLSDN NW10 .... 87 F2
Crews St POP/IOD E14 .... 104 A5
Crewys Rd CRICK NW2 .... 53 F4
   PECK SE15 .... 120 B5
Crichton St VX/NE SW8 * 116 C1
Cricketers Ms BAL SW12 .... 134 B5
   WAND/EARL SW18 .... 132 B5
Cricketers Wy SYD SE26 .... 156 C5
Cricketfield Rd CLPT E5 .... 78 B1
Cricklade Av BRXS/STRHM SW2 .... 153 E2
Cricklewood Broadway CRICK NW2 .... 71 D1
Cricklewood La CRICK NW2 .... 71 D1
Cridland St SRTFD E15 .... 81 F5
Crieff Rd WAND/EARL SW18 .... 132 C4
Criffel Av BRXS/STRHM SW2 .... 153 D2
Crimscott St STHWK SE1 .... 49 D3
Crimsworth Rd VX/NE SW8 .... 117 D3
Crinan St IS N1 .... 9 D1
Cringle St VX/NE SW8 .... 116 C3
Cripplegate St BARB EC2Y * 23 E2
Crispian Cl WLSDN NW10 .... 69 E1
Crispin St WCHPL E1 .... 25 E3
Crisp Rd HMSMTH W6 .... 112 C1
Cristowe Rd FUL/PGN SW6 * 113 F5
Criterion Ms ARCH N19 .... 57 D4
Crockerton Rd TOOT SW17 .... 151 F2
Crockham Wy ELTH/MOT SE9 .... 162 A4
Croft Cl CHST BR7 .... 161 F5
Croftdown Rd KTTN NW5 .... 56 A5
Crofters Ct DEPT SE8 .... 103 E5
Crofters Wy CAMTN NW1 .... 75 D5
Crofton Av CHSWK W4 .... 111 D3
Crofton Gate Wy BROCKY SE4 .... 139 E5
Crofton Park Rd BROCKY SE4 .... 139 F4
Crofton Rd CMBW SE5 .... 119 E4
   PLSTW E13 .... 94 B3
Croft St DEPT SE8 .... 103 E4
   WCHPL E1 .... 102 A1
The Croft WLSDN NW10 .... 87 F1
Croft Wy BFN/LL DA15 .... 163 E3
Crogsland Rd CAMTN NW1 .... 74 A4
Cromartie Rd ARCH N19 .... 57 D2
Cromarty Vls BAY/PAD W2 * 27 E1
Crombie Ms BTSEA SW11 * 115 E5
Crombie Rd BFN/LL DA15 .... 162 C3
Crome Rd WLSDN NW10 .... 69 E3
Cromer Rd LEY E10 .... 63 D2
Cromer St STPAN WC1H 9 D4
Cromer Ter HACK E8 .... 78 A2
Cromer Villas Rd WAND/EARL SW18 * 131 F4
Cromford Rd PUT/ROE SW15 .... 131 F3
Crompton St BAY/PAD W2 .... 16 A1

Cromwell Av HGT N6 .... 56 B3
   HMSMTH W6 .... 112 B1
Cromwell Cl CHSWK W4 * 110 B1
Cromwell Crs ECT SW5 .... 38 A4
Cromwell Gdns SKENS SW7 .... 40 B4
Cromwell Gv HMSMTH W6 .... 100 C4
Cromwell Ms SKENS SW7 * 40 A4
Cromwell Pl ACT W3 .... 98 C2
   HGT N6 * 56 B3
   MORT/ESHN SW14 .... 128 C1
   SKENS SW7 .... 40 B4
Cromwell Rd BRXN/ST SW9 .... 118 B4
   ECT SW5 .... 38 B4
   FSTGT E7 .... 82 C4
   SKENS SW7 .... 39 D4
   WIM/MER SW19 .... 150 A5
Crondace Rd FUL/PGN SW6 .... 114 A4
Crondall St IS N1 .... 12 B1
Cronin St PECK SE15 .... 119 F3
Crooke Rd DEPT SE8 .... 121 F1
Crookham Rd FUL/PGN SW6 .... 113 F4
Crookston Rd ELTH/MOT SE9 .... 144 A1
Croombs Rd CAN/RD E16 .... 94 C4
Crooms Hill GNWCH SE10 .... 123 D3
Croom's Hill Gv GNWCH SE10 .... 122 C5
Cropley Ct IS N1 * 12 A1
Cropley St IS N1 .... 12 A1
Cropthorne Ct MV/WKIL W9 .... 3 F4
Crosby Rd FSTGT E7 .... 82 A5
Crosby Rw STHWK SE1 .... 48 A1
Crosby Sq HDTCH EC3A 25 E5
Crosby Wk HACK E8 .... 77 F5
Crosier Cl BKHTH/KID SE3 .... 125 E4
Crosland Pl BTSEA SW11 .... 134 A1
Crossbrook Rd BKHTH/KID SE3 .... 125 E5
Crossfield Est DEPT SE8 .... 122 A3
Crossfield Rd HAMP NW3 .... 73 D3
Crossfield St DEPT SE8 .... 122 A3
Crossford St BRXN/ST SW9 .... 117 F5
Cross Keys Cl MHST W1U 18 B3
Cross La MON EC3R 36 C2
Crosslet St WALW SE17 .... 48 B4
Crosslet V GNWCH SE10 .... 122 B4
Crossley St HOLWY N7 .... 76 A3
Crossmead ELTH/MOT SE9 .... 161 F1
Crossness Rd BARK IG11 .... 97 F2
Cross Rd CMBW SE5 .... 119 E5
   IS N1 .... 11 E5
Cross St BARN SW13 .... 111 E5
   IS N1 .... 76 B5
Crosswaite Av HNHL SE24 .... 137 D2
Crosswall TWRH EC3N 37 E1
Crossway STNW/STAM N16 .... 77 E2
Crossways Ter CLPT E5 .... 78 C1
The Crossways WBLY HA9 .... 50 A4
The Crossway ELTH/MOT SE9 .... 162 A3
Croston St HACK E8 .... 78 A5
Crouch Cft ELTH/MOT SE9 .... 162 A3
Crouch End Hl CEND/HSY/T N8 .... 57 D2
Crouch Hall Rd CEND/HSY/T N8 .... 57 D1
Crouch Hl CEND/HSY/T N8 .... 57 E2
Crouch Rd WLSDN NW10 .... 69 D4
Crouchmans Cl SYD SE26 .... 155 F3
Crowborough Rd TOOT SW17 .... 152 A5
Crowder St WCHPL E1 .... 102 B1
Crowfoot Cl HOM E9 .... 79 F2
   THMD SE28 .... 109 E2
Crowhurst Cl BRXN/ST SW9 .... 118 A5
Crowland Ter IS N1 .... 77 D4
Crowline Wk IS N1 * 76 C3
Crowmarsh Gdns FSTH SE23 .... 138 C5
Crown Cl BOW E3 .... 80 A5
   KIL/WHAMP NW6 .... 72 B3
Crown Ct HOL/ALD WC2B 21 D5
Crowndale Rd CAMTN NW1 .... 8 B2
Crownfield Rd SRTFD E15 .... 81 D2
Crownhill Rd WLSDN NW10 .... 69 F5
Crown La STRHM/NOR SW16 .... 154 A3
Crown Lane Gdns
   STRHM/NOR SW16 * 154 A3
Crown Office Rw EMB EC4Y 34 A1
Crown Pas STJS SW1Y 31 F4
Crown Pl KTTN NW5 .... 74 B3
   SDTCH EC2A 24 C1
Crownstone Rd BRXS/STRHM SW2 .... 136 A3
Crown St ACT W3 .... 98 B2
   CMBW SE5 .... 118 C3
Crown Ter CRICK NW2 * 71 D1
Crown Vls ACT W3 * 98 C3
Crown Woods La WOOL/PLUM SE18 ...... 126 B5
Crown Woods Wy ELTH/MOT SE9 .... 145 D3
Crows Rd BARK IG11 .... 84 B3
   BOW E3 .... 93 D2
Crowther Cl FUL/PGN SW6 .... 113 F2

Crowthorne Cl *WAND/EARL* SW18.... 131 F5
Crowthorne Rd *NKENS* W10 .... 89 D5
Croxley Rd *MV/WKIL* W9................. 89 F2
Croxted Cl *DUL* SE21 .... 136 C5
Croxted Ms *HNHL* SE24 .... 136 C4
Croxted Rd *DUL* SE21 .... 155 D2
Croyde Cl *BFN/LL* DA15 .... 145 D5
Croydon Rd *PLSTW* E13 .... 93 F3
Crozier Ter *HOM* E9 .... 79 D2
Crucifix La *STHWK* SE1 .... 36 C5
Cruden St *IS* N1 .... 76 B5
Cruikshank St *FSBYW* WC1X 10 A3
Cruikshank Rd *SRTFD* E15 .... 81 E1
Crusoe Ms *STNW/STAM* N16 .... 59 D4
Crutched Friars *TWRH* EC3N 37 D1
Crutchley Rd *CAT* SE6 .... 159 E2
Crystal Palace Park Rd *SYD* SE26.. 156 A5
Crystal Palace Rd *EDUL* SE22 .... 137 F4
Cuba St *POP/IOD* E14 .... 104 A3
Cubitt St *FSBYW* WC1X 9 F4
Cubitt Ter *CLAP* SW4 .... 134 C1
Cudham St *CAT* SE6 .... 140 B5
Cudworth St *WCHPL* E1 .... 90 B3
Cuff Crs *ELTH/MOT* SE9 .... 143 D5
Culford Gdns *CHEL* SW3 .... 41 E5
Culford Gv *IS* N1 .... 77 E3
Culford Ms *IS* N1 .... 77 D3
Culford Rd *IS* N1 .... 77 E4
Culling Rd *BERM/RHTH* SE16 .... 102 C4
Cullingworth Rd *WLSDN* NW10 ..... 70 B2
Culloden Cl *BERM/RHTH* SE16 ...... 120 A1
Culloden St *POP/IOD* E14 .... 92 C5
Cullum St *FENCHST* EC3M 36 C1
Culmore Rd *PECK* SE15 .... 120 B3
Culross St *MYFR/PKLN* W1K 30 A2
Culverden Rd *BAL* SW12 .... 152 C3
Culverhouse Gdns *STRHM/NOR* SW16. 153 F4
Culverley Rd *CAT* SE6 .... 158 B1
Culvert Pl *BTSEA* SW11 .... 116 A5
Culvert Rd *BTSEA* SW11 .... 115 F5
Culworth St *STJWD* NW8 .... 4 C2
Cumberland Av *WELL* DA16 .... 145 E1
    WLSDN NW10 .... 86 B2
Cumberland Cl *HACK* E8 .... 77 F3
Cumberland Crs *WKENS* W14 .... 101 E5
Cumberland Gdns *FSBYW* WC1X 9 F3
Cumberland Ga *BAY/PAD* W2 .... 29 E1
    CAMTN NW1 .... 6 C3
Cumberland Market *CAMTN* NW1 .... 7 D3
Cumberland Ms *LBTH* SE11 .... 118 A1
Cumberland Pk *ACT* W3 .... 98 C1
Cumberland Pl *CAMTN* NW1 .... 6 C3
    CAT SE6 .... 159 F2
Cumberland Rd *ACT* W3 .... 98 C1
    BARN SW13 .... 111 F4
    MNPK E12 .... 83 D1
    PLSTW E13 .... 94 B4
    RCH/KEW TW9 .... 110 A4
Cumberland St *PIM* SW1V 116 B1
Cumberland Ter *CAMTN* NW1 .... 6 C2
Cumberland Terrace Ms *CAMTN* NW1. 6 C2
Cumbrian Gdns *CRICK* NW2 .... 53 D4
Cumming St *IS* N1 .... 9 F2
Cumnor Cl *BRXN/ST* SW9 * 117 F5
Cunard Rd *WLSDN* NW10 .... 87 D2
Cundy Rd *CAN/RD* E16 .... 94 C5
Cundy St *BGVA* SW1W 42 B5
Cunningham St *STJWD* NW8 .... 4 A5
Cunnington St *CHSWK* W4 .... 98 C4
Cupar Rd *BTSEA* SW11 .... 116 A4
Cupola Cl *BMLY* BR1 .... 160 B5
Cureton St *PIM* SW1P 117 D1
Curlew Cl *THMD* SE28 .... 97 E1
Curlew St *STHWK* SE1 .... 37 E5
Curness St *LEW* SE13 .... 140 C2
Curnick's La *WNWD* SE27 .... 154 C4
Curran Av *BFN/LL* DA15 .... 145 F3
Curricle St *ACT* W3 .... 99 E2
Currie Hill Cl *WIM/MER* SW19 ..... 149 F4
Cursitor St *FLST/FETLN* EC4A 22 A4
Curtain Pl *SDTCH* EC2A 13 D4
Curtain Rd *SDTCH* EC2A 24 C1
Curtis Dr *ACT* W3 .... 87 D5
Curtis Field Rd *STRHM/NOR* SW16. 153 F4
Curtis St *STHWK* SE1 .... 49 E4
Curtis Wy *STHWK* SE1 .... 49 E4
The Curve *SHB* W12 .... 100 A1
Curwen Av *FSTGT* E7 .... 82 B1
Curwen Rd *SHB* W12 .... 100 A3
Curzon Crs *BARK* IG11 .... 97 F2
    WLSDN NW10 .... 69 E4
Curzon St *MYFR/PKLN* W1K 30 B4

Custom House Reach
  BERM/RHTH SE16 * 103 F4
Cutcombe Rd *CMBW* SE5 .... 118 C5
Cuthberga Cl *BARK* IG11 .... 84 C4
Cuthbert St *BAY/PAD* W2 .... 16 A1
Cutlers Gardens Ar *LVPST* EC2M 25 D4
Cutler St *HDTCH* EC3A 25 D4
The Cut *STHWK* SE1 .... 34 B5
Cygnet Cl *WLSDN* NW10 .... 69 D2
Cygnet St *WCHPL* E1 .... 13 F5
Cynthia St *IS* N1 .... 9 F2
Cypress Cl *CLPT* E5 .... 60 A4
Cypress Gdns *BROCKY* SE4 .... 139 E3
Cypress Pl *FITZ* W1T 19 F1
Cypress Tree Cl *BFN/LL* DA15 ..... 163 F1
Cyprus Cl *FSBYPK* N4 .... 58 A1
Cyprus Pl *BETH* E2 .... 90 C1
    EHAM E6 .... 108 A1
Cyprus St *BETH* E2 .... 90 C1
Cyrena Rd *EDUL* SE22 .... 137 F4
Cyrus St *FSBYE* EC1V 11 D5
Czar St *DEPT* SE8 .... 122 A1

D

Dabin Crs *GNWCH* SE10 .... 122 C4
Dacca St *DEPT* SE8 .... 121 F2
Dace Rd *BOW* E3 .... 80 A5
Dacre Gdns *LEW* SE13 .... 141 E2
Dacre Pk *LEW* SE13 .... 141 E1
Dacre Pl *LEW* SE13 .... 141 E1
Dacre Rd *PLSTW* E13 .... 82 B5
    WAN E11 .... 63 F3
Dacres Est *FSTH* SE23 * 157 D3
Dacres Rd *FSTH* SE23 .... 157 D3
Dacre St *STJSPK* SW1H 44 A2
Daffodil Gdns *IL* IG1 .... 84 B2
Daffodil St *SHB* W12 .... 99 F1
Dafforne Rd *TOOT* SW17 .... 151 F3
Dagenham Rd *LEY* E10 .... 61 F3
Dagmar Gdns *WLSDN* NW10 .... 89 D1
Dagmar Pas *IS* N1 .... 76 B5
Dagmar Rd *CMBW* SE5 .... 119 E4
    FSBYPK N4 .... 58 A2
Dagmar Ter *IS* N1 .... 76 B5
Dagnall St *BTSEA* SW11 .... 115 F5
Dagnan Rd *BAL* SW12 .... 134 B5
Dagonet Rd *BMLY* BR1 .... 160 A5
Dahlia Gdns *IL* IG1 .... 84 B3
Daines Cl *MNPK* E12 .... 65 F5
Dainford Cl *BMLY* BR1 .... 159 D5
Dairsie Rd *ELTH/MOT* SE9 .... 144 A1
Dairy Cl *WLSDN* NW10 .... 70 A5
Dairyman Cl *CRICK* NW2 .... 53 D5
Daisy La *FUL/PGN* SW6 .... 132 A1
Dakin Pl *WCHPL* E1 .... 91 E4
Dalberg Rd *BRXS/STRHM* SW2 ..... 136 A3
Dalby Rd *WAND/EARL* SW18 .... 132 C2
Dalby St *KTTN* NW5 .... 74 B3
Dalebury Rd *TOOT* SW17 .... 151 F2
Dale Cl *BKHTH/KID* SE3 .... 142 A1
Dalehame Gdns *HAMP* NW3 .... 73 D1
Dalehame Ms *HAMP* NW3 .... 73 D3
Dalemain Ms *CAN/RD* E16 .... 106 A2
Dale Rd *KTTN* NW5 .... 74 A2
    WLSDN NW10 .... 118 E2
Daleside Rd *STRHM/NOR* SW16 .... 152 B5
Dale St *CHSWK* W4 .... 111 E1
Dale Rw *NTGHL* W11 .... 89 E5
Dalgarno Gdns *NKENS* W10 .... 88 A3
Dalgarno Wy *NKENS* W10 .... 88 C3
Dalkeith Rd *DUL* SE21 .... 154 C1
    IL IG1 .... 66 C5
Dallas Rd *HDN* NW4 .... 52 A2
    SYD SE26 .... 156 B4
Dallinger Rd *LEE/GVPK* SE12 ...... 141 F4
Dalling Rd *HMSMTH* W6 .... 100 B4
Dallington St *FSBYE* EC1V 11 C5
Dallington St *FSBYE* EC1V 11 D5
Dalin Rd *WOOL/PLUM* SE18 .... 126 B3
Dalmain Rd *FSTH* SE23 .... 157 D1
Dalmeny Av *HOLWY* N7 .... 75 D1
Dalmeny Rd *ARCH* N19 .... 57 D1
    HOLWY N7 .... 75 D1
Dalmeyer Rd *WLSDN* NW10 .... 69 F3

Dalmore Rd *DUL* SE21................. 154 C2
Dalrymple Rd *BROCKY* SE4......... 139 E2
Dalston La *HACK* E8.................... 77 F3
Dalton St *WNWD* SE27................ 154 B2
Dalwood St *CMBW* SE5............... 119 E4
Dalyell Rd *BRXN/ST* SW9........... 135 F1
Damask Crs *CAN/RD* E16............ 93 E3
Damer Ter *WBPTN* SW10............ 114 C3
Dames St *IS* N1.......................... 11 E1
Damien St *WCHPL* E1................. 90 B4
Damsel Ct *BERM/RHTH* SE16 *.... 102 A3
Danbury St *IS* N1....................... 11 D1
Danby St *PECK* SE15................... 137 F1
Dancer Rd *FUL/PGN* SW6............ 113 F4
   RCH/KEW TW9....................... 128 A1
Dando Crs *BKHTH/KID* SE3......... 142 B1
Dandridge Cl *GNWCH* SE10......... 123 F1
Danebury Av *PUT/ROE* SW15...... 129 F5
Daneby Rd *CAT* SE6................... 158 C3
Danecroft Rd *HNHL* SE24........... 136 C5
Danehurst St *FUL/PGN* SW6....... 113 E4
Danemere St *PUT/ROE* SW15...... 130 C1
Dane Pl *BOW* E3........................ 91 E1
Dane Rd *IL* IG1.......................... 84 C2
Danescombe *LEE/GVPK* SE12..... 160 A1
Danesdale Rd *HOM* E9............... 79 E3
Dane St *GINN* WC1R.................. 21 E3
Daneswood Av *CAT* SE6............. 158 C3
Daneville Rd *CMBW* SE5............ 119 D4
Dangan Rd *WAN* E11.................. 64 A1
Daniel Bolt Cl *POP/IOD* E14........ 92 B4
Daniel Gdns *PECK* SE15............. 119 F3
Daniel Pl *HDN* NW4................... 52 B1
Daniel's Rd *PECK* SE15.............. 138 C1
Dan Leno Wk *FUL/PGN* SW6 *..... 114 B3
Dansey Pl *SOHO/SHAV* W1D...... 32 A1
Dante Pl *LBTH* SE11................... 46 C4
Danube St *CHEL* SW3................. 15 D5
Danvers St *CHEL* SW3................ 115 D2
Daphne St *WAND/EARL* SW18..... 132 C4
Daplyn St *WCHPL* E1................. 90 A4
D'Arblay St *SOHO/CST* W1F....... 19 F5
Darell Rd *RCH/KEW* TW9............ 128 A1
Darenth Rd *STNW/STAM* N16..... 59 F2
Darfield Rd *BROCKY* SE4............ 139 F3
Darfield Wy *NKENS* W10............. 101 D1
Darfur St *PUT/ROE* SW15........... 131 D1
Darien Rd *BTSEA* SW11.............. 133 D1
Darlan Rd *FUL/PGN* SW6............ 113 F3
Darley Rd *BTSEA* SW11.............. 133 F4
Darling Rd *BROCKY* SE4............. 140 A1
Darling Rw *WCHPL* E1................ 90 B3
Darlington Rd *WNWD* SE27......... 154 B5
Darnley Rd *HACK* E8.................. 78 B3
Darnley Ter *NTGHL* W11............. 101 D2
Darrell Rd *EDUL* SE22............... 138 A3
Darren Cl *FSBYPK* N4................. 57 F2
Darsley Dr *VX/NE* SW8............... 117 D4
Dartford St *WALW* SE17............. 118 C1
Dartmoor Wk *POP/IOD* E14 *....... 104 A5
Dartmouth Cl *NTGHL* W11........... 89 F2
Dartmouth Gv *GNWCH* SE10....... 122 C4
Dartmouth Hill *GNWCH* SE10...... 122 C4
Dartmouth Park Av *KTTN* NW5.... 56 B5
Dartmouth Park Hl *KTTN* NW5..... 56 B5
Dartmouth Park Rd *KTTN* NW5.... 56 B5
Dartmouth Pl *CHSWK* W4............ 111 E2
   FSTH SE23............................. 156 C2
Dartmouth Rd *CRICK* NW2........... 71 D3
   HDN NW4............................... 52 A1
   SYD SE26............................... 156 B3
Dartmouth Rw *GNWCH* SE10....... 122 C5
Dartmouth St *STJSPK* SW1H....... 44 A3
Dartmouth Ter *GNWCH* SE10....... 123 D4
Dartrey Wk *WBPTN* SW10 *......... 114 C5
Dart St *NKENS* W10.................... 89 F2
Darville Rd *STNW/STAM* N16....... 59 F5
Darwell Cl *EHAM* E6................... 96 A1
Darwin Rd *WELL* DA16............... 145 F1
Darwin St *WALW* SE17............... 48 B4
Dashwood Rd *CEND/HSY/T* N8.... 57 F1
Dassett Rd *WNWD* SE27............. 154 B5
Datchelor Pl *CMBW* SE5 *.......... 119 D4
Datchet Rd *CAT* SE6................... 157 F3
Date St *WALW* SE17.................. 118 C1
Daubeney Rd *CLPT* E5................ 79 F1
Dault Rd *WAND/EARL* SW18........ 132 C4
Davenant Rd *ARCH* N19.............. 57 D4
Davenant St *WCHPL* E1.............. 90 A4
Davenport Rd *CAT* SE6............... 140 B4
Daventry Av *WALTH* E17............. 62 A1

Daventry St *CAMTN* NW1............ 16 C2
Davern Cl *GNWCH* SE10............. 105 F5
Davey Cl *HOLWY* N7................... 75 F4
Davey Rd *HOM* E9...................... 80 A4
Davey St *PECK* SE15.................. 119 F2
Davidge St *STHWK* SE1............... 46 C1
David Ms *MHST* W1U.................. 17 F2
Davidson Gdns *VX/NE* SW8......... 117 E3
David's Rd *FSTH* SE23................ 156 C1
David St *SRTFD* E15................... 81 D3
Davies La *WAN* E11.................... 63 E4
Davies Ms *MYFR/PKLN* W1K....... 30 C1
Davies St *MYFR/PKLN* W1K........ 30 C1
Davis Rd *ACT* W3....................... 99 F2
Davis St *PLSTW* E13................... 94 B1
Davisville Rd *SHB* W12................ 100 A3
Dawes Rd *FUL/PGN* SW6............ 113 F5
Dawes St *WALW* SE17................ 119 D1
Dawlish Av *WAND/EARL* SW18.... 150 B2
Dawlish Dr *GDMY/SEVK* IG3....... 85 F1
Dawlish Rd *CRICK* NW2.............. 71 D3
   LEY E10................................. 62 C4
Dawnay Gdns *WAND/EARL* SW18. 151 D2
Dawnay Rd *WAND/EARL* SW18.... 150 C2
Dawn Crs *SRTFD* E15................. 81 D5
Dawpool Rd *CRICK* NW2............. 51 F4
Dawson Av *BARK* IG11................ 85 F4
Dawson Cl *WOOL/PLUM* SE18...... 108 C5
Dawson Gdns *BARK* IG11............ 85 F4
Dawson Pl *BAY/PAD* W2.............. 26 A1
Dawson Rd *CRICK* NW2............... 70 C2
Dawson St *BETH* E2.................... 13 F4
Daylesford Av *PUT/ROE* SW15.... 130 A2
Daysbrook Rd *BRXS/STRHM* SW2. 153 F1
Days La *BFN/LL* DA15................. 145 E5
Dayton Gv *PECK* SE15................ 120 C4
Deacon Ms *IS* N1....................... 77 D4
Deacon Rd *CRICK* NW2............... 70 A3
Deacons Ter *IS* N1 *................... 76 C5
Deacon Wy *WALW* SE17.............. 47 F4
Deal Porters Wy *BERM/RHTH* SE16 102 C4
Deals Gtwy *LEW* SE13................ 122 B4
Deal St *WCHPL* E1..................... 90 A4
Dealtry Rd *PUT/ROE* SW15......... 130 C2
Dean Cl *BERM/RHTH* SE16 *........ 103 D2
Deal Wk *BRXN/ST* SW9............... 118 A3
Dean Bradley St *WEST* SW1P...... 44 C3
Dean Cl *BERM/RHTH* SE16.......... 103 D2
   HOM E9................................. 78 C2
Deancross St *WCHPL* E1............. 90 C5
Deanery Ms *MYFR/PKLN* W1K *... 30 B3
Deanery Rd *SRTFD* E15.............. 81 E3
Deanery St *MYFR/PKLN* W1K...... 30 B3
Dean Farrar St *STJSPK* SW1H..... 44 B2
Deanhill Ct *MORT/ESHN* SW14 *.. 128 B2
Deanhill Rd *MORT/ESHN* SW14.... 128 B2
Dean Rd *CRICK* NW2................... 70 C3
Dean Ryle St *WEST* SW1P........... 44 C4
Dean's Blds *WALW* SE17............. 48 B5
Deans Cl *CHSWK* W4.................. 110 B2
Dean's Ct *STP* EC4M.................. 23 D5
Deanscroft Av *CDALE/KGS* NW9... 50 C4
Deans Gate Cl *FSTH* SE23........... 157 D5
Dean's Ms *CAVSQ/HST* W1G *...... 19 D4
Dean Stanley St *WEST* SW1P....... 44 C3
Dean St *FSTG* E7....................... 82 A2
   SOHO/SHAV W1D.................... 20 A4
Deans Yd *WEST* SW1P................ 44 B2
Dean Trench St *WEST* SW1P........ 44 C3
Deason St *SRTFD* E15................ 80 C5
De Barowe Ms *HBRY* N5............. 76 B1
De Beauvoir Crs *IS* N1............... 77 E5
De Beauvoir Rd *IS* N1 *.............. 77 E5
De Beauvoir Sq *IS* N1................ 77 E4
De Beauvoir Sq *IS* N1................. 77 E4
Debnams Rd *BERM/RHTH* SE16... 102 C5
Decima St *STHWK* SE1............... 48 C2
Deck Cl *BERM/RHTH* SE16.......... 103 D2
De Crespigny Pk *CMBW* SE5....... 119 D5
Deeley Rd *VX/NE* SW8................ 117 D4
Deepdale *WIM/MER* SW19........... 149 D3
Deepdene Gdns *BRXS/STRHM* SW2. 135 F5
Deepdene Rd *HNHL* SE24............ 136 C2
Deerbrook Rd *HNHL* SE24........... 154 B1
Deerdale Rd *HNHL* SE24............. 136 C2
Deerhurst Rd *KIL/WHAMP* NW6.... 71 D4
   STRHM/NOR SW16.................. 153 F5
Deeside Rd *TOOT* SW17............. 151 D3
Dee St *POP/IOD* E14.................. 92 C5
Defence Cl *THMD* SE28.............. 109 E2
Defoe Av *RCH/KEW* TW9............ 110 A3
Defoe Pl *TOOT* SW17................. 151 E2
Defoe Rd *BERM/RHTH* SE16........ 103 F3

STNW/STAM N16	59	E4
De Frene Rd SYD SE26	157	D4
Degema Rd CHST BR7	162	B5
Dehar Crs CDALE/KGS NW9	51	F2
De Haviland Dr WOOL/PLUM SE18	126	B1
De Havilland Rd EDGW HA8	67	D3
Dekker Rd DUL SE21	137	E4
Delacourt Rd BKHTH/KID SE3	124	B3
Delafield Rd CHARL SE7	124	B1
Delaford Rd BERM/RHTH SE16	120	B1
Delaford St FUL/PGN SW6	113	E3
Delamere Rd BAY/PAD W2	15	E3
Delamere Ter BAY/PAD W2	15	D2
Delancey Pas CAMTN NW1	4	B5
Delancey St CAMTN NW1	74	B5
De Laune St LBTH SE11	118	B2
Delaware Rd MV/WKIL W9	2	C5
Delawyk Crs HNHL SE24	137	D4
Delhi St IS N1	75	E5
Delia St WAND/EARL SW18	132	B5
Delius Gv SRTFD E15	92	C1
Della Pth CLPT E5	60	A5
Dell Cl SRTFD E15	81	D5
Dellow Cl GNTH/NBYPK IG2	67	D2
Dellow St WCHPL E1	102	B1
Dell's Ms PIM SW1V *	43	F5
Delme Crs BKHTH/KID SE3	124	B3
Deloraine St DEPT SE8	122	A4
Delorme St HMSMTH W6	113	D2
Delta Est BETH E2 *	90	A2
Delta St BETH E2 *	90	A2
Delverton Rd WALW SE17	118	B1
Delvino Rd FUL/PGN SW6	114	A4
Demeta Cl WBLY HA9	50	C5
De Montfort Pde		
STRHM/NOR SW16 *	153	E3
De Montfort Rd STRHM/NOR SW16	153	E3
De Morgan Rd FUL/PGN SW6	132	B1
Dempster Rd WAND/EARL SW18	132	C3
Denbigh Cl NTGHL W11	101	F1
Denbigh Pl PIM SW1V *	116	C1
Denbigh Rd EHAM E6	95	D2
NTGHL W11	101	F1
Denbigh St PIM SW1V	43	E5
Denbigh Ter NTGHL W11	101	F1
Dendy St BAL SW12	152	A1
Dene Cl BROCKY SE4	139	E1
Denehurst Gdns ACT W3	98	B2
HDN NW4	52	C1
RCHPK/HAM TW10	128	A2
Denewood Rd HGT N6	55	E1
Dengie Wk IS N1 *	76	C5
Denham Ct GNTH/NBYPK IG2	66	C1
Denham Wy BARK IG11	85	E5
Denholme Rd MV/WKIL W9	89	F2
Denman Rd PECK SE15	119	F4
Denman St SOHO/SHAV W1D	31	F2
Denmark Gv IS N1	10	A1
Denmark Hl CMBW SE5	119	D5
HNHL SE24	137	D2
Denmark Rd CMBW SE5	118	C4
KIL/WHAMP NW6	89	F1
Denmark St LSQ/SEVD WC2H	20	B5
PLSTW E13	94	B4
WAN E11	63	E5
Denne Ter HACK E8	77	F5
Dennett's Gv NWCR SE14	121	D5
Dennett's Rd NWCR SE14	121	D4
Densham Rd SRTFD E15	81	E5
Denton St WAND/EARL SW18	132	B4
Denton Wy CLPT E5	61	D5
Dents Rd BTSEA SW11	133	F4
Denver Rd STNW/STAM N16	59	E2
Denyer St CHEL SW3	41	D4
Denzil Rd WLSDN NW10	69	F2
Deodar Rd PUT/ROE SW15	131	E2
Depot Ap CRICK NW2	71	D1
Depot St CMBW SE5	119	D2
Deptford Br DEPT SE8	122	A4
Deptford Broadway NWCR SE14	122	A4
Deptford Church St DEPT SE8	122	A3
Deptford Gn DEPT SE8	122	A3
Deptford High St DEPT SE8	122	A2

Deptford Market DEPT SE8 *	122	A3
Deptford Whf DEPT SE8	103	F5
De Quincey Ms CAN/RD E16	106	A2
Derby Ga WHALL SW1A	32	C5
Derby Hl FSTH SE23	156	C2
Derby Hill Crs FSTH SE23	156	C2
Derby Rd FSTGT E7	83	D4
HOM E9	79	D5
MORT/ESHN SW14	128	B2
Derbyshire St BETH E2	90	A2
Dereham Pl SDTCH EC2A	13	D5
Dereham Rd BARK IG11	85	F3
Derek Av WBLY HA9	68	B4
Derek Walcott Cl HNHL SE24	136	B3
Dericote St HACK E8	78	A5
Derifall Cl EHAM E6	95	F4
Dering St OXSTW W1C	18	C5
Derinton Rd TOOT SW17	152	A4
Dermody Gdns LEW SE13	141	D3
Dermody Rd LEW SE13	141	D3
Deronda Rd HNHL SE24	154	B1
Derrick Gdns CHARL SE7	106	C4
Derry St KENS W8	38	C1
Dersingham Av MNPK E12	83	F1
Dersingham Rd CRICK NW2	53	E5
Derwent Av PUT/ROE SW15	147	E4
Derwent Gv EDUL SE22	137	F2
Derwent Rd CDALE/KGS NW9	51	E1
Derwent St GNWCH SE10	123	E1
Derwentwater Rd ACT W3	98	C2
Desenfans Rd DUL SE21	137	E4
Desford Rd CAN/RD E16	93	E3
Desmond St NWCR SE14	121	E2
Desmond Tutu Dr FSTH SE23	157	F1
Despard Rd ARCH N19	56	C3
Desvignes Dr LEW SE13	141	D4
Detling Rd BMLY BR1	160	A5
Detmold Rd CLPT E5	60	B4
Devalls Cl EHAM E6	108	A1
Devas Rd RYNPK SW20	149	F4
Devas St BOW E3	92	B3
Devenay Rd SRTFD E15	81	F4
De Vere Gdns IL IG1	65	F3
KENS W8	39	E1
Deverell St STHWK SE1	48	A3
De Vere Ms KENS W8	39	E2
Devereux Ct TPL/STR WC2R	34	A1
Devereux La BARN SW13	112	B3
Devereux Rd BTSEA SW11	133	F4
Devizes St IS N1	77	D5
Devon Gdns FSBYPK N4	58	B1
Devonhurst Pl CHSWK W4 *	111	D1
Devonia Rd IS N1	11	D1
Devonport Gdns IL IG1	65	E4
Devonport Rd SHB W12	100	B2
Devonport St WCHPL E1	90	C5
Devons Est BOW E3	92	B2
Devons Rd BARK IG11	85	E5
BOW E3	92	B3
Devonshire Cl CAVSQ/HST W1G	18	C2
SRTFD E15	81	E1
Devonshire Dr GNWCH SE10	122	B4
Devonshire Gdns CHSWK W4	110	C3
Devonshire Gv PECK SE15	120	B2
Devonshire Ms CHSWK W4	111	E1
Devonshire Ms South		
CAVSQ/HST W1G	18	C2
Devonshire Ms West CAVSQ/HST W1G	18	B1
Devonshire Pl CAVSQ/HST W1G	18	B1
CRICK NW2	54	A5
KENS W8 *	38	C3
Devonshire Place Ms		
CAVSQ/HST W1G	18	B1
Devonshire Rd CAN/RD E16	94	B5
CHSWK W4	111	E1
ELTH/MOT SE9	161	E2
FSTH SE23	139	D5
GNTH/NBYPK IG2	67	D2
WALTH E17	62	A1
Devonshire Rw LVPST EC2M	25	D3
Devonshire Row Ms GTPST W1W	19	D3
Devonshire Sq LVPST EC2M	25	D4
Devonshire St CAVSQ/HST W1G	18	B2
CHSWK W4	111	E1
Devonshire Ter BAY/PAD W2	15	F5
EDUL SE22 *	138	A2
Devons Rd BOW E3	92	A4
Devon St PECK SE15	120	B2
De Walden St CAVSQ/HST W1G	18	B3
Dewar St PECK SE15	138	A1
Dewberry Gdns EHAM E6	95	D4
Dewberry St POP/IOD E14	92	C4

Dewey La *BRXS/STRHM* SW2	136	A4
Dewey Rd *IS* N1	10	A1
Dewey St *TOOT* SW17	151	D5
Dewhurst Rd *HMSMTH* W6	101	D4
Dewsbury Rd *WLSDN* NW10	70	A2
D'Eynsford Rd *CMBW* SE5	119	D4
Diadem Ct *SOHO/CST* W1F	20	A4
Diamond St *CMBW* SE5	119	E3
WLSDN NW10	69	D3
Diamond Ter *GNWCH* SE10	122	C3
Diana Cl *DEPT* SE8	121	F2
Dibden St *IS* N1	76	C5
Dicey Av *CRICK* NW2	70	C2
Dickens Est *BERM/RHTH* SE16 *	102	A4
Dickens Ms *EC1M*	22	C1
Dickenson Rd *CEND/HSY/T* N8	57	F2
Dickens St *EHAM* E6	95	D1
Dickens St *STHWK* SE1	47	F2
Dickson House *CHARL* SE7 *	125	E3
Dickson Rd *ELTH/MOT* SE9	143	E1
Didsbury Cl *EHAM* E6	88	C4
Digby Crs *FSBYPK* N4	58	C3
Digby Rd *BARK* IG11	85	F4
HOM E9	79	D3
Digby St *BETH* E2	90	C2
Diggon St *WCHPL* E1	91	D4
Dighton Rd *WAND/EARL* SW18	132	C3
Dignum St *IS* N1	10	A1
Digswell St *HOLWY* N7 *	76	A3
Dilhorne Cl *LEE/GVPK* SE12	160	B3
Dilke St *CHEL* SW3	115	F2
Dillwyn Cl *SYD* SE26	157	E4
Dilton Gdns *PUT/ROE* SW15	148	A1
Dimes Pl *HMSMTH* W6	100	B5
Dimond Cl *FSTGT* E7	82	A1
Dimsdale Dr *CDALE/KGS* NW9	50	C3
Dimsdale Wk *PLSTW* E13	82	A5
Dimson Crs *BOW* E3	92	A3
Dingle Gdns *POP/IOD* E14 *	104	A3
Dingle La *STRHM/NOR* SW16	153	D2
Dingley Pl *FSBYE* EC1V	11	F4
Dingley Rd *FSBYE* EC1V	11	E4
Dingwall Gdns *GLDGN* NW11	54	A1
Dingwall Rd *WAND/EARL* SW18	132	C5
Dinmont St *BETH* E2	90	B1
Dinsdale Rd *BKHTH/KID* SE3	123	F2
Dinsmore Rd *BAL* SW12	134	B5
Dirleton Rd *SRTFD* E15	81	F5
Disbrowe Rd *HMSMTH* W6	113	E2
Discovery Wk *WAP* E1W	102	B1
Disney Pl *STHWK* SE1	35	F5
Disney St *STHWK* SE1	35	F5
Disraeli Rd *FSTGT* E7	82	A3
PUT/ROE SW15	131	E2
WLSDN NW10	86	C1
Diss St *BETH* E2	13	E3
Distaff La *BLKFR* EC4V	35	E1
Distillery La *HMSMTH* W6	112	C1
Distillery Rd *HMSMTH* W6	112	C1
Distin St *LBTH* SE11	46	A5
Ditchburn St *POP/IOD* E14	104	C1
Dittisham Rd *ELTH/MOT* SE9	161	E4
Dixon Cl *EHAM* E6	95	F5
Dixon Rd *NWCR* SE14	121	E4
Dixon Wy *WLSDN* NW10	69	E4
Dobell Rd *ELTH/MOT* SE9	143	F3
Dobree Av *WLSDN* NW10	70	B4
Dobson Cl *KIL/WHAMP* NW6	73	D4
Dockers Tanner Rd *POP/IOD* E14	104	A5
Dockhead *STHWK* SE1	49	F1
Dock Hill Av *BERM/RHTH* SE16	103	D3
Dockland St *CAN/RD* E16	108	A2
Dockley Rd *BERM/RHTH* SE16	102	A4
Dock Rd *CAN/RD* E16	105	F1
Dockside Rd *CAN/RD* E16	107	D1
Dock St *WCHPL* E1	102	A1
Doctors Cl *SYD* SE26	156	C5
Docwra's Blds *IS* N1	77	E3
Dodbrooke Rd *WNWD* SE27	154	A3
Doddington Gv *WALW* SE17	118	B2
Doddington Pl *LBTH* SE11	118	B2
Dodson St *STHWK* SE1	46	B1
Dod St *POP/IOD* E14	92	A5
Doggett Rd *CAT* SE6	140	A5
Dog Kennel Hl *CMBW* SE5	137	E1
Dog La *WLSDN* NW10	69	E1
Doherty Rd *PLSTW* E13	94	A3
Dolben Ct *DEPT* SE8 *	105	F5
Dolben St *STHWK* SE1 *	35	D4
Dolby Rd *FUL/PGN* SW6	113	F5
Dolland St *LBTH* SE11	117	F1

Dollis Hill Av *CRICK* NW2	52	B5
Dollis Hill Est *CRICK* NW2 *	52	A5
Dollis Hill La *CRICK* NW2	69	F1
Dolman Rd *CHSWK* W4	99	D5
Dolman St *CLAP* SW4	135	F2
Dolphin Cl *BERM/RHTH* SE16	103	D3
Dolphin La *POP/IOD* E14	104	B1
Dolphin Sq *BMSBY* WC1N	116	C1
PIM SW1V	116	C1
Dombey St *BMSBY* WC1N	21	E2
Dome Hill Pk *SYD* SE26	155	F4
Domett Cl *CMBW* SE5	137	D2
Domingo St *FSBYE* EC1V	11	E5
Dominica Cl *PLSTW* E13	95	D2
Dominion St *LVPST* EC2M	24	B2
Domonic Dr *ELTH/MOT* SE9	162	B3
Donald Rd *PLSTW* E13	82	B5
Donaldson Rd *KIL/WHAMP* NW6	71	F5
WOOL/PLUM SE18	126	A4
Doncaster Gdns *FSBYPK* N4 *	58	C1
Donegal St *IS* N1	9	F2
Doneraile St *FUL/PGN* SW6	113	D5
Dongola Rd *PLSTW* E13	94	B2
WCHPL E1	91	F4
Dongola Rd West *PLSTW* E13	94	B2
Donkey Aly *EDUL* SE22	138	C1
Donne Pl *CHEL* SW3	41	D4
Donnington Rd *WLSDN* NW10	70	B5
Donoghue Cots *POP/IOD* E14 *	91	E4
Don Phelan Cl *CMBW* SE5	119	D4
Doon St *STHWK* SE1	34	A3
Dorando Cl *SHB* W12 *	100	B3
Doran Gv *WOOL/PLUM* SE18	127	E3
Dora Rd *WIM/MER* SW19	150	A5
Dora St *POP/IOD* E14	91	F5
Dora Wy *BRXN/ST* SW9	118	A5
Dorchester Ct *CRICK* NW2	52	C5
HNHL SE24	136	C3
Dorchester Dr *HNHL* SE24	136	C3
Dorchester Gv *CHSWK* W4	111	E2
Dorchester Pde *STRHM/NOR* SW16 *	153	E2
Dordrecht Rd *ACT* W3	99	E2
Dore Av *MNPK* E12	84	A2
Doreen Av *CDALE/KGS* NW9	51	D3
Doria Rd *FUL/PGN* SW6	113	F5
Doric Wy *CAMTN* NW1	8	A3
Doris Rd *FSTGT* E7	82	A4
Dorking Cl *DEPT* SE8	121	F2
Dorlcote Rd *WAND/EARL* SW18	133	D5
Dorman Wy *STJWD* NW8	73	D5
Dormay St *WAND/EARL* SW18	132	B3
Dormer Cl *SRTFD* E15	81	F3
Dornberg Cl *BKHTH/KID* SE3	124	A3
Dornberg Rd *BKHTH/KID* SE3 *	124	B3
Dorncliffe Rd *FUL/PGN* SW6	113	E5
Dornfell St *KIL/WHAMP* NW6	71	F5
Dornton Rd *BAL* SW12	152	B2
Dorothy Rd *BTSEA* SW11	133	F1
Dorrell Pl *BRXN/ST* SW9	136	A1
Dorrington St *HCIRC* EC1N	22	A2
Dorrit St *STHWK* SE1 *	35	F5
Dors Cl *CDALE/KGS* NW9	51	D3
Dorset Av *WELL* DA16	145	F2
Dorset Blds *EMB* EC4Y *	22	C5
Dorset Cl *CAMTN* NW1	17	E2
Dorset Ms *KTBR* SW1X	42	C2
Dorset Pl *SRTFD* E15	81	D3
Dorset Ri *EMB* EC4Y	22	C5
Dorset Rd *ELTH/MOT* SE9	161	D2
FSTGT E7	82	C4
VX/NE SW8	117	F3
Dorset Sq *CAMTN* NW1	17	E1
Dorset St *MHST* W1U	17	F3
Dorton Cl *PECK* SE15	119	E3
Dorville Crs *HMSMTH* W6	100	B4
Dorville Rd *LEE/GVPK* SE12	142	A3
Dothill Rd *WOOL/PLUM* SE18	127	D5
Doughty Ms *BMSBY* WC1N	21	E1
Doughty St *BMSBY* WC1N	9	E5
Douglas Est *IS* N1	76	C3
Douglas Ms *CRICK* NW2	53	E5
Douglas Pth *POP/IOD* E14	122	C1
Douglas Rd *POP/IOD* E14 *	122	C1
IS N1	76	C4
KIL/WHAMP NW6	71	F5
Douglas Rd North *IS* N1	76	C3
Douglas Rd South *IS* N1 *	76	C3
Douglas St *WEST* SW1P	44	A5
Douglas Wy *DEPT* SE8	122	A3
NWCR SE14	121	F3
Doulton Ms *KIL/WHAMP* NW6 *	72	B3

Dounesforth Gdns WAND/EARL SW18..	150	B1
Douro Pl KENS W8	39	D2
Douro St BOW E3	92	A1
Douthwaite Sq WAP E1W	102	A2
Dove Ap EHAM E6	95	E4
Dove Cl PLUM SE18 *	24	A5
Dovedale Rd EDUL SE22	138	B3
Dovehouse Md BARK IG11	97	D1
Dovehouse St CHEL SW3	115	D1
Dove Ms ECT SW5	39	E5
Dover Cl CRICK NW2	53	D4
Dovercourt Est IS N1	77	D3
Dovercourt Rd DUL SE22	137	E4
Doverfield Rd BRXS/STRHM SW2	135	E4
Dover House Rd PUT/ROE SW15	130	A2
Dove Rd IS N1	77	D3
Dover Rd MNPK E12	64	C5
WOOL/PLUM SE18	126	B5
Dover St CONDST W1S	31	D2
Dover Ter RCH/KEW TW9 *	110	A5
Dover Yd MYFR/PICC W1J	31	A5
Doves Yd IS N1	76	A5
Doveton St WCHPL E1	90	C3
Dowanhill Rd CAT SE6	159	D1
Dowdeswell Cl PUT/ROE SW15	129	E2
Dowdney Cl KTTN NW5	74	C2
Dowgate Hl CANST EC4R	36	A1
Dowland St NKENS W10	89	E2
Dowlas St CMBW SE5	119	E3
Downderry Rd BMLY BR1	159	D3
Downend WOOL/PLUM SE18	126	B3
Downer's Cots CLAP SW4 *	134	C2
Downfield Cl MV/WKIL W9	14	C1
Downham La BMLY BR1	159	D5
Downham Rd IS N1	77	D4
Downham Wy BMLY BR1	159	E5
Downings EHAM E6	96	A5
Downing St WHALL SW1A	32	C5
Downleys Cl ELTH/MOT SE9	161	E2
Downman Rd ELTH/MOT SE9	143	E1
Down Pl HMSMTH W6	100	B5
Downs Av CHST BR7	161	F5
Downs Court Rd HACK E8 *	78	B2
Downsell Rd SRTFD E15	81	D1
Downsfield Rd WALTH E17	61	E1
Downshall Av GDMY/SEVK IG3	67	E1
Downshire Hl HAMP NW3	73	E1
Downside Crs HAMP NW3	73	E2
Downs La CLPT E5	78	B1
Downs Park Rd HACK E8	78	A2
Downs Rd CLPT E5	78	A1
Down St MYFR/PICC W1J	30	C4
Dowson Cl CMBW SE5 *	137	D2
Doyce St STHWK SE1	35	E5
Doyle Gdns WLSDN NW10	70	B5
D'Oyley St BGVA SW1W	42	A4
Doynton St ARCH N19 *	56	B4
Draco Ga PUT/ROE SW15 *	130	C1
Draco St WALW SE17	118	C4
Dragonfly Cl PLSTW E13	94	B2
Dragon Rd LBTH SE11	45	F5
PECK SE15	119	E2
Dragoon Rd DEPT SE8	121	E1
Dragor Rd WLSDN NW10	86	C2
Drake Cl BERM/RHTH SE16	103	D3
Drakefell Rd NWCR SE14	121	D5
Drakefield Rd TOOT SW17	152	A3
Drake Rd BROCKY SE4	140	A1
CRICK NW2		
Drakes Ctyd KIL/WHAMP NW6	71	F4
Drake St FSBYW WC1X	21	E3
Draper Est STHWK SE1	47	D4
Draper Pl IS N1	76	B5
Drapers Rd SRTFD E15	80	C1
Drappers Wy BERM/RHTH SE16	102	A5
Drawell Cl WOOL/PLUM SE18	127	E1
Draycot Rd WAN E11	64	B1
Draycott Av CHEL SW3	41	D5
CRICK NW2	53	D5
Draycott Pl CHEL SW3	41	E5
Draycott Ter CHEL SW3	41	E4
Drayford Cl MV/WKIL W9	89	F3
Dray Gdns BRXS/STRHM SW2	135	F3
Draymans Ms PECK SE15	119	F5
Drayson Ms KENS W8	38	B1
Drayton Cl IL IG1	67	D3
Drayton Gdns WBPTN SW10	114	C1
Drayton Pk HBRY N5	76	A2
Drayton Park Ms HOLWY N7 *	76	A2
Drayton Rd WAN E11	63	D3
WLSDN NW10	69	F5
Dreadnought St GNWCH SE10	105	E4
Dresden Cl KIL/WHAMP NW6	72	B3
Dresden Rd ARCH N19	56	C3
Dressington Av BROCKY SE4	140	C3
Drewery Ct BKHTH/KID SE3 *	141	E1
Drew Rd CAN/RD E16	107	E2
Drews Cots STRHM/NOR SW16 *	153	D3
Drewstead Rd STRHM/NOR SW16	153	D2
Driffield Rd BOW E3	91	E1
The Drive ACT W3	86	C5
BARK IG11	85	F4
GLDGN NW11	53	E2
HOLWY N7	75	F3
IL IG1	65	E1
WBLY HA9	50	C4
Dr Johnson Av TOOT SW17	152	B3
Droitwich Cl SYD SE26	156	A3
Dromore Rd PUT/ROE SW15	131	E4
Droop St NKENS W10	89	E3
Drovers Pl PECK SE15	120	B3
Drovers Wy HOLWY N7	75	E3
Druce Rd DUL SE21	137	E4
Druid St STHWK SE1	37	D5
Drummond Crs CAMTN NW1	8	A3
Drummond Ga PIM SW1V	117	D1
Drummond Rd BERM/RHTH SE16	102	B4
WAN E11	64	B1
Drummond St CAMTN NW1	7	F2
Drum St WCHPL E1	25	F4
Drury La HOL/ALD WC2B	20	C4
Drury Wy WLSDN NW10	69	D2
Dryad St PUT/ROE SW15	131	D1
Dryburgh Rd PUT/ROE SW15	130	B1
Dryden Cl CLAP SW4	135	D5
Dryden Rd WELL DA16	127	F4
WIM/MER SW19		
Dryfield Cl WLSDN NW10	68	C3
Drylands Rd CEND/HSY/T N8	57	F1
Drysdale Dwellings HACK E8 *	77	F2
Drysdale Pl IS N1	13	D4
Drysdale St IS N1	13	D4
Dublin Av HACK E8	78	A5
Ducal St BETH E2	13	F4
Du Cane Cl SHB W12 *	88	C5
Du Cane Rd SHB W12	88	A5
Duchess Ms CAVSQ/HST W1G	19	D3
Duchess of Bedford's Wk KENS W8	101	F3
Duchess St REGST W1B	19	D3
Duchy St STHWK SE1	34	B3
Ducie St CLAP SW4	135	E2
Duckett Rd FSBYPK N4	58	B1
Duckett St WCHPL E1	91	D4
Duck La SOHO/CST W1F	20	A5
Du Cros Rd ACT W3	99	E2
Dudden Hill La WLSDN NW10	69	F1
Dudden Hill Pde WLSDN NW10 *	69	F1
Duddington Cl ELTH/MOT SE9	161	D4
Dudley Rd IL IG1	66	B1
KIL/WHAMP NW6	89	E1
Dudley St BAY/PAD W2 *	16	A3
Dudlington Rd CLPT E5	60	C4
Dudmaston Ms CHEL SW3	115	D1
Dudrich Ms EDUL SE22	137	F3
Dufferin Av STLK EC1Y	23	F1
Dufferin St STLK EC1Y	23	F1
Duff St POP/IOD E14	92	B5
Dufour's Pl SOHO/CST W1F	19	F5
Dugard Wy LBTH SE11	46	C4
Dugolly Av WBLY HA9	50	B5
Duke Humphrey Rd BKHTH/KID SE3	123	E4
The Dukes of Wellington Av		
WOOL/PLUM SE18	108	B4
Duke of Wellington Pl KTBR SW1X	42	B1
Duke of York Sq CHEL SW3	115	F1
Duke of York St STJS SW1Y	31	F3
Duke Rd CHSWK W4	111	D1
Duke's Av CHSWK W4	111	D1
Dukes Ga CHSWK W4 *	98	C5
Duke's Ms MHST W1U	18	B4
Duke's Pl HDTCH EC3A	25	E5
Dukes Point HGT N6	56	B3
Dukes Rd ACT W3	86	A3
EHAM E6	84	A5
Duke's Rd CAMTN NW1	8	B4
Dukesthorpe Rd SYD SE26	157	D4
Duke St MHST W1U	18	B4

MYFR/PKLN W1K	18	B5
Duke Street HI *STHWK* SE1	36	B3
Duke Street St James's		
MYFR/PICC W1J	31	F3
Duke's Yd *MYFR/PKLN* W1K	30	B1
Dulas St *FSBYPK* N4	57	F3
Dulford St *NTGHL* W11	101	E1
Dulka Rd *BTSEA* SW11	133	F3
Dulverton Rd *ELTH/MOT* SE9	162	C2
Dulwich Common *DUL* SE21	155	D1
The Dulwich Oaks *DUL* SE21 *	155	F3
Dulwich Rd *HNHL* SE24	136	A3
Dulwich Village *DUL* SE21	137	D4
Dulwich Wood Av *NRWD* SE19	155	F3
Dulwich Wood Pk *NRWD* SE19	155	E4
Dumbarton Rd *BRXS/STRHM* SW2	135	E4
Dumbreck Rd *ELTH/MOT* SE9	144	A2
Dumont Rd *STNW/STAM* N16	59	E5
Dumpton Pl *CAMTN* NW1	74	A4
Dunbar Rd *FSTGT* E7	82	A3
Dunbar St *WNWD* SE27	154	C3
Dunblane Rd *ELTH/MOT* SE9	143	E1
Dunboyne Rd *HAMP* NW3	73	F2
Dunbridge St *BETH* E2	90	A3
Duncan Gv *ACT* W3	87	E5
Duncan Rd *HACK* E8	78	B5
Duncan St *IS* N1	10	C1
Duncan Ter *IS* N1	10	C2
Dunch St *WCHPL* E1	90	B5
Duncombe HI *FSTH* SE23	139	E4
Duncombe Rd *ARCH* N19	57	D3
Duncrievie Rd *LEW* SE13	141	D4
Duncroft *WOOL/PLUM* SE18	127	E3
Dundalk Rd *BROCKY* SE4	139	E1
Dundas Rd *PECK* SE15	120	C5
Dundee Rd *PLSTW* E13	94	B1
Dundee St *WAP* E1W	102	B2
Dundee Whf *POP/IOD* E14	103	F1
Dundonald Cl *EHAM* E6	95	E5
Dundonald Rd *WLSDN* NW10	71	D5
Dunedin Rd *IL* IG1	66	C3
LEY E10	62	B5
Dunelm St *WCHPL* E1	91	D5
Dunfield Rd *CAT* SE6	158	B5
Dunford Rd *HOLWY* N7	75	F1
Dungarvan Av *PUT/ROE* SW15	130	A2
Dunkery Rd *ELTH/MOT* SE9	161	D4
Dunkirk St *WNWD* SE27 *	154	C4
Dunlace Rd *CLPT* E5	78	C2
Dunloe St *BETH* E2	13	E2
Dunlop Pl *BERM/RHTH* SE16	49	F3
Dunmore Rd *KIL/WHAMP* NW6	71	E5
Dunmow Rd *SRTFD* E15	81	D1
Dunmow Wk *IS* N1 *	76	C5
Dunnage Crs *BERM/RHTH* SE16	103	E5
Dunnock Rd *EHAM* E6	95	E5
Dunn St *HACK* E8	77	F2
Dunollie Pl *KTTN* NW5	74	C2
Dunollie Rd *KTTN* NW5	74	C2
Dunoon Gdns *FSTH* SE23 *	139	D5
Dunoon Rd *FSTH* SE23	138	C5
Dunraven Rd *SHB* W12	100	A2
Dunraven St *MYFR/PKLN* W1K	29	F1
Dunsany Rd *HMSMTH* W6	101	D4
Dunsford Wy *PUT/ROE* SW15	130	B5
Dunsmure Rd *STNW/STAM* N16	59	E3
Dunstable Ms *CAVSQ/HST* W1G	18	B2
Dunstan Houses *WCHPL* E1 *	90	C4
Dunstan Rd *GLDGN* NW11	53	F3
Dunstan's Gv *EDUL* SE22	138	B4
Dunstan's Rd *EDUL* SE22	138	A5
Dunster Cl *MON* EC3R	36	C1
Dunster Dr *CDALE/KGS* NW9	50	C3
Dunster Gdns *KIL/WHAMP* NW6	71	F4
Dunsterville Wy *STHWK* SE1	48	B1
Dunston Rd *BTSEA* SW11	116	A5
HACK E8	77	F5
Dunston St *HACK* E8	77	F5
Dunton Rd *LEY* E10	49	E5
STHWK SE1		
Duntshill Rd *WAND/EARL* SW18	150	B1
Dunvegan Rd *ELTH/MOT* SE9	143	F2
Dunworth Ms *NTGHL* W11	89	F5
Duplex Ride *KTBR* SW1X	41	F1
Dupree Rd *CHARL* SE7	124	B1
Durand Gdns *BRXN/ST* SW9	117	F4
Durand Wy *WLSDN* NW10	68	C4
Durant St *BETH* E2	90	A1
Durban Rd *CNTH/NBYPK* IG2	67	E3
SRTFD E15	93	E2
WNWD SE27	154	C4

Durfey Pl *CMBW* SE5	119	D3
Durford Crs *PUT/ROE* SW15	148	A1
Durham HI *BMLY* BR1	159	F4
Durham House St *CHCR* WC2N *	33	D2
Durham Pl *CHEL* SW3 *	115	F1
Durham Ri *WOOL/PLUM* SE18	126	C1
Durham Rd *CAN/RD* E16	93	E3
HOLWY N7	57	F4
MNPK E12	83	F1
Durham Rw *WCHPL* E1	91	D4
Durham St *LBTH* SE11	117	F1
Durham Ter *BAY/PAD* W2	14	C4
Durham Yd *BETH* E2	90	B2
Durley Rd *STNW/STAM* N16	59	E3
Durlston Rd *CLPT* E5	60	A4
Durning Rd *NRWD* SE19	155	D5
Durnsford Av *WIM/MER* SW19	150	A2
Durnsford Rd *WIM/MER* SW19	150	A3
Durrell Rd *FUL/PGN* SW6	113	E4
Durrington Rd *CLPT* E5	79	E1
Dursley Cl *BKHTH/KID* SE3	124	C5
Dursley Gdns *BKHTH/KID* SE3	125	D4
Dursley Rd *BKHTH/KID* SE3	124	C5
Durward St *WCHPL* E1	90	B4
Durweston Ms *MHST* W1U *	17	F2
Durweston St *MBLAR* W1H	17	E3
Dutch Yd *WAND/EARL* SW18	132	A5
Duthie St *POP/IOD* E14	104	C1
Dutton St *GNWCH* SE10	122	C4
Dye House La *BOW* E3	80	A5
Dyer's Blds *FLST/FETLN* EC4A	22	A3
Dyers Hall Rd *WAN* E11	63	D4
Dyer's La *PUT/ROE* SW15	130	B1
Dylan Rd *HNHL* SE24	136	B2
Dylways *CMBW* SE5	137	D2
Dymock St *FUL/PGN* SW6	132	B1
Dyneley Rd *LEE/GVPK* SE12	160	C4
Dyne Rd *KIL/WHAMP* NW6	71	F4
Dynevor Rd *STNW/STAM* N16	59	E5
Dynham Rd *KIL/WHAMP* NW6	72	A4
Dyott St *RSQ* WC1B	20	B3
Dysart St *SDTCH* EC2A	24	B1
Dyson Rd *SRTFD* E15	81	F3
WAN E11	63	E1

E

Eade Rd *FSBYPK* N4	58	C2
Eagle Ct *BERM/RHTH* SE16	120	B1
FARR EC1M	22	C1
Eagle House Ms *CLAP* SW4	134	C3
Eagle Ms *IS* N1	77	E3
Eagle Pl *WBPTN* SW10	114	C1
Eaglesfield Rd *WOOL/PLUM* SE18	126	B4
Eagle St *HHOL* WC1V	21	E3
Eagle Wharf Rd *IS* N1	11	F1
Eagling Cl *BOW* E3	92	A2
Ealdham Sq *ELTH/MOT* SE9	142	C2
Ealing Rd *BOW* E3	92	B2
Eamont St *STJWD* NW8	4	C1
Eardley Crs *ECT* SW5	114	A1
Earldom Rd *PUT/ROE* SW15	130	C2
Earlham Gv *FSTGT* E7	81	F2
Earlham St *LSO/SEVD* WC2H	20	B5
Earl Ri *WOOL/PLUM* SE18	127	D1
Earl Rd *MORT/ESHN* SW14	128	C2
Earl's Court Gdns *ECT* SW5	38	C5
Earl's Court Rd *KENS* W8	38	A3
Earl's Court Sq *ECT* SW5	114	B1
Earlsferry Wy *IS* N1	75	E4
Earlsfield Rd *WAND/EARL* SW18	150	C1
Earlshall Rd *ELTH/MOT* SE9	143	F2
Earlsmead Rd *WLSDN* NW10	88	C2
Earls Ms *WAND/EARL* SW18	132	C5
Earls Ter *KENS* W8	101	F1
Earlsthorpe Ms *BAL* SW12	134	A4
Earlsthorpe Rd *SYD* SE26	157	D4
Earlstoke Est *FSBYE* EC1V	10	C3
Earlstoke St *FSBYE* EC1V	10	C3
Eariston Gv *HOM* E9	78	B5
Earl St *SDTCH* EC2A	24	C2
Earls Wk *KENS* W8	38	A3
Earlswood St *GNWCH* SE10	123	E1
Early Ms *CAMTN* NW1	74	B5
Earnshaw St *NOXST/BSQ* WC1A	20	B4
Earsby St *WKENS* W14	101	E3
East Acton Ar *ACT* W3 *	87	F5
East Acton La *ACT* W3	99	D1
East Arbour St *WCHPL* E1	91	D5

East Av *EHAM* E6 .... 83 E4
East Bank *STNW/STAM* N16 .... 59 E2
Eastbourne Av *ACT* W3 .... 87 D5
Eastbourne Gdns *MORT/ESHN* SW14 ... 128 C1
Eastbourne Ms *BAY/PAD* W2 .... 15 F4
Eastbourne Rd *CHSWK* W4 .... 110 C2
   EHAM E6 .... 96 A2
   SEVS/STOTM N15 .... 59 E1
   SRTFD E15 .... 81 E5
Eastbourne Ter *BAY/PAD* W2 .... 15 F4
Eastbrook Rd *BKHTH/KID* SE3 .... 124 B4
Eastbury Av *BARK* IG11 .... 85 D5
Eastbury Gv *CHSWK* W4 .... 111 E1
Eastbury Rd *EHAM* E6 .... 96 A3
Eastbury Sq *BARK* IG11 .... 85 F5
Eastbury Ter *WCHPL* E1 .... 91 D3
Eastcastle St *GTPST* W1W 19 E4
Eastcheap *FENCHST* EC3M 36 B1
East Churchfield Rd *ACT* W3 .... 99 D2
East Cl *EA* W5 .... 86 A3
Eastcombe Av *CHARL* SE7 .... 124 B2
Eastcote Rd *WELL* DA16 .... 127 D5
Eastcote St *BRXN/ST* SW9 .... 111 F5
East Cross Route *HOM* E9 .... 79 F3
Eastdown Pk *LEW* SE13 .... 141 D2
East Dulwich Gv *EDUL* SE22 .... 137 E3
East Dulwich Rd *EDUL* SE22 .... 137 F2
Eastern Av *GDMY/SEVK* IG3 .... 67 E1
   WAN E11 .... 65 E3
Eastern Gtwy *CAN/RD* E16 .... 106 C1
Eastern Rd *BROCKY* SE4 .... 140 A2
   PLSTW E13 .... 94 B3
Easternville Gdns *GNTH/NBYPK* IG2 ... 66 C1
East Ferry Rd *POP/IOD* E14 .... 104 B5
Eastfields Av *WAND/EARL* SW18 .... 132 A2
Eastfields Rd *ACT* W3 .... 86 C4
Eastfield St *POP/IOD* E14 .... 91 E4
East Ham Manor Wy *EHAM* E6 .... 96 A5
East Harding St *FLST/FETLN* EC4A 22 B4
East Heath Rd *HAMP* NW3 .... 55 D5
East Hl *WAND/EARL* SW18 .... 132 C5
   WBLY HA9 .... 50 A4
East India Dock Rd *POP/IOD* E14 .... 104 A1
Eastlake Rd *CMBW* SE5 .... 118 B5
Eastlands Crs *EDUL* SE22 .... 137 F4
East La *BERM/RHTH* SE16 .... 102 A3
Eastlea Ms *CAN/RD* E16 .... 93 E5
Eastleigh Cl *CRICK* NW2 .... 51 E5
Eastman Rd *ACT* W3 .... 99 D3
Eastmearn Rd *WNWD* SE27 .... 154 B2
Eastmoor Pl *CHARL* SE7 .... 107 D4
Eastmoor St *CHARL* SE7 .... 107 D4
East Mount St *WCHPL* E1 * 90 B4
Eastney St *GNWCH* SE10 .... 123 D1
Eastnor Rd *ELTH/MOT* SE9 .... 162 C1
Easton St *FSBYW* WC1X 10 A5
East Parkside *GNWCH* SE10 .... 105 E3
East Pas *STBT* EC1A 23 E2
East Poultry Av *FARR* EC1M 22 C3
East Rd *CHEL* SW3 .... 116 A1
   IS N1 .... 12 B3
   SRTFD E15 .... 82 A5
East Rochester Wy *BFN/LL* DA15 .... 145 E3
   ELTH/MOT SE9 .... 145 E3
East Rw *WKENS* W14 .... 14 A1
East Sheen Av *MORT/ESHN* SW14 .... 129 D2
East Smithfield *WAP* E1W 37 F2
East St *BARK* IG11 .... 84 C4
   WALW SE17 .... 48 C5
East Surrey Gv *PECK* SE15 .... 119 F3
East Tenter St *WCHPL* E1 .... 25 F5
East Ter *BFN/LL* DA15 * 163 E1
East V *ACT* W3 * 99 F2
Eastview Av *WOOL/PLUM* SE18 .... 127 E3
Eastway *BOW* E3 .... 79 E5
   LEY E10 .... 78 A5
Eastwood Cl *HOLWY* N7 .... 76 A2
Eaton Cl *BGVA* SW1W 42 A4
Eaton Dr *BRXN/ST* SW9 .... 136 B2
Eaton Ga *BGVA* SW1W 42 A4
Eaton La *BGVA* SW1W 43 D3
Eaton Ms North *KTBR* SW1X 42 B4
Eaton Ms South *BGVA* SW1W 42 B4
Eaton Ms West *BGVA* SW1W 42 B4
Eaton Pl *KTBR* SW1X 42 A3
Eaton Rw *BGVA* SW1W 42 C4
Eaton Sq *BGVA* SW1W 42 C3
Eaton Ter *BGVA* SW1W 42 A4
   BOW E3 * 91 E2
Eaton Terrace Ms *BGVA* SW1W 42 A4
Eatonville Rd *TOOT* SW17 .... 151 F2

Eatonville Vls *TOOT* SW17 .... 151 F2
Ebbisham Dr *VX/NE* SW8 .... 117 F2
Ebbsfleet Rd *CRICK* NW2 .... 71 E2
Ebdon Wy *BKHTH/KID* SE3 .... 142 B1
Ebenezer St *IS* N1 .... 12 A3
Ebley Cl *PECK* SE15 .... 119 F2
Ebner St *WAND/EARL* SW18 .... 132 B3
Ebor St *WCHPL* E1 .... 13 E5
Ebsworth St *FSTH* SE23 .... 139 D5
Eburne Rd *HOLWY* N7 .... 57 E5
Ebury Br *BGVA* SW1W 116 B1
Ebury Bridge Rd *BGVA* SW1W 116 A1
Ebury Ms *BGVA* SW1W 42 A4
Ebury Ms East *BGVA* SW1W 42 C4
Ebury Sq *BGVA* SW1W 42 C5
Ebury St *BGVA* SW1W 42 B5
Ecclesbourne Rd *IS* N1 .... 76 C4
Eccles Rd *BTSEA* SW11 .... 133 F2
Eccleston Ms *KTBR* SW1X 42 B3
Eccleston Pl *BGVA* SW1W 42 C5
Eccleston Sq *PIM* SW1V 43 D5
Eccleston Square Ms *PIM* SW1V 43 D5
Eccleston St *BGVA* SW1W 42 B3
Eckford St *IS* N1 .... 10 A1
Eckstein Rd *BTSEA* SW11 .... 133 E2
Eclipse Rd *PLSTW* E13 .... 94 B4
Ector Rd *CAT* SE6 .... 159 E2
Edans Ct *SHB* W12 .... 99 F3
Edbrooke Rd *MV/WKIL* W9 .... 14 A1
Eddiscombe Rd *FUL/PGN* SW6 .... 113 F5
Eddystone Rd *BROCKY* SE4 .... 139 E5
Edenbridge Cl *BERM/RHTH* SE16 * 120 B1
Edenbridge Rd *HOM* E9 .... 79 D4
Eden Cl *HAMP* NW3 .... 54 A4
   KENS W8 .... 38 B2
Edenham Wy *NKENS* W10 .... 89 F3
Edenhurst Av *FUL/PGN* SW6 .... 131 F1
Eden Rd *WNWD* SE27 .... 154 B5
Edensor Gdns *CHSWK* W4 .... 111 E3
Edensor Rd *CHSWK* W4 .... 111 E3
Eden Wy *BOW* E3 .... 79 F5
Edgar Kail Wy *CMBW* SE5 .... 137 E1
Edgarley Ter *FUL/PGN* SW6 * 113 E4
Edgar Rd *BOW* E3 .... 92 B2
Edgar Wallace Cl *PECK* SE15 .... 119 E3
Edgebury *CHST* BR7 .... 162 B4
Edgecote Cl *ACT* W3 .... 98 C2
Edgefield Av *BARK* IG11 .... 85 F4
Edge Hl *WOOL/PLUM* SE18 .... 126 B2
Edgehill Rd *CHST* BR7 .... 162 C3
Edgeley La *CLAP* SW4 .... 135 D1
Edgeley Rd *CLAP* SW4 .... 134 C1
Edgel St *WAND/EARL* SW18 .... 132 B2
Edge Point Cl *STRHM/NOR* SW16 .... 154 B5
Edgepoint Cl *WNWD* SE27 * 154 B5
Edge St *KENS* W8 .... 26 B3
Edgeworth Rd *ELTH/MOT* SE9 .... 142 C3
Edgware Rd *BAY/PAD* W2 .... 16 A1
   CRICK NW2 .... 52 C4
Edgware Road Wy *CRICK* NW2 .... 51 F4
Edinburgh Cl *BETH* E2 .... 90 C1
Edinburgh Ga *KTBR* SW1X 29 E5
Edinburgh Rd *PLSTW* E13 .... 94 B1
Edison Gv *WOOL/PLUM* SE18 .... 127 F3
Edison Rd *CEND/HSY/T* N8 .... 57 D1
   WELL DA16 .... 127 F4
Edis St *CAMTN* NW1 .... 74 A5
Edith Cavell Wy *WOOL/PLUM* SE18 .... 125 E4
Edith Gv *WBPTN* SW10 .... 114 C2
Edithna St *BRXN/ST* SW9 .... 135 F1
Edith Nesbit Ws *ELTH/MOT* SE9 .... 143 E2
Edith Neville Cots *CAMTN* NW1 * 8 A3
Edith Rd *EHAM* E6 .... 83 D4
   SRTFD E15 .... 81 D2
   WKENS W14 .... 101 E5
Edith Rw *FUL/PGN* SW6 .... 114 B4
Edith St *BETH* E2 .... 13 F1
Edith Ter *WBPTN* SW10 * 114 C3
Edith Vls *WKENS* W14 .... 101 F5
Edith Yd *WBPTN* SW10 .... 115 D3
Edmeston Cl *HOM* E9 .... 79 E3
Edmund Halley Wy *CNWCH* SE10 .... 105 E3
Edmund Hurst Dr *EHAM* E6 .... 96 B4
Edmund St *CMBW* SE5 .... 119 D3
Edna St *BTSEA* SW11 .... 115 E4
Edric Rd *NWCR* SE14 .... 121 D3
Edward Cl *CRICK* NW2 * 71 D1
Edward Ct *CAN/RD* E16 .... 94 A4
Edwardes Pl *WKENS* W14 .... 101 F4
Edwardes Sq *KENS* W8 .... 38 A3

Edward Mann Cl East *WCHPL* E1 * 91 D5
Edward Mann Cl West *WCHPL* E1 * 91 D5
Edward Ms *CAMTN* NW1 * 7 D5
Edward Pl *DEPT* SE8 .... 121 F2
Edward Rd *CHST* BR7 .... 162 B5
Edward's Cots *IS* N1 * 76 B4
Edward's La *STNW/STAM* N16 .... 59 D4
Edwards Ms *IS* N1 .... 76 B4
Edward Sq *IS* N1 .... 75 F5
Edward St *CAN/RD* E16 .... 94 A3
NWCR SE14 .... 121 E3
Edward's Wy *BROCKY* SE4 .... 140 A3
Edward Temme Av *SRTFD* E15 .... 81 F4
Edward Tyler Rd *LEE/GVPK* SE12 .... 160 B2
Edwin Av *EHAM* E6 .... 96 A1
Edwin Hall Pl *LEW* SE13 .... 141 D4
Edwin's Md *HOM* E9 .... 79 E1
Edwin St *CAN/RD* E16 .... 94 A4
WCHPL E1 .... 90 C5
Effie Pl *FUL/PGN* SW6 .... 114 A3
Effie Rd *FUL/PGN* SW6 .... 114 A3
Effingham Rd *LEE/GVPK* SE12 .... 141 A3
Effort St *TOOT* SW17 .... 151 D5
Effra Pde *BRXS/STRHM* SW2 .... 136 A3
Effra Rd *BRXS/STRHM* SW2 .... 136 A3
Egbert St *CAMTN* NW1 .... 74 A5
Egerton Crs *CHEL* SW3 .... 41 D4
Egerton Dr *GNWCH* SE10 .... 122 B4
Egerton Gdns *CHEL* SW3 .... 40 C3
GDMY/SEVK IG3 .... 67 F5
WLSDN NW10 .... 70 C1
Egerton Gardens Ms *CHEL* SW3 .... 41 D3
Egerton Pl *CHEL* SW3 * 41 D3
Egerton Rd *STNW/STAM* N16 .... 59 F2
Egerton Ter *CHEL* SW3 .... 41 D3
Egham Rd *PLSTW* E13 .... 94 B4
Eglantine Rd *WAND/EARL* SW18 .... 132 C3
Eglinton HI *WOOL/PLUM* SE18 .... 126 B2
Eglinton Rd *WOOL/PLUM* SE18 .... 126 A2
Egliston Ms *PUT/ROE* SW15 .... 130 C1
Egliston Rd *PUT/ROE* SW15 .... 130 C1
Eglon Ms *CAMTN* NW1 .... 73 F4
Egmont St *NWCR* SE14 .... 121 D3
Egremont Rd *WNWD* SE27 .... 154 A3
Eider Cl *SRTFD* E15 .... 81 D2
Eighth Av *MNPK* E12 .... 83 F1
Eisenhower Dr *EHAM* E6 .... 95 E4
Elaine Cl *KTTN* NW5 .... 74 A2
Elam Cl *CMBW* SE5 .... 118 B5
Elam St *CMBW* SE5 .... 118 A5
Eland Rd *BTSEA* SW11 .... 133 F1
Elba Pl *WALW* SE17 * 47 F4
Elbe St *FUL/PGN* SW6 .... 114 C5
Elborough St *WAND/EARL* SW18 .... 150 A1
Elbury Dr *CAN/RD* E16 .... 94 A5
Elcho St *BTSEA* SW11 .... 115 E3
Elcot Av *PECK* SE15 .... 120 B3
Elder Cl *BFN/LL* DA15 .... 163 F1
Elderfield Rd *HACK* E8 .... 79 D1
Elderflower Wy *SRTFD* E15 .... 81 E4
Elder Rd *WNWD* SE27 .... 154 C5
Eldersie Rd *ELTH/MOT* SE9 .... 144 A5
Elder St *WCHPL* E1 .... 25 E2
Elderton Rd *SYD* SE26 .... 157 E4
Elder Wk *IS* N1 .... 76 B5
Eldon Gv *HAMP* NW3 .... 73 D2
Eldon Rd *KENS* W8 .... 39 D3
Eldon St *LVPST* EC2M 24 B3
Eldon Wy *WLSDN* NW10 .... 86 B1
Eleanor Cl *BERM/RHTH* SE16 .... 103 D3
Eleanor Gv *BARN* SW13 .... 129 E1
Eleanor Rd *HACK* E8 .... 78 B3
SRTFD E15 .... 81 F3
Eleanor St *BOW* E3 .... 92 A2
Electric Av *BRXN/ST* SW9 .... 136 A3
Electric La *BRXN/ST* SW9 * 136 A3
Elephant & Castle *STHWK* SE1 .... 47 D4
Elephant La *BERM/RHTH* SE16 .... 102 C3
Elephant Rd *WALW* SE17 .... 47 E4
Elfindale Rd *HNHL* SE24 .... 136 C3
Elford Cl *BKHTH/KID* SE3 .... 142 C5
Elfort Rd *HBRY* N5 .... 76 A1
Elfrida Crs *CAT* SE6 .... 158 A4
Elf Rw *WAP* E1W 102 C1
Elgar Av *WLSDN* NW10 .... 69 D3
Elgar Cl *DEPT* SE8 .... 122 A3
PLSTW E13 .... 94 C1
Elgar St *BERM/RHTH* SE16 .... 103 E3
Elgin Av *MV/WKIL* W9 .... 2 C5
SHB W12 .... 100 A3
Elgin Cl *SHB* W12 .... 100 B3

Elgin Crs *NTGHL* W11 .... 101 E1
Elgin Est *MV/WKIL* W9 .... 14 A1
Elgin Ms *NTGHL* W11 .... 89 E5
Elgin Ms North *MV/WKIL* W9 .... 3 D3
Elgin Ms South *MV/WKIL* W9 .... 3 D4
Elgin Rd *GDMY/SEVK* IG3 .... 67 E3
Elgood Cl *NTGHL* W11 .... 101 E1
Elias Ms *IS* N1 .... 10 C2
Elia Ms *VX/NE* SW8 .... 118 A2
Elias Pl *VX/NE* SW8 .... 118 A2
Elia St *IS* N1 .... 10 C2
Elibank Rd *ELTH/MOT* SE9 .... 144 C1
Elim St *STHWK* SE1 .... 48 C2
Elim Wy *PLSTW* E13 .... 93 F2
Eliot Bank *FSTH* SE23 .... 156 B2
Eliot Gdns *PUT/ROE* SW15 .... 130 A2
Eliot HI *LEW* SE13 .... 122 C5
Eliot Ms *STJWD* NW8 .... 3 E2
Eliot Pk *LEW* SE13 .... 122 C5
Eliot Pl *BKHTH/KID* SE3 .... 123 E5
Eliot V *BKHTH/KID* SE3 .... 123 D5
Elizabeth Av *IL* IG1 .... 67 D4
Elizabeth Barnes Ct *FUL/PGN* SW6 * .. 76 C4
Elizabeth Br *BGVA* SW1W 114 B5
Elizabeth Cl *MV/WKIL* W9 * 42 C3
Elizabeth Fry Pl *WOOL/PLUM* SE18 ... 15 F1
Elizabeth Gdns *ACT* W3 .... 125 E4
Elizabeth Ms *HAMP* NW3 .... 99 F2
Elizabeth Rd *EHAM* E6 .... 73 E3
Elizabeth Sq *BERM/RHTH* SE16 .... 83 D5
Elizabeth St *BGVA* SW1W 103 E1
Elkington Rd *PLSTW* E13 .... 42 B4
Elkstone Rd *NKENS* W10 .... 94 B3
Ellaline Rd *HMSMTH* W6 .... 89 F4
Ella Ms *HAMP* NW3 .... 113 D2
Elland Rd *PECK* SE15 .... 73 F1
Ella Rd *CEND/HSY/T* N8 .... 138 C2
Ellenborough Pl *PUT/ROE* SW15 .... 57 E2
Ellen St *WCHPL* E1 * 130 A2
Ellerby St *FUL/PGN* SW6 .... 90 A5
Ellerdale Cl *HAMP* NW3 .... 113 D4
Ellerdale Rd *HAMP* NW3 .... 72 C2
Ellerdale St *LEW* SE13 .... 72 C2
Ellerslie Rd *SHB* W12 .... 140 B2
Ellerton Rd *BARN* SW13 .... 100 B2
WAND/EARL SW18 .... 112 A4
Ellery Rd *PECK* SE15 .... 151 D1
Ellery St *PECK* SE15 .... 120 B5
Ellesmere Rd *BOW* E3 .... 91 E1
WLSDN NW10 .... 70 A2
Ellesmere St *POP/IOD* E14 .... 92 B5
Ellingfort Rd *HACK* E8 .... 78 C4
Ellingham Rd *SHB* W12 .... 100 A3
SRTFD E15 .... 81 D2
Ellington Rd *HOLWY* N7 .... 76 A3
Elliott Cl *SRTFD* E15 .... 81 E4
Elliott Rd *BRXN/ST* SW9 .... 118 B1
CHSWK W4 .... 99 E5
Elliott's Pl *IS* N1 .... 76 B5
Elliott Sq *HAMP* NW3 .... 73 E4
Elliott's Rw *LBTH* SE11 .... 47 D4
Ellis Cl *ELTH/MOT* SE9 .... 162 C2
WLSDN NW10 .... 70 C3
Ellora Rd *STRHM/NOR* SW16 .... 153 D5
Ellsworth St *BETH* E2 * 90 B2
Elm Bank Gdns *BARN* SW13 .... 111 E5
Elmbourne Rd *TOOT* SW17 .... 152 B3
Elmbridge Wk *HACK* E8 * 78 A4
Elmbrook Gdns *ELTH/MOT* SE9 .... 144 B1
Elm Cl *WAN* E11 .... 64 B1
Elmcourt Rd *WNWD* SE27 .... 154 B2
Elmcroft Av *BFN/LL* DA15 .... 145 E5
GLDGN NW11 .... 53 F2
Elmcroft Crs *GLDGN* NW11 .... 53 D2
Elmcroft St *CLPT* E5 .... 78 C1
Elmdene Rd *WOOL/PLUM* SE18 .... 126 B3
Elmer Rd *CAT* SE6 .... 140 C5
Elmfield Rd *TOOT* SW17 .... 152 B2
WALTH E17 .... 61 D1
Elmfield Wy *MV/WKIL* W9 .... 14 A2
Elm Friars Wk *CAMTN* NW1 .... 75 D4
Elm Gn *ACT* W3 .... 87 E5
Elmgreen Cl *SRTFD* E15 .... 81 E5
Elm Gv *CEND/HSY/T* N8 .... 57 F1
CRICK NW2 .... 71 D1
PECK SE15 .... 120 A5

Elm Grove Rd *BARN* SW13 ... 112 A5
Elm Hall Gdns *WAN* E11 ... 64 B1
Elmhurst Rd *ELTH/MOT* SE9 ... 161 E2
　FSTGT E7 ... 82 B4
Elmhurst St *CLAP* SW4 ... 135 D1
Elmington Est *CMBW* SE5 ... 118 C3
Elmington Rd *CMBW* SE5 ... 119 D4
Elmira St *LEW* SE13 ... 140 B1
Elm La *CAT* SE6 ... 157 F2
Elmley St *WOOL/PLUM* SE18 ... 109 D3
Elmore Rd *WAN* E11 ... 62 C5
Elmore St *IS* N1 ... 77 D4
Elm Pk *BRXS/STRHM* SW2 ... 135 E4
Elm Park Gdns *WBPTN* SW10 ... 115 D1
Elm Park La *CHEL* SW3 ... 115 D1
Elm Park Rd *CHEL* SW3 ... 115 D2
　LEY E10 ... 61 E3
Elm Pl *WBPTN* SW7 ... 115 D1
Elm Rd *FSTGT* E7 ... 81 F5
　MORT/ESHN SW14 ... 128 C1
　WAN E11 ... 63 D4
Elm Rw *HAMP* NW3 ... 54 C5
Elmscott Rd *BMLY* BR1 ... 159 E5
Elms Crs *CLAP* SW4 ... 134 C4
Elmshaw Rd *PUT/ROE* SW15 ... 130 A3
Elmside Rd *WBLY* HA9 ... 50 A5
Elms Ms *BAY/PAD* W2 ... 28 A1
Elms Rd *CLAP* SW4 ... 134 C3
Elmstead Av *CHST* BR7 ... 161 F5
Elmstead Rd *GDMY/SEVK* IG3 ... 67 E4
The Elms *BARN* SW13 ... 129 F1
　TOOT SW17 * ... 152 A3
Elmstone Rd *FUL/PGN* SW6 ... 114 A4
Elm St *FSBYW* WC1X ... 21 F1
Elm Ter *CRICK* NW2 ... 54 A5
Elmton Wy *CLPT* E5 ... 60 A5
Elm Tree Cl *STJWD* NW8 ... 4 A3
Elm Tree Ct *CHARL* SE7 * ... 124 C2
Elm Tree Rd *STJWD* NW8 ... 4 A3
Elm Wk *HAMP* NW3 ... 54 A4
Elm Wy *WLSDN* NW10 ... 69 E1
Elmwood Rd *CHSWK* W4 ... 110 C2
　HNHL SE24 ... 137 D3
Elmworth Gv *DUL* SE21 ... 155 D2
Elnathan Ms *MV/WKIL* W9 ... 15 D1
Elphinstone St *HBRY* N5 ... 76 B1
Elrington Rd *HACK* E8 ... 78 A3
Elsa Cots *POP/IOD* E14 * ... 91 E4
Elsa St *WCHPL* E1 * ... 91 E4
Elsdale St *HOM* E9 ... 78 C3
Elsden Ms *BETH* E2 * ... 90 C1
Elsenham St *WAND/EARL* SW18 ... 149 F1
Elsham Rd *WAN* E11 ... 63 E5
　WKENS W14 ... 101 E3
Elsham Ter *WKENS* W14 * ... 101 E3
Elsie Lane Ct *BAY/PAD* W2 ... 14 B3
Elsiemaud Rd *BROCKY* SE4 ... 140 C2
Elsinore Gdns *CRICK* NW2 * ... 53 E5
Elsinore Rd *FSTH* SE23 ... 157 F1
Elsinore Wy *RCH/KEW* TW9 ... 128 B3
Elsley Rd *BTSEA* SW11 ... 133 F1
Elspeth Rd *BTSEA* SW11 ... 133 F2
Elsted St *WALW* SE17 ... 48 B5
Elstow Rd *ELTH/MOT* SE9 ... 143 F5
Elstree Gdns *IL* IG1 ... 84 C2
Elswick Rd *LEW* SE13 ... 122 B5
Elswick St *FUL/PGN* SW6 ... 114 C5
Elsworthy Rd *HAMP* NW3 ... 73 E4
Elsworthy Ri *HAMP* NW3 ... 73 E5
Elsworthy Ter *HAMP* NW3 ... 73 E4
Elsynge Rd *WAND/EARL* SW18 ... 133 D3
Eltham Gn *ELTH/MOT* SE9 ... 142 C3
Eltham Green Rd *ELTH/MOT* SE9 ... 142 C3
Eltham High St *ELTH/MOT* SE9 ... 143 E3
Eltham Hl *ELTH/MOT* SE9 ... 143 D3
Eltham Palace Rd *ELTH/MOT* SE9 ... 142 C4
Eltham Park Gdns *ELTH/MOT* SE9 ... 144 A3
Eltham Rd *ELTH/MOT* SE9 ... 142 C3
Elthiron Rd *FUL/PGN* SW6 ... 114 A4
Elthorne Rd *ARCH* N19 ... 57 D4
　CDALE/KGS NW9 ... 51 D2
Elthorne Wy *CDALE/KGS* NW9 ... 51 D3
Elthruda Rd *LEW* SE13 ... 141 D4
Eltisley Rd *IL* IG1 ... 84 B1
Elton Pl *STNW/STAM* N16 ... 77 E2
Eltringham St *WAND/EARL* SW18 ... 132 C2
Elvaston Ms *SKENS* SW7 ... 39 F3
Elvaston Pl *SKENS* SW7 ... 39 E3
Elveden Pl *WLSDN* NW10 ... 86 A1

Elveden Rd *WLSDN* NW10 ... 86 A1
Elver Gdns *BETH* E2 ... 90 A2
Elverson Ms *DEPT* SE8 * ... 121 F3
Elverson Rd *DEPT* SE8 ... 122 B5
Elverton St *WEST* SW1P ... 44 A4
Elvino Rd *SYD* SE26 ... 157 D5
Elvis Rd *CRICK* NW2 ... 70 C3
Elwin St *BETH* E2 ... 90 A2
Elwood St *HBRY* N5 ... 58 B5
Elwyn Gdns *LEE/GVPK* SE12 ... 142 A5
Ely Cots *VX/NE* SW8 * ... 117 F3
Elyne Rd *FSBYPK* N4 ... 58 A1
Ely Pl *HCIRC* EC1N ... 22 B3
Ely Rd *LEY* E10 ... 62 C1
Elysium Pl *FUL/PGN* SW6 ... 113 F5
Elysium St *FUL/PGN* SW6 ... 113 F5
Elystan Pl *CHEL* SW3 ... 115 E1
Elystan St *CHEL* SW3 ... 40 C5
Elystan Wk *IS* N1 ... 76 A5
Emanuel Av *ACT* W3 ... 86 C5
Embankment *PUT/ROE* SW15 ... 131 D1
Embankment Gdns *CHEL* SW3 ... 115 F2
Embankment Pl *CHCR* WC2N ... 33 D3
Embleton Rd *BERM/RHTH* SE16 ... 102 A3
Emblem Ct *EDUL* SE22 ... 138 A3
Embleton Rd *LEW* SE13 ... 140 B2
Emden Cl *FUL/PGN* SW6 ... 114 B4
Emden St *FUL/PGN* SW6 ... 114 B4
Emerald Cl *CAN/RD* E16 ... 95 E5
Emerald St *BMSBY* WC1N ... 21 F2
Emerson Rd *IL* IG1 ... 66 A2
Emerson St *STHWK* SE1 ... 35 E3
Emery Hill St *WEST* SW1P ... 43 F5
Emery St *STHWK* SE1 ... 46 B2
Emily St *CAN/RD* E16 ... 93 F5
Emlyn Rd *SHB* W12 ... 99 E5
Emmanuel Rd *BAL* SW12 ... 152 C1
Emma Rd *PLSTW* E13 ... 93 F1
Emma St *BETH* E2 ... 90 B1
Emmott Cl *GLDGN* NW11 ... 54 C1
　WCHPL E1 ... 91 E3
Emperor's Ga *SKENS* SW7 ... 39 E4
Empire Pde *WBLY* HA9 * ... 50 A5
Empire Sq *STHWK* SE1 ... 48 A1
Empire Wharf Rd *POP/IOD* E14 ... 105 D5
Empress Av *IL* IG1 ... 66 A4
　MNPK E12 ... 64 C4
Empress Pl *FUL/PGN* SW6 ... 114 A1
Empress St *WALW* SE17 ... 118 C2
Empson St *BOW* E3 ... 92 B3
Emsworth St *BRXS/STRHM* SW2 ... 153 F2
Emu Rd *VX/NE* SW8 ... 116 B5
Enbrook St *NKENS* W10 ... 89 E2
Enclave Ct *FSBYE* EC1V ... 11 D5
Endeavour Wy *WIM/MER* SW19 ... 150 B4
Endell St *LSQ/SEVD* WC2H ... 20 C4
Enderby St *GNWCH* SE10 ... 123 E1
Endlesham Rd *BAL* SW12 ... 134 A5
Endsleigh Gdns *IL* IG1 ... 65 F3
　STPAN WC1H ... 8 A5
Endsleigh Pl *STPAN* WC1H ... 8 B5
Endsleigh St *STPAN* WC1H ... 8 B5
Endwell Rd *BROCKY* SE4 ... 121 F4
Endymion Rd *BRXS/STRHM* SW2 ... 135 F4
　FSBYPK N4 ... 58 B2
Energen Cl *WLSDN* NW10 ... 69 E5
Enfield Rd *ACT* W3 ... 98 B3
　IS N1 ... 77 E4
Enford St *CAMTN* NW1 ... 17 D3
Engadine St *WAND/EARL* SW18 ... 149 F1
Engate St *LEW* SE13 ... 140 C2
Engineer Cl *WOOL/PLUM* SE18 ... 126 A2
Engineers Wy *WBLY* HA9 ... 68 A1
England's La *HAMP* NW3 ... 73 F3
Englefield Rd *IS* N1 ... 77 D4
Engleheart Rd *CAT* SE6 ... 140 B5
Englewood Rd *BAL* SW12 ... 134 B4
English St *BOW* E3 ... 91 F3
Enid St *BERM/RHTH* SE16 ... 49 F2
Enmore Gdns *MORT/ESHN* SW14 ... 129 D3
Enmore Rd *PUT/ROE* SW15 ... 130 C2
Ennersdale Rd *LEW* SE13 ... 141 D3
Ennismore Av *CHSWK* W4 ... 99 E5
Ennismore Gdns *SKENS* SW7 ... 40 B2
Ennismore Gardens Ms *SKENS* SW7 ... 40 B3
Ennismore Ms *SKENS* SW7 ... 40 C1
Ennismore St *SKENS* SW7 ... 40 C2
Ennis Rd *FSBYPK* N4 ... 58 B1
　WOOL/PLUM SE18 ... 127 D2
Ensign St *WCHPL* E1 ... 102 A1
Enslin Rd *ELTH/MOT* SE9 ... 144 A4
Ensor Ms *SKENS* SW7 ... 115 D1
Enterprise Wy *WAND/EARL* SW18 ... 132 A2

WLSDN NW10	**87**	F2
Enterprize Wy DEPT SE8 *	**103**	F5
Entrance to Strand Underpass		
(northbound only) TPL/STR WC2R	**33**	F2
Epcot Ms WLSDN NW10 *	**89**	D2
Epirus Ms FUL/PGN SW6	**114**	A3
Epirus Rd FUL/PGN SW6	**113**	F3
Epping Cl POP/IOD E14	**104**	A5
Epping Pl IS N1	**76**	A3
Epple Rd FUL/PGN SW6	**113**	F4
LEY E10	**62**	C1
Epworth St SDTCH EC2A	**24**	D1
Equity Sq BETH E2	**15**	F4
Erasmus St WEST SW1P	**44**	B5
Erconwald St SHB W12	**87**	F5
Erebus Dr THMD SE28	**108**	C4
Eresby Pl KIL/WHAMP NW6	**72**	A4
Erica St SHB W12	**100**	A1
Eric Clarke La EHAM E6	**96**	B3
Eric Est BOW E3	**91**	F3
Eric Rd FSTGT E7	**82**	A1
WLSDN NW10	**69**	F5
Eric St BOW E3	**91**	F3
Eridge Rd CHSWK W4	**99**	D4
Erindale WOOL/PLUM SE18	**127**	D2
Erindale Ter WOOL/PLUM SE18	**127**	D2
Erlanger Rd NWCR SE14	**121**	D4
Erlich Cots WCHPL E1 *	**90**	C4
Ermine Rd LEW SE13	**140**	B1
SEVS/STOTM N15	**59**	F1
Ermington Rd ELTH/MOT SE9	**162**	C3
Ernald Av EHAM E6	**95**	E1
Ernest Av WNWD SE27	**154**	B4
Ernest Gdns CHSWK W4	**110**	B2
Ernest St WCHPL E1	**91**	D3
Ernshaw Pl PUT/ROE SW15	**131**	F3
Erpingham Rd PUT/ROE SW15	**130**	C1
Errington Rd MV/WKIL W9	**89**	F3
Errol St STLK EC1Y	**23**	F1
Erskine Ms HAMP NW3 *	**73**	F4
Erskine Rd HAMP NW3	**73**	F4
Erwood Rd CHARL SE7	**125**	E1
Esam Wy STRHM/NOR SW16	**154**	A5
Escreet Gv WOOL/PLUM SE18	**108**	A5
Esher Rd GDMY/SEVK IG3	**67**	E5
Esk Rd PLSTW E13	**94**	B3
Esmar Crs CDALE/KGS NW9	**52**	A2
Esmeralda Rd STHWK SE1	**102**	A5
Esmond Gdns CHSWK W4 *	**99**	D5
Esmond Rd CHSWK W4	**99**	D4
KIL/WHAMP NW6	**71**	F5
Esmond St PUT/ROE SW15	**131**	E2
Esparto St WAND/EARL SW18	**132**	B5
Essendine Rd MV/WKIL W9	**2**	B5
Essex Ct BARN SW13	**111**	F5
EMB EC4Y *	**22**	A5
Essex Gdns FSBYPK N4	**58**	B1
Essex Park Ms ACT W3	**99**	D3
Essex Pl CHSWK W4	**98**	C5
Essex Place Sq CHSWK W4 *	**99**	D5
Essex Rd ACT W3	**98**	C1
BARK IG11	**85**	D4
CHSWK W4	**99**	D5
IS N1	**76**	B5
LEY E10	**62**	C1
MNPK E12	**83**	E2
WALTH E17	**61**	E1
WLSDN NW10	**69**	E4
Essex Rd South WAN E11	**63**	D2
Essex St FSTGT E7	**81**	F5
TPL/STR WC2R	**22**	A5
Essex Vls KENS W8	**38**	A1
Essex Whf CLPT E5 *	**61**	D4
Essian St WCHPL E1	**91**	E4
Estate Wy LEY E10	**61**	F3
Estcourt Rd FUL/PGN SW6	**113**	F3
Estelle Rd HAMP NW3	**73**	F1
Esterbrooke St WEST SW1P	**44**	A3
Este Rd BTSEA SW11	**133**	E1
Esther Rd WAN E11	**63**	E2
Estoria Cl BRXS/STRHM SW2	**136**	A5
Eswyn Rd TOOT SW17	**151**	F4
Etchingham Rd SRTFD E15	**80**	C1
Eternit Wk FUL/PGN SW6	**112**	C4
Ethelbert St BAL SW12	**152**	B1
Ethelburga St BTSEA SW11 *	**115**	E4
Ethelden Rd SHB W12	**100**	B2
Ethelred Est LBTH SE11	**46**	A5
Ethel Rd CAN/RD E16	**106**	B1
Ethel St WALW SE17 *	**47**	F5

Etheridge Rd CRICK NW2	**52**	C2
Etherow St EDUL SE22	**138**	A4
Etherstone Rd STRHM/NOR SW16	**154**	A4
Ethnard Rd PECK SE15	**120**	B2
Etloe Rd LEY E10	**62**	A4
Eton Av HAMP NW3	**73**	E4
Eton Cl WAND/EARL SW18	**132**	B5
Eton College Rd HAMP NW3	**73**	F5
Eton Garages HAMP NW3	**73**	E5
Eton Gv LEW SE13	**141**	E1
Eton Pl HAMP NW3	**74**	A4
Eton Ri HAMP NW3 *	**73**	F5
Eton Rd HAMP NW3	**73**	F5
IL IG1	**84**	C1
Eton Vls HAMP NW3	**73**	F5
Etta St DEPT SE8	**121**	F2
Ettrick St POP/IOD E14	**92**	C5
Eugenia Rd BERM/RHTH SE16	**120**	C1
Europa Pl FSBYE EC1V	**11**	E4
Europe Rd WOOL/PLUM SE18	**107**	F4
Eustace Pl WOOL/PLUM SE18	**107**	F5
Eustace Rd EHAM E6	**95**	E2
FUL/PGN SW6	**114**	A3
Euston Centre CAMTN NW1	**7**	E5
Euston Rd CAMTN NW1	**7**	E5
STPAN WC1H	**8**	C3
Euston Sq CAMTN NW1	**8**	A4
Euston St CAMTN NW1	**7**	F5
Evan Cook Cl PECK SE15	**120**	C4
Evandale Rd BRXN/ST SW9	**118**	A5
Europa Pl FSBYE EC1V	**74**	B1
Evans Cl HACK E8	**77**	F3
Evans Rd CAT SE6	**159**	E2
Evanston Gdns REDBR IG4	**65**	E1
Evelina Rd PECK SE15	**138**	C1
Eveline Lowe Est BERM/RHTH SE16	**102**	A4
Evelyn Denington Rd EHAM E6	**95**	E3
Evelyn Est DEPT SE8	**121**	E2
Evelyn Gdns SKENS SW7	**114**	C1
Evelyn Rd CAN/RD E16	**106**	A2
WIM/MER SW19	**150**	B5
Evelyn St DEPT SE8	**121**	F2
Evelyn Wk IS N1	**12**	A2
Evenwood Cl PUT/ROE SW15 *	**131**	E3
Everatt Cl WAND/EARL SW18	**131**	F4
Everdon Rd BARN SW13	**112**	A2
Everest Pl POP/IOD E14	**92**	C4
Everest Rd ELTH/MOT SE9	**143**	E5
Evergreen Sq HACK E8	**77**	F4
Everilda St IS N1 *	**75**	F5
Evering Rd STNW/STAM N16	**59**	F5
Everington St HMSMTH W6	**113**	D3
Everitt Rd WLSDN NW10	**87**	D2
Everleigh St FSBYPK N4	**57**	F5
Eve Rd SRTFD E15	**93**	E1
WAN E11	**81**	E1
Evershed Wk CHSWK W4	**98**	C4
Eversholt St CAMTN NW1	**7**	F3
Evershot Rd FSBYPK N4	**57**	F3
Eversleigh Rd BTSEA SW11	**133**	F1
EHAM E6	**83**	D5
Eversley Av WBLY HA9	**50**	A4
Eversley Pk WIM/MER SW19	**148**	B5
Eversley Rd CHARL SE7	**124**	B2
Everthorpe Rd PECK SE15	**137**	F1
Everton Blds CAMTN NW1	**7**	E4
Evesham Rd SRTFD E15	**81**	F4
Evesham St NTGHL W11	**101**	D1
Evesham Wk BRXN/ST SW9	**118**	A5
Evesham Wy BTSEA SW11	**134**	A1
Ewald Rd FUL/PGN SW6	**113**	F5
Ewart Pl BOW E3 *	**91**	F1
Ewart Rd FSTH SE23	**139**	D5
Ewe Cl HOLWY N7	**75**	E3
Ewelme Rd FSTH SE23	**156**	C1
Ewen Crs BRXS/STRHM SW2	**136**	A5
Ewer St STHWK SE1	**35**	E4
Ewhurst Cl WCHPL E1	**90**	C4
Ewhurst Rd BROCKY SE4	**139**	F4
Exbury Rd CAT SE6	**158**	A2
Excel Ct LSQ/SEVD WC2H	**32**	B2
Excel Marina CAN/RD E16	**106**	A1
Excel Waterfront CAN/RD E16	**106**	B1
Exchange Ar LVPST EC2A	**24**	C3
Exchange Ct COVGDN WC2E *	**33**	D2
Exchange Sq SDTCH EC2A *	**25**	D2
Exeter Cl EHAM E6	**95**	F5
Exeter Gdns IL IG1	**65**	F3
Exeter Ms FUL/PGN SW6	**114**	A3
Exeter Pde CRICK NW2 *	**71**	E3
Exeter Rd CAN/RD E16	**94**	A4
CRICK NW2	**71**	E2

WELL DA16	127	F5
Exeter St COVGDN WC2E	33	D1
Exeter Wy SE14	121	F5
Exford Gdns LEE/GVPK SE12	160	B1
Exford Rd LEE/GVPK SE12	160	B2
Exhibition Grounds WBLY HA9 *	68	B1
Exhibition Rd SKENS SW7	40	B1
Exmoor St NKENS W10	89	D3
Exmouth Market CLKNW EC1R	10	A5
Exmouth Ms HACK E8 *	7	F4
Exmouth Pl HACK E8	78	B5
Exmouth St WCHPL E1	90	C5
Exning Rd CAN/RD E16	93	E3
Exon St WALW SE17	48	C5
Exton Rd WLSDN NW10	68	C4
Exton St STHWK SE1	34	A4
Eyhurst Cl CRICK NW2	52	A4
Eylewood Rd WNWD SE27	154	C5
Eynella Rd DUL SE21	137	F5
Eynham Rd SHB W12	88	C5
Eynsford Rd GDMY/SEVK IG3	67	E4
Eyot Gdns HMSMTH W6	111	F1
Eyre Street Hl CLKNW EC1R	22	A1
Eythorne Rd BRXN/ST SW9	118	A4
Ezra St BETH E2	13	F3

F

Fabian Rd FUL/PGN SW6	113	F5
Fabian St EHAM E6	95	F3
The Facade FSTH SE23 *	156	C2
Factory Pl POP/IOD E14	122	C1
Factory Rd CAN/RD E16	107	D2
Fairacres PUT/ROE SW15	129	F2
Fairbank Est IS N1	13	A2
Fairbridge Rd ARCH N19	57	D4
Fairby Rd LEE/GVPK SE12	142	B3
Fairchild Cl BTSEA SW11	115	D1
Fairchild Pl SDTCH EC2A	25	D1
Fairchild St SDTCH EC2A	25	D1
Fairclough St WCHPL E1	90	A5
Faircross Av BARK IG11	84	C3
Fairdale Gdns PUT/ROE SW15	130	B2
Fairfax Gdns BKHTH/KID SE3	124	C4
Fairfax Ms CAN/RD E16	106	B2
PUT/ROE SW15	130	C2
Fairfax Pl KIL/WHAMP NW6	72	C4
WKENS W14	101	E4
Fairfax Rd CHSWK W4	99	E4
KIL/WHAMP NW6	72	C4
WKENS W14	101	E4
Fairfield Av HDN NW4	52	B1
Fairfield Cl BFN/LL DA15	145	E4
Fairfield Ct WAND/EARL SW18	132	B3
Fairfield Gv CHARL SE7	125	D2
Fairfield Rd BOW E3	92	A1
IL IG1	84	B3
Fairfields CAT SE6	140	B5
Fairfield St WAND/EARL SW18	132	B3
Fairfoot Rd BOW E3 *	92	A3
Fairhazel Gdns KIL/WHAMP NW6	72	B5
Fairholme Rd IL IG1	65	F2
WKENS W14	113	E1
Fairholt Rd STNW/STAM N16	59	D3
Fairholt St SKENS SW7	41	D2
Fairland Rd SRTFD E15	81	F5
Fairlawn CHARL SE7	124	C3
Fairlawn Av CHSWK W4	98	C5
Fairlawn Ct CHARL SE7 *	124	C3
Fairlawn Dr CHSWK W4	98	C5
Fairlawn Pk SYD SE26	157	E5
Fairlie Gdns FSTH SE23	138	C5
Fairlight Av WLSDN NW10	87	E1
Fairlight Rd TOOT SW17	151	D4
Fairlop Pl STJWD NW8	4	B4
Fairlop Rd WAN E11	63	D2
Fairmead Rd ARCH N19	57	E5
Fairmile Av STRHM/NOR SW16	153	D5
Fairmount Rd BRXS/STRHM SW2	135	F4
Fairoak Dr ELTH/MOT SE9	145	D3
Fairstead Wk IS N1 *	76	C5
Fair St STHWK SE1	37	D5
Fairthorn Rd CHARL SE7	124	A1
Fairview Cl SYD SE26	157	A1
Fairview Pl BRXS/STRHM SW2	135	F5
Fairview Rd SEVS/STOTM N15	59	F1
Fairway CLGDN SW11	54	C2
Fairway Gdns IL IG1	84	C2
The Fairway ACT W3	87	E5
Fairweather Rd STNW/STAM N16	60	A1
Fairwyn Rd SYD SE26	157	E3
Fakruddin St WCHPL E1	90	A3
Falaize Av IG1	84	B1
Falconberg Ct SOHO/SHAV W1D *	20	A4
Falcon Cl CHSWK W4	110	B2
Falcon Ct IS N1	11	D2
Falcon Gv BTSEA SW11	133	E1
Falcon La BTSEA SW11	133	E1
Falcon Rd BTSEA SW11	133	E1
Falcon St PLSTW E13	94	A3
Falcon Ter BTSEA SW11 *	133	E1
Falcon Wy POP/IOD E14	104	B5
Falconwood Av WELL DA16	127	D5
Falconwood Pde WELL DA16	145	E2
Falkirk St IS N1	12	D2
Falkland Pl KTTN NW5	74	C2
Falkland Rd KTTN NW5	74	C2
Fallow Ct BERM/RHTH SE16 *	120	A1
Falmouth Cl LEE/GVPK SE12	141	F3
Falmouth Rd STHWK SE1	47	F3
Falmouth St SRTFD E15	81	D2
Fambridge Cl SYD SE26	157	F4
Fane St WKENS W14	113	F2
Fann St FARR EC1M	23	E1
STLK EC1Y	23	E1
Fanshawe Av BARK IG11	84	C3
Fanshaw St IS N1	12	C3
Fanthorpe St PUT/ROE SW15	130	C1
Faraday Cl HOLWY N7	75	F3
Faraday Rd ACT W3	98	C1
NKENS W10	89	E4
SRTFD E15	81	F3
Faraday Wy WOOL/PLUM SE18	107	D4
Fareham St SOHO/CST W1F *	20	A4
Faringford Rd SRTFD E15	81	E4
Farjeon Rd BKHTH/KID SE3	125	D4
Farleigh Pl STNW/STAM N16	77	F1
Farleigh Rd STNW/STAM N16	77	F1
Farley Dr GDMY/SEVK IG3	67	E3
Farley Ms CAT SE6	140	C5
Farley Rd CAT SE6	140	C5
Farlington Pl PUT/ROE SW15	130	B5
Farlow Rd PUT/ROE SW15	131	D1
Farlton Rd WAND/EARL SW18	132	B5
Farm Av CRICK NW2	53	E5
STRHM/NOR SW16	153	E3
Farm Cl FUL/PGN SW6 *	114	A3
Farmcote Rd LEE/GVPK SE12	160	A1
Farmdale Rd CHARL SE7	124	A1
Farmer Rd LEY E10	62	B3
Farmers Rd CMBW SE5	118	B3
Farmfield Rd BMLY BR1	159	E5
Farmilo Rd WALTH E17	62	A2
Farmland Wk CHST BR7	162	B5
Farm La FUL/PGN SW6	114	A2
Farm Pl KENS W8	26	A3
Farm Rd WLSDN NW10	69	D5
Farmstead Rd CAT SE6	158	B4
Farm St MYFR/PICC W1J	30	C2
The Farm WIM/MER SW19 *	131	D5
Farnaby Rd ELTH/MOT SE9	142	A4
Farnan Rd STRHM/NOR SW16	153	E5
Farnborough Ct WBLY HA9	50	A4
Farnborough Wy PECK SE15 *	119	E3
Farncombe St BERM/RHTH SE16	102	C5
Farnell Ms ECT SW5	114	B1
Farnell Pl ACT W3	98	B1
Farnham Pl STHWK SE1	35	D4
Farnham Rd GDMY/SEVK IG3	67	F1
Farnham Royal LBTH SE11	117	D1
Faroe Rd WKENS W14	101	D4
Farquhar Rd NRWD SE19	155	F5
WIM/MER SW19	150	A3
Farrance St POP/IOD E14	92	A5
Farren Rd FSTH SE23	157	E2
Farrier Rd NTHLT UB5	84	A4
Farrier Wk WBPT SW10	74	B4
Farringdon La CLKNW EC1R	22	B1
Farringdon Rd CLKNW EC1R	22	A1
Farringdon St FLST/FETLN EC4A	22	C4
Farrins Rents BERM/RHTH SE16	103	E2
Farrow La NWCR SE14	120	C3
Farrow Pl BERM/RHTH SE16	103	E4
Farthingale St SRTFD E15	81	D4
Farthing Aly STHWK SE1 *	102	A3
Farthing Flds WAP E1W	102	B2
Fashion St WCHPL E1	25	E3
Fassett Rd HACK E8	78	A3
Fassett Sq HACK E8	78	A3
Fauconberg Rd CHSWK W4	110	C2
Faulkner St NWCR SE14	120	C4

Faunce St *WALW* SE17 .... 118 B2
Favart Rd *FUL/PGN* SW6 .... 114 A4
Faversham Rd *CAT* SE6 .... 139 F5
Fawcett Cl *BTSEA* SW11 .... 115 D5
 STRHM/NOR SW16 .... 154 A4
Fawcett Est *CLPT* E5 * 60 A3
Fawcett Rd *WLSDN* NW10 .... 69 F4
Fawcett St *WBPTN* SW10 .... 114 C2
Fawe Park Rd *PUT/ROE* SW15 .... 131 F2
Fawe St *POP/IOD* E14 .... 94 A5
Fawley Rd *KIL/WHAMP* NW6 .... 72 B2
Fawnbrake Av *HNHL* SE24 .... 136 B3
Fawn Rd *PLSTW* E13 .... 94 C1
Fawood Av *WLSDN* NW10 .... 69 D5
Faygate Rd *BRXS/STRHM* SW2 .... 153 F2
Fayland Av *STRHM/NOR* SW16 .... 152 C5
Fearon St *GNWCH* SE10 .... 124 A1
Feathers Pl *GNWCH* SE10 .... 123 D2
Featherstone Av *FSTH* SE23 .... 156 B1
Featherstone St *STLK* EC1Y 12 A5
Featley Rd *BRXN/ST* SW9 .... 136 B1
Feeny Cl *WLSDN* NW10 .... 69 F1
Felbridge Cl *STRHM/NOR* SW16 .... 154 A4
Felbrigge Rd *GDMY/SEVK* IG3 .... 67 F3
Felday Rd *LEW* SE13 .... 140 B4
Felden St *FUL/PGN* SW6 .... 113 F4
Feldman Cl *STNW/STAM* N16 .... 60 C5
Felgate Ms *HMSMTH* W6 .... 100 B5
Felhampton Rd *ELTH/MOT* SE9 .... 162 B3
Felix Av *CEND/HSY/T* N8 .... 57 E1
Felix Pl *BRXS/STRHM* SW2 .... 136 A3
Felixstowe Rd *WLSDN* NW10 .... 88 B2
Felix St *BETH* E2 * 90 A1
Fellbrigg Rd *EDUL* SE22 .... 137 F3
Fellbrigg St *WCHPL* E1 * 90 B3
Fellows Rd *HAMP* NW3 .... 73 D4
Felltram Wy *CHARL* SE7 .... 124 A1
Felmersham Cl *CLAP* SW4 .... 135 E2
Felsberg Rd *BRXS/STRHM* SW2 .... 135 F5
Felsham Ms *PUT/ROE* SW15 .... 131 D1
Felsham Rd *PUT/ROE* SW15 .... 130 C1
Felspar Cl *WOOL/PLUM* SE18 .... 127 F1
Felstead Rd *HOM* E9 .... 80 A3
 WAN E11 .... 64 A1
Felstead St *HOM* E9 .... 79 F3
Felsted Rd *CAN/RD* E16 .... 95 D5
Felton Lea *SCUP* DA14 .... 163 F5
Felton Rd *BARK* IG11 .... 97 E1
Felton St *IS* N1 .... 77 D5
Fenchurch Av *FENCHCH* EC3M 24 C5
Fenchurch Blds *FENCHST* EC3M 25 D5
Fenchurch Pl *FENCHST* EC3M * 37 D1
Fenchurch St *FENCHST* EC3M 36 C1
Fendall St *STHWK* SE1 .... 49 D2
Fendt Cl *CAN/RD* E16 .... 93 F3
Fenelon Pl *WKENS* W14 .... 101 F3
Fen Gv *BFN/LL* DA15 .... 145 F4
Fenham Rd *PECK* SE15 .... 120 A3
Fennel Cl *CAN/RD* E16 .... 93 E3
Fennell St *WOOL/PLUM* SE18 .... 126 A2
Fenner Cl *BERM/RHTH* SE16 .... 102 B5
Fenner Sq *BTSEA* SW11 * 133 D1
Fenning St *STHWK* SE1 .... 36 C5
Fenn St *HOM* E9 .... 79 D2
Fen St *CAN/RD* E16 .... 105 F1
Fentiman Rd *VX/NE* SW8 .... 117 F2
Fenton Cl *BRXN/ST* SW9 * 117 F1
 CHST BR7 .... 161 F5
 HACK E8 .... 77 F5
Fenton's Av *PLSTW* E13 .... 94 B2
Fenton St *WCHPL* E1 .... 90 B5
Fenwick Gv *PECK* SE15 .... 138 A1
Fenwick Pl *BRXN/ST* SW9 .... 135 E1
Fenwick Rd *PECK* SE15 .... 138 A1
Ferdinand Pl *CAMTN* NW1 .... 74 A4
Ferdinand St *CAMTN* NW1 .... 74 A4
Ferguson Dr *ACT* W3 .... 87 D5
Ferguson's Cl *POP/IOD* E14 .... 104 A3
Fergus Rd *HBRY* N5 .... 76 B2
Fermor Rd *FSTH* SE23 .... 157 E1
Fermoy Rd *MV/WKIL* W9 .... 89 F3
Fernbank Ms *BAL* SW12 .... 134 B4
Fernbrook Rd *LEW* SE13 .... 141 E4
Ferncliff Rd *HACK* E8 .... 78 A2
Fern Cl *IS* N1 .... 12 C5
Fern Ct *NWCR* SE14 .... 121 D5
Ferncroft Av *HAMP* NW3 .... 54 A5
Ferndale Rd *CLAP* SW4 .... 135 E2
 FSTGT E7 .... 82 B4
 SEVS/STOTM N15 .... 59 F1
 WAN E11 .... 63 F4
Ferndale St *EHAM* E6 .... 108 B1

Ferndene Rd *HNHL* SE24 .... 136 C2
Ferndown Rd *ELTH/MOT* SE9 .... 143 D5
Fernhead Rd *MV/WKIL* W9 .... 89 F2
Fernhill St *CAN/RD* E16 .... 107 F2
Fernholme Rd *PECK* SE15 .... 139 D3
Fernhurst Rd *FUL/PGN* SW6 .... 113 E4
Fernlea Rd *BAL* SW12 .... 152 B1
Fernleigh Cl *MV/WKIL* W9 .... 89 F2
Fernsbury St *FSBYW* WC1X 10 A4
Fernshaw Cl *WBPTN* SW10 * 114 C2
Fernshaw Rd *WBPTN* SW10 .... 114 C2
Fernside *GLDGN* NW11 .... 54 A4
Fernside Rd *BAL* SW12 .... 151 F1
Ferns Rd *SRTFD* E15 .... 81 E3
Fern St *BOW* E3 .... 92 A3
Ferntower Rd *HBRY* N5 .... 77 D2
Fern Wk *BERM/RHTH* SE16 .... 120 A1
Fernways *IL* IG1 .... 66 B5
Fernwood Av *STRHM/NOR* SW16 ..... 153 D4
Ferranti Cl *WOOL/PLUM* SE18 .... 107 D4
Ferrers Rd *STRHM/NOR* SW16 .... 153 D5
Ferrey Ms *BRXN/ST* SW9 .... 118 A5
Ferriby Cl *IS* N1 .... 76 A4
Ferrier St *WAND/EARL* SW18 .... 132 B2
Ferrings *DUL* SE21 .... 155 E2
Ferris Rd *EDUL* SE22 .... 138 A2
Ferron Rd *CLPT* E5 .... 60 B5
Ferry La *BARN* SW13 .... 111 F2
Ferry Rd *BARN* SW13 .... 112 A3
Ferry St *POP/IOD* E14 .... 122 C1
Festing Rd *PUT/ROE* SW15 .... 131 D1
Festoon Wy *CAN/RD* E16 .... 107 D1
Fetter La *FLST/FETLN* EC4A 22 C2
Finch Cl *DEPT* SE8 .... 122 A3
Field Cl *CRICK* NW2 .... 52 A4
Field Cots *FUL/PGN* SW6 * 113 F5
Field Ct *GINN* WC1R 21 F3
Fieldgate St *WCHPL* E1 .... 90 A4
Fieldhouse Rd *BAL* SW12 .... 152 C1
Fielding Rd *CHSWK* W4 .... 99 D4
 WKENS W14 .... 101 D4
The Fieldings *FSTH* SE23 .... 156 C1
Field Rd *FSTGT* E7 .... 82 A1
 HMSMTH W6 .... 113 E1
Fields Est *HACK* E8 * 78 A4
Fieldside Rd *BMLY* BR1 .... 159 D5
Field St *FSBYW* WC1X 9 E3
Fieldview *WAND/EARL* SW18 .... 151 E1
Field Wy *WLSDN* NW10 .... 68 C4
Fieldway Crs *HBRY* N5 .... 76 A2
Fife Rd *CAN/RD* E16 .... 94 A4
 MORT/ESHN SW14 .... 128 C3
Fife Ter *IS* N1 .... 9 F1
Fifield Pth *FSTH* SE23 .... 157 D3
Fifth Av *MNPK* E12 .... 83 F1
 NKENS W10 .... 89 E3
Fifth Wy *WBLY* HA9 .... 50 C4
Fig Tree Cl *WLSDN* NW10 * 69 E5
Filey Av *STNW/STAM* N16 .... 60 A3
Fillebrook Rd *WAN* E11 .... 63 D3
Filmer Chambers *FUL/PGN* SW6 * 113 F4
Filmer Rd *FUL/PGN* SW6 .... 113 F4
Finborough Rd *WBPTN* SW10 .... 114 B2
Finch Av *WNWD* SE27 .... 155 D4
Finch La *BANK* EC3V 24 B5
Finchley Pl *STJWD* NW8 .... 4 A1
Finchley Rd *GLDGN* NW11 .... 54 A1
 HAMP NW3 .... 72 A1
 STJWD NW8 .... 73 D5
Finch Ms *PECK* SE15 * 119 F4
Finchs Ct *POP/IOD* E14 * 104 B1
Finden Rd *FSTGT* E7 .... 82 B2
Findhorn St *POP/IOD* E14 .... 92 C5
Findon Cl *WAND/EARL* SW18 .... 132 A4
Findon Rd *SHB* W12 .... 100 A3
Fingal St *GNWCH* SE10 .... 123 F1
Finland Rd *BROCKY* SE4 .... 139 E1
Finland St *BERM/RHTH* SE16 .... 103 E4
Finlay St *FUL/PGN* SW6 .... 113 D4
Finnis St *BETH* E2 .... 90 B2
Finsbury Av *LVPST* EC2M * 24 B3
Finsbury Circ *LVPST* EC2M 24 B3
Finsbury Est *CLKNW* EC1R 10 B4
Finsbury Market *SDTCH* EC2A 24 C1
Finsbury Park Av *FSBYPK* N4 .... 58 C1
Finsbury Park Rd *FSBYPK* N4 .... 58 B4
Finsbury Pavement *LVPST* EC2M 24 B2
Finsbury Sq *SDTCH* EC2A 24 B1
Finsbury St *STLK* EC1Y 24 A2
Finsen Rd *CMBW* SE5 .... 136 C2
Finstock Rd *NKENS* W10 .... 89 D5
Firbank Cl *CAN/RD* E16 .... 95 D4

Firbank Rd *PECK* SE15	120	B5
Fircroft Rd *TOOT* SW17	151	F3
Firecrest Dr *HAMP* NW3	54	B5
Firefly Gdns *EHAM* E6	95	E3
Fir Grove Rd *BRXN/ST* SW9 *	118	A3
Firhill Rd *CAT* SE6	158	A3
Firle Pl *WAND/EARL* SW18	132	C5
Firs Av *MORT/ESHN* SW14	128	C2
Firsby Rd *STNW/STAM* N16	59	F3
Firs Cl *FSTH* SE23	139	D5
Firside Gv *BFN/LL* DA15	163	F1
First Av *ACT* W3	99	F2
MNPK E12	83	E1
MORT/ESHN SW14	111	E5
NKENS W10	89	F3
PLSTW E13	94	A2
First Dr *WLSDN* NW10	68	C4
First St *CHEL* SW3	41	D4
First Wy *WBLY* HA9	68	B1
Firth Gdns *FUL/PGN* SW6	113	E4
Fir Tree Cl *STRHM/NOR* SW16	152	B5
Fir Trees Cl *STRHM/NOR* SW16	153	D3
Fishermans Dr *BERM/RHTH* SE16	103	D3
Fishers Cl *STRHM/NOR* SW16	153	D3
Fishers Ct *NWCR* SE14	121	D4
Fisher's La *CHSWK* W4	99	D5
Fisher St *CAN/RD* E16	94	A4
RSQ WC1B	21	E3
Fisherton St *STJWD* NW8	16	A1
Fishguard Wy *BARK/RD* E16	108	B2
Fishponds Rd *TOOT* SW17	151	E4
Fish Street Hl *MON* EC3R	36	B2
Fisons Rd *CAN/RD* E16	106	A2
Fitzalan St *LBTH* SE11	45	F4
Fitzgeorge Av *WKENS* W14	101	E5
Fitzgerald Av *MORT/ESHN* SW14	129	E1
Fitzgerald Rd *MORT/ESHN* SW14	129	D1
Fitzhardinge St *MBLAR* W1H	18	A4
Fitzhugh Gv *WAND/EARL* SW18	133	D4
Fitzjames Av *WKENS* W14	101	E5
Fitz-James Av *WKENS* W14	101	E5
Fitzjohn's Av *HAMP* NW3	73	D2
Fitzmaurice Pl *MYFR/PICC* W1J *	31	D3
Fitzneal St *SHB* W12	87	F5
Fitzroy Cl *HGT* N6	55	F3
Fitzroy Crs *CHSWK* W4 *	111	D3
Fitzroy Ms *FITZ* W1T	19	E1
Fitzroy Pk *HGT* N6	55	F4
Fitzroy Rd *CAMTN* NW1	74	A5
Fitzroy Sq *FITZ* W1T	19	E1
Fitzroy St *CAMTN* NW1	19	E1
FITZ W1T	19	E2
Fitzwarren Gdns *HGT* N6	56	C3
Fitzwilliam Ms *CAN/RD* E16	106	A1
Fitzwilliam Rd *CLAP* SW4	134	C1
Five Oak Ms *BMLY* BR1	160	A3
Fiveways Cnr *ELTH/MOT* SE9	162	B2
Fiveways Rd *BRXN/ST* SW9	118	A5
Fladbury Rd *SEVS/STOTM* N15	59	D1
Fladgate Rd *WAN* E11	63	E1
Flamborough St *POP/IOD* E14	91	E5
Flamborough Wk *POP/IOD* E14 *	91	E5
Flamsted Av *WBLY* HA9	68	A3
Flamsteed Rd *CHARL* SE7	125	E1
Flanchford Rd *SHB* W12	99	F4
Flanders Rd *CHSWK* W4	99	E5
EHAM E6	95	F1
Flanders Wy *HOM* E9	79	D3
Flank St *WCHPL* E1	102	A1
Flask Wk *HAMP* NW3	72	C1
Flavell Ms *GNWCH* SE10	123	E1
Flaxman Rd *CMBW* SE5	118	B5
Flaxman Ter *STPAN* WC1H	8	B4
Flaxton Rd *WOOL/PLUM* SE18	127	D4
Fleece Wk *HOLWY* N7 *	75	E3
Fleet Pl *FLST/FETLN* EC4A	22	C4
Fleet Rd *HAMP* NW3	73	E2
Fleet Sq *FSBYW* WC1X	9	G4
Fleet St *EMB* EC4Y	22	A5
Fleet Street Hl *WCHPL* E1 *	90	A3
Fleet Ter *CAT* SE6 *	140	C5
Fleetwood Cl *CAN/RD* E16	95	D4
Fleetwood Rd *WLSDN* NW10	70	A2
Fleetwood St *STNW/STAM* N16	59	E4
Fleming Cl *MV/WKIL* W9	14	A1
WBPTN SW10 *	114	C2
Fleming St *WALW* SE17	118	B2
Flempton Rd *LEY* E10	61	D3
Fletcher Cl *EHAM* E6	108	B1
Fletcher La *LEY* E10	62	C2
Fletcher Rd *CHSWK* W4	98	C4
Fletcher St *WCHPL* E1	102	A1
Fletching Rd *CHARL* SE7	125	D2
CLPT E5	60	C5
Fleur De Lis St *WCHPL* E1	25	D1
Fleur Gates *WIM/MER* SW19	131	D5
Flimwell Cl *BMLY* BR1	159	E5
Flint Cl *SRTFD* E15	81	E3
Flintmill Crs *BKHTH/KID* SE3	125	E5
ELTH/MOT SE9	143	E1
Flinton St *WALW* SE17	119	E1
Flint St *WALW* SE17	48	B5
Flitcroft St *LSO/SEVD* WC2H	20	B5
Flock Mill Pl *WAND/EARL* SW18	150	B1
Flockton St *BERM/RHTH* SE16	102	A3
Flodden Rd *CMBW* SE5	118	C4
Flood St *CHEL* SW3	115	E1
Flood Wk *CHEL* SW3	115	E2
Flora Cl *POP/IOD* E14	92	B5
Flora Gdns *HMSMTH* W6	100	B5
Floral Pl *IS* N1	77	D2
Floral St *COVGDN* WC2E	33	D1
Florence Elson Cl *MNPK* E12	84	A1
Florence Gdns *CHSWK* W4	110	C2
Florence Rd *CHSWK* W4	99	D4
EHAM E6	82	C5
FSBYPK N4	57	F2
NWCR SE14	121	F4
PLSTW E13	94	A1
Florence St *CAN/RD* E16	93	F3
IS N1	76	B4
Florence Ter *NWCR* SE14	121	F4
Florence Vis *HGT* N6 *	56	B2
Florence Wy *BAL* SW12	151	F1
Florfield Rd *HACK* E8	78	B3
Florian Rd *PUT/ROE* SW15	131	E2
Florida Rd *BETH* E2	90	A2
Floris Pl *CLAP* SW4	134	C1
Floss St *PUT/ROE* SW15	112	C5
Flower & Dean Wk *WCHPL* E1	25	F3
Flower Ms *GLDGN* NW11	53	E1
Flowerpot Cl *SEVS/STOTM* N15	59	F1
Flowers Cl *CRICK* NW2	51	F5
Flowers Ms *ARCH* N19	56	C4
Floyd Rd *CHARL* SE7	124	C1
Fludyer St *LEW* SE13	141	E2
Foley St *GTPST* W1W	19	E3
Folgate St *WCHPL* E1	25	D1
Foliot St *SHB* W12	87	F5
Folkestone Rd *EHAM* E6	96	A1
Follett St *POP/IOD* E14	92	C5
Folly Wall *POP/IOD* E14	104	C3
Fontarabia Rd *BTSEA* SW11	134	A2
Fontenoy Rd *BAL* SW12	152	B2
Fonthill Ms *FSBYPK* N4	57	F4
Fonthill Rd *FSBYPK* N4	57	F4
Fontley Wy *PUT/ROE* SW15	130	A5
The Footpath *PUT/ROE* SW15	130	A5
Footscray Rd *ELTH/MOT* SE9	162	B1
Forbes Cl *CRICK* NW2	52	A5
Forbes St *WCHPL* E1	90	A5
Forburg Rd *STNW/STAM* N16	60	A3
Fordel Rd *CAT* SE6	159	D1
Fordham St *WCHPL* E1	90	A5
Fordingley Rd *MV/WKIL* W9	89	F2
Fordmill Rd *CAT* SE6	158	A2
Ford Rd *BOW* E3	91	E1
Fords Park Rd *CAN/RD* E16	94	A5
Ford Sq *WCHPL* E1	90	B4
Ford St *BOW* E3	79	E5
CAN/RD E16	93	F5
Fordwych Rd *CRICK* NW2	71	E2
Fordyce Rd *LEW* SE13	141	D4
Foreland St *WOOL/PLUM* SE18	109	D5
Foreshore *DEPT* SE8	121	F1
Forest Cl *KIL/WHAMP* NW6	71	E4
Forest Dr *MNPK* E12	65	D5
Forest Dr East *WAN* E11	63	D2
Forest Dr West *WAN* E11	62	C2
Forester Rd *PECK* SE15	138	B2
Forest Gld *WAN* E11	63	E1
Forest Gv *HACK* E8	77	F3
Forest Hill Rd *EDUL* SE22	138	C4
Forestholme Cl *FSTH* SE23	156	C2
SYD SE26 *	156	C2
Forest La *FSTGT* E7	82	A2
Forest St *BARB* EC2Y	24	A3
Forest Rd *FSTGT* E7	82	A1
HACK E8	77	F3
RCH/KEW TW9	110	A3
Forest Side *FSTGT* E7	82	B1
Forest St *FSTGT* E7	82	A2
Forest Vw *WAN* E11	63	F2

Forest View Rd *MNPK* E12	83 E1
Forest Wy *BFN/LL* DA15	145 D5
Forfar Rd *BTSEA* SW11	116 A4
Forge PI *CAMTN* NW1	74 A3
Formosa St *MV/WKIL* W9	15 D1
Formunt CI *CAN/RD* E16	93 F4
Forres Gdns *GLDGN* NW11	54 A1
Forrester Pth *SYD* SE26	156 C4
Forset St *MBLAR* W1H	17 D4
Forster Rd *BRXS/STRHM* SW2	135 E5
WALTH E17	61 E1
Forston St *IS* N1	11 E1
Forsyth Gdns *WALW* SE17	118 B2
Forsythia CI *IL* IG1	84 B2
Fortess Gv *KTTN* NW5	74 C1
Fortess Rd *KTTN* NW5	74 C2
Fortess Wk *KTTN* NW5	74 B2
Forthbridge Rd *BTSEA* SW11	134 A2
Fortis CI *CAN/RD* E16	94 C5
Fortnam Rd *ARCH* N19	57 D4
Fort Rd *STHWK* SE1	49 F5
Fortrose CI *POP/IOD* E14	93 D5
Fortrose Gdns *BRXS/STRHM* SW2	153 E1
Fort St *CAN/RD* E16	106 B2
WCHPL E1	19 F4
Fortuna CI *HOLWY* N7 *	75 F3
Fortunegate Rd *WLSDN* NW10	69 E5
Fortune Green Rd *KIL/WHAMP* NW6	72 A2
Fortune PI *STHWK* SE1	120 A1
Fortune St *STLK* EC1Y	23 F1
Fortune Wy *WLSDN* NW10	88 C2
Forty Acre La *CAN/RD* E16	94 A4
Forty La *WBLY* HA9	50 B4
Forum CI *BOW* E3	80 A5
Forum Magnum Sq *STHWK* SE1	33 E5
Fosbury Ms *BAY/PAD* W2	27 D2
Foscote Ms *MV/WKIL* W9	14 B1
Foscote Rd *HDN* NW4	52 B1
Foskett Rd *FUL/PGN* SW6	113 F5
Fossdene Rd *CHARL* SE7	124 B5
Fossil Rd *LEW* SE13	140 A1
Foss Rd *TOOT* SW17	151 D4
Foster La *CITYW* EC2V	23 E4
Foster Rd *ACT* W3	99 E1
CHSWK W4	111 D1
PLSTW E13	94 A3
Fosters CI *CHST* BR7	161 F5
Fothergill CI *PLSTW* E13	82 A5
Fouberts PI *SOHO/CST* W1F *	19 E5
Foubert's PI *SOHO/CST* W1F	19 E5
Foulden Rd *STNW/STAM* N16	77 F1
Foulden Ter *STNW/STAM* N16	77 F1
Foulis Ter *SKENS* SW7	40 A5
Foulser Rd *TOOT* SW17	151 F3
Foundation PI *ELTH/MOT* SE9 *	144 A3
Founder CI *EHAM* E6	96 B3
Foundry CI *BERM/RHTH* SE16	103 E2
Foundry Ms *CAMTN* NW1	7 F5
Foundry PI *WAND/EARL* SW18 *	132 B5
Fountain Dr *NRWD* SE19	155 F4
Fountain Green Sq *BERM/RHTH* SE16	102 A3
Fountain Ms *HAMP* NW3	73 F3
Fountain Rd *BRXN/ST* SW9	118 A4
TOOT SW17	151 D5
Fountayne Rd *STNW/STAM* N16	60 A4
Fount St *VX/NE* SW8	117 D5
Four Seasons CI *BOW* E3	92 A1
Fournier St *WCHPL* E1	25 E2
Fourth Av *MNPK* E12	83 F1
NKENS W10	89 E3
Fourth Wy *WBLY* HA9	68 B1
Fowey CI *WAP* E1W	102 B2
Fowler CI *BTSEA* SW11	133 D1
Fowler Rd *FSTGT* E7	82 A1
IS N1	76 B5
Fownes St *BTSEA* SW11	133 E1
Foxberry Rd *BROCKY* SE4	139 E2
Foxborough Gdns *BROCKY* SE4	140 A4
Foxbourne Rd *TOOT* SW17	152 A2
Fox CI *CAN/RD* E16	94 A4
WCHPL E1	90 C3
Foxcroft Rd *WOOL/PLUM* SE18	126 B4
Foxes DI *BKHTH/KID* SE3	142 A1
Foxglove Pth *THMD* SE28	109 E5
Foxglove St *ACT* W3	99 F1
Foxham Rd *ARCH* N19	57 D5
Foxhole Rd *ELTH/MOT* SE9	143 E3
Fox Hollow CI *WOOL/PLUM* SE18	127 E1
Foxholt Gdns *WLSDN* NW10	68 C5
Fox & Knot St *FARR* EC1M *	23 D2
Foxley CI *HACK* E8	78 A2
Foxley Rd *CMBW* SE5	118 A3

Foxley Sq *BRXN/ST* SW9 *	118 B3
Foxmore St *BTSEA* SW11	115 F4
Fox Rd *CAN/RD* E16	93 F4
Foxwell St *BROCKY* SE4	139 E1
Foxwood Rd *BKHTH/KID* SE3	141 F2
Foyle Rd *BKHTH/KID* SE3	123 F2
Framfield Rd *HBRY* N5	76 B2
Framlingham Crs *ELTH/MOT* SE9	161 E4
Frampton Park Rd *HOM* E9	78 C3
Frampton St *STJWD* NW8	16 B1
Francemary Rd *LEW* SE13	140 A3
Frances St *WOOL/PLUM* SE18	107 F5
Franche Court Rd *TOOT* SW17	150 C3
Francis Av *IL* IG1	67 D4
Francis Barber CI	
STRHM/NOR SW16 *	153 F4
Francis Bentley Ms *CLAP* SW4	134 C1
Franciscan Rd *TOOT* SW17	152 A4
Francis Chichester Wy *BTSEA* SW11 *	116 A4
Francis Ms *LEE/GVPK* SE12 *	141 F4
Francis Rd *LEY* E10	62 C4
Francis St *SRTFD* E15	81 E2
WEST SW1P	43 F4
Francis Ter *ARCH* N19	56 C5
Francis Wk *IS* N1	75 F5
Franconia Rd *CLAP* SW4	134 C3
Frank Burton CI *CHARL* SE7	124 B1
Frank Dixon CI *DUL* SE21	137 E1
Frank Dixon Wy *DUL* SE21	155 E1
Frankfurt Rd *HNHL* SE24	136 C5
Frankham St *DEPT* SE8	122 A3
Frankland CI *BERM/RHTH* SE16	102 B4
Frankland Rd *SKENS* SW7	40 A3
Franklin CI *LEW* SE13	122 B4
WNWD SE27	154 B3
Franklin PI *GNWCH* SE10	122 B4
Franklin Sq *WKENS* W14	113 F1
Franklins Rw *CHEL* SW3	115 E1
Franklin's Rw *CHEL* SW3	115 F1
Franklin St *BOW* E3	92 B2
SEVS/STOTM N15	59 E1
Franklyn Rd *WLSDN* NW10	69 F4
Fransfield Gv *SYD* SE26	156 B3
Fraser CI *CHSWK* W4	111 E1
Frazier St *STHWK* SE1	46 A1
Frean St *BERM/RHTH* SE16	102 A4
Freda Corbett CI *PECK* SE15	120 A3
Frederica St *BAY/PAD* W2	29 D1
Frederick Crs *BRXN/ST* SW9	118 B3
Frederick PI *WOOL/PLUM* SE18	126 B1
Frederick Rd *WALW* SE17	118 B2
Frederick's PI *LOTH* EC2R *	24 A5
Frederick Sq *BERM/RHTH* SE16 *	103 E1
Frederick's Rw *FSBYE* EC1V	10 C3
Frederick St *FSBYW* WC1X	9 F4
Frederick Ter *HACK* E8 *	77 F4
Frederic Ms *KTBR* SW1X *	42 A1
Freedom St *BTSEA* SW11	115 F5
Freegrove Rd *HOLWY* N7	75 E2
Freeling St *IS* N1	75 F4
Freemantle St *WALW* SE17	119 E1
Freemasons Rd *CAN/RD* E16	94 B4
Freke Rd *BTSEA* SW11	134 A1
Fremont St *HOM* E9	78 B5
French PI *SDTCH* EC2A	13 D4
Frendsbury Rd *BROCKY* SE4	139 E2
Frensham Dr *PUT/ROE* SW15	148 A2
Frensham Rd *ELTH/MOT* SE9	163 D2
Frensham St *PECK* SE15	120 A2
Frere St *BTSEA* SW11	115 E5
Freshfield Av *HACK* E8	77 F4
Freshfield CI *LEW* SE13	141 D2
Freshford St *TOOT* SW17	150 C3
Fresh Wharf Rd *BARK* IG11	84 B5
Freston Rd *NKENS* W10	101 D1
Frewin Rd *WAND/EARL* SW18	151 D1
Friar Ms *WNWD* SE27	154 B3
Friars Av *PUT/ROE* SW15	147 F5
Friars CI *IL* IG1	67 D3
STHWK SE1 *	35 D3
Friars Gdns *ACT* W3	87 D3
Friars Md *POP/IOD* E14	104 C4
Friars Ms *ELTH/MOT* SE9	144 A3
Friars Place La *ACT* W3	99 D1
Friars Rd *EHAM* E6	83 D5
Friars Wy *ACT* W3	87 D3
Friary Est *PECK* SE15 *	120 A3
Friary Park Ct *ACT* W3 *	86 C5
Friary Rd *ACT* W3	86 C5
PECK SE15	120 A3
Friday St *STP* EC4M	35 E1

Frideswide Pl *KTTN* NW5 .... 74 C2
Friendly Pl *LEW* SE13 .... 122 B4
Friendly St *DEPT* SE8 .... 122 A4
Friendly Street Ms
DEPT SE8 .... 122 A5
Friendship Wy *SRTFD* E15 * 80 C5
Friend St *FSBYE* EC1V 10 C5
Frigate Ms *DEPT* SE8 .... 122 A2
Frimley Cl *WIM/MER* SW19 .... 149 E2
Frimley Rd *GDMY/SEVK* IG3 .... 67 E5
Frimley Wy *WCHPL* E1 * 91 D3
Frinton Ms *CNTH/NBYPK* IG2 .... 66 A1
Frinton Rd *EHAM* E6 .... 95 D2
SEVS/STOTM N15 .... 59 E1
Friston St *FUL/PGN* SW6 .... 114 B5
Frith Rd *WAN* E11 .... 80 C1
Frith St *SOHO/SHAV* W1D 20 A5
Frithville Gdns *SHB* W12 .... 100 C2
Frobisher Crs *BARB* EC2Y * 23 F2
Frobisher Gdns *LEY* E10 * 62 B1
Frobisher Rd *EHAM* E6 .... 95 F5
Frith St *FSTT* 37 F2
Frogley Rd *EDUL* SE22 .... 137 D3
Frogmore *WAND/EARL* SW18 .... 132 A3
Frogmore Est *HBRY* N5 * 76 C1
Frognal *HAMP* NW3 .... 72 C2
Frognal Cl *HAMP* NW3 .... 72 C2
Frognal Gdns *HAMP* NW3 .... 72 C1
Frognal La *HAMP* NW3 .... 72 B2
Frognal Man *HAMP* NW3 * 72 C1
Frognal Pde *HAMP* NW3 .... 72 C3
Frognal Ri *HAMP* NW3 .... 72 C1
Frognal Wy *HAMP* NW3 .... 72 C1
Froissart Rd *ELTH/MOT* SE9 .... 143 E5
Frome St *IS* N1 .... 11 E1
Fromows Cnr *CHSWK* W4 * 110 C1
Frostic Wk *WCHPL* E1 .... 25 F3
Froude St *VX/NE* SW8 .... 116 B5
Fryday Grove Ms *BAL* SW12 .... 134 C5
Fryent Cl *KTN/HRWW/WS* HA3 .... 50 A1
Fryent Crs *CDALE/KGS* NW9 .... 51 E1
Fryent Flds *CDALE/KGS* NW9 .... 51 E1
Fryent Gv *CDALE/KGS* NW9 .... 51 E1
Fryent Wy *CDALE/KGS* NW9 .... 50 A1
Frying Pan Aly *WCHPL* E1 .... 25 D3
Fry Rd *EHAM* E6 .... 83 D4
WLSDN NW10 .... 69 F5
Fulbourne St *WCHPL* E1 .... 90 B4
Fulbrook Ms *ARCH* N19 .... 74 C1
Fulbrook Rd *ARCH* N19 .... 74 C1
Fulford St *BERM/RHTH* SE16 .... 102 B3
Fulham Broadway
FUL/PGN SW6 .... 114 A3
Fulham Est *FUL/PGN* SW6 .... 114 A2
Fulham High St *FUL/PGN* SW6 .... 113 E5
Fulham Palace Rd
FUL/PGN SW6 .... 113 D3
Fulham Park Gdns
FUL/PGN SW6 .... 113 F5
Fulham Park Rd *FUL/PGN* SW6 .... 113 E5
Fulham Rd *FUL/PGN* SW6 .... 113 F5
WBPTN SW10 .... 115 D1
Fuller Cl *BETH* E2 * 90 A3
Fullerton Rd
WAND/EARL SW18 .... 132 C3
Fullwood Pl *GINN* WC1R 21 F3
Fullwood's Ms *IS* N1 .... 12 B3
Fulmead St *FUL/PGN* SW6 .... 114 B4
Fulmer Rd *CAN/RD* E16 .... 95 D4
Fulthorp Rd *BKHTH/KID* SE3 .... 123 F5
Fulton Rd *WBLY* HA9 .... 50 A5
Fulwood Wk
WIM/MER SW19 .... 149 E1
Furber Rd *HMSMTH* W6 .... 100 B4
Furley Rd *PECK* SE15 .... 120 A1
Furlong Rd *HOLWY* N7 .... 76 A3
Furmage St
WAND/EARL SW18 .... 132 B5
Furneaux Av *WNWD* SE27 .... 154 B5
Furness Rd *FUL/PGN* SW6 .... 114 B5
WLSDN NW10 .... 88 A1
Furnival St *FLST/FETLN* EC4A 22 A4
Furrow La *HOM* E9 .... 78 C2
Further Green Rd *LEW* SE13 .... 141 E5
Furzedown Dr *TOOT* SW17 .... 152 B5
Furzedown Rd *TOOT* SW17 .... 152 B5
Furzefield Rd *BKHTH/KID* SE3 .... 124 B2
Furze St *BOW* E3 .... 92 A4
Fye Foot La *BLKFR* EC4V * 35 F1
Fyfield Rd *BRXN/ST* SW9 .... 136 A1
Fynes St *WEST* SW1P 44 A4

G

Gable Ct *SYD* SE26 .... 156 B4
Gables Cl *CMBW* SE5 .... 119 E4
LEE/GVPK SE12 .... 160 A1
Gabriel St *FSTH* SE23 .... 139 D5
Gad Cl *PLSTW* E13 .... 94 B2
Gadsbury Cl *CDALE/KGS* NW9 .... 51 F1
Gadwall Cl *CAN/RD* E16 .... 94 B5
Gage Rd *CAN/RD* E16 .... 93 E4
Gage St *BMSBY* WC1N 21 D2
Gainford St *IS* N1 .... 76 A5
Gainsborough Av *MNPK* E12 .... 84 A2
Gainsborough Ct *SHB* W12 .... 100 C3
Gainsborough Gdns
GLDGN NW11 .... 53 F2
HAMP NW3 .... 55 D5
Gainsborough Ms *DUL* SE21 .... 154 C1
SYD SE26 .... 156 B3
Gainsborough Rd *CHSWK* W4 .... 99 F5
SRTFD E15 .... 93 E2
WAN E11 .... 63 E2
Gainsborough St *HOM* E9 .... 79 F3
Gainsford St *STHWK* SE1 .... 37 E4
Gairloch Rd *CMBW* SE5 .... 119 E5
Gaisford St *KTTN* NW5 .... 74 C3
Gaitskell Rd *ELTH/MOT* SE9 .... 162 C1
Gaitskell Wy *STHWK* SE1 * 35 E5
Galahad Rd *BMLY* BR1 .... 160 A3
Galata Rd *BARN* SW13 .... 112 A3
Galatea Sq *PECK* SE15 * 138 B1
Galbraith St *POP/IOD* E14 .... 104 C4
Galena Rd *HMSMTH* W6 .... 100 B5
Galesbury Rd *WAND/EARL* SW18 .... 132 C4
Gales Gdns *BETH* E2 .... 90 B2
Gale St *BOW* E3 .... 92 A4
Galgate Cl *WIM/MER* SW19 .... 149 D1
Galleon Cl *BERM/RHTH* SE16 .... 102 C3
The Galleries *IS* N1 * 11 D1
Gallery Rd *DUL* SE21 .... 155 D1
Galleywall Rd *BERM/RHTH* SE16 .... 102 B5
Gallia Rd *HBRY* N5 .... 76 B2
Gallions Rd *CAN/RD* E16 .... 108 B1
CHARL SE7 .... 106 B5
Gallions View Rd *THMD* SE28 .... 109 E3
Gallon Cl *CHARL* SE7 .... 106 C5
Gallosson Rd *WOOL/PLUM* SE18 .... 109 E3
Galloway Rd *SHB* W12 .... 100 A2
Gallus Sq *BKHTH/KID* SE3 .... 142 B1
Galsworthy Av *POP/IOD* E14 .... 91 E4
Galsworthy Crs *BKHTH/KID* SE3 .... 124 C4
Galsworthy Rd *CRICK* NW2 .... 71 E1
Galton St *NKENS* W10 .... 89 E3
Galveston Rd *PUT/ROE* SW15 .... 131 F3
Galway Cl *BERM/RHTH* SE16 * 120 B1
Galway St *FSBYE* EC1V 11 F4
Gambetta St *VX/NE* SW8 .... 116 B5
Gambia St *STHWK* SE1 .... 35 D4
Gamble Rd *TOOT* SW17 .... 151 E4
Gamlen Rd *PUT/ROE* SW15 .... 131 D2
Gamuel Cl *WALTH* E17 .... 62 A1
Gandhi Cl *WALTH* E17 .... 62 A1
Gandolfi St *CMBW* SE5 .... 119 E2
PECK SE15 * 119 E2
Ganton St *REGST* W1B 31 E1
Gap Rd *WIM/MER* SW19 .... 150 A5
Garage Rd *ACT* W3 .... 86 A5
Garbutt Pl *MHST* W1U * 18 B2
Garden Cl *LEE/GVPK* SE12 .... 160 B3
PUT/ROE SW15 .... 130 B5
Garden Ct *CHSWK* W4 .... 98 C4
EMB EC4Y * 34 A1
Garden Flats *HMSMTH* W6 * 113 D2
Garden La *BRXS/STRHM* SW2 .... 153 F1
Garden Pl *HACK* E8 .... 77 F5
Garden Rw *RCH/KEW* TW9 .... 128 C3
STJWD NW8 .... 3 F3
Garden St *WCHPL* E1 .... 91 D4
Garden Studios *BAY/PAD* W2 * 15 E3
Garden Ter *PIM* SW1V * 117 D1
Garden Wk *SDTCH* EC2A 12 C5
Garden Wy *WLSDN* NW10 .... 68 C3
Gardiner House *CHARL* SE7 * 125 E3
Gardner Cl *WAN* E11 .... 64 B1
Gardner Rd *PLSTW* E13 .... 94 B3

Gardners La *BLKFR* EC4V **35** E1
Gardnor Rd *HAMP* NW3 ..... **73** D1
Gard St *FSBYE* EC1V **11** D3
Gareth Gv *BMLY* BR1 ..... **160** A4
Garfield Ms *BTSEA* SW11 ..... **134** B1
Garfield Rd *BTSEA* SW11 ..... **134** A1
PLSTW E13 ..... **93** F3
Garford St *POP/IOD* E14 ..... **104** A1
Garibaldi St *WOOL/PLUM* SE18 ..... **109** E5
Garland Rd *WOOL/PLUM* SE18 ..... **127** D3
Garlick Hl *BLKFR* EC4V **35** F1
Garlies Rd *FSTH* SE23 ..... **157** E5
Garlinge Rd *CRICK* NW2 ..... **71** F3
Garnault Ms *CLKNW* EC1R **10** B4
Garnault Pl *CLKNW* EC1R **10** B4
Garner St *BETH* E2 ..... **90** A1
Garnet Rd *WLSDN* NW10 ..... **69** E5
Garnet St *WAP* E1W **102** C4
Garnett Cl *ELTH/MOT* SE9 ..... **143** F1
Garnett Rd *HAMP* NW3 ..... **73** F2
Garnham St *STNW/STAM* N16 ..... **59** F4
Garnies Cl *PECK* SE15 ..... **119** F3
Garrad's Rd *STRHM/NOR* SW16 ..... **153** D3
Garrard Cl *CHST* BR7 ..... **162** B5
Garrard Wk *WLSDN* NW10 * **69** E5
Garratt La *TOOT* SW17 ..... **150** C3
Garratt Ter *TOOT* SW17 ..... **151** E4
Garrett Cl *ACT* W3 ..... **87** D4
Garrett St *STLK* EC1Y **11** E5
Garrick Av *GLDGN* NW11 ..... **53** E1
Garrick Dr *WAND/EARL* SW18 ..... **132** C2
Garrick Dr *THMD* SE28 ..... **109** D4
Garrick Rd *CDALE/KGS* NW9 ..... **51** F1
RCH/KEW TW9 ..... **110** A5
Garrick St *COVGDN* WC2E **32** C1
Garrick Yd *CHCR* WC2N **32** C1
Garrison Cl *WOOL/PLUM* SE18 ..... **126** A3
Garrison Rd *BOW* E3 ..... **80** A5
Garsdale Ter *WKENS* W14 * **113** F1
Garside Cl *THMD* SE28 ..... **109** D4
Garsington Ms *BROCKY* SE4 ..... **139** F1
Garter Wy *BERM/RHTH* SE16 ..... **103** D3
Garthorne Rd *FSTH* SE23 ..... **139** D5
Garth Rd *CHSWK* W4 ..... **111** D3
CRICK NW2 ..... **53** F4
Gartmoor Gdns *WIM/MER* SW19 ..... **149** F1
Gartmore Rd *GDMY/SEVK* IG3 ..... **67** F3
Garton Pl *WAND/EARL* SW18 ..... **132** C4
Gartons Wy *BTSEA* SW11 ..... **132** C1
Garvary Rd *CAN/RD* E16 ..... **94** B5
Garway Rd *BAY/PAD* W2 ..... **14** C5
Gascoigne Pl *BETH* E2 ..... **13** E3
Gascoigne Rd *BARK* IG11 ..... **84** C5
Gascony Av *KIL/WHAMP* NW6 ..... **72** A4
Gascoyne Rd *HOM* E9 ..... **79** D4
Gaselee St *POP/IOD* E14 ..... **104** C1
Gasholder Pl *LBTH* SE11 ..... **117** F1
Gaskarth Rd *BAL* SW12 ..... **134** B4
Gaskell Rd *HGT* N6 ..... **55** F1
Gaskell St *CLAP* SW4 ..... **117** E5
Gaskin St *IS* N1 ..... **76** B5
Gaspar Cl *ECT* SW5 * **39** D4
Gaspar Ms *ECT* SW5 ..... **39** D4
Gassiot Rd *TOOT* SW17 ..... **151** F4
Gastein Rd *HMSMTH* W6 ..... **113** D2
Gataker St *BERM/RHTH* SE16 ..... **102** B4
Gatcombe Rd *ARCH* N19 ..... **57** D5
Gateforth St *STJWD* NW8 ..... **16** C1
Gatehouse Sq *STHWK* SE1 ..... **35** F3
Gateley Rd *BRXN/ST* SW9 ..... **135** F1
Gate Ms *SKENS* SW7 ..... **41** D1
Gates Ct *WALW* SE17 * **118** C5
Gateside Rd *TOOT* SW17 ..... **151** E3
Gate St *LINN* WC2A **21** E4
Gateway *WALW* SE17 * **118** C2
Gateway Ar *IS* N1 * **10** C1
Gateway Gdns *EHAM* E6 ..... **95** F2
Gateway Ms *HACK* E8 * **77** F2
Gathorne Rd *BETH* E2 ..... **91** D1
Gatliff Cl *BGVA* SW1W * **116** A1
Gatliff Rd *BGVA* SW1W **116** A1
Gatonby St *PECK* SE15 ..... **119** F4
Gatton Rd *TOOT* SW17 ..... **151** E4
Gatwick Rd *WAND/EARL* SW18 ..... **131** F5
Gauden Cl *CLAP* SW4 ..... **135** D1
Gauden Rd *CLAP* SW4 ..... **135** D1
Gaumont Ter *SHB* W12 * **100** C3
Gaunt St *STHWK* SE1 ..... **47** D2
Gautrey Rd *PECK* SE15 ..... **120** C5
Gavel St *WALW* SE17 * **48** B4
Gaverick St *POP/IOD* E14 ..... **104** A5
Gavestone Crs *LEE/GVPK* SE12 ..... **142** B5

Gavestone Rd *LEE/GVPK* SE12 ..... **142** B5
Gawber St *BETH* E2 ..... **90** C2
Gawsworth Cl *SRTFD* E15 ..... **81** F2
Gay Cl *CRICK* NW2 ..... **70** B2
Gayfere St *WEST* SW1P **44** C5
Gayford Rd *SHB* W12 ..... **99** F3
Gayhurst Rd *HACK* E8 ..... **78** A4
Gaynesford Rd *FSTH* SE23 ..... **157** D2
Gay Rd *SRTFD* E15 ..... **93** D1
Gay St *PUT/ROE* SW15 ..... **131** D1
Gayton Crs *HAMP* NW3 ..... **73** D1
Gayton Rd *HAMP* NW3 ..... **73** D1
Gayville Rd *BTSEA* SW11 ..... **133** F4
Gaywood Cl *BRXS/STRHM* SW2 ..... **153** F1
Gaywood St *STHWK* SE1 ..... **47** D3
Gaza St *WALW* SE17 ..... **118** B3
Gearing Cl *TOOT* SW17 ..... **152** A4
Geary Rd *WLSDN* NW10 ..... **70** A2
Geary St *HOLWY* N7 ..... **75** F2
Gedling Pl *STHWK* SE1 ..... **49** E2
Geere Rd *SRTFD* E15 ..... **81** F5
Gees Ct *MHST* W1U **18** B5
Gee St *FSBYE* EC1V **11** E5
Geffrye Est *IS* N1 ..... **13** D2
Geffrye St *BETH* E2 ..... **13** E1
Geldart Rd *PECK* SE15 ..... **120** B3
Geldeston Rd *CLPT* E5 ..... **60** A4
Gellatly Rd *NWCR* SE14 ..... **120** C5
General Gordon Pl *WOOL/PLUM* SE18.. **108** B4
General Wolfe Rd *GNWCH* SE10 ..... **123** D4
Genesta Rd *WOOL/PLUM* SE18 ..... **126** B2
Geneva Dr *BRXN/ST* SW9 ..... **136** A2
Genoa Av *PUT/ROE* SW15 ..... **130** C3
Geoffrey Cl *CMBW* SE5 ..... **118** C5
Geoffrey Gdns *EHAM* E6 ..... **95** E1
Geoffrey Rd *BROCKY* SE4 ..... **139** F1
George Beard Rd *DEPT* SE8 ..... **103** F5
George Downing Est
STNW/STAM N16 ..... **59** F4
George La *LEW* SE13 ..... **140** C4
George Lowe Ct *BAY/PAD* W2 ..... **14** C2
George Mathers Rd *LBTH* SE11 * **46** C4
George Ms *BRXN/ST* SW9 ..... **118** A5
CAMTN NW1 ..... **7** F3
George Rw *BERM/RHTH* SE16 ..... **102** A3
Georges Rd *HOLWY* N7 ..... **75** F3
George's Rd *HOLWY* N7 ..... **75** F2
George St *BARK* IG11 ..... **84** C4
CAN/RD E16 ..... **93** F5
MBLAR W1H **17** E4
Georgetown Cl *NRWD* SE19 ..... **155** E5
Georgette Pl *GNWCH* SE10 ..... **122** C5
George Wyver Cl *WIM/MER* SW19 ..... **131** E5
George Yd *BANK* EC3V **24** B5
MYFR/PKLN W1K **30** B1
Georgiana St *CAMTN* NW1 ..... **74** C5
Georgian Ct *WBLY* HA9 ..... **68** A3
Georgina Gdns *BETH* E2 * **13** F3
Geraint Rd *BMLY* BR1 ..... **160** A3
Geraldine Rd *CHSWK* W4 ..... **110** A2
WAND/EARL SW18 ..... **132** C3
Geraldine St *LBTH* SE11 ..... **46** C3
Gerald Rd *BGVA* SW1W **42** B4
CAN/RD E16 ..... **93** F5
Gerards Rd *BARN* SW13 ..... **111** F4
Gerards Cl *BERM/RHTH* SE16 ..... **120** C2
Gerda Rd *ELTH/MOT* SE9 ..... **162** B2
Germander Wy *SRTFD* E15 ..... **93** E2
Gernon Rd *BOW* E3 ..... **91** E1
Geron Wy *CRICK* NW2 ..... **52** C4
Gerrard Pl *SOHO/SHAV* W1D * **32** B1
Gerrard Rd *IS* N1 ..... **10** C1
Gerrard St *SOHO/SHAV* W1D **32** A1
Gerridge St *STHWK* SE1 ..... **46** B1
Gertrude St *WBPTN* SW10 ..... **114** C2
Gervase St *WBLY* HA9 ..... **50** C5
Gervase St *PECK* SE15 ..... **120** B5
Ghent St *CAT* SE6 ..... **158** A2
Ghent Wy *HACK* E8 ..... **77** F3
Giant Arches Rd *HNHL* SE24 ..... **136** C5
Gibbins Rd *SRTFD* E15 ..... **80** C4
Gibbon Rd *ACT* W3 ..... **99** E1
PECK SE15 ..... **120** C5
Gibbons Rd *WLSDN* NW10 ..... **69** D3
Gibbon Wk *PUT/ROE* SW15 * **130** B2
Gibbs Cl *NRWD* SE19 ..... **155** D5
Gibbs Gn *WKENS* W14 ..... **113** F1
Gibbs Gn *WKENS* W14 ..... **113** F1
Gibbs Sq *NRWD* SE19 * **155** D5
Gibraltar Wk *BETH* E2 ..... **13** F4
Gibson Cl *WCHPL* E1 ..... **90** C3
Gibson Gdns *STNW/STAM* N16 * **59** F4

Gibson Rd *LBTH* SE11 .... 45 F5
Gibson Sq *IS* N1 .... 76 A3
Gibson St *GNWCH* SE10 .... 123 E1
Gideon Rd *BTSEA* SW11 .... 134 A1
Giesbach Rd *ARCH* N19 .... 56 C4
Giffin St *DEPT* SE8 .... 122 A3
Gifford Rd *WLSDN* NW10 .... 69 E4
Gifford St *IS* N1 .... 75 E4
Gift La *SRTFD* E15 .... 81 E5
Gilbert Cl *WOOL/PLUM* SE18 .... 125 F4
Gilbert Pl *NOXST/BSQ* WC1A 20 C3
Gilbert Rd *LBTH* SE11 .... 46 B4
Gilbert St *MYFR/PKLN* W1K 18 B5
SRTFD E15 .... 81 E1
Gilbeys Yd *CAMTN* NW1 .... 151 E4
Gilbourne Rd *WOOL/PLUM* SE18 .... 127 F2
Gilda Crs *STNW/STAM* N16 .... 60 A3
Gildea Cl *GTPST* W1W 19 D3
Gilden Crs *KTTN* NW5 .... 74 A2
Gildersome St *WOOL/PLUM* SE18 .... 126 A3
Giles Coppice *NRWD* SE19 .... 155 F4
Gilkes Crs *DUL* SE21 .... 137 E4
Gilkes Pl *DUL* SE21 .... 137 E4
Gill Av *CAN/RD* E16 .... 94 A5
Gillender St *BOW* E3 .... 92 C3
Gillespie Rd *HBRY* N5 .... 58 A5
Gillett Av *EHAM* E6 .... 95 E4
Gillett Pl *HACK* E8 .... 77 F2
Gillett St *STNW/STAM* N16 .... 77 F2
Gillian St *LEW* SE13 .... 140 B3
Gillies St *KTTN* NW5 .... 74 A2
Gillingham Rd *CRICK* NW2 .... 53 E5
Gillingham Rw *PIM* SW1V 43 E4
Gillingham St *PIM* SW1V 43 D5
Gillison Wk *BERM/RHTH* SE16 * 102 A4
Gillman Dr *SRTFD* E15 .... 81 E5
Gill St *POP/IOD* E14 .... 91 F5
Gilmore Rd *LEW* SE13 .... 141 D1
Gilpin Av *MORT/ESHN* SW14 .... 129 D2
Gilpin Cl *BAY/PAD* W2 .... 15 F3
Gilpin Rd *CLPT* E5 .... 79 E1
Gilstead Rd *FUL/PGN* SW6 .... 114 B5
Gilston Rd *WBPTN* SW10 .... 114 C1
Gilton Rd *CAT* SE6 .... 159 E3
Giltspur St *STBT* EC1A 23 D1
Gipsy Hl *NRWD* SE19 .... 155 E5
Gipsy La *PUT/ROE* SW15 .... 130 A1
Gipsy Rd *WNWD* SE27 .... 155 D4
Gipsy Road Gdns *WNWD* SE27 .... 154 C4
Giralda Cl *CAN/RD* E16 .... 95 D4
Giraud St *POP/IOD* E14 .... 92 B5
Girdlers Rd *WKENS* W14 .... 101 E4
Girdwood Rd *WAND/EARL* SW18 .... 131 E5
Gironde Rd *FUL/PGN* SW6 .... 113 F3
Girton Rd *SYD* SE26 .... 157 D5
Gissing Wk *IS* N1 .... 76 A4
Gittens Cl *BMLY* BR1 .... 159 F4
Gladding Rd *MNPK* E12 .... 83 D1
Glades more Rd *SEVS/STOTM* N15 .... 124 C3
The Glade *CHARL* SE7 .... 77 F3
SHB W12 .... 100 B3
Gladiator St *FSTH* SE23 .... 139 E4
Glading Ter *STNW/STAM* N16 .... 59 F5
Gladsmuir Rd *ARCH* N19 .... 56 C2
Gladstone Av *MNPK* E12 .... 83 E4
Gladstone Ms *KIL/WHAMP* NW6 * 71 F4
Gladstone Pde *CRICK* NW2 * 52 C5
Gladstone Park Gdns *CRICK* NW2 .... 52 B5
Gladstone Rd *CHSWK* W4 * 99 D4
Gladstone St *STHWK* SE1 .... 46 C2
Gladstone Ter *VX/NE* SW8 * 116 B4
WNWD SE27 * 154 C4
Gladwell Rd *CEND/HSY/T* N8 .... 57 F1
Gladwyn Rd *PUT/ROE* SW15 .... 131 F1
Gladys Rd *KIL/WHAMP* NW6 .... 72 A4
Glaisher St *DEPT* SE8 .... 122 A2
Glamis Pl *WAP* E1W 102 C1
Glamis Rd *WAP* E1W 102 C1
Glanville Rd *BRXS/STRHM* SW2 .... 135 E3
Glasbrook Rd *ELTH/MOT* SE9 .... 143 D5
Glaserton Rd *STNW/STAM* N16 .... 59 E2
Glasgow Rd *PLSTW* E13 .... 94 B1
Glasgow Ter *PIM* SW1V 116 C1
Glaskin Ms *HOM* E9 .... 79 E3
Glasshill St *STHWK* SE1 .... 35 D5
Glasshouse Flds *WAP* E1W 103 D1
Glasshouse St *REGST* W1B 31 F2
Glasshouse Wk *LBTH* SE11 .... 117 E1
Glasshouse Yd *FARR* EC1M 23 E1
Glass St *BETH* E2 * 90 B3

Glass Yd *WOOL/PLUM* SE18 .... 108 A4
Glastonbury Pl *WCHPL* E1 .... 90 C5
Glastonbury St *KIL/WHAMP* NW6 .... 71 F2
Glaucus St *BOW* E3 .... 92 B4
Glazbury Rd *WKENS* W14 .... 101 E5
Glazebrook Cl *DUL* SE21 .... 155 D2
Glebe Cl *CHSWK* W4 * 111 E1
Glebe Ct *BKHTH/KID* SE3 * 141 E1
Glebelands Av *GNTH/NBYPK* IG2 .... 67 D2
Glebelands Cl *CMBW* SE5 .... 137 E1
Glebe Pl *CHEL* SW3 .... 115 E2
Glebe Rd *BARN* SW13 .... 112 A5
HACK E8 * 77 F4
WLSDN NW10 .... 70 A3
Glebe St *CHSWK* W4 .... 111 D1
STRHM/NOR SW16 * 153 D4
Gledhow Gdns *ECT* SW5 .... 39 E5
Gledstanes Rd *WKENS* W14 .... 113 E1
Glegg Pl *PUT/ROE* SW15 * 131 D2
Glenaffric Av *POP/IOD* E14 .... 104 C5
Glen Albyn Rd *WIM/MER* SW19 .... 149 D2
Glenalvon Wy *WOOL/PLUM* SE18 .... 107 F5
Glenarm Rd *CLPT* E5 .... 78 C1
Glenavon Rd *SRTFD* E15 .... 81 E4
Glenbarr Cl *ELTH/MOT* SE9 .... 144 B1
Glenbrook Rd *KIL/WHAMP* NW6 .... 72 A2
Glenburnie Rd *TOOT* SW17 .... 151 E3
Glencairne Cl *CAN/RD* E16 .... 95 D4
Glencoe Av *GNTH/NBYPK* IG2 .... 67 E2
Glendale Cl *ELTH/MOT* SE9 .... 144 A1
Glendale Dr *WIM/MER* SW19 .... 149 F5
Glendall St *BRXN/ST* SW9 .... 135 F1
Glendarvon St *PUT/ROE* SW15 .... 131 D1
Glendower Gdns *MORT/ESHN* SW14 .... 129 D1
Glendower Pl *SKENS* SW7 .... 40 A4
Glendower Rd *MORT/ESHN* SW14 .... 129 D1
Glendun Rd *ACT* W3 .... 99 E1
Gleneagle Ms *STRHM/NOR* SW16 .... 153 D5
Gleneagle Rd *STRHM/NOR* SW16 .... 153 D5
Gleneagles Cl *BERM/RHTH* SE16 * 120 B1
Gleneldon Ms *STRHM/NOR* SW16 .... 153 E5
Gleneldon Rd *STRHM/NOR* SW16 .... 153 E4
Glenelg Rd *BRXS/STRHM* SW2 .... 135 E3
Glenesk Rd *ELTH/MOT* SE9 .... 144 A2
Glenfarg Rd *CAT* SE6 .... 159 D1
Glenfield Rd *BAL* SW12 .... 152 C1
Glenfinlas Wy *CMBW* SE5 .... 118 B3
Glenforth St *GNWCH* SE10 .... 106 C5
Glengall Br *POP/IOD* E14 .... 104 B4
Glengall Gv *POP/IOD* E14 .... 104 B4
Glengall Rd *KIL/WHAMP* NW6 .... 71 F5
PECK SE15 .... 119 F2
Glengall Ter *PECK* SE15 .... 119 F2
Glengarnock Av *POP/IOD* E14 .... 104 C5
Glengarry Rd *EDUL* SE22 .... 137 E2
Glenhead Cl *ELTH/MOT* SE9 .... 144 B1
Glenhouse Rd *ELTH/MOT* SE9 .... 144 A3
Glenhurst Av *KTTN* NW5 .... 74 A1
Glenilla Rd *HAMP* NW3 .... 73 E3
Glenister Rd *GNWCH* SE10 .... 123 F1
Glenlea Rd *ELTH/MOT* SE9 .... 144 A3
Glenloch Rd *HAMP* NW3 .... 73 E3
Glenluce Rd *BKHTH/KID* SE3 .... 142 B1
Glenluge Rd *BKHTH/KID* SE3 .... 124 A2
Glenlyon Rd *ELTH/MOT* SE9 .... 144 A3
Glenmere Rw *LEE/GVPK* SE12 .... 141 F4
Glenmore Rd *HAMP* NW3 .... 73 E3
WELL DA16 .... 127 F2
Glennie Rd *WNWD* SE27 .... 154 A3
Glenny Rd *BARK* IG11 .... 84 C3
Glenparke Rd *FSTGT* E7 .... 82 B3
Glen Rd *PLSTW* E13 .... 94 C3
Glenrosa St *FUL/PGN* SW6 .... 114 C5
Glenroy St *SHB* W12 .... 88 B4
Glensdale Rd *BROCKY* SE4 .... 139 F1
Glenshiel Rd *ELTH/MOT* SE9 .... 144 A3
Glentanner Wy *TOOT* SW17 .... 151 D5
Glentham Cots *BARN* SW13 * 112 A2
Glentham Gdns *BARN* SW13 .... 112 A2
Glentham Rd *BARN* SW13 .... 112 A2
Glenthorne Rd *HMSMTH* W6 .... 100 B5
Glenton Rd *LEW* SE13 .... 141 E2
Glentworth St *CAMTN* NW1 .... 17 F1
Glenure Rd *ELTH/MOT* SE9 .... 144 A3
Glenville Gv *DEPT* SE8 .... 121 F3
Glenville Ms *WAND/EARL* SW18 .... 132 B5
Glenwood Av *CDALE/KGS* NW9 .... 51 E3
Glenwood Gv *CDALE/KGS* NW9 .... 50 C3
Glenwood Rd *CAT* SE6 .... 157 F1
Glenworth Av *POP/IOD* E14 .... 105 D5
Gliddon Dr *CLPT* E5 .... 78 B1

Gliddon Rd *WKENS* W14 .... 101 E5
Globe Pond Rd *BERM/RHTH* SE16 ... 103 E2
Globe Rd *BETH* E2 .... 90 C1
SRTFD E15 .... 81 F2
WCHPL E1 .... 90 C2
Globe Ter *SE1* 48 A1
Globe Ter *BETH* E2 .... 90 C2
Gloucester Av *BFN/LL* DA15 .... 163 E2
CAMTN NW1 .... 74 A4
WELL DA16 .... 145 F3
Gloucester Circ *CNWCH* SE10 ... 122 C5
Gloucester Cl *WLSDN* NW10 .... 69 D4
Gloucester Ct *RCH/KEW* TW9 * ... 110 A3
Gloucester Crs *CAMTN* NW1 .... 74 B5
Gloucester Dr *FSBYPK* N4 .... 58 B4
Gloucester Gdns *BAY/PAD* W2 ... 15 D4
GLDGN NW11 .... 53 F2
IL IG1 .... 65 E2
Gloucester Ga *CAMTN* NW1 .... 6 B1
Gloucester Gate Br *CAMTN* NW1 * 74 B5
Gloucester Gate Ms *CAMTN* NW1 .. 6 C1
Gloucester Ms *BAY/PAD* W2 .... 15 F5
LEY E10 .... 62 A2
Gloucester Ms West *BAY/PAD* W2 15 E5
Gloucester Pl *CAMTN* NW1 .... 5 E5
MHST W1U 17 F3
Gloucester Place Ms *MHST* W1U .. 17 F4
Gloucester Rd *ACT* W3 .... 98 C3
LEY E10 .... 62 A2
MNPK E12 .... 65 F5
RCH/KEW TW9 .... 110 A3
SKENS W7 .... 39 E2
BETH E2 .... 78 A5
Gloucester Sq *BAY/PAD* W2 .... 16 B5
Gloucester St *PIM* SW1V 116 C1
Gloucester Ter *BAY/PAD* W2 .... 15 D4
Gloucester Wk *KENS* W8 .... 26 B5
Gloucester Wy *CLKNW* EC1R 10 B2
Glycena Rd *BTSEA* SW11 .... 133 F1
Glynde Ms *CHEL* SW3 .... 41 F3
Glynde St *BROCKY* SE4 .... 139 F4
Glyndon Rd *WOOL/PLUM* SE18 ... 108 C5
Glynfield Rd *WLSDN* NW10 .... 69 E4
Glyn Rd *CLPT* E5 .... 79 D1
Glyn St *LBTH* SE11 .... 117 F1
Glynwood Ct *FSTH* SE23 .... 156 C2
Godalming Rd *POP/IOD* E14 .... 92 B4
Godbold Rd *SRTFD* E15 .... 93 E3
Goddard Pl *ARCH* N19 .... 56 C5
Goddards Wy *IL* IG1 .... 67 D3
Godfrey Hl *WOOL/PLUM* SE18 ... 107 E5
Godfrey Rd *WOOL/PLUM* SE18 ... 107 F5
Godfrey St *CHEL* SW3 .... 115 E1
SRTFD E15 .... 92 C1
Goding St *LBTH* SE11 .... 117 E1
Godley Rd *WAND/EARL* SW18 ... 151 D1
Godliman St *BLKFR* EC4V 23 D5
Godman Rd *PECK* SE15 * 120 B5
Godolphin Pl *ACT* W3 .... 99 D1
Godolphin Rd *SHB* W12 .... 100 B3
Godson St *IS* N1 .... 10 A1
Godwin Cl *IS* N1 .... 11 F1
Godwin Rd *FSTGT* E7 .... 82 B1
Goffers Rd *BKHTH/KID* SE3 .... 123 E4
Golborne Gdns *NKENS* W10 * 89 E3
Golborne Ms *NKENS* W10 .... 89 E4
Golborne Rd *NKENS* W10 .... 89 E4
Goldcrest Cl *CAN/RD* E16 .... 95 D4
Golden Cross Ms *NTGHL* W11 * ... 89 F5
Golden Hind Pl *DEPT* SE8 * 103 F5
Golden Jubilee Br *STHWK* SE1 ... 33 E5
Golden La *STLK* EC1Y 11 E5
Golden Lane Est *STLK* EC1Y 23 E1
Golden Plover Cl *CAN/RD* E16 ... 94 A5
Golden Sq *SOHO/CST* W1F 31 F1
Golden Yd *HAMP* NW3 .... 72 C1
Golders Gdns *GLDGN* NW11 .... 53 E2
Golders Green Crs *GLDGN* NW11 . 53 F2
Golders Green Rd *GLDGN* NW11 .. 53 E1
Golders Hl *HAMP* NW3 * 54 B4
Golderslea *GLDGN* NW11 * 54 A3
Golders Manor Dr *GLDGN* NW11 . 53 D1
Golders Park Cl *GLDGN* NW11 ... 54 B4
Golders Wy *GLDGN* NW11 .... 53 F2
Goldfinch Rd *THMD* SE28 .... 109 D4
Goldhawk Ms *SHB* W12 .... 100 B3
Goldhawk Rd *HMSMTH* W6 .... 99 F5
SHB W12 .... 100 A4
Goldhurst Ter *KIL/WHAMP* NW6 .. 72 B4
Golding St *WCHPL* E1 .... 90 A5
Goldington Crs *CAMTN* NW1 .... 7 F1
Goldington St *CAMTN* NW1 .... 8 A1

Goldman Cl *BETH* E2 .... 90 A3
Goldney Rd *MV/WKIL* W9 .... 14 A1
Goldsboro' Rd *VX/NE* SW8 .... 117 D3
Goldsmid St *WOOL/PLUM* SE18 ... 127 E1
Goldsmith Av *ACT* W3 .... 99 D1
MNPK E12 .... 83 E3
Goldsmith Pl *KIL/WHAMP* NW6 * .. 72 B5
Goldsmith Rd *ACT* W3 .... 99 D2
LEY E10 .... 62 B3
PECK SE15 .... 120 A4
Goldsmiths Cl *ACT* W3 * 99 D2
Goldsmith's Rw *BETH* E2 .... 90 B1
Goldsmith St *CITYW* EC2V 23 F4
Goldsworthy Gdns *BERM/RHTH* SE16 102 C5
Goldwing Cl *CAN/RD* E16 .... 94 A5
Golfe Rd *IL* IG1 .... 67 D5
Gollogly Ter *CHARL* SE7 .... 124 C1
Gomm Rd *BERM/RHTH* SE16 ...... 102 C4
Gondar Gdns *CRICK* NW2 .... 71 F2
Gonson St *DEPT* SE8 .... 122 B2
Gonston Cl *WIM/MER* SW19 .... 149 E2
Gonville St *FUL/PGN* SW6 .... 131 E1
Goodall Rd *WAN* E11 .... 62 C5
Goodey Rd *BARK* IG11 .... 85 F4
Goodge Pl *FITZ* W1T 19 F3
Goodge St *FITZ* W1T 19 F3
Goodhall St *WLSDN* NW10 .... 87 E2
Goodinge Cl *HOLWY* N7 .... 75 E2
Goodinge Rd *HOLWY* N7 .... 75 E3
Goodman Crs *BRXS/STRHM* SW2 153 D2
Goodman Rd *LEY* E10 .... 62 C2
Goodman's Yd *TWRH* EC3N 37 E1
Goodrich Rd *EDUL* SE22 .... 137 F4
Goodson Rd *WLSDN* NW10 .... 69 E4
Goodway Gdns *POP/IOD* E14 ...... 93 D5
Goodwin Cl *BERM/RHTH* SE16 ... 49 F1
Goodwin Rd *SHB* W12 .... 100 A3
Goodwins Ct *CHCR* WC2N 32 C1
Goodwin St *FSBYPK* N4 .... 58 A4
Goodwood Rd *NWCR* SE14 .... 121 E3
Goosander Wy *THMD* SE28 .... 109 D4
Gooseley La *EHAM* E6 .... 96 A2
Gophir La *CANST* EC4R * 36 A1
Gopsall St *IS* N1 .... 77 D5
Gordon Av *MORT/ESHN* SW14 ... 129 E2
Gordonbrock Rd *BROCKY* SE4 ... 140 A3
Gordon Cl *WALTH* E17 .... 62 A1
Gordondale Rd *WIM/MER* SW19 . 150 A2
Gordon Gv *CMBW* SE5 .... 118 B5
Gordon House Rd *KTTN* NW5 ...... 74 A1
Gordon Pl *KENS* W8 .... 26 B5
Gordon Rd *BARK* IG11 .... 85 E5
BFN/LL DA15 .... 145 E3
CHSWK W4 .... 110 B2
IL IG1 .... 67 D5
PECK SE15 .... 120 B5
SRTFD E15 .... 80 C1
WAN E11 .... 64 A1
Gordon Sq *STPAN* WC1H 8 A5
Gordon St *PLSTW* E13 .... 94 A2
STPAN WC1H 8 A5
Gorefield Pl *KIL/WHAMP* NW6 ..... 2 A1
Gore Rd *HOM* E9 .... 78 C5
Gore St *SKENS* SW7 .... 39 F2
Gorham Pl *NTGHL* W11 .... 101 E1
Goring St *HDTCH* EC3A 25 D4
Gorleston St *WKENS* W14 .... 101 E5
Gorman Rd *WOOL/PLUM* SE18 ... 107 F5
Gorse Cl *CAN/RD* E16 .... 94 A5
Gorse Ri *TOOT* SW17 .... 152 A5
Gorst Rd *BTSEA* SW11 .... 133 F4
WLSDN NW10 .... 86 C3
Gorsuch Pl *BETH* E2 .... 13 E3
Gorsuch St *BETH* E2 .... 13 E3
Gosberton Rd *BAL* SW12 .... 151 F1
Gosfield St *GTPST* W1W 19 D2
Goslett Yd *SOHO/SHAV* W1D 20 B4
Gosling Wy *BRXN/ST* SW9 .... 118 A4
Gosport Wy *PECK* SE15 .... 119 F3
Gossage Rd *WOOL/PLUM* SE18 .. 127 D1
Gosset St *BETH* E2 .... 90 A2
Gossington Cl *CHST* BR7 .... 162 B4
Gosterwood St *DEPT* SE8 .... 121 E2
Goswell Pl *FSBYE* EC1V 11 D4
Goswell Rd *FSBYE* EC1V 11 D3
Gottfried Ms *KTTN* NW5 .... 74 C1
Goudhurst Rd *BMLY* BR1 .... 159 E5
Gough Rd *SRTFD* E15 .... 81 F1
Gough Sq *FLST/FETLN* EC4A 22 B4
Gough St *FSBYW* WC1X 9 F5
Gould Ter *HACK* E8 .... 78 B2

Goulston St *WCHPL* E1	25 E4
Goulton Rd *CLPT* E5	78 B2
Gourock Rd *ELTH/MOT* SE9	144 A3
Govan St *BETH* E2	78 A5
Govier Cl *SRTFD* E15	81 E4
Gowan Av *FUL/PGN* SW6	113 E4
Gowan Rd *WLSDN* NW10	70 B4
Gower Cl *CLAP* SW4	134 C4
Gower Ms *GWRST* WC1E	20 B3
Gower Pl *GWRST* WC1E	7 F5
Gower Rd *FSTGT* E7	82 A3
Gower St *GWRST* WC1E	20 A1
Gower's Wk *WCHPL* E1	90 A5
Gowlett Rd *PECK* SE15	138 A1
Gowrie Rd *BTSEA* SW11	134 A1
Gracechurch St *BANK* EC3V	36 B1
Grace Cl *ELTH/MOT* SE9	161 D3
Gracedale Rd *STRHM/NOR* SW16	152 B5
Gracefield Gdns *STRHM/NOR* SW16	153 E5
Grace Jones Cl *HACK* E8	77 F3
Grace Pl *BOW* E3	92 B2
Graces Aly *WCHPL* E1 *	102 A1
Graces Ms *STJWD* NW8 *	3 F2
Grace's Rd *CMBW* SE5	119 D5
Grace's Rd *CMBW* SE5	119 E5
Grace St *BOW* E3	92 B2
The Gradient *SYD* SE26	156 A4
Graduate Pl *STHWK* SE1	48 C3
Graemesdyke Av *MORT/ESHN* SW14	128 B1
Grafton Crs *CAMTN* NW1	74 B3
Grafton Gdns *FSBYPK* N4	58 C1
Grafton Ms *FITZ* W1T	19 E1
Grafton Pl *CAMTN* NW1	8 A4
Grafton Rd *ACT* W3	98 C1
Grafton Rd *KTTN* NW5	74 A2
Grafton Sq *CLAP* SW4	134 C1
Grafton St *CONDST* W1S	31 D2
Grafton Ter *HAMP* NW3	73 F2
Grafton Wy *FITZ* W1T	19 E2
Grafton Yd *KTTN* NW5	74 B3
Graham Rd *CHSWK* W4	99 D4
Graham Rd *HACK* E8	78 A3
Graham Rd *HDN* NW4	52 B1
Graham Rd *PLSTW* E13	94 A3
Graham St *IS* N1	11 D2
Graham Ter *BGVA* SW1W	42 A5
Gramer Cl *WAN* E11	63 D4
Grampian Gdns *CRICK* NW2	53 E3
Gramsci Wy *CAT* SE6	158 B3
Granada St *TOOT* SW17	151 F5
Granard Av *PUT/ROE* SW15	130 B3
Granard Rd *BTSEA* SW11	133 F5
Granary Rd *WCHPL* E1	90 B3
Granary Sq *IS* N1	76 A3
Granary St *CAMTN* NW1	75 D5
Granby Cl *ELTH/MOT* SE9	123 F5
Granby Rd *ELTH/MOT* SE9	108 B4
Granby St *BETH* E2	13 F5
Granby Ter *CAMTN* NW1	7 E2
Grand Av *FARR* EC1M *	23 D2
Grand Av *WBLY* HA9	68 A2
Grand Av East *WBLY* HA9	68 B2
Grand Depot Rd *WOOL/PLUM* SE18	126 A1
Grandison Rd *BTSEA* SW11	133 F3
Grand Junction Whf *IS* N1 *	11 E2
Grand Pde *FSBYPK* N4 *	58 B1
Grand Pde *MORT/ESHN* SW14 *	128 C2
Grand Pde *WBLY* HA9 *	50 B4
Grand Union Canal Wk *MV/WKIL* W9	14 B2
Grand Union Canal Wk *NKENS* W10	88 C3
Grand Union Canal Wk *WLSDN* W10	86 B3
Grand Union Cl *MV/WKIL* W9	89 F4
Grand Union Crs *HACK* E8 *	78 A5
Grand Union Wk *CAMTN* NW1 *	74 B4
Grand Wk *WCHPL* E1 *	91 E3
Granfield St *BTSEA* SW11	115 D4
Grangecourt Rd *STNW/STAM* N16	59 D3
Grange Gdns *HAMP* NW3	54 B5
Grange Gv *IS* N1	76 C3
Grangehill Pl *ELTH/MOT* SE9	143 F1
Grangehill Rd *ELTH/MOT* SE9	143 F2
Grange Houses *HBRY* N5 *	76 C1
Grange La *DUL* SE21	155 F2
Grangemill Rd *CAT* SE6	158 A3
Grangemill Wy *CAT* SE6	158 A2
Grange Park Rd *LEY* E10	62 B3
Grange Pl *KIL/WHAMP* NW6	72 A4
Grange Rd *BARN* SW13	112 A4
Grange Rd *CHSWK* W4	110 B1
Grange Rd *HGT* N6	56 A1
Grange Rd *IL* IG1	84 C1
Grange Rd *LEY* E10	62 A3
Grange Rd *PLSTW* E13	93 F2
Grange Rd *STHWK* SE1	49 D5
Grange Rd *WLSDN* NW10	70 B3
Grange St *IS* N1 *	77 D5
The Grange *ALP/SUD* HA0	68 A4
The Grange *WKENS* W14 *	101 F5
Grange Wk *STHWK* SE1	49 D2
Grange Walk Ms *STHWK* SE1 *	49 D3
Grangeway *KIL/WHAMP* NW6	72 A4
Grangewood St *EHAM* E6	83 D5
Grange Yd *STHWK* SE1	49 E3
Granite St *WOOL/PLUM* SE18	127 E1
Granleigh Rd *WAN* E11	63 E4
Gransden Av *HACK* E8	78 B4
Gransden Rd *SHB* W12	99 F3
Grantbridge St *IS* N1	11 D1
Grantham Pl *MYFR/PKLN* W1K	30 C4
Grantham Rd *BRXN/ST* SW9	135 E1
Grantham Rd *CHSWK* W4	111 E3
Grantley St *WCHPL* E1	66 A5
Grant Rd *BTSEA* SW11	133 D1
Grant St *IS* N1	10 A1
Grant St *PLSTW* E13	94 A2
Grant Ter *STNW/STAM* N16 *	60 A2
Grantully Rd *MV/WKIL* W9	2 C4
Granville Ar *BRXN/ST* SW9 *	136 A3
Granville Gv *LEW* SE13	140 C1
Granville Pk *LEW* SE13	140 C1
Granville Pl *FUL/PGN* SW6 *	114 B3
Granville Pl *MBLAR* W1H	18 A5
Granville Rd *CEND/HSY/T* N8	57 F1
Granville Rd *CRICK* NW2	53 F4
Granville Rd *IL* IG1	66 B3
Granville Rd *KIL/WHAMP* NW6	2 A2
Granville Rd *WALTH* E17	62 B1
Granville Rd *WAND/EARL* SW18	131 F5
Granville Sq *PECK* SE15	119 E3
Granville St *FSBYW* WC1X	9 F4
Grape La *LSQ/SEVD* WC2H	20 C1
Graphite Sq *LBTH* SE11	117 F2
Grasgarth Cl *ACT* W3	98 C1
Grasmere Av *ACT* W3	98 C1
Grasmere Rd *PLSTW* E13	94 A1
Grasmere Rd *PUT/ROE* SW15	147 D4
Grasmere Rd *STRHM/NOR* SW16	153 F5
Grasshaven Wy *THMD* SE28	109 F2
Grassmount *FSTH* SE23	156 B2
Grately Wy *PECK* SE15 *	119 E3
Gratton Rd *WKENS* W14	101 E4
Gratton Ter *CRICK* NW2	53 D5
Gravel La *WCHPL* E1	25 E4
Gravelwood Cl *CHST* BR7	162 C3
Gravenel Gdns *TOOT* SW17 *	151 E5
Graveney Rd *TOOT* SW17	151 E4
Gravesend Rd *SHB* W12	100 A1
Grayling Cl *CAN/RD* E16	93 D4
Grayling Rd *STNW/STAM* N16	59 D4
Grayling Sq *BETH* E2 *	90 A2
Grayshott Rd *BTSEA* SW11	134 A1
Grazebrook Rd *STNW/STAM* N16	59 D4
Great Brownings *DUL* SE21	155 F4
Great Castle St *REGST* W1B	19 E4
Great Central St *CAMTN* NW1	17 E2
Great Central Wy *WBLY* HA9	68 C2
Great Chapel St *SOHO/SHAV* W1D	20 A4
Great Chart St *BTSEA* SW11	132 C1
Great Chertsey Rd *CHSWK* W4	111 D4
Great Church La *HMSMTH* W6	113 D1
Great College St *WEST* SW1P	44 C2
Great Cross Av *GNWCH* SE10	123 E3
Great Cumberland Ms *MBLAR* W1H *	17 E5
Great Cumberland Pl *MBLAR* W1H..	17 E4
Great Dover St *STHWK* SE1	48 A2
Great Eastern Rd *SRTFD* E15	81 D4
Great Eastern St *SDTCH* EC2A	12 C4
Great Eastern Whf *BTSEA* SW11	115 E3
Greatfield Av *EHAM* E6	95 F3
Greatfield Cl *ARCH* N19	74 C1
Greatfield Cl *BROCKY* SE4	140 A2
Greatfields Rd *BARK* IG11	85 D5
Great George St *STJSPK* SW1H	44 B1
Great Guildford St *STHWK* SE1	35 F2
Great Harry Dr *ELTH/MOT* SE9	162 A3
Great James St *BMSBY* WC1N	21 E1
Great Marlborough St *REGST* W1B	19 E5
Great Maze Pond *STHWK* SE1	36 B4
Great New St *FLST/FETLN* EC4A *	22 B4

Greatorex St WCHPL E1........................ 90 A4
Great Ormond St BMSBY WC1N........... 21 D2
Great Percy St FSBYW WC1X............... 9 F3
Great Peter St WEST SW1P................. 44 A3
Great Portland St GTPST W1W........... 19 D2
Great Pulteney St SOHO/CST W1F...... 31 F1
Great Queen St HOL/ALD WC2B......... 21 D4
Great Russell St NOXST/BSQ WC1A..... 20 C3
  RSO WC1B................................... 20 B4
Great St Thomas Apostle
  BLKFR EC4V.............................. 35 F1
Great Scotland Yd WHALL SW1A......... 32 C4
Great Smith St WEST SW1P.............. 44 B2
Great Spilmans EDUL SE22............... 137 E3
Great Suffolk St STHWK SE1............. 35 D4
Great Sutton St FSBYE EC1V............. 23 D1
Great Swan Aly LOTH EC2R.............. 24 A4
Great Titchfield St GTPST W1W........ 19 D2
Great Tower St MON EC3R................ 36 C1
Great Trinity La BLKFR EC4V............ 35 F1
Great Turnstile HHOL WC1V............. 21 F3
Great Western Rd NTGHL W11........... 89 F4
Great West Rd HMSMTH W6............ 112 B1
Great West Road Chiswick
  CHSWK W4................................. 111 F1
Great West Road Ellesmere Rd
  CHSWK W4................................. 110 C2
Great West Road Hogarth La
  CHSWK W4................................. 111 D2
Great Winchester St OBST EC2N....... 24 B4
Great Windmill St SOHO/SHAV W1D... 32 A2
Greaves Cl BARK IG11.................... 85 D4
Greaves Cots POP/IOD E14 *........... 91 E4
Greaves Pl TOOT SW17................... 151 E4
Grebe Cl STGT E7......................... 81 F2
Greek St SOHO/SHAV W1D.............. 20 B5
Greenacres ELTH/MOT SE9............. 144 A4
Green Acres SCUP DA14 *.............. 163 F4
Greenacre Sq BERM/RHTH SE16 *.... 103 D3
Green Arbour Ct STP EC4M............. 22 C4
Greenaway Gdns HAMP NW3........... 72 B1
Green Bank WAP E1W.................... 102 B2
Greenbay Rd CHARL SE7................. 125 D3
Greenberry St STJWD NW8.............. 4 C1
Green Chain Wk BMLY BR1.............. 158 C5
  CHARL SE7............................... 107 D5
  ELTH/MOT SE9.......................... 144 B3
  ELTH/MOT SE9.......................... 161 D5
  WOOL/PLUM SE18....................... 125 F2
Green Cl CDALE/KGS NW9............... 50 C1
  GLDGN NW11............................. 54 C2
Greencoat Pl WEST SW1P............... 43 F4
Greencoat Rw WEST SW1P.............. 43 F3
Greencroft Gdns KIL/WHAMP NW6... 72 B4
Green Dl EDUL SE22...................... 137 E3
Green Dragon La WCHPL E1............ 90 A4
Greenend Rd CHSWK W4................ 99 E3
Greenfield Man DEPT SE8 *............. 121 F1
Greenfield Cl ELTH/MOT SE9............ 161 E3
Greenfield Gdns CRICK NW2............ 53 E4
Greenfield Rd WCHPL E1................ 90 A4
Greengate St PLSTW E13................ 94 B1
Greenham Cl STHWK SE1................ 46 A1
Greenhill HAMP NW3..................... 73 D1
  WBLY HA9................................. 50 B4
Green Hl WOOL/PLUM SE18............. 125 F1
Greenhill Gv MNPK E12.................. 85 E1
Greenhill Pk WLSDN NW10.............. 69 E5
Greenhill Rd WLSDN NW10.............. 69 E5
Greenhill's Rents FARR EC1M *........ 22 C2
Greenhills Ter IS N1...................... 77 D5
Greenhill Ter WOOL/PLUM SE18....... 125 F1
Greenhill Wy WBLY HA9.................. 50 B4
Greenhithe Cl BFN/LL DA15............ 145 E3
Greenholm Rd ELTH/MOT SE9.......... 144 B3
Green Hundred Rd PECK SE15......... 120 A2
Greenhurst Rd WNWD SE27............. 154 A5
Greenland Ms DEPT SE8................. 121 D1
Greenland Pl CAMTN NW1............... 74 B5
Greenland Quay BERM/RHTH SE16... 103 D5
Greenland Rd CAMTN NW1.............. 74 B5
Greenland St CAMTN NW1............... 74 B5
Green La ELTH/MOT SE9................. 162 A1
  IL IG1.................................... 67 D4
Green Lanes FSBYPK N4................. 58 B2
  HBRY N5.................................. 58 C5
Greenlaw St WOOL/PLUM SE18........ 108 A4
Greenleaf Cl BRXS/STRHM SW2 *..... 136 A5
Greenleaf Rd EHAM E6................... 82 C5
Greenlink Wk RCH/KEW TW9........... 110 B4
Greenman St IS N1....................... 76 C4
Greenoak Wy WIM/MER SW19.......... 149 D4

Greenock Rd ACT W3.................... 98 B4
Greenroof Wy GNWCH SE10........... 105 F4
Greens Ct NTGHL W11 *................. 101 F2
Green's Ct SOHO/CST W1F............. 32 A1
Greens Rd WOOL/PLUM SE18.......... 108 B5
Greenside Cl CAT SE6................... 159 D2
Greenside Rd SHB W12................. 100 A4
Greenslade Rd BARK IG11............. 85 D4
Greenstead Gdns PUT/ROE SW15... 130 A3
Greenstone Ms WAN E11............... 64 A1
Green St FSTGT E7....................... 82 B2
  MYFR/PKLN W1K........................ 29 F1
Greenstreet Hill NWCR SE14 *........ 139 D1
Green Ter CLKNW EC1R................. 10 B4
The Green ACT W3...................... 87 E5
  SRTFD E15............................. 81 F5
  WAN E11................................. 64 B1
  WELL DA16.............................. 145 E2
  WIM/MER SW19......................... 149 D5
Greenvale Rd ELTH/MOT SE9.......... 143 F2
Greenview Cl ACT W3................... 99 E2
Green Wk STHWK SE1................... 48 C5
Green Wy ELTH/MOT SE9.............. 143 D5
Greenway Cl FSBYPK N4............... 58 C4
Greenway Ct IL IG1..................... 66 A3
  SRTFD E15.............................. 93 E1
Greenwell St GTPST W1W.............. 19 D1
Greenwich Church St GNWCH SE10 *. 122 C2
Greenwich Crs EHAM E6................ 95 E4
Greenwich Foot Tnl GNWCH SE10... 122 C1
Greenwich Hts CHARL SE7 *.......... 125 F1
Greenwich High Rd GNWCH SE10.... 122 B3
Greenwich House LEW SE13........... 141 D4
Greenwich Park St GNWCH SE10..... 123 D2
Greenwich Quay DEPT SE8............ 122 B2
Greenwich South St GNWCH SE10... 122 B4
Greenwood Pl KTTN NW5............... 74 B2
Greenwood Rd HACK E8................ 78 A2
  PLSTW E13............................. 93 F1
Greenwood Ter WLSDN NW10......... 69 D5
Green Yd FSBYW WC1X................. 9 F5
Greet St STHWK SE1.................... 34 B4
Greg Cl LEY E10......................... 62 C1
Gregor Ms BKHTH/KID SE3............ 124 A3
Gregory Crs ELTH/MOT SE9........... 143 D5
Gregory Pl KENS W8.................... 26 C5
Greig Ter WALW SE17................... 118 B2
Grenada Rd BKHTH/KID SE3.......... 124 C3
Grenade St POP/IOD E14.............. 103 F1
Grenadier St CAN/RD E16............. 108 A2
Grenard Ct PECK SE15 *.............. 120 A3
Grendon Gdns WBLY HA9............. 50 A4
Grendon St STJWD NW8................ 4 C5
Grenfell Rd NTGHL W11............... 101 D1
Grenville Ms ARCH N19................. 57 E3
Grenville Pl SKENS SW7............... 39 E4
Grenville Rd ARCH N19................ 57 E3
Grenville St BMSBY WC1N............. 21 D1
Gresham Gdns GLDGN NW11......... 53 E3
Gresham Rd BRXN/ST SW9............ 136 A1
  CAN/RD E16............................ 94 B5
  EHAM E6................................ 95 F1
  WLSDN NW10.......................... 69 D2
Gresham St CITYW EC2V............... 23 E4
Gresham Wy WIM/MER SW19......... 150 A3
Gresley Cl WALTH E17.................. 61 E1
Gresley Rd ARCH N19.................. 56 C3
Gressenhall Rd WAND/EARL SW18.. 131 F4
Gresse St FITZ W1T..................... 20 A3
Greswell St FUL/PGN SW6............ 113 D4
Greville Ms KIL/WHAMP NW6......... 72 B5
Greville Pl KIL/WHAMP NW6.......... 3 D1
Greville St HCIRC EC1N................ 22 B3
Grey Cl GLDGN NW11.................. 54 C1
Greycoat Pl WEST SW1P............... 44 A3
Greycoat St WEST SW1P.............. 44 A3
Greycot Rd BECK BR3.................. 158 A5
Grey Eagle St WCHPL E1.............. 25 F1
Greyhound Rd HMSMTH W6.......... 113 D2
  WLSDN NW10.......................... 88 B2
Greyladies Gdns GNWCH SE10 *.... 122 C5
Greystead Rd FSTH SE23.............. 138 C5
Grierson Rd FSTH SE23............... 139 E4
Griffin Cl WLSDN NW10............... 70 B2
Griffin Manor Wy THMD SE28....... 109 D4
Griffin Rd WOOL/PLUM SE18........ 127 D1
Griffin Wy THMD SE28................. 109 E4
Griggs Ap IL IG1........................ 66 C4
Griggs Cl IL IG1......................... 85 E1
Grigg's Pl STHWK SE1................. 49 D3

Griggs Rd *LEY* E10 .... 62 C1
Grimsby Cl *CAN/RD* E16 .... 108 B2
Grimsby St *WCHPL* E1 .... 25 F1
Grimshaw Cl *HGT* N6 * 56 A2
Grimston Rd *FUL/PGN* SW6 .... 113 F5
Grimwade Cl *PECK* SE15 .... 120 B5
Grindal St *STHWK* SE1 .... 46 A1
Grinling Pl *DEPT* SE8 .... 122 A2
Grinstead Rd *DEPT* SE8 .... 121 E1
Grittleton Av *WBLY* HA9 .... 68 B3
Grittleton Rd *MV/WKIL* W9 .... 2 A5
Grizedale Ter *FSTH* SE23 * 156 B2
Grocers' Hall Ct *LOTH/CE2R* * 24 A5
Groombridge Rd *HOM* E9 .... 79 D4
Groom Crs *WAND/EARL* SW18 .... 133 D5
Groomfield Cl *TOOT* SW17 .... 152 A4
Groom Pl *KTBR* SW1X 42 B2
Grosmont Rd *WOOL/PLUM* SE18 .... 127 F1
Grosse Wy *PUT/ROE* SW15 .... 130 B4
Grosvenor Av *HBRY* N5 .... 76 C2
  MORT/ESHN SW14 .... 129 E1
Grosvenor Br *VX/NE* SW8 .... 116 B2
Grosvenor Cots *KTBR* SW1X 42 A4
Grosvenor Crs *KTBR* SW1X 42 A1
Grosvenor Crescent Ms *KTBR* SW1X 42 A1
Grosvenor Gdns *BCVA* SW1W 43 D3
  CRICK NW2 .... 70 C3
  GLDGN NW11 .... 53 F1
  MORT/ESHN SW14 .... 129 E1
Grosvenor Gardens Ms East
  BCVA SW1W * 43 D2
Grosvenor Gardens Ms North
  BCVA SW1W * 42 C3
Grosvenor Ga *MYFR/PKLN* W1K 29 F2
Grosvenor Hl *MYFR/PKLN* W1K 30 C1
Grosvenor Pde *EA* W5 * 98 A2
Grosvenor Pk *CMBW* SE5 .... 118 C3
Grosvenor Pl *KTBR* SW1X 30 B5
Grosvenor Rd *CHSWK* W4 .... 110 C5
  EHAM E6 .... 83 D5
  FSTGT E7 .... 82 B3
  IL IG1 .... 66 C5
  LEY E10 .... 62 C3
  PIM SW1V 116 C2
Grosvenor Sq *MYFR/PKLN* W1K 30 B1
Grosvenor St *MYFR/PKLN* W1K 30 B1
Grosvenor Ter *CMBW* SE5 .... 118 B3
Grosvenor Wharf Rd *POP/IOD* E14 .... 105 D5
Grote's Bldgs *BKHTH/KID* SE3 * 123 E5
Grote's Pl *BKHTH/KID* SE3 .... 123 E5
Groton Rd *WAND/EARL* SW18 .... 150 B3
Grotto Ct *STHWK* SE1 * 35 E5
Grotto Pas *MHST* W1U 18 A2
Grove Cl *FSTH* SE23 .... 157 D1
Grove Cots *CHEL* SW3 * 115 E2
Grove Crescent Rd *SRTFD* E15 .... 81 D4
Grovedale Rd *ARCH* N19 .... 57 D4
Grove Dwellings *WCHPL* E1 * 90 C4
Grove End *KTTN* NW5 .... 74 B1
Grove End Rd *STJWD* NW8 .... 4 A2
Grove Gdns *STJWD* NW8 .... 5 D1
Grove Green Rd *WAN* E11 .... 62 C5
Grove Hill Rd *CMBW* SE5 .... 137 E1
Groveland Ct *STP* EC4M * 24 A6
Grovelands Cl *CMBW* SE5 .... 119 E5
Grovelands Rd *SEVS/STOTM* N15 .... 60 A1
Grove La *CMBW* SE5 .... 119 D4
Grove Ms *HMSMTH* W6 .... 100 C4
Grove Pk *CMBW* SE5 .... 119 E5
Grove Park Br *CHSWK* W4 .... 110 B3
Grove Park Gdns *CHSWK* W4 .... 110 B3
Grove Park Rd *CHSWK* W4 .... 110 B3
  ELTH/MOT SE9 .... 161 E3
Grove Park Ter *CHSWK* W4 .... 110 B3
Grove Pl *ACT* W3 .... 98 C2
  BAL SW12 .... 134 B4
  HAMP NW3 .... 55 D5
Grove Rd *ACT* W3 .... 98 C2
  BARN SW13 .... 111 F5
  BOW E3 .... 91 E1
  CRICK NW2 .... 70 C3
  HOM E9 .... 79 D5
  WAN E11 .... 63 F2
Groveside Cl *ACT* W3 .... 86 A5
Grove St *BERM/RHTH* SE16 .... 103 F5
Grove Ter *KTTN* NW5 .... 56 B5
Grove Terrace Ms *KTTN* NW5 * 56 B5
The Grove *FSBYPK* N4 .... 57 F2
  GLDGN NW11 .... 53 E2
  HGT N6 .... 56 A3

Grove V *EDUL* SE22 .... 137 E2
Groveway *BRXN/ST* SW9 .... 117 F4
Grove Wy *WBLY* HA9 .... 68 C2
Grummant Rd *PECK* SE15 .... 119 F4
Grundy St *POP/IOD* E14 .... 92 B5
Guardian Ct *BKHTH/KID* SE3 * 136 B5
Gubyon Av *HNHL* SE24 .... 136 C5
Guernsey Gv *HNHL* SE24 .... 136 C5
Guernsey Rd *IS* N1 .... 76 C3
  LEY E10 .... 63 D3
Guibal Rd *LEE/GVPK* SE12 .... 142 A5
Guildford Gv *GNWCH* SE10 .... 122 B4
Guildford Rd *EHAM* E6 .... 95 E5
  GDMY/SEVK IG3 .... 67 E4
  VX/NE SW8 .... 117 E4
Guildhall Blds *CITYW* EC2V * 23 F4
Guildhall Yd *CITYW* EC2V * 23 F4
Guildhouse St *PIM* SW1V 43 E5
Guild Rd *CHARL* SE7 .... 125 D1
Guilford Pl *BMSBY* WC1N 21 E1
Guilford St *BMSBY* WC1N 21 E1
Guinness Cl *HOM* E9 .... 79 E4
Guinness Sq *STHWK* SE1 * 48 C3
Guinness Trust *STNW/STAM* N16 * 59 F3
Guinness Trust Est *CHEL* SW3 * 41 E5
Guion Rd *FUL/PGN* SW6 .... 113 F5
Gulland Wk *IS* N1 * 76 C3
Gulliver Rd *BFN/LL* DA15 .... 163 D2
Gulliver St *BERM/RHTH* SE16 .... 105 F4
Gunmakers La *BOW* E3 .... 79 E5
Gunnell Cl *SYD* SE26 * 156 A4
Gunner La *WOOL/PLUM* SE18 .... 126 A1
Gunnersbury Ave *ACT* W3 .... 98 A4
Gunnersbury Avenue (North Circular
  Road) *ACT* W3 .... 98 A5
Gunnersbury Cl *CHSWK* W4 .... 110 B1
Gunnersbury Crs *ACT* W3 .... 98 A3
Gunnersbury Gdns *ACT* W3 .... 98 A3
Gunnersbury La *ACT* W3 .... 98 A3
Gunnersbury Ms *CHSWK* W4 .... 110 B1
Gunners Rd *WAND/EARL* SW18 .... 151 D2
Gunning St *WOOL/PLUM* SE18 .... 109 E5
Gunstor Rd *STNW/STAM* N16 * 77 E1
Gun St *WCHPL* E1 .... 25 E3
Gunter Gv *WBPTN* SW10 .... 114 C2
Gunterstone Rd *WKENS* W14 .... 113 E1
Gunthorpe St *WCHPL* E1 .... 25 F3
Gunton Rd *CLPT* E5 .... 60 B5
Gunwhale Cl *BERM/RHTH* SE16 .... 103 D2
Gunyard Ms *WOOL/PLUM* SE18 * 125 E3
Gurdon Rd *CHARL* SE7 .... 124 A1
Gurney Cl *BARK* IG11 .... 84 B3
Gurney Rd *FUL/PGN* SW6 .... 132 C1
  SRTFD E15 .... 81 E2
Guthrie St *CHEL* SW3 .... 115 E1
Gutter La *CITYW* EC2V 23 E4
Guy Barnett Gv *BKHTH/KID* SE3 * 142 A1
Guyscliff Rd *LEW* SE13 .... 140 C3
Guy St *STHWK* SE1 .... 36 B5
Gwalior Rd *PUT/ROE* SW15 .... 131 D2
Gwendolen Av *PUT/ROE* SW15 .... 131 D3
Gwendoline Av *PLSTW* E13 .... 82 B5
Gwendwr Rd *WKENS* W14 .... 113 E1
Gwyn Cl *FUL/PGN* SW6 .... 114 C3
Gwynne Rd *BTSEA* SW11 .... 115 D5
Gwynne Whf *CHSWK* W4 .... 111 F2
Gylcote Cl *CMBW* SE5 .... 137 D2
Gyllyngdune Gdns *GDMY/SEVK* IG3 .... 67 F5
Gywnne Pl *FSBYW* WC1X 9 F4

H

Haarlem Rd *WKENS* W14 .... 101 D4
Haberdasher Pl *IS* N1 .... 12 B3
Haberdasher St *IS* N1 .... 12 B3
Habington Cl *CMBW* SE5 * 119 D3
Habitat Cl *PECK* SE15 .... 120 B5
Hackford Rd *BRXN/ST* SW9 .... 117 F4
Hackford Wk *BRXN/ST* SW9 .... 117 F4
Hackney Gv *HACK* E8 * 78 B3
Hackney Rd *BETH* E2 .... 13 E5
Hackney Wick *HOM* E9 .... 79 F3
Hadden Rd *THMD* SE28 .... 109 E4
Haddington Rd *BMLY* BR1 .... 159 D5
Haddo St *GNWCH* SE10 .... 122 B2
Hadleigh Cl *WCHPL* E1 .... 90 C3
Hadleigh St *BETH* E2 .... 90 C3
Hadley Gdns *CHSWK* W4 .... 111 D1

Hadley St *KTTN* NW5	74	B3
Hadrian Cl *BOW* E3	80	A5
Hadrian Est *BETH* E2 *	90	A1
Hadrian St *GNWCH* SE10	123	E1
Hadyn Park Rd *SHB* W12	100	A3
Hafer Rd *BTSEA* SW11	133	F2
Hafton Rd *CAT* SE6	159	E1
Haggerston Rd *HACK* E8	77	F4
Hague St *BETH* E2	90	A2
Ha-Ha Rd *WOOL/PLUM* SE18	125	F2
Haig East *PLSTW* E13	94	A2
Haig Rd West *PLSTW* E13	94	C2
Hailsham Av *BRXS/STRHM* SW2	153	F2
Haimo Rd *ELTH/MOT* SE9	143	D3
Hainault Bldgs *LEY* E10 *	62	C3
Hainault Rd *WAN* E11	62	C1
Hainault St *ELTH/MOT* SE9	162	B1
IL IG1	66	B4
Hainford Cl *PECK* SE15	139	D2
Haining Cl *CHSWK* W4	110	A1
Hainthorpe Rd *WNWD* SE27	154	B3
Hainton Cl *WCHPL* E1	90	B5
Halberd Ms *CLPT* E5	60	B4
Halcomb St *IS* N1	77	E5
Halcrow St *WCHPL* E1 *	90	B4
Haldane Pl *WAND/EARL* SW18	150	B1
Haldane Rd *EHAM* E6	95	D2
FUL/PGN SW6	113	D3
Haldon Rd *WAND/EARL* SW18	131	F4
Hale Gdns *ACT* W3	98	A2
Hale House *WOOL/PLUM* SE18 *	125	E3
Hale Rd *EHAM* E6	95	E3
Hales St *DEPT* SE8	122	A3
Hale St *POP/IOD* E14	104	B1
Halesworth Rd *LEW* SE13	140	B1
Haley Rd *HDN* NW4	52	C1
Half Moon Crs *IS* N1	9	F1
Half Moon La *HNHL* SE24	136	C4
Half Moon Pas *WCHPL* E1	25	F5
Half Moon St *MYFR/PICC* W1J	31	D3
Halford Rd *FUL/PGN* SW6	114	A2
Halfway St *BFN/LL* DA15	163	E1
Haliday Wk *IS* N1	77	D3
Halifax St *SYD* SE26	156	B3
Halkin Ar *KTBR* SW1X *	42	A1
Halkin Ms *KTBR* SW1X *	42	A2
Halkin Pl *KTBR* SW1X	42	A2
Halkin St *KTBR* SW1X	42	B1
Hallam Cl *CHST* BR7	161	F5
Hallam Ms *GTPST* W1W	19	D2
Hallam Rd *BARN* SW13	130	B1
Hallam St *GTPST* W1W	19	D2
Hall Dr *SYD* SE26	156	C5
Halley Gdns *LEW* SE13	141	D2
Halley Rd *FSTGT* E7	82	C3
Halley St *POP/IOD* E14	91	E4
Hallfield Est *BAY/PAD* W2	15	D5
Hall Ga *STJWD* NW8	3	F4
Halliford St *IS* N1	76	C4
Halliwell Rd *BRXS/STRHM* SW2	135	F4
Hall Oak Wk *KIL/WHAMP* NW6	71	F3
Hall Pl *BAY/PAD* W2	16	A1
Hall Rd *EHAM* E6	83	F5
MV/WKIL W9	3	F4
SRTFD E15	81	D1
Hall St *FSBYE* EC1V	11	D3
Hallsville Rd *CAN/RD* E16	93	F5
The Hall *BKHTH/KID* SE3	142	A1
Hall Vw *ELTH/MOT* SE9	161	D2
Hallywell Crs *EHAM* E6	95	F4
Halons Rd *ELTH/MOT* SE9	144	A5
Halpin Pl *WALW* SE17	48	B5
Halsbrook Rd *BKHTH/KID* SE3	142	C1
Halsbury Rd *SHB* W12	100	B2
Halsey St *CHEL* SW3	41	E4
Halsham Crs *BARK* IG11	85	E3
Halsmere Rd *CMBW* SE5	118	B4
Halston Cl *BTSEA* SW11	133	F4
Halstow Rd *GNWCH* SE10	124	A1
WLSDN NW10	89	D2
Halton Cross St *IS* N1 *	76	B5
Halton Rd *IS* N1	76	B5
Hambalt Rd *CLAP* SW4	134	C3
Hambledon *WALW* SE17 *	119	D2
Hambledon Cl *DUL* SE21	155	F1
Hambledon Rd *WAND/EARL* SW18	131	F5
Hambledown Rd *BFN/LL* DA15 *	145	D5
Hamble St *FUL/PGN* SW6	132	B1
Hameway *EHAM* E6	96	A3
Hamfrith Rd *SRTFD* E15	81	F3
Hamilton Cl *BERM/RHTH* SE16	103	E3
STJWD NW8	4	A4
Hamilton Gdns *STJWD* NW8	3	F3
Hamilton Ms *MYFR/PICC* W1J	30	C5
Hamilton Pk *HBRY* N5	76	B1
Hamilton Pk West *HBRY* N5	76	B1
Hamilton Pl *MYFR/PKLN* W1K	30	B2
Hamilton Rd *CHSWK* W4	99	E4
CLDGN NW11	53	D2
IL IG1	84	B1
SRTFD E15	93	E2
WLSDN NW10	70	A2
WNWD SE27	155	D4
Hamilton St *DEPT* SE8	122	A2
Hamilton Ter *STJWD* NW8	3	E2
Hamlea Cl *LEE/GVPK* SE12	142	A3
Hamlet Cl *LEW* SE13	141	E2
Hamlet Gdns *HMSMTH* W6	100	A5
Hamlet Sq *CRICK* NW2	53	E5
Hamlets Wy *BOW* E3	91	F3
The Hamlet *CMBW* SE5	137	D1
Hamlet Wy *STHWK* SE1	48	B1
Hammersmith Br *HMSMTH* W6	112	B1
Hammersmith Bridge Rd *BARN* SW13	112	B2
Hammersmith Broadway *HMSMTH* W6	100	C5
Hammersmith Br *HMSMTH* W6 *	112	C2
Hammersmith F/O *HMSMTH* W6	112	C1
Hammersmith Gv *HMSMTH* W6	100	C4
Hammersmith Rd *HMSMTH* W6	101	D5
Hammersmith Ter *HMSMTH* W6 *	112	A1
Hammett St *TWRH* EC3N	37	E1
Hammond St *KTTN* NW5	74	C3
Hamond Sq *IS* N1	13	E1
Ham Park Rd *SRTFD* E15	81	F4
Hampden Cl *CAMTN* NW1	8	B2
Hampden Gurney St *MBLAR* W1H	17	E5
Hampden Rd *ARCH* N19	57	D4
Hampshire Hog La *HMSMTH* W6 *	100	B5
Hampshire St *KTTN* NW5	75	D3
Hampson Wy *VX/NE* SW8	117	F4
Hampstead Gdns *CLDGN* NW11	54	A1
Hampstead Ga *HAMP* NW3	72	C2
Hampstead Gn *HAMP* NW3	73	E2
Hampstead Gv *HAMP* NW3	72	E1
Hampstead Hill Gdns *HAMP* NW3	73	E1
Hampstead La *HGT* N6	55	F2
Hampstead Rd *CAMTN* NW1	7	E4
Hampstead Sq *HAMP* NW3	54	C5
Hampstead Wy *CLDGN* NW11	54	A1
Hampton Cl *KIL/WHAMP* NW6	2	A2
Hampton Ct *IS* N1	76	B3
Hampton Rd *FSTGT* E7	82	B2
IL IG1	84	C1
WAN E11	63	D3
Hampton St *WALW* SE17	47	D5
Ham Shades Cl *BFN/LL* DA15	163	F3
Ham Yd *SOHO/SHAV* W1D *	32	A1
Hanameel St *CAN/RD* E16	106	A2
Hanbury Dr *WAN* E11	63	F2
Hanbury Rd *ACT* W3	98	B3
Hanbury St *WCHPL* E1	25	F1
WCHPL E1	90	A1
Hancock Rd *BOW* E3	92	C2
Handa Wk *IS* N1	76	C3
Hand Ct *HHOL* WC1V	21	F3
Handel St *BMSBY* WC1N	8	C5
Handen Rd *LEE/GVPK* SE12	141	E3
Handforth Rd *BRXN/ST* SW9	118	A3
IL IG1	66	B5
Handley Gv *CRICK* NW2	53	D5
Handley Rd *HOM* E9	78	C4
Handtrough Wy *BARK* IG11	96	B1
Hanford Cl *WAND/EARL* SW18	150	A1
Hanger Gn *EA* W5	86	A3
Hanger View Wy *ACT* W3	86	A5
Hankey Pl *STHWK* SE1	48	B1
Hanley Gdns *FSBYPK* N4	57	F3
Hanley Rd *FSBYPK* N4	57	E3
Hanmer Wk *HOLWY* N7	57	F4
Hannah Cl *WLSDN* NW10	68	C1
Hannah Mary Wy *STHWK* SE1 *	102	A5
Hannay La *ARCH* N19	57	D2
Hannell Rd *FUL/PGN* SW6	113	E3
Hannen Rd *WNWD* SE27 *	154	B3
Hannibal Rd *WCHPL* E1	90	C4
Hannington Rd *CLAP* SW4	134	B1
Hanover Av *CAN/RD* E16	106	A2
Hanover Cl *RCH/KEW* TW9	110	A3
Hanover Dr *CHST* BR7	162	C4
Hanover Gdns *LBTH* SE11	118	A2
Hanover Pk *PECK* SE15	120	A4
Hanover Pl *COVGDN* WC2E	21	D5

Hanover Rd *WLSDN* NW10	70	C4
Hanover Sq *CONDST* W1S	19	D5
Hanover Steps *BAY/PAD* W2 *	17	D5
Hanover St *CONDST* W1S	19	D5
Hanover Ter *CAMTN* NW1	5	E4
Hanover Yd *IS* N1 *	11	D1
Hansard Ms *WKENS* W14	101	D3
Hans Crs *KTBR* SW1X	41	E2
Hansler Rd *EDUL* SE22	137	F3
Hanson Cl *BAL* SW12	134	B5
MORT/ESHN SW14	128	C1
Hans Pl *KTBR* SW1X	41	E2
Hans Rd *CHEL* SW3	41	E2
Hans St *KTBR* SW1X	41	F3
Hanway Pl *FITZ* W1T	20	A4
Hanway St *FITZ* W1T	20	A4
Harben Pde *HAMP* NW3 *	73	D4
Harben Rd *KIL/WHAMP* NW6	72	C4
Harberson Rd *BAL* SW12	152	B1
SRTFD E15		
Harberton Rd *ARCH* N19	56	C3
Harbet Rd *BAY/PAD* W2	16	B5
Harbinger Rd *POP/IOD* E14	104	B5
Harbledown Rd *FUL/PGN* SW6	114	A4
Harbord Cl *CMBW* SE5	119	D5
Harbord St *FUL/PGN* SW6	113	D4
Harborough Av *BFN/LL* DA15	145	E5
Harborough Rd *STRHM/NOR* SW16	153	F4
Harbour Av *WBPTN* SW10	114	C4
Harbour Exchange Sq *POP/IOD* E14.	136	C1
Harbour Yd *CMBW* SE5	136	C1
Harbour Yd *WBPTN* SW10 *	114	C4
Harbridge Av *PUT/ROE* SW15	129	F5
Harbut Rd *BTSEA* SW11	133	D2
Harcombe Rd *STNW/STAM* N16	59	E5
Harcourt Av *MNPK* E12	83	F1
Harcourt Blds *EMB* EC4Y *	34	A1
Harcourt Rd *BROCKY* SE4	139	F2
SRTFD E15		
Harcourt St *MBLAR* W1H	93	F1
Harcourt Ter *WBPTN* SW10	114	B1
Hardel Wk *BRXS/STRHM* SW2	136	A5
Hardens Manorway		
WOOL/PLUM SE18	107	D4
Harders Rd *PECK* SE15	120	B5
Hardess St *HNHL* SE24	136	C1
Hardie Cl *WLSDN* NW10	69	D2
Harding Cl *WALW* SE17	118	C2
Hardinge Rd *WLSDN* NW10	70	C5
WOOL/PLUM SE18	108	B4
Hardinge St *WCHPL* E1	90	C5
Harding Crs *WOOL/PLUM* SE18.	108	C4
Hardman Rd *CHARL* SE7	124	B1
Hardwicke Ms *FSBYW* WC1X *	9	F4
Hardwicke Rd *CHSWK* W4	98	C5
Hardwicke St *BARK* IG11	84	C5
Hardwick St *CLKNW* EC1R	10	B4
Hardwick's Wy *WAND/EARL* SW18	132	A3
Hardwidge St *STHWK* SE1	36	A5
Hardy Av *CAN/RD* E16	106	A2
Hardy Cl *BERM/RHTH* SE16	103	D3
Hardy Cots *GNWCH* SE10	123	D2
Hardy Rd *BKHTH/KID* SE3	123	F2
Harebell Dr *EHAM* E6	96	A4
Hare & Billet Rd *BKHTH/KID* SE3	123	D4
Hare Ct *EMB* EC4Y *	22	A5
Harecourt Rd *IS* N1	76	C3
Haredale Rd *HNHL* SE24	136	C2
Haredon Cl *FSTH* SE23	138	C5
Harefield Ms *BROCKY* SE4	139	F1
Harefield Rd *BROCKY* SE4	139	F1
Hare Marsh *BETH* E2	90	A3
Hare Rw *BETH* E2	90	B1
Hare St *WOOL/PLUM* SE18	108	A4
Hare Wk *IS* N1	13	D2
Harewood Av *CAMTN* NW1	17	D1
Harewood Pl *CONDST* W1S	19	D5
Harewood Rw *CAMTN* NW1	17	D2
Harfield Gdns *CMBW* SE5 *	137	E1
Harford St *WCHPL* E1	91	E3
Hargood Rd *BKHTH/KID* SE3	124	C4
Hargrave Pk *ARCH* N19	56	C4
Hargrave Pl *KTTN* NW5	75	D2
Hargrave Rd *ARCH* N19	56	C4
Hargwyne St *BRXN/ST* SW9	135	F1
Haringey Pk *CEND/HSY/T* N8	57	E1
Harland Av *BFN/LL* DA15	163	D5
Harland Rd *LEE/GVPK* SE12	160	A1
Harlescott Rd *PECK* SE15	139	D2
Harlesden Gdns *WLSDN* NW10	69	F5
Harlesden Rd *WLSDN* NW10	70	A4
WLSDN NW10	70	A5
Harleyford Rd *LBTH* SE11	117	F2
Harleyford St *LBTH* SE11	118	A2
Harley Gdns *WBPTN* SW10	114	C1
Harley Gv *BOW* E3	91	F2
Harley Pl *CAVSQ/HST* W1G	18	C4
Harley Rd *HAMP* NW3	73	D4
WLSDN NW10	87	E1
Harley St *CAVSQ/HST* W1G	18	C1
Harley Vls *WLSDN* NW10 *	87	E1
Harlinger St *WOOL/PLUM* SE18	107	E4
Harman Cl *CRICK* NW2	53	E5
STHWK SE1	120	A1
Harman Dr *BFN/LL* DA15	145	F4
CRICK NW2	53	E5
Harmony Pl *STHWK* SE1	119	F1
Harmood Gv *CAMTN* NW1	74	B4
Harmood St *CAMTN* NW1	74	B3
Harmsworth St *STHWK* SE5	46	B3
Harmsworth St *WALW* SE17	118	B1
Harold Rd *PLSTW* E13	82	B5
WAN E11	63	E3
Harpenden Rd *MNPK* E12	87	D2
WNWD SE27	64	C4
Harper Rd *EHAM* E6	154	B2
STHWK SE1	95	F5
Harp Island Cl *WLSDN* NW10	47	F2
Harp La *MON* EC3R	51	D4
Harpley Sq *WCHPL* E1	36	C2
Harpour Rd *BARK* IG11	90	C3
Harpsden St *BTSEA* SW11	84	C3
Harpur Ms *BMSBY* WC1N	116	A4
Harpur St *BMSBY* WC1N	21	E2
Harraden Rd *BKHTH/KID* SE3	21	E2
Harrier Ms *THMD* SE28	124	C4
Harriet Cl *HACK* E8	109	D3
Harriet Tubman Cl *BRXS/STRHM* SW2..	78	A5
Harriet Wk *KTBR* SW1X	136	A5
Harrington Cl *WLSDN* NW10	41	F1
Harrington Ct *NKENS* W10 *	51	D5
Harrington Gdns *SKENS* SW7	89	F2
Harrington Hl *CLPT* E5	39	D5
Harrington Rd *SKENS* SW7	60	B3
WAN E11	40	A4
Harrington Sq *CAMTN* NW1	63	E3
Harrington St *CAMTN* NW1	7	E1
Harrington Wy *WOOL/PLUM* SE18	7	E2
Harriott Cl *GNWCH* SE10	107	D4
Harrison Rd *WLSDN* NW10	105	F5
Harrison St *STPAN* WC1H	69	D5
Harris St *CMBW* SE5	9	D4
WALTH E17	119	D3
Harroway Rd *BTSEA* SW11	61	F2
Harrowby St *MBLAR* W1H	115	D5
Harrowgate Rd *HOM* E9	17	D4
Harrow Gn *WAN* E11	79	E3
Harrow La *POP/IOD* E14	63	E5
Harrow Pl *WCHPL* E1	104	C1
Harrow Rd *IL* IG1	25	D4
MV/WKIL W9	84	C1
WAN E11	14	A1
WLSDN NW10	63	F5
Harrow Road F/O *BAY/PAD* W2	88	B2
Harrow St *CAMTN* NW1 *	16	B3
Hart Gv *EA* W5	17	D2
Hartham Cl *HOLWY* N7	98	A2
Hartham Rd *HOLWY* N7	75	E2
Harting Rd *ELTH/MOT* SE9	75	E2
Hartington Rd *CAN/RD* E16	161	E4
CHSWK W4	94	B5
VX/NE SW8	110	B3
WALTH E17	117	E4
Hartismere Rd *FUL/PGN* SW6	61	E1
Hartlake Rd *HOM* E9	113	F5
Hartland Rd *CAMTN* NW1 *	79	D3
KIL/WHAMP NW6	74	B4
SRTFD E15	89	F1
Hartland Road Arches *CAMTN* NW1 *	81	F4
Hartley Av *EHAM* E6	74	A4
Hartley Rd *WAN* E11	83	E5
Hartley St *BETH* E2	63	F4
Hartmann Rd *CAN/RD* E16	90	C2
Hartnoll St *HOLWY* N7	107	D2
Harton Rd *DEPT* SE8	75	F2
Hartshorn Gdns *EHAM* E6	122	A4
Harts La *BARK* IG11	96	A3
Hart's La *NWCR* SE14	84	D4
	121	E3

Hartsmead Rd *ELTH/MOT SE9* 161 F2
Hart St *MON* EC3R 37 D1
Hartswood Gdns *SHB* W12 * 99 F4
Hartswood Rd *SHB* W12 .... 99 F3
Hartsworth Cl *PLSTW* E13 .... 93 F1
Hartville Rd *WOOL/PLUM* SE18 .... 109 E5
Hartwell Cl *BRXS/STRHM* SW2 .... 135 F1
Hartwell St *HACK* E8 .... 77 F3
Harvard Hl *CHSWK* W4 .... 110 B1
Harvard Rd *CHSWK* W4 .... 110 B1
   LEW SE13 .... 140 C3
Harvey Gdns *CHARL* SE7 .... 124 C1
Harvey Rd *CMBW* SE5 .... 119 D4
   IL IG1 .... 84 B2
   WAN E11 .... 63 E3
Harvey St *IS* N1 .... 77 D5
Harvington Wk *HACK* E8 * 78 A4
Harvist Rd *KIL/WHAMP* NW6 .... 89 E1
Harwood Ms *FUL/PGN* SW6 .... 114 B3
Harwood Rd *FUL/PGN* SW6 .... 114 A3
Hascombe Ter *CMBW* SE5 * 119 D5
Haseley End *FSTH* SE23 * 138 C5
Haselrigge Rd *CLAP* SW4 .... 135 D2
Haseltine Rd *SYD* SE26 .... 157 F4
Hasker St *CHEL* SW3 .... 41 D4
Haslam Cl *IS* N1 .... 76 A4
Haslam St *PECK* SE15 .... 119 F4
Haslemere Av *HDN* NW4 .... 53 D1
   WAND/EARL SW18 .... 150 B2
Haslemere Rd *CEND/HSY/T* N8 .... 57 E2
   GDMY/SEVK IG3 .... 67 F4
Hassard St *BETH* E2 .... 13 F2
Hassendean Rd *BKHTH/KID* SE3 ...... 124 B2
Hassett Rd *HOM* E9 .... 79 D3
Hassocks Cl *SYD* SE26 .... 156 B3
Hassop Rd *CRICK* NW2 .... 71 D1
Hasted Rd *CHARL* SE7 .... 125 D1
Hastings Cl *PECK* SE15 * 120 A3
Hastings St *STPAN* WC1H 8 C4
Hastings Rd *WOOL/PLUM* SE18 .... 108 C4
Hatcham Park Ms *NWCR* SE14 .... 121 D4
Hatcham Park Rd *NWCR* SE14 .... 121 D4
Hatcham Rd *PECK* SE15 .... 120 C2
Hatchard Rd *ARCH* N19 .... 57 D4
Hatchers Ms *STHWK* SE1 * 49 D1
Hatcliffe Cl *BKHTH/KID* SE3 .... 141 F1
Hatcliffe St *GNWCH* SE10 .... 123 F1
Hatfield Cl *BKHTH/KID* SE3 * 124 A3
Hatfield Rd *CHSWK* W4 .... 99 D3
   SRTFD E15 .... 81 E2
Hatfields *STHWK* SE1 .... 34 B3
Hathaway Crs *MNPK* E12 .... 83 F3
Hatherley Gdns *CEND/HSY/T* N8 ...... 57 E1
   EHAM E6 .... 95 D2
Hatherley Gv *BAY/PAD* W2 .... 14 C4
Hatherley St *WEST* SW1P 43 F5
Hathern Gdns *ELTH/MOT* SE9 .... 162 A4
Hathorne Cl *PECK* SE15 .... 120 B5
Hathorne Ter *ARCH* N19 * 57 D5
Hathway St *PECK* SE15 .... 120 C5
Hatley Rd *FSBYPK* N4 .... 57 F4
Hat & Mitre Ct *FARR* EC1M 23 D1
Hatteraick St *BERM/RHTH* SE16 ...... 102 C3
Hatton Cl *WOOL/PLUM* SE18 .... 127 D3
Hatton Gdn *HCIRC* EC1N 22 B2
Hatton Pl *HCIRC* EC1N 22 B1
Hatton Rw *STJWD* NW8 * 16 B1
Hatton St *STJWD* NW8 .... 16 B1
Hatton Wall *HCIRC* EC1N 22 A2
Haunch of Venison Yd *OXSTW* W1C * 18 C5
Havannah St *POP/IOD* E14 .... 104 A3
Havelock Cl *SHB* W12 * 100 B1
Havelock Rd *WIM/MER* SW19 .... 150 C5
Havelock St *IS* N1 .... 75 E5
Havelock Ter *VX/NE* SW8 .... 116 B3
Havelock Wk *FSTH* SE23 .... 156 C1
Haven Cl *ELTH/MOT* SE9 .... 161 F3
   WIM/MER SW19 .... 149 D3
Havens Ms *BOW* E3 .... 91 F4
Haven St *CAMTN* NW1 .... 74 B4
The Haven *RCH/KEW* TW9 .... 128 A1
Havenwood *WBLY* HA9 .... 50 B5
Haverfield Gdns *RCH/KEW* TW9 .... 110 A3
Haverfield Rd *BOW* E3 .... 91 E2
Haverhill Rd *BAL* SW12 .... 152 C1
Havering St *WCHPL* E1 .... 91 D5
Haversham Pl *HGT* N6 .... 55 F4
Haverstock Hl *HAMP* NW3 .... 73 E3
Haverstock Pl *FSBYE* EC1V 10 B3
Haverstock Rd *KTTN* NW5 .... 74 A2

Haverstock St *IS* N1 .... 11 D2
Havil St *CMBW* SE5 .... 119 E4
Hawarden Gv *HNHL* SE24 .... 136 C5
Hawarden Hl *CRICK* NW2 .... 52 A5
Hawbridge Rd *WAN* E11 .... 63 D3
Hawes St *IS* N1 .... 76 B4
Hawgood St *BOW* E3 .... 92 A4
Hawke Pl *BERM/RHTH* SE16 * 103 D3
Hawkesbury Rd *PUT/ROE* SW15 ...... 130 B3
Hawkesfield Rd *FSTH* SE23 .... 157 E2
Hawkins Rd *WLSDN* NW10 .... 69 E4
Hawkins Ter *CHARL* SE7 .... 125 E1
Hawkins Wy *CAT* SE6 .... 158 A5
Hawkley Gdns *WNWD* SE27 .... 154 B2
Hawkshaw Cl *BRXS/STRHM* SW2 ..... 135 E5
Hawkshead Rd *CHSWK* W4 .... 99 E4
   WLSDN NW10 .... 69 F4
Hawkslade Rd *PECK* SE15 .... 139 D3
Hawksley Rd *STNW/STAM* N16 .... 59 D5
Hawks Ms *GNWCH* SE10 * 122 C3
Hawksmoor Cl *EHAM* E6 .... 95 E5
   WOOL/PLUM SE18 .... 127 E1
Hawksmoor Ms *WCHPL* E1 .... 102 B1
Hawksmoor St *HMSMTH* W6 .... 113 D2
Hawkstone Est *BERM/RHTH* SE16 ... 102 C5
Hawkstone Rd *BERM/RHTH* SE16 ... 102 C5
Hawkwell Wk *IS* N1 * 76 C5
Hawkwood Mt *CLPT* E5 .... 60 B3
Hawley Crs *CAMTN* NW1 .... 74 B4
Hawley Ms *CAMTN* NW1 * 74 B4
Hawley Rd *CAMTN* NW1 .... 74 B4
Hawstead Rd *CAT* SE6 .... 140 B4
Hawthorn Crs *TOOT* SW17 .... 152 A5
Hawthorne Av *BOW* E3 .... 79 F5
Hawthorne Cl *IS* N1 .... 77 E3
Hawthorne Gv *CDALE/KGS* NW9 ...... 50 C2
Hawthorn Rd *WLSDN* NW10 .... 70 A4
Hawthorn Ter *BFN/LL* DA15 .... 145 F4
Hawthorn Wk *NKENS* W10 .... 89 E3
Hawtrey Rd *HAMP* NW3 .... 73 E4
Hay Cl *SRTFD* E15 .... 81 E4
Haycroft Gdns *WLSDN* NW10 .... 70 A5
Haycroft Rd *BRXS/STRHM* SW2 .... 135 E5
Hay Currie St *POP/IOD* E14 .... 92 B5
Hayday Rd *CAN/RD* E16 .... 94 A3
Hayden's Pl *NTGHL* W11 .... 89 F5
Haydon Park Rd *WIM/MER* SW19 .... 150 A5
Haydon's Rd *WIM/MER* SW19 .... 150 B5
Haydon St *TWRH* EC3N 37 E1
Haydon Wk *WCHPL* E1 .... 25 E5
Haydon Wy *WAND/EARL* SW18 .... 132 C2
Hayes Gv *EDUL* SE22 .... 137 F1
Hayes Pl *CAMTN* NW1 .... 17 D1
Hayfield Pas *WCHPL* E1 .... 90 C3
Haygarth Pl *WIM/MER* SW19 .... 149 D5
Hay Hl *MYFR/PICC* W1J 31 D2
Hayles St *LBTH* SE11 .... 46 C4
Hayling Cl *STNW/STAM* N16 .... 77 E2
Haymarket *STJS* SW1Y 32 A2
Haymerle Rd *PECK* SE15 .... 120 A2
Haynes Cl *BKHTH/KID* SE3 .... 141 E1
Hayne St *STBT* EC1A 23 D2
Hay's La *STHWK* SE1 .... 36 C3
Hay's Ms *MYFR/PICC* W1J 30 C2
Hayst St *BETH* E2 .... 78 A5
Hayter Rd *BRXS/STRHM* SW2 .... 135 E3
Hayton Cl *HACK* E8 .... 77 F3
Hayward Gdns *PUT/ROE* SW15 .... 130 C4
Hayward's Pl *CLKNW* EC1R * 22 C1
Hazelbank Rd *CAT* SE6 .... 159 D2
Hazelbourne Rd *BAL* SW12 .... 134 B4
Hazeldean Rd *WLSDN* NW10 .... 69 D4
Hazeldon Rd *BROCKY* SE4 .... 139 E3
Hazel Gv *SYD* SE26 .... 157 D4
Hazelhurst Rd *TOOT* SW17 .... 150 C4
Hazellville Rd *ARCH* N19 .... 57 D2
Hazelmere Rd *KIL/WHAMP* NW6 ...... 71 F5
Hazel Rd *SRTFD* E15 * 81 E2
   WLSDN NW10 .... 88 B2
Hazel Wy *STHWK* SE1 .... 49 E4
Hazelwood Cl *CLPT* E5 .... 61 E5
Hazlebury Rd *FUL/PGN* SW6 .... 114 B5
Hazledene Rd *CHSWK* W4 .... 110 C2
Hazlewell Rd *PUT/ROE* SW15 .... 130 C3
Hazlewood Crs *NKENS* W10 .... 89 E5
Hazlitt Ms *WKENS* W14 * 101 E4
Hazlitt Rd *WKENS* W14 .... 101 E4
Headcorn Rd *BMLY* BR1 .... 159 F5
Headfort Pl *KTBR* SW1X 42 B1
Headington Rd *WAND/EARL* SW18 .. 150 C1
Headlam Rd *CLAP* SW4 .... 135 D4
Headlam St *WCHPL* E1 .... 90 B3

Headley Dr *GNTH/NBYPK* IG2	66 B1
Heads Ms *NTGHL* W11	14 A5
Head St *WCHPL* E1	91 D5
Heald St *NWCR* SE14	121 F4
Healey St *CAMTN* NW1 *	74 B3
Hearne Rd *CHSWK* W4	110 A1
Hearn's Blds *WALW* SE17	48 B5
Hearnshaw St *POP/IOD* E14	91 E5
Hearn St *SDTCH* EC2A	25 D1
Hearnville Rd *BAL* SW12	152 A1
Heath Brow *HAMP* NW3	54 C5
Heath Cl *GLDGN* NW11	54 B2
Heathcote St *BMSBY* WC1N	9 E5
Heath Dr *HAMP* NW3	72 B1
Heathedge *SYD* SE26 *	156 B2
Heatherbank *ELTH/MOT* SE9	125 F5
Heather Cl *EHAM* E6	96 A5
LEW SE13	141 D4
VX/NE SW8	134 B1
Heather Gdns *GLDGN* NW11	53 E1
Heather Park Dr *ALP/SUD* HA0	68 A4
Heather Rd *CRICK* NW2	51 F4
LEE/GVPK SE12	160 A2
Heather Wk *NKENS* W10	89 E3
Heatherwood Cl *MNPK* E12	64 B4
Heathfield Av *WAND/EARL* SW18	133 D5
Heathfield Cl *CAN/RD* E16	95 D4
Heathfield Gdns *CHSWK* W4	110 C1
GLDGN NW11	53 D1
WAND/EARL SW18	133 D4
Heathfield Pk *CRICK* NW2	70 C3
Heathfield Rd *ACT* W3	98 B3
WAND/EARL SW18	132 C4
Heathfield Sq *WAND/EARL* SW18	133 D5
Heathfield Ter *CHSWK* W4	110 C1
WOOL/PLUM SE18	127 E2
Heathgate *GLDGN* NW11	54 B1
Heathgate Pl *HAMP* NW3	73 F1
Heath Hurst Rd *HAMP* NW3	73 E1
Heathland Rd *STNW/STAM* N16	59 E3
Heath La *BKHTH/KID* SE3	123 D5
Heathlee Rd *BKHTH/KID* SE3	141 F2
Heathman's Rd *FUL/PGN* SW6	113 F4
Heath Md *WIM/MER* SW19	149 D3
Heath Ri *PUT/ROE* SW15	131 D4
Heath Rd *VX/NE* SW8	116 B5
Heathside *HAMP* NW3	73 D1
Heathstan Rd *SHB* W12	88 A5
Heath St *HAMP* NW3	72 C1
Heathview Gdns *PUT/ROE* SW15	130 C5
Heath Vis *WAND/EARL* SW18 *	150 C1
WOOL/PLUM SE18	127 F1
Heathville Rd *ARCH* N19	57 E2
Heathwall St *BTSEA* SW11	133 F1
Heathway *BKHTH/KID* SE3	123 A3
Heathwood Gdns *CHARL* SE7	107 E5
Heaton Rd *PECK* SE15	138 B1
Heaven Tree Cl *IS* N1	76 C2
Heaver Rd *BTSEA* SW11 *	133 D1
Heavitree Cl *WOOL/PLUM* SE18	127 D1
Heavitree Rd *WOOL/PLUM* SE18	127 D1
Hebdon Rd *TOOT* SW17	151 E3
Heber Rd *CRICK* NW2	71 D2
EDUL SE22	137 F4
Hebron Rd *HMSMTH* W6	100 B4
Heckfield Pl *FUL/PGN* SW6	114 A3
Heckford St *WAP* E1W	103 D1
Hector St *WOOL/PLUM* SE18 *	109 E5
Heddington Gv *HOLWY* N7	75 F2
Heddon St *CONDST* W1S	31 E2
Hedger's Gv *HOM* E9 *	79 E3
Hedger St *LBTH* SE11	46 C4
Hedgley St *LEE/GVPK* SE12	141 F3
Hedingham Cl *IS* N1	76 C3
Hedley Rw *HBRY* N5	77 D2
Heenan Cl *BARK* IG11	84 C3
Heidegger Crs *BARN* SW13	112 B3
Heigham Rd *EHAM* E6	83 E4
The Heights *CHARL* SE7	124 C1
Heiron St *WALW* SE17	118 B2
Helby Rd *CLAP* SW4	135 D4
Helder St *LEE/GVPK* SE12	141 F5
Helena Pl *HACK* E8	78 B5
Helena Rd *PLSTW* E13	93 F1
WLSDN NW10	70 B2
Helena Sq *BERM/RHTH* SE16.	103 E1
Helenslea Av *GLDGN* NW11	53 F3
Helen's Pl *BETH* E2	90 C2
Helen St *WOOL/PLUM* SE18 *	108 B5
Helix Gdns *BRXS/STRHM* SW2	135 F4
Helix Rd *BRXS/STRHM* SW2	135 F4
Hellings St *WAP* E1W	102 A2

Helme Cl *WIM/MER* SW19	149 F5
Helmet Rw *FSBYE* EC1V	11 F5
Helmore Rd *BARK* IG11	85 F4
Helmsley Pl *HACK* E8	78 B4
Helmsley St *HACK* E8	78 B5
Helperby Rd *WLSDN* NW10	69 E4
Helsinki Sq *BERM/RHTH* SE16	103 E4
Helvetia St *CAT* SE6	157 F2
Hemans St *VX/NE* SW8	117 D3
Hemingford Rd *IS* N1	75 F5
Hemlock Rd *SHB* W12	99 F1
Hemming St *WCHPL* E1	90 A3
Hemmingway Cl *KTTN* NW5	74 A1
Hemp Wk *WALW* SE17	48 B4
Hemstal Rd *KIL/WHAMP* NW6	72 A4
Hemsworth St *IS* N1	12 C1
Henchman St *SHB* W12	87 F5
Henderson Cl *WLSDN* NW10	68 C3
Henderson Dr *STJWD* NW8	4 A5
Henderson Rd *FSTGT* E7	82 C5
WAND/EARL SW18	133 E5
Hendham Rd *TOOT* SW17	151 E2
Hendon Park Rw *GLDGN* NW11 *	53 F1
Hendon Wy *CRICK* NW2	53 D2
Hendre Rd *STHWK* SE1	49 D5
Hendrick Av *BAL* SW12	133 F4
Heneage La *HDTCH* EC3A	25 D5
Heneage St *WCHPL* E1	25 F2
Henfield Cl *ARCH* N19	56 C3
Hengist Rd *LEE/GVPK* SE12	142 B5
Hengrave Rd *FSTH* SE23	138 C5
Henley Cl *BERM/RHTH* SE16 *	102 C3
Henley Dr *STHWK* SE1	49 F4
Henley Rd *CAN/RD* E16	107 F3
IL IG1	84 C1
WLSDN NW10	70 C5
Henley St *BTSEA* SW11	116 A5
Hennel Cl *FSTH* SE23	156 B1
Henniker Gdns *EHAM* E6	95 D2
Henniker Ms *CHEL* SW3	115 D2
Henniker Rd *SRTFD* E15	81 D2
Henning St *BTSEA* SW11	115 E4
Henrietta Cl *DEPT* SE8	122 A2
Henrietta Ms *BMSBY* WC1N	9 D5
Henrietta Pl *CAVSQ/HST* W1G	18 C4
Henrietta St *COVGDN* WC2E	33 D1
SRTFD E15	80 C2
Henriques St *WCHPL* E1	90 A5
Henry Addington Cl *EHAM* E6	96 B4
Henry Cooper Wy *ELTH/MOT* SE9	161 D3
Henry Dickens Ct *NTGHL* W11	101 D1
Henry Doulton Dr *TOOT* SW17	152 A4
Henry Jackson Rd *PUT/ROE* SW15	131 D1
Henry Rd *EHAM* E6	95 E1
FSBYPK N4	58 C3
Henryson Rd *BROCKY* SE4	140 A3
Henry Tate Ms *STRHM/NOR* SW16	154 A5
Henshall St *IS* N1	77 D3
Henshaw St *WALW* SE17	48 A4
Henslowe Rd *EDUL* SE22	138 A3
Henson Av *CRICK* NW2	70 C2
Henstridge Pl *STJWD* NW8	4 C1
Henty Cl *BTSEA* SW11	115 E3
Henty Wk *PUT/ROE* SW15	130 B5
Henwick Rd *ELTH/MOT* SE9	143 D1
Hepscott Rd *HOM* E9	80 A3
Heralds Pl *LBTH* SE11	46 C4
Herald St *BETH* E2	90 B3
Herbal Hl *CLKNW* EC1R	22 B1
Herbert Crs *KTBR* SW1X	41 F2
Herbert Gdns *CHSWK* W4	110 B2
WLSDN NW10	88 B1
Herbert Ms *BRXS/STRHM* SW2	136 A4
Herbert Rd *WOOL/PLUM* SE18	126 B2
Herbert Rd *CDALE/KGS* NW9	52 A1
GDMY/SEVK IG3	67 E4
MNPK E12	83 E1
WALTH E17	62 F2
WOOL/PLUM SE18	126 B3
Herbert St *KTTN* NW5	74 A3
PLSTW E13	94 A1
Herbrand St *BMSBY* WC1N	8 C5
Hercules Pl *HOLWY* N7	57 E5
Hercules Rd *STHWK* SE1	45 F5
Hercules St *HOLWY* N7	57 E5
Hereford Gdns *IL* IG1	65 E2
Hereford Ms *BAY/PAD* W2	14 B4
Hereford Pl *NWCR* SE14	121 F3
Hereford Retreat *PECK* SE15	120 A3
Hereford Rd *ACT* W3	98 C1
BAY/PAD W2	14 B5
BOW E3	91 F1

Hereford Sq SKENS SW7 .... 39 F5
Hereford St BETH E2 .... 90 A3
Heretage CI BRXN/ST SW9 .... 136 B1
Hereward Rd TOOT SW17 .... 151 E4
Heritage PI WAND/EARL SW18 * 133 D4
Herlwyn Gdns TOOT SW17 .... 151 F4
Hermes CI MV/WKIL W9 .... 14 A1
Hermes Dr BRXS/STRHM SW2 .... 135 F3
Hermes St IS N1 .... 10 A2
Hermitage Gdns CRICK NW2 .... 54 A5
Hermitage La CRICK NW2 .... 54 A5
Hermitage Rd FSBYPK N4 .... 58 A5
Hermitage Rw HACK E8 * 78 A2
Hermitage St BAY/PAD W2 .... 16 A3
The Hermitage BARN SW13 * 111 F4
    FSTH SE23 .... 156 C1
    LEW SE13 * 122 C5
Hermitage Wall WAP E1W 102 A3
Hermit PI KIL/WHAMP NW6 .... 72 A5
Hermit Rd CAN/RD E16 .... 93 F3
Hermit St FSBYE EC1V 10 C3
Herndon Rd WAND/EARL SW18 ...... 132 B4
Herne CI WLSDN NW10 .... 69 D2
Herne HI HNHL SE24 .... 136 C5
Herne PI HNHL SE24 .... 136 B4
Heron CI WLSDN NW10 .... 69 E3
Heron Crs SCUP DA14 .... 163 E4
Herondale Av WAND/EARL SW18 .... 151 F1
Heron Dr FSBYPK N4 .... 58 C4
Herongate Rd MNPK E12 .... 64 C4
Heron Ms IL IG1 .... 66 B4
Heron PI BERM/RHTH SE16 .... 103 E2
Heron Quays POP/IOD E14 .... 104 A2
Herons Lea HGT N6 * 55 F2
Herrick Rd HBRY N5 .... 58 C5
Herries St WEST SW1P 44 A5
Herringham Rd CHARL SE7 .... 106 C4
Hersant CI WLSDN NW10 .... 70 A5
Herschell Rd FSTH SE23 .... 139 E5
Hersham CI PUT/ROE SW15 .... 130 A5
Hershell Ct MORT/ESHN SW14 * 128 B2
Hertford Av MORT/ESHN SW14 ...... 129 D3
Hertford PI FITZ W1T 19 E1
Hertford Rd BARK IG11 .... 84 A4
    GNTH/NBYPK IG2 .... 67 E1
    IS N1 .... 77 E5
Hertford St MYFR/PICC W1J 30 C3
Hertslet Rd HOLWY N7 .... 57 F5
Hertsmere Rd POP/IOD E14 .... 104 A1
Hesewall CI CLAP SW4 .... 116 C5
Hesketh PI NTGHL W11 .... 89 E1
Hesketh Rd FSTGT E7 .... 64 A5
Heslop Rd BAL SW12 .... 151 F1
Hesper Ms ECT SW5 .... 114 B1
Hesperus Crs POP/IOD E14 .... 104 B3
Hessel St WCHPL E1 .... 90 B5
Hestercombe Av FUL/PGN SW6 ..... 113 E5
Hester Rd BTSEA SW11 .... 115 E3
Hester Ter RCH/KEW TW9 .... 128 A1
Heston St NWCR SE14 .... 121 F4
Hetherington Rd CLAP SW4 .... 135 E2
Hetley Rd SHB W12 .... 100 B2
Hevelius CI CNWCH SE10 .... 123 F1
Hever Cft ELTH/MOT SE9 .... 162 A4
Heverham Rd WOOL/PLUM SE18 ... 109 E5
Hewer St NKENS W10 .... 89 D4
Hewetts Quay BARK IG11 .... 84 B5
Hewett St SDTCH EC2A 25 D1
Hewison St BOW E3 .... 91 F1
Hewlett Rd BOW E3 .... 91 E1
The Hexagon HGT N6 .... 55 F3
Hexal Rd CAT SE6 .... 159 E3
Hexham Rd WNWD SE27 .... 154 C1
Heybridge Wy LEY E10 .... 61 D2
Heyford Av VX/NE SW8 .... 117 E3
Heyford Ter VX/NE SW8 .... 117 E3
Heygate Est WALW SE17 .... 47 F4
Heygate St WALW SE17 .... 47 E5
Heysham La HAMP NW3 .... 54 B5
Heysham Rd SEVS/STOTM N15 ...... 59 D1
Heythorp St WAND/EARL SW18 ..... 149 F2
Heyworth Rd CLPT E5 .... 78 B1
    SRTFD E15 .... 81 F1
Hibbert Rd WALTH E17 .... 61 F2
Hibbert St BTSEA SW11 .... 132 C1
Hichisson Rd PECK SE15 .... 138 B3
Hicken Rd BRXS/STRHM SW2 .... 135 F3
Hickin CI CHARL SE7 .... 107 D5
Hickin St POP/IOD E14 .... 104 C4

Hickling Rd IL IG1 .... 84 B2
Hickman CI CAN/RD E16 .... 95 D4
Hicks CI BTSEA SW11 .... 133 E1
Hicks St DEPT SE8 .... 121 E1
Hide PI WEST SW1P 44 A5
Highbank PI WAND/EARL SW18 * ... 150 B1
Highbank Wy CEND/HSY/T N8 .... 58 A1
Highbridge Rd BARK IG11 .... 84 B5
Highbrook Rd BKHTH/KID SE3 ...... 143 D5
Highbury Cnr IS N1 .... 76 B3
Highbury Crs HBRY N5 .... 76 A2
Highbury Est HBRY N5 .... 76 C3
Highbury Gra GDMY/SEVK IG3 ..... 67 E4
Highbury Gra HBRY N5 .... 76 B1
Highbury Gv HBRY N5 .... 76 B2
Highbury HI HBRY N5 .... 76 B3
Highbury New Pk HBRY N5 .... 76 B3
Highbury Pk HBRY N5 .... 76 B1
Highbury PI HBRY N5 .... 76 B3
Highbury Qd HBRY N5 .... 58 C5
Highbury Rd WIM/MER SW19 .... 149 E5
Highbury Station Rd IS N1 * 76 A3
Highbury Ter HBRY N5 .... 76 B2
Highbury Terrace Ms HBRY N5 ..... 76 B2
Highclere St SYD SE26 .... 157 E4
Highcombe CHARL SE7 .... 124 B2
Highcombe CI ELTH/MOT SE9 .... 161 D1
Highcroft Gdns GLDGN NW11 .... 53 F1
Highcroft Rd ARCH N19 .... 57 E2
Highcross Wy PUT/ROE SW15 .... 148 A1
Highdown Rd PUT/ROE SW15 .... 130 B4
Highfield Av GLDGN NW11 .... 53 D2
Highfield CI LEW SE13 .... 141 D3
Highfield Gdns GLDGN NW11 .... 53 E1
Highfield Rd ACT W3 .... 86 B4
    GLDGN NW11 * 53 E1
Highfields Gv HGT N6 .... 56 A3
Highgate Av HGT N6 .... 56 A2
Highgate HI HGT N6 .... 56 A3
Highgate High St HGT N6 .... 56 A3
Highgate Hi ARCH N19 .... 56 B3
Highgate Rd KTTN NW5 .... 56 A5
Highgate Spinney CEND/HSY/T N8 * 57 D1
Highgate Wk FSTH SE23 .... 156 C1
Highgate West HI HGT N6 .... 56 A3
High Gv WOOL/PLUM SE18 .... 127 D5
High Hill Ferry CLPT E5 .... 60 B3
High Holborn HHOL WC1V 21 D4
Highland Cft BECK BR3 .... 158 B5
Highlands Av ACT W3 .... 98 C1
Highlands CI FSBYPK N4 .... 57 E2
Highlands Gdns IL IG1 .... 65 F3
Highlands Heath PUT/ROE SW15 ... 130 C5
Highland Ter LEW SE13 * 140 B1
High Level Dr SYD SE26 .... 156 A4
Highlever Rd NKENS W10 .... 88 C4
Highmead WOOL/PLUM SE18 .... 127 F3
Highmore Rd BKHTH/KID SE3 ...... 123 E5
High Mt HDN NW4 .... 52 A1
The High Pde STRHM/NOR SW16 * . 153 E3
High Park Rd RCH/KEW TW9 .... 110 A4
High Point ELTH/MOT SE9 .... 162 B3
High Rd GDMY/SEVK IG3 .... 67 E4
    IL IG1 .... 66 B1
    LEY E10 .... 62 B1
    WLSDN NW10 .... 69 E3
High Road Leyton LEY E10 .... 62 B4
High Road Leytonstone WAN E11 ... 63 E3
Highstone Av WAN E11 .... 64 A1
High St ACT W3 .... 98 C2
    PLSTW E13 .... 94 A1
    SRTFD E15 .... 92 C1
    WAN E11 .... 64 B1
    WIM/MER SW19 .... 149 D5
High Street Harlesden WLSDN NW10 . 69 E5
High Street Ms WIM/MER SW19 ..... 149 E5
High St North EHAM E6 .... 83 E5
    EHAM E6 .... 83 E3
High St South EHAM E6 .... 95 F1
    MNPK E12 .... 83 E3
High Timber St BLKFR EC4V 35 F1
High Trees BRXS/STRHM SW2 .... 154 A1
The Highway WAP E1W 102 C3
    WCHPL E1 .... 102 A1
Highwood CI EDUL SE22 .... 156 A1
Highwood Rd ARCH N19 .... 57 E5
Highworth St CAMTN NW1 * 17 D2
Hilary CI FUL/PGN SW6 * 114 B3
Hilary Rd SHB W12 .... 99 F1
Hilborough Rd HACK E8 .... 77 F4

Hilda Lockert Wk *BRXN/ST* SW9	118	B5
Hilda Rd *CAN/RD* E16	95	E3
EHAM E6	83	D4
Hilda Ter *BRXN/ST* SW9 *	118	A5
Hildreth St *BAL* SW12	152	B1
Hildyard Rd *FUL/PGN* SW6	114	A2
Hiley Rd *WLSDN* NW10	88	C2
Hilgrove Rd *KIL/WHAMP* NW6	72	C4
Hillbeck Cl *PECK* SE15	120	C3
Hillbrook Rd *TOOT* SW17	151	F3
Hillbury Rd *TOOT* SW17	152	B3
Hill Cl *CHST* BR7	162	B5
CRICK NW2	52	B5
GLDGN NW11	54	A1
Hillcourt Rd *EDUL* SE22	138	B4
Hillcrest *HGT* N6	56	A2
HNHL SE24 *	137	D2
Hillcrest Cl *SYD* SE26	156	A4
Hill Crest Gdns *CRICK* NW2	52	A5
Hillcrest Rd *ACT* W3	98	A2
BMLY BR1	160	A4
Hillcroft Rd *EHAM* E6	96	B4
Hill Dr *WBLY* HA9	50	B3
Hilldrop Crs *HOLWY* N7	75	D2
Hilldrop Est *HOLWY* N7	75	D2
Hilldrop La *HOLWY* N7	75	D2
Hilldrop Rd *HOLWY* N7	75	D2
Hill End *WOOL/PLUM* SE18	126	A4
Hillersdon Av *BARN* SW13	112	A5
Hillery Cl *WALW* SE17	48	B5
Hill Farm Rd *NKENS* W10	88	C4
Hillfield Rd *KIL/WHAMP* NW6	71	F2
Hill Gardens Craven *BAY/PAD* W2 *	27	E1
KENS W8	26	A3
Hillgate Pl *BAL* SW12	134	B4
KENS W8	26	A3
Hillgate St *KENS* W8	26	A3
Hill House Rd *STRHM/NOR* SW16	153	F5
Hilliard's Ct *WAP* E1W *	102	C2
Hillier Rd *BTSEA* SW11	133	F4
Hillingdon St *WALW* SE17	118	B2
Hillman Dr *NKENS* W10	88	C3
Hillman St *HACK* E8	78	B3
Hillmarton Rd *HOLWY* N7	75	D2
Hillmarton Ter *HOLWY* N7 *	75	E2
Hillmead Dr *BRXN/ST* SW9	136	B2
Hillmore Gv *SYD* SE26	157	D5
Hillreach *WOOL/PLUM* SE18	125	F1
Hill Ri *FSTH* SE23	156	B1
Hillrise Rd *ARCH* N19	57	E2
Hill Rd *STJWD* NW8	3	F2
Hillsboro Rd *EDUL* SE22	137	E3
Hillside *WLSDN* NW10	69	D5
Hillside *STJWD* NW8	3	D1
Hillside Gdns *BRXS/STRHM* SW2 *	154	A2
HGT N6	56	A1
Hillside Gdns *BRXS/STRHM* SW2	153	F2
SEVS/STOTM N15	59	E1
Hillsleigh Rd *KENS* W8	101	F2
Hills Pl *SOHO/SHAV* W1D	19	E5
Hillstowe St *CLPT* E5	60	C4
Hill St *MYFR/PICC* W1J	30	C3
Hilltop Av *WLSDN* NW10	68	C3
Hilltop Cots *SYD* SE26 *	156	B4
Hilltop Rd *KIL/WHAMP* NW6	72	A4
Hillview Crs *IL* IG1	66	B2
Hill View Dr *THMD* SE28	109	E2
WELL DA16	127	E5
Hillview Rd *CHST* BR7	162	A5
HGT N6	56	A4
Hillway *CDALE/KGS* NW9	51	E3
HGT N6	56	A4
Hillworth Rd *BRXS/STRHM* SW2	136	A5
Hillyard Rd *BRXN/ST* SW9	118	A4
Hillyfield Cl *HOM* E9	79	E2
Hilly Flds *BROCKY* SE4 *	140	A2
Hilly Fields Crs *BROCKY* SE4	140	A2
Hilsea St *CLPT* E5	78	C1
Himley Rd *TOOT* SW17	152	A3
Hinckley Rd *PECK* SE15	138	A2
Hind Ct *FLST/FETLN* EC4A	22	B5
Hinde Ms *MHST* W1U *	18	B4
Hinde St *MHST* W1U	18	B4
Hind Gv *POP/IOD* E14	92	A5
Hindmans Rd *EDUL* SE22	138	A3
Hindmarsh Cl *WCHPL* E1 *	102	A1
Hindrey Rd *CLPT* E5	78	B2
Hindsley's Pl *FSTH* SE23	156	C2
Hinstock Rd *WOOL/PLUM* SE18	126	C3
Hinton Cl *ELTH/MOT* SE9	144	B1
Hinton Rd *HNHL* SE24	136	C1
Hippodrome Pl *NTGHL* W11	101	E1
Hitcham Rd *WALTH* E17	61	F3
Hithe Gv *BERM/RHTH* SE16	102	C4
Hither Farm Rd *BKHTH/KID* SE3	142	C1
Hitherfield Rd *STRHM/NOR* SW16	153	F2
Hither Green La *LEW* SE13	140	C5
Hitherwood Dr *NRWD* SE19	155	F4
Hoadly Rd *STRHM/NOR* SW16	153	D3
Hobart Pl *BGVA* SW1W	42	C3
Hobbes Wk *PUT/ROE* SW15	130	B5
Hobbs Pl *IS* N1 *	77	E5
Hobbs Place Est *IS* N1	12	C1
Hobbs Rd *WNWD* SE27	154	C2
Hobday St *POP/IOD* E14	92	B5
Hobsons Pl *WCHPL* E1 *	90	C1
Hobury St *WBPTN* SW10	114	C2
Hocker St *BETH* E2 *	13	E4
Hockley Av *EHAM* E6	95	E1
Hockley Ms *BARK* IG11	97	E1
Hocroft Av *CRICK* NW2	53	F5
Hocroft Rd *CRICK* NW2	71	F1
Hocroft Wk *CRICK* NW2	53	F5
Hodes Rw *HAMP* NW3	75	F1
Hodford Rd *GLDGN* NW11	53	F3
Hodister Cl *CMBW* SE5	118	C3
Hodnet Gv *BERM/RHTH* SE16	102	C5
Hoffmann Sq *IS* N1 *	12	B3
Hofland Rd *WKENS* W14	101	E4
Hogan Ms *BAY/PAD* W2	16	A2
Hogarth Cl *CAN/RD* E16	95	D4
Hogarth Pl *ECT* SW5	38	C5
Hogarth Rd *ECT* SW5	38	C5
Hogarth Ter *CHSWK* W4 *	111	E2
Hogshead Pas *WAP* E1W *	102	B1
Holbeach Gdns *BFN/LL* DA15	145	E4
Holbeach Rd *CAT* SE6	140	A5
Holbeck Rw *PECK* SE15	120	A3
Holbein Ms *BGVA* SW1W	41	F3
Holbein Pl *BGVA* SW1W	42	A5
Holberton Gdns *WLSDN* NW10	88	B2
Holborn *HCIRC* EC1N	22	A3
Holborn Circ *HCIRC* EC1N	22	B3
Holborn Pl *HHOL* WC1V	21	E3
Holborn Rd *PLSTW* E13	94	B4
Holborn Viad *STBT* EC1A	22	C3
Holbrooke Ct *HOLWY* N7	57	E5
Holbrook Rd *SRTFD* E15	93	F1
Holburn *GINN* WC1R	22	A3
Holburne Cl *BKHTH/KID* SE3	124	C4
Holburne Gdns *BKHTH/KID* SE3	125	D4
Holburne Rd *BKHTH/KID* SE3	124	C4
Holcombe Rd *IL* IG1	66	A2
Holcombe St *HMSMTH* W6	112	B1
Holcroft Rd *HOM* E9	78	C4
Holden Av *CDALE/KGS* NW9	50	C5
Holdenby Rd *BROCKY* SE4	139	E5
Holden St *BTSEA* SW11	116	A5
Holdernesse Rd *TOOT* SW17	151	F3
Holderness Wy *WNWD* SE27	154	B5
Holford Ms *FSBYW* WC1X *	9	E3
Holford Rd *HAMP* NW3	54	C5
Holford St *FSBYW* WC1X	10	A3
Holford Yd *FSBYW* WC1X *	10	A2
Holgate Av *BTSEA* SW11	133	D1
Holgate Rd *CHARL* SE7	107	D4
Holland Dr *FSTH* SE23	157	E3
Holland Gdns *WKENS* W14	101	E4
Holland Gv *BRXN/ST* SW9	118	A3
Holland Pk *NTCHL* W11	101	F2
Holland Park Av *GDMY/SEVK* IG3	67	E1
NTCHL W11	101	E2
Holland Park Gdns *WKENS* W14	101	E3
Holland Park Ms *NTGHL* W11	101	F1
Holland Park Rd *NTGHL* W11	101	F2
Holland Park Ter *NTGHL* W11 *	101	E2
Holland Pas *IS* N1	76	C5
Holland Pl *KENS* W8	26	C5
Holland Rd *EHAM* E6	83	E2
SRTFD E15	93	E2
WKENS W14	101	D5
WLSDN NW10	70	A5
Holland St *KENS* W8	38	B1
STHWK SE1	35	D3
Holland Villas Rd *WKENS* W14	101	E3
Hollar Rd *STNW/STAM* N16	59	F5
Hollen St *SOHO/CST* W1F	19	D5
Holles St *CAVSQ/HST* W1C	19	D3
Holley Rd *ACT* W3	99	E3
Holliday Sq *BTSEA* SW11 *	133	D1
Hollies Av *BFN/LL* DA15	163	F3
Hollies Rd *EA* W5	110	A3
Hollies Wy *BAL* SW12 *	134	A5
Hollingbourne Rd *HNHL* SE24	136	C3
Hollington Rd *EHAM* E6	95	F2
Holloway Rd *ARCH* N19	57	D4
EHAM E6	95	F2
HOLWY N7	75	F1

WAN E11	63	D5
Hollybush Gdns *BETH* E2	90	B2
Hollybush Hl *WAN* E11	63	F1
Hollybush Pl *BETH* E2	90	B2
Hollybush St *PLSTW* E13	95	F2
Holly Bush W *HAMP* NW3 *	72	C1
Holly Cl *WLSDN* NW10	69	E4
Hollycroft Av *HAMP* NW3	54	A5
Hollydale Rd *PECK* SE15	120	C5
Hollydown Wy *WAN* E11	63	D5
Holly Gv *CDALE/KGS* NW9	50	C2
PECK SE15	119	F5
Holly Hedge Ter *LEW* SE13	140	C3
Holly Hl *HAMP* NW3	72	C1
Holly Lodge Gdns *HGT* N6	56	A4
Holly Ms *WBPTN* SW10 *	114	C1
Holly Mt *HAMP* NW3 *	72	C1
Hollymount Cl *GNWCH* SE10	122	C4
Holly Pk *FSBYPK* N4	57	E2
WAN E11	63	D5
Holly Rd *CHSWK* W4	99	D5
LEE/GVPK SE12	160	B3
Holly St *HACK* E8	77	F4
Hollytree Cl *WIM/MER* SW19	149	D1
Hollyview Cl *HDN* NW4	52	A1
Holly Vis *HMSMTH* W6 *	100	B4
Holly Wk *HAMP* NW3	72	C1
Hollywood Ms *WBPTN* SW10 *	114	C2
Hollywood Rd *WBPTN* SW10	114	C2
Holman Rd *BTSEA* SW11	115	D5
Holmbury Vw *CLPT* E5	60	B5
Holmbush Rd *PUT/ROE* SW15	131	F4
Holmcote Gdns *HBRY* N5	76	C2
Holmdale Rd *CHST* BR7	162	C5
KIL/WHAMP NW6	72	A2
Holmdale Ter *SEVS/STOTM* N15	59	E1
Holmdene Av *HNHL* SE24	136	C3
Holmead Rd *FUL/PGN* SW6	114	B3
Holme Lacey Rd *LEE/GVPK* SE12	141	F4
Holme Rd *EHAM* E6	83	E5
Holmes Cl *EDUL* SE22	138	A2
Holmesdale Av *MORT/ESHN* SW14	128	B1
Holmesdale Rd *HGT* N6	56	B2
Holmesley Rd *FSTH* SE23	139	E4
Holmes Rd *KTTN* NW5	74	B2
Holmes Ter *STHWK* SE1	34	A5
Holmewood Gdns *BRXS/STRHM* SW2	135	F5
Holmewood Rd *BRXS/STRHM* SW2	135	E5
Holmleigh Rd *STNW/STAM* N16	59	E3
Holm Oak Cl *PUT/ROE* SW15	131	F4
Holmshaw Cl *SYD* SE26	157	E4
Holmside Rd *BAL* SW12	134	A4
Holmwood Rd *GDMY/SEVK* IG3	67	A4
Holmwood Vis *CHARL* SE7	124	C1
Holne Cha *EFNCH* N2	54	C1
Holness Rd *SRTFD* E15	81	F3
Holroyd Rd *PUT/ROE* SW15	130	C2
Holstock Rd *IL* IG1	66	C4
Holsworthy Sq *FSBYW* WC1X *	21	F1
Holton St *WCHPL* E1	91	D3
Holt Rd *CAN/RD* E16	107	E2
Holwood Pl *CLAP* SW4	135	D2
Holyhead Cl *BOW* E3	92	A2
Holyoake Ct *BERM/RHTH* SE16	103	E3
Holyoak Rd *LBTH* SE11 *	46	C4
Holyport Rd *FUL/PGN* SW6	112	C5
Holyrood Ms *CAN/RD* E16	106	A2
Holyrood St *STHWK* SE1	36	C4
Holywell Cl *BERM/RHTH* SE16 *	120	B1
BKHTH/KID SE3	124	C2
Holywell La *SDTCH* EC2A	13	D5
Holywell Rw *SDTCH* EC2A	24	C1
Homecroft Rd *SYD* SE26	156	C5
Homefield Cl *WLSDN* NW10	68	C3
Homefield Rd *CHSWK* W4	99	F5
Homefield St *IS* N1 *	12	C2
Homeleigh Rd *PECK* SE15	139	D3
Home Park Rd *WIM/MER* SW19	149	F4
Homer Dr *POP/IOD* E14	104	A5
Home Rd *BTSEA* SW11	115	D5
Homer Rd *HOM* E9	79	E3
Homer Rw *CAMTN* NW1	3	D3
Homer St *MBLAR* W1H	17	D3
Homerton High St *HOM* E9	79	D2
Homerton Rd *HOM* E9	79	F2
Homerton Rw *HOM* E9	78	C2
Homerton Ter *HOM* E9	79	D2
Homestall Rd *EDUL* SE22	138	C3
Homestead Pk *CRICK* NW2	51	F5
Homestead Rd *FUL/PGN* SW6	113	D3
Honduras St *FSBYE* EC1V	11	E5
Honeybourne Rd *KIL/WHAMP* NW6	72	B2
Honeybrook Rd *BAL* SW12	134	C5
Honeyman Cl *CRICK* NW2	71	D4
Honeywell Rd *BTSEA* SW11	133	E4
Honeywood Rd *WLSDN* NW10	87	F1
Honiton Gdns *PECK* SE15 *	120	C5
Honiton Rd *KIL/WHAMP* NW6	89	F1
WELL DA16	127	F5
Honley Rd *CAT* SE6	140	F5
Honor Oak Pk *FSTH* SE23	138	C5
Honor Oak Ri *FSTH* SE23	138	C4
Honor Oak Rd *FSTH* SE23	156	C1
Hood Av *MORT/ESHN* SW14	128	C3
Hook La *WELL* DA16	145	F2
Hooper Rd *CAN/RD* E16	94	A5
Hooper's Ms *ACT* W3	98	C2
Hope Cl *IS* N1	76	C3
LEE/GVPK SE12	160	B3
Hopedale Rd *CHARL* SE7	124	B2
Hopefield Av *KIL/WHAMP* NW6	89	E1
Hope Gdns *ACT* W3	98	B3
Hope La *ELTH/MOT* SE9	162	B3
Hope Sq *LVPST* EC2M *	24	C3
Hope St *BTSEA* SW11	133	D1
Hopetoun St *WCHPL* E1 *	25	F3
Hopewell St *CMBW* SE5	119	D5
Hopewell Yd *CMBW* SE5	119	D5
Hop Gdns *CHCR* WC2N	32	C2
Hopgood St *SHB* W12	100	C2
Hopkins Ms *SRTFD* E15	81	F5
Hopkins St *SOHO/CST* W1F	19	F5
Hopping La *IS* N1 *	76	B3
Hop St *GNWCH* SE10	105	F5
Hopton Pde *STRHM/NOR* SW16 *	153	E5
Hopton Rd *STRHM/NOR* SW16	153	E5
WOOL/PLUM SE18	108	B4
Hoptons Gdns *STHWK* SE1 *	35	D3
Hopton St *STHWK* SE1	35	D2
Hopwood Cl *TOOT* SW17	150	C3
Hopwood Rd *WALW* SE17	119	D2
Hopwood Wk *HACK* E8 *	78	A4
Horace Rd *FSTF* E7	82	B1
Horatio Pl *POP/IOD* E14	104	C3
Horatio St *BETH* E2	13	F2
Horbury Crs *NTGHL* W11	26	A2
Horbury Ms *NTGHL* W11	101	F1
Horder Rd *FUL/PGN* SW6	113	E4
Hordle Prom East *PECK* SE15	119	F3
Hordle Prom North *PECK* SE15	119	F3
Hordle Prom West *PECK* SE15	119	E3
Horley Rd *ELTH/MOT* SE9	161	E4
Hormead Rd *MV/WKIL* W9	89	F3
Hornbeam Cl *IL* IG1	85	D2
LBTH SE11	46	A4
Hornbeam Sq *BOW* E3	79	F5
Hornby Cl *HAMP* NW3	73	D4
Horncastle Cl *LEE/GVPK* SE12	142	A5
Horncastle Rd *LEE/GVPK* SE12	142	A5
Horndean Cl *PUT/ROE* SW15	148	A1
Horne House *CHARL* SE7 *	124	B2
Horne Wy *PUT/ROE* SW15	112	C5
Hornfair Rd *CHARL* SE7	125	D2
Horniman Dr *FSTH* SE23	156	B1
Horniman Gdns *FSTH* SE23 *	156	B1
Horning Cl *ELTH/MOT* SE9	161	E4
Horn La *ACT* W3	98	C1
GNWCH SE10	106	A5
Horn Link Wy *GNWCH* SE10	106	A4
Horn Park Cl *LEE/GVPK* SE12	142	B3
Horn Park La *LEE/GVPK* SE12	142	B3
Horns Cft *BARK* IG11	85	E4
Hornsey Chambers *CLPT* E5 *	60	B4
Hornsey La *HGT* N6	56	C2
Hornsey Lane Est *ARCH* N19	57	D2
Hornsey Lane Gdns *HGT* N6	56	C2
Hornsey Ri *ARCH* N19	57	D2
Hornsey Rise Gdns *ARCH* N19	57	D2
Hornsey Rd *ARCH* N19	57	D2
HOLWY N7	57	F5
Hornsey St *HOLWY* N7	75	F2
Hornshay St *PECK* SE15	120	C2
Hornton Pl *KENS* W8	38	B1
Hornton St *KENS* W8	26	B5
Horsa Rd *LEE/GVPK* SE12	142	C5
Horseferry Pl *GNWCH* SE10	122	C2
Horseferry Rd *POP/IOD* E14	103	E1
WEST SW1P	44	A3
Horse Guards Av *WHALL* SW1A	32	C4

Horse Guards Rd WHALL SW1A........ 32 B4
Horse Leaze EHAM E6........ 66 B5
Horsell Rd HBRY N5........ 76 A2
Horselydown La STHWK SE1........ 37 F3
Horseshoe Cl POP/IOD E14........ 52 B4
POP/IOD E14........ 122 C1
Horseshoe Ms BRXS/STRHM SW2........ 135 E2
Horse Yd IS N1 *........ 76 B5
Horsfeld Gdns ELTH/MOT SE9........ 143 E5
Horsfeld Rd ELTH/MOT SE9........ 143 D5
Horsford Rd BRXS/STRHM SW2........ 135 F3
Horsley St WALW SE17........ 119 D2
Horsman St CMBW SE5........ 118 C2
Horsmonden Rd BROCKY SE4........ 139 F5
Hortensia Rd WBPTN SW10........ 114 C2
Horticultural Pl CHSWK W4 *........ 111 D1
Horton Av CRICK NW2........ 71 E1
Horton Rd HACK E8........ 78 B1
Horton St LEW SE13........ 140 B1
Hosack Rd TOOT SW17........ 151 F2
Hoser Av LEE/GVPK SE12........ 160 A2
Hosier La STBT EC1A........ 22 C3
Hoskin's Cl CAN/RD E16........ 94 C5
Hoskins St GNWCH SE10........ 123 D1
Hospital Rd LEY E10........ 63 D1
Hospital Wy LEW SE13........ 141 D4
Hotham Rd PUT/ROE SW15........ 130 C1
Hotham St SRTFD E15........ 81 E5
Hothfield Pl BERM/RHTH SE16........ 102 C4
Hotspur St LBTH SE11 *........ 118 A1
Houghton Cl HACK E8 *........ 77 F3
Houghton St LINN WC2A *........ 21 F5
Houndsditch HDTCH EC3A........ 25 D4
Houseman Wy CMBW SE5........ 119 D3
Houston Rd FSTH SE23........ 157 E2
Hoveden Rd CRICK NW2........ 71 D2
Howard Cl ACT W3........ 86 B5
CRICK NW2 *........ 71 E1
Howard Rd BARK IG11........ 85 D5
CRICK NW2........ 71 D1
EHAM E6........ 95 F1
IL IG1........ 84 B1
SEVS/STOTM N15........ 59 E1
STNW/STAM N16........ 77 D1
WAN E11........ 63 E5
Howard's La PUT/ROE SW15........ 130 C2
Howard's Rd PLSTW E13........ 94 A2
Howards Yd WAND/EARL SW18........ 132 B5
Howbury Rd PECK SE15........ 138 C1
Howden Cl PECK SE15........ 138 A1
Howell Wk STHWK SE1........ 47 D5
Howerd Wy WOOL/PLUM SE18........ 125 E4
Howgate Rd MORT/ESHN SW14........ 129 D1
Howick Pl WESTW SW1E........ 43 F3
Howie St BTSEA SW11........ 115 E3
Howitt Cl HAMP NW3........ 73 E3
Howitt Rd HAMP NW3........ 73 E3
Howland Ms East FITZ W1T........ 19 F2
Howland St FITZ W1T........ 19 F2
Howland Wy BERM/RHTH SE16........ 103 E3
Howletts Rd HNHL SE24........ 136 C4
Howley Pl BAY/PAD W2........ 15 F2
Howsman Rd BARN SW13........ 112 A2
Howson Rd BROCKY SE4........ 139 E2
How's St BETH E2........ 13 E1
Hoxton Market IS N1........ 12 C4
Hoxton Sq IS N1........ 12 C4
Hoxton St IS N1........ 13 D1
Hoylake Rd ACT W3........ 87 E5
Hoyland Cl PECK SE15 *........ 120 B3
Hoyle Rd TOOT SW17........ 151 E5
Hoy St CAN/RD E16........ 93 F5
Hubbard Rd WNWD SE27........ 154 C4
Hubbard St SRTFD E15........ 81 E5
Hubert Gv BRXN/ST SW9........ 135 E1
Hubert Rd EHAM E6........ 95 D2
Huddart St BOW E3........ 91 F4
Huddleston Cl BETH E2 *........ 90 C1
Huddlestone Rd CRICK NW2........ 70 B3
FSTGT E7........ 81 F1
Huddleston Rd HOLWY N7........ 56 C5
Hudson Cl SHB W12 *........ 100 B1
Hudson Rd WOOL/PLUM SE18........ 126 C1
Huggin Hl BLKFR EC4V........ 35 F3
Huggins Pl BRXS/STRHM SW2........ 155 F1
Hughan Rd SRTFD E15........ 81 D2
Hughes Ter CAN/RD E16 *........ 93 F4
Hugh Gaitskell Cl FUL/PGN SW6 *........ 113 F2
Hugh Ms PIM SW1V........ 43 D5
Hugh Pl WEST SW1P........ 44 A4
Hugh St PIM SW1V........ 43 D5
Hugon Rd FUL/PGN SW6........ 132 B1
Hugo Rd ARCH N19........ 74 C1
Huguenot Pl WAND/EARL SW18........ 132 C3
WCHPL E1........ 25 F2
Huitt Sq BTSEA SW11........ 133 D1
Hullbridge Ms IS N1........ 77 D5
Hull Cl BERM/RHTH SE16 *........ 103 D2
Hull St FSBYE EC1V........ 11 E4
Hulme Pl STHWK SE1........ 47 F1
Hulse Av BARK IG11........ 85 D3
Humber Dr NKENS W10........ 89 D3
Humber Rd BKHTH/KID SE3........ 124 A2
CRICK NW2........ 52 B4
Humberstone Rd PLSTW E13........ 94 C2
Humbolt Rd HMSMTH W6........ 113 E2
Humphrey St STHWK SE1........ 119 F1
Hungerford Rd HOLWY N7........ 75 D3
Hungerford St WCHPL E1 *........ 90 B5
Hunsdon Rd NWCR SE14........ 121 D3
Hunslett St BETH E2 *........ 90 C1
Hunt Cl BKHTH/KID SE3 *........ 124 A5
NTGHL W11........ 101 D2
Hunter Cl BAL SW12........ 152 A1
STHWK SE1........ 48 B3
Hunter St CMBW SE5 *........ 137 D2
Hunters Meadow NRWD SE19........ 155 E4
Hunters Gv IL IG11........ 84 B2
Hunter St BMSBY WC1N........ 9 D5
Huntingdon Gdns CHSWK W4........ 110 C3
Huntingdon St CAN/RD E16........ 93 F5
IS N1........ 76 A4
Huntingfield Rd PUT/ROE SW15........ 130 A4
Huntley St GWRST WC1E........ 19 F1
Hunton St WCHPL E1........ 90 A4
Hunts Cl BKHTH/KID SE3........ 124 A5
Hunt's La SRTFD E15........ 92 C1
Huntsman St WALW SE17........ 48 C5
Huntspill St TOOT SW17........ 150 C3
Hunts Slip Rd DUL SE21........ 155 E2
Huntsworth Ms CAMTN NW1........ 5 E5
Hurdwick Pl CAMTN NW1 *........ 7 E1
Hurley Crs BERM/RHTH SE16........ 103 D2
Hurlingham Gdns FUL/PGN SW6........ 131 F1
Hurlingham Pk FUL/PGN SW6 *........ 131 F1
Hurlingham Rd FUL/PGN SW6........ 113 F5
Hurlingham Sq FUL/PGN SW6 *........ 132 A1
Hurlock St HBRY N5........ 58 B5
Huron Rd TOOT SW17........ 151 F3
Hurren Cl BKHTH/KID SE3........ 141 E1
Hurricane House WOOL/PLUM SE18 *........ 125 E3
Hurry Cl SRTFD E15........ 81 E4
Hurst Av HGT N6........ 56 C2
Hurstbourne Gdns BARK IG11........ 85 D3
Hurstbourne Rd FSTH SE23........ 157 E1
Hurst Cl GLDGN NW11........ 54 B1
Hurstdene Gdns SEVS/STOTM N15........ 59 E2
Hurst St HNHL SE24........ 136 B4
Hurstway Rd NTGHL W11........ 101 D1
Hurstway Wk NTGHL W11........ 101 D1
Huson Cl HAMP NW3 *........ 73 E4
Hutching's St POP/IOD E14........ 104 A3
Hutchins Cl SRTFD E15........ 80 C4
Hutton St EMB EC4Y........ 22 B5
Huxbear St BROCKY SE4........ 139 F3
Huxley Rd LEY E10........ 62 C4
WELL DA16........ 145 F1
Huxley St NKENS W10........ 89 E2
Hyacinth Cl IL IG1........ 84 B3
Hyacinth Rd PUT/ROE SW15........ 148 A1
Hyde Farm Ms BAL SW12........ 153 D1
Hyde La BTSEA SW11........ 115 E4
Hyde Park Cnr MYFR/PICC W1J........ 30 B5
Hyde Park Crs BAY/PAD W2........ 16 C5
Hyde Park Gdns BAY/PAD W2........ 28 B1
Hyde Park Gardens Ms BAY/PAD W2........ 28 B1
Hyde Park Ga SKENS SW7........ 39 E1
Hyde Park Gate Ms SKENS SW7 *........ 39 F1
Hyde Park Pl BAY/PAD W2........ 29 D1
Hyde Park Sq BAY/PAD W2........ 16 C5
Hyde Park Square Ms BAY/PAD W2........ 16 C5
Hyde Park St BAY/PAD W2........ 28 C1
Hyderabad Wy SRTFD E15........ 81 E4
Hyde Rd IS N1........ 77 E5
Hyde's Pl IS N1........ 76 B4
Hyde St DEPT SE8........ 122 A2
Hydethorpe Rd BAL SW12........ 152 C1
Hyde V GNWCH SE10........ 122 C3
Hylton St WOOL/PLUM SE18........ 109 F5
Hyndewood FSTH SE23 *........ 157 D3
Hyndman St PECK SE15........ 120 B2
Hyson Rd BERM/RHTH SE16........ 120 B1
Hythe Rd WLSDN NW10........ 87 F2

I

Ibbotson Av *CAN/RD* E16 .... **93** F5
Ibbott St *WCHPL* E1 .... **90** C3
Ibis La *CHSWK* W4 .... **110** C4
Ibsley Gdns *PUT/ROE* SW15 .... **148** A1
Iceland Rd *BOW* E3 .... **80** A5
Ickburgh Est *CLPT* E5 .... **60** B4
Ickburgh Rd *CLPT* E5 .... **60** B5
Ickleton Rd *ELTH/MOT* SE9 .... **161** E4
Ida St *POP/IOD* E14 .... **92** C5
Idmiston Rd *SRTFD* E15 .... **81** F2
WNWD SE27 .... **154** C3
Idol La *MON* EC3R **36** C2
Idonia St *DEPT* SE8 .... **121** F3
Iffley Rd *HMSMTH* W6 .... **100** B4
Ifield Rd *WBPTN* SW10 .... **114** B2
Ilbert St *NKENS* W10 .... **89** E2
Ilchester Gdns *BAY/PAD* W2 .... **26** C1
Ilchester Pl *WKENS* W14 .... **101** F4
Ildersly Gv *DUL* SE21 .... **155** D2
Ilderton Rd *PECK* SE15 .... **120** C2
Ilex Rd *WLSDN* NW10 .... **69** F3
Ilex Wy *STRHM/NOR* SW16 .... **154** B5
Ilford Hl *IL* IG1 .... **66** A5
MNPK E12 .... **83** F1
Ilford La *IL* IG1 .... **84** B1
Ilfracombe Rd *BMLY* BR1 .... **159** F5
Iliffe St *WALW* SE17 .... **118** B1
Iliffe Yd *WALW* SE17 .... **118** B1
Ilkley Rd *CAN/RD* E16 .... **94** C4
Ilminster Gdns *BTSEA* SW11 .... **133** E2
Imber St *IS* N1 .... **77** D5
Imperial Av *STNW/STAM* N16 * **77** E1
Imperial Cl *CRICK* NW2 .... **70** B2
Imperial College Rd *SKENS* SW7 .... **40** A3
Imperial Crs *FUL/PGN* SW6 .... **114** C3
Imperial Ms *EHAM* E6 .... **95** D1
Imperial Rd *FUL/PGN* SW6 .... **114** B4
Imperial Sq *FUL/PGN* SW6 .... **114** B4
Imperial St *BOW* E3 .... **92** C2
Imperial Wy *CHST* BR7 .... **162** C3
Imre Cl *SHB* W12 .... **100** B3
Inca Dr *ELTH/MOT* SE9 .... **144** B5
Inchmery Rd *CAT* SE6 .... **158** B2
Independent Pl *HACK* E8 .... **77** F2
Independents Rd
BKHTH/KID SE3 .... **141** E1
Inderwick Rd *CEND/HSY/T* N8 .... **57** F1
Indescon Ct *POP/IOD* E14 .... **104** B3
India Wy *SHB* W12 .... **100** B1
Indigo Ms *POP/IOD* E14 * **104** C1
STNW/STAM N16 .... **59** D3
Indus Rd *CHARL* SE7 .... **124** C3
Infant House *WOOL/PLUM* SE18 * **125** E3
Ingal Rd *PLSTW* E13 .... **94** A3
Ingate Pl *VX/NE* SW8 .... **116** B4
Ingatestone Rd *MNPK* E12 .... **64** C3
Ingelow Rd *VX/NE* SW8 .... **116** B5
Ingersoll Rd *SHB* W12 .... **100** B2
Ingestre Pl *SOHO/CST* W1F **19** E5
Ingestre Rd *FSTGT* E7 .... **82** A1
KTTN NW5 .... **74** B1
Ingham Rd *KIL/WHAMP* NW6 .... **72** A1
Inglebert St *CLKNW* EC1R **10** A3
Ingleborough St *BRXN/ST* SW9 .... **118** A5
Ingleby Rd *HOLWY* N7 .... **57** F5
IL IG1 .... **66** B3
Ingleby Wy *CHST* BR7 .... **162** A5
Ingledew Rd *WOOL/PLUM* SE18 .... **127** D1
Inglefield Sq *WAP* E1W * **102** B2
Inglemere Rd *FSBYE* EC1V **11** F4
Ingleside Gv *BKHTH/KID* SE3 .... **123** F2
Inglethorpe St *FUL/PGN* SW6 .... **113** D4
Ingleton St *BRXN/ST* SW9 .... **118** A5
Inglewood Cl *POP/IOD* E14 .... **104** A5
Inglewood Rd *KIL/WHAMP* NW6 .... **72** A2
Inglis St *CMBW* SE5 .... **118** B4
Ingram Av *GLDGN* NW11 .... **54** C2
Ingram Cl *LBTH* SE11 .... **45** E4
Ingrave St *BTSEA* SW11 .... **133** D1
Ingress St *CHSWK* W4 .... **111** E1
Inigo Jones Rd *CHARL* SE7 .... **125** D3
Inkerman Rd *KTTN* NW5 .... **74** B3
Inman Rd *WAND/EARL* SW18 .... **132** C5
WLSDN NW10 .... **69** E5
Inner Cir *CAMTN* NW1 .... **6** A4
Inner Park Rd *WIM/MER* SW19 .... **149** D2
Innes Gdns *PUT/ROE* SW15 .... **130** B4

Innes St *PECK* SE15 .... **119** E3
Inniskilling Rd *PLSTW* E13 .... **94** C1
Inskip Cl *LEY* E10 .... **62** B4
Institute Pl *HACK* E8 .... **78** B2
Integer Gdns *WAN* E11 * **63** D2
Inver Ct *BAY/PAD* W2 .... **15** D5
Inverforth Cl *HAMP* NW3 .... **54** C4
Inverine Rd *CHARL* SE7 .... **124** B1
Invermore Pl *WOOL/PLUM* SE18 .... **108** C5
Inverness Gdns *KENS* W8 .... **26** C4
Inverness Ms *BAY/PAD* W2 .... **27** D1
Inverness Pl *BAY/PAD* W2 .... **27** D1
Inverness St *CAMTN* NW1 .... **74** B5
Inverness Ter *BAY/PAD* W2 .... **15** D5
Inverton Rd *PECK* SE15 .... **139** D2
Invicta Cl *CHST* BR7 .... **162** A5
Invicta Plaza *STHWK* SE1 .... **34** C3
Invicta Rd *BKHTH/KID* SE3 .... **124** A3
Inville Rd *WALW* SE17 .... **119** D1
Inworth St *BTSEA* SW11 .... **115** E5
Inworth Wk *IS* N1 * **76** C5
Iona Cl *CAT* SE6 .... **140** A5
Ireland Cl *EHAM* E6 .... **95** F4
Irene Rd *FUL/PGN* SW6 .... **114** A4
Ireton St *BOW* E3 .... **92** A3
Iris Cl *EHAM* E6 .... **95** E4
Iron Bridge Cl *WLSDN* NW10 .... **69** E3
Iron Mill Pl *WAND/EARL* SW18 .... **132** B4
Iron Mill Rd *WAND/EARL* SW18 .... **132** B4
Ironmonger La *CITYW* EC2V **24** A5
Ironmonger Rw *FSBYE* EC1V **11** F4
Ironmongers Pl *POP/IOD* E14 .... **104** A5
Ironside Cl *BERM/RHTH* SE16 .... **103** D3
Irvine Cl *POP/IOD* E14 .... **92** B4
Irving Gv *BRXN/ST* SW9 .... **117** F5
Irving Ms *IS* N1 .... **76** C3
Irving Rd *WKENS* W14 .... **101** D4
Irving St *LSQ/SEVD* WC2H **32** B2
Irwell Est *BERM/RHTH* SE16 .... **102** C3
Irwin Av *WOOL/PLUM* SE18 .... **127** E3
Irwin Gdns *WLSDN* NW10 .... **70** B5
Isaac Wy *STHWK* SE1 * **48** A1
Isabella Ms *IS* N1 * **77** E3
Isabella Rd *HOM* E9 .... **78** C2
Isabella St *STHWK* SE1 .... **35** D5
Isabel St *BRXN/ST* SW9 .... **117** F4
Isambard Ms *POP/IOD* E14 .... **104** C4
Isambard Pl *BERM/RHTH* SE16 .... **102** C2
Isis Cl *PUT/ROE* SW15 .... **130** C2
Isis St *WAND/EARL* SW18 .... **150** C2
Island Rd *BERM/RHTH* SE16 .... **103** D5
Island Rw *POP/IOD* E14 .... **91** F5
Isla Rd *WOOL/PLUM* SE18 .... **126** C5
Islay Wk *IS* N1 * **76** C3
Islay Whf *POP/IOD* E14 * **92** C4
Isledon Rd *HOLWY* N7 .... **58** A5
Islington Gn *IS* N1 .... **76** B5
Islington High St *IS* N1 .... **10** C1
Islington Park Ms *IS* N1 .... **76** B4
Islington Park St *IS* N1 .... **76** A4
Islip St *KTTN* NW5 .... **74** C2
Ismailia Rd *FSTGT* E7 .... **82** B4
Isom Cl *PLSTW* E13 .... **94** B2
Ivanhoe Rd *CMBW* SE5 .... **137** F1
Ivatt Pl *WKENS* W14 .... **113** F1
Iveagh Av *WLSDN* NW10 .... **86** A1
Iveagh Cl *HOM* E9 .... **79** D5
WLSDN NW10 .... **86** A1
Ive Farm Cl *LEY* E10 .... **62** A4
Ive Farm La *LEY* E10 .... **62** A4
Iveley Rd *CLAP* SW4 .... **116** C5
Iverna Ct *KENS* W8 .... **38** B2
Iverna Gdns *KENS* W8 .... **38** B2
Iverson Rd *KIL/WHAMP* NW6 .... **71** F3
Ives Rd *CAN/RD* E16 .... **93** E4
Ives St *CHEL* SW3 .... **41** D4
Ivimey St *BETH* E2 * **90** A2
Ivor Gv *ELTH/MOT* SE9 .... **162** B1
Ivor Pl *CAMTN* NW1 .... **17** E1
Ivor St *CAMTN* NW1 .... **74** C4
Ivorydown *BMLY* BR1 .... **160** A4
Ivy Church La *WALW* SE17 .... **119** E1
Ivydale Rd *BERM/RHTH* SE16 .... **120** A1
Ivy Crs *CHSWK* W4 .... **98** C5
Ivydale Rd *PECK* SE15 .... **139** D3
Ivyday Gv *STRHM/NOR* SW16 .... **153** E3
Ivy Gdns *CEND/HSY/T* N8 .... **57** E1
Ivymount Rd *WNWD* SE27 .... **154** A3
Ivy Rd *BROCKY* SE4 .... **139** F2
CAN/RD E16 .... **94** A5
CRICK NW2 .... **70** C1

TOOT SW17 .... **151** E5
WALTH E17 .... **62** A1
Ivy St IS N1 .... **12** C1
Ixworth Pl *CHEL* SW3 .... **40** C5

J

Jacaranda Gv *HACK* E8 .... **77** F4
Jack Clow Rd *SRTFD* E15 .... **93** E1
Jack Cornwell St *MNPK* E12 .... **84** A1
Jack Dash Wy *EHAM* E6 .... **95** E3
Jackman Ms *WLSDN* NW10 .... **51** E5
Jackman St *HACK* E8 .... **78** B5
Jackson Cl *HOM* E9 .... **79** D4
   HOLWY N7 .... **75** F1
Jackson Rd *BARK* IG11 .... **85** D5
Jackson's La *HGT* N6 .... **56** A2
Jackson St *WOOL/PLUM* SE18 .... **126** A3
Jack Walker Ct *HBRY* N5 .... **76** B1
Jacob St *STHWK* SE1 .... **37** F5
Jacob's Well Ms *MHST* W1U **18** B4
Jacqueline Creft Ter *HGT* N6 * **56** A1
Jade Cl *CAN/RD* E16 .... **95** D5
   CRICK NW2 .... **53** D2
Jade Ter *KIL/WHAMP* NW6 * **72** C4
Jaffe Rd *IL* IG1 .... **66** C3
Jaggard Wy *BAL* SW12 .... **133** F5
Jago Cl *WOOL/PLUM* SE18 .... **126** C2
Jago Wk *CMBW* SE5 .... **119** D3
Jamaica Rd *BERM/RHTH* SE16 .... **102** A4
   STHWK SE1 .... **90** C4
Jamaica St *WCHPL* E1 .... **90** F4
James Av *CRICK* NW2 .... **70** C2
James Cl *CLDGN* NW11 * **53** E1
   PLSTW E13 .... **94** A1
James Collins Cl *MV/WKIL* W9 .... **89** F3
James Joyce Wk *BRXN/ST* SW9 .... **136** B2
James La *WAN* E11 .... **62** C2
Jameson St *KENS* W8 .... **26** B3
James St *BARK* IG11 .... **84** C4
   COVGDN WC2E **33** D1
   MHST W1U **18** B5
Jamestown Rd *CAMTN* NW1 .... **74** B5
Jamestown Wy *POP/IOD* E14 .... **105** D3
James Voller Wy *WCHPL* E1 .... **90** C5
Jamuna Cl *POP/IOD* E14 .... **91** E4
Jane St *WCHPL* E1 .... **90** B5
Janet St *POP/IOD* E14 .... **104** A4
Janeway Pl *BERM/RHTH* SE16 .... **102** B3
Janeway Rd *BERM/RHTH* SE16 .... **102** A3
Janson Cl *SRTFD* E15 .... **81** E2
   WLSDN NW10 .... **51** D5
Janson Rd *SRTFD* E15 .... **81** E2
Jardine Rd *WAP* E1W **103** D1
Jarrett Cl *BRXS/STRHM* SW2 .... **154** B1
Jarrow Rd *BERM/RHTH* SE16 .... **102** C5
Jarrow Wy *HOM* E9 .... **79** F1
Jarvis Rd *EDUL* SE22 .... **137** E2
Jasmine Cl *IL* IG1 .... **84** B2
Jasmine Ct *LEE/GVPK* SE12 .... **142** A4
Jason Wk *ELTH/MOT* SE9 .... **161** F3
Jasper Rd *CAN/RD* E16 .... **95** D5
Jay Gdns *CHST* BR7 .... **161** F4
Jay Ms *SKENS* SW7 .... **39** F1
Jebb Av *BRXS/STRHM* SW2 .... **135** E4
Jebb St *BOW* E3 .... **92** A1
Jedburgh Rd *PLSTW* E13 .... **94** C2
Jedburgh St *BTSEA* SW11 .... **134** A2
Jeddo Ms *SHB* W12 .... **99** F3
Jeddo Rd *SHB* W12 .... **99** F3
Jeffrey's Pl *CAMTN* NW1 .... **74** C4
Jeffreys Rd *CLAP* SW4 .... **117** E3
Jeffrey's St *CAMTN* NW1 .... **74** B4
Jeger Av *BETH* E2 .... **77** F5
Jeken Rd *ELTH/MOT* SE9 .... **142** C2
Jelf Rd *BRXS/STRHM* SW2 .... **136** A3
Jenkins La *BARK* IG11 .... **96** B3
Jenkins Rd *PLSTW* E13 .... **94** B3
Jenner Av *ACT* W3 .... **87** D4
Jenner Pl *BARN* SW13 .... **112** B2
Jenner Rd *STNW/STAM* N16 .... **59** F4
Jennifer Rd *BMLY* BR1 .... **159** F5
Jennings Rd *EDUL* SE22 .... **137** F4
Jenny Hammond Cl *WAN* E11 .... **63** F5
Jephson Rd *FSTGT* E7 .... **82** C5
Jephson St *CMBW* SE5 .... **119** D4
Jephtha Rd *WAND/EARL* SW18 .... **132** A4
Jerdan Pl *FUL/PGN* SW6 .... **114** A3

Jeremiah St *POP/IOD* E14 .... **92** B5
Jermyn St *ST/JS* SW1Y **31** E3
Jerningham Rd *NWCR* SE14 .... **121** E5
Jerome St *WCHPL* E1 .... **25** E2
Jerrard St *LEW* SE13 .... **140** B1
Jerrold St *IS* N1 * **13** D2
Jersey Rd *CAN/RD* E16 .... **94** C4
   IL IG1 .... **84** B1
   LEY E10 .... **63** D3
Jersey St *BETH* E2 .... **90** B1
Jerusalem Pas *CLKNW* EC1R **22** C1
Jervois House *WOOL/PLUM* SE18 * **125** E5
Jesmond Dene *HAMP* NW3 * **72** C3
Jessam Av *CLPT* E5 .... **60** B3
Jesse Rd *LEY* E10 .... **62** B5
Jessica Rd *WAND/EARL* SW18 .... **132** C4
Jessop Sq *POP/IOD* E14 * **104** A2
Jessup Cl *WOOL/PLUM* SE18 .... **108** C5
Jevington Wy *LEE/GVPK* SE12 .... **160** B1
Jewry St *TWRH* EC3N **25** E5
Jews Rw *WAND/EARL* SW18 .... **132** B2
Jews Wk *SYD* SE26 .... **156** B4
Jeymer Av *WLSDN* NW10 .... **70** B2
Jeypore Rd *WAND/EARL* SW18 .... **132** C5
Jim Bradley Cl *WOOL/PLUM* SE18 .... **108** A5
Joan Crs *ELTH/MOT* SE9 .... **143** D5
Joan St *STHWK* SE1 .... **34** C4
Jocelyn St *PECK* SE15 .... **120** A4
Jockey's Flds *FSBYW* WC1X **21** F2
Jodrell Rd *BOW* E3 .... **79** F5
Johanna St *STHWK* SE1 * **46** A1
John Adam St *CHCR* WC2N **33** D3
John Aird Ct *BAY/PAD* W2 .... **15** F2
John Archer Wy *WAND/EARL* SW18 .... **133** D4
John Ashby Cl *BRXS/STRHM* SW2 .... **135** E4
John Burns Dr *BARK* IG11 .... **85** E5
John Campbell Rd *STNW/STAM* N16 .... **77** E2
John Carpenter St *EMB* EC4Y **34** B1
John Felton Rd *BERM/RHTH* SE16 * **102** A3
John Fisher St *WCHPL* E1 .... **37** F1
John Harrison Wy *BERM/RHTH* SE16 .... **103** D4
John Islip St *WEST* SW1P **44** C5
John Maurice Cl *WALW* SE17 .... **48** A1
John McKenna Wk
   BERM/RHTH SE16 * **102** A4
John Parker Sq *BTSEA* SW11 * **133** D1
John Penn St *LEW* SE13 .... **122** B4
John Prince's St *CAVSQ/HST* W1G **19** D4
John Rennie Wk *WAP* E1W **102** B1
John Roll Wy *BERM/RHTH* SE16 .... **102** A4
John Ruskin St *CMBW* SE5 .... **118** B3
John Silkin La *DEPT* SE8 .... **121** D1
John's Ms *BMSBY* WC1N **21** F1
John Smith Av *FUL/PGN* SW6 .... **113** F3
John Smith Ms *POP/IOD* E14 .... **105** D3
Johnson Cl *HACK* E8 .... **78** A5
Johnson Rd *WLSDN* NW10 .... **69** B5
Johnson's Cl *CAR* SM5 .... **22** B5
Johnson's Pl *PIM* SW1V **116** C1
Johnson St *WCHPL* E1 .... **90** C5
Johnsons Wy *WLSDN* NW10 .... **86** B3
John Spencer Sq *IS* N1 * **76** B3
Johns Pl *WCHPL* E1 .... **90** B5
Johnston Cl *BRXN/ST* SW9 .... **117** F4
Johnstone Rd *EHAM* E6 .... **95** F2
Johnstone Ter *CRICK* NW2 .... **53** D5
John St *BMSBY* WC1N **21** F1
   SRTFD E15 .... **81** F5
John Trundle Highwalk *BARB* EC2Y * **23** E2
John Wesley Cl *EHAM* E6 * **95** F2
John Williams Cl *NWCR* SE14 .... **121** D2
John Wilson St *WOOL/PLUM* SE18 .... **108** A5
John Wooley Cl *LEW* SE13 * **141** E2
Joiners Arms Yd *CMBW* SE5 * **119** D4
Joiner St *STHWK* SE1 .... **36** B4
Jonathan St *LBTH* SE11 .... **117** F1
Jones Rd *PLSTW* E13 .... **94** B3
Joseph Av *ACT* W3 .... **87** D5
Joseph Hardcastle Cl *NWCR* SE14 .... **121** D3
Josephine Av *BRXS/STRHM* SW2 .... **135** E3
Joseph Powell Cl *BAL* SW12 .... **134** C4
Joseph Ray Rd *WAN* E11 .... **63** E4
Joseph St *BOW* E3 .... **91** F4
Joseph Trotter Cl *CLKNW* EC1R **10** B4
Joshua St *POP/IOD* E14 .... **92** C5
Joslings Cl *SHB* W12 .... **100** A1
Joubert St *BTSEA* SW11 .... **115** F5
Jowett St *PECK* SE15 .... **119** F5
Jubilee Cl *CDALE/KGS* NW9 .... **51** D1
   WLSDN NW10 .... **87** E1
Jubilee Gdns *STHWK* SE1 * **33** F4

Jubilee Pl *CHEL* SW3 .... 115 E1
Jubilee St *WCHPL* E1 .... 90 C5
Jubilee Ter *FUL/PGN* SW6 * 113 E6
The Jubilee *CNWCH* SE10 * 122 B3
Jude St *STPAN* WC1H 8 C4
Jude St *CAN/RD* E16 .... 93 F5
Judges' Wk *HAMP* NW3 .... 54 C5
Julian Av *ACT* W3 .... 98 B1
Julian Pl *POP/IOD* E14 .... 122 B1
Julian Tayler Pth *FSTH* SE23 * 156 B2
Juliette Rd *PLSTW* E13 .... 94 A1
Julius Nyerere Cl *IS* N1 * 75 F5
Junction Ap *BTSEA* SW11 .... 133 E1
  LEW SE13 .... 140 C1
Junction Ms *BAY/PAD* W2 .... 16 C4
Junction Pl *BAY/PAD* W2 * 16 B4
Junction Rd *ARCH* N19 .... 56 C5
  PLSTW E13 .... 82 B5
Juniper Crs *CAMTN* NW1 .... 74 A4
Juniper Dr *WAND/EARL* SW18 ...... 132 C2
Juniper La *EHAM* E6 .... 95 E4
Juniper Rd *IL* IG1 .... 84 A1
Juniper St *WCHPL* E1 * 102 C1
Juno Wy *NWCR* SE14 .... 121 D2
Jupiter Wy *HOLWY* N7 .... 75 F3
Jupp Rd *SRTFD* E15 .... 81 D4
Jupp Rd West *SRTFD* E15 .... 81 D5
Justice Wk *CHEL* SW3 .... 115 G2
Jutland Cl *ARCH* N19 .... 57 E3
Jutland Rd *CAT* SE6 .... 140 C5
  PLSTW E13 .... 94 A3
Juxon St *LBTH* SE11 .... 45 F4

Kellino St *TOOT* SW17 .... 151 F4
Kellner Rd *THMD* SE28 .... 109 F4
Kell St *STHWK* SE1 .... 47 D2
Kelly Av *PECK* SE15 .... 119 F3
Kelly Cl *WLSDN* NW10 .... 51 D5
Kelly Ms *MV/WKIL* W9 .... 89 F4
Kelly St *CAMTN* NW1 .... 74 B3
Kelman Cl *CLAP* SW4 .... 117 D5
Kelmore Gv *EDUL* SE22 .... 138 A2
Kelmscott Gdns *SHB* W12 .... 100 A4
Kelmscott Rd *BTSEA* SW11 .... 133 E3
Kelross Rd *HBRY* N5 .... 76 B1
Kelsall Cl *BKHTH/KID* SE3 .... 124 B5
Kelsall Ms *RCH/KEW* TW9 .... 110 B4
Kelsey St *BETH* E2 .... 90 A3
Kelso Pl *KENS* W8 .... 38 C5
Kelvedon Rd *FUL/PGN* SW6 .... 113 F3
Kelvin Gv *SYD* SE26 .... 156 B3
Kelvington Rd *PECK* SE15 .... 139 D3
Kelvin Rd *HBRY* N5 .... 76 B1
Kember St *IS* N1 .... 75 F1
Kemble Rd *FSTH* SE23 .... 157 D1
Kemble St *HOL/ALD* WC2B 21 E5
Kemerton Rd *CMBW* SE5 .... 136 C1
Kemey's St *HOM* E9 .... 79 E2
Kemnal Rd *CHST* BR7 .... 163 D3
Kempe Rd *KIL/WHAMP* NW6 .... 89 D1
Kemplay Rd *HAMP* NW3 .... 73 D1
Kemps Dr *POP/IOD* E14 .... 104 A1
Kempsford Gdns *ECT* SW5 .... 114 A4
Kempsford Rd *LBTH* SE11 .... 46 B5
Kempson Rd *FUL/PGN* SW6 .... 114 A4
Kempthorne Rd *DEPT* SE8 .... 103 E3
Kempton Rd *EHAM* E6 .... 83 F5
Kempt St *WOOL/PLUM* SE18 .... 126 A2
Kemsing Rd *GNWCH* SE10 .... 124 A1
Kenbury St *CMBW* SE5 .... 118 C5
Kenchester Cl *VX/NE* SW8 .... 117 E3
Kendal Av *BARK* IG11 .... 85 E5
Kendal Cl *BRXN/ST* SW9 .... 118 B3
Kendal Ct *ACT* W3 .... 86 A4
Kendale Rd *BMLY* BR1 .... 159 E5
Kendall Pl *MHST* W1U 18 A3
Kendall Rd *WOOL/PLUM* SE18 .... 125 E4
Kendal Rd *WLSDN* NW10 .... 70 A1
Kendal Steps *BAY/PAD* W2 * 17 D5
Kendal St *BAY/PAD* W2 .... 17 D5
Kender St *NWCR* SE14 .... 120 C3
Kendoa Rd *CLAP* SW4 .... 135 D2
Kendrick Ms *SKENS* SW7 .... 40 A4
Kendrick Pl *SKENS* SW7 .... 40 A5
Kenilford Rd *BAL* SW12 .... 134 B5
Kenilworth Av *WIM/MER* SW19 .... 150 A5
Kenilworth Gdns *GDMY/SEVK* IG3 ...... 67 F4
  WOOL/PLUM SE18 .... 126 B5
Kenilworth Rd *BOW* E3 .... 91 E1
  KIL/WHAMP NW6 .... 71 F5
Kenley Wk *NTGHL* W11 * 101 E1
Kenlor Rd *TOOT* SW17 .... 151 D5
Kenmere Gdns *ALP/SUD* HA0 ...... 68 A5
Kenmont Gdns *WLSDN* NW10 .... 88 B2
Kenmure Rd *HACK* E8 .... 78 B2
Kenmure Yd *HACK* E8 * 78 B2
Kennacraig Cl *CAN/RD* E16 .... 106 B2
Kennard Rd *SRTFD* E15 .... 81 D4
Kennard St *BTSEA* SW11 .... 116 A4
  CAN/RD E16 .... 107 F2
Kennedy Cl *PLSTW* E13 .... 94 A1
Kennedy Rd *BARK* IG11 .... 85 E5
Kennedy Wk *WALW* SE17 .... 48 B5
Kennet Cl *BTSEA* SW11 .... 133 D2
Kenneth Av *IL* IG1 .... 84 B1
Kenneth Crs *CRICK* NW2 .... 70 B2
Kenneth More Rd *IL* IG1 .... 66 B5
Kennet Rd *MV/WKIL* W9 .... 89 F3
Kennet St *WAP* E1W 102 A2
Kennett Wharf La *BLKFR* EC4V 35 F1
Kenning St *BERM/RHTH* SE16 .... 102 C3
Kennings Wy *LBTH* SE11 .... 118 A1
Kennington La *LBTH* SE11 .... 117 F1
Kennington Ov *LBTH* SE11 .... 117 F2
Kennington Park Gdns *LBTH* SE11 ...... 118 B2
Kennington Park Pl *LBTH* SE11 ...... 118 A2
Kennington Park Rd *LBTH* SE11 ...... 118 A2
Kennington Rd *LBTH* SE11 .... 46 A3
Kenrick Pl *MHST* W1U 18 A2
Kensal Rd *NKENS* W10 * 89 E3
Kensal Wnf *NKENS* W10 * 89 E3
Kensington Av *MNPK* E12 .... 83 E3
Kensington Church Ct *KENS* W8 ...... 38 C1

Kambala Rd *BTSEA* SW11 .... 115 D5
Kangley Bridge Rd *SYD* SE26 .... 157 F5
Kara Wy *CRICK* NW2 .... 71 D1
Karen Ct *ELTH/MOT* SE9 .... 142 C3
Kashgar Rd *WOOL/PLUM* SE18 ...... 127 F1
Kashmir Rd *CHARL* SE7 .... 125 D3
Kassala Rd *BTSEA* SW11 .... 115 F5
Katherine Cl *BERM/RHTH* SE16 ...... 103 D2
Katherine Gdns *ELTH/MOT* SE9 ...... 143 D2
Katherine Rd *FSTGT* E7 .... 82 C3
Katherine Sq *NTGHL* W11 * 101 E2
Kathleen Av *ACT* W3 .... 86 C4
Kathleen Rd *BTSEA* SW11 .... 133 F1
Kay Rd *BRXN/ST* SW9 .... 117 E5
Kay St *BETH* E2 .... 90 A1
  SRTFD E15 .... 81 D4
Kean St *HOL/ALD* WC2B 21 E5
Keats Av *CAN/RD* E16 .... 106 B2
Keats Cl *STHWK* SE1 .... 49 E5
Keats Est *STNW/STAM* N16 * 59 F4
Keats Gv *HAMP* NW3 .... 73 E1
Keats Rd *WELL* DA16 .... 127 E4
Keble Pl *BARN* SW13 .... 112 B3
Keble St *TOOT* SW17 .... 150 C4
Kedleston Wk *BETH* E2 .... 90 B2
Keeble Cl *WOOL/PLUM* SE18 * 126 B2
Keedonwood Rd *BMLY* BR1 .... 159 E4
Keel Cl *BERM/RHTH* SE16 .... 103 D2
Keeley Rd *ELTH/MOT* SE9 .... 143 D3
Keeley Rd *WCHPL* WC2B 21 E5
Keeling Rd *ELTH/MOT* SE9 .... 143 D3
Keemor Cl *WOOL/PLUM* SE18 ...... 126 A3
Keens Cl *STRHM/NOR* SW16 ...... 153 D5
Keen's Yd *IS* N1 .... 76 B3
The Keep *BKHTH/KID* SE3 .... 124 A5
Keesey St *WALW* SE17 .... 119 E3
Keeton's Rd *BERM/RHTH* SE16 ...... 102 B4
Keevil Dr *WIM/MER* SW19 ...... 131 D5
Keighley Cl *HOLWY* N7 .... 75 E1
Keightley Dr *ELTH/MOT* SE9 ...... 162 C1
Keildon Rd *BTSEA* SW11 .... 133 F2
Keir Hardie Est *CLPT* E5 * 60 B3
Keith Connor Ct *VX/NE* SW8 ...... 134 B1
Keith Gv *SHB* W12 .... 100 A3
Keith Rd *BARK* IG11 .... 97 D1
Kelbrook Rd *BKHTH/KID* SE3 ...... 125 E5
Kelceda Cl *CRICK* NW2 .... 52 A4
Kelfield Gdns *NKENS* W10 .... 89 D5
Kelfield Ms *NKENS* W10 .... 89 D4
Kelland Rd *PLSTW* E13 .... 94 A3
Kellaway Rd *BKHTH/KID* SE3 ...... 124 C5
Keller Crs *MNPK* E12 .... 83 D1
Kellerton Rd *LEW* SE13 .... 141 E3
Kellett Rd *BRXS/STRHM* SW2 ...... 136 A2

Kensington Church St *KENS* W8	26	B3
Kensington Church Wk *KENS* W8 *	26	C5
Kensington Ct *KENS* W8	39	D1
Kensington Court Gdns *KENS* W8 *	39	D2
Kensington Court Ms *KENS* W8 *	39	D2
Kensington Court Pl *KENS* W8	39	D2
Kensington Gdns *KENS* W8	65	F3
Kensington Gardens Sq *BAY/PAD* W2	14	C5
Kensington Ga *KENS* W8	39	E2
Kensington Hall Gdns *WKENS* W14 *	113	F1
Kensington High St *KENS* W8	38	B2
Kensington Ml *KENS* W8	26	B3
Kensington Palace *KENS* W8 *	27	D4
Kensington Palace Gdns *KENS* W8	26	C5
Kensington Park Gdns *NTGHL* W11	101	F1
Kensington Park Ms *NTGHL* W11	89	F5
Kensington Park Rd *NTGHL* W11	89	F5
Kensington Pl *KENS* W8	26	A4
Kensington Rd *KENS* W8	39	D1
Kensington Sq *KENS* W8	38	C1
Kent Av *WELL* DA16	145	F3
Kent House Rd *SYD* SE26	157	E5
Kentish Town Rd *CAMTN* NW1	74	B4
Kentlea Rd *THMD* SE28	109	E2
Kentmere Rd *WOOL/PLUM* SE18	109	H3
Kenton Rd *HOM* E9	79	D3
Kenton St *STPAN* WC1H	8	C5
Kent Pas *CAMTN* NW1	5	E5
Kent Rd *CHSWK* W4	98	C4
RCH/KEW TW9	110	A3
Kent St *BETH* E2	13	F1
PLSTW E13	94	B2
Kent Ter *CAMTN* NW1	5	D4
Kent View Gdns *GDMY/SEVK* IG3	67	E4
Kentwell Cl *BROCKY* SE4 *	139	D2
Kentwode Gn *BARN* SW13	112	A3
Kent Yd *SKENS* SW7	41	D1
Kenward Rd *ELTH/MOT* SE9	142	C3
Ken Wy *WBLY* HA9	50	C4
Kenway Rd *ECT* SW5	38	C5
Kenwood Cl *HAMP* NW3	55	D3
Kenwood Rd *HGT* N6	55	F1
Kenworthy Rd *HOM* E9	79	E2
Kenwyn Dr *CRICK* NW2	51	E5
Kenwyn Rd *CLAP* SW4	135	D2
CHARL SE7	125	D3
Kenya Rd *CHARL* SE7	125	D3
Kenyon St *FUL/PGN* SW6	113	D4
Keogh Rd *SRTFD* E15	81	E3
Kepler Rd *CLAP* SW4	135	E2
Keppel Rd *BETH* E2	88	E4
EHAM E6	83	B5
Keppel St *GWRST* WC1E	20	B2
Kerbela St *BETH* E2	90	A3
Kerbey St *POP/IOD* E14	92	B5
Kerfield Crs *CMBW* SE5	119	D4
Kerfield Pl *CMBW* SE5	119	D4
Kerrison Rd *BTSEA* SW11	133	E1
SRTFD E15	81	D5
Kerry Cl *CAN/RD* E16	94	B5
Kerry Pth *NWCR* SE14	121	F2
Kerry Rd *NWCR* SE14	121	F2
Kersfield Rd *PUT/ROE* SW15	131	D4
WAND/EARL SW18	131	E5
Kershaw Cl *WAND/EARL* SW18	133	D4
Kersley Ms *BTSEA* SW11	115	F4
Kersley Rd *STNW/STAM* N16	59	F5
Kersley St *BTSEA* SW11	115	F5
Kerwick Cl *HOLWY* N7	75	F4
Keslake Rd *KIL/WHAMP* NW6	89	D1
Keston Rd *PECK* SE15	138	A1
Kestrel Av *EHAM* E6	95	E4
HNHL SE24	136	B3
Kestrel Cl *WLSDN* NW10	69	D2
Kestrel Pl *NWCR* SE14 *	121	E2
Keswick Av *PUT/ROE* SW15	147	E5
Keswick Rd *PUT/ROE* SW15	131	E3
Kett Gdns *BRXS/STRHM* SW2	135	F3
Kettlebaston Rd *LEY* E10	61	F3
Kew Br *RCH/KEW* TW9	110	A2
Kew Bridge Arches *CHSWK* W4 *	110	A2
Kew Bridge Ct *BTFD* TW8	110	A1
Kew Gn *RCH/KEW* TW9	110	A2
Kew Meadow Pth *RCH/KEW* TW9	110	B3
Kew Riverside Pk *RCH/KEW* TW9	110	B3
Key Cl *WCHPL* E1	90	B3
Keyes Rd *CRICK* NW2	71	D2
Keymer Rd *BRXS/STRHM* SW2	153	F2
Keynsham Gdns *ELTH/MOT* SE9	143	E3
Keynsham Rd *ELTH/MOT* SE9	143	D3
Keystone Crs *IS* N1	9	D2
Keyworth Cl *CLPT* E5	79	E3
Keyworth St *STHWK* SE1	47	D2
Kezia St *DEPT* SE8	121	E1
Khama Rd *TOOT* SW17	151	E4
Khartoum Rd *IL* IG1	84	B2
PLSTW E13	94	B2
TOOT SW17	151	D4
Khyber Rd *BTSEA* SW11	115	E5
Kibworth St *VX/NE* SW8	117	F3
Kidbrooke Gdns *BKHTH/KID* SE3	124	A4
Kidbrooke Gv *BKHTH/KID* SE3	124	A3
Kidbrooke La *ELTH/MOT* SE9	143	E2
Kidbrooke Park Cl *BKHTH/KID* SE3	124	B4
Kidbrooke Park Rd *BKHTH/KID* SE3	124	B5
LEE/GVPK SE12	142	B5
Kidbrooke Wy *BKHTH/KID* SE3	124	B3
Kidderpore Av *HAMP* NW3	72	A1
Kidderpore Gdns *HAMP* NW3	72	A1
Kidd Pl *CHARL* SE7	125	E1
Kiffen St *SDTCH* EC2A	12	B5
Kilburn Br *KIL/WHAMP* NW6	72	A5
Kilburn High Rd *KIL/WHAMP* NW6	72	A4
Kilburn La *NKENS* W10	89	D2
Kilburn Park Rd *KIL/WHAMP* NW6	2	A4
Kilburn Pl *KIL/WHAMP* NW6	72	A5
Kilburn Priory *STJWD* NW6	72	B5
Kilburn Sq *KIL/WHAMP* NW6	72	A5
Kilburn V *KIL/WHAMP* NW6	72	A5
Kildare Gdns *BAY/PAD* W2	14	B4
Kildare Rd *CAN/RD* E16	94	A4
Kildare Ter *BAY/PAD* W2	14	B4
Kildoran Rd *CLAP* SW4	135	E3
Kilgour Rd *FSTH* SE23	139	E4
Kilkie St *FUL/PGN* SW6	114	C5
Killarney Rd *WAND/EARL* SW18	132	C4
Killearn Rd *CAT* SE6	159	D1
Killick St *IS* N1	9	E1
Killieser Av *BRXS/STRHM* SW2	153	E2
Killip Cl *CAN/RD* E16	93	F5
Killowen Rd *HOM* E9	79	D3
Killyon Rd *VX/NE* SW8	116	C5
Kilmaine Rd *FUL/PGN* SW6	113	E3
Kilmarsh Rd *HMSMTH* W6	100	C5
Kilmington Rd *BARN* SW13	112	A2
Kilmorie Rd *FSTH* SE23	157	E1
Kilner St *POP/IOD* E14	92	A4
Kiln Ms *TOOT* SW17	151	D5
Kiln Pl *KTTN* NW5	74	A1
Kilravock St *NKENS* W10	89	E2
Kimbell Gdns *FUL/PGN* SW6	113	E4
Kimbell Pl *BKHTH/KID* SE3	142	C2
Kimberley Av *EHAM* E6	95	E1
GNTH/NBYPK IG2	67	D2
PECK SE15	120	B5
Kimberley Ct *KIL/WHAMP* NW6	71	E4
Kimberley Rd *BRXN/ST* SW9	117	E5
CAN/RD E16	93	E3
KIL/WHAMP NW6	71	E5
WAN E11	63	D4
Kimber Rd *WAND/EARL* SW18	132	A5
Kimbolton Cl *LEE/GVPK* SE12	141	F4
Kimmeridge Gdns *ELTH/MOT* SE9	161	E4
Kimmeridge Rd *ELTH/MOT* SE9	161	E4
Kimpton Rd *CMBW* SE5	119	D4
Kinburn St *BERM/RHTH* SE16	103	D3
Kincaid Rd *PECK* SE15	120	B3
Kincardine Gdns *MV/WKIL* W9 *	14	A1
Kinder St *WCHPL* E1	90	B5
Kingdon Rd *KIL/WHAMP* NW6	72	A3
King Edward II Ms *BERM/RHTH* SE16	102	B3
King Edward Rd *LEY* E10	62	B3
King Edward's Gdns *ACT* W3	98	A2
King Edward's Rd *ACT* W3	98	A2
BARK IG11	85	D5
HACK E8	78	B5
King Edward St *STBT* EC1A	23	E4
King Edward Wk *STHWK* SE1	46	B2
Kingfield St *POP/IOD* E14	104	C5
Kingfisher Ms *LEW* SE13	140	B3
Kingfisher St *EHAM* E6	95	E4
Kingfisher Wy *WLSDN* NW10	69	D2
King Garth Ms *FSTH* SE23	156	C2
King George Av *CAN/RD* E16	94	C5
GNTH/NBYPK IG2	67	D1
King George St *GNWCH* SE10	122	C3
Kingham Cl *NTGHL* W11	101	E3
WAND/EARL SW18	132	C5
King Henry's Reach *HMSMTH* W6	112	C2

King Henry's Rd *HAMP* NW3 .... 73 E4
King Henry St *STNW/STAM* N16 .... 77 E2
King Henry's Wk *IS* N1 .... 77 E3
King Henry Ter *WAP* E1W * 102 B1
Kinghorn St *STBT* EC1A 23 E3
King James Ct *STHWK* SE1 .... 47 D1
King James St *STHWK* SE1 .... 47 D1
King John Ct *SDTCH* EC2A 13 D5
King John St *WCHPL* E1 .... 91 D4
King John's Wk *ELTH/MOT* SE9 .... 143 E5
Kinglake Est *WALW* SE17 .... 119 E4
Kinglake St *WALW* SE17 .... 119 E1
Kinglet Cl *FSTGT* E7 .... 82 A3
Kingly Ct *REGST* W1B * 31 F1
Kingly St *REGST* W1B 19 E5
King & Queen St *ELTH/MOT* SE9 ..... 161 E4
King & Queen St *WALW* SE17 .... 118 C1
King & Queen Whf
   BERM/RHTH SE16 * 103 D2
Kingsand Rd *LEE/GVPK* SE12 .... 160 A2
Kings Av *BAL* SW12 .... 153 D1
   CLAP SW4 .... 135 E4
King's Bench St *STHWK* SE1 .... 35 D5
King's Bench Wk *EMB* EC4Y * 34 B1
Kingsbridge Ct *POP/IOD* E14 .... 104 A4
Kingsbridge Rd *BARK* IG11 .... 97 D1
   NKENS W10 .... 88 C5
Kingsbury Rd *IS* N1 .... 77 E3
Kingsbury Ter *IS* N1 .... 77 E3
Kingsclere Cl *PUT/ROE* SW15 .... 130 C4
Kingscliffe Gdns *WIM/MER* SW19 ... 149 F1
Kings Cl *LEY* E10 .... 62 B2
King's College Rd *HAMP* NW3 * 73 D4
Kingscote Rd *CHSWK* W4 .... 99 D4
Kingscote St *BLKFR* EC4V 34 C1
Kings Ct *PLSTW* E13 .... 85 D5
King's Ct *STHWK* SE1 * 35 D5
Kingscourt Rd *STRHM/NOR* SW16 ... 153 D3
Kings Crs *FSBYPK* N4 .... 58 C5
Kingscroft Rd *CRICK* NW2 .... 71 F3
King's Cross Br *IS* N1 * 9 D3
King's Cross Rd *FSBYW* WC1X 9 E5
Kingsdale Gdns *NTGHL* W11 .... 101 D2
Kingsdale Rd *WOOL/PLUM* SE18 ..... 127 F2
Kingsdown Av *ACT* W3 .... 99 E1
Kingsdown Cl *BERM/RHTH* SE16 * ... 120 B1
   NKENS W10 .... 89 D5
Kingsdown Rd *ARCH* N19 .... 57 E5
   WAN E11 .... 63 E5
Kings Dr *WBLY* HA9 .... 50 B4
Kings Farm Av *RCHPK/HAM* TW10 .. 128 A2
Kingsford St *KTTN* NW5 .... 73 F2
Kingsford Wy *EHAM* E6 .... 95 F4
Kings Gdns *IL* IG1 .... 67 D3
   KIL/WHAMP NW6 .... 72 A4
Kingsgate *WBLY* HA9 .... 50 C5
Kingsgate Est *IS* N1 .... 77 E3
Kingsgate Pl *KIL/WHAMP* NW6 ...... 72 A4
Kingsgate Rd *KIL/WHAMP* NW6 ..... 72 A4
Kingsground *ELTH/MOT* SE9 .... 143 D5
Kings Hall Rd *LEW* SE13 .... 140 C1
King's Hwy *WOOL/PLUM* SE18 .... 127 F2
Kingshold Rd *HOM* E9 .... 78 C4
Kingsholm Gdns *ELTH/MOT* SE9 .... 143 D2
Kingshurst Rd *LEE/GVPK* SE12 ...... 142 A5
Kingsland Gn *STNW/STAM* N16 ...... 77 E3
Kingsland High St *HACK* E8 .... 77 E3
Kingsland Pas *HACK* E8 .... 77 E3
Kingsland Rd *BETH* E2 .... 13 D2
   HACK E8 .... 77 F4
   PLSTW E13 .... 94 C2
Kingslawn Cl *PUT/ROE* SW15 .... 130 B3
Kingsley Ms *IL* IG1 .... 66 B4
   KENS W8 .... 39 E5
   WAP E1W * 102 B1
Kingsley Pl *HGT* N6 .... 56 A2
Kingsley Rd *FSTGT* E7 .... 82 A4
   KIL/WHAMP NW6 .... 71 F5
   WIM/MER SW19 .... 150 B5
Kingsley St *BTSEA* SW11 .... 133 F1
Kingsley Wy *EFNCH* N2 .... 54 C1
Kingsley Wood Dr *ELTH/MOT* SE9 .. 161 F5
Kings Ml *HMSMTH* W6 * 100 C5
Kingsmead *WOOL/PLUM* SE18 ...... 107 F5
Kingsmead Av *CDALE/KGS* NW9 .... 51 D2
Kingsmead Rd *BRXS/STRHM* SW2 .. 154 A2
Kingsmead Wy *CLPT* E5 .... 79 E1
Kingsmere Cl *PUT/ROE* SW15 .... 117 E5
Kingsmere Pk *CDALE/KGS* NW9 .... 50 C3
Kingsmere Pl *STNW/STAM* N16 * ... 59 D3

Kingsmere Rd *WIM/MER* SW19 ..... 149 D2
King's Ms *BMSBY* WC1N 21 F1
   CLAP SW4 .... 135 E3
Kingsmill Ter *STJWD* NW8 .... 4 B1
King's Orch *ELTH/MOT* SE9 .... 143 E4
Kings Pde *SHB* W12 * 100 A4
   WLSDN NW10 * 70 C5
Kings Pas *WAN* E11 * 63 E2
Kings Pl *CHSWK* W4 .... 110 C1
King's Pl *STHWK* SE1 .... 47 E1
King Sq *FSBYE* EC1V 11 E4
King's Quay *WBPTN* SW10 * 114 C4
Kings Reach *WHALL* SW1A 33 D4
Kings Ride Ga *RCHPK/HAM* TW10 .. 128 A2
Kings Rd *CHEL* SW3 .... 115 D2
   WLSDN NW10 .... 70 B4
King's Rd *BARK* IG11 .... 84 C4
   FUL/PGN SW6 .... 114 B4
   MORT/ESHN SW14 .... 129 D1
   PLSTW E13 .... 82 C5
   WAN E11 .... 63 E2
King's Scholars' Pas *PIM* SW1V 43 E3
King Stairs Cl *BERM/RHTH* SE16 ... 102 B3
King's Ter *CAMTN* NW1 .... 74 C5
Kingsthorpe Rd *SYD* SE26 .... 157 D4
Kingston Hl *KUTN/CMB* KT2 .... 146 C5
Kingston Hill Pl *KUTN/CMB* KT2 .... 146 C4
Kingston La *IL* IG1 .... 84 C1
   PUT/ROE SW15 .... 148 B1
Kingston Sq *NRWD* SE19 .... 155 D5
Kingston V *PUT/ROE* SW15 .... 147 D4
Kingstown St *CAMTN* NW1 .... 73 F5
King St *ACT* W3 .... 98 B2
   CITYW EC2V 23 F5
   COVGDN WC2E 32 C1
   HMSMTH W6 .... 100 A5
   PLSTW E13 .... 94 A3
   WHALL SW1A 31 F4
King Street Cloisters *HMSMTH* W6 * 100 B5
Kingswater Pl *BTSEA* SW11 .... 115 E3
Kingsway *HOL/ALD* WC2B 21 E5
   MORT/ESHN SW14 .... 128 B1
Kingsway Pde *STNW/STAM* N16 * ... 59 D5
Kingsway Pl *CLKNW* EC1R * 10 B3
Kingswear Rd *KTTN* NW5 .... 56 B5
Kingswood Av *KIL/WHAMP* NW6 .... 71 E5
   VX/NE SW8 .... 117 E5
Kingswood Cl *LEW* SE13 .... 141 D4
Kingswood Dr *DUL* SE21 .... 155 E4
Kingswood Pl *LEW* SE13 .... 141 E2
Kingswood Rd *BRXS/STRHM* SW2 .. 135 E4
   CHSWK W4 .... 98 C4
   WAN E11 .... 63 E2
   WBLY HA9 .... 50 A5
Kingswood Ter *CHSWK* W4 .... 98 C4
Kings Yd *PUT/ROE* SW15 * 131 D2
   SRTFD E15 * 80 A3
Kingthorpe Rd *WLSDN* NW10 .... 69 D4
Kingthorpe Ter *WLSDN* NW10 * 69 D4
Kingweston Cl *CRICK* NW2 .... 53 E5
Kingwood Rd *FUL/PGN* SW6 .... 113 E3
Kinlet Rd *WOOL/PLUM* SE18 .... 126 C3
Kinloch Dr *CDALE/KGS* NW9 .... 51 E2
Kinloch St *HOLWY* N7 .... 57 F5
Kinnaird Av *CHSWK* W4 .... 110 C3
Kinnear Rd *SHB* W12 .... 99 F3
Kinnerton Pl North *KTBR* SW1X * ... 41 F1
Kinnerton Pl South *KTBR* SW1X * ... 41 F1
Kinnerton St *KTBR* SW1X 42 A1
Kinnerton Yd *KTBR* SW1X * 42 A1
Kinnoul Rd *HMSMTH* W6 .... 113 E2
Kinsale Rd *PECK* SE15 .... 138 A1
Kinveachy Gdns *CHARL* SE7 .... 125 E1
Kinver Rd *SYD* SE26 .... 156 C4
Kipling Est *STHWK* SE1 .... 48 B1
Kipling St *STHWK* SE1 .... 48 B1
Kippington Dr *ELTH/MOT* SE9 .... 161 D1
Kirby Est *BERM/RHTH* SE16 * 102 B4
Kirby Gv *STHWK* SE1 .... 36 C5
Kirby St *HCIRC* EC1N 22 B2
Kirkdale *SYD* SE26 .... 156 B2
Kirkdale Cnr *SYD* SE26 * 156 C4
Kirkdale Rd *WAN* E11 .... 63 E3
Kirkham Rd *EHAM* E6 .... 95 E5
Kirkham St *WOOL/PLUM* SE18 ...... 127 E2
Kirkland Cl *BFN/LL* DA15 .... 145 E4
Kirkland Wk *HACK* E8 .... 77 F3
Kirk La *WOOL/PLUM* SE18 .... 126 C2
Kirkmichael Rd *POP/IOD* E14 .... 92 C5

Kirk Rd *WALTH* E17.......................... 61 F1
Kirkside Rd *BKHTH/KID* SE3................. 124 A2
Kirkstall Gdns *BRXS/STRHM* SW2......... 153 D1
Kirkstall Rd *BRXS/STRHM* SW2............. 153 E1
Kirkwall Pl *BETH* E2 *...................... 90 C2
Kirkwood Rd *PECK* SE15.................... 120 B5
Kirtley Rd *SYD* SE26....................... 157 E4
Kirtling St *VX/NE* SW8...................... 116 C3
Kirton Cl *CHSWK* W4........................ 99 D5
Kirton Gdns *BETH* E2........................ 13 F4
Kirton Ldg *WAND/EARL* SW18 *........... 132 B4
Kirton Rd *PLSTW* E13....................... 95 D1
Kirwyn Wy *CMBW* SE5....................... 118 C3
Kitcat Ter *BOW* E3.......................... 92 A3
Kitchener Rd *FSTGT* E7..................... 82 B3
Kite Pl *BETH* E2 *.......................... 90 A2
Kite Yd *BTSEA* SW11 *...................... 115 F4
Kitson Rd *BARN* SW13...................... 112 A4
CMBW SE5.................................. 118 C3
Kitto Rd *NWCR* SE14....................... 121 D5
Kiver Rd *ARCH* N19......................... 77 F1
Kiwi Ter *EHAM* E6.......................... 96 A2
Klea Av *CLAP* SW4.......................... 134 C4
Knapdale Cl *FSTH* SE23.................... 156 B2
Knapmill Rd *CAT* SE6...................... 158 A2
Knapmill Wy *CAT* SE6...................... 158 A2
Knapp Cl *WLSDN* NW10.................... 69 E3
Knapp Rd *BOW* E3.......................... 92 A3
Knaresborough Dr *WAND/EARL* SW18... 150 B1
Knaresborough Pl *ECT* SW5............... 38 C3
Knatchbull Rd *CMBW* SE5................. 118 B5
WLSDN NW10.............................. 69 D5
Knebworth Rd *STNW/STAM* N16 *........ 77 E1
Kneller Rd *BROCKY* SE4.................... 139 E2
Knighten St *WAP* E1W...................... 102 B2
Knighthead Point *POP/IOD* E14 *......... 104 A3
Knightland Rd *CLPT* E5.................... 60 B4
Knighton Park Rd *SYD* SE26.............. 157 D5
Knighton Rd *FSTGT* E7..................... 64 A5
Knightrider Ct *BLKFR* EC4V *............. 35 D1
Knightrider St *BLKFR* EC4M............... 35 D1
Knightsbridge *SKENS* SW7................ 41 D1
Knightsbridge Gn *KTBR* SW1X *.......... 41 E1
Knights Hl *WNWD* SE27.................... 154 B5
Knight's Hill Sq *WNWD* SE27 *........... 154 B5
Knights Rd *CAN/RD* E16.................... 106 A2
Knights Wk *LBTH* SE11..................... 46 C5
Knivet Rd *FUL/PGN* SW6................... 114 A2
Knockholt Rd *ELTH/MOT* SE9.............. 143 D3
The Knole *ELTH/MOT* SE9.................. 162 A4
Knoll Rd *WAND/EARL* SW18............... 132 B5
Knollys Cl *STRHM/NOR* SW16 *.......... 154 B5
Knolly's Cl *STRHM/NOR* SW16............ 154 A5
Knolly's Rd *STRHM/NOR* SW16........... 154 A5
Knottisford St *BETH* E2.................... 91 D2
Knotts Green Ms *LEY* E10................. 62 B1
Knotts Green Rd *LEY* E10.................. 62 B1
Knowle Cl *BRXN/ST* SW9.................. 136 A1
Knowles Hill Crs *LEW* SE13............... 141 D3
Knowsley Rd *BTSEA* SW11................. 115 F5
Knox Rd *FSTGT* E7........................... 82 A3
Knox St *CAMTN* NW1........................ 17 E2
Knoyle St *NWCR* SE14...................... 121 E2
Kohat Rd *WIM/MER* SW19................. 150 B5
Kossuth St *GNWCH* SE10.................. 123 E1
Kramer Ms *ECT* SW5 *..................... 114 A1
Kreedman Wk *HACK* E8 *.................. 78 A2
Kylemore Cl *EHAM* E6..................... 95 D1
Kylemore Rd *KIL/WHAMP* NW6............ 72 A4
Kynance Ms *SKENS* SW7................... 39 D3
Kynance Pl *KENS* SW6...................... 39 E3
Kynaston Rd *BMLY* BR1.................... 160 A5
STNW/STAM N16............................ 59 E5
Kyrle Rd *BTSEA* SW11...................... 134 A4
Kyverdale Rd *STNW/STAM* N16 *......... 59 F2

Ladas Rd *WNWD* SE27...................... 154 C5
Ladbroke Crs *NTGHL* W11.................. 89 E1
Ladbroke Gdns *NTGHL* W11................ 101 F1
Ladbroke Gv *NKENS* W10................... 89 D3
NTGHL W11.................................. 101 F1
Ladbroke Ms *NTGHL* W11................... 101 E2
Ladbroke Rd *NTGHL* W11................... 101 F2
Ladbroke Sq *NTGHL* W11................... 101 F1
Ladbroke Ter *NTGHL* W11................... 101 F1
Ladbroke Wk *NTGHL* W11................... 101 F2
Ladderstile Ride *KUTN/CMB* KT2......... 146 B5
Ladycroft Rd *LEW* SE13.................... 140 B1
Lady Margaret Rd *KTTN* NW5.............. 74 C2
Ladyship Ter *EDUL* SE22 *................. 138 B5
Ladysmith Av *EHAM* E6..................... 95 E1
Ladysmith Rd *CAN/RD* E16................. 93 F2
ELTH/MOT SE9.............................. 144 A4
Lady Somerset Rd *KTTN* NW5.............. 74 B1
Ladywell Cl *BROCKY* SE4.................. 140 A3
Ladywell Rd *LEW* SE13..................... 140 A3
Ladywell St *SRTFD* E15.................... 81 F5
Ladywell Water Tower *BROCKY* SE4 *.... 139 F1
Lafone St *STHWK* SE1....................... 37 E5
Lagado Ms *BERM/RHTH* SE16.............. 103 D2
Lainson St *WAND/EARL* SW18.............. 132 A5
Lairdale Cl *DUL* SE21........................ 154 C1
Lairs Cl *HOLWY* N7 *........................ 75 E3
Laitwood Rd *BAL* SW12..................... 152 B1
Lakedale Rd *WOOL/PLUM* SE18............ 127 E1
Lake House Rd *WAN* E11.................... 64 A5
Lake Rd *LEY* E10............................ 62 B2
WIM/MER SW19.............................. 149 F5
Lakeside Rd *WKENS* W14................... 101 D4
Lakeside Wy *WBLY* HA9..................... 68 A1
Lake View Est *BOW* E3 *.................... 91 D1
Lakeview Rd *WNWD* SE27.................. 154 A5
Lakis Cl *HAMP* NW3......................... 72 C1
Laleham Rd *CAT* SE6....................... 140 C5
Lalor St *FUL/PGN* SW6..................... 113 E5
Lambarde Av *ELTH/MOT* SE9.............. 162 A4
Lamberhurst Rd *WNWD* SE27............. 154 A4
Lambert Av *RCH/KEW* TW9................. 128 A1
Lambert Jones Ms *BARB* EC2Y *.......... 23 E2
Lambert Rd *BRXS/STRHM* SW2........... 135 E3
CAN/RD E16................................. 94 B5
Lambert St *IS* N1............................ 76 A4
Lambeth Br *WEST* SW1P................... 45 D4
Lambeth High St *STHWK* SE1............. 45 F5
Lambeth Hl *BLKFR* EC4V.................... 35 E1
Lambeth Palace Rd *STHWK* SE1.......... 46 A3
Lambeth Rd *STHWK* SE1.................... 45 F4
PECK SE15................................... 119 F5
Lambeth Wk *LBTH* SE11.................... 45 F4
Lamb La *HACK* E8........................... 78 B4
Lamble St *KTTN* NW5....................... 74 A1
Lambolle Pl *HAMP* NW3..................... 73 E3
Lambolle Rd *HAMP* NW3.................... 73 E3
Lambourn Cl *KTTN* NW5 *.................. 74 C1
Lambourne Av *WIM/MER* SW19............ 149 F4
Lambourne Gdns *BARK* IG11............... 85 F4
Lambourne Gv *BERM/RHTH* SE16......... 121 D1
Lambourne Pl *BKHTH/KID* SE3............ 124 B4
Lambourne Rd *BARK* IG11.................. 85 E4
GDMY/SEVK IG3............................. 67 E4
WAN E11..................................... 62 C2
Lambourn Rd *VX/NE* SW8.................. 134 B1
Lambrook Ter *FUL/PGN* SW6.............. 113 E4
Lamb's Conduit Pas *FSBYW* WC1X *..... 21 E2
Lamb's Conduit St *BMSBY* WC1N......... 21 E1
Lambscroft Av *ELTH/MOT* SE9............ 160 C5
Lambs Gv *BARK* IG11 *..................... 85 E4
Lambs Ms *IS* N1 *........................... 76 B5
Lamb's Pas *STLK* EC1Y.................... 24 A1
Lamb St *WCHPL* E1.......................... 25 E2
Lambton Pl *NTGHL* W11 *.................. 101 F1
Lambton Rd *ARCH* N19..................... 57 D2
Lamb Wk *STHWK* SE1....................... 48 C1
Lamerock Rd *BMLY* BR1.................... 159 F4
Lamerton St *DEPT* SE8..................... 122 A2
Lamington St *HMSMTH* W6................ 100 B5
Lamlash St *LBTH* SE11..................... 46 C4
Lammas Rd *HOM* E9........................ 79 D4
LEY E10...................................... 61 E4
Lammermoor Rd *BAL* SW12 *.............. 134 B5
Lamont Rd *WBPTN* SW10.................... 115 D2
Lamont Road Pas *WBPTN* SW10 *......... 115 D2
Lamorbey Cl *BFN/LL* DA15 *............... 163 F2
Lampard Gv *STNW/STAM* N16............. 59 F3
Lampern Sq *BETH* E2 *..................... 90 A2
Lampeter Sq *HMSMTH* W6................. 113 E2
Lamplighter Cl *WCHPL* E1.................. 90 C3

L

Laburnum Cl *ALP/SUD* HA0................. 68 A5
PECK SE15................................... 120 C3
Laburnum Gv *CDALE/KGS* NW9........... 50 C2
Laburnum Rd *ELTH/MOT* SE9 *............ 144 A3
Laburnum St *BETH* E2....................... 13 E1
Laceback Ct *BFN/LL* DA15.................. 145 F5
Lacewing Cl *PLSTW* E13..................... 94 A2
Lacey Av *BOW* E3............................ 92 A1
Lackington St *SDTCH* EC2A................. 24 B2
Lacon Rd *EDUL* SE22........................ 138 A2
Lacy Rd *PUT/ROE* SW15.................... 131 D2

Lampmead Rd LEE/GVPK SE12 .... 141 E3
Lamport Cl WOOL/PLUM SE18 .... 107 F5
Lampton House Cl WIM/MER SW19 ...... 149 D4
Lanark Av MV/WKIL W9 .... 3 F5
Lanark Pl MV/WKIL W9 .... 3 E5
Lanbury Rd PECK SE15 .... 139 D2
Lancashire Ct MYFR/PKLN W1K 30 C1
Lancaster Av BARK IG11 .... 85 E4
WIM/MER SW19 .... 149 D5
WNWD SE27 .... 154 B2
Lancaster Ct BAY/PAD W2 .... 27 F1
Lancaster Dr HAMP NW3 .... 73 E3
POP/IOD E14 .... 104 C2
Lancaster Gdns WIM/MER SW19 .... 149 E5
Lancaster Ga BAY/PAD W2 .... 27 E2
Lancaster Gv HAMP NW3 .... 73 E3
Lancaster House WOOL/PLUM SE18 * . 125 E3
Lancaster Ms BAY/PAD W2 .... 27 F1
WAND/EARL SW18 * 132 B3
Lancaster Pl COVGDN WC2E 33 E1
TPL/STR WC2R 33 E1
WIM/MER SW19 .... 149 D5
Lancaster Rd FSBYPK N4 .... 58 A2
FSTGT E7 .... 82 A4
NKENS W10 .... 89 D5
WAN E11 .... 63 E4
WIM/MER SW19 .... 149 D5
WLSDN NW10 .... 69 F2
Lancaster Stables HAMP NW3 * 73 E3
Lancaster Ter BAY/PAD W2 .... 28 A1
Lancaster West NTGHL W11 * 89 F2
Lacefield NKENS W10 .... 89 F2
Lancell St STNW/STAM N16 .... 59 E4
Lancelot Pl SKENS SW7 .... 41 E1
Lancer Sq KENS W8 .... 26 C5
Lancey Cl CHARL SE7 .... 107 D5
Lanchester Wy NWCR SE14 .... 120 C4
Lancing Rd CROY/NA/BYPK IG2 .... 67 D1
Lancing St CAMTN NW1 .... 8 A4
Landcroft Rd EDUL SE22 .... 137 E4
Landells Rd EDUL SE22 .... 137 F4
Landford Rd PUT/ROE SW15 .... 130 C1
Landgrove Rd WIM/MER SW19 .... 150 A5
Landleys Flds HOLWY N7 * 75 D2
Landmann Wy NWCR SE14 .... 121 D2
Landon Pl KTBR SW1X 41 E2
Landons Cl POP/IOD E14 .... 104 C2
Landor Rd BRXN/ST SW9 .... 135 E1
Landor Wk SHB W12 .... 100 A3
Landridge Rd FUL/PGN SW6 .... 113 E5
Landrock Rd CEND/HSY/T N8 .... 57 E1
Landseer Av MNPK E12 .... 84 A2
Landseer Rd ARCH N19 .... 57 E5
Landstead Rd WOOL/PLUM SE18 ...... 127 D3
Lane Cl CRICK NW2 .... 52 B5
Lane Ms MNPK E12 .... 65 F5
Lanercost Rd BRXS/STRHM SW2 .... 154 A2
Laneside CHST BR7 .... 162 B5
The Lane BKHTH/KID SE3 .... 142 A1
STJWD NW8 .... 3 E2
Laneway PUT/ROE SW15 .... 130 B3
Lanfranc Rd BOW E3 .... 91 E1
Lanfrey Pl WKENS W14 .... 113 F1
Langbourne Av HGT N6 .... 56 A4
Langbrook Rd BKHTH/KID SE3 .... 143 D1
Langdale Cl MORT/ESHN SW14 .... 128 B2
Langdale Rd CNWCH SE10 .... 122 C5
Langdale St WCHPL E1 * 90 B5
Langdon Ct WLSDN NW10 .... 69 E5
Langdon Crs EHAM E6 .... 96 A1
Langdon Dr CDALE/KGS NW9 .... 50 C3
Langdon House WOOL/PLUM SE18 * .. 125 E3
Langdon Park Rd HGT N6 .... 56 B2
Langdon Rd MORT/ESHN SW14 .... 128 C3
EHAM E6 .... 84 A5
Langdon Shaw SCUP DA14 .... 163 F5
Langdon Wy STHWK SE1 .... 102 A5
Langford Cl HACK E8 .... 78 A2
SEVS/STOTM N15 .... 59 E1
STJWD NW8 .... 3 F1
Langford Gn CMBW SE5 .... 137 E1
Langford Pl STJWD NW8 .... 3 F2
Langford Rd FUL/PGN SW6 .... 114 B5
Langham Dr CHSWK W4 .... 111 E5
REGST W1B 19 D3
Langham St GTPST W1W 19 E3
REGST W1B 19 D3
Langholm Cl BAL SW12 .... 135 D5
Langland Gdns HAMP NW3 .... 72 B2
Langler Rd WLSDN NW10 .... 88 C3
Langley Ct COVGDN WC2E 32 C1

Langley Crs WAN E11 .... 64 B2
Langley Dr ACT W3 .... 98 B3
WAN E11 .... 64 B2
Langley La VX/NE SW8 .... 117 E2
Langley St LSQ/SEVD WC2H 20 C5
Langmead St WNWD SE27 .... 154 B4
Langroyd Rd TOOT SW17 .... 151 F2
Langside Av PUT/ROE SW15 .... 130 A2
Langston Hughes Cl HNHL SE24 * 136 B2
Lang St WCHPL E1 .... 90 C2
Langthorn Ct LOTH EC2R * 24 B4
Langthorne Rd WAN E11 .... 63 D5
Langthorne St FUL/PGN SW6 .... 113 D4
Langton Av EHAM E6 .... 96 A2
Langton Cl FSBYW WC1X 9 F4
Langton Ri EDUL SE22 .... 138 B5
Langton Rd BRXN/ST SW9 .... 118 B3
CRICK NW2 .... 52 C5
Langton St WBPTN SW10 .... 114 C2
Langtry Rd EDUL SE24 .... 72 B5
Langtry Wk STJWD NW8 .... 72 C5
Lanhill Rd MV/WKIL W9 .... 2 A5
Lanier Rd LEW SE13 .... 140 C4
Lannoy Rd ELTH/MOT SE9 .... 162 C1
Lanrick Rd POP/IOD E14 .... 93 D4
Lansbury Cl WLSDN NW10 .... 68 C2
Lansbury Gdns POP/IOD E14 * 93 D5
Lanscombe Wk VX/NE SW8 * 117 E3
Lansdowne Dr HACK E8 .... 78 A4
Lansdowne Gdns VX/NE SW8 .... 117 E3
Lansdowne Gv WLSDN NW10 .... 69 E1
Lansdowne Hl WNWD SE27 .... 154 B3
Lansdowne La CHARL SE7 .... 125 D1
Lansdowne Ms CHARL SE7 .... 125 D1
NTGHL W11 .... 101 F2
Lansdowne Pl STHWK SE1 .... 48 B2
Lansdowne Ri NTGHL W11 .... 101 E1
Lansdowne Rd GDMY/SEVK IG3 .... 67 F3
HACK E8 .... 78 A3
NTGHL W11 .... 101 E1
WALTH E17 .... 62 A1
WAN E11 .... 63 F4
Lansdowne Ter BMSBY WC1N 21 D1
Lansdowne Wk NTGHL W11 .... 101 E2
Lansdowne Wy VX/NE SW8 .... 117 E4
Lansdowne Wood Cl WNWD SE27 ..... 154 B3
Lansdown Rd FSTGT E7 .... 82 C4
Lantern Cl PUT/ROE SW15 .... 130 A2
Lanterns Ct POP/IOD E14 .... 104 A4
Lant St STHWK SE1 .... 35 E5
Lanvanor Rd PECK SE15 .... 120 C5
Lapford Cl MV/WKIL W9 * 89 F3
Lapse Wood Wk FSTH SE23 .... 156 B1
Lapwing Ter FSTGT E7 .... 83 D2
Lapworth Ct BAY/PAD W2 .... 15 D2
Lara Cl LEW SE13 .... 140 C4
DEPT SE8 .... 121 F2
Larch Av ACT W3 .... 99 E2
Larch Cl BAL SW12 .... 152 B2
DEPT SE8 .... 121 F2
Larch Dr CHSWK W4 * 110 A1
Larches Av MORT/ESHN SW14 .... 129 D2
Larch Gv BFN/LL DA15 .... 163 F1
Larch Rd CRICK NW2 .... 70 C1
LEY E10 .... 62 A4
Larchwood Rd ELTH/MOT SE9 .... 162 B2
Larcom St WALW SE17 .... 47 F5
Larden Rd ACT W3 .... 99 E3
Larissa St WALW SE17 * 119 D1
Larkbere Rd SYD SE26 .... 157 E4
Larkfield Rd SCUP DA14 .... 163 F3
Larkhall La CLAP SW4 .... 117 D5
Larkhall Ri CLAP SW4 .... 134 C1
Larkhill Ter WOOL/PLUM SE18 * 126 A3
Lark Rw BETH E2 .... 78 C5
Larnach Rd HMSMTH W6 .... 113 D2
Larpent Av PUT/ROE SW15 .... 130 C3
Lascelles Cl WAN E11 .... 63 D4
Lassa Rd ELTH/MOT SE9 .... 143 E3
Lassell St CNWCH SE10 .... 123 D1
Lasseter Pl BKHTH/KID SE3 .... 123 E2
Latchmere Rd BTSEA SW11 .... 115 F5
Latchmere St BTSEA SW11 .... 115 F5
Latham Ct EHAM E6 .... 95 E5
Latham Rd EHAM E6 .... 83 F4
Latimer Av EHAM E6 .... 83 F5
Latimer Pl NKENS W10 .... 88 C4
Latimer Rd FSTGT E7 .... 82 B1
NKENS W10 .... 88 C4
SEVS/STOTM N15 .... 59 E1

Latona Rd *PECK* SE15	120	A2
Lattimer Pl *CHSWK* W4	111	E3
Lauderdale Pde *MV/WKIL* W9 *	2	C1
Lauderdale Pl *BARB* EC2Y *	23	F5
Lauderdale Rd *MV/WKIL* W9 *	3	D4
Laud St *LBTH* SE11	117	F1
Launcelot Rd *BMLY* BR1	160	A4
Launcelot St *STHWK* SE1	46	A1
Launceston Pl *KENS* W8	39	E1
Launch St *POP/IOD* E14	104	C4
Laundress Ga *ACT* W3 *	98	B3
Laundress La *STNW/STAM* N16	60	A5
Laundry Ms *FSTH* SE23	139	D5
Laundry Rd *HMSMTH* W6	113	E2
Laura Pl *CLPT* E5	74	D3
Laura Ter *FSBYPK* N4 *	58	B4
Laurel Bank Gdns *FUL/PGN* SW6	113	F5
Laurel Cl *TOOT* SW17	151	E5
Laurel Gv *SYD* SE26	157	D5
Laurel Rd *BARN* SW13	112	A5
The Laurels *BRXN/ST* SW9 *	118	B3
Laurel St *HACK* E8	77	F3
Laurence Ms *SHB* W12	100	A3
Laurence Pountney HI *CANST* EC4R	36	A1
Laurence Pountney La *CANST* EC4R	36	A1
Laurie Gv *NWCR* SE14	121	E4
Laurier Rd *KTTN* NW5	56	B5
Lauriston Rd *HOM* E9	79	D4
Lausanne Rd *PECK* SE15	120	C4
Lavender Av *CDALE/KGS* NW9	50	C3
Lavender Cl *CLPT* E5	60	B3
Lavender Gdns *BTSEA* SW11	133	F2
Lavender Gv *HACK* E8	78	A4
Lavender HI *BTSEA* SW11	133	E1
Lavender Pl *IL* IG1	84	B2
Lavender Rd *BERM/RHTH* SE16	103	E2
BTSEA SW11	133	D1
Lavender Sweep *BTSEA* SW11	133	F2
Lavender Ter *BTSEA* SW11 *	133	E1
Lavender Wk *BTSEA* SW11	133	F1
Lavengro Rd *WNWD* SE27	154	C2
Lavenham Rd *WAND/EARL* SW18	149	E2
Lavers Rd *STNW/STAM* N16	59	E5
Laverstoke Gdns *PUT/ROE* SW15	129	F5
Laverton Ms *ECT* SW5 *	39	D5
Laverton Pl *ECT* SW5	39	D5
Lavidge Rd *ELTH/MOT* SE9	161	E2
Lavina Gv *IS* N1	9	E1
Lavington Cl *HOM* E9	79	F3
Lavington St *STHWK* SE1	35	D4
Lawford Rd *CHSWK* W4	110	C3
IS N1	77	E4
KTTN NW5	74	C3
Lawless St *POP/IOD* E14 *	104	B1
Lawley St *CLPT* E5	78	C1
Lawn Crs *RCH/KEW* TW9	110	A5
Lawn House Cl *POP/IOD* E14	104	C3
Lawn La *VX/NE* SW8	117	E2
Lawn Rd *HAMP* NW3	73	F2
Lawns Ct *WBLY* HA9 *	50	A4
The Lawns *BKHTH/KID* SE3 *	141	F1
Lawn Ter *BKHTH/KID* SE3	141	F1
Lawrence Av *MNPK* E12	84	B2
WLSDN NW10	69	D5
Lawrence Bldgs *STNW/STAM* N16	59	F1
Lawrence La *CITYW* EC2V	23	F5
Lawrence Pl *IS* N1 *	75	E5
Lawrence Rd *EHAM* E6	83	E5
PLSTW E13	82	B5
Lawrence St *CAN/RD* E16	93	F4
CHEL SW3	115	E2
Lawrence Wy *WLSDN* NW10	50	C5
Lawrie Park Av *SYD* SE26	156	B5
Lawrie Park Crs *SYD* SE26	156	B5
Lawrie Park Gdns *SYD* SE26	156	B5
Lawson Cl *CAN/RD* E16	94	C4
IL IG1	85	D2
WIM/MER SW19	149	D3
Lawson Rd *LEY* E10	62	C5
Lawton Rd *BOW* E3	91	E2
LEY E10	62	C5
Laxcon Cl *WLSDN* NW10	69	D2
Laxley Cl *CMBW* SE5	118	B3
Laxton Pl *CAMTN* NW1	7	E5
Layard Rd *BERM/RHTH* SE16	102	B5
Layard Sq *BERM/RHTH* SE16	102	B5
Laycock St *IS* N1	76	A3
Layer Gdns *ACT* W3	98	A1
Layfield Cl *HDN* NW4	52	B2
Layfield Crs *HDN* NW4	52	B2
Layfield Rd *HDN* NW4	52	B2
Laystall St *FSBYW* WC1X	22	A1
Layton Pl *RCH/KEW* TW9	110	A4
Layzell Wk *ELTH/MOT* SE9	161	D1
Lazenby Ct *COVGDN* WC2E *	32	C1
Leabank Sq *HOM* E9	80	A3
Leabank Vw *SEVS/STOTM* N15	60	A5
Leabourne Rd *STNW/STAM* N16	60	B1
Lea Bridge Rd *LEY* E10	61	D4
Leacroft Av *BAL* SW12	135	F5
Leadale Rd *STNW/STAM* N16	60	A1
Leadenhall Pl *BANK* EC3V	24	C5
Leadenhall St *BANK* EC3V	24	C5
Leader Av *MNPK* E12	84	A2
The Leadings *WBLY* HA9	50	C5
Leaf Gv *WNWD* SE27	154	A5
Leafy Oak Rd *LEE/GVPK* SE12	160	C4
Leagrave St *CLPT* E5	60	C5
Lea Hall Gdns *LEY* E10 *	62	A3
Lea Hall Rd *LEY* E10	62	A3
Leahurst Rd *LEW* SE13	141	D3
Leake St *STHWK* SE1	33	F5
Lealand Rd *SEVS/STOTM* N15	59	F1
Leaming Cl *MNPK* E12	83	E2
Leamington Av *BMLY* BR1	160	C5
Leamington Cl *BMLY* BR1	160	C5
Leamington Gdns *GDMY/SEVK* IG3	67	F4
Leamington Pk *ACT* W3	87	D4
Leamington Road Vls *NTGHL* W11	89	F4
Leamore St *HMSMTH* W6	100	B5
Leamouth Rd *EHAM* E6	95	E5
POP/IOD E14	93	D5
Leander Rd *BRXS/STRHM* SW2	135	F4
Learoyd Gdns *EHAM* E6	108	A1
Leas Dl *ELTH/MOT* SE9	162	A3
Leaside Rd *CLPT* E5	60	C3
Leasowes Rd *LEY* E10	62	A3
Leatherdale St *WCHPL* E1 *	91	D2
Leather Gdns *SRTFD* E15	81	E5
Leatherhead Cl *STNW/STAM* N16	59	E3
Leather La *HCIRC* EC1N	22	A2
Leathermarket Ct *STHWK* SE1	48	C1
Leathermarket St *STHWK* SE1	48	C1
Leather Rd *BERM/RHTH* SE16 *	103	D5
Leather St *WAP* E1W	103	D1
Leathwaite Rd *BTSEA* SW11	133	F2
Leathwell Rd *DEPT* SE8	122	B5
Lea Valley Rd *CLPT* E5	60	B2
Leaway *CLPT* E5	60	C3
Lebanon Gdns *WAND/EARL* SW18	132	A4
Lebanon Rd *WAND/EARL* SW18	132	A3
Lebrun Sq *BKHTH/KID* SE3	142	B2
Lechmere Rd *CRICK* NW2	70	B3
Leckford Rd *WAND/EARL* SW18	150	C2
Leckhampton Pl *BRXS/STRHM* SW2	136	A5
Lecky St *SKENS* SW7	115	D1
Leconfield Av *BARN* SW13	129	F1
Leconfield Rd *HBRY* N5	77	D1
Leda Rd *WOOL/PLUM* SE18	107	F4
Ledbury Ms North *NTGHL* W11	26	A1
Ledbury Ms West *NTGHL* W11	26	A1
Ledbury Rd *NTGHL* W11	89	F5
Ledbury St *PECK* SE15	120	A3
Leechcroft Av *BFN/LL* DA15	145	F3
Lee Church St *LEW* SE13	141	E2
Lee Conservancy Rd *HOM* E9	79	F2
Leeds Rd *IL* IG1	67	D5
Lee High Rd *LEW* SE13	141	D2
Leeke St *FSBYW* WC1X	9	E3
Leeland Wy *WLSDN* NW10	69	D1
Lee Pk *BKHTH/KID* SE3	141	F2
Lee Rd *BKHTH/KID* SE3	141	F2
Leeside Crs *GLDGN* NW11	53	E1
Leeson Rd *HNHL* SE24 *	136	A3
Lees Pl *MYFR/PKLN* W1K	30	A1
Lee St *HACK* E8	77	F5
Lee Ter *BKHTH/KID* SE3	141	E1
Leeway *DEPT* SE8	121	F1
Leewood Cl *LEE/GVPK* SE12	142	B5
Lefevre Wk *BOW* E3	79	F5
Leffern Rd *SHB* W12	100	A3
Lefroy Rd *SHB* W12	99	F3
Legard Rd *HBRY* N5	58	B5
Legatt Rd *ELTH/MOT* SE9	143	D3
Leggatt Rd *SRTFD* E15	80	C1
Legge St *LEW* SE13	140	C3
Leghorn Rd *WLSDN* NW10	88	A1
WOOL/PLUM SE18	127	D1
Legion Cl *IS* N1	76	A3
Legion Ter *BOW* E3	80	A5
Leicester Gdns *GDMY/SEVK* IG3	67	E2
Leicester Pl *LSQ/SEVD* WC2H *	32	B1
Leicester Rd *WLSDN* NW10	69	D4

Leicester Sq *LSQ/SEVD* WC2H ... 32 B2
Leicester St *LSQ/SEVD* WC2H ... 32 B2
Leigham Av *STRHM/NOR* SW16 ... 153 E3
Leigham Cl *STRHM/NOR* SW16 ... 154 A3
Leigham Court Rd *STRHM/NOR* SW16 . 153 F3
Leigham Hall Pde
  STRHM/NOR SW16 * ... 153 E3
Leigham V *STRHM/NOR* SW16 ... 154 A3
Leigh Gdns *WLSDN* NW10 ... 88 C1
Leigh Orchard Cl *STRHM/NOR* SW16 . 153 F3
Leigh Rd *EHAM* E6 ... 84 A4
  HBRY N5 ... 76 B1
  LEY E10 ... 62 C2
Leigh St *STPAN* WC1H ... 8 C5
Leighton Av *MNPK* E12 ... 84 A2
Leighton Crs *KTTN* NW5 ... 74 C2
Leighton Gdns *WLSDN* NW10 ... 88 C1
Leighton Gv *KTTN* NW5 ... 74 C2
Leighton Pl *KTTN* NW5 ... 74 C2
Leighton Rd *KTTN* NW5 ... 74 C2
Leila Parnell Pl *CHARL* SE7 ... 124 C2
Leinster Av *MORT/ESHN* SW14 ... 128 C1
Leinster Gdns *BAY/PAD* W2 ... 15 E5
Leinster Ms *BAY/PAD* W2 ... 27 E2
Leinster Pl *BAY/PAD* W2 ... 15 E5
Leinster Sq *BAY/PAD* W2 ... 26 B1
Leinster Ter *BAY/PAD* W2 ... 27 E1
Leith Cl *CDALE/KGS* NW9 ... 51 D3
Leithcote Gdns *STRHM/NOR* SW16 . 153 F3
Leithcote Pth *STRHM/NOR* SW16 ... 153 F4
Leith Yd *KIL/WHAMP* NW6 * ... 72 A5
Lelitia Cl *CAN/RD* E16 ... 78 A5
Leman St *WCHPL* E1 ... 25 F3
Le May Av *LEE/GVPK* SE12 ... 160 B3
Lemmon Rd *GNWCH* SE10 ... 123 F2
Lemna Rd *WAN* E11 ... 63 E2
Lemonwell Dr *ELTH/MOT* SE9 ... 146 A1
Lemsford Cl *SEVS/STOTM* N15 ... 60 A1
Lena Gdns *HMSMTH* W6 ... 100 C4
Lendal Ter *CLAP* SW4 ... 135 D1
Len Freeman Pl *FUL/PGN* SW6 ... 113 F2
Lennon Rd *CRICK* NW2 ... 70 C2
Lennox Gdns *IL* IG1 ... 65 F3
  KTBR SW1X ... 41 E3
  WLSDN NW10 ... 69 F1
Lennox Gardens Ms *KTBR* SW1X ... 41 E4
Lennox Rd *FSBYPK* N4 ... 57 F4
  WALTH E17 ... 61 E2
Lens Rd *FSTGT* E7 ... 82 C4
Lenthall Rd *HACK* E8 ... 77 F4
Lenthorp Rd *GNWCH* SE10 ... 105 F5
Lentmead Rd *BMLY* BR1 ... 159 F3
Lenton St *WOOL/PLUM* SE18 ... 109 D5
Lenton Ter *FSBYPK* N4 * ... 58 B5
Leof Crs *CAT* SE6 ... 158 B5
Leonard Ct *KENS* W8 * ... 58 A2
Leonard Pl *STNW/STAM* N16 ... 77 E1
Leonard Rd *FSTGT* E7 ... 82 A1
Leonard St *CAN/RD* E16 ... 107 E2
  SDTCH EC2A ... 12 C3
Leontine Cl *PECK* SE15 ... 120 A3
Leopold Av *WIM/MER* SW19 ... 149 E5
Leopold Ms *HOM* E9 ... 78 C5
Leopold Rd *WIM/MER* SW19 ... 149 F4
  WLSDN NW10 ... 69 E4
Leopold St *BOW* E3 ... 91 F4
Leo St *PECK* SE15 ... 120 B3
Leppoc Rd *CLAP* SW4 ... 135 D3
Leroy St *STHWK* SE1 ... 48 C4
Lerry Cl *WKENS* W14 ... 113 F2
Lescombe Cl *FSTH* SE23 ... 157 E3
Lescombe Rd *FSTH* SE23 ... 157 E3
Leslie Rd *CAN/RD* E16 ... 94 B5
  WAN E11 ... 81 D1
Lessar Av *CLAP* SW4 ... 134 C3
Lessingham Av *TOOT* SW17 ... 151 F4
Lessing St *FSTH* SE23 ... 139 E5
Lester Av *SRTFD* E15 ... 93 E3
Leswin Pl *STNW/STAM* N16 ... 59 F5
Leswin Rd *STNW/STAM* N16 ... 59 F5
Letchford Gdns *WLSDN* NW10 ... 88 A2
Letchford Ms *WLSDN* NW10 * ... 88 A2
Letchworth St *TOOT* SW17 ... 151 F4
Letterstone Rd *FUL/PGN* SW6 ... 113 F3
Lettice St *FUL/PGN* SW6 ... 113 F5
Lett Rd *SRTFD* E15 ... 81 D4
Levana Cl *WIM/MER* SW19 ... 149 E1
Levehurst Wy *CLAP* SW4 ... 117 E3
Levendale Rd *FSTH* SE23 ... 157 E2
Leven Rd *POP/IOD* E14 ... 92 C4
Leverett St *CHEL* SW3 ... 41 D4

Leverholme Gdns *ELTH/MOT* SE9 ... 162 A4
Lever St *FSBYE* EC1V ... 11 E4
Leverton Pl *KTTN* NW5 ... 74 C2
Leverton St *KTTN* NW5 ... 74 C2
Levett Gdns *GDMY/SEVK* IG3 ... 85 F1
Levett Rd *BARK* IG11 ... 85 E3
Lewesdon Cl *WIM/MER* SW19 ... 149 D1
Leweston Pl *STNW/STAM* N16 ... 59 F2
Lewgars Av *CDALE/KGS* NW9 ... 50 C1
Lewin Rd *MORT/ESHN* SW14 ... 129 D1
Lewis Crs *WLSDN* NW10 ... 69 D2
Lewis Gdns *SEVS/STOTM* N15 ... 59 F2
Lewis Gv *LEW* SE13 ... 140 B4
Lewisham High St *LEW* SE13 ... 140 B4
Lewisham Hi *LEW* SE13 ... 122 C5
Lewisham Pk *LEW* SE13 ... 140 B4
Lewisham Rd *LEW* SE13 ... 122 C5
Lewisham Wy *BROCKY* SE4 ... 121 F5
Lewis Pl *HACK* E8 ... 78 A2
Lewis St *CAMTN* NW1 ... 74 B4
Lexden Rd *ACT* W3 ... 98 B1
Lexham Gdns *KENS* W8 ... 38 B4
Lexham Ms *KENS* W8 ... 38 B4
Lexington St *SOHO/CST* W1F ... 19 F5
Lexton Gdns *BAL* SW12 ... 153 D1
Leyborne Pk *RCH/KEW* TW9 ... 110 A4
Leybourne Rd *CAMTN* NW1 * ... 74 B4
  WAN E11 ... 63 D3
Leybourne St *CAMTN* NW1 ... 74 B4
Leyburn House *CHARL* SE7 * ... 125 E3
Leyden St *WCHPL* E1 ... 25 E3
Leydon Cl *BERM/RHTH* SE16 ... 103 D2
Leyes Rd *CAN/RD* E16 ... 106 C1
Leyland Rd *LEE/GVPK* SE12 ... 141 F3
Leylang Rd *NWCR* SE14 ... 121 D3
Leysdown Rd *ELTH/MOT* SE9 ... 161 E2
Leysfield Rd *SHB* W12 ... 100 A3
Leyspring Rd *WAN* E11 ... 63 F3
Ley St *GNTH/NBYPK* IG2 ... 66 C2
  IL IG1 ... 66 B4
Leythe Rd *ACT* W3 ... 98 C3
Leyton Gra *LEY* E10 ... 62 A4
Leyton Green Rd *LEY* E10 ... 62 C1
Leyton Park Rd *LEY* E10 ... 62 C4
Leyton Rd *SRTFD* E15 ... 80 C2
Leytonstone Rd *SRTFD* E15 ... 81 E3
Leywick St *SRTFD* E15 ... 93 E1
Liardet St *NWCR* SE14 ... 121 E2
Liberia Rd *HBRY* N5 ... 76 B3
Liberty St *BRXN/ST* SW9 ... 117 F4
Libra Rd *BOW* E3 ... 79 F5
  PLSTW E13 ... 94 A1
Library Pde *WLSDN* NW10 * ... 69 E5
Library St *STHWK* SE1 ... 47 D1
Lichfield Rd *BOW* E3 ... 91 E2
  CRICK NW2 ... 71 E1
  EHAM E6 ... 95 D2
Lidcote Gdns *BRXN/ST* SW9 * ... 118 A5
Liddell Gdns *WLSDN* NW10 ... 88 C1
Liddell Rd *KIL/WHAMP* NW6 ... 72 A3
Liddington Rd *SRTFD* E15 ... 81 F5
Liddon Rd *PLSTW* E13 ... 94 B2
Liden Cl *LEY* E10 ... 61 F2
Lidfield Rd *STNW/STAM* N16 ... 77 D1
Lidgate Rd *CMBW* SE5 * ... 119 D3
Lidlington Pl *CAMTN* NW1 ... 7 F2
Lidyard Rd *ARCH* N19 ... 56 C3
Liffler Rd *WOOL/PLUM* SE18 ... 127 E1
Lifford St *PUT/ROE* SW15 ... 131 D2
Lighter Cl *BERM/RHTH* SE16 ... 103 E5
Lighterman Ms *WCHPL* E1 ... 91 D5
Lighterman's Rd *POP/IOD* E14 ... 104 A3
Ligonier St *BETH* E2 ... 13 E5
Lilac Pl *LBTH* SE11 ... 45 E5
Lilac St *SHB* W12 ... 100 A1
Lilburne Gdns *ELTH/MOT* SE9 ... 143 E3
Lilburne Rd *ELTH/MOT* SE9 ... 143 E3
Lilestone St *STJWD* NW8 ... 4 C5
Lilford Rd *CMBW* SE5 ... 118 B5
Lilian Barker Cl *LEE/GVPK* SE12 ... 142 A3
Lilley Cl *WAP* E1W ... 102 A2
Lillian Av *ACT* W3 ... 98 A3
Lillian Rd *BARN* SW13 ... 112 A2
Lillie Rd *FUL/PGN* SW6 ... 113 D2
Lillieshall Rd *CLAP* SW4 ... 134 B1
Lillie Yd *FUL/PGN* SW6 ... 114 A2
Lillington Gardens Est *PIM* SW1V ... 43 F5
Lily Cl *WKENS* W14 ... 101 E5
Lily Pl *FARR* EC1M ... 22 B2
Lily Rd *WALTH* E17 ... 62 A1
Lilyville Rd *FUL/PGN* SW6 ... 113 F4

Limburg Rd *BTSEA* SW11 .... **133** E2
Limeburner La *STP* EC4M **102** A2
Lime CI *WAP* E1W **102** A2
Lime Gv *BFN/LL* DA15 .... **145** E4
  SHB W12 .... **100** C3
Limeharbour *POP/IOD* E14 .... **104** B4
Limehouse *POP/IOD* E14 .... **104** A1
Limehouse Cswy *POP/IOD* E14 .... **103** F1
Limehouse Link (Tunnel)
  POP/IOD E14 .... **103** F1
Lime Kiln Dr *CHARL* SE7 .... **124** B2
Limerick CI *BAL* SW12 .... **134** C5
Limerston St *WBPTN* SW10 .... **114** C2
Limes Av *BARN* SW13 .... **111** F5
  GLDGN NW11 .... **53** E2
Limes Field Rd *MORT/ESHN* SW14 .... **129** E1
Limesford Rd *PECK* SE15 .... **139** D2
Limes Gdns *WAND/EARL* SW18 .... **132** A4
Limes Gv *LEW* SE13 .... **140** C2
The Limes *CMBW* SE5 * **137** E1
  WAND/EARL SW18 .... **132** A4
Lime St *FENCHST* EC3M **36** C1
Lime Street Pas *BANK* EC3V * **24** C5
Limes Wk *PECK* SE15 * **138** C2
Limetree St *BRXS/STRHM* SW2 .... **153** F1
Lime Tree Ter *CAT* SE6 * **157** F1
Lime Wk *SRTFD* E15 * **81** E5
Limpsfield Av *WIM/MER* SW19 .... **149** D2
Linacre CI *PECK* SE15 .... **138** B1
Linacre Rd *CRICK* NW2 .... **70** B3
Linchmere Rd *LEE/GVPK* SE12 .... **141** F5
Lincoln Av *WIM/MER* SW19 .... **149** D3
Lincoln Est *BOW* E3 .... **92** A3
Lincoln Gdns *IL* IG1 .... **65** E2
Lincoln Ms *KIL/WHAMP* NW6 .... **71** F5
Lincoln Rd *FSTGT* E7 .... **83** D3
  PLSTW E13 .... **94** B3
Lincoln's Inn Flds *LINN* WC2A **21** E4
Lincoln St *CHEL* SW3 .... **41** E5
  WAN E11 .... **63** E4
Lincombe Rd *BMLY* BR1 .... **159** E5
Lindal Rd *BROCKY* SE4 .... **139** F3
Linden Av *WLSDN* NW10 .... **89** D1
Linden Gdns *BAY/PAD* W2 .... **26** B2
  CHSWK W4 .... **111** D3
Linden Gv *PECK* SE15 .... **138** B3
Linden Ms *BAY/PAD* W2 .... **26** B2
  IS N1 .... **77** D2
The Lindens *CHSWK* W4 .... **110** C4
Linden Wk *ARCH* N19 .... **56** B4
Lindfield Gdns *HAMP* NW3 .... **72** C3
Lindfield St *POP/IOD* E14 .... **92** A5
Lindisfarne Rd *MOIT* SW19 .... **79** E1
Lindley Est *PECK* SE15 * **120** A3
Lindley Pl *RCH/KEW* TW9 .... **110** A4
Lindley Rd *LEY* E10 .... **62** C4
Lindley St *WCHPL* E1 .... **90** C4
Lindore Rd *BTSEA* SW11 .... **133** F2
Lindo St *PECK* SE15 .... **120** C5
Lindrop St *FUL/PGN* SW6 .... **114** C5
Lindsay Sq *PIM* SW1V **117** D1
Lindsell St *GNWCH* SE10 .... **122** C4
Lindsey Ms *IS* N1 .... **76** C4
Lindsey St *FARR* EC1M **23** D2
Lind St *DEPT* SE8 .... **122** B5
Lindway *WNWD* SE27 .... **154** B5
Linford St *VX/NE* SW8 .... **116** C4
Lingards Rd *LEW* SE13 .... **140** C2
Lingey CI *BFN/LL* DA15 .... **163** F2
Lingfield CI *ENC/FH* EN2 * **117** E5
Lingham St *BRXN/ST* SW9 .... **117** E5
Ling Rd *CAN/RD* E16 .... **94** A4
Lingwell Rd *TOOT* SW17 .... **151** E3
Lingwood Rd *CLPT* E5 .... **60** A2
Linhope St *CAMTN* NW1 .... **5** E5
Links Rd *ACT* W3 .... **86** A5
  CRICK NW2 .... **51** F4
Link St *HOM* E9 .... **78** C3
Links Yd *WCHPL* E1 .... **25** F2
The Link *ACT* W3 .... **86** B5
  CRICK NW2 .... **52** A3
Linkway *FSBYPK* N4 .... **58** C2
Linkwood Wk *CAMTN* NW1 .... **75** D4
Linnell CI *GLDGN* NW11 .... **54** B1
Linnell Dr *GLDGN* NW11 .... **54** B1
Linnell Rd *CMBW* SE5 .... **119** E5
Linnet Ms *BAL* SW12 .... **134** A5
Linom Rd *CLAP* SW4 .... **135** E2
Linscott Rd *CLPT* E5 .... **78** C1
Linsdell Rd *BARK* IG11 .... **84** C5
Linsey St *BERM/RHTH* SE16 .... **102** A4

Linstead St *KIL/WHAMP* NW6 .... **72** A4
Linstead Wy *WAND/EARL* SW18 .... **131** E5
Lintaine CI *HMSMTH* W6 * **113** E2
Linthorpe Rd *STNW/STAM* N16 .... **59** E2
Linton CI *CHARL* SE7 .... **124** C1
Linton Gdns *EHAM* E6 .... **95** E5
Linton Gv *WNWD* SE27 .... **154** B5
Linton Rd *BARK* IG11 .... **84** C4
Linton St *IS* N1 .... **76** C5
Linver Rd *FUL/PGN* SW6 .... **113** F5
Lionel Gdns *ELTH/MOT* SE9 .... **143** D5
Lionel Ms *NKENS* W10 * **89** E4
Lionel Rd *ELTH/MOT* SE9 .... **143** D3
Lion Gate Ms *WAND/EARL* SW18 .... **132** A5
Lion Mills *BETH* E2 * **90** A1
Lion Rd *EHAM* E6 .... **95** F4
Lions CI *LEE/GVPK* SE12 .... **160** C3
Liphook Crs *FSTH* SE23 .... **138** C5
Lipton Rd *WCHPL* E1 .... **91** D5
Lisburne Rd *HAMP* NW3 .... **73** F1
Lisford St *PECK* SE15 .... **119** F4
Lisgar Ter *WKENS* W14 .... **101** F5
Liskeard Gdns *BKHTH/KID* SE3 .... **123** F4
Liston Rd *CLAP* SW4 .... **134** C1
Lisle CI *TOOT* SW17 .... **152** B4
Lisle St *LSQ/SEVD* WC2H **32** B1
Lismore CI *WIM/MER* SW19 * **149** F5
Lismore Circ *KTTN* NW5 .... **73** F2
Lismore Wk *IS* N1 * **76** C3
Lissenden Gdns *KTTN* NW5 .... **74** A1
Lisson Gv *STJWD* NW8 .... **4** B5
Lisson St *CAMTN* NW1 .... **16** C2
Lister CI *ACT* W3 .... **87** D4
Lister Rd *WAN* E11 .... **63** E3
Liston Rd *CLAP* SW4 .... **134** C1
Listowel CI *BRXN/ST* SW9 .... **118** A3
Listria Pk *STNW/STAM* N16 .... **59** E4
Litchfield Av *SRTFD* E15 * **81** E3
Litchfield Gdns *WLSDN* NW10 .... **70** A3
Litchfield St *LSQ/SEVD* WC2H **32** B1
Lithos Rd *HAMP* NW3 .... **72** B3
Little Albany St *CAMTN* NW1 .... **7** D5
Little Argyll St *REGST* W1B * **19** E5
Little Birches *BFN/LL* DA15 .... **163** F3
The Little Boltons *WBPTN* SW10 .... **114** B1
Little Britain *STBT* EC1A **23** D3
Little Brownings *FSTH* SE23 .... **156** B2
Littlebury Rd *CLAP* SW4 * **135** D1
Little Chester St *KTBR* SW1X * **42** C2
Little Cloisters *WEST* SW1P * **44** C2
Littlecombe CI *PUT/ROE* SW15 * **131** D4
Littlecote CI *WIM/MER* SW19 .... **131** D5
Little Cottage Pl *GNWCH* SE10 * **122** B3
Littlecroft *ELTH/MOT* SE9 .... **144** A1
Little Deans Yd *WEST* SW1P * **44** C2
Little Dimocks *BAL* SW12 .... **152** B2
Little Dorrit Ct *STHWK* SE1 .... **35** F5
Little Edward St *CAMTN* NW1 * **7** D3
Little Essex St *TPL/STR* WC2R * **34** A1
Littlefield CI *ARCH* N19 * **74** C1
Little George St *WEST* SW1P * **44** C1
Little Green St *KTTN* NW5 * **74** B1
Little Heath *CHARL* SE7 .... **125** E2
Little Ilford La *MNPK* E12 .... **83** F1
Little Marlborough St *REGST* W1B * **19** E5
Littlemede *ELTH/MOT* SE9 .... **161** F5
Littlemoor Rd *IL* IG1 .... **67** D5
Little Newport St *LSQ/SEVD* WC2H **32** B1
Little Portland St *REGST* W1B **19** D4
Little Russell St *NOXST/BSQ* WC1A **20** C3
Little St James's St *WHALL* SW1A **31** E4
Little St Leonards *MORT/ESHN* SW14 .... **128** C1
Little Smith St *WEST* SW1P * **44** B2
Little Somerset St *TWRH* EC3N **25** E5
Little Titchfield St *GTPST* W1W **19** E3
Littleton St *WAND/EARL* SW18 .... **150** C2
Little Trinity La *BLKFR* EC4V * **35** F1
Little Turnstile *HHOL* WC1V * **21** D4
Littlewood *LEW* SE13 .... **140** C3
Livermere Rd *HACK* E8 .... **77** F5
Liverpool Gv *WALW* SE17 .... **119** D1
Liverpool Rd *CAN/RD* E16 .... **93** E4
  IS N1 .... **76** A5
  LEY E10 .... **62** C1
Liverpool St *LVPST* EC2M **24** C3
Livesey CI *THMD* SE28 .... **108** C4
Livesey Pl *STHWK* SE1 .... **120** A2
Livingstone Rd *BTSEA* SW11 .... **133** D1
  WALTH E17 .... **62** B1

Lizard St *FSBYE* EC1V 11 F4
Lizban St *BKHTH/KID* SE3 .... 124 B3
Llanelly Rd *CRICK* NW2 .... 53 F4
Llanover Rd *WOOL/PLUM* SE18 .. 126 A3
Llanvanor Rd *CRICK* NW2 .... 53 F4
Llewellyn St *BERM/RHTH* SE16.... 102 A3
Lloyd Baker St *FSBYW* WC1X 10 A4
Lloyd Rd *EHAM* E6 .... 83 F5
Lloyd's Av *FENCHST* EC3M 25 D5
Lloyd's Pl *BKHTH/KID* SE3 * 123 E5
Lloyd Sq *FSBYW* WC1X 10 A3
Lloyd's Rw *CLKNW* EC1R 10 D4
Lloyd St *FSBYW* WC1X 10 A3
Lloyd Vls *BROCKY* SE4 .... 122 A5
Loampit HI *LEW* SE13 .... 122 A5
Loampit V *LEW* SE13 .... 140 B1
Loanda Cl *HACK* E8 .... 77 F5
Loats Rd *BRXS/STRHM* SW2 ...... 135 E4
Locarno Rd *ACT* W3 .... 98 C3
Lochaber Rd *LEW* SE13 .... 141 E2
Lochaline St *HMSMTH* W6 .... 112 C2
Lochinvar St *BAL* SW12 .... 134 B5
Lochnagar St *POP/IOD* E14 .... 92 C4
Lock Cha *BKHTH/KID* SE3 .... 141 E1
Lockesfield Pl *POP/IOD* E14 .... 104 B5
Lockgate Cl *HOM* E9 .... 79 F2
Lockhart Cl *HOLWY* N7 .... 75 F3
Lockhart St *BOW* E3 .... 91 F3
Lockhurst St *CLPT* E5 .... 79 D1
Lockington Rd *VX/NE* SW8 .... 116 B4
Lockmead Rd *LEW* SE13 .... 140 C1
    SEVS/STOTM N15 .... 60 A1
Locksley Rd *POP/IOD* E14 .... 91 F5
Locksley St *POP/IOD* E14 .... 91 F4
Lockton St *NTGHL* W11 .... 101 D1
Lockwood Cl *SYD* SE26 .... 157 D4
Lockwood St *BERM/RHTH* SE16.. 102 B4
Lockyer St *STHWK* SE1 * 48 B1
Locton Gn *BOW* E3 * 79 F5
Loddiges Rd *HOM* E9 .... 78 C4
Loder St *PECK* SE15 .... 120 C3
Lodge Ms *HBRY* N5 * 76 C1
Lodge Rd *STJWD* NW8 .... 4 B3
The Lodge *SHB* W12 * 101 D3
Loftie St *BERM/RHTH* SE16 .... 102 A3
Lofting Rd *IS* N1 .... 76 A4
Loftus Rd *BARK* IG11 .... 84 C5
    SHB W12 .... 100 B2
Loftus Vls *SHB* W12 * 100 B2
Logan Ms *KENS* W8 .... 38 A4
Logan Pl *ECT* SW5 .... 38 A4
Lolesworth Cl *WCHPL* E1 .... 25 F3
Lollard St *LBTH* SE11 * 45 F4
Loman St *STHWK* SE1 .... 35 D5
Lomas Dr *HACK* E8 * 77 F4
Lombard Av *GDMY/SEVK* IG3 .... 67 E3
Lombard La *EMB* EC4Y 22 B5
Lombard Rd *BTSEA* SW11 .... 115 D5
Lombard St *BANK* EC3V 24 B5
Lombard Wall *CHARL* SE7 .... 106 B4
Lombardy Pl *BAY/PAD* W2 .... 26 C2
Lomond Gv *CMBW* SE5 .... 119 D3
Loncroft Rd *CMBW* SE5 .... 119 E2
Londesborough Rd *STNW/STAM* N16. 77 E1
London Br *CANST* EC4R 36 B2
London Bridge St *STHWK* SE1 ... 36 B3
London Bridge Wk *STHWK* SE1 * . 36 B3

London City Airport Link
    CAN/RD E16 .... 105 F1
London Flds *HACK* E8 .... 78 B4
London Fields East Side *HACK* E8. 78 B4
London Fields West Side *HACK* E8. 78 A4
London Fruit Ex *WCHPL* E1 * 25 F3
London La *HACK* E8 .... 78 B4
London Ms *BAY/PAD* W2 .... 16 B5
London Rd *BARK* IG11 .... 84 B4
    FSTH SE23 .... 156 C1
    PLSTW E13 .... 94 A1
    STHWK SE1 .... 47 D2
London Stile *CHSWK* W4 .... 110 A3
London St *BAY/PAD* W2 .... 16 A4
    FENCHST EC3M * 37 D1
London Ter *BETH* E2 * 90 A1
London Wall *CITYW* EC2Y 23 F3
London Wall Blds *LVPST* EC2M 24 B3
Long Acre *LSQ/SEVD* WC2H 32 C1
Longbeach Rd *BTSEA* SW11 .... 133 F1
Longbridge Rd *BARK* IG11 .... 85 D3
Longbridge Wy *CAT* SE6 .... 140 C3
Longcroft *ELTH/MOT* SE9 .... 162 A3
Longdown Rd *CAT* SE6 .... 158 A4

Long Dr *ACT* W3 .... 87 E5
Longfellow Rd *WALTH* E17 .... 61 F1
    WCHPL E1 * 91 E2
Longfellow Wy *STHWK* SE1 * 49 F5
Longfield Crs *SYD* SE26 .... 156 C3
Longfield Dr *MORT/ESHN* SW14.. 128 B3
Longfield St *STHWK* SE1 .... 49 F4
Longfield St *WAND/EARL* SW18 .. 132 A5
Longford St *CAMTN* NW1 .... 7 D5
Longhedge St *BTSEA* SW11 .... 116 A5
Longhurst Rd *LEW* SE13 .... 141 E3
Longlands Park Crs *BFN/LL* DA15 . 163 E3
Longlands Rd *BFN/LL* DA15 .... 163 E3
Long La *STBT* EC1A 23 D2
    STHWK SE1 .... 48 B1
Longley St *STHWK* SE1 .... 102 A5
Longley Wy *CRICK* NW2 .... 52 C5
Long Mark Rd *CAN/RD* E16 .... 95 D5
Longmarsh La *THMD* SE28 .... 109 E2
Long Meadow *KTTN* NW5 .... 75 D3
Longmeadow Rd *BFN/LL* DA15 ... 163 E1
Longmead Rd *TOOT* SW17 .... 151 F5
Longmoore St *PIM* SW1V 43 E5
Long Pond Rd *BKHTH/KID* SE3 .. 123 E4
Long Reach Rd *BARK* IG11 .... 97 F3
Longridge Rd *ECT* SW5 .... 38 A5
Long Rd *CLAP* SW4 .... 134 C2
Longshore *DEPT* SE8 .... 103 F5
Longstaff Crs *WAND/EARL* SW18. 132 A4
Longstaff Rd *WAND/EARL* SW18 . 132 A4
Longstone Av *WLSDN* NW10 .... 69 F4
Longstone Rd *TOOT* SW17 .... 152 B5
Long St *BETH* E2 .... 13 E2
Longton Av *SYD* SE26 .... 156 A4
Longton Gv *SYD* SE26 .... 156 B4
Longville Rd *LBTH* SE11 .... 46 C4
Long Wk *STHWK* SE1 .... 49 D2
    WOOL/PLUM SE18 .... 126 B3
Longwood Dr *PUT/ROE* SW15 .... 130 A4
Long Yd *BMSBY* WC1N 21 E1
Lonsdale Av *EHAM* E6 .... 95 D3
Lonsdale Cl *EHAM* E6 .... 95 E3
    ELTH/MOT SE9 .... 161 D3
Lonsdale Crs *GNTH/NBYPK* IG2 .. 66 B1
Lonsdale Ms *NTGHL* W11 .... 89 C5
    RCH/KEW TW9 * 110 A4
Lonsdale Pl *IS* N1 .... 76 A4
Lonsdale Rd *BARN* SW13 .... 111 F3
    CHSWK W4 .... 99 F5
    KIL/WHAMP NW6 .... 71 F5
    NTGHL W11 .... 89 C5
    WAN E11 .... 63 F2
Lonsdale Sq *IS* N1 * 76 A4
Loraine Cots *HOLWY* N7 * 75 F1
Loraine Rd *CHSWK* W4 .... 110 B2
    HOLWY N7 .... 75 F1
Lord Hills Rd *BAY/PAD* W2 .... 15 D2
Lord Holland La *BRXN/ST* SW9 * 118 A5
Lord Napier Pl *HMSMTH* W6 .... 112 A1
Lord North St *WEST* SW1P 44 C3
Lord Roberts Ms *FUL/PGN* SW6 * 114 B3
Lordship Gv *STNW/STAM* N16 ..... 59 D4
Lordship La *EDUL* SE22 .... 137 F4
Lordship Pk *STNW/STAM* N16 ...... 59 D4
Lordship Park Ms *STNW/STAM* N16 . 58 C4
Lordship Pl *CHEL* SW3 .... 115 E2
Lordship Rd *STNW/STAM* N16 ..... 59 D3
Lordship Ter *STNW/STAM* N16 .... 59 D4
Lords Cl *DUL* SE21 .... 154 C2
Lords Vw *STJWD* NW8 .... 4 C3
Lord Warwick St *WOOL/PLUM* SE18. 107 F4
Lorenzo St *FSBYW* WC1X 9 E3
Loris Rd *HMSMTH* W6 .... 100 C3
Lorne Cl *STJWD* NW8 .... 5 D4
Lorne Gdns *NTGHL* W11 .... 101 D3
Lorne Rd *FSBYPK* N4 .... 57 F5
    FSTGT E7 .... 82 B1
Lorn Rd *BRXN/ST* SW9 .... 117 F5
Lorrimore Rd *WALW* SE17 .... 118 B2
Lorrimore Sq *WALW* SE17 .... 118 B2
Lothair Rd North *FSBYPK* N4 .... 58 B1
Lothair Rd South *FSBYPK* N4 ...... 58 A2
Lothbury *LOTH* EC2R 24 A4
Lothian Rd *BRXN/ST* SW9 .... 118 B3
Lothrop St *NKENS* W10 .... 89 E2
Lots Rd *WBPTN* SW10 .... 114 C3
Loudoun Rd *STJWD* NW8 .... 72 C5
Loughborough Pk *BRXN/ST* SW9. 136 B2
Loughborough Rd *BRXN/ST* SW9. 118 A5

Loughborough St *LBTH* SE11...... 117 F1
Lough Rd *HOLWY* N7...... 75 F2
Louisa Cl *HOM* E9...... 78 C4
Louisa St *WCHPL* E1...... 91 D4
Louis Cl *CHST* BR7...... 161 F4
Louise Bennett Cl *HNHL* SE24 *...... 136 B2
Louise Rd *SRTFD* E15...... 81 E3
Louisville Rd *TOOT* SW17...... 152 A3
Louvaine Rd *BTSEA* SW11...... 133 D2
Lovage Ap *EHAM* E6...... 95 E4
Lovat Cl *CRICK* NW2...... 51 F5
Lovat La *FENCHST* EC3M...... 36 C1
Lovegrove St *STHWK* SE1...... 120 A1
Lovegrove Wk *POP/IOD* E14...... 105 F5
Lovelace Gn *ELTH/MOT* SE9...... 143 F1
Lovelace Rd *DUL* SE21...... 154 C2
Love La *CITYW* EC2V...... 23 F4
    WOOL/PLUM SE18...... 108 A5
Lovelinch Cl *STHWK* SE15...... 120 C2
Lovell Pl *BERM/RHTH* SE16...... 103 E4
Loveridge Ms *KIL/WHAMP* NW6...... 71 F3
Loveridge Rd *KIL/WHAMP* NW6...... 71 F3
Lovetts Pl *WAND/EARL* SW18...... 132 C2
Lovett Wy *WLSDN* NW10...... 68 C2
Love Wk *CMBW* SE5...... 119 D5
Lowbrook Rd *IL* IG1...... 84 B1
Lowden Rd *HNHL* SE24...... 136 B2
Lowe Av *CAN/RD* E16...... 94 A4
Lowell St *POP/IOD* E14...... 91 E2
Lower Addison Gdns *WKENS* W14...... 101 E3
Lower Belgrave St *BGVA* SW1W...... 42 C3
Lower Clapton Rd *HACK* E8...... 78 B2
Lower Clarendon Wk *NTGHL* W11 *...... 89 E5
Lower Common South
    PUT/ROE SW15...... 130 B1
Lower Grosvenor Pl *BGVA* SW1W...... 42 C2
Lower James St *SOHO/CST* W1F *...... 31 F1
Lower John St *SOHO/CST* W1F *...... 31 F1
Lower Lea Crossing *POP/IOD* E14...... 105 E1
Lower Marsh *STHWK* SE1...... 46 A1
Lower Merton Ri *HAMP* NW3...... 73 E4
Lower Richmond Rd *PUT/ROE* SW15...... 130 C1
    RCH/KEW TW9...... 128 A1
Lower Rd *BERM/RHTH* SE16...... 102 C3
Lower Robert St *CHCR* WC2N...... 33 D2
Lower Sloane St *BGVA* SW1W...... 41 F5
Lower Ter *HAMP* NW3...... 54 C5
Lower Thames St *MON* EC3R...... 36 C2
Lowfield Rd *ACT* W3...... 86 C5
    KIL/WHAMP NW6...... 72 A4
Low Hall La *WALTH* E17...... 61 E1
Lowndes Cl *KTBR* SW1X *...... 42 B3
Lowndes Ct *SOHO/CST* W1F *...... 19 E5
Lowndes Ms *STRHM/NOR* SW16...... 153 E2
Lowndes Pl *KTBR* SW1X *...... 42 A3
Lowndes Sq *KTBR* SW1X...... 41 F1
Lowndes St *KTBR* SW1X...... 41 F2
Lowood St *WCHPL* E1...... 102 B1
Lowther Hl *FSTH* SE23...... 139 E5
Lowther Man *BARN* SW13 *...... 112 A4
Lowther Rd *BARN* SW13...... 111 F4
    HOLWY N7 *...... 76 A2
Lowth Rd *CMBW* SE5...... 118 C5
Loxford Av *EHAM* E6...... 95 D1
Loxford La *IL* IG1...... 84 C2
Loxford Rd *BARK* IG11...... 84 B3
Loxham St *STPAN* WC1H *...... 9 D4
Loxley Cl *SYD* SE26...... 157 E5
Loxley Rd *WAND/EARL* SW18...... 151 D1
Loxton Rd *FSTH* SE23...... 157 D1
Lubbock St *NWCR* SE14...... 120 C3
Lucas Av *PLSTW* E13...... 82 B5
Lucas Sq *GLDGN* NW11...... 54 A1
Lucas St *BROCKY* SE4...... 122 A5
Lucerne Ms *KENS* W8 *...... 26 B3
Lucerne Rd *HBRY* N5...... 76 B1
Lucey Rd *BERM/RHTH* SE16...... 102 A4
Lucey Wy *BERM/RHTH* SE16...... 102 A4
Lucien Rd *TOOT* SW17...... 152 A4
    WIM/MER SW19...... 150 B2
Lucknow St *WOOL/PLUM* SE18...... 127 E3
Lucorn Cl *LEE/GVPK* SE12...... 141 F4
Ludgate Broadway *BLKFR* EC4V *...... 22 C5
Ludgate Circ *STP* EC4M...... 22 C5
Ludgate Hl *STP* EC4M...... 22 C5
Ludgate Sq *STP* EC4M...... 23 D5
Ludlow St *FSBYE* EC1V *...... 11 E5
Ludovick Wk *PUT/ROE* SW15...... 129 E2
Luffman Rd *LEE/GVPK* SE12...... 160 B3
Lugard Rd *PECK* SE15...... 120 B5

Lugg Ap *MNPK* E12...... 66 A5
Luke St *SDTCH* EC2A...... 12 C5
Lukin St *WCHPL* E1...... 90 C5
Lullingstone Cl *LEW* SE13...... 141 D4
Lulot Gdns *ARCH* N19...... 56 B4
Lulworth Rd *ELTH/MOT* SE9...... 161 E2
    PECK SE15 *...... 120 B5
    WELL DA16...... 127 F5
Lumley Flats *BGVA* SW1W *...... 116 A1
Lumley St *OXSTW* W1C...... 18 B5
Lundy Wk *IS* N1 *...... 76 C3
Lupin Cl *BRXS/STRHM* SW2...... 154 B2
Lupton Cl *LEE/GVPK* SE12...... 160 B4
Lupton St *KTTN* NW5...... 74 C1
Lupus St *PIM* SW1V...... 116 B1
Lurgan Av *HMSMTH* W6...... 113 D2
Lurline Gdns *BTSEA* SW11...... 116 A4
Lushington Rd *CAT* SE6...... 158 B5
    WLSDN NW10...... 88 B1
Lushington Ter *HACK* E8 *...... 78 A2
Luther King Cl *WALTH* E17...... 61 E1
Luton Pl *GNWCH* SE10...... 122 C3
Luton Rd *PLSTW* E13...... 94 A3
Luton St *STJWD* NW8...... 16 B1
Luttrell Av *PUT/ROE* SW15...... 130 B3
Lutwyche Rd *FSTH* SE23...... 157 F2
Luxborough St *MHST* W1U...... 18 A2
Luxemburg Ms *SRTFD* E15...... 81 E2
Luxemburg Gdns *HMSMTH* W6...... 101 D5
Luxfield Rd *ELTH/MOT* SE9...... 161 E1
Luxford St *BERM/RHTH* SE16...... 103 D5
Luxmore St *BROCKY* SE4...... 121 F4
Luxor St *CMBW* SE5...... 136 C1
Lyall Av *DUL* SE21...... 155 E4
Lyall Ms *KTBR* SW1X...... 42 A3
Lyall Ms West *KTBR* SW1X *...... 42 A3
Lyall St *KTBR* SW1X...... 42 A3
Lyal Rd *BOW* E3...... 91 E1
Lycett Pl *SHB* W12...... 100 A3
Lydd Cl *BFN/LL* DA15...... 163 E3
Lydden Gv *WAND/EARL* SW18...... 132 B5
Lydden Rd *WAND/EARL* SW18...... 132 B5
Lydeard Rd *EHAM* E6...... 83 F4
Lydford Cl *STNW/STAM* N16...... 77 E2
Lydford Rd *MV/WKIL* W9...... 71 D3
    MV/WKIL W9...... 89 F3
Lydhurst Av *BRXS/STRHM* SW2...... 153 F2
Lydney Cl *WIM/MER* SW19...... 149 E2
Lydon Rd *CLAP* SW4...... 134 C1
Lydstep Rd *CHST* BR7...... 162 A4
Lyford Rd *WAND/EARL* SW18...... 133 D5
Lyford St *WOOL/PLUM* SE18...... 107 F5
Lygon Pl *BGVA* SW1W *...... 42 C3
Lyham Cl *BRXS/STRHM* SW2...... 135 E4
Lyham Rd *BRXS/STRHM* SW2...... 135 E4
Lyme Farm Rd *LEE/GVPK* SE12...... 142 A2
Lyme Gv *HOM* E9...... 78 C4
Lymer Av *NRWD* SE19...... 155 F5
Lyme St *CAMTN* NW1...... 74 C4
Lyme Ter *CAMTN* NW1...... 74 C4
Lyminge Gdns *WAND/EARL* SW18...... 151 E1
Lyminge Gdns *WAND/EARL* SW18...... 151 E1
Lymington Rd *KIL/WHAMP* NW6 *...... 72 B3
Lympstone Gdns *PECK* SE15...... 120 A3
Lynbrook Gv *PECK* SE15...... 119 D5
Lyncourt *BKHTH/KID* SE3...... 123 D5
Lyncroft Gdns *KIL/WHAMP* NW6...... 72 A2
Lyndale *CRICK* NW2...... 53 F5
Lyndale Av *CRICK* NW2...... 53 F5
Lyndale Cl *BKHTH/KID* SE3...... 123 F2
Lyndhurst Cl *WLSDN* NW10...... 51 D5
Lyndhurst Dr *LEY* E10...... 62 C2
Lyndhurst Gdns *BARK* IG11...... 85 E5
    GNTH/NBYPK IG2...... 67 D1
    HAMP NW3...... 73 D2
Lyndhurst Gv *CMBW* SE5...... 119 D5
Lyndhurst Rd *HAMP* NW3...... 73 D2
Lyndhurst Rd *PECK* SE15...... 119 F4
Lyndhurst Ter *HAMP* NW3...... 73 D2
Lyndhurst Wy *PECK* SE15...... 119 F4
Lyndon Av *BFN/LL* DA15...... 145 E3
Lyndon Yd *TOOT* SW17...... 150 B4
Lyneham Wy *CLPT* E5 *...... 79 E2
Lynette Av *CLAP* SW4...... 134 B4
Lynford Gdns *CDMY/SEVK* IG3...... 67 F4
Lyn Ms *STNW/STAM* N16 *...... 77 F1
Lynmouth Rd *STNW/STAM* N16...... 59 F3
    WALTH E17...... 61 E1
Lynn Ms *WAN* E11...... 63 E4
Lynn Rd *BAL* SW12...... 134 B5
    GNTH/NBYPK IG2...... 67 D2

WAN E11	63	E4
Lynsted Gdns *ELTH/MOT* SE9	143	D2
Lynton Cl *WLSDN* NW10	69	E2
Lynton Crs *GNTH/NBYPK* IG2	66	B1
Lynton Est *STHWK* SE1	49	F5
Lynton Rd *ACT* W3	98	A1
KIL/WHAMP NW6	71	F5
STHWK SE1	49	F5
Lynton Ter *ACT* W3 *	86	C5
Lynwood Rd *TOOT* SW17	151	F3
Lyons Pl *STJWD* NW8	16	A1
Lyon St *IS* N1	75	F4
Lyons Wk *WKENS* W14	101	E5
Lyric Ms *SYD* SE26	156	C4
Lyric Rd *BARN* SW13	111	F4
Lysander Gv *ARCH* N19	57	D3
Lysander Ms *ARCH* N19 *	57	E3
Lysias Rd *BAL* SW12	134	A4
Lysia St *FUL/PGN* SW6	113	D3
Lysons Wk *PUT/ROE* SW15 *	130	A3
Lytcott Gv *EDUL* SE22	137	F3
Lytham St *WALW* SE17	119	D1
Lytton Cl *LEY* E10	62	B5
Lyttelton Cl *HAMP* NW3	73	E4
Lytton Gv *PUT/ROE* SW15	131	D1
Lytton Rd *WAN* E11	63	D2
Lyveden Rd *BKHTH/KID* SE3	124	B3

M

Mabledon Pl *CAMTN* NW1	8	B4
Mablethorpe Rd *FUL/PGN* SW6	113	E3
Mabley St *HOM* E9	79	E2
Macarthur Cl *FSTGT* E7	82	A3
WBLY HA9	68	B3
Macarthur Ter *CHARL* SE7 *	125	D2
Macaulay Rd *CLAP* SW4	134	B1
EHAM E6	95	D1
Macbean St *WOOL/PLUM* SE18	108	A4
Macbeth St *HMSMTH* W6	112	A4
Macclesfield Br *STJWD* NW8	5	D1
Macclesfield Rd *FSBYE* EC1V	11	E3
Macclesfield St *SOHO/SHAV* W1D *	32	B1
Macdonald Rd *ARCH* N19	56	C4
FSTGT E7	82	A1
Macduff Rd *BTSEA* SW11	116	A4
Mace Cl *WAP* E1W	102	B2
Mace St *BETH* E2	91	D1
Macfarlane Rd *SHB* W12	100	C2
Mac Farren Pl *CAMTN* NW1 *	18	B1
Macgregor Rd *CAN/RD* E16	94	C4
Machell Rd *PECK* SE15	138	C1
Mackay Rd *VX/NE* SW8	134	B1
Mackennal St *STJWD* NW8	5	D2
Mackenzie Cl *SHB* W12	100	B1
Mackenzie Rd *HOLWY* N7	75	F3
Mackeson Rd *HAMP* NW3 *	73	F1
Mackie Rd *BRXS/STRHM* SW2	136	A5
Mackintosh La *HOM* E9	79	E2
Macklin St *HOL/ALD* WC2B *	21	D4
Macks Rd *BERM/RHTH* SE16	102	A4
Mackworth St *CAMTN* NW1	7	E3
Maclean Rd *FSTH* SE23	139	E4
Macleod House *CHARL* SE7 *	125	E3
Macleod St *WALW* SE17	118	C1
Maclise Rd *WKENS* W14	101	E4
Macoma Rd *WOOL/PLUM* SE18	127	D2
Macoma Ter *WOOL/PLUM* SE18	127	D2
Maconochies Rd *POP/IOD* E14 *	122	B1
Macquarie Wy *POP/IOD* E14	104	B5
Macroom Rd *MV/WKIL* W9	89	F2
Maddams St *BOW* E3	92	B3
Maddock Wy *WALW* SE17	118	B2
Maddox St *CONDST* W1S	31	D1
Madeira Rd *STRHM/NOR* SW16	153	E5
WAN E11	63	D3
Madeline Gv *IL* IG1	85	D5
Madge Gill Wy *EHAM* E6 *	83	E5
Madinah Rd *HACK* E8	78	A2
Madras Pl *HOLWY* N7	76	A3
Madras Rd *IL* IG1	84	B1
Madrid Rd *BARN* SW13	112	A4
Madron St *WALW* SE17	119	E1
Mafeking Av *EHAM* E6	95	D1
GNTH/NBYPK IG2	67	D2
Mafeking Rd *CAN/RD* E16	93	F3
Magazine Ga *BAY/PAD* W2 *	29	D3
Magdala Av *ARCH* N19	56	C4

Magdalene Gdns *EHAM* E6	96	A3
Magdalen Rd *WAND/EARL* SW18	150	C1
Magdalen St *STHWK* SE1	36	C4
Magee St *LBTH* SE11	118	C1
Magellan Bvd *EHAM* E6	108	C1
Magellan Pl *POP/IOD* E14	104	A5
Magnin Cl *HACK* E8	78	A5
Magnolia Cl *LEY* E10	62	A4
Magnolia Pl *CLAP* SW4 *	135	E3
Magnolia Rd *CHSWK* W4	110	B2
Magnolia Whf *CHSWK* W4 *	110	B2
Magpie Cl *FSTGT* E7	81	F2
Magpie Pl *NWCR* SE14 *	121	E2
Magri Wk *WCHPL* E1	90	C4
Maguire St *STHWK* SE1	37	F5
Mahogany Cl *BERM/RHTH* SE16	103	E2
Maida Av *BAY/PAD* W2	15	F2
Maida V *MV/WKIL* W9	3	D2
STJWD NW8	4	A5
Maiden La *CAMTN* NW1	75	D4
COVGDN WC2E *	33	D1
STHWK SE1	35	D5
Maiden Rd *SRTFD* E15	81	E4
Maidenstone Hl *GNWCH* SE10	122	C4
Maidstone Buildings Ms *STHWK* SE1 *	35	F4
Main Barracks *WOOL/PLUM* SE18 *	125	F1
Mainridge Rd *CHST* BR7	162	A4
Main Rd *SCUP* DA14	163	E5
Maismore St *PECK* SE15	120	A2
Maitland Cl *GNWCH* SE10	122	B3
Maitland Park Rd *HAMP* NW3	73	F3
Maitland Park Vis *HAMP* NW3	73	F3
Maitland Rd *SRTFD* E15	81	F2
SYD SE26	157	E5
Majendie Rd *WOOL/PLUM* SE18	127	D1
Major Cl *BRXN/ST* SW9	136	B1
Major Rd *BERM/RHTH* SE16	102	A4
SRTFD E15	80	C2
Makepeace Av *HGT* N6	56	A4
Makins St *CHEL* SW3	41	D5
Malabar St *POP/IOD* E14	104	A3
Malam Gdns *POP/IOD* E14 *	104	B1
Malbrook Rd *PUT/ROE* SW15	130	B2
Malcolm Pl *BETH* E2	90	C3
Malcolm Rd *WCHPL* E1	90	C3
Malden Pl *KTTN* NW5	74	A2
Malden Rd *KTTN* NW5	73	F2
IS N1	76	C5
Maldon Cl *CMBW* SE5	137	E1
Maldon Rd *ACT* W3	98	C1
Malet St *GWRST* WC1E	20	A1
Maley Av *WNWD* SE27	154	B2
Malfort Rd *CMBW* SE5	137	E1
Malham Rd *FSTH* SE23	157	D1
Mallams Ms *BRXN/ST* SW9	136	A1
Mallard Wy *CDALE/KGS* NW9	50	C2
Mall Chambers *KENS* W8 *	26	B3
Mallet Rd *LEW* SE13	141	D4
Mallinson Rd *BTSEA* SW11	133	E5
Mallord St *CHEL* SW3	115	D2
Mallory Cl *BROCKY* SE4	139	E2
POP/IOD E14	92	B3
Mallory Ct *LEE/GVPKSE12	142	B5
Mallory St *STJWD* NW8	17	D1
Mallow St *FSBYE* EC1V	12	A5
The Mall *MORT/ESHN* SW14	128	C3
WHALL SW1A	31	E5
Mall Vis *HMSMTH* W6 *	112	B1
CAN/RD E16	93	E4
Malmesbury Rd *BOW* E3	91	F1
Malmesbury Ter *CAN/RD* E16	93	F4
Malmesbury West Est *BOW* E3 *	91	F2
Malpas Rd *BROCKY* SE4	121	F5
HACK E8	78	B3
Malta Rd *LEY* E10	62	A3
Malta St *FSBYE* EC1V	10	C5
Maltby St *STHWK* SE1	49	E1
Malthouse Pl *CHSWK* W4 *	111	F2
Maltings Cl *BOW* E3	92	C3
Maltings Pl *FUL/PGN* SW6	114	B4
STHWK SE1	37	D5
Malton Ms *NKENS* W10 *	89	E5
WOOL/PLUM SE18	127	E2
Malton Rd *NKENS* W10	89	E5
Malton St *WOOL/PLUM* SE18	127	E2
Maltravers St *TPL/STR* WC2R	33	F1
Malt St *STHWK* SE1	120	A2
Malva Cl *WAND/EARL* SW18	132	B3
Malvern Cl *NKENS* W10	89	F4
Malvern Rd *GDMY/SEVK* IG3	85	F1
Malvern Gdns *CRICK* NW2	53	E1
Malvern Ms *KIL/WHAMP* NW6	2	A4

Malvern Pl *MV/WKIL* W9 *	89 F2
Malvern Rd *EHAM* E6	83 E5
HACK E8	78 A4
KIL/WHAMP NW6	2 A3
MV/WKIL W9 *	89 F2
WAN E11	63 E4
Malvern Ter *IS* N1	75 A5
Malwood Rd *BAL* SW12	134 B4
Malyons Rd *LEW* SE13	140 B3
Malyons Ter *LEW* SE13	140 B3
Managers St *POP/IOD* E14	104 C2
Manaton Cl *PECK* SE15	138 B1
Manbey Gv *SRTFD* E15	81 E5
Manbey Park Rd *SRTFD* E15	81 E5
Manbey Rd *SRTFD* E15	81 E5
Manbey St *SRTFD* E15	81 E5
Manbre Rd *CAN* W6	112 C2
Manbrough Av *EHAM* E6	96 A2
Manchester Dr *CAN/RD* E16	94 B5
Manchester Dr *NKENS* W10 *	89 E3
Manchester Gv *POP/IOD* E14	122 C1
Manchester Ms *MHST* W1U	18 A3
Manchester Rd *POP/IOD* E14	122 C1
SEVS/STOTM N15	59 D1
Manchester Sq *MBLAR* W1H	18 A4
Manchester St *MHST* W1U	18 A4
Manchuria Rd *BTSEA* SW11	134 A4
Manciple St *STHWK* SE1	48 B1
Mandalay Rd *CLAP* SW4	135 D4
Mandela Cl *WLSDN* NW10	68 C4
Mandela Rd *CAN/RD* E16	94 A5
Mandela St *BRXN/ST* SW9	118 A3
CAMTN NW1	74 C5
Mandela Wy *STHWK* SE1	49 D4
Mandeville Cl *MHST* W1U	18 D4
Mandeville St *CLPT* E5	61 E5
Mandrake Rd *TOOT* SW17	151 F3
Mandrake Wy *SRTFD* E15 *	81 E4
Mandrell Rd *BRXS/STRHM* SW2	135 E3
Manette St *LSQ/SEVD* WC2H	20 B5
Manfred Rd *PUT/ROE* SW15	131 F3
Manger Rd *HOLWY* N7	75 E3
Manilla St *POP/IOD* E14	104 A1
Manley St *STNW/STAM* N16	59 F5
Manley St *CAMTN* NW1	74 A5
Manningford Cl *FSBYE* EC1V *	11 F2
Manningtree Cl *WIM/MER* SW19	149 E1
Manningtree St *WCHPL* E1	90 A5
Manor Av *BROCKY* SE4	121 F5
Manorbrook *BKHTH/KID* SE3	142 A2
Manor Ct *ACT* W3 *	98 A5
Manor Est *BERM/RHTH* SE16	102 B5
Manorfield Cl *ARCH* N19	74 C1
Manor Gdns *ACT* W3	98 A5
CLAP SW4 *	116 C5
HOLWY N7	57 E5
Manor Gv *PECK* SE15	120 C2
RCH/KEW TW9	128 A2
Manor Hall Gdns *LEY* E10	62 A3
Manor House Dr *KIL/WHAMP* NW6	71 D4
Manor La *LEE/GVPK* SE12	141 E4
Manor Lane Ter *LEW* SE13	141 E2
Manor Ms *BROCKY* SE4	121 F5
KIL/WHAMP NW6	2 B1
Manor Mt *FSTH* SE23	156 C1
Manor Pde *STNW/STAM* N16 *	59 F4
Manor Pk *LEW* SE13	141 D3
Manor Park Rd *MNPK* E12	83 D1
WLSDN NW10	69 E5
Manor Pl *WALW* SE17	118 B1
Manor Rd *BARK* IG11	85 F3
BFN/LL DA15	163 F5
CAN/RD E16	93 E4
LEY E10	62 A2
SRTFD E15	81 E3
STNW/STAM N16	59 E3
Manresa Rd *CHEL* SW3	115 D1
Mansard Beeches *TOOT* SW17	152 A5
Mansell Rd *ACT* W3	99 D2
Mansell St *WCHPL* E1	25 F5
Mansergh Cl *CHARL* SE7	125 E3
Manse Rd *STNW/STAM* N16	59 F5
Mansfield Ms *CAVSQ/HST* W1G	18 C3
Mansfield Rd *ACT* W3	86 B3
HAMP NW3	73 F2
IL IG1	84 A4
WAN E11	64 B1
Mansfield St *CAVSQ/HST* W1G	18 C3
Mansford St *BETH* E2	90 A1
Mansion Cl *BRXN/ST* SW9	118 A4
Mansion Gdns *HAMP* NW3	54 B5

Mansion House Pl *MANHO* EC4N *	24 A5
Mansion House St *MANHO* EC4N	24 A5
The Mansions *ECT* SW5 *	114 B1
Manson Ms *SKENS* SW7	39 F5
Manson Pl *SKENS* SW7	40 A5
Manstone Rd *CRICK* NW2	71 E2
Manthorpe Rd *WOOL/PLUM* SE18	126 C1
Mantilla Rd *TOOT* SW17	152 A4
Mantle Rd *BROCKY* SE4	139 E1
Mantle Wy *SRTFD* E15	81 E4
Mantua St *BTSEA* SW11	133 D1
Mantus Cl *WCHPL* E1	90 C3
Mantus Rd *WCHPL* E1	90 C3
Manville Gdns *TOOT* SW17	152 B2
Manville Rd *TOOT* SW17	152 B1
Manwood Rd *BROCKY* SE4	139 F3
Manwood St *CAN/RD* E16	107 F2
Many Gates *BAL* SW12	152 B2
Mapesbury Ms *CDALE/KGS* NW9	52 A1
Mapesbury Rd *CRICK* NW2	71 E3
Mapeshill Pl *CRICK* NW2	70 C3
Mape St *BETH* E2	90 B3
Maple Av *ACT* W3	99 E2
Maple Cl *CLAP* SW4	135 D4
STNW/STAM N16	60 A1
Maple Ct *HACK* E8 *	78 A3
Maplecroft Cl *EHAM* E6	95 D5
Mapledene Est *HACK* E8 *	78 A4
Mapledene Rd *HACK* E8	77 F4
Maple Gv *CDALE/KGS* NW9	50 C2
Maple Leaf Dr *BFN/LL* DA15	163 F1
Maple Leaf Sq *BERM/RHTH* SE16 *	103 D3
Maple Ms *KIL/WHAMP* NW6 *	2 C1
STRHM/NOR SW16	153 F5
Maple Pl *FITZ* W1T	19 F2
Maple Rd *WAN* E11	63 E1
Maples Pl *WCHPL* E1 *	90 B4
Maplestead Rd *BRXS/STRHM* SW2	135 F5
Maple St *BETH* E2	90 A1
FITZ W1T	19 E2
Mapleton Crs *WAND/EARL* SW18	132 B4
Mapleton Rd *WAND/EARL* SW18	132 A4
Maple Tree Pl *BKHTH/KID* SE3	125 E4
Maple Wk *NKENS* W10 *	89 D3
Maplin Rd *CAN/RD* E16	94 A5
Maplin St *BOW* E3	91 F2
Marabou Cl *MNPK* E12	83 E2
Marathon Wy *THMD* SE28	109 F2
Marban Rd *MV/WKIL* W9	89 F2
Marble Cl *ACT* W3	98 B2
Marble Dr *CRICK* NW2	53 D2
Marble Quay *WAP* E1W	37 F3
Marbrook Ct *LEE/GVPK* SE12	160 C5
Marcella Rd *BRXN/ST* SW9	118 A5
Marchant Rd *WAN* E11	63 D4
Marchant St *NWCR* SE14	121 E2
Marchbank Rd *WKENS* W14	113 F2
Marchmont St *BMSBY* WC1N	8 C5
Marchwood Cl *CMBW* SE5	119 E3
Marcia Rd *STHWK* SE1	49 D5
Marcilly Rd *WAND/EARL* SW18	133 D3
Marconi Rd *LEY* E10	62 A3
Marcon Pl *HACK* E8	78 B3
Marco Rd *HMSMTH* W6	100 B4
Marcus Garvey Ms *EDUL* SE22	138 B4
Marcus Garvey Wy *HNHL* SE24	136 A2
Marcus St *SRTFD* E15	81 E5
WAND/EARL SW18	132 B4
Marcus Ter *WAND/EARL* SW18	132 B4
Marden Sq *BERM/RHTH* SE16	102 B4
Marder Rd *WEA* W13	95 E1
Mare St *HACK* E8	78 B5
Margaret Gardner Dr *ELTH/MOT* SE9	161 F2
Margaret Ingram Cl *FUL/PGN* SW6 *	113 F2
Margaret Rd *STNW/STAM* N16 *	59 F3
Margaret Rutherford Pl *BAL* SW12	152 C1
Margaret St *CTPST* W1W	19 E4
Margaretta Ter *CHEL* SW3	115 E2
Margaretting Rd *MNPK* E12	64 C4
Margaret Wy *REDBR* IG4	65 E1
Margate Rd *BRXS/STRHM* SW2	135 E3
Margery Park Rd *FSTGT* E7	82 A3
Margery St *CLKNW* EC1R	10 A4
Margin Dr *WIM/MER* SW19	149 D5
Margravine Gdns *HMSMTH* W6	113 D1
Margravine Rd *HMSMTH* W6	113 D2
Marham Gdns *WAND/EARL* SW18	151 E1
Maria Cl *STHWK* SE1	102 A5
Marian Pl *BETH* E2	90 B1
Marian St *BETH* E2 *	90 B1

Marian Wy *WLSDN* NW10............... 69 F4
Maria Ter *WCHPL* E1 *.................... 91 D4
Marie Curie *CMBW* SE5 *................ 119 E4
Marie Lloyd Wk *HACK* E8 *............. 78 A4
Marigold Av *STHWK* SE1 *.............. 34 C2
Marigold St *BERM/RHTH* SE16....... 102 B3
Marina Dr *WELL* DA16..................... 127 E5
Marine *WOOL/PLUM* SE18............. 107 F5
Mariner Rd *MNPK* E12..................... 84 A1
Mariners Ms *POP/IOD* E14.............. 105 D5
Marine St *BERM/RHTH* SE16........... 102 A4
Marion Ms *DUL* SE21...................... 155 D3
Marischal Rd *LEW* SE13.................. 141 D1
Maritime Quay *POP/IOD* E14.......... 122 A1
Maritime St *BOW* E3....................... 91 F5
Marius Rd *TOOT* SW17................... 152 A2
Marjorie Gv *BTSEA* SW11............... 133 F2
Market Est *HOLWY* N7.................... 75 E3
Market Ms *MYFR/PICC* W1J........... 30 C4
Market Pde *LEY* E10 *..................... 62 B1
STNW/STAM N16 *...................... 60 A5
Market Pl *ACT* W3........................... 98 C2
BERM/RHTH SE16 *..................... 102 A5
GTPST W1W............................... 19 E4
Market Rd *HOLWY* N7..................... 75 E3
RCH/KEW TW9............................ 128 A1
Market Sq *EHAM* E6........................ 95 F1
WOOL/PLUM SE18...................... 108 A5
The Market *PECK* SE15................... 120 A5
Market Yard Ms *STHWK* SE1........... 48 C2
Markham Sq *CHEL* SW3................... 115 F1
Markham Sq *CHEL* SW3................... 115 F1
Markham St *CHEL* SW3................... 115 F1
Markhouse Av *WALTH* E17............... 61 E1
Markhouse Rd *WALTH* E17............... 61 E1
Mark La *MON* EC3R........................ 37 D1
Markmanor Av *WALTH* E17............... 61 E2
Marksbury Av *RCH/KEW* TW9.......... 128 A1
Mark St *SDTCH* EC2A..................... 12 C5
SRTFD E15................................. 81 E4
Markwade Cl *MNPK* E12.................. 65 D3
Markwell Cl *SYD* SE26.................... 156 A4
Marlborough Av *HACK* E8............... 78 A5
WALTH SE17 *............................ 47 D5
Marlborough Ct *REGST* W1B *.......... 31 F1
Marlborough Crs *CHSWK* W4.......... 99 D4
Marlborough Ga *BAY/PAD* W2......... 28 A3
Marlborough Gv *STHWK* SE1........... 120 A1
Marlborough La *CHARL* SE7........... 124 C2
Marlborough Ms *BRXS/STRHM* SW2.. 135 F2
Marlborough Pde *FSBYPK* N4 *........ 58 C3
Marlborough Pl *STJWD* NW8............ 3 E2
Marlborough Rd *ARCH* N19.............. 57 E4
CHSWK W4................................ 110 C1
FSTGT E7.................................. 82 C4
SRTFD E15 *.............................. 81 E1
WHALL SW1A............................. 31 F4
WOOL/PLUM SE18...................... 108 B4
Marlborough St *CHEL* SW3.............. 40 C5
Marlborough Yd *ARCH* N19............. 57 D4
Marler Rd *FSTH* SE23..................... 157 F1
Marley Rd *BERM/RHTH* SE16 *........ 103 D5
The Marlowes *STJWD* NW8.............. 73 D5
Marlow Rd *EHAM* E6....................... 95 F2
Marlow Wy *BERM/RHTH* SE16......... 103 D3
Marl Rd *WAND/EARL* SW18.............. 132 B2
Marlton St *GNWCH* SE10................. 123 F1
Marlwood Cl *BFN/LL* DA15.............. 163 E2
Marmadon Rd *WOOL/PLUM* SE18.... 109 F5
Marmion Ms *BTSEA* SW11 *............. 134 A1
Marmion Rd *BTSEA* SW11............... 134 A1
Marmont Rd *PECK* SE15.................. 120 A4
Marmora Rd *EDUL* SE22.................. 138 C4
Marne St *NKENS* W10...................... 89 E2
Marney Rd *BTSEA* SW11.................. 134 A2
Marnfield Crs *BRXS/STRHM* SW2..... 153 F1
Marnham Av *CRICK* NW2.................. 71 E1
Marnock Rd *BROCKY* SE4................ 139 F3
Maroon St *POP/IOD* E14.................. 91 E4
Maroons Wy *CAT* SE6..................... 158 A5
Marquess Gv *IS* N1......................... 77 D3
Marquess Rd North *IS* N1 *............. 76 C3
Marquess Rd South *IS* N1 *............ 76 C3
Marquis Rd *CAMTN* NW1................. 75 D3
FSBYPK N4................................. 57 F3
Marrick Cl *PUT/ROE* SW15.............. 130 A3
Marriott Rd *FSBYPK* N4................... 57 F3
SRTFD E15................................. 81 E5
Marriotts Cl *CDALE/KGS* NW9......... 51 F1

Marryat Pl *WIM/MER* SW19.............. 149 E4
Marryat Rd *WIM/MER* SW19............. 149 D5
Marryfields Wy *CAT* SE6.................. 140 B5
Marsala Rd *LEW* SE13..................... 140 B2
Marsden Rd *PECK* SE15................... 137 F1
Marsden St *KTTN* NW5.................... 74 A3
Marshall Cl *WAND/EARL* SW18......... 132 C4
Marshall Rd *LEY* E10....................... 80 B1
Marshalls Gv *WOOL/PLUM* SE18...... 107 F5
Marshall's Pl *BERM/RHTH* SE16....... 49 F3
Marshall St *SOHO/CST* W1F............ 19 F5
Marshalsea Rd *STHWK* SE1............. 35 F5
Marsham Cl *CHST* BR7 *................. 162 B5
Marsham St *WEST* SW1P................. 44 B4
Marshbrook Cl *BKHTH/KID* SE3....... 124 C2
Marsh Dr *CDALE/KGS* NW9.............. 51 F1
Marshfield St *POP/IOD* E14............. 104 C4
Marsh Hl *HOM* E9.......................... 79 E2
Marsh La *LEY* E10........................... 61 F4
Marsh St *POP/IOD* E14 *................. 104 C5
Marsh Wall *POP/IOD* E14................ 104 A5
Marsland Cl *WALW* SE17................. 118 B3
Marston Cl *KIL/WHAMP* NW6........... 72 C4
Martaban Rd *STNW/STAM* N16........ 59 E4
Martara Ms *WALW* SE17.................. 118 C1
Martello St *HACK* E8....................... 78 B4
Martello Ter *HACK* E8 *.................. 78 B4
Martell Rd *DUL* SE21...................... 155 D3
Martel Pl *HACK* E8 *...................... 77 F3
Martha Rd *SRTFD* E15..................... 81 E3
Martha's Blds *FSBYE* EC1V............. 12 A5
Martha St *WCHPL* E1...................... 90 C5
Martin Bowes Rd *ELTH/MOT* SE9.... 144 A5
Martindale *MORT/ESHN* SW14......... 128 C3
Martindale Av *CAN/RD* E16............. 106 A1
Martindale Rd *BAL* SW12................ 134 B5
Martineau Rd *HBRY* N5.................... 76 B1
Martin La *CANST* EC4R................... 36 C1
Martins Pl *THMD* SE28................... 109 E2
The Martins *SYD* SE26.................... 156 B5
Martin St *THMD* SE28..................... 109 E2
Martins Wk *THMD* SE28.................. 109 E2
Martlett Ct *HOL/ALD* WC2B............. 21 D5
Marton Cl *CAT* SE6......................... 158 A3
Marton Rd *STNW/STAM* N16 *......... 59 E4
Martys Yd *HAMP* NW3 *................. 73 D1
Marvels Cl *LEE/GVPK* SE12............. 160 B2
Marvels La *LEE/GVPK* SE12............. 160 B2
Marville Rd *FUL/PGN* SW6.............. 113 F3
Marvin St *HACK* E8 *..................... 78 B3
Mary Adelaide Cl *PUT/ROE* SW15.... 147 E3
Mary Ann Blds *DEPT* SE8................ 122 A2
Maryat Sq *FUL/PGN* SW6............... 113 E4
Marybank *WOOL/PLUM* SE18.......... 107 F5
Mary Datchelor Cl *CMBW* SE5......... 119 D4
Maryland Pk *SRTFD* E15................. 81 E2
Maryland Rd *MV/WKIL* W9............... 14 B1
SRTFD E15................................ 81 D2
Maryland Sq *SRTFD* E15................. 81 E2
Marylands Rd *MV/WKIL* W9............. 14 B1
Maryland St *SRTFD* E15.................. 81 D2
Maryland Wk *IS* N1 *..................... 8 B1
Mary Lawrenson Pl *BKHTH/KID* SE3.. 123 F3
Marylebone F/O *BAY/PAD* W2......... 16 C3
Marylebone High St *CAVSQ/HST* W1G.. 18 B3
Marylebone La *MHST* W1U............... 18 B4
Marylebone Ms *CAVSQ/HST* W1G.... 18 B3
Marylebone Pas *GTPST* W1W........... 19 F4
Marylebone Rd *MBLAR* W1H............ 17 D2
Marylebone St *CAVSQ/HST* W1G..... 18 B3
Marylee Wy *LBTH* SE11................... 45 F5
Maryon Gv *CHARL* SE7................... 107 E5
Maryon Ms *HAMP* NW3................... 73 E1
Maryon Rd *CHARL* SE7................... 107 E5
Mary Pl *NTGHL* W11....................... 101 E1
Mary Seacole Cl *HACK* E8............... 77 F5
Mary St *CAN/RD* E16....................... 93 F4
IS N1.. 76 C5
Mary Ter *CAMTN* NW1.................... 74 C5
Masbro' Rd *WKENS* W14.................. 101 D4
Mascalls Rd *CHARL* SE7.................. 124 C2
Mascotts Cl *CRICK* NW2.................. 52 B5
Masefield Gdns *EHAM* E6................ 96 A3
Mashie Rd *ACT* W3......................... 87 F5
Maskall Cl *BRXS/STRHM* SW2.......... 154 A1
Maskell Rd *TOOT* SW17.................. 150 C3
Maskelyne Cl *BTSEA* SW11............. 115 E4
Mason Cl *BERM/RHTH* SE16............ 120 A1
CAN/RD E16.............................. 106 A1
Mason Ct *WBLY* HA9 *.................... 50 A4
Mason's Arms Ms *CONDST* W1S *.... 19 D5
Mason's Av *CITYW* EC2V................. 24 A4

Masons HI *WOOL/PLUM* SE18 ...... 108 B5
Mason's PI *FSBYE* EC1V 11 D3
Mason St *WALW* SE17 ...... 48 B5
Masons Yd *FSBYE* EC1V 11 E5
  STJS SW1Y 31 F3
Massie Rd *HACK* E8 ...... 78 A3
Massingberd Wy *TOOT* SW17 ...... 152 B4
Massinger St *WALW* SE17 ...... 48 C5
Massingham St *WCHPL* E1 ...... 91 D3
Masterman Rd *EHAM* E6 ...... 95 E2
Masters Dr *BERM/RHTH* SE16 ...... 120 B1
Master's St *WCHPL* E1 ...... 91 D4
Mast House Ter *POP/IOD* E14 ...... 104 A5
Masthouse Ter *POP/IOD* E14 ...... 104 A5
Mast Leisure Pk *POP/IOD* E14 ...... 104 A5
Mast Quay *WOOL/PLUM* SE18 ...... 107 F4
Matcham Rd *WAN* E11 ...... 63 E5
Matchless Dr *WOOL/PLUM* SE18 ...... 126 A3
Matham Gv *EDUL* SE22 ...... 137 F2
Matheson Rd *WKENS* W14 ...... 101 F5
Mathews Av *EHAM* E6 ...... 96 A1
Mathews Park Av *SRTFD* E15 ...... 81 F3
Mathews Yd *LSQ/SEVD* WC2H * 20 C5
Mathieson Ct *STHWK* SE1 ...... 47 D1
Matilda Gdns *BOW* E3 ...... 92 A1
Matilda St *IS* N1 ...... 75 D2
Matlock Cl *HNHL* SE24 ...... 136 C2
Matlock Rd *LEY* E10 ...... 62 C1
Matlock St *POP/IOD* E14 ...... 91 E5
Matthew Cl *NKENS* W10 * 89 D3
Matthews St *BTSEA* SW11 ...... 115 E5
Matthias Rd *STNW/STAM* N16 ...... 77 D2
Mattingly Wy *PECK* SE15 ...... 119 E3
Mattison Rd *FSBYPK* N4 ...... 58 A1
Maud Cashmore Wy
  WOOL/PLUM SE18 ...... 107 F4
Maude Rd *CMBW* SE5 ...... 119 E5
Maud Gdns *BARK* IG11 ...... 97 F1
  PLSTW E13 ...... 93 F1
Maudlins Gn *WAP* E1W * 102 A2
Maud Rd *LEY* E10 ...... 62 C5
  PLSTW E13 ...... 93 F1
Maudslay Rd *ELTH/MOT* SE9 ...... 143 F1
Maud St *CAN/RD* E16 ...... 93 F4
Maud Wilkes Cl *KTTN* NW5 ...... 74 C2
Mauleverer Rd *BRXS/STRHM* SW2 ...... 135 E3
Maundeby Wk *WLSDN* NW10 * 69 E2
Maunsel St *WEST* SW1P 44 A4
Maurice St *SHB* W12 ...... 88 B5
Mauritius Rd *GNWCH* SE10 ...... 105 E5
Maury Rd *STNW/STAM* N16 ...... 60 A4
Maverton Rd *BOW* E3 * 80 A5
Mawbey PI *STHWK* SE1 ...... 119 F5
Mawbey Rd *STHWK* SE1 ...... 119 F1
Mawbey St *VX/NE* SW8 ...... 117 E3
Mawson La *CHSWK* W4 * 111 F2
Maxey Rd *WOOL/PLUM* SE18 ...... 108 C5
Maxilla Wk *NKENS* W10 * 89 D5
Maxted Rd *PECK* SE15 ...... 137 F1
Maxwell Rd *FUL/PGN* SW6 ...... 114 B3
Maya Cl *PECK* SE15 ...... 120 B5
Mayall Cl *STHWK* SE1 ...... 35 E5
Mayall Rd *HNHL* SE24 ...... 136 B3
Maybourne Rd *SYD* SE26 ...... 156 B5
Maybury Ms *HGT* N6 ...... 56 C2
Maybury Rd *PLSTW* E13 ...... 94 C3
Maybury St *TOOT* SW17 ...... 151 E5
Mayday Gdns *BKHTH/KID* SE3 ...... 125 E5
Mayerne Rd *ELTH/MOT* SE9 ...... 143 D3
Mayesbrook Rd *BARK* IG11 ...... 85 F5
Mayeswood Rd *LEE/GVPK* SE12 ...... 160 C4
Mayfair Av *IL* IG1 ...... 65 F4
Mayfair Ms *CAMTN* NW1 * 73 F4
Mayfair PI *MYFR/PICC* W1J * 31 D3
Mayfield Av *CHSWK* W4 ...... 99 E5
  HACK E8 ...... 77 F3
Mayfield Gdns *HDN* NW4 ...... 53 D1
Mayfield Rd *ACT* W3 ...... 98 B1
  CEND/HSY/T N8 ...... 57 F1
  HACK E8 ...... 77 F4
  PLSTW E13 ...... 93 F3
  SHB W12 ...... 99 E3
Mayfields *WBLY* HA9 ...... 50 A4
Mayfields Cl *WBLY* HA9 ...... 50 A4
Mayflower Cl *BERM/RHTH* SE16 ...... 103 D5
Mayflower Rd *BRXN/ST* SW9 ...... 135 E1
Mayflower St *BERM/RHTH* SE16 ...... 102 C3
Mayford Cl *BAL* SW12 ...... 133 F5
Mayford Rd *BAL* SW12 ...... 133 F5
Maygood St *IS* N1 ...... 9 F1

Maygrove Rd *KIL/WHAMP* NW6 ...... 71 F3
Mayhill Rd *CHARL* SE7 ...... 124 B2
Maynard Cl *FUL/PGN* SW6 ...... 114 B3
Maynards Quay *WAP* E1W * 102 C1
Mayola Rd *CLPT* E5 ...... 78 C1
Mayo Rd *WLSDN* NW10 ...... 69 E5
Mayow Rd *SYD* SE26 ...... 157 D4
Mayplace La *WOOL/PLUM* SE18 ...... 126 B2
May Rd *PLSTW* E13 ...... 94 A1
May's Buildings Ms *GNWCH* SE10 ...... 123 D3
Mays Ct *CHCR* WC2N 32 C2
Maysoule Rd *BTSEA* SW11 ...... 133 D2
May St *WKENS* W14 ...... 113 F1
Mayston Sk *HOLWY* N7 ...... 57 F5
Maytree Wk *BRXS/STRHM* SW2 * 154 A2
Mayville Est *STNW/STAM* N16 * 77 E2
Mayville Rd *IL* IG1 ...... 84 B2
  WAN E11 ...... 63 E4
Maze Hl *GNWCH* SE10 ...... 123 E2
Mazenod Av *KIL/WHAMP* NW6 ...... 72 A4
Maze Rd *RCH/KEW* TW9 ...... 110 A3
McAuley Cl *ELTH/MOT* SE9 ...... 144 A3
  STHWK SE1 ...... 46 A2
McCall Cl *CLAP* SW4 ...... 117 E5
McCall Crs *CHARL* SE7 ...... 125 E1
McCoid Wy *STHWK* SE1 ...... 47 E1
McCrone Ms *HAMP* NW3 ...... 73 D3
McCullum Rd *BOW* E3 ...... 79 F5
McDermott Cl *BTSEA* SW11 ...... 115 E5
McDermott Rd *PECK* SE15 ...... 138 A1
McDougall Ct *RCH/KEW* TW9 ...... 110 A5
McDowall Cl *CAN/RD* E16 ...... 94 A4
McDowall Rd *CMBW* SE5 ...... 118 C4
McEwan Wy *SRTFD* E15 ...... 81 D5
McGrath Rd *SRTFD* E15 ...... 81 F2
McGregor Rd *NTGHL* W11 ...... 89 F5
McKerrell Rd *PECK* SE15 ...... 120 A4
McLeod's Ms *SKENS* SW7 ...... 39 D3
McMillan St *DEPT* SE8 ...... 122 A2
McNeil Rd *CMBW* SE5 ...... 119 E5
McNicol Dr *WLSDN* NW10 ...... 86 C1
Mead Cl *CAMTN* NW1 ...... 74 A4
Meadcroft Rd *LBTH* SE11 ...... 118 A2
Meade Cl *CHSWK* W4 ...... 110 A2
Meadowbank *BKHTH/KID* SE3 ...... 141 F1
  HAMP NW3 ...... 73 F4
Meadowbank Cl *FUL/PGN* SW6 ...... 112 C3
Meadowbank Rd *CDALE/KGS* NW9 ...... 51 D2
Meadow Cl *BARK* IG11 ...... 85 F4
  CAT SE6 ...... 158 A5
  CHST BR7 ...... 162 B5
  HOM E9 ...... 79 F2
Meadowcourt Rd *BKHTH/KID* SE3 ...... 141 F2
Meadow Garth *WLSDN* NW10 ...... 68 C3
Meadow La *LEE/GVPK* SE12 ...... 160 B3
Meadow Ms *VX/NE* SW8 ...... 117 F2
Meadow PI *CHSWK* W4 * 111 E5
  VX/NE SW8 ...... 117 E3
Meadow Rd *BARK* IG11 ...... 85 F4
  VX/NE SW8 ...... 117 F2
Meadow Rw *STHWK* SE1 ...... 47 E5
Meadows Cl *LEY* E10 ...... 62 A4
Meadowside *BKHTH/KID* SE3 ...... 142 C2
Meadowsweet Cl *CAN/RD* E16 ...... 95 D4
Meadowview Rd *CAT* SE6 ...... 158 A4
Mead PI *HOM* E9 ...... 78 C3
Mead Plat *WLSDN* NW10 ...... 68 C3
Mead Rw *STHWK* SE1 ...... 46 A2
Meads La *GDMY/SEVK* IG3 ...... 67 F2
Meadway *GDMY/SEVK* IG3 ...... 85 E1
  GLDGN NW11 ...... 54 B1
Meadway Cl *GLDGN* NW11 ...... 54 B1
The Meadway *BKHTH/KID* SE3 ...... 123 D5
Meanley Rd *MNPK* E12 ...... 83 E2
Meard St *SOHO/CST* W1F 20 A5
Meath Crs *BETH* E2 ...... 91 D2
Meath Rd *IL* IG1 ...... 66 C5
  SRTFD E15 ...... 93 F1
Mecklenburgh PI *BMSBY* WC1N 9 E5
Mecklenburgh Sq *BMSBY* WC1N 9 E5
Mecklenburgh St *BMSBY* WC1N 9 E5
Medburn St *CAMTN* NW1 ...... 8 A1
Medcroft Gdns *MORT/ESHN* SW14 ...... 128 C2
Medebourne Cl *BKHTH/KID* SE3 ...... 142 A1
Medfield St *PUT/ROE* SW15 ...... 130 A5
Medhurst Cl *BOW* E3 ...... 91 E1
Medhurst Dr *BMLY* BR1 ...... 159 E5
Median Rd *CLPT* E5 ...... 78 C2
Medina Rd *HOLWY* N7 ...... 58 A5
Medlar St *CMBW* SE5 ...... 118 C4

Medley Rd *KIL/WHAMP* NW6............ 72 A3
Medora Rd *BRXS/STRHM* SW2........ 135 F4
Medusa Rd *CAT* SE6...................... 140 B4
Medway Cl *IL* IG1........................... 84 C2
Medway Rd *BOW* E3........................ 91 E1
Medway St *WEST* SW1P................. 48 A3
Medwin St *CLAP* SW4.................... 135 F2
Meerbrook Rd *BKHTH/KID* SE3...... 142 C1
Meeson Rd *SRTFD* E15................... 81 F4
Meeson St *CLPT* E5........................ 79 E1
Meeting Field Pth *HOM* E9 *........... 78 C3
Meeting House Aly *WAP* E1W........ 102 B2
Meeting House La *PECK* SE15........ 120 B4
Mehetabel Rd *HOM* E9.................... 78 C3
Meister Cl *IL* IG1............................ 67 D3
Melanda Cl *CHST* BR7................... 161 F5
Melbourne Gv *EDUL* SE22............. 137 E2
CAT SE6.. 140 C5
Melbourne Pl *HOL/ALD* WC2B....... 21 F5
Melbourne Rd *EHAM* E6................. 83 F5
IL IG1.. 66 B3
LEY E10... 62 B2
Melbourne Sq *BRXN/ST* SW9....... 118 A4
Melbourne Ter *EDUL* SE22 *.......... 137 E2
FUL/PGN SW6............................... 114 B3
Melbury Ct *KENS* W8.................... 101 F4
Melbury Rd *CMBW* SE5.................. 119 E3
Melbury Rd *WKENS* W14................ 101 F4
Melbury Ter *CAMTN* NW1.............. 17 D1
Melcombe Pl *CAMTN* NW1............. 17 E2
Melcombe St *CAMTN* NW1............. 17 F1
Meldon Cl *FUL/PGN* SW6 *............ 114 B4
Melfield Gdns *CAT* SE6................. 158 B4
Melford Rd *BARK* IG11................... 85 E3
Melford Rd *EDUL* SE22.................. 156 A1
EHAM E6.. 95 F3
IL IG1.. 67 D4
WAN E11.. 63 E4
Melgund Rd *HBRY* N5.................... 76 A2
Melina Pl *STJWD* NW8................... 2 B3
Melina Rd *SHB* W12....................... 100 B3
Melior Pl *STHWK* SE1 *................. 36 C5
Melior St *STHWK* SE1.................... 36 B5
Meliot Rd *CAT* SE6......................... 159 D2
Melling St *WOOL/PLUM* SE18....... 127 E2
Mellison Rd *TOOT* SW17............... 151 E5
Melliss Av *RCH/KEW* TW9............. 110 B4
Mellitus St *SHB* W12..................... 87 F5
Mells Crs *ELTH/MOT* SE9.............. 161 F4
Mell St *GNWCH* SE10..................... 123 E1
Melody La *HBRY* N5....................... 76 B2
Melody Rd *WAND/EARL* SW18....... 132 C3
Melon Pl *KENS* W8 *...................... 26 B5
Melon Rd *PECK* SE15...................... 120 A4
WAN E11... 63 E5
Melrose Av *CRICK* NW2................. 70 C4
Melrose Av *WIM/MER* SW19.......... 149 F2
Melrose Cl *LEE/GVPK* SE12.......... 160 A1
Melrose Gdns *HMSMTH* W6.......... 100 C4
Melrose Rd *BARN* SW13................. 111 F5
WAND/EARL SW18......................... 131 F4
Melrose Ter *HMSMTH* W6.............. 100 C3
Melthorpe Gdns *BKHTH/KID* SE3... 125 D4
Melton Ct *DEPT* SE8....................... 103 F5
Melville Pl *IS* N1............................ 76 C4
Melville Rd *BARN* SW13................. 112 A4
WLSDN NW10................................ 69 D4
Melville Villas Rd *ACT* W3 *.......... 99 D2
Memel St *STLK* EC1Y..................... 23 E1
Memorial Av *SRTFD* E15................ 93 E2
Mendip Cl *SYD* SE26...................... 156 C4
Mendip Dr *CRICK* NW2................... 53 E4
Mendip Houses *BETH* E2 *............. 90 C2
Mendip Rd *BTSEA* SW11................ 132 C1
Mendora Rd *FUL/PGN* SW6........... 113 E3
Menelik Rd *CRICK* NW2................. 71 E1
Menotti St *BETH* E2 *..................... 90 A3
Mentmore Ter *HACK* E8.................. 78 B4
Meon Rd *ACT* W3........................... 98 C3
Mepham St *STHWK* SE1................. 33 F4
Merbury Cl *LEW* SE13.................... 140 C3
Merbury Rd *THMD* SE28................ 109 D2
Merbury St *WOOL/PLUM* SE18...... 108 B4
Mercator Rd *LEW* SE13.................. 141 D2
Merceron Houses *BETH* E2 *......... 90 C2
Merceron St *WCHPL* E1.................. 90 B3

Mercers Cl *GNWCH* SE10.............. 105 F5
Mercers Cots *WCHPL* E1 *............. 91 E5
Mercers Ms *ARCH* N19................... 75 D1
Mercers Pl *HMSMTH* W6................ 100 C5
Mercers Rd *ARCH* N19................... 57 D5
Merchant Dr *LSQ/SEVD* WC2H...... 20 C5
Merchant St *BOW* E3..................... 91 F2
Merchiston Rd *CAT* SE6................. 159 D2
Merchland Rd *ELTH/MOT* SE9....... 162 C1
Mercia Gv *LEW* SE13..................... 140 C1
Mercier Rd *PUT/ROE* SW15........... 131 E3
Mercury Wy *NWCR* SE14............... 121 D2
Mercy Ter *LEW* SE13..................... 140 B3
Mere Cl *WIM/MER* SW19................ 131 D5
Meredith Av *CRICK* NW2............... 70 C2
Meredith Ms *BROCKY* SE4............ 139 F2
Meredith St *CLKNW* EC1R............. 10 C4
PLSTW E13..................................... 94 A2
Meredyth Rd *BARN* SW13.............. 112 A5
Meretone Cl *BROCKY* SE4............. 139 E2
Mereworth Dr *WOOL/PLUM* SE18... 126 B3
Meridian Rd *CHARL* SE7................ 125 D3
Meridian Sq *SRTFD* E15................ 81 D4
Merifield Rd *ELTH/MOT* SE9.......... 142 C2
Merivale Rd *PUT/ROE* SW15......... 131 E2
Merley Ct *CDALE/KGS* NW9.......... 50 C3
Merlin Rd *MNPK* E12...................... 83 D4
Merlin St *FSBYW* WC1X................. 10 A4
Mermaid Ct *STHWK* SE1................ 36 A5
Merredene St *BRXS/STRHM* SW2... 135 F4
Merriam Av *HOM* E9....................... 79 F3
Merrick Sq *STHWK* SE1................. 48 A2
Merrilees Rd *BFN/LL* DA15........... 145 E5
Merriman Rd *BKHTH/KID* SE3....... 124 C4
Merrington Rd *FUL/PGN* SW6........ 114 A2
Merritt Rd *BROCKY* SE4................. 139 F3
Merrow St *WALW* SE17.................. 119 D1
Merrow Wk *WALW* SE17................. 119 D1
Merryfield *BKHTH/KID* SE3............ 123 F5
Merthyr Ter *BARN* SW13................ 112 B2
Merton Av *CHSWK* W4.................... 99 F5
Merton La *HGT* N6.......................... 73 F4
Merton Ri *HAMP* NW3.................... 73 E4
Merton Rd *BARK* IG11.................... 85 E4
GDMY/SEVK IG3............................ 67 F2
WAND/EARL SW18......................... 150 A1
Mertoun Ter *MBLAR* W1H *............ 17 E4
Mertins Rd *PECK* SE15.................. 139 D2
Meru Cl *KTTN* NW5........................ 74 A1
Mervan Rd *BRXS/STRHM* SW2...... 136 A2
Mervyn Av *ELTH/MOT* SE9............ 162 C3
Messaline Av *ACT* W3.................... 86 C5
Messent Rd *ELTH/MOT* SE9.......... 142 C5
Messeter Pl *ELTH/MOT* SE9.......... 144 A4
Messina Av *KIL/WHAMP* NW6........ 72 A2
Meteor St *BTSEA* SW11................. 134 A2
Methley St *LBTH* SE11.................... 118 A1
Methwold Rd *NKENS* W10.............. 88 C3
Metropolitan Cl *POP/IOD* E14........ 92 A4
Metropolitan Whf *WAP* E1W *........ 102 C2
Mews North *BGVA* SW1W.............. 42 C3
Mews South *PIM* SW1V................... 116 C1
Mews St *WAP* E1W......................... 37 F3
Mexfield Rd *PUT/ROE* SW15......... 131 F3
Meymott St *STHWK* SE1................. 34 C4
Meynell Crs *HOM* E9...................... 79 D4
Meynell Gdns *HOM* E9................... 79 D4
Meynell Rd *HOM* E9....................... 79 D4
Meyrick Rd *BTSEA* SW11............... 133 D1
WLSDN NW10................................ 70 A2
Miah Ter *WAP* E1W *...................... 102 A3
Micawber St *IS* N1.......................... 11 E3
Michael Rd *FUL/PGN* SW6............. 114 B4
WAN E11... 63 E3
Michaels Cl *LEW* SE13................... 141 E1
Micheldever Rd *LEE/GVPK* SE12... 141 E4
Michel Wk *WOOL/PLUM* SE18....... 126 C1
Michigan Av *MNPK* E12.................. 83 E1
Micklethwaite Rd *FUL/PGN* SW6... 114 B2
Middle Dartrey Wk *WBPTN* SW10 *.. 114 C3
Middlefield *STJWD* NW8................. 73 D5
Middle Park Av *ELTH/MOT* SE9..... 143 D5
Middle Rd *PLSTW* E13................... 94 A1
Middle Rw *NKENS* W10................... 89 E3
Middlesex Pl *HOM* E9.................... 78 C4
Middlesex St *WCHPL* E1................. 25 D3
Middle St *STBT* EC1A..................... 23 E2
Middle Temple La *EMB* EC4Y......... 22 A5
Middleton Dr *BERM/RHTH* SE16..... 103 D3
Middleton Gdns *GNTH/NBYPK* IG2.. 66 B1
Middleton Gv *HOLWY* N7............... 75 E2

Middleton Ms *HOLWY* N7 .... 75 E2
Middleton Pl *TPPST* W1W 19 E5
Middleton Rd *GLDGN* NW11 .... 54 A2
  HACK E8 .... 77 F4
Middleton St *BETH* E2 .... 90 B2
Middle Yd *STHWK* SE1 .... 36 B3
Midford Pl *FITZ* W1T * 19 F1
Midholm *WBLY* HA9 .... 50 A3
Midhope St *STPAN* WC1H 9 D4
Midhurst Wy *CLPT* E5 .... 78 A1
Midland Arches *CRICK* NW2 * 52 B4
Midland Crs *HAMP* NW3 .... 72 C3
Midland Rd *CAMTN* NW1 .... 8 B2
  LEY E10 .... 62 C2
Midland Ter *CRICK* NW2 .... 53 D5
  WLSDN NW10 .... 87 E3
Midlothian Rd *BOW* E3 .... 91 F3
Midmoor Rd *BAL* SW12 .... 152 C1
Midship Cl *BERM/RHTH* SE16 * 103 D2
Midship Point *POP/IOD* E14 * 104 A3
Midstrath Rd *WLSDN* NW10 .... 69 E1
Midwood Cl *CRICK* NW2 .... 52 A5
Milborne Gv *WBPTN* SW10 .... 114 C1
Milborne St *HOM* E9 .... 78 C3
Milborough Crs *LEE/GVPK* SE12 .... 141 E4
Milcote St *STHWK* SE1 .... 46 C1
Mildenhall Rd *CLPT* E5 .... 78 C1
Mildmay Av *IS* N1 .... 77 D3
Mildmay Gv North *IS* N1 .... 77 D2
Mildmay Gv South *IS* N1 .... 77 D2
Mildmay Pk *IS* N1 .... 77 D2
Mildmay Pl *STNW/STAM* N16 * 77 E2
  IS N1 .... 66 B5
Mildmay Rd *IS* N1 .... 77 D3
Mildmay St *IS* N1 .... 77 D3
Mile End Pl *WCHPL* E1 .... 91 D5
Mile End Rd *WCHPL* E1 .... 90 C4
Miles Dr *THMD* SE28 .... 109 E2
Miles St *VX/NE* SW8 .... 117 E2
Milfoil St *SHB* W12 .... 100 A1
Milford La *TPL/STR* WC2R 34 A1
Milford Ms *STRHM/NOR* SW16 .... 153 F3
Milk St *BMLY* BR1 .... 160 B5
  CAN/RD E16 .... 108 B2
  CITYW EC2V 23 F4
Milkwell Yd *CMBW* SE5 .... 118 C4
Milkwood Rd *HNHL* SE24 .... 136 B5
Milk Yd *WAP* E1W 102 C1
Millais Av *MNPK* E12 .... 84 A2
Millais Rd *WAN* E11 .... 80 C1
Millard Cl *STNW/STAM* N16 .... 77 E2
Millard Rd *DEPT* SE8 .... 121 F1
Millars Meadow *BKHTH/KID* SE3 * 142 C4
Millbank *WEST* SW1P 44 C4
Millbank Est *WEST* SW1P 44 B5
Millbank Wy *LEE/GVPK* SE12 .... 142 A3
Millbrook Av *ELTH/MOT* SE9 .... 145 D2
Millbrook Rd *BRXN/ST* SW9 .... 136 B1
Millennium Br *STHWK* SE1 .... 35 E2
Millennium Cl *CAN/RD* E16 .... 94 A5
Millennium Dr *POP/IOD* E14 .... 105 D4
Millennium Pl *BETH* E2 * 90 B1
Millennium Sq *STHWK* SE1 .... 37 E5
Millennium Wy *GNWCH* SE10 .... 105 E5
Millennium Whf *POP/IOD* E14 .... 105 D5
Miller Cl *BMLY* BR1 .... 160 A5
Miller's Av *HACK* E8 .... 77 F2
Miller's Ct *CHSWK* W4 .... 111 F1
Miller's Ter *HACK* E8 .... 77 F2
Miller St *CAMTN* NW1 .... 7 F1
Miller's Wy *HMSMTH* W6 .... 100 B2
Millfield La *HGT* N6 .... 55 F4
Millfield Pl *HGT* N6 .... 56 A4
Millfields Rd *CLPT* E5 .... 78 C1
Mill Gdns *SYD* SE26 .... 156 B4
Millgrove St *BTSEA* SW11 .... 116 B4
Millharbour *POP/IOD* E14 .... 104 B4
Mill Hl *BARN* SW13 .... 130 A1
Mill Hill Gv *ACT* W3 * 98 B2
Mill Hill Rd *ACT* W3 .... 98 B3
  BARN SW13 .... 130 B1
Mill Hill Ter *ACT* W3 .... 98 B2
Millhouse Pl *WNWD* SE27 .... 154 B4
Millicent Rd *LEY* E10 * 61 F3
Milligan St *POP/IOD* E14 .... 103 F1
Mill La *CRICK* NW2 .... 71 E2
  WOOL/PLUM SE18 .... 126 A1
Millman Ms *BMSBY* WC1N * 21 E1
Millman Pl *BMSBY* WC1N 21 E1
Millman St *BMSBY* WC1N 21 E1

Millmark Gv *NWCR* SE14 .... 121 E5
Mill Pl *POP/IOD* E14 .... 91 E5
Mill Pond Cl *VX/NE* SW8 .... 117 D3
Millpond Est *BERM/RHTH* SE16 * 102 B3
Mill Rd *CAN/RD* E16 .... 106 B2
  IL IG1 .... 66 A5
Mills Gv *POP/IOD* E14 .... 92 C4
Millshot Cl *FUL/PGN* SW6 .... 112 C4
Millshott Cl *WHALL* SW1A * 32 B3
Mills Rw *CHSWK* W4 .... 99 D5
Millstone Cl *SRTFD* E15 .... 81 D3
Millstream Rd *STHWK* SE1 .... 49 E3
Mill St *CONDST* W1S 31 D1
  STHWK SE1 .... 49 F1
Millwall Dock Rd *POP/IOD* E14 .... 104 A4
Millwood St *NKENS* W10 .... 89 E4
Mill Yd *WCHPL* E1 .... 102 A1
Milman Rd *KIL/WHAMP* NW6 .... 89 D1
Milman's St *WBPTN* SW10 .... 115 D2
Milne Gdns *ELTH/MOT* SE9 .... 143 E3
Milner Pl *IS* N1 .... 76 A5
Milner Rd *SRTFD* E15 .... 93 E2
Milner Sq *IS* N1 * 76 A4
Milner St *CHEL* SW3 .... 41 E4
Milnthorpe Rd *CHSWK* W4 .... 111 D2
Milo Rd *EDUL* SE22 .... 137 F4
Milroy Wk *STHWK* SE1 .... 34 B3
Milson Rd *WKENS* W14 .... 101 E4
Milton Av *EHAM* E6 .... 83 D4
  HGT N6 .... 56 C2
  WLSDN NW10 .... 69 D5
Milton Cl *EFNCH* N2 .... 54 C1
  STHWK SE1 .... 49 E5
Milton Ct *BARB* EC2Y 24 A2
Milton Court Rd *NWCR* SE14 .... 121 E2
Milton Crs *GNTH/NBYPK* IG2 .... 66 C2
Milton Gv *STNW/STAM* N16 .... 77 D1
Milton Pk *HGT* N6 .... 56 C2
Milton Rd *ACT* W3 .... 99 D2
  CDALE/KGS NW9 * 52 A2
  HGT N6 .... 56 C2
  HNHL SE24 .... 136 B3
  MORT/ESHN SW14 .... 129 D1
  WELL DA16 .... 127 F4
Milton St *BARB* EC2Y 24 A2
Milverton Gdns *GDMY/SEVK* IG3 * 67 F4
Milverton Rd *KIL/WHAMP* NW6 .... 70 C4
Milverton St *LBTH* SE11 .... 118 A1
Milverton Wy *ELTH/MOT* SE9 .... 162 A4
Milward St *WCHPL* E1 .... 90 B4
Mimosa St *FUL/PGN* SW6 .... 113 F4
Minard Rd *CAT* SE6 .... 141 E5
Mina Rd *STHWK* SE1 .... 119 E1
Mincing La *MON* EC3R 36 C1
Minehead Rd *STRHM/NOR* SW16 .... 153 F5
Mineral Cl *WOOL/PLUM* SE18 .... 109 E5
Minera Ms *BGVA* SW1W 42 B4
Minerva Cl *BRXN/ST* SW9 .... 118 A3
  SCUP DA14 .... 163 E4
Minerva Rd *WLSDN* NW10 .... 86 C3
Minerva St *BETH* E2 .... 90 B1
Minet Av *WLSDN* NW10 .... 87 E1
Minet Gdns *WLSDN* NW10 .... 87 E1
Minet Rd *BRXN/ST* SW9 .... 118 B5
Minford Gdns *WKENS* W14 .... 101 D3
Ming St *POP/IOD* E14 * 104 A1
Ministry Wy *ELTH/MOT* SE9 .... 161 F2
Minnow Wk *WALW* SE17 .... 49 D5
Minories *TWRH* EC3N 25 E5
Minshull St *VX/NE* SW8 * 117 D4
Minson Rd *HOM* E9 .... 79 D5
Minstead Gdns *PUT/ROE* SW15 .... 129 F5
Minster Ct *MON* EC3R * 36 C1
Minster Rd *CRICK* NW2 .... 71 E2
Mintern St *IS* N1 .... 12 B1
Minton Ms *KIL/WHAMP* NW6 .... 72 B3
Mint St *STHWK* SE1 .... 35 E5
Mirabel Rd *FUL/PGN* SW6 .... 113 F3
Miranda Cl *WCHPL* E1 .... 90 C4
Miranda Rd *ARCH* N19 .... 56 C5
Mirfield St *CHARL* SE7 .... 107 D4
Miriam Rd *WOOL/PLUM* SE18 .... 127 E1
Mission Pl *PECK* SE15 .... 120 A4
Mitali Pas *WCHPL* E1 .... 90 A5
Mitcham La *STRHM/NOR* SW16 .... 152 C5
Mitcham Rd *EHAM* E6 .... 95 E2
  GDMY/SEVK IG3 .... 67 F2
  TOOT SW17 .... 151 F4
Mitchellbrook Wy *WLSDN* NW10 .... 69 D3
Mitchell St *FSBYE* EC1V 11 E5
Mitchell Wy *WLSDN* NW10 .... 68 C3

Mitchison Rd *IS* N1 .... 77 D3
Mitford Rd *ARCH* N19 .... 57 E4
Mitre Rd *SRTFD* E15 .... 93 E1
  STHWK SE1 .... 34 B5
Mitre Sq *HDTCH* EC3A 25 C5
Mitre St *HDTCH* EC3A 25 D5
The Mitre *POP/IOD* E14 .... 103 F1
Mitre Wy *NKENS* W10 .... 88 B4
Moat Ct *ELTH/MOT* SE9 * 143 F4
Moat Dr *PLSTW* E13 .... 94 C1
Moat Pl *ACT* W3 .... 86 B5
  BRXN/ST SW9 .... 135 F1
Moberly Rd *CLAP* SW4 .... 155 D5
Modbury Gdns *KTTN* NW5 .... 74 A3
Model Cots *MORT/ESHN* SW14 .... 128 C3
Model Farm Cl *ELTH/MOT* SE9 .... 161 E3
Moffat Rd *TOOT* SW17 .... 151 E4
Mohmmad Khan Rd *WAN* E11 * 63 F1
Moiety Rd *POP/IOD* E14 .... 104 A3
Moira Rd *ELTH/MOT* SE9 .... 143 F2
Molescroft *ELTH/MOT* SE9 .... 162 C3
Molesford Rd *FUL/PGN* SW6 * 114 A4
Molesworth St *LEW* SE13 .... 140 C1
Molly Huggins Cl *BAL* SW12 .... 134 C5
Molyneux Dr *TOOT* SW17 .... 152 B4
Molyneux St *MBLAR* W1H 17 D3
Monarch Dr *CAN/RD* E16 .... 95 D4
Monarch Ms *STRHM/NOR* SW16 .... 154 B5
Monarch Wy *CNTH/NBYPK* IG2 .... 67 D1
Mona Rd *PECK* SE15 .... 120 C5
Mona St *CAN/RD* E16 .... 93 F4
Monck's Rw *WAND/EARL* SW18 * 131 F4
Monck St *WEST* SW1P 44 B3
Monclar Rd *CMBW* SE5 .... 137 D2
Moncorvo Cl *SKENS* SW7 .... 40 C5
Moncrieff St *PECK* SE15 .... 120 A5
Monday Aly *STNW/STAM* N16 .... 59 F5
Monega Rd *FSTGT* E7 .... 82 C3
Monier Rd *BOW* E3 .... 80 A4
Monk Dr *CAN/RD* E16 .... 95 D4
Monks Dr *ACT* W3 .... 86 A4
Monks Pk *WBLY* HA9 .... 68 B3
Monks Park Gdns *WBLY* HA9 .... 68 B3
Monk St *WOOL/PLUM* SE18 .... 108 A5
Monk Ter *FSTH* SE23 .... 157 F2
Monkton Rd *WELL* DA16 .... 115 F5
Monkton St *LBTH* SE11 .... 48 B4
Monkwell Sq *BARB* EC2Y 23 F3
Monmouth Cl *CHSWK* W4 .... 99 D4
Monmouth Pl *BAY/PAD* W2 .... 14 B5
Monmouth Rd *BAY/PAD* W2 .... 14 B5
  EHAM E6 .... 95 F2
Monmouth St *LSQ/SEVD* WC2H 20 C5
Monnery Rd *ARCH* N19 .... 56 C5
Monnow Rd *STHWK* SE1 .... 120 A1
Monroe Dr *MORT/ESHN* SW14 .... 128 B3
Monsell Rd *FSBYPK* N4 .... 58 B5
Monson Rd *NWCR* SE14 .... 121 D3
  WLSDN NW10 .... 88 A1
Montacute Rd *CAT* SE6 .... 139 F5
Montague Av *BROCKY* SE4 .... 139 F2
Montague Cl *STHWK* SE1 .... 36 A3
Montague Gdns *EA* W5 .... 98 A1
Montague Pl *CWRST* WC1E 20 B2
Montague Rd *HACK* E8 .... 78 A2
  WAN E11 .... 63 F4
Montague Sq *PECK* SE15 .... 120 C3
Montague St *RSQ* WC1B 20 C2
  STBT EC1A 23 E3
Montagu Man *MHST* W1U 17 E4
Montagu Ms North *MBLAR* W1H 17 F3
Montagu Ms South *MBLAR* W1H 17 F4
Montagu Ms West *MBLAR* W1H 17 E4
Montagu Pl *MBLAR* W1H 17 E3
Montagu Rw *MBLAR* W1H 52 A1
Montagu Rw *MBLAR* W1U 17 F3
Montagu Sq *MBLAR* W1H 17 F3
Montagu St *MBLAR* W1H 17 F4
Montaigne Cl *WEST* SW1P 44 B5
Montana Gdns *SYD* SE26 .... 157 F5
Montana Rd *TOOT* SW17 .... 152 A3
Montbelle Rd *ELTH/MOT* SE9 .... 162 B3
Montcalm Rd *CHARL* SE7 .... 125 D3
Montclare St *BETH* E2 .... 13 E4
Monteagle Av *BARK* IG11 .... 84 C3
Monteagle Wy *PECK* SE15 .... 138 B1
Montefiore St *VX/NE* SW8 .... 116 B5
Montem Rd *FSTH* SE23 .... 139 F5
Montem St *FSBYPK* N4 .... 57 F5
Montesquieu Ter *CAN/RD* E16 * 93 F5
Montford Pl *LBTH* SE11 .... 118 A1

Montfort Pl *WIM/MER* SW19 .... 149 D1
Montgomerie Ms *FSTH* SE23 .... 138 C5
Montgomery Cl *BFN/LL* DA15 .... 145 E3
Montgomery Rd *CHSWK* W4 .... 98 C5
Montgomery St *POP/IOD* E14 .... 104 B2
Montholme Rd *BTSEA* SW11 .... 133 F4
Monthorpe Rd *WCHPL* E1 .... 90 A4
Montolieu Gdns *PUT/ROE* SW15 .... 130 B3
Montpelier Gdns *EHAM* E6 .... 95 D2
Montpelier Gv *KTTN* NW5 .... 74 C2
Montpelier Ms *SKENS* SW7 .... 41 D2
Montpelier Pl *SKENS* SW7 * 41 D2
  WCHPL E1 .... 90 C5
Montpelier Ri *GLDGN* NW11 .... 53 E2
Montpelier Rd *PECK* SE15 .... 120 B4
Montpelier Rw *BKHTH/KID* SE3 .... 123 F5
Montpelier Sq *SKENS* SW7 .... 41 D2
Montpelier St *SKENS* SW7 .... 41 D2
Montpelier Ter *SKENS* SW7 .... 41 D1
Montpelier V *BKHTH/KID* SE3 * 123 F5
Montpelier Wk *SKENS* SW7 .... 41 D1
Montpelier Wy *GLDGN* NW11 .... 53 E2
Montreal Rd *IL* IG1 .... 33 E1
Montreal Rd *IL* IG1 .... 66 C2
Montrell Rd *BRXS/STRHM* SW2 .... 153 E1
Montrose Av *KIL/WHAMP* NW6 .... 89 E5
  WELL DA16 .... 145 D1
Montrose Cl *WELL* DA16 .... 145 F1
Montrose Pl *KTBR* SW1X 42 B1
Montrose Vls *HMSMTH* W6 * 112 A1
Montrose Wy *FSTH* SE23 .... 157 D1
Montserrat Cl *NRWD* SE19 .... 155 D5
Montserrat Rd *PUT/ROE* SW15 .... 131 E2
Monza St *WAP* E1W 102 C1
Moodkee St *BERM/RHTH* SE16 .... 102 C4
Moody St *WCHPL* E1 .... 91 D2
Moon Ct *LEE/GVPK* SE12 * 142 A2
Moon St *IS* N1 .... 76 B5
Moorcroft Rd *STRHM/NOR* SW16 .... 153 E3
Moordown *WOOL/PLUM* SE18 .... 126 A4
Moore Cl *MORT/ESHN* SW14 .... 128 C1
Moore Park Rd *FUL/PGN* SW6 .... 114 B3
Moore St *CHEL* SW3 .... 41 E4
Moorey Cl *SRTFD* E15 .... 81 F5
Moorfields *LVPST* EC2M 24 A3
Moorfields Highwalk *BARB* EC2Y 24 A3
Moorgate *LOTH* EC2R 24 A4
Moorgate Pl *LOTH* EC2R * 24 A4
Moorhead Wy *BKHTH/KID* SE3 .... 142 B1
Moorhouse Rd *BAY/PAD* W2 .... 14 A4
The Moorings *CHSWK* W4 * 110 A2
Moorland Rd *BRXN/ST* SW9 .... 136 B2
Moor La *BARB* EC2Y 24 A3
Moorside Rd *BMLY* BR1 .... 159 E4
Moor St *SOHO/SHAV* W1D 20 B5
Morant St *POP/IOD* E14 .... 104 A1
Mora Rd *CRICK* NW2 .... 70 C1
Mora St *FSBYE* EC1V 11 F4
Morat St *BRXN/ST* SW9 .... 117 F4
Moravian Pl *WBPTN* SW10 * 115 D2
Moravian St *BETH* E2 .... 90 C1
Moray Ms *HOLWY* N7 .... 57 F4
Moray Rd *HOLWY* N7 .... 57 F4
Morcambe St *WALW* SE17 .... 47 F5
Mordaunt Rd *WLSDN* NW10 .... 69 D5
Mordaunt St *BRXN/ST* SW9 .... 135 F1
Morden Cl *LEW* SE13 .... 122 C5
Morden La *LEW* SE13 .... 122 C5
Morden Rd *BKHTH/KID* SE3 .... 124 A5
Morden Road Ms *BKHTH/KID* SE3 .... 124 A5
Morden St *LEW* SE13 .... 122 B4
Morden Wharf Rd *GNWCH* SE10 .... 105 E4
Mordon Rd *GDMY/SEVK* IG3 .... 67 F2
Mordred Rd *CAT* SE6 .... 159 E2
Morecambe Cl *WCHPL* E1 * 91 D4
Morecambe St *POP/IOD* E14 .... 122 B1
More Cl *CAN/RD* E16 .... 93 F5
  WKENS W14 .... 101 D5
Moreland Cots *BOW* E3 * 92 A1
Moreland St *FSBYE* EC1V 11 D3
Morella Rd *BTSEA* SW11 .... 133 F5
More London Riverside *STHWK* SE1 .... 37 D4
Moremead Rd *CAT* SE6 .... 157 F4
Morena St *CAT* SE6 .... 140 B5
Moresby Rd *CLPT* E5 .... 60 B3
Mores Gdn *CHEL* SW3 * 115 D2
Moreton Cl *CLPT* E5 .... 60 C4
  SEVS/STOTM N15 .... 59 D1
Moreton Pl *SEVS/STOTM* N15 .... 59 D1
Moreton Pl *PIM* SW1V 116 C1
Moreton St *PIM* SW1V 117 D1
Moreton Ter *PIM* SW1V 116 C1

Moreton Terrace Ms North
  PIM SW1V 116 C1
Moreton Terrace Ms South
  PIM SW1V 116 C1
Morgan Rd *HOLWY* N7 .... 76 A2
  NKENS W10 .... 89 F4
Morgan St *BOW* E3 .... 91 E2
  CAN/RD E16 .... 95 F4
Moriatry CI *HOLWY* N7 .... 75 E1
Morie St *WAND/EARL* SW18 .... 132 B2
Morieux Rd *LEY* E10 .... 61 F3
Moring Rd *TOOT* SW17 * 152 A4
Morkyns Wk *DUL* SE21 .... 155 E3
Morland CI *GLDGN* NW11 .... 54 B3
Morland Est *HACK* E8 * 78 A4
Morland Gdns *WLSDN* NW10 .... 69 D4
Morland Ms *IS* N1 .... 76 A4
Morland Rd *IL* IG1 .... 66 B4
Morley Rd *BARK* IG11 .... 140 C2
  LEY E10 .... 62 C3
  SRTFD E15 .... 93 F1
Morley St *STHWK* SE1 .... 46 B1
Morna Rd *CMBW* SE5 .... 118 C5
Morning La *HOM* E9 .... 78 C3
Mornington Av *IL* IG1 .... 66 A2
  WKENS W14 .... 101 F5
Mornington Crs *CAMTN* NW1 ... 7 E1
Mornington Gv *BOW* E3 .... 92 A2
Mornington Ms *CMBW* SE5 .... 118 C4
Mornington PI *CAMTN* NW1 .... 7 D1
Mornington Rd *NWCR* SE14 .... 121 F3
  WAN E11 .... 63 F3
Mornington St *CAMTN* NW1 .... 7 D1
Mornington Ter *CAMTN* NW1 ...... 74 B5
Morocco St *STHWK* SE1 .... 48 C1
Morpeth Gv *HOM* E9 .... 79 D5
Morpeth Rd *HOM* E9 .... 78 C5
Morpeth St *BETH* E2 .... 91 D2
Morpeth Ter *WEST* SW1P 43 E5
Morrab Gdns *GDMY/SEVK* IG3 .... 67 F5
Morrells Yd *LBTH* SE11 .... 118 A1
Morris Av *MNPK* E12 .... 83 F2
Morris Bishop Ter *HGT* N6 * 56 A1
Morris Gdns *WAND/EARL* SW18 .. 132 A5
Morrish Rd *BRXS/STRHM* SW2 ... 135 E3
Morrison St *BTSEA* SW11 .... 134 A1
Morris PI *FSBYPK* N4 * 58 A4
Morris Rd *POP/IOD* E14 .... 92 B4
  SRTFD E15 .... 81 E1
Morris St *WCHPL* E1 .... 90 B5
Morse CI *PLSTW* E13 .... 94 A2
Morshead Rd *MV/WKIL* W9 .... 2 B4
Mortham St *SRTFD* E15 .... 81 E5
Mortimer CI *CRICK* NW2 .... 53 F5
  STRHM/NOR SW16 .... 153 D2
Mortimer Crs *KIL/WHAMP* NW6 . 72 B5
Mortimer PI *KIL/WHAMP* NW6 .. 72 B5
Mortimer Rd *EHAM* E6 .... 95 F2
  IS N1 .... 77 D4
  WLSDN NW10 .... 88 C2
Mortimer Sq *NTGHL* W11 .... 101 D1
Mortimer St *GTPST* W1W 19 D4
Mortimer Ter *KTTN* NW5 * 74 B1
Mortlake High St *MORT/ESHN* SW14 .. 129 D1
Mortlake Rd *CAN/RD* E16 .... 94 B5
  IL IG1 .... 84 C1
  MORT/ESHN SW14 .... 128 B1
  RCH/KEW TW9 .... 110 A3
Morton Cl *CLAP* SW4 .... 135 D4
  WCHPL E1 .... 90 C5
Morton Ms *ECT* SW5 .... 38 C5
Morton PI *STHWK* SE1 .... 46 A3
Morton Rd *IS* N1 .... 76 C4
  SRTFD E15 .... 81 F4
Morval Rd *BRXS/STRHM* SW2 .... 136 A3
Morven Rd *TOOT* SW17 .... 151 F3
Morville St *BOW* E3 .... 92 A1
Morwell St *RSQ* WC1B 20 A3
Moscow PI *BAY/PAD* W2 .... 26 C1
Moscow Rd *BAY/PAD* W2 .... 26 C1
Mossbury Rd *BTSEA* SW11 ...... 133 E1
Moss CI *WCHPL* E1 .... 90 A4
Mossford St *BOW* E3 .... 91 F3
Mossop St *CHEL* SW3 .... 41 D4
Mostyn Gdns *WLSDN* NW10 .... 89 D2
Mostyn Gv *BOW* E3 .... 91 F1
Mostyn Rd *BRXN/ST* SW9 .... 118 A4
Motcomb St *KTBR* SW1X 42 A2
The Mothers Sq *CLPT* E5 * 78 B1
Moth House *WOOL/PLUM* SE18 * .. 125 E5
Motley St *VX/NE* SW8 .... 116 C5

Mottingham Gdns *ELTH/MOT* SE9 ... 161 D1
Mottingham La *LEE/GVPK* SE12 .... 160 C1
Mottingham Rd *ELTH/MOT* SE9 ..... 161 E3
Moulins Rd *HOM* E9 .... 78 C4
Moundfield Rd *STNW/STAM* N16 .. 60 A1
Mountacre CI *SYD* SE26 .... 155 F4
Mount Adon Pk *EDUL* SE22 .... 138 A5
Montague PI *POP/IOD* E14 .... 104 C1
Mount Angelus Rd *PUT/ROE* SW15 . 129 F5
Mount Ash Rd *SYD* SE26 .... 156 B3
Mountbatten CI *NRWD* SE19 .... 155 E5
  WOOL/PLUM SE18 .... 127 E2
Mount Dr *WBLY* HA9 .... 50 C4
Mountearl Gdns *STRHM/NOR* SW16 . 153 F3
Mount Ephraim La
  STRHM/NOR SW16 .... 153 D3
Mount Ephraim Rd
  STRHM/NOR SW16 .... 153 D3
Mountfield CI *CAT* SE6 .... 141 D5
Mountfield Rd *EHAM* E6 .... 96 A1
Mountfield Ter *CAT* SE6 * 141 D5
Mountfort Crs *IS* N1 .... 76 A4
Mountfort Ter *IS* N1 .... 76 A4
Mount Gdns *SYD* SE26 .... 156 B5
Mountgrove Rd *HBRY* N5 .... 58 C5
Mount Mills *FSBYE* EC1V 11 D4
Mount Nod Rd *STRHM/NOR* SW16 . 153 F3
Mount PI *ACT* W3 * 98 B2
Mount Pleasant *FSBYW* WC1X .. 21 F1
  WNWD SE27 .... 154 C4
Mount Pleasant Crs *FSBYPK* N4 * . 57 F2
Mount Pleasant HI *CLPT* E5 .... 60 B4
Mount Pleasant La *CLPT* E5 .... 60 B3
Mount Pleasant PI *WOOL/PLUM* SE18 . 109 D5
  WLSDN NW10 .... 70 C4
Mount Pleasant Vls *FSBYPK* N4 . 57 F2
Mount Rd *CRICK* NW2 .... 52 B5
  HDN NW4 .... 52 A1
  IL IG1 .... 84 B2
  WIM/MER SW19 .... 150 A2
Mount Rw *MYFR/PKLN* W1K 30 C2
Mounts Pond Rd *BKHTH/KID* SE3 . 123 D5
  LEW SE13 .... 123 D5
The Mount Sq *HAMP* NW3 * 54 C5
Mount St *MYFR/PKLN* W1K 30 A2
Mount Ter *WCHPL* E1 .... 90 B4
The Mount *CLPT* E5 * 60 B4
  HAMP NW3 .... 72 C1
  WBLY HA9 .... 50 C4
Mountview CI *HAMP* NW3 * 54 C3
Mount View Rd *FSBYPK* N4 .... 57 F2
Mount Vls *WNWD* SE27 .... 154 B3
Moxon CI *PLSTW* E13 .... 93 F1
Moxon St *MHST* W1U 18 A3
Moye CI *BETH* E2 .... 78 A5
Moyers Rd *LEY* E10 .... 62 B1
Moylan Rd *HMSMTH* W6 .... 113 E2
Moyne PI *WLSDN* NW10 .... 86 A2
Moyser Rd *STRHM/NOR* SW16 .. 152 B5
Mozart St *NKENS* W10 .... 89 F2
Muirdown Av *MORT/ESHN* SW14 . 128 C2
Muir Dr *WAND/EARL* SW18 .... 133 D4
Muirfield *ACT* W3 .... 99 E1
Muirfield CI *BERM/RHTH* SE16 * ... 120 B1
Muirfield Crs *POP/IOD* E14 .... 104 B4
Muirkirk Rd *CAT* SE6 .... 158 C1
Muir Rd *CLPT* E5 .... 60 A5
Muir St *CAN/RD* E16 .... 107 F2
Mulberry CI *CHEL* SW3 * 115 D2
  STRHM/NOR SW16 .... 152 C4
Mulberry Ms *NWCR* SE14 .... 121 F4
Mulberry PI *ELTH/MOT* SE9 ...... 143 D2
  HMSMTH W6 .... 112 A1
Mulberry Rd *HACK* E8 .... 77 F4
Mulberry St *WCHPL* E1 .... 90 A5
Mulberry Wk *CHEL* SW3 .... 115 D2
Mulgrave Rd *WKENS* W14 .... 113 F2
  WLSDN NW10 .... 69 F1
  WOOL/PLUM SE18 .... 107 F5
Mulkern Rd *ARCH* N19 .... 57 D3
Mullins Pth *MORT/ESHN* SW14 .. 129 D1
Mull Wk *IS* N1 .... 76 C3
Mulready St *STJWD* NW8 .... 16 C1
Multi Wy *ACT* W3 .... 99 E3

Multon Rd WAND/EARL SW18	133	D5
Mumford Ct CITYW EC2V	23	F4
Mumford Mills CNWCH SE10	122	A3
Mumford Rd HNHL SE24	136	B3
Muncaster Rd CLAP SW4	133	F2
Muncies Ms CAT SE6	158	C2
Mundania Rd EDUL SE22	138	B4
Munden St WKENS W14	101	E5
Mundford Rd CLPT E5	60	C4
Mundon Gdns IL IG1	67	D3
Mund St WKENS W14	113	F1
Mundy St IS N1	12	C1
Munroe Ter WBPTN SW10	115	D3
Munro Ms WKENS W10	89	E4
Munro Ter WBPTN SW10	115	D2
Munro Wy CLPT E5	78	A1
Munster Ct FUL/PGN SW6	113	F5
Munster Ms FUL/PGN SW6 *	113	F3
Munster Rd FUL/PGN SW6	113	E3
Munster Sq CAMTN NW1	7	D4
Munton Rd WALW SE17	47	F4
Murchison Rd LEY E10	62	C4
Murdock Cl CAN/RD E16	93	F5
Murdock St PECK SE15	120	B2
Muriel St IS N1	75	F5
Murillo Rd LEW SE13	141	D2
Murphy St STHWK SE1	46	A1
Murray Cl THMD SE28	109	E1
Murray Gv IS N1	12	A2
Murray House WOOL/PLUM SE18 *	125	E3
Murray Sq CAN/RD E16	94	A5
Murray Sq CAMTN NW1	75	D4
Murray Ter HAMP NW3	72	C1
Musard Rd HMSMTH W6	113	E2
Musbury St WCHPL E1	90	C5
Muscatel Pl CMBW SE5	119	E4
Muschamp Rd PECK SE15	137	F1
Muscovy St MON EC3R	37	D2
Museum St NOXST/BSQ WC1A	20	C4
Museum Wy ACT W3	98	A3
Musgrave Crs FUL/PGN SW6	114	A3
Musgrove Rd NWCR SE14	121	D4
Musjid Rd BTSEA SW11	115	D5
Muston Rd CLPT E5	60	B4
Muswell Hill Rd HGT N6	56	A1
Mutrix Rd KIL/WHAMP NW6	72	A5
Mutton Pl CAMTN NW1	74	A3
Myatt Rd BRXN/ST SW9	118	B4
Mycenae Rd BKHTH/KID SE3	124	A2
Myddelton Pas CLKNW EC1R	10	B3
Myddelton Sq CLKNW EC1R	10	B3
Myddelton St CLKNW EC1R	10	B4
Myddleton Av FSBYPK N4	58	B4
Myers La NWCR SE14	121	D2
Mylis Cl SYD SE26	156	B4
Mylne Cl HMSMTH W6 *	112	A1
Mylne St IS N1	10	A2
Myrdle St WCHPL E1	90	A5
Myron Pl LEW SE13	140	C1
Myrtle Aly WOOL/PLUM SE18	108	A4
Myrtleberry Cl HACK E8 *	77	F3
Myrtle Rd ACT W3	98	C2
EHAM E6	83	E5
IL IG1	66	B4
WALTH E17	61	E1
Myrtle St IS N1	12	C2
Myrtle Wk IS N1	12	C2
Mysore Rd BTSEA SW11	133	F2
Myton Rd DUL SE21	155	D3

N

Nadine St CHARL SE7	124	C1
Nairne Gv HNHL SE24	137	D3
Nairn St POP/IOD E14	92	C4
Namba Roy Cl STRHM/NOR SW16	153	F4
Nankin St POP/IOD E14	92	A5
Nansen Rd BTSEA SW11	134	A2
Nantes Cl WAND/EARL SW18	132	C2
Nant Rd CRICK NW2	53	F4
Nant St BETH E2	90	B2
Naoroji St IS N1	10	A4
Napier Av FUL/PGN SW6	131	F1
POP/IOD E14	122	A1
Napier Cl DEPT SE8	121	F3
Napier Ct LEE/GVPK SE12	160	B2
Napier Gv IS N1	11	F2
Napier Pl WKENS W14	101	F4
Napier Rd EHAM E6	83	F1
SRTFD E15	93	E1
WAN E11	63	E5
WKENS W14	101	F4
WLSDN NW10	88	B2
Napier Ter IS N1	76	B5
Napoleon Rd CLPT E5	60	B5
Narbonne Av CLAP SW4	134	C5
Narborough St FUL/PGN SW6	114	B5
Narcissus Rd KIL/WHAMP NW6	72	A2
Narford Rd CLPT E5	60	A5
Narrow Boat Cl THMD SE28	109	D3
Narrow St ACT W3	98	B2
POP/IOD E14	103	E1
Nascot St SHB W12	88	C5
Naseby Cl KIL/WHAMP NW6 *	72	C4
Nash Rd BROCKY SE4	139	E2
Nash St CAMTN NW1	7	D3
Nasmyth St HMSMTH W6	100	B4
Nassau Rd BARN SW13	111	F4
Nassau St GTPST W1W	19	E3
Nassington Rd HAMP NW3	73	E1
Natal Rd IL IG1	66	C1
Nathaniel Cl WCHPL E1	25	F3
Nathan Wy THMD SE28	109	F4
National Ter BERM/RHTH SE16 *	102	B3
Naval Rw POP/IOD E14	104	C1
Navarino Gv HACK E8	78	A3
Navarino Rd HACK E8	78	A3
Navarre Rd EHAM E6	95	E1
Navarre St BETH E2	13	E5
Navy St CLAP SW4	135	D1
Nayim Pl HACK E8	78	B3
Naylor Rd PECK SE15	120	B3
Nazareth Cl PECK SE15	120	B5
Nazrul St BETH E2	13	E4
Nealden St BRXN/ST SW9	135	F1
Neal St LSO/SEVD WC2H	20	C5
Neal Ter FSTH SE23	157	D1
Neal Yd LSO/SEVD WC2H	20	C5
Neasden Cl WLSDN NW10	69	D2
Neasden La WLSDN NW10	51	D5
Neate St CMBW SE5	119	F2
Neathouse Pl PIM SW1V	43	E4
Neatscourt Rd EHAM E6	95	D4
Neckinger BERM/RHTH SE16	49	F2
Neckinger Est BERM/RHTH SE16	49	F2
Neckinger St STHWK SE1	49	F1
Nectarine Wy LEW SE13	122	B5
Needham Rd NTGHL W11	14	A5
Needleman St BERM/RHTH SE16	103	D3
Neeld Crs WBLY HA9	68	A2
Neils Yd LSO/SEVD WC2H *	20	C5
Nelgarde Rd CAT SE6	140	A5
Nella Rd HMSMTH W6	113	D2
Nelldale Rd BERM/RHTH SE16	102	B5
Nello James Gdns WNWD SE27	155	D4
Nelson Gdns BETH E2	90	A2
Nelson Mandela Rd BKHTH/KID SE3	142	C1
Nelson Pl IS N1	11	D2
Nelson Rd GNWCH SE10	122	C2
Nelson Sq STHWK SE1	34	C5
Nelsons Rw CLAP SW4	135	D2
Nelson St CAN/RD E16	105	F1
EHAM E6	84	A5
WCHPL E1	90	A5
Nelson Ter FSBYE EC1V	11	D2
Nemoure Rd ACT W3	98	C1
Nepaul Rd BTSEA SW11	115	E5
Nepean St PUT/ROE SW15	130	A4
Neptune St BERM/RHTH SE16	102	C4
Nesbit Cl BKHTH/KID SE3	141	E1
Nesbit Rd ELTH/MOT SE9	143	D2
Nesham St WAP E1W	102	A2
Ness St BERM/RHTH SE16	102	A4
Netheravon Rd CHSWK W4	99	F5
Netheravon Rd South CHSWK W4	111	F2
Netherby Rd FSTH SE23	138	C5
Netherfield Gdns BARK IG11	85	D3
Netherfield Rd TOOT SW17	152	A3
Netherford Rd VX/NE SW8	116	C5
Netherhall Gdns HAMP NW3	72	C2
Netherhall Wy HAMP NW3	72	C2
Netherleigh Cl HGT N6	56	B3
Netherton Gv WBPTN SW10	114	C2
Netherton Rd SEVS/STOTM N15	59	D1
Netherwood Pl HMSMTH W6 *	101	D4
Netherwood Rd WKENS W14	101	D4

Netherwood St KIL/WHAMP NW6 .... 71 F4
Netley St CAMTN NW1 .... 7 E4
Nettleden Av WBLY HA9 .... 68 A3
Nettlefold Pl WNWD SE27 .... 154 B3
Nettleton Rd NWCR SE14 .... 121 D1
Neuchatel Rd CAT SE6 .... 157 F2
Nevada St GNWCH SE10 .... 122 C3
Nevern Pl ECT SW5 .... 38 B5
Nevern Rd ECT SW5 .... 38 A5
Nevern Sq ECT SW5 .... 38 A5
Neville Cl ACT W3 .... 98 C5
    BFN/LL DA15 .... 163 F4
    CAMTN NW1 .... 8 B2
    KIL/WHAMP NW6 .... 89 F1
    PECK SE15 .... 120 A3
    WAN E11 .... 63 F5
Neville Dr EFNCH N2 .... 54 C1
Neville Gill Cl WAND/EARL SW18 .... 132 A4
Neville Pl FSTGT E7 .... 82 A4
    KIL/WHAMP NW6 * 89 F1
Neville St SKENS SW7 .... 115 D1
Neville Ter SKENS SW7 * 115 D1
Nevill Rd STNW/STAM N16 .... 77 E1
Nevinson Cl WAND/EARL SW18 .... 133 D4
Nevis Rd TOOT SW17 .... 152 A2
New Acres Rd THMD SE28 .... 109 E1
Newark Crs WLSDN NW10 .... 87 D2
Newark Knok EHAM E6 .... 96 A5
Newark St WCHPL E1 .... 90 B4
Newbold Cots WCHPL E1 * 90 C5
New Bond St MYFR/PICC W1J 31 D1
New Bridge St EMB EC4V 22 C5
New Broad St LVPST EC2M 24 B3
Newburgh Rd ACT W3 .... 98 C2
Newburgh St SOHO/CST W1F 19 E5
New Burlington Ms CONDST W1S * ... 31 E1
New Burlington Pl CONDST W1S * 31 E1
New Burlington St CONDST W1S 31 E1
Newburn St LBTH SE11 .... 117 F1
Newbury Ms KTTN NW5 .... 74 A3
Newbury Rd GNTH/NBYPK IG2 .... 67 D3
Newbury St STBT EC1A 23 E2
New Butt La DEPT SE8 .... 122 A4
Newby Pl POP/IOD E14 .... 104 C1
Newby St VX/NE SW8 .... 134 B1
Newcastle Cl FLST/FETLN EC4A 22 C4
Newcastle Pl BAY/PAD W2 .... 16 B3
Newcastle Rw CLKNW EC1R 22 B1
New Cavendish St CAVSQ/HST W1G .. 18 B3
New Change STP EC4M 23 E5
New Charles St FSBYE EC1V 11 D3
New Church Rd CMBW SE5 .... 118 C3
New City Rd PLSTW E13 .... 94 C2
New College Ms IS N1 * 76 A4
New College Pde HAMP NW3 * 72 C3
Newcombe St KENS W8 * 26 B3
Newcome Gdns STRHM/NOR SW16 .. 153 E4
Newcomen Rd BTSEA SW11 .... 133 D1
    WAN E11 * 63 F5
Newcomen St STHWK SE1 .... 36 A5
New Compton St LSQ/SEVD WC2H *.. 20 B5
Newcourt St EMB EC4Y * 34 A1
Newcourt St STJWD NW8 .... 4 C2
New Crane Pl WAP E1W * 102 C2
New Crescent Yd WLSDN NW10 * 87 F1
New Cross Rd NWCR SE14 .... 120 C3
Newdigate STRHM/NOR SW16 * 154 A4
Newell St POP/IOD E14 .... 104 A1
New End HAMP NW3 .... 72 C1
New End Sq HAMP NW3 .... 73 D1
Newent Cl PECK SE15 .... 119 E3
New Era Est IS N1 * 77 E5
New Ferry Ap WOOL/PLUM SE18 ..... 108 A4
New Fetter La FLST/FETLN EC4A 22 B4
Newfield Cl HDN NW4 .... 52 A5
Newgate St STBT EC1A 23 D4
New Globe Wk STHWK SE1 .... 35 E3
New Goulston St WCHPL E1 .... 25 D4
New Green Pl BRXS/STRHM SW2 .... 136 A5
Newham's Rw STHWK SE1 .... 49 D1
Newham Wy CAN/RD E16 .... 93 F4
    EHAM E6 .... 95 E3
Newhaven Gdns ELTH/MOT SE9 ..... 143 D2
Newhaven La CAN/RD E16 .... 94 A4
Newick Rd CLPT E5 .... 60 B5
Newington Barrow Wy HOLWY N7 ... 57 F5
Newington Butts WALW SE17 .... 47 D5
Newington Cswy STHWK SE1 .... 47 E2
Newington Gn IS N1 .... 77 D2
Newington Green Rd IS N1 .... 77 D2

New Inn Broadway SDTCH EC2A * 13 D5
New Inn Sq SDTCH EC2A * 13 D5
New Inn St SDTCH EC2A 13 D5
New Inn Yd SDTCH EC2A 13 D5
New Kent Rd WALW SE17 .... 47 F4
New King's Rd FUL/PGN SW6 .... 114 A4
New King St DEPT SE8 .... 122 A2
Newland Ct WBLY HA9 * 50 A2
Newlands Quay WAP E1W 102 C1
Newland St CAN/RD E16 .... 107 E2
Newling St BETH E2 .... 13 E5
Newling Est BETH E2 .... 13 E5
New London St MON EC3R * 37 D1
New Lydenburg St CHARL SE7 .... 106 C2
Newlyn Rd WELL DA16 .... 127 F5
Newman Rd PLSTW E13 .... 94 B2
Newman's Rw LINN WC2A 21 F3
Newman St FITZ W1T 19 F3
Newmarsh Rd THMD SE28 .... 109 F2
New Mount St SRTFD E15 .... 81 D4
Newnham Ter STHWK SE1 .... 46 A2
New North Pl SDTCH EC2A 12 C5
New North Rd IS N1 .... 12 B2
New North St BMSBY WC1N 21 E2
Newnton Cl FSBYPK N4 .... 59 D2
New Oxford St NOXST/BSQ WC1A ... 20 B4
New Park Rd BRXS/STRHM SW2 ...... 135 E5
New Place Sq BERM/RHTH SE16 * ... 102 B4
New Plaistow Rd SRTFD E15 .... 81 E5
Newport Av PLSTW E13 .... 94 B3
    POP/IOD E14 .... 105 D1
Newport Cl ISLG/SEVD WC2H 32 B1
Newport Pl SOHO/SHAV W1D * 32 B1
Newport Rd ACT W3 .... 98 C3
    BARN SW13 .... 112 A4
    LEY E10 .... 63 D4
Newport St LBTH SE11 .... 45 E5
Newquay Rd CAT SE6 .... 158 B2
New Quebec St MBLAR W1H 17 F5
New River Wy FSBYPK N4 .... 59 D2
New Rd GDMY/SEVK IG3 .... 67 E4
    WCHPL E1 .... 90 A4
New Row CHCR WC2N 32 C1
New Spring Gardens Wk
    STHWK SE1 * 117 E1
New Sq LINN WC2A 21 F4
Newstead Rd LEE/GVPK SE12 .... 141 F5
Newstead Wy WIM/MER SW19 .... 149 D4
New St LVPST EC2M 25 D3
New Street HI BMLY BR1 .... 160 B5
New Street Sq FLST/FETLN EC4A 22 B4
Newton Av ACT W3 .... 98 C3
Newton Cl WALTH E17 .... 61 E1
Newton Gv CHSWK W4 .... 99 E4
Newton Pl POP/IOD E14 .... 104 A5
Newton Rd BAY/PAD W2 .... 14 B5
    CRICK NW2 .... 70 C1
    SRTFD E15 .... 81 D2
Newton St HOL/ALD WC2B 21 D4
Newton's Yd WAND/EARL SW18 ...... 132 A3
New Tower Bldgs WAP E1W * 102 B2
Newtown St BTSEA SW11 .... 116 B4
New Union Cl POP/IOD E14 .... 104 C4
New Union St BARB EC2Y 24 A3
New Wanstead WAN E11 .... 64 A1
New Wharf Rd IS N1 .... 9 D1
Niagara Cl IS N1 .... 11 F1
Nicholas La MANHO EC4N 36 B1
Nicholas Pas WCHPL E1 * 90 C3
Nicholay Rd ARCH N19 .... 57 D3
Nichollsfield Wk HOLWY N7 .... 75 E2
Nicholl St BETH E2 .... 78 A5
Nichols Cl FSBYPK N4 * 58 A3
Nicholson House CHARL SE7 * 125 E3
Nicholson St STHWK SE1 .... 34 C4
Nickols Wk WAND/EARL SW18 .... 132 B2
Nicoll Pl HDN NW4 .... 52 A1
Nicoll Rd WLSDN NW10 .... 69 E5
Nicosia Rd WAND/EARL SW18 .... 133 E5
Niederwald Rd SYD SE26 .... 157 E4
Nigel Ms IL IG1 .... 84 B1
Nigel Playfair Av HMSMTH W6 .... 100 B5
Nigel Rd FSTGT E7 .... 82 C2
    PECK SE15 .... 138 A1
Nigeria Rd CHARL SE7 .... 124 C3
Nightingale Cl CHSWK W4 .... 110 C2
Nightingale Gv LEW SE13 .... 141 D3
Nightingale La BAL SW12 .... 134 A4
Nightingale Ms LBTH SE11 .... 46 B4
Nightingale Pl WBPTN SW10 .... 114 C2
    WOOL/PLUM SE18 .... 126 A2
Nightingale Rd CLPT E5 .... 60 B5

WLSDN NW10 .... 87 F1
Nightingale Sq BAL SW12 .... 134 A5
Nightingale V WOOL/PLUM SE18 .... 126 A2
Nightingale Wk WOOL/PLUM SE18 .... 136 B4
Nightingale Wy EHAM E6 .... 95 E4
Nile Cl STNW/STAM N16 .... 59 F5
Nile Rd PLSTW E13 .... 94 C1
Nile St IS N1 .... 12 A3
Nile Ter PECK SE15 .... 119 F1
Nimrod Pas IS N1 * 77 E3
Nina Mackay Cl SRTFD E15 * 81 E5
Nine Acres Cl MNPK E12 .... 83 E2
Nine Elms La VX/NE SW8 .... 116 C3
Nithdale Rd WOOL/PLUM SE18 .... 126 B5
Niton Rd RCH/KEW TW9 * 128 A1
Niton St FUL/PGN SW6 .... 113 D5
No1 St WOOL/PLUM SE18 .... 108 B4
No2 St WOOL/PLUM SE18 .... 108 B4
Noble St CITYW EC2V 23 E4
Noel Rd ACT W3 .... 86 A5
    EHAM E6 .... 95 E5
    IS N1 .... 6 A5
Noel St SOHO/CST W1F 19 F5
Nolan Wy CLPT E5 .... 78 A1
Norbiton Rd POP/IOD E14 .... 91 F5
Norbroke St SHB W12 .... 99 F1
Norburn St NKENS W10 .... 89 E4
Norcott Rd STNW/STAM N16 .... 60 A4
Norcroft Gdns EDUL SE22 .... 138 A5
Norfolk Av SEVS/STOTM N15 .... 59 E1
Norfolk Crs BAY/PAD W2 .... 16 A4
    BFN/LL DA15 .... 145 E5
Norfolk House Rd STRHM/NOR SW16 ...... 153 D5
Norfolk Ms NKENS W10 .... 89 E4
Norfolk Pl BAY/PAD W2 .... 16 B4
Norfolk Rd BARK IG11 .... 85 E4
    EHAM E6 .... 83 E5
    GDMY/SEVK IG3 .... 67 E3
    STJWD NW8 .... 73 D5
    WLSDN NW10 .... 69 E4
Norfolk Rw STHWK SE1 .... 45 E4
Norfolk Sq BAY/PAD W2 .... 16 B5
Norfolk Square Ms BAY/PAD W2 * 16 B5
Norgrove St BAL SW12 .... 152 A1
Norland Pl NTGHL W11 .... 101 E2
Norland Rd NTGHL W11 .... 101 D2
Norland Sq NTGHL W11 .... 101 E2
Norley V PUT/ROE SW15 .... 148 A1
Norlington Rd LEY E10 .... 62 C3
Normanby Cl PUT/ROE SW15 .... 131 D5
Normanby Rd WLSDN NW10 .... 69 F2
Normand Gdns WKENS W14 * 113 E2
Normand Ms WKENS W14 .... 113 E2
Normand Rd WKENS W14 .... 113 E2
Normandy Cl SYD SE26 .... 157 E3
Normandy Rd BRXN/ST SW9 .... 118 A4
Normandy Ter CAN/RD E16 .... 94 B3
Norman Gv BOW E3 .... 91 E1
Normanhurst Rd BRXS/STRHM SW2 .... 153 F2
Norman Rd EHAM E6 .... 95 E4
    GNWCH SE10 .... 122 B5
    IL IG1 .... 84 B2
    WAN E11 .... 63 E4
Normans Cl WLSDN NW10 .... 69 D3
Normans Md WLSDN NW10 .... 69 D3
Norman St FSBYE EC1V 11 E4
Norman Ter KIL/WHAMP NW6 * 71 F2
Normanton Av WAND/EARL SW18 .... 150 A2
Normanton St SELH SE23 .... 157 D2
Norman Wy ACT W3 .... 86 B4
Normington Cl STRHM/NOR SW16 .... 154 A5
Norris St STJS SW1Y 32 A3
Norroy Rd PUT/ROE SW15 .... 131 D2
Norstead Pl PUT/ROE SW15 .... 148 A2
North Access Rd WALTH E17 .... 61 D1
North Acton Rd WLSDN NW10 .... 87 D1
Northampton Gv IS N1 .... 77 D2
Northampton Pk IS N1 .... 76 C3
Northampton Rd CLKNW EC1R 10 B5
Northampton Rw CLKNW EC1R * 10 C4
Northampton Sq FSBYE EC1V 10 C4
Northampton St IS N1 .... 76 C4
North Audley St MYFR/PKLN W1K 30 A1
North Av RCH/KEW TW9 .... 110 A4
North Bank STJWD NW8 .... 4 C4
North Birkbeck Rd WAN E11 .... 63 D5
Northbourne Rd CLAP SW4 .... 135 D2
Northbrook Rd IL IG1 .... 66 A4
    LEW SE13 .... 141 D3
Northburgh St FSBYE EC1V 23 D1
North Carriage Dr BAY/PAD W2 .... 29 D1

The North Colonnade POP/IOD E14 .... 108 B2
Northcote Rd BTSEA SW11 .... 133 E2
    SCUP DA14 .... 163 E4
    WLSDN NW10 .... 69 E4
Northcourt FITZ W1T 19 F2
North Crs CAN/RD E16 .... 93 D5
    GWRST WC1E 20 A2
North Cross Rd EDUL SE22 .... 137 F3
Northdene Gdns SEVS/STOTM N15 .... 59 E1
Northdown St IS N1 .... 9 E2
North Dr STRHM/NOR SW16 .... 152 B1
North End NWMS NW3 .... 54 C4
North End Av HAMP NW3 .... 54 C4
North End Crs WKENS W14 .... 101 F5
North End Rd FUL/PGN SW6 .... 114 A3
    GLDGN NW11 .... 54 A3
    HAMP NW3 .... 50 A5
    WKENS W14 .... 101 E5
North End Wy HAMP NW3 .... 54 C4
Northern Relief Rd BARK IG11 * 84 C4
North Eyot Gdns HMSMTH W6 * 111 F1
Northey St POP/IOD E14 .... 103 E1
Northfield Rd EHAM E6 .... 83 F3
    STNW/STAM N16 .... 59 E2
Northfields WAND/EARL SW18 .... 132 A2
Northfields Rd ACT W3 .... 86 C4
Northgate Dr CDALE/KGS NW9 .... 51 E1
North Gower St CAMTN NW1 .... 7 E4
North Gv HGT N6 .... 56 A2
North Hl HGT N6 .... 55 F1
North Hill Av HGT N6 .... 55 F1
Northiam St HACK E8 .... 78 B5
Northington St BMSBY WC1N 21 E2
Northlands St CMBW SE5 .... 118 C5
North Lodge Cl PUT/ROE SW15 * 131 D3
North Ms BMSBY WC1N 21 F1
Northolme Rd HBRY N5 .... 76 C1
Northover BMLY BR1 .... 159 F4
North Pk ELTH/MOT SE9 .... 143 F4
North Pas WAND/EARL SW18 .... 132 A3
North Peckham Est PECK SE15 .... 119 F3
North Pole Rd SHB W12 .... 88 C4
Northport St IS N1 .... 77 D5
North Ri BAY/PAD W2 * 17 D5
North Rd GDMY/SEVK IG3 .... 67 E4
    HGT N6 .... 56 A2
    HOLWY N7 .... 75 E3
    RCH/KEW TW9 .... 110 A5
    WOOL/PLUM SE18 .... 109 E5
North Rw MYFR/PKLN W1K 29 F1
North Several BKHTH/KID SE3 * 123 D5
North Side Wandsworth Common
    WAND/EARL SW18 .... 132 C3
North Sq GLDGN NW11 .... 54 A1
Northstead Rd BRXS/STRHM SW2 .... 154 A2
North St BARK IG11 .... 84 B4
    CLAP SW4 .... 134 B1
    PLSTW E13 .... 94 B1
North Tenter St WCHPL E1 .... 25 F5
North Ter SKENS SW7 .... 40 C4
Northumberland Aly
    FENCHST EC3M * 25 D5
Northumberland Av CHCR WC2N 32 C3
    MNPK E12 .... 64 C3
    WELL DA16 .... 145 E2
Northumberland Pl BAY/PAD W2 .... 14 A4
Northumberland Rd EHAM E6 .... 95 E4
    WALTH E17 .... 62 A2
Northumberland St CHCR WC2N 32 C3
Northumbria St POP/IOD E14 .... 92 A5
North Verbena Gdns HMSMTH W6 * 112 A1
North Vw WIM/MER SW19 .... 148 B5
Northview Crs WLSDN NW10 .... 69 F1
Northview Pde HOLWY N7 * 57 E5
North Vls CAMTN NW1 .... 75 D3
Northway CR CMBW SE5 .... 136 C1
Northways Pde HAMP NW3 * 73 D4
North Wharf Rd BAY/PAD W2 .... 16 A3
Northwick Cl STJWD NW8 .... 4 A5
Northwick Ter STJWD NW8 .... 4 A5
Northwold Rd STNW/STAM N16 .... 60 A4
Northwood Rd FSTH SE23 .... 157 F1
    HGT N6 .... 56 B2

North Woolwich Rd *CAN/RD* E16...... 105 F2
North Worple Wy *MORT/ESHN* SW14.. 129 F1
Norton Folgate *WCHPL* E1.............. 25 D1
Norton Rd *LEY* E10....................... 61 F3
Norval Gn *BRXN/ST* SW9 *.............. 138 A1
Norway Ga *BERM/RHTH* SE16.......... 105 E4
Norway Pl *POP/IOD* E14................. 91 F5
Norway St *GNWCH* SE10................ 122 B2
Norwich Rd *FSTGT* E7................... 82 A2
Norwich Rd *FLST/FETLN* EC4A.......... 22 A4
Norwood Cl *CRICK* NW2................. 53 E5
Norwood High St *WNWD* SE27........ 154 B3
Norwood Park Rd *WNWD* SE27......... 154 B2
Norwood Rd *WNWD* SE27............... 154 B2
Notley St *CMBW* SE5................... 119 D3
Notting Barn Rd *NKENS* W10........... 89 D3
Nottingdale Sq *NTGHL* W11 *.......... 101 E2
Nottingham Av *CAN/RD* E16........... 94 C4
Nottingham Ct *LSQ/SEVD* WC2H....... 20 C5
Nottingham Pl *CAMTN* NW1........... 18 A1
Nottingham Rd *LEY* E10................ 62 C1
Nottingham Rd *TOOT* SW17............ 151 F1
Nottingham St *MHST* W1U............. 18 A2
Nottingham Ter *CAMTN* NW1.......... 18 A1
Notting Hill Ga *NTGHL* W11............ 26 B3
Novar Rd *ELTH/MOT* SE9............... 162 C1
Novello St *FUL/PGN* SW6.............. 114 A4
Nowell Rd *BARN* SW13................. 111 F2
Noyna Rd *TOOT* SW17................... 151 F3
Nubia Wy *BMLY* BR1.................... 159 E4
Nuding Cl *LEW* SE13................... 140 A1
Nugent Rd *ARCH* N19.................. 57 E3
Nugent Ter *STJWD* NW8................. 3 F2
Nunhead Crs *PECK* SE15............... 138 B1
Nunhead Gv *PECK* SE15................ 138 B1
Nunhead La *PECK* SE15................ 138 B1
Nunnington Cl *ELTH/MOT* SE9......... 161 E3
Nursery Cl *BROCKY* SE4................ 121 F5
Nursery Cl *PUT/ROE* SW15............ 131 D3
Nursery La *BETH* E2.................... 77 F5
Nursery La *FSTGT* E7................... 82 A3
Nursery La *NKENS* W10................. 88 C4
Nursery Rd *BRXN/ST* SW9 *............ 135 F2
Nursery Rd *HOM* E9.................... 78 C3
Nursery Rw *WALW* SE17............... 48 A5
Nutbourne St *NKENS* W10.............. 89 D2
Nutbrook St *PECK* SE15................ 137 F1
Nutcroft Rd *PECK* SE15................ 120 B3
Nutfield Gdns *GDMY/SEVK* IG3....... 67 F4
Nutfield Rd *CRICK* NW2................ 52 A4
Nutfield Rd *EDUL* SE22................ 137 E3
Nutfield Rd *SRTFD* E15................ 80 C1
Nutford Pl *MBLAR* W1H................ 17 D4
Nuthatch Gdns *THMD* SE28............ 109 D3
Nuthurst Av *BRXS/STRHM* SW2........ 153 F2
Nutley Ter *HAMP* NW3.................. 73 D3
Nutmeg Cl *CAN/RD* E16................ 93 D3
Nutmeg La *POP/IOD* E14................ 93 D5
Nuttall St *IS* N1........................ 13 D1
Nutt St *PECK* SE15...................... 119 E3
Nutwell St *TOOT* SW17................. 151 E5
Nyanza St *WOOL/PLUM* SE18........... 127 D2
Nylands Av *RCH/KEW* TW9............. 110 A5
Nynehead St *NWCR* SE14.............. 121 E3
Nyon Gv *CAT* SE6....................... 157 F2
Nyton Cl *ARCH* N19.................... 57 E3

O

Oakbank Gv *HNHL* SE24................ 136 C2
Oakbrook Cl *BMLY* BR1................. 160 B4
Oakbury Rd *FUL/PGN* SW6............. 114 B5
Oak Cottage Cl *CAT* SE6............... 159 E1
Oak Crs *CAN/RD* E16................... 93 E4
Oakcroft Rd *LEW* SE13................ 123 D5
Oakdale Rd *FSBYPK* N4................ 58 C1
Oakdale Rd *FSTGT* E7.................. 82 B4
Oakdale Rd *PECK* SE15................ 138 B1
Oakdale Rd *STRHM/NOR* SW16....... 153 E5
Oakdale Rd *WAN* E11................... 63 D4
Oakdene Av *CHST* BR7.................. 162 A5
Oakden St *LBTH* SE11.................. 46 B4
Oakeshott Av *HGT* N6.................. 56 A4
Oakey La *STHWK* SE1.................. 46 A2
Oakfield Rd *EHAM* E6................... 83 E5
Oakfield Rd *FSBYPK* N4................ 58 A1
Oakfield Rd *IL* IG1..................... 66 B5
Oakfield Rd *WIM/MER* SW19........... 149 E3
Oakfields Rd *GLDGN* NW11............ 53 E1

North Woolwich Rd *CAN/RD* E16...... 105 F2
Oakford Rd *KTTN* NW5.................. 74 C1
Oak Hall Rd *WAN* E11................... 63 F1
Oakham Cl *CAT* SE6 *.................. 157 F2
Oakhill Av *HAMP* NW3................. 72 B1
Oak Hill Pk *HAMP* NW3................. 72 B1
Oak Hill Park Ms *HAMP* NW3.......... 72 C1
Oakhill Pl *PUT/ROE* SW15............. 132 A3
Oakhill Rd *PUT/ROE* SW15............. 131 F2
Oak Hill Wy *HAMP* NW3................ 54 C5
Oak Hill Wy *HAMP* NW3................ 72 B1
Oakhurst Gv *EDUL* SE22............... 138 A2
Oakington Manor Dr *WBLY* HA9....... 68 A2
Oakington Rd *MV/WKIL* W9............ 2 B5
Oakington Wy *CEND/HSY/T* N8........ 57 E1
Oakland Rd *SRTFD* E15................. 81 E1
Oaklands Av *BFN/LL* DA15............. 145 F5
Oaklands Av *IS* N1..................... 13 D1
Oaklands Gv *SHB* W12.................. 100 A2
Oaklands Ms *CRICK* NW2............... 71 D1
Oaklands Pk *IL* IG1.................... 66 C4
Oaklands Pl *CLAP* SW4 *............... 135 D2
Oaklands Rd *CRICK* NW2............... 71 D1
Oaklands Rd *MORT/ESHN* SW14....... 129 D1
Oak La *POP/IOD* E14.................... 103 F1
Oakley Av *BARK* IG11................... 85 F4
Oakley Cl *EHAM* E6..................... 95 E5
Oakley Cl *FSBYE* EC1V *................ 11 D2
Oakley Crs *FSBYE* EC1V *............... 11 D2
Oakley Dr *CAT* SE6...................... 141 D4
Oakley Dr *ELTH/MOT* SE9.............. 163 D1
Oakley Gdns *CHEL* SW3................. 115 E2
Oakley Pl *STHWK* SE1................... 119 F1
Oakley Rd *IS* N1........................ 77 D4
Oakley Sq *CAMTN* NW1................. 7 F1
Oakley St *CHEL* SW3.................... 115 E2
Oakley Yd *BETH* E2 *................... 13 F5
Oakmead Rd *BAL* SW12................. 152 A4
Oak Park Gdns *WIM/MER* SW19........ 149 D1
Oakridge La *BMLY* BR1................. 159 D5
Oakridge Rd *BMLY* BR1................. 159 E4
Oaks Av *NRWD* SE19.................... 155 E5
Oaksford Av *SYD* SE26................. 156 B3
Oakshade Rd *BMLY* BR1................ 159 D4
Oakshaw Rd *WAND/EARL* SW18....... 132 B5
The Oaks *WOOL/PLUM* SE18........... 126 C1
Oak Tree Gdns *BMLY* BR1.............. 160 B5
Oaktree Gv *IL* IG1...................... 85 D2
Oak Tree Rd *STJWD* NW8............... 4 B4
Oakview Rd *CAT* SE6................... 158 B5
Oak Village *KTTN* NW5................. 74 A1
Oak Vis *GLDGN* NW11 *................ 53 F1
Oak Wy *ACT* W3......................... 99 E2
Oakways *ELTH/MOT* SE9................ 144 B4
Oakwood Cl *LEW* SE13................. 141 D5
Oakwood Ct *WKENS* W14............... 101 F4
Oakwood Gdns *GDMY/SEVK* IG3....... 67 F4
Oakwood La *WKENS* W14............... 101 F4
Oakworth Rd *NKENS* W10............... 88 C4
Oat La *CITYW* EC2V..................... 23 E4
Oban Cl *PLSTW* E13.................... 94 C3
Oban Rd *PLSTW* E13.................... 94 C2
Oban St *POP/IOD* E14.................. 93 D5
Oberstein Rd *BTSEA* SW11............ 133 D2
Oborne Cl *HNHL* SE24................. 136 B3
Observatory Gdns *KENS* W8............ 26 A5
Observatory Rd *MORT/ESHN* SW14.... 128 C2
Observatory Rd *SKENS* SW7............ 40 B2
Occupation La *WOOL/PLUM* SE18..... 126 B4
Occupation Rd *WALW* SE17............ 118 C5
Ocean Est *WCHPL* E1................... 91 D3
Ocean St *WCHPL* E1.................... 91 D4
Ockendon Ms *IS* N1 *.................. 77 D3
Ockendon Rd *IS* N1.................... 77 D3
Ockley Rd *STRHM/NOR* SW16.......... 153 E4
Octagon Ar *LVPST* EC2M *.............. 24 C3
Octavia Ms *CRICK* NW2 *............... 70 B3
Octavia Rd *BTSEA* SW11............... 115 E4
Octavius St *DEPT* SE8.................. 122 A3
Odell Cl *BARK* IG11.................... 85 F4
Odell Wk *LEW* SE13.................... 140 B1
Odeon Pde *ELTH/MOT* SE9 *........... 143 E2
Odeon Pde *ELTH/MOT* SE9 *
     HOLWY N7 *....................... 57 E5
Odessa Rd *FSTGT* E7.................... 81 F1
Odessa Rd *WLSDN* NW10................ 88 A1
Odessa St *BERM/RHTH* SE16........... 105 F4
Odger St *BTSEA* SW11.................. 115 F5
Odhams Wk *LSQ/SEVD* WC2H *......... 20 C5
Odsey Vls *FSBYPK* N4 *................. 58 A1
Offa's Md *HOM* E9...................... 79 E1
Offenham Rd *ELTH/MOT* SE9........... 161 F4
Offerton Rd *CLAP* SW4................. 134 C1

Offley Rd *BRXN/ST* SW9...............118 A3
Offord Rd *IS* N1...........................75 F4
Offord St *HOLWY* N7.....................75 F4
Ogilby St *WOOL/PLUM* SE18........107 F5
Oglander Rd *PECK* SE15..............137 F2
Ogle St *GTPST* W1W.....................19 E2
Ohio Rd *PLSTW* E13.......................93 F3
Oil Mill La *HMSMTH* W6...............112 A1
Okeburn Rd *TOOT* SW17..............152 A5
Okehampton Rd *WLSDN* NW10......70 C5
Olaf St *NTGHL* W11.......................101 D1
Old Bailey *STP* EC4M....................23 D5
Old Barrack Yd *KTBR* SW1X...........30 A5
Old Bellgate Whf *POP/IOD* E14....104 A4
Old Bethnal Green Rd *BETH* E2.....90 B2
Old Bond St *CONDST* W1S.............31 E2
Old Brewery Ms *HAMP* NW3...........73 D1
Old Broad St *LVPST* EC2M.............24 C4
  OBST EC2N.....................................24 B4
Old Bromley Rd *BMLY* BR1...........159 D5
Old Brompton Rd *ECT* SW5...........114 B1
Old Blds *LINN* WC2A.....................22 B2
Old Burlington St *CONDST* W1S.....31 E1
Oldbury Pl *MHST* W1U....................18 B2
Old Castle St *WCHPL* E1................25 E4
Old Cavendish St *OXSTW* W1C.......18 C5
Old Church La *CDALE/KGS* NW9.....50 C4
Old Church Rd *WCHPL* E1 *..............91 D5
Old Church St *CHEL* SW3..............115 D1
Old Compton St *SOHO/SHAV* W1D...32 A1
Old Court Pl *KENS* W8...................26 C5
Old Dairy Ms *BAL* SW12...............152 A1
  KTTN NW5 *......................................74 B3
Old Devonshire Rd *BAL* SW12......134 B5
Old Dock Cl *RCH/KEW* TW9..........110 A2
Old Dover Rd *BKHTH/KID* SE3.......124 A3
Old Farm Av *BFN/LL* DA15............163 D1
Old Farm Rd *BFN/LL* DA15............163 D1
Old Farm Rd West *BFN/LL* DA15...163 D2
Oldfield Gv *BERM/RTHTH* SE16.....103 D5
Oldfield Ms *HGT* N6.......................56 C2
Oldfield Rd *ACT* W3.......................99 F3
  STNW/STAM N16..............................59 E5
  WLSDN NW10...................................69 F4
Old Fish Street Hl *BLKFR* EC4V *.....35 E1
Old Fleet La *FLST/FETLN* EC4A......22 B4
Old Ford Lock *BOW* E3 *................80 A4
Old Ford Rd *BETH* E2.....................90 C1
  BOW E3...79 E5
Old Forge Ms *SHB* W12................100 B3
Old Forge Rd *ARCH* N19................57 D2
Old Gloucester St *BMSBY* WC1N....21 D2
Oldham Ter *ACT* W3.......................98 C2
Oldhill St *STNW/STAM* N16.............60 A3
Old Hospital Cl *BAL* SW12............151 F1
Old House Cl *WIM/MER* SW19........149 E5
Old Jamaica Rd *BERM/RTHTH* SE16...102 A4
Old James St *PECK* SE15.............138 B1
Old Jewry *LOTH* EC2R.....................24 A5
Old Kent Rd *PECK* SE15................120 B2
  STHWK SE1..48 C4
Old Manor Wy *CHST* BR7..............161 F5
Old Market Sq *BETH* E2.................13 E3
Old Marylebone Rd *CAMTN* NW1....17 D3
Old Mill Rd *WOOL/PLUM* SE18.....127 D2
Old Mitre Ct *EMB* EC4Y *...............22 B5
Old Montague St *WCHPL* E1...........90 A4
Old Nichol St *BETH* E2...................13 E5
Old North St *FSBYW* WC1X *...........21 E2
Old Oak Common La *ACT* W3..........99 F1
  WLSDN NW10...................................85 E1
Old Oak La *WLSDN* NW10...............87 F2
Old Oak Rd *ACT* W3.......................99 F1
The Old Orch *HAMP* NW3...............73 F1
Old Palace Yd *WHALL* SW1A..........44 C2
Old Paradise St *LBTH* SE11............45 E4
Old Park Av *BAL* SW12..................134 A4
Old Park La *MYFR/PKLN* W1K.........30 B4
Old Pearson St *GNWCH* SE10........122 B3
Old Post Office La *BKHTH/KID* SE3...142 B1
Old Pye St *WEST* SW1P..................44 A2
Old Quebec St *MBLAR* W1H............17 F5
Old Queen St *STJSPK* SW1H...........44 B1
Oldridge Rd *BAL* SW12.................134 A5
Old Rd *LEW* SE13.........................141 E2
Old Royal Free Pl *IS* N1 *...............76 A5
Old Royal Free Sq *IS* N1 *.............76 A5
Old Schools Crs *FSTGT* E7...............81 F3
Old Seacoal La *STP* EC4M.............22 C5
Old South Lambeth Rd *VX/NE* SW8 *...117 E3
Old Sq *LINN* WC2A.........................21 F4
Old Stable Ms *HBRY* N5..................58 C5
Oldstead Rd *BMLY* BR1................159 D4
Old St *FSBYE* EC1V.........................11 E5
  PLSTW E13.......................................94 B1
  STLK EC1Y..12 B5
Old Town *CLAP* SW4....................134 C1
Old Tramyard *WOOL/PLUM* SE18...109 E5
Old Woolwich Rd *GNWCH* SE10....123 D2
Old York Rd *WAND/EARL* SW18.....132 B3
O'Leary Sq *WCHPL* E1....................90 C4
Olga St *BOW* E3.............................91 E1
Olinda Rd *STNW/STAM* N16............59 F1
Oliphant St *NKENS* W10..................89 E2
Oliver Cl *CHSWK* W4.....................110 B2
Oliver Gdns *EHAM* E6.....................95 E4
Oliver Ms *PECK* SE15....................120 A5
Olive Rd *CRICK* NW2.......................70 C1
  PLSTW E13.......................................94 C2
Oliver Rd *LEY* E10..........................62 B5
Oliver's Yd *STLK* EC1Y....................12 B5
Ollerton Gn *BOW* E3.......................79 F5
Ollgar Cl *SHB* W12..........................99 F2
Olliffe St *POP/IOD* E14.................104 C4
Olney St *STHWK* SE1.......................46 B1
Olney Rd *WALW* SE17...................118 B2
Olven Rd *WOOL/PLUM* SE18.........126 C3
Olympia Wy *WKENS* W14...............101 E4
Olympic Wy *WBLY* HA9....................50 A5
Olympus Sq *CLPT* E5........................60 B5
Oman Av *CRICK* NW2.......................70 C2
O'Meara St *STHWK* SE1...................35 F4
Omega Pl *IS* N1..............................9 D2
Omega St *NWCR* SE14..................121 F4
Ommaney Rd *NWCR* SE14.............121 D4
Ondine Rd *PECK* SE15...................137 F2
Onega Gn *BERM/RTHTH* SE16........103 E4
One Tree Cl *FSTH* SE23.................138 C4
Ongar Rd *FUL/PGN* SW6................114 A2
Onra Rd *WALTH* E17.........................62 A2
Onslow Cl *NKENS* W10....................89 F2
Onslow Crs *SKENS* SW7.................40 A5
Onslow Gdns *SKENS* SW7..............40 A5
Onslow Ms East *SKENS* SW7..........40 A5
Onslow Ms West *SKENS* SW7.........40 A5
Onslow Sq *SKENS* SW7...................40 A5
Onslow St *CLKNW* EC1R *...............22 B3
Ontario St *STHWK* SE1....................47 D3
Ontario Wy *POP/IOD* E14..............104 A1
Onyx Ms *SRTFD* E15.......................81 E3
Opal Cl *CAN/RD* E16........................95 D5
Opal Ms *IL* IG1................................66 B4
  KIL/WHAMP NW6..............................71 F5
Opal St *LBTH* SE11..........................46 C5
Openview *WAND/EARL* SW18........132 B1
Oppenheim Rd *LEW* SE13.............122 C5
Oppidans Rd *HAMP* NW3.................73 F4
Orange Gv *WAN* E11........................63 E5
Orange Pl *BERM/RTHTH* SE16.......102 C4
Orangery La *ELTH/MOT* SE9..........143 F5
Orange St *LSQ/SEVD* WC2H............32 B2
  WAP E1W...102 A2
Oransay Rd *IS* N1............................76 C3
Oratory La *CHEL* SW3 *.................115 D1
Orbain Rd *FUL/PGN* SW6...............113 F4
Orbel St *BTSEA* SW11...................115 E4
Orb St *WALW* SE17..........................48 A5
Orchard Cl *CRICK* NW2...................52 A5
  FSTH SE23......................................138 C4
  IS N1..76 C4
  NKENS W10.......................................89 E4
Orchard Dr *BKHTH/KID* SE3..........123 E5
Orchard Hl *LEW* SE13....................122 B4
Orchard Ms *IS* N1...........................77 D4
  TOOT SW17.....................................150 C5
Orchard Pl *POP/IOD* E14...............105 E1
Orchard Ri *RCHPK/HAM* TW10......128 B2
Orchard Ri East *BFN/LL* DA15.......145 E3
Orchard Rd *HGT* N6.........................56 B2
  RCH/KEW TW9..................................128 A1
  SCUP DA14......................................163 E4
Orchardson St *STJWD* NW8.............16 A1
Orchard Sq *WKENS* W14 *.............101 F4
Orchard St *MBLAR* W1H..................18 A5
Orchard Ter *WLSDN* NW10 *............69 F1
The Orchard *BKHTH/KID* SE3 *.....123 D5
  CHSWK W4.......................................99 D5
Orchid Cl *EHAM* E6..........................83 E5
  LEW SE13..141 D3
Orchid St *SHB* W12........................100 A1
Orde Hall St *BMSBY* WC1N *............21 E2
Ordell Rd *BOW* E3...........................91 F1
Ordnance Crs *GNWCH* SE10..........105 E3

Ordnance Hl *STJWD* NW8	73	D5
Ordnance Ms *STJWD* NW8	4	B1
Ordnance Rd *CAN/RD* E16	93	F4
WOOL/PLUM SE18	126	A2
Oregano Dr *POP/IOD* E14	93	D5
Oregon Av *MNPK* E12	83	F1
Orestes Ms *KIL/WHAMP* NW6	72	A2
Orford Rd *CAT* SE6	158	B3
Oriel Ct *HAMP* NW3	72	C1
Oriel Dr *BARN* SW13	112	C2
Oriel Rd *HOM* E9	79	D3
Oriental Rd *CAN/RD* E16	107	D2
Orient St *LBTH* SE11	46	C4
Orient Wy *CLPT* E5	61	D5
LEY E10	62	A4
Orissa Rd *WOOL/PLUM* SE18	127	E1
Orkney St *BTSEA* SW11	116	A5
Orlando Rd *CLAP* SW4	134	C1
Orleston Ms *HOLWY* N7	76	A3
Orleston Rd *HOLWY* N7	76	A3
Ormanton Rd *SYD* SE26	156	A4
Orme Ct *BAY/PAD* W2	26	C2
Orme Court Ms *BAY/PAD* W2 *	26	C2
Orme La *BAY/PAD* W2	26	C2
Ormeley Rd *BAL* SW12	134	B5
Orme Sq *BAY/PAD* W2	26	C2
Orme Square Ga *BAY/PAD* W2	26	C2
Ormiston Gv *SHB* W12	100	A2
Ormiston Rd *GNWCH* SE10	124	A1
Ormond Cl *BMSBY* WC1N	21	D2
Ormonde Ct *STJWD* NW8 *	73	D5
Ormonde Ga *CHEL* SW3	115	F1
Ormonde Pl *BGVA* SW1W	42	B3
Ormonde Rd *STNW/STAM* SW14	128	B1
Ormonde Ter *STJWD* NW8	73	F5
Ormond Rd *ARCH* N19	57	E3
Ormond Yd *STJS* SW1Y	31	F1
Ormsby Pl *STNW/STAM* N16	59	F5
Ormsby St *BETH* E2	13	E1
Ormside St *PECK* SE15	120	C1
Ornan Rd *HAMP* NW3	73	C2
Oronsay Wk *IS* N1 *	76	C3
Orpheus St *CMBW* SE5	119	D4
Orsett Ms *BAY/PAD* W2	15	D4
Orsett St *LBTH* SE11	117	F1
Orsett Ter *BAY/PAD* W2	15	E4
Orsman Rd *IS* N1	77	E5
Orton St *WAP* E1W	102	A2
Orville Rd *BTSEA* SW11	115	D5
Orwell Rd *PLSTW* E13	94	C1
Osbaldeston Rd *STNW/STAM* N16	60	A4
Osbert St *WEST* SW1P	44	A5
Osborn Cl *HACK* E8	78	A5
Osborne Rd *ACT* W3	98	B5
CRICK NW2	70	B3
FSBYPK N4	58	A3
FSTGT E7	82	B2
HOM E9	79	F3
LEY E10	62	B5
Osborne Ter *TOOT* SW17 *	152	A5
Osborn La *FSTH* SE23	139	E5
Osborn St *BKHTH/KID* SE3	141	F2
Osborn Ter *BKHTH/KID* SE3	141	F2
Oscar Faber Pl *IS* N1 *	77	E4
Oscar St *BROCKY* SE4	122	A5
Oseney Crs *KTTN* NW5	74	C3
Osiers Rd *WAND/EARL* SW18	132	A2
Osier Wy *LEY* E10	62	B5
Oslac Rd *CAT* SE6	158	B5
Oslo Sq *BERM/RHTH* SE16	103	E4
Osman Rd *HMSMTH* W6 *	100	C4
Osmund St *SHB* W12	87	F5
Osnaburgh St *CAMTN* NW1	7	D5
Osnaburgh Ter *CAMTN* NW1	7	D5
Osprey Cl *EHAM* E6	95	E4
Osprey Est *BERM/RHTH* SE16	103	D5
Ospringe Rd *KTTN* NW5	74	C1
Ossian Rd *FSBYPK* N4	57	F2
Ossier Ms *CHSWK* W4	111	F1
Ossington Blds *MHST* W1U *	18	A2
Ossington Cl *BAY/PAD* W2 *	26	B2
Ossington St *BAY/PAD* W2	26	B1
Ossory Rd *STHWK* SE1	120	A1
Ossulston St *CAMTN* NW1	8	B1
Ostade Rd *BRXS/STRHM* SW2	135	F5
Osten Ms *SKENS* SW7	39	D5
Osterley Rd *STNW/STAM* N16	77	E1
Oswald's Md *HOM* E9	79	E1
Oswald St *CLPT* E5	61	D5
Oswald Ter *CRICK* NW2 *	52	C5

Osward Rd *BAL* SW12	151	F2
Oswin St *LBTH* SE11	47	D4
Oswyth Rd *CMBW* SE5	119	E5
Otford Crs *BROCKY* SE4	139	F4
Othello Cl *LBTH* SE11	118	B1
Otis St *BOW* E3	92	C2
Otley Dr *GNTH/NBYPK* IG2	66	B1
Otley Rd *CAN/RD* E16	94	C5
Otley Ter *CLPT* E5	60	C4
Ottaway St *CLPT* E5	60	A5
Otterden St *CAT* SE6	158	A4
Otto Cl *CAT* SE6	157	F5
SYD SE26	156	B2
Otto St *WALW* SE17	118	B2
Oulton Crs *BARK* IG11	85	F3
Ouseley Rd *BAL* SW12	134	A5
Outer Cir *CAMTN* NW1	5	D2
Outgate Rd *WLSDN* NW10	69	F4
Outram Pl *IS* N1	75	E5
Outram Rd *EHAM* E6	83	E5
Outwich St *HDTCH* EC3A *	25	D4
Oval Pl *VX/NE* SW8	117	F4
Oval Rd *CAMTN* NW1	74	B5
The Oval *BETH* E2	90	B1
Oval Wy *LBTH* SE11	117	F1
Overbury Rd *FSBYPK* N4	57	F2
Overbury St *CLPT* E5	79	D1
Overcliff Rd *BROCKY* SE4	140	A1
Overdown Rd *CAT* SE6	158	A4
Overhill Rd *EDUL* SE22	138	A5
Overlea Rd *CLPT* E5	60	A2
Overmead *ELTH/MOT* SE9	145	D5
Overstone Rd *HMSMTH* W6	100	C5
Overton Cl *WLSDN* NW10	68	C3
Overton Dr *WAN* E11	64	B2
Overton Rd *BRXN/ST* SW9	118	A5
LEY E10	61	E3
Ovex Cl *POP/IOD* E14	104	C4
Ovington Gdns *CHEL* SW3	41	D3
Ovington Ms *CHEL* SW3	41	D3
Ovington Sq *CHEL* SW3	41	D3
Ovington St *CHEL* SW3	41	D3
Owens Ms *WAN* E11	63	E4
Owen's Rw *FSBYE* EC1V	10	C3
Owen St *FSBYE* EC1V	10	B2
Owen Wy *WLSDN* NW10	68	C3
Owgan Cl *CMBW* SE5	119	D3
Oxberry Av *FUL/PGN* SW6	113	E5
Oxendon St *SOHO/SHAV* W1D *	32	A2
Oxenford St *PECK* SE15	137	F1
Oxestalls Rd *DEPT* SE8	121	E1
Oxford Cl *OXSTW* W1C	18	A5
Oxford Gdns *CHSWK* W4	110	A1
NKENS W10	89	D5
Oxford Ga *HMSMTH* W6	101	D5
Oxford Rd *FSBYPK* N4	58	A3
IL IG1	84	C1
KIL/WHAMP NW6	2	B1
PUT/ROE SW15	131	E2
SRTFD E15	81	D3
Oxford Rd North *CHSWK* W4	110	B1
Oxford Rd South *CHSWK* W4	110	A1
Oxford Sq *BAY/PAD* W2	16	C5
Oxford St *OXSTW* W1C	18	A5
SOHO/SHAV W1D	19	E4
Oxgate Court Pde *CRICK* NW2 *	52	B4
Oxgate Gdns *CRICK* NW2	52	B5
Oxgate La *CRICK* NW2	52	B4
Oxleas *EHAM* E6	96	B5
Oxleas Cl *WELL* DA16	127	D5
Oxley Cl *STHWK* SE1	119	F1
Oxleys Rd *CRICK* NW2	52	B5
Oxonian St *EDUL* SE22	137	F2
Oyster Catchers Cl *CAN/RD* E16	94	B5
Oyster Rw *WCHPL* E1	90	C5
Ozolins Wy *CAN/RD* E16	93	F5

P

Pablo Neruda *HNHL* SE24	136	B2
Pace Pl *WCHPL* E1	90	B5
Pacific Rd *CAN/RD* E16	94	A5
Packington Sq *IS* N1	76	C5
Packington St *IS* N1	76	B5
Packmores Rd *ELTH/MOT* SE9	145	D3
Padbury Ct *BETH* E2	13	F4
Paddenswick Rd *HMSMTH* W6	100	A4

Paddington Gn *BAY/PAD* W2 .... **16** A3
Paddington St *MHST* W1U **18** A2
Paddock Cl *BERM/RHTH* SE3 .... **142** A1
   SYD SE26 .... **157** D4
Paddock Rd *CRICK* NW2 .... **52** A5
The Paddocks *WBLY* HA9 .... **50** B4
Paddock Wy *PUT/ROE* SW15 .... **130** C5
Padfield Rd *BRXN/ST* SW9 .... **136** C1
Pagden St *VX/NE* SW8 .... **116** B4
Pageant Crs *BERM/RHTH* SE16 .... **103** F2
Page Av *WBLY* HA9 .... **50** C5
Page Rd *WEST* SW1P **44** B4
Pages Wk *STHWK* SE1 .... **49** D3
Pages Yd *CHSWK* W4 * **48** C4
Pages Yd *CHSWK* W4 * **111** E2
Paget's Yd *CHSWK* W4 .... **111** E2
Paget Ri *WOOL/PLUM* SE18 .... **126** A3
Paget Rd *IL* IG1 .... **84** B1
   STNW/STAM N16 .... **59** D3
Paget St *FSBYE* EC1V **10** C3
Pagitts Gv *BKHTH/KID* SE3 .... **123** D5
Pagnell St *NWCR* SE14 .... **121** E2
Pagoda Gdns *BKHTH/KID* SE3 .... **123** D5
Pagoda Gv *WNWD* SE27 .... **154** C3
Paignton Rd *SEVS/STOTM* N15 .... **59** E1
Painsthorpe Rd *STNW/STAM* N16 .... **59** E1
Painters Ms *BERM/RHTH* SE16 .... **102** A5
Pakeman St *HOLWY* N7 .... **57** F5
Pakenham Cl *BAL* SW12 .... **152** A1
Pakenham St *FSBYW* WC1X **9** F4
Palace Av *KENS* W8 .... **27** D4
Palace Cl *HOM* E9 .... **79** F3
Palace Ct *BAY/PAD* W2 .... **26** C1
Palace Gardens Ms *KENS* W8 .... **26** C3
Palace Gardens Ter *KENS* W8 .... **26** B3
Palace Ga *KENS* W8 .... **39** E1
Palace Gn *KENS* W8 .... **26** C4
Palace Ms *FUL/PGN* SW6 .... **113** F3
Palace Pl *BGVA* SW1W **43** D1
Palace Rd *BRXS/STRHM* SW2 .... **153** F1
Palace St *WESTW* SW1E **43** D2
Palace Vw *LEE/GVPK* SE12 .... **160** A2
Palamos Rd *LEY* E10 .... **62** A3
Palatine Av *STNW/STAM* N16 .... **77** E1
Palatine Rd *STNW/STAM* N16 .... **77** E1
Palemead Cl *FUL/PGN* SW6 .... **113** D4
Palermo Rd *WLSDN* NW10 .... **88** A1
Palewell Common Dr
   MORT/ESHN SW14 .... **129** D3
Palewell Pk *MORT/ESHN* SW14 .... **129** D3
Palfrey Pl *VX/NE* SW8 .... **117** F3
Palgrave Gdns *CAMTN* NW1 .... **5** D5
Palgrave Rd *SHB* W12 .... **99** F4
Palissy St *BETH* E2 .... **13** E4
Pallet Wy *WOOL/PLUM* SE18 .... **125** E4
Palliser Rd *WKENS* W14 .... **113** E1
Pall Ml *STJS* SW1Y **32** A4
Pall Ml East *STJS* SW1Y **32** A4
Pall Ml Pl *STJS* SW1Y **31** F4
Palm Cl *LEY* E10 .... **62** B5
Palmer Av *HOLWY* N7 .... **76** A2
Palmer Rd *PLSTW* E13 .... **94** B3
Palmers Rd *BETH* E2 .... **91** D1
   MORT/ESHN SW14 .... **128** C1
Palmerston Crs *WOOL/PLUM* SE18 .... **126** C2
Palmerston Rd *ACT* W3 .... **98** C4
   FSTGT E7 .... **82** B2
   KIL/WHAMP NW6 .... **71** F4
   MORT/ESHN SW14 .... **128** C2
Palmerston Wy *VX/NE* SW8 * **116** B3
Palmer St *STJSPK* SW1H **43** F2
Pancras La *MANHO* EC4N **23** F5
Pancras Rd *CAMTN* NW1 .... **8** A1
Pancras Wy *BOW* E3 .... **92** A1
Pandian Wy *KTTN* NW5 .... **75** D3
Pandora Rd *KIL/WHAMP* NW6 .... **72** A3
Panfield Ms *GNTH/NBYPK* IG2 .... **66** A1
Pangbourne Av *NKENS* W10 * **88** C4
Pankhurst Av *CAN/RD* E16 .... **106** B2
Pankhurst Cl *NWCR* SE14 .... **121** D3
Panmure Cl *HBRY* N5 .... **76** B1
Panmure Rd *SYD* SE26 .... **156** B5
Pansy Gdns *SHB* W12 .... **100** A1
Panther Dr *WLSDN* NW10 .... **69** D2
Panton St *STJS* SW1Y **32** B2
Paper Blds *EMB* EC4Y * **34** B1
Papillons Wk *BKHTH/KID* SE3 .... **124** A5
Papworth Gdns *HOLWY* N7 .... **75** F2
Papworth Wy *BRXS/STRHM* SW2 .... **136** A5
Parade Ms *BRXS/STRHM* SW2 .... **154** B2
Parade Ter *CDALE/KGS* NW9 * **52** A1
The Parade *BROCKY* SE4 * **121** F4

BTSEA SW11 * **133** D2
EDUL SE22 * **137** E1
FSBYPK N4 * **58** A4
RCH/KEW TW9 * **128** A1
Paradise Pas *HOLWY* N7 .... **156** B4
Paradise Rd *CLAP* SW4 .... **75** F2
Paradise Rw *BETH* E2 * **117** E5
Paradise St *BERM/RHTH* SE16 .... **90** B2
Paradise Wk *CHEL* SW3 .... **102** B3
Paragon Cl *CAN/RD* E16 .... **115** F2
Paragon Ms *STHWK* SE1 .... **94** A5
Paragon Pl *BKHTH/KID* SE3 .... **48** D4
Paragon Rd *HACK* E8 .... **125** F5
The Paragon *BKHTH/KID* SE3 .... **78** B3
Parbury Rd *FSTH* SE23 .... **125** F5
Pardoe Rd *LEY* E10 .... **139** E3
Pardoner St *STHWK* SE1 .... **62** B2
Pardon St *FSBYE* EC1V **48** B2
Parfett St *WCHPL* E1 .... **11** D5
Parfrey St *HMSMTH* W6 .... **90** A4
Parham Dr *GNTH/NBYPK* IG2 .... **112** C2
Paris Gdn *STHWK* SE1 .... **66** B3
Parish Gate Dr *BFN/LL* DA15 .... **34** C3
Parish Whf *WOOL/PLUM* SE18 .... **145** E4
Park Ap *BERM/RHTH* SE16 * **107** E5
Park Av *CRICK* NW2 .... **102** C4
   EHAM E6 .... **70** B3
   GLDGN NW11 .... **84** A5
   IL IG1 .... **54** B5
   MORT/ESHN SW14 .... **66** A3
   SRTFD E15 .... **129** D2
Park Av North *WLSDN* NW10 .... **81** E3
Park Cl *CRICK* NW2 .... **70** B2
   HOM E9 .... **52** A5
   SKENS SW7 * **78** C5
   WKENS W14 .... **41** E1
Park Ct *DUL* SE21 * **101** F4
Park Crs *REGST* W1B **155** D3
Park Crescent Ms East *GTPST* W1W **18** C1
Park Crescent Ms West
   CAVSQ/HST W1G **18** C1
Parkcroft Rd *LEE/GVPK* SE12 .... **141** F5
Parkdale Rd *WOOL/PLUM* SE18 .... **127** E1
Park Dr *ACT* W3 .... **98** A4
   CHARL SE7 .... **125** E1
   GLDGN NW11 .... **54** B3
   MORT/ESHN SW14 .... **129** D3
Park End *HAMP* NW3 .... **75** E1
Parker Cl *CAN/RD* E16 .... **107** E2
Parker Ms *HOL/ALD* WC2B * **21** D4
Parke Rd *BARN* SW13 .... **112** A4
Parker's Rw *STHWK* SE1 .... **49** F1
Parker St *CAN/RD* E16 .... **107** E2
   HOL/ALD WC2B **21** D4
Parker Ter *FSTH* SE23 .... **157** E2
Parkfield Av *MORT/ESHN* SW14 .... **129** E2
Parkfield Rd *NWCR* SE14 .... **121** F4
   WLSDN NW10 .... **70** A4
Parkfields *PUT/ROE* SW15 .... **130** C2
Parkfields Av *CDALE/KGS* NW9 .... **51** D3
Parkfield St *IS* N1 .... **10** B1
Parkgate *BKHTH/KID* SE3 .... **141** F1
Parkgate Gdns *MORT/ESHN* SW14 .... **129** D3
Parkgate Ms *HGT* N6 .... **56** C2
Parkgate Rd *BTSEA* SW11 .... **115** E3
Park Gv *SRTFD* E15 .... **82** A5
Park Hall Rd *DUL* SE21 * **155** D2
Parkham St *BTSEA* SW11 .... **115** D4
Park HI *CLAP* SW4 .... **135** D3
   FSTH SE23 .... **156** B2
Parkhill Rd *BFN/LL* DA15 .... **163** E3
   HAMP NW3 .... **73** F2
Park Hill Wk *HAMP* NW3 .... **73** F2
Parkholme Rd *HACK* E8 .... **78** A3
Parkhouse St *CMBW* SE5 .... **119** D3
Parkhurst Rd *HOLWY* N7 .... **75** E1
   MNPK E12 .... **84** A1
Parklands *HGT* N6 .... **56** B2
Parklands Cl *GNTH/NBYPK* IG2 .... **66** C2
   MORT/ESHN SW14 .... **128** C3
Parklands Rd *STRHM/NOR* SW16 .... **152** B5
Park La *MYFR/PICC* W1J **30** D1
   OXSTW W1C **29** F1
   SRTFD E15 * **82** C1
Parkmead *PUT/ROE* SW15 .... **130** B4
Park Ms *GNWCH* SE10 * **123** F1
   NKENS W10 .... **89** E1
Park Pde *ACT* W3 * **98** A4
   WLSDN NW10 .... **87** F1

Park Piazza *LEW* SE13 .... 141 D4
Park Pl *ACT* W3 .... 98 A5
  IS N1 .... 77 D5
  POP/IOD E14 .... 104 A2
  WHALL SW1A 31 E4
Park Place Vls *BAY/PAD* W2 .... 15 F2
Park Rise Rd *BTSEA* SE23 .... 157 E1
Park Rd *CDALE/KGS* NW9 .... 51 D2
  CEND/HSY/T N8 .... 57 E1
  CHSWK W4 .... 111 D3
  HDN NW4 .... 52 B1
  IL IG1 .... 67 D5
  LEY E10 .... 62 A3
  MNPK E12 .... 64 B3
  SRTFD E15 .... 82 A5
  STJWD NW8 .... 5 D4
  WLSDN NW10 * 69 E5
Park Rd East *ACT* W3 .... 98 C3
Park Rd North *ACT* W3 .... 98 B5
  CHSWK W4 .... 111 D2
Park Rw *GNWCH* SE10 .... 123 D2
Park Royal Rd *WLSDN* NW10 .... 86 C2
Parkside *BKHTH/KID* SE3 .... 123 F3
Park Side *CRICK* NW2 .... 52 A5
Parkside *WIM/MER* SW19 .... 149 D5
Parkside Av *WIM/MER* SW19 .... 149 D5
Parkside Crs *HOLWY* N7 .... 58 A5
Parkside Est *HOM* E9 * 79 D5
Parkside Gdns *WIM/MER* SW19 .... 149 D5
Park St *BTSEA* SW11 .... 116 A4
Park Sq East *CAMTN* NW1 .... 6 C5
Park Square Ms *CAMTN* NW1 .... 18 C1
Park Sq West *CAMTN* NW1 .... 6 C5
Parkstead Rd *FUL/PGN* SW6 .... 130 A3
Parkstone Rd *PECK* SE15 * 130 A5
Park St *MYFR/PKLN* W1K 30 A2
  STHWK SE1 .... 35 E3
The Park *GLDGN* NW11 .... 54 B3
  HGT N6 .... 56 A2
  SCUP DA14 .... 163 F5
Parkthorne Rd *BAL* SW12 .... 135 D5
Park Vw *ACT* W3 .... 86 C4
  WBLY HA9 .... 68 B2
Park View Est *HBRY* N5 * 76 A3
Park View Rd *CRICK* NW2 .... 69 F1
  ELTH/MOT SE9 .... 162 B1
Park Village East *CAMTN* NW1 .... 6 C1
Park Village West *CAMTN* NW1 .... 6 C1
Park Vls *TOOT* SW17 * 151 E5
Parkville Rd *FUL/PGN* SW6 .... 113 F3
Park Vis *GNWCH* SE10 .... 123 D2
Park Vista Apartments *CAN/RD* E16 .... 93 F2
Parkway *WEPTN* SW10 .... 114 C2
Parkwat Crs *SRTFD* E15 .... 81 D2
Parkway *CAMTN* NW1 .... 74 B5
  GDMY/SEVK IG3 .... 67 F5
Park West Pl *BAY/PAD* W2 .... 17 D4
Parkwood Ms *HGT* N6 .... 56 B1
Parkwood Rd *WIM/MER* SW19 .... 149 F5
Parliament Ct *WCHPL* E1 * 25 D3
Parliament Hl *HAMP* NW3 .... 73 E1
Parliament Hill Flds *KTTN* NW5 * 56 A5
Parliament Ms *MORT/ESHN* SW14 .... 110 C5
Parliament Sq *WEST* SW1P 44 C1
Parliament St *WHALL* SW1A 32 C5
Parma Crs *BTSEA* SW11 .... 133 F2
Parmiter St *BETH* E2 .... 90 B1
Parnell Cl *SHB* W12 .... 100 B4
Parnell Rd *BOW* E3 .... 79 F5
Parnham St *POP/IOD* E14 * 91 E5
Parolles Rd *ARCH* N19 .... 56 C5
Parr Rd *EHAM* E6 .... 83 D5
Parr St *IS* N1 .... 12 A1
Parry Av *EHAM* E6 .... 95 F5
Parry Pl *WOOL/PLUM* SE18 .... 108 B5
Parry Rd *NKENS* W10 .... 89 E2
Parry St *VX/NE* SW8 .... 117 E2
Parsifal Rd *KIL/WHAMP* NW6 .... 72 A2
Parsonage St *POP/IOD* E14 .... 104 C5
Parsons Gn *FUL/PGN* SW6 .... 114 A4
Parsons Green La *FUL/PGN* SW6 .... 114 A4
Parsons Rd *PLSTW* E13 .... 94 C1
Parthenia Rd *FUL/PGN* SW6 .... 114 B3
Partington Cl *ARCH* N19 .... 57 D3
Partridge Cl *CAN/RD* E16 .... 95 D4
Partridge Gn *ELTH/MOT* SE9 .... 162 A3
Partridge Rd *SCUP* DA14 .... 163 E3
Partridge Sq *EHAM* E6 .... 95 D4
Pascal St *VX/NE* SW8 .... 117 D3
Pascoe Rd *LEW* SE13 .... 141 D3
Pasley Cl *WALW* SE17 .... 118 B1

Passey Pl *ELTH/MOT* SE9 .... 143 F4
Passfield Dr *POP/IOD* E14 .... 92 B4
Passmore St *BCVA* SW1W 42 B5
Paston Crs *LEE/GVPK* SE12 .... 142 B5
Pastor St *LBTH* SE11 .... 47 D4
Pasture Rd *CAT* SE6 .... 159 E1
Patcham Ter *VX/NE* SW8 .... 116 B4
Paternoster Sq *STP* EC4M 23 D5
Pater St *KENS* W8 .... 38 A3
Patience Rd *BTSEA* SW11 .... 115 E5
Patio Cl *CLAP* SW4 .... 135 E4
Patmore St *VX/NE* SW8 .... 116 C4
Patmos Rd *BRXN/ST* SW9 .... 118 B3
Paton Cl *BOW* E3 .... 92 A2
Patrick Rd *PLSTW* E13 .... 94 C2
Patriot Sq *BETH* E2 .... 90 B1
Patrol Pl *CAT* SE6 .... 140 B4
Patshull Pl *KTTN* NW5 .... 74 C3
Patshull Rd *KTTN* NW5 .... 74 C3
Pattenden Rd *CAT* SE6 .... 157 F1
Patten Rd *WAND/EARL* SW18 .... 133 E5
Patterdale Rd *PECK* SE15 .... 120 C3
Pattina Wk *BERM/RHTH* SE16 .... 103 E2
Pattison Rd *CRICK* NW2 .... 54 A5
Paul Cl *SRTFD* E15 .... 81 E4
Paulet Rd *CMBW* SE5 .... 118 B5
Paulet Wy *WLSDN* NW10 .... 69 E4
Paul Julius Cl *POP/IOD* E14 .... 105 D1
Paul Robeson Cl *EHAM* E6 .... 96 A2
Paul St *SDTCH* EC2A 12 C5
  SRTFD E15 .... 81 E5
Paultons Sq *CHEL* SW3 .... 115 D2
Paultons St *CHEL* SW3 .... 115 D2
Pauntley St *ARCH* N19 .... 56 C3
Paveley Dr *BTSEA* SW11 .... 115 E5
Paveley St *STJWD* NW8 .... 5 D4
The Pavement *CLAP* SW4 .... 134 C2
  WAN E11 * 62 C3
  WNWD SE27 * 154 C4
Pavilion Pde *SHB* W12 * 88 C5
Pavilion Rd *IL* IG1 .... 65 F2
  KTBR SW1X 41 F1
Pavilion Sq *KTBR* SW1X 41 F3
Pavillion Sq *TOOT* SW17 .... 151 E3
Pavillion Ter *SHB* W12 * 88 C5
Pawsey Cl *PLSTW* E13 .... 82 A5
Paxton Rd *CHSWK* W4 .... 111 E2
  FSTH SE23 .... 157 E5
Paxton Ter *PIM* SW1V 116 B2
Payne Rd *BOW* E3 .... 80 C5
Paynell Ct *BKHTH/KID* SE3 .... 141 E5
Payne Rd *BOW* E3 .... 92 B1
Paynesfield Av *MORT/ESHN* SW14 .... 129 D1
Payne St *DEPT* SE8 .... 121 F2
Paynes Wk *HMSMTH* W6 .... 112 B2
Peabody Av *PIM* SW1V 116 B1
Peabody Cl *GNWCH* SE10 .... 122 B4
  PIM SW1V 116 B1
Peabody Cots *HNHL* SE24 .... 136 C5
Peabody Est *BTSEA* SW11 * 133 E2
  CHEL SW3 * 115 C2
  CLKNW EC1R * 21 D1
  CMBW SE5 * 119 D4
  FUL/PGN SW6 * 114 A2
  HMSMTH W6 * 112 C1
  HNHL SE24 * 136 B5
  NKENS W10 * 88 B4
  STHWK SE1 * 34 B3
  STLK EC1Y * 23 F1
Peabody Hl *DUL* SE21 .... 154 B3
Peabody Sq *IS* N1 * 76 C5
Peabody Ter *CLKNW* EC1R * 22 B1
Peace Gv *WBLY* HA9 .... 50 B5
Peace St *WOOL/PLUM* SE18 .... 126 A2
Peach Gv *WAN* E11 .... 63 D5
Peach Rd *NKENS* W10 .... 89 D2
Peachum Rd *BKHTH/KID* SE3 .... 123 F2
Peacock St *WALW* SE17 .... 47 D5
Peacock Yd *WALW* SE17 .... 47 D5
Peak Hl *SYD* SE26 .... 156 C4
Peak Hill Av *SYD* SE26 .... 156 C4
Peak Hill Gdns *SYD* SE26 * 156 C4
The Peak *SYD* SE26 .... 156 C4
Pearcefield Av *FSTH* SE23 .... 156 C1
Pear Cl *NWCR* SE14 .... 121 F3
Pearcroft Rd *WAN* E11 .... 63 D4
Peardon St *VX/NE* SW8 .... 134 A1
Pearfield Rd *FSTH* SE23 .... 157 F3
Pearl Cl *CRICK* NW2 .... 53 D2
  EHAM E6 .... 96 A5
Pearl St *WAP* E1W 102 B2

Pearman St *STHWK* SE1	46	B2
Pear Pl *STHWK* SE1	34	A5
Pear Rd *WAN* E11	63	D5
Pearscroft Ct *FUL/PGN* SW6	114	B4
Pearscroft Rd *FUL/PGN* SW6	114	B5
Pearse St *PECK* SE15	119	E2
Pearson's *NWCR* SE14	122	A4
Pearson's Rd *NWCR* SE14 *	122	A4
Pear Tree Cl *BETH* E2	13	E1
Pear Tree Ct *CLKNW* EC1R	22	B1
Peartree La *WAP* E1W *	102	C1
Pear Tree St *FSBYE* EC1V	11	D5
Peartree Wy *GNWCH* SE10	106	A5
Peary Pl *BETH* E2	90	C2
Peatfield Cl *BFN/LL* DA15	163	E3
Peckarmans Wd *SYD* SE26	156	A5
Peckett Sq *HBRY* N5 *	76	C1
Peckford Pl *BRXN/ST* SW9	118	A5
Peckham High St *PECK* SE15	119	E3
Peckham High St *PECK* SE15	120	A4
Peckham Hill St *PECK* SE15	120	A3
Peckham Park Rd *PECK* SE15	120	A3
Peckham Rd *CMBW* SE5	119	E4
Peckham Rye *EDUL* SE22	138	A2
Pecks Yd *WCHPL* E1 *	25	E2
Peckwater St *KTTN* NW5	74	C2
Pedlars Wk *HOLWY* N7 *	75	E2
Pedley St *WCHPL* E1	25	F1
Pedro St *CLPT* E5	61	D5
Peek Crs *WIM/MER* SW19	149	D5
Peel Gv *BETH* E2	90	C1
Peel Pas *KIL/WHAMP* NW6	2	A4
Peel Prec *KIL/WHAMP* NW6 *	89	F1
Peel St *KENS* W8	26	A4
Peerless St *FSBYE* EC1V	12	A4
Pegasus Cl *STNW/STAM* N16 *	77	D1
Pegasus Pl *FUL/PGN* SW6 *	114	A4
LBTH SE11	118	A2
Pegley Gdns *LEE/GVPK* SE12	160	A2
Pegwell St *WOOL/PLUM* SE18	127	E3
Pekin St *POP/IOD* E14	92	A5
Peldon Wk *IS* N1 *	76	B5
Pelham Av *BARK* IG11	85	F5
Pelham Cl *CMBW* SE5	137	E1
Pelham Crs *SKENS* SW7	40	C5
Pelham Pl *SKENS* SW7	40	C5
Pelham Rd *IL* IG1	67	D4
Pelham St *SKENS* SW7	40	B4
Pelier St *WALW* SE17	118	C2
Pelinore Rd *CAT* SE6	159	E2
Pellant Rd *FUL/PGN* SW6	113	F3
Pellatt Rd *EDUL* SE22	137	F3
Pellerin Rd *STNW/STAM* N16	77	E2
Pelling St *POP/IOD* E14	91	F5
Pellipar Rd *WOOL/PLUM* SE18	125	F1
Pelly Rd *PLSTW* E13	94	A1
SRTFD E15	82	A5
Pelter St *BETH* E2	13	E3
Pelton Rd *GNWCH* SE10	123	E1
Pember Rd *WLSDN* NW10	89	D2
Pemberton Gdns *ARCH* N19	56	C5
Pemberton Rd *EA* W5	78	B4
Pemberton Rw *FLST/FETLN* EC4A		
Pemberton Ter *ARCH* N19	56	C5
Pembridge Crs *NTGHL* W11	101	F1
Pembridge Gdns *BAY/PAD* W2	26	A2
Pembridge Ms *NTGHL* W11	26	A1
Pembridge Pl *NTGHL* W11	26	B1
Pembridge Rd *NTGHL* W11	26	A2
Pembridge Sq *BAY/PAD* W2	26	A2
Pembridge Vls *BAY/PAD* W2	26	A1
Pembroke Av *IS* N1	75	E5
Pembroke Cl *KTBR* SW1X	42	B1
Pembroke Gdns *KENS* W8	101	F4
Pembroke Gardens Cl *KENS* W8	101	F4
Pembroke Ms *KENS* W8	38	A3
Pembroke Pl *KENS* W8	38	A3
Pembroke Rd *EHAM* E6	95	F4
GDMY/SEVK IG3	67	F3
Pembroke Sq *KENS* W8	38	A3
Pembroke St *IS* N1	75	E4
Pembroke Ter *STJWD* NW8 *	73	D5
Pembroke Vls *KENS* W8	38	A3
Pembroke Wk *KENS* W8	38	A4
Pembrook Ms *BTSEA* SW11 *	133	D2
Pembry Cl *BRXN/ST* SW9	118	A4
Pembury Cl *CLPT* E5	78	B2
Pembury Rd *CLPT* E5	78	B2
Pemell Cl *WCHPL* E1	90	C3
Penally Pl *IS* N1	77	D5
Penang St *WAP* E1W	102	B2
Penarth St *PECK* SE15	120	C2
Penberth Rd *CAT* SE6	158	A5
Pencombe Ms *NTGHL* W11	101	F1
Pencraig Wy *PECK* SE15	120	B2
Penda's Md *HOM* E9	79	E1
Pendennis Rd *STRHM/NOR* SW16	153	E4
Penderry Ri *CAT* SE6	159	D2
Penderyn Wy *HOLWY* N7	75	D1
Pendlebury House *CHARL* SE7 *	125	D3
Pendragon Rd *BMLY* BR1	160	A3
Pendrell Rd *NWCR* SE14	139	E1
Pendrell St *WOOL/PLUM* SE18	127	D2
Pendulum Ms *HACK* E8 *	77	F2
Penerley Rd *CAT* SE6	158	B1
Penfold Pl *BAY/PAD* W2	16	C2
Penfold St *STJWD* NW8	16	B1
Penford Gdns *ELTH/MOT* SE9	143	D2
Penford St *CMBW* SE5	118	B5
Penge Rd *PLSTW* E13	82	C4
Penhall Rd *CHARL* SE7	107	D5
Peninsular Park Rd *CHARL* SE7	124	A1
Penmon Rd *WOOL/PLUM* SE18	119	F2
Pennant Ms *KENS* W8	38	C4
Pennard Rd *SHB* W12	100	C3
Penner Cl *WIM/MER* SW19	149	E2
Pennethorne Cl *HOM* E9	78	C5
Pennethorne Rd *PECK* SE15	120	B3
Pennine Dr *CRICK* NW2	53	D4
Pennine La *CRICK* NW2	53	E4
Pennine Pde *CRICK* NW2 *	53	E4
Pennington St *WAP* E1W	102	B1
Pennington Wy *LEE/GVPK* SE12	160	B2
Penn Rd *HOLWY* N7	75	E2
Penny Ms *WAND/EARL* SW18	132	A3
Pennymoor Wk *MV/WKIL* W9	89	F3
Penny Rd *WLSDN* NW10	86	B2
Pennyroyal Av *EHAM* E6	96	A5
Penpoll Rd *HACK* E8	78	B3
Penrhyn Crs *MORT/ESHN* SW14	128	C2
Penrith Cl *PUT/ROE* SW15	131	E3
Penrith Pl *WNWD* SE27	154	B2
Penrose Gv *WALW* SE17	118	C1
Penrose St *WALW* SE17	118	C1
Penryn St *CAMTN* NW1	8	A1
Penry St *STHWK* SE1	49	D5
Pensbury Pl *VX/NE* SW8	116	C5
Pensbury St *VX/NE* SW8	116	C5
Pensford Av *RCH/KEW* TW9	110	A5
Penshurst Rd *HOM* E9	79	D4
Pentland Cl *GLDGN* NW11	53	E4
Pentland Rd *KIL/WHAMP* NW6	2	A3
Pentland St *WAND/EARL* SW18	132	C4
Pentlow St *PUT/ROE* SW15	112	C5
Pentney Rd *BAL* SW12	152	C1
Penton Gv *IS* N1	10	A2
Penton Pl *WALW* SE17	47	D5
Penton Ri *FSBYW* WC1X	9	F3
Penton St *IS* N1	10	A1
Pentonville Rd *IS* N1	9	E2
Pentridge St *PECK* SE15	119	F3
Penwith Rd *WAND/EARL* SW18	150	B2
Penywern Rd *ECT* SW5	114	A1
Penzance Pl *NTGHL* W11	101	E2
Penzance St *NTGHL* W11	101	E2
Peony Gdns *SHB* W12	100	A1
Pepler Ms *CMBW* SE5	119	F1
Peploe Rd *KIL/WHAMP* NW6	89	D1
Pepper Cl *EHAM* E6	96	A4
Peppermead Sq *LEW* SE13	140	A3
Peppermint Pl *WAN* E11	63	E5
Pepper St *POP/IOD* E14	104	B4
STHWK SE1	35	E5
Peppie Cl *STNW/STAM* N16	59	E4
Pepys Crs *CAN/RD* E16	106	A2
Pepys Est *DEPT* SE8	103	E5
Pepys Park Est *DEPT* SE8	103	F5
Pepys Rd *NWCR* SE14	121	D5
Pepys St *TWRH* EC3N	37	D1
Perceval Av *HAMP* NW3	73	E2
Perch St *HACK* E8	77	F1
Percival Rd *MORT/ESHN* SW14	128	C3
Percival St *FSBYE* EC1V	10	C5
Percy Ms *FITZ* W1T	20	A3
Percy Rd *CAN/RD* E16	93	E4
SHB W12	100	A3
WAN E11	63	E2
Percy St *FITZ* W1T	20	A3
Peregrine Cl *WLSDN* NW10	69	D2
Peregrine Ct *WELL* DA16	127	F4
Perham Rd *WKENS* W14	113	E1

Peridot St *EHAM* E6	95	E4
Perifield *DUL* SE21	154	C1
Periton Rd *ELTH/MOT* SE9	143	D2
Perkin's Rents *WEST* SW1P	44	A1
Perkins Sq *STHWK* SE1	35	F3
Perks Cl *BKHTH/KID* SE3	123	E5
Perpins Rd *ELTH/MOT* SE9	145	E4
Perran Rd *BRXS/STRHM* SW2	154	B2
Perrers Rd *HMSMTH* W6	100	B4
Perrin's Ct *HAMP* NW3	72	C1
Perrin's Wk *HAMP* NW3	72	C1
Perry Av *ACT* W3	87	D5
Perry Ct *SEVS/STOTM* N15	59	E1
Perryfield Wy *CDALE/KGS* NW9	51	F1
Perry Hl *CAT* SE6	157	F2
Perrymans Farm Rd *GNTH/NBYPK* IG2	67	D1
Perrymead St *FUL/PGN* SW6	114	A4
Perryn Rd *ACT* W3	99	D1
BERM/RHTH SE16	102	B4
Perry Ri *FSTH* SE23	157	E3
Perry V *FSTH* SE23	156	C2
Perry Rd *CAT* SE6	139	E3
Perseverance Pl *BRXN/ST* SW9	118	A3
Perth Av *CDALE/KGS* NW9	51	E2
Perth Rd *BARK* IG11	97	D1
FSBYPK N4	58	A3
GNTH/NBYPK IG2	66	B1
LEY E10	61	E3
PLSTW E13	94	B1
Perth Ter *GNTH/NBYPK* IG2	66	C2
Peter Av *WLSDN* NW10	70	B4
Peterboat Cl *GNWCH* SE10	105	E5
Peterborough Ms *FUL/PGN* SW6	114	A5
Peterborough Rd *FUL/PGN* SW6	114	A5
Peterborough Vls *FUL/PGN* SW6	114	B4
Petergate *BTSEA* SW11	132	C2
Peters Cl *WELL* DA16	127	E2
Petersfield Ri *PUT/ROE* SW15	148	B1
Petersfield Rd *ACT* W3	98	C3
Petersham La *SKENS* SW7	39	E2
Petersham Ms *SKENS* SW7	39	E3
Petersham Pl *SKENS* SW7	39	E3
Peter's Hl *BLKFR* EC4V	35	E1
Peterstow Cl *WIM/MER* SW19	149	E3
Peter St *SOHO/CST* W1F	32	A1
Petherton Rd *HBRY* N5	76	C2
Petiver Cl *HOM* E9	78	C4
Petley Rd *HMSMTH* W6	112	C2
Peto Pl *CAMTN* NW1	7	D5
Peto St North *CAN/RD* E16	93	F5
Petrie Cl *CRICK* NW2	71	F3
Petros Gdns *KIL/WHAMP* NW6	72	B2
Petro St South *CAN/RD* E16	105	F1
Pettacre Cl *THMD* SE28	108	C4
Petticoat La *WCHPL* E1	25	D3
Petticoat Sq *WCHPL* E1	25	E4
Petticoat Tower *WCHPL* E1 *	25	E4
Pettiward Cl *PUT/ROE* SW15	130	C2
Pettman Crs *THMD* SE28	109	D4
Pett St *WOOL/PLUM* SE18	107	E5
Petty France *WESTW* SW1E	43	F2
Petty Wales *MON* EC3R	37	D2
Petworth St *BTSEA* SW11	115	E4
Petyt Pl *CHEL* SW3 *	115	E2
Petyward *CHEL* SW3	41	D5
Pevensey Rd *FSTGT* E7	82	A1
TOOT SW17	151	D4
Peverel *EHAM* E6	96	A5
Peyton Pl *GNWCH* SE10	122	C3
Pheasant Cl *CAN/RD* E16	94	B5
Phelp St *WALW* SE17	119	D2
Phene St *CHEL* SW3	115	E2
Philbeach Gdns *ECT* SW5	114	A1
Philchurch Pl *WCHPL* E1	90	A5
Philimore Cl *WOOL/PLUM* SE18	127	E1
Philippa Gdns *ELTH/MOT* SE9	143	D3
Philip St *PLSTW* E13	94	A3
Philip Wk *PECK* SE15	138	A1
Phillimore Gdns *KENS* W8	38	A1
WLSDN NW10	70	C5
Phillimore Gardens Cl *KENS* W8 *	38	A2
Phillimore Pl *KENS* W8	38	A1
Phillimore Wk *KENS* W8	38	A2
Phillipp St *IS* N1	77	E5
Philpot La *FENCHST* EC3M	36	C1
Philpot St *WCHPL* E1 *	90	B5
Phineas Pett Rd *ELTH/MOT* SE9	143	F1
Phipp's Ms *BGVA* SW1W	42	C3
Phipp St *SDTCH* EC2A	12	C3
Phoebeth Rd *LEW* SE13	140	A3
Phoenix Cl *HACK* E8 *	77	F5
Phoenix Ct *POP/IOD* E14	104	A5
Phoenix Pl *FSBYW* WC1X	9	F5
Phoenix Rd *CAMTN* NW1	8	A3
Phoenix St *LSQ/SEVD* WC2H	20	B5
Phoenix Wharf Rd *STHWK* SE1	49	F1
Physic Pl *CHEL* SW3	115	F2
Piccadilly *MYFR/PICC* W1J	31	E3
Piccadilly Ar *STJS* SW1Y	31	E3
Piccadilly Circ *REGST* W1B	31	F2
Pickard St *FSBYE* EC1V	11	D3
Pickering Av *EHAM* E6	96	A1
Pickering Ms *BAY/PAD* W2	15	D4
Pickering Pl *WHALL* SW1A *	31	F4
Pickering St *IS* N1	76	B5
Pickets St *BAL* SW12	134	A5
Pickwick Rd *DUL* SE21	137	D5
Pickwick St *STHWK* SE1	47	E1
Pickworth Cl *VX/NE* SW8 *	117	E3
Picton Pl *MHST* W1U	18	B5
Picton St *CMBW* SE5	119	D3
Pied Bull Yd *IS* N1 *	76	B5
Piedmont Rd *WOOL/PLUM* SE18	127	D1
Piermont Rd *EDUL* SE22	138	B3
Pierrepoint Ar *IS* N1 *	10	C1
Pierrepoint Rd *ACT* W3	98	B1
Pierrepoint Rw *IS* N1	10	C1
Pier Rd *CAN/RD* E16	107	F3
Pier St *POP/IOD* E14	104	C5
Pier Ter *WAND/EARL* SW18	132	B2
Pier Wy *THMD* SE28	109	D4
Pigott St *POP/IOD* E14	92	A5
Pilgrims Cl *BMLY* BR1	160	B5
Pilgrimage St *STHWK* SE1	48	A1
Pilgrim Hl *WNWD* SE27	154	C4
Pilgrim's La *HAMP* NW3	73	D1
Pilgrims Ms *POP/IOD* E14	105	D1
Pilgrim St *BLKFR* EC4V *	22	C5
Pilgrims Wy *ARCH* N19	57	D3
WBLY HA9	50	B3
Pilkington Rd *PECK* SE15	120	B5
Pilot Cl *DEPT* SE8	121	F2
Pilsden Cl *WIM/MER* SW19 *	149	E1
Pilton Pl *WALW* SE17	118	C1
Pimlico Rd *BGVA* SW1W	116	A1
Pinchin & Johnsons Yd *WCHPL* E1 *	102	A1
Pinchin St *WCHPL* E1	102	A1
Pincott Pl *BROCKY* SE4	139	D1
Pindar St *SDTCH* EC2A	24	C2
Pindock Ms *MV/WKIL* W9	15	D1
Pine Apple Ct *WESTW* SW1E *	43	E2
Pine Av *SRTFD* E15	81	D2
Pine Cl *LEY* E10	62	A4
Pinefield Cl *POP/IOD* E14 *	104	A1
Pine Gv *FSBYPK* N4	57	F3
WIM/MER SW19	149	F5
Pinelands Cl *BKHTH/KID* SE3 *	123	F3
Pinelees Ct *MORT/ESHN* SW14 *	128	C2
Pinemartin Cl *CRICK* NW2	52	C5
Pine Rd *CRICK* NW2	70	C1
Pine Tree Wy *LEW* SE13	140	B1
Pinewood Av *BFN/LL* DA15	163	E1
Pinewood Rd *STRHM/NOR* SW16	153	E4
Pinnell Rd *ELTH/MOT* SE9	143	D2
Pintail Cl *EHAM* E6	95	E4
Pinto Cl *BKHTH/KID* SE3	142	B2
Pioneer Cl *BOW* E3	92	B4
SHB W12	88	B5
Pioneer St *PECK* SE15	120	A4
Pioneer Wy *SHB* W12	88	C5
Piper Cl *HOLWY* N7	75	F3
Piper Wy *IL* IG1	67	D3
Pippin Cl *CRICK* NW2	52	A5
Pipright Rd *WAND/EARL* SW18	149	F1
Pirie St *CAN/RD* E16	106	B2
Pitchford St *SRTFD* E15	81	D4
Pitfield St *IS* N1	12	C3
Pitfield Wy *WLSDN* NW10	68	C3
Pitfold Rd *LEE/GVPK* SE12	142	A4
Pitman St *CMBW* SE5	118	C5
Pitsea Pl *WCHPL* E1	91	D5
Pitsea St *WCHPL* E1	91	D5
Pitt Crs *WIM/MER* SW19	150	B4
Pittman Gdns *IL* IG1	84	C2
Pitts Head Ms *MYFR/PICC* W1J	30	B4
Pitt St *KENS* W8	38	B5
Pixley St *POP/IOD* E14	91	F5
Plaistow Gv *SRTFD* E15	81	F5
Plaistow Park Rd *PLSTW* E13	94	B1
Plaistow Rd *PLSTW* E13	94	A1

SRTFD E15 ... 81 F5
Plane St SYD SE26 ... 156 B3
Plaintain Gdns WAN E11 * ... 63 D5
Plaintain Pl STHWK SE1 ... 36 A5
Plantation La FENCHST EC3M ... 36 C1
The Plantation BKHTH/KID SE3 ... 124 A5
Plashet Gv EHAM ... 82 C5
Plashet Rd FSTGT E13 ... 82 A5
Plassy Rd CAT SE6 ... 140 B5
Platina St SDTCH EC2A ... 12 D5
Plato Rd BRXS/STRHM SW2 ... 135 E2
Platt's La HAMP NW3 ... 54 A5
Platt St CAMTN NW1 ... 8 A1
Playfair St HMSMTH W6 * ... 112 C1
Playfield Crs EDUL SE22 ... 137 E3
Playford Rd FSBYPK N4 ... 57 F3
Playgreen Wy CAT SE6 ... 158 A4
Playhouse Ct STHWK SE1 * ... 35 E5
Playhouse Yd BLKFR EC4V ... 22 C5
Pleasance Rd PUT/ROE SW15 ... 130 B3
The Pleasance PUT/ROE SW15 ... 130 B2
Pleasant Pl IS N1 ... 76 B4
Plender St CAMTN NW1 ... 74 C5
Plesney Rd ARCH N19 ... 75 D1
Plevna Crs SEVS/STOTM N15 ... 59 E1
Plevna St POP/IOD E14 ... 104 C4
Pleydell Av HMSMTH W6 ... 99 F4
Pleydell Est FSBYE EC1V * ... 11 F4
Pleydell St EMB EC4Y ... 22 B5
Plimsoll Cl POP/IOD E14 ... 92 B5
Plimsoll Rd FSBYPK N4 ... 58 B5
Plough La EDUL SE22 ... 137 F4
Plough La WIM/MER SW19 ... 150 B5
Ploughmans Cl CAMTN NW1 ... 75 D5
Plough Pl FLST/FETLN EC4A ... 22 A4
Plough St BTSEA SW11 ... 133 D1
Plough St WCHPL E1 * ... 90 A5
Plough Ter BTSEA SW11 ... 133 D2
Plough Wy BERM/RHTH SE16 ... 103 D5
Plough Wy DEPT SE8 ... 103 D5
Plough Wy SDTCH EC2A ... 25 D1
Plover Wy BERM/RHTH SE16 ... 103 E4
Plowden Blds EMB EC4Y * ... 34 A1
Plumbers Rw WCHPL E1 ... 90 A4
Plumbridge St GNWCH SE10 * ... 122 C4
Plum La WOOL/PLUM SE18 ... 126 B3
Plummer Rd CLAP SW4 ... 135 D5
Plumstead Common Rd WOOL/PLUM SE18 ... 126 B2
Plumstead High St WOOL/PLUM SE18 ... 109 F5
Plumstead Rd WOOL/PLUM SE18 ... 108 C5
Plumtree Ct FLST/FETLN EC4A ... 22 B4
Plymouth Rd CAN/RD E16 ... 94 A4
Plymouth Whf POP/IOD E14 ... 105 D5
Plympton Av KIL/WHAMP NW6 ... 71 F4
Plympton Pl STJWD NW8 * ... 16 C1
Plympton Rd KIL/WHAMP NW6 ... 71 F4
Plympton St STJWD NW8 ... 16 C1
Pocock St STHWK SE1 ... 34 C5
Podmore Rd WAND/EARL SW18 ... 132 C3
Poets Ms HNHL SE24 ... 136 B3
Poet's Rd HBRY N5 ... 77 D2
Point Cl GNWCH SE10 ... 122 C4
Pointers Cl POP/IOD E14 ... 122 B1
Point Hl GNWCH SE10 ... 122 C4
Point Pl WBLY HA9 ... 68 B4
Point Pleasant WAND/EARL SW18 ... 132 A2
Poland St SOHO/SHAV W1D ... 19 F4
Polebrook Rd BKHTH/KID SE3 ... 142 C1
Polecroft La CAT SE6 ... 157 F2
Pollard Cl CAN/RD E16 ... 106 A1
Pollard Cl HOLWY N7 ... 75 F1
Pollard Rw BETH E2 ... 90 A2
Pollard St BETH E2 * ... 90 A2
Pollen St CONDST W1S ... 19 D5
Pollitt Dr STJWD NW8 ... 4 A5
Polperro Ms LBTH SE11 ... 46 B4
Polsted Rd CAT SE6 ... 139 F5
Polthorne Gv WOOL/PLUM SE18 ... 108 C5
Polworth Rd STRHM/NOR SW16 ... 153 E5
Polygon Rd CAMTN NW1 ... 8 A2
The Polygon CLAP SW4 * ... 134 C2
Polytechnic St WOOL/PLUM SE18 ... 108 A5
Pomell Wy WCHPL E1 ... 25 E4
Pomeroy St NWCR SE14 ... 120 C3
Pomfret Rd CMBW SE5 ... 136 B1
Pomoja La ARCH N19 ... 57 E4
Pond Cl BKHTH/KID SE3 ... 124 A5
Pond Cots DUL SE21 ... 155 E1
Ponder St HOLWY N7 * ... 75 F4
Pond Farm Est CLPT E5 * ... 60 C5
Pond Md DUL SE21 ... 137 D4

Pond Pl CHEL SW3 ... 40 C5
Pond Rd BKHTH/KID SE3 ... 141 F1
SRTFD E15 ... 81 F5
Pond St HAMP NW3 ... 73 E2
Ponler St WCHPL E1 ... 90 B5
Ponsard Rd WLSDN NW10 ... 88 B2
Ponsford St HOM E9 ... 78 C3
Ponsonby Pl WEST SW1P ... 117 D1
Ponsonby Rd PUT/ROE SW15 ... 130 B5
Ponsonby Ter WEST SW1P ... 117 D1
Pontefract Rd BMLY BR1 ... 160 A5
Ponton Rd VX/NE SW8 ... 117 D3
Pont St KTBR SW1X ... 41 E3
Pont Street Ms KTBR SW1X ... 41 E3
Pool Cl BECK BR3 ... 158 A5
Pool Ct CAT SE6 ... 158 A2
Poole Rd HOM E9 ... 79 D3
Pooles Bldgs FSBYW WC1X ... 22 A1
Pooles La WBPTN SW10 ... 114 C3
Pooles Pk FSBYPK N4 ... 58 A4
Poole St IS N1 ... 77 D5
Pooley Dr MORT/ESHN SW14 ... 128 C1
Poolmans St BERM/RHTH SE16 ... 103 D3
Poonah St WCHPL E1 ... 90 C5
Pope's Rd BRXN/ST SW9 * ... 136 A2
Pope St STHWK SE1 ... 49 D1
Popham Gdns RCH/KEW TW9 * ... 128 B1
Popham Rd IS N1 ... 76 C5
Popham St IS N1 ... 76 C5
Poplar Bath St POP/IOD E14 ... 104 B1
Poplar Cl HOM E9 ... 79 F2
Poplar Gv HMSMTH W6 ... 99 F4
Poplar Gv WBLY HA9 ... 50 C5
Poplar High St POP/IOD E14 ... 104 B1
Poplar Ms SHB W12 ... 100 C2
Poplar Pl BAY/PAD W2 ... 26 C1
Poplar Rd HNHL SE24 ... 136 C2
Poplars Rd WALTH E17 ... 62 B1
Poplar Wk HNHL SE24 ... 136 C2
Poppleton Rd WAN E11 ... 63 E1
Porchester Garden Ms BAY/PAD W2 * ... 15 D5
Porchester Gdns BAY/PAD W2 ... 27 D1
Porchester Ga BAY/PAD W2 * ... 27 E2
Porchester Pl BAY/PAD W2 ... 17 D5
Porchester Rd BAY/PAD W2 ... 15 D4
Porchester Sq BAY/PAD W2 ... 15 D4
Porchester Square Ms BAY/PAD W2 * ... 15 D4
Porchester Ter BAY/PAD W2 ... 15 E5
Porchester Ter North BAY/PAD W2 ... 15 D4
Porcupine Cl ELTH/MOT SE9 ... 161 E2
Porden Rd BRXS/STRHM SW2 ... 135 F2
Porlock St STHWK SE1 ... 36 B5
Portal Cl WNWD SE27 ... 154 A3
Portal Wy ACT W3 ... 87 D4
Portbury Cl PECK SE15 ... 120 A4
Portchester Cl HNHL SE24 ... 136 C2
Portchester Ga BAY/PAD W2 * ... 27 E2
Portelet Rd WCHPL E1 ... 91 D2
Porten Houses WKENS W14 * ... 101 E4
Porten Rd WKENS W14 ... 101 E4
Porter Rd EHAM E6 ... 95 F5
Porter Sq ARCH N19 ... 57 E3
Porter St MHST W1U ... 17 F2
Porter St STHWK SE1 ... 35 F3
Porters Wk WAP E1W * ... 102 B1
Porteus Rd BAY/PAD W2 ... 15 F3
Portgate Cl MV/WKIL W9 ... 89 F3
Porthcawe Rd SYD SE26 ... 157 E4
Portia Wy BOW E3 ... 91 F5
The Porticos CHEL SW3 * ... 115 D2
Portinscale Rd PUT/ROE SW15 ... 131 E3
Portland Av STNW/STAM N16 ... 59 F3
Portland Crs ELTH/MOT SE9 ... 161 E2
Portland Gdns FSBYPK N4 ... 58 B1
Portland Gv VX/NE SW8 ... 117 F4
Portland Ms SOHO/CST W1F ... 19 F5
Portland Pl REGST W1B ... 18 C1
Portland Ri FSBYPK N4 ... 58 B3
Portland Rd BMLY BR1 ... 160 C4
Portland Rd ELTH/MOT SE9 ... 161 E2
Portland Rd NTGHL W11 ... 101 E1
Portland Sq WAP E1W ... 102 B1
Portland St WALW SE17 ... 119 D1
Portman Av MORT/ESHN SW14 ... 129 D1
Portman Cl MBLAR W1H ... 18 A4
Portman Ga CAMTN NW1 ... 17 D1
Portman Ms South MBLAR W1H ... 18 A5
Portman Sq MBLAR W1H ... 17 F4
Portman St MBLAR W1H ... 18 A5
Portmeers Cl WALTH E17 * ... 61 F1

Portnall Rd *MV/WKIL* W9	89	F2
Portobello Ct *NTGHL* W11 *	101	F1
Portobello Ms *NTGHL* W11 *	26	A2
Portobello Rd *NKENS* W10	89	E4
NTGHL W11	101	F1
Portpool La *FSTGT* E7	22	A2
Portree Rd *POP/IOD* E14	93	D5
Portsdown Av *GLDGN* NW11	53	F1
Portsdown Ms *GLDGN* NW11	53	F1
Portsea Ms *BAY/PAD* W2	17	D5
Portsea Pl *BAY/PAD* W2	17	D5
Portside Rd *VX/NE* SW8	116	C5
Portsmouth Ms *CAN/RD* E16	106	B1
Portsmouth Rd *PUT/ROE* SW15	130	B5
Portsmouth St *LINN* WC2A	21	E4
Portsoken St *TWRH* EC3N	37	E1
Portugal St *LINN* WC2A	21	F5
Portway *SRTFD* E15	81	F5
Portway Gdns *WOOL/PLUM* SE18	125	D4
The Postern *BARB* EC2Y *	23	F3
Post Office Ap *FSTGT* E7	82	B2
Post Office Wy *VX/NE* SW8	117	D3
Postway Ms *IL* IG1	66	B5
Potier St *STHWK* SE1	48	B3
Potterne Cl *WIM/MER* SW19	131	D5
Potters Cl *PECK* SE15 *	119	E3
Potters Flds *STHWK* SE1	37	D4
Potters Rd *FUL/PGN* SW6	115	E3
Pottery La *NTGHL* W11	101	E2
Pottery St *BERM/RHTH* SE16 *	102	B3
Pott St *BETH* E2	90	B2
Poulett Rd *EHAM* E6	95	F1
Poultry *LOTH* EC2R	24	A5
Pound La *WLSDN* NW10	70	A3
Pound Park Rd *CHARL* SE7	107	D5
Pound Pl *ELTH/MOT* SE9	144	A4
Pountney Rd *BTSEA* SW11	134	A1
Powell Rd *CLPT* E5	60	B5
Power Rd *CHSWK* W4	98	A5
Powerscroft Rd *CLPT* E5	78	C1
Powis Gdns *GLDGN* NW11	53	F2
NTGHL W11	89	F5
Powis Ms *NTGHL* W11	89	F5
Powis Ms *BMSBY* WC1N	21	D1
Powis Rd *BOW* E3	92	B2
Powis Sq *NTGHL* W11	89	F5
Powis St *WOOL/PLUM* SE18	108	A4
Powis Ter *NTGHL* W11	89	F5
Powlett Pl *CAMTN* NW1 *	74	A4
Pownall Rd *HACK* E8	78	A5
Pownsett Ter *IL* IG1 *	84	C2
Powster Rd *BMLY* BR1	160	A5
Poynders Rd *CLAP* SW4	134	C4
Poynings Rd *ARCH* N19	56	C5
Poyntz Rd *BTSEA* SW11	115	F5
Poyser St *BETH* E2	90	B1
Praed Ms *BAY/PAD* W2	16	B4
Praed St *BAY/PAD* W2	16	B4
Pragel St *PLSTW* E13	94	B1
Pragnell Rd *LEE/GVPK* SE12	160	B2
Prague Pl *BRXS/STRHM* SW2	135	E3
Prah Rd *FSBYPK* N4	58	A4
Prairie St *VX/NE* SW8	116	A5
Pratt Ms *CAMTN* NW1	74	C5
Pratt St *CAMTN* NW1	74	C5
Pratt Wk *LBTH* SE11	45	F4
Prayle Gv *CRICK* NW2	53	D3
Prebend Gdns *HMSMTH* W6	99	F5
Prebend St *IS* N1	76	C5
Premiere Pl *POP/IOD* E14 *	104	A1
Premier Park Rd *WLSDN* NW10	86	B1
Prendergast Rd *BKHTH/KID* SE3	141	E1
Prentis Rd *STRHM/NOR* SW16	153	D4
Prentiss Ct *CHARL* SE7	107	D5
Prescot St *WCHPL* E1	37	F1
Prescott Pl *CLAP* SW4	135	D1
Presentation Ms *BRXS/STRHM* SW2	135	F2
Presidents Dr *WAP* E1W	102	B2
President St *FSBYE* EC1V *	11	E3
Press Rd *WLSDN* NW10	51	D5
Prestage Wy *POP/IOD* E14	104	C1
Prestbury Rd *FSTGT* E7	82	C4
Prestbury Sq *ELTH/MOT* SE9	161	F4
Prested Rd *BTSEA* SW11	133	D2
Preston Cl *STHWK* SE1	48	C4
Preston Gdns *IL* IG1	65	E1
WLSDN NW10 *	69	E3
Preston Pl *CRICK* NW2	70	A3
Preston Rd *WAN* E11	63	E1
Preston's Rd *POP/IOD* E14	104	C1
Prestwich Ter *CLAP* SW4 *	135	D3
Prestwood St *IS* N1 *	11	F2
Pretoria Pde *BROCKY* SE4 *	122	A5
Pretoria Rd *CAN/RD* E16	93	F2
IL IG1	84	B1
LEY E10	63	D3
Price Cl *TOOT* SW17	151	E2
Price's St *STHWK* SE1	35	D4
Prideaux Pl *ACT* W3	99	D1
FSBYW WC1X	9	F3
Prideaux Rd *BRXN/ST* SW9	135	F1
Priestfield Rd *FSTH* SE23	157	E3
Priestlands Park Rd *SCUP* DA14	163	F3
Priestley Cl *STNW/STAM* N16 *	59	F2
Priestley Wy *CRICK* NW2	52	A3
Priests Br *MORT/ESHN* SW14	129	E1
Prima Rd *BRXN/ST* SW9	118	A3
Primrose Cl *BOW* E3	92	A1
CAT SE6	158	C5
Primrose Gdns *HAMP* NW3	73	E3
Primrose Hill *EMB* EC4Y	22	B5
Primrose Hill Rd *HAMP* NW3	73	F4
Primrose Hill Studios *CAMTN* NW1	74	A5
Primrose Ms *CAMTN* NW1 *	73	F4
Primrose Rd *LEY* E10	62	B3
Primrose Sq *HOM* E9	78	C4
Primrose St *SDTCH* EC2A	24	C2
Primrose Wk *NWCR* SE14	121	E3
Primula St *SHB* W12	100	A1
Prince Albert Rd *CAMTN* NW1	74	A5
STJWD NW8	4	C3
Prince Arthur Rd *HAMP* NW3	72	C1
Prince Charles Dr *HDN* NW4	52	C2
Prince Charles Rd *BKHTH/KID* SE3	123	F4
Prince Consort Rd *SKENS* SW7	40	A2
Princedale Rd *NTGHL* W11	101	E2
Prince Edward Rd *HOM* E9	79	F3
Prince George Rd *STNW/STAM* N16	77	E1
Prince Henry Rd *CHARL* SE7	125	D3
Prince Imperial Rd *WOOL/PLUM* SE18	125	F4
Prince John Rd *ELTH/MOT* SE9	143	E5
Princelet St *WCHPL* E1	25	F2
Prince of Orange La *GNWCH* SE10 *	122	C3
Prince of Wales Dr *BTSEA* SW11	115	E4
Prince of Wales Pas *CAMTN* NW1 *	7	F4
Prince of Wales Rd *BKHTH/KID* SE3	123	F4
CAN/RD E16	94	C5
KTTN NW5	74	A3
Prince of Wales Ter *CHSWK* W4	111	E1
KENS W8	39	D1
Prince Regent La *PLSTW* E13	94	B2
Prince Regent Ms *CAMTN* NW1 *	7	F4
Prince Rupert Rd *ELTH/MOT* SE9	143	F2
Princes Ar *MYFR/PICC* W1J	31	F3
Princes Av *ACT* W3	98	A4
Princes Cl *FSBYPK* N4	58	B3
Princes Ct *WAP* E1W	102	B1
Princes Gdns *ACT* W3	86	A5
SKENS SW7	40	B2
Princes Ga *SKENS* SW7	40	B2
Princes Ga *SKENS* SW7	40	C1
Princes Gate Ct *SKENS* SW7	40	A1
Princes Gate Ms *SKENS* SW7	40	B2
Princes Ms *HMSMTH* W6 *	112	B1
Prince's Ms *BAY/PAD* W2	26	C1
Princes Park Av *GLDGN* NW11	53	E1
Princes Pl *NTGHL* W11	101	E2
Princes Ri *LEE* SE13	122	C4
Princes Riverside Rd		
BERM/RHTH SE16	103	D2
Prince's Rd *MORT/ESHN* SW14	129	D1
Princess Crs *FSBYPK* N4	58	B4
Princess Alice Wy *THMD* SE28	109	D3
Princess Louise Cl *BAY/PAD* W2	16	B2
Princess May Rd *STNW/STAM* N16	77	D4
Princess Ms *HAMP* NW3	73	D3
Prince's Rd *BAY/PAD* W2	26	B1
Princess Rd *CAMTN* NW1	74	A5
KIL/WHAMP NW6	2	A2
Princess St *STHWK* SE1	47	D3
Princes St *REGST* W1B	19	D5
Prince's St *LOTH* EC2R	24	A5
Prince's Ter *PLSTW* E13	82	B5
Princes Wy *WIM/MER* SW19	149	E1
Prince's Yd *IS* N1	75	F5
NTGHL W11	101	E2
Princethorpe Rd *SYD* SE26	157	D4
Princeton St *GINN* WC1R	21	E3
Pringle Gdns *STRHM/NOR* SW16	152	C4
Printers Inn Ct *FLST/FETLN* EC4A	22	A4
Printing House Yd *BETH* E2 *	13	D4

Priolo Rd *CHARL* SE7 ..... 124 C1
Prior Bolton St N1 ..... 76 B3
Prioress Rd *WNWD* SE27 ..... 154 B3
Prioress St *STHWK* SE1 ..... 48 B3
Prior Rd *IL* IG1 ..... 66 A5
Prior St *GNWCH* SE10 ..... 122 C5
Priory Av *CHSWK* W4 ..... 99 E4
Priory Ct *BLKFR* EC4V * 23 D5
  VX/NE SW8 ..... 117 D4
Priory Gdns *BARN* SW13 ..... 129 F1
  CHSWK W4 * 99 E4
  HGT N6 ..... 56 B1
Priory Green Est N1 ..... 5 E3
Priory Gv *VX/NE* SW8 ..... 117 E4
Priory La *PUT/ROE* SW15 ..... 129 F3
Priory Leas *ELTH/MOT* SE9 * 161 E1
Priory Pk *BKHTH/KID* SE3 ..... 141 F1
Priory Park Rd *KIL/WHAMP* NW6 ..... 71 F5
Priory Rd *BARK* IG11 ..... 91 D1
  CHSWK W4 ..... 99 D4
  EHAM E6 ..... 83 D5
  KIL/WHAMP NW6 ..... 72 B4
  RCH/KEW TW9 ..... 110 A2
Priory St *BOW* E3 ..... 92 B2
Priory Ter *KIL/WHAMP* NW6 ..... 72 B5
The Priory *BKHTH/KID* SE3 ..... 141 F1
Priory Wk *WBPTN* SW10 ..... 114 C1
Pritchard's Rd *BETH* E2 ..... 90 A1
Priter Rd *BERM/RHTH* SE16 * 102 A4
Probert Rd *BRXS/STRHM* SW2 ..... 136 A3
Probyn Rd *BRXS/STRHM* SW2 ..... 154 B2
Procter St *GINN* WC1R 21 E3
Promenade Approach Rd *CHSWK* W4. ..... 111 E3
The Promenade *CHSWK* W4 ..... 111 E4
Prospect Cl *SYD* SE26 ..... 156 B4
Prospect Cots *WAND/EARL* SW18. ..... 132 A2
Prospect Pl *CHSWK* W4 ..... 111 D1
  CRICK NW2 ..... 53 F5
  WAP E1W 102 C2
Prospect Rd *CRICK* NW2 ..... 53 F5
Prospect St *BERM/RHTH* SE16 ..... 102 B3
Prospect V *WOOL/PLUM* SE18 ..... 107 F1
Prospero Rd *ARCH* N19 ..... 57 D3
Protea Cl *CAN/RD* E16 ..... 93 F5
Prothero Rd *FUL/PGN* SW6 ..... 113 E3
Prout Gv *WLSDN* NW10 ..... 69 E1
Prout Rd *CLPT* E5 ..... 60 B5
Provence St N1 ..... 11 E1
Providence Cl *HOM* E9 * 79 D5
Providence Pl *MYFR/PKLN* W1K 30 B1
Providence Row Cl *BETH* E2 ..... 90 B2
Providence Sq *STHWK* SE1 * 36 C5
Providence Yd *BETH* E2 * 90 A2
Provost Est N1 ..... 12 A3
Provost Rd *HAMP* NW3 ..... 73 F4
Provost St *FSBYE* EC1V 12 A4
  IS N1 ..... 12 A2
Prowse Pl *CAMTN* NW1 ..... 74 C4
Prusom St *WAP* E1W 102 B2
Pudding La *MON* EC3R 36 B1
Pudding Mill La *SRTFD* E15 ..... 80 B5
Puddle Dock *BLKFR* EC4V 35 D3
Pulborough Rd *WAND/EARL* SW18. ..... 131 F5
Pulford St *SEVS/STOTM* N15 ..... 59 D1
Pulleyns Av *EHAM* E6 ..... 95 E2
Pullman Gdns *PUT/ROE* SW15 ..... 130 C4
Pullman Ms *LEE/GVPK* SE12 ..... 160 B3
Pullman Pl *ELTH/MOT* SE9 ..... 143 E3
Pulross Rd *BRXN/ST* SW9 ..... 135 F1
Pulteney Cl *BOW* E3 ..... 79 F5
Pulton Pl *FUL/PGN* SW6 ..... 114 A3
Puma Ct *WCHPL* E1 * 25 E2
Pump Ct *EMB* EC4Y * 22 A5
Pump House Ms *WCHPL* E1 * 102 A1
Pumping Station Rd *CHSWK* W4. ..... 111 E3
Pump La *NWCR* SE14 ..... 120 C3
Punderson's Gdns *BETH* E2 ..... 90 B2
Purbeck Dr *CRICK* NW2 ..... 53 D4
Purbrook St *STHWK* SE1 ..... 49 D2
Purcell Crs *FUL/PGN* SW6 ..... 113 D2
Purcell Ms *WLSDN* NW10 * 69 E4
Purcell St *IS* N1 ..... 12 C1
Purcers Cross Rd *FUL/PGN* SW6 ..... 113 F4
Purchese St *CAMTN* NW1 ..... 8 A1
Purdy St *BOW* E3 ..... 92 B3
Purelake Ms *LEW* SE13 * 141 E1
Purley Av *CRICK* NW2 ..... 53 E4
Purley Pl *IS* N1 ..... 76 B4
Purneys Rd *ELTH/MOT* SE9 ..... 143 D2
Purrett Rd *WOOL/PLUM* SE18 ..... 127 F1
Pursers Cross Rd *FUL/PGN* SW6 * 113 F4

Purves Rd *WLSDN* NW10. ..... 88 B2
Putney Br *PUT/ROE* SW15 ..... 131 E1
Putney Bridge Ap *FUL/PGN* SW6... ..... 131 E1
Putney Bridge Rd *PUT/ROE* SW15 ..... 131 E1
Putney Common *PUT/ROE* SW15 ..... 130 C1
Putney Ex *PUT/ROE* SW15 * 131 D2
Putney Heath *PUT/ROE* SW15 ..... 130 B4
Putney Heath La *PUT/ROE* SW15 ..... 131 D4
Putney High St *PUT/ROE* SW15 ..... 131 E2
Putney Hl *PUT/ROE* SW15 ..... 130 C5
Putney Park Av *PUT/ROE* SW15 ..... 130 A2
Putney Park La *PUT/ROE* SW15 ..... 130 B2
Pymers Md *DUL* SE21 ..... 154 C1
Pyrland Rd *HBRY* N5 ..... 77 D2
Pyrmont Gv *WNWD* SE27 ..... 154 B3
Pyrmont Rd *CHSWK* W4 ..... 110 A2
Pytchley Rd *EDUL* SE22 ..... 137 E1

Q

The Quadrangle *BAY/PAD* W2 ..... 16 C4
  HNHL SE24 * 136 C3
  WBPTN SW10 * 114 C4
Quadrant Ar *REGST* W1B 31 F2
Quadrant Gv *KTTN* NW5 ..... 73 F2
The Quadrant *NKENS* W10 * 89 D2
Quaggy Wk *BKHTH/KID* SE3 ..... 142 A2
Quainton St *WLSDN* NW10 ..... 51 D5
Quakers Pl *FSTGT* E7 ..... 83 D2
Quaker St *WCHPL* E1 ..... 25 E1
Quality Ct *LINN* WC2A 22 A4
Quantock Gdns *CRICK* NW2 ..... 53 D4
Quarley Wy *PECK* SE15 ..... 120 A5
Quarrendon St *FUL/PGN* SW6 ..... 114 A4
Quarry Rd *WAND/EARL* SW18 ..... 132 C4
Quay House *POP/IOD* E14 * 104 A3
Quebec Ms *MBLAR* W1H 17 F5
Quebec Rd *GNTH/NBYPK* IG2 ..... 66 C2
Quebec Wy *BERM/RHTH* SE16 ..... 103 D5
Queen Anne Ms *CAVSQ/HST* W1G 19 D3
Queen Anne Rd *HOM* E9 ..... 79 D3
Queen Anne's Gdns *CHSWK* W4 ..... 99 E3
Queen Anne's Ga *STJSPK* SW1H 44 A1
Queen Anne's Gv *CHSWK* W4 ..... 99 E4
Queen Anne St *CAVSQ/HST* W1G 19 D4
Queen Anne Ter *WAP* E1W * 102 B1
Queen Caroline Est *HMSMTH* W6 ..... 112 C1
Queen Caroline St *HMSMTH* W6 ..... 112 C1
Queen Elizabeth Blds *EMB* EC4Y * 34 A1
Queen Elizabeth College
  GNWCH SE10 ..... 122 C3
Queen Elizabeth's Cl
  STNW/STAM N16 ..... 59 D3
Queen Elizabeth St *STHWK* SE1 ..... 37 D5
Queen Elizabeth's Wk
  STNW/STAM N16 ..... 59 D3
Queen Elizabeth Wk *BARN* SW13 ..... 112 A4
Queenhithe *BLKFR* EC4V 35 F2
Queen Isabella Wy *STBT* EC1A 23 D4
Queen Margaret's Gv *IS* N1 ..... 77 E2
Queen Mother Ga *MYFR/PICC* W1J.. ..... 30 B4
Queensberry Ms West *SKENS* SW7 *... ..... 40 A4
Queensberry Pl *MNPK* E12. ..... 83 D2
  SKENS SW7 ..... 40 A4
Queensberry Wy *SKENS* SW7 * 40 A4
Queensborough Ms *BAY/PAD* W2 *... ..... 27 E1
Queensborough Pas *BAY/PAD* W2 *.. ..... 27 E1
Queensborough Studios
  BAY/PAD W2 * 27 E1
Queensborough Ter *BAY/PAD* W2 ..... 27 D1
Queensbridge Rd *HACK* E8 ..... 77 F3
Queensbury Rd *CDALE/KGS* NW9 ..... 51 D2
Queensbury St *IS* N1 ..... 76 C4
Queens Circ *VX/NE* SW8 ..... 116 B3
Queen's Club Gdns *WKENS* W14 ..... 113 E2
Queens Club Ter *WKENS* W14 * 113 F2
Queen's Crs *KTTN* NW5 ..... 74 A2
Queenscroft Rd *ELTH/MOT* SE9 ..... 143 E5
Queensdale Crs *NTGHL* W11. ..... 101 D2
Queensdale Pl *NTGHL* W11. ..... 101 E2
Queensdale Rd *NTGHL* W11. ..... 101 D2
Queensdale Wk *NTGHL* W11. ..... 101 E2
Queens Down Rd *CLPT* E5. ..... 78 B1
Queens Dr *LEY* E10. ..... 62 A2
Queen's Dr *FSBYPK* N4. ..... 58 B4
Queen's Elm Sq *WBPTN* SW10. ..... 115 D1
Queen's Gdns *BAY/PAD* W2 * 27 E1
Queens Garth *FSTH* SE23 * 156 C2
Queens Ga *SKENS* SW7 ..... 39 F1

Queen's Ga *SKENS* SW7 — 39 F1
Queensgate Gdns *PUT/ROE* SW15 — 130 B2
Queen's Gate Gdns *SKENS* SW7 — 39 E3
Queen's Gate Ms *SKENS* SW7 — 39 E2
Queensgate Pl *KIL/WHAMP* NW6 — 72 A4
Queen's Gate Pl *SKENS* SW7 — 39 F3
Queen's Gate Place Ms *SKENS* SW7 — 39 F3
Queen's Gate Ter *SKENS* SW7 — 39 E3
Queen's Gro *STJWD* NW8 — 73 D5
Queen's Head St *IS* N1 — 76 B5
Queensland Rd *HOLWY* N7 — 76 A1
Queensmead *STJWD* NW8 — 73 D5
Queensmere Cl *WIM/MER* SW19 — 149 D2
Queensmere Rd *WIM/MER* SW19 — 149 D2
Queen's Ms *BAY/PAD* W2 — 26 C1
Queensmill Rd *FUL/PGN* SW6 — 113 D3
Queens Pde *CRICK* NW2 * — 70 C3
Queen Sq *BMSBY* WC1N — 21 D1
Queen's Ride *PUT/ROE* SW15 — 130 A2
Queen's Rd *BARK* IG11 — 84 C4
MORT/ESHN SW14 — 129 D1
PECK SE15 — 120 C4
PLSTW E13 — 82 B5
RCHPK/HAM TW10 — 146 A5
WALTH E17 — 61 F1
WAN E11 — 63 E2
WIM/MER SW19 — 150 B5
Queen's Rd West *PLSTW* E13 — 94 A1
Queen's Rw *WALW* SE17 — 119 D2
Queens Ter *PLSTW* E13 — 82 B5
WCHPL E1 * — 90 C5
Queen's Ter *STJWD* NW8 — 73 D5
Queensthorpe Ms *SYD* SE26 * — 157 D4
Queensthorpe Rd *SYD* SE26 — 157 D4
Queenstown Rd *VX/NE* SW8 — 116 B5
SToN SO C3
STP SW20 — 23 F5
Queen St *MYFR/PICC* W1J — 30 C3
STP SW20 — 23 F5
Queen Street Pl *CANST* EC4R — 35 F2
Queensville Rd *BAL* SW12 — 135 D5
The Queens Wk *STHWK* SE1 — 39 F3
Queensway *BAY/PAD* W2 — 15 D4
Queen's Whf *HMSMTH* W6 — 112 C1
Queenswood Gdns *WAN* E11 — 64 A3
Queenswood Rd *BFN/LL* DA15 — 145 F3
FSTH SE23 — 157 E3
Queen's Wood Rd *HGT* N6 — 56 B1
Queen's Yd *FITZ* W1T — 19 F1
Queen Victoria St *BLKFR* EC4V — 34 C1
MANHO EC4N — 23 F5
Queen Victoria Ter *WAP* E1W * — 102 B1
Quemerford Rd *HOLWY* N7 — 75 F2
Quentin Pl *LEW* SE13 — 141 E1
Quentin Rd *LEW* SE13 — 141 E1
Quernmore Rd *FSBYPK* N4 — 58 A1
Querrin St *FUL/PGN* SW6 — 114 C5
Quex Ms *KIL/WHAMP* NW6 — 72 A5
Quex Rd *KIL/WHAMP* NW6 — 72 A5
Quick Rd *CHSWK* W4 — 111 E1
Quick St *IS* N1 — 11 D2
Quicksword *HAMP* NW3 — 73 E4
Quill St *FSBYPK* N4 — 58 A5
Quilp St *STHWK* SE1 — 35 E5
Quilters Pl *ELTH/MOTSE9* — 162 C1
Quilter St *BETH* E2 — 90 A2
WOOL/PLUM SE18 — 127 F1
Quince Rd *LEW* SE13 — 122 B5
Quinnell Cl *WOOL/PLUM* SE18 — 127 F1
Quinton Rd *WAND/EARL* SE18 — 150 C2
Quixley St *POP/IOD* E14 — 105 D1
Quorn Rd *EDUL* SE22 — 137 F2

Rabbit Rw *KENS* W8 * — 26 B3
Rabbits Rd *MNPK* E12 — 83 E1
Raby St *POP/IOD* E14 * — 91 E5
Racton Rd *FUL/PGN* SW6 — 114 A2
Radbourne Cl *CLPT* E5 — 79 D1
Radbourne Rd *BAL* SW12 — 134 C5
Radcliffe Av *WLSDN* NW10 — 88 A1
Radcliffe Rd *STHWK* SE1 — 49 D2
Radcliffe Sq *PUT/ROE* SW15 — 131 D4
Radcot St *LBTH* SE11 — 118 A1
Raddington Rd *NKENS* W10 — 89 E4
Radfield Wy *BFN/LL* DA15 — 145 D5
Radford Est *WLSDN* NW10 * — 87 E2
Radford Rd *LEW* SE13 — 140 C4
Radford Wy *BARK* IG11 — 97 F2
Radipole Rd *FUL/PGN* SW6 — 113 F4
Radland Rd *CAN/RD* E16 — 94 A5
Radlet Av *SYD* SE26 — 156 B3
Radlett Cl *FSTGT* E7 — 81 F3
Radlett Pl *STJWD* NW8 — 73 E5
Radley Av *GDMY/SEVK* IG3 — 85 F1
Radley Ct *BERM/RHTH* SE16 — 103 D3
Radley Ms *KENS* W8 — 38 B3
Radley Sq *CLPT* E5 * — 60 C4
Radley Ter *CAN/RD* E16 * — 93 F4
Radlix Rd *LEY* E10 — 62 A3
Radnor Ms *BAY/PAD* W2 — 16 B5
Radnor Pl *BAY/PAD* W2 — 16 C5
Radnor Rd *KIL/WHAMP* NW6 — 71 E5
PECK SE15 — 120 A3
Radnor St *FSBYE* EC1V — 11 F4
Radnor Ter *WKENS* W14 — 101 F5
Radnor Wk *CHEL* SW3 — 115 E3
Radstock St *BTSEA* SW11 * — 115 E3
Raeburn Cl *GLDGN* NW11 — 54 C1
Raeburn Rd *BFN/LL* DA15 — 145 E4
Raeburn St *BRXS/STRHM* SW2 — 135 E2
Raglan Rd *WOOL/PLUM* SE18 — 126 C1
Raglan St *KTTN* NW5 — 74 B3
Ragley Cl *ACT* W3 — 98 C3
Railey Ms *KTTN* NW5 — 74 C2
Railton Rd *HNHL* SE24 — 136 A3
Railway Ap *FSBYPK* N4 — 58 A1
STHWK SE1 — 36 B3
Railway Av *BRXN/ST* SW9 * — 136 A2
Railway Av *BERM/RHTH* SE16 — 102 C3
Railway Cots *HMSMTH* W6 * — 100 C3
SRTFD E15 * — 93 E1
WIM/MER SW19 * — 150 B4
Railway Gv *NWCR* SE14 — 121 F3
Railway Ri *EDUL* SE22 — 137 E2
Railway Side *BARN* SW13 — 129 E1
Railway Station Whf *LEY* E10 * — 61 E3
Railway St *IS* N1 — 9 D2
Railway Ter *LEW* SE13 — 140 B5
Rainborough Cl *WAP* E1W — 68 C3
Rainbow Av *POP/IOD* E14 — 122 B1
Rainbow Quay *BERM/RHTH* SE16 — 103 E4
Rainbow St *CMBW* SE5 — 119 E3
Raine St *WAP* E1W — 102 B2
Rainham Cl *BTSEA* SW11 — 133 E4
Rainham Rd *WLSDN* NW10 — 88 C2
Rainhill Wy *BOW* E3 — 92 A2
Rainsborough Av *DEPT* SE8 — 103 E5
Rainsford Rd *WLSDN* NW10 — 86 B2
Rainsford St *BAY/PAD* W2 — 16 C4
Rainton Rd *CHARL* SE7 — 124 A1
Rainville Rd *HMSMTH* W6 — 112 C2
Raleigh Gdns *BRXS/STRHM* SW2 — 135 F4
Raleigh Ms *IS* N1 — 76 B5
Raleigh St *IS* N1 — 76 B5
Ralston St *CHEL* SW3 — 115 F1
Ramac Wy *CHARL* SE7 — 106 B5
Rambler Cl *STRHM/NOR* SW16 — 152 C4
Rame Cl *TOOT* SW17 — 152 A5
Ramillies Cl *BRXS/STRHM* SW2 — 135 E4
Ramillies Pl *SOHO/CST* W1F — 19 E5
Ramillies Rd *CHSWK* W4 — 99 D4
Ramillies St *SOHO/SHAV* W1D — 19 E5
Rampart St *WCHPL* E1 — 90 B5
Rampayne St *PIM* SW1V — 117 D1
Ramsay Rd *ACT* W3 — 98 C4
FSTGT E7 — 81 F1
Ramsdale Rd *TOOT* SW17 — 152 A5
Ramsden Ga *BAL* SW12 * — 134 B5
Ramsden Rd *BAL* SW12 — 134 A5
Ramsey Cl *CDALE/KGS* NW9 — 51 F1
Ramsey St *BETH* E2 — 90 A3
Ramsey Wk *IS* N1 — 77 D3
Ramsgate Cl *CAN/RD* E16 — 106 B2
Ramsgate St *HACK* E8 * — 77 F3
Rancliffe Gdns *ELTH/MOT* SE9 — 143 E2
Rancliffe Rd *EHAM* E6 — 95 E1
Randall Av *CRICK* NW2 — 51 E4
Randall Cl *BTSEA* SW11 — 115 E4
Randall Pl *GNWCH* SE10 — 122 C3
Randall Rd *LBTH* SE11 — 117 F1
Randall Rw *LBTH* SE11 — 45 E5
Randell's Rd *IS* N1 — 75 E5
Randisbourne Gdns *CAT* SE6 * — 158 B3
Randlesdown Rd *CAT* SE6 — 158 A4
Randolph Ap *CAN/RD* E16 — 94 C5
Randolph Av *MV/WKIL* W9 — 2 C2
Randolph Cl *KUTN/CMB* KT2 * — 146 C5
Randolph Crs *MV/WKIL* W9 — 15 E1

Randolph Gdns KIL/WHAMP NW6 ... 2 C2
Randolph Ms MV/WKIL W9 ... 15 F1
Randolph Rd MV/WKIL W9 ... 15 E1
Ranelagh Av BARN SW13 ... 112 A5
   FUL/PGN SW6 ... 131 F1
Ranelagh Gdns CHSWK W4 ... 110 C3
   FUL/PGN SW6 ... 131 E1
   IL IG1 ... 86 A3
Ranelagh Gv BCVA SW1W ... 116 A1
Ranelagh Rd EHAM E6 ... 84 A5
   PIM SW1V ... 116 C1
   SRTFD E15 ... 81 E5
   WLSDN NW10 ... 87 F1
Rangefield Rd BMLY BR1 ... 152 B5
Rangeworthy Pl BFN/LL DA15 ... 163 F5
Rangoon St TWRH EC3N * ... 25 C3
Ranmere St BAL SW12 ... 152 B1
Rannoch Rd HMSMTH W6 ... 112 C2
Rannock Av CDALE/KGS NW9 ... 51 D2
Ransom Rd CHARL SE7 ... 106 C5
Ranston St CAMTN NW1 ... 16 C2
Ranulf Rd CRICK NW2 ... 71 F1
Ranwell Cl BOW E3 * ... 79 F5
Raphael St SKENS SW7 ... 41 E1
Rastell Av BRXS/STRHM SW2 ... 153 D2
Ratcliffe Cl LEE/GVPK SE12 ... 142 A5
Ratcliffe Cross St WCHPL E1 * ... 91 D5
Ratcliffe La POP/IOD E14 ... 91 E5
Ratcliff Rd FSTGT E7 ... 82 C2
Rathbone Market CAN/RD E16 ... 93 F4
Rathbone Pl FITZ W1T ... 20 A3
Rathbone St CAN/RD E16 ... 93 F4
   FITZ W1T ... 19 F3
Rathfern Rd CAT SE6 ... 157 F1
Rathgar Rd BRXN/ST SW9 ... 136 B1
Rathmell Dr CLAP SW4 ... 135 D4
Rathmore Rd CHARL SE7 ... 106 B4
Rattray Rd BRXS/STRHM SW2 ... 136 A2
Raul Rd PECK SE15 ... 120 A3
Raveley St KTTN NW5 ... 74 C1
Ravelston Crs ELTH/MOT SE9 ... 161 F3
Ravenet St BTSEA SW11 ... 116 B4
Ravenfield Rd TOOT SW17 ... 151 F3
Ravenhill Rd PLSTW E13 ... 82 C5
Ravenna Rd PUT/ROE SW15 ... 131 D3
Raven Rw WCHPL E1 ... 90 B4
Ravensbourne Pk CAT SE6 ... 140 A5
Ravensbourne Park Crs CAT SE6 ... 139 F5
Ravensbourne Pl LEW SE13 ... 122 B5
Ravensbourne Rd CAT SE6 ... 139 F5
Ravensbury Rd WAND/EARL SW18 ... 150 B2
Ravensbury Ter WAND/EARL SW18 ... 150 B2
Ravenscar Rd BMLY BR1 ... 159 E4
Ravenscourt Av HMSMTH W6 ... 100 A5
Ravenscourt Gdns HMSMTH W6 ... 99 F5
Ravenscourt Pk HMSMTH W6 ... 100 A5
Ravenscourt Pl HMSMTH W6 ... 100 B5
Ravenscourt Sq HMSMTH W6 ... 100 A4
Ravenscroft Av GLDGN NW11 ... 53 F2
Ravenscroft Cl CAN/RD E16 ... 94 A4
Ravenscroft Rd CAN/RD E16 ... 94 A4
   CHSWK W4 ... 98 C5
Ravenscroft St BETH E2 ... 13 F2
Ravensdale Rd STNW/STAM N16 ... 59 F2
Ravensdon St LBTH SE11 ... 118 A1
Ravenshaw St KIL/WHAMP NW6 ... 71 F2
Ravenslea Rd BAL SW12 ... 133 F5
Ravensleigh Gdns BMLY BR1 ... 160 A5
Ravensmede Wy CHSWK W4 ... 99 F5
Ravens Ms LEE/GVPK SE12 ... 142 A3
Ravenstone Rd CDALE/KGS NW9 * ... 51 F1
Ravenstone St BAL SW12 ... 152 A1
Ravens Wy LEE/GVPK SE12 ... 142 A3
Ravenswood Rd BAL SW12 ... 134 B5
Ravensworth Rd ELTH/MOT SE9 ... 161 F4
   WLSDN NW10 * ... 88 B2
Ravey St SDTCH EC2A ... 12 C5
Ravine Gv WOOL/PLUM SE18 ... 127 E2
Raw Pinter Cl STNW/STAM N16 ... 59 E2
Rawlings Crs WBLY HA9 ... 50 B5
Rawlings St CHEL SW3 ... 41 E4
Rawreth Wk IS N1 * ... 76 B5
Rawson St BTSEA SW11 ... 116 A4
Rawsthorne Cl CAN/RD E16 ... 107 F2
Rawstone Pl FSBYE EC1V * ... 10 C3
Rawstorne St FSBYE EC1V ... 10 C3
Ray Bell Ct BROCKY SE4 * ... 121 F1
Raydon St ARCH N19 ... 56 B1
Rayford Av LEE/GVPK SE12 ... 141 F5
Rayleas Cl WOOL/PLUM SE18 ... 126 B4
Rayleigh Rd CAN/RD E16 ... 106 B2

Raymere Gdns WOOL/PLUM SE18 ... 127 D3
Raymond Blds GINN WC1R * ... 21 F2
Raymond Cl SYD SE26 ... 156 C5
Raymond Rd GNTH/NBYPK IG2 ... 67 D2
   PLSTW E13 ... 82 C4
Raymouth Rd BERM/RHTH SE16 ... 102 B5
Rayner's Rd PUT/ROE SW15 ... 131 E3
Raynes Av WAN E11 ... 64 C2
Raynham Rd HMSMTH W6 ... 100 B5
Raynor Pl IS N1 ... 76 C5
Reachview Cl CAMTN NW1 ... 74 C4
Reading La HACK E8 ... 78 B3
Reads Cl IL IG1 ... 66 B5
Reapers Cl CAMTN NW1 ... 75 D5
Reardon Pth WAP E1W ... 102 B2
Reardon St WAP E1W ... 102 B2
Reaston St NWCR SE14 ... 120 C3
Reckitt Rd CHSWK W4 ... 111 E1
Record St PECK SE15 ... 120 C2
Recovery St TOOT SW17 ... 151 F5
Recreation Rd SYD SE26 ... 157 D4
Rectar Pl ARCH N19 ... 56 B4
Rector St IS N1 ... 76 C5
Rectory Field Crs CHARL SE7 ... 124 C5
Rectory Gv CLAP SW4 ... 134 C1
Rectory La TOOT SW17 ... 152 A5
Rectory Orch WIM/MER SW19 ... 149 E4
Rectory Pl WOOL/PLUM SE18 ... 108 A5
Rectory Rd BARN SW13 ... 112 A5
   MNPK E12 ... 83 F2
   STNW/STAM N16 ... 59 F5
Rectory Sq WCHPL E1 ... 91 D4
Reculver Rd BERM/RHTH SE16 ... 121 D1
Red Anchor Cl CHEL SW3 ... 115 D2
Red Pl BAY/PAD W2 ... 14 C5
Redan St WKENS W14 ... 101 D4
Redan Ter CMBW SE5 ... 118 B5
Red Barracks Rd WOOL/PLUM SE18 ... 107 F5
Redberry Gv SYD SE26 ... 156 C5
Redbridge Gdns CMBW SE5 ... 119 E3
Redbridge La East REDBR IG4 ... 65 D1
Redbridge La West WAN E11 ... 64 B1
Redburn St CHEL SW3 ... 115 F2
Redcar St CMBW SE5 ... 118 C3
Redcastle Cl WAP E1W ... 102 C1
Redchurch St BETH E2 ... 13 E3
Redcliffe Gdns IL IG1 ... 66 A3
   WBPTN SW10 ... 114 B1
Redcliffe Ms WBPTN SW10 ... 114 B1
Redcliffe Pl WBPTN SW10 ... 114 C2
Redcliffe Rd WBPTN SW10 ... 114 C1
Redcliffe Sq WBPTN SW10 ... 114 B2
Redcliffe St WBPTN SW10 * ... 114 B2
Redcliffe Rd PLSTW E13 ... 82 C5
Redcross Wy STHWK SE1 ... 35 F5
Reddins Rd PECK SE15 ... 120 A3
Rede Pl BAY/PAD W2 ... 14 B3
Redesdale St CHEL SW3 ... 115 F2
Redfern Rd CAT SE6 ... 140 C5
   WLSDN NW10 ... 69 E4
Redfield La ECT SW5 ... 38 C4
Redford Wk IS N1 * ... 76 B5
Redgate Ter PUT/ROE SW15 ... 131 E4
Redgrave Rd PUT/ROE SW15 ... 131 D1
Redgrave Ter BETH E2 * ... 90 A2
Redhall Ter EA W5 * ... 98 A1
Red Hl CHST BR7 ... 162 A5
Redhill St CAMTN NW1 ... 7 D3
Red House Sq IS N1 * ... 76 C4
Redington Gdns HAMP NW3 ... 72 B1
Redington Rd HAMP NW3 ... 54 B5
Redlands Wy BRXS/STRHM SW2 ... 135 E5
Red Lion Cl WALW SE17 * ... 119 D2
Red Lion Ct FLST/FETLN EC4A ... 22 B4
Red Lion La WOOL/PLUM SE18 ... 126 A4
Red Lion Pl WOOL/PLUM SE18 * ... 126 A4
Red Lion Rw WALW SE17 ... 118 C2
Red Lion Sq GINN WC1R ... 21 E3
   WAND/EARL SW18 * ... 132 A3
Red Lion St GINN WC1R ... 21 E3
Red Lion Yd MYFR/PKLN W1K * ... 30 A1
Redman's Rd WCHPL E1 ... 90 C4
Redmead La WAP E1W ... 102 A2
Redmore Rd HMSMTH W6 ... 100 B5
Red Pl MYFR/PKLN W1K ... 30 A1
Red Post Hl HNHL SE24 ... 137 D3
Redriffe Rd PLSTW E13 ... 81 D5
Redriff Rd BERM/RHTH SE16 ... 103 E4
Redruth Rd HOM E9 ... 78 C5

Redstart Cl *EHAM* E6................................95 E4
  NWCR SE14 *..121 E3
Redvers St *IS* N1................................13 D3
Redwald Rd *CLPT* E5................................79 D1
Redwing Ms *WLSDN* SE5................................118 C5
Redwood Cl *BERM/RHTH* SE16................103 E2
  BOW E3................................92 A1
Redwood Ms *VX/NE* SW8................................134 B1
Reece Ms *SKENS* SW7................................40 A4
Reed Cl *CAN/RD* E16................................94 A4
  LEE/GVPK SE12................................142 A3
Reedham St *PECK* SE15 *................................120 A5
Reedholm Vls *STNW/STAM* N16................77 D1
Reed Pl *BTSEA* SW11................................133 E2
  CLAP SW4................................135 D2
Reed's Pl *CAMTN* NW1................................74 C4
Reedworth St *LBTH* SE11................................46 B5
Reesland Cl *MNPK* E12................................84 A3
Rees St *IS* N1................................76 C5
Reets Farm Cl *CDALE/KGS* NW9................51 E1
Reeves Av *CDALE/KGS* NW9................................51 D2
Reeves Ms *MYFR/PKLN* W1K................................30 A2
Reeves Rd *BOW* E3................................92 B5
  WOOL/PLUM SE18................................126 B2
Reform St *BTSEA* SW11................................115 F5
Regal Cl *WCHPL* E1................................90 A4
Regal La *CAMTN* NW1................................74 A5
Regal Rw *PECK* SE15................................120 C4
Regan Wy *IS* N1................................12 C2
Regency Cl *KTTN* NW5 *................................58 B5
Regency Ms *WLSDN* NW10................................70 A3
Regency Pde *HAMP* NW3 *................................73 D4
Regency Pl *WEST* SW1P *................................44 A4
Regency St *WEST* SW1P................................44 B5
Regency Ter *HGT* N6 *................................55 F1
  SKENS SW7 *................................115 D1
Regeneration Rd *BERM/RHTH* SE16....103 D5
Regent Pde *STNW/STAM* N16 *................77 E1
Regent Pl *WIM/MER* SW19................................150 C5
Regent Rd *HNHL* SE24................................136 B4
Regents Bridge Gdns *VX/NE* SW8 *................117 E2
Regents Ms *STJWD* NW8................................3 F1
Regent's Park Rd *CAMTN* NW1................73 F5
Regent's Park Ter *CAMTN* NW1................74 B5
Regents Plaza *KIL/WHAMP* NW6 *................2 C1
Regent Sq *BOW* E3................................92 B2
  STPAN WC1H................................9 D4
Regent's Rw *BETH* E2................................78 A5
Regent St *CHSWK* W4................................110 A1
  REGST W1B................................19 D4
  STJS SW1Y................................32 A2
  WLSDN NW10................................89 D2
Regents Whf *IS* N1 *................................9 E1
Regent Whf *IS* N1 *................................9 E1
Reginald Rd *DEPT* SE8................................122 A4
  FSTGT E7................................82 A3
Reginald Sq *DEPT* SE8................................122 A4
Regina Rd *FSBYPK* N4................................57 F3
Regis Rd *KTTN* NW5................................74 B2
Regnart Blds *CAMTN* NW1................................7 F4
Reidhaven Rd *WOOL/PLUM* SE18................109 E5
Reigate Rd *BMLY* BR1................................160 A2
  GDMY/SEVK IG3................................67 F4
Reighton Rd *CLPT* E5................................60 A5
Reinckendorf Av *ELTH/MOT* SE9................144 C3
Reindeer Cl *PLSTW* E15................................82 A5
Reizel Cl *STNW/STAM* N16................................59 F3
Relay Rd *SHB* W12................................100 C1
Relf Rd *PECK* SE15................................138 A1
Reliance Ar *BRXN/ST* SW9 *................136 A2
Relton Ms *SKENS* SW7................................41 D2
Rembrandt Cl *BGVA* SW1W *................116 A1
  POP/IOD E14................................105 D3
Rembrandt Rd *LEW* SE13................................141 E2
Remington Rd *EHAM* E6................................95 E5
  SEVS/STOTM N15................................59 D1
Remington St *IS* N1................................11 D2
Remnant St *HOL/ALD* WC2B................21 E4
Remus Rd *BOW* E3................................80 A4
Renaissance Wk *GNWCH* SE10................105 F4
Rendlesham Rd *CLPT* E5................................78 A1
Renforth St *BERM/RHTH* SE16................102 C5
Renfrew Cl *EHAM* E6................................108 A1
Renfrew Rd *LBTH* SE11................................46 C4
Rennell St *LEW* SE13................................140 C1
Rennets Cl *ELTH/MOT* SE9................................145 D3
Rennets Wood Rd *ELTH/MOT* SE9......145 D3
Rennie Est *BERM/RHTH* SE16................102 B5
Rennie St *STHWK* SE1................................34 C3
Renters Av *HDN* NW4................................52 C1
Renton Cl *BRXS/STRHM* SW2 *................135 F4
Rephidim St *STHWK* SE1................................48 B3

Replingham Rd *WAND/EARL* SW18......149 F1
Reporton Rd *FUL/PGN* SW6................................113 E4
Repository Rd *WOOL/PLUM* SE18......125 F2
Repton St *POP/IOD* E14................................91 E5
Reservoir Rd *BROCKY* SE4................................121 E5
Restell Cl *BKHTH/KID* SE3................................123 E2
Reston Pl *KENS* W8................................39 E1
Restons Crs *ELTH/MOT* SE9................................145 D4
Reston Wy *CAN/RD* E16................................107 D1
Retford St *IS* N1................................13 D2
Retreat Pl *HOM* E9................................78 C3
The Retreat *MORT/ESHN* SW14................129 E1
Reunion Rw *WAP* E1W *................................102 B1
Reveley Sq *BERM/RHTH* SE16................103 E3
Revell Ri *WOOL/PLUM* SE18................................127 F2
Revelon Rd *BROCKY* SE4................................139 E2
Revelstoke Rd *WAND/EARL* SW18......150 A2
  WIM/MER SW19................................149 E4
Reventlow Rd *ELTH/MOT* SE9................162 C1
Reverdy Rd *STHWK* SE1................................102 A5
Review Rd *CRICK* NW2................................51 F4
Rewell St *FUL/PGN* SW6 *................................114 C3
Rex Pl *MYFR/PKLN* W1K................................30 B5
Reydon Av *WAN* E11................................64 C1
Reynard Pl *NWCR* SE14 *................................121 E2
Reynola Gdns *CHARL* SE7................................124 B1
Reynolds Av *MNPK* E12................................84 A2
Reynolds Cl *GLDGN* NW11................................54 B2
Reynolds Pl *BKHTH/KID* SE3................................124 B3
Reynolds Rd *CHSWK* W4................................98 C4
  PECK SE15................................138 C3
Rheidol Ms *IS* N1................................11 E1
Rheidol Ter *IS* N1................................11 D1
Rhoda St *BETH* E2................................13 F5
Rhodesia Rd *BRXN/ST* SW9................................117 E5
  WAN E11................................63 D4
Rhodes St *HOLWY* N7................................75 F2
Rhodeswell Rd *POP/IOD* E14................91 E4
Rhondda Gv *BOW* E3................................91 E2
Rhyl St *KTTN* NW5................................74 A3
Ribblesdale Rd *STRHM/NOR* SW16....153 D5
Ricardo St *POP/IOD* E14................................92 B5
Ricards Rd *WIM/MER* SW19................149 E5
Richard Cl *WOOL/PLUM* SE18................107 E5
Richard House Dr *CAN/RD* E16................95 D5
Richardson Cl *HACK* E8 *................................77 F5
Richardson Rd *SRTFD* E15 *................93 E1
Richardson's Ms *FITZ* W1T................................19 E1
Richard's Pl *CHEL* SW3................................41 D4
Richard St *WCHPL* E1................................90 B5
Richbell Pl *FSBYW* WC1X................................21 E2
Richborne Ter *VX/NE* SW8................................117 F5
Richborough Rd *CRICK* NW2................71 D1
Riches Rd *IL* IG1................................66 C4
Richford Ga *HMSMTH* W6................................100 C4
Richford Rd *SRTFD* E15................................81 F5
Richford St *HMSMTH* W6................................100 C3
Richmond Av *IS* N1................................75 F5
  SOHO/SHAV W1D................................20 A5
Richmond Blds *SOHO/SHAV* W1D................20 A5
Richmond Cl *WALTH* E17................................61 F1
Richmond Crs *IS* N1................................75 F5
Richmond Gv *IS* N1................................76 B4
Richmond Ms *SOHO/SHAV* W1D................20 A5
Richmond Park Rd
  MORT/ESHN SW14................................128 C3
Richmond Pl *WOOL/PLUM* SE18................108 C5
Richmond Rd *FSTGT* E7................................82 B2
  HACK E8................................77 F4
  IL IG1................................66 C5
  SEVS/STOTM N15................................59 E1
  WAN E11................................63 D4
Richmond Rd *PLSTW* E13................................94 A1
Richmond Ter *WHALL* SW1A................32 C5
Richmond Wy *SHB* W12................................101 D3
  WAN E11................................64 A4
Richmount Gdns *BKHTH/KID* SE3................142 A1
Rich St *POP/IOD* E14................................103 F1
Rickard Cl *BRXS/STRHM* SW2................154 A1
Rickett St *FUL/PGN* SW6................................114 A2
Rickman St *WCHPL* E1................................90 C3
Rick Roberts Wy *SRTFD* E15................81 D5
Rickthorne Rd *ARCH* N19 *................................57 E4
Riddons Rd *LEE/GVPK* SE12................160 C3
Rideout St *WOOL/PLUM* SE18................107 F5
Rider Cl *BFN/LL* DA15................................145 E4
Ridgdale St *BOW* E3................................92 B1
Ridge Cl *BKHTH/KID* SE3................................142 C2
Ridge Ct *THMD* SE28................................109 D3
Ridge Hl *GLDGN* NW11................................53 E3
Ridge Rd *CEND/HSY/T* N8................................57 F1

CRICK NW2	53	F5
Ridgeway Dr BMLY BR1	160	B4
Ridgeway East BFN/LL DA15	145	F3
The Ridgeway ACT W3	98	A4
GLDGN NW11	53	F3
Ridgeway Rd BFN/LL DA15	145	E3
Ridgeway West BFN/LL DA15	145	E3
Ridgewell Cl IS N1	76	C5
SYD SE26	157	F4
Ridgmount Gdns GWRST WC1E	20	A2
Ridgmount Rd WAND/EARL SW18	132	B3
Ridgmount St GWRST WC1E	20	A2
Ridgway Rd BRXN/ST SW9	136	B1
Ridgwell Rd CAN/RD E16	94	C4
Riding House St REGST W1B	19	D4
Ridings Cl HGT N6	56	C2
The Riding GLDGN NW11	53	F2
Ridley Cl BARK IG11	82	C1
Ridley Rd FSTGT E7	77	F2
HACK E8	77	F2
WLSDN NW10	88	A1
Riefield Rd ELTH/MOT SE9	144	C2
Riffel Rd CRICK NW2	52	C2
Rifle St POP/IOD E14	92	B4
Rigault Rd FUL/PGN SW6	113	E5
Rigby Ms IL IG1	66	A4
Rigden St POP/IOD E14	92	B5
Rigeley Rd WLSDN NW10	88	A3
Rigg Ap LEY E10	61	D5
Rigge Pl CLAP SW4	135	D2
Riggindale Rd STRHM/NOR SW16	153	D5
Riley Rd STHWK SE1	49	E2
Riley St WBPTN SW10	115	D3
Rinaldo Rd BAL SW12	134	B3
Ringcroft St HOLWY N7	76	A2
Ringford Rd WAND/EARL SW18	131	F3
Ringlet Cl CAN/RD E16	94	B4
Ringmer Av FUL/PGN SW6	113	E4
Ringmore Ri FSTH SE23	138	B5
Ring Rd SHB W12	100	C2
Ringstead Rd CAT SE6	140	B5
Ringwood Gdns PUT/ROE SW15	148	A2
Ringwood Rd WALTH E17	61	F1
Ripley Gdns MORT/ESHN SW14	129	D1
Ripley Ms WAN E11	63	E1
Ripley Rd CAN/RD E16	94	C5
GDMY/SEVK IG3	67	E4
Ripon Gdns IL IG1	65	E1
Ripon Rd WOOL/PLUM SE18	126	B2
Ripple Rd BARK IG11	84	C4
Ripplevale Gv IS N1	75	F4
Rippolson Rd WOOL/PLUM SE18	127	F1
Risborough St STHWK SE1	35	D5
Risdon St BERM/RHTH SE16	102	C3
Riseldine Rd FSTH SE23	139	E4
The Rise WLSDN NW10	51	D5
Risinghill St IS N1	10	A1
Rita Rd VX/NE SW8	117	E3
Ritchie St IS N1	10	B1
Ritherdon Rd TOOT SW17	152	A2
Ritson Rd HACK E8	77	F3
Ritter St WOOL/PLUM SE18	126	A2
Rivaz Pl HOM E9	78	C3
Riverbank Rd BMLY BR1	160	A3
River Barge Cl POP/IOD E14	104	C3
River Cl WAN E11	64	C1
Rivercourt Rd HMSMTH W6	100	B5
Riverdale Dr WAND/EARL SW18	150	B1
Riverdale Rd WOOL/PLUM SE18	127	F1
River Pl IS N1	66	A5
River Rd BARK IG11	97	E2
Riversdale Rd HBRY N5	58	B5
Riverside CHARL SE7	106	B4
HDN NW4	52	B2
RCH/KEW TW9	110	A2
Riverside Cl CLPT E5	60	C3
Riverside Dr CHSWK W4	111	D3
GLDGN NW11 *	53	E1
Riverside Gdns HMSMTH W6	112	B1
Riverside Rd IL IG1	66	B5
SEVS/STOTM N15	60	A1
SRTFD E15	92	C1
TOOT SW17	150	B4
Riverside Yd TOOT SW17	150	B3
River St CLKNW EC1R	10	A3
River Ter HMSMTH W6	112	B1
Riverton Cl MV/WKIL W9 *	89	F2
Riverview Gdns BARN SW13	112	B2
Riverview Gv CHSWK W4	110	B2
Riverview Pk CAT SE6	158	A2
Riverview Rd CHSWK W4	110	B3
River Wy GNWCH SE10	105	F4
Rivington Pl FSBYE EC1V	13	D1
Rivington St SDTCH EC2A	13	D4
Rivington Wk HACK E8 *	78	A5
Rixon St HOLWY N7	58	A5
Rixsen Rd MNPK E12	83	E2
Roach Rd BOW E3	80	A4
Roads Pl ARCH N19	57	E4
Roan St GNWCH SE10	122	C2
Robert Adam St MHST W1U	18	A4
Roberta St BETH E2	90	A2
Robert Cl MV/WKIL W9	15	F1
Robert Dashwood Wy WALW SE17	47	E5
Robert Keen Cl PECK SE15	120	A4
Robert Lowe Cl NWCR SE14	121	D5
Roberts Cl ELTH/MOT SE9	163	D1
Roberts Ct WLSDN NW10	69	E3
Roberts House WOOL/PLUM SE18 *	125	E3
Roberts Ms KTBR SW1X *	42	A3
Robertson St VX/NE SW8	116	B5
Robert's Pl CLKNW EC1R *	10	B5
Robert Sq LEW SE13	140	C2
Robert St CAMTN NW1	7	D4
CHCR WC2N	33	D2
WOOL/PLUM SE18	109	D5
Robeson St BOW E3	91	F4
Robina Cl BXLYHN DA7	145	F5
Robin Gv HGT N6	56	A4
Robin Hood Gdns POP/IOD E14 *	104	C1
Robin Hood La POP/IOD E14	104	C1
PUT/ROE SW15	147	E3
Robin Hood Rd PUT/ROE SW15	147	E4
Robin Hood Wy PUT/ROE SW15	147	E3
Robinia Crs LEY E10	62	B4
Robinson Cl WAN E11	63	E5
Robinson Rd BETH E2	90	C1
PUT/ROE SW15	115	F2
Robinswood Ms HBRY N5	76	B2
Robinwood Pl PUT/ROE SW15	147	D4
Robsart St BRXN/ST SW9	117	F5
Robson Av WLSDN NW10	70	A4
Robson Rd EHAM E6	95	E5
Robson Rd WNWD SE27	154	B3
Rocastle Rd BROCKY SE4	139	E3
Rochdale Rd WALTH E17	62	A2
Rochdale Wy DEPT SE8	122	A3
Rochelle Cl BTSEA SW11	133	D2
Rochelle St BETH E2	13	E4
Rochemont Wk HACK E8 *	77	F5
Rochester Av PLSTW E13	82	C5
Rochester Gdns IL IG1	65	F2
Rochester Ms CAMTN NW1	74	C3
Rochester Pl CAMTN NW1	74	C3
Rochester Rd CAMTN NW1	74	C3
Rochester Rw WEST SW1P	43	F4
Rochester Sq CAMTN NW1	74	C4
Rochester St WEST SW1P	44	A3
Rochester Ter CAMTN NW1	74	C3
Rochester Wk STHWK SE1 *	36	A5
Rochester Wy BKHTH/KID SE3	124	B4
ELTH/MOT SE9	143	E2
Rochester Way Relief Rd		
ELTH/MOT SE9	143	E3
Rochford Cl EHAM E6	95	D1
Rochford Wk HACK E8 *	78	A4
Rock Av MORT/ESHN SW14	129	D1
Rockbourne Rd FSTH SE23	157	D1
Rockell's Pl EDUL SE22	138	B4
Rock Grove Wy BERM/RHTH SE16	102	A5
Rockhall Rd CRICK NW2	71	D1
Rockhampton Rd STRHM/NOR SW16	154	A4
Rock Hl DUL SE21	155	F4
Rockingham Cl PUT/ROE SW15	129	F2
Rockingham St STHWK SE1	47	E3
Rockland Rd PUT/ROE SW15	131	E2
Rockley Rd SHB W12	100	D3
Rockmount Rd WOOL/PLUM SE18	127	F1
Rocks La BARN SW13	130	A1
Rock St FSBYPK N4	58	A4
Rockwell Gdns NRWD SE19	155	E4
Rocliffe St IS N1	11	D1
Rocombe Crs FSTH SE23	138	C5
Rocque La BKHTH/KID SE3	141	F1
Rodborough Rd GLDGN NW11	54	A3
Rodenhurst Rd CLAP SW4	134	C5
Roden St HOLWY N7	57	F5
IL IG1	66	A5
Roderick Rd HAMP NW3	73	F1
Roding Ms WAP E1W	102	A2
Roding Rd CLPT E5	79	D1
EHAM E6	96	B4
Rodmarton St MHST W1U	17	F3

Rodmere St *GNWCH* SE10	123	E1
Rodney Pl *STHWK* SE1	47	F4
Rodney Rd *WALW* SE17	47	F5
Rodney St *IS* N1	9	F2
Rodway Rd *PUT/ROE* SW15	130	A5
Rodwell Rd *EDUL* SE22	137	F4
Roedean Crs *PUT/ROE* SW15	129	E3
Roehampton Cl *PUT/ROE* SW15	130	A2
Roehampton Ga *PUT/ROE* SW15	129	E4
Roehampton High St *PUT/ROE* SW15..	130	A5
Roehampton La *PUT/ROE* SW15	148	B1
Roehampton V *PUT/ROE* SW15	147	F3
Roffey St *POP/IOD* E14	104	C3
Rogers Rd *CAN/RD* E16	95	F5
TOOT SW17	151	D4
Roger St *BMSBY* WC1N	21	F1
Rojack Rd *FSTH* SE23	157	D1
Rokeby Rd *BROCKY* SE4	121	F5
Rokeby St *SRTFD* E15	81	E5
Rokesby Cl *WELL* DA16	127	D5
Roland Gdns *SKENS* SW7	31	D5
Roland Ms *WCHPL* E1 *	91	D4
Roland Wy *SKENS* SW7	114	C1
WALW SE17	119	D1
Rollins St *PECK* SE15	120	C2
Rollit St *HOLWY* N7	76	A2
Rolls Blds *FLST/FETLN* EC4A *	22	B4
Rollscourt Av *HNHL* SE24	136	C3
Rolls Rd *STHWK* SE1	119	F1
Rolt St *DEPT* SE8	121	F2
NWCR SE14	121	E2
Romanfield Rd *BRXS/STRHM* SW2	98	B3
Romanfield Rd *BRXS/STRHM* SW2	135	F5
Roman Rd *BETH* E2	91	D1
BOW E3	79	F5
CHSWK W4	99	E5
CRICK NW2	52	C5
EHAM E6	95	E3
IL IG1	84	B5
Roman St *HOLWY* N7 *	75	D4
Romberg Rd *TOOT* SW17	152	A3
Romborough Gdns *LEW* SE13	140	C3
Romborough Wy *LEW* SE13	140	C3
Romero Cl *BRXN/ST* SW9	135	F1
Romero Sq *BKHTH/KID* SE3	142	C2
Romeyn Rd *STRHM/NOR* SW16	153	F3
Romford Rd *FSTGT* E7	82	C2
MNPK E12	83	E1
SRTFD E15	81	F3
Romford St *WCHPL* E1	90	A4
Romilly Rd *FSBYPK* N4	58	B4
Romilly St *SOHO/SHAV* W1D	32	B1
Rommany Rd *WNWD* SE27	155	D4
Romney Cl *GLDGN* NW11	54	C3
NWCR SE14	120	C3
Romney Rd *GNWCH* SE10	122	C2
WOOL/PLUM SE18	108	C4
Romney Rw *CRICK* NW2 *	53	D4
Romney St *WEST* SW1P	44	B3
Romola Rd *HNHL* SE24	154	B1
Ronald Av *SRTFD* E15	93	E2
Ronalds Rd *HBRY* N5	76	A2
Ronaldstone Rd *BFN/LL* DA15	145	E4
Rona Rd *HAMP* NW3	74	A1
Rona Wk *IS* N1 *	77	D3
Rondu Rd *CRICK* NW2	71	E2
Ron Leighton Wy *EHAM* E6	83	E5
Ronver Rd *LEE/GVPK* SE12	160	A1
Rood La *FENCHST* EC3M	36	C1
Rook Cl *WBLY* HA9	50	B5
Rookery Cl *CLAP* SW4	134	C2
Rookstone Rd *TOOT* SW17	151	F5
Rookwood Rd *STNW/STAM* N16	60	A2
Rootes Dr *NKENS* W10	89	D3
Ropemaker Rd *BERM/RHTH* SE16	103	E3
Ropemaker's Flds *POP/IOD* E14 *	103	F1
Ropemaker St *BARB* EC2Y	24	A2
Roper La *STHWK* SE1	49	D1
Ropers Orch *CHEL* SW3 *	115	E2
Roper St *ELTH/MOT* SE9	143	F3
Ropery St *BOW* E3	91	F3
Rope St *BERM/RHTH* SE16	103	E4
Ropewalk Gdns *WCHPL* E1	90	A5
Ropewalk Ms *HACK* E8 *	77	F4
Rope Yard Rails *WOOL/PLUM* SE18	108	B4
Ropley St *BETH* E2	90	A1
Rosa Alba Ms *HBRY* N5	76	C1
Rosaline Rd *FUL/PGN* SW6	113	E3
Rosaline Ter *FUL/PGN* SW6 *	113	E3
Rosamond St *SYD* SE26	156	B3
Rosamond Vls *MORT/ESHN* SW14 *	129	D2
Rosary Gdns *SKENS* SW7	39	F5

Rosary Ga *BTSEA* SW11	116	B3
Rosaville Rd *FUL/PGN* SW6	113	F3
Roscoe St *STLK* EC1Y	23	F1
Rose Aly *LVPST* EC2M *	25	D3
STHWK SE1 *	35	F3
Rosebank Est *BOW* E3	91	F1
Rosebank Gdns *ACT* W3 *	87	D5
BOW E3	91	E1
Rosebank Rd *WALTH* E17	62	A1
Rosebank Wk *CAMTN* NW1 *	75	D4
Rosebank Wy *ACT* W3	87	D5
Roseberry Gdns *FSBYPK* N4	58	B1
Roseberry Pl *HACK* E8	77	F3
Roseberry St *BERM/RHTH* SE16	102	B5
Rosebery Av *BFN/LL* DA15	145	E5
CLKNW EC1R	22	A1
MNPK E12	83	D3
Rosebery Ct *CLKNW* EC1R *	10	A5
Rosebery Rd *CLAP* SW4	135	E4
Rosebury Rd *FUL/PGN* SW6	114	B5
Rose Ct *WCHPL* E1	25	E3
Rosecroft Av *HAMP* NW3	54	A5
Rose Croft Gdns *CRICK* NW2	52	A5
Rose & Crown Yd *STJS* SW1Y *	31	F4
Rosedale Rd *FSTGT* E7	82	C2
Rosedene Av *STRHM/NOR* SW16	153	F3
Rosedene Ter *LEY* E10	62	B4
Rosefield Rd *HMSMTH* W6	113	D2
Rosefield Av *POP/IOD* E14	104	A1
Rosefield Gdns *POP/IOD* E14	104	A1
Rosehart Ms *NTGHL* W11	14	A5
Rosehill Rd *WAND/EARL* SW18	132	C4
Rose Joan Ms *KIL/WHAMP* NW6	72	A1
Roseleigh Av *HBRY* N5	76	B1
Rosemary Dr *POP/IOD* E14	93	D5
Rosemary La *MORT/ESHN* SW14	128	C1
Rosemary Rd *PECK* SE15	119	F3
TOOT SW17	150	C3
WELL DA16	127	F4
Rosemary St *IS* N1	77	D5
Rosemead *CDALE/KGS* NW9	51	F2
Rosemont Rd *ACT* W3	98	B1
HAMP NW3	72	C3
Rosemoor St *CHEL* SW3	41	E5
Rosenau Crs *BTSEA* SW11	115	E4
Rosenau Rd *BTSEA* SW11	115	E4
Rosendale Rd *DUL* SE21	154	C2
HNHL SE24	136	C5
Roseneath Pl *STRHM/NOR* SW16	154	A4
Roseneath Rd *BTSEA* SW11	134	A4
Rosenthal Rd *CAT* SE6	140	B4
Rosenthorpe Rd *PECK* SE15	139	D3
Roserton St *POP/IOD* E14	104	C3
Rose Sq *CHEL* SW3 *	40	B1
Rose Sq *COVGDN* WC2E *	32	C1
Rosethorn Cl *BAL* SW12	134	C5
Rosetta Cl *VX/NE* SW8	117	E3
Roseveare Rd *LEE/GVPK* SE12	160	C4
Roseway *DUL* SE21	137	D4
Rose Wy *LEE/GVPK* SE12	142	A3
Rosher Cl *SRTFD* E15	81	D4
Rosina St *HOM* E9	79	D3
Roskell Rd *PUT/ROE* SW15	131	D1
Roslin Rd *ACT* W3	98	B4
Roslin Wy *BMLY* BR1	160	A5
Rosmead Rd *NTGHL* W11	14	A5
Rosoman Pl *CLKNW* EC1R *	10	B5
Rosoman St *CLKNW* EC1R	10	B4
Rossdale Dr *CDALE/KGS* NW9	50	B3
Rossdale Rd *PUT/ROE* SW15	130	C2
Rosse Ms *BKHTH/KID* SE3	124	B4
Rossendale St *CLPT* E5	60	B4
Rossendale Wy *CAMTN* NW1	74	C5
Rossetti Ms *STJWD* NW8	73	D5
Rossetti Rd *BERM/RHTH* SE16	120	B1
Ross House *CHARL* SE7 *	125	E3
Rossington St *CLPT* E5	60	A4
Rossiter Rd *BAL* SW12	152	B1
Rosslyn Av *BARN* SW13	129	E1
Rosslyn HI *HAMP* NW3	73	D2
Rosslyn Park Ms *HAMP* NW3	73	D2
Rosslyn Rd *BARK* IG11	85	D4
Rossmore Cl *CAMTN* NW1 *	17	D1
Rossmore Rd *CAMTN* NW1	5	D5
Ross Wy *ELTH/MOT* SE9	143	E1
Rostella Rd *TOOT* SW17	151	D4
Rostrevor Av *SEVS/STOTM* N15	59	F1
Rostrevor Rd *FUL/PGN* SW6	113	F4
WIM/MER SW19	150	A5
Rotary St *STHWK* SE1	46	C2
Rothbury Cots *GNWCH* SE10 *	105	F3
Rothbury Rd *HOM* E9	79	F4

Rotherfield St *IS* N1 .... 76 C4
Rotherham Wk *STHWK* SE1 * 35 D4
Rotherhithe New Rd
  BERM/RHTH SE16 .... 120 B1
Rotherhithe Old Rd
  BERM/RHTH SE16 .... 103 D5
Rotherhithe St *BERM/RHTH* SE16 .... 102 B3
Rotherwick Rd *GLDGN* NW11 .... 54 A2
Rotherwood Rd *PUT/ROE* SW15 ...... 131 D1
Rothery St *IS* N1 .... 76 B5
Rothesay Av *RCHPK/HAM* TW10 ...... 128 B2
Rothesay Rd *FSTGT* E7 .... 48 C2
Rothsay St *STHWK* SE1. ....
Rothschild Rd *CHSWK* W4 .... 98 C5
Rothschild St *WNWD* SE27 .... 154 B4
Rothwell St *CAMTN* NW1 .... 73 F5
Rotten Row *BAY/PAD* W2 .... 29 D5
Rotterdam Dr *POP/IOD* E14. .... 104 C4
Rouel Rd *BERM/RHTH* SE16 .... 102 A4
Roundel Cl *BROCKY* SE4 .... 139 F2
Roundhay Cl *FSTH* SE23 .... 157 D2
Round Hl *SYD* SE26. .... 156 B2
Roundtable Rd *BMLY* BR1. .... 159 F3
Roundwood Pk *WLSDN* NW10 * 70 A5
Roundwood Rd *WLSDN* NW10 .... 69 E3
Roundwood Ter *STNW/STAM* N16 .... 59 E2
Rounton Rd *BOW* E3. .... 92 A3
Roupell Rd *BRXS/STRHM* SW2 .... 153 F1
Roupell St *STHWK* SE1 *. 34 B4
Rousden St *CAMTN* NW1 .... 74 C1
Rouse Gdns *DUL* SE21. .... 155 E4
Routemaster Cl *PLSTW* E15 .... 94 B2
Routh Rd *WAND/EARL* SW18 .... 133 E5
Routh St *EHAM* E6. .... 95 F4
Rowallan Rd *FUL/PGN* SW6 .... 113 E3
Rowan Cl *IL* IG1. .... 85 D2
Rowan Rd *HMSMTH* W6. .... 101 D5
Rowan Ter *HMSMTH* W6. .... 101 D5
Rowan Wk *EFNCH* N2. .... 54 C1
  NKENS W10 *. 89 E3
Rowberry Cl *FUL/PGN* SW6 .... 113 D3
Rowcross St *STHWK* SE1 .... 119 F1
Rowditch La *BTSEA* SW11 .... 116 A5
Rowdon Av *WLSDN* NW10 .... 70 B4
Rowe Gdns *BARK* IG11 .... 97 F1
Rowe La *HOM* E9. .... 78 C2
Rowena Crs *BTSEA* SW11 .... 115 E5
Rowfant Rd *TOOT* SW17 .... 152 A2
Rowhill Rd *CLPT* E5 .... 78 B1
Rowington Cl *BAY/PAD* W2 .... 14 C2
Rowland Gv *SYD* SE26. .... 156 B3
Rowland Hill St *HAMP* NW3 .... 72 C2
Rowlands Cl *HGT* N6 *. 56 A1
Rowley Cots *WKENS* W14 * 101 F5
Rowley Gdns *FSBYPK* N4. .... 58 B2
Rowley Wy *STJWD* NW8 .... 72 C5
Rowntree Clifford Cl *PLSTW* E13 .... 94 B3
Rowntree Cl *KIL/WHAMP* NW6 * 72 A3
Rowse Cl *SRTFD* E15. .... 80 C3
Rowstock Gdns *HOLWY* N7 .... 75 D3
Rowton Rd *WOOL/PLUM* SE18 .... 126 C3
Roxburgh Rd *WNWD* SE27 .... 154 B5
Roxby Pl *FUL/PGN* SW6. .... 114 A2
Roxley Rd *LEW* SE13 .... 140 B4
Roxwell Rd *SHB* W12. .... 100 A3
Royal Albert Wy *CAN/RD* E16 .... 107 D1
Royal Ar *CONDST* W1S. 31 E2
Royal Arsenal West
  WOOL/PLUM SE18 * 126 A1
Royal Av *CHEL* SW3. .... 115 F1
Royal Circ *WNWD* SE27 .... 154 B4
Royal Cl *DEPT* SE8. .... 121 F2
  STNW/STAM N16 .... 59 E3
  WIM/MER SW19 .... 149 D2
Royal College St *CAMTN* NW1. .... 74 C4
Royal Ar *BANK* EC3V 24 B5
  ELTH/MOT SE9 * 161 F1
Royal Crs *GNTH/NBYPK* IG2. .... 67 D3
  NTGHL W11 *. 101 D3
Royal Crescent Ms *NTGHL* W11. ...... 101 D3
Royal Docks Rd *EHAM* E6. .... 96 B4
Royal Herbert Pavilions
  WOOL/PLUM SE18 * 125 F4
Royal Hl *GNWCH* SE10. .... 122 C3
Royal Hospital Rd *CHEL* SW3. .... 115 F2
Royal Ms *BAL* SW12. .... 134 B5
Royal Mint Pl *WCHPL* E1. .... 37 F1
Royal Mint St *WCHPL* E1. .... 37 F1
Royal Naval Pl *NWCR* SE14 .... 121 F3
Royal Oak Pl *EDUL* SE22. .... 138 B4
Royal Oak Rd *HACK* E8. .... 78 B3

Royal Oak Yd *STHWK* SE1. .... 48 C1
Royal Opera Ar *STJS* SW1Y *. 32 A3
Royal Orchard Cl *WAND/EARL* SW18.. 131 E5
Royal Pde *BKHTH/KID* SE3. .... 123 F5
  FUL/PGN SW6 *. 113 E5
Royal Pl *GNWCH* SE10. .... 122 C3
Royal Rd *CAN/RD* E16 .... 94 C5
  LBTH SE11 .... 118 B2
Royal St *STHWK* SE1 .... 45 F2
Royal Victor Pl *BOW* E3. .... 91 D1
Roycraft Av *BARK* IG11 .... 97 F1
Roycroft Cl *BRXS/STRHM* SW2 * 154 A1
Roydene Rd *WOOL/PLUM* SE18 ...... 127 E2
Roy Sq *POP/IOD* E14. .... 103 E1
Royston Gdns *IL* IG1 .... 65 D1
Royston St *BETH* E2 .... 90 C1
Rozel Rd *VX/NE* SW8. .... 116 C5
Rubens St *CAT* SE6 .... 157 F2
Ruby Cl *PECK* SE15. .... 120 B2
  WLSDN NW10. .... 68 C4
Ruby Triangle *PECK* SE15 * 120 B2
Ruckholt Cl *LEY* E10. .... 62 B5
Ruckholt Rd *LEY* E10. .... 62 C5
Rucklidge Av *WLSDN* NW10. .... 87 F1
Rudall Crs *HAMP* NW3. .... 73 D1
Ruddington Cl *CLPT* E5. .... 79 F1
Ruddstreet Cl *WOOL/PLUM* SE18 .... 108 B5
Rudgwick Ter *STJWD* NW8 * 73 E5
Rudloe Rd *BAL* SW12. .... 134 C5
Rudolf Pl *VX/NE* SW8. .... 117 E2
Rudolph Rd *KIL/WHAMP* NW6 .... 2 B2
  PLSTW E13. .... 93 F1
Rufford St *IS* N1. .... 75 E5
Rufford Street Ms *IS* N1 .... 75 E4
Rufus St *FSBYE* EC1V. 12 C4
Rugby Rd *CHSWK* W4 .... 99 E3
Rugby St *BMSBY* WC1N 21 E1
Rugg St *POP/IOD* E14. .... 104 A1
Ruislip St *TOOT* SW17. .... 151 F4
Rumbold Rd *FUL/PGN* SW6 .... 114 B3
Rum Cl *WAP* E1W. 102 B1
Rumsey Rd *BRXN/ST* SW9 .... 135 F1
Runbury Cir *CDALE/KGS* NW9 .... 51 D4
Runcorn Pl *NTGHL* W11. .... 101 E1
Rupack St *BERM/RHTH* SE16 * 102 C3
Rupert Ct *SOHO/SHAV* W1D. 32 A1
Rupert Gdns *BRXN/ST* SW9 .... 118 B5
Rupert Rd *ARCH* N19. .... 57 D5
  CHSWK W4 .... 99 E4
  KIL/WHAMP NW6 .... 89 F1
Rupert St *SOHO/SHAV* W1D *. 32 A1
Rusbridge Cl *HACK* E8 .... 78 A2
Ruscoe Rd *CAN/RD* E16 .... 93 F5
Rusham Rd *BAL* SW12 .... 133 F4
Rushbrook Rd *ELTH/MOT* SE9 .... 162 C2
Rush Common Ms *BRXS/STRHM* SW2.. 135 E4
Rushcroft Rd *BRXS/STRHM* SW9 ..... 136 A2
Rushey Gn *CAT* SE6. .... 140 B5
Rushey Md *BROCKY* SE4 .... 140 A3
Rushford Rd *BROCKY* SE4 .... 139 F4
Rushgrove St *WOOL/PLUM* SE18. .... 107 F5
Rush Hill Ms *BTSEA* SW11 * 134 A1
Rush Hill Rd *BTSEA* SW11 .... 134 A1
Rushmead *BETH* E2. .... 90 B2
Rushmere Pl *WIM/MER* SW19. .... 149 D5
Rushmore Rd *CLPT* E5. .... 78 C1
Rusholme Gv *NRWD* SE19. .... 155 F5
Rusholme Rd *PUT/ROE* SW15. .... 131 D4
Rushton St *IS* N1. .... 12 B1
Rushworth St *STHWK* SE1 .... 35 D5
Ruskin Av *MNPK* E12. .... 83 E3
  RCH/KEW TW9 .... 110 A3
Ruskin Cl *GLDGN* NW11 .... 54 B1
Ruskin Wk *HNHL* SE24. .... 136 C3
Rusper Cl *CRICK* NW2. .... 52 C5
Russell Cl *BKHTH/KID* SE3. .... 124 C3
  CHSWK W4. .... 111 F2
  WLSDN NW10. .... 68 C4
Russell Ct *WHALL* SW1A. 31 F4
Russell Gdns *GLDGN* NW11 .... 53 E1
  WKENS W14 *. 101 E4
Russell Gardens Ms *WKENS* W14. .... 101 E4
Russell Gv *BRXN/ST* SW9 .... 118 A4
Russell Kerr Cl *CHSWK* W4 * 110 C3
Russell Pde *GLDGN* NW11 * 53 E1
Russell Pl *HAMP* NW3. .... 73 E2
Russell Rd *CAN/RD* E16 .... 94 A5
  CDALE/KGS NW9 .... 51 F1
  CEND/HSY/T N8 .... 57 D1
  WALTH E17 .... 62 B1
  WKENS W14 .... 101 E4
Russell Sq *RSQ* WC1B. 20 B1

Russell St *HOL/ALD* WC2B	33	D1
Russell Yd *PUT/ROE* SW15	131	E2
Russet Crs *HOLWY* N7 *	75	F2
Russia Dock Rd *BERM/RHTH* SE16 *	103	E2
Russia La *BETH* E2	90	C1
Russia Rw *CITYW* EC2V	23	F5
Rusthall Av *CHSWK* W4	99	D4
Ruston Ms *NTGHL* W11 *	89	E5
Ruston Rd *WOOL/PLUM* SE18	107	E4
Ruston St *BOW* E3	79	F1
Rust Sq *CMBW* SE5	119	D3
Rutford Rd *STRHM/NOR* SW16	155	E5
Rutherford St *WEST* SW1P		
Rutherford Wy *WBLY* HA9	50	A5
Ruthin Cl *CDALE/KGS* NW9	51	E1
Ruthin Rd *BKHTH/KID* SE3	124	A2
Ruthven St *HOM* E9	79	D5
Rutland Av *MORT/ESHN* SW14	128	B1
Rutland Cl *SKENS* SW7	41	D1
Rutland Gdns *FSBYPK* N4	58	B1
SKENS SW7	41	D1
Rutland Gardens Ms *SKENS* SW7	41	D1
Rutland Ga *SKENS* SW7	40	C1
Rutland Gate Ms *SKENS* SW7 *	40	C1
Rutland Gv *HMSMTH* W6	112	B1
Rutland Ms *SKENS* SW7 *	40	C2
Rutland Ms South *SKENS* SW7 *		
Rutland Pk *CAT* SE6	157	F2
CRICK NW2	70	C3
Rutland Pl *FARR* EC1M *	23	D2
Rutland Rd *FSTGT* E7	83	D4
HOM E9	79	D5
IL IG1	84	B1
WALTH E17	62	A1
Rutland St *SKENS* SW7	41	D2
Rutland Wk *CAT* SE6	157	F2
Rutley Cl *WALW* SE17	118	B2
Rutt's Ter *NWCR* SE14	121	D4
Ruvigny Gdns *PUT/ROE* SW15	131	D1
Ryan Cl *BKHTH/KID* SE3	142	B2
Rycuilff Sq *BKHTH/KID* SE3	123	F5
Rydal Gdns *PUT/ROE* SW15	147	E5
Rydal Rd *STRHM/NOR* SW16	153	D5
Ryder St *STJS* SW1Y	31	F3
Ryder Yd *STJS* SW1Y	31	F3
Ryde Vale Rd *BAL* SW12	152	B2
Rydon St *IS* N1	76	C5
Rydston Cl *HOLWY* N7	75	F4
Ryecotes Md *DUL* SE21	155	E1
Ryecroft Rd *LEW* SE13	140	C3
Ryecroft St *FUL/PGN* SW6	114	B4
Ryedale *EDUL* SE22	138	B4
Rye Hill Pk *PECK* SE15	138	C2
Ryelands Crs *LEE/GVPK* SE12	142	C4
Rye La *PECK* SE15	120	A5
Rye Rd *PECK* SE15	139	D2
Rye Wk *PUT/ROE* SW15	131	D3
Ryfold Rd *WIM/MER* SW19	150	A3
Rylandes Rd *CRICK* NW2	52	A5
Ryland Rd *KTTN* NW5 *	74	B3
Rylett Crs *SHB* W12	99	F4
Rylett Rd *SHB* W12	99	F3
Rylston Rd *FUL/PGN* SW6	113	F2
Rymer St *HNHL* SE24	136	B4
Rymill St *CAN/RD* E16	108	A2
Rysbrack St *CHEL* SW3	41	E2

S

Sabbarton St *CAN/RD* E16	93	F5
Sabine Rd *BTSEA* SW11	133	F1
Sable St *IS* N1	76	B4
Sach Rd *CLPT* E5	60	D4
Sackville Rd *STRHM/NOR* SW16	153	E3
Sackville Gdns *IL* IG1	65	E3
Sackville St *CONDST* W1S	31	E2
Sadlers Gate Ms *PUT/ROE* SW15	130	C1
Saffron Av *POP/IOD* E14	105	D1
Saffron Hl *HCIRC* EC1N	22	B2
Saffron St *HCIRC* EC1N	22	B2
Sage Cl *WCHPL* E1	95	F4
Sage Ms *EDUL* SE22	137	F3
Sage Wy *FSBYW* WC1X	102	C1
Sage Wy *FSBYW* WC1X	9	D4
Saigasso Cl *CAN/RD* E16	95	D5
Sail St *LBTH* SE11	45	F4
Sainfoin Rd *TOOT* SW17	152	A2
Sainsbury Rd *NRWD* SE19	155	E5

St Agnes Cl *HOM* E9 *	78	C5
St Agnes Pl *LBTH* SE11	118	B2
St Agnes Well *STLK* EC1Y	12	B5
St Aidan's Rd *EDUL* SE22	138	B4
St Albans Av *CHSWK* W4	99	D4
St Alban's Av *EHAM* E6	95	F2
St Albans Gv *KENS* W8	39	D2
St Albans La *GLDGN* NW11	54	A3
St Alban's Ms *BAY/PAD* W2	16	B2
St Alban's Pl *IS* N1	76	B5
St Albans Rd *GDMY/SEVK* IG3	67	F3
St Alban's Rd *KTTN* NW5	56	A5
WLSDN NW10	69	E5
St Alban's St *STJS* SW1Y	32	A2
St Albans Ter *HMSMTH* W6	113	E2
St Alphage Gdns *BARB* EC2Y	23	F3
St Alphage Highwalk *BARB* EC2Y	23	F3
St Alphonsus Rd *CLAP* SW4	134	C2
St Amunds Cl *CAT* SE6	158	A4
St Andrews Cl *BERM/RHTH* SE16 *	120	B1
St Andrew's Cl *CRICK* NW2	52	B5
St Andrew's Ct *WAND/EARL* SW18	150	C2
St Andrew's Dr *STNW/STAM* N16	59	D3
St Andrews Ms *BAL* SW12	153	D1
BKHTH/KID SE3	124	A3
St Andrew's Ms *STNW/STAM* N16	59	E3
St Andrew's Pl *CAMTN* NW1	6	C5
St Andrew's Rd *CDALE/KGS* NW9	51	D5
St Andrew's Rd *ACT* W3	87	E5
GLDGN NW11	53	F1
IL IG1	65	F2
PLSTW E13	94	B2
WAN E11	63	E1
WKENS W14	113	E2
WLSDN NW10	70	B3
St Andrew's Sq *NTGHL* W11 *	89	E5
St Andrew St *HCIRC* EC1N	22	B3
St Andrews Wy *BOW* E3	92	B3
St Anne's Cl *HGT* N6	56	A5
St Annes Pas *SOHO/CST* W1F	20	A5
St Anne's Pas *POP/IOD* E14 *	91	F5
St Anne's Rd *LEY* E10	63	D4
St Anne's Rw *POP/IOD* E14	91	F5
St Anne St *POP/IOD* E14	91	F5
St Ann's Crs *WAND/EARL* SW18	132	B4
St Ann's Gdns *KTTN* NW5	74	A3
St Ann's Hl *WAND/EARL* SW18	132	B3
St Ann's Park Rd *WAND/EARL* SW18	132	C4
St Anns Rd *BARN* SW13 *	111	F5
St Ann's Rd *BARK* IG11	84	C5
NTGHL W11	101	D1
St Ann's St *WEST* SW1P	44	B2
St Ann's Ter *STJWD* NW8	4	B1
St Ann's Vls *NTGHL* W11	101	D2
St Anthonys Cl *TOOT* SW17	151	E2
St Anthony's Cl *WAP* E1W *	102	A2
St Antony's Rd *FSTGT* E7	82	B4
St Asaph Rd *BROCKY* SE4	139	D1
St Aubyn's Av *WIM/MER* SW19	149	F5
St Augustine's Rd *CAMTN* NW1	75	D4
St Austell Rd *LEW* SE13	122	C5
St Awdry's Rd *BARK* IG11	85	D4
St Barnabas Cl *EDUL* SE22	137	E2
St Barnabas Rd *WALTH* E17	62	A1
St Barnabas St *BCVA* SW1W	116	A1
St Barnabas Ter *HOM* E9	79	D2
St Barnabas Vls *VX/NE* SW8	117	E4
St Bartholomew's Cl *SYD* SE26	156	C4
St Bartholomew's Rd *EHAM* E6	83	E5
St Benets Cl *TOOT* SW17	151	E2
St Bernards Cl *WNWD* SE27	155	D4
St Bernard's Rd *EHAM* E6	83	D5
St Botolph St *WCHPL* EC3N	25	E4
St Bride St *FLST/FETLN* EC4A	22	C4
St Catherines Cl *TOOT* SW17 *	151	E2
St Catherine's Dr *NWCR* SE14	121	D5
St Catherines Ms *CHEL* SW3	41	E4
St Chad's Pl *FSBYW* WC1X	9	D3
St Chad's St *STPAN* WC1H	9	D3
St Charles Pl *NKENS* W10	89	E4
St Charles Sq *NKENS* W10	89	D4
St Christopher's Pl *MHST* W1U	18	B5
St Clair Rd *PLSTW* E13	94	B1
St Clare St *TWRH* EC3N	25	E5
St Clements La *LINN* WC2A	21	F5
St Clements St *HOLWY* N7	76	A4
St Clements Yd *EDUL* SE22 *	137	F3
St Cloud Rd *WNWD* SE27	154	C4

St Crispins CI *HAMP* NW3........... 73 E1
St Cross St *HCIRC* EC1N............. 22 D2
St Cuthbert's Rd *CRICK* NW2......... 71 F3
St Cyprian's St *TOOT* SW17......... 151 E1
St Davids CI *BERM/RHTH* SE16 *..... 120 B1
   WBLY HA9........................ 50 C5
St Davids Ms *BOW* E3 *............. 91 F2
St David's PI *HDN* NW4............. 52 B2
St Davids Sq *POP/IOD* E14.......... 122 B1
St Denis Rd *WNWD* SE27............ 154 C4
St Dionis Rd *FUL/PGN* SW6......... 113 F5
   MNPK E12........................ 65 F4
St Donatt's Rd *NWCR* SE14......... 121 F4
St Dunstan's Av *ACT* W3............ 99 D1
St Dunstan's Gdns *ACT* W3.......... 99 D1
St Dunstan's HI *MON* EC3R *........ 36 C3
St Dunstan's La *MON* EC3R *........ 36 C2
St Dunstans Rd *FSTGT* E7........... 82 B3
St Dunstan's Rd *HMSMTH* W6........ 113 D1
St Edmunds CI *TOOT* SW17.......... 151 E2
St Edmund's Rd *IL* IG1............. 65 F1
St Edmunds Sq *BARN* SW13.......... 112 C2
St Edward's CI *GLDGN* NW11........ 54 A1
St Elmo Rd *SHB* W12................ 99 F3
St Elmos Rd *BERM/RHTH* SE16....... 105 E3
St Erkenwald Ms *BARK* IG11........ 85 D5
St Erkenwald Rd *BARK* IG11........ 85 D5
St Ervans Rd *NKENS* W10........... 89 E4
St Faith's Rd *DUL* SE21............ 154 B1
St Fillans Rd *CAT* SE6............. 158 C1
St Francis Rd *EDUL* SE22........... 137 E2
St Francis Wy *IL* IG1.............. 85 D1
St Gabriel's CI *WAN* E11........... 64 B3
St Gabriel's Rd *CRICK* NW2......... 71 D2
St George's Av *FSTGT* E7........... 82 B4
   HOLWY N7......................... 75 D1
St George's Circ *STHWK* SE1........ 46 C1
St Georges CI *VX/NE* SW8.......... 116 C4
St George's CI *GLDGN* NW11........ 53 F1
St George's Dr *PIM* SW1V........... 43 D5
St Georges Flds *BAY/PAD* W2........ 29 D1
St George's Gv *TOOT* SW17......... 151 D5
St George's La *MON* EC3R *......... 36 C3
St Georges Ms *CHSWK* W4 *......... 110 C2
   DEPT SE8......................... 103 F5
St George's Ms *CAMTN* NW1......... 73 F4
St Georges Pde *CAT* SE6 *.......... 157 F2
St Georges Rd *CHSWK* W4........... 99 D3
St George's Rd *FSTGT* E7........... 82 B4
   GLDGN NW11...................... 53 F1
   IL IG1........................... 65 F2
   LEY E10.......................... 62 C5
   STHWK SE1........................ 46 C3
St George's Ct *STP* EC4M *......... 22 C4
St George's Sq *FSTGT* E7........... 82 B4
   PIM SW1V......................... 117 D1
St George's Square Ms *PIM* SW1V.... 117 D1
St Georges Ter *PECK* SE15 *........ 120 A3
St George's Ter *CAMTN* NW1........ 73 F4
St George Ste *CONDST* W1S.......... 31 D1
St George's Wy *PECK* SE15......... 119 E2
St Gerards CI *CLAP* SW4........... 134 C3
St German's PI *BKHTH/KID* SE3...... 124 A4
St German's Rd *FSTH* SE23......... 157 E1
St Giles Churchyard *BARB* EC2Y *... 23 F5
St Giles Circ *SOHO/SHAV* W1D....... 20 B4
St Giles Ct *LSQ/SEVD* WC2H *....... 20 B4
St Giles High St *LSQ/SEVD* WC2H.... 20 B4
St Giles Pas *LSQ/SEVD* WC2H........ 20 B5
St Giles Rd *CMBW* SE5............. 119 D4
St Gothard Rd *WNWD* SE27.......... 155 D4
St Helena Rd *BERM/RHTH* SE16...... 105 D5
St Helena St *FSBYW* WC1X *......... 10 A4
St Helen's Gdns *NKENS* W10........ 89 D5
St Helens PI *LEY* E10............. 61 E2
St Helen's PI *HDTCH* EC3A.......... 24 C4
St Helen's Rd *IL* IG1............. 65 F1
St Hellier's Rd *LEY* E10.......... 62 B1
St Hildas CI *KIL/WHAMP* NW6 *...... 71 D5
   TOOT SW17....................... 151 E1
St Hilda's Rd *BARN* SW13.......... 112 B2
St Hughes CI *TOOT* SW17........... 151 E1
St James *STJWD* NW8............... 5 E1
St James' Ct *WESTW* SW1E *......... 43 F2
St James Ms *POP/IOD* E14.......... 104 C4
St James' Rd *SRTFD* E15........... 81 F2
St James's *NWCR* SE14............. 121 E4
St James's Av *BETH* E2............ 90 C1
St James's Chambers *STJS* SW1Y *... 31 F5
St James's CI *TOOT* SW17 *......... 151 F2
   WOOL/PLUM SE18.................. 126 C1

St James's Ct *WESTW* SW1E.......... 43 F2
St James's Dr *BRXN/ST* SW9......... 136 A1
St James's Dr *BAL* SW12........... 151 F1
   TOOT SW17........................ 151 F1
St James's Gdns *CAMTN* NW1 *....... 7 E4
   NTGHL W11........................ 101 D2
St James's Gv *BTSEA* SW11......... 115 F5
St James's Market *STJS* SW1Y *..... 32 A2
St James's PI *WHALL* SW1A......... 31 E4
St James's Rd *BERM/RHTH* SE16...... 120 A1
   STHWK SE1........................ 120 A1
St James's Sq *STJS* SW1Y.......... 32 A3
St James's St *WHALL* SW1A......... 31 E5
St James's Terrace Ms *STJWD* NW8... 73 F5
St James St *HMSMTH* W6............ 112 C1
St James Ter *BAL* SW12 *.......... 152 A1
St James Wk *CLKNW* EC1R........... 10 C5
St John's Av *PUT/ROE* SW15........ 131 D3
   WLSDN NW10....................... 69 F5
St John's Church Rd *HOM* E9 *...... 79 D2
St John's CI *FUL/PGN* SW6 *........ 114 A3
St John's Crs *BRXN/ST* SW9........ 136 A1
St John's Dr *WAND/EARL* SW18....... 150 B1
St John's Gdns *NTGHL* W11.......... 101 E1
St John's Gv *ARCH* N19............ 56 C4
   BARN SW13....................... 111 F5
St John's HI *BTSEA* SW11.......... 133 E2
St John's Hill Gv *BTSEA* SW11..... 133 D2
St John's La *FARR* EC1M........... 22 C1
St John's Pk *BKHTH/KID* SE3....... 124 A3
St John's PI *FARR* EC1M........... 22 C1
St Johns Rd *GNTH/NBYPK* IG2....... 67 E2
St John's Rd *BARK* IG11........... 85 E5
   BTSEA SW11...................... 133 E2
   CAN/RD E16...................... 94 A5
   EHAM E6......................... 83 E5
   GLDGN NW11...................... 53 F1
   SEVS/STOTM N15.................. 59 E1
St John's Sq *FARR* EC1M........... 22 C1
   FSBYE EC1V...................... 22 C1
St John's Ter *FSTGT* E7........... 82 B3
   NKENS W10....................... 89 D3
   WOOL/PLUM SE18.................. 126 C2
St John St *FSBYE* EC1V............ 10 B2
St John's V *BROCKY* SE4........... 122 A5
St Johns VIs *KENS* W8............. 39 D3
St John's VIs *ARCH* N19........... 57 D4
St John's Wy *ARCH* N19............ 57 D4
St John's Wood High St *STJWD* NW8.. 4 B2
St John's Wood Pk *STJWD* NW8....... 73 D5
St John's Wood Rd *STJWD* NW8....... 4 A5
St John's Wood Ter *STJWD* NW8...... 4 C1
St Josephs CI *NKENS* W10.......... 89 E4
St Joseph's St *VX/NE* SW8 *........ 116 B4
St Joseph's V *BKHTH/KID* SE3...... 123 D5
St Jude's Rd *BETH* E2............. 90 B1
St Jude St *STNW/STAM* N16......... 77 E2
St Julian's CI *STRHM/NOR* SW16.... 154 A4
St Julian's Farm Rd *WNWD* SE27.... 154 A4
St Julian's Rd *KIL/WHAMP* NW6..... 71 F4
St Katharine's Prec *CAMTN* NW1 *... 6 C1
St Katharine's Wy *WAP* E1W........ 37 F3
St Katherines Wk *NTGHL* W11 *...... 101 D1
St Keverne Rd *ELTH/MOT* SE9....... 161 E4
   ELTH/MOT SE9.................... 143 F5
St Kilda's Rd *STNW/STAM* N16...... 59 D3
St Kitts Ter *NRWD* SE19........... 150 A5
St Laurence's CI *KIL/WHAMP* NW6... 71 D5
St Lawrence Cots *POP/IOD* E14 *.... 104 C2
St Lawrence St *POP/IOD* E14....... 104 C2
St Lawrence Ter *NKENS* W10........ 89 E4
St Lawrence Wy *BRXN/ST* SW9....... 118 A5
St Leonards Gdns *IL* IG1.......... 84 C2
St Leonards Rd *MORT/ESHN* SW14.... 128 C1
St Leonard's Rd *POP/IOD* E14...... 92 C5
   WLSDN NW10...................... 87 D3
St Leonard's Sq *KTTN* NW5......... 74 A4
St Leonard's St *BOW* E3........... 92 B2
St Leonards Ter *CHEL* SW3......... 42 B5
St Loo Av *CHEL* SW3............... 115 E2
St Louis Rd *WNWD* SE27............ 154 C4
St Lucia Dr *SRTFD* E15............ 81 F1
St Luke's Av *CLAP* SW4............ 135 D2
   IL IG1.......................... 84 B2
St Luke's Est *FSBYE* EC1V......... 12 A4
St Luke's Ms *NTGHL* W11........... 89 F5
St Luke's Rd *NTGHL* W11........... 89 F4
St Lukes's CI *FSBYE* EC1V......... 11 F5
St Luke's Rd *CAN/RD* E16.......... 93 F5
St Luke's St *CHEL* SW3............ 115 E1
St Lukes Yd *MV/WKIL* W9 *......... 89 F1
St Margarets *BARK* IG11........... 85 D5

KUTN/CMB KT2 *	146	C5
St Margarets Av BFN/LL DA15	163	D3
St Margarets Ct PUT/ROE SW15 *	130	B2
St Margaret's Crs PUT/ROE SW15 *	130	B3
St Margaret's Gv WAN E11	63	F5
WOOL/PLUM SE18	126	C2
St Margarets La KENS W8.	38	C4
St Margarets Ms KUTN/CMB KT2 *	146	C5
St Margaret's Rd BROCKY SE4	139	F2
MNPK E12	64	C4
WLSDN NW10	88	C2
St Margaret's Ter WOOL/PLUM SE18.	115	E6
St Margaret St WEST SW1P	44	C1
WHALL SW1A	44	C1
St Marks Cl FUL/PGN SW6.	114	A4
St Mark's Crs CAMTN NW1	74	A5
St Marks Ga HOM E9	79	E4
St Mark's Gv WBPTN SW10 *	114	B5
St Mark's Pl NTGHL W11	89	E5
St Mark's Ri HACK E8	77	F2
St Mark's Rd KENS W10.	89	D5
St Mark's Sq CAMTN NW1	74	A5
St Mark St WCHPL E1	13	K5
St Marks Vls FSBYPK N4 *	57	F4
St Martin's Av EHAM E6.	95	D1
St Martin's Cl CAMTN NW1	74	D1
St Martins Ct CHCR WC2N	32	C1
St Martin's La CHCR WC2N	32	C1
St Martin's le Grand STBT EC1A	12	D3
St Martin's Pl CHCR WC2N	32	C2
St Martin's Rd BRXN/ST SW9	117	F5
St Martin's St LSQ/SEVD WC2H *	32	B2
St Martin's Wy TOOT SW17	150	D3
St Mary Abbot's Pl KENS W8.	101	F4
St Mary Abbots Ter WKENS W14 *	101	F4
St Mary At Hl MON EC3R.	36	C2
St Mary Axe HDTCH EC3A	24	C5
St Marychurch St BERM/RHTH SE16.	102	C3
St Mary Graces Ct WCHPL E1 *	37	F2
St Mary Newington Cl WALW SE17 *	119	E1
St Marys BARK IG11	78	C1
St Mary's Ap MNPK E12	83	F2
St Mary's Av WAN E11.	64	B1
St Marys Ct HMSMTH W6	99	F4
St Marys Est BERM/RHTH SE16 *	102	C3
St Mary's Gdns LBTH SE11	46	B4
St Marys Ga KENS W8.	38	C5
St Mary's Gv BARN SW13	130	B1
CHSWK W4	110	B2
IS N1	76	B3
St Mary's Man BAY/PAD W2.	15	F2
St Mary's Ms KIL/WHAMP NW6 *	72	B4
St Mary's Pth IS N1 *	76	B5
WCHPL E1 *	90	A5
St Marys Pl KENS W8.	38	C5
St Marys Rd IL IG1.	66	C4
St Mary's Rd GLDGN NW11	53	E2
LEY E10.	62	C5
PECK SE15	120	C4
PLSTW E13	94	B1
WIM/MER SW19	149	E5
WLSDN NW10.	69	E5
St Mary's Sq BAY/PAD W2.	16	A2
St Mary's Ter BAY/PAD W2.	16	A2
St Mary St WOOL/PLUM SE18 *	114	D3
St Mary St WEST SW1P	44	A2
St Mary's Wk LBTH SE11	46	B4
St Matthews Rd SRTFD E15	81	F4
St Matthew's Rd BRXS/STRHM SW2	135	F3
St Matthew's Rw BETH E2	90	A2
St Matthew St WEST SW1P	44	A2
St Maur Rd FUL/PGN SW6	113	F4
St Merryn Cl WOOL/PLUM SE18	127	D3
St Michael's Aly BANK EC3V	24	A5
St Michael's Av WBLY HA9	68	A3
St Michaels Ct CAN/RD E16	95	D4
St Michael's Gdns NKENS W10	89	E4
St Michael's Ms BETH E2	42	A5
St Michael's Gv BRXN/ST SW9	117	F5
CRICK NW2	70	C1
St Michaels St BAY/PAD W2	16	B4
St Michaels Ter HGT N6	56	A3
St Mildred's Ct LOTH EC2R *	24	A5
St Mildreds Rd CAT SE6	141	E5
St Nicholas Rd WOOL/PLUM SE18	127	F1
St Nicholas St DEPT SE8.	121	F4
St Norbert Rd BROCKY SE4	139	E2
St Olaf's Rd FUL/PGN SW6	113	E3
St Olave's Rd EHAM E6	84	A5
St Oswald's Pl LBTH SE11	117	F1
St Oswulf St WEST SW1P *	44	B5
St Pancras Gdns CAMTN NW1 *	75	D5

St Pancras Station Forecourt
CAMTN NW1 *	8	C3
St Pancras Wy CAMTN NW1	74	C4
St Paul's Av BERM/RHTH SE16 *	103	D2
CRICK NW2	70	B3
St Paul's Church Yd STP EC4M	23	C5
St Pauls Crs CAMTN NW1	75	D3
St Paul's Dr SRTFD E15	81	D2
St Pauls Ms CAMTN NW1	75	D3
St Paul's Pl IS N1	77	D3
St Pauls Rd BARK IG11	84	C5
St Paul's Rd IS N1	76	B3
St Pauls Ter WALW SE17 *	118	B2
St Paul St IS N1	76	C5
St Paul's Wy POP/IOD E14.	91	F4
St Peter's Av BETH E2	90	A1
St Petersburgh Ms BAY/PAD W2	26	C1
St Petersburgh Pl BAY/PAD W2	26	C1
St Peters Cl TOOT SW17	151	E2
St Peter's Cl BETH E2	90	A1
St Peters Ct BKHTH/KID SE3 *	141	F3
St Peter's Gdns WNWD SE27	154	A3
St Peter's Gv HMSMTH W6.	100	A5
St Peter's Pl MV/WKIL W9	14	C1
St Peter's Rd HMSMTH W6 *	112	A1
St Peter's Sq BETH E2 *	90	A1
HMSMTH W6.	100	A5
St Peter's Ter FUL/PGN SW6.	113	E3
St Peter's Vls HMSMTH W6	100	A5
St Peter's Wy IS N1	77	E4
St Philip Sq VX/NE SW8 *	116	B5
St Philip's Rd HACK E8	78	A3
St Philip St VX/NE SW8.	116	B5
St Philip's Wy IS N1	76	C5
St Quentin Rd WELL DA16	145	F1
St Quintin Av NKENS W10.	88	C4
St Quintin Gdns NKENS W10	88	C4
St Quintin Rd PLSTW E13.	94	B2
St Raphael's Wy WLSDN NW10	68	D3
St Rule St VX/NE SW8	116	C5
St Saviour's Est STHWK SE1	49	E2
St Saviour's Rd BRXS/STRHM SW2	135	F3
Saints Cl WNWD SE27	154	B4
Saints Dr FSTGT E7	83	G2
St Silas Pl KTTN NW5	74	A3
St Simon's Av PUT/ROE SW15	130	C3
St Stephen's Av SHB W12	100	B2
St Stephens Cl STJWD NW8	73	E5
St Stephen's Crs BAY/PAD W2	14	B4
St Stephen's Gdns BAY/PAD W2	14	A4
St Stephen's Gv LEW SE13	140	C1
St Stephen's Ms BAY/PAD W2 *	14	B3
St Stephens Pde WHALL SW1A.	32	C5
St Stephen's Rd BOW E3	79	E5
EHAM E6.	82	C4
St Stephen's Ter VX/NE SW8	117	F3
St Stephen's Wk SKENS SW7 *	39	E4
St Swithin's La MANHO EC4N.	36	A1
St Swithun's Rd LEW SE13 *	141	D3
St Theresas Cl HOM E9.	80	A1
St Thomas Gdns IL IG1	84	C3
St Thomas Rd CAN/RD E16.	94	A5
St Thomas Rd CHSWK W4	110	C3
St Thomas's Gdns KTTN NW5.	74	A3
St Thomas's Pl HOM E9.	78	C4
St Thomas's Rd FSBYPK N4.	58	A4
WLSDN NW10.	69	E5
St Thomas's Sq HOM E9	78	B4
St Thomas St STHWK SE1	36	G4
St Thomas's Wy FUL/PGN SW6.	113	F5
St Vincent Cl WNWD SE27	154	B5
St Vincent St MHST W1U	18	B3
St Winefride's Av MNPK E12	83	F2
Salamanca Pl STHWK SE1	45	E5
Salamanca St STHWK SE1	45	E5
Salcombe Rd STNW/STAM N16.	77	F2
WALTH E17	61	F2
Salcott Rd BTSEA SW11	133	E3
Salehurst Rd BROCKY SE4	139	F4
Salem Pl BAY/PAD W2.	26	C3
Sale Pl BAY/PAD W2	16	C3
Sale St BETH E2	90	A3
Salford Rd BRXS/STRHM SW2	153	D1
Salisbury Av BARK IG11	85	D4
Salisbury Cl WALW SE17	48	A4
Salisbury Ct EMB EC4Y	22	C5
Salisbury Pavement FUL/PGN SW6 *	114	A3
Salisbury Pl BRXN/ST SW9	118	B3
MBLAR W1H.	17	E2
Salisbury Rd FSTGT E7	82	A3

GDMY/SEVK IG3	67	E4
LEY E10.	62	C4
MNPK E12	83	D2
Salisbury Sq EMB EC4Y *	22	B5
Salisbury St ACT W3	98	C3
STJWD NW8.	16	B1
Salisbury Ter PECK SE15	138	C1
Salisbury Wk ARCH N19	56	C4
Sally Murray Cl MNPK E12	84	A1
Salmen Rd PLSTW E13	93	F1
Salmon La POP/IOD E14	91	E5
Salmon Ms KIL/WHAMP NW6 *	72	A2
Salmon St CDALE/KGS NW9.	50	B3
POP/IOD E14 *	91	F5
Salomons Rd PLSTW E13	94	C4
Salop Rd WALTH E17	61	D1
Saltcoats Rd CHSWK W4	99	E3
Saltcroft Cl WBLY HA9	50	B3
Salter Rd BERM/RHTH SE16	103	D2
Salters' Hall Ct MANHO EC4N *	36	A1
Salters Rd NKENS W10	89	D3
Salters Rw IS N1 *	77	D3
Salter St POP/IOD E14.	104	A1
WLSDN NW10	88	A2
Salterton Rd HOLWY N7	57	E5
Saltley Cl EHAM E6	95	E5
Saltoun Rd BRXS/STRHM SW2	136	A2
Saltram Crs MV/WKIL W9	2	C4
Saltwell St POP/IOD E14	104	A1
Saltwood Gv WALW SE17 *	119	D1
Salusbury Rd KIL/WHAMP NW6	89	F1
Salvador TOOT SW17	151	E1
Salvin Rd PUT/ROE SW15.	131	D1
Salway Rd SRTFD E15	81	D3
Samantha Cl WALTH E17	61	F2
Sam Bartram Cl CHARL SE7	124	C1
Samels Ct HMSMTH W6	112	A1
Samford St STJWD NW8	16	C1
Samira Cl WALTH E17	61	D1
Sampson St WAP E1W *	102	B2
Samson St PLSTW E13	94	C1
Samuel Cl HACK E8	77	F5
NWCR SE14.	121	D2
WOOL/PLUM SE18	107	E5
Samuel St BERM/RHTH SE16.	107	F5
Sancroft Cl CRICK NW2	52	B5
Sancroft St LBTH SE11	118	A1
Sanctuary Ms HACK E8	77	F3
Sanctuary St STHWK SE1	47	F1
The Sanctuary WEST SW1P	44	B2
Sandall Rd KTTN NW5	74	C3
Sandal St SRTFD E15	81	E5
Sandalwood Cl WCHPL E1	91	E3
Sandbach Pl WOOL/PLUM SE18	108	C5
Sandbourne Rd NWCR SE14.	121	D3
Sandbrook Rd STNW/STAM N16.	59	E5
Sandby Gn ELTH/MOT SE9	143	E1
Sandell St STHWK SE1 *	34	A5
Sanderson Cl KTTN NW5 *	74	B1
Sanderstead Av GLDGN NW11	53	E4
Sanderstead Cl BAL SW12	134	C5
Sanderstead Rd LEY E10	61	E3
Sandford Rd EHAM E6	95	F2
Sandford Rw WALW SE17	119	D1
Sandford St FUL/PGN SW6.	114	B3
Sandgate La WAND/EARL SW18.	151	E1
Sandgate St PECK SE15	120	B2
The Sandhills WBPTN SW10 *	114	C2
Sandhurst Dr GDMY/SEVK IG3	85	F1
Sandhurst Market CAT SE6 *	158	C1
Sandhurst Pde CAT SE6 *	158	C1
Sandhurst Rd BFN/LL DA15.	163	F5
CAT SE6.	159	D1
Sandifer Dr CRICK NW2	53	D5
Sandilands Rd FUL/PGN SW6.	114	B4
Sandison St PECK SE15	137	F1
Sandland St BMSBY WC1R	21	F3
Sandling Ri ELTH/MOT SE9	162	A3
Sandlings Ct PECK SE15	120	B5
Sandmere Rd CLAP SW4	135	E2
Sandown Ct SYD SE26 *	156	B3
Sandpiper Ct BERM/RHTH SE16.	103	F3
Sandpit Pl CHARL SE7	125	E1
Sandpit Rd BMLY BR1	159	E5
Sandridge St ARCH N19	56	C4
Sandringham Cl WIM/MER SW19	149	D1
Sandringham Dr WELL DA16.	127	E5
Sandringham Gdns CEND/HSY/T N8	55	F2
Sandringham Rd BARK IG11.	85	F3
BMLY BR1.	160	A5
CRICK NW2.	70	B2

FSTGT E7.	82	C2
GLDGN NW11	53	E2
HACK E8.	77	F2
LEY E10.	63	D2
Sandrock Rd LEW SE13.	140	A1
Sands End La FUL/PGN SW6.	114	B4
Sandstone La CAN/RD E16.	106	B1
Sandstone Pl ARCH N19	56	B4
Sandstone Rd LEE/GVPK SE12.	160	B2
Sandtoft Rd CHARL SE7	124	B2
Sandwell Crs KIL/WHAMP NW6	72	A5
Sandy Cl ROCH/KEW TW9	110	A5
Sandycombe Rd RICH/KEW TW9	110	A5
Sandy Hill Av WOOL/PLUM SE18	126	B1
Sandy Hill La WOOL/PLUM SE18	108	B5
Sandyhill Rd IL IG1	84	B1
Sandy Hill Rd WOOL/PLUM SE18	126	B1
Sandy Rd HAMP NW3.	54	B4
Sandy's Rw WCHPL E1	25	D3
Sanford La STNW/STAM N16.	59	F4
Sanford St NWCR SE14.	121	F1
Sanford Ter STNW/STAM N16.	59	F5
Sangley Rd CAT SE6.	140	B5
Sangora Rd BTSGEA SW11	133	D2
Sansom Rd WAN E11 *	63	F4
Sansom St CMBW SE5.	119	D3
Sans Wk CLKNW EC1R	10	C5
Santley Cl CLAP SW4	135	E1
Santos Rd WAND/EARL SW18.	132	A3
Saperton Wk LBTH SE11.	45	F4
Sapphire Rd DEPT SE8.	103	E5
WLSDN NW10	68	C4
Saracen's Head Yd FENCHST EC3M.	25	D5
Saracen St POP/IOD E14.	92	A5
Saratoga Rd CLPT E5	78	C1
Sardinia St HOL/ALD WC2B.	21	E5
Sarre Rd CRICK NW2	71	E1
Sarsfeld Rd BAL SW12	151	F1
Sartor Rd PECK SE15	139	D2
Sarum Ter BOW E3 *	91	F3
Satanita Cl CAN/RD E16.	95	D5
Satchwell Rd BETH E2	90	A2
Sattar Ms STNW/STAM N16 *	59	D5
Sauls Gn WAN E11.	63	E5
Saunders Cl IL IG1.	67	D3
POP/IOD E14 *	103	F1
Saunders Ness Rd POP/IOD E14.	105	D5
Saunders Rd WOOL/PLUM SE18.	127	F1
Saunders St LBTH SE11.	46	A4
Savage Gdns EHAM E6.	95	F5
TWRH EC3N.	37	D1
Savanah Cl PECK SE15.	119	F3
Savernake Rd HAMP NW3	73	F1
Savile Rw CONDST W1S.	31	F1
Saville Rd CAN/RD E16.	107	E2
CHSWK W4.	99	D4
Savona St VX/NE SW8	116	C3
Savoy Cl SRTFD E15	81	E5
Savoy Ct TPL/STR WC2R *	33	D2
Savoy Hl TPL/STR WC2R *	33	E2
Savoy Ms BRXN/ST SW9	135	E1
Savoy Pl CHCR WC2N.	33	D2
Savoy Rw TPL/STR WC2R	33	E1
Savoy St TPL/STR WC2R.	33	E2
Savoy Steps TPL/STR WC2R *	33	E2
Savoy Wy TPL/STR WC2R	33	E2
Sawkins Cl WIM/MER SW19	149	D2
Sawley Rd SHB W12	100	A2
Sawyer's Hl MORT/ESHN SW14.	128	C5
Sawyer St STHWK SE1	35	E5
Saxby Rd BRXS/STRHM SW2	135	E5
Saxham Rd BARK IG11.	85	E5
Saxon Cl WALTH E17	62	A2
Saxon Dr ACT W3	86	B5
Saxonfield Cl BRXS/STRHM SW2	135	F5
Saxon Rd BOW E3.	91	F1
EHAM E6.	95	F3
IL IG1.	84	B3
WBLY HA9	50	C5
Saxton Cl LEW SE13.	141	D1
Sayes Court St DEPT SE8.	121	F1
Scala St FITZ W1T	19	F2
Scandrett St WAP E1W *	102	B2
Scarba Wk IS N1	77	D3
Scarborough Rd FSBYPK N4.	57	F3
WAN E11	63	D5
Scarborough St WCHPL E1	25	F5
Scarlet Rd CAT SE6.	159	E3
Scarsbrook Rd BKHTH/KID SE3.	143	D1
Scarsdale Pl KENS W8 *	38	C2
Scarsdale Vls KENS W8	38	B3
Scarth Rd BARN SW13.	129	F1

Scawen Rd *DEPT* SE8	121 E1
Scawfell St *BETH* E2	13 F2
Sceptre Rd *BETH* E2	90 C2
Scholars Rd *BAL* SW12	152 C1
Scholefield Rd *ARCH* N19	57 D4
Schonfeld Sq *STNW/STAM* N16	59 D4
Schoolbank Rd *GNWCH* SE10	105 F5
Schoolhouse La *WAP* E1W *	103 D1
School Rd *MNPK* E12	83 F1
WLSDN NW10	87 D3
School Sq *GNWCH* SE10	105 F4
Schooner Cl *BERM/RHTH* SE16	103 D3
POP/IOD E14	105 D4
Schubert Rd *PUT/ROE* SW15	131 F3
Sclater St *WCHPL* E1	13 E5
Scoble Pl *STNW/STAM* N16	77 F1
Scoles Crs *BRXS/STRHM* SW2	154 A1
Scoresby St *STHWK* SE1	34 C4
Scotia Rd *BRXS/STRHM* SW2	136 A5
Scotsdale Rd *LEE/GVPK* SE12	142 B3
Scotswood St *CLKNW* EC1R *	10 B5
Scott Av *PUT/ROE* SW15	131 E4
Scott Ellis Gdns *STJWD* NW8	4 A4
Scott Lidgett Crs *BERM/RHTH* SE16	102 A3
Scotts Pas *WOOL/PLUM* SE18 *	114 C1
Scott's Rd *LEY* E10	62 C5
SHB W12	100 B5
Scott St *WCHPL* E1	90 B3
Scott's Yd *MANHO* EC4N	36 A1
Scoulding Rd *CAN/RD* E16	93 F5
Scouler St *POP/IOD* E14	105 D1
Scout Ap *WLSDN* NW10	69 E1
Scovell Crs *STHWK* SE1 *	47 E1
Scovell Rd *STHWK* SE1	47 E1
Scriven St *HACK* E8	77 F5
Scrooby St *CAT* SE6	140 B4
Scrubs La *WLSDN* NW10	88 A2
Scrutton Cl *BAL* SW12	135 D5
Scrutton St *SDTCH* EC2A	24 C1
Scutari Rd *EDUL* SE22	138 B3
Scylla Rd *PECK* SE15	138 B1
Seabright St *BETH* E2	90 B2
Seacole Cl *ACT* W3	87 D5
Seaford St *STPAN* WC1H	9 D4
Seaforth Crs *HBRY* N5	76 C2
Seaforth Pl *WESTW* SW1E	43 F2
Seager Blds *DEPT* SE8 *	122 A4
Seager Pl *BOW* E3	91 F4
Seagrave Cl *WCHPL* E1 *	91 D4
Seagrave Rd *FUL/PGN* SW6	114 A2
Seagry Rd *WAN* E11	64 A1
Seagull La *CAN/RD* E16	106 A1
Seal St *HACK* E8	77 F1
Searles Cl *BTSEA* SW11	115 E3
Searles Dr *EHAM* E6	96 A4
Searles Rd *STHWK* SE1	48 B4
Sears St *CMBW* SE5	119 D3
Seaton Av *GDMY/SEVK* IG3	85 E2
Seaton Cl *LBTH* SE11	118 B1
PLSTW E13	94 A3
PUT/ROE SW15	130 B5
Sebastian St *FSBYE* EC1V	11 D4
Sebbon St *IS* N1	76 B4
Sebert Rd *FSTGT* E7	82 B2
Secker St *STHWK* SE1	34 A4
Second Av *ACT* W3	99 F2
MNPK E12	83 F1
MORT/ESHN SW14	111 E1
NKENS W10	89 E3
PLSTW E13	94 A2
Second Wy *WBLY* HA9	68 B1
Sedan Wy *WALW* SE17	119 E1
Sedding St *KTBR* SW1X	42 A4
Seddon St *FSBYW* WC1X	9 E4
Sedgebrook Rd *BKHTH/KID* SE3	125 D5
Sedgeford Rd *SHB* W12	99 F2
Sedgehill Rd *CAT* SE6	158 A5
Sedgeway *CAT* SE6	159 F1
Sedgmoor Pl *CMBW* SE5	119 F3
Sedgwick Rd *LEY* E10	62 C4
Sedgwick St *HOM* E9	79 D2
Sedleigh Rd *WAND/EARL* SW18	131 F4
Sediescombe Rd *FUL/PGN* SW6	113 F3
Sedley Pl *OXSTW* W1C	18 C5
Sednem Ct *PECK* SE15	120 A5
Seeley Dr *DUL* SE21	155 E4
Seelig Av *CDALE/KGS* NW9	52 A2
Seething La *TWRH* EC3N	37 D1
Sefton St *PUT/ROE* SW15	112 C5
Sekforde St *CLKNW* EC1R	22 C1
Selbie Av *WLSDN* NW10	69 F2
Selborne Av *MNPK* E12	84 A1
Selborne Rd *CMBW* SE5	119 D5
IL IG1	66 A4
Selby Rd *PLSTW* E13	94 B4
WAN E11	63 E5
Selby St *WCHPL* E1	90 A3
Selden Rd *PECK* SE15	120 C5
Selhurst Cl *WIM/MER* SW19	149 D1
Selkirk Rd *TOOT* SW17	151 E4
Sellincourt Rd *TOOT* SW17	151 E5
Sellons Av *WLSDN* NW10	69 F5
Selsdon Rd *CRICK* NW2	51 F4
PLSTW E13	82 C5
WAN E11	64 A2
WNWD SE27	154 B3
Selsdon Wy *POP/IOD* E14	104 B4
Selsea Pl *STNW/STAM* N16	77 E2
Selsey St *BOW* E3	92 A4
Selwood Pl *SKENS* SW7	115 D1
Selwood Ter *SKENS* SW7	115 D1
Selworthy Rd *CAT* SE6	157 F3
Serbin Cl *LEY* E10	62 C2
Selwyn Av *GDMY/SEVK* IG3	67 F1
Selwyn Rd *BOW* E3	91 F1
PLSTW E13	82 B5
WLSDN NW10	69 E5
Semley Pl *BGVA* SW1W	42 B5
Senate St *PECK* SE15	120 C5
Senior St *BAY/PAD* W2	14 C2
Senlac Rd *LEE/GVPK* SE12	160 B1
Senrab St *WCHPL* E1	91 D5
Sentamu Cl *HNHL* SE24	154 B1
Serbin Cl *LEY* E10	62 C2
Serenaders Rd *BRXN/ST* SW9	118 A5
Serjeant's Inn *EMB* EC4Y *	22 B5
Serle St *LINN* WC2A	21 F4
Sermon La *BLKFR* EC4V	23 E5
Serpentine Rd *BAY/PAD* W2	29 D4
Service Route No 1 *SRTFD* E15	81 D4
Service Route No 2 *SRTFD* E15	81 D4
Service Route No 3 *SRTFD* E15	81 D3
Setchell Est *STHWK* SE1	49 E4
Setchell Rd *STHWK* SE1	49 E4
Setchell Wy *STHWK* SE1	49 E4
Seth St *BERM/RHTH* SE16	102 C3
Settles St *WCHPL* E1	90 A5
Settrington Rd *FUL/PGN* SW6	114 B5
Seven Dials *LSO/SEVD* WC2H	20 C5
Seven Kings Rd *GDMY/SEVK* IG3	67 E3
Sevenoaks Rd *BROCKY* SE4	139 F4
Seven Sisters Rd *FSBYPK* N4	58 B4
HOLWY N7	57 F5
SEVS/STOTM N15	59 D1
Seven Stars Yd *WCHPL* E1	25 E2
Seventh Av *MNPK* E12	83 F1
Severnake Cl *POP/IOD* E14	104 A5
Severn Av *NKENS* W10	89 E2
Severn Wy *WLSDN* NW10	69 F2
Severus Rd *BTSEA* SW11	133 E2
Seville Ms *IS* N1	77 E4
Seville St *KTBR* SW1X	41 F1
Sevington Rd *HDN* NW4	52 B1
Sevington St *MV/WKIL* W9	14 C1
Sewardstone Rd *BETH* E2	90 C1
Seward St *FSBYE* EC1V	11 D5
Sewdley St *CLPT* E5	61 D5
Sewell St *PLSTW* E13	94 A2
Sextant Av *POP/IOD* E14	105 D5
Seymour Gdns *BROCKY* SE4	139 D1
IL IG1	65 F3
Seymour Ms *MBLAR* W1H	18 A4
Seymour Pl *MBLAR* W1H	17 E4
Seymour Rd *CHSWK* W4	98 C5
EHAM E6	83 D5
LEY E10	61 F5
WAND/EARL SW18	131 F5
WIM/MER SW19	149 D3
Seymour St *BAY/PAD* W2	17 E5
WOOL/PLUM SE18	108 C4
Seymour Wk *WBPTN* SW10	114 C2
Seyssel St *POP/IOD* E14	104 C5
Shaa Rd *ACT* W3	99 D1
Shackleton Cl *FSTH* SE23	156 B2
Shacklewell La *HACK* E8	77 F1
Shacklewell Rd *STNW/STAM* N16	77 F1
Shacklewell Rw *HACK* E8	77 F1
Shacklewell St *BETH* E2	13 F5
Shad Thames *STHWK* SE1	37 E4
Shadwell Gdns *WCHPL* E1 *	102 C1
Shadwell Pierhead *WAP* E1W	102 C1
Shaftesbury Av *LSO/SEVD* WC2H	20 C4
SOHO/SHAV W1D	32 A1
Shaftesbury Gdns *WLSDN* NW10	87 E3
Shaftesbury Ms *CLAP* SW4	134 C3

KENS W8 *	38 B3
Shaftesbury Pl *BARB* EC2Y *	23 E3
Shaftesbury Rd *ARCH* N19	57 E3
FSTGT E7	82 C4
LEY E10	62 A3
The Shaftesburys *BARK* IG11	96 C1
Shaftesbury St *IS* N1	11 F2
Shaftesbury Ter *HMSMTH* W6 *	99 F5
Shafteswood Ct *TOOT* SW17	151 E3
Shafto Ms *KTBR* SW1X	41 E3
Shafton Ms *HOM* E9 *	79 D5
Shafton Rd *HOM* E9	79 D5
Shakespeare Av *WLSDN* NW10	68 C5
Shakespeare Crs *MNPK* E12	83 F4
WLSDN NW10	69 D5
Shakespeare Rd *ACT* W3	98 C2
HNHL SE24	136 B3
Shakespeare Ter *RCH/KEW* TW9 *	128 A1
Shakspeare St *STNW/STAM* N16	77 E1
Shakspeare St *STNW/STAM* N16	77 E1
Shalbourne Sq *HOM* E9	79 F5
Shalcomb St *WBPTN* SW10	114 C2
Shaldon Dr *MRDN* SM4	161 D4
Shalfleet Dr *NKENS* W10	101 D1
Shalford Ct *IS* N1	10 C1
Shalimar Gdns *ACT* W3	98 C1
Shalimar Rd *ACT* W3	98 C1
Shallons Rd *ELTH/MOT* SE9	162 B4
Shalstone Rd *MORT/ESHN* SW14	128 B1
Shamrock St *CLAP* SW4	135 D1
Shandon Rd *CLAP* SW4	134 C4
Shand St *STHWK* SE1	37 D5
Shandy St *WCHPL* E1	91 D4
Shannon Cl *CRICK* NW2	53 D5
Shannon Gv *BRXN/ST* SW9	135 F2
Shannon Pl *STJWD* NW8	5 D1
Shardcroft Av *HNHL* SE24	136 B3
Shardeloes Rd *BROCKY* SE4 *	139 F3
NWCR SE14	121 F5
Shard's Sq *PECK* SE15	120 A2
Sharon Gdns *HOM* E9	78 C5
Sharon Rd *CHSWK* W4	111 D1
Sharples Hall St *CAMTN* NW1	73 F4
Sharratt St *PECK* SE15	120 C2
Sharsted St *WALW* SE17	118 B1
Shavers Pl *MYFR/PICC* W1J	32 A2
Shawbrooke Rd *ELTH/MOT* SE9	143 D2
Shawbury Rd *EDUL* SE22	137 F3
Shaw Crs *POP/IOD* E14	91 E5
Shawfield St *CHEL* SW3	115 E1
Shaw Rd *BMLY* BR1	159 F5
EDUL SE22	137 E2
Shaw's Cots *FSTH* SE23	157 E3
Shearling Wy *HOLWY* N7	75 E3
Shearman Rd *BKHTH/KID* SE3	141 F5
Sheen Common Dr	
RCHPK/HAM TW10	128 A2
Sheen Court Rd *RCHPK/HAM* TW10	128 A2
Sheenewood *SYD* SE26	156 B5
Sheen Ga *MORT/ESHN* SW14	129 D4
Sheen Gate Gdns *MORT/ESHN* SW14	128 C2
Sheen Gv *IS* N1	76 A5
Sheen La *MORT/ESHN* SW14	128 C2
Sheen Wd *MORT/ESHN* SW14	128 C3
Sheepcote La *BTSEA* SW11	115 F5
Sheep La *HACK* E8	78 B5
Sheerwater Rd *CAN/RD* E16	95 D4
Sheffield St *LINN* WC2A *	21 E5
Sheffield Ter *KENS* W8	26 A5
Shelduck Cl *SRTFD* E15	81 F2
Shelford Pl *STNW/STAM* N16	59 D5
Shelgate Rd *BTSEA* SW11	133 F3
Shelley Av *MNPK* E12	83 E3
Shelley Cl *PECK* SE15	120 B5
Shelley Dr *WELL* DA16	127 E4
Shellgrove Rd *STNW/STAM* N16 *	77 E2
Shellness Rd *CLPT* E5	78 B2
Shell Rd *LEW* SE13	140 B1
Shellwood Rd *BTSEA* SW11	115 F5
Shelmerdine Cl *BOW* E3	92 A4
Shelton St *LSQ/SEVD* WC2H *	20 C5
Shenfield St *IS* N1	13 D2
Shenley Rd *CMBW* SE5	119 E4
Shepherdess Pl *FSBYE* EC1V	11 F3
Shepherdess Wk *IS* N1	11 F1
Shepherd Market *MYFR/PICC* W1J	30 C4
Shepherd's Bush Gn *SHB* W12	100 C3
Shepherd's Bush Market *SHB* W12	100 C3
Shepherd's Bush Pl *SHB* W12 *	101 D3
Shepherd's Bush Rd *HMSMTH* W6	100 C4
Shepherd's Cl *HGT* N6	56 B1
Shepherd's Hl *HGT* N6	56 B1
Shepherds La *THMD* SE28	109 E2
Shepherd's La *HOM* E9	79 D2
Shepherd's Leas *ELTH/MOT* SE9	144 C3
Shepherds Pl *MYFR/PICC* W1K	30 A1
Shepherds St *MYFR/PICC* W1J	30 C4
Shepherds Wk *CRICK* NW2	52 A4
Sheppard Dr *BERM/RHTH* SE16	120 B1
Sheppard St *CAN/RD* E16	93 F3
Shepperton Rd *IS* N1	77 D5
Sheppey Wk *IS* N1	76 C4
Shepton Houses *BETH* E2 *	90 C2
Sherard Rd *ELTH/MOT* SE9	143 E3
Sheraton St *SOHO/CST* W1F *	20 A5
Sherborne La *MANHO* EC4N	36 A1
Sherborne St *IS* N1	77 D5
Sherboro Rd *SEVS/STOTM* N15	59 F1
Sherbrooke Rd *FUL/PGN* SW6	113 E3
Sherbrooke Ter *FUL/PGN* SW6 *	113 E3
Sherfield Gdns *PUT/ROE* SW15	129 F4
Sheridan Ms *WAN* E11	64 B1
Sheridan Rd *FSTGT* E7	63 F5
MNPK E12	83 E2
Sheridan Wk *GLDGN* NW11	54 A1
Sheringham Av *MNPK* E12	83 F2
Sheringham Dr *BARK* IG11	85 F2
Sherington Rd *HOLWY* N7	76 A3
Sherington Rd *BKHTH/KID* SE3	124 B2
Sherlock Ms *MHST* W1U	18 A2
Sherrard Rd *FSTGT* E7	82 C3
Sherrick Green Rd *WLSDN* NW10	70 B2
Sherriff Rd *KIL/WHAMP* NW6	72 A3
Sherry Ms *BARK* IG11	85 D4
Sherwin Rd *NWCR* SE14	121 D4
Sherwood Ct *MBLAR* W1H	17 E3
Sherwood Gdns *BARK* IG11	85 D4
BERM/RHTH SE16	120 A1
POP/IOD E14	104 A5
Sherwood Rd *WELL* DA16	145 E1
Sherwood St *SOHO/CST* W1F	31 F1
Shetland Rd *BOW* E3	91 F1
Shifford Pth *FSTH* SE23	157 D3
Shillibeer Pl *MBLAR* W1H	17 D3
Shillingford St *IS* N1	76 B5
Shinfield St *SHB* W12	88 C5
Shipka Rd *BAL* SW12	152 B1
Ship La *MORT/ESHN* SW14	128 C1
Shipman Rd *CAN/RD* E16	94 B5
FSTH SE23	157 D2
Ship & Mermaid Rw *STHWK* SE1 *	36 B5
Ship St *DEPT* SE8	122 A4
Ship Tavern Pas *BANK* EC3V	36 C1
Shipton St *BETH* E2	13 F3
Shirburn Cl *FSTH* SE23	138 C5
Shirbutt St *POP/IOD* E14	104 A1
Shirebrook Rd *BKHTH/KID* SE3	125 D5
Shirehall Cl *HDN* NW4	53 D1
Shirehall Gdns *HDN* NW4	53 D1
Shirehall La *HDN* NW4	53 D1
Shirehall Pk *HDN* NW4	53 D1
Shirland Ms *MV/WKIL* W9	2 B5
Shirland Rd *MV/WKIL* W9	2 B5
Shirley Gdns *BARK* IG11	85 E3
Shirley Gv *BTSEA* SW11	134 A1
Shirley Rd *BFN/LL* DA15	163 E5
CHSWK W4	99 D5
SRTFD E15	81 E4
Shirley St *CAN/RD* E16	93 F5
Shirlock Rd *HAMP* NW3	73 F1
Shobroke Cl *CRICK* NW2	52 B4
Shoebury Rd *EHAM* E6	83 F4
Shoe La *FLST/FETLN* EC4A	22 B4
Shooters Hill Rd *BKHTH/KID* SE3	124 A4
GNWCH SE10	123 E4
Shoot-Up Hl *CRICK* NW2	71 E3
Shops *SYD* SE26 *	157 D5
Shoreditch High St *WCHPL* E1	25 D2
Shoreham Cl *WAND/EARL* SW18	132 B3
Shore Pl *HOM* E9	78 C4
Shore Rd *HOM* E9	78 C4

Shore Wy *BRXN/ST* SW9 .... 118 A5
Shorncliffe Rd *STHWK* SE1 .... 119 F1
Shorndean St *CAT* SE6 .... 158 C1
Shorrolds Rd *FUL/PGN* SW6 .... 114 A1
Shorter St *TWRH* EC3N 37 F1
Shortlands *HMSMTH* W6 .... 101 D5
WAN E11 .... 63 E4
Shortlands Rd *LEY* E10 .... 62 B2
Short Rd *CHSWK* W4 .... 111 E2
WAN E11 .... 63 E4
Shorts Gdns *LSQ/SEVD* WC2H * 20 C5
Short St *STHWK* SE1 .... 34 B5
Shortway *ELTH/MOT* SE9 .... 143 E1
Shottendane Rd *FUL/PGN* SW6 * ... 114 A4
Shottery Cl *ELTH/MOT* SE9 .... 161 E5
Shottfield Av *MORT/ESHN* SW14 .... 129 E2
Shoulder of Mutton Aly
   POP/IOD E14 .... 103 E1
Shouldham St *MBLAR* W1H 17 D3
Shrapnel Cl *WOOL/PLUM* SE18 ..... 125 F3
Shrapnel Rd *ELTH/MOT* SE9 .... 143 F1
Shrewsbury Av *MORT/ESHN* SW14 .. 128 C2
   WLSDN NW10 .... 69 D5
Shrewsbury La *WOOL/PLUM* SE18 .. 126 B4
Shrewsbury Ms *BAY/PAD* W2 .... 14 A4
Shrewsbury Rd *BAY/PAD* W2 .... 14 A3
   FSTGT E7 .... 83 E4
Shrewsbury St *NKENS* W10 .... 88 C3
Shroffold Rd *BMLY* BR1 .... 159 E4
Shroton St *CAMTN* NW1 .... 16 C2
Shrubbery Rd *STRHM/NOR* SW16 ... 153 E4
Shruband Rd *HACK* E8 .... 78 A5
   LEY E10 .... 62 A2
Shrublands Cl *SYD* SE26 .... 156 C3
Shrubsall Cl *ELTH/MOT* SE9 .... 161 E1
Shubbery Cl *IS* N1 .... 76 C5
Shuna Wk *IS* N1 * 77 D3
Shurland Gdns *PECK* SE15 * 119 F5
Shuters Sq *WKENS* W14 * 113 F1
Shuttle Cl *BFN/LL* DA15 .... 145 F5
Shuttle St *WCHPL* E1 .... 90 A3
Shuttleworth Rd *BTSEA* SW11 ...... 115 D5
Sibella Rd *CLAP* SW4 .... 117 D5
Sibley Gv *EHAM* E6 .... 83 E4
   MNPK E12 .... 83 E1
Sibthorpe Rd *LEE/GVPK* SE12 ...... 142 B5
Sicilian Av *NOXST/BSQ* WC1A * 21 D3
Sidbury St *FUL/PGN* SW6 .... 113 E4
Sidcup By-Pass Rd *SCUP* DA14 .... 161 F4
Sidcup Rd *ELTH/MOT* SE9 .... 161 D1
   LEE/GVPK SE12 .... 142 B3
Siddons La *CAMTN* NW1 .... 17 F1
Siddons Rd *FSTH* SE23 .... 157 E2
Sidewood Rd *ELTH/MOT* SE9 .... 163 D1
Sidford Pl *STHWK* SE1 .... 45 F3
Sidings Rd *HOLWY* N7 .... 76 A1
The Sidings *WAN* E11 * 62 C5
Sidmouth Pde *CRICK* NW2 * 70 C4
Sidmouth Rd *CRICK* NW2 .... 70 C4
   LEY E10 .... 62 C4
   PECK SE15 .... 119 F4
Sidmouth St *STPAN* WC1H 9 D4
Sidney Eison Wy *EHAM* E6 .... 96 A4
Sidney Gv *FSBYE* EC1V 10 C2
Sidney Rd *BRXN/ST* SW9 .... 117 F5
   FSTGT E7 .... 64 C5
Sidney Sq *WCHPL* E1 * 90 C5
Sidney St *WCHPL* E1 .... 90 B5
Sidworth St *HACK* E8 .... 78 B4
Siebert Rd *BKHTH/KID* SE3 .... 124 A2
Siemens Rd *WOOL/PLUM* SE18 ..... 107 D4
Sienna Ter *CRICK* NW2 .... 52 A4
Sigdon Rd *HACK* E8 .... 78 A2
Signmakers Yd *CAMTN* NW1 * 74 B5
Silbury St *IS* N1 * 12 A3
Silesia Bdgs *HACK* E8 .... 78 B4
Silex St *STHWK* SE1 .... 47 D1
Silk Cl *LEE/GVPK* SE12 .... 142 A3
Silkin Ms *PECK* SE15 .... 120 A3
Silk Mills Pth *LEW* SE13 .... 140 C1
Silk St *BARB* EC2Y 23 F2
Silver Birch Cl *CAT* SE6 .... 157 F3
Silverbirch Wk *HAMP* NW3 * 73 F1
Silver Cl *NWCR* SE14 * 121 E3
Silver Crs *CHSWK* W4 .... 98 B5
Silverdale *SYD* SE26 .... 156 C4
Silverdale Dr *ELTH/MOT* SE9 ...... 161 C2
Silver Dene *PUT/ROE* SW15 * 130 C3
Silvermere Rd *CAT* SE6 .... 140 A4
Silver Pl *SOHO/CST* W1F 19 F5
Silver Rd *LEW* SE13 .... 140 B1
   NKENS W10 .... 101 D1
Silverthorne Rd *VX/NE* SW8 .... 116 B5

Silverton Rd *HMSMTH* W6 .... 113 D3
Silvertown Wy *CAN/RD* E16 .... 105 F1
Silver Wk *BERM/RHTH* SE16 .... 103 F2
Silvester Rd *EDUL* SE22 .... 137 F3
Silvester St *STHWK* SE1 .... 48 A1
Silwood Rd *BERM/RHTH* SE16 ...... 121 D1
Simmons Rd *WOOL/PLUM* SE18 .... 126 B1
Simms Rd *STHWK* SE1 .... 102 A5
Simnel Rd *LEE/GVPK* SE12 .... 142 B5
Simon Cl *NTGHL* W11 .... 101 F1
Simonds Rd *LEY* E10 .... 62 A4
Simons Wk *SRTFD* E15 .... 81 D2
Simpson Dr *ACT* W3 .... 87 D5
Simpson's Rd *POP/IOD* E14 .... 104 B1
Simpson St *BTSEA* SW11 .... 115 E5
Simrose Ct *WAND/EARL* SW18 ..... 132 A5
Sinclair Gdns *WKENS* W14 .... 101 F5
Sinclair Gv *GLDGN* NW11 .... 53 D1
Sinclair Rd *WKENS* W14 .... 101 E4
Singer St *FSBYE* EC1V 12 B4
Sir Abraham Dawes Cots
   PUT/ROE SW15 * 131 E2
Sir Alexander Cl *ACT* W3 .... 99 F1
Sirdar Rd *NTGHL* W11 .... 101 D1
Sir John Kirk Cl *CMBW* SE5 .... 118 C3
Sir Thomas More Est *CHEL* SW3 ... 115 D2
Sise La *MANHO* EC4N * 24 A5
Sisley Rd *BARK* IG11 .... 85 E5
Sispara Gdns *WAND/EARL* SW18 ... 131 F4
Sissinghurst Cl *BMLY* BR1 .... 159 E5
Sister Mabel's Wy *PECK* SE15 * 120 A3
Sisters Av *BTSEA* SW11 .... 133 F2
Sistova Rd *BAL* SW12 .... 152 B1
Sisulu Pl *BRXN/ST* SW9 .... 136 A1
Siward Rd *TOOT* SW17 .... 150 C3
Sixth Av *MNPK* E12 .... 83 F1
   NKENS W10 .... 89 E3
Skardu Rd *CRICK* NW2 .... 71 E2
Skeena Hi *WAND/EARL* SW18 ...... 131 E5
Skeffington Rd *EHAM* E6 .... 83 F5
Skeffington St *WOOL/PLUM* SE18 .. 108 C4
Skelbrook St *WAND/EARL* SW18 ... 150 B2
Skelgill Rd *PUT/ROE* SW15 .... 131 F2
Skelley Rd *SRTFD* E15 .... 81 F4
Skelton Cl *HACK* E8 * 77 F3
Skelton Rd *FSTGT* E7 .... 82 A3
Skelton's La *LEY* E10 .... 62 B2
Skelwith Rd *HMSMTH* W6 .... 112 C2
Sketchley Gdns *BERM/RHTH* SE16 . 121 D1
Skiers St *SRTFD* E15 .... 81 E5
Skiffington Cl *BRXS/STRHM* SW2 .. 154 A1
Skinner Pl *BGVA* SW1W * 42 A5
Skinners La *BLKFR* EC4V 35 F1
Skinner St *CLKNW* EC1R 10 C5
   FSBYE EC1V 10 C4
Skipsey Av *EHAM* E6 .... 95 F2
Skipworth Rd *HOM* E9 .... 78 C5
Skylines *POP/IOD* E14 .... 104 C3
Skylines Village *POP/IOD* E14 * 104 C3
Sladebrook Rd *BKHTH/KID* SE3 .... 143 D1
Sladedale Rd *WOOL/PLUM* SE18 ... 127 D1
Slades Dr *ELTH/MOT* SE9 .... 162 C4
The Slade *WOOL/PLUM* SE18 ...... 127 E2
Slade Wk *WALW* SE17 .... 118 B2
Slagrove Pl *LEW* SE13 .... 140 A3
Slaidburn St *WBPTN* SW10 .... 114 C2
Slaithwaite Rd *LEW* SE13 .... 140 C2
Slaney Pl *HOLWY* N7 * 76 A2
Sleaford St *VX/NE* SW8 .... 116 C3
Slievemore Cl *CLAP* SW4 * 135 D1
Slingsby Pl *LSQ/SEVD* WC2H 32 C1
Slippers Pl *BERM/RHTH* SE16 ...... 102 B4
Sloane Av *CHEL* SW3 .... 41 D5
Sloane Ct East *CHEL* SW3 .... 116 A1
Sloane Ct West *CHEL* SW3 .... 116 A1
Sloane Gdns *BGVA* SW1W 42 A5
Sloane Sq *BGVA* SW1W 41 F5
Sloane St *KTBR* SW1X 41 F3
Sloane Ter *KTBR* SW1X 41 F4
Slough La *CDALE/KGS* NW9 .... 50 C1
Sly St *WCHPL* E1 * 90 B5
Smallbrook Ms *BAY/PAD* W2 ...... 16 A5
Smalley Cl *STNW/STAM* N16 ...... 59 F5
Smallwood Rd *TOOT* SW17 .... 151 D4
Smart's Pl *NOXST/BSQ* WC1A 21 D4
Smart St *BETH* E2 .... 91 D2
Smeaton Rd *WAND/EARL* SW18 ... 132 A5
Smeaton St *WAP* E1W 102 B2
Smedley St *VX/NE* SW8 .... 117 D5
Smeed Rd *BOW* E3 .... 80 A4
Smiles Pl *LEW* SE13 .... 122 C5

Smith Cl *BERM/RHTH* SE16 .... 103 D2
Smithfield St *STBT* EC1A 22 C5
Smith's Ct *SOHO/SHAV* W1D * 32 A1
Smith Sq *WEST* SW1P 44 C3
Smith St *CHEL* SW3 .... 115 F1
Smith Ter *CHEL* SW3 .... 115 F1
Smithwood Cl *WIM/MER* SW19 ...... 149 E1
Smithy St *WCHPL* E1 .... 90 Q4
Smugglers Wy *WAND/EARL* SW18 .... 118 A3
Smyrks Rd *WALW* SE17 * 119 E1
Smyrk's Rd *WALW* SE17 .... 119 E1
Smyrna Rd *KIL/WHAMP* NW6 .... 72 A4
Smythe St *POP/IOD* E14 .... 104 B1
Snarsgate St *NKENS* W10 .... 88 C4
Sneath Av *GLDGN* NW11 .... 53 F2
Sneyd Rd *CRICK* NW2 .... 70 C2
Snowberry Cl *SRTFD* E15 .... 81 D1
Snowbury Rd *FUL/PGN* SW6 .... 114 B5
Snowden Dr *CDALE/KGS* NW9 .... 51 E1
Snow Hl *STBT* EC1A 22 C3
Snowsfields *STHWK* SE1 .... 36 B5
Snowshill Rd *MNPK* E12 .... 83 E2
Soames St *PECK* SE15 .... 137 F1
Soho St *SOHO/SHAV* W1D 20 A4
Soho St *SOHO/SHAV* W1D 20 A4
Sojourner-Truth Cl *HACK* E8 .... 78 B3
Solander Gdns *WCHPL* E1 .... 102 B1
Solebay St *WCHPL* E1 .... 91 E3
Solent Pl *PLSTW* E13 .... 94 A2
Solent Rd *KIL/WHAMP* NW6 .... 72 A2
Solna Av *PUT/ROE* SW15 .... 130 C5
Solomon's Pas *PECK* SE15 .... 138 B2
Solon New Rd *CLAP* SW4 .... 135 E2
Solon Rd *BRXS/STRHM* SW2 .... 135 E2
Solway Cl *HACK* E8 .... 77 F3
Solway Rd *EDUL* SE22 .... 138 A2
Somali Rd *CRICK* NW2 .... 71 F1
Somerby Rd *BARK* IG11 .... 85 D4
Somerfield Rd *FSBYPK* N4 .... 58 B4
Somerfield St *BERM/RHTH* SE16 ... 121 D1
Somerford Gv *STNW/STAM* N16 .... 77 F1
Somerford Wy *BERM/RHTH* SE16 ... 103 F1
Somerleyton Rd *BRXN/ST* SW9 ..... 136 A2
Somers Cl *CAMTN* NW1 .... 8 A1
Somers Pl *BRXS/STRHM* SW2 .... 135 F5
Somers Rd *BRXS/STRHM* SW2 .... 135 F4
Somerset Av *WELL* DA16 .... 145 E5
Somerset Gdns *HGT* N6 .... 56 A2
                LEW SE13 .... 122 B5
Somerset Rd *CHSWK* W4 .... 99 D4
                WIM/MER SW19 .... 149 D3
Somerset Sq *WKENS* W14 * 101 E4
Somers Pl *BRXS/STRHM* SW2 .... 135 F5
Somers Rd *BRXS/STRHM* SW2 .... 135 F4
Somerton Av *RCH/KEW* TW9 .... 128 B1
Somerton Rd *CRICK* NW2 .... 53 D5
                PECK SE15 .... 138 B2
Somertrees Av *LEE/GVPK* SE12 .... 160 C1
Somerville Av *BARN* SW13 .... 112 C2
Somerville Cl *BRXN/ST* SW9 .... 117 F4
Sonderburg Rd *HOLWY* N7 .... 57 F4
Sondes St *WALW* SE17 .... 119 D2
Sonia Gdns *WLSDN* NW10 .... 69 F1
Soper Cl *FSTH* SE23 .... 157 D1
Sophia Cl *HOLWY* N7 .... 76 C1
                LEY E10 .... 62 B3
Sophia Rd *CAN/RD* E16 .... 94 B4
Sophia Sq *BERM/RHTH* SE16 .... 103 F1
Sopwith Wy *VX/NE* SW8 .... 116 B3
Sorrel Gdns *EHAM* E6 .... 95 E4
Sorrel La *POP/IOD* E14 .... 93 D5
Sorrell Cl *BRXN/ST* SW9 * 118 A5
                NWCR SE14 .... 121 E5
Sotheby Rd *HBRY* N5 .... 76 C1
Sotheran Cl *HACK* E8 .... 78 A5
Soudan Rd *BTSEA* SW11 .... 115 F4
Souldern Rd *WKENS* W14 * 101 D4
South Access Rd *LEY* E10 .... 61 D2
South Africa Rd *SHB* W12 .... 100 B1
Southall Pl *STHWK* SE1 .... 48 A1
Southampton Blds *LINN* WC2A * ... 22 A3
Southampton Ms *CAN/RD* E16 ...... 106 A2
Southampton Pl *NOXST/BSQ* WC1A .. 21 D3
Southampton Rd *HAMP* NW3 .... 73 F2
Southampton Rw *BMSBY* WC1N 20 C2
Southampton St *COVGDN* WC2E 33 D1
Southam St *NKENS* W10 .... 89 E3
Southampton St *MYFR/PKLN* W1K ... 30 B2
South Av *RCH/KEW* TW9 * 110 A5
South Bank *STHWK* SE1 .... 34 B2
South Birkbeck Rd *WAN* E11 .... 63 D5

South Black Lion La *HMSMTH* W6 .. 112 A1
South Bolton Gdns *WBPTN* SW10 ... 114 B1
Southborough Rd *HOM* E9 .... 78 C5
Southbourne Gdns *IL* IG1 .... 85 D3
                LEE/GVPK SE12 .... 142 B3
South Carriage Dr *KTBR* SW1X 29 F5
                SKENS SW7 .... 40 C1
Southchurch Rd *EHAM* E6 .... 95 F1
South Cl *HGT* N6 .... 56 B1
The South Colonnade *POP/IOD* E14. 104 A2
Southcombe St *WKENS* W14 .... 101 E5
Southcote Rd *ARCH* N19 .... 74 C1
South Crs *CAN/RD* E16 .... 93 D5
Southcroft Av *WELL* DA16 .... 145 E1
South Croxted Rd *DUL* SE21 .... 155 D5
Southdean Gdns *WIM/MER* SW19 .. 149 F2
South Eaton Pl *BGVA* SW1W 42 B4
South Edwardes Sq *KENS* W8 ...... 101 F4
South End *KENS* W8 .... 39 D2
Southend La *ELTH/MOT* SE9 .... 144 B4
Southend Crs *ELTH/MOT* SE9 ...... 144 A4
Southend La *SYD* SE26 .... 157 F4
Southend Rd *EHAM* E6 .... 83 F4
South End Rd *HAMP* NW3 .... 73 E1
South End Rw *KENS* W8 .... 39 D2
Southerngate Wy *NWCR* SE14 ...... 121 E3
Southern Gv *BOW* E3 .... 91 F2
Southern Rd *PLSTW* E13 .... 94 B1
Southern St *IS* N1 .... 9 E1
Southern Wy *GNWCH* SE10 .... 105 E5
Southerton Rd *HMSMTH* W6 * 100 C5
South Esk Rd *FSTGT* E7 .... 82 C3
Southey Rd *BRXN/ST* SW9 .... 118 A4
Southfield Rd *CHSWK* W4 .... 99 D3
Southfields Ms *WAND/EARL* SW18 * 132 A4
Southfields Rd *WAND/EARL* SW18 .. 132 A4
South Gdns *WBLY* HA9 * 50 A4
Southgate Gv *IS* N1 .... 77 D4
Southgate Rd *IS* N1 .... 77 D4
South Gate Rd *MNPK* E12 .... 65 D5
South Gv *HGT* N6 .... 56 A3
South Hill Pk *HAMP* NW3 .... 73 E1
South Hill Park Gdns *HAMP* NW3 ... 73 E1
Southill St *POP/IOD* E14 .... 92 B5
South Island Pl *BRXN/ST* SW9 ..... 117 F3
South Kensington Station Ar
                SKENS SW7 .... 40 B4
South Lambeth Pl *VX/NE* SW8 ...... 117 F2
South Lambeth Rd *VX/NE* SW8 ..... 117 E3
Southland Rd *WOOL/PLUM* SE18 ... 127 F4
Southlands Dr *WIM/MER* SW19 ..... 149 D2
Southmead Rd *WIM/MER* SW19 ..... 149 E1
South Molton La *MYFR/PKLN* W1K .. 18 C5
South Molton Rd *CAN/RD* E16 ...... 94 A5
South Molton St *MYFR/PKLN* W1K .. 18 C5
Southmoor Wy *HOM* E9 .... 79 F3
South Oak Rd *STRHM/NOR* SW16 .. 153 F4
Southold Ri *ELTH/MOT* SE9 .... 161 F3
Southolm St *BTSEA* SW11 .... 116 B4
Southover *BMLY* BR1 .... 160 A5
South Pde *CHEL* SW3 .... 115 D1
                CHSWK W4 .... 99 D5
South Park Crs *CAT* SE6 .... 159 E1
                IL IG1 .... 67 D5
South Park Dr *GDMY/SEVK* IG3 ..... 85 E2
South Park Rd *FUL/PGN* SW6 .... 132 B1
South Park Rd *IL* IG1 .... 85 D1
South Park Ter *IL* IG1 .... 67 D5
South Pl *LVPST* EC2M 24 B3
South Place Ms *LVPST* EC2M 24 B3
Southport Rd *WOOL/PLUM* SE18 ... 109 D5
South Ri *BAY/PAD* W2 * 28 D1
South Rd *FSTH* SE23 .... 157 D2
South Rw *BKHTH/KID* SE3 .... 124 A5
South Sea St *BERM/RHTH* SE16 .... 103 F4
South Side *HMSMTH* W6 .... 99 F4
Southspring *BFN/LL* DA15 .... 145 D5
South Sq *GINN* WC1R 22 A3
Southvale Rd *BKHTH/KID* SE3 ...... 123 E5
Southview Av *WLSDN* NW10 .... 69 F2
Southview Cl *TOOT* SW17 .... 152 A5
South View Crs *GNTH/NBYPK* IG2 .. 66 B1
Southview Rd *BMLY* BR1 .... 159 D4
South Vls *CAMTN* NW1 .... 75 D3
Southville *VX/NE* SW8 .... 117 D4
Southwark Br *CANST* EC4R 35 F2

Southwark Bridge Rd *STHWK* SE1 .... 47 D2
Southwark Park Est
   BERM/RHTH SE16 * 102 B5
Southwark Park Rd
   BERM/RHTH SE16 .... 49 H4
Southwark St *STHWK* SE1 .... 35 D3
Southwater Cl *POP/IOD* E14 .... 91 F5
Southway *GLDGN* NW11 .... 54 B1
South Wy *WBLY* HA9 .... 68 A2
Southway Cl *SHB* W12 .... 100 B3
Southwell Gdns *SKENS* SW7 .... 39 E4
Southwell Grove Rd *WAN* E11 .... 63 E4
Southwell Rd *CMBW* SE5 .... 136 C1
South West India Dock Entrance
   POP/IOD E14 .... 104 C3
Southwest Rd *WAN* E11 .... 63 D3
South Wharf Rd *BAY/PAD* W2 .... 16 A4
Southwick Ms *BAY/PAD* W2 .... 16 B4
Southwick Pl *BAY/PAD* W2 .... 16 C5
Southwick St *BAY/PAD* W2 .... 16 C4
Southwick Yd *BAY/PAD* W2 * 17 D5
Southwold Rd *CLPT* E5 .... 60 B4
Southwood Av *HGT* N6 .... 56 B3
Southwood La *HGT* N6 .... 56 A2
Southwood Lawn Rd *HGT* N6 .... 56 A2
Southwood Pk *HGT* N6 .... 56 B2
Southwood Rd *ELTH/MOT* SE9 .... 162 B2
Southwood Smith St *IS* N1 * 76 B5
South Worple Wy *MORT/ESHN* SW14 .... 129 D1
Southy Ms *CMBW* SE16 .... 106 A2
Sovereign Cl *WAP* E1W 102 B1
Sovereign Crs *BERM/RHTH* SE16 .... 103 E1
Sovereign Ms *BETH* E2 * 13 E1
Sovereign Pk *WLSDN* NW10 .... 86 B3
Sowerby Cl *ELTH/MOT* SE9 .... 143 F3
Spafield St *CLKNW* EC1R 10 B5
Spa Green Est *CLKNW* EC1R * 10 B3
Spalding Rd *HDN* NW4 .... 52 C1
   TOOT SW17 .... 152 B5
Spanby Rd *BOW* E3 .... 92 A3
Spaniards Cl *GLDGN* NW11 .... 54 C3
Spaniards End *HAMP* NW3 .... 54 C3
Spaniards Rd *HAMP* NW3 .... 54 C4
Spanish Rd *MHST* W1U * 18 B4
Spanish Rd *WAND/EARL* SW18 .... 132 C3
Sparke Ter *CAN/RD* E16 * 93 F5
Sparks Cl *ACT* W3 .... 87 D5
Spa Rd *BERM/RHTH* SE16 .... 51 F5
Sparrows La *ELTH/MOT* SE9 .... 144 C5
Sparsholt Rd *ARCH* N19 .... 57 F5
   BARK IG11 .... 85 E5
Sparta St *GNWCH* SE10 .... 122 C4
Spearman St *WOOL/PLUM* SE18 * 126 A2
Spear Ms *ECT* SW5 .... 38 A5
Spears Rd *ARCH* N19 .... 57 E5
Spectrum Pl *WALW* SE17 .... 119 D1
Spedan Cl *HAMP* NW3 .... 54 B5
Speedwell St *DEPT* SE8 .... 122 A3
Speedy Pl *STPAN* WC1H 8 C4
Spekehill *ELTH/MOT* SE9 .... 161 F3
Speldhurst Rd *CHSWK* W4 .... 99 D4
   HOM E9 .... 79 D4
Spellbrook Wk *IS* N1 * 76 C5
Spelman St *WCHPL* E1 .... 90 A4
Spence Cl *BERM/RHTH* SE16 .... 103 F3
Spencer Dr *EFNCH* N2 .... 54 C1
Spencer Gdns *MORT/ESHN* SW14 .... 128 C3
Spencer Ms *CLAP* SW4 .... 117 E4
   HMSMTH W6 .... 113 E2
Spencer Pk *WAND/EARL* SW18 .... 133 D3
Spencer Pl *IS* N1 .... 76 B4
   WEST SW1P 43 F3
Spencer Rd *KTTN* NW5 .... 57 E1
Spencer Rd *ACT* W3 .... 98 C2
   BTSEA SW11 .... 133 D2
   CHSWK W4 .... 110 C3
   EHAM E6 .... 83 D5
   GDMY/SEVK IG3 .... 67 F3
Spencer St *FSBYE* EC1V 10 C4
Spencer Wk *PUT/ROE* SW15 .... 131 D2
Spenser Gv *STNW/STAM* N16 .... 77 E1
Spenser Ms *DUL* SE21 .... 155 D1
Spenser Rd *HNHL* SE24 .... 136 B4
Spenser St *WESTW* SW1E 43 F2
Spensley Wk *STNW/STAM* N16 .... 59 D5
Speranza St *WOOL/PLUM* SE18 .... 127 F1
Spert St *POP/IOD* E14 .... 103 E1
Spey Rd *POP/IOD* E14 .... 92 C4
Spezia Rd *WLSDN* NW10 .... 88 A1
Spicer Cl *BRXN/ST* SW9 .... 118 B5
Spindle Cl *WOOL/PLUM* SE18 .... 107 E4

Spindrift Av *POP/IOD* E14 .... 104 B5
Spinel Cl *WOOL/PLUM* SE18 .... 127 F1
Spinney Gdns *NRWD* SE19 .... 155 F5
The Spinney *BARN* SW13 * 112 B2
   STRHM/NOR SW16 .... 152 C3
Spirit Quay *WAP* E1W 102 A2
Spital Sq *WCHPL* E1 .... 25 D2
Spital St *WCHPL* E1 .... 90 A4
Spital Yd *WCHPL* E1 * 25 D2
Spitfire House *WOOL/PLUM* SE18 * 125 E3
Spode Wk *KIL/WHAMP* NW6 * 72 B2
Sportsbank St *CAT* SE6 .... 140 C5
Sportsman Pl *BETH* E2 .... 78 A5
Spratt Hall Rd *WAN* E11 .... 64 A1
Spray St *WOOL/PLUM* SE18 .... 108 B5
Sprimont Pl *CHEL* SW3 .... 115 F1
Springall St *PECK* SE15 .... 120 B3
Springbank Rd *LEW* SE13 .... 141 E4
Springbank Wk *CAMTN* NW1 .... 75 D4
Springdale Rd *STNW/STAM* N16 .... 77 D1
Springfield *CLPT* E5 .... 60 B3
Springfield Gdns *CLPT* E5 .... 60 B3
Springfield Gv *CHARL* SE7 .... 124 C2
Springfield La *KIL/WHAMP* NW6 .... 72 B5
Springfield Ri *SYD* SE26 .... 156 B5
Springfield Rd *EHAM* E6 .... 83 F4
   SRTFD E15 * 93 E2
   STJWD NW8 .... 72 C5
   SYD SE26 .... 156 B5
   WALTH E17 .... 61 F1
   WIM/MER SW19 .... 149 F5
Springfield Wk *KIL/WHAMP* NW6 .... 72 B5
Spring Gdns *HBRY* N5 .... 76 C2
   WHALL SW1A 32 C3
Spring Gv *CHSWK* W4 .... 110 A3
Spring Hl *CLPT* E5 .... 60 A2
   SYD SE26 .... 156 C4
Springhill Cl *CMBW* SE5 .... 137 D1
Spring La *CLPT* E5 .... 60 B3
Spring Ms *MHST* W1U * 17 F2
Springpark Dr *FSBYPK* N4 .... 58 C3
Spring Pl *BARK* IG11 .... 96 C1
   KTTN NW5 .... 74 A2
Springrice Rd *LEW* SE13 .... 140 C4
Spring St *BAY/PAD* W2 .... 16 A5
Spring Tide Cl *PECK* SE15 * 120 A4
Springvale Ter *WKENS* W14 .... 101 D4
Spring Wk *WCHPL* E1 .... 90 A4
Springwater Cl *WOOL/PLUM* SE18 * 126 A4
Springwell Av *WLSDN* NW10 .... 69 F5
Springwell Rd *STRHM/NOR* SW16 .... 153 F4
Springwood Cl *BOW* E3 .... 92 A1
Sprowston Ms *FSTGT* E7 .... 82 A2
Sprowston Rd *FSTGT* E7 .... 82 A2
Sprules Rd *BROCKY* SE4 .... 121 E5
Spurgeon St *STHWK* SE1 .... 48 A5
Spurling Rd *EDUL* SE22 * 137 F2
Spur Rd *BARK* IG11 .... 96 C2
   STHWK SE1 .... 34 A5
   WHALL SW1A 43 E1
Spurstowe Rd *HACK* E8 .... 78 B3
Spurstowe Ter *HACK* E8 .... 78 A2
The Square *HMSMTH* W6 .... 112 C5
   IL IG1 .... 66 A2
Squarey St *TOOT* SW17 .... 150 C3
Squire Gdns *STJWD* NW8 .... 4 A4
Squires Ct *WIM/MER* SW19 .... 150 A4
Squire's Mt *HAMP* NW3 .... 55 D5
The Squirrels *LEW* SE13 .... 141 D1
Squirries St *BETH* E2 .... 90 A2
Stable Ms *WNWD* SE27 .... 154 C5
Stables Wy *LBTH* SE11 .... 118 A1
Stable Wk *IS* N1 .... 9 D1
Stable Wy *NKENS* W10 .... 88 C5
Stable Yard Rd *WHALL* SW1A 31 F4
Stacey Pth *HOLWY* N7 .... 58 A5
   LSO/SEVD WC2H 20 B5
Stackhouse St *KTBR* SW1X 41 E2
Stacey Pth *CMBW* SE5 * 119 E3
Stadium Rd *HDN* NW4 .... 52 B2
   WOOL/PLUM SE18 .... 125 F3
Stadium St *WBPTN* SW10 .... 114 C3
Staffa Rd *LEY* E10 .... 61 E3
Stafford Cl *KIL/WHAMP* NW6 .... 2 A4
   WALTH E17 .... 61 F1
Stafford Pl *WESTW* SW1E 43 E2
Stafford Rd *BOW* E3 .... 91 F1
   FSTGT E7 .... 82 C4
   KIL/WHAMP NW6 .... 2 A3
   SCUP DA14 .... 163 E4
Staffordshire St *PECK* SE15 .... 120 A4
Stafford St *CONDST* W1S 31 E3

Stafford Ter *KENS* W8 .... 38 A2
Stag La *PUT/ROE* SW15 .... 147 F3
Stag Pl *WESTW* SW1E 43 E2
Stainer St *STHWK* SE1 .... 36 B4
Staines Rd *IL* IG1 .... 85 D1
Stainforth Rd *CNTH/NBYPK* IG2 .... 67 D2
Staining La *CITYW* EC2V 23 F4
Stainsby Pl *POP/IOD* E14 * 92 A5
Stainsby Rd *POP/IOD* E14 .... 92 A5
Stainton Rd *CAT* SE6 .... 141 D5
Stalbridge St *CAMTN* NW1 .... 17 D2
Stalham St *BERM/RHTH* SE16 .... 102 B4
Stamford Brook Av *HMSMTH* W6 .... 99 F1
Stamford Brook Gdns *HMSMTH* W6 .... 99 F1
Stamford Brook Rd *HMSMTH* W6 .... 99 F1
Stamford Cl *HAMP* NW3 * 54 C5
Stamford Cots *WBPTN* SW10 * 114 B5
Stamford Gv East *STNW/STAM* N16 .... 60 A3
Stamford Gv West *STNW/STAM* N16 .... 60 A3
Stamford Hl *STNW/STAM* N16 .... 59 F3
Stamford Rd *EHAM* E6 .... 83 E5
    IS N1 .... 77 E4
Stamford St *STHWK* SE1 .... 34 A3
Stamp Pl *BETH* E2 .... 13 E2
Stanborough Pas *HACK* E8 .... 77 F3
Stanbridge Rd *PUT/ROE* SW15 .... 130 C1
Stanbury Ct *HAMP* NW3 * 73 F3
Stanbury Rd *PECK* SE15 .... 120 B4
Standard Pl *SDTCH* EC2A 13 D4
Standard Rd *WLSDN* NW10 .... 86 C5
Standen Rd *WAND/EARL* SW18 .... 132 A5
Standish Rd *HMSMTH* W6 .... 100 A5
Stane Gv *VX/NE* SW8 .... 117 D5
Stane Wy *WOOL/PLUM* SE18 .... 125 D3
Stanford Pl *WALW* SE17 .... 48 C5
Stanford Rd *KENS* W8 .... 39 D5
Stanford St *PIM* SW1V 44 A5
Stanhope Cl *BERM/RHTH* SE16 * 103 D3
    HGT N6 .... 56 B1
    IL IG1 .... 65 F3
    SKENS SW7 .... 39 F4
Stanhope Ga *BAY/PAD* W2 .... 29 E1
    MYFR/PKLN W1K 30 B4
Stanhope Ms East *SKENS* SW7 .... 39 F4
Stanhope Ms South *SKENS* SW7 .... 39 F5
Stanhope Ms West *SKENS* SW7 .... 39 F4
Stanhope Pde *CAMTN* NW1 .... 7 D5
Stanhope Pl *BAY/PAD* W2 .... 17 E5
Stanhope Rd *HGT* N6 .... 56 C1
Stanhope Rw *MYFR/PICC* W1J * 30 C4
Stanhope St *CAMTN* NW1 .... 7 E3
Stanhope Ter *BAY/PAD* W2 .... 28 C1
Stanier Cl *WKENS* W14 .... 113 F1
Stanlake Rd *SHB* W12 .... 100 C2
Stanlake Vls *SHB* W12 .... 100 C2
Stanley Av *BARK* IG11 .... 97 F2
Stanley Cl *ELTH/MOT* SE9 .... 162 C1
    VX/NE SW8 .... 117 F2
Stanley Gdns *ACT* W3 * 99 E3
    CRICK NW2 .... 70 C2
    NTGHL W11 .... 101 F1
Stanley Gv *VX/NE* SW8 .... 116 A5
Stanley Pas *CAMTN* NW1 .... 8 B2
Stanley Rd *ACT* W3 .... 98 B4
    IL IG1 .... 67 D4
    MNPK E12 .... 83 D2
    MORT/ESHN SW14 .... 128 B2
    WALTH E17 .... 62 B1
Stanley St *DEPT* SE8 .... 121 F2
Stanley Ter *ARCH* N19 * 57 E4
Stanmer St *BTSEA* SW11 .... 115 E4
Stanmore Rd *WAN* E11 .... 63 F3
    IS N1 .... 75 F3
Stanmore St *IS* N1 .... 75 E4
Stannard Ms *HACK* E8 * 78 A3
Stannard Rd *HACK* E8 .... 78 A3
Stannary Pl *LBTH* SE11 .... 118 A1
Stannary St *LBTH* SE11 .... 118 A1
Stansbury Sq *NKENS* W10 .... 89 D2
Stansfeld Rd *CAN/RD* E16 .... 95 D5
Stansfield Rd *BRXN/ST* SW9 .... 135 C1
Stanstead Gv *CAT* SE6 .... 157 F1
Stanstead Rd *FSTH* SE23 .... 157 D1
Stanswood Gdns *CMBW* SE5 .... 119 E3
Stanthorpe Cl *STRHM/NOR* SW16 * 153 D5
Stanthorpe Rd *STRHM/NOR* SW16 .... 153 D5
Stanton Rd *BARN* SW13 .... 111 F5
Stanton St *PECK* SE15 .... 120 A4
Stanton Wy *SYD* SE26 .... 157 F4
Stanway Gdns *ACT* W3 .... 98 A2

Stanway St *IS* N1 .... 13 D1
Stanwick Rd *WKENS* W14 .... 101 F5
Stanworth St *STHWK* SE1 .... 49 E1
Staplefield Cl *BRXS/STRHM* SW2 * 153 E1
Stapleford Cl *WIM/MER* SW19 .... 131 E5
Staplehurst Rd *LEW* SE13 .... 141 E3
Staple Inn *HHOL* WC1V 22 A3
Staples Cl *BERM/RHTH* SE16 .... 103 E2
Staple St *STHWK* SE1 .... 48 B1
Stapleton Hall Rd *FSBYPK* N4 .... 57 F2
Stapleton Rd *TOOT* SW17 .... 152 A3
Stapley Rd *STNW/STAM* N16 * 77 E1
Starboard Wy *POP/IOD* E14 .... 104 A4
Starcross St *CAMTN* NW1 .... 7 F4
Starfield Rd *SHB* W12 .... 100 A3
Star La *CAN/RD* E16 .... 93 F2
Star Pl *WAP* E1W 37 F2
Star Rd *WKENS* W14 .... 113 F2
Star Yd *LINN* WC2A 22 A4
Statham Gv *STNW/STAM* N16 .... 59 D5
Station Ap *BKHTH/KID* SE3 .... 142 B1
    CAMTN NW1 * 18 A1
    FSTGT E7 .... 82 B1
    FUL/PGN SW6 * 131 E1
    GLDGN NW11 * 53 D2
    RCH/KEW TW9 .... 110 A4
    STRHM/NOR SW16 .... 157 F5
    SYD SE26 .... 157 F5
    WAN E11 * 81 E1
    WELL DA16 .... 127 F5
    WLSDN NW10 .... 87 F2
Station Approach Rd *CHSWK* W4 .... 110 C4
Station Ar *GTPST* W1W * 19 D1
Station Av *RCH/KEW* TW9 .... 110 A4
Station Chambers *EA* W5 * 86 A3
Station Crs *BKHTH/KID* SE3 .... 124 A1
Stationers Hall Ct *STP* EC4M * 23 D5
Station Gdns *CHSWK* W4 .... 110 C3
Station Pde *ACT* W3 * 86 A5
    BAL SW12 * 152 A1
    BARK IG11 .... 84 C4
    CHSWK W4 * 110 C3
    CLPT E5 * 60 B5
    CRICK NW2 .... 70 C3
    EHAM E6 * 83 E4
    PLSTW E13 * 94 C5
    RCH/KEW TW9 .... 110 A2
Station Pas *PECK* SE15 .... 120 C4
Station Pl *FSBYPK* N4 .... 58 A4
Station Ri *WNWD* SE27 .... 154 B2
Station Rd *BARN* SW13 .... 111 F5
    HDN NW4 .... 52 A1
    HOLWY N7 .... 66 B4
    IL IG1 .... 66 C4
    LEW SE13 .... 140 C1
    MNPK E12 .... 83 D1
    WALTH E17 .... 61 E1
    WLSDN NW10 .... 87 F1
Station St *SRTFD* E15 .... 81 D4
Station Ter *CMBW* SE5 .... 118 C4
    WLSDN NW10 .... 89 D1
Staunton St *DEPT* SE8 .... 121 F2
Staveley Cl *HOLWY* N7 * 75 E1
    PECK SE15 .... 120 C4
Staveley Gdns *CHSWK* W4 .... 111 D4
Staveley Rd *CHSWK* W4 .... 110 C2
Staverton Rd *CRICK* NW2 .... 70 C4
Stave Yard Rd *BERM/RHTH* SE16 .... 103 E2
Stavordale Rd *HBRY* N5 .... 76 A1
Stayners Rd *WCHPL* E1 .... 91 D3
Stead St *WALW* SE17 .... 48 A5
Stean St *HACK* E8 .... 77 F5
Stebondale St *POP/IOD* E14 .... 122 C1
Steedman St *WALW* SE17 .... 47 E5
Steele Rd *CHSWK* W4 .... 98 B4
    WAN E11 .... 81 E1
    WLSDN NW10 .... 86 C1
Steele's Ms North *HAMP* NW3 * 73 F3
Steele's Ms South *HAMP* NW3 * 73 F3
Steele's Rd *HAMP* NW3 .... 73 F3
Steeles Studios *HAMP* NW3 * 73 F3
Steel's La *WCHPL* E1 .... 90 C5
Steep Hl *STRHM/NOR* SW16 .... 153 D3
Steeple Cl *FUL/PGN* SW6 .... 131 E1
    WIM/MER SW19 .... 149 E4
Steeple Wk *IS* N1 * 76 C5
Steerforth St *WAND/EARL* SW18 .... 150 B2
Steers Wy *BERM/RHTH* SE16 .... 103 E3
Stellman Cl *CLPT* E5 .... 59 E5
Stephan Cl *HACK* E8 .... 78 A5

Stephendale Rd FUL/PGN SW6...... 132 B1
Stephen Ms FITZ W1T....... 20 A3
Stephen Pl CLAP SW4....... 134 C1
Stephenson Cl WELL DA16....... 127 F5
Stephenson St CAN/RD E16....... 93 E3
WLSDN NW10....... 87 E2
Stephenson Wy CAMTN NW1....... 7 G3
Stephen's Rd SRTFD E15....... 81 E5
Stephen St FITZ W1T....... 20 A3
Stepney Cswy WCHPL E1....... 91 D5
Stepney Gn WCHPL E1....... 90 C4
Stepney High St WCHPL E1....... 91 D4
Stepney Wy WCHPL E1....... 90 B4
Sterling Cl WLSDN NW10....... 70 A4
Sterling Gdns NWCR SE14....... 121 E2
Sterling St SKENS SW7....... 41 D1
Sterndale Rd HMSMTH W14 *....... 101 D4
Sterne St SHB W12....... 101 D3
Sternhall La PECK SE15....... 138 A1
Sternhold Av BRXS/STRHM SW2....... 153 D2
Sterry Rd BARK IG11....... 85 F5
Sterry St STHWK SE1....... 48 A1
Steucers La FSTH SE23....... 157 E1
Steve Biko La CAT SE6....... 158 A4
Steve Biko Rd HOLWY N7....... 58 A5
Stevedore St WAP E1W....... 90 B2
Stevenage Rd EHAM E6....... 84 A3
FUL/PGN SW6....... 113 D4
Stevens Av HOM E9....... 78 C3
Stevenson Crs BERM/RHTH SE16....... 120 A1
Stevens St STHWK SE1....... 49 D2
Steventon Rd SHB W12....... 99 F1
Stewart Cl CDALE/KGS NW9 *....... 50 C1
CHST BR7....... 162 B5
Stewart's Gv CHEL SW3....... 115 D1
Stewart's La VX/NE SW8....... 116 B3
VX/NE SW8....... 116 C4
Stewart St POP/IOD E14....... 104 C3
Stew La BLKFR EC4V....... 35 E1
Steyne Rd ACT W3....... 98 B2
Steyning Gv ELTH/MOT SE9....... 161 F4
Stile Hall Gdns CHSWK W4....... 110 A1
Stillingfleet Rd BARN SW13....... 112 A3
Stillington St WEST SW1P....... 43 F4
Stillness Rd FSTH SE23....... 139 E4
Stirling Cl SCUP DA14....... 163 E4
Stirling Rd ACT W3....... 98 B5
BRXN/ST SW9....... 117 E5
PLSTW E13....... 94 B1
St John's Est IS N1....... 12 B2
STHWK SE1....... 37 E5
St Martin-in-the-Fields CHCR WC2N *....... 32 C2
Stockfield Rd STRHM/NOR SW16....... 153 F3
Stockholm Rd BERM/RHTH SE16....... 120 C4
Stockholm Wy WAP E1W....... 102 A2
Stockhurst Cl PUT/ROE SW15....... 112 C5
Stock Orchard Crs HOLWY N7 *....... 75 F1
Stock Orchard St HOLWY N7....... 75 F2
Stocks Pl POP/IOD E14....... 103 F1
Stock St PLSTW E13....... 94 A1
Stockwell Av BRXN/ST SW9....... 135 F1
Stockwell Gdns BRXN/ST SW9....... 117 F4
Stockwell Gn BRXN/ST SW9....... 117 F5
Stockwell La BRXN/ST SW9....... 117 F5
Stockwell Park Crs BRXN/ST SW9....... 117 F5
Stockwell Park Rd BRXN/ST SW9....... 117 F4
Stockwell Park Wk BRXN/ST SW9....... 135 F1
Stockwell Rd BRXN/ST SW9....... 117 F5
Stockwell Ter CNWCH SE10....... 122 C2
Stofield Gdns ELTH/MOT SE9....... 161 D3
Stoford Cl WIM/MER SW19....... 149 E1
Stokenchurch St FUL/PGN SW6....... 114 B4
Stoke Newington Church St
STNW/STAM N16....... 59 D5
Stoke Newington Common
STNW/STAM N16....... 59 F4
Stoke Newington High St
STNW/STAM N16....... 59 F5
Stoke Newington Rd HACK E8....... 77 F2
Stoke Pl WLSDN NW10....... 87 F2
Stokesley St SHB W12....... 87 F5
Stokes Rd EHAM E6....... 95 E3
Stoll Cl CRICK NW2....... 52 C5
Stondon Pk FSTH SE23....... 139 E4
Stonebridge Pk WLSDN NW10....... 69 D4
Stonebridge Wy WBLY HA9....... 68 B3
Stone Blds LINN WC2A *....... 21 F3
Stonechat Sq EHAM E6....... 95 E4
Stone Cl CLAP SW4....... 116 C5
Stonecutter St FLST/FETLN EC4A *....... 22 C4

Stonefield St IS N1....... 76 A5
Stonehall Wy CHARL SE7 *....... 125 D3
Stonehall Av IL IG1....... 65 E1
Stone Hall Gdns KENS W8 *....... 38 C3
Stone Hall Pl KENS W8 *....... 38 C3
Stonehill Cl MORT/ESHN SW14....... 129 D3
Stonehill Rd CHSWK W4....... 110 A1
MORT/ESHN SW14....... 128 C3
Stonehills Ct DUL SE21....... 155 E5
Stone House Ct LVPST EC2M....... 25 D4
Stoneleigh Pl NTGHL W11....... 101 D1
Stoneleigh St NTGHL W11....... 101 D1
Stoneleigh Ter ARCH N19....... 56 B4
Stonell's Rd TOOT SW17....... 150 C3
Stonenest St FSBYPK N4....... 57 F3
Stones End St STHWK SE1....... 47 E1
Stonewall EHAM E6....... 96 A4
Stoney Aly WOOL/PLUM SE18....... 126 A5
Stoneyard La POP/IOD E14....... 104 B1
Stoneycroft Cl LEE/GVPK SE12....... 141 F5
Stoney La HDTCH EC3A....... 25 D4
Stoney St STHWK SE1....... 36 A5
Stonhouse St CLAP SW4....... 134 C1
Stonnell's Rd BTSEA SW11....... 133 F3
Stonor Rd WKENS W14....... 101 F5
Stopes St PECK SE15....... 119 F3
Stopford Rd PLSTW E13....... 82 A5
WALW SE17....... 118 B1
Store Rd CAN/RD E16....... 108 A3
Storers Quay POP/IOD E14....... 105 D5
Store St GWRST WC1E....... 20 A5
SRTFD E15....... 81 D2
Storey Rd HGT N6....... 55 F1
Storey's Ga STJSPK SW1H....... 44 A1
Stories Ms CMBW SE5 *....... 119 E5
Stories Rd CMBW SE5....... 137 E1
Stork Rd FSTGT E7....... 81 F3
Storks Rd BERM/RHTH SE16 *....... 102 A4
Stormont Rd BTSEA SW11....... 134 A2
HGT N6....... 55 F2
Story St IS N1....... 75 F4
Stothard St WCHPL E1....... 90 C3
Stott Cl WAND/EARL SW18....... 133 D4
Stoughton Cl LBTH SE11....... 45 F5
PUT/ROE SW15....... 148 A1
Stourcliffe St MBLAR W1H....... 17 D3
Stourhead Cl WIM/MER SW19....... 131 D5
Stour Rd BOW E3....... 80 A4
Stowage DEPT SE8....... 122 B2
The Stowage DEPT SE8....... 122 A2
Stowe Rd SHB W12....... 100 B3
Stracey Rd WLSDN NW10....... 69 D5
Stradbroke Rd HBRY N5....... 76 C1
Stradella Rd HNHL SE24....... 155 D4
Strafford Rd ACT W3....... 98 C3
Strafford St POP/IOD E14....... 104 A3
Strahan Rd BOW E3....... 91 E1
Straightsmouth CNWCH SE10....... 122 C3
Strait Rd EHAM E6....... 107 E1
Straker's Rd EDUL SE22....... 138 B2
Strand CHCR WC2N....... 33 D2
Strand Dr RCH/KEW TW9....... 110 A3
Strandfield Cl WOOL/PLUM SE18....... 127 E1
Strand-on-the-Green CHSWK W4....... 110 A2
Strangways Ter WKENS W14....... 101 F4
Stranraer Wy IS N1....... 75 E4
Strasburg Rd BTSEA SW11....... 116 A4
Stratford Gv PUT/ROE SW15....... 131 D2
Stratford Pl OXSTW W1C....... 18 C5
Stratford Rd KENS W8....... 38 B3
PLSTW E13....... 82 A5
Stratford Studios KENS W8 *....... 38 B4
Stratford Vls CAMTN NW1....... 74 C4
Strathan Cl WAND/EARL SW18....... 131 E4
Strathaven Rd LEE/GVPK SE12....... 142 B4
Strathblaine Rd BTSEA SW11....... 133 D3
Strathbrook Rd STRHM/NOR SW16....... 153 F4
Strathdale STRHM/NOR SW16....... 153 F5
Strathearn Pl BAY/PAD W2....... 28 C1
Strathearn Rd WIM/MER SW19....... 150 A5
Stratheden Rd BKHTH/KID SE3....... 124 A4
Strathfield Gdns BARK IG11....... 85 D3
Strathleven Rd BRXS/STRHM SW2....... 135 E3
Strathmore Rd WIM/MER SW19....... 150 A3
Strathnairn St STHWK SE1....... 102 A5
Strathray Gdns HAMP NW3 *....... 73 E3
Strath Ter BTSEA SW11....... 133 E2
Strathville Rd WAND/EARL SW18....... 150 A2
Strattondale St POP/IOD E14....... 104 C4
Stratton Dr BARK IG11....... 85 E2
Stratton St MYFR/PICC W1J....... 31 D3

Strauss Rd *CHSWK* W4 * 99 D3
Streakes Field Rd *CRICK* NW2 .... 52 A4
Streamline Ms *EDUL* SE22 .... 156 B1
Streatfeild Av *EHAM* E6 .... 85 F5
Streatham Av *STRHM/NOR* SW16 * 153 E2
Streatham Cl *STRHM/NOR* SW16 * 153 E2
Streatham Common North
  STRHM/NOR SW16 .... 153 E5
Streatham Ct *STRHM/NOR* SW16 .... 153 E3
Streatham Rd *STRHM/NOR* SW16 * 153 E4
Streatham High Rd
  STRHM/NOR SW16 .... 155 H5
Streatham Hl *BRXS/STRHM* SW2 .... 153 E1
Streatham Pl *BRXS/STRHM* SW2 .... 135 E1
Streatham Rd *SRTFD* E15 .... 20 C4
Streathbourne Rd *TOOT* SW17 .... 152 A2
Streatleigh Pde *STRHM/NOR* SW16 * 153 E2
Streatley Pl *HAMP* NW3 .... 73 D1
Streatley Rd *KIL/WHAMP* NW6 .... 71 F4
Streetfield Ms *BKHTH/KID* SE3 .... 124 A5
Streimer Rd *SRTFD* E15 .... 92 C1
Strelley Wy *ACT* W3 .... 99 E1
Strickland Rw *WAND/EARL* SW18 .... 133 D5
Strickland St *DEPT* SE8 .... 122 A5
Stride Rd *PLSTW* E13 .... 93 F1
Strode Rd *FSTGT* E7 .... 82 A1
  FUL/PGN SW6 .... 113 D3
  WLSDN NW10 .... 70 A3
Strone Rd *FSTGT* E7 .... 82 C3
Strongbow Crs *ELTH/MOT* SE9 .... 143 F3
Strongbow Rd *ELTH/MOT* SE9 .... 143 F3
Stronsa Rd *SHB* W12 .... 99 F5
Stroud Crs *PUT/ROE* SW15 .... 147 F3
Stroud Green Rd *FSBYPK* N4 .... 57 F3
Stroud Rd *WIM/MER* SW19 .... 150 A3
Strout's Pl *BETH* E2 .... 13 E3
Strutton Gd *CDALE/KGS* SW1H 44 A2
Strype St *WCHPL* E1 .... 25 E3
Stuart Av *CDALE/KGS* NW9 .... 50 C2
Stuart Rd *ACT* W3 .... 98 C2
  BARK IG11 .... 85 F5
  KIL/WHAMP NW6 .... 2 A4
  PECK SE15 .... 138 C2
  WIM/MER SW19 .... 150 A3
Stubbs Dr *BERM/RHTH* SE16 .... 120 B1
Stucley Pl *CAMTN* NW1 .... 74 B4
Studdridge St *FUL/PGN* SW6 .... 114 A5
Studd St *IS* N1 .... 76 B5
Studholme Ct *HAMP* NW3 * 72 A1
Studholme St *PECK* SE15 .... 120 B4
Studio Pl *KTBR* SW1X 41 F1
Studland St *BFN/LL* DA15 .... 163 F3
Studland St *SYD* SE26 .... 157 D5
Studland St *HMSMTH* W6 .... 100 B5
Studley Cl *CLPT* E5 .... 79 E2
Studley Dr *REDBR* IG4 .... 65 D1
Studley Rd *CLAP* SW4 .... 117 E4
  FSTGT E7 .... 82 B3
Stukeley Rd *FSTGT* E7 .... 82 B4
Stukeley St *HOL/ALD* WC2B 21 D4
Sturdy Rd *PECK* SE15 .... 120 B5
Sturgeon Rd *WALW* SE17 .... 118 C1
Sturgess Av *HDN* NW4 .... 52 B2
Sturge St *STHWK* SE1 .... 47 E1
Sturmer Wy *HOLWY* N7 .... 75 F2
Sturry St *POP/IOD* E14 .... 92 B5
Sturt St *IS* N1 .... 11 F2
Stutfield St *WCHPL* E1 .... 90 A5
Styles Gdns *BRXN/ST* SW9 .... 136 B1
Sudbourne Rd *BRXS/STRHM* SW2 .... 135 E3
Sudbrooke Rd *BAL* SW12 .... 133 F4
Sudbury *EHAM* E6 .... 96 A5
Sudbury Crs *BMLY* BR1 .... 160 A5
Sudbury Rd *BARK* IG11 .... 85 F2
Sudeley St *IS* N1 .... 11 D2
Sudlow Rd *WAND/EARL* SW18 .... 132 A2
Sudrey St *STHWK* SE1 .... 47 E1
Suffolk La *CANST* EC4R 36 A1
Suffolk Rd *BARK* IG11 .... 85 D4
  BARN SW13 .... 111 F3
  GDMY/SEVK IG3 .... 67 E1
  PLSTW E13 .... 93 F2
  SEVS/STOTM N15 .... 59 D1
  WLSDN NW10 .... 69 E4
Suffolk St *FSTGT* E7 .... 82 A2
  STJS SW1Y 32 B3
Sulina Rd *BRXS/STRHM* SW2 .... 135 E5
Sulivan Ct *FUL/PGN* SW6 .... 114 A5
Sulivan Rd *FUL/PGN* SW6 .... 132 A1
Sullivan Av *CAN/RD* E16 .... 95 D4
Sullivan Cl *BTSEA* SW11 .... 133 D1
Sullivan Rd *LBTH* SE11 .... 46 B4
Sultan St *CMBW* SE5 .... 118 C3
Sumatra Rd *KIL/WHAMP* NW6 .... 72 A3
Sumburgh Rd *BAL* SW12 .... 134 A4
Summerfield Av *KIL/WHAMP* NW6 .... 89 E1
Summerfield St *LEE/GVPK* SE12 .... 141 F5
Summerhouse Rd *STNW/STAM* N16 ...... 59 E4
Summerlands Av *ACT* W3 .... 98 C1
Summerley St *WAND/EARL* SW18 .... 150 B2
Summersby Rd *HGT* N6 .... 56 B1
Summers Cl *WBLY* HA9 .... 50 B3
Summers St *CLKNW* EC1R 22 A1
Summerstown *TOOT* SW17 .... 150 C3
Summit Est *STNW/STAM* N16 * 60 A2
Sumner Av *PECK* SE15 * 119 E4
Sumner Pl *SKENS* SW7 .... 40 B5
Sumner Place Ms *SKENS* SW7 .... 40 B5
Sumner Rd *PECK* SE15 .... 119 F4
Sumner St *STHWK* SE1 .... 35 E3
Sumpter Cl *HAMP* NW3 .... 72 C3
Sunbeam Crs *NKENS* W10 .... 88 C3
Sunbeam Rd *WLSDN* NW10 .... 86 C3
Sunbury Av *MORT/ESHN* SW14 .... 129 D2
Sunbury La *BTSEA* SW11 .... 115 D4
Sunbury St *WOOL/PLUM* SE18 .... 107 F4
Suncroft Pl *SYD* SE26 .... 156 C3
Sunderland Mt *FSTH* SE23 * 157 D2
Sunderland Rd *FSTH* SE23 .... 157 D1
Sunderland Ter *BAY/PAD* W2 .... 14 C4
Sundew Av *SHB* W12 .... 100 A1
Sundorne Rd *CHARL* SE7 .... 124 B1
Sundridge Av *WELL* DA16 .... 127 D5
Sunfields Pl *BKHTH/KID* SE3 .... 124 B3
Sun in Sands Rbt *BKHTH/KID* SE3 .... 124 B3
Sun La *BKHTH/KID* SE3 .... 124 B3
Sunlight Sq *BETH* E2 .... 90 B2
Sunningdale Av *ACT* W3 * 99 E1
  BARK IG11 .... 85 D5
Sunningdale Cl *BERM/RHTH* SE16 * 120 B1
Sunningdale Gdns *KENS* W8 .... 38 B3
Sunninghill Ct *ACT* W3 * 98 C3
Sunninghill Rd *LEW* SE13 .... 122 B5
Sunny Crs *WLSDN* NW10 .... 68 C4
Sunnydale Rd *LEE/GVPK* SE12 .... 142 B3
Sunnydene St *SYD* SE26 .... 157 E4
Sunnyhill Cl *CLPT* E5 .... 79 E1
Sunnyhill Rd *STRHM/NOR* SW16 .... 153 E4
Sunnymead Rd *CDALE/KGS* NW9 .... 51 D2
  PUT/ROE SW15 .... 130 B3
Sunnyside *CAT* SE6 * 139 F5
  CRICK NW2 .... 53 F5
Sunnyside Rd *ARCH* N19 .... 57 D2
  IL IG1 .... 66 C5
  LEY E10 .... 62 A3
Sun Pas *BERM/RHTH* SE16 * 102 A4
Sunray Av *HNHL* SE24 .... 137 D2
Sun Rd *WKENS* W14 .... 113 F1
Sunset Rd *HNHL* SE24 .... 136 C2
  WIM/MER SW19 .... 148 B5
Sun St *SDTCH* EC2A 24 B2
Sun Street Pas *LVPST* EC2M 24 C3
Surma Cl *WCHPL* E1 .... 90 A3
Surrey La *BTSEA* SW11 .... 115 E4
Surrey Canal Rd *PECK* SE15 .... 120 C2
Surrey Crs *CHSWK* W4 .... 110 A1
Surrey Gdns *FSBYPK* N4 .... 58 C1
Surrey Gv *WALW* SE17 .... 119 E1
Surrey La *BTSEA* SW11 .... 115 E4
Surrey Ms *WNWD* SE27 .... 155 E4
Surrey Mt *FSTH* SE23 .... 156 B1
Surrey Quays Rd *BERM/RHTH* SE16 ...... 102 C4
Surrey Rd *BARK* IG11 .... 85 E4
  PECK SE15 .... 139 D3
Surrey Rw *STHWK* SE1 .... 34 C5
Surrey Sq *WALW* SE17 .... 119 E1
Surrey St *PLSTW* E13 .... 94 B2
  TPL/STR WC2R 33 F1
Surrey Ter *WALW* SE17 .... 49 D5
Surrey Water Rd *BERM/RHTH* SE16 .... 103 D2
Surr St *HOLWY* N7 .... 75 E2
Susannah St *POP/IOD* E14 .... 92 B5
Susan Rd *BKHTH/KID* SE3 .... 124 B5
Sussex Cl *ARCH* N19 * 57 E4
  REDBR IG4 .... 65 F1
Sussex Gdns *BAY/PAD* W2 .... 16 A3
Sussex Ms East *BAY/PAD* W2 * 28 B1

Sussex Ms West *BAY/PAD* W2........... 28 B1
Sussex Pl *BAY/PAD* W2...................... 16 B5
   CAMTN NW1.................................. 5 E5
   HMSMTH W6.................................. 112 C1
Sussex Rd *EHAM* E6......................... 96 A1
Sussex Sq *BAY/PAD* W2..................... 28 B1
Sussex St *PIM* SW1V........................ 116 B1
   PLSTW E13.................................. 94 B2
Sussex Wy *ARCH* N19....................... 57 D3
Sutcliffe Rd *WOOL/PLUM* SE18.......... 127 E2
   MV/WKIL W9................................. 14 B1
   WELL DA16................................... 145 D2
Sutherland Av *MV/WKIL* W9................ 14 B1
Sutherland Gdns *MORT/ESHN* SW14... 129 F3
Sutherland Gv *STWD/EARL* SW18........ 131 F5
Sutherland Pl *BAY/PAD* W2................ 14 A4
Sutherland Rd *BOW* E3...................... 91 F1
   CHSWK W4.................................... 111 D2
Sutherland Rw *PIM* SW1V.................. 116 B1
Sutherland Sq *WALW* SE17................ 118 C1
Sutherland St *PIM* SW1V.................. 116 B1
Sutherland Wk *WALW* SE17................ 118 C1
Sutlej Rej *CHARL* SE7...................... 124 C3
Sutterton St *HOLWY* N7.................... 75 F3
Sutton Cl *CHSWK* W4........................ 110 C2
Sutton Ct *CHSWK* W4........................ 110 C2
Sutton Court Rd *CHSWK* W4............... 110 C2
   PLSTW E13.................................. 94 C2
Sutton Dwelling Est *CHEL* SW3........... 115 E1
Sutton Est *IS* N1 *............................ 76 B4
The Sutton Est *IS* N1 *...................... 76 B4
Sutton La *FARR* EC1M........................ 23 E1
Sutton La North *CHSWK* W4............... 110 C1
Sutton La South *CHSWK* W4............... 110 C2
Sutton Pl *HOM* E9.............................. 78 C2
Sutton Rd *BARK* IG11........................ 97 E1
   PLSTW E13.................................. 93 F3
Sutton Rw *SOHO/SHAV* W1D.............. 20 A4
Sutton Sq *HOM* E9............................ 78 C2
Sutton St *WCHPL* E1.......................... 90 C5
Sutton Wy *NKENS* W10....................... 88 C4
   STLK EC1Y.................................... 23 F1
Swaby Rd *WAND/EARL* SW18............... 150 C2
Swaffield Rd *WAND/EARL* SW18........... 132 C5
Swain's La *HGT* N6.............................. 56 A5
Swainson Rd *ACT* W3.......................... 99 F3
Swain St *STJWD* NW8........................ 16 B1
Swallands Rd *CAT* SE6........................ 158 A3
Swallow Cl *NWCR* SE14...................... 120 C4
Swallow Dr *WLSDN* NW10................... 69 D5
Swallowfield Rd *CHARL* SE7............... 124 B1
Swallow Gdns *STRHM/NOR* SW16........ 153 D5
Swallow Pl *REGST* W1B *..................... 19 D5
Swallow St *EHAM* E6.......................... 95 E4
   REGST W1B.................................. 31 F2
Swanage Rd *WAND/EARL* SW18........... 132 C4
Swan Ap *EHAM* E6............................ 95 E4
Swandon Wy *WAND/EARL* SW18......... 132 B2
Swanfield St *BETH* E2........................ 13 E4
Swan La *CANST* EC4R......................... 36 A2
Swan Md *STHWK* SE1......................... 48 C3
Swan Ms *BRXN/ST* SW9..................... 117 F5
Swan Pas *WCHPL* E1 *......................... 37 F2
Swan Pl *BARN* SW13.......................... 111 F5
Swan Rd *BERM/RHTH* SE16................ 102 C3
   WOOL/PLUM SE18.......................... 107 D4
Swanscombe Rd *CHSWK* W4............... 111 E1
   NTGHL W11.................................. 101 D2
Swanton Gdns *WIM/MER* SW19.......... 149 D1
Swan Wk *CHEL* SW3........................... 115 F2
Swanwick Cl *PUT/ROE* SW15.............. 129 F5
Swan Yd *IS* N1.................................. 76 B3
Swaton Rd *BOW* E3............................ 92 A3
Swedenbourg Gdns *WCHPL* E1........... 102 A1
Sweden Ga *BERM/RHTH* SE16............ 103 E5
Sweeney Crs *STHWK* SE1.................. 49 F1
Swete St *PLSTW* E13......................... 94 A1
Sweyn Pl *BKHTH/KID* SE3................. 124 A5
Swift Cl *FUL/PGN* SW6...................... 113 E4
Swinbrook Rd *NKENS* W10.................. 89 E4
Swinburne Rd *PUT/ROE* SW15........... 130 A2
Swindon Cl *GDMY/SEVK* IG3............... 67 E4
Swindon St *SHB* W12 *....................... 100 B2
Swinford Gdns *BRXN/ST* SW9............. 136 B1
Swingate La *WOOL/PLUM* SE18.......... 127 E3
Swinnerton St *HOM* E9....................... 79 E2
Swinton Cl *WBLY* HA9........................ 50 B3
Swinton Pl *FSBYW* WC1X................... 9 E3
Swinton St *FSBYW* WC1X................... 9 E3
Swithland Gdns *ELTH/MOT* SE9.......... 161 F4
Sybil Ms *FSBYPK* N4.......................... 58 B1
Sybil Phoenix Cl *DEPT* SE8............... 121 D1

Sybourn St *WALTH* E17...................... 61 F2
Sycamore Cl *BFN/LL* DA15................. 145 F4
   BOW E3...................................... 79 F5
Sycamore Cl *ACT* W3.......................... 99 E2
   CAN/RD E16................................ 93 E3
Sycamore Gdns *SHB* W12................... 100 B3
Sycamore Gv *CAT* SE6........................ 140 C4
   CDALE/KGS NW9............................ 50 C2
Sycamore Ms *CLAP* SW4.................... 134 C1
Sycamore St *FSBYE* EC1V.................. 23 E1
Sycamore Wk *NKENS* W10................... 89 E3
Sydcote *DUL* SE21 *.......................... 154 C2
Sydenham Av *SYD* SE26..................... 156 B5
Sydenham Cots *LEE/GVPK* SE12 *....... 160 C5
Sydenham Hl *SYD* SE26..................... 156 A3
Sydenham Pk *SYD* SE26..................... 156 C3
Sydenham Park Rd *SYD* SE26............. 156 C3
Sydenham Ri *FSTH* SE23.................... 156 B2
Sydenham Rd *SYD* SE26..................... 157 D5
Sydenham Station Ap *SYD* SE26......... 156 C4
Sydmons Ct *FSTH* SE23 *................... 138 C5
Sydner Rd *STNW/STAM* N16............... 77 F1
Sydney Cl *SKENS* SW7....................... 40 B5
Sydney Ms *SKENS* SW7...................... 40 B5
Sydney Pl *SKENS* SW7....................... 40 B5
Sydney Rd *SCUP* DA14....................... 163 E4
   WAN E11..................................... 64 B1
Sydney St *CHEL* SW3......................... 115 E1
Sylvan Gv *CRICK* NW2....................... 71 D1
   PECK SE15.................................. 120 B2
Sylvan Rd *FSTGT* E7......................... 82 A3
   IL IG1.. 66 C4
Sylvan Ter *PECK* SE15 *.................... 120 B3
Sylvester Pth *HACK* E8 *.................... 78 B3
Sylvester Rd *HACK* E8 *..................... 78 B3
   WALTH E17 *................................ 61 F2
Sylvia Gdns *WBLY* HA9...................... 68 B4
Symes Ms *CAMTN* NW1...................... 7 E1
Symington Ms *HOM* E9...................... 79 D2
Symister Ms *IS* N1............................ 12 C1
Symons Cl *PECK* SE15....................... 120 C5
Symons St *CHEL* SW3........................ 41 F5
   KTBR SW1X................................. 41 F5
Symphony Ms *NKENS* W10.................. 89 E2

T

Tabard Garden Est *STHWK* SE1........... 36 A5
Tabard St *STHWK* SE1........................ 48 A1
Tabernacle Av *PLSTW* E13................. 94 A3
Tabernacle St *SDTCH* EC2A............... 24 B1
Tableer Av *CLAP* SW4........................ 154 C1
Tabley Rd *HOLWY* N7........................ 75 E1
Tabor Rd *HMSMTH* W6....................... 100 B4
Tachbrook St *PIM* SW1V.................... 43 F5
Tack Ms *BROCKY* SE4........................ 140 A1
Tadema Rd *WBPTN* SW10.................. 114 C3
Tadmor St *SHB* W12.......................... 101 D2
Tadworth Rd *CRICK* NW2................... 52 A4
Taeping St *POP/IOD* E14.................... 104 B5
Tait Ct *BOW* E3................................ 79 F5
Tait St *WCHPL* E1............................ 90 B5
Talacre Rd *KTTN* NW5....................... 74 A3
Talbot Ct *BANK* EC3V....................... 36 A2
Talbot Pl *BKHTH/KID* SE3................. 123 E5
Talbot Rd *BAY/PAD* W2..................... 14 B4
   EDUL SE22.................................. 137 E2
   EHAM E6..................................... 95 F1
   FSTGT E7.................................... 82 A3
   HGT N6....................................... 56 A1
   NTGHL W11................................. 89 F5
Talbot Sq *BAY/PAD* W2...................... 16 A5
Talbot Wk *NTGHL* W11....................... 89 E5
   WLSDN NW10 *............................ 69 E3
Talbot Yd *STHWK* SE1........................ 36 A4
Talcott Pth *BRXS/STRHM* SW2 *......... 154 C1
Talfourd Pl *PECK* SE15...................... 119 F4
Talfourd Rd *PECK* SE15..................... 119 F4
Talgarth Rd *WKENS* W14................... 113 E1
Talisman Sq *SYD* SE26...................... 156 A4
Tallack Rd *LEY* E10........................... 61 F3
Tallis Cl *CAN/RD* E16........................ 94 B5
Tallis Gv *CHARL* SE7......................... 124 B2
Tallis St *EMB* EC4Y.......................... 34 B1
Tallis Vw *WLSDN* NW10..................... 69 D3
Talmage Cl *FSTH* SE23...................... 138 C5
Talma Rd *BRXS/STRHM* SW2............. 136 A2
Talwin St *BOW* E3............................. 92 B2
Tamar Cl *BOW* E3 *........................... 79 F5

Tamarind Yd *WAP* E1W	102	A2
Tamarisk Sq *SHB* W12	99	F1
Tamar St *CHARL* SE7	107	E5
Tamworth St *FUL/PGN* SW6	114	A2
Tancred Rd *FSBYPK* N4	58	E1
Tanfield Av *CRICK* NW2	69	F1
Tangier Rd *RCHPK/HAM* TW10	128	A2
Tangley Gv *PUT/ROE* SW15	129	F5
Tanhouse Fld *KTTN* NW5 *	75	D2
Tankerton Houses *STPAN* WC1H *	9	D4
Tankerton St *STPAN* WC1H	9	D4
Tankridge Rd *CRICK* NW2	52	B4
The Tanneries *WCHPL* E1 *	90	C3
Tanner's HI *DEPT* SE8	122	A4
Tanners Ms *DEPT* SE8	121	F4
Tanner St *IG1*	84	C3
STHWK SE1	49	D1
Tannington Ter *HBRY* N5	58	A5
Tannsfeld Rd *SYD* SE26	157	D5
Tansley Cl *HOLWY* N7	75	D2
Tanswell St *STHWK* SE1 *	46	A1
Tansy Cl *EHAM* E6	96	A5
Tantallon Rd *BAL* SW12	152	A1
Tant Av *CAN/RD* E16	93	F5
Tanza Rd *HAMP* NW3	73	F1
Taplow St *IS* N1	11	F2
Tappesfield Rd *PECK* SE15	139	F1
Tapp St *WCHPL* E1	90	B3
Tara Ms *CEND/HSY/T* N8	57	E1
Taransay Wk *IS* N1	77	D3
Tara Ter *BROCKY* SE4 *	139	E1
Tarbert Rd *EDUL* SE22	137	E3
Tarbert Wk *WCHPL* E1 *	102	C1
Tarleton Gdns *FSTH* SE23	156	B1
Tarling Rd *CAN/RD* E16	93	F5
Tarling St *WCHPL* E1	90	B5
Tarn St *STHWK* SE1	47	E3
Tarnwood Pk *ELTH/MOT* SE9	161	F1
Tarragon Cl *NWCR* SE14	121	E3
Tarrant Pl *MBLAR* W1H	17	E3
Tarriff Crs *DEPT* SE8	103	F5
Tarrington Cl *STRHM/NOR* SW16	153	D4
Tarver Rd *WALW* SE17	118	B1
Tarves Wy *GNWCH* SE10	122	B3
Tasker Rd *HAMP* NW3	73	F2
Tasman Rd *BRXN/ST* SW9	135	E1
Tasso Rd *HMSMTH* W6	113	E2
Tate Rd *CAN/RD* E16	107	F2
Tatham Pl *STJWD* NW8	4	B1
Tatnell Rd *FSTH* SE23	139	E4
Tattersall Cl *ELTH/MOT* SE9	143	E2
Tatton Crs *CLPT* E5	59	F2
Tatum Rd *WLSDN* NW10	68	C4
Tatum St *WALW* SE17	48	B5
Tauheed Cl *FSBYPK* N4	58	C4
Taunton Ms *CAMTN* NW1	17	E1
Taunton Pl *CAMTN* NW1	5	D5
Taunton Rd *LEE/GVPK* SE12	141	E3
Taverners Cl *NTGHL* W11	101	E2
Taverner Sq *HBRY* N5 *	76	C1
Tavistock Cl *STNW/STAM* N16 *	77	E2
Tavistock Ct *COVGDN* WC2E *	33	D1
Tavistock Crs *NTGHL* W11	89	F4
Tavistock Gdns *GDMY/SEVK* IG3	85	E1
Tavistock Ms *NTGHL* W11 *	89	F5
Tavistock Pl *STPAN* WC1H	8	B5
Tavistock Rd *FSBYPK* N4	59	D1
NTGHL W11	89	F4
SRTFD E15	81	F3
WLSDN NW10	87	F1
Tavistock Sq *STPAN* WC1H	8	B5
Tavistock St *COVGDN* WC2E	33	D1
Tavistock Ter *ARCH* N19	57	D5
Taviton St *STPAN* WC1H	8	A5
Tavy Cl *LBTH* SE11	118	A3
Tawny Wy *BERM/RHTH* SE16	103	D5
Taybridge Rd *BTSEA* SW11	134	A1
Tayburn Cl *POP/IOD* E14	92	C5
Taylor Av *RCH/KEW* TW9	110	B5
Taylor Cl *DEPT* SE8	121	F2
Taylor's Blds *WOOL/PLUM* SE18	108	B5
Taylors Cl *SCUP* DA14	163	H4
Taylor's Gn *ACT* W3 *	87	E5
Taylors La *WLSDN* NW10	69	E3
SYD SE26	156	B4
WLSDN NW10	69	E4
Taymount Ri *FSTH* SE23	156	B2
Tayport Cl *IS* N1	75	F4
Teak Cl *BERM/RHTH* SE16	103	E2
Teal Cl *CAN/RD* E16	95	D4
Teale St *BETH* E2	90	A1
Teasel Crs *THMD* SE28	109	E2
Teasel Wy *SRTFD* E15	93	E2
Tedworth Gdns *CHEL* SW3 *	115	F1
Tedworth Sq *CHEL* SW3	115	F1
Teesdale Cl *BETH* E2	90	A1
Teesdale Rd *WAN* E11	63	F1
Teesdale St *BETH* E2	90	B1
Teesdale Yd *BETH* E2 *	90	B1
The Tee *ACT* W3	87	E5
Teign Ms *ELTH/MOT* SE9	161	E2
Teignmouth Cl *CLAP* SW4	135	D2
Teignmouth Rd *CRICK* NW2	71	D2
Telegraph HI *HAMP* NW3	72	B5
Telegraph Ms *GDMY/SEVK* IG3	67	F3
Telegraph Pas *BRXS/STRHM* SW2	135	E5
Telegraph Pl *POP/IOD* E14	104	B5
Telegraph Rd *PUT/ROE* SW15	130	B5
Telegraph St *LOTH* EC2R	24	A2
Telephone Pl *WKENS* W14 *	113	F2
Telferscot Rd *BAL* SW12	153	D1
Telford Av *BRXS/STRHM* SW2	153	D1
Telford Cl *WALTH* E17	61	E2
Telford Rd *CDALE/KGS* NW9	51	F1
ELTH/MOT SE9	163	D2
NKENS W10	89	E4
Telfords Yd *WAP* E1W *	102	A1
Telford Ter *PIM* SW1V *	116	C2
Telford Wy *ACT* W3	87	E4
Telham Rd *EHAM* E6	96	A1
Tell Gv *EDUL* SE22	137	F2
Tellson Av *WOOL/PLUM* SE18	125	E4
Temeraire St *BERM/RHTH* SE16	102	C3
Tempelhof Av *HDN* NW4	52	C3
Temperley Rd *BAL* SW12	134	A5
Templars Av *GLDGN* NW11	53	F1
Templar St *CMBW* SE5	118	B5
Temple Av *EMB* EC4Y	34	B1
Temple Cl *THMD* SE28	108	C4
WAN E11	63	E2
Templecombe Rd *HOM* E9	78	C5
Temple Dwellings *BETH* E2 *	90	B1
Temple Fortune La *GLDGN* NW11	53	F1
Temple Gdns *EMB* EC4Y *	34	A1
GLDGN NW11	53	F1
Temple Gv *GLDGN* NW11	54	A1
Temple La *EMB* EC4Y	22	B5
Templemead Cl *ACT* W3	87	E5
Temple Mills La *LEY* E10	80	B1
SRTFD E15	81	D1
Temple Pl *TPL/STR* WC2R	33	F1
Temple Rd *CHSWK* W4	98	C4
CRICK NW2	70	C1
EHAM E6	83	E5
Temple Sheen Rd *MORT/ESHN* SW14	128	C2
Temple St *BETH* E2	90	B1
Templeton Cl *STNW/STAM* N16 *	77	E2
Templeton Pl *ECT* SW5	38	B5
Templeton Rd *FSBYPK* N4	59	D1
Templewood Av *HAMP* NW3	54	B5
Templewood Gdns *HAMP* NW3	54	B5
Temple Yd *BETH* E2	90	A2
Tenbury Cl *FSTGT* E7	83	D2
Tenbury Ct *BAL* SW12	153	D1
Tench St *WAP* E1W *	102	A1
Tenda Rd *STHWK* SE1	102	B5
Tenham Av *BRXS/STRHM* SW2	153	D2
Tenison Wy *STHWK* SE1	34	A4
Tenniel Cl *BAY/PAD* W2	15	E5
Tennis St *STHWK* SE1	36	A5
Tennyson Av *MNPK* E12	83	E4
WAN E11	64	A2
Tennyson Cl *WELL* DA16	127	F4
Tennyson Rd *KIL/WHAMP* NW6	71	F5
LEY E10	62	B3
SRTFD E15	81	E4
WALTH E17	61	F1
Tennyson St *VX/NE* SW8	116	C5
Tenterden Cl *ELTH/MOT* SE9	161	F4
Tenterden St *CONDST* W1S	19	D5
Tenter Gnd *WCHPL* E1	25	E3
Tent St *WCHPL* E1	90	B3
Teredo St *LEW* SE13	122	B5
Terling Cl *WAN* E11	63	F5
Terling Wk *IS* N1 *	76	C5
Terminus Pl *BGVA* SW1W	43	D3
Terrace Gdns *BARN* SW13	111	F5
Terrace Rd *HOM* E9	79	D4
PLSTW E13	82	A5
The Terrace *BARN* SW13	111	E5
BETH E2 *	90	B1
DEPT SE8 *	103	F5
FSTH SE23 *	139	E5
KIL/WHAMP NW6	72	A5

Terrace Vls *HMSMTH* W6 * | 112 A1
Terrapin Rd *TOOT* SW17 | 152 B3
Terretts Pl *IS* N1 | 76 B4
Terrick St *SHB* W12 | 88 B5
Testerton Rd *NTGHL* W11 * | 101 D1
Testerton Wk *NTGHL* W11 * | 100 D1
Tetbury Pl *IS* N1 | 76 B5
Tetcott Rd *WBPTN* SW10 | 114 C3
Teversham La *VX/NE* SW8 | 117 E4
Teviot St *POP/IOD* E14 | 92 C4
Tewkesbury Av *FSTH* SE23 | 156 B1
Tewkesbury Rd *SEVS/STOTM* N15 | 59 D2
Tewson Rd *WOOL/PLUM* SE18 | 127 E1
Thackeray Av *HACK* E8 | 78 A3
Thackeray Rd *EHAM* E6 | 95 D1
VX/NE SW8 | 117 D3
Thackeray St *KENS* W8 | 39 D2
Thakeham Cl *SYD* SE26 | 156 B5
Thalia Cl *GNWCH* SE10 | 123 D2
Tham Cl *HNHL* SE24 | 136 B1
Thame Rd *BERM/RHTH* SE16 | 103 D5
Thames Av *WBPTN* SW10 | 114 C4
Thames Bank *MORT/ESHN* SW14 | 110 C5
Thames Cir *POP/IOD* E14 | 104 A5
Thames Crs *CHSWK* W4 | 111 E3
Thames Pth *BERM/RHTH* SE16 | 103 F4
BOW E3 | 22 B1
BTSEA SW11 | 132 C1
CHARL SE7 | 106 C4
CHEL SW3 | 116 A2
CLPT E5 | 61 D5
GNWCH SE10 | 122 C2
HOM E9 | 79 F4
POP/IOD E14 | 104 A4
RCH/KEW TW9 | 110 B3
SRTFD E15 | 92 B1
TPL/STR WC2R | 33 F2
TWRH EC3N | 37 D3
VX/NE SW8 | 117 D2
Thames Pl *PUT/ROE* SW15 | 131 D1
Thames Quay *WBPTN* SW10 * | 114 C1
Thames Rd *CAN/RD* E16 | 107 D2
CHSWK W4 | 110 C5
Thames St *GNWCH* SE10 | 122 B2
Thames Village *CHSWK* W4 | 110 C4
Thanet St *STPAN* WC1H | 8 C4
Thane Vls *HOLWY* N7 | 57 F5
Thant Cl *LEY* E10 | 62 B5
Thavies Inn *FLST/FETLN* EC4A | 22 B4
Thaxted Rd *ELTH/MOT* SE9 | 162 C4
Thaxton Rd *WKENS* W14 | 113 F2
Thayer St *MHST* W1U | 18 B4
Theatre Sq *SRTFD* E15 | 81 D3
Theatre St *BTSEA* SW11 | 133 F1
Theberton St *IS* N1 | 76 A5
Theed St *STHWK* SE1 | 34 A4
The Green *WIM/MER* SW19 | 149 D5
Theobald Rd *WALTH* E17 | 61 F2
Theobald's Rd *GINN* WC1R * | 21 E2
Theobald St *STHWK* SE1 | 48 A3
Theodore Rd *LEW* SE13 | 141 D4
Therapia Rd *EDUL* SE22 | 138 C4
Theresa Rd *HMSMTH* W6 | 100 A5
Thermopylae Ga *POP/IOD* E14 | 104 B5
Theseus Wk *IS* N1 | 11 D2
Thessaly Rd *VX/NE* SW8 | 117 D4
Theydon Rd *CLPT* E5 | 60 C4
Theydon St *WALTH* E17 | 61 F3
Third Av *ACT* W3 | 99 F2
MNPK E12 | 83 E1
NKENS W10 | 89 E2
PLSTW E13 | 94 A2
Third Wy *WBLY* HA9 | 68 B1
Thirleby Rd *WEST* SW1P | 43 F5
Thirlmere Rd *STRHM/NOR* SW16 | 153 D4
Thirsk Rd *BTSEA* SW11 | 134 A1
Thistle Gv *WBPTN* SW10 * | 114 C1
Thistlewaite Rd *CLPT* E5 | 60 B5
Thistlewood Cl *HOLWY* N7 | 57 F4
Thomas Baines Rd *BTSEA* SW11 | 133 D1
Thomas Cribb Ms *EHAM* E6 | 95 F5
Thomas Dean Rd *SYD* SE26 * | 157 F4
Thomas Dinwiddy Rd *LEE/GVPK* SE12 | 160 B2
Thomas Doyle St *STHWK* SE1 | 46 C2
Thomas' La *CAT* SE6 | 140 B5
Thomas Moore St *WAP* E1W * | 102 A1
Thomas More St *WAP* E1W * | 102 A1
Thomas North St *CAN/RD* E16 * | 93 F4
Thomas Pl *KENS* W8 | 38 C3
Thomas Rd *POP/IOD* E14 | 91 F5
Thomas St *WOOL/PLUM* SE18 | 108 A5

Thompson Av *CMBW* SE5 | 118 C3
RCH/KEW TW9 | 128 B1
Thompson Cl *IL* IG1 | 66 C4
Thompson Rd *EDUL* SE22 | 137 F4
Thompson's Av *CMBW* SE5 * | 118 C3
Thorburn Sq *STHWK* SE1 | 102 A5
Thoresby St *IS* N1 | 11 F3
Thornbury Cl *STNW/STAM* N16 | 77 E2
Thornbury Rd *CLAP* SW4 | 135 E4
Thornbury Sq *HGT* N6 | 56 C5
Thornby Rd *CLPT* E5 | 60 C5
Thorncliffe Rd *CLAP* SW4 | 135 D4
Thorncombe Rd *EDUL* SE22 | 137 E3
Thorncroft St *VX/NE* SW8 | 117 E3
Thorndean St *WAND/EARL* SW18 | 150 C2
Thorndike Cl *WBPTN* SW10 | 114 C3
Thorndike Rd *IS* N1 | 77 D3
Thorndike St *PIM* SW1V * | 44 A5
Thorne Cl *CAN/RD* E16 | 94 A5
WAN E11 | 81 E1
Thorne Rd *VX/NE* SW8 | 117 E3
Thorne St *BARN* SW13 | 129 E1
Thorney Crs *BTSEA* SW11 * | 115 D3
Thorney Hedge Rd *CHSWK* W4 | 98 B5
Thorney St *WEST* SW1P | 44 C4
Thornfield Rd *SHB* W12 | 100 B3
Thornford Rd *LEW* SE13 | 140 C3
Thorngate Rd *MV/WKIL* W9 | 2 B5
Thorngrove Rd *PLSTW* E13 | 82 B5
Thornham Gv *SRTFD* E15 | 81 D2
Thornham St *GNWCH* SE10 | 122 B2
Thornhaugh St *STPAN* WC1H | 20 B1
Thornhill Av *WOOL/PLUM* SE18 | 127 E3
Thornhill Bridge Whf *IS* N1 * | 75 F5
Thornhill Crs *IS* N1 | 75 F4
Thornhill Gdns *BARK* IG11 | 85 E4
LEY E10 | 62 B4
Thornhill Gv *IS* N1 | 75 F4
Thornhill Rd *IS* N1 | 75 F4
LEY E10 | 62 B4
Thornhill Sq *IS* N1 | 75 F5
Thornlaw Rd *WNWD* SE27 | 154 A4
Thornsbeach Rd *CAT* SE6 | 158 C1
Thornsett Rd *WAND/EARL* SW18 | 150 C2
Thornton Av *BRXS/STRHM* SW2 | 153 D1
CHSWK W4 | 99 E5
Thornton Gdns *BAL* SW12 | 153 D1
Thornton Pl *MBLAR* W1H | 17 E2
Thornton Rd *BAL* SW12 | 135 D5
BMLY BR1 | 160 A5
IL IG1 | 84 B1
MORT/ESHN SW14 | 129 D1
WAN E11 | 63 D4
Thornton St *BRXN/ST* SW9 | 118 A5
Thorntree Rd *CHARL* SE7 | 125 D1
Thornville St *DEPT* SE8 | 122 A4
Thornwood Rd *LEW* SE13 | 141 E3
Thorogood Gdns *FSBYPK* N4 | 81 E2
Thorold Rd *IL* IG1 | 66 B4
Thorparch Rd *VX/NE* SW8 | 117 D4
Thorpebank Rd *SHB* W12 | 100 A2
Thorpe Cl *NKENS* W10 | 89 E5
SYD SE26 * | 157 D4
Thorpe Rd *TOOT* SW17 | 151 E4
Thorpedale Rd *FSBYPK* N4 | 57 F3
Thorpe St *BARK* IG11 | 85 D4
EHAM E6 | 95 E3
FSTGT E7 | 64 A5
SEVS/STOTM N15 | 59 E1
Thorpewood Av *SYD* SE26 | 156 B2
Thorsden Wy *NRWD* SE19 * | 155 E5
Thorverton Rd *CRICK* NW2 | 53 E5
Thoydon Rd *BOW* E3 | 91 E1
Thrale Rd *STRHM/NOR* SW16 | 152 C5
Thrale St *STHWK* SE1 | 35 F4
Thrasher Cl *HACK* E8 * | 7 F5
Thrawl St *WCHPL* E1 | 25 F3
Threadneedle St *LOTH* EC2R | 24 A5
Three Colts La *BETH* E2 | 90 B3
Three Colt St *POP/IOD* E14 * | 103 F1
Three Kings Yd *MYFR/PKLN* W1K | 30 C1
Three Mill La *BOW* E3 | 92 C2
Three Oak La *STHWK* SE1 | 37 E5
Threshers Pl *NTGHL* W11 | 101 E1
Thriffwood *SYD* SE26 | 156 C3
Throckmorten Rd *CAN/RD* E16 | 94 B5
Throgmorton Av *OBST* EC2N | 24 B4
Throgmorton St *OBST* EC2N | 24 B4
Thrush St *WALW* SE17 | 118 C1
Thurbarn Rd *CAT* SE6 | 158 B5
Thurland Rd *BERM/RHTH* SE16 | 102 A4
Thurlby Rd *WNWD* SE27 | 154 A4

Thurleigh Av *BAL* SW12 .... 134 A4
Thurleigh Rd *BAL* SW12 .... 133 F4
Thurlestone Av *GDMY/SEVK* IG3 .. 85 F1
Thurlestone Rd *WNWD* SE27 ...... 154 A3
Thurloe Cl *SKENS* SW7 .... 40 C4
Thurloe Pl *SKENS* SW7 .... 40 B4
Thurloe Place Ms *SKENS* SW7 * ... 40 B4
Thurloe Sq *SKENS* SW7 .... 40 B4
Thurloe St *SKENS* SW7 .... 40 B4
Thurlow Hl *DUL* SE21 .... 154 C1
Thurlow Park Rd *DUL* SE21 .... 154 B2
Thurlow Rd *HAMP* NW3 .... 73 D2
Thurlow St *WALW* SE17 .... 119 E1
Thurlow Ter *KTTN* NW5 .... 73 F2
Thurlow Wk *WALW* SE17 .... 119 E1
Thursley Gdns *WIM/MER* SW19 ... 149 D2
Thursley Rd *ELTH/MOT* SE9 ...... 161 F3
Thurso St *TOOT* SW17 .... 151 D4
Thurston Rd *DEPT* SE8 .... 122 B5
Tibbatt's Rd *BOW* E3 .... 92 B3
Tibbenham Pl *CAT* SE6 .... 158 A2
Tibberton Sq *IS* N1 * 76 C4
Tibbets Cl *WIM/MER* SW19 .... 149 D1
Tibbet's Ride *PUT/ROE* SW15 .... 131 D5
Tiber Cl *BOW* E3 .... 80 A5
Tiber Gdns *IS* N1 .... 75 E5
Tichurst Rd *FSTH* SE23 .... 157 E2
Tidal Basin Rd *CAN/RD* E16 ...... 105 F1
Tideswell Rd *PUT/ROE* SW15 ..... 130 C2
Tideway Wk *VX/NE* SW8 * 116 C3
Tidey St *BOW* E3 .... 92 A4
Tidford Rd *WELL* DA16 .... 127 F5
Tidworth Rd *BOW* E3 .... 92 A2
Tierney Rd *BRXS/STRHM* SW2 ... 153 E1
Tierney Ter *BRXS/STRHM* SW2 * . 153 E1
Tiger Wy *CLPT* E5 .... 78 B1
Tilbrook Rd *BKHTH/KID* SE3 ..... 142 C1
Tilbury Cl *PECK* SE15 .... 119 F3
Tilbury Rd *EHAM* E6 .... 95 F1
   LEY E10 .... 62 C2
Tildesley Rd *PUT/ROE* SW15 ..... 130 C4
Tilehurst Rd *WAND/EARL* SW18 .. 151 D1
Tile Kiln La *HGT* N6 .... 56 B3
Tileyard Rd *HOLWY* N7 .... 75 E4
Tilia Rd *CLPT* E5 .... 78 B1
Tilia Wk *BRXN/ST* SW9 .... 136 B2
Tiller Rd *POP/IOD* E14 .... 104 A4
Tillett Cl *WLSDN* NW10 .... 68 C3
Tillett Wy *BETH* E2 .... 90 A2
Tilling Rd *CRICK* NW2 .... 52 B3
Tillman St *WCHPL* E1 .... 90 B5
Tilloch St *IS* N1 * 75 F4
Tilney Gdns *IS* N1 .... 77 D3
Tilney Rd *MYFR/PKLN* W1K * 30 B3
Tilson Cl *CMBW* SE5 .... 119 E5
Tilson Gdns *BRXS/STRHM* SW2 .. 135 E5
Tilston Rd *WAN* E11 .... 63 F5
Tilton St *FUL/PGN* SW6 .... 113 E2
The Tiltwood *ACT* W3 .... 98 C1
Tilt Yard Ap *ELTH/MOT* SE9 ..... 143 F4
Timbercroft La *WOOL/PLUM* SE18 117 F2
Timberland Cl *PECK* SE15 * 120 A3
Timberland Rd *WCHPL* E1 * 90 B5
Timber Mill Wy *CLAP* SW4 .... 135 D1
Timber Pond Rd *BERM/RHTH* SE16 103 D3
Timber St *FSBYE* EC1V * 11 E5
Timberwharf Rd *SEVS/STOTM* N15 60 A1
Time Sq *HACK* E8 * 77 F2
Timothy Cl *CLAP* SW4 .... 134 C3
Tindal St *BRXN/ST* SW9 .... 118 B4
Tinniswood Cl *HBRY* N5 .... 76 A2
   HOLWY N7 * 76 A2
Tinsley Rd *WCHPL* E1 .... 90 C4
Tintagel Crs *EDUL* SE22 .... 137 F2
Tintern Cl *PUT/ROE* SW15 .... 131 E3
Tintern St *CLAP* SW4 .... 135 E2
Tinto Rd *CAN/RD* E16 .... 94 A4
Tinworth St *STHWK* SE1 .... 117 F1
Tipthorpe Rd *BTSEA* SW11 .... 134 A1
Tisdall Pl *WALW* SE17 .... 48 B5
Titchborne Rw *BAY/PAD* W2 * ... 17 D5
Titchfield Rd *STJWD* NW8 .... 73 E5
Titchwell Rd *WAND/EARL* SW18 .. 133 D5
Tite St *GHEL* SW3 .... 115 F2
Titmuss St *SHB* W12 * 100 B3
Tiverton Rd *SEVS/STOTM* N15 ... 59 D1
   WLSDN NW10 .... 71 D5
Tiverton St *STHWK* SE1 .... 47 E2
Tivoli Gdns *WOOL/PLUM* SE18 ... 107 E5
Tivoli Rd *WNWD* SE27 .... 154 C5

Tobago St *POP/IOD* E14 .... 104 A3
Tobin Cl *HAMP* NW3 .... 73 E4
Toby La *WCHPL* E1 .... 91 E3
Tokenhouse Yd *LOTH* EC2R 24 A4
Token Yd *PUT/ROE* SW15 .... 131 E2
Tokyngton Av *WBLY* HA9 .... 68 A3
Toland Sq *PUT/ROE* SW15 .... 130 A3
Tollbridge Cl *NKENS* W10 .... 89 D3
Tollet St *WCHPL* E1 .... 91 D3
Tollgate Dr *DUL* SE21 .... 155 D1
Tollgate Gdns *KIL/WHAMP* NW6 . 2 C1
Tollgate Rd *CAN/RD* E16 .... 94 C4
Tollhouse Wy *ARCH* N19 .... 56 C4
Tollington Pk *FSBYPK* N4 .... 57 F4
Tollington Pl *FSBYPK* N4 .... 57 F4
Tollington Rd *HOLWY* N7 .... 75 F1
Tollington Wy *HOLWY* N7 .... 57 E5
Tolmer's Sq *CAMTN* NW1 .... 7 F5
Tolpaide Av *PLSTW* E13 .... 82 C5
Tolpuddle St *IS* N1 .... 10 A1
Tolsford Rd *HACK* E8 .... 78 B2
Tom Cribb Rd *THMD* SE28 .... 109 D4
   WOOL/PLUM SE18 .... 108 C4
Tom Groves Cl *SRTFD* E15 .... 81 D2
Tom Hood Cl *SRTFD* E15 .... 81 D2
Tom Jenkinson Rd *CAN/RD* E16 . 106 A2
Tomlin's Gv *BOW* E3 .... 92 A2
Tomlinson Cl *BETH* E2 .... 13 F4
   CHSWK W4 .... 110 B1
Tomlins Orch *BARK* IG11 .... 84 C5
Tomlin's Ter *POP/IOD* E14 .... 91 F5
Tom Mann Cl *BARK* IG11 .... 85 E5
Tom Nolan Cl *SRTFD* E15 .... 93 E1
Tompion St *FSBYE* EC1V 10 C4
Tom Smith Cl *GNWCH* SE10 ...... 123 E2
Tonbridge St *STPAN* WC1H 8 C4
Tonsley Hl *WAND/EARL* SW18 .... 132 B3
Tonsley Pl *WAND/EARL* SW18 .... 132 B3
Tonsley Rd *WAND/EARL* SW18 ... 132 B3
Tonsley St *WAND/EARL* SW18 .... 132 B3
Took's Ct *FLST/FETLN* EC4A 22 A4
Tooley St *STHWK* SE1 .... 36 B5
Tooting Bec Gdns *STRHM/NOR* SW16 153 D4
Tooting Bec Rd *TOOT* SW17 ...... 152 A3
Tooting Gv *TOOT* SW17 .... 151 E5
Tooting High St *TOOT* SW17 ...... 151 E4
Topham St *CLKNW* EC1R * 10 A5
Topley St *ELTH/MOT* SE9 .... 142 C2
Topmast Point *POP/IOD* E14 * ... 104 A3
Topsham Rd *TOOT* SW17 .... 151 F3
Torbay Rd *KIL/WHAMP* NW6 ...... 71 F4
Torbay St *CAMTN* NW1 * 74 B4
Torcross Dr *FSTH* SE23 .... 156 C2
Tor Gdns *KENS* W8 .... 26 A5
Tor Gv *THMD* SE28 .... 109 E2
Tormount Rd *WOOL/PLUM* SE18 . 127 E2
Toronto Av *MNPK* E12 .... 83 F1
Toronto Rd *IL* IG1 .... 66 B3
Torquay St *BAY/PAD* W2 .... 14 C3
Torrens Rd *BRXS/STRHM* SW2 ... 135 F3
   SRTFD E15 .... 81 F3
Torrens Sq *SRTFD* E15 .... 81 F3
Torrens St *FSBYE* EC1V 10 C1
Torres Sq *POP/IOD* E14 .... 122 A1
Torrey Dr *BRXN/ST* SW9 .... 118 A5
Torriano Av *KTTN* NW5 .... 75 D2
Torriano Cots *KTTN* NW5 .... 75 D2
Torriano Ms *KTTN* NW5 .... 74 C2
Torridge Gdns *PECK* SE15 .... 138 C2
Torridon Rd *CAT* SE6 .... 159 D1
Torrington Pl *FITZ* W1T 19 F2
   WAP E1W 102 A2
Torrington Sq *STPAN* WC1H 20 B1
Torwood Rd *PUT/ROE* SW15 ...... 130 A3
Tothill St *STJSPK* SW1H 44 A1
Tottan Ter *WCHPL* E1 .... 91 D5
Tottenham Court Rd *FITZ* W1T ... 19 F1
Tottenham Ms *FITZ* W1T * 19 F2
Tottenham Rd *IS* N1 .... 77 E3
Tottenham St *FITZ* W1T 19 F3
Totterdown St *TOOT* SW17 .... 151 F4
Toucan Cl *WLSDN* NW10 .... 86 A2
Toulmin St *STHWK* SE1 .... 47 E1
Toulon St *CMBW* SE5 .... 118 C3
Tournay Rd *FUL/PGN* SW6 .... 113 F3
Toussaint Wk *BERM/RHTH* SE16 . 102 A4
Tower Br *WAP* E1W 37 E3
Tower Bridge Ap *TWRH* EC3N 37 E3
Tower Bridge Rd *STHWK* SE1 ..... 48 C3
Tower Blds *WAP* E1W * 102 B2
Tower Cl *HAMP* NW3 .... 73 D2

Tower Ct LSO/SEVD WC2H *	20	C5
Tower Hamlets Rd FSTGT E7	81	F1
Tower Hl TWRH EC3N	37	E2
Tower Hill Ter MON EC3R	37	E2
Tower Ms CLPT E5	79	E1
Tower Mill Rd CMBW SE5 *	119	E3
Tower Pl MON EC3R	37	D2
Tower Rd WLSDN NW10	70	A4
Tower Royal MANHO EC4N *	35	F1
Tower St LSO/SEVD WC2H	20	C5
Towncourt Pth FSBYPK N4	58	C3
Townhall Av CHSWK W4	111	D1
Town Hall Pde BRXS/STRHM SW2 *	135	F2
Town Hall Rd BTSEA SW11	133	F1
Townley Ct SRTFD E15	81	F3
Townley Rd EDUL SE22	137	E5
Townley St WALW SE17 *	119	D1
Townmead Rd FUL/PGN SW6	132	B1
RCH/KEW TW9	110	B5
Town Quay BARK IG11	84	B5
Townsend La CDALE/KGS NW9	51	D2
Townsend Ms WAND/EARL SW18	150	C2
Townsend Rd STJWD NW8	5	D1
WOOL/PLUM SE18	108	B4
Townsend St WALW SE17	48	B5
Townsend Yd HGT N6	4	C1
Townshend Est STJWD NW8	4	C1
Townshend Rd CHST BR7	162	B5
STJWD NW8	73	E5
Towton Rd WNWD SE27	154	C2
Toynbec Cl BR7	162	B4
Toynbee St WCHPL E1	25	E3
Toyne Wy HGT N6	55	F1
Tracey Av CRICK NW2 *	70	C2
Trader Rd EHAM E6	96	B5
Tradescant Rd VX/NE SW8	117	E3
Trading Estate Rd WLSDN NW10 *	86	C3
Trafalgar Av PECK SE15	119	F4
Trafalgar Chambers CHEL SW3 *	115	D1
Trafalgar Gdns WCHPL E1	91	D4
Trafalgar Gv GNWCH SE10	123	D2
Trafalgar Ms HOM E9 *	79	F3
Trafalgar Rd GNWCH SE10	123	E1
Trafalgar Sq STJS SW1Y *	32	B5
Trafalgar St WALW SE17	119	D1
Trafalgar Wy POP/IOD E14	104	C1
Trahorn Cl WCHPL E1	90	A3
Tranby Ms HOM E9	79	D2
Tranmere Rd WAND/EARL SW18	150	C2
Tranquil Pas BKHTH/KID SE3 *	123	F5
Tranquil V BKHTH/KID SE3	123	E5
Transept St CAMTN NW1	16	C3
Transom Cl BERM/RHTH SE16	103	E5
Transom Sq POP/IOD E14	122	B1
Tranton Rd BERM/RHTH SE16	102	B4
Travers Rd HOLWY N7	58	A5
Treadgold St NTGHL W11	101	D1
Treadway St BETH E2	90	B1
Treaty St IS N1	75	F5
Trebeck St MYFR/PICC W1J	30	C2
Trebovir Rd ECT SW5	114	A1
Treby St BOW E3	91	F3
Trecastle Wy HOLWY N7	75	D1
Tredegar Rd BOW E3	91	F1
Tredegar Sq BOW E3	91	F2
Tredegar Ter BOW E3	91	F2
Trederwen Rd HACK E8	78	A5
Tredown Rd SYD SE26	156	C5
Tredwell Rd WNWD SE27	154	B4
Treen Av BARN SW13	129	E1
Tree Rd CAN/RD E16	94	C5
Treewall Gdns BMLY BR1	160	B4
Trefoil Rd WAND/EARL SW18	132	C3
Tregaron Av CEND/HSY/T N8	57	E2
Tregarvon Rd BTSEA SW11	134	A2
Trego Rd HOM E9	80	A4
Tregothnan Rd BRXN/ST SW9	135	E1
Tregunter Rd WBPTN SW10	114	C2
Treherne Ct BRXN/ST SW9 *	118	B4
Trehern Rd MORT/ESHN SW14	129	D1
Trehurst St CLPT E5	79	F1
Trelawney Est HOM E9 *	78	C3
Trelawn Rd BRXS/STRHM SW2	136	A3
LEY E10	62	C5
Trellis Sq BOW E3	91	F2
Treloar Gdns HNHL SE24 *	136	B4
Tremadoc Rd CLAP SW4	135	D2
Tremaine Cl BROCKY SE4	122	A5
Tremlett Gv ARCH N19	56	C5
Tremlett Ms ARCH N19	56	C5
Trenchard St GNWCH SE10	123	D1
Trenholme Ct VX/NE SW8 *	117	E2
Trenmar Gdns WLSDN NW10	88	B2
Trentham St WAND/EARL SW18	150	A1
Trent Rd BRXS/STRHM SW2	135	F3
Trerose Ct WAND/EARL SW18 *	132	B5
Tresco Gdns GDMY/SEVK IG3	67	F4
Tresco Rd PECK SE15	138	B2
Tresham Crs STJWD NW8	4	C5
Tresham Rd BARK IG11	85	F4
Tressell Cl IS N1	76	B4
Tressillian Crs BROCKY SE4	140	A1
Tressillian Rd BROCKY SE4	140	A1
Trevanion Rd WKENS W14	113	E1
Trevelyan Av MNPK E12	83	F1
Trevelyan Gdns WLSDN NW10 *	70	C5
Trevelyan Rd SRTFD E15	81	E1
Treveris St STHWK SE1	35	D4
Treverton St NKENS W10	89	D3
Treville St PUT/ROE SW15	130	B5
Treviso Rd FSTH SE23	157	D2
Trevithick St DEPT SE8	122	A2
Trevor Pl SKENS SW7	41	D1
Trevor Sq SKENS SW7	41	D1
Trevor St SKENS SW7	41	D1
Trewint St WAND/EARL SW18	150	C2
Trewsbury Rd SYD SE26	157	D5
Triangle Pl CLAP SW4	135	D2
Triangle Rd HACK E8	78	B5
The Triangle HACK E8	78	B5
Triangle Wy ACT W3	98	A4
Trident Pl CHEL SW3 *	115	D2
Trident St BERM/RHTH SE16	103	D5
Trigon Rd VX/NE SW8	117	F3
Trilby Rd FSTH SE23	157	D2
Trim St NWCR SE14	121	F2
Trinder Rd ARCH N19	57	E3
Tring Av WBLY HA9	68	A3
Trinidad St POP/IOD E14	103	F3
Trinity Buoy Whf POP/IOD E14 *	105	E1
Trinity Church Rd BARN SW13	112	B2
Trinity Church Sq STHWK SE1	47	F2
Trinity Cl CLAP SW4 *	134	C2
HACK E8 *	77	F3
LEW SE13	141	D2
WAN E11	63	E4
Trinity Ct ELTH/MOT SE9	144	B4
Trinity Crs TOOT SW17	151	F2
Trinity Est DEPT SE8	121	F1
Trinity Gdns BRXN/ST SW9	135	F2
CAN/RD E16	93	F4
Trinity Gn WCHPL E1 *	90	C4
Trinity Gv GNWCH SE10	122	C4
Trinity Ri BRXS/STRHM SW2	136	B5
Trinity Rd TOOT SW17	151	F2
WAND/EARL SW18	133	D4
Trinity Sq TWRH EC3N	37	D2
Trinity St CAN/RD E16	94	A4
STHWK SE1	47	F1
Trinity Wy ACT W3	99	E1
Trio Pl STHWK SE1	47	F1
Tristan Sq BKHTH/KID SE3	141	E1
Tristram Rd BMLY BR1	159	F4
Triton Rd DUL SE21	155	D5
Triumph Rd EHAM E6	95	F5
Troon Cl BERM/RHTH SE16 *	120	B1
Troon St WCHPL E1	91	E5
Trossachs Rd EDUL SE22	137	E3
Trothy Rd STHWK SE1	102	A5
Trott St BTSEA SW11	115	D4
Troughton Rd CHARL SE7	124	B1
Troutbeck Rd NWCR SE14	121	E4
Trouville Rd CLAP SW4	134	C4
Trowbridge Rd HOM E9	79	F3
Troy Ct KENS W8	38	A2
Troy Town PECK SE15	138	A1
Truman's Rd STNW/STAM N16	77	E2
Trumpington Rd FSTGT E7	81	F1
Trump St CITYW EC2V	23	F5
Trundle St STHWK SE1	35	E5
Trundley's Rd DEPT SE8	121	D1
Trundley's Ter DEPT SE8	103	F5
Truro Gdns IL IG1	65	E2
Truro St KTTN NW5	74	A3
Trusedale Rd EHAM E6	95	F5
Truslove Rd WNWD SE27	154	A5
Trussley Rd HMSMTH W6	100	C4
Tryon Crs HOM E9	78	C5
Tryon St CHEL SW3	115	F1
Tuam Rd WOOL/PLUM SE18	127	D2
Tubbs Rd WLSDN NW10	87	F1
Tudor Cl BRXS/STRHM SW2 *	135	F4
CDALE/KGS NW9	50	C4
HAMP NW3	73	E2

HGT N6	56	C2
Tudor Ct *ELTH/MOT* SE9 *	143	E2
WALTH E17	61	F2
Tudor Ct North *WBLY* HA9	68	A2
Tudor Ct South *WBLY* HA9	68	A2
Tudor Est *WLSDN* NW10 *	86	B1
Tudor Gdns *ACT* W3	86	A5
BARN SW13	129	E1
CDALE/KGS NW9	50	C4
Tudor Gv *HOM* E9	78	C4
Tudor Ms *WLSDN* NW10	70	A3
Tudor Pde *ELTH/MOT* SE9 *	143	E2
Tudor Rd *BARK* IG11	85	F4
HACK E8	78	B5
PLSTW E13	82	C5
Tudor St *EMB* EC4Y	34	B1
Tudor Wy *ACT* W3	98	A3
Tudway Rd *BKHTH/KID* SE3	142	C2
Tufnell Park Rd *HOLWY* N7	75	D1
Tufton St *WEST* SW1P	44	C3
Tugboat St *THMD* SE28	109	E3
Tugela St *CAT* SE6	157	F2
Tulip Cl *EHAM* E6	95	E4
Tulip Gdns *IL* IG1	84	B5
Tulse HI *BRXS/STRHM* SW2	154	B1
Tulsemere Rd *WNWD* SE27	154	C2
Tunis Rd *SHB* W12	100	C2
Tunley Gn *POP/IOD* E14	91	F4
Tunley Rd *TOOT* SW17	152	A2
WLSDN NW10	69	E5
Tunmarsh La *PLSTW* E13	94	B2
Tunnan Leys *EHAM* E6	96	A5
Tunnel Av *GNWCH* SE10	124	A1
Tunnel Rd *BERM/RHTH* SE16	102	C3
Tunstall Rd *BRXN* SW9	135	F2
Tunworth Cl *CDALE/KGS* NW9	50	C1
Tunworth Crs *PUT/ROE* SW15	129	F4
Tupelo Rd *LEY* E10	62	B4
Tuppy St *THMD* SE28	108	C4
Turene St *WAND/EARL* SW18	132	C2
Turin St *BETH* E2	90	A2
Turks Rw *CHEL* SW3	115	F1
Turle Rd *FSBYPK* N4 *	75	D3
Turlewray Cl *FSBYPK* N4	57	F3
Turley Cl *SRTFD* E15	81	E5
Turnagain La *FLST/FETLN* EC4A *	22	C4
Turnberry Cl *BERM/RHTH* SE16 *	120	B1
Turnchapel Ms *CLAP* SW4	134	B1
Turner Cl *BRXN/ST* SW9	118	B4
GLDGN NW11	54	B1
Turner Dr *GLDGN* NW11	54	B1
Turner's Rd *BOW* E3	91	F4
Turner St *CAN/RD* E16	93	F5
WCHPL E1	90	B4
Turner's Wd *GLDGN* NW11	54	C3
Turneville Rd *WKENS* W14	113	F1
Turney Rd *DUL* SE21	136	C5
Turnham Green Ter *CHSWK* W4	99	E5
Turnham Rd *BROCKY* SE4	139	E3
Turnmill St *FARR* EC1M	23	B1
Turnpike Cl *DEPT* SE8	121	F3
Turnstone Cl *PLSTW* E13	94	A2
Turpentine La *PIM* SW1V	116	A3
Turpin Cl *WAP* E1W	103	D1
Turpins Yd *CRICK* NW2 *	52	B4
GNWCH SE10	122	C5
Turquand St *WALW* SE17	47	F5
Turret Gv *CLAP* SW4	134	C1
Turville St *BETH* E2	13	E5
Tuscan Rd *WOOL/PLUM* SE18	127	D5
Tuskar St *GNWCH* SE10	123	E5
Tweedmouth Rd *PLSTW* E13	94	B1
Twelvetrees Crs *BOW* E3	92	C3
Twickenham Rd *WAN* E11	63	D4
Twig Folly Cl *BETH* E2	91	D1
Twig Folly Whf *BETH* E2 *	91	D1
Twilley St *WAND/EARL* SW18	132	B5
Twine Ct *WCHPL* E1	102	C1
Twine Ter *BOW* E3 *	91	F3
Twisden Rd *KTTN* NW5	74	B1
Twybridge Wy *WLSDN* NW10	68	C4
Twycross Ms *GNWCH* SE10	105	E5
Twyford Av *ACT* W3	98	A1
Twyford Crs *ACT* W3	98	A2
Twyford Rd *IL* IG1	84	C2
Twyford St *IS* N1	75	F5
Tyas Rd *CAN/RD* E16	93	F3
Tyburn Wy *MBLAR* W1H	29	F1
Tyers Ga *STHWK* SE1	48	C1
Tyers St *LBTH* SE11	117	F1
Tyers Ter *LBTH* SE11	117	F1
Tylehurst Gdns *IL* IG1	84	C2
Tyler Cl *BETH* E2	13	E1
Tyler St *GNWCH* SE10	123	E1
Tylney Av *NRWD* SE19	155	F5
Tylney Rd *FSTGT* E7	82	C1
Tyndale Ter *IS* N1	76	B4
Tyndale Ter *IS* N1	76	B4
Tyndall Rd *LEY* E10	62	C4
WELL DA16	145	F1
Tyneham Cl *BTSEA* SW11	134	A1
Tyneham Rd *BTSEA* SW11	116	A5
Tynemouth Cl *EHAM* E6	96	B5
Tynemouth Rd *WOOL/PLUM* SE18	127	E1
Tynemouth St *FUL/PGN* SW6	114	C5
Tyne St *WCHPL* E1	25	H4
Tynsdale Rd *WLSDN* NW10	69	E4
Type St *BETH* E2	91	D1
Tyrawley Rd *FUL/PGN* SW6	114	B4
Tyrone Rd *EHAM* E6	95	F1
Tyron Wy *SCUP* DA14	163	E4
Tyrrell Rd *EDUL* SE22	138	A2
Tyrrel Wy *CDALE/KGS* NW9	51	F2
Tyrwhitt Rd *BROCKY* SE4	140	A1
Tysoe St *FSBYW* WC1X *	10	A4
Tyson Gdns *FSTH* SE23 *	138	C5
Tyson Rd *FSTH* SE23	138	C5
Tyssen Rd *STNW/STAM* N16 *	59	F5
Tyssen St *HACK* E8	77	F3
IS N1	13	D1
Tytherton Rd *ARCH* N19	57	D5

U

Uamvar St *POP/IOD* E14	92	B3
Udall St *WEST* SW1P	43	F5
Uffington Rd *WLSDN* NW10	70	A5
WNWD SE27	154	A4
Ufford St *STHWK* SE1	34	B5
Ufton Rd *IS* N1	77	E4
Uhura Sq *STNW/STAM* N16 *	59	E5
Ullathorne Rd *STRHM/NOR* SW16	152	C4
Ullin St *POP/IOD* E14	92	C4
Ullswater Cl *PUT/ROE* SW15 *	147	D4
Ullswater Crs *PUT/ROE* SW15	147	D4
Ullswater Rd *BARN* SW13	112	A3
WNWD SE27	154	B3
Ulster Pl *CAMTN* NW1	18	C1
Ulundi Rd *BKHTH/KID* SE3	123	E2
Ulva Rd *PUT/ROE* SW15	131	D2
Ulverscroft Rd *EDUL* SE22	138	A3
Ulysses Rd *KIL/WHAMP* NW6	71	F2
Umberston St *WCHPL* E1	90	A5
Umbria St *PUT/ROE* SW15	130	A4
Umfreville Rd *FSBYPK* N4	58	B1
Undercliff Rd *LEW* SE13	140	A1
Underhill Rd *EDUL* SE22	138	A4
Underhill St *CAMTN* NW1	74	B5
Undershaft *HDTCH* EC3A	24	C5
Undershaw Rd *BMLY* BR1	159	E3
Underwood Rd *WCHPL* E1	90	A3
IS N1	11	F3
Underwood St *IS* N1	11	F3
The Underwood *ELTH/MOT* SE9 *	161	F2
Undine Rd *POP/IOD* E14	104	B5
Undine St *TOOT* SW17	151	F5
Union Ct *WAN* E11	81	D1
Union Ct *CLAP* SW4	117	E5
OBST EC2N	24	C4
Union Dr *WCHPL* E1 *	91	E3
Union Gv *VX/NE* SW8	117	D5
Union Pk *GNWCH* SE10 *	123	F1
Union Rd *CLAP* SW4	117	D5
Union Sq *IS* N1	76	C5
Union St *STHWK* SE1	35	D4
Union Wk *BETH* E2	13	E5
Unity Cl *NRWD* SE19	154	C5
WLSDN NW10	70	A3
Unity Ms *CAMTN* NW1	8	A1
Unity Wy *WOOL/PLUM* SE18	107	D4
University St *FITZ* W1T	19	E4
University Wy *CAN/RD* E16	108	A1
Unwin Cl *PECK* SE15	120	A2
Unwin Rd *SKENS* SW7	40	B2
Upbrook Ms *BAY/PAD* W2	15	F5
Upcerne Rd *WBPTN* SW10	114	C5
Upgrove Manor Wy *BRXS/STRHM* SW2 *	163	F3
Uphall Rd *IL* IG1	84	B2
Upham Park Rd *CHSWK* W4	99	E5
Upland Rd *EDUL* SE22	138	A5

PLSTW E13...... **94** A3
Uplands Cl *MORT/ESHN* SW14...... **128** B3
   WOOL/PLUM SE18...... **126** B2
Upney La *BARK* IG11...... **85** F4
Upnor Wy *WALW* SE17...... **119** E1
Uppark Dr *GNTH/NBYPK* IG2...... **66** C1
Upper Addison Gdns
   WKENS W14...... **101** E3
Upper Bank St *POP/IOD* E14...... **104** B3
Upper Bardsey Wk *IS* N1 *...... **76** C3
Upper Belgrave St *KTBR* SW1X...... **42** B2
Upper Berenger Wk
   WBPTN SW10 *...... **115** D3
Upper Berkeley St *MBLAR* W1H...... **17** E5
Upper Blantyre Wk *WBPTN* SW10 *...... **115** D3
Upper Brockley Rd *BROCKY* SE4...... **121** F5
Upper Brook St *MYFR/PKLN* W1K...... **30** A1
Upper Caldy Wk *IS* N1 *...... **76** C3
Upper Camelford Wk
   NTGHL W11 *...... **89** E5
Upper Cheyne Rw *CHEL* SW3...... **115** E2
Upper Clapton Rd *CLPT* E5...... **60** B4
Upper Clarendon Wk *NTGHL* W11 *...... **89** E5
Upper Dengie Wk *IS* N1 *...... **76** C3
Upper Dartrey Wk *WBPTN* SW10 *...... **114** C3
Upper Grosvenor St
   MYFR/PKLN W1K...... **30** A2
Upper Gnd *STHWK* SE1...... **34** A3
Upper Gulland Wk *IS* N1 *...... **76** C3
Upper Handa Wk *IS* N1 *...... **77** D3
Upper Harley St *CAMTN* NW1...... **18** B1
Upper Hawkwell Wk *IS* N1 *...... **76** C5
Upper John St *SOHO/CST* W1F...... **31** F1
Upper Lismore Wk *IS* N1 *...... **76** C3
Upper Ldg *KENS* W8 *...... **27** D4
Upper Ml *HMSMTH* W6...... **112** A1
Upper Marsh *STHWK* SE1...... **45** F2
Upper Montagu St *MBLAR* W1H...... **17** E2
Upper North St *POP/IOD* E14...... **92** A4
Upper Park Rd *HAMP* NW3...... **75** F3
Upper Phillimore Gdns *KENS* W8...... **38** A1
Upper Ramsey Wk *IS* N1 *...... **77** D3
Upper Rawreth Wk *IS* N1 *...... **76** C5
Upper Richmond Rd
   PUT/ROE SW15...... **130** B2
Upper Richmond Rd West
   MORT/ESHN SW14...... **129** D2
   RCHPK/HAM TW10...... **128** A3
Upper Rd *PLSTW* E13...... **94** A2
Upper St Martin's La
   LSQ/SEVD WC2H...... **20** C5
Upper Sheppey Wk *IS* N1...... **76** C3
Upper St *IS* N1...... **10** B1
Upper Tachbrook St *PIM* SW1V...... **43** E4
Upper Talbot St *NTGHL* W11 *...... **89** E5
Upper Ter *HAMP* NW3...... **54** C5
Upper Thames St *BLKFR* EC4V...... **35** E1
Upper Tollington Pk *SCUP* DA14...... **58** A3
Upperton Rd East *PLSTW* E13...... **94** C2
Upperton Rd West *PLSTW* E13...... **94** C2
Upper Tooting Pk *TOOT* SW17...... **151** F2
Upper Tooting Rd *TOOT* SW17...... **151** F4
Upper Tulse Hl *BRXS/STRHM* SW2...... **135** F5
Upper Whistler Wk
   WBPTN SW10 *...... **114** C3
Upper Wimpole St
   CAVSQ/HST W1G...... **18** B2
Upper Woburn Pl *STPAN* WC1H...... **8** B5
Upstall St *CMBW* SE5...... **118** B4
Upton Av *FSTGT* E7...... **82** A3
Upton Cl *CRICK* NW2...... **53** E5
Upton La *FSTGT* E7...... **82** A4
Upton Park Rd *FSTGT* E7...... **82** B4
Upton Rd *WOOL/PLUM* SE18...... **126** C2
Upwood Rd *LEE/GVPK* SE12...... **142** A4
Urban Ms *FSBYPK* N4...... **58** B2
Urlwin St *CMBW* SE5...... **118** C2
Urlwin Wk *BRXN/ST* SW9...... **118** A4
Urmston Dr *WIM/MER* SW19...... **149** E1
Ursula Ms *FSBYPK* N4...... **58** B3
Ursula St *BTSEA* SW11...... **115** E4
Urswick Rd *CLPT* E5...... **78** C2
Usborne Ms *VX/NE* SW8...... **117** F3
Usher Rd *BOW* E3...... **79** F1
Usk Rd *BTSEA* SW11...... **132** C2
Usk St *BETH* E2...... **91** D2
Uverdale Rd
   WBPTN SW10 *...... **114** C3
Uxbridge Rd *SHB* W12...... **100** A3
Uxbridge St *KENS* W8...... **26** A3
   NTGHL W11 *...... **26** B3

V

Vale Cl *MV/WKIL* W9...... **3** E4
Vale Cots *PUT/ROE* SW15 *...... **147** E3
Vale Ct *ACT* W3...... **99** F2
Vale Crs *PUT/ROE* SW15...... **147** E4
Vale End *EDUL* SE22...... **137** F2
Vale Gv *ACT* W3...... **99** D2
   FSBYPK N4...... **58** C2
Vale La *ACT* W3...... **86** A4
Valentia Pl *BRXN/ST* SW9...... **136** A2
Valentine Rd *HOM* E9 *...... **54** C5
Valentine Rd *HOM* E9 *...... **79** D3
Valentines Rd *IL* IG1...... **66** B3
Vale of Health *HAMP* NW3...... **54** C5
Valerian Wy *SRTFD* E15...... **93** E2
Vale Ri *GLDGN* NW11...... **53** F3
Vale Rd *FSBYPK* N4...... **58** C2
   FSTGT E7...... **82** B5
Vale Rw *HBRY* N5...... **58** B5
Vale Royal *HOLWY* N7...... **75** E4
Vale St *DUL* SE21...... **155** D3
Valeswood Rd *BMLY* BR1...... **159** D3
Vale Ter *FSBYPK* N4...... **58** C1
The Vale *ACT* W3...... **99** D2
   CHEL SW3...... **115** D2
   GLDGN NW11...... **53** D5
   SHB W12...... **99** F2
Valetta Gv *PLSTW* E13...... **94** A1
Valetta Rd *ACT* W3...... **99** E3
Valette St *HACK* E8 *...... **78** B3
Valiant Wy *EHAM* E6...... **95** F4
Vallance Rd *WCHPL* E1...... **90** A3
Valleyfield Rd *STRHM/NOR* SW16...... **153** F5
Valley Gv *CHARL* SE7...... **124** C1
Valley Rd *STRHM/NOR* SW16...... **153** F4
Valliere Rd *WLSDN* NW10...... **88** A2
Valliers Wood Rd *BFN/LL* DA15...... **163** D1
Valmar Rd *CMBW* SE5...... **118** C4
Val McKenzie Av *HOLWY* N7...... **58** A5
Valnay St *TOOT* SW17...... **151** F5
Valonia Gdns *WAND/EARL* SW18...... **131** F4
Vambery Rd *WOOL/PLUM* SE18...... **126** C2
Vanbrugh Hl *BKHTH/KID* SE3...... **123** F2
Vanbrugh Hl *GNWCH* SE10...... **123** E1
Vanbrugh Pk *BKHTH/KID* SE3...... **123** F3
Vanbrugh Park Rd
   BKHTH/KID SE3...... **123** F3
Vanbrugh Park Rd West
   BKHTH/KID SE3...... **123** F3
Vanbrugh Ter *BKHTH/KID* SE3...... **123** F4
Vanburgh Cl *CAN/RD* E16...... **95** D4
Vancouver Rd *FSTH* SE23...... **157** E2
Vanderbilt Rd *WAND/EARL* SW18...... **150** B1
Vanderbilt Vls *WIM* SW12 *...... **101** D3
Vandome Cl *CAN/RD* E16...... **94** B5
Vandon St *STJSPK* SW1H...... **43** F2
Vandyke Cl *PUT/ROE* SW15...... **131** D4
Vandyke Cross *ELTH/MOT* SE9...... **143** E3
Vandy St *SDTCH* EC2A...... **24** C1
Vane Cl *HAMP* NW3...... **73** D2
Vanguard Cl *CAN/RD* E16...... **94** A4
Vanguard St *DEPT* SE8...... **122** A4
Vanneck Sq *PUT/ROE* SW15 *...... **130** A3
Vanoc Gdns *BMLY* BR1...... **160** A4
Vansittart Rd *FSTGT* E7...... **82** A1
Vansittart St *NWCR* SE14...... **121** E3
Vanston Pl *FUL/PGN* SW6...... **114** A3
   Vantage Pl *KENS* W8...... **38** B3
Vant Rd *TOOT* SW17...... **151** F5
Varcoe Rd *BERM/RHTH* SE16...... **120** B1
Vardens Rd *BTSEA* SW11...... **133** D2
Varden St *WCHPL* E1...... **90** B5
Vardon Cl *ACT* W3...... **87** D5
Varley Rd *CAN/RD* E16...... **94** B5
Varna Rd *FUL/PGN* SW6...... **113** E3
Varndell St *CAMTN* NW1...... **7** E5
Varsity Rw *MORT/ESHN* SW14...... **110** C3
Vartry Rd *SEVS/STOTM* N15...... **59** E1
Vassall Rd *BRXN/ST* SW9...... **118** A3
Vauban Est *BERM/RHTH* SE16...... **49** F3
Vauban St *BERM/RHTH* SE16...... **49** F3
Vaughan Av *HMSMTH* W6...... **99** F5
Vaughan Est *BETH* E2 *...... **13** F3
Vaughan Gdns *IL* IG1...... **65** F2
Vaughan Rd *CMBW* SE5...... **118** C5
   SRTFD E15...... **81** F3
   WELL DA16...... **127** F5
Vaughan St *BERM/RHTH* SE16...... **103** F3

Vaughan Wy *WAP* E1W 102 A3
Vaughan Williams Cl *DEPT* SE8 .. 122 A3
Vauxhall Br *VX/NE* SW8 .... 117 E1
Vauxhall Bridge Rd *PIM* SW1V 43 E3
Vauxhall Gv *VX/NE* SW8 .... 117 F2
Vauxhall St *LBTH* SE11 .... 117 F1
Vauxhall Wk *LBTH* SE11 .... 117 F1
Vawdrey Cl *WCHPL* E1 .... 90 C3
Veda Rd *LEW* SE13 .... 140 A2
Venables St *STJWD* NW8 .... 16 B1
Vencourt Pl *HMSMTH* W6 .... 100 A5
Venetian Rd *CMBW* SE5 .... 118 C5
Venetia Rd *FSBYPK* N4 .... 134 C2
Venn St *CLAP* SW4 .... 129 E1
Ventnor Gdns *BARK* IG11 .... 85 E3
Ventnor Rd *NWCR* SE14 .... 121 D3
Venue St *POP/IOD* E14 .... 92 B4
Venus Rd *WOOL/PLUM* SE18 .... 107 F4
Vera Lynn Cl *FSTGT* E7 .... 82 A1
Vera Rd *FUL/PGN* SW6 .... 113 E4
Verbena Cl *CAN/RD* E16 .... 93 E3
Verbena Gdns *HMSMTH* W6 .... 112 A1
Verdant La *CAT* SE6 .... 159 E1
Verdun Rd *BARN* SW13 .... 111 F3
Vereker Rd *WKENS* W14 * 113 E1
Vere St *CAVSQ/HST* W1G 18 C5
Vermont Rd *WAND/EARL* SW18 .... 132 B4
Verney Rd *BERM/RHTH* SE16 ...... 120 B1
Verney St *WLSDN* NW10 .... 51 D5
Verney Wy *BERM/RHTH* SE16 ...... 120 B1
Vernham Rd *WOOL/PLUM* SE18 .... 126 C2
Vernon Av *MNPK* E12 .... 83 F1
Vernon Pl *FSBYW* WC1X 21 D3
Vernon Rd *FSBYW* WC1X 9 F3
Vernon Rd *BOW* E3 .... 91 F1
GDMY/SEVK IG3 .... 67 F5
MORT/ESHN SW14 .... 129 D1
SRTFD E15 .... 81 D4
WAN E11 .... 63 E3
Vernon Sq *FSBYW* WC1X 9 F3
Vernon St *WKENS* W14 .... 101 E5
Vernon Yd *NTGHL* W11 .... 101 F1
Verona Ct *CHSWK* W4 .... 111 D1
Veronica Rd *TOOT* SW17 .... 152 B3
Verran Rd *BAL* SW12 * 134 B5
Verulam Av *WALTH* E17 .... 61 F1
Verulam Ct *CDALE/KGS* NW9 * 52 A2
Verulam St *FSBYW* WC1X 22 A2
Vespan Rd *SHB* W12 .... 100 A3
Vesta Rd *BROCKY* SE4 .... 121 F5
Vestris Rd *FSTH* SE23 .... 157 D2
Vestry Ms *CMBW* SE5 .... 119 E4
Vestry Rd *CMBW* SE5 .... 119 E4
Vestry St *IS* N1 .... 12 A3
Vevey St *CAT* SE6 .... 157 F2
Viaduct Pl *BETH* E2 * 90 B2
Viaduct St *BETH* E2 .... 90 B2
Vian St *LEW* SE13 .... 140 B1
Vibart Gdns *BRXS/STRHM* SW2 .... 135 F5
Vibart Wk *IS* N1 * 75 E5
Vicarage Crs *BTSEA* SW11 .... 115 D5
Vicarage Dr *BARK* IG11 .... 84 C4
MORT/ESHN SW14 .... 129 D1
Vicarage Gdns *KENS* W8 * 26 B5
Vicarage Gv *CMBW* SE5 .... 119 D4
Vicarage La *EHAM* E6 .... 95 F2
IL IG1 .... 67 D3
SRTFD E15 .... 81 D3
Vicarage Ms *CHSWK* W4 * 111 E2
Vicarage Pk *WOOL/PLUM* SE18 .... 126 C1
Vicarage Rd *HDN* NW4 .... 52 A1
LEY E10 .... 62 B2
MORT/ESHN SW14 .... 128 C3
SRTFD E15 .... 81 F4
WOOL/PLUM SE18 .... 126 C1
Vicarage Wk *BTSEA* SW11 .... 115 D4
Vicarage Wy *WLSDN* NW10 .... 51 D5
Vicar's Cl *HOM* E9 .... 82 A5
SRTFD E15 .... 81 F3
Vicars HI *LEW* SE13 .... 140 B2
Vicar's Rd *KTTN* NW5 .... 74 A2
Viceroy Rd *VX/NE* SW8 .... 117 E4
Victoria Ar *WESTW* SW1E 43 D3
Victoria Av *EHAM* E6 .... 83 D5
WBLY HA9 .... 68 B3
Victoria Cots *WCHPL* E1 * 90 A4
Victoria Dock Rd *CAN/RD* E16 .... 93 F5
Victoria Dr *WIM/MER* SW19 ...... 149 D1
Victoria Emb *EMB* EC4Y 34 B1
TPL/STR WC2R 33 E2

Victoria Embankment Gdns
WHALL SW1A 45 D1
CHCR WC2N * 33 D2
Victoria Ga *BAY/PAD* W2 .... 28 B1
Victoria Gv *KENS* W8 .... 39 E2
Victoria Grove Ms *BAY/PAD* W2 ... 28 C2
Victoria Ms *KIL/WHAMP* NW6 ...... 72 A5
WAND/EARL SW18 .... 150 C1
Victorian Gv *STNW/STAM* N16 ..... 59 E5
Victorian Rd *STNW/STAM* N16 ..... 59 E5
Victoria Pde *RCH/KEW* TW9 * 110 A4
Victoria Park Rd *HOM* E9 .... 78 C5
Victoria Park Sq *BETH* E2 .... 90 C2
Victoria Park Studios *HOM* E9 * .. 78 C3
Victoria Ri *CLAP* SW4 .... 134 B1
Victoria Rd *ACT* W3 .... 87 D4
BARK IG11 .... 84 B3
BFN/LL DA15 .... 163 F5
CHST BR7 .... 162 A5
FSBYPK N4 .... 57 F2
KENS W8 .... 39 E3
KIL/WHAMP NW6 .... 89 F1
MORT/ESHN SW14 .... 129 D1
PLSTW E13 .... 94 A1
WAN E11 .... 81 D1
WLSDN NW10 .... 87 E3
Victoria Sq *BGVA* SW1W 43 D2
Victoria St *SRTFD* E15 .... 81 E4
WESTW SW1E 43 E5
Victoria Ter *FSBYPK* N4 .... 58 A5
Victoria Wy *CHARL* SE7 .... 124 B1
Victoria Yd *WCHPL* E1 * 90 A5
Victor Rd *WLSDN* NW10 .... 88 B2
Victory Pl *WALW* SE17 .... 47 F4
Victory Wy *BERM/RHTH* SE16 ..... 103 E5
Vigilant Cl *SYD* SE26 .... 156 A4
Vigo St *CONDST* W1S 31 F2
Viking Cl *BOW* E3 .... 91 E1
Viking Gdns *EHAM* E6 .... 95 E4
Viking Pl *LEY* E10 .... 61 F3
Village Cl *HAMP* NW3 * 73 D2
Village Ms *CDALE/KGS* NW9 * 51 D4
Village Mt *HAMP* NW3 * 73 D1
The Village *CHARL* SE7 .... 124 C2
Village Wy *DUL* SE21 .... 137 D4
WLSDN NW10 .... 69 D1
Villa Rd *BRXN/ST* SW9 .... 136 A1
Villas Rd *WOOL/PLUM* SE18 ...... 108 C5
Villa St *WALW* SE17 .... 119 D1
Villiers Cl *LEY* E10 .... 62 A4
Villiers Rd *CRICK* NW2 .... 70 A3
Villiers St *CHCR* WC2N 33 D3
Vincennes Est *WNWD* SE27 * 155 D4
Vincent Cl *BFN/LL* DA15 .... 163 E1
Vincent Dr *CRICK* NW2 * 51 E5
Vincent Pde *FSBYPK* N4 * 57 E5
Vincent Rd *ACT* W3 .... 98 C4
WOOL/PLUM SE18 .... 108 B5
Vincents Cl *BERM/RHTH* SE16 .... 103 E5
Vincent Sq *WEST* SW1P 43 F4
Vincent St *CAN/RD* E16 .... 94 A4
WEST SW1P 44 A4
Vincent Ter *IS* N1 .... 10 C1
Vince St *FSBYE* EC1V 12 B1
Vine Cl *CLPT* E5 .... 78 A1
Vine Cots *WCHPL* E1 * 90 C5
Vine Ct *WCHPL* E1 .... 90 A4
Vine Gdns *IL* IG1 .... 84 C2
Vinegar St *WAP* E1W 102 B2
Vinegar Yd *STHWK* SE1 .... 36 C5
Vine HI *CLKNW* EC1R 22 A1
Vine La *STHWK* SE1 .... 37 F5
The Vineries *CAT* SE6 * 158 A1
Vine Rd *BARN* SW13 .... 129 F1
SRTFD E15 .... 81 F4
Vine Sq *WKENS* W14 * 113 E1
Vine St *MYFR/PICC* W1J 31 F2
TWRH EC3N 25 E3
Vine Street Br *FARR* EC1M 22 B1
Vine Yd *STHWK* SE1 .... 35 F5
Vineyard Cl *CAT* SE6 .... 158 A1
Vineyard Hill Rd *WIM/MER* SW19 .. 150 A4
Vineyard Ms *CLKNW* EC1R * 10 A5
Vineyard Pth *MORT/ESHN* SW14 ... 129 D1
Vineyard Wk *CLKNW* EC1R 10 A5
Viney Rd *LEW* SE13 .... 140 B1
Vining St *BRXS/STRHM* SW2 ...... 136 A2

Viola Sq *SHB* W12......................................99 F1
Violet Cl *CAN/RD* E16................................93 E3
   DEPT SE8....................................121 F2
Violet Hl *STJWD* NW8..................................3 E2
Violet Rd *BOW* E3.....................................92 B3
   WALTH E17...............................62 A1
Violet St *BETH* E2....................................90 B5
Virgil St *STHWK* SE1................................45 F2
Virginia Rd *BETH* E2.................................13 E4
Virginia St *WCHPL* E1 *............................102 A1
Viscount Dr *EHAM* E6.................................95 F4
Viscount St *BARB* EC2Y..............................23 E1
The Vista *ELTH/MOT* SE9...........................143 D4
Vivian Av *WBLY* HA9..................................68 A3
Vivian Gdns *WBLY* HA9...............................68 A2
Vivian Rd *BOW* E3......................................91 E1
Vixen Cl *PECK* SE15.................................138 B1
Vixen Ms *HACK* E8 *..................................77 F5
Voce Rd *WOOL/PLUM* SE18..........................127 D5
Voltaire Rd *CLAP* SW4..............................135 D1
Volt Av *WLSDN* NW10..................................87 D2
Voluntary Pl *WAN* E11...............................64 A1
Vorley Rd *ARCH* N19.................................56 C4
Voss St *BETH* E2.......................................90 A2
Vulcan Cl *EHAM* E6....................................96 A3
Vulcan Ter *BROCKY* SE4............................121 F5
Vulcan Wy *HOLWY* N7..................................75 F3
Vyner Rd *ACT* W3......................................99 D1
Vyner St *BETH* E2.....................................90 B1

W

Wadding St *WALW* SE17...............................48 A5
Waddington Rd *SRTFD* E15...........................81 D2
Waddington St *SRTFD* E15...........................81 D3
Wade House *STHWK* SE1 *..........................102 A3
Wade Rd *CAN/RD* E16.................................94 C5
Wadeson St *BETH* E2.................................90 B1
Wade's Pl *POP/IOD* E14.............................104 B1
Wadham Gdns *HAMP* NW3.............................73 E4
Wadham Rd *PUT/ROE* SW15..........................131 D2
Wadhurst Rd *CHSWK* W4..............................99 D4
Wadley Rd *WAN* E11...................................63 E2
Wager St *BOW* E3.......................................91 F3
Waghorn Rd *PLSTW* E13..............................82 C5
Waghorn St *PECK* SE15.............................138 A1
Wagner St *PECK* SE15...............................120 C3
Wainford Cl *WIM/MER* SW19.......................149 D1
Waite Davies Rd *LEE/GVPK* SE12.................141 F5
Waite St *CMBW* SE5..................................119 D2
Waithman St *STP* EC4M...............................22 C5
Wakefield Gdns *IL* IG1..............................65 E1
Wakefield Ms *STPAN* WC1H............................8 C4
Wakefield St *BMSBY* WC1N.............................9 D5
   EHAM E6.....................................83 E5
Wakeham St *IS* N1.....................................77 D3
Wakehurst Rd *BTSEA* SW11.........................133 E3
Wakeling Rd *WCHPL* E1 *............................91 E5
Wakelin Rd *SRTFD* E15...............................93 E1
Wakeman Rd *WLSDN* NW10...........................88 C2
Wakering Rd *BARK* IG11..............................84 C3
Wakerly Cl *EHAM* E6..................................95 F5
Wakley St *FSBYE* EC1V...............................10 C3
Walberswick St *VX/NE* SW8........................117 E3
Walbrook *MANHO* EC4N................................36 A1
Walburgh St *WCHPL* E1 *.............................90 B5
Walcorde Av *WALW* SE17..............................47 F4
Walcot Sq *LBTH* SE11.................................46 B4
Walcott St *WEST* SW1P *.............................43 F4
Waldeck Gv *WNWD* SE27.............................154 B3
Waldeck Rd *CHSWK* W4..............................110 A2
   MORT/ESHN SW14........................128 C1
Waldemar Av *FUL/PGN* SW6.........................114 A5
Waldemar Rd *WIM/MER* SW19.......................150 A5
Walden Av *CHST* BR7.................................161 F4
Waldenshaw Rd *FSTH* SE23.........................156 C1
Walden St *WCHPL* E1 *...............................90 B5
Waldo Cl *CLAP* SW4.................................134 C3
Waldo Rd *WLSDN* NW10...............................88 A1
Waldram Crs *FSTH* SE23............................156 C1
Waldram Park Rd *FSTH* SE23......................157 D1
Waldron Ms *CHEL* SW3.............................115 D2
Waldron Rd *WAND/EARL* SW18......................150 C3
Walerand Rd *LEE/GVPK* SE12.......................122 C5
Wales Cl *PECK* SE15................................120 B3
Wales Farm Rd *ACT* W3..............................87 D4
Waley St *WCHPL* E1 *.................................91 D4
Walford Rd *STNW/STAM* N16..........................77 E1

Walham Green Ct *FUL/PGN* SW6 *.................114 B3
Walham Gv *FUL/PGN* SW6............................114 A3
Walham Yd *FUL/PGN* SW6............................114 A3
Walkden Rd *CHST* BR7..............................162 A4
Walker Cl *WOOL/PLUM* SE18.......................108 C5
Walker's Ct *SOHO/CST* W1F...........................32 A1
Walkerscroft Md *CAT* SE6.........................158 B2
   DUL SE21....................................154 C1
Wallace Rd *IS* N1.....................................76 C3
Wallbutton Rd *BROCKY* SE4........................121 E5
Wallcote Av *CRICK* NW2...............................53 D3
Wall End Rd *EHAM* E6.................................84 A4
Waller Rd *NWCR* SE14...............................121 D4
Wallflower St *SHB* W12..............................99 F1
Wallgrave Rd *ECT* SW5...............................38 B4
Wallingford Av *NKENS* W10..........................89 D4
Wallington Rd *GDMY/SEVK* IG3......................67 F2
Wallis Cl *BTSEA* SW11..............................133 D1
Wallis Rd *HOM* E9.....................................79 F3
Wallorton Gdns *MORT/ESHN* SW14.................129 D2
Wallside *BARB* EC2Y *................................23 F3
Wall St *IS* N1...77 D3
Wallwood Rd *WAN* E11................................63 D2
Wallwood St *POP/IOD* E14...........................91 F4
Walmer Pl *MBLAR* W1H *..............................17 E2
Walmer Rd *NTGHL* W11..............................101 E1
Walmer Ter *WOOL/PLUM* SE18.....................108 C5
Walm La *CRICK* NW2..................................71 D2
Walnut Cl *DEPT* SE8.................................121 F2
Walnut Gdns *SRTFD* E15.............................81 E4
Walnut Rd *LEY* E10...................................62 A4
Walnut Tree Cl *BARN* SW13........................111 F4
Walnut Tree Rd *GNWCH* SE10 *....................123 E1
Walnut Tree Wlk *LBTH* SE11..........................46 A4
Walpole Gdns *CHSWK* W4............................110 C1
Walpole Ms *STJWD* NW8...............................3 F5
Walpole Rd *EHAM* E6..................................82 C4
Walpole St *CHEL* SW3...............................115 F1
Walsham Cl *STNW/STAM* N16..........................60 A3
Walsham Rd *NWCR* SE14.............................121 D5
Walsingham Rd *CLPT* E5 *............................60 A5
Walter Rodney Cl *MNPK* E12.........................83 F3
Walter St *BETH* E2....................................91 D2
Walters Wy *FSTH* SE23.............................139 D4
Walter Ter *WCHPL* E1................................91 D5
Walterton Rd *MV/WKIL* W9.............................89 F3
Waltham Av *CDALE/KGS* NW9..........................50 A1
Walton Av *WBLY* HA9..................................50 B5
Walton Cl *CRICK* NW2................................52 B4
   VX/NE SW8................................117 E3
Walton Dr *WLSDN* NW10..............................69 D3
Walton Gdns *ACT* W3.................................86 B4
Walton Pl *CHEL* SW3..................................41 F2
Walton Rd *MNPK* E12..................................84 A1
   PLSTW E13................................94 C1
Walton Vis *IS* N1 *....................................77 E4
Walton Wy *ACT* W3.....................................86 B4
Walt Whitman Cl *HNHL* SE24 *....................136 B2
Walworth Pl *WALW* SE17............................118 C1
Walworth Rd *STHWK* SE1.............................47 E4
Wanborough Dr *PUT/ROE* SW15....................148 B1
Wandle Rd *TOOT* SW17...............................151 E2
Wandle Wy *WAND/EARL* SW18.......................150 B1
Wandsworth Br *WAND/EARL* SW18..................132 C1
Wandsworth Bridge Rd
   FUL/PGN SW6..............................114 B4
Wandsworth Common West Side
   WAND/EARL SW18.........................132 C3
Wandsworth High St
   WAND/EARL SW18.........................132 A3
Wandsworth Rd *VX/NE* SW8.........................134 B1
Wanless Rd *HNHL* SE24.............................136 C1
Wanley Rd *CMBW* SE5................................137 D2
Wanlip Rd *PLSTW* E13.................................94 B3
Wansbeck Rd *HOM* E9..................................79 F4
Wansdown Pl *FUL/PGN* SW6........................114 B3
Wansey St *WALW* SE17...............................47 F5
Wanstead La *IL* IG1..................................65 E1
Wanstead Park Av *MNPK* E12........................65 D4
Wanstead Park Rd *IL* IG1...........................65 E3
Wanstead Pl *WAN* E11.................................64 A1
Wantage Rd *LEE/GVPK* SE12........................141 F3
Wapping Dock St *WAP* E1W *.......................102 B2
Wapping High St *WAP* E1W.........................102 A2
Wapping La *WAP* E1W................................102 B1
Wapping Wall *WAP* E1W.............................102 C2
Warbeck Rd *SHB* W12................................100 B2
Warburton Cl *IS* N1 *................................77 E3

Warburton Rd *HACK* E8 .... 78 B5
Warburton St *HACK* E8 .... 78 B5
Wardalis Gv *NWCR* SE14 * 120 C3
Warden Rd *KTTN* NW5 .... 74 A3
Wardens Gv *STHWK* SE1 .... 35 E4
Wardle St *HOM* E9 .... 79 D2
Wardley St *WAND/EARL* SW18 .... 132 B5
Wardo Av *FUL/PGN* SW6 .... 113 E4
Wardour Ms *SOHO/CST* W1F 19 F5
Wardour St *SOHO/CST* W1F 19 F4
Ward Rd *ARCH* N19 .... 56 C5
  SRTFD E15 * 81 D5
Wardrobe PI *BLKFR* EC4V * 23 D5
Wards Rd *GNTH/NBYPK* IG2 .... 67 D2
Wards Wharf Ap *CAN/RD* E16 .... 107 D2
Warepoint Dr *THMD* SE28 .... 109 D3
Warfield Rd *WLSDN* NW10 .... 89 D2
Warfield Yd *WLSDN* NW10 * 89 D2
Wargrave Av *SEVS/STOTM* N15 .... 59 F1
Warham St *WLSDN* NW10 * 118 B3
Waring St *WNWD* SE27 .... 154 C4
Warland Rd *WOOL/PLUM* SE18 .... 127 D3
Warley St *BETH* E2 .... 91 D2
Warlock Rd *MV/WKIL* W9 .... 89 F3
Warlters Cl *HOLWY* N7 * 75 E1
Warlters Rd *HOLWY* N7 .... 75 E1
Warltersville Rd *ARCH* N19 .... 57 E2
Warming Cl *CLPT* E5 * 61 D5
Warmington Rd *HNHL* SE24 .... 136 C4
Warmington St *PLSTW* E13 .... 94 A3
Warndon St *BERM/RHTH* SE16 .... 102 C5
Warneford St *HOM* E9 .... 78 B5
Warner Cl *CDALE/KGS* NW9 .... 51 F2
  SRTFD E15 .... 81 E2
Warner PI *BETH* E2 .... 90 A1
Warner Rd *CMBW* SE5 .... 118 C4
Warner St *CLKNW* EC1R 22 A1
Warner Ter *POP/IOD* E14 * 92 A4
Warner Yd *CLKNW* EC1R 22 A1
Warple Ms *ACT* W3 * 99 E3
Warple Wy *ACT* W3 .... 99 E3
Warren Lane Ga *WOOL/PLUM* SE18 .... 108 B4
Warren Av *RCHPK/HAM* TW10 .... 128 B2
  WAN E11 * 63 D5
Warren Ct *CHARL* SE7 .... 124 C1
Warrender Rd *ARCH* N19 .... 56 C5
The Warren Dr *WAN* E11 .... 64 C2
Warren La *WOOL/PLUM* SE18 .... 108 B4
Warren Ms *FITZ* W1T * 19 E1
Warren Rd *CRICK* NW2 .... 51 F4
  LEY E10 .... 62 C5
  WAN E11 .... 64 C1
Warren St *FITZ* W1T 19 E1
The Warren *MNPK* E12 .... 83 E1
Warriner Gdns *BTSEA* SW11 .... 115 F4
Warrington Crs *MV/WKIL* W9 .... 15 E1
Warrington Gdns *MV/WKIL* W9 .... 15 E1
Warrington PI *POP/IOD* E14 * 104 C2
Warrior Sq *MNPK* E12 .... 84 A1
Warspite Rd *WOOL/PLUM* SE18 .... 107 E4
Warton Rd *SRTFD* E15 .... 80 C5
Warwall *EHAM* E6 .... 96 B5
Warwick Av *MV/WKIL* W9 .... 15 D1
Warwick Ct *HHOL* WC1V 21 F3
Warwick Crs *BAY/PAD* W2 .... 15 E1
Warwick Dr *PUT/ROE* SW15 .... 130 B1
Warwick Gdns *IL* IG1 .... 66 B3
  WKENS W14 .... 101 F4
Warwick Gv *CLPT* E5 .... 60 B3
Warwick House St *STJS* SW1Y 32 B3
Warwick La *STP* EC4M 23 D4
Warwick PI *MV/WKIL* W9 .... 15 E2
Warwick PI North *PIM* SW1V * 43 E5
Warwick Rd *ECT* SW5 .... 38 A5
  MNPK E12 .... 83 E2
  SRTFD E15 .... 81 E5
  WKENS W14 .... 101 F5
Warwick Rw *WESTW* SW1E 43 E2
Warwick Sq *PIM* SW1V 43 E5
  STP EC4M * 23 D4
Warwick Square Ms *PIM* SW1V 43 E5
Warwick St *REGST* W1B 31 F1
Warwick Ter *WOOL/PLUM* SE18 .... 127 D2
Warwick Wy *PIM* SW1V 43 E5
Warwick Yd *STLK* EC1Y * 23 F1
Washington Av *MNPK* E12 .... 83 E1
Washington Cl *BOW* E3 .... 92 B2
Washington Rd *BARN* SW13 .... 112 A3
  EHAM E6 .... 95 F1
Wastdale Rd *FSTH* SE23 .... 157 D1
Watchfield Ct *CHSWK* W4 * 110 C1

Waterbank Rd *CAT* SE6 .... 158 B2
Watercress PI *IS* N1 .... 77 E1
Waterfield Cots *MORT/ESHN* SW14 * 128 B2
Waterford Rd *FUL/PGN* SW6 .... 114 B3
Waterford Wy *WLSDN* NW10 .... 70 B2
The Water Gdns *BAY/PAD* W2 .... 16 C4
Watergate *EMB* EC4Y * 34 C1
Watergate St *DEPT* SE8 .... 122 A2
Waterhouse Cl *HAMP* NW3 .... 73 D2
Wateridge Cl *POP/IOD* E14 .... 104 A4
Water La *CAMTN* NW1 .... 74 B4
  CDMY/SEVK IG3 .... 67 F3
  NWCR SE14 .... 120 C3
  SRTFD E15 .... 81 E3
Waterloo Br *IS/TPL/STR* WC2R 33 E2
Waterloo Cl *HOM* E9 .... 78 C2
Waterloo Gdns *BETH* E2 .... 90 C1
Waterloo PI *RCH/KEW* TW9 .... 110 A2
  STJS SW1Y 32 A3
Waterloo Rd *CRICK* NW2 .... 52 A4
  EHAM E6 .... 82 C4
  FSTGT E7 .... 81 F2
  LEY E10 .... 62 A2
  STHWK SE1 .... 33 F3
Waterloo Ter *IS* N1 .... 76 B4
Waterlow Rd *ARCH* N19 .... 56 C3
Waterman St *PUT/ROE* SW15 .... 131 D1
Waterman Wy *WAP* E1W 102 B2
Watermeadow La *FUL/PGN* SW6 .... 114 C5
Watermead Rd *CAT* SE6 .... 158 C4
Water Ms *PECK* SE15 .... 138 C2
Watermint Quay *STNW/STAM* N16 .... 60 A2
Water's Edge *FUL/PGN* SW6 * 113 D4
Waterside *WALTH* E17 .... 60 C1
Waterside Cl *BERM/RHTH* SE16 .... 102 A3
  BOW E3 .... 79 F5
  THMD SE28 .... 109 F2
Waterside Ct *LEW* SE13 * 141 E3
Waterside Wy *TOOT* SW17 .... 150 C4
Waterson St *BETH* E2 .... 13 D3
Waters Rd *CAT* SE6 .... 159 E3
Water St *TPL/STR* WC2R 34 A1
Waterway Av *LEW* SE13 .... 140 B5
Waterworks La *CLPT* E5 .... 61 D4
Waterworks Rd *BRXS/STRHM* SW2 .... 135 E4
Watford Cl *BTSEA* SW11 .... 115 E4
Watford Rd *CAN/RD* E16 .... 94 A4
Watkin Rd *WBLY* HA9 .... 50 B3
Watkinson Rd *HOLWY* N7 .... 75 F5
Watling Ct *STP* EC4M 23 F5
Watling St *PECK* SE15 .... 119 E2
  STP EC4M 23 F5
Watlington Gv *SYD* SE26 .... 157 E5
Watney Market *WCHPL* E1 .... 90 B5
Watney Rd *MORT/ESHN* SW14 .... 128 C1
Watney St *WCHPL* E1 .... 90 B5
Watson Av *EHAM* E6 .... 84 A4
Watson Cl *STNW/STAM* N16 .... 77 D2
Watson's Ms *CAMTN* NW1 .... 17 D3
Watson's Ms *CAMTN* NW1 .... 122 A3
Wattisfield Rd *CLPT* E5 .... 60 C5
Wattsdown Cl *PLSTW* E13 .... 82 A5
Watts Gv *BOW* E3 .... 92 A4
Watts St *PECK* SE15 .... 119 F4
  WAP E1W 102 B2
Wat Tyler Rd *GNWCH* SE10 .... 122 C5
Wavell Dr *BFN/LL* DA15 .... 145 E4
Wavel Ms *KIL/WHAMP* NW6 .... 72 B4
Wavel PI *SYD* SE26 .... 155 F4
Wavendon Av *CHSWK* W4 .... 111 D1
Waveney Av *PECK* SE15 .... 138 B2
Waveney Cl *WAP* E1W 102 A2
Waverley Crs *WOOL/PLUM* SE18 .... 127 D2
Waverley Gdns *BARK* IG11 .... 97 E1
  EHAM E6 .... 95 E4
Waverley PI *FSBYPK* N4 * 58 B3
  STJWD NW8 .... 4 A1
Waverley Rd *CEND/HSY/T* N8 .... 57 D1
  WOOL/PLUM SE18 .... 126 C1
Waverton Rd *WAND/EARL* SW18 .... 132 C5
Waverton St *MYFR/PKLN* W1K 30 B3
Wavertree Rd *BRXS/STRHM* SW2 .... 153 F1
Waxlow Rd *WLSDN* NW10 .... 86 C1
Wayford St *BTSEA* SW11 .... 115 E5
Wayland Av *HACK* E8 .... 78 A2
Waylett PI *WNWD* SE27 .... 154 B3
Waynflete Sq *NKENS* W10 .... 101 D1
Waynflete St *WAND/EARL* SW18 .... 150 C2
Wayside *GLDGN* NW11 .... 53 E3
  MORT/ESHN SW14 .... 128 C2
Wayside Gv *ELTH/MOT* SE9 .... 161 F4
Wayside Ms *GNTH/NBYPK* IG2 .... 66 A1

Weald Cl *BERM/RHTH* SE16	120	B1
Weald Sq *CLPT* E5 *	60	B4
Weardale Rd *LEW* SE13	141	D2
Wear Pl *BETH* E2	90	B2
Wearside Rd *LEW* SE13	140	B2
Weatherley Cl *BOW* E3	91	F4
Weaver Cl *EHAM* E6	108	B1
Weaver's La *STHWK* SE1 *	37	D4
Weavers Ter *FUL/PGN* SW6 *	114	A2
Weaver St *WCHPL* E1	90	A3
Weavers Wy *CAMTN* NW1	75	D5
Weaver Wk *WNWD* SE27	154	B4
Webb Cl *NKENS* W10	88	C3
Webber Rw *STHWK* SE1	46	B1
Webber St *STHWK* SE1	34	B5
Webb Est *CLPT* E5 *	60	A2
Webb Pl *WLSDN* NW10	87	F2
Webb Rd *BKHTH/KID* SE3	123	F2
Webb's Rd *BTSEA* SW11	133	F5
Webb St *STHWK* SE1	48	C3
Webster Rd *BERM/RHTH* SE16	102	A4
WAN E11	62	C5
Wedderburn Rd *BARK* IG11	73	D2
HAMP NW3	55	D5
Wedgwood Wk *KIL/WHAMP* NW6 *	72	B2
Wedlake St *NKENS* W10	89	E3
Wedmore Gdns *ARCH* N19	57	E4
Wedmore Ms *ARCH* N19	57	D5
Wedmore St *ARCH* N19	57	D5
Weech Rd *KIL/WHAMP* NW6	72	A1
Weedington Rd *KTTN* NW5	74	A2
Weekley Sq *BTSEA* SW11 *	133	D1
Weigall Rd *LEE/GVPK* SE12	142	A4
Weighhouse St *MYFR/PKLN* W1K	30	B1
Weimar St *PUT/ROE* SW15	131	E1
Weir Rd *BAL* SW12	152	C1
WIM/MER SW19	150	B3
Weirs Pas *CAMTN* NW1	8	B3
Weiss Rd *PUT/ROE* SW15	131	D1
Welbeck Av *BMLY* BR1	160	A4
Welbeck Rd *EHAM* E6	95	D2
Welbeck St *CAVSQ/HST* W1G	18	B3
Welbeck Wy *CAVSQ/HST* W1G	18	C4
Welby Ct *PLSTW* E13	94	C1
Welby St *CMBW* SE5	118	B4
Welfare Rd *SRTFD* E15	81	E4
Welford Cl *CLPT* E5	61	D5
Welford Pl *WIM/MER* SW19	149	E4
Welham Rd *TOOT* SW17	152	A5
Welland Ms *WAP* E1W *	102	A2
Welland St *GNWCH* SE10	122	C2
Well Cl *STRHM/NOR* SW16	153	F4
Wellclose Sq *WCHPL* E1	102	A1
Wellclose St *WCHPL* E1	102	A1
Well Cottage Cl *WAN* E11	64	C2
Well Ct *STP* EC4M	23	F5
Weller St *STHWK* SE1	35	E5
Wellesley Av *HMSMTH* W6	100	B4
Wellesley Cl *CHARL* SE7 *	124	C1
Wellesley Ct *MV/WKIL* W9	3	E3
Wellesley Pl *CAMTN* NW1 *	8	A4
KTTN NW5	74	A2
Wellesley Rd *CHSWK* W4	110	A1
IL IG1	66	B4
KTTN NW5	74	A2
WALTH E17	62	A1
Wellesley Ter *IS* N1	11	F3
Wellfield Rd *STRHM/NOR* SW16	153	E4
Wellfit St *HNHL* SE24	136	B1
Wellgarth Rd *GLDGN* NW11	54	B3
Well Hall Pde *ELTH/MOT* SE9 *	143	F2
Well Hall Rd *ELTH/MOT* SE9	143	F2
Wellington Av *SEVS/STOTM* N15	60	A1
Wellington Cl *NTGHL* W11	14	A5
NWCR SE14	121	D2
Wellington Gdns *CHARL* SE7	124	C1
Wellington Gv *GNWCH* SE10	123	D3
Wellington Ms *CHARL* SE7	124	C2
EDUL SE22	138	A2
HOLWY N7	75	F3
STRHM/NOR SW16	153	D3
Wellington Park Est *CRICK* NW2 *	52	A4
Wellington Pl *STJWD* NW8	4	B5
Wellington Rd *EHAM* E6	83	F5
FSTGT E7	81	F1
LEY E10	61	E3
NKENS W10 *	89	D2
STJWD NW8	4	B2
WIM/MER SW19	150	A2
Wellington Rw *BETH* E2	13	F3
Wellington Sq *CHEL* SW3	115	F1
IS N1 *	75	E5
Wellington St *COVGDN* WC2E	33	D1
WOOL/PLUM SE18	108	A5
Wellington Ter *BAY/PAD* W2	26	B2
WAP E1W *	102	B2
Wellington Wy *BOW* E3	92	A2
Welling La *MORT/ESHN* SW14	145	D1
Welling La *MORT/ESHN* SW14	111	E4
Wellmeadow Rd *CAT* SE6	159	E1
LEW SE13	141	E4
Well Rd *HAMP* NW3	55	D5
Wells Dr *CDALE/KGS* NW9	51	D3
Wells Gdns *IL* IG1	65	E2
Wells House Rd *WLSDN* NW10	87	E4
Wellside Gdns *MORT/ESHN* SW14	128	C2
Wells Ms *FITZ* W1T *	19	F3
Wells Park Rd *SYD* SE26	156	A3
Wells Pl *CMBW* SE5	119	E3
WAND/EARL SW18	132	C5
Wellspring Crs *WBLY* HA9	50	B4
Wells Ri *STJWD* NW8	73	F5
Wells Rd *SHB* W12	100	C3
Wells Sq *FSBYW* WC1X	9	E4
Wells St *GTPST* W1W	19	E3
Wellstead Rd *EHAM* E6	96	A1
Wells Ter *FSBYPK* N4	58	A4
Well St *HOM* E9	78	C4
SRTFD E15	81	E3
Well Wy *SKENS* SW7	40	A2
WALW SE17	119	D2
Well Wk *HAMP* NW3	55	D5
Welsford St *STHWK* SE1	120	A1
Welsh Cl *PLSTW* E13	94	A1
Welshpool St *HACK* E8 *	78	A5
Welstead Wy *CHSWK* W4	99	F4
Weltje Rd *HMSMTH* W6	112	A1
Welton Rd *WOOL/PLUM* SE18	127	E3
Welwyn St *BETH* E2	90	C2
Wembley Wy *WBLY* HA9	68	B3
Wembury Ms *HGT* N6	56	B2
Wembury Rd *HGT* N6	56	B2
Wemyss Rd *BKHTH/KID* SE3	123	F5
Wendell Rd *SHB* W12	99	F3
Wendon St *BOW* E3	79	F5
Wendover Rd *ELTH/MOT* SE9	143	D1
WLSDN NW10	87	F1
Wenlock Rd *IS* N1	11	F2
Wenlock St *IS* N1	11	F2
Wennington Rd *BOW* E3	91	D1
Wensley Cl *ELTH/MOT* SE9	143	F4
Wentland Cl *CAT* SE6	159	D2
Wentland Rd *CAT* SE6	159	D2
Wentworth Crs *PECK* SE15	120	A3
Wentworth Ms *BOW* E3	91	E3
Wentworth Rd *GLDGN* NW11	53	F1
MNPK E12	83	D1
Wentworth St *WCHPL* E1	25	E4
Wernbrook St *WOOL/PLUM* SE18	126	C2
Werrington St *CAMTN* NW1	7	F2
Werter Rd *PUT/ROE* SW15	131	E2
Wesleyan Pl *KTTN* NW5	74	B1
Wesley Av *CAN/RD* E16	106	A2
WLSDN NW10	87	D2
Wesley Cl *HOLWY* N7	57	F4
LBTH SE11	118	B1
WALW SE17	47	D5
Wesley Rd *LEY* E10	62	C2
WLSDN NW10	86	C5
Wesley Sq *NTGHL* W11	89	D5
Wesley St *CAVSQ/HST* W1G	18	B3
Wessex Cl *GDMY/SEVK* IG3	67	E1
Wessex Gdns *GLDGN* NW11	53	E3
Wessex St *BETH* E2	90	C2
Wessex Wy *GLDGN* NW11	53	E2
Wesson Md *CMBW* SE5 *	118	C3
Westacott Cl *ARCH* N19	57	D3
West Arbour St *WCHPL* E1	90	C5
West Bank *BARK* IG11	84	B5
STNW/STAM N16	59	E2
Westbere Rd *CRICK* NW2	71	E1
Westbourne Av *ACT* W3	87	D5
Westbourne Crs *BAY/PAD* W2	28	A1
Westbourne Crescent Ms		
BAY/PAD W2	28	A1
Westbourne Dr *FSTH* SE23	157	D1
Westbourne Gdns *BAY/PAD* W2	14	C4
Westbourne Ga *BAY/PAD* W2	28	A1
Westbourne Gv *NTGHL* W11	14	A5
Westbourne Grove Ms *NTGHL* W11	14	A4
Westbourne Grove Ter *BAY/PAD* W2	14	C4
Westbourne Park Rd *BAY/PAD* W2	14	B4
NTGHL W11	14	A4

Westbourne Park Vls *BAY/PAD* W2 .... 14 B3
Westbourne Rd *HOLWY* N7 .... 75 F3
Westbourne St *BAY/PAD* W2 .... 28 A1
Westbourne Ter *BAY/PAD* W2 .... 15 E3
Westbourne Terrace Ms *BAY/PAD* W2 .. 15 E4
Westbourne Terrace Rd *BAY/PAD* W2 .. 15 E3
Westbridge Cl *SHB* W12 .... 100 A2
Westbridge Rd *BTSEA* SW11 .... 115 D4
Westbrooke Rd *BFN/LL* DA15 .... 163 D2
Westbrook Rd *BKHTH/KID* SE3 .... 124 A4
Westbrook Rd *BARK* IG11 .... 85 D5
　　　FSTGT E7 .... 82 B2
　　　IL IG1 .... 66 A4
Westbury Ter *FSTGT* E7 .... 82 B3
West Carriage Dr *BAY/PAD* W2 .... 28 A4
West Central St *LSQ/SEVD* WC2H 20 C3
Westcombe Hl *BKHTH/KID* SE3 .... 124 A2
Westcombe Park Rd *BKHTH/KID* SE3 . 123 E2
Westcote Rd *STRHM/NOR* SW16 ...... 152 C5
Westcott Cl *SEVS/STOTM* N15 .... 59 F1
Westcott House *POP/IOD* E14 * 104 A1
Westcott Rd *WALW* SE17 .... 118 B2
Westcroft Cl *CRICK* NW2 .... 71 E1
Westcroft Ms *HMSMTH* W6 * 100 A5
Westcroft Sq *HMSMTH* W6 .... 100 A5
Westcroft Wy *CRICK* NW2 .... 71 E1
West Cross Route *NTGHL* W11 .... 101 D2
Westdale Rd *WOOL/PLUM* SE18 ...... 126 B2
Westdean Av *LEE/GVPK* SE12 .... 160 B1
Westdean Cl *WAND/EARL* SW18 .... 132 B4
Westdown Rd *CAT* SE6 .... 140 A5
　　　SRTFD E15 .... 80 C1
West Dr *STRHM/NOR* SW16 .... 152 B4
West Eaton Pl *BGVA* SW1W 42 A4
West Eaton Place Ms *KTBR* SW1X 42 A4
West Ella Rd *WLSDN* NW10 .... 69 E4
West End Cl *WLSDN* NW10 .... 68 C4
West End La *KIL/WHAMP* NW6 .... 72 A3
　　　KIL/WHAMP NW6 .... 72 A5
Westerdale Rd *GNWCH* SE10 .... 124 A1
Westerham Rd *LEY* E10 .... 62 B1
Westerley Crs *SYD* SE26 * 157 F5
Western Av *EA* W5 .... 86 A3
　　　GLDGN NW11 .... 53 D1
Western Gdns *EA* W5 .... 98 A1
Western Gtwy *CAN/RD* E16 .... 106 A1
Western La *BAL* SW12 .... 134 A5
Western Ms *MV/WKIL* W9 .... 89 F3
Western Pl *BERM/RHTH* SE16 .... 102 C3
Western Rd *BRXN/ST* SW9 .... 136 A1
　　　PLSTW E13 .... 82 B5
　　　WLSDN NW10 .... 86 C3
Western Ter *HMSMTH* W6 * 112 A1
Westernville Gdns *GNTH/NBYPK* IG2 . 66 C2
Western Wy *THMD* SE28 .... 109 D4
　　　THMD SE28 .... 109 E5
Westferry Circ *POP/IOD* E14 .... 104 A2
Westferry Rd *POP/IOD* E14 .... 104 A4
Westfield Cl *FUL/PGN* SW6 .... 114 C3
　　　WBPTN SW10 .... 114 C3
Westfields *BARN* SW13 .... 129 F1
Westfields Av *BARN* SW13 .... 129 E1
Westfields Rd *ACT* W3 .... 86 B4
Westfield St *WOOL/PLUM* SE18 ...... 107 D4
Westfield Wy *WCHPL* E1 .... 91 E2
West Gdns *WAP* E1W 91 F1
Westgate St *HACK* E8 .... 78 B5
Westgate Ter *WBPTN* SW10 .... 114 B1
West Gv *GNWCH* SE10 .... 122 C4
Westgrove La *GNWCH* SE10 .... 122 C4
West Halkin St *KTBR* SW1X 42 A2
West Hallowes *ELTH/MOT* SE9 .... 161 D1
West Ham La *SRTFD* E15 .... 81 D4
West Hampstead Ms
　　　KIL/WHAMP NW6 .... 72 B3
West Harding St *FLST/FETLN* EC4A * . 22 A4
Westhay Gdns *MORT/ESHN* SW14 ... 128 B3
West Heath Av *GLDGN* NW11 .... 54 A5
West Heath Cl *HAMP* NW3 .... 54 A5
West Heath Dr *GLDGN* NW11 .... 54 A5
West Heath Gdns *HAMP* NW3 .... 54 A3
West Heath Rd *HAMP* NW3 .... 54 A4
West Hl *PUT/ROE* SW15 .... 131 E4
　　　WAND/EARL SW18 .... 132 A3
　　　WIM/MER SW19 .... 131 D5
Westhill Pk *HGT* N6 .... 55 F4
West Hill Rd *WAND/EARL* SW18 ...... 131 F4
Westhorne Av *ELTH/MOT* SE9 .... 142 C4
Westhorpe Rd *PUT/ROE* SW15 .... 130 C1
West House Cl *WIM/MER* SW19 ...... 149 E1
Westhurst Dr *CHST* BR7 .... 162 B5
West India Av *POP/IOD* E14 .... 104 A3

West India Dock Rd *POP/IOD* E14.... 104 B1
Westland Pl *FSBYE* EC1V 12 A3
Westlands Ter *BAL* SW12 .... 134 C4
West La *BERM/RHTH* SE16 .... 102 B3
Westleigh Av *PUT/ROE* SW15 .... 130 C3
West Lodge Av *ACT* W3 .... 98 A2
West Lodge Rd *ACT* W3 * 98 A2
Westmead *PUT/ROE* SW15 .... 130 B5
West Mersea Cl *CAN/RD* E16 .... 106 B2
West Ms *PIM* SW1V 45 D5
Westminster Br *WHALL* SW1A 45 D1
Westminster Bridge Rd *WHALL* SW1A . 45 D1
Westminster Gdns *BARK* IG11 .... 97 E1
Westmoor St *CHARL* SE7 .... 107 D5
Westmoreland Av *WELL* DA16 .... 145 E1
Westmoreland Pl *PIM* SW1V * 116 B1
Westmoreland Rd *BARN* SW13 .... 111 F4
　　　WALW SE17 .... 119 D2
Westmoreland St *CAVSQ/HST* W1G .. 18 B3
Westmoreland Ter *PIM* SW1V 116 B1
Westmorland Cl *MNPK* E12 .... 65 D4
Westmorland Rd *WALTH* E17 .... 62 A1
Weston Pk *CEND/HSY/T* N8 .... 57 E1
Weston Ri *FSBYW* WC1X 9 F5
Weston Rd *CHSWK* W4 .... 98 C4
Weston St *STHWK* SE1 .... 48 B2
Weston Wk *HACK* E8 .... 78 B4
Westover Hl *HAMP* NW3 .... 54 A4
Westover Rd *WAND/EARL* SW18 ..... 132 C4
West Pk *ELTH/MOT* SE9 .... 161 E2
West Park Av *RCH/KEW* TW9 .... 110 A4
West Park Rd *RCH/KEW* TW9 .... 110 A4
West Parkside *GNWCH* SE10 .... 105 E5
West Pl *WIM/MER* SW19 .... 148 C5
Westport Rd *PLSTW* E13 .... 94 B3
Westport St *WCHPL* E1 .... 91 D5
West Poultry Av *FARR* EC1M 22 C3
West Quarters *SHB* W12 .... 88 A5
West Ri *BAY/PAD* W2 * 29 D1
West Rd *CHEL* SW3 .... 115 F2
　　　CLAP SW4 .... 135 D3
　　　SRTFD E15 .... 81 F5
West Rw *NKENS* W10 .... 89 E3
Westrow Dr *BARK* IG11 .... 85 F3
Westrow Gdns *GDMY/SEVK* IG3 ..... 67 F4
West Side Common *WIM/MER* SW19 . 148 C5
West Smithfield *STBT* EC1A 22 C3
West Sq *LBTH* SE11 .... 46 C3
West St *BETH* E2 .... 90 B1
　　　LSQ/SEVD WC2H 20 B5
　　　WAN E11 .... 63 E5
West Temple Sheen
　　　MORT/ESHN SW14 .... 128 B3
West Tenter St *WCHPL* E1 .... 25 F5
West Ter *BFN/LL* DA15 * 163 E4
Westview Cl *NKENS* W10 .... 88 C5
　　　WLSDN NW10 .... 69 F2
Westville Rd *SHB* W12 .... 100 A3
West Warwick Pl *PIM* SW1V * 43 E5
Westway *BAY/PAD* W2 .... 15 E3
　　　NKENS W10 .... 89 F4
　　　SHB W12 .... 100 A1
West Wy *WLSDN* NW10 .... 69 D1
Westwick Gdns *HMSMTH* W6 .... 101 D3
Westwood Gdns *BARN* SW13 .... 129 F1
Westwood Hl *SYD* SE26 .... 156 A5
Westwood Pk *FSTH* SE23 .... 138 B5
Westwood Pl *SYD* SE26 * 156 A5
Westwood Rd *BARN* SW13 .... 129 F1
　　　GDMY/SEVK IG3 .... 67 F3
Wetherby Gdns *ECT* SW5 .... 39 E5
Wetherby Ms *ECT* SW5 .... 114 B1
Wetherby Pl *SKENS* SW7 .... 39 E5
Wetherden St *WALTH* E17 .... 61 F2
Wetherell Rd *HOM* E9 .... 79 D5
Wexford Rd *BAL* SW12 .... 133 F5
Weybourne St *WAND/EARL* SW18 ... 150 C2
Weybridge Ct *BERM/RHTH* SE16 * ... 120 B1
Weydown Cl *WIM/MER* SW19 .... 149 E1
Weyhill Rd *WCHPL* E1 * 90 A5
Weyman Rd *BKHTH/KID* SE3 .... 124 C4
Weymouth Cl *EHAM* E6 .... 96 B5
Weymouth Ms *CAVSQ/HST* W1G 18 C2
Weymouth St *CAVSQ/HST* W1G 18 B2
Weymouth Ter *BETH* E2 .... 13 F1
Weymouth Vls *FSBYPK* N4 * 57 F4
Whadcoat St *FSBYPK* N4 .... 58 A4
Whales Yd *SRTFD* E15 * 81 D4
Wharfdale St *WBPTN* SW10 .... 114 B1
Wharfedale St *WBPTN* SW10 .... 114 B1
Wharf La *POP/IOD* E14 .... 91 F5

Wharf Pl *BETH* E2	78	A5	
Wharf Rd *IS* N1	11	E2	
SRTFD E15	81	E5	
Wharfside Rd *POP/IOD* E14	93	E5	
Wharf St *CAN/RD* E16	93	E4	
Wharf Ter *PUT/ROE* SW15	131	E1	
Wharton Rd *WLSDN* NW10	69	E5	
Wharton Cots *FSBYW* WC1X *	9	F4	
Wharton St *FSBYW* WC1X	9	F4	
Whateley Rd *EDUL* SE22	137	F3	
Whatman Rd *FSTH* SE23	139	D5	
Wheastone Rd *NKENS* W10 *	89	E4	
Wheatlands Rd *TOOT* SW17	154	A3	
Wheatley St *CAVSQ/HST* W1G	18	B3	
Wheat Sheaf Cl *POP/IOD* E14	104	A5	
Wheatsheaf La *FUL/PGN* SW6	112	C3	
VX/NE SW8	117	E3	
Wheatsheaf Ter *FUL/PGN* SW6 *	113	F5	
Wheatstone Rd *NKENS* W10	89	E4	
Wheeler Gdns *IS* N1	75	E5	
Wheeler La *WCHPL* E1	25	E2	
Wheelers Cross *BARK* IG11	97	D1	
Wheelwright St *HOLWY* N7	75	F1	
Wheler St *WCHPL* E1	25	E1	
Whellock Rd *CHSWK* W4	99	E4	
Whetstone Pk *LINN* WC2A	21	E4	
Whetstone Rd *BKHTH/KID* SE3	124	C5	
Whewell Rd *ARCH* N19	57	E4	
Whichcote St *STHWK* SE1 *	34	A4	
Whidborne Cl *DEPT* SE8	122	A5	
Whidborne St *STPAN* WC1H	9	D4	
Whinchat Rd *THMD* SE28	109	D4	
Whinfell Cl *STRHM/NOR* SW16	153	D5	
Whinyates Rd *ELTH/MOT* SE9	143	E1	
Whiskin St *CLKNW* EC1R	10	C4	
Whistlers Av *BTSEA* SW11 *	115	D5	
Whistler St *HBRY* N5	76	B1	
Whistler Wk *WBPTN* SW10 *	114	C3	
Whiston Rd *BETH* E2	13	E1	
Whitbread Rd *BROCKY* SE4	139	E2	
Whitburn Rd *LEW* SE13	140	B3	
Whitby Av *WLSDN* NW10	86	B2	
Whitby Rd *WOOL/PLUM* SE18	107	F5	
Whitby St *WCHPL* E1	13	E5	
Whitcher Cl *NWCR* SE14	121	E2	
Whitcher Pl *CAMTN* NW1	74	C3	
Whitchurch Rd *NTGHL* W11	101	D1	
Whitcomb St *SOHO/SHAV* W1D	32	A1	
Whitcome Ms *RCH/KEW* TW9	110	B4	
Whiteadder Wy *POP/IOD* E14	104	B5	
Whitear Wk *SRTFD* E15	81	D3	
Whitebeam Cl *VX/NE* SW8 *	117	F3	
White Bear Pl *HAMP* NW3 *	72	C1	
White Bear Yd *CLKNW* EC1R *	22	A1	
Whitechapel High St *TWRH* EC3N	25	F4	
Whitechapel Rd *WCHPL* E1	90	A5	
White City Cl *SHB* W12	100	C1	
White City Rd *SHB* W12	100	B1	
White Conduit St *IS* N1	10	B1	
Whitecross St *STLK* EC1Y	11	F5	
Whitefield Av *CRICK* NW2	52	C2	
Whitefield Cl *PUT/ROE* SW15	131	E4	
Whitefoot La *BMLY* BR1	159	D4	
Whitefoot Ter *BMLY* BR1	159	F5	
Whitefriars St *EMB* EC4Y	22	B5	
Whitehall *WHALL* SW1A	32	C4	
Whitehall Ct *WHALL* SW1A	32	C4	
Whitehall Gdns *ACT* W3	98	A2	
CHSWK W4	110	B2	
WHALL SW1A	32	C4	
Whitehall Pk *ARCH* N19	56	C3	
Whitehall Park Rd *CHSWK* W4	110	B2	
Whitehall Pl *WHALL* SW1A	32	C4	
White Hart Av *WOOL/PLUM* SE18...	109	F4	
White Hart La *BARN* SW13	111	E5	
White Hart Rd *WOOL/PLUM* SE18	109	F5	
White Hart St *LBTH* SE11	118	A1	
White Hart Yd *STHWK* SE1 *	36	A4	
Whitehaven St *STJWD* NW8	16	C1	
Whitehead Cl *WAND/EARL* SW18	132	C5	
Whiteheads Gv *CHEL* SW3	41	D5	
Whiteheads Gv *CHEL* SW3	115	E1	
White Horse La *CHST* BK7	162	A4	
White Horse La *WCHPL* E1	91	D3	
White Horse Ms *EHAM* E6	95	F2	
Whitehorse Rd *WCHPL* E1	91	E4	
White Horse Rd *WCHPL* E1	91	E5	
White Horse St *MYFR/PICC* W1J	31	D4	
White Kennett St *HDTCH* EC3A	25	D4	
Whitelands Crs *WAND/EARL* SW18...	131	E5	
Whitelegg Rd *PLSTW* E13	93	F1	
Whiteley Rd *NRWD* SE19	155	D5	
White Lion Ct *LOTH* EC2R	24	C5	
PECK SE15 *	120	C2	
White Lion Hl *BLKFR* EC4V	35	D1	
White Lion St *IS* N1	10	A2	
White Lodge Cl *EFNCH* N2	55	D1	
White Lyon Ct *STBT* EC1A	23	D2	
White Oak Gdns *BFN/LL* DA15	145	F5	
White Post La *HOM* E9	79	F4	
White Post St *NWCR* SE14	120	C3	
White Rd *SRTFD* E15	81	E4	
Whites Av *GNTH/NBYPK* IG2	67	E1	
White's Grounds *STHWK* SE1	37	D5	
White's Grounds Est *STHWK* SE1	37	D5	
White's Rw *WCHPL* E1	25	E3	
White's Sq *CLAP* SW4	135	D2	
Whitestone La *HAMP* NW3	54	C5	
Whitestone Wk *HAMP* NW3	54	B5	
Whitethorn St *BOW* E3	92	A3	
White Tower Wy *WCHPL* E1	91	E4	
Whitfield Pl *FITZ* W1T	19	E1	
Whitfield Rd *EHAM* E6	82	C4	
GNWCH SE10	123	D4	
Whitfield St *FITZ* W1T	19	F2	
Whitgift St *STHWK* SE1	45	E4	
Whitings Wy *EHAM* E6	96	A4	
Whitlock Dr *WIM/MER* SW19	131	E5	
Whitman Rd *WCHPL* E1	91	E3	
Whitmore Est *IS* N1	77	E5	
Whitmore Gdns *WLSDN* NW10	88	A1	
Whitmore Rd *IS* N1	77	E5	
Whitnell Wy *PUT/ROE* SW15 *	130	C3	
Whitney Rd *LEY* E10	62	A2	
Whittaker Rd *EHAM* E6	82	A4	
Whittaker St *BCVA* SW1W	42	A5	
Whitta Rd *MNPK* E12	83	D1	
Whittell Gdns *SYD* SE26	156	C3	
Whittingstall Rd *FUL/PGN* SW6	113	F4	
Whittington Av *BANK* EC3V	24	C5	
Whittle Cl *WALTH* E17	61	E1	
Whittlesey St *STHWK* SE1	34	B4	
Whitwell Rd *PLSTW* E13	94	A2	
Whitworth Rd *WOOL/PLUM* SE18	126	A3	
Whitworth St *GNWCH* SE10	123	E1	
Whorlton Rd *PECK* SE15	138	A1	
Whyteville Rd *FSTGT* E7	82	B1	
Wickersley Rd *BTSEA* SW11	116	A5	
Wickers Oake *NRWD* SE19	155	F4	
Wicker St *WCHPL* E1 *	90	A5	
Wickford St *WCHPL* E1	90	C3	
Wickham Cl *WCHPL* E1	90	C4	
Wickham Gdns *BROCKY* SE4	139	F1	
Wickham Ms *BROCKY* SE4	121	F5	
Wickham Rd *BROCKY* SE4	139	F1	
Wickham St *LBTH* SE11	117	F1	
WELL DA16	127	E5	
Wick La *BOW* E3	92	A1	
Wickliffe Gdns *WBLY* HA9	50	A4	
Wicklow St *FSBYW* WC1X	9	E3	
Wick Rd *HOM* E9	79	D3	
Wicks Cl *LEE/GVPK* SE12	160	C1	
Wickwood St *CMBW* SE5	118	B5	
Widdenham Rd *HOLWY* N7	75	F1	
Widdin St *SRTFD* E15	81	E4	
Widecombe Rd *ELTH/MOT* SE9	161	E5	
Widegate St *WCHPL* E1	25	D3	
Widgeon Cl *CAN/RD* E16	94	B5	
Widley Rd *MV/WKIL* W9	2	B4	
Wigginton Av *WBLY* HA9	68	A3	
Wigmore Pl *MHST* W1U *	18	C4	
Wigmore St *MHST* W1U	18	A4	
Wigram Rd *WAN* E11	64	C1	
Wigston Rd *PLSTW* E13	94	B3	
Wigton Pl *LBTH* SE11	118	A1	
Wilberforce Ms *CLAP* SW4	135	D2	
Wilberforce Rd *CDALE/KGS* NW9	52	A1	
FSBYPK N4	58	B4	
Wilbraham Pl *KTBR* SW1X	42	A4	
Wilby Ms *NTGHL* W11	101	F1	
Wilcox Cl *VX/NE* SW8	117	E3	
Wilcox Rd *VX/NE* SW8	117	E3	
Wild Ct *HOL/ALD* WC2B	21	E4	
Wildcroft Rd *PUT/ROE* SW15	130	C5	
Wilde Cl *HACK* E8	78	A5	
Wilde Pl *WAND/EARL* SW18	133	D5	
Wilderness Ms *CLAP* SW4	134	B2	
Wilderton Rd *STNW/STAM* N16	59	E2	
Wildfell Rd *CAT* SE6	140	B5	
Wild Goose Dr *NWCR* SE14	120	C4	
Wild Hatch *GLDGN* NW11	54	A1	
Wild's Rents *STHWK* SE1	48	C2	
Wild St *HOL/ALD* WC2B	21	D5	

Wildwood Cl *LEE/GVPK* SE12 .... 141 F5
Wildwood Gv *HAMP* NW3 .... 54 C3
Wildwood Ri *GLDGN* NW11 .... 54 C3
Wildwood Rd *GLDGN* NW11 .... 54 C3
Wildwood Ter *HAMP* NW3 .... 54 C3
Wilfred St *WESTW* SW1E 43 E2
Wilfrid Gdns *ACT* W3 .... 86 C4
Wilkes St *WCHPL* E1 .... 25 F2
Wilkinson Rd *CAN/RD* E16 .... 94 C5
Wilkinson St *VX/NE* SW8 .... 117 F3
Wilkinson Wy *CHSWK* W4 .... 99 D3
Wilkin St *KTTN* NW5 .... 74 A3
Wilkin Street Ms *KTTN* NW5 .... 74 A3
Wilks Pl *IS* N1 .... 13 D2
Willan Wall *CAN/RD* E16 .... 105 F1
Willard St *VX/NE* SW8 .... 134 B1
Willcott Rd *ACT* W3 .... 98 B2
Will Crooks Gdns *ELTH/MOT* SE9 .... 143 D2
Willenfield Rd *WLSDN* NW10 .... 86 B1
Willenhall Rd *WOOL/PLUM* SE18 .... 126 B1
Willersley Av *BFN/LL* DA15 .... 163 F1
Willersley Cl *BFN/LL* DA15 .... 163 F1
Willesden La *KIL/WHAMP* NW6 .... 71 D4
Willes Rd *KTTN* NW5 .... 74 B3
William Barefoot Dr *ELTH/MOT* SE9 162 A3
William Cl *LEW* SE13 .... 140 C1
William Ellis Wy *BERM/RHTH* SE16 * 102 A4
William Gdns *PUT/ROE* SW15 .... 130 B3
William Guy Gdns *BOW* E3 .... 92 B2
William IV St *CHCR* WC2N 32 C2
William Margrie Cl *PECK* SE15 * 120 A5
William Ms *KTBR* SW1X 41 F1
William Morley Cl *EHAM* E6 .... 83 D5
William Morris Wy *FUL/PGN* SW6 ... 132 C1
William Rd *CAMTN* NW1 .... 7 E4
William's Blds *WCHPL* E1 * 90 C3
Williams Cl *CEND/HSY/T* N8 * 57 D1
FUL/PGN SW6 .... 113 E5
William St *BARK* IG11 .... 84 C4
KTBR SW1X 41 F1
LEY E10 .... 62 B1
Willingham Cl *KTTN* NW5 .... 74 C2
Willingham Ter *KTTN* NW5 * 74 C2
Willington Rd *BRXN/ST* SW9 .... 135 E1
Willis Rd *SRTFD* E15 .... 81 F5
Willis St *POP/IOD* E14 .... 92 B5
Willoughby Rd *HAMP* NW3 .... 73 D1
Willoughby Wy *CHARL* SE7 .... 106 B5
Willow Av *BARN* SW13 .... 111 F5
Willow Bridge Rd *IS* N1 .... 76 C3
Willowbrook Est *PECK* SE15 * 119 F3
Willowbrook Rd *PECK* SE15 .... 119 F2
Willow Cl *CAT* SE6 .... 159 F1
Willowdene *HGT* N6 * 55 F2
Willowfields Cl *WOOL/PLUM* SE18 127 E1
Willow La *WOOL/PLUM* SE18 .... 107 F5
Willow Pl *WEST* SW1P 43 F4
Willow Rd *HAMP* NW3 .... 73 D1
Willows Ter *WLSDN* NW10 * 87 F1
Willow St *SDTCH* EC2A 12 C5
Willow Tree Cl *BOW* E3 .... 79 E5
WAND/EARL SW18 .... 150 B1
Willow V *SHB* W12 .... 100 A2
Willow Wk *STHWK* SE1 .... 48 C5
Willow Wy *NTGHL* W11 .... 101 D1
SYD SE26 .... 156 B3
Will Rd *KTTN* NW5 .... 74 B3
Wilman Gv *HACK* E8 .... 78 A4
Wilmer Gdns *IS* N1 .... 13 D1
Wilmer Lea Cl *SRTFD* E15 .... 80 C4
Wilmer Pl *STNW/STAM* N16 .... 59 F4
Wilmington Av *CHSWK* W4 .... 111 D3
Wilmington Gdns *BARK* IG11 .... 85 D4
Wilmington Sq *FSBYW* WC1X 10 A4
Wilmington St *FSBYW* WC1X 10 A4
Wilmot Cl *PECK* SE15 * 120 A3
Wilmot Pl *CAMTN* NW1 .... 74 C4
Wilmot Rd *LEY* E10 .... 62 B4
Wilmot St *BETH* E2 .... 90 B3
Wilmount St *WOOL/PLUM* SE18 ..... 108 B5
Wilna Rd *WAND/EARL* SW18 .... 132 C5
Wilsham St *NTGHL* W11 .... 101 D2
Wilshaw St *NWCR* SE14 .... 122 A4
Wilson Gv *BERM/RHTH* SE16 .... 102 B3
Wilson Rd *CMBW* SE5 .... 119 D2
IL IG1 .... 65 F2
PLSTW E13 .... 95 D2
Wilson's Pl *POP/IOD* E14 .... 91 F5
Wilson's Rd *HMSMTH* W6 .... 113 D1
Wilson St *LVPST* EC2M 24 B2
Wilton Wk *CHSWK* W4 * 99 F5
Wilton Av *CHSWK* W4 .... 111 E1
Wilton Crs *KTBR* SW1X 42 A1
Wilton Est *HACK* E8 * 78 A3
Wilton Ms *HACK* E8 * 78 B3
KTBR SW1X 42 B2
Wilton Pl *KTBR* SW1X 30 A5
Wilton Rd *PIM* SW1V 43 D3
Wilton Rw *KTBR* SW1X 42 A1
Wilton Sq *IS* N1 .... 77 D5
Wilton St *KTBR* SW1X 42 C2
Wilton Ter *KTBR* SW1X 42 A2
Wilton Vls *IS* N1 .... 77 D5
Wilton Wy *HACK* E8 .... 78 A3
Wiltshire Cl *CHEL* SW3 .... 41 D5
Wiltshire Gdns *FSBYPK* N4 .... 58 C1
Wiltshire Rd *BRXN/ST* SW9 .... 136 A1
Wiltshire Rw *IS* N1 .... 77 D5
Wimbart Rd *BRXS/STRHM* SW2 * ... 135 F5
Wimbledon Park Side *PUT/ROE* SW15. 148 B1
Wimbledon Park Rd *WIM/MER* SW19. 149 E3
WIM/MER SW19 .... 149 E3
Wimbledon Rd *TOOT* SW17 .... 150 C4
Wimbolt St *BETH* E2 .... 90 A2
Wimborne Cl *LEE/GVPK* SE12 .... 141 F3
Wimbourne St *IS* N1 .... 12 A1
Wimpole Ms *CAVSQ/HST* W1G 18 C2
Wimpole St *CAVSQ/HST* W1G 18 C4
Winans Wk *BRXN/ST* SW9 .... 118 A5
Wincanton Rd *WAND/EARL* SW18 .. 131 F5
Winchcomb Gdns *ELTH/MOT* SE9 .. 143 D1
Winchelsea Cl *PUT/ROE* SW15 ...... 131 D3
Winchelsea Rd *FSTGT* E7 .... 82 A1
WLSDN NW10 .... 69 D5
Winchendon Rd *FUL/PGN* SW6 ...... 113 F5
Winchester Av *KIL/WHAMP* NW6 ..... 71 E4
Winchester Cl *LBTH* SE11 * 47 D5
Winchester Pl *HACK* E8 .... 77 F2
HGT N6 .... 56 B3
Winchester Rd *HAMP* NW3 .... 73 D4
HGT N6 .... 56 B3
IL IG1 .... 67 D5
Winchester Sq *STHWK* SE1 .... 36 A3
Winchester St *ACT* W3 .... 98 C2
PIM SW1V 116 B1
Winchester Wk *STHWK* SE1 .... 36 A3
Winchfield Rd *SYD* SE26 .... 157 E5
Wincott St *LBTH* SE11 .... 46 B4
Wincrofts Dr *ELTH/MOT* SE9 .... 145 D2
Windermere Av *KIL/WHAMP* NW6 ..... 71 D5
Windermere Rd *ARCH* N19 * 56 C4
PUT/ROE SW15 .... 147 E4
Winders Rd *BTSEA* SW11 .... 115 E5
Windfield Cl *SYD* SE26 .... 157 D4
Windlass Pl *DEPT* SE8 .... 103 E5
Windlesham Gv *WIM/MER* SW19 .... 149 D1
Windley Cl *FSTH* SE23 .... 156 C2
Windmill Cl *LEW* SE13 * 122 C5
STHWK SE1 * 102 A5
Windmill Dr *CLAP* SW4 .... 134 B3
CRICK NW2 .... 53 E5
Windmill Hl *HAMP* NW3 * 54 C5
Windmill La *SRTFD* E15 .... 81 D3
Windmill Pas *CHSWK* W4 * 99 E5
Windmill Rd *CHSWK* W4 .... 99 E5
WAND/EARL SW18 .... 133 D4
WIM/MER SW19 .... 148 B5
Windmill Rw *LBTH* SE11 * 118 A1
Windmill St *FITZ* W1T 20 A3
Windmill Wk *STHWK* SE1 * 34 B4
Windrose Cl *BERM/RHTH* SE16 ...... 103 D3
Windrush Cl *BTSEA* SW11 * 133 D2
CHSWK W4 .... 110 C3
HACK E8 .... 78 A4
Windrush La *FSTH* SE23 .... 157 D3
Windrush Rd *WLSDN* NW10 .... 69 D5
Windsor Cl *CHST* BR7 .... 162 A5
WNWD SE27 .... 154 C4
Windsor Crs *WBLY* HA9 .... 50 A5
Windsor Gdns *MV/WKIL* W9 .... 14 A1
Windsor Gv *WNWD* SE27 .... 154 C4
Windsor Ms *CAT* SE6 .... 158 C1
CRICK NW2 .... 70 B3
Windsor Rd *CRICK* NW2 .... 70 B3
FSTGT E7 .... 82 B2
HOLWY N7 .... 57 E5
IL IG1 .... 84 C1
LEY E10 .... 62 B4
WAN E11 .... 64 A3

Windsor St *IS* N1	76	B5
Windsor Ter *IS* N1	11	F3
Windsor Wk *CMBW* SE5	119	D5
Windsor Wy *WKENS* W14	101	D5
Windspoint Dr *PECK* SE15	120	B2
Windus Rd *STNW/STAM* N16	59	F3
Wine Cl *WAP* E1W	102	C1
Wine Office Ct *FLST/FETLN* EC4A	22	B4
Winforton St *GNWCH* SE10	122	C4
Winfrith Rd *WAND/EARL* SW18	132	C5
Wingate Rd *HMSMTH* W6	100	B4
IL IG1	84	B2
Wingfield Ms *PECK* SE15	138	A1
Wingfield St *SRTFD* E15	81	E2
Wingfield St *PECK* SE15	138	A1
Wingford Rd *BRXS/STRHM* SW2	135	E4
Wingmore Rd *HNHL* SE24	136	C1
Wingrave Rd *HMSMTH* W6	112	C2
Wingrove Rd *CAT* SE6	159	E2
Winifred St *CAN/RD* E16	107	F2
Winifred Ter *PLSTW* E13	94	A1
Winkley St *BETH* E2	90	B1
Winlaton Rd *BMLY* BR1	159	D4
Winn Common Rd *WOOL/PLUM* SE18	127	E2
Winnett St *SOHO/SHAV* W1D	32	A1
Winnington Cl *EFNCH* N2	55	D1
Winnington Rd *EFNCH* N2	55	D2
Winn Rd *LEE/GVPK* SE12	160	A1
Winscombe St *KTTN* NW5	56	B5
Winsford Rd *CAT* SE6	157	F5
Winsham Gv *BTSEA* SW11	134	A3
Winslade Rd *BRXS/STRHM* SW2	135	E3
Winsland Ms *BAY/PAD* W2	16	A4
Winsland St *BAY/PAD* W2	16	A4
Winsley St *GTPST* W1W	19	E4
Winslow Cl *WLSDN* NW10	51	E5
Winslow Rd *HMSMTH* W6	112	C3
Winsor Ter *EHAM* E6	96	A4
Winstanley Rd *BTSEA* SW11	133	D1
Winston Av *CDALE/KGS* NW9	51	E2
Winston Rd *STNW/STAM* N16	77	D1
Winston Wy *IL* IG1	66	B5
Winter Av *EHAM* E6	83	E5
Winterbourne Rd *CAT* SE6	157	F1
Winterbrook Rd *HNHL* SE24	136	C4
Winterfold Cl *WIM/MER* SW19	149	E2
Winterstoke Rd *FSTH* SE23	157	F1
Winterton Pl *WBPTN* SW10	114	C2
Winterwell Rd *BRXS/STRHM* SW2	135	E3
Winthorpe Rd *PUT/ROE* SW15	131	E2
Winthrop St *WCHPL* E1	90	B4
Winton Wy *STRHM/NOR* SW16	154	A5
Wiseman Rd *LEY* E10	62	A4
Wise Rd *SRTFD* E15	80	C5
Wiseton Rd *TOOT* SW17	151	E1
Wishart Rd *BKHTH/KID* SE3	125	D3
Wisley Rd *BTSEA* SW11	133	F3
Wisteria Cl *IL* IG1	84	B2
Wisteria Rd *LEW* SE13	141	D2
Witanhurst La *HGT* N6	56	A3
Witan St *BETH* E2	90	B2
Witherington Rd *HBRY* N5 *	76	A2
Witherston Wy *ELTH/MOT* SE9	162	A2
Withycombe Rd *WIM/MER* SW19	131	D5
Witley Rd *ARCH* N19	56	C4
Witney Pth *FSTH* SE23	157	D3
Wittersham Rd *BMLY* BR1	159	F5
Wivenhoe Cl *PECK* SE15	138	A1
Wix's La *CLAP* SW4	134	B2
Woburn Pl *STPAN* WC1H	8	C5
Woburn Sq *STPAN* WC1H	20	B1
Woburn Wk *STPAN* WC1H *	8	B4
Wodeham Gdns *WCHPL* E1	90	A4
Wodehouse Av *CMBW* SE5	119	F4
Woking Cl *PUT/ROE* SW15	129	F2
Wolfe Crs *BERM/RHTH* SE16	103	D3
CHARL SE7	125	D1
Wolferton Rd *MNPK* E12	83	F1
Wolfington Rd *WNWD* SE27	154	B4
Wolfram Cl *LEW* SE13	141	E3
Wolftencroft Cl *BTSEA* SW11	133	E1
Wollaston Cl *STHWK* SE1	47	D4
Wolseley Av *WAND/EARL* SW18	150	A2
Wolseley Gdns *CHSWK* W4	110	B2
Wolseley Rd *CEND/HSY/T* N8	57	D1
CHSWK W4	98	C5
FSTGT E7	82	B4
Wolseley St *STHWK* SE1	49	F1
Wolsey Av *EHAM* E6	96	A2
Wolsey Ct *ELTH/MOT* SE9 *	143	F4
Wolsey Ms *KTTN* NW5	74	C3
Wolsey Rd *IS* N1	77	D2
Wolsey St *WCHPL* E1	90	C4
Wolverley St *BETH* E2 *	90	B2
Wolverton Gdns *HMSMTH* W6	101	D5
Womersley Rd *CEND/HSY/T* N8	57	F1
Wontner Cl *IS* N1	76	C4
Wontner Rd *BAL* SW12	151	F2
Woodbank Rd *BMLY* BR1	159	F3
Woodberry Down *FSBYPK* N4	58	C3
Woodberry Gv *FSBYPK* N4	58	C2
Woodbine Pl *WAN* E11	64	A1
Woodbine Rd *BFN/LL* DA15	163	E1
Woodbine Ter *HOM* E9 *	78	C3
Woodborough Rd *PUT/ROE* SW15	130	B2
Woodbourne Av *STRHM/NOR* SW16	153	D3
Woodbridge Cl *HOLWY* N7	57	F4
Woodbridge Rd *BARK* IG11	85	F2
Woodbridge St *CLKNW* EC1R	10	C5
Woodbury Gdns *LEE/GVPK* SE12	160	B3
Woodbury St *TOOT* SW17	151	E5
Woodchester Sq *BAY/PAD* W2	14	C2
Woodchurch Rd *KIL/WHAMP* NW6	72	A4
Wood Cl *BETH* E2	90	A3
CDALE/KGS NW9	51	D2
Woodcocks *CAN/RD* E16	94	C4
Woodcombe Av *FSTH* SE23	156	C5
Woodcote Pl *WNWD* SE27 *	154	B5
Woodcote Rd *WAN* E11	64	A2
Woodcroft *ELTH/MOT* SE9	161	F3
Woodcroft Ms *DEPT* SE8	103	E5
Wood Dene *PECK* SE15 *	120	B4
Wooden Bridge Ter *WNWD* SE27 *	154	B3
Wooder Gdns *FSTGT* E7	81	F1
Woodfall Rd *FSBYPK* N4	58	A3
Woodfall St *CHEL* SW3	115	F1
Woodfarrs *CMBW* SE5	137	D2
Wood Fld *HAMP* NW3 *	73	F2
Woodfield Av *STRHM/NOR* SW16	153	D3
Woodfield Cl *WNWD* SE27 *	154	B5
Woodfield La *STRHM/NOR* SW16	153	D3
Woodfield Pl *MV/WKIL* W9	89	F4
Woodfield Rd *MV/WKIL* W9	89	F4
Woodford Rd *FSTGT* E7	82	B1
Woodger Rd *SHB* W12	100	B3
Woodget Cl *EHAM* E6	95	E5
Woodgrange Rd *FSTGT* E7	82	A2
Woodhall Av *DUL* SE21	155	F3
Woodhall Dr *DUL* SE21	155	F3
Woodham Rd *CAT* SE6	158	C3
Woodhatch Cl *EHAM* E6	95	E4
Woodheyes Rd *WLSDN* NW10	69	E2
Woodhill *WOOL/PLUM* SE18	107	E5
Woodhouse Cl *EDUL* SE22	138	A2
Woodhouse Gv *FSTGT* E7	82	B3
Woodhouse Rd *WAN* E11	63	F5
Woodhurst Rd *ACT* W3	98	C2
Woodington Cl *ELTH/MOT* SE9	144	A4
Woodland Cl *CDALE/KGS* NW9	50	C1
Woodland Crs *BERM/RHTH* SE16	103	D3
GNWCH SE10	123	E2
Woodland Gv *GNWCH* SE10	123	E1
Woodland Ms *STRHM/NOR* SW16	153	E3
Woodland Rd *NRWD* SE19	155	E5
Woodlands *GLDGN* NW11	53	E1
Woodlands Av *ACT* W3	98	B2
BFN/LL DA15	163	E1
WAN E11	64	B3
Woodlands Park Rd *GNWCH* SE10	123	E2
Woodlands Rd *BARN* SW13	129	F1
IL IG1	66	C5
WAN E11	63	E4
Woodlands St *LEW* SE13	141	D5
The Woodlands *BRXN/ST* SW9 *	135	F1
LEW SE13	141	D5
Woodland St *HACK* E8 *	77	F3
Woodlands Wy *PUT/ROE* SW15	131	F3
Woodland Ter *CHARL* SE7	107	F5
Woodland Wk *HAMP* NW3	73	E2
Wood La *CDALE/KGS* NW9	51	D2
HGT N6	56	B1
SHB W12	100	C1
Woodlawn Cl *PUT/ROE* SW15	131	F3
Woodlawn Rd *FUL/PGN* SW6	113	D3
Woodlea Rd *STNW/STAM* N16	59	E5
Woodleigh Gdns *STRHM/NOR* SW16	153	E3
Woodman Ms *RCH/KEW* TW9	110	B4
Woodmans Gv *WLSDN* NW10	69	F2
Woodman Rd *CAN/RD* E16	108	A2

Woodmere *ELTH/MOT* SE9 .... 143 F5
Woodmere Av *BRYLDS* KT5 .... 134 A1
Woodmill Rd *CLPT* E5 .... 60 C4
Woodnook Rd *STRHM/NOR* SW16... 152 B5
Woodpecker Ms *LEW* SE13 .... 141 D2
Woodriffe Rd *WAN* E11 .... 63 D2
Wood Rd *WLSDN* NW10 .... 68 C4
Woodrow *WOOL/PLUM* SE18 .... 107 F5
Woodrush Cl *NWCR* SE14 .... 121 E3
Woodseer St *WCHPL* E1 .... 25 F2
Woodsford Sq *WKENS* W14 .... 101 E5
Woodside *WIM/MER* SW19 .... 94 C5
Woodside Av *CHST* BR7 .... 162 C5
Woodside Crs *BFN/LL* DA15 * 163 E3
Woodside Pde *BFN/LL* DA15 * 163 E3
Woodside Rd *BFN/LL* DA15 .... 163 E3
   PLSTW E13 .... 94 C3
Woodsome Ms *MYFR/PKLN* W1K 29 F1
Woodsome Rd *KTTN* NW5 .... 56 A5
Woodspring Rd *WIM/MER* SW19.... 149 E2
Wood's Rd *PECK* SE15 .... 120 B4
Woodstock Av *GLDGN* NW11 .... 53 E2
Woodstock Gv *SHB* W12 .... 101 D3
Woodstock Ms *CAVSQ/HST* W1G.... 18 B3
Woodstock Rd *CHSWK* W4 .... 99 E5
   FSBYPK N4 .... 58 A3
   FSTGT E7 .... 82 C4
   GLDGN NW11 .... 53 F2
Woodstock St *CAN/RD* E16 .... 95 F5
   OXSTW W1C 18 C5
Woodstock Ter *POP/IOD* E14 .... 104 B1
Wood St *BARB* EC2Y 23 F3
   CAN/RD E16 .... 106 B1
   CHSWK W4 .... 111 E1
   CITYW EC2V 23 F4
Woodsyre *SYD* SE26 .... 155 F4
Wood Ter *CRICK* NW2 * 51 F4
Woodthorpe Rd *PUT/ROE* SW15 .. 130 B2
Wood V *FSTH* SE23 .... 156 B1
Woodvale Av *GLDGN* NW11 .... 53 D5
Woodview Cl *PUT/ROE* SW15 ...... 147 D4
Woodville Cl *LEE/GVPK* SE12 .... 142 A3
Woodville Rd *GLDGN* NW11 .... 53 E2
   KIL/WHAMP NW6 * 89 F1
   STNW/STAM N16 .... 77 E2
   WAN E11 .... 63 F3
Woodville St *WOOL/PLUM* SE18 .. 107 E5
Woodwarde Rd *EDUL* SE22 .... 137 E4
Woodwell St *WAND/EARL* SW18 .. 132 C3
Wood Wharf *GNWCH* SE10 .... 122 B2
Woodyard Cl *KTTN* NW5 .... 74 A2
Woodyard La *DUL* SE21 .... 137 E5
Woodyates Rd *LEE/GVPK* SE12 .... 142 A4
Woolacombe Rd *BKHTH/KID* SE3... 124 C5
Wooler St *WALW* SE17 .... 119 D1
Woolf Ms *STPAN* WC1H * 8 C5
Woollaston Rd *FSBYPK* N4 .... 58 B1
Woolmead Av *CDALE/KGS* NW9... 52 A2
Woolmore St *POP/IOD* E14 .... 104 C1
Woolneigh St *FUL/PGN* SW6 .... 132 B1
Woolridge Wy *HOM* E9 * 78 C4
Woolstaplers Wy *BERM/RHTH* SE16.. 102 A4
Woolstone Rd *FSTH* SE23 .... 157 E2
Woolwich Church St
   WOOL/PLUM SE18 .... 107 D5
Woolwich Common
   WOOL/PLUM SE18 .... 126 A2
Woolwich Foot Tnl *CAN/RD* E16 ... 108 A3
Woolwich High St *WOOL/PLUM* SE18.. 108 A4
Woolwich Manorway *CAN/RD* E16.. 108 B3
Woolwich Manor Wy *EHAM* E6 ...... 95 F5
Woolwich New Rd *WOOL/PLUM* SE18.. 108 B5
   WOOL/PLUM SE18 .... 126 A1
Woolwich Rd *CHARL* SE7 .... 106 C5
   GNWCH SE10 .... 124 A1
Wooster Gdns *POP/IOD* E14 .... 93 D5
Wootton St *STHWK* SE1 .... 34 B5
Worcester Cl *CRICK* NW2 .... 52 A5
Worcester Dr *CHSWK* W4 .... 99 E4
Worcester Gdns *IL* IG1 .... 65 E2
Worcester Ms *MNPK* E12 .... 65 F5
   WIM/MER SW19 .... 149 F5
Wordsworth Av *MNPK* E12 .... 83 E4
Wordsworth Pl *HAMP* NW3 .... 73 F2
Wordsworth Rd *STHWK* SE1 .... 49 E5
   STNW/STAM N16 .... 77 E1
   WELL DA16 .... 127 E4
Worfield St *BTSEA* SW11 .... 115 E3
Worgan St *BERM/RHTH* SE16 ...... 103 D4

Worland Rd *SRTFD* E15 .... 81 E4
Worlds End *SRTFD* E15 * 117 F1
Worlds End Est *WBPTN* SW10 * .. 115 D5
Worlds End Pas *WBPTN* SW10 * .. 115 D3
Worlidge St *HMSMTH* W6 .... 112 C1
Worlingham Rd *EDUL* SE22 .... 137 F2
Wormholt Rd *SHB* W12 .... 100 A2
Wormholt Ter *SHB* W12 * 100 A2
Wormwood St *OBST* EC2N 24 C4
Wornington Rd *NKENS* W10 .... 89 E4
Woronzow Rd *STJWD* NW8 .... 73 D5
Worple St *MORT/ESHN* SW14 ...... 129 D1
Worship St *SDTCH* EC2A 24 B1
Worslade Rd *TOOT* SW17 .... 151 D4
Worsley Bridge Rd *SYD* SE26 .... 157 F5
Worsley Gv *CLPT* E5 .... 78 A1
Worsley Rd *WAN* E11 .... 81 E1
Worsopp Dr *CLAP* SW4 .... 134 C3
Worth Gv *WALW* SE17 * 119 D1
Worthing Cl *SRTFD* E15 .... 81 E5
Wortley Rd *EHAM* E6 .... 83 D4
Wotton Rd *CRICK* NW2 .... 70 C1
   DEPT SE8 .... 121 F2
Wouldham Rd *CAN/RD* E16 .... 93 F5
Wragby Rd *WAN* E11 * 63 E5
Wray Crs *FSBYPK* N4 .... 57 E4
Wrekin Rd *WOOL/PLUM* SE18 ...... 126 C3
Wren Av *CRICK* NW2 .... 70 C1
Wren Cl *CAN/RD* E16 .... 93 F5
Wren Ms *LEW* SE13 * 141 E2
Wren Rd *CMBW* SE5 .... 119 D4
Wren St *FSBW* WC1X 9 F5
Wrentham Av *WLSDN* NW10 .... 89 D1
Wrenthorpe Rd *BMLY* BR1 .... 159 E4
Wrexham Rd *BOW* E3 .... 92 A1
Wricklemarsh Rd *BKHTH/KID* SE3.. 124 B5
Wrigglesworth St *NWCR* SE14 .... 121 D3
Wright Cl *LEW* SE13 .... 141 D2
Wright's La *KENS* W8 .... 38 C2
Wrights Pl *WLSDN* NW10 * 68 C3
Wright's Rd *BOW* E3 .... 91 F1
Wrotham Rd *CAMTN* NW1 * 74 C4
Wrottesley Rd *WLSDN* NW10 .... 88 A1
   WOOL/PLUM SE18 .... 126 C2
Wroughton Rd *BTSEA* SW11 .... 133 F4
Wroxton Rd *PECK* SE15 .... 120 B5
Wulfstan St *SHB* W12 .... 87 F5
Wyatt Dr *BARN* SW13 .... 112 B2
Wyatt Park Rd *BRXS/STRHM* SW2.. 153 F2
Wyatt Rd *FSTGT* E7 .... 82 A3
   HBRY N5 .... 58 C5
Wybert St *CAMTN* NW1 .... 7 D5
Wyborne Wy *WLSDN* NW10 .... 68 C4
Wychcombe Studios *HAMP* NW3 *.. 73 F3
Wycherley Cl *BKHTH/KID* SE3 ..... 123 E5
Wychwood End *HGT* N6 .... 56 C2
Wycliffe Cl *WELL* DA16 .... 127 F4
Wycliffe Rd *BTSEA* SW11 .... 116 A5
Wyclif St *FSBYE* EC1V 10 C4
Wycombe Gdns *GLDGN* NW11 ...... 53 F4
Wycombe Pl *WAND/EARL* SW18 .. 132 C4
Wycombe Rd *ALP/SUD* HA0 .... 68 A5
Wycombe Sq *KENS* W8 .... 26 A4
Wydeville Manor Rd *LEE/GVPK* SE12.. 160 B4
Wye St *BTSEA* SW11 .... 133 D1
Wyfold Rd *FUL/PGN* SW6 .... 113 D3
Wyke Rd *BOW* E3 .... 80 A4
Wyldes Cl *GLDGN* NW11 .... 54 C3
Wyld Wy *WBLY* HA9 .... 68 B3
Wyleu St *FSTH* SE23 .... 139 E5
Wyllen Cl *WCHPL* E1 .... 90 C3
Wymering Rd *MV/WKIL* W9 .... 2 B4
Wymond St *PUT/ROE* SW15 .... 130 C1
Wynan Rd *POP/IOD* E14 .... 122 B1
Wyncham Av *BFN/LL* DA15 .... 163 E1
Wyndale Av *CDALE/KGS* NW9 .... 50 A1
Wyndcliff Rd *CHARL* SE7 .... 124 B2
Wyndham Crs *KTTN* NW5 .... 56 C5
Wyndham Est *CMBW* SE5 .... 118 C3
Wyndham Ms *MBLAR* W1H 17 E3
Wyndham Pl *MBLAR* W1H 17 E3
Wyndham Rd *CMBW* SE5 .... 118 C3
   EHAM E6 .... 83 D4
Wyndham St *CAMTN* NW1 .... 17 E2
Wyndham Yd *MBLAR* W1H * 17 E3
Wyneham Rd *HNHL* SE24 .... 137 D3
Wynell Rd *FSTH* SE23 .... 157 D3
Wynford Rd *IS* N1 .... 9 E1
Wynford Wy *ELTH/MOT* SE9 .... 161 F3
Wynne Rd *BRXN/ST* SW9 .... 118 A5
Wynnstay Gdns *KENS* W8 .... 38 B2
Wynter St *BTSEA* SW11 .... 132 C2

Wynton Pl *ACT* W3	86	B5
Wynyard Ter *LBTH* SE11 *	117	F1
Wynyatt St *FSBYE* EC1V	10	C3
Wythburn Pl *MBLAR* W1H	17	E5
Wythes Rd *CAN/RD* E16	107	E2
Wythfield Rd *ELTH/MOT* SE9	143	F4
Wyvil Rd *VX/NE* SW8	117	E3
Wyvis St *POP/IOD* E14	92	B4

Y

Yabsley St *POP/IOD* E14	104	C2
Yalding Rd *BERM/RHTH* SE16	102	A4
Yardley St *FSBYW* WC1X	10	A4
Yarmouth Pl *MYFR/PICC* W1J	30	C4
Yarrow Crs *EHAM* E6	95	E4
Yateley St *WOOL/PLUM* SE18	107	D4
Yeate St *IS* N1	7	D4
Yeatman Rd *HGT* N6	55	F1
Yeats Cl *LEW* SE13	123	D5
WLSDN NW10	69	E3
Yeldham Rd *HMSMTH* W6	113	D1
Yeldham Vls *HMSMTH* W6 *	113	D1
Yelverton Rd *BTSEA* SW11	115	D5
Yeoman Cl *EHAM* E6	108	B1
Yeoman's Rw *CHEL* SW3	41	D3
Yeoman St *BERM/RHTH* SE16	103	E5
Yeoman's Yd *WCHPL* E1	37	F1
Yeo St *BOW* E3	92	B4
Yerbury Rd *ARCH* N19	57	D5
Yewfield Rd *WLSDN* NW10	69	F3
Yew Gv *CRICK* NW2	71	D1
Yew Tree Cl *LEW* SE13	140	F1
Yew Tree Rd *SHB* W12	99	F1
Yoakley Rd *STNW/STAM* N16	59	E4
Yoke Cl *HOLWY* N7	75	E3
Yolande Gdns *ELTH/MOT* SE9	143	E3
Yonge Pk *HOLWY* N7	58	A5
York Av *BFN/LL* DA15	163	E2
MORT/ESHN SW14	128	C3
York Br *CAMTN* NW1	6	A5
York Blds *CHCR* WC2N	33	D2
York Cl *CMBW* SE5 *	118	C5
EHAM E6	95	F5
York Ga *CAMTN* NW1	18	B1
York Gv *PECK* SE15	120	C4

York Hl *WNWD* SE27	154	B3
York House Pl *KENS* W8	26	C5
Yorkland Av *WELL* DA16	145	E5
York Ms *IL* IG1	66	C4
KTTN NW5	74	B2
York Pde *CDALE/KGS* NW9 *	52	A1
York Pl *BTSEA* SW11	132	C1
IL IG1	66	A4
York Ri *KTTN* NW5	56	B5
York Rd *ACT* W3	86	C5
BTSEA SW11	132	C2
FSTGT E7	82	A3
IL IG1	66	A5
LEY E10	62	C5
STHWK SE1	33	F5
Yorkshire Cl *STNW/STAM* N16	59	E5
Yorkshire Grey Yd *GINN* WC1R *	21	E5
Yorkshire Rd *POP/IOD* E14	91	E5
York Sq *POP/IOD* E14	91	E5
York St *MBLAR* W1H	17	E3
MHST W1U	17	F2
York Street Chambers *MHST* W1U *	17	F2
York Ter East *CAMTN* NW1	18	B1
York Ter West *CAMTN* NW1	18	A1
Yorkton St *BETH* E2	90	A1
York Wy *HOLWY* N7	75	D3
York Way Ct *IS* N1	75	E5
York Way Est *HOLWY* N7	75	E3
Young Rd *CAN/RD* E16	94	C5
Young St *KENS* W8	38	C1
Yoxley Ap *GNTH/NBYPK* IG2	66	C1
Yoxley Dr *GNTH/NBYPK* IG2	66	C1
Yukon Rd *BAL* SW12	134	B5

Z

Zampa Rd *BERM/RHTH* SE16	120	C1
Zander Ct *BETH* E2	90	A2
Zangwill Rd *BKHTH/KID* SE3	125	D4
Zealand Rd *BOW* E3	91	E1
Zennor Rd *BAL* SW12	152	C1
Zenoria St *EDUL* SE22	137	F2
Zetland St *POP/IOD* E14	92	C4
Zoar St *STHWK* SE1	35	E3
Zoffany St *ARCH* N19	57	D4

Index - featured places

02 Centre		
HAMP NW3	72	C3
2 Willow Road (NT)		
HAMP NW3	73	E1
7/7 Memorial		
MYFR/PKLN W1K	30	B4
30 St Mary Axe		
HDTCH EC3A	25	D5
41 Hotel		
BGVA SW1W	43	F2
51 Buckingham Gate		
WESTW SW1E	43	F2
Abbey Business Centre		
VX/NE SW8	116	C4
Abbey Christian School for the		
English Language		
STJWD NW8	3	F2
Abbey College London		
BAY/PAD W2	14	B5
Abbey Lane Commercial Estate		
SRTFD E15	93	D1
Abbey Medical Centre		
STJWD NW8	72	B5
Abbey Park Industrial Estate		
BARK IG11	96	B1
Abbey Road ⊖		
SRTFD E15	93	D1
Abbey Road Health Centre		
SRTFD E15	81	E5
Abbey Road Studios		
STJWD NW8	3	F2
Abbey Sports Centre		
BARK IG11	84	C5
Abbey Trading Estate		
SYD SE26	157	E5

Abbey Wharf		
Industrial Estate		
BARK IG11	97	D2
ABC Cinema		
PUT/ROE SW15	131	E1
Abercorn Place School		
CAMTN NW1	17	D2
Abercorn School		
MBLAR W1H	17	E3
STJWD NW8	3	F2
Aberdeen Wharf		
WAP E1W	102	B2
Abingdon House School		
KENS W8	38	B2
Abney Park Cemetery		
STNW/STAM N16	59	E4
Acacia Business Centre		
WAN E11	63	E5
The Academy at Peckham		
PECK SE15	119	F4
The Academy School		
HAMP NW3	73	D1
Acland Burghley School		
KTTN NW5	74	B1
Acton Business Centre		
WLSDN NW10	87	D3
Acton Central ⊖		
ACT W3	99	D2
Acton Central		
Industrial Estate		
ACT W3	98	B1
Acton Health Centre		
ACT W3	98	C2
Acton High School		
ACT W3	98	A3

Acton Hospital
ACT W3 .... 98 A3

Acton Lane Medical Centre
CHSWK W4 .... 98 C3

Acton Main Line ≠
ACT W3 .... 86 C5

Acton Park Industrial Estate
ACT W3 .... 99 D3

Acton Superbowl
ACT W3 .... 86 A4

Acton Swimming Baths
ACT W5 .... 98 C2

Acton Town ⊖
ACT W5 .... 98 A3

Adams Bridge Business Centre
WBLY HA9 .... 68 B2

Adamsrill Primary School
SYD SE26 .... 157 E3

Addey & Stanhope School
NWCR SE14 .... 121 F4

Addison Primary School
WKENS W14 .... 101 D4

Adelphi Theatre
COVGDN WC2E 33 C2

Admiral Hyson
Industrial Estate
STHWK SE1 .... 102 B5

Admiralty Arch
STJS SW1Y 32 B3

The Adult College of Barking
& Dagenham
BARK IG11 .... 85 E3

Africa Centre
COVGDN WC2E 33 D1

Aga Khan University
CAN/RD E16 .... 93 F4
RSQ WC1B 20 B3

Agnew's
CONDST W1S 31 E3

Agora Shopping Centre
PECK SE15 .... 120 A5

AHA International
London Centre
BMSBY WC1N 21 F2

Airedale Physiotherapy Clinic
CHSWK W4 .... 111 F1

Aksaray Sports Club
STNW/STAM N16 .... 77 D1

Albany Centre & Theatre
DEPT SE8 .... 121 F3

Albemarle Primary School
WIM/MER SW19 .... 149 E2

Albert Memorial
SKENS SW7 .... 28 A5

Albion College
RSQ WC1B 20 C3

Albion Health Centre
WCHPL E1 .... 90 B4

Albion J & I School
BERM/RHTH SE16 .... 102 C3

Albion Street Health Centre
BERM/RHTH SE16 .... 102 C3

Alchemea
IS N1 .... 76 B5

The Alchemy Gallery
CLKNW EC1R 10 A5

Alderbrook Primary School
BAL SW12 .... 134 B5

Aldersbrook County
Secondary School
MNPK E12 .... 64 C3

Aldersbrook Primary School
MNPK E12 .... 64 B3

Alderwood Primary School
ELTH/MOT SE9 .... 145 D4

Aldgate ⊖
TWRH EC3N 25 E5

Aldgate Bus Station
HDTCH EC3A 25 E4

Aldgate East ⊖
WCHPL E1 .... 25 F4

Aldwych Theatre
HOL/ALD WC2B 21 E5

Al Falah Boys School
CLPT E5 .... 60 B5

Alfred Salter Primary School
BERM/RHTH SE16 .... 103 D3

Allen Edwards Primary School
CLAP SW4 .... 117 E4

The All England Lawn Tennis &
Croquet Club
WIM/MER SW19 .... 149 D3

Allergy Clinic
CAVSQ/HST W1G 18 C3

Alleyns Junior School
EDUL SE22 .... 137 E3

Allfarthing JMI School
WAND/EARL SW18 .... 132 C4

All Saints ⊖
POP/IOD E14 .... 92 B5

All Saints CE Primary School
BKHTH/KID SE3 .... 123 E5
CRICK NW2 .... 53 F5
FUL/PGN SW6 .... 113 E5
PUT/ROE SW15 .... 130 C1

All Souls CE Primary School
GTPST W1W 19 E3

Allum Medical Centre
WAN E11 .... 63 D2

Alma Primary School
BERM/RHTH SE16 .... 102 A5

Almeida Theatre
IS N1 .... 76 B4

Alpine Business Centre
EHAM E6 .... 96 A4

Al-Risaala Boys Secondary School
BAL SW12 .... 152 B1

Al Sadiq & Al-Zahra High School
KIL/WHAMP NW6 .... 71 E5

Alscot Road Industrial Estate
STHWK SE1 .... 49 F4

Altmore Infant School
EHAM E6 .... 83 F4

The Alton School
PUT/ROE SW15 .... 129 F5

Ambler Primary School
FSBYPK N4 .... 58 B5

AMC Business Centre
WLSDN NW10 .... 86 B2

American Intercontinental University
MHST W1U 18 B3

AMF Bowling
LEW SE13 .... 140 C1

Ampthill Square Medical Centre
CAMTN NW1 .... 7 F2

Anchorage Point Industrial Estate
CHARL SE7 .... 106 C4

Anchor Retail Park
WCHPL E1 .... 90 C3

AndAZ Hotel
LVPST EC2M 24 C3

Andover Medical Centre
HOLWY N7 .... 57 F5

Angel ⊖
IS N1 .... 10 C1

Angerstein Business Park
GNWCH SE10 .... 106 A5

Anglian Industrial Estate
BARK IG11 .... 97 F3

Annemount School
EFNCH N2 .... 54 C1

Anson Primary School
CRICK NW2 .... 71 D2

Apex Hotel
MON EC3R 37 D1

Apex Industrial Estate
WLSDN NW10 .... 87 F3

Apex Primary School
IL IG1 .... 66 A4

Apollo Theatre
SOHO/SHAV W1D 32 A1

Apollo Victoria Theatre
PIM SW1V 43 E3

Apostolic Nuncio
WIM/MER SW19 .... 148 C3

Apsley House,
The Wellington Museum
KTBR SW1X 30 B5

Aquarius Business Park
CRICK NW2 .... 52 A3

Aquarius Golf Club
EDUL SE22 .... 138 C3

Arcadia University
BAY/PAD W2 .... 26 C2

Archbishop Sumners CE
Primary School
LBTH SE11 .... 46 B5

Archbishop Tenison's School
VX/NE SW8 .... 117 F2

Arches Leisure Centre
GNWCH SE10 .... 123 D2

Architecture Association
School of Architecture
RSQ WC1B 20 A3

Archway ⊖
ARCH N19 ....56 C4
Archway Business Centre
ARCH N19 ....57 D5
Archway Leisure Centre
ARCH N19 ....56 C4
Arena Estate
FSBYPK N4 ....58 B1
Argyle Primary School
STPAN WC1H 9 D4
Arklow Trading Estate
NWCR SE14 ....121 E2
Armourers & Braziers' Hall
LOTH EC2R 24 A3
Arndale Health Centre
WAND/EARL SW18 ....132 A4
Arnhem Wharf
  Primary School
POP/IOD E14 ....103 F4
Arnold House School
STJWD NW8 ....4 A1
Arsenal ⊖
HBRY N5 ....58 A5
Arsenal FC
  (Emirates Stadium)
HOLWY N7 ....76 A1
The Arts Educational School
CHSWK W4 ....99 E5
Arts Theatre
LSQ/SEVD WC2H 32 B1
Ashburnham Primary School
WBPTN SW10 ....115 D3
Ashby Mill
BRXS/STRHM SW2 ....135 E4
Ashby Mill School
CLAP SW4 ....135 E3
Ashcroft Technology Academy
PUT/ROE SW15 ....131 F3
Ashleigh Commercial Estate
CHARL SE7 ....106 C5
Ashmead Primary School
BROCKY SE4 ....122 A5
Ashmole Primary School
VX/NE SW8 ....117 F2
Ashmount Primary School
ARCH N19 ....57 D2
Aspen House School
LBTH SE11 ....118 B2
Aspen House Secondary &
  Primary School
BRXS/STRHM SW2 ....153 E1
Associated Newspapers Offices
BERM/RHTH SE16 ....103 D4
Atheney Primary School
CAT SE6 ....158 A3
Athenaeum Hotel
MYFR/PICC W1J 30 C4
Athena Medical Centre
CLPT E5 ....78 C1
Atherton Leisure Centre
SRTFD E15 ....81 F3
Athlone House Hospital
HGT N6 ....55 F3
Atlantic House
  (Richmond American
  International University)
KENS W8 ....39 E2
Atlas Business Centre
CRICK NW2 ....52 B4
Atlas Transport Estate
BTSEA SW11 ....114 C5
Attlee Youth &
  Community Centre
WCHPL E1 ....25 F3
Australia House
HOL/ALD WC2B 21 F5
Avenue Pre-Preparatory School
HGT N6 ....56 B2
Avenue Primary School
MNPK E12 ....83 E1
Avondale Park Primary School
NTGHL W11 ....101 D1
Avon Trading Estate
WKENS W14 ....101 F5
Axis Business Centre
SRTFD E15 ....80 B5
The Aylesham Centre
PECK SE15 ....120 A4
Azhar Academy
FSTGT E7 ....82 A3
B6 Sixth Form College
CLPT E5 ....60 B5

Bacon's College
BERM/RHTH SE16 ....103 E2
Baden Powell House
SKENS SW7 ....39 F4
Baglioni Hotel
KENS W8 ....39 E1
Bakers Hall
MON EC3R 37 D2
Baker Street ⊖
CAMTN NW1 ....17 F1
Balaam Leisure Centre
PLSTW E13 ....94 A3
Bales College
NKENS W10 ....89 D2
Balham ≷ ⊖
BAL SW12 ....152 B1
Balham Girls Preparatory
  Secondary School
TOOT SW17 ....151 F3
Balham Health Centre
BAL SW12 ....152 B2
Balham Leisure Centre
TOOT SW17 ....152 A2
Balmoral Trading Estate
BARK IG11 ....97 F3
Baltic Exchange
HDTCH EC3A 25 D4
Bangabandhu Primary School
BETH E2 ....90 C2
Bank ⊖
LOTH EC2R 24 A5
Bank of England Extension
CITYW EC2V 23 E5
Bank of England (& Museum)
LOTH EC2R 24 A5
Bankside Gallery
STHWK SE1 ....35 D2
Bankside Jetty
STHWK SE1 ....35 E2
Bannockburn Primary School
WOOL/PLUM SE18 ....109 F5
The Banqueting House, Whitehall
WHALL SW1A 32 C4
Barbara Speake
  Theatre School
ACT W3 ....99 E1
Barber Surgeons' Hall
BARB EC2Y 23 F3
Barbican ⊖
FARR EC1M 23 D2
Barbican Cinema
BARB EC2Y 23 E2
Barbican Exhibition Halls
BARB EC2Y 23 F2
The Barbican
BARB EC2Y 23 E2
Barbican Theatre
BARB EC2Y 23 F2
Barclay Primary School
LEY E10 ....63 D1
Baring Primary School
LEE/GVPK SE12 ....142 A5
Baring Road Medical Centre
BMLY BR1 ....160 A2
Barkantine Clinic
POP/IOD E14 ....104 A3
Barking ≷ ⊖
BARK IG11 ....84 C4
Barking Abbey
  Comprehensive School (Lower)
IL IG1 ....85 D2
Barking Abbey
  Comprehensive School (Upper)
BARK IG11 ....85 F3
Barking Abbey Industrial Estate
BARK IG11 ....84 B5
Barking Abbey School
BARK IG11 ....85 F3
Barking Hospital
BARK IG11 ....85 F4
Barking Industrial Park
BARK IG11 ....85 F5
Barlby Primary School
NKENS W10 ....89 D3
Barn Croft Primary School
WALTH E17 ....61 E1
Barn Elms Athletics Track
BARN SW13 ....112 B5
Barn Elms Sports Centre
BARN SW13 ....112 C4
Barn Elms Water Sports Centre
PUT/ROE SW15 ....112 C5

Barnes ≥
BARN SW13 ....**130** A1
Barnes Bridge ≥
BARN SW13 ....**111** E5
Barnes Hospital
MORT/ESHN SW14 ....**129** E1
Barnes Primary School
BARN SW13 ....**129** E1
Barnes Sports Club
BARN SW13 ....**111** F4
Barnet College
HDN NW4 ....**52** A1
Barnsbury Complex
HOLWY N7 ....**76** A4
Barnsbury School for Girls
IS N1 ....**76** A3
Barons Court ⊖
WKENS W14 ....**113** E1
Barons Court Theatre
WKENS W14 ....**113** E1
Barratt Industrial Park
BOW E3 ....**92** C3
Barrow Hill Junior School
STJWD NW8 ....**4** C2
Barton House Health Centre
STNW/STAM N16 ....**59** D5
Bassett House School
NKENS W10 ....**89** D5
Bath Factory Estate
HNHL SE24 ....**136** C4
Battersea Arts Centre (BAC)
BTSEA SW11 ....**133** F1
Battersea Business Centre
BTSEA SW11 ....**134** A1
Battersea Dogs' Home
VX/NE SW8 ....**116** B3
Battersea Park ≥
BTSEA SW11 ....**116** B3
Battersea Power Station
(under redevelopment)
VX/NE SW8 ....**116** B3
Battersea Sports Centre
BTSEA SW11 ....**133** D1
Battersea Technology College
BTSEA SW11 ....**115** F4
Battersea Tutorial College
TOOT SW17 ....**152** A2
Bayswater ⊖
BAY/PAD W2 ....**27** C1
BBC Broadcasting House
REGST W1B **19** D3
BBC Media Village
SHB W12 ....**100** C1
BBC Studios
MV/WKIL W9 ....**2** C5
BBC Television Centre
SHB W12 ....**100** C1
BBC Worldwide
SHB W12 ....**88** C5
Beatrice Tate School
BETH E2 ....**90** B2
Beatrix Potter
Primary School
WAND/EARL SW18 ....**150** C1
The Beaufort Hotel
CHEL SW3 ....**41** E3
Beaumont Primary School
LEY E10 ....**62** C1
Beaver College
BAY/PAD W2 ....**26** C2
Beckenham Hill ≥
CAT SE6 ....**158** C5
Beckford Primary School
KIL/WHAMP NW6 ....**71** F2
Beckton ⊖
EHAM E6 ....**96** A4
Beckton Park ⊖
EHAM E6 ....**107** F1
Beckton Ski Centre
EHAM E6 ....**96** A3
Beckton Special School
CAN/RD E16 ....**95** D4
Beckton Triangle Retail Park
EHAM E6 ....**96** B2
Bective House Clinic
PUT/ROE SW15 ....**131** F2
Bedford Hotel
RSQ WC1B **21** D2
Beechwood School
STRHM/NOR SW16 ....**153** E3
The Beehive School
ARCH N19 ....**57** D2

Beis Hamedrash Elyon
GLDGN NW11 ....**53** E2
Beis Malka Girls School
STNW/STAM N16 ....**59** F3
Beis Rochel D'Satmar Girls School
STNW/STAM N16 ....**59** E2
Bellamy's Wharf
BERM/RHTH SE16 ....**103** D2
Bellenden Primary School
PECK SE15 ....**138** A1
Bellenden Road Business Centre
PECK SE15 ....**119** F5
Bellenden Road Retail Park
PECK SE15 ....**119** F4
Bellerbys College
DEPT SE8 ....**122** B2
Belleville Primary School
BTSEA SW11 ....**133** F3
Belle Vue Cinema
WLSDN NW10 ....**70** B4
Bell Industrial Estate
CHSWK W4 ....**98** C5
Bellingham ≥
CAT SE6 ....**158** B3
Bellingham Trading Estate
CAT SE6 ....**158** B3
Belmont Primary School
LEY E10 ....**62** C1
Belmont Primary School
CHSWK W4 ....**99** D5
Belsize Park ⊖
HAMP NW3 ....**73** E2
Belvedere Day Hospital
WLSDN NW10 ....**70** A5
Benedict House
Preparatory School
BFN/LL DA15 ....**163** F4
Ben Jonson Primary School
WCHPL E1 ....**91** E3
Benthal Primary School
STNW/STAM N16 ....**60** A5
The Bentley Kempinski Hotel
SKENS SW7 ....**39** E5
Bentworth Primary School
SHB W12 ....**88** B5
Ben Uri Gallery, London Jewish
Museum of Art
STJWD NW8 ....**72** B5
Beormund School
STHWK SE1 ....**48** A1
Berger Primary School
HOM E9 ....**79** D3
The Berkeley Hotel
KTBR SW1X **30** A5
Berlitz School of Languages
HHOL WC1V **21** F3
Bermondsey ⊖
BERM/RHTH SE16 ....**102** A4
Bermondsey Town Hall
STHWK SE1 ....**49** E3
Bermondsey Trading Estate
BERM/RHTH SE16 ....**120** C1
Berrymede Infant School
ACT W3 ....**98** B3
Berrymede Junior School
ACT W3 ....**98** B3
Bertram House School
TOOT SW17 ....**152** A2
Bessemer Grange J & I School
HNHL SE24 ....**137** D3
Bessemer Park Industrial Estate
BRXN/ST SW9 ....**136** B2
Best Western Lodge Hotel
PUT/ROE SW15 ....**131** F3
Best Western Mostyn Hotel
MBLAR W1H **17** F5
Best Western Phoenix Hotel
BAY/PAD W2 ....**26** C1
Bethnal Green ≥
WCHPL E1 ....**90** B1
Bethnal Green ⊖
WCHPL E1 ....**90** C2
Bethnal Green Technology College
BETH E2 ....**13** F4
The Betty Layward School
STNW/STAM N16 ....**59** D5
Bevington Primary School
NKENS W10 ....**89** E4
BFI London IMAX Cinema
STHWK SE1 ....**33** F4
Big Ben
WHALL SW1A **45** D1

Bigland Green Primary School
WCHPL E1.....................................90 B5

Billingsgate Fish Market
POP/IOD E14.............................104 B2

Birkbeck College
GWRST WC1E................................20 B1
RSQ WC1B....................................20 B3

Bishop Challoner Catholic Collegiate School
WCHPL E1.....................................90 C5

Bishop Challoner Girls School
WCHPL E1...................................102 A1

Bishop Gilpin Primary School
WIM/MER SW19.........................149 F5

Bishopsgate Institute
LVPST EC2M................................25 D3

Bishop Thomas Grant School
STRHM/NOR SW16....................153 F5

Blackfen Medical Centre
BFN/LL DA15..............................145 F3

Blackfriars ⇌
BLKFR EC4V.................................34 C1

Blackfriars Millennium Pier
EMB EC4Y....................................34 B1

Blackfriars Pier
BLKFR EC4V.................................35 D1

Blackheath ⇌
BKHTH/KID SE3.........................141 F1

Blackheath Bluecoat School
BKHTH/KID SE3.........................124 B3

Blackheath Business Estate
GNWCH SE10.............................122 C4

The Blackheath Clinic
BKHTH/KID SE3.........................142 A1

Blackheath High School GDST
BKHTH/KID SE3.........................123 F5

Blackheath High Senior School
BKHTH/KID SE3.........................124 A3

Blackheath Hospital
BKHTH/KID SE3.........................141 F1

Blackheath Preparatory School
BKHTH/KID SE3.........................124 A4

Blackheath RFC (The Rectory Field)
BKHTH/KID SE3.........................124 B3

Blackwall ⊖
POP/IOD E14.............................104 C1

Blackwall Trading Estate
POP/IOD E14...............................93 D4

Blake College
GTPST W1W..................................19 E2

Blanche Nevile School
HGT N6...55 F5

Blessed Sacrament RC Primary School
IS N1...75 F5

Bloomfield Clinic Guys
STHWK SE1...................................36 B5

Bloomsbury International
NOXST/BSQ WC1A.......................21 D3

Bloomsbury Theatre
GWRST WC1E................................8 A5

Blossoms Inn Medical Centre
BLKFR EC4V.................................35 F1

Blue Gate Fields Infant School
WCHPL E1...................................102 C1

Blyth's Wharf
POP/IOD E14.............................103 E1

BMI Medical Centre
CAVSQ/HST W1G........................18 B3

Bnois Jerusalem Girls School
STNW/STAM N16........................59 D2

The Bob Hope Theatre
ELTH/MOT SE9...........................143 F4

Bodywise Natural Health Centre
BETH E2.......................................90 C2

Boleyn Cinema
EHAM E6.......................................95 D1

Bolingbroke Hospital
BTSEA SW11...............................133 E3

Bolingbroke Primary School
BTSEA SW11...............................115 D4

Bond Street ⊖
OXSTW W1C.................................18 B5

Bonner Primary School
BETH E2.......................................91 D1

Bonneville Primary School
CLAP SW4...................................134 C4

Bonnington Hotel
RSQ WC1B....................................21 D2

Bonus Pastor Catholic College
BMLY BR1....................................159 D4

Borough ⊖
STHWK SE1...................................47 F1

Borough Market
STHWK SE1...................................36 A3

Borthwick Wharf
DEPT SE8....................................122 A1

Bousfield Primary School
WBPTN SW10.............................114 C1

Boutcher CE Primary School
STHWK SE1...................................49 E5

Bowater House
SKENS SW7..................................41 E1

Bow Church ⊖
BOW E3...92 A2

Bow Junior & Youth Centre
BOW E3...91 F4

Bowling Club
STRHM/NOR SW16....................153 E3

Bow Road ⊖
BOW E3...92 A2

Bow Secondary School
BOW E3...92 A1

Bow Triangle Business Centre
BOW E3...92 A3

BPP Law School
HHOL WC1V..................................21 E3

Brackenbury Health Centre
HMSMTH W6..............................100 B4

Brackenbury Primary School
HMSMTH W6..............................100 B4

Brady Recreation Centre
WCHPL E1.....................................90 A4

Braincroft Primary School
CRICK NW2...................................51 F5

Bramah's Tea & Coffee Museum
STHWK SE1...................................35 F4

Brampton Manor School
EHAM E6.......................................95 D3

Brampton Primary School
EHAM E6.......................................95 E2

Brandlehow Primary School
PUT/ROE SW15..........................131 F2

Branollys Health Centre
PLSTW E13...................................94 B3

Brecknock Primary School
HOLWY N7....................................75 D3

Bredinghurst School
PECK SE15.................................138 C2

Brent Adult College
WLSDN NW10...............................69 D5

Brent Arts Council
CRICK NW2...................................52 A5

Brent Child & Family Clinic
WLSDN NW10...............................69 F2

Brent Cross ⊖
CRICK NW2...................................53 D2

Brent Cross Shopping Centre
HDN NW4......................................52 C2

Brentfield Medical Centre
WLSDN NW10...............................69 D3

Brentfield Primary School
WLSDN NW10...............................69 D3

Brent Knoll School
FSTH SE23..................................157 D3

Brent Trading Estate
WLSDN NW10...............................69 E2

Brewers' Hall
CITYW EC2V..................................23 F3

Brewery Industrial Estate
IS N1...11 E2

Brick Lane Music Hall
CAN/RD E16...............................107 D2

Brick Lane Music House
WCHPL E1.....................................25 F1

Bricklayer Arms Industrial Estate
STHWK SE1...................................49 E5

The Bridewell Theatre
EMB EC4Y.....................................22 C5

The Bridge Academy
BETH E2.......................................77 F5

Bridge Lane Theatre
BTSEA SW11...............................115 E4

The Bridge Leisure Centre
SYD SE26....................................157 F5

Bridge Park Business & Leisure Centre
WLSDN NW10...............................68 B4

The Bridge School
ARCH N19.....................................56 C4
HOLWY N7....................................75 D3

Bright Sparks Montessori School
WKENS W14................................101 D3

Brindishe Primary School
  LEE/GVPK SE12.................................141 F3
Britain & London Visitor Centre
  STJS SW1Y......................................32 A3
Britannia Business Centre
  CRICK NW2......................................71 D1
Britannia Leisure Centre
  IS N1..77 D5
Britannia Village Primary School
  CAN/RD E16....................................106 B2
The British American Drama Academy
  CAMTN NW1......................................21 F4
  SRTFD E15......................................93 D1
British Cartoon Centre
  BMSBY WC1N.....................................21 D1
British College of Osteopathy
  HAMP NW3.......................................72 C3
British Dental Association
  CAVSQ/HST W1G..................................18 C3
British Library
  CAMTN NW1.......................................8 B3
British Medical Association
  STPAN WC1H......................................8 B5
British Museum
  RSQ WC1B.......................................20 C3
British Telecom Tower
  GTPST W1W......................................19 E2
British Transport Police Station
  WBLY HA9.......................................50 A4
Brixton ≷ ⊖
  BRXN/ST SW9...................................136 A2
Brixton Academy
  BRXN/ST SW9...................................136 A1
Brixton Recreation Centre
  BRXN/ST SW9...................................136 A1
Broadgate
  LVPST EC2M.....................................24 B2
Broadgate Ice Arena
  LVPST EC2M.....................................24 B3
Broadhurst School
  KIL/WHAMP NW6..................................72 C4
Broadwater Primary School
  TOOT SW17.....................................151 D4
Broadway Retail Park
  CRICK NW2......................................71 D1
Broadway Shopping Centre
  HMSMTH W6.....................................112 C1
Broadway Squash & Fitness Centre
  HMSMTH W6.....................................101 D5
Brocklebank Health Centre
  WAND/EARL SW18................................132 B5
Brocklebank Industrial Estate
  GNWCH SE10....................................106 A5
Brockley ≷ ⊖
  BROCKY SE4....................................139 E1
Brockley Cross Business Centre
  BROCKY SE4....................................139 E1
Brockley Primary School
  BROCKY SE4....................................139 F3
Brockwell Lido
  HNHL SE24.....................................136 B4
Bromley by Bow ⊖
  BOW E3...92 B3
Bromley Road Retail Park
  CAT SE6.......................................158 B2
Brompton Cemetery
  WBPTN SW10....................................114 B2
Brompton Medical Centre
  ECT SW5.......................................114 B1
Brompton Oratory
  SKENS SW7......................................40 C3
Bromyard Leisure Centre
  ACT W3...99 E2
Brondesbury ⊖
  KIL/WHAMP NW6..................................71 F4
Brondesbury College for Boys
  KIL/WHAMP NW6..................................71 D4
Brondesbury Park ⊖
  KIL/WHAMP NW6..................................71 E5
Brook Community Primary School
  HACK E8..78 A2
Brookfield Primary School
  HGT N6...56 B4
Brooklands Primary School
  BKHTH/KID SE3.................................142 A1
Brookmarsh Trading Estate
  DEPT SE8......................................122 B3
Broomsleigh Business Park
  SYD SE26......................................157 F5
Broomwood Hall Lower School
  BAL SW12......................................133 F4
  STRHM/NOR SW16................................153 D3

Broomwood Hall Upper School
  BAL SW12......................................134 A5
Brown's Hotel
  MYFR/PICC W1J..................................31 D2
Brunel Gallery
  STPAN WC1H.....................................20 B1
Brunel Engine House
  BERM/RHTH SE16................................102 C3
Brunel University
  GLDGN NW11.....................................53 D1
Brunswick Housing &
  Shopping Centre
  BMSBY WC1N......................................9 D5
Brunswick Medical Centre
  BMSBY WC1N......................................8 C5
Brunswick Park Primary School
  CMBW SE5......................................119 D3
BT Centre
  STBT EC1A......................................23 E4
Buckingham Palace
  WHALL SW1A.....................................43 E1
Buckingham Road Cemetery
  IL IG1...67 D4
Building Centre
  GWRST WC1E.....................................20 A3
Burbage School
  IS N1..12 C1
Burdett Coutts CE
  Primary School
  WEST SW1P......................................44 A3
Burgess Business Park
  CMBW SE5......................................119 D3
Burgess Park Tennis Centre
  CMBW SE5......................................118 C2
Burlington Danes School
  SHB W12..88 B5
Burney Street Clinic
  GNWCH SE10....................................122 C3
Burnley Road Clinic
  WLSDN NW10.....................................70 A2
Burns Hotel
  ECT SW5..38 C5
Burnt Ash Primary School
  BMLY BR1......................................160 A5
Burntwood School
  TOOT SW17.....................................151 D2
Burwell Industrial Estate
  LEY E10..61 E3
Bush House (BBC)
  HOL/ALD WC2B...................................21 E5
Bush Industrial Estate
  ARCH N19.......................................56 C5
  WLSDN NW10.....................................87 D3
The Business Design Centre
  IS N1..76 A5
Bute House Preparatory
  School for Girls
  HMSMTH W6.....................................100 C5
Butlers Wharf
  STHWK SE1......................................37 F4
Butler's Wharf Business Centre
  STHWK SE1......................................37 F5
Butler's Wharf Pier
  STHWK SE1......................................37 F4
Butterfly Sports Club
  ELTH/MOT SE9..................................144 B4
Buzzard Creek Industrial Estate
  BARK IG11......................................97 F2
Byam Shaw School of Art
  ARCH N19.......................................56 C4
Bygrove Primary School
  POP/IOD E14....................................92 B5
Cabot Place
  POP/IOD E14...................................104 A2
Cadogan Pier
  CHEL SW3......................................115 E2
Caledonian Market
  STHWK SE1......................................49 D2
Caledonian Road ⊖
  HOLWY N7.......................................75 E2
Caledonian Road & Barnsbury ≷
  HOLWY N7.......................................75 F4
Cally Pool
  IS N1..75 F5
Calverton Primary School
  CAN/RD E16.....................................95 D5
Camberwell Business Centre
  CMBW SE5......................................119 D3
Camberwell College of Arts
  CMBW SE5......................................119 E4
Camberwell Leisure Centre
  CMBW SE5......................................119 D4

Camberwell New Cemetery
PECK SE15...............................139 D4
Camberwell Trading Estate
CMBW SE5..............................118 B5
Cambridge Heath ⇌
BETH E2...................................90 B1
Cambridge School
HMSMTH W6.........................100 B5
Cambridge Theatre
LSQ/SEVD WC2H......................20 C5
Camden Arts Centre
HAMP NW3..............................72 B2
Camden House Clinic
BKHTH/KID SE3......................123 E5
Camden Market
CAMTN NW1............................74 A4
Camden Mews
Day Hospital
CAMTN NW1............................74 C4
Camden People's Theatre
CAMTN NW1...............................7 E4
Camden Road ⇌
CAMTN NW1............................74 C4
Camden School for Girls
KTTN NW5...............................74 C3
Camden Theatre
CAMTN NW1...............................7 E1
Camden Town ⊖
CAMTN NW1............................74 B5
Camden Town Hall &
St Pancras Library
CAMTN NW1...............................8 C3
Camelot Primary School
PECK SE15.............................120 B3
Cameron House School
CHEL SW3..............................115 D2
Camperdown House
WCHPL E1................................25 F5
Canada House
STJS SW1Y..............................32 B3
Canada Place
POP/IOD E14.........................104 A2
Canada Square
POP/IOD E14.........................104 A2
Canada Water ⊖
BERM/RHTH SE16..................102 C4
Canada Water Retail Park
BERM/RHTH SE16..................103 D4
Canada Wharf Museum
BERM/RHTH SE16..................103 F2
Canal Cafe Theatre
BAY/PAD W2...............................15 D2
Canary Riverside
BERM/RHTH SE16..................103 F2
Canary Wharf ⊖
POP/IOD E14.........................104 A2
Canary Wharf Pier
POP/IOD E14.........................103 F2
Canberra Primary School
SHB W12.................................100 B1
Cann Hall Primary School
WAN E11...................................63 F5
The Canning School
ECT SW5...................................38 C4
KENS W8...................................38 A1
Canning Town ⇌ ⊖
POP/IOD E14............................93 E5
Cannon Sports Club
CANST EC4R..............................35 F1
Cannon Street ⇌ ⊖
CANST EC4R..............................36 A2
Cannon Trading Estate
WBLY HA9..................................68 B1
Cannon Wharf
Business Centre
DEPT SE8................................103 E5
Canon Barnett Primary School
WCHPL E1..................................25 F4
Canonbury ⊖
HBRY N5....................................76 C2
Canonbury Business Centre
IS N1...76 C5
Canonbury Primary School
IS N1...76 B3
Canon Palmer RC High School
IL IG1...67 E3
Canterbury Industrial Estate
NWCR SE14.............................121 D2
Cantium Retail Park
STHWK SE1.............................120 A2
Capital City Academy
WLSDN NW10............................70 B5

The Capital Hotel
CHEL SW3..................................41 E1
Capital Radio
LSQ/SEVD WC2H......................32 B2
Capital Wharf
WAP E1W.................................102 A2
Cardinal Hinsley College
WLSDN NW10............................70 A5
Cardinal Pole RC School
HOM E9.....................................79 E3
Cardinal Pole RC Secondary
Lower School
HOM E9.....................................79 D4
The Cardinal Vaughan
Memorial School
WKENS W14.............................101 E3
Cardwell Primary School
WOOL/PLUM SE18..................107 F5
Carlton House
STJS SW1Y..............................32 A4
Carlton Primary School
KTTN NW5.................................74 A2
Carlton Vale Infant School
MV/WKIL W9..............................89 F2
Carlyle's House (NT)
CHEL SW3................................115 E2
Carnwath Road Industrial Estate
FUL/PGN SW6..........................132 B1
Carpenters' Hall
OBST EC2N................................24 B3
Carpenters Primary School
SRTFD E15................................80 C5
The Cartoon Museum
RSQ WC1B.................................20 C3
Cassidy Medical Centre
FUL/PGN SW6..........................114 A3
Castlecombe Primary School
ELTH/MOT SE9.......................161 E5
Castle Industrial Estate
WALW SE17................................47 E4
Catford ⇌
CAT SE6...................................140 A5
Catford Bridge ⇌
CAT SE6...................................140 A5
Catford Cricket & Sports Club
CAT SE6...................................158 B1
Catford Cyphers CC
CAT SE6...................................157 F2
Catford High School
CAT SE6...................................159 D3
Catford Trading Estate
CAT SE6...................................158 B2
Catford Wanderers Sports Club
CAT SE6...................................158 C4
Cathall Leisure Centre
WAN E11...................................63 D5
Cavendish College
FITZ W1T...................................20 A2
Cavendish Hotel
STJS SW1Y................................31 F3
Cavendish Primary School
CHSWK W4..............................111 E3
Cavendish School
BERM/RHTH SE16..................102 C5
The Cavendish School
CAMTN NW1..............................74 B5
Caxton Hall
STJSPK SW1H............................44 A2
Cayley Primary School
WCHPL E1..................................91 E4
The Cedar School
FSTGT E7...................................82 C3
Cedar Way Industrial Estate
CAMTN NW1..............................75 D4
Cenotaph
WHALL SW1A.............................32 C5
Central Business Centre
WLSDN NW10............................69 E2
Central Foundation Boys School
SDTCH EC2A..............................12 B3
Central Foundation Girls
School (Lower)
BOW E3.......................................91 E2
Central Foundation Girls
School (Upper)
BOW E3.......................................91 F2
Central Hall
STJSPK SW1H............................44 B1
Central London Golf Club
TOOT SW17.............................151 D2
Central London Markets
STBT EC1A.................................22 C3

Central Middlesex Hospital
WLSDN NW10............**86** C2
Central Park Primary School
EHAM E6............**95** D1
Central St Martins College of Art & Design
RSQ WC1B............**21** E3
Central School of Ballet
CLKNW EC1R............**22** B1
Central School of Fashion
GTPST W1W............**19** E3
Central School of Speech & Drama
HAMP NW3............**73** D4
Central YMCA
ELTH/MOT SE9............**161** D2
The Centre Performing Arts College
WOOL/PLUM SE18............**107** D4
Centre Point
LSO/SEVD WC2H............**20** B4
Chalcot School
CAMTN NW1............**74** B3
Chalk Farm ⊖
HAMP NW3............**74** A4
Chalkhill Primary School
WBLY HA9............**50** B5
The Chamberlain Hotel
TWRH EC3N............**37** E1
Chambers Wharf
BERM/RHTH SE16............**102** A3
Chancery Court Hotel
HHOL WC1V............**21** E3
Chancery Lane ⊖
FSBYW WC1X............**22** A3
Channelsea Business Centre
SRTFD E15............**93** D1
Channel Tunnel Rail Link
SRTFD E15............**80** C3
Channing School
HGT N6............**56** B3
Chapman Park Industrial Estate
WLSDN NW10............**69** F3
Charing Cross ⇌ ⊖
CHCR WC2N............**33** D3
Charing Cross Hospital
HMSMTH W6............**113** D2
Charing Cross Hotel
CHCR WC2N............**32** C2
The Charles Dickens Museum
BMSBY WC1N............**21** E1
Charles Dickens Primary School
STHWK SE1............**47** E1
Charles Edward Brooke School (Lower School)
CMBW SE5............**118** B4
Charles Edward Brooke School (Upper School)
BRXN/ST SW9............**118** B4
Charlotte Sharman Primary School
LBTH SE11............**46** C3
Charlotte Turner Primary School
DEPT SE8............**122** A2
Charlton ⇌
CHARL SE7............**124** C1
Charlton Athletic FC (The Valley)
CHARL SE7............**124** C1
Charlton Health & Fitness Centre
CHARL SE7............**124** C1
Charlton House
CHARL SE7............**125** D2
Charlton Manor Junior School
CHARL SE7............**125** D3
Charlton RFC
ELTH/MOT SE9............**144** B5
Charlton School
CHARL SE7............**125** E2
Charter Clinic
CHEL SW3............**115** F1
Charterhouse
FARR EC1M............**23** D1
Charteris Road Sports Centre
HAMP NW3............**73** E2
KIL/WHAMP NW6............**71** F5
Charter Nightingale Hospital & Counselling Centre
CAMTN NW1............**17** D2
The Charter School
HNHL SE24............**137** D3
Chase Road Trading Estate
WLSDN NW10............**87** D3
Chelsea Bridge Business Centre
VX/NE SW8............**116** B3

Chelsea Centre & Theatre
WBPTN SW10............**114** C3
Chelsea Cinema
CHEL SW3............**115** E1
The Chelsea Club Leisure Centre
FUL/PGN SW6............**114** B2
Chelsea College of Art & Design
CHEL SW3............**115** E1
FUL/PGN SW6............**114** C5
SHB W12............**100** D3
WEST SW1P............**117** E1
Chelsea FC (Stamford Bridge)
FUL/PGN SW6............**114** B3
Chelsea Fire Station
CHEL SW3............**115** E1
Chelsea Group of Children
WBPTN SW10............**114** C3
Chelsea Independent College
FUL/PGN SW6............**114** B3
Chelsea Leisure Centre
CHEL SW3............**115** E1
Chelsea Old Town Hall
CHEL SW5............**115** E1
Chelsea Physic Garden
CHEL SW3............**115** F2
Chelsea & Westminster Hospital
WBPTN SW10............**114** C2
Chelsea Wharf
WBPTN SW10............**115** D3
Cherry Garden Pier
BERM/RHTH SE16............**102** B3
Cherry Garden School
BERM/RHTH SE16............**102** A5
Cherry Orchard Primary School
CHARL SE7............**124** C3
The Chesterfield Mayfair Hotel
MYFR/PICC W1J............**30** C3
Chesterton Primary School
BTSEA SW11............**116** A4
Chestnut Grove School
BAL SW12............**152** A1
Cheyne Centre
CHEL SW3............**115** D2
Childeric Primary School
NWCR SE14............**121** E3
Childs Hill Clinic
CRICK NW2............**53** F4
Childs Hill Primary School
CRICK NW2............**53** E5
Chiltonian Industrial Estate
LEE/GVPK SE12............**141** F4
Chimnocks Wharf
POP/IOD E14............**103** E1
Chisenhale Primary School
BOW E3............**91** E1
Chislehurst Cemetery
CHST BR7............**163** E5
Chiswick ⇌
CHSWK W4............**110** C3
Chiswick & Bedford Park Preparatory School
CHSWK W4............**99** E5
Chiswick Business Park
CHSWK W4............**98** B5
Chiswick Community School
CHSWK W4............**111** D3
Chiswick House
CHSWK W4............**111** D2
Chiswick Moran Hotel
CHSWK W4............**110** B1
Chiswick Park ⊖
CHSWK W4............**98** C5
Chrisp Street Health Centre
POP/IOD E14............**92** B5
Christ Church Bentinck CE Primary School
CAMTN NW1............**16** C2
Christ Church Brondesbury CE J & I School
KIL/WHAMP NW6............**71** E3
Christchurch CE Primary School
HAMP NW3............**55** D5
WCHPL E1............**25** F3
Christ Church CE Primary School
BRXN/ST SW9............**118** A4
BRXS/STRHM SW2............**153** F1
BTSEA SW11............**133** E1
CHEL SW3............**115** F2
FSTH SE23............**157** D2
WOOL/PLUM SE18............**126** A4

Christchurch Industrial Centre
STHWK SE1...........................**34** C3

Christ Church School
CAMTN NW1...........................**7** D2

Christopher Hatton Primary School
FSBYW WC1X...........................**22** A1

Christ the King RC Primary School
FSBYPK N4...........................**57** F3

Christ the King Sixth Form College
LEW SE13...........................**141** D1

Chrysalis Theatre
BAL SW12...........................**152** A1

Chrysanthemum Clinic
CHSWK W4...........................**110** C3

Chrysolyte Independent
Christian School
STHWK SE1...........................**48** B2

Church Down Adult School
LEE/GVPK SE12...........................**160** A2

Church End Medical Centre
WLSDN NW10...........................**69** E3

Church House
WEST SW1P...........................**44** B2

Churchill Clinic
STHWK SE1...........................**46** B2

Churchill Gardens Primary School
PIM SW1V...........................**116** C1

Churchill Museum & Cabinet
War Rooms
STJSPK SW1H...........................**32** B5

Church Stairs
BERM/RHTH SE16...........................**102** B3

Cineworld
CHEL SW3...........................**115** D2
CRICK NW2...........................**52** B3
HMSMTH W6...........................**100** B5
SOHO/SHAV W1D...........................**32** A2
WBPTN SW10...........................**115** D1

Citigroup Tower
POP/IOD E14...........................**104** B2

City Business Centre
BERM/RHTH SE16...........................**102** B3

City Business College
FSBYE EC1V...........................**11** D4

City Central Estate
FSBYE EC1V...........................**11** E4

City College of Higher Education
IS N1...........................**12** B3

City & Guilds of London Art School
LBTH SE11...........................**118** A1

City Health Centre
FSBYE EC1V...........................**12** A5

City & Islington College
FSBYE EC1V...........................**11** F4
FSBYPK N4...........................**58** B4
HBRY N5...........................**76** A3
HOLWY N7...........................**75** E1
STLK EC1Y...........................**24** A1

City & Islington Sixth Form College
FSBYE EC1V...........................**10** C2

City Literary College
HHOL WC1V...........................**21** D4

City of East London College
WCHPL E1...........................**90** A5

City of London Academy
STHWK SE1...........................**120** A1

City of London Academy Islington
IS N1...........................**10** A5

The City of London Academy
EDUL SE22...........................**138** A3

City of London Cemetery
MNPK E12...........................**65** E4

City of London Club
OBST EC2N...........................**24** C4

City of London College
WCHPL E1...........................**90** A5

City of London Crematorium
MNPK E12...........................**65** D5

City of London School
BLKFR EC4V...........................**35** D1

City of London School for Girls
BARB EC2Y...........................**23** E2

City of London School Sports Ground
LEE/GVPK SE12...........................**160** C2

City of Westminster College
BAY/PAD W2...........................**16** A2
MV/WKIL W9...........................**2** B4

City of Westminster
Vehicle Pound
MYFR/PKLN W1K...........................**29** F2

City Thameslink ≥
FLST/FETLN EC4A...........................**22** C4

City University
FSBYE EC1V...........................**11** D5
IS N1...........................**11** E2
STBT EC1A...........................**23** E3
WCHPL E1...........................**90** B4

City University Business School
BARB EC2Y...........................**23** F2

Civil Service Sports Ground
CHSWK W4...........................**111** E4
LEE/GVPK SE12...........................**142** C3

Clapham Common ⊖
CLAP SW4...........................**134** C2

Clapham Common Clinic
CLAP SW4...........................**135** D2

Clapham High Street ≥ ⊖
CLAP SW4...........................**135** D1

Clapham Junction ≥ ⊖
BTSEA SW11...........................**133** D2

Clapham Manor Primary School
CLAP SW4...........................**134** C1

Clapham Manor Street
Public Baths
CLAP SW4...........................**135** D1

Clapham North ⊖
CLAP SW4...........................**135** E1

Clapham North Business Centre
CLAP SW4...........................**135** D1

Clapham Picture House
CLAP SW4...........................**134** C2

Clapham South ⊖
CLAP SW4...........................**134** B4

Clapton ≥
CLPT E5...........................**60** B4

Clapton Girls Technology College
CLPT E5...........................**78** C1

Clara Grant Primary School
BOW E3...........................**92** A3

Claremont Clinic
FSTGT E7...........................**82** C2

Claremont Primary School
CRICK NW2...........................**53** D4

Claremont Way Industrial Estate
CRICK NW2...........................**52** C3

Clarence House
WHALL SW1A...........................**31** F5

Claridge's Hotel
MYFR/PKLN W1K...........................**30** C1

Cleopatra's Needle
CHCR WC2N...........................**33** E3

Clerkenwell Heritage Centre
FARR EC1M...........................**22** C1

Clerkenwell Parochial CE
Primary School
CLKNW EC1R...........................**10** A4

Cleveland Primary School
IL IG1...........................**84** B1

Cleves Primary School
EHAM E6...........................**83** D5

Clink Exhibition
STHWK SE1...........................**36** A3

Clissold Leisure Centre
STNW/STAM N16...........................**59** D5

Clissold Park Natural Health Centre
STNW/STAM N16...........................**59** E4

Clock Museum
CITYW EC2V...........................**23** F4

Cloisters Business Centre
VX/NE SW8...........................**116** B3

Clore Gallery
WEST SW1P...........................**44** C5

Clothworkers' Hall
FENCHST EC3M...........................**37** D1

Clouster's Green
WAP E1W...........................**102** A2

Cobbold Estate
WLSDN NW10...........................**69** F3

Cobourg Primary School
CMBW SE5...........................**119** D2

Cochrane Theatre
GINN WC1R...........................**21** D3

The Cockpit Theatre
STJWD NW8...........................**16** C1

Coldharbour Industrial Estate
CMBW SE5...........................**118** C5

Coldharbour Leisure Centre
ELTH/MOT SE9...........................**161** F2

Coldharbour Sports Ground
ELTH/MOT SE9...........................**162** A2

Colebrooke Primary School
IS N1...........................**10** C1

Colegrave School
SRTFD E15...........................**81** D2

Coleridge Primary School
HGT N6 .... 57 D2
Colfe's Preparatory School
LEE/GVPK SE12 .... 142 A4
Colfe's Senior School
LEE/GVPK SE12 .... 142 A4
Coliseum Theatre
CHCR WC2N 32 C2
College of Arms
BLKFR EC4V 23 E5
College of Business & Technology
FSTGT E7 .... 82 A2
College of Central London
SDTCH EC2A 12 C5
College of Fuel Technology
HGT N6 .... 56 A1
The College of Law
FITZ W1T 20 A3
LINN WC2A 22 A4
College of North West London
KIL/WHAMP NW6 .... 72 A5
WBLY HA9 .... 50 A5
WLSDN NW10 .... 69 F2
College of Organists
FLST/FETLN EC4A 22 B3
College Park School
BAY/PAD W2 .... 14 B5
Collingwood Business Centre
ARCH N19 .... 57 E5
Collins Method School
CRICK NW2 .... 70 C3
The Colonnades Shopping Centre
BGVA SW1W 42 C4
Columbia Primary School
BETH E2 .... 13 F3
Colvestone Primary School
HACK E8 .... 77 F2
Colville Primary School
NTGHL W11 .... 89 F5
Comber Grove Primary School
CMBW SE5 .... 118 C3
Comedy Theatre
STJS SW1Y 32 A2
Comelle House Trading Estate
DEPT SE8 .... 121 E1
Commonwealth Institute
WKENS W14 .... 101 F4
Community Arts Centre
GNWCH SE10 .... 122 B3
Community Centre (Island
History Trust)
POP/IOD E14 .... 104 C5
Community College & School
GNWCH SE10 .... 122 C3
The Community College
HACK E8 .... 78 B5
Complementary
Health Centre
LEE/GVPK SE12 .... 141 E4
Concord Business Centre
ACT W3 .... 86 B4
Conduit House
GNWCH SE10 .... 123 D3
Connaught House School
BAY/PAD W2 .... 17 D5
Connaught School for Girls
WAN E11 .... 63 E3
Consort Clinic
PECK SE15 .... 138 B1
Consulate General of Monaco
SKENS SW7 .... 40 A4
Consulate General of the
Republic of Guinea Bissau
KENS W8 .... 39 E2
Consulate of Burkina Faso
BTSEA SW11 .... 132 C1
Consulate of Chile
CAVSQ/HST W1G 18 C1
Consulate of Colombia
GTPST W1W 19 E4
Consulate of Eritrea
IS N1 .... 10 B1
Consulate of Guinea
MYFR/PKLN W1K 30 A2
Consulate of Panama
MYFR/PICC W1J 30 C4
Convent of Jesus & Mary
Infant School
CRICK NW2 .... 70 C3
Convent of Jesus & Mary
Language College
WLSDN NW10 .... 69 F5

Convoy's Wharf
DEPT SE8 .... 122 A1
Conway Medical Centre
WOOL/PLUM SE18 .... 127 D1
Conway Primary School
WOOL/PLUM SE18 .... 109 E5
Coopers' Hall
LVPST EC2M 25 D3
Coopers Lane Primary School
LEE/GVPK SE12 .... 160 A2
Copenhagen Primary School
IS N1 .... 18 C3
Copthorne Tara Hotel
KENS W8 .... 38 C2
Cordwainers College
HACK E8 .... 78 C4
Coronet Cinema
NTGHL W11 .... 26 A3
Corpus Christi RC Primary School
BRXS/STRHM SW2 .... 135 F3
Corus Hotel
BAY/PAD W2 .... 28 A1
Cosmopolitan College
IS N1 .... 9 E2
Courtauld Institute of Art
TPL/STR WC2R 33 F2
Courtfield Medical Centre
ECT SW5 .... 39 D5
Covent Garden ⊖
COVGDN WC2E 32 C1
Covent Garden Flower Market
VX/NE SW8 .... 117 D2
Covent Garden Medical Centre
LSQ/SEVD WC2H 20 C5
Crafts Council
IS N1 .... 10 B2
Crampton Primary School
WALW SE17 .... 47 D5
Cranbrook College
IL IG1 .... 66 A4
Cranbrook Primary School
IL IG1 .... 65 F2
The Craven Clinic
HMSMTH W6 .... 100 B5
Craven Park Health Centre
WLSDN NW10 .... 69 D5
Craven Park Medical Centre
WLSDN NW10 .... 69 D5
Crawford Primary School
CMBW SE5 .... 118 C4
Creekmouth Industrial Estate
BARK IG11 .... 97 F3
Creek Road Health Centre
DEPT SE8 .... 122 A2
Creek Road Industrial Estate
DEPT SE8 .... 122 B2
Crewe House
MYFR/PICC W1J 30 C3
Cricklefield Stadium
IL IG1 .... 67 E4
Cricklewood ⇌
CRICK NW2 .... 53 D5
Cricklewood Trading Estate
CRICK NW2 .... 53 E5
Criterion Theatre
MYFR/PICC W1J 31 F2
Crofton Leisure Centre
BROCKY SE4 .... 140 A4
Crofton Park ⇌
BROCKY SE4 .... 139 F3
Cromwell Business Centre
BARK IG11 .... 97 E3
Cromwell Hospital
ECT SW5 .... 38 C4
Crossharbour ⊖
POP/IOD E14 .... 104 B4
Crossways Academy
BROCKY SE4 .... 121 E5
Crouch Hill ⇌
FSBYPK N4 .... 57 F2
Crouch Hill Recreation Centre
CEND/HSY/T N8 .... 57 E2
Crown Close Business Centre
BOW E3 .... 80 A5
Crowndale Health Centre
CAMTN NW1 .... 7 F1
Crowne Plaza
CAN/RD E16 .... 106 A1
Crown Lane Primary School
WNWD SE27 .... 154 C4
Crown Moran Hotel
CRICK NW2 .... 71 D1

Crown Woods School
ELTH/MOT SE9 .... **144** C3
Crusader Industrial Estate
FSBYPK N4 .... **58** C1
Crystal Palace FC Soccer &
Sports Centre
BRXN/ST SW9 .... **135** F1
Cubitt Town Infant School
POP/IOD E14 .... **104** C4
Culloden Primary School
POP/IOD E14 .... **93** D5
Cumberland Business Park
WLSDN NW10 .... **86** B2
The Cumberland Hotel
FITZ W1T **20** A4
OXSTW W1C **17** F5
Cumberland Park Industrial Estate
WLSDN NW10 .... **88** A2
The Cumming Museum
WALW SE17 .... **47** E5
Curwen Primary School
PLSTW E13 .... **94** A1
Curzon Mayfair Cinema
MYFR/PICC W1J **30** C4
Curzon Soho Cinema
SOHO/SHAV W1D **32** B1
Custom House
MON EC3R **36** C2
Custom House for ExCeL ⊖
CAN/RD E16 .... **106** B1
Cutlers' Hall
STP EC4M **23** D4
Cutty Sark
GNWCH SE10 .... **122** C2
Cutty Sark Clipper Ship
GNWCH SE10 .... **122** C2
Cygnet Clinic Beckton
EHAM E6 .... **96** B4
Cygnus Business Centre
WLSDN NW10 .... **69** F2
Cyprus ⊖
CAN/RD E16 .... **108** A1
Cyprus College of Art
WNWD SE27 .... **154** B4
Cyril Jackson Primary School
POP/IOD E14 .... **103** F1
Daily Telegraph
Newspaper Offices
POP/IOD E14 .... **104** A4
Dali Universe
STHWK SE1 .... **33** E5
Dallington School
FSBYE EC1V **11** D5
Dalmain Primary School
FSTH SE23 .... **157** E1
Dalston Junction ⊖
HACK E8 .... **77** F3
Dalston Kingsland ⊖
IS N1 .... **77** E3
Damilola Taylor Centre
PECK SE15 .... **119** F3
Darell Primary School
RCH/KEW TW9 .... **128** A1
Darwin Centre
SKENS SW7 .... **40** A3
Datapoint Business Centre
BOW E3 .... **93** D3
Daubeney Primary School
CLPT E5 .... **79** E1
The David Beckham Academy
GNWCH SE10 .... **105** F3
David Game College
KENS W8 .... **26** A3
David Lloyd Leisure Centre
SKENS SW7 .... **39** D4
Davies Laing & Dick College
BAY/PAD W2 .... **26** C2
Davies Lane Primary School
WAN E11 .... **63** F4
Davies's College
STHWK SE1 .... **36** A5
Dawlish Primary School
LEY E10 .... **62** C4
Days Hotel
BAY/PAD W2 .... **16** B5
STHWK SE1 .... **46** A3
Days Inn
PIM SW1V **116** C1
Days Lane Primary School
BFN/LL DA15 .... **145** F4
Dean College of London
HOLWY N7 .... **57** F5

Deansfield Primary School
ELTH/MOT SE9 .... **144** A1
Delta Wharf
GNWCH SE10 .... **105** D3
Denmark Hill ≈ ⊖
CMBW SE5 .... **137** D1
Department for Environment,
Food & Rural Affairs
CHCR WC2N **32** C3
Department for Transport
WEST SW1P **44** B4
Department of Art & Design (London
Metropolitan University)
WCHPL E1 .... **25** F4
Department of Economics (London
Metropolitan University)
TWRH EC3N **25** E5
Department of Education
STJSPK SW1H **44** B1
Department of Health
WHALL SW1A **32** C5
Department of Trade & Industry
STJSPK SW1H **44** B2
Deptford ≈
DEPT SE8 .... **122** A3
Deptford Bridge ⊖
DEPT SE8 .... **122** A4
Deptford Business Centre
NWCR SE14 .... **121** D1
Deptford Green School
NWCR SE14 .... **121** F3
Deptford Park Business Centre
DEPT SE8 .... **121** E1
Deptford Park Primary School
DEPT SE8 .... **121** E1
Deptford Trading Estate
DEPT SE8 .... **121** E1
Dersingham Infant School
MNPK E12 .... **83** F2
Derwentwater Primary School
ACT W3 .... **98** C2
Design Centre Chelsea Harbour
FUL/PGN SW6 .... **114** C4
Design Museum
STHWK SE1 .... **37** F4
Devonshire Hospital
MHST W1U **18** B2
Devonshire House
Preparatory School
HAMP NW3 .... **72** C2
Devons Road ⊖
BOW E3 .... **92** B3
Diamond College
SOHO/SHAV W1D **20** B4
Diana Princess of Wales
Memorial Fountain
BAY/PAD W2 .... **28** B4
Discovery Business Park
BERM/RHTH SE16 .... **102** A4
Discovery Primary School
THMD SE28 .... **109** F2
Docklands Medical Centre
POP/IOD E14 .... **104** A5
Docklands Sailing &
Watersports Centre
POP/IOD E14 .... **104** A4
Dockmaster's House
POP/IOD E14 .... **104** A1
Dock Offices
BERM/RHTH SE16 .... **102** C4
Dockyard Industrial Estate
WOOL/PLUM SE18 .... **107** E4
Dog Kennel Hill Primary School
EDUL SE22 .... **137** E1
Dollis Hill ⊖
WLSDN NW10 .... **70** A2
Dolphin School
BTSEA SW11 .... **133** E3
The Dominie
BTSEA SW11 .... **115** F4
Donmar Warehouse Theatre
LSQ/SEVD WC2H **20** C5
Donnington Primary School
WLSDN NW10 .... **70** B4
The Dorchester Hotel
MYFR/PKLN W1K **30** B3
Dorma Trading Park
LEY E10 .... **61** D3
Dorset Road Infant School
ELTH/MOT SE9 .... **161** E2
Dorset Square Hotel
CAMTN NW1 .... **17** E2

Douglas Bader Foundation
PUT/ROE SW15................................**130** A4
Downderry Primary School
BMLY BR1.....................................**159** E4
Downham Health Centre
BMLY BR1.....................................**159** E4
Downsell Primary School
SRTFD E15....................................**81** D1
Downshall Primary School
CNTH./NBYPK IG2.............................**67** E2
Downsview School
CLPT E5.......................................**78** D1
Drapers Hall
LOTH EC2R....................................**24** B4
Drapers Sports Ground
SRTFD E15....................................**80** C1
The Draycott Hotel
CHEL SW3.....................................**41** F4
Drayton Park ≥
HOLWY N7.....................................**76** A2
Drayton Park Primary School
HBRY N5.......................................**76** A2
DRCA Business Centre
BTSEA SW11...................................**116** A4
Drew Primary School
CAN/RD E16....................................**107** E2
Drill Hall
GWRST WC1E...................................**20** A2
Dr Johnson's House
FLST/FETLN EC4A..............................**22** B4
Drury Lane Theatre
WLSDN NW10...................................**69** D1
Duchess Theatre
COVGDN WC2E..................................**33** E1
Duff Miller College
SKENS SW7....................................**39** F4
Duke of York Column
STJS SW1Y.....................................**32** B4
Duke of York Theatre
CHCR WC2N....................................**32** C2
Dukes Hotel
WHALL SW1A...................................**31** E4
Dulverton Primary School
ELTH/MOT SE9..................................**163** D2
Dulwich College
DUL SE21......................................**155** E1
Dulwich College Track
DUL SE21......................................**155** E1
Dulwich Hamlet FC
EDUL SE22.....................................**137** E2
Dulwich Hamlet Junior School
HNHL SE24.....................................**137** D4
Dulwich Hospital
EDUL SE22.....................................**137** E2
Dulwich Leisure Centre
EDUL SE22.....................................**138** A2
Dulwich Medical Centre
EDUL SE22.....................................**138** A3
Dulwich Picture Gallery
DUL SE21......................................**137** E5
Dulwich & Sydenham Hill Golf Club
DUL SE21......................................**156** A1
Dulwich Village CE Infant School
DUL SE21......................................**137** E4
Dunbar Wharf
POP/IOD E14...................................**103** F1
Duncombe Primary School
ARCH N19......................................**57** E3
Dundee Wharf
POP/IOD E14...................................**103** F1
Dunraven School
STRHM/NOR SW16..............................**153** F3
Durand Primary School
BRXN/ST SW9...................................**117** F4
Durands Wharf
BERM/RHTH SE16...............................**103** F3
Dyslexia Teaching Centre
ECT SW5.......................................**114** B1
Eaglesfield School
WOOL/PLUM SE18...............................**126** A4
Ealdham Primary School
ELTH/MOT SE9..................................**142** C2
Ealing, Hammersmith &
West London College
ACT W3...**98** B2
WKENS W14.....................................**101** D5
Earlham Primary School
FSTGT E7......................................**81** F2
Earl's Court ⊖
ECT SW5.......................................**38** B5
Earl's Court Exhibition Centre
FUL/PGN SW6...................................**114** A1

Earlsfield ≥
WAND/EARL SW18...............................**150** C1
Earlsfield Primary School
WAND/EARL SW18...............................**150** C2
Earth Galleries
SKENS SW7....................................**40** B3
East Acton ⊖
SHB W12.......................................**87** F5
East Acton Primary School
ACT W3...**99** E1
East Beckton District Centre
EHAM E6.......................................**95** F5
Eastbury Comprehensive School
BARK IG11......................................**85** E5
Eastbury Primary School
BARK IG11......................................**85** F4
Eastcote Primary School
WELL DA16.....................................**145** D1
East Dulwich ≥
EDUL SE22.....................................**137** E2
East End Computing &
Business College
WCHPL E1......................................**90** B5
Eastgate Business Park
LEY E10..**61** E3
East Greenwich Christ Church CE
Primary School
GNWCH SE10...................................**105** E5
East Ham ⊖
EHAM E6.......................................**83** E4
East Ham Industrial Estate
EHAM E6.......................................**95** D3
East Ham Jewish Cemetery
EHAM E6.......................................**95** E2
East Ham Leisure Centre
EHAM E6.......................................**83** F5
East Ham Memorial Hospital
EHAM E6.......................................**83** D4
East Ham Nature Reserve
EHAM E6.......................................**95** F3
East India ⊖
POP/IOD E14...................................**105** D1
Eastlea Community Centre
CAN/RD E16....................................**93** F3
Eastlea Community School
CAN/RD E16....................................**93** E3
East London Business College
WAN E11..**63** F3
East London Cemetery
PLSTW E13.....................................**93** F2
East London Crematorium
SRTFD E15.....................................**93** F2
East London RFC
EHAM E6.......................................**95** F4
East London RUFC
SRTFD E15.....................................**93** F1
Eastman Dental Hospital
FSBYW WC1X...................................**9** E5
East Putney ⊖
PUT/ROE SW15.................................**131** E3
East Sheen Cemetery
RCHPK/HAM TW10...............................**128** A3
East Sheen Primary School
MORT/ESHN SW14...............................**129** E2
East Wickham Primary School
WELL DA16.....................................**127** F4
Eaton Square Preparatory School
BGVA SW1W.....................................**42** C4
Eden College
STHWK SE1.....................................**47** D2
Eden High School
FUL/PGN SW6...................................**113** F4
Eden Medical Centre
WKENS W14.....................................**101** F5
Edgebury Primary School
CHST BR7......................................**162** C4
Edge Business Centre
CRICK NW2.....................................**52** B4
Edgware College
KIL/WHAMP NW6................................**72** C3
Edgware Road ⊖
CAMTN NW1.....................................**16** C3
Edith Neville Primary School
CAMTN NW1.....................................**8** A2
Edmund Waller Primary School
NWCR SE14.....................................**121** D5
Education Centre
WOOL/PLUM SE18...............................**126** B1
Edward Wilson Primary School
BAY/PAD W2....................................**14** C2
Effra Road Retail Park
BRXS/STRHM SW2...............................**136** A3

The Egerton House Hotel
CHEL SW3 .... **41** D3
Eglinton Junior School
WOOL/PLUM SE18 .... **126** A2
Eglinton Primary School
WOOL/PLUM SE18 .... **126** A3
Eleanor Palmer Primary School
KTTN NW5 .... **74** C1
Eleanor Smith Special School
PLSTW E13 .... **94** A1
Electric Cinema
NTGHL W11 .... **89** F5
Elephant & Castle ⇌ ⊖
STHWK SE1 .... **47** E4
Elephant & Castle Leisure Centre
LBTH SE11 .... **47** D4
Elephant & Castle Shopping Centre
STHWK SE1 .... **47** D3
Elfrida Primary School
CAT SE6 .... **158** B4
Eliot Bank Primary School
FSTH SE23 .... **156** B2
Elizabeth Selby Infant School
BETH E2 .... **90** A2
Elizabeth Trading Estate
NWCR SE14 .... **121** D2
Ellen Wilkinson Primary School
CAN/RD E16 .... **95** D4
Ellerslie Square Industrial Estate
BRXS/STRHM SW2 .... **135** E2
Elm Court School
WNWD SE27 .... **154** B2
The Elmgreen School
WNWD SE27 .... **154** B2
Elmhurst Primary School
FSTGT E7 .... **82** B4
Elm Wood Primary School
DUL SE21 .... **155** D3
Elsdale Street Health Centre
HOM E9 .... **78** C4
Elsley School
BTSEA SW11 .... **134** A1
Eltham ⇌
ELTH/MOT SE9 .... **143** F2
Eltham Bus Station
ELTH/MOT SE9 .... **143** F3
Eltham CE Primary School
ELTH/MOT SE9 .... **143** F3
Eltham College Junior School
ELTH/MOT SE9 .... **161** D1
Eltham College Senior School
ELTH/MOT SE9 .... **161** D2
Eltham Crematorium
ELTH/MOT SE9 .... **145** D2
Eltham Green School
ELTH/MOT SE9 .... **143** D4
Eltham Health Clinic
ELTH/MOT SE9 .... **143** E3
Eltham Health & Fitness Centre
ELTH/MOT SE9 .... **144** A4
Eltham Hill Technical College
ELTH/MOT SE9 .... **143** E4
Eltham Palace
ELTH/MOT SE9 .... **143** E5
Eltham Pools
ELTH/MOT SE9 .... **143** E3
Eltham Warren Golf Club
ELTH/MOT SE9 .... **144** B3
Elverson Road ⊖
DEPT SE8 .... **122** B5
Emanuel School
BTSEA SW11 .... **133** D3
Embankment ⊖
CHCR WC2N **33** D3
Embankment Pier
CHCR WC2N **33** E3
Embassy of Afghanistan
SKENS SW7 .... **40** A1
Embassy of Albania
BCVA SW1W **43** D3
Embassy of Algeria
NTGHL W11 .... **101** E2
Embassy of Angola
MYFR/PKLN W1K **30** A2
Embassy of Argentina
MYFR/PKLN W1K **30** C1
Embassy of Armenia
KENS W8 .... **38** C2
Embassy of Austria
KTBR SW1X **42** A2
Embassy of Bahrain
SKENS SW7 .... **39** E3

Embassy of Belarus
KENS W8 .... **39** D1
Embassy of Belgium
KTBR SW1X **42** B3
Embassy of Bolivia
BCVA SW1W **42** B3
Embassy of Bosnia-Herzegovina
CAVSQ/HST W1G **19** D4
Embassy of Brazil
MYFR/PKLN W1K **30** A1
Embassy of Bulgaria
SKENS SW7 .... **39** F2
Embassy of Cameroon
NTGHL W11 .... **101** E2
Embassy of China
CAVSQ/HST W1G **18** C2
Embassy of Costa Rica
BAY/PAD W2 .... **27** F1
Embassy of Cote d'Ivoire
KTBR SW1X **42** B2
Embassy of Croatia
GTPST W1W **19** D1
Embassy of Cuba
LSQ/SEVD WC2H **20** C4
**Embassy of Democratic
Republic of the Congo**
KTBR SW1X **41** F3
Embassy of Denmark
KTBR SW1X **41** E2
**Embassy of
Dominican Republic**
BAY/PAD W2 .... **15** D5
Embassy of Ecuador
KTBR SW1X **41** E2
Embassy of Egypt
MYFR/PICC W1J **30** C4
Embassy of Estonia
SKENS SW7 .... **39** F1
Embassy of Ethiopia
KTBR SW1X **40** B1
Embassy of Finland
KTBR SW1X **42** A2
Embassy of France
KTBR SW1X **29** F5
Embassy of Gabon
SKENS SW7 .... **39** F3
Embassy of Georgia
KENS W8 .... **38** C1
Embassy of Germany
KTBR SW1X **42** A2
Embassy of Ghana
HGT N6 .... **56** B3
Embassy of Greece
NTGHL W11 .... **101** F2
Embassy of Guatemala
WBPTN SW10 .... **114** B2
Embassy of Honduras
MBLAR W1H **17** F2
Embassy of Hungary
KTBR SW1X **42** B3
Embassy of Iceland
KTBR SW1X **42** A4
Embassy of Indonesia
MYFR/PKLN W1K **30** B2
Embassy of Iraq
SKENS SW7 .... **39** F2
Embassy of Ireland
KTBR SW1X **42** C1
Embassy of Israel
KENS W8 .... **27** D5
Embassy of Italy
MYFR/PKLN W1K **30** B1
Embassy of Jordan
KENS W8 .... **38** A1
Embassy of Krygyzstan
MBLAR W1H **17** E3
Embassy of Kuwait
KTBR SW1X **29** F5
Embassy of Latvia
CAMTN NW1 .... **18** A1
Embassy of Lebanon
KENS W8 .... **26** C3
Embassy of Liberia
BAY/PAD W2 .... **27** E3
Embassy of Lithuania
MBLAR W1H **17** E3
Embassy of Luxembourg
KTBR SW1X **42** A1
Embassy of Mexico
MYFR/PICC W1J **30** C4
Embassy of Mongolia
KENS W8 .... **39** D1

Embassy of Morocco
SKENS SW7................................39 E4
Embassy of Mozambique
FITZ W1T................................19 E1
Embassy of Myanmar
MYFR/PICC W1J................................30 C3
Embassy of Nepal
KENS W8................................26 C3
Embassy of Netherlands
SKENS SW7................................39 F1
Embassy of Norway
KTBR SW1X................................42 B2
Embassy of Paraguay
SKENS SW7................................39 D3
Embassy of Peru
KTBR SW1X................................41 F2
Embassy of Philippines
KENS W8................................26 C4
Embassy of Poland
CAVSQ/HST W1G................................18 C2
Embassy of Portugal
KTBR SW1X................................42 A1
Embassy of Qatar
MYFR/PKLN W1K................................30 B4
Embassy of Romania
KENS W8................................26 C5
Embassy of Russian Federation
KENS W8................................26 C4
Embassy of Saudi Arabia
MYFR/PICC W1J................................30 C3
Embassy of Senegal
CRICK NW2................................70 C4
Embassy of Slovak Republic
KENS W8................................26 C3
Embassy of Slovenia
MHST W1U................................18 C4
Embassy of Spain
KTBR SW1X................................42 B2
Embassy of Sudan
WHALL SW1A................................31 E4
Embassy of Sweden
MBLAR W1H................................17 E3
Embassy of Switzerland
MBLAR W1H................................17 E3
Embassy of Syria
KTBR SW1X................................42 A1
Embassy of Thailand
SKENS SW7................................39 F3
Embassy of the Holy See
WIM/MER SW19................................148 C3
Embassy of the US
MYFR/PKLN W1K................................30 A1
Embassy of Turkey
KTBR SW1X................................42 B1
Embassy of Turkmenistan
FITZ W1T................................19 E3
Embassy of Ukraine
NTGHL W11................................101 E2
Embassy of United Arab Emirates
BAY/PAD W2................................28 B5
Embassy of Uruguay
SKENS SW7................................41 D2
Embassy of Uzbekistan
NTGHL W11................................101 F2
Embassy of Venezuela
SKENS SW7................................40 B3
Embassy of Vietnam
KENS W8................................39 D2
Embassy of Yemen
SKENS SW7................................40 A4
Emery Theatre
POP/IOD E14................................92 B5
Emmanuel CE Primary School
KIL/WHAMP NW6................................72 A2
Empire Cinema
LSQ/SEVD WC2H................................32 B1
English Martyrs RC Primary School
WALW SE17................................48 A5
Ensham Secondary School
TOOT SW17................................151 E3
Enterprise Business Park
POP/IOD E14................................104 B3
Enterprise Industrial Estate
BERM/RHTH SE16................................120 C1
Eric Liddell Sports Centre
ELTH/MOT SE9................................161 D2
Eridge House Preparatory School
FUL/PGN SW6................................113 F5
Ernest Bevin College
TOOT SW17................................151 E3
Eros
MYFR/PICC W1J................................32 A2

Essendine Primary School
KIL/WHAMP NW6................................2 B4
Essex Primary School
MNPK E12................................85 E3
Essex Road ≷
IS N1................................76 C4
Ethelburga GM School
BTSEA SW11................................115 E4
Euro Business Centre
SRTFD E15................................81 F5
Euro Freightliner Terminal ≷
WLSDN NW10................................87 E2
Eurolink Business Centre
BRXS/STRHM SW2................................136 A2
European Business
School London
SDTCH EC2A................................12 C5
European College of
Business Management
CAMTN NW1................................6 A5
European School of Economics
KTBR SW1X................................42 B1
European Vocational College
HDTCH EC3A................................25 D5
Euro Way School London
FSBYPK N4................................58 B2
Euston ≷ ⊖ ⊖
CAMTN NW1................................8 A4
Euston Centre University
of Westminster
CAMTN NW1................................7 E5
Euston Square ⊖
CAMTN NW1................................7 F5
Euston Tower
CAMTN NW1................................7 E5
Evans Business Centre
CRICK NW2................................52 A5
Eveline Day School
TOOT SW17................................151 F2
Eveline Lowe Primary School
PECK SE15................................119 F1
Evendine College
SOHO/SHAV W1D................................20 A4
Everyman Belsize Park Cinema
HAMP NW3................................73 E2
Everyman Cinema
HAMP NW3................................72 C1
ExCeL Exhibition Centre
CAN/RD E16................................106 B1
Exchange Square
SDTCH EC2A................................24 C2
The Exchange
IL IG1................................66 B4
Express by Holiday Inn
CAN/RD E16................................93 F5
GNTH/NBYPK IG2................................67 D1
HMSMTH W6................................100 B5
PIM SW1V................................116 C1
SDTCH EC2A................................12 C4
STHWK SE1................................35 D3
WAND/EARL SW18................................132 B2
WAP E1W................................103 D1
Faircharm Trading Estate
DEPT SE8................................122 B3
The Faircross Complementary
Medical Centre
BARK IG11................................85 E3
Fairlawn Primary School
FSTH SE23................................138 C5
Fairley House School
PIM SW1V................................44 A5
Fairways Business Park
LEY E10................................61 E4
Falconbrook Primary School
BTSEA SW11................................115 D5
Falcon Business Centre
BTSEA SW11................................133 E2
Falcon Park Industrial Estate
WLSDN NW10................................69 E2
Falconwood ≷
ELTH/MOT SE9................................145 D1
Falkner House School
SKENS SW7................................114 C1
Family Records Centre
FSBYW WC1X................................10 A4
Fanmakers' Hall
LVPST EC2M................................24 C3
The Fan Museum
GNWCH SE10................................122 C3
Faraday Building
BLKFR EC4V................................23 D5

Farm Lane Trading Estate
FUL/PGN SW6 ... 114 A2
Farringdon ⇄ ⊖
FARR EC1M ... 22 B2
Fenchurch Street ⇄
FENCHST EC3M ... 37 D1
Fenstanton J & I School
BRXS/STRHM SW2 ... 154 A1
Fenton House
HAMP NW3 ... 54 C5
Ferrier Industrial Estate
WAND/EARL SW18 ... 132 B2
Festival Pier
STHWK SE1 ... 33 F3
Financial Times
STHWK SE1 ... 35 F3
Financial Times Newspaper Offices
POP/IOD E14 ... 92 C5
Finchley Road ⊖
KIL/WHAMP NW6 ... 72 C3
Finchley Road & Frognal ⊖
KIL/WHAMP NW6 ... 72 B2
Finsbury Circus Medical Centre
LVPST EC2M ... 24 B3
Finsbury Health Centre
CLKNW EC1R ... 10 A5
Finsbury Leisure Centre
FSBYE EC1V ... 11 F4
Finsbury Park ⇄ ⊖
FSBYPK N4 ... 58 A4
Finsbury Park Track
FSBYPK N4 ... 58 A4
Finton House School
TOOT SW17 ... 151 F2
Fircroft Primary School
TOOT SW17 ... 151 F2
Fire Brigade Museum
STHWK SE1 ... 35 E5
Firepower Royal Artillery Museum
WOOL/PLUM SE18 ... 108 B4
Fisher Athletic FC
BERM/RHTH SE16 ... 103 D2
Fishmonger's Hall
CANST EC4R ... 36 A2
Fitness Unlimited Leisure Centre
BOW E3 ... 92 A1
Fitzrovia Medical Centre
FITZ W1T ... 19 E1
Fitzroy Nuffield Hospital
MBLAR W1H ... 17 E4
Five Bridges School
LBTH SE11 ... 117 F1
Flamsteed House Museum
GNWCH SE10 ... 123 D3
Flaxman Sports Centre
CMBW SE5 ... 118 C5
Fleet Primary School
HAMP NW3 ... 73 F2
Fleming Lab Museum
BAY/PAD W2 ... 16 B4
Flora Gardens Primary School
HMSMTH W6 ... 100 B5
Florence Nightingale Museum
STHWK SE1 ... 45 E1
Flutters Leisure Centre
FUL/PGN SW6 ... 114 A3
The Ford College
CONDST W1S ... 19 D5
Foreign & Commonwealth Office
WHALL SW1A ... 32 B5
Foreland Medical Centre
NTGHL W11 ... 101 E1
Forest Business Park
LEY E10 ... 61 D2
Forest Gate ⇄
FSTGT E7 ... 82 A2
Forest Gate Community School
FSTGT E7 ... 82 A2
Forest Hill ⇄ ⊖
FSTH SE23 ... 156 C2
Forest Hill Business Centre
FSTH SE23 ... 156 C2
Forest Hill Industrial Estate
FSTH SE23 ... 156 C2
Forest Hill Pools
SYD SE26 ... 156 C2
Forest Hill School
FSTH SE23 ... 157 D3
Forest House Business Centre
WAN E11 ... 63 F2
The Former Health Centre
CHARL SE7 ... 107 D5

Forster Park Primary School
CAT SE6 ... 159 E3
Fortune Theatre
HOL/ALD WC2B ... 21 D5
Fossdene Primary School
CHARL SE7 ... 124 B1
The Foundling Museum
BMSBY WC1N ... 9 D5
The Fountain Studios
WBLY HA9 ... 68 A3
Fountayne Road Health Centre
STNW/STAM N16 ... 60 A4
Four Seasons Hotel
BERM/RHTH SE16 ... 103 F2
MYFR/PKLN W1K ... 30 C5
Foxfield Primary School
WOOL/PLUM SE18 ... 126 C1
Fox Primary School
KENS W8 ... 26 A4
Franciscan Primary School
TOOT SW17 ... 152 A4
Francis Holland School
BGVA SW1W ... 42 A5
CAMTN NW1 ... 17 E1
Frank Barnes Primary School
STJWD NW8 ... 73 D4
Free Trade Wharf
WAP E1W ... 103 D1
Freightliners City Farm
HOLWY N7 ... 75 F3
The French Institute
SKENS SW7 ... 40 A4
Fresh Wharf Estate
BARK IG11 ... 84 B5
Freuchen Medical Centre
WLSDN NW10 ... 87 F1
Freud Museum
HAMP NW3 ... 73 D3
Friars Primary Foundation School
STHWK SE1 ... 34 C5
Friends House
CAMTN NW1 ... 8 A4
Frogmore Industrial Estate
HBRY N5 ... 76 C1
WLSDN NW10 ... 86 C2
Fryent Country Park
KTN/HRWW/WS HA3 ... 50 A2
Fryent Medical Centre
CDALE/KGS NW9 ... 50 C2
Fryent Primary School
CDALE/KGS NW9 ... 50 C2
Fulham Broadway ⊖
FUL/PGN SW6 ... 114 A3
Fulham Cemetery
FUL/PGN SW6 ... 113 D3
Fulham Clinic
HMSMTH W6 ... 113 E2
Fulham Cross Girls Secondary School
FUL/PGN SW6 ... 113 D3
Fulham FC (Craven Cottage)
PUT/ROE SW15 ... 112 C4
Fulham Medical Centre
FUL/PGN SW6 ... 114 B3
Fulham Palace
FUL/PGN SW6 ... 113 D5
Fulham Pools
FUL/PGN SW6 ... 113 F2
Fulham Preparatory School
WKENS W14 ... 113 E2
Fulham Pre-Preparatory School
FUL/PGN SW6 ... 113 E5
Fulham Preparatory School
FUL/PGN SW6 ... 113 E5
Fulham Primary School
FUL/PGN SW6 ... 114 A2
Fuller Smith & Turner Sports Club
CHSWK W4 ... 111 E4
Furness Primary School
WLSDN NW10 ... 88 A1
Future Business College
CONDST W1S ... 19 D5
Gainsborough Primary School
HOM E9 ... 79 F3
SRTFD E15 ... 93 E2
Gallions Mount Primary School
WOOL/PLUM SE18 ... 127 F1
Gallions Primary School
EHAM E6 ... 96 B5
Gallions Reach ⊖
EHAM E6 ... 96 B5

Gallions Reach Shopping Park
 EHAM E6...96 B4
Gants Hill ⊖
 GNTH/NBYPK IG2.............................66 A1
Gants Hill Medical Centre
 GNTH/NBYPK IG2.............................66 A1
Gardener Industrial Estate
 SYD SE26..157 E5
Garden House School
 BGVA SW1W....................................116 A1
Garratt Park
 Secondary Special School
 WAND/EARL SW18..........................150 C3
Garrick Theatre
 LSQ/SEVD WC2H...............................32 C2
Gascoigne Primary School
 BARK IG11...84 C5
Gate Cinema
 KENS W8...26 A3
Gatehouse School
 BETH E2...91 D1
The Gatehouse Theatre
 HGT N6..56 A2
The Gate Theatre
 NTGHL W11.......................................26 A3
Gateway
 EHAM E6..96 B3
Gateway Business Centre
 WOOL/PLUM SE18..........................108 C4
Gateway Industrial Estate
 WLSDN NW10.....................................87 F2
Gatton School
 TOOT SW17......................................151 E4
Gayhurst Primary School
 HACK E8..78 A4
Geffrye Museum
 BETH E2...13 D2
Gemini Business Estate
 NWCR SE14......................................121 D1
General Medical Clinics
 WCHPL E1..25 E2
Genesis Cinema
 WCHPL E1..90 C3
Geoffrey Chaucer
 Technology College
 STHWK SE1..48 A3
The Geoffrey Lloyd Foulkes Clinic
 IL IG1...66 A4
George Eliot J & I School
 STJWD NW8.......................................72 C5
George Greens School
 POP/IOD E14....................................122 C1
George Mitchell School
 LEY E10..62 B3
George Tomlinson
 Primary School
 WAN E11...63 E3
Germal College
 FSBYPK N4...58 A3
Gibbs Green Special School
 WKENS W14.....................................113 F1
The Gielgud Theatre
 SOHO/CST W1F..................................32 A1
Giffin Business Centre
 DEPT SE8...122 A3
Gilbert Collection
 TPL/STR WC2R...................................33 F1
Gillespie Primary School
 HBRY N5...58 B5
Gipsy Hill ₴
 NRWD SE19......................................155 E5
Girdlers' Hall
 CITYW EC2V.......................................23 F3
Gladstone Medical Centre
 CRICK NW2...69 F1
Gladstone Park Primary School
 WLSDN NW10.....................................70 A2
Glaziers/Scientific Instrument
 Makers Hall
 STHWK SE1..36 A3
Gleen Lecky Health Centre
 PUT/ROE SW15................................131 D2
Glenbrook Primary School
 CLAP SW4..135 D4
Glenham College
 IL IG1...66 B4
Globe Academy
 STHWK SE1..48 A3
Globe Primary School
 BETH E2...90 C2
Globe Wharf
 BERM/RHTH SE16............................103 D1

Gloucester Primary School
 PECK SE15.......................................119 E3
Gloucester Road ⊖
 SKENS SW7..39 E4
Godolphin & Latymer School
 HMSMTH W6....................................100 B5
Godwin Junior School
 FSTGT E7...82 B1
Goethe Institute
 SKENS SW7..40 B2
Golborne Medical Centre
 NKENS W10..89 F3
Golden Hinde Educational Trust
 STHWK SE1..36 A2
Golders Green ⊖
 GLDGN NW11.....................................54 A2
Golders Green Crematorium
 GLDGN NW11.....................................54 A2
Golders Green Health Centre
 GLDGN NW11.....................................54 B3
Golders Hill Health Centre
 GLDGN NW11.....................................54 C1
Golders Hill School
 GLDGN NW11.....................................54 A2
Goldhawk Industrial Estate
 SHB W12..100 B4
Goldhawk Road ⊖
 SHB W12..100 C3
Goldsmiths Hall
 STBT EC1A..23 E4
Goldsmiths University of London
 BROCKY SE4.....................................139 F1
 DEPT SE8...122 A4
 LEW SE13...141 E2
 NWCR SE14......................................121 D1
Goodge St ⊖
 FITZ W1T..19 F2
Goodinge Health Centre
 HOLWY N7...75 E3
Goodrich J & I School
 EDUL SE22.......................................138 A4
Good Shepherd RC
 Primary School
 BMLY BR1...159 F4
The Good Shepherd RC
 Primary School
 SHB W12..99 F3
Goose Green Primary School
 EDUL SE22.......................................137 F2
Goose Green Trading Estate
 EDUL SE22.......................................138 A2
Gordonbrock Primary School
 BROCKY SE4.....................................140 A3
Gordon Hospital
 WEST SW1P..44 A5
Gordon Infant School
 IL IG1...67 D5
Gordon Primary School
 ELTH/MOT SE9.................................143 F2
The Goring Hotel
 BGVA SW1W.......................................43 D2
Gospel Oak ⊖
 HAMP NW3...74 A1
Gower House School
 CDALE/KGS NW9................................50 C4
Grace Theatre at the Latchmere
 BTSEA SW11.....................................115 F3
Grafton Primary School
 HOLWY N7...57 E5
Granard Primary School
 PUT/ROE SW15................................130 B4
Granby Sports Club
 CHST BR7...161 E5
Grande Vitesse Industrial Centre
 STHWK SE1..35 D4
Grand Union Industrial Estate
 WLSDN NW10.....................................86 B2
The Grange City Hotel
 TWRH EC3N.......................................37 E1
The Grange Museum
 CRICK NW2...69 F1
Grange Primary School
 CAN/RD E16.......................................93 E3
 STHWK SE1..48 C3
Grange Whitehall Hotel
 RSQ WC1B..20 C3
Grangewood Independent School
 FSTGT E7...83 D4
Granville Road Industrial Estate
 CRICK NW2...53 F4
Grasmere Primary School
 STNW/STAM N16...............................77 D1

Grazebrook Primary School
STNW/STAM N16..........................59 E4

Great Chapel Street Medical Centre
SOHO/SHAV W1D.........................20 A4

**Greater London Authority
Headquarters (City Hall)**
STHWK SE1...................................37 D4

Great Jubilee Wharf
WAP E1W.....................................102 C2

Great Portland Street ⊖
GTPST W1W....................................19 D1

Great Scotland Yard
WHALL SW1A...............................32 C3

Greek School of London
ACT W3...98 B1

Greenacres Primary School
ELTH/MOT SE9............................162 A2

Greenfield Medical Centre
CRICK NW2...................................53 E5

Greenfields Junior School
SHB W12.......................................99 F1

Greengate Medical Centre
PLSTW E13...................................94 B2

Greenheath Business Centre
BETH E2..90 B2

Greenhill Park Medical Centre
WLSDN NW10...............................69 E5

Greenland Pier
BERM/RHTH SE16........................103 F4

Green Lane Business Park
ELTH/MOT SE9............................162 A2

Greenmead Primary School
PUT/ROE SW15...........................130 B3

Green Park ⊖
MYFR/PICC W1J...........................31 D4

Greenshields Industrial Estate
CAN/RD E16................................106 A2

Greenside Primary School
SHB W12......................................100 A3

Greenslade Primary School
WOOL/PLUM SE18.......................127 D2

Greenvale School
FSTH SE23...................................157 E3

Greenwich ≠ ⊖
GNWCH SE10...............................122 B3

Greenwich Centre Business Park
DEPT SE8.....................................122 B3

Greenwich Cinema
GNWCH SE10...............................122 C3

Greenwich Community College
WOOL/PLUM SE18.......................108 B5
WOOL/PLUM SE18.......................127 D2

Greenwich Industrial Estate
CHARL SE7..................................106 B5
GNWCH SE10...............................122 B5

Greenwich Natural Health Centre
GNWCH SE10...............................122 C3

Greenwich Pier
GNWCH SE10...............................122 C1

Greenwich School of Management
GNWCH SE10...............................122 C3

Greenwich Theatre & Art Gallery
GNWCH SE10...............................123 D3

Greenwood Theatre
STHWK SE1...................................36 B5

Gresham College
HCIRC EC1N..................................22 A3

Gresham Way Industrial Estate
WIM/MER SW19...........................150 B3

Grey Coat Hospital School for Girls
WEST SW1P...................................44 A3

The Greycoat Hospital
WEST SW1P...................................44 A5

Griffen Manor School
WOOL/PLUM SE18.......................127 E4

Grinling Gibbons Primary School
DEPT SE8.....................................121 F2

Grocers' Hall
CITYW EC2V..................................24 A5

Grosvenor House Hotel
MYFR/PKLN W1K...........................30 A2

Grove Health Centre
KENS W8..26 B3

The Grove Health Centre
SHB W12......................................100 B3

Grove House (Froebel College)
PUT/ROE SW15...........................129 F4

**Grove House Primary School for
Deaf Children**
WNWD SE27................................154 B2

Grove Medical Centre
DEPT SE8.....................................103 E5

The Grove Medical Centre
ARCH N19......................................57 D4

Grove Park ≠
BMLY BR1.....................................160 A3

Grove Park Primary School
CHSWK W4...................................110 C2

Guardian Angels RC Primary School
BOW E3..91 E3

Guardian Newspapers
POP/IOD E14...............................104 B3

Guards' Chapel & Museum
STJSPK SW1H................................44 A1

Gunnersbury ⊖ ⊖
CHSWK W4...................................110 B1

Gunnersbury Cemetery
BTFD TW8......................................98 A5

Gunnersbury Park Museum
ACT W3...98 A4

Guy's Hospital
STHWK SE1...................................36 B4

**Guys Kings & Thomas Medical School
(Kings College London)**
STHWK SE1...................................35 E3

Gwyn Jones Primary School
WAN E11..63 D2

GX Superbowl
EHAM E6.......................................96 A4

Gypsy Moth IV
GNWCH SE10...............................122 C2

Haberdashers Askes Hatcham College
NWCR SE14..................................121 D5

**Haberdashers Askes
Knights Academy**
BMLY BR1.....................................160 A4

Haberdashers' Hall
STBT EC1A.....................................22 C3

Hackney Business Centre
HACK E8...78 B3

Hackney Central ⊖
HACK E8...78 B3

Hackney City Farm
BETH E2..90 A1

Hackney Community College
IS N1..12 C2

Hackney Downs ≠
HACK E8...78 A2

Hackney Empire Variety Theatre
HACK E8...78 B3

**Hackney Free &
Parochial CE School**
HOM E9..78 C3

The Hackney Museum
HACK E8...78 B3

Hackney Sports Centre
HOM E9..80 A1

Hackney Wick ⊖
HOM E9..80 A3

The Haelan Clinic
CEND/HSY/T N8.............................57 E1

Haggerston ⊖
HACK E8...77 E4

Haggerston School
BETH E2...13 F1

Haggerston Swimming Pool
BETH E2...77 F5

Hague Primary School
BETH E2...90 B3

Haimo Primary School
ELTH/MOT SE9............................143 D3

The Hale Clinic
CAMTN NW1..................................19 D1

Half Moon Theatre
WCHPL E1......................................91 D3

The Halkin Hotel
KTBR SW1X....................................42 B1

Halley Primary School
POP/IOD E14.................................91 E4

Hallfield Clinic
BAY/PAD W2..................................15 E5

Hallfield Infant School
BAY/PAD W2..................................15 D5

Hallmark Trading Estate
WBLY HA9......................................68 C1

The Hall School
HAMP NW3.....................................73 D3

**Hall School Wimbledon
Junior Department**
PUT/ROE SW15...........................148 A3

Hallsville Primary School
CAN/RD E16..................................94 A4

Halstow Primary School
GNWCH SE10...............................123 F1

Hambledon Clinic
CMBW SE5 ....137 D1
Hamer Indoor Market
BOW E3 ....91 F1
Hamilton Road Industrial Estate
WNWD SE27 ....155 D4
Hammersmith ⊖
HMSMTH W6 ....100 C5
Hammersmith Apollo
HMSMTH W6 ....112 C1
Hammersmith Cemetery
HMSMTH W6 ....113 D1
Hammersmith Hospital
SHB W12 ....88 A5
Hammersmith Industrial Estate
HMSMTH W6 ....112 C2
Hammersmith New Cemetery
RCH/KEW TW9 ....110 B5
Hammersmith Physiotherapy &
  Sports Injury Clinic
HMSMTH W6 ....100 C5
Hammersmith &
  West London College
WKENS W14 ....101 E5
WKENS W14 ....113 E1
Hampden Gurney School
MBLAR W1H 17 D1
The Hampshire School
SKENS SW7 ....40 C1
Hampstead ⊖
HAMP NW3 ....72 C1
Hampstead College of Fine Art
  & Humanities
HAMP NW3 ....73 E3
Hampstead CC
KIL/WHAMP NW6 ....72 B2
Hampstead Golf Club
GLDGN NW11 ....54 C2
Hampstead Heath ⊖
HAMP NW3 ....73 E1
Hampstead Medical Centre
HAMP NW3 ....72 C1
Hampstead Parochial CE School
HAMP NW3 ....72 C1
Hampstead School
CRICK NW2 ....71 E1
The Hampstead School of Art
HAMP NW3 ....72 A1
Hampstead School of English
KIL/WHAMP NW6 ....72 A1
Hampstead Theatre
HAMP NW3 ....73 D4
Handel's House
MYFR/PKLN W1K 30 C1
Hanover Primary School
IS N1 ....11 D1
Hanover Trading Estate
HOLWY N7 ....75 E2
Hanover West Industrial Estate
WLSDN NW10 ....86 C2
Harbinger Primary School
POP/IOD E14 ....104 A5
Harborough School
ARCH N19 ....57 D4
Hargrave Park Primary School
ARCH N19 ....56 C4
Harlesden ⊖ ⊖
WLSDN NW10 ....87 D1
Harlesden Primary School
WLSDN NW10 ....87 E1
Harley Medical Centre
CAVSQ/HST W1G 19 D4
The Harley Medical Centre
CANST EC4R 35 F1
Harley Street Clinic
CAVSQ/HST W1G 18 C3
The Harley Street Clinic
CAVSQ/HST W1G 18 C2
Harp Business Centre
CRICK NW2 ....52 A4
Harringay ⊖
FSBYPK N4 ....58 A1
Harringay Green Lanes ⊖
FSBYPK N4 ....58 B1
Harrington Hill Primary School
CLPT E5 ....60 B3
Harris Academy Bermondsey
STHWK SE1 ....49 F4
Harris Academy Falconwood
WELL DA16 ....145 E2
Harris Girls Academy
EDUL SE22 ....138 C3

Harrodian School
BARN SW13 ....111 F3
Harrods Store
CHEL SW3 ....41 E2
Harrow Road Health Centre
BAY/PAD W2 ....14 B2
Harry Gosling Primary School
WCHPL E1 ....90 A5
Hartley Primary School
EHAM E6 ....83 E5
Haseltine Primary School
SYD SE26 ....157 F4
Haslemere Industrial Estate
WAND/EARL SW18 ....150 A3
Hastings Clinic
BRXS/STRHM SW2 ....135 F3
Hatcham Mews Business Centre
NWCR SE14 ....121 D3
Haverstock School
HAMP NW3 ....74 A3
Hawkesdown House School
KENS W8 ....26 B4
Hawkins Clinic
PUT/ROE SW15 ....131 D2
Hawley Infant School
CAMTN NW1 ....74 B4
Haydons Road ⊖
WIM/MER SW19 ....150 C5
Haymerle School
PECK SE15 ....120 A2
Hays Galleria
STHWK SE1 ....36 C3
Hayward Gallery
STHWK SE1 ....33 F4
Hazeldene Medical Centre
WBLY HA9 ....68 B3
Headstart Montessori School
TOOT SW17 ....150 C4
The Health Clinic
SKENS SW7 ....40 B4
Healy Medical Centre
CLPT E5 ....60 B3
The Heart Hospital
CAVSQ/HST W1G 18 B3
Heathbrook Primary School
VX/NE SW8 ....116 C5
Heathfield House School
CHSWK W4 ....110 C1
Heath House Preparatory School
BKHTH/KID SE3 ....123 F5
Heathmere Primary School
PUT/ROE SW15 ....148 A1
Heathside Preparatory School
HAMP NW3 ....72 C1
Heathside Preparatory
  School (Lower)
HAMP NW3 ....72 C1
Heathside Preparatory
  School (Upper)
HAMP NW3 ....72 C1
Heber Primary School
EDUL SE22 ....137 F4
Heckford Street
  Business Centre
WAP E1W 103 D1
Hedges & Butler Estate
SRTFD E15 ....92 C1
Helena Road Clinic
WLSDN NW10 ....70 B1
Heliport Industrial Estate
BTSEA SW11 ....115 D5
Helston Court Business Centre
WIM/MER SW19 ....148 B5
Hendon ⊖
HDN NW4 ....52 A1
Hendon FC
CRICK NW2 ....53 D4
Hendon Youth Sports Centre
CRICK NW2 ....53 D2
Henry Cavendish
  Primary School
BAL SW12 ....152 C1
Henry Compton School
FUL/PGN SW6 ....113 D4
Henry Fawcett Primary School
LBTH SE11 ....118 A2
Henwick Primary School
ELTH/MOT SE9 ....143 D1
Herbert Morrison Primary School
VX/NE SW8 ....117 E3
Hereward House School
HAMP NW3 ....73 E3

Her Majestys' Theatre
STJS SW1Y **32** B3

Hermitage Primary School
WAP E1W **102** A2

Herne Hill ⇄
HNHL SE24 ....**136** B3

Herne Hill School
HNHL SE24 ....**136** C3

Herne Hill Stadium
(Cycle Centre)
HNHL SE24 ....**137** D4

Heron Industrial Estate
SRTFD E15 ....**92** B1

Heron Quays ⊖
POP/IOD E14 ....**104** A2

Heronsgate Primary School
THMD SE28 ....**109** D4

Heron Trading Estate
ACT W3 ....**86** B4

Heythrop College
KENS W8 ....**38** C2

Higgs Industrial Estate
HNHL SE24 ....**136** B3

Highbury Fields School
HBRY N5 ....**76** B1

Highbury Grove School
HBRY N5 ....**76** C2

Highbury & Islington ⇄ ⊖ ⊖
IS N1 ....**76** A3

Highbury Park Clinic
HBRY N5 ....**76** B3

Highbury Pool
HBRY N5 ....**76** B3

Highbury Quadrant
Primary School
HBRY N5 ....**76** C1

Highbury Square development
HBRY N5 ....**58** B5

High Commission of Angola
MHST W1U **17** F3

High Commission of Antigua
& Barbuda
MHST W1U **18** A4

High Commission of Bahamas
MYFR/PICC W1J **30** B3

High Commission of Bangladesh
SKENS SW7 ....**39** F2

High Commission of Barbados
FITZ W1T **20** A4

High Commission of Belize
CAVSQ/HST W1G **19** D4

High Commission of Botswana
OXSTW W1C **18** C5

High Commission of Brunei
KTBR SW1X **42** A2

High Commission of Canada
MYFR/PKLN W1K **30** B1

High Commission of Cyprus
MYFR/PKLN W1K **30** A1

High Commission of Dominica
ECT SW5 ....**39** D5

High Commission of Fiji
SKENS SW7 ....**39** E1

High Commission of Grenada
ECT SW5 ....**114** B1

High Commission of Guyana
BAY/PAD W2 ....**26** C3

High Commission of Jamaica
SKENS SW7 ....**40** A1

High Commission of Kenya
CAVSQ/HST W1G **18** C2

High Commission of Lesotho
KTBR SW1X **42** A2

High Commission of Malawi
MYFR/PKLN W1K **30** C1

High Commission of Malaysia
KTBR SW1X **42** B1

High Commission of Maldives
MHST W1U **18** A2

High Commission of Malta
CONDST W1S **31** F2

High Commission of Mauritius
SKENS SW7 ....**39** F3

High Commission of Namibia
CAVSQ/HST W1G **19** D3

High Commission of New Zealand
STJS SW1Y **32** A3

High Commission of Nigeria
CHCR WC2N **32** C3
EMB EC4Y **22** B5

High Commission of Pakistan
KTBR SW1X **41** F2

High Commission of Papua
New Guinea
STJS SW1Y **31** F3

High Commission of St Vincent &
the Grenadines
KENS W8 ....**39** D1

High Commission of Seychelles
MHST W1U **17** F2

High Commission of Sierra Leone
REGST W1B **19** E4

High Commission of Singapore
KTBR SW1X **41** F1

High Commission of South Africa
CHCR WC2N **32** C3

High Commission of Sri Lanka
BAY/PAD W2 ....**28** B1

High Commission of Swaziland
WESTW SW1E **43** E2

High Commission of the Gambia
KENS W8 ....**39** D1

High Commission of Tonga
MBLAR W1H **17** D3

High Commission of Trinidad
& Tobago
KTBR SW1X **42** A2

High Commission of Uganda
CHCR WC2N **32** B3

High Commission of Zambia
KENS W8 ....**39** E1

High Commission of Zimbabwe
CHCR WC2N **32** C2

Highfield School
WAND/EARL SW18 ....**133** E5

Highgate ⊖
HGT N6 ....**56** B1

Highgate Cemetery
HGT N6 ....**56** A3

Highgate Golf Club
EFNCH N2 ....**55** E1

Highgate Junior School
HGT N6 ....**55** F1

Highgate Private Hospital
HGT N6 ....**55** F1

Highgate School
HGT N6 ....**55** F2

Highlands J & I School
IL IG1 ....**65** F3

Highlands Primary School
IL IG1 ....**65** F3

Highshore School
PECK SE15 ....**119** F4

High Street Kensington ⊖
KENS W8 ....**38** C1

High View Primary School
BTSEA SW11 ....**133** D2

The Highway Trading Centre
WAP E1W **103** D1

Hillbrook Primary School
TOOT SW17 ....**151** F4

Hill House International Junior School
KTBR SW1X **41** F3

Hill House
Preparatory School
CHEL SW3 ....**115** E2

Hill House School
KTBR SW1X **41** E3

Hill Mead Infant School
BRXN/ST SW9 ....**136** B2

Hillmead Primary School
BRXN/ST SW9 ....**136** B2

Hilly Fields Medical Centre
BROCKY SE4 ....**140** A3

Hilton Docklands Pier
BERM/RHTH SE16 ....**103** F2

Hinley Clinic
LBTH SE11 ....**46** B5

Hispaniola
WHALL SW1A **33** D4

Hitherfield Primary School
STRHM/NOR SW16 ....**154** A2

Hither Green ⇄
LEW SE13 ....**141** E4

Hither Green Cemetery
CAT SE6 ....**159** F2

Hither Green Primary School
LEW SE13 ....**141** D4

HM Prison
BRXS/STRHM SW2 ....**135** E4
HOLWY N7 ....**75** E1
SHB W12 ....**88** A5
THMD SE28 ....**109** E4
WAND/EARL SW18 ....**133** D5

HMS President
EMB EC4Y **34** B1
Hogarth Business Park
CHSWK W4 .... **111** E5
Hogarth Industrial Estate
WLSDN NW10 .... **88** A3
Hogarth's House
CHSWK W4 .... **111** D2
Holbeach Primary School
CAT SE6 .... **140** A5
Holborn ⊖
HHOL WC1V **21** D4
Holborn College
WOOL/PLUM SE18 .... **107** D5
**Holborn College
Independent School**
HMSMTH W6 .... **112** C1
Holborn Medical Centre
BMSBY WC1N **21** E1
Holborn Town Hall
HHOL WC1V **21** D4
Holiday Inn
CAMTN NW1 .... **74** B4
FSBYW WC1X **9** F4
Holland House
WKENS W14 .... **101** F3
Holland Park ⊖
NTGHL W11 .... **101** F2
**Holland Park
Pre-Preparatory School**
WKENS W14 .... **101** F4
Holland Park School
KENS W8 .... **101** F3
Holland Park Theatre
WKENS W14 .... **101** F3
Holland Street Clinic
KENS W8 .... **38** B1
Holloway Road ⊖
HOLWY N7 .... **75** F2
Holloway School
HOLWY N7 .... **75** D2
Hollydale Primary School
PECK SE15 .... **120** C5
Hollywood Bowl
BERM/RHTH SE16 .... **103** D4
The Holme
CAMTN NW1 .... **5** F4
Holmleigh Primary School
STNW/STAM N16 .... **59** F3
Holocaust Memorial Garden
KTBR SW1X **29** F5
Holy Cross RC Primary School
CAT SE6 .... **158** C1
Holy Family RC Primary School
BKHTH/KID SE3 .... **142** B2
POP/IOD E14 .... **104** A1
Holy Ghost RC Primary School
BAL SW12 .... **133** F5
Holy Trinity CE Primary School
BRXS/STRHM SW2 .... **135** F5
KIL/WHAMP NW6 .... **72** C3
KTBR SW1X **42** A4
RCHPK/HAM TW10 .... **128** A2
SYD SE26 .... **156** C2
Holy Trinity In St Silas
CAMTN NW1 .... **74** B4
Holy Trinity Primary School
HACK E8 .... **77** F3
Holy Trinity School
CHEL SW3 .... **41** F4
Home Office
WEST SW1P **44** B3
Homerton ⊖
HOM E9 .... **79** D2
Homerton University Hospital
HOM E9 .... **79** D2
Homoeopathic Health Centre
PLSTW E13 .... **94** A3
Honeywell Primary School
BTSEA SW11 .... **133** F4
Honor Oak Crematorium
FSTH SE23 .... **139** D3
Honor Oak Gallery
FSTH SE23 .... **139** D3
Honor Oak Health Centre
BROCKY SE4 .... **139** E2
Honor Oak Park ⇌ ⊖
FSTH SE23 .... **139** D4
Honourable Artillery Company
STLK EC1Y **24** A1
Hopewell School
BARK IG11 .... **85** D3

Horizon Industrial Estate
PECK SE15 .... **120** A2
Horizon School
STNW/STAM N16 .... **77** E1
The Horniman Museum & Gardens
FSTH SE23 .... **156** B1
Horniman Primary School
FSTH SE23 .... **156** B1
Horn Park Primary School
LEE/GVPK SE12 .... **142** B5
Hornsby House School
BAL SW12 .... **152** A1
Hornsey Rise Health Centre
ARCH N19 .... **57** D2
Horn Stairs
BERM/RHTH SE16 .... **103** F2
Horse Guards Parade
WHALL SW1A **32** B4
Hospital of St John & St Elizabeth
STJWD NW8 .... **4** A2
The Hotel Russell
RSQ WC1B **20** C1
Hotham Primary School
PUT/ROE SW15 .... **131** D2
House of Detention
CLKNW EC1R **10** B5
Houses of Parliament
WHALL SW1A **45** D1
Howland Quay
BERM/RHTH SE16 .... **103** D4
Hoxton ⊖
BETH E2 .... **13** E2
Hoxton Hall Community Theatre
IS N1 .... **12** C1
HQS Wellington (Master Mariners)
TPL/STR WC2R **34** B2
HSBC Tower
POP/IOD E14 .... **104** B2
The Humana Wellington Hospital
STJWD NW8 .... **4** B3
Humber Trading Estate
CRICK NW2 .... **52** B4
Hunterian Museum
LINN WC2A **21** F4
Hunter Street Health Centre
STPAN WC1H **8** C5
Huntsman Sports Club
BKHTH/KID SE3 .... **142** A5
Hurlingham Business Park
FUL/PGN SW6 .... **132** A1
Hurlingham House
FUL/PGN SW6 .... **132** A1
Hurlingham Private School
PUT/ROE SW15 .... **131** F2
Huron University
RSQ WC1B **20** C2
Hyatt Carlton Tower Hotel
KTBR SW1X **41** F3
Hyatt Regency-The Churchill
MBLAR W1H **17** F4
Hyde Park Corner ⊖
KTBR SW1X **30** C3
Hyleford School
IL IG1 .... **85** E2
Hythe Road Industrial Estate
WLSDN NW10 .... **88** A3
Ian Mikardo High School
BOW E3 .... **92** B2
Ibis Hotel
CAMTN NW1 .... **7** F4
CAN/RD E16 .... **106** A4
FUL/PGN SW6 .... **114** A2
GNWCH SE10 .... **122** C2
POP/IOD E14 .... **104** C1
SRTFD E15 .... **81** E3
WBLY HA9 .... **68** A2
Ibstock Place School
PUT/ROE SW15 .... **129** E4
ICA Cinema
STJS SW1Y **32** B3
Ickburgh School
CLPT E5 .... **60** B5
Ihlara Sport FC
HBRY N5 .... **76** C3
Ilderton Primary School
PECK SE15 .... **120** C2
Ilford ⇌
IL IG1 .... **66** A5
Ilford Business Centre
IL IG1 .... **66** B4
Ilford Golf Club
IL IG1 .... **65** F3

Ilford Medical Centre
IL IG1 .... 66 B5

Ilford Preparatory School
GDMY/SEVK IG3 .... 67 F3

Ilford Retail Park
IL IG1 .... 66 C4

Ilford Swimming Pool
IL IG1 .... 67 D4

Ilford Ursuline High School
IL IG1 .... 66 B4

Ilford Ursuline Preparatory School
IL IG1 .... 66 B4

Iman Zakaria Academy
FSTGT E7 .... 82 B2

Imperial College
PUT/ROE SW15 .... 113 D5
SKENS SW7 .... 115 D1

Imperial College of London
SKENS SW7 .... 40 A1

Imperial College of Science
FUL/PGN SW6 .... 114 A2

Imperial College of Science
& Technology
SKENS SW7 .... 40 B1

Imperial College of Science
Technology & Medicine
SKENS SW7 .... 39 F2

Imperial College
School of Medicine
PIM SW1V 117 D1

Imperial War Museum
STHWK SE1 .... 46 B3

Imperial War Museum Annexe
LBTH SE11 .... 46 B3

Imperial Wharf ⇄ ⊖
FUL/PGN SW6 .... 114 C4

Inchbald School of Design
BGVA SW1W 42 B4

India House
HOL/ALD WC2B 33 E1

Infant College
IL IG1 .... 66 A4

Inner London Sessions House
(Crown Court)
STHWK SE1 .... 47 E2

Innholders Hall
CANST EC4R 36 A1

Inns of Court & Chancery
TPL/STR WC2R 22 A5

Inns of Court Law School
GINN WC1R 21 F2

Institute of Education University
of London
RSQ WC1B 20 B1

Instituto Espanol
Canada Blanch
NKENS W10 .... 89 E4

Intercontinental Hotel
MYFR/PICC W1J 30 B5

International Community School
CAMTN NW1 .... 18 A1

International Medical Centre
ECT SW5 .... 38 C3

International School of London
ACT W3 .... 98 A5

Invicta Industrial Estate
SRTFD E15 .... 92 C2

Invicta Primary School
BKHTH/KID SE3 .... 124 A2

IQRA Independent School
BRXN/ST SW9 .... 136 A1

Ironmonger Row Baths
FSBYE EC1V 11 E4

Ironmongers Hall
STBT EC1A 23 E3

Islamia Girls School
KIL/WHAMP NW6 .... 71 E5

Islamic College for
Advanced Studies
WLSDN NW10 .... 70 B4

The Islamic Grammar School
WAND/EARL SW18 .... 131 F5

Island Clinic
POP/IOD E14 .... 104 C3

Island Gardens ⊖
POP/IOD E14 .... 104 C5

Islington Arts & Media School
FSBYPK N4 .... 57 F3

Islington Business Centre
IS N1 .... 76 C5

Islington Green Medical Centre
IS N1 .... 76 B5

Islington Green School
IS N1 .... 76 B5

Islington Tennis Centre
HOLWY N7 .... 75 E3

Islington Town Hall
IS N1 .... 76 B4

Ismaili Centre
SKENS SW7 .... 40 B4

Italia Conti Academy of Theatre Arts
BRXN/ST SW9 .... 135 E1
FARR EC1M 23 E1

Italian Hospital
PIM SW1V 43 E4

Ivydale Primary School
PECK SE15 .... 139 D2

Jack Taylor School
STJWD NW8 .... 72 C5

Jack Tizard School
SHB W12 .... 100 C1

Jacques Prevert School
HMSMTH W6 .... 101 D5

Jamahiriya School
CHEL SW3 .... 115 E2

James Allens
Preparatory Girls School
HNHL SE24 .... 137 D3

Jamestown Mental Health Centre
HAMP NW3 .... 73 F4

James Wolfe Primary School
GNWCH SE10 .... 122 B3

Jamiatul Ummah School
WCHPL E1 .... 90 B5

Janet Adegoke Leisure Centre
SHB W12 .... 100 A1

The Japanese School
ACT W3 .... 98 A1

Japan Green Medical Centre
ACT W3 .... 98 B2

Jenner Health Centre
FSTH SE23 .... 157 E1

Jenny Hammond Primary School
WAN E11 .... 81 E1

Jermyn Street Theatre
MYFR/PICC W1J 31 F2

Jessop Primary School
HNHL SE24 .... 136 B2

Jewel Tower
WEST SW1P 44 C2

Jewish Cemetery
GLDGN NW11 .... 54 A1

Jewish Community Theatre
HNHL SE24 .... 137 D1

Jewish Free School
KTTN/HRWW/WS HA3 .... 50 A1
KTTN NW5 .... 75 D3

The Jewish Museum
CAMTN NW1 .... 74 B5

Johanna Primary School
STHWK SE1 .... 46 A1

John Ball Primary School
BKHTH/KID SE3 .... 123 E5

John Betts Primary School
HMSMTH W6 .... 100 A4

John Burns Primary School
BTSEA SW11 .... 116 A5

John Dixon Clinic
BERM/RHTH SE16 .... 102 B4

John Donne Primary School
PECK SE15 .... 120 B4

John F Kennedy School
CAN/RD E16 .... 95 D4

John F Kennedy Special School
SRTFD E15 .... 81 E5

John Keble CE Primary School
WLSDN NW10 .... 87 F1

John Kelly Girls
Technology College
CRICK NW2 .... 51 F5

John Orwell Sports Centre
WAP E1W 102 A2

John Paul II RC School
WIM/MER SW19 .... 131 D5

John Perryn Primary School
ACT W3 .... 87 E5

John Roan Lower School
BKHTH/KID SE3 .... 123 F3

John Roan School
BKHTH/KID SE3 .... 123 E3

John Ruskin Primary School
WALW SE17 .... 118 C2

John Scott Health Centre
FSBYPK N4 .... 58 C3

John Scurr Primary School
WCHPL E1...**90** C3
John Smith House
WALW SE17..**47** E5
John Stainer Primary School
BROCKY SE4..**139** E1
Joseph Lancaster
Primary School
STHWK SE1..**47** F3
Jubilee Market
COVGDN WC2E..**33** D1
Jubilee Primary School
BRXS/STRHM SW2...**136** A4
Julians Primary School
STRHM/NOR SW16..**154** A4
Jumeirah Carlton Tower Hotel
KTBR SW1X..**41** F2
Jumeirah Lowndes Hotel
KTBR SW1X..**41** F2
Juno Way Industrial Estate
NWCR SE14...**121** D2
Jurys Clifton-Ford Hotel
MHST W1U..**18** B3
Jurys Great Russell Street
RSQ WC1B..**20** B4
Jurys Inn Chelsea
FUL/PGN SW6...**114** C4
Jurys Inn Islington
IS N1..**10** A2
Jurys Kensington Hotel
SKENS SW7...**40** A5
JVC Business Park
CRICK NW2..**52** A3
Kaizen Primary School
PLSTW E13...**94** B3
Kangley Business Centre
SYD SE26..**157** F5
Katella Trading Estate 10a
BARK IG11...**97** E2
Katherine Road Medical Centre
FSTGT E7...**82** C3
Keats House
HAMP NW3..**73** D1
Keen Students
Supplementary School
WCHPL E1...**90** A4
Keir Hardie Primary School
CAN/RD E16..**94** A4
Kelmscott Community Centre
WALTH E17..**61** F1
Kelmscott Leisure Centre
WALTH E17..**61** F1
Kelmscott School
WALTH E17..**61** F1
Ken Barrington Centre
LBTH SE11...**117** F2
Kender Primary School
NWCR SE14...**120** C4
Kenmont Primary School
WLSDN NW10..**88** A2
Kenneth More Theatre
IL IG1...**66** C5
Kennington
LBTH SE11..**118** B1
Kensal Green ≷ ⊖ ⊖
WLSDN NW10..**88** C2
Kensal Green Cemetery
WLSDN NW10..**88** B2
Kensal Rise ⊖
WLSDN NW10..**88** C1
Kensal Rise Primary School
KIL/WHAMP NW6...**89** D1
Kensington & Chelsea College
NKENS W10...**89** E3
Kensington & Chelsea Town Hall
KENS W8..**38** B1
Kensington Business Centre
SKENS SW7...**41** D2
Kensington & Chelsea College
KENS W8...**26** A5
NTGHL W11..**101** F3
WBPTN SW10..**114** C3
The Kensington Clinic
KENS W8..**38** C3
Kensington House Hotel
KENS W8..**39** E1
Kensington Leisure Centre
NTGHL W11..**101** D1
Kensington Market
KENS W8..**38** C1
Kensington (Olympia) ≷ ⊖ ⊖
WKENS W14...**101** E4

Kensington Palace State Apartments
& Royal Ceremonial Dress Collection
KENS W8..**27** D4
Kensington Park School
REGST W1B...**19** D2
Kensington Preparatory School
FUL/PGN SW6...**113** F4
Kensington Primary School
MNPK E12...**85** F3
Kensington School of Business
HCIRC EC1N..**22** B2
Kensington Wharf
WBPTN SW10..**115** D3
Kentish Town ≷ ⊖
KTTN NW5...**74** C2
Kentish Town CE Primary School
KTTN NW5...**74** C2
Kentish Town Health Centre
KTTN NW5...**74** C3
Kentish Town Industrial Estate
KTTN NW5...**74** B2
Kentish Town Sports Centre
KTTN NW5...**74** A3
Kentish Town West ⊖
KTTN NW5...**74** B3
Kent Park Industrial Estate
PECK SE15..**120** B2
Kenwood House
HAMP NW3..**55** E3
Kew Gardens ≷ ⊖
RCH/KEW TW9...**110** A3
Kew Gardens ≷ ⊖
RCH/KEW TW9...**110** A4
Kew Retail Park
RCH/KEW TW9...**110** B4
Kew Riverside Primary School
RCH/KEW TW9...**110** B5
Keyplan & Roxburghe College
FITZ W1T..**19** F1
Keyworth Primary School
WALW SE17...**118** B1
Kidbrooke ≷
BKHTH/KID SE3...**142** C1
Kidbrooke Park Primary School
BKHTH/KID SE3...**124** C5
Kidbrooke School
BKHTH/KID SE3...**125** D5
Kilburn ⊖
CRICK NW2..**71** E3
Kilburn High Road ⊖
KIL/WHAMP NW6...**72** B5
Kilburn Park ⊖
KIL/WHAMP NW6...**2** B1
Kilburn Park Junior School
KIL/WHAMP NW6...**2** A2
Killick Street Medical Centre
IS N1..**9** E1
Kilmorie Primary School
FSTH SE23..**157** E2
King Alfred School
GLDGN NW11...**54** B3
King Edward VII
Hospital for Officers
MHST W1U..**18** B2
King Fahad Academy
ACT W3...**99** E1
The Kingfisher Medical Centre
DEPT SE8..**121** F2
King George V ⊖
CAN/RD E16...**108** A2
King George VI Youth Hostel
KENS W8...**101** F3
Kingham Industrial Estate
WLSDN NW10..**87** D2
King & Queen Wharf
BERM/RHTH SE16...**103** D1
Kings Avenue School
CLAP SW4...**135** E3
Kingsbury Trading Estate
CDALE/KGS NW9..**50** C1
Kings College (Hampstead Campus)
HAMP NW3..**72** A1
King's College Hospital
CMBW SE5...**136** C3
Kings College London
CMBW SE5...**119** D5
HOL/ALD WC2B..**21** D5
STHWK SE1..**35** D3
STHWK SE1..**35** F4
TPL/STR WC2R..**33** E1
Kings College London - Humanities
WEST SW1P...**43** F4

Kings College London - Law
TPL/STR WC2R **33** F1
Kings College London
(Waterloo Campus)
STHWK SE1 .... **34** A4
Kings College School of Medicine
& Dentistry
CMBW SE5 .... **119** D5
DUL SE21 .... **137** D4
King's Cross ≠ ⊖
IS N1 .... **9** D2
King's Cross St Pancras ⊖
IS N1 .... **8** C3
Kingsdale School
DUL SE21 .... **155** E3
Kingsford Community School
PLSTW E13 .... **94** C3
Kingsgate Primary School
KIL/WHAMP NW6 .... **2** A4
Kings Hall Leisure Centre
CLPT E5 .... **78** C2
Kings Head Theatre
IS N1 .... **76** A5
Kingsland College of Business Studies
SRTFD E15 .... **93** D1
Kingsland Health Centre
HACK E8 .... **77** F4
Kingsland Shopping Centre
HACK E8 .... **77** F3
Kings Mall Shopping Centre
HMSMTH W6 .... **100** C5
Kingsmead Primary School
CLPT E5 .... **79** E1
Kings Private Clinic
GDMY/SEVK IG3 .... **67** F3
MHST W1U **18** A2
Kings Stairs
BERM/RHTH SE16 .... **102** B3
Kingston University
KUTN/CMB KT2 .... **147** D5
PUT/ROE SW15 .... **147** F2
King Street College
HMSMTH W6 .... **100** C5
Kingsway College
CAMTN NW1 .... **7** E5
KTTN NW5 .... **74** B3
STPAN WC1H **9** E4
Kingswood Primary School
WNWD SE27 .... **155** D4
Kisharon School
GLDGN NW11 .... **53** F1
K+K Hotel George
ECT SW5 .... **38** B5
KLC School of Design
WBPTN SW10 .... **114** C4
Knightsbridge ⊖
SKENS SW7 .... **41** E1
Knightsbridge Barracks
SKENS SW7 .... **41** D1
Knightsbridge Medical Centre
KTBR SW1X **41** F2
Knightsbridge School
KTBR SW1X **41** E3
Knowledge Point School
HOLWY N7 .... **75** F3
Kobi Nazrul Primary School
WCHPL E1 .... **90** A5
Kubrick Business Estate
FSTGT E7 .... **82** B1
Laban Centre for
Movement & Dance
DEPT SE8 .... **122** B3
Ladbroke Grove ⊖
NTGHL W11 .... **89** E5
Lady Margaret School
FUL/PGN SW6 .... **114** A4
Ladywell ≠
LEW SE13 .... **140** B3
Ladywell Arena
LEW SE13 .... **140** B4
Ladywell Cemetery
BROCKY SE4 .... **139** F3
Ladywell Leisure Centre
LEW SE13 .... **140** C3
Laker Industrial Estate
BECK BR3 .... **157** F5
Lambeth Academy
CLAP SW4 .... **134** C3
Lambeth Cemetery
TOOT SW17 .... **150** C5
Lambeth College
BRXS/STRHM SW2 .... **135** F3

CLAP SW4 .... **134** C3
STHWK SE1 .... **37** D4
STRHM/NOR SW16 .... **155** E2
VX/NE SW8 .... **117** D4
Lambeth Crematorium
TOOT SW17 .... **150** C4
Lambeth Hospital
BRXN/ST SW9 .... **135** E1
Lambeth North ⊖
STHWK SE1 .... **46** A2
Lambeth Palace
STHWK SE1 .... **45** E3
Lambs Court
POP/IOD E14 .... **103** E1
Lammas School
LEY E10 .... **61** F3
The Lanark Medical Centre
MV/WKIL W9 .... **3** D3
Lancaster Gate ⊖
BAY/PAD W2 .... **28** A1
Lancaster House
WHALL SW1A **31** E5
The Landmark Hotel
CAMTN NW1 .... **17** E2
The Lanesborough Hotel
KTBR SW1X **30** A5
Langbourne Primary School
DUL SE21 .... **155** E3
Langdon Park ⊖
POP/IOD E14 .... **92** B4
Langdon Park School
POP/IOD E14 .... **92** B5
Langdon School
EHAM E6 .... **96** B1
Langford Primary School
FUL/PGN SW6 .... **114** B5
Langham Hotel
CAVSQ/HST W1G **19** D4
Langthorne Health Centre
WAN E11 .... **63** D5
Langthorne Hospital
WAN E11 .... **81** D1
Lansbury Lawrence
Primary School
POP/IOD E14 .... **92** B5
Lansdowne College
BAY/PAD W2 .... **26** C2
Lansdowne School
BRXN/ST SW9 .... **135** F1
La Retraite RC Girls School
BAL SW12 .... **134** C5
Lark Hall Primary School
CLAP SW4 .... **117** D5
Larmenier & Sacred Catholic
Primary School
HMSMTH W6 .... **101** D5
La Sainte Union Catholic
Secondary School
HGT N6 .... **56** A5
La Sainte Union Convent School
KTTN NW5 .... **56** B5
Latchmere Leisure Centre
BTSEA SW11 .... **115** F5
Lathom Junior School
EHAM E6 .... **83** E4
Latimer Road ⊖
NTGHL W11 .... **101** F1
The Latymer
Preparatory School
HMSMTH W6 .... **112** A1
Latymer Upper School
HMSMTH W6 .... **100** A5
Launcelot Primary School
BMLY BR1 .... **160** A4
Lauriston Primary School
HOM E9 .... **79** D5
Lawdale Junior School
BETH E2 .... **90** A2
Lawrence Trading Estate
GNWCH SE10 .... **105** E5
Lawrence University
SKENS SW7 .... **39** F5
Lawrence Wharf
BERM/RHTH SE16 .... **103** F2
Laycock Primary School
IS N1 .... **76** A3
Leadenhall Market
BANK EC3V **24** C5
Lea Park Trading Estate
LEY E10 .... **61** F2
Leathermarket Gardens
STHWK SE1 .... **48** C1

Leathersellers Sports Ground
  LEE/GVPK SE12 ....142 C5
Leathers Hall
  HDTCH EC3A 24 C4
L'Ecoles Des Petits School
  FUL/PGN SW6 ....114 B5
Lee ⇌
  LEE/GVPK SE12 ....142 A4
Lee Manor Primary School
  LEW SE13 ....141 E4
Leeside Court
  BERM/RHTH SE16 ....103 D2
Lee Valley Ice Centre
  LEY E10 ....61 D4
Leicester Square ⊖
  LSQ/SEVD WC2H 32 B1
Leighton House Museum
  WKENS W14 ....101 F4
Lena Gardens Primary School
  HMSMTH W6 ....100 C4
Leopold Primary School
  WLSDN NW10 ....69 F4
Leopold Street Clinic
  BOW E3 ....91 F4
The Levin Hotel
  KTBR SW1X 41 E2
Lewisham ⇌ ⊖
  DEPT SE8 ....122 B5
Lewisham Bridge
  Primary School
  LEW SE13 ....140 B1
Lewisham Business Centre
  NWCR SE14 ....121 D2
Lewisham Centre
  LEW SE13 ....140 C2
Lewisham College
  BROCKY SE4 ....122 A5
Lewisham Crematorium
  CAT SE6 ....159 F2
Lewisham Lions Centre
  BERM/RHTH SE16 ....120 C1
Leyton Business Centre
  LEY E10 ....61 F4
Leyton FC
  LEY E10 ....61 F3
Leyton Industrial Village
  LEY E10 ....61 D2
Leyton Leisure Centre
  LEY E10 ....62 B2
Leyton Midland Road ⊖
  LEY E10 ....62 C3
Leyton Orient FC
  (Matchroom Stadium)
  LEY E10 ....62 B5
Leytonstone High Road ⊖
  WAN E11 ....63 E3
Leytonstone School
  WAN E11 ....63 E1
Leyton VI Form College
  LEY E10 ....63 D1
Leyton Youth Sports Ground
  LEY E10 ....62 B3
The Liberty City Clinic
  SDTCH EC2A 12 C5
Library & Community Centre
  BTSEA SW11 ....133 D1
L'Ile Aux Enfants
  KTTN NW5 ....74 A2
Lilian Baylis Technology School
  LBTH SE11 ....117 F1
Lillian Bishop School of English
  SKENS SW7 ....40 A4
Limehouse ⇌ ⊖
  WCHPL E1 ....91 E5
Limehouse Hoie Stairs
  BERM/RHTH SE16 ....103 F2
Lincoln's Inn
  LINN WC2A 21 F4
Linden Lodge School
  WIM/MER SW19 ....149 E1
Linford Christie Stadium
  SHB W12 ....88 A4
Linley Sambourne House
  KENS W8 ....38 A1
Linnet House Clinic
  STJWD NW8 ....4 C2
Lion House School
  PUT/ROE SW15 ....131 D2
Lisson Grove Health Centre
  STJWD NW8 ....4 C5
Lister Community School
  PLSTW E13 ....94 B1

The Lister Hospital
  BGVA SW1W 116 B1
Lister House Clinic
  CAVSQ/HST W1G 18 C4
Little Ilford School
  MNPK E12 ....83 F2
Little Venice Medical Centre
  MV/WKIL W9 ....15 F1
Little Wandsworth School
  TOOT SW17 ....152 A2
Liverpool Street ⇌ ⊖
  LVPST EC2M 24 C3
Livesey Museum for Children
  PECK SE15 ....120 B2
The Livity School
  BRXS/STRHM SW2 ....135 E3
Lloyd's of London
  FENCHST EC3M 24 C5
Lloyds Register CC
  DUL SE21 ....155 D1
Locks View Court
  POP/IOD E14 ....103 E1
Lombard Business Centre
  BTSEA SW11 ....115 D5
Lombard Business Park
  WAND/EARL SW18 ....133 D4
Lombard Trading Estate
  CHARL SE7 ....106 B5
London Academy of Music &
  Dramatic Art
  KENS W8 ....38 A4
London Aquarium
  WHALL SW1A 45 E1
London Bridge ⇌ ⊖
  STHWK SE1 ....36 B4
London Bridge City Pier
  STHWK SE1 ....36 C3
London Bridge Hospital
  STHWK SE1 ....36 B3
London Bridge Hotel
  STHWK SE1 ....36 A4
London Bridge Sports Centre
  CANST EC4R 36 A2
London Business School
  CAMTN NW1 ....5 E5
The London Canal Museum
  IS N1 ....9 D1
London Capital College
  CAMTN NW1 ....74 B5
London Centre of
  Contemporary Music
  STHWK SE1 ....35 F4
London Chest Hospital
  BETH E2 ....90 C1
London Chinese Dance School
  CAN/RD E16 ....93 D4
  REGST W1B 19 D2
London City Airport
  CAN/RD E16 ....107 E2
London City Airport ⊖
  CAN/RD E16 ....107 E2
London City College (English
  Language Institute) & Schiller
  International University
  STHWK SE1 ....33 F4
London City Mission
  STHWK SE1 ....37 D5
The London Clinic
  CAVSQ/HST W1G 18 B1
London College of Business &
  Computer Services
  CLAP SW4 ....135 D2
London College of Business
  & Computing
  BETH E2 ....90 B1
London College of
  Communication
  LBTH SE11 ....47 D3
London College of Fashion
  CAVSQ/HST W1G 19 D4
  MHST W1U 18 B4
  MYFR/PKLN W1K 18 C5
  SDTCH EC2A 13 D5
London College of Further Education
  LBTH SE11 ....46 C5
London College of Higher Education
  CLAP SW4 ....134 B1
London Commodity Exchange
  WAP E1W 37 E2
London Contemporary Dance School
  CAMTN NW1 ....8 B4
  PLSTW E13 ....93 F2

London Cornish RFC
PUT/ROE SW15 .... 147 F3
The London Dungeon
STHWK SE1 .... 36 B4
London Esthetique
CAVSO/HST W1G 19 D4
POP/IOD E14 .... 93 E5
London Eye
STHWK SE1 .... 33 E5
London Eye Clinic
CAVSO/HST W1G 18 C3
London Fields ⇌
HACK E8 .... 78 B4
London Fields Lido
HACK E8 .... 78 B4
London Fields Primary School
HACK E8 .... 78 B5
London Film Academy
FUL/PGN SW6 .... 114 A3
London Film School
LSQ/SEVD WC2H 20 C5
London Foot Hospital
FITZ W1T 19 E1
London Gender Clinic
HDN N12 .... 52 B1
London Group Business Park
CRICK NW2 .... 51 F3
London Heart Clinic
CAVSO/HST W1G 18 C3
The London Industrial Estate
EHAM E6 .... 96 A4
London Industrial Park
EHAM E6 .... 96 B4
London International College
POP/IOD E14 .... 93 E5
SOHO/SHAV W1D 19 F4
The London Irish
Youth Theatre
HGT N6 .... 56 B3
London Islamic School/
Madrasah
WCHPL E1 .... 90 B5
London Ladies & Girls FC
CAT SE6 .... 158 B5
London Lighthouse
NTGHL W11 .... 89 E4
London Living Theatre
SYD SE26 .... 157 D4
London Marriott Hotel
HAMP NW3 .... 73 E4
MYFR/PKLN W1K 30 B1
OXSTW W1C 29 F1
STHWK SE1 .... 33 E5
London Marriott West India
Quay Hotel
POP/IOD E14 .... 104 C3
London Metrocity College
BOW E3 .... 92 A2
London Metropolitan University
LVPST EC2M 24 B3
WCHPL E1 .... 25 E4
WCHPL E1 .... 90 A5
London Natural
Therapy School
POP/IOD E14 .... 105 E1
SOHO/SHAV W1F 31 F1
London Nautical School
STHWK SE1 .... 34 B3
London Nutrition Clinic
MHST W1U 18 A2
London Open College
FSBYE EC1V 11 D3
London Oratory School
FUL/PGN SW6 .... 114 A3
London School of Economics
CLKNW EC1R 10 B4
HHOL WC1V 20 C4
HOL/ALD WC2B 21 E5
STHWK SE1 .... 35 E3
London School of Hygiene &
Tropical Medicine
GWRST WC1E 20 B2
London Scottish Golf Club
WIM/MER SW19 .... 148 B3
London Silver Vaults
LINN WC2A 22 A3
London South Bank University
STHWK SE1 .... 47 D2
London Stock Exchange
STBT EC1A 23 D4
London's Transport Museum
HOL/ALD WC2B 33 D1

The London Television Centre
STHWK SE1 .... 34 A3
London Tourist Board &
Convention Centre
BGVA SW1W 42 C2
London Toy & Model Museum
BAY/PAD W2 .... 27 F1
London Underwriting Centre
MON EC3R 36 C1
London Wall
BARB EC2Y 23 E3
London Weather Centre
HICRC EC1N 22 A2
The London Welbeck Hospital
CAVSO/HST W1G 18 B3
London Welsh School
CRICK NW2 .... 70 C3
London West Crematorium
WLSDN NW10 .... 88 B3
London Wetland Centre
BARN SW13 .... 112 B4
Longlands Primary School
BFN/LL DA15 .... 163 E3
Long Lane AFC
BKHTH/KID SE3 .... 124 C5
Lord Chancellors Department
WEST SW1P 44 B3
Lord Lister Health Centre
FSTGT E7 .... 82 A1
Lord's Tour & MCC Museum
ST/JWD NW8 .... 4 A4
Lord Williamson School
NKENS W10 .... 89 E4
Loughborough Junction ⇌
CMBW SE5 .... 118 B5
Loughborough Primary School
CMBW SE5 .... 118 B5
Lovell's Wharf
GNWCH SE10 .... 123 D1
Lower Clapton Health Centre
CLPT E5 .... 78 C2
Lower Place Business Centre
WLSDN NW10 .... 86 C1
Lower Sydenham ⇌
SYD SE26 .... 157 F5
Lower Sydenham Industrial Estate
SYD SE26 .... 157 F5
Low Hall Sports Ground
LEY E10 .... 61 D1
Lowther Primary School
BARN SW13 .... 112 A2
Loxford School of Science
& Technology
IL IG1 .... 85 D2
Lubavitch Boys Primary School
CLPT E5 .... 59 F2
Lubavitch House School (Senior Girls)
STNW/STAM N16 .... 59 E2
Lucas Vale Primary School
DEPT SE8 .... 122 A4
Lutomer House Business Centre
POP/IOD E14 .... 104 B2
Lux Cinema
IS N1 .... 12 C4
Lycee Francais
SKENS SW7 .... 40 A4
Lycee Francais Charles De Gaulle
BTSEA SW11 .... 134 B2
The Lyceum Theatre
COVGDN WC2E 33 E1
Lyndhurst House Preparatory School
HAMP NW3 .... 73 D2
Lyndhurst Primary School
CMBW SE5 .... 119 D5
Lyon Business Park
BARK IG11 .... 97 E1
Lyric Theatre
SOHO/SHAV W1D 32 A1
Lyric Theatre Hammersmith
HMSMTH W6 .... 100 C5
Macaulay CE Primary School
CLAP SW4 .... 134 B2
Madame Tussauds & the
London Auditorium
CAMTN NW1 .... 17 F1
Madni Girls School
WCHPL E1 .... 90 B5
Madrasah-e-Darue Qirat
Majidiah School
WCHPL E1 .... 102 B1
Mahatma Gandhi Industrial Estate
BRXN/ST SW9 .... 136 B1

Maida Vale ⊖
MV/WKIL W9 .... 3 D4
Maida Vale Medical Centre
MV/WKIL W9 .... 2 C4
Malham Road Industrial Estate
FSTH SE23 .... 157 D1
Mall Galleries
STJS SW1Y 32 B3
Malmaison Charterhouse
Square Hotel
FARR EC1M 23 D2
Malmesbury Primary School
BOW E3 .... 91 F2
Malorees Junior School
KIL/WHAMP NW6 .... 71 D4
Mandarin Oriental Hotel
KTBR SW1X 29 F5
The Mandeville Hotel
MHST W1U 18 B4
Mandeville Primary School
CLPT E5 .... 61 E5
Manor Brook Medical Centre
BKHTH/KID SE3 .... 124 B5
Manorfield Primary School
POP/IOD E14 .... 92 B4
Manor House ⊖
FSBYPK N4 .... 58 C3
Manor Infant School
BARK IG11 .... 85 F3
Manor Park ⇌
MNPK E12 .... 83 D1
Manor Park Cemetery
FSTGT E7 .... 83 D1
Manor Park Crematorium
FSTGT E7 .... 82 C1
Manor Park Methodist School
MNPK E12 .... 83 E1
Manor Primary School
SRTFD E15 .... 93 E1
Manor Special School
WLSDN NW10 .... 89 D1
Mansion House ⊖
STP EC4M 35 F1
Mapledown School
CRICK NW2 .... 53 D2
Maples Business Centre
IS N1 .... 76 A4
Marble Arch ⊖
OXSTW W1C 17 F5
Maria Fidelis Convent School
CAMTN NW1 .... 7 F4
Maria Montessori Childrens House
HAMP NW3 .... 73 D2
Marion Richardson
Primary School
WCHPL E1 .... 91 D5
Maritime Greenwich College
DEPT SE8 .... 122 A3
Maritime Industrial Estate
CHARL SE7 .... 106 B5
Maritime Museum
GNWCH SE10 .... 105 E5
Marlborough CC
DUL SE21 .... 156 A1
Marlborough Day Hospital
STJWD NW8 .... 3 E1
Marlborough House
STJS SW1Y 31 F4
Marlborough Primary School
CHEL SW3 .... 41 D5
Marlborough Trading Estate
RCH/KEW TW9 .... 110 B4
Marlowe Business Centre
NWCR SE14 .... 121 E3
Marner Primary School
BOW E3 .... 92 B3
Marriott Hotel
ECT SW5 .... 38 C4
KIL/WHAMP NW6 .... 2 C1
MBLAR W1H 17 D4
Marsh Gate Business Centre
SRTFD E15 .... 92 C1
Martan College
HOL/ALD WC2B 21 D1
Marvels Lane Primary School
LEE/GVPK SE12 .... 160 C4
Mary Boone School
WKENS W14 .... 101 E5
Maryland ⇌
SRTFD E15 .... 81 E2
Maryland Industrial Estate
SRTFD E15 .... 81 E2

Maryland Primary School
SRTFD E15 .... 81 E2
Marylebone ⇌ ⊖
CAMTN NW1 .... 17 D1
Marylebone Health Centre
CAMTN NW1 .... 18 B1
Maudlin's Green
WAP E1W 37 F3
The Maudsley Hospital
CMBW SE5 .... 119 D5
Maughan Library (Kings College)
LINN WC2A 22 A4
Mawbrey Brough Health Centre
VX/NE SW8 .... 117 E3
Mayflower Primary School
POP/IOD E14 .... 92 A5
Maytime School
IL IG1 .... 66 A5
Mayville J & P School
WAN E11 .... 63 E5
Maze Hill ⇌
GNWCH SE10 .... 123 E2
McKay Trading Estate
NKENS W10 .... 89 E3
MDQ Majidiah School
WCHPL E1 .... 102 B1
Meadowgate School
BROCKY SE4 .... 139 D1
Meadowside Leisure Centre
BKHTH/KID SE3 .... 142 C2
The Medical Centre
WAND/EARL SW18 .... 132 B4
Medical Express Clinic
CAVSQ/STQM W1G 18 C2
Mednurs Clinic
SEVS/STOTM N15 .... 59 D1
Melcombe Primary School
HMSMTH W6 .... 113 D2
Melia White House Hotel
CAMTN NW1 .... 7 D5
Mellish Industrial Estate
WOOL/PLUM SE18 .... 107 D4
Memorial Hospital
WOOL/PLUM SE18 .... 126 A5
Menorah Grammar School
GLDGN NW11 .... 53 E2
Menorah High School for Girls
CRICK NW2 .... 51 F5
Menorah Primary School
GLDGN NW11 .... 53 E2
MERC Education
WOOL/PLUM SE18 .... 108 B5
Mercers' Hall
CITYW EC2V 23 F5
The Merchant Taylors Hall
BANK EC3V 24 B5
Mercure London City
Bankside Hotel
STHWK SE1 .... 35 E4
Meridian Clinic
BRXN/ST SW9 .... 135 F1
Meridian Locality Mental
Health Centre
CHARL SE7 .... 124 C2
Meridian Primary School
GNWCH SE10 .... 123 D1
Meridian Sports Club
CHARL SE7 .... 125 E3
Meridian Trading Estate
CHARL SE7 .... 106 B5
Merlin Primary School
BMLY BR1 .... 160 A3
Merlin School
PUT/ROE SW15 .... 131 D3
Mermaid Theatre
BLKFR EC4V 35 D1
Merton Road Industrial Estate
WAND/EARL SW18 .... 132 A5
The Method Studio
FSBYW WC1X 21 E2
Metropolitan Business Centre
IS N1 .... 77 E4
Metropolitan Hospital
STHWK SE1 .... 46 B2
The Metropolitan Hotel
MYFR/PKLN W1K 30 C4
Metropolitan Police
STJWD NW8 .... 4 C2
Metropolitan Tabernacle
STHWK SE1 .... 47 D4
Metro Trading Centre
WBLY HA9 .... 68 B1

Michael Faraday Primary School
WALW SE17............................119 D1
Michael Manley Industrial Estate
VX/NE SW8............................116 C4
Michael Sobell Sinai School
KTN/HRWW/WS HA3...................50 A1
The Michael Tippett School
LBTH SE11.............................46 B5
Middle Park Primary School
ELTH/MOT SE9.......................143 D5
Middle Row Primary School
NKENS W10............................89 E3
Middlesex CCC
(Lord's Cricket Ground)
STJWD NW8................................4 B3
Middlesex Hospital
Medical School
FITZ W1T...............................19 F2
Middlesex Hospital Nurses Home
GTPST W1W............................19 E2
Middlesex Hospital School
of Physiotherapy
FITZ W1T...............................19 F2
Middlesex Hospital Sports Ground
CHST BR7.............................163 F5
Middlesex University
ARCH N19..............................56 C3
GLDGN NW11.........................54 B3
Midway Mission Hospital
BETH E2................................13 E4
Mile End ⊖
BOW E3.................................91 F3
Mile End & Bow Business Centre
WCHPL E1..............................90 B4
Mile End Hospital
WCHPL E1..............................91 D2
Mile End Stadium
POP/IOD E14..........................91 F4
Miles Coverdale Primary School
SHB W12.............................100 C3
Milestone Hotel
KENS W8................................39 D1
Military Barracks
WOOL/PLUM SE18..................126 A1
Millbank Millennium Pier
WEST SW1P............................44 C5
Millbank Primary School
WEST SW1P............................44 B5
Millbank Tower
WEST SW1P............................44 C5
Millennium Arena
BTSEA SW11.........................116 A3
Millennium Bailey's Hotel
SKENS SW7............................39 E4
Millennium Balloon
STHWK SE1............................37 D4
Millennium & Copthorne
Hotels at Chelsea FC
FUL/PGN SW6.......................114 B3
Millennium Dance 2000
Theatre School
HAMP NW3.............................73 E2
Millennium Gloucester Hotel
ECT SW5................................39 D5
Millennium Harbour
POP/IOD E14.........................103 F3
Millennium Hotel
KTBR SW1X.............................41 F1
Millennium Hotel London Mayfair
MYFR/PKLN W1K....................30 B2
Millennium Quay
DEPT SE8.............................122 B2
Millennium Wharf
POP/IOD E14.........................105 D4
Millfields Primary School
CLPT E5.................................78 C1
Mill Lane Medical Centre
KIL/WHAMP NW6.....................72 A2
Mill Street Clinic
STHWK SE1.............................37 F5
Mill Trading Estate
WLSDN NW10..........................86 B1
The Mill Trading Estate
WLSDN NW10..........................86 C2
Millwall FC (The New Den)
BERM/RHTH SE16...................120 C1
Milton Natural Health Centre
HGT N6..................................56 C2
Ministry of Defence
WHALL SW1A...........................32 C4
Mint Business Park
CAN/RD E16............................94 A4

Mitchell Brook Primary School
WLSDN NW10..........................69 D3
Mitre Bridge Industrial Park
NKENS W10............................88 B3
Mitre House Hotel
BAY/PAD W2...........................16 A5
Moatbridge School
ELTH/MOT SE9.......................143 D4
The Moat School
FUL/PGN SW6........................113 E5
Moberly Sports & Education Centre
WLSDN NW10..........................89 D2
Monega Primary School
MNPK E12...............................83 D2
The Montague on the Gardens Hotel
RSQ WC1B..............................20 C2
Montbelle Primary School
ELTH/MOT SE9......................162 A4
The Montcalm-Hotel Nikko
MBLAR W1H............................17 F5
Montem Primary School
HOLWY N7...............................57 F5
Monument ⊖
MANHO EC4N..........................36 B1
The Monument
CANST EC4R............................36 B1
Moorfields Eye Hospital
FSBYE EC1V............................12 A4
Moorgate ⇄ ⊖
BARB EC2Y.............................24 A3
Mora Primary School
CRICK NW2..............................70 C1
Morden College Homes
BKHTH/KID SE3.....................124 A5
Morden Mount Primary School
LEW SE13.............................122 B5
Moreland Primary School
FSBYE EC1V............................11 D3
Morley College
LBTH SE1.............................118 A2
STHWK SE1.............................46 B2
Morningside Primary School
HOM E9..................................78 C3
Mornington Crescent ⊖
CAMTN NW1..............................7 E1
Mornington Sports & Fitness Centre
CAMTN NW1.............................74 B5
Morpeth School
BETH E2.................................90 C2
Mortimer Road Clinic
WLSDN NW10..........................88 C2
Mortimer School
STRHM/NOR SW16..................153 D2
Mortlake ⇄
MORT/ESHN SW14..................128 C1
Mortlake Cemetery
MORT/ESHN SW14..................129 E1
Mortlake Crematorium
RCH/KEW TW9.......................110 B5
Mosiah Foundation
Supplementary School
STNW/STAM N16......................59 E3
Mossbourne Community Academy
HACK E8.................................78 A1
The Mother & Baby Clinic
HOM E9..................................78 C3
Mottingham ⇄
ELTH/MOT SE9......................161 F1
Mottingham Community
Health Clinic
ELTH/MOT SE9......................161 E4
Mottingham Primary School
ELTH/MOT SE9......................161 F3
Mount Carmel RC Technical College
for Girls
ARCH N19..............................57 D3
The Movieum of London
STHWK SE1.............................33 E5
Mowlem Primary School
BETH E2.................................90 C1
MPR Eurotots School
KIL/WHAMP NW6.....................71 D4
MSP Business Centre
WBLY HA9...............................68 B1
Mudchute ⊖
POP/IOD E14.........................104 B5
Mudchute City Farm
POP/IOD E14.........................104 C5
Mulberry Business Centre
BERM/RHTH SE16...................103 D3
Mulberry House School
CRICK NW2..............................71 E2

Mulberry School for Girls
WCHPL E1 .... **90** B5
Mulgrave Primary School
WOOL/PLUM SE18 .... **108** A5
Munroe Centre
STHWK SE1 .... **36** B5
Museum in Docklands
POP/IOD E14 .... **104** A1
Museum of Fulham Palace
FUL/PGN SW6 .... **113** D5
Museum of Garden History
STHWK SE1 .... **45** D3
Museum of London
BARB EC2Y **23** E3
Museum of London Archaeology
IS N1 .... **30** A1
Museum of the Artillery in
the Rotunda
CHARL SE7 .... **125** E1
Museum of the Order of St John
FARR EC1M **23** D1
Myatt Garden Primary School
BROCKY SE4 .... **121** F5
Myatts Field Clinic
BRXN/ST SW9 .... **118** B4
N1 Shopping Centre
IS N1 .... **10** B1
Nags Head Shopping Centre
HOLWY N7 .... **75** F1
Naima Jewish
Preparatory School
KIL/WHAMP NW6 .... **2** C1
The National Archives
RCH/KEW TW9 .... **110** B3
National Army Museum
CHEL SW3 .... **115** F2
National Film Theatre
STHWK SE1 .... **33** F3
National Gallery
LSQ/SEVD WC2H **32** B2
National Hospital for Neurology
& Neurosurgery
RSQ WC1B **20** C1
National Maritime Museum
GNWCH SE10 .... **123** D2
National Portrait Gallery
LSQ/SEVD WC2H **32** B2
National Temperance Hospital
CAMTN NW1 .... **7** E3
National Tennis Centre
PUT/ROE SW15 .... **129** E3
National Youth Theatre
Great Britain
HOLWY N7 .... **57** E5
The Natural History Museum
SKENS SW7 .... **40** A3
Natural Therapy Clinic
TOOT SW17 .... **152** B5
Neasden ⊖
WLSDN NW10 .... **69** E2
Negus Sixth Form Centre
WOOL/PLUM SE18 .... **127** D2
Nelson Dock Museum
BERM/RHTH SE16 .... **103** F2
Nelson Primary School
EHAM E6 .... **96** A1
Nelson's Column
STJS SW1Y **32** B3
Neo Clinic
PIM SW1V **43** E4
The New Ambassadors Theatre
LSQ/SEVD WC2H **20** B5
New Atlas Wharf
POP/IOD E14 .... **103** F4
The New Aylesbury Medical Centre
WALW SE17 .... **119** D1
Newbury Park ⊖
GNTH/NBYPK IG2 .... **67** D1
Newbury Park Health Centre
GNTH/NBYPK IG2 .... **67** D1
The New Business Centre
WLSDN NW10 .... **87** F2
New Caledonian Wharf
BERM/RHTH SE16 .... **103** F4
New Chiswick Pool
CHSWK W4 .... **111** E3
New City Primary School
PLSTW E13 .... **94** C2
New Connaught Rooms
HOL/ALD WC2B **21** D4
New Covent Garden Market
VX/NE SW8 .... **117** D3

New Crane Wharf
WAP E1W **102** C2
New Cross ⇌ ⊖
NWCR SE14 .... **121** F3
New Cross Gate ⇌ ⊖
NWCR SE14 .... **121** E3
New Cross Sports Arena
NWCR SE14 .... **121** E3
New Eltham ⇌
ELTH/MOT SE9 .... **162** B1
New End Primary School
HAMP NW3 .... **72** C1
New End Theatre
HAMP NW3 .... **54** C5
New England Industrial Estate
BARK IG11 .... **96** C1
Newfield Primary School
WLSDN NW10 .... **69** F4
Newham City Farm
CAN/RD E16 .... **95** D5
Newham College of
Further Education
EHAM E6 .... **95** F1
SRTFD E15 .... **81** E4
Newham Leisure Centre
PLSTW E13 .... **94** C3
Newham Medical Centre
PLSTW E13 .... **94** C1
Newham Sixth Form College
PLSTW E13 .... **94** B3
Newham Training & Education Centre
SRTFD E15 .... **81** E3
New Hope Christian School
EDUL SE22 .... **137** F2
New Horizons Computer
Learning Centre
FSBYE EC1V **12** A4
Newington Court Business Centre
STHWK SE1 .... **47** E3
Newington Green Primary School
STNW/STAM N16 .... **77** E2
Newington Industrial Estate
WALW SE17 .... **47** D5
New Kings Primary School
FUL/PGN SW6 .... **113** F5
New London Theatre
LSQ/SEVD WC2H **21** D4
New North Community School
IS N1 .... **76** C4
Newport School
LEY E10 .... **62** C4
New Rush Hall School
IL IG1 .... **66** C4
New School
FUL/PGN SW6 .... **113** F4
New Scotland Yard
STJSPK SW1H **44** A2
News International Offices
WAP E1W **102** B1
New Spitalfields Market
LEY E10 .... **80** A1
Newton Medical Centre
BAY/PAD W2 .... **14** C4
Newton Preparatory School
VX/NE SW8 .... **116** B3
New Woodlands School
BMLY BR1 .... **159** E4
N H Harrington Hall Hotal
SKENS SW7 .... **39** E5
Nightingale Clinic
PLSTW E13 .... **94** C1
Nightingale Primary School
CLPT E5 .... **60** A5
WOOL/PLUM SE18 .... **126** B2
Nightingale School
TOOT SW17 .... **151** D3
Noel Coward Theatre
CHCR WC2N **32** C1
Noor Ul Islam Primary School
LEY E10 .... **62** C4
Norland Place School
NTGHL W11 .... **101** E2
Norlington School
LEY E10 .... **63** D3
Normand Croft Community School
WKENS W14 .... **113** F2
Norman Shaw Building (MP's Offices)
WHALL SW1A **32** C5
North Acton ⊖
WLSDN NW10 .... **87** D3

North Acton Business Park
ACT W3 .... 87 D5
North Beckton Primary School
EHAM E6 .... 95 F3
North Bridge House
HAMP NW3 .... 72 C3
North Bridge House Preparatory School
CAMTN NW1 .... 74 B5
North Bridge House School
HAMP NW3 .... 73 D3
Northbrook CE School
LEE/GVPK SE12 .... 141 E3
Northbury Primary School
BARK IG11 .... 84 B3
North Dulwich ≷
HNHL SE24 .... 137 D3
Northfields Industrial Estate
ALP/SUD HA0 .... 68 A3
Northfields Prospect Business Centre
PUT/ROE SW15 .... 131 F2
Northgate Clinic
CDALE/KGS NW9 .... 51 E1
North Greenwich ⊖
GNWCH SE10 .... 105 E3
North Kensington Video-Drama Project
NKENS W10 .... 89 E5
North London School of Physiotherapy
ARCH N19 .... 56 C3
North London Tutorial College
HDN NW4 .... 52 C1
North Pole Depot
WLSDN NW10 .... 87 F3
North Sheen ≷
RCH/KEW TW9 .... 128 A2
The North Street Health Centre
CLAP SW4 .... 134 C1
Northview Primary School
WLSDN NW10 .... 69 E1
North West London Jewish Primary School
CRICK NW2 .... 71 E4
North West London Medical Centre
MV/WKIL W9 .... 3 E2
North Westminster Community Secondary School
MV/WKIL W9 .... 2 B5
Northwold Primary School
CLPT E5 .... 60 A4
Northwood Primary School
CLPT E5 .... 60 A4
Norwegian/British Monument
BAY/PAD W2 .... 28 C3
Norwood School
NRWD SE19 .... 154 C5
Notre Dame RC Girls School
STHWK SE1 .... 46 C2
Notre Dame RC Primary School
WOOL/PLUM SE18 .... 126 B2
Notre Dame University
LSQ/SEVD WC2H 32 B2
Notting Hill Gate ⊖
BAY/PAD W2 .... 26 B3
Novello Theatre
HOL/ALD WC2B 33 E1
Novotel
CAMTN NW1 .... 8 B3
CAN/RD E16 .... 106 B1
GNWCH SE10 .... 122 E3
TWRH EC3N 37 D1
STHWK SE1 .... 35 F4
STHWK SE1 .... 45 E4
Novotel London West
HMSMTH W6 .... 113 D1
NTGB Sports Ground
EHAM E6 .... 84 A3
Nunhead ≷
PECK SE15 .... 138 C1
The O2
POP/IOD E14 .... 105 D2
Oakfield Preparatory School
DUL SE21 .... 155 D2
Oakington Manor School
WBLY HA9 .... 68 B2
Oaklands Secondary School
BETH E2 .... 90 A2
Oak Lodge School
BAL SW12 .... 133 F5
Oak Tree Medical Centre
GDMY/SEVK IG3 .... 67 E4

Oakwood Business Park
WLSDN NW10 .... 87 D2
Oasis Sports Centre
LSQ/SEVD WC2H 20 C4
Obstetrics Hospital
GWRST WC1E 19 F1
Odeon Cinema
BAY/PAD W2 .... 17 E5
BERM/RHTH SE16 .... 103 D4
CAMTN NW1 .... 74 B5
ELTH/MOT SE9 .... 143 E2
FITZ W1T 20 A5
HAMP NW3 .... 73 D4
HOLWY N7 .... 57 E5
KENS W8 .... 38 A3
LSQ/SEVD WC2H 32 B2
STJS SW1Y 32 A2
STRHM/NOR SW16 .... 153 E3
Odeon Covent Garden Cinema
LSQ/SEVD WC2H 20 B5
Odeon Wardour Street Cinema
SOHO/SHAV W1D 32 A1
Odessa Infant School
FSTGT E7 .... 82 A2
Old Admiralty
STJS SW1Y 32 B4
Old Barnes Cemetery
BARN SW13 .... 112 B5
Old Bellgate Wharf
POP/IOD E14 .... 103 F4
Old Brocklelans Sports Ground
LEE/GVPK SE12 .... 142 A3
Old Cemetery
EDUL SE22 .... 138 B4
Old Colfeian Sports Club
LEE/GVPK SE12 .... 142 A3
Old Curiosity Shop
LINN WC2A 21 E4
Old Ford Primary School
BOW E3 .... 91 F1
Oldhill Medical Centre
STNW/STAM N16 .... 59 F3
Old Jamaica Business Estate
BERM/RHTH SE16 .... 49 F2
Old Oak Primary School
SHB W12 .... 87 F5
Old Operating Theatre & Herb Garret Museum
STHWK SE1 .... 36 A4
Old Palace Primary School
BOW E3 .... 92 B2
Old Royal Naval College
GNWCH SE10 .... 123 D1
Old Royal Observatory Greenwich
GNWCH SE10 .... 123 D3
Old Spitalfields Market Hall
WCHPL E1 .... 25 E2
Old Street ≷ ⊖
FSBYE EC1V 12 A4
Old Sun Wharf
POP/IOD E14 .... 103 F3
Old Treasury
WHALL SW1A 32 C5
Old Vic Theatre
STHWK SE1 .... 34 B5
Old War Office
WHALL SW1A 32 C4
Olga Primary School
BOW E3 .... 91 E1
Oliver Business Park
WLSDN NW10 .... 86 C1
Oliver Goldsmith Primary School
CMBW SE5 .... 119 F4
Oliver House Preparatory School
CLAP SW4 .... 134 B4
Olympia
WKENS W14 .... 101 E4
Olympic Industrial Estate
WBLY HA9 .... 68 A1
Olympic Retail Park
WBLY HA9 .... 68 A1
Olympic Site under development
SRTFD E15 .... 80 B2
Olympic Trading Estate
WBLY HA9 .... 68 B1
One Aldwych Hotel
COVGDN WC2E 33 E1
On Sai Clinic
ECT SW5 .... 38 C5
The Open University
FSBYW WC1X 9 E3

HAMP NW3...............................**72** A1
Ophaboom Theatre
WLSDN NW10..........................**88** B1
Optimax Laser Eye Clinic
HAMP NW3...............................**72** C3
Orchard Business Centre
BECK BR3................................**157** F5
The Orchard Health Centre
BARK IG11...............................**96** C1
Orchard House School
CHSWK W4..............................**99** D5
Orchard J & I School
HOM E9.................................**78** C4
The Orchard School
BRXS/STRHM SW2.....................**153** F1
Orient Industrial Park
LEY E10.................................**62** A4
Orion Business Centre
NWCR SE14.............................**121** D1
Osier Industrial Estate
WAND/EARL SW18.....................**132** A3
Osmani Primary School
WCHPL E1..............................**90** A4
Our Lady of Dolours RC
Primary School
BAY/PAD W2............................**14** C2
Our Lady of Grace RC
Junior School
CRICK NW2.............................**52** B5
Our Lady of Grace
RC Primary School
CHARL SE7..............................**124** B2
Our Lady of Lourdes RC
Primary School
WAN E11................................**63** F1
WLSDN NW10...........................**68** C5
Our Lady of the Rosary RC School
ELTH/MOT SE9.........................**145** E4
Our Lady of the
Sacred Heart School
HOLWY N7..............................**75** F2
Our Lady of Victories RC
Primary School
PUT/ROE SW15.........................**131** D2
SKENS SW7.............................**39** F5
Our Lady Queen of Heaven RC
Primary School
PUT/ROE SW15.........................**131** D5
Our Lady RC Primary School
POP/IOD E14............................**91** F5
Our Lady & St Joseph
Primary School
IS N1....................................**77** E3
Our Lady & St Philip Neri
Infants School
FSTH SE23...............................**157** D3
Our Lady & St Philip Neri RC
Primary School
SYD SE26...............................**157** E4
Our Ladys RC Primary School
CAMTN NW1............................**74** C5
Oval ⊖
LBTH SE11..............................**118** A2
Oval Business Centre
LBTH SE11..............................**117** F1
Oval House Theatre
LBTH SE11..............................**118** A2
Oxford Circus ⊖
REGST W1B.............................**19** D4
Oxford Gardens Primary School
NKENS W10............................**89** D5
Oxford House College
SOHO/SHAV W1D......................**20** A4
Oxo Tower Wharf
STHWK SE1.............................**34** B2
Paddington ⇌ ⊖
BAY/PAD W2............................**16** A1
Paddington Academy
MV/WKIL W9...........................**14** B1
Paddington Bowling & Sports Club
MV/WKIL W9............................**2** C5
Paddington Community Hospital
MV/WKIL W9...........................**14** A2
Paddington Green Primary School
BAY/PAD W2............................**16** A4
Paddington Recreation Ground
Athletics Track
KIL/WHAMP NW6.......................**2** B3
Paddock Primary School
BTSEA SW11...........................**134** A2
Paddock School
PUT/ROE SW15.........................**129** F2

Pain Relief Clinic
HDN NW4................................**52** B1
Paint Pots Montessori School
WBPTN SW10...........................**114** C2
Pakeman Primary School
HOLWY N7..............................**57** F5
Palace of Westminster
WHALL SW1A...........................**45** D1
Palace Theatre
SOHO/SHAV W1D......................**32** B1
Palladium Theatre
SOHO/CST W1F........................**19** E5
Panorama Pier
STHWK SE1.............................**35** E2
Paray House School
FUL/PGN SW6...........................**113** F5
Parayhouse School
WBPTN SW10...........................**114** C3
Parent Infant Centre
HAMP NW3...............................**72** C2
Park Royal Business Park
WLSDN NW10...........................**86** A2
Park Business Centre
KIL/WHAMP NW6........................**2** A4
Parkes Hotel
CHEL SW3................................**41** D2
Parkfield Industrial Estate
BTSEA SW11............................**116** A5
Parkfield JMI School
HDN NW4................................**52** B2
Parkgate House School
CLAP SW4...............................**134** A2
Park Hall Trading Estate
WNWD SE27............................**154** C3
Park House Medical Centre
KIL/WHAMP NW6.......................**89** E1
Park Medical Centre
BERM/RHTH SE16......................**103** D5
Park Mews Small Business Centre
HNHL SE24.............................**136** C4
Park Plaza County Hall Hotel
STHWK SE1.............................**33** F5
Park Primary School
SRTFD E15..............................**81** F4
Park Royal ⊖
EA W5..................................**86** A3
Park Royal Business Centre
WLSDN NW10...........................**87** D3
Park School for Girls
IL IG1...................................**66** A4
Parkside Business Estate
DEPT SE8...............................**121** F2
Parkside Clinic
NTGHL W11.............................**89** E5
Parkside Health
NTGHL W11.............................**89** E5
Parkside Hospital
WIM/MER SW19........................**149** D3
Park Walk Primary School
WBPTN SW10...........................**115** D2
Parkwood Primary School
FSBYPK N4.............................**58** B4
Parliament Hill
Fields Athletics Track
HAMP NW3...............................**73** E3
Parliament Hill Lido
HAMP NW3...............................**74** A1
Parliament Hill School
KTTN NW5...............................**74** A1
Parmiter Industrial Centre
BETH E2................................**90** B1
Parsons Green ⊖
FUL/PGN SW6...........................**114** A4
Parsons Green Health Clinic
FUL/PGN SW6...........................**114** A4
Pastoria Hotel
LSQ/SEVD WC2H.......................**32** B2
Patent Office
FLST/FETLN EC4A......................**22** A3
PCMS London
SRTFD E15..............................**93** D1
Peace Pagoda
CHEL SW3................................**115** F3
The Peacock Theatre
HOL/ALD WC2B........................**21** E5
Peckham Park Primary School
PECK SE15.............................**120** A3
The Peckham Pulse Health &
Leisure Centre
PECK SE15.............................**120** A4
Peckham Rye ⇌ ⊖
PECK SE15.............................**120** A5

Pembridge Hall Preparatory
School Girls
BAY/PAD W2 ....**26** B1

Pendragon Secondary School
BMLY BR1 ....**160** A3

Percival David Foundation of
Chinese Art
STPAN WC1H **8** B5

Perrymount Primary School
FSTH SE23 ....**157** D2

The Petchy Academy
HACK E8 ....**77** F2

Peterborough Primary School
FUL/PGN SW6 ....**114** A5

Peter Hills School
BERM/RHTH SE16 ....**103** D2

Peterley Business Centre
BETH E2 ....**90** B1

Peter Pan Statue
BAY/PAD W2 ....**28** A3

Petrie Museum of
Egyptian Archaeology
GWRST WC1E **20** A1

Pewterers' Hall
CITYW EC2V **23** F3

Phoenix Business Centre
POP/IOD E14 ....**92** A4

Phoenix High School
SHB W12 ....**100** A1

Phoenix Leisure Centre
CAT SE6 ....**140** B5

Phoenix School
HAMP NW3 ....**73** D3

Phoenix Secondary & Primary School
BOW E3 ....**91** F2

Phoenix Theatre
LSQ/SEVD WC2H **20** B5

Physical Energy Statue
BAY/PAD W2 ....**28** A4

Piccadilly Circus ⊖
MYFR/PICC W1J **32** A2

Piccadilly Theatre
SOHO/SHAV W1D **32** A1

Picture House Cinema
SRTFD E15 ....**81** D3

Pilgrims Way J & I School
PECK SE15 ....**120** C2

Pilot Industrial Centre
WLSDN NW10 ....**87** E3

Pimlico ⊖
PIM SW1V **117** D1

Pimlico Academy
PIM SW1V **116** C1

Plaisterers Hall
STBT EC1A **23** E3

Plaistow ⊖
SRTFD E15 ....**93** F1

Plaistow Hospital
PLSTW E13 ....**94** B1

Plaistow Primary School
PLSTW E13 ....**94** B1

Plantation House
Medical Centre
LOTH EC2R **24** B4

Plashet Jewish Cemetery
MNPK E12 ....**83** D3

Plashet Road Medical Centre
FSTGT E7 ....**82** B4

Plashet School
EHAM E6 ....**83** E4

Players Theatre
CHCR WC2N **33** D3

The Playhouse
CHCR WC2N **33** D3

Pleasance Theatre
HOLWY N7 ....**75** E3

Plumcroft Primary School
WOOL/PLUM SE18 ....**126** C2

Plumstead ⇌
WOOL/PLUM SE18 ....**109** D5

Plumstead Leisure Centre
WOOL/PLUM SE18 ....**127** F1

Plumstead Manor School
WOOL/PLUM SE18 ....**127** D1

The Pointer School
BKHTH/KID SE3 ....**124** A4

Police Cadet School
WAN E11 ....**64** A3

The Polish Institute &Sikorski Museum
SKENS SW7 ....**40** B1

Pontoon Dock ⊖
CAN/RD E16 ....**106** B2

Pooles Park Primary School
FSBYPK N4 ....**57** F4

Pope John Primary School
SHB W12 ....**100** B1

Pop In Business Centre
WBLY HA9 ....**68** B2

Poplar ⊖
POP/IOD E14 ....**104** B1

Poplar Business Park
POP/IOD E14 ....**104** A3

Poplar Coroners Court
POP/IOD E14 ....**104** B1

Pop Up Theatre
CLKNW EC1R **10** B2

Porchester Leisure Centre
BAY/PAD W2 ....**14** C4

Portcullis House
WHALL SW1A **45** D1

Portico City Learning Centre
CLPT E5 ....**78** C1

The Portland Hospital
REGST W1B **19** D1

Portland Place School
REGST W1B **19** D2

The Portman Clinic
HAMP NW3 ....**73** D3

Portobello Market
NKENS W10 ....**89** E4

Portobello Medical Centre
NTGHL W11 ....**89** E5

Portway Primary School
SRTFD E15 ....**82** A5

Pound Park Nursery School
CHARL SE7 ....**125** D1

Powergate Business Park
WLSDN NW10 ....**87** D2

Premier Cinema
PECK SE15 ....**120** A5

Prendergast Ladywell Fields College
BROCKY SE4 ....**140** A4

Prendergast School
BROCKY SE4 ....**140** A2

Primrose Hill School
CAMTN NW1 ....**74** A3

Primrose Montessori School
HBRY N5 ....**58** C5

Prince Charles Cinema
LSQ/SEVD WC2H **32** B1

Prince Edward Theatre
SOHO/SHAV W1D **20** A5

Prince of Wales Theatre
STJS SW1Y **32** A2

Prince Regent ⊖
CAN/RD E16 ....**106** C1

Princes College
NOXST/BSQ WC1A **20** C4

Princes Court Business Centre
WAP E1W **102** B3

Princess Frederica CE J & I School
WLSDN NW10 ....**88** B1

Princess Grace Hospital
MHST W1U **18** A1

Princess Louise Hospital
NKENS W10 ....**88** C4

Princess May Primary School
STNW/STAM N16 ....**77** E2

The Princess Royal Distribution Centre
WLSDN NW10 ....**68** B5

Prior Weston Primary School
STLK EC1Y **23** F1

Priory CE Primary School
WIM/MER SW19 ....**150** B5

Privy Council
STJS SW1Y **32** A4

Privy Council Office
WHALL SW1A **32** C4

Prospect House School
PUT/ROE SW15 ....**131** D5

Proteus School
KIL/WHAMP NW6 ....**72** B4

Proud Gallery
CHCR WC2N **32** C2

PS Tattershall Castle
WHALL SW1A **33** D4

Pudding Mill Lane ⊖
SRTFD E15 ....**80** B5

Pumphouse Educational Museum
BERM/RHTH SE16 ....**103** E2

Purdy Hicks Gallery
STHWK SE1 ....**34** C3

Putney ⇌
PUT/ROE SW15 ....**131** D2

Putney Animal Hospital
PUT/ROE SW15 ....131 D2
Putney Arts Theatre
PUT/ROE SW15 ....131 D2
Putney Bridge ⊖
FUL/PGN SW6 ....131 E1
Putney Exchange Shopping Centre
PUT/ROE SW15 ....131 D2
Putney High School
PUT/ROE SW15 ....131 D3
Putney Leisure Centre
PUT/ROE SW15 ....130 C2
Putney Lower Common Cemetery
BARN SW13 ....112 B5
Putneymead Medical Centre
PUT/ROE SW15 ....130 C2
Putney Park School
PUT/ROE SW15 ....130 B2
Putney School of Art
PUT/ROE SW15 ....131 E2
Putney Town Social & Bowls Club
PUT/ROE SW15 ....112 C5
Putney Vale Cemetery
PUT/ROE SW15 ....148 A2
Putney Vale Crematorium
PUT/ROE SW15 ....148 A2
Pylon Trading Estate
CAN/RD E16 ....93 D3
Quadrant Business Park
KIL/WHAMP NW6 ....71 E5
Quality Hotel
WBLY HA9 ....68 A1
Quebec Industrial Estate
BERM/RHTH SE16 ....103 E3
Queen Charlotte's &
Chelsea Hospital
SHB W12 ....88 B5
Queen Elizabeth College
KENS W8 ....26 A5
Queen Elizabeth Conference Centre
WEST SW1P 44 B1
Queen Elizabeth Hall
STHWK SE1 ....33 E3
Queen Elizabeth Hospital
WOOL/PLUM SE18 ....125 F2
Queen Elizabeth II School
MV/WKIL W9 ....89 F3
Queenhithe Stairs
BLKFR EC4V 35 E2
Queen Mary College
WCHPL E1 ....91 D3
Queen Mary's Hospital
HAMP NW3 ....54 C5
Queen Mary's University Hospital
PUT/ROE SW15 ....130 A4
Queen Mother Sports Centre
PIM SW1V 43 E4
Queensbridge Primary School
HACK E8 ....77 F4
Queensbridge Sports Centre
HACK E8 ....77 F4
Queen's Club
WKENS W14 ....113 E1
Queens College London
CAVSQ/HST W1G 18 C3
Queens College Preparatory School
CAVSQ/HST W1G 18 C2
The Queen's Gallery
BGVA SW1W 43 D1
Queens Gate School
SKENS SW7 ....40 A4
The Queens House
GNWCH SE10 ....123 D2
Queens Ice Rink & Bowl
BAY/PAD W2 ....27 D2
Queens Manor Primary School
FUL/PGN SW6 ....112 C3
Queensmill School
FUL/PGN SW6 ....114 A5
Queens Park ⊖ ⊖
KIL/WHAMP NW6 ....89 F1
Queens Park Community School
WLSDN NW10 ....70 C5
Queens Park Health Centre
NKENS W10 ....89 E2
Queens Park Primary School
NKENS W10 ....89 E2
Queens Park Rangers FC
(Loftus Road Stadium)
SHB W12 ....100 B2
Queen's Road Peckham ≹ ⊖
PECK SE15 ....120 B4

Queens Theatre
SOHO/SHAV W1D 32 A1
Queenstown Road Battersea ≹
VX/NE SW8 ....116 B4
Queensway ⊖
BAY/PAD W2 ....27 D2
Queen Victoria Memorial
WHALL SW1A 43 E1
Quintin Kynaston School
Technology College
STJWD NW8 ....73 D5
Ouuwat UL Islam Girl's School
FSTGT E7 ....82 A3
Radcliffe College
SOHO/SHAV W1D 19 E5
Radisson Edwardian
Berkshire Hotel
OXSTW W1C 18 C5
Radisson Edwardian Grafton Hotel
CAMTN NW1 ....7 E5
Radisson Edwardian
Hampshire Hotel
LSQ/SEVD WC2H 32 B2
Radisson Edwardian
Kenilworth Hotel
RSQ WC1B 20 B3
Radisson Edwardian
Marlborough Hotel
RSQ WC1B 20 B3
Radisson Edwardian Mayfair Hotel
MYFR/PICC W1J 31 D2
Radisson Edwardian
Mountbatten Hotel
LSQ/SEVD WC2H 20 C5
Radisson Edwardian Vanderbilt Hotel
SKENS SW7 ....39 F4
Radisson SAS Portman Hotel
MBLAR W1H 17 F4
Railton Road Clinic
HNHL SE24 ....136 B3
Rainbow Quay
BERM/RHTH SE16 ....103 E4
Rainbow School for
Autistic Children
WAND/EARL SW18 ....150 C2
Raines Foundation School
BETH E2 ....90 B2
Ramac Industrial Estate
CHARL SE7 ....124 A1
Ramada Encore Hotel
ACT W3 ....87 D4
Ramada Hotel
BAY/PAD W2 ....26 C2
Randal Cremer Primary School
BETH E2 ....13 E1
Ranelagh Gardens (site of Chelsea
Flower Show)
CHEL SW5 ....116 A1
Ranelagh Primary School
SRTFD E15 ....93 E1
Rangefield Primary School
BMLY BR1 ....159 E5
Ransomes Dock Business Centre
BTSEA SW11 ....115 E3
The Rathbone Education Centre
CAN/RD E16 ....93 F4
Rathbow Clinic
BAY/PAD W2 ....16 B1
Rathfern Primary School
FSTH SE23 ....157 F1
Ravensbourne College of Design
& Communication
CHST BR7 ....162 A5
Ravenscourt Park ⊖
HMSMTH W6 ....100 A5
Ravenscourt Park
Preparatory School
HMSMTH W6 ....100 A5
Ravenscroft Medical Centre
GLDGN NW11 ....53 F2
Ravenscroft Primary School
CAN/RD E16 ....94 A3
Ravenstone Preparatory School
SKENS SW7 ....39 F3
Ravenstone Primary School
BAL SW12 ....152 A1
RCA Sculpture School
BTSEA SW11 ....115 E3
Reay Primary School
BRXN/ST SW9 ....118 A3
Records Office
CLKNW EC1R 10 B5

Rectory Road ⇌
STNW/STAM N16 .... **60** A5
Redbridge ⊖
REDBR IG4 .... **65** D1
Redbridge Museum
IL IG1 .... **66** B5
Redcliffe School
WBPTN SW10 .... **114** C2
Redhill Junior School
CHST BR7 .... **162** B5
Redlands Primary School
WCHPL E1 .... **90** C4
Redriff Primary School
BERM/RHTH SE16 .... **103** E3
Regent Clinic
CAVSQ/HST W1G **18** C3
Regent's Park ⊖
CAMTN NW1 .... **18** C1
Regent's Park Barracks
CAMTN NW1 .... **6** C2
Regent's Park Clinic
CAMTN NW1 .... **5** E5
Regent's Park Medical Centre
CAMTN NW1 .... **7** D3
Regent's Park Open Air Theatre
CAMTN NW1 .... **6** A4
Regent's Park Track
STJWD NW8 .... **5** E1
Renoir Cinema
BMSBY WC1N **9** D5
Reynolds Sports Centre
ACT W3 .... **98** A3
Rhyl Primary School
KTTN NW5 .... **74** A3
RIBA Library Drawings &
Manuscript Collection
MBLAR W1H **17** F4
Ricards Lodge High School
WIM/MER SW19 .... **149** F4
Richard Atkins Primary School
BRXS/STRHM SW2 .... **135** E5
Richard Cloudesley School
STLK EC1Y **23** E1
Richard Cobden
Primary School
CAMTN NW1 .... **74** C5
Rich Industrial Estate
STHWK SE1 .... **49** D3
Richmond American
International University
KENS W8 .... **38** C1
Richmond Park Golf Club
PUT/ROE SW15 .... **129** E5
Richmond Park National
Nature Reserve
RCHPK/HAM TW10 .... **147** E2
Rio Cinema
HACK E8 .... **77** F2
Ripple Infant School
BARK IG11 .... **85** E5
The Ritz Hotel
WHALL SW1A **31** E3
Ritzy Cinema
BRXN/ST SW9 .... **136** A2
Riverbank Park Plaza Hotel
STHWK SE1 .... **45** E5
River House Montessori School
POP/IOD E14 .... **104** A2
Riverley Primary School
LEY E10 .... **62** A3
River Place Health Centre
IS N1 .... **76** C4
River Road Business Park
BARK IG11 .... **97** E2
Riversdale Primary School
WAND/EARL SW18 .... **150** A1
Riverside Business Centre
WAND/EARL SW18 .... **150** B1
Riverside Community Health Care
WKENS W14 .... **101** D4
Riverside Primary School
BERM/RHTH SE16 .... **102** A3
Riverside Quarter
WAND/EARL SW18 .... **132** A2
Riverside Studios Cinema
HMSMTH W6 .... **112** C1
Riverston School
LEE/GVPK SE12 .... **142** A3
RNLI Lifeboat Station
TWRH EC3N **37** D3
Robert Blair Primary School
HOLWY N7 .... **75** E3

Robert Browning
Primary School
WALW SE17 .... **119** D1
Robin Hood Primary School
KUTN/CMB KT2 .... **147** D5
Robinsfield Infant School
STJWD NW8 .... **4** B1
The Roche School
WAND/EARL SW18 .... **132** A3
Rockliffe Manor Primary School
WOOL/PLUM SE18 .... **127** F2
The Rockwell Hotel
ECT SW5 .... **38** C4
Roehampton Church School
PUT/ROE SW15 .... **130** B5
Roehampton Recreation Centre
PUT/ROE SW15 .... **129** F5
Roehampton University
(Digby Stuart College)
PUT/ROE SW15 .... **129** F3
Roehampton University
(Froebel College)
PUT/ROE SW15 .... **129** F4
Roehampton University
(Southlands College)
PUT/ROE SW15 .... **129** F3
Roehampton University
(Whitelands College)
PUT/ROE SW15 .... **129** F5
Rokeby School
SRTFD E15 .... **81** D4
Roman Bath
TPL/STR WC2R **33** F1
Roman Road Primary School
EHAM E6 .... **95** D3
Ronald Rose Primary School
PUT/ROE SW15 .... **131** D5
Rood Lane Medical Centre
FENCHST EC3M **36** C1
Roosevelt Memorial
MYFR/RKLN W1K **30** B1
Ropery Business Park
CHARL SE7 .... **106** C5
Rosary RC Primary School
HAMP NW3 .... **73** E2
Rose McAndrew Clinic
BRXN/ST SW9 .... **117** F5
Rosemead Preparatory School
DUL SE21 .... **154** C2
Rosendale Primary School
DUL SE21 .... **136** C5
Rose Theatre Exhibition
STHWK SE1 .... **35** E3
Rosetta Primary School
CAN/RD E16 .... **94** B4
Rosslyn Park RFC
PUT/ROE SW15 .... **129** F2
Rotherhead Primary School
IS N1 .... **76** C5
Rotherhithe ⊖
BERM/RHTH SE16 .... **102** C3
Rotherhithe Civic Centre
BERM/RHTH SE16 .... **102** C3
Rotherhithe Primary School
BERM/RHTH SE16 .... **102** C5
The Roundhouse Theatre
CAMTN NW1 .... **74** A4
Rowley Park Industrial Park
ACT W3 .... **98** B4
Roxwell Trading Park
LEY E10 .... **61** E2
Royal Academy of Arts
MYFR/PICC W1J **31** E2
Royal Academy of Dance
BTSEA SW11 .... **115** E4
Royal Academy of Dramatic Art
GWRST WC1E **20** A2
Royal Academy of Music
CAMTN NW1 .... **18** B1
Royal Albert ⊖
CAN/RD E16 .... **107** E1
Royal Albert Hall
SKENS SW7 .... **40** A1
Royal Arsenal
WOOL/PLUM SE18 .... **108** B4
The Royal Ballet School
(White Lodge)
RCHPK/HAM TW10 .... **147** D1
Royal Ballet Upper School
COVGDN WC2E **21** D5

Royal Blackheath Golf Club
ELTH/MOT SE9................................143 F5
Royal Brompton Hospital
CHEL SW3......................................115 D1
Royal College of Anaesthetists
RSQ WC1B.......................................20 C2
Royal College of Art
SKENS SW7.....................................39 F1
Royal College of Music
SHB W12.......................................100 A4
SKENS SW7.....................................40 A2
Royal College of Nursing
IS N1...76 B5
Royal College of Obstetricians
& Gynaecologists
CAMTN NW1.......................................5 E5
Royal College of Ophthalmologists
CAMTN NW1......................................18 A1
Royal College of Paediatrics &
Child Health
GTPST W1W......................................19 D2
The Royal College of Pathology
STJS SW1Y......................................32 A4
Royal College of Physicians
CAMTN NW1.......................................6 C5
Royal College of Surgeons
LINN WC2A......................................21 F4
Royal College of
Veterinary Surgeons
WEST SW1P......................................44 C4
Royal Courts of Justice
LINN WC2A......................................21 F5
Royal Court Theatre
BGVA SW1W......................................42 A5
Royal Court Young Peoples Theatre
NKENS W10......................................89 E4
The Royal Dock
Community School
CAN/RD E16.....................................94 C5
Royal Docks Medical Centre
EHAM E6..96 A5
Royal Exchange
BANK EC3V......................................24 B5
Royal Festival Hall
STHWK SE1......................................33 E4
Royal Free Hospital
HAMP NW3.......................................73 E2
Royal Garden Hotel
KENS W8..27 D5
Royal Geographical Society
SKENS SW7......................................40 A1
The Royal Horseguards Hotel
WHALL SW1A.....................................33 D4
Royal Horticultural Society New Hall
WEST SW1P......................................44 A3
Royal Horticultural Society Old Hall
WEST SW1P......................................44 A4
Royal Hospital Chelsea
CHEL SW3......................................115 F1
Royal Hospital for Neuro-disability
PUT/ROE SW15.................................131 E4
Royal Hospital & Home
PUT/ROE SW15.................................130 B5
Royal Hospital Museum
CHEL SW3......................................116 A1
Royal Institute of British Architects
REGST W1B......................................19 D2
Royal Institution's Faraday Museum
MYFR/PICC W1J..................................31 D2
Royal Lancaster Hotel
BAY/PAD W2.....................................28 B2
Royal London Homeopathic Hospital
BMSBY WC1N.....................................21 D2
Royal Marsden Hospital
CHEL SW3......................................115 D1
The Royal Mews
BGVA SW1W......................................43 D2
Royal Mint Court
TWRH EC3N......................................37 F2
Royal National Orthopaedic Hospital
GTPST W1W......................................19 D1
Royal National Theatre
STHWK SE1......................................34 A3
Royal National Throat Nose &
Ear Hospital
FSBYW WC1X......................................9 E3
Royal Oak ⊖
BAY/PAD W2.....................................15 D3
Royal Opera House
COVGDN WC2E....................................21 D5
The Royal School
HAMP NW3.......................................73 D1

Royal Society of Arts
CHCR WC2N......................................33 D2
Royal Veterinary College
CAMTN NW1......................................75 D1
Royal Victoria ⊖
CAN/RD E16....................................106 A1
Royal Victoria Docks
Watersports Centre
CAN/RD E16....................................106 A1
Royal Wimbledon Golf Club
WIM/MER SW19..................................148 B5
RSPCA Animal Hospital
FSBYPK N4......................................57 F4
Rudolph Steiner Hall
CAMTN NW1.......................................5 E5
Rufus Business Centre
WIM/MER SW19..................................150 B2
Rushey Green Primary School
CAT SE6.......................................158 B1
Rushmore Primary School
CLPT E5..78 C1
Ruskin House School
HNHL SE24.....................................136 C3
Russell Square ⊖
STPAN WC1H.....................................20 C1
Rye Oak Primary School
PECK SE15.....................................138 B1
Sacred Heart Catholic Primary School
PUT/ROE SW15..................................130 A3
Sacred Heart High School
HMSMTH W6.....................................100 C5
Sacred Heart RC Infant School
BTSEA SW11....................................115 E5
Sacred Heart RC School
CMBW SE5......................................118 C4
Sacred Heart School
HOLWY N7.......................................75 F2
Saddlers Hall
CITYW EC2V.....................................23 F4
Sadler's Wells Theatre
CLKNW EC1R.....................................10 B3
Sai Medical Centre
POP/IOD E14...................................104 C1
St Agnes RC Primary School
BOW E3...92 A2
CRICK NW2......................................53 E5
St Aidans Primary School
FSBYPK N4......................................58 A2
St Aidans RC Primary School
IL IG1...67 D3
St Albans CE Primary School
HCIRC EC1N.....................................22 A2
St Albans Health Clinic
HGT N6...56 A5
St Alfege with St Peter CE
Primary School
CNWCH SE10....................................122 C2
St Aloysius College
HGT N6...56 C3
St Aloysius RC Infant School
CAMTN NW1.......................................7 F2
St Aloysius RC Junior School
CAMTN NW1.......................................8 A3
St Andrew & Francis CE JMI School
CRICK NW2......................................70 A3
St Andrews Greek School
CAMTN NW1......................................74 B3
St Andrews Primary School
BRXN/ST SW9...................................117 F5
IS N1..75 F5
St Andrews School
WLSDN NW10.....................................70 B4
St Angelas Ursuline School
FSTGT E7.......................................82 B3
St Annes CE Primary School
WAND/EARL SW18................................132 B3
St Annes RC Primary School
LBTH SE11.....................................117 F2
St Anne's Trading Estate
POP/IOD E14....................................91 F5
St Anselms RC Primary School
TOOT SW17.....................................152 A3
St Anthonys RC Primary School
EDUL SE22.....................................138 A4
St Anthony's School (Junior House)
HAMP NW3.......................................73 D2
St Anthony's School (Senior House)
HAMP NW3.......................................72 C2
St Antonys RC Primary School
FSTGT E7.......................................82 A4
St Augustines CE High School
KIL/WHAMP NW6...................................2 B2

St Augustines Primary School
KIL/WHAMP NW6 .... 2 B1
St Augustines RC Primary School
CAT SE6 .... 158 B5
WKENS W14 .... 113 E2
St Barnabas & St Philip's CE
Primary School
KENS W8 .... 38 A3
St Bartholomews CE Primary School
SYD SE26 .... 156 C4
St Bartholomews Hospital
STBT EC1A 23 D3
St Bartholomews Medical School
FARR EC1M 23 D1
St Bartholomews & Royal London
School of Medicine
FARR EC1M 23 E2
St Bartholomew's the Great
STBT EC1A 23 D3
St Barts & the Royal London Hospital
WCHPL E1 .... 90 B4
St Bedes RC Infant School
BAL SW12 .... 153 D1
St Bernadette Catholic Junior School
BAL SW12 .... 134 C5
St Bonaventures School
FSTGT E7 .... 82 A4
St Boniface RC Primary School
TOOT SW17 .... 151 F5
St Cecilias CE School
WAND/EARL SW18 .... 131 F5
St Charles Hospital
NKENS W10 .... 89 D4
St Charles Primary School
NKENS W10 .... 89 D4
St Christinas RC Preparatory School
STJWD NW8 .... 5 D1
St Christophers School
HAMP NW3 .... 73 D2
St Clement Danes CE
Primary School
HOL/ALD WC2B 21 E5
St Clement & St James CE
Primary School
NTGHL W11 .... 101 D2
St Clements Hospital
BOW E3 .... 91 F2
St Cuthbert with St Mattias CE
Primary School
ECT SW5 .... 114 A1
St Dominics RC Primary School
HAMP NW3 .... 73 F2
HOM E9 .... 79 E3
St Dunstans College
CAT SE6 .... 157 F1
St Edmunds RC Primary School
POP/IOD E14 .... 104 A5
St Edwards RC JMI School
STJWD NW8 .... 16 C1
St Elizabeths RC Primary School
BETH E2 .... 90 C1
St Eugene de Mazenod RC
Primary School
KIL/WHAMP NW6 .... 72 A4
St Faiths CE School
WAND/EARL SW18 .... 132 B3
St Francesca Cabrini
Primary School
FSTH SE23 .... 138 C4
St Francis of Assisi Primary School
NKENS W10 .... 101 D1
St Francis RC Primary School
PECK SE15 .... 120 A2
SRTFD E15 .... 81 E2
St Francis Xavier College
BAL SW12 .... 134 B4
St Gabriels CE Primary School
PIM SW1V 116 C1
St George's Cathedral
STHWK SE1 .... 46 B2
St Georges CE Primary School
CMBW SE5 .... 119 E3
VX/NE SW8 .... 116 C4
St Georges College
HOLWY N7 .... 58 A5
St Georges Elizabethan Theatre
HOLWY N7 .... 75 D1
St Georges Hanover Square CE
Primary School
MYFR/PKLN W1K 30 B2
St Georges Hospital
TOOT SW17 .... 151 E5
St Georges RC School
MV/WKIL W9 .... 3 D2
St Georges University of London
TOOT SW17 .... 151 D5
St George the Martyr CE
Primary School
BMSBY WC1N 21 E1
St George Wharf
VX/NE SW8 .... 117 E2
St Gildas RC Junior School
CEND/HSY/T N8 .... 57 E2
St Giles College London Central
RSQ WC1B 21 D2
St Helens RC Primary School
BRXN/ST SW9 .... 136 A1
CAN/RD E16 .... 93 F3
St Ignatius RC Primary School
SEVS/STOTM N15 .... 59 E1
St James CE J & I School
BERM/RHTH SE16 .... 102 A4
St James CE Primary School
NWCR SE14 .... 121 E4
St James CE Junior School
FSTGT E7 .... 81 F2
St James Independent
School for Girls
NTGHL W11 .... 26 A1
St James Independent School for
Senior Girls
WKENS W14 .... 101 E5
St James Independent Schools for
Juniors & Girls
WKENS W14 .... 101 E5
St James & Lucie Clayton College
SKENS SW7 .... 39 D5
St James's Palace
WHALL SW1A 31 F4
St James's Park ⊖
STJSPK SW1 .... 44 A2
St James the Great RC Primary School
PECK SE15 .... 119 F4
St Joachims RC Primary School
CAN/RD E16 .... 94 C5
St Joan of Arc RC Primary School
HBRY N5 .... 76 B1
St John of Jerusalem CE
Primary School
HOM E9 .... 78 C4
St Johns ⇌
DEPT SE8 .... 122 A5
St Johns Angell Town CE
Primary School
BRXN/ST SW9 .... 118 A5
St Johns CE Primary School
BETH E2 .... 90 C1
St John's CE Walham Green
Primary School
FUL/PGN SW6 .... 113 E4
St John's Concert Hall
WEST SW1P 44 C3
St Johns Highbury Vale CE
Primary School
HBRY N5 .... 76 B1
St John's Hospital Day Centre
BTSEA SW11 .... 133 D2
St John's Lodge
CAMTN NW1 .... 6 A3
St Johns RC Primary School
BERM/RHTH SE16 .... 103 E3
St Johns & St Clements
CE J & I School
PECK SE15 .... 138 A1
St Johns Upper Holloway CE
Primary School
ARCH N19 .... 56 C4
St Johns Walworth
CE Primary School
WALW SE17 .... 47 E5
St Johns Way Medical Centre
ARCH N19 .... 57 D3
St John's Wood ⊖
STJWD NW8 .... 4 A1
St Johns Wood
Pre-Preparatory School
STJWD NW8 .... 4 C3
St John the Baptist CE Primary School
BMLY BR1 .... 158 C4
St John the Baptist VA CE
Primary School
IS N1 .... 12 C2
St John the Divine CE Primary School
CMBW SE5 .... 118 B3

St John the Evangelist RC Primary
IS N1 .... **10** C1
St Josephs Catholic Infant School
LEY E10 .... **61** F3
St Josephs Catholic Junior School
CMBW SE5 .... **118** C3
St Josephs Convent School
WAN E11 .... **64** A1
St Josephs Primary School
WAND/EARL SW18 .... **132** A3
St Josephs RC Junior School
LEY E10 .... **62** A3
St Josephs RC Primary School
ARCH N19 .... **56** B3
BARK IG11 .... **84** C5
BERM/RHTH SE16 .... **102** C4
CHEL SW3 .... **41** G5
DEPT SE8 .... **122** A5
GNWCH SE10 .... **123** E1
HOL/ALD WC2B **3** E5
MV/WKIL W9 .... **3** E5
STHWK SE1 .... **35** F5
STHWK SE1 .... **102** A3
WLSDN NW10 .... **69** E4
St Judes CE Primary School
HNHL SE24 .... **136** B4
STHWK SE1 .... **46** C3
St Judes & St Pauls CE Primary School
IS N1 .... **77** E2
St Katharine Pier
WAP E1W **37** F3
St Katherine
TPL/STR WC2R **33** F2
St Lawrence University
BMSBY WC1N **21** F1
St Leonards CE Primary School
STRHM/NOR SW16 .... **153** D5
St Leonards Hospital
IS N1 .... **13** D1
St Lukes CE Primary School
CAN/RD E16 .... **93** F5
FSBYE EC1V **11** F4
MV/WKIL W9 .... **89** F1
POP/IOD E14 .... **105** D5
WNWD SE27 .... **154** C5
St Luke's Health Centre
CAN/RD E16 .... **93** F5
St Lukes Hospital for the Clergy
FITZ W1T **19** E1
St Margarets CE Primary School
WOOL/PLUM SE18 .... **126** C2
St Margarets Clitherow RC
Primary School
WBLY HA9 .... **50** C5
St Margarets Primary School
BARK IG11 .... **84** B5
St Margarets School
HAMP NW3 .... **72** B1
St Marks CE Primary School
ARCH N19 .... **57** E4
LBTH SE11 .... **117** F2
St Marks Industrial Estate
CAN/RD E16 .... **107** D2
St Martin-in-the-Fields
CHCR WC2N **32** C2
St Martin in the Fields High School
BRXS/STRHM SW2 .... **154** B1
St Martins Hospital
MYFR/PKLN W1K **30** A1
St Martins School of Art
SOHO/SHAV W1D **20** B5
St Martins Theatre
LSQ/SEVD WC2H **32** B1
St Mary Abbots CE
Primary School
KENS W8 .... **38** C1
St Mary Abbots Church Hall
KENS W8 .... **26** C5
The St Marylebone CE School
MHST W1U **18** B2
St Mary Magdalene CE
Primary School
MV/WKIL W9 .... **14** C1
WOOL/PLUM SE18 .... **107** F5
St Mary Magdalen
RC Junior School
CRICK NW2 .... **70** B3
St Mary Magdalens Catholic
Primary School
BROCKY SE4 .... **139** E2
St Mary Magdalens Primary School
MORT/ESHN SW14 .... **129** D1

St Mary of the Angels RC
Primary School
NTGHL W11 .... **14** A4
St Mary & St Michael
Primary School
WCHPL E1 .... **90** C5
St Marys Bryanston Square CE
Primary School
MBLAR W1H **17** D2
St Mary's Cemetery
BTSEA SW11 .... **133** E3
St Marys CE Primary School
IS N1 .... **76** B4
LEW SE13 .... **140** B3
St Mary's CE Primary School
PUT/ROE SW15 .... **131** D1
STNW/STAM N16 .... **59** D4
WLSDN NW10 .... **69** E3
St Marys Hospital
BAY/PAD W2 .... **16** B4
St Marys Hospital Medical School
BAY/PAD W2 .... **16** B4
St Marys Kilburn Primary School
KIL/WHAMP NW6 .... **72** A5
St Marys Primary School
WKENS W14 .... **101** D4
St Mary's RC Primary School
CHSWK W4 .... **111** E1
CLAP SW4 .... **134** C3
ELTH/MOT SE9 .... **144** B3
KIL/WHAMP NW6 .... **2** A1
NKENS W10 .... **89** E3
VX/NE SW8 .... **116** B4
St Marys School
HAMP NW3 .... **72** C2
St Mary's Western Eye Hospital
MBLAR W1H **17** E2
St Matthew Academy
LEW SE13 .... **141** D1
St Matthias CE Primary School
BETH E2 .... **13** E5
STNW/STAM N16 .... **77** E2
St Michael & All Angels
CE Academy
CMBW SE5 .... **118** B3
St Michaels CE Primary School
HGT N6 .... **56** A2
WAND/EARL SW18 .... **151** F5
St Michaels RC Primary School
EHAM E6 .... **95** F1
St Michaels RC Secondary School
BERM/RHTH SE16 .... **102** A3
St Michaels Sydenham CE
Primary School
SYD SE26 .... **157** E4
The St Michael Steiner School
WAND/EARL SW18 .... **132** A3
St Monica's RC Primary School
IS N1 .... **12** C3
St Nicholas
Preparatory School
SKENS SW7 .... **40** B1
St Nicholas School
CDALE/KGS NW9 .... **50** C4
St Olaves Preparatory School
ELTH/MOT SE9 .... **162** B2
St Pancras Hospital
CAMTN NW1 .... **75** D5
St Pancras International ≠ ⊖
CAMTN NW1 .... **8** C2
St Pancras International
Youth Hostel
CAMTN NW1 .... **8** B3
St Patricks Church School
STHWK SE1 .... **34** A4
St Patricks Infants School
WAP E1W **102** B2
St Patricks
International School
SOHO/SHAV W1D **19** F4
St Patricks Primary School
KTTN NW5 .... **74** B3
St Patricks RC Primary School
WOOL/PLUM SE18 .... **109** D5
St Paul's ⊖
STP EC4M **23** E4
St Paul's Cathedral
STP EC4M **23** E5
St Paul's Cathedral School
STP EC4M **23** E5
St Pauls CE Primary School
HAMP NW3 .... **73** E4

WALW SE17 ....118 B1
WCHPL E1 ....102 A1

St Pauls Girls School
HMSMTH W6 ....101 D5
St Paul's Primary School
HMSMTH W6 ....112 C1
St Pauls Road Medical Centre
IS N1 ....76 B3
St Pauls School
BARN SW13 ....112 B1
St Pauls Steiner School
IS N1 ....77 D3
St Pauls Way Community School
BOW E3 ....92 A4
St Pauls with St Lukes CE
Primary School
BOW E3 ....91 F4
St Pauls with St Michaels CE School
HACK E8 ....78 A5
St Peter & St Pauls Primary School
FSBYE EC1V 10 C5
St Peters CE Primary School
HMSMTH W6 ....112 A1
MV/WKIL W9 ....14 A1
WALW SE17 ....119 D1
WAP E1W 102 C2
St Peter's Church
KTBR SW1X 42 C2
St Peter's Hospital
COVGDN WC2E 33 D1
St Peters RC Primary School
WOOL/PLUM SE18 ....126 B1
St Philips School
SKENS SW7 ....39 F5
St Phillips Infant School
SYD SE26 ....156 B4
St Quintins Health Centre
NKENS W10 ....88 C4
St Raphaels Way Medical Centre
WLSDN NW10 ....68 C2
St Robert Southwell RC
Primary School
CDALE/KGS NW9 ....50 C1
St Savior & St Mary Overy
STHWK SE1 ....35 F5
St Saviour & St Olaves School
STHWK SE1 ....48 B3
St Saviours CE Primary School
HNHL SE24 ....136 C1
MV/WKIL W9 ....15 D1
POP/IOD E14 ....92 B4
WALTH E17 ....61 F2
St Saviours RC Primary School
LEW SE13 ....140 C2
St Scholasticas RC Primary School
CLPT E5 ....60 A5
St Stephens CE Primary School
BAY/PAD W2 ....14 B3
DEPT SE8 ....122 A5
SHB W12 ....100 B2
St Stephens CE School
VX/NE SW8 ....117 C1
St Stephens Primary School
EHAM E6 ....82 C4
St Thomas CE Primary School
NKENS W10 ....89 E3
St Thomas' Hospital
STHWK SE1 ....45 E2
St Thomas More RC Primary School
ELTH/MOT SE9 ....143 E1
St Thomas More RC School
CHEL SW3 ....41 E4
ELTH/MOT SE9 ....144 A4
St Thomas of Canterbury RC
Primary School
FUL/PGN SW6 ....113 F3
St Thomas the Apostle College
PECK SE15 ....120 C4
St Ursulas Convent School
GNWCH SE10 ....123 D3
St Vincent de Paul RC Primary
WEST SW1P 43 E3
St Vincents Catholic
Primary School
ELTH/MOT SE9 ....161 E4
St Vincent's RC Primary School
MHST W1U 18 A3
St Walter & St John Sports Ground
TOOT SW17 ....151 E1
St William of York Primary School
FSTH SE23 ....139 E5
FSTH SE23 ....157 E1

St Winefrides Catholic Primary School
MNPK E12 ....83 F2
St Winifreds Catholic Junior School
LEE/GVPK SE12 ....141 F4
St Winifreds RC Infant School
LEW SE13 ....141 E3
SS Angelas & Bonaventures Sixth
Form Centre
FSTGT E7 ....82 B3
SS Mary & Pancras CE
Primary School
CAMTN NW1 ....8 A2
SS Peter & Pauls RC Primary School
IL IG1 ....67 D5
Salisbury Primary School
MNPK E12 ....83 D2
Salters' Hall
BARB EC2Y 23 F3
Salusbury Primary School
KIL/WHAMP NW6 ....71 E5
Samuel Jones Industrial Estate
PECK SE15 ....119 E3
Samuel Rhodes School
IS N1 ....76 A5
Sandgate Trading Estate
BERM/RHTH SE16 ....120 B1
Sandhurst Primary School
CAT SE6 ....141 E5
Sandringham Primary School
FSTGT E7 ....82 C3
Sapcote Trading Centre
WLSDN NW10 ....69 F2
Sarah Bonnell School
SRTFD E15 ....81 E3
Sarum Hall School
HAMP NW3 ....73 E4
Satmer Trust School
STNW/STAM N16 ....60 A4
Savoy Pier
TPL/STR WC2R 33 E2
The Savoy
TPL/STR WC2R 33 D2
Savoy Theatre
TPL/STR WC2R 33 E2
Sayer Clinics
MBLAR W1H 17 F5
Scarsdale Place Medical Centre
KENS W8 ....38 C2
School of Oriental & African Studies
GWRST WC1E 20 B1
Schomberg House
STJS SW1Y 31 F4
School of English
GLDGN NW11 ....54 A3
School of Islamic Republic Iran
KIL/WHAMP NW6 ....2 A2
The School of Pharmacy
BMSBY WC1N 9 D5
Science Museum
SKENS SW7 ....40 B3
Science Museum IMAX Cinema
SKENS SW7 ....40 A3
The Science Museum Library
SKENS SW7 ....40 A2
Scott Wilkie Primary School
CAN/RD E16 ....94 C5
Screen on Baker Street Cinema
MHST W1U 17 F2
Screen on the Green Cinema
IS N1 ....76 A5
Sebright Primary School
BETH E2 ....90 A1
Sedgehill School
CAT SE6 ....158 B3
Sedgewick Centre
WCHPL E1 ....25 F4
The Selfridge Hotel
MBLAR W1H 18 B5
Selwyn Primary School
PLSTW E13 ....82 A5
Sergeant Industrial Estate
WAND/EARL SW18 ....132 B4
Serpentine Gallery
BAY/PAD W2 ....28 B4
Serpentine Lido & Cafe
SKENS SW7 ....28 C5
Servite RC Primary School
WBPTN SW10 ....114 C2
Seven Islands Leisure Centre
BERM/RHTH SE16 ....102 C4
Seven Kings ⇌
GDMY/SEVK IG3 ....67 E3

Seven Kings Health Centre
CDMY/SEVK IG3..........................**67** E3
Seven Kings High School
GNTH/NBYPK IG2.......................**67** D2
Seven Mills Primary School
POP/IOD E14...........................**104** A3
Seymour Gardens Medical Centre
IL IG1...................................**65** F3
Seymour Leisure Centre
MBLAR W1H.............................**17** E3
Shaare Zedek Medical Centre
GLDGN NW11............................**53** F1
Shacklewell Primary School
HACK E8.................................**77** F1
Shadwell ↔ ⊖
WCHPL E1..............................**102** B1
Shadwell Dock Stairs
WAP E1W...............................**103** D1
Shaftesbury Hospital
LSQ/SEVD WC2H.........................**20** C5
Shaftesbury Park
  Primary School
BTSEA SW11............................**134** A1
Shaftesbury Primary School
FSTGT E7..............................**82** C4
Shaftesbury Theatre
LSQ/SEVD WC2H.........................**20** C4
Shahjalal Medical Centre
WCHPL E1..............................**90** A5
Shakespeare Business Centre
BRXN/ST SW9..........................**136** B1
Shakespeare's Globe Theatre
  & Exhibition
STHWK SE1.............................**35** E3
The Shamrock Sports Club
ACT W3.................................**86** C5
Shapla Primary School
WCHPL E1.............................**102** A1
Sheen Lane Health Centre
MORT/ESHN SW14......................**128** C1
Sheen Lawn Tennis & Squash Club
MORT/ESHN SW14......................**128** C3
Sheen Mount Primary School
RCHPK/HAM TW10......................**128** B3
Sheen Sports Centre
MORT/ESHN SW14......................**129** E2
Shell Centre
STHWK SE1.............................**33** F4
Shelley School
CLAP SW4.............................**134** C1
Shene School
MORT/ESHN SW14......................**129** E2
Shepherd's Bush ⇌ ⊖ ⊖
SHB W12...............................**101** D3
Shepherd's Bush CC
ACT W3.................................**99** E1
Shepherd's Bush Empire
SHB W12..............................**100** C3
Shepherd's Bush Market ⊖
SHB W12..............................**100** C2
Sheraton Belgravia Hotel
KTBR SW1X.............................**42** A3
Sheraton Park Tower Hotel
KTBR SW1X.............................**29** F5
Sheringdale Primary School
WAND/EARL SW18......................**149** F1
Sheringham Junior School
MNPK E12..............................**83** F1
Sherington Primary School
CHARL SE7............................**124** B2
Sherlock Holmes Hotel
MHST W1U.............................**17** E1
Sherlock Holmes Museum
CAMTN NW1............................**17** E1
Shooters Hill Golf Club
WOOL/PLUM SE18.....................**126** C4
Shooters Hill Post 16 Campus
WOOL/PLUM SE18.....................**126** A3
The Shopping Hall
EHAM E6...............................**83** E5
Shore Business Centre
HOM E9................................**78** C4
Shoreditch Comprehensive School
IS N1..................................**13** D2
Shoreditch High Street ⊖
WCHPL E1..............................**25** E1
Showcase Newham Cinema
BARK IG11.............................**96** C2
Shrewsbury Road Health Centre
FSTGT E7..............................**83** D4
Sidcup Sports Club
SCUP DA14............................**163** F4

Simon Marks Jewish Primary School
STNW/STAM N16........................**59** F3
Sion College
EMB EC4Y.............................**34** B1
Sion Manning RC Girls School
NKENS W10............................**89** D4
Sir Francis Drake Primary School
DEPT SE8............................**121** E1
Sir James Barrie School
VX/NE SW8............................**116** C4
Sir John Cass Foundation School
HDTCH EC3A...........................**25** D5
Sir John Cass Found/Redcoat School
WCHPL E1..............................**91** D4
Sir John Heron Primary School
MNPK E12.............................**83** F1
Sir John Lillie Primary School
HMSMTH W6...........................**113** E2
Sir John Soane's Museum
LINN WC2A.............................**21** E4
Sir Thomas Abney Primary School
STNW/STAM N16........................**59** D2
Sir William Burrough
  Primary School
POP/IOD E14...........................**91** E5
Site of Greenwich Hospital
GNWCH SE10...........................**123** F1
Six Bridges Trading Estate
STHWK SE1...........................**120** A1
Skillion Business Park
BARK IG11.............................**97** F2
Skinners Co Lower Girls School
CLPT E5................................**60** B3
Skinners Companys
  School for Girls
STNW/STAM N16........................**59** E2
Slade School of Fine Art
STPAN WC1H.............................**8** B4
Sleaford Industrial Estate
VX/NE SW8............................**116** C3
Sloane Square ⊖
BGVA SW1W.............................**42** A5
Smallwood Primary School
TOOT SW17............................**151** D4
SMA Medical Centre
LEY E10................................**62** B2
Smithy Street School
WCHPL E1..............................**90** C4
Snowsfields Primary School
STHWK SE1............................**36** C5
Sobell Leisure Centre
HOLWY N7.............................**57** F5
Sobell Medical Centre
HOLWY N7.............................**76** A1
Sofitel St James Hotel
STJS SW1Y............................**32** A3
Soho Parish CE Primary School
SOHO/CST W1V.........................**32** A1
Solent Road Health Centre
KIL/WHAMP NW6.......................**72** A3
Somerset House
COVGDN WC2E.........................**33** E1
Somers Town Community
  Sports Centre
CAMTN NW1.............................**7** F2
Sorsby Health Centre
CLPT E5................................**79** D1
South Acton ⊖
ACT W3................................**98** B4
South Bank Business Centre
VX/NE SW8............................**117** D2
Southbank International
  School Hampstead
HAMP NW3.............................**72** C3
Southbank International
  School Kensington
NTGHL W11...........................**101** F1
Southbank International
  School Westminster
BAY/PAD W2...........................**26** B2
South Bank University
STHWK SE1............................**46** C1
STHWK SE1............................**47** F3
South Bermondsey ⇌
BERM/RHTH SE16......................**120** C1
South Camden
  Community School
CAMTN NW1.............................**7** F2
South Chelsea College
BRXN/ST SW9.........................**136** B2
South Eastern U...
HOLWY N...

Southern Road Primary School
PLSTW E13 ....**94** B1
Southfield First & Middle School
CHSWK W4 ....**99** E3
Southfield Medical Centre
CHSWK W4 ....**99** D3
Southfields ⊖
WAND/EARL SW18 ....**149** F1
The Southfields Clinic
WAND/EARL SW18 ....**132** A4
Southfields Community College
WAND/EARL SW18 ....**150** A1
Southgate Road Medical Centre
IS N1 ....**77** D4
South Grove Primary School
WALTH E17 ....**61** E1
South Hampstead ⊖
STJWD NW8 ....**72** C4
South Hampstead CC
CRICK NW2 ....**70** C4
South Hampstead High School
HAMP NW3 ....**73** D3
South Kensington ⊖
SKENS SW7 ....**40** B4
South Lewisham Health Centre
CAT SE6 ....**158** C4
South London Gallery
CMBW SE5 ....**119** E4
The South London Natural
Health Centre
CLAP SW4 ....**134** C2
South London Theatre
WNWD SE27 ....**154** C3
Southmead Primary School
WIM/MER SW19 ....**149** E1
South Park Business Centre
IL IG1 ....**67** E4
South Park Clinic
IL IG1 ....**85** E1
South Park Primary School
GDMY/SEVK IG3 ....**67** E5
South Quay ⊖
POP/IOD E14 ....**104** B3
South Quay Plaza
POP/IOD E14 ....**104** B3
South Rise Primary School
WOOL/PLUM SE18 ....**127** D1
Southside Industrial Estate
VX/NE SW8 ....**116** C3
Southside Shopping Centre
WAND/EARL SW18 ....**132** B4
South Thames College
PUT/ROE SW15 ....**129** F4
PUT/ROE SW15 ....**131** D3
TOOT SW17 ....**151** E5
WAND/EARL SW18 ....**132** B3
Southwark ⊖
STHWK SE1 ....**34** C3
Southwark Bridge Stairs
BLKFR EC4V **35** E2
Southwark Cathedral
STHWK SE1 ....**36** A3
Southwark College
BERM/RHTH SE16 ....**102** B4
CMBW SE5 ....**119** E3
STHWK SE1 ....**34** B5
STHWK SE1 ....**49** D2
Southwark Park
Primary School
BERM/RHTH SE16 ....**102** B4
Southwark Park Sports Centre
BERM/RHTH SE16 ....**102** C5
Southwark Sports Ground
DUL SE21 ....**155** F1
South_____ Primary School
C_____ **60** C4
So_____ Hospital
....**56** A2
_____tre Cinema
....**103** F5
....**102** A5
....**29** F1
....**8** B3
....**27** F3
...._____ E4

Spitalfields Health Centre
WCHPL E1 ....**25** F3
Springfield Christian School
CAT SE6 ....**157** F3
Springfield Community
Primary School
SEVS/STOTM N15 ....**60** A1
Springfield Hospital
TOOT SW17 ....**151** E3
Springfield Primary School
VX/NE SW8 ....**117** D3
The Stables Gallery & Art Centre
CRICK NW2 ....**70** A1
Stadium Business Centre
WBLY HA9 ....**50** B5
Stadium Industrial Estate
WBLY HA9 ....**68** B2
Stadium Retail Park
WBLY HA9 ....**50** A5
The Stafford Hotel
WHALL SW1A **31** E4
Stamford Brook ⊖
CHSWK W4 ....**99** F5
Stamford Clinic
HMSMTH W6 ....**100** A5
Stamford Hill ⊜
SEVS/STOTM N15 ....**59** E1
Stamford Hill Primary School
SEVS/STOTM N15 ....**59** D1
Standard Industrial Estate
CAN/RD E16 ....**107** E3
CAN/RD E16 ....**107** F3
Stanton Square Industrial Estate
SYD SE26 ....**157** F4
Staple Inn Buildings
HHOL WC1V **22** A3
Staples Corner Business Park
CRICK NW2 ....**52** A3
Star Lane ⊜
CAN/RD E16 ....**93** D3
Star Primary School
CAN/RD E16 ....**93** E3
Stationers Hall
STP EC4M **23** D5
Stationery Office
HOL/ALD WC2B **21** E4
Stebon Primary School
POP/IOD E14 ....**91** F4
Stephen Hawking Primary
Special School
POP/IOD E14 ....**91** E5
Stepney Day Hospital
WCHPL E1 ....**90** C5
Stepney Green ⊖
WCHPL E1 ....**91** D3
Stepney Greencoat CE
Primary School
POP/IOD E14 ....**91** F5
Stepney Green College
WCHPL E1 ....**91** D4
Stewart Headlam
Primary School
WCHPL E1 ....**90** B3
Stillness Primary School
FSTH SE23 ....**139** E4
Stockwell ⊖
CLAP SW4 ....**117** E5
Stockwell Park School
BRXN/ST SW9 ....**117** F4
Stockwell Primary School
BRXN/ST SW9 ....**135** F1
Stoke Newington ⇌
STNW/STAM N16 ....**59** F4
Stonebridge Park ⇌ ⊖
ALP/SUD HA0 ....**68** A4
The Stonebridge Primary School
(London Welsh School)
WLSDN NW10 ....**68** C5
Stonebridge Shopping Centre
WLSDN NW10 ....**69** D5
Stone Lake Retail Park
CHARL SE7 ....**106** C5
Strand on the Green J & I School
CHSWK W4 ....**110** A2
Strand Palace Hotel
COVGDN WC2E **33** D1
Stratford ⇌ ⊖ ⊜
SRTFD E15 ....**80** C3
Stratford College
SRTFD E15 ....**81** E4
Stratford High Street ⊖
SRTFD E15 ....**81** D5

~~University~~

Stratford International ≥ ⊖
  SRTFD E15 .... 80 C3
Stratford School
  FSTGT E7 .... 82 A4
Stratford Shopping Centre
  SRTFD E15 .... 81 D4
Strawberry Fields School
  NTGHL W11 .... 14 B5
Streatham ≥
  STRHM/NOR SW16 .... 153 D5
Streatham Cemetery
  TOOT SW17 .... 151 E3
Streatham Clapham
  High School
  STRHM/NOR SW16 .... 152 C3
  BRXS/STRHM SW2 .... 153 F1
Streatham Hill ≥
  STRHM/NOR SW16 .... 153 E2
Streatham Ice Rink
  STRHM/NOR SW16 .... 153 E3
Streatham Leisure Centre
  STRHM/NOR SW16 .... 153 E2
Streatham Swimming Pool
  STRHM/NOR SW16 .... 153 E2
Streatham Wells Primary School
  BRXS/STRHM SW2 .... 153 F2
Stroud Green Primary School
  FSBYPK N4 .... 58 A3
The Study Preparatory School
  WIM/MER SW19 .... 149 D5
Sudbourne Primary School
  BRXS/STRHM SW2 .... 135 F3
Sulivan Primary School
  FUL/PGN SW6 .... 114 A5
Sunnyhill Primary School
  STRHM/NOR SW16 .... 153 F4
Surrey CCC (The Oval)
  LBTH SE11 .... 117 F2
Surrey Docks Farm
  BERM/RHTH SE16 .... 103 F3
Surrey Docks Health Centre
  BERM/RHTH SE16 .... 103 E3
Surrey Docks Watersports Centre
  BERM/RHTH SE16 .... 103 E4
Surrey Quays ⊖
  BERM/RHTH SE16 .... 103 D5
Surrey Quays Leisure Park
  BERM/RHTH SE16 .... 103 D4
Surrey Quays Shopping Centre
  BERM/RHTH SE16 .... 103 D4
Surrey Square Primary School
  WALW SE17 .... 119 E1
Sussex Hotel
  OXSTW W1C 18 A5
Sussex House School
  KTBR SW1X 41 E4
Sutcliffe Park Athletics Track
  LEE/GVPK SE12 .... 142 B3
Sutton House
  HACK E8 .... 78 C2
Swaffield Primary School
  WAND/EARL SW18 .... 132 C4
Swaminarayan School
  WLSDN NW10 .... 69 D3
Swan Business Centre
  CHSWK W4 .... 99 C3
Swan Lane Pier
  CANST EC4R 36 C4
Swanlea School
  WCHPL E1 .... 90 B3
Swedish School
  BARN SW13 .... 112 A2
Swiss Cottage ⊖
  KIL/WHAMP NW6 .... 73 D4
Swiss Cottage Hotel
  HAMP NW3 .... 73 D4
Swiss Cottage Leisure Centre
  HAMP NW3 .... 73 D4
Swiss Cottage School
  STJWD NW8 .... 73 D5
Swissotel the Howard
  TPL/STR WC2R 33 F1
Sybourn Infant School
  LEY E10 .... 61 E3
The Sybourn Junior School
  WALTH E17 .... 61 F2
Sydenham ≥
  SYD SE26 .... 156 C5
Sydenham Girls School
  SYD SE26 .... 156 B3
Sydenham High Junior School
  SYD SE26 .... 156 B4
Sydenham High School
  Sports Ground
  CAT SE6 .... 158 A5
Sydenham High Senior School
  SYD SE26 .... 156 B5
Sydenham Hill ≥
  DUL SE21 .... 155 E3
Syracuse University
  NTGHL W11 .... 101 F1
Tabard Theatre
  CHSWK W4 .... 99 E5
Tabernacle School
  NTGHL W11 .... 101 D2
Talmud Torah School
  STNW/STAM N16 .... 59 D2
Tate Britain
  WEST SW1P 44 C3
Tate Modern
  STHWK SE1 .... 35 D3
Tavistock Clinic
  HAMP NW3 .... 73 D3
Tawhid Boys School
  STNW/STAM N16 .... 59 F4
Tayyibah Girls School
  STNW/STAM N16 .... 60 A3
Telferscot Primary School
  BAL SW12 .... 152 C1
Temple ⊖
  TPL/STR WC2R 33 F1
Temple Grove Hatcham School
  NWCR SE14 .... 121 D3
Temple of Bacchus
  CMBW SE5 .... 118 C5
Temple of Mithras
  MANHO EC4N 24 A5
Terence McMillan Stadium
  PLSTW E13 .... 94 C3
Thames Barrier
  CAN/RD E16 .... 107 D3
Thames Barrier Information &
  Learning Centre
  CHARL SE7 .... 107 D4
Thames Christian College
  BTSEA SW11 .... 133 D1
Thames House
  WEST SW1P 44 C4
Thameside Industrial Estate
  CAN/RD E16 .... 107 D2
Thames View Clinic
  BARK IG11 .... 97 F1
Thames Water Tower
  NTGHL W11 .... 101 D3
Theatre de l'Ange Fou International
  School of Corporeal Mime
  ARCH N19 .... 57 D3
Theatre for Mankind
  FSBYPK N4 .... 57 F3
Theatre Museum
  Library & Archive
  COVGDN WC2E 33 D1
Theatre of the Dispossessed
  WIM/MER SW19 .... 149 D1
Theatre Royal
  HOL/ALD WC2B 21 D5
  SRTFD E15 .... 81 D3
Theatre Royal Haymarket
  STJS SW1Y 32 B2
Theodore McLeary
  Primary School
  EDUL SE22 .... 137 F2
Thistle Hotel
  BAY/PAD W2 .... 27 E2
  BGVA SW1W 43 D3
  CAMTN NW1 .... 7 F4
  FITZ W1T 19 E4
  FSBYE EC1V 11 E4
  HOXST/BSQ WC1A 20 C3
  WESTW SW1E 43 D3
Thistle Marble Arch Hotel
  MBLAR W1H 17 F5
Thistle Piccadilly Hotel
  SOHO/SHAV W1D 32 B2
Thomas Buxton Infant School
  WCHPL E1 .... 90 A3
Thomas Fairchild Primary School
  IS N1 .... 12 A1
Thomas Francis Academy
  BRXN/ST SW9 .... 136 B2
Thomas Gamuel Primary School
  WALTH E17 .... 62 A1
Thomas Jones Primary School
  NTGHL W11 .... 89 E5

Thomas London Independent
  Day School
  KENS W8 ....**39** D2
Thomas Road Industrial Estate
  POP/IOD E14 ....**92** A4
Thomas's Fulham
  FUL/PGN SW6 ....**132** B1
Thomas's Preparatory School
  BTSEA SW11 ....**133** F3
Thomas Tallis School
  BKHTH/KID SE3 ....**142** B1
Thornhill Primary School
  IS N1 ....**76** A4
Thorntree Primary School
  CHARL SE7 ....**125** D1
Three Mills Heritage Centre
  BOW E3 ....**92** C3
Thurston Industrial Estate
  LEW SE13 ....**140** B1
Tibetan Buddhist Centre
  WALW SE17 ....**118** C1
Tidemill Primary School
  DEPT SE8 ....**122** A3
Tideway Industrial Estate
  VX/NE SW8 ....**116** C2
Tiller Centre (Swimming Baths)
  POP/IOD E14 ....**104** A4
Tiller Leisure Centre
  POP/IOD E14 ....**104** A4
Timbercroft Primary School
  WOOL/PLUM SE18 ....**127** E3
Tiverton Primary School
  SEVS/STOTM N15 ....**59** D1
Tobacco Dock
  WAP E1W **102** B1
Tokyngton Community Centre
  WBLY HA9 ....**68** B2
Toldos School
  STNW/STAM N16 ....**59** D3
Tollgate
  DUL SE21 ....**155** E2
Tollgate Primary School
  PLSTW E13 ....**94** C3
Tom Hood School
  WAN E11 ....**63** F5
Tooting Bec ⊖
  TOOT SW17 ....**152** A3
Tooting Bec Athletics Track
  TOOT SW17 ....**152** B4
Tooting Broadway ⊖
  TOOT SW17 ....**151** E5
Tooting Leisure Centre
  TOOT SW17 ....**151** D4
Torah Vodaas
  GLDGN NW11 ....**53** F4
Torriano Junior School
  KTTN NW5 ....**74** C2
Torridon Primary School
  CAT SE6 ....**159** D2
Total Health Clinic
  SHB W12 ....**100** B3
Tottenham Court Road ⊖
  SOHO/SHAV W1D **20** A4
Tower 42
  OBST EC2N **24** C4
The Tower Bridge Exhibition
  STHWK SE1 ....**37** E4
Tower Bridge Primary School
  STHWK SE1 ....**37** E5
Tower Bridge Wharf
  WAP E1W **102** A2
Tower Gateway ⊖
  TWRH EC3N **37** E1
Tower Hamlets College
  POP/IOD E14 ....**104** B1
  WCHPL E1 ....**90** C4
Tower Hill ⊖
  TWRH EC3N **37** E2
The Tower Hotel
  WAP E1W **37** F3
Tower Medical Centre
  WCHPL E1 ....**90** A5
Tower Millennium Pier
  TWRH EC3N **37** D3
Tower of London
  TWRH EC3N **37** E2
Towers Business Park
  WBLY HA9 ....**68** B1
Tower Stairs
  MON EC3R **36** C2
Townmead Business Centre
  FUL/PGN SW6 ....**114** C5

Townsend Industrial Estate
  WLSDN NW10 ....**68** C5
Townsend Primary School
  WALW SE17 ....**48** B4
Toynbee Theatre &
  Curtain Theatre
  WCHPL E1 ....**25** E3
Trade Union Congress
  NOXST/BSQ WC1A **20** B4
Trafalgar Business Centre
  BARK IG11 ....**97** F3
Trafalgar Square
  STJS SW1Y **32** B3
Tramshed Theatre
  WOOL/PLUM SE18 ....**108** B5
Trans Atlantic College
  BETH E2 ....**13** D1
Transport for London Lost
  Property Office
  CAMTN NW1 ....**17** F1
Transport House
  WEST SW1P **44** C3
Travelodge
  ACT W5 ....**86** A3
  BTSEA SW11 ....**132** C1
  CAMTN NW1 ....**17** D2
  CAN/RD E16 ....**107** D2
  FSBYW WC1X **9** F3
  IL IG1 ....**66** B5
  LSQ/SEVD WC2H **20** C4
  POP/IOD E14 ....**93** D5
  REDBR IG4 ....**65** F1
  STPAN WC1H **9** D3
  WCHPL E1 ....**25** E4
  WLSDN NW10 ....**86** A1
Treasury
  WHALL SW1A **44** C1
The Treehouse School
  BMSBY WC1N **9** E5
Trevor Roberts School
  HAMP NW3 ....**73** D4
Tricycle Theatre
  KIL/WHAMP NW6 ....**71** F4
Trident Business Centre
  TOOT SW17 ....**151** F5
Trinity Business Centre
  BERM/RHTH SE16 ....**103** F3
Trinity College Centre
  PECK SE15 ....**119** E3
Trinity College London
  STHWK SE1 ....**117** E1
Trinity College of Music
  GNWCH SE10 ....**122** C2
  MHST W1U **18** B3
Trinity Hospital
  GNWCH SE10 ....**123** D1
Trinity House
  TWRH EC3N **37** D1
Trinity St Marys
  Primary School
  BAL SW12 ....**152** A1
Tripcock Point
  Development Site
  THMD SE28 ....**109** F1
Trocadero
  SOHO/SHAV W1D **32** A2
Trojan Business Centre
  WLSDN NW10 ....**69** F3
True Buddha School
  IS N1 ....**75** F5
TS Queen Mary
  TPL/STR WC2R **33** E2
TTMH Belz Day School
  STNW/STAM N16 ....**60** A2
Tudor Lodge Health Centre
  WIM/MER SW19 ....**149** D1
Tufnell Park ⊖
  KTTN NW5 ....**74** B1
Tufnell Park Primary School
  HOLWY N7 ....**75** D1
Tuke School
  PECK SE15 ....**120** B4
Tulse Hill ≠
  WNWD SE27 ....**154** B2
Tunnel Avenue Trading Estate
  GNWCH SE10 ....**105** D3
Turney School
  DUL SE21 ....**136** C5
Turnham Green ⊖
  CHSWK W4 ....**99** E5
Turnham Primary School
  BROCKY SE4 ....**139** E2

Turtle Key Arts Centre
FUL/PGN SW6 ....**114** A2

Twenty Nevern Square Hotel
ECT SW5 ....**38** B5

Twyford CE High School
ACT W3 ....**98** A2

Twyford Sports Centre
ACT W3 ....**98** B2

Tyburn Infant School
STJWD NW8 ....**4** B5

The Type Museum
BRXN/ST SW9 ....**117** F4

Tyssen Primary School
STNW/STAM N16 ....**60** A3

UCI Cinema
BAY/PAD W2 ....**15** D5

UCI Empire Cinema
LSQ/SEVD WC2H **32** B2

UCI Filmworks Cinema
GNWCH SE10 ....**105** F5

UK Passport Office
..................................**43** D4

Unicorn Theatre
STHWK SE1 ....**37** D5

United Medical & Dental Schools
STHWK SE1 ....**45** E2

Unity College
KTTN NW5 ....**74** B1

**University Church of
Christ the King**
STPAN WC1H **20** A1

University College Hospital
CAMTN NW1 ....**7** F5
HAMP NW3 ....**73** D3

University College London
FITZ W1T **19** F1
GWRST WC1E **20** A1
STPAN WC1H **8** A5

**University College London,
Astor College**
FITZ W1T **19** F2

**University College London
Medical School**
FITZ W1T **19** E2

University College School
HAMP NW3 ....**72** C2

University Hospital Lewisham
LEW SE13 ....**140** B3

University of California
WHALL SW1A **31** E4

University of East London
CAN/RD E16 ....**108** A1
PLSTW E13 ....**94** B2
SRTFD E15 ....**81** D5

University of Greenwich
ELTH/MOT SE9 ....**145** D4
GNWCH SE10 ....**123** D1
WOOL/PLUM SE18 ....**108** A5

**University of Greenwich
(Mansion Site)**
ELTH/MOT SE9 ....**144** C4

**University of Greenwich
Sports Ground**
ELTH/MOT SE9 ....**143** E2

University of London
BAY/PAD W2 ....**16** A5
BMSBY WC1N **21** D1
CLKNW EC1R **10** B5
FITZ W1T **20** A4
GWRST WC1E **20** B2
MBLAR W1H **17** D4
STHWK SE1 ....**36** A4
STPAN WC1H **8** A5

University of the Arts London
MYFR/PKLN W1K **18** C5

University of Westminster
CAMTN NW1 ....**7** E5
CAVSQ/HST W1G **19** D4
CHSWK W4 ....**110** C4
GTPST W1W **19** D2

**University of Westminster
- Environment**
MHST W1U **18** A2

**University of Westminster
(Faculty of Engineering & Science)**
FITZ W1T **19** F2

Uphall Primary School
IL IG1 ....**84** B2

Upney ⊖
BARK IG11 ....**85** F4

Upper Holloway ⊖
ARCH N19 ....**57** D4

Upper Montagu Street Clinic
CAMTN NW1 ....**17** E2

**Upper Tooting Independent
High School**
TOOT SW17 ....**151** E2

Upton Cross Primary School
PLSTW E13 ....**82** B5

Upton Lane Medical Centre
FSTGT E7 ....**82** B3

Upton Park ⊖
PLSTW E13 ....**82** C5

The Urdang Academy
LSQ/SEVD WC2H **20** C5

The Vale Medical Centre
FSTH SE23 ....**157** E2

Valentine High School
GNTH/NBYPK IG2 ....**66** A1

Vale Park Industrial
ACT W3 ....**99** E3

The Vale School
SKENS SW7 ....**39** E3

Valmar Trading Estate
CMBW SE5 ....**118** C4

V & A Museum of Childhood
BETH E2 ....**90** C2

Vanbrugh Theatre
GWRST WC1E **20** A1

Vanguard Trading Estate
SRTFD E15 ....**80** C5

Vaudeville Theatre
COVGDN WC2E **33** D1

Vauxhall ⇌ ⊖
VX/NE SW8 ....**117** E2

Vauxhall Primary School
LBTH SE11 ....**117** F1

**Vernon House
Special School**
WLSDN NW10 ....**68** C2

Vicarage Fields Health Clinic
BARK IG11 ....**84** C4

**The Vicarage Field
Shopping Centre**
BARK IG11 ....**84** C4

Vicarage Primary School
EHAM E6 ....**95** F2

Victoria ⇌ ⊖
PIM SW1V **43** D4

Victoria & Albert Museum
SKENS SW7 ....**40** B3

Victoria Bus Station
PIM SW1V **43** D3

Victoria Chiropractic Clinic
SKENS SW7 ....**41** E1

Victoria Coach Station
BGVA SW1W **42** C5

Victoria Industrial Estate
ACT W3 ....**87** D4

Victoria Medical Centre
PIM SW1V **43** F5

Victoria Palace Theatre
BGVA SW1W **43** D3

Victoria Park Industrial Centre
HOM E9 ....**79** F4

Victoria Park Plaza Hotel
PIM SW1V **43** E4

**Victoria Place
Shopping Centre**
BGVA SW1W **43** D4

Victoria Rail/Air Terminal
PIM SW1V **43** D4

Victoria Wharf
POP/IOD E14 ....**103** E1

Victoria Wharf Industrial Estate
DEPT SE8 ....**121** E1

Victory Primary School
WALW SE17 ....**47** F4

The Village School
HAMP NW3 ....**73** F3

The Vines School
BTSEA SW11 ....**134** A2

Vinopolis, City of Wine
STHWK SE1 ....**35** F3

Vinters' Hall
BLKFR EC4V **35** F1

V I P Trading Estate
CHARL SE7 ....**106** C5

Virginia Primary School
BETH E2 ....**13** E4

Visage School of Hair & Beauty
ELTH/MOT SE9 ....**144** A5

Vision College of Technology
HOM E9 ....**80** A3

Vittoria Primary School
   IS N1...**76** A5
Voyager Business Estate
   BERM/RHTH SE16.................**102** A4
Vue Cinema
   ACT W3.................................**86** A3
   FUL/PGN SW6.......................**114** A5
   HAMP NW3.............................**72** C3
   LSQ/SEVD WC2H....................**32** B1
   SHB W12.............................**101** D3
Waldorf School of SW London
   BAL SW12............................**152** C2
Waldron Health Centre & Surgery
   NWCR SE14..........................**121** F3
The Wallace Centre
   DEPT SE8............................**122** B2
The Wallace Collection
   MHST W1U..............................**18** A4
Walmer Road Clinic
   NTGHL W11..........................**101** E1
Walm Lane Clinic
   CRICK NW2............................**71** D2
Walnut Tree Walk
   Primary School
   LBTH SE11............................**46** A4
Walworth Academy
   STHWK SE1..........................**119** E1
Walworth Lower Secondary School
   WALW SE17..........................**119** D1
Walworth Town Hall
   WALW SE17............................**47** E5
Wandle Recreation Centre
   WAND/EARL SW18...................**132** B4
Wandsworth Adult College
   BTSEA SW11.........................**116** A4
   TOOT SW17..........................**151** E2
Wandsworth Cemetery
   WAND/EARL SW18...................**150** C1
Wandsworth Common ≥
   TOOT SW17..........................**133** E5
Wandsworth Road ≥ ⊖
   VX/NE SW8..........................**116** C5
Wandsworth Town ≥
   WAND/EARL SW18...................**132** B2
Wandsworth Trading Estate
   WAND/EARL SW18...................**132** B5
Wanstead ⊖
   WAN E11..............................**64** B1
Wanstead CC
   WAN E11..............................**64** B2
Wanstead Golf Club
   WAN E11..............................**64** B2
Wanstead High School
   WAN E11..............................**64** C1
Wanstead Leisure Centre
   WAN E11..............................**64** C1
Wanstead Park ⊖
   FSTGT E7............................**82** B1
Wapping ⊖
   WAP E1W............................**102** C2
Wapping Wharf
   WAP E1W............................**102** C2
Warren Street ⊖
   CAMTN NW1.............................**7** E5
Warwick Avenue ⊖
   MV/WKIL W9..........................**15** E1
Warwick Dubbing Theatre
   SOHO/CST W1F.......................**20** A5
Warwick Estate
   BAY/PAD W2..........................**15** D3
Warwick Leadlay Gallery
   GNWCH SE10.........................**122** C2
The Washington Mayfair Hotel
   MYFR/PICC W1J......................**31** D3
Waterfront Leisure Centre
   WOOL/PLUM SE18...................**108** A4
Watergate School
   CAT SE6.............................**158** B5
Waterloo ≥ ⊖
   STHWK SE1............................**34** A5
Waterloo East ≥
   STHWK SE1............................**34** B4
Waterloo Health Centre
   STHWK SE1............................**46** A1
Waterloo School of English
   NOXST/BSQ WC1A....................**20** C3
The Watermans Hall
   MON EC3R............................**36** C2
Water Rats Theatre
   STPAN WC1H............................**9** D3
Waterside Primary School
   WOOL/PLUM SE18...................**127** D1

Watersports Centre
   STNW/STAM N16.......................**58** C3
Wavelengths Leisure Pool & Library
   DEPT SE8...........................**122** A3
Waverley Lower
   Secondary School
   EDUL SE22..........................**138** B3
Waxchandlers' Hall
   CITYW EC2V..........................**23** F4
Webber Douglas Academy of
   Dramatic Art
   SKENS SW7...........................**39** F5
Webster Graduate Studies Center
   CAMTN NW1.............................**5** F5
Welbeck Clinic
   CRICK NW2............................**54** A5
Welfare Clinic
   HGT N6..............................**56** A1
Wellcome Institute
   CAMTN NW1.............................**8** A5
Welling Medical Centre
   WELL DA16..........................**145** F2
Wellington Arch
   MYFR/PICC W1J......................**30** B5
Wellington Barracks
   WESTW SW1E..........................**43** F1
Wellington Primary School
   BOW E3..............................**92** A2
Wembley Arena
   WBLY HA9............................**68** A1
Wembley Exhibition Halls
   WBLY HA9............................**68** A1
Wembley Park ⊖
   WBLY HA9............................**50** A5
Wembley Park Business Centre
   WBLY HA9............................**50** B5
Wembley Stadium
   WBLY HA9............................**68** A1
Wembley Stadium ≥
   WBLY HA9............................**68** A2
Wembley Stadium Industrial Estate
   WBLY HA9............................**50** A5
Wendell Park Primary School
   SHB W12.............................**99** F3
Wentworth Tutorial College
   GLDGN NW11..........................**53** D1
The Wernher Collection at
   Ranger's House
   GNWCH SE10.........................**123** D4
Wesley's Chapel, House & Museum
   STLK EC1Y...........................**12** A5
Wessex Gardens Primary School
   GLDGN NW11..........................**53** E3
West 12 Shopping & Leisure Centre
   SHB W12............................**101** D3
West Acton ⊖
   ACT W3..............................**86** A5
West Acton Primary School
   ACT W3..............................**86** B5
West Beckton Health Centre
   CAN/RD E16..........................**94** C4
Westbourne Green Sports Complex
   BAY/PAD W2..........................**14** B3
Westbourne Park ⊖
   NKENS W10..........................**89** F4
Westbridge College
   BTSEA SW11.........................**115** E4
West Brompton ≥ ⊖ ⊖
   ECT SW5............................**114** A1
The Westbury Hotel
   CONDST W1S..........................**31** D1
Westcombe Park ≥
   BKHTH/KID SE3......................**124** A1
West Dulwich ≥
   DUL SE21...........................**155** D1
Western Avenue Business Park
   ACT W3..............................**86** A3
Western Trading Estate
   WLSDN NW10.........................**86** C3
Westferry ⊖
   POP/IOD E14........................**103** F1
Westfield London
   SHB W12............................**100** C2
Westfields Primary School
   BARN SW13.........................**111** F5
Westfield Stratford City
   development
   SRTFD E15...........................**80** C3
Westgate Business Centre
   NKENS W10..........................**89** E3
West Ham ≥ ⊖
   SRTFD E15...........................**93** E2

West Ham ⊖
  BOW E3...93 D2
West Ham Church Primary School
  SRTFD E15......................................81 F5
West Ham Lane Clinic
  SRTFD E15......................................81 E5
West Hampstead ⇌ ⊖ ⊖
  KIL/WHAMP NW6..............................72 A3
West Hampstead Clinic
  KIL/WHAMP NW6..............................72 A4
West Hampstead Thameslink ⇌
  KIL/WHAMP NW6..............................72 A3
West Ham United FC (Upton Park)
  PLSTW E13......................................95 D1
West Hendon Clinic
  CDALE/KGS NW9..............................51 F1
West Hill Primary School
  WAND/EARL SW18..........................132 A3
West India Pier
  POP/IOD E14..................................103 F3
West India Quay ⊖
  POP/IOD E14..................................104 A1
West India Shopping Centre
  POP/IOD E14..................................104 A2
West Kensington ⊖
  WKENS W14....................................113 F1
Westland Heliport
  BTSEA SW11..................................133 F1
West Lodge Preparatory School
  BFN/LL DA15..................................163 F3
West London Tamil School
  WLSDN NW10...................................87 F1
Westminster ⊖
  WHALL SW1A....................................45 D1
Westminster Abbey
  WEST SW1P......................................44 C2
Westminster Abbey Choir School
  WEST SW1P......................................44 B2
Westminster Academy
  BAY/PAD W2.....................................14 B3
Westminster Bridge Park Plaza Hotel
  STHWK SE1......................................45 E1
Westminster Business Square
  LBTH SE11......................................117 F1
Westminster Cathedral
  WESTW SW1E....................................43 E3
Westminster Cathedral Choir School
  WEST SW1P......................................43 F3
Westminster Cathedral RC
  Primary School
  PIM SW1V.......................................117 D1
Westminster City Hall
  WESTW SW1E....................................43 F3
Westminster City School
  WESTW SW1E....................................43 F2
Westminster Hall
  WHALL SW1A....................................45 D1
Westminster Industrial Estate
  WOOL/PLUM SE18..........................107 D4
Westminster Kingsway College
  CAMTN NW1.......................................7 E4
  WEST SW1P......................................43 F4
Westminster Natural Health Centre
  PIM SW1V..43 E5
Westminster Pier
  WHALL SW1A....................................45 D1
Westminster School
  WEST SW1P......................................44 C2
Westminster Theatre
  WESTW SW1E....................................43 E2
Westminster Under School
  WEST SW1P......................................44 A5
Westmoor Community Clinic
  PUT/ROE SW15...............................130 A5
West Norwood ⇌
  WNWD SE27....................................154 B4
West Norwood Clinic
  WNWD SE27....................................154 C2
West Norwood Crematorium
  WNWD SE27....................................154 C3
West One Shopping Centre
  MYFR/PKLN W1K................................18 B5
Westpoint Trading Estate
  ACT W3..86 B4
West Silvertown ⊖
  CAN/RD E16....................................106 A2
West Thamesmead Business Park
  THMD SE28.....................................109 F4
West Twyford Primary School
  WLSDN NW10....................................86 A1
Westway Business Centre
  BAY/PAD W2.....................................14 C3

Westway Sports Centre
  NKENS W10......................................89 D5
Westwood College
  WELL DA16.....................................145 D2
Westwood Primary School
  WELL DA16.....................................145 E2
Wetherby Preparatory School
  BAY/PAD W2.....................................26 B1
Whaddon House Clinic
  CMBW SE5......................................137 E1
Whipps Cross Hospital
  LEY E10..63 D1
Whitechapel ⊖
  WCHPL E1..90 B4
Whitechapel Art Gallery
  WCHPL E1..25 F4
Whitechapel Sports Centre
  WCHPL E1..90 A4
White City ⊖
  SHB W12...100 C1
Whitefield School
  CRICK NW2.......................................53 D2
Whitehall Theatre
  WHALL SW1A....................................32 B3
The White House
  Preparatory School
  BAL SW12......................................153 D1
White House Preparatory
  & Kindergarten
  BAL SW12......................................153 D1
Whiteleys Shopping Centre
  BAY/PAD W2.....................................14 C5
Whitmore Primary School
  IS N1..12 B1
Whittington Hospital
  ARCH N19...56 B4
Wigmore Hall
  CAVSQ/HST W1G..............................18 C4
Wigram House (University
  of Westminster)
  WEST SW1P......................................44 A3
Wilberforce Primary School
  NKENS W10......................................89 E2
Willesden Centre for
  Health & Care
  WLSDN NW10....................................70 A4
Willesden Green ⊖
  CRICK NW2.......................................70 C3
Willesden Junction ⊖ ⊖
  WLSDN NW10....................................87 F2
Willesden Medical Centre
  CRICK NW2.......................................70 B3
Willesden Sports Centre
  WLSDN NW10....................................70 B5
Willesden Sports Stadium
  WLSDN NW10....................................70 B5
William Davies Primary School
  FSTGT E7...83 D3
William Ellis School
  KTTN NW5..56 A5
William Hogarth School
  CHSWK W4......................................111 E2
William Morris Academy
  HMSMTH W6....................................113 D1
William Patten Primary School
  STNW/STAM N16................................59 F4
William Tyndale Primary School
  IS N1..76 B4
Willow Brook Primary
  LEY E10..62 A3
Willow Business Park
  SYD SE26.......................................156 C3
Wimbledon Common Golf Club
  WIM/MER SW19...............................148 B5
Wimbledon (Gap Road) Cemetery
  WIM/MER SW19...............................150 B4
Wimbledon Lawn Tennis Museum
  WIM/MER SW19...............................149 E3
Wimbledon Park ⊖
  WIM/MER SW19...............................150 A3
Wimbledon Park Athletics Track
  WIM/MER SW19...............................149 F2
Wimbledon Park Golf Club
  WIM/MER SW19...............................149 F3
Wimbledon Park
  Primary School
  WIM/MER SW19...............................150 A2
Wimbledon Stadium
  WIM/MER SW19...............................150 B4
Wimbledon Stadium
  Business Centre
  WIM/MER SW19...............................150 B3

Winchcombe Business Centre
PECK SE15 .... 119 E2
Winfield House
CAMTN NW1 .... 5 D3
Wingfield Primary School
BKHTH/KID SE3 .... 142 A1
Winsor Primary School
EHAM E6 .... 96 A5
Winston Churchill's Britain at
War Experience
STHWK SE1 .... 36 B4
Winston Way Primary School
IL IG1 .... 66 B5
Winton Primary School
IS N1 .... 9 E2
The Women's Library
WCHPL E1 .... 25 E4
Woodberry Down Centre
FSBYPK N4 .... 58 C3
Woodberry Down
Community Primary
FSBYPK N4 .... 58 C2
Woodfield School
CDALE/KGS NW9 .... 51 E3
Woodgrange Infant School
FSTGT E7 .... 82 B1
Woodgrange Park ⊖
FSTGT E7 .... 83 D2
Woodgrange Park Cemetery
MNPK E12 .... 83 D1
Woodhill Primary School
CHARL SE7 .... 107 E5
Woodlands J & I School
IL IG1 .... 85 D1
Woodlands Medical Centre
LEW SE13 .... 141 D4
Wood Lane ⊖
SHB W12 .... 100 C1
Wood Lane School
FUL/PGN SW6 .... 114 C4
Wood Wharf
POP/IOD E14 .... 104 B2
Wood Wharf Business Park
POP/IOD E14 .... 104 C3
Woolmore Primary School
POP/IOD E14 .... 104 C1
Woolwich Arsenal ⇌ ⊖
WOOL/PLUM SE18 .... 108 B5
Woolwich Dockyard ⇌
WOOL/PLUM SE18 .... 107 F5
Worlds End Place
WBPTN SW10 .... 114 C3
World Spiritual University
WLSDN NW10 .... 70 A4

World University Service
STLK EC1Y 24 A1
Wormholt Park Primary School
SHB W12 .... 100 A1
Wyborne Primary School
ELTH/MOT SE9 .... 162 B1
Wykeham Primary School
WLSDN NW10 .... 51 D5
Wyndham Grand Hotel
WBPTN SW10 .... 114 C4
Wyndhams Theatre
CHCR WC2N 32 B1
Wyvil Primary School
VX/NE SW8 .... 117 E3
Yale University Press
HAMP NW3 .... 73 E1
Yerbury Primary School
ARCH N19 .... 57 D5
Yeshivo Horomo
Talmudical College
STNW/STAM N16 .... 59 D3
Yesodey Hatorah
Jewish Boys School
SEVS/STOTM N15 .... 59 F2
Yesodey Hatorah
School For Girls
STNW/STAM N16 .... 59 F2
Yetev Lev Day School for Boys
STNW/STAM N16 .... 60 A3
YMCA Leisure Centre
RSQ WC1B 20 B4
York Clinic
STHWK SE1 .... 36 A4
York Hall
BETH E2 .... 90 B1
York Water Gate
CHCR WC2N 33 D3
Young Actors Theatre
IS N1 .... 75 F5
Young England RFC
VX/NE SW8 .... 117 F3
Young Vic Theatre
STHWK SE1 .... 34 B5
Zennor Road Industrial Estate
BAL SW12 .... 152 C1
The Zetter Hotel
FARR EC1M 22 C1
Ziam Trading Estate
CLPT E5 .... 60 C3
ZSL London Zoo
CAMTN NW1 .... 6 A1

Acknowledgements

Schools address data provided by Education Direct

Petrol station information supplied by Johnsons

Garden centre information provided by:

Garden Centre Association ● Britains best garden centres

Wyevale Garden Centres ❀

The boundary of the London Congestion Charging Zone and Low Emission Zone supplied by
⊖ Transport for London

The statement on the front cover of this atlas is sourced, selected and quoted
from a reader comment and feedback form received in 2004